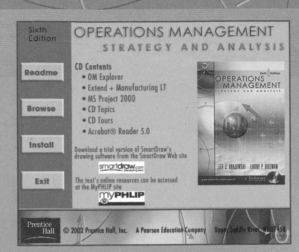

FREE STUDENT CD-ROM

PACKAGED FREE WITH EVERY NEW COPY OF THE TEXT!

THIS EXCITING CD-ROM CONTAINS:

OM Explorer—OM Explorer is a complete software decision-support package designed specifically for this text. The revised version has the look and feel of an Excel worksheet environment. Over 66 tutorials provide coaching for all of the difficult analytical methods presented in the text. The package also contains 40 powerful routines to solve problems often encountered in practice.

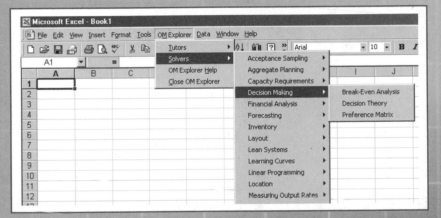

Microsoft Project (120-Day Evaluation) Software—This package is used extensively in practice to manage projects. The package can be used to solve the problems and the case at the end of Chapter 4 in addition to any problems or cases the instructor may add.

Extend + Manufacturing Software/Simulation Cases—Eleven challenging case problems have been prepared using Extend simulation models. Students use the models to answer questions regarding the cases.

CD-ROM Tours—Virtual tours of the Lower Florida Keys Hospital and Chaparral Steel.

CD-ROM Topics—These topics include: Learning Curve Analysis, Measuring Output Rates, Acceptance Sampling Plans, and Financial Analysis.

Link to MyPHLIP Web site.

Link to Lecture Notes—These notes are summaries, in outline form, of the material in each chapter and supplement.

Link to SmartDraw Web site.

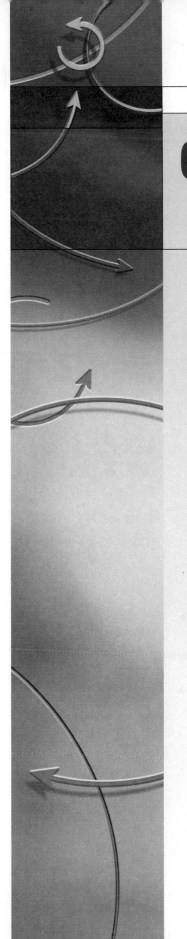

OPERATIONS MANAGEMENT

STRATEGY AND ANALYSIS

SIXTH EDITION

OPERATIONS MANAGEMENT

STRATEGY AND ANALYSIS

SIXTH EDITION

LEE J. KRAJEWSKI
University of Notre Dame

LARRY P. RITZMAN
Boston College

Prentice Hall
Upper Saddle River, NJ 07458

Library of Congress Cataloging-in-Publication Data

Krajewski, Lee J.
    Operations management: strategy and analysis / Lee J. Krajewski, Larry P. Ritzman.—
6th ed.
        p. cm.
    Includes bibliographical references and index.
    ISBN: 0-201-61545-2
    1. Production management.   I. Ritzman, Larry P. II. Title.

TS155 .K788 2001
658.5—dc21   2001033855

Exective Editor: Tom Tucker
Editor-in-Chief: P.J. Boardman
Assistant Editor: Jennifer Surich
Developmental Editor: Ronald Librach
Media Project Manager: Nancy Welcher
Marketing Manager: Debbie Clare
Marketing Assistant: Brian Rappelfeld
Managing Editor (Production): Cynthia Regan
Production Assistant: Dianne Falcone
Permissions Coordinator: Suzanne Grappi
Associate Director, Manufacturing: Vincent Scelta
Production Manager: Arnold Vila
Design Manager: Patricia Smythe
Designer: Blair Brown
Cover Design/Cover Illustration: Blair Brown
Interior Design/Illustration (Interior): Proof Positive
Manager, Print Production: Christy Mahon
Composition: Progressive Information Technologies
Full-Service Project Management: Progressive Publishing Alternatives
Printer/Binder: Courier/Westford

10 9 8 7 6 5 4 3 2 1
ISBN 0-201-61545-2

Dedicated with love
to our Families

Judie Krajewski
Gary
Lori and Dan; Aubrey
Carrie and Jon
Selena and Jeff
Virginia and Jerry
Virginia and Larry

Barbara Ritzman
Karen and Matt; Kristin and Alayna
Lisa and Todd; Cody, Cole, and Taylor
Kathryn and Paul
Mildred and Ray

ABOUT THE AUTHORS

LEE J. KRAJEWSKI is the William R. and F. Cassie Daley Professor of Manufacturing Strategy at the University of Notre Dame. Prior to joining Notre Dame, Lee was a faculty member at The Ohio State University, where he received the University Alumni Distinguished Teaching Award and the College of Business Outstanding Faculty Research Award. He initiated the Center for Excellence in Manufacturing Management and served as its director for four years. In addition, he received the National President's Award and the National Award of Merit of the American Production and Inventory Control Society. He served as President Elect of the Decision Sciences Institute and was elected a Fellow of the Institute in 1988.

Lee's career spans more than thirty-two years of research and education in the field of operations management. He has designed and taught courses at both graduate and undergraduate levels on topics such as manufacturing strategy, introduction to operations management, operations design, and manufacturing planning and control systems.

Lee served as the editor of *Decision Sciences,* was the founding editor of the *Journal of Operations Management* (1980–1983), and has served on several editorial boards. Widely published himself, Lee has contributed numerous articles to such journals as *Decision Sciences,* the *Journal of Operations Management, Management Science, Harvard Business Review,* and *Interfaces,* to name just a few. He has received five best-paper awards. Lee's areas of specialization include manufacturing strategy, manufacturing planning and control systems, supply-chain management, and master production scheduling.

LARRY P. RITZMAN is the Thomas J. Galligan, Jr. Professor in Operations and Strategic Management at Boston College. He previously served at The Ohio State University for twenty-three years, where he acted as department chairperson and received several awards for both teaching and research. He received his doctorate at Michigan State University, having had prior industrial experience at the Babcock and Wilcox Company. Over the years, he has been privileged to teach and learn more about operations management with numerous students at all levels—undergraduate, MBA, executive MBA, and doctorate.

Particularly active in the Decision Sciences Institute, Larry has served as Council Coordinator, Publications Committee Chair, Track Chair, Vice President, Board Member, Executive Committee Member, Doctoral Consortium Coordinator, and President. He was elected a Fellow of the Institute in 1987 and earned the Distinguished Service Award in 1996. He has received three best-paper awards. He is a frequent reviewer, discussant, and session chair for several other professional organizations.

Larry's areas of particular expertise are operations strategy, production and inventory systems, forecasting, multistage manufacturing, disaggregation, scheduling, and layout. An active researcher, Larry's publications have appeared in such journals as *Decision Sciences, Journal of Operations Management, Production and Operations Management, Harvard Business Review,* and *Management Science.* He has served in various editorial capacities for several journals.

Brief Contents

Contents

(handwritten margin notes: "Capacity management", "Global Operations")

Lean Process

PREFACE

Operations Management: Strategy and Analysis, Sixth Edition, continues its hallmark reputation for innovation in presenting operations management as a powerful tool for achieving organizational objectives and gaining competitive advantage. Our goal is to help students become effective managers in today's competitive, global environment. First, because many students who take this course will go on to become managers in service and manufacturing organizations in a variety of departments and functional areas, we focus on processes—the fundamental unit of work in all organizations. It is all about processes! This unifying theme opens up the topics in operations management to all students, regardless of their majors or career paths. They discover the challenge of both managing and understanding the interrelatedness of activities throughout the organization, and how the operations function fits into the organization. Second, we seek to help students discover the excitement of the dynamic field of operations management (OM). We engage them by offering a wealth of interesting examples at numerous service and manufacturing firms that bring operations alive, presenting new technologies for enhancing decision making and data gathering, and including realistic cases that encourage open debate of important issues. Third, to put the subject in appropriate context, we want students to gain an understanding of what managers do about processes, to realize that operations management involves many cross-functional links, and to learn more about the tools that managers can use to make better operating decisions.

PHILOSOPHY OF OPERATIONS MANAGEMENT: STRATEGY AND ANALYSIS

A Balanced Perspective. The Sixth Edition blends the latest in strategic issues with proven analytic techniques. It reflects our philosophy that OM texts should address both the "big picture" strategic issues and also the analytic tools that facilitate decision making. It is not just about "concepts" or just about "numbers," but recognizes both dimensions. Strategic and managerial issues have been woven into the fabric of each chapter to emphasize that management decisions about operations and processes should be consistent with corporate strategies shared by managers in all functional areas. Tools and techniques, including computer models and Internet capabilities, are also woven into the text as ways to solve problems and develop tactics that help achieve the firm's overall goals and strategies. We also continue to provide a balanced treatment of manufacturing and services throughout the text, and give special recognition to service provider processes of with an S icon in the margin. This approach not only reflects the remarkable growth of the service sector in the global economy, but also helps the student view how designing and managing processes are fundamental to all activities throughout any organization.

Operations Management Within the Whole Firm. Our message to students is clear: This text presents practical approaches to solve operations problems, and the solutions to those problems can and do make a difference in a firm's competitiveness. New to the Sixth Edition are interdisciplinary perspectives that begin and end each chapter, giving students a better appreciation for how operations relates throughout the whole business.

Active Learning. Motivating students to learn and apply OM concepts to processes is an important ingredient to a successful course. In the Sixth Edition, we have retained several popular and time-tested features that give students a deeper understanding of realistic business issues and enable them to become active participants in and out of the classroom. For example, *OM Explorer* tutors, end-of-chapter cases, and experiential exercises involve the students in actually applying the concepts and theories explained in the text. New to the Sixth Edition are the *Extend* and *SimQuick* simulators. The multiple activities available at the textbook's Web site expand learning beyond the textbook and the classroom; they include Internet activities, tours, *OM Explorer* computer assignments, and previews of the latest "industrial strength" commercial software now used in practice. Such features recognize the rapid growth of information technology, which is significantly reshaping processes around the world.

ORGANIZATION

We have chosen to organize the text so that it moves from strategic choices to tactical decisions. Chapter 1 is an introductory chapter on the meaning and role of processes and operations. It demonstrates the role of processes in every phase of businesses and functional areas, and then explores how to manage processes to provide a competitive advantage for the firm. It also shows how trends in productivity, service operations, global competition, quality, technology, and environmental concerns are broadening the scope and increasing the importance of operations management in all organizations.

Part 1 (Strategic Choices) consists of one chapter and one supplement. Chapter 2 discusses key issues in customer-driven operations strategy that affect a company's future. Competitive priorities (for individual processes and even major business units), global strategies, service and manufacturing strategies, and new technologies such as e-commerce are important pillars of operations strategy. So is how these choices relate to customer needs and corporate strategy. Identifying the pattern of decisions—and how the pattern should vary by situation—is demonstrated with detailed tours of two real organizations: a hospital and a steel company.

Part 2 (Process) consists of three chapters and one supplement. Chapter 3 looks at important choices about processes, which are fundamental to all activities that produce goods and services. Key decisions include process choice, outsourcing, flexibility, customer involvement, and automation. These decisions, and how they are related, are described for processes of both manufacturers and service providers. We cover economies of scope and job design, and then provide a systematic approach to improving processes that includes both reengineering and process improvement. Chapter 4 focuses on project processes, so common in everyday life as well as in business. While projects can be large or small, unique or routine, they all require special approaches to manage them effectively. Chapter 5 turns to another important issue in designing processes: the use of technology. Every process uses one or more technologies. The increasing role of information technology is given particular attention, including its components, e-commerce, the Internet and World Wide Web, and enterprise resource planning (ERP). Strategic issues, such as first-mover considerations and implementation guidelines, are also covered.

Part 3 (Quality) consists of two chapters. Quality issues underlie all processes and work activities. Chapter 6 reflects current thought on quality management, including teamwork, continuous improvement through TQM, benchmarking, quality function deployment, and basic tools for data analysis. Chapter 7 shows how inspection and statistical methods can be combined to monitor and measure the capability of the process to produce goods or services to specification.

Part 4 (Capacity, Location, and Layout) consists of three chapters and two supplements. This part focuses on decisions that require long-term commitments about the process. Managers must help determine the process's capacity, where to locate new facilities (including global operations), and how to organize the layout of the processes within a facility. Discussion of these decisions completes our coverage of how to design processes for service providers and manufacturers.

Part 5 (Operating Decisions) consists of seven chapters and three supplements. This part deals with operating the processes after they have been designed. Chapters 11–17 examine the issues that managers face as they coordinate quarter-to-quarter and day-to-day issues in concert with an overall operations strategy. Topics include the supply-chain management and how to coordinate the internal and external supply chain, forecasting demand, managing inventory, controlling output and work-force levels over time, planning resource levels, managing lean systems and deciding which elements of just-in-time techniques to implement, scheduling the use of resources, and establishing priorities of work to be done.

The seven supplements interspersed in the text provide more in-depth coverage of techniques, including decision making, computer-integrated manufacturing, waiting lines, simulation, special inventory models, linear programming, and master production scheduling. Many of the supplements apply to multiple chapters, not simply to the chapter that they follow. Even more supplements are accessible on the Student CD-ROM packaged free with every new copy of the textbook. They cover learning curve analysis, measuring output rates, acceptance sampling plans, and financial analysis. Each topical supplement is complete within itself and includes a full problem set when appropriate. This arrangement makes incorporating this important material into courses easy and pedagogically effective for instructors.

The text aims at core-curriculum courses at the undergraduate and graduate levels. It covers all the basic topics in the area of operations management and allows the instructor to challenge the students at the appropriate level for their academic maturity. The book can be used in many ways, depending on the course objectives. It offers considerable flexibility in order, depth of coverage (qualitative or quantitative), and level (undergraduate or graduate). Thus instructors will find that the organization of the text allows smooth adaptation to various course syllabi. Once Chapters 1 and 2 have been covered, instructors can easily rearrange chapters and supplements to suit their individual course and teaching needs. The truth is that there is too much content in operations management to cover in one course. Thus the instructor will assign some materials and not others. Sequencing of materials depends on the orientation of your instructor, and what topics have already been covered in your program. We designed the book to be used flexibly, regardless of the orientation.

CHANGES FOR THE SIXTH EDITION

Following are highlights of content changes made to enhance coverage of the ever-changing field of operations management. These changes are based on extensive feedback from professors and students. All of these changes support the overall text philosophy.

- **NEW! Increased Emphasis on Processes.** Beginning in Chapter 1, we put increased emphasis on the central role of processes. Making decisions about processes naturally leads to issues in the various chapters on competitive priorities, technology, project management, quality, capacity, layout, supply-chain management, and the like. We wanted to create a better "buy-in" for a course in operations management. Our new focus on processes does just that, because students understand that processes underlie activities throughout the organization, not just in one functional area.

- **NEW! Managing Technology.** We significantly upgraded the chapters on managing technology, incorporating the latest developments in e-commerce (both B2B and B2C) and enterprise resource planning (ERP). Together, a chapter, case, and video on technology management explore the stages of technology development, the challenges of choosing and implementing new technology, and how technology can create a competitive advantage (Chapter 5, Managing Technology). These topics are developed further throughout in many Managerial Practices and business examples throughout the text.

- **NEW! Updated Coverage of Supply-Chain Management.** Chapter 11 on supply-chain management has been given a major face-lift. It brings out many of the newer things going on with supply chains, while building on the base provided in the last edition. New sections include managing the customer interface, and managing the supplier interface. The section on e-purchasing is rewritten to include catalog hubs, exchanges, and auctions. Other important additions include postponement, channel assembly, and green purchasing (Chapter 11, Supply-Chain Management).

- **NEW! Process Management for Services.** Chapter 3, Process Management, has been given a major revision. The parts on service processes are strengthened with a new paradigm on how process choice relates with customization and volume. It now has more of a "how to" slant to revising processes, and there is more emphasis on flowcharting and simulation. Having a link to the SmartDraw Web site where students can download a trial version and Extend+ Manufacturing LT software on the Student CD-ROM adds a new dimension to process analysis.

- **NEW! Across the Organization.** Focusing on processes allows us to expand our coverage of cross-functional perspectives. Each chapter begins and ends with a discussion of how the chapter topic is important to professionals in a variety of disciplines. In every chapter, cross-functional connections link operations management to accounting, finance, human resources, marketing, and management information systems. (See pages 29 and 58.)

- **NEW! Early Coverage of Project Management.** Chapter 4, Managing Project Processes, has been moved to the front of the text for two reasons: It is a topic of interest to all students regardless of their functional area emphasis, and it allows for some problem solving early in the outline. It focuses on the management of project processes. Having Microsoft Project (120-day evaluation) software available on the Student CD-ROM allows students to gain experience with advanced commercial software for project management.

- **NEW! Resource Planning.** Chapter 15, Resource Planning, has been renamed and its scope broadened. There is a completely new section on resource planning for services, including resources such as financial assets, human resources, equipment and inventories.

- **NEW! Student CD-ROM.** This CD-ROM is packaged free with each new copy of the text. It contains OM Explorer, Extend+ Manufacturing LT software with simulation cases, Microsoft Project (120-day evaluation) software, a link to the SmartDraw Web site, CD-ROM Topics, CD-ROM tours of the Lower Florida Keys Hospital and Chaparral Steel, and a link to the MyPhlip Web site with additional student and faculty resources.

TUTOR

- **NEW! OM Explorer.** This complete decision-support software package is designed *specifically for this text*. It has the look and feel of an Excel worksheet environment, and works with Excel 2000 and Excel 97. There are two drop-down menus that are user friendly—one for Tutors and one for Solvers. The 66 *Tutors* provide coaching for all of the difficult analytical methods presented in the text. They extend self-testing opportunities beyond the printed page. The Tutor icon shown in the margin flags all Tutor applications in the textbook. The package also contains 40 powerful *Solvers,* general-purpose routines to solve problems often encountered in practice. Both Tutors and Solvers can be used extensively for the problems at the end of each chapter.

- **NEW! Microsoft Project (120-day evaluation) Software.** This package is quite popular in practice for managing projects. The package can be used to solve the problems and the case at the end of Chapter 4 in addition to any problems or cases the instructor may add.

- **NEW! Link to SmartDraw Web site.** Students can download a trial version of this software which allows them to draw complex process flow charts, organizational charts, and other diagrams and figures to support their analysis of problems in the text or provided by their instructor.

- **NEW! SimQuick.** This simulation software is Excel-based and easy-to-use, and the manual and program can be bundled with this text at a 50% discount. To order this package, use ISBN 0-13-072122-0.

- **NEW! Simulation Cases.** In-depth demonstrations of the simulation package Extend+ Manufacturing LT are integrated into three key chapters and one supplement. Additional challenging case problems are included at the end of nine chapters and two supplements, and are available on the Student CD-ROM. The students use the models to answer questions regarding the cases. These cases support our thrust in active learning. Extend + Manufacturing LT is a student version of the graphic simulation program Extend, and pre-existing models are provided on the Student CD-ROM. For instructors ordering SimQuick, an optional simulation package, eight case problems are provided.

- **NEW! OM Explorer and Internet Activities.** This element appears at the end of most chapters, directing students to the text's Web site, where interesting Internet activities, virtual plant tours, and Tutor exercises using OM Explorer can be found. The Internet has become a critical tool for success in business. Students can get online to build research skills and reinforce their understanding of operations management concepts. Future business graduates will use the Internet to find and share information in ways we cannot even imagine today. The Web site is designed to take advantage of Internet resources and provide a host of integrated Internet applications to show students the possibilities the World Wide Web offers for understanding operations management.

- **NEW! CD-ROM Topics.** Additional CD-ROM topics contains the following supplements: Learning Curve Analysis, Measuring Output Rates, Acceptance Sampling Plans, and Financial Analysis.

- **NEW! Screen Captures and Photos.** The sixth edition includes 46 screen captures demonstrating the use of OM Explorer, Microsoft Project, Extend, and SmartDraw. The text integrates these packages into the analysis of meaningful problems. There are also 80 photos which give the reader a better visual understanding of the different business examples.

- **NEW! Company URLs.** The URLs are now provided for all companies featured in the Opening Vignettes and Managerial Practices, allowing students to explore them more fully beyond what is said in the text.
- **NEW! Margin Items.** Three new margin items will be included in the sixth edition:
  1. *Definitions*—Short definitions of boldfaced terms are provided for easy reference.
  2. *Service icon*—This icon indicates coverage of a service application.
  3. *CD-ROM icons*—This icon will indicate where a software application can be used. The icons may indicate a Tutor alongside an example, or OM Explorer, SmartDraw, Extend, or Microsoft Project alongside a problem.
- **NEW! JIT Program.** The sixth edition can be obtained in the form of customized publishing the JIT program of Prentice Hall.
- **NEW! MyPHLIP Web site.** This content-rich, interactive Web site for students and professors includes: *In the News* articles with discussion questions, Internet exercises, Virtual Plant tours, an Interactive study guide (true/false, multiple choice, and essay questions) and more. In the faculty resource section instructors can download the Instructor's Resource Manual, Instructor's Solutions Manual, and answers to all the *In the News* articles and Internet exercises. The New MyPhlip Web site also allows instructor's to personalize their Web site with some additional content, personal notes and reminders, send messages to individual students or all students linked to their courses, check out links to articles in today's business news, and much more. Go to http://www.prenhall.com/krajewski.
- **NEW! WebCT, Blackboard, and CourseCompass.** Prentice Hall now makes its class-tested online course content available in WebCT, Blackboard, and CourseCompass. Instructors receive easy-to-use design templates, communication, testing, and course management tools. To learn more, contact your local Prentice Hall representation or go to http://www.prenhall.com/demo for a quick preview of our online solutions.

CONTEMPORARY COVERAGE

Following are highlights of the other key features of the text.

- **Interactive Teaching Approach.** Motivating students to learn and apply operations management concepts within the context of the firm is an important aspect of the learning process. The sixth edition of *Operations Management* offers a variety of creative teaching and learning tools that actively engage students and reinforce their understanding of operations management.
- **Experiential Learning Exercises.** There are three experiential learning exercises: Min-Yo Garment Company (Chapter 2), SPC with a Coin Catapult (Chapter 7), and Sonic Distributors (Chapter 11). Each of these experiences is an in-class simulation exercise that actively involves the students. Team-based discussion questions reinforce student learning. Each exercise has been thoroughly tested in class and proven to be a valuable learning tool.
- **Cases.** All chapters end with at least one case that can either serve as a basis for classroom discussion or provide an important capstone problem to the chapter, challenging students to grapple with the issues of the chapter in a less

structured and more comprehensive way. Many of the cases can be used as in-class exercises without prior student preparation.

- **Chapter Opening Vignettes.** Each chapter opens with an example of how a company actually dealt with the specific operations issues addressed in the chapter. (See page 92, for example.)

- **Questions from Managers.** In the margins are questions linked to the material being presented. These voices from the real world highlight key concepts and permit a quick review of concepts being presented. (See page 96, for example.)

- **The Big Picture.** Four, full-color, two-page spreads present the layouts of the Lower Florida Keys Hospital (pp. 52–53), Chaparral Steel (pp. 56–57), King Soopers Bakery (pp. 100–101), and the Coors Field baseball stadium (pp. 162–163) to reinforce concepts.

- **Managerial Practices.** Boxed inserts show operations management in action at various firms. Balanced between service and manufacturing organizations, these inserts present current examples of how companies—successfully or unsuccessfully—meet the operations challenges facing them. Almost all of the Managerial Practices have been replaced or refreshed to assure up-to-date coverage. (See page 94, for example.)

- **Examples.** Numerous Examples throughout the chapter are a very popular feature designed to help students understand the quantitative material. Whenever a new technique is presented, an Example is immediately provided to walk the student through the solution. Usually there is a companion computerized Tutor, indicated by an icon with the Tutor number, to afford another learning opportunity to try out the new technique. The sixth edition has added the feature of a "Decision Point" to conclude an Example, which focuses on the decision implications for managers (NEW!). (See page 122, for example.)

- **Solved Problems.** At the end of each chapter, detailed solutions demonstrate how to solve problems with the techniques presented in the chapter. These solved problems reinforce basic concepts and serve as models for students to refer to when doing the problems that follow. (See pages 129–131, for example.)

- **Text Web Site.** The Web site (http://www.prenhall.com/krajewski) is a great starting point for operations management resources and features a range of student and instructor resources.

ENHANCED INSTRUCTIONAL SUPPORT SYSTEM

- **Instructor's Solutions Manual.** Updated by the authors, so as to keep it current and eliminate any errors, the **Solutions Manual** provides complete solutions to all discussion questions, problems, and notes for each case and experiential exercise in the text. Selected computer screen captures are included to illustrate the different software capabilities available. Each case note includes a brief synopsis of the case, a description of the purposes for using the case, recommendations for analysis and goals for student learning from the case, and detailed teaching suggestions for assigning and discussing the case with students. Each element of the Solutions Manual was checked and rechecked, and then Professor Vijay Gupta reviewed it again to eliminate any lingering flaws. The Solutions Manual is intended for instructors who may in turn choose to share parts of it with students, possibly through WebCT. An electronic version of the entire manual, written is MS Word, is provided on the Instructor's Resource CD-ROM.

- **Instructor's Resource Manual.** The Instructor's Manual includes:
  - Sample course outlines.
  - A summary of the various ancillaries that accompany the text.
  - Annotated Lecture Notes for each chapter and supplement which summarizes, in outline form, the material of each chapter and supplement.
  - In-class exercises called "Applications."
  - Solutions to the in-class Applications are supplied as transparency masters (and available electronically on the Instructor's Resource CD-ROM).
  - Miniature reproductions of the PowerPoint slides available on the Instructor's Resource CD-ROM.

- **Instructor's Resource CD-ROM.** The Instructor's Resource CD-ROM provides the electronic files for the entire Solutions Manual (in MS Word), the Annotated Lecture Notes (in MS Word), in-class Applications (in MS Word), and solutions to the Applications (in PowerPoint). Providing these materials as MS Word and PowerPoint files (NEW!), rather than pdf files, allows the instructor to customize portions of the material and provide them to their students as appropriate. It also provides the **PowerPoint Lecture Presentation** that has been updated and enriched by Jeff Heyl of Lincoln University in New Zealand. *Test Manager,* the computerized test bank with its online testing component, is another important component on the CD-ROM.

- **Test Bank and Computerized Test Bank.** Professor Ross Fink of Bradley University Foster College of Business has made a major overhaul of the Test Bank. Containing nearly 2,000 items, the Test Bank includes a balance of conceptual and technique-oriented questions. Short-answer and essay questions are included in each chapter to test students' conceptual understanding of the material and critical-thinking skills. The Test Bank is available in Prentice Hall's test generating software, *Test Manager.* It allows the instructor to pick and choose questions, revising them as necessary, and create customized exams.

- **Video Package.** Designed *specifically for this text,* this video package contains the following videos: *TQM at Christchurch Parkroyal, Process Choice at the King Soopers Bakery, Queuing at First Bank Villa Italia, Inventory and Textbooks, Service Scheduling at Air New Zealand* (NEW!), *Project Management at Nantucket Nectars* (NEW!), *and Managing Information Technology at Prentice Hall* (NEW!). The videos provide pedagogical value in that they incorporate summary "bullet point" screens and interviews with managers regarding significant issues.

ACKNOWLEDGMENTS

We wish to thank various people at Prentice Hall who made up the publishing team. Those most closely involved with the project and for whom we hold the greatest admiration include Tom Tucker, Executive Editor, who supervised the overall project and was always ready to lend a helping hand as we made the transition from Addison Wesley Longman after the merger; Ron Librach, Development Editor, whose creative publishing insight of some key chapter revisions and ability to coordinate the convoluted flow of manuscript were much appreciated; Jennifer Surich, Assistant Editor, who coordinated several print ancillaries and videos; Nancy Welcher, Multimedia

Project Manager, who produced all Internet and CD-ROM materials; Cynthia Regan, Managing Editor, who managed to assemble an excellent product from a seemingly endless array of components; Pamela Rockwell, Copy Editor, who knows how to turn our prose into much better material; Diane Austin, Photo Researcher, who created a wealth of great photo options for the text; Beverly Amer, whose talents in creating two new videos augment the already impressive library that Jeff Heyl created earlier; and Debbie Clare, Senior Marketing Manager, whose promotional efforts make all the work of the publishing team worthwhile. We are especially appreciative of the work done by KMT Software Inc., particularly by Richard Cranford and Jim Kinlan, whose computer skills and perseverance won the day in creating the new *OM Explorer* software.

We also thank our colleagues who provided extremely useful guidance for the sixth edition. They include the following:

Xin (James) He
South Carolina State

Jeffrey L. Rummel
University of Connecticut

Ceasar Douglas
Grand Valley State University

Sarah McComb
University of Massachusetts, Amherst

W. Blaker Bolling
Marshall University

Muzaffar A. Shaikh
Florida Institute of Technology

Billy M. Thorton
Colorado State University

Girish Shambu
Canisius College

We are also indebted to Ross Fink at Bradley University Foster College of Business who did a masterful job on the Test Manager and the Interactive Study Guide, to Vijay Gupta for his outstanding work making sure that the Solutions Manual was fully accurate, and to Tom Wood at James Madison University who did great work on the *Instructor's Resource Manual*. Special thanks go to John Gallaugher of Boston College who gave us invaluable and extensive insight on e-commerce and the needed revisions to the Managing Technology. Kudos also go to Larry Miele of Boston College, who creatively pulled together the various materials that went into the *OM Explorer and Internet Activities* sections, and updated an experiential exercise and case. Brooke Saladin's cases continue to make it easy for instructors to add interest and excitement to their classes. We also are endebted to Robert Klassen, University of Western Ontario, for the models and cases using the Extend simulator, and to David Hartvigsen, University of Notre Dame, for the cases using *SimQuick* simulator and the original materials for the Software Previews. Two graduate students at Boston College also provided valued input. Maryann Symanowicz and Michelle Beretvas Mittlesteadt were marvelous in spotting errors in the *Solutions Manual* and OM Explorer software. Michelle had the particular skills and steadfastness to find just the right company examples to illustrate important concepts in an interesting and educational way, even when publication due dates were pressing.

We also gratefully acknowledge Cheryl Pauley, University of Notre Dame, for her expert help in typing and proofing manuscript, searching the Web, creating figures, and for being understanding when deadlines loomed. We also thank Sarv Devaraj and Jerry Wei for their suggestions and moral support during the project.

Finally, we thank out families for putting up with our days of seclusion even when the weather was nice. Our wives, Judie and Barb, have provided the love, stability, and encouragement that we needed while we were "with book" for our sixth time.

Lee J. Krajewski
University of Notre Dame

Larry P. Ritzman
Boston College

1

Operations as a Competitive Weapon

Across the Organization

Operations as a competitive weapon is important to . . .

- ☐ **accounting,** which prepares financial and cost accounting information that aids operations managers in designing and operating production systems.
- ☐ **finance,** which manages the cash flows and capital investment requirements that are created by the operations function.
- ☐ **human resources,** which hires and trains employees to match process needs, location decisions, and planned production levels.
- ☐ **management information systems,** which develops information systems and decision support systems for operations managers.
- ☐ **marketing,** which helps create the demand that operations must satisfy, link customer demand with staffing and production plans, and keep the operations function focused on satisfying customers' needs.
- ☐ **operations,** which designs and operates processes to give the firm a sustainable competitive advantage.

Learning Goals

After reading this chapter, you will be able to . . .

1. describe operations in terms of inputs, processes, outputs, information flows, suppliers and customers.
2. explain the meaning of nested processes.
3. identify the set of decisions that operations managers make.
4. describe operations as a function alongside finance, accounting, marketing, and human resources.
5. explain how operations management is fundamental to both manufacturers and service providers.
6. describe the differences and similarities between manufacturing and service organizations.
7. discuss trends in operations management, including service sector growth; productivity changes; global competition; and competition based on quality, time, and technology.
8. discuss the need for operations management to develop and maintain both intraorganizational and interorganizational relationships.
9. give examples of how operations can be used as a competitive weapon.

Two companies—one in manufacturing and the other in services—operate in the same industry and provide vivid examples of the role of operations management in different types of firms. The K2 Corporation (www.k2sports.com), named for the world's second-highest mountain, is a world-class manufacturer of ski equipment and uses operations management as a competitive weapon. The way that management handles new product introductions, manufacturing processes, job designs, capacities, inventory levels, and schedules is a key to how well it implements the company's overall strategies.

The K2 Corporation uses the latest technologies in its products and processes. Building on its recently developed shaped ski design, K2 introduced Smart Ski Technology in 1996. This technology, originally developed for jet aircraft by the defense industry, dampens ski vibration. The Triaxial braiding process, used in the manufacturing process, also improves ski performance. To support the company's competitive efforts, operations devotes some facilities to high-volume stock items and others to low-volume customized products. Consistent quality, an important part of K2's competitive plan, is the responsibility of each operator at each workstation; operators are trained to monitor critical quality measures. To handle product variety, K2 installed general-purpose machinery to allow easy changeovers from one product to another. Production and machine maintenance are managed carefully because the plant runs at full capacity. The company prepares for heavy seasonal sales with a production plan that calls for building finished goods inventories from January to May.

In the service sector, a skier begins her descent at a ski resort. The last decade has been good to Breckenridge, where then number of skier visits grew by more than 50 percent since the 1990–91 ski season to over 1.4 million visits in 1999–2000.

S The ski industry includes a competitive service sector, with numerous mountain resorts for both beginners and skilled athletes. Operations management also plays an important role in this segment of the ski market. Vail Resorts (www.vail.com), in Colorado, offers four full-service resorts with many skiable mountains. It also provides services such as ski lessons, snowmobiles, ice skating, child care, retail offerings, and a variety of restaurants and social events.

Vail Resorts' operations are carefully designed for each service. For example, lifts are designed for high-volume, low-cost operations. The more elegant restaurants are designed for low-volume, high-quality meals. Extensive off-season promotions help stabilize demand. Scheduled events must begin on time, and careful capacity planning keeps costs down and service quality high. The company recently invested $74 million to expand capacity and strengthen its long-term commitment to quality.

Each of its four resorts has created its own market. For example, Breckenridge's location next to a classic mining town attracts European skiers seeking a "Western" experience. Although the resorts operate independently on most dimensions, the group collaborates in the high-payoff areas of supplies procurement, integrated information systems, and interchangeable lift ticketing.

These two companies are making operations management a key weapon in gaining competitive advantage. So it is with many of the real company examples presented in this text.

A ski being manufactured using the patented Triaxial Braiding™ process at K2's manufacturing facility. This technology makes the ski from an interlocking braid of lightweight fibers woven tightly around the core at a precise 38 degrees angle. The end results is a strong, lightweight ski with optimum torsional stiffness, giving skiers greater turn response with less effort, while keeping a sensitive feel for the snow.

OPERATIONS MANAGEMENT DEALS WITH processes that produce goods and services that people use every day. *Processes* are the fundamental activities that organizations use to do work and achieve their goals. Manufacturers of skis, steel, and computers have processes throughout every phase of their businesses and every functional area. So do ski resorts, health care providers, banks, and retailers. Examples of processes include:

- ❏ the process at Vail Resorts to schedule its facilities and events,
- ❏ the Triaxial braiding process at K2 Corporation to manufacture skis,
- ❏ the inventory ordering process at a firm that designs and produces orthopedic braces,
- ❏ the on-line, order-fulfillment process at an e-commerce communications provider,
- ❏ the process at an organization's internal consulting department to select and prioritize new projects,
- ❏ the process at a company with several downtown facilities to transport employees from outlying parking areas,
- ❏ the application process at a business school to gather information and communicate with applicants,
- ❏ the sales-generating process at a manufacturer, beginning when a prospective client is identified and ending when the company is offered or declined the job,
- ❏ the purchase-ordering process at a public relations agency serving clients in high technology, e-business, and health care,
- ❏ the order-fulfillment process at an importer and distributor of merchandise to retail stores,
- ❏ the process at a nonprofit performing arts organization to schedule its function rooms and the process at a nonprofit organization that schedules transportation services for seniors and individuals with disabilities,
- ❏ the payment-dispute process at a large PC software company, which involves sales, customer order entry, and credit,
- ❏ the corporate real estate process at a large insurance and financial services firm to help customers renew an existing lease or negotiate a lease at a new site, and
- ❏ the patient care process used by a hospital's cardiac catheterization laboratory.

What processes have you been involved with?

Every organization, whether public or private, manufacturing or service, must manage processes and the operations where these processes are performed. Managing processes so as to add the most value for customers is the focus of this book. We explore with you the role of managing processes within the total organization. We explain what managers of processes do, the decisions they make, and some of the tools and concepts that they can use. By selecting appropriate techniques and strategies, managers can design and operate processes to give companies a competitive edge. Helping you understand how to make operations a competitive weapon begins with the last section of this chapter and continues throughout the book.

WHAT IS A PROCESS?

A **process** is any activity or group of activities that takes one or more inputs, transforms and adds value to them, and provides one or more outputs for its customers. The type of processes may vary. For example, at a factory a primary process would be a physical or chemical change of raw materials into products. But there also are many nonmanufacturing processes at a factory, such as order fulfillment, making due-date promises to customers, and inventory control. At an airline, a primary process would be the movement of passengers and their luggage from one location to another, but there are also processes for making reservations, checking in passengers, and scheduling crews.

As Figure 1.1 illustrates, processes have inputs and customer outputs. Inputs include human resources (workers and managers), capital (equipment and facilities), purchased materials and services, land, and energy. The numbered circles represent operations through which services, products, or customers pass and where processes are performed. The arrows represent flows and can cross because one job or customer can have different requirements (and thus a different flow pattern) than the next job or customer. Processes provide outputs—often services (which can take the form of information)—to their "customers." Both manufacturing and service organizations now realize that every process and every person in an organization has customers. Some are **external customers,** who may be either end users or intermediaries (such as manufacturers, wholesalers, or retailers) buying the firm's finished products and services. Others are **internal customers** who may be one or more other employees who rely on inputs from earlier processes in order to perform processes in the next office, shop, or department. Either way, processes must be managed with the customer in mind.

Inputs and outputs vary, depending on the service or product provided. For example, inputs at a jewelry store include merchandise, the store building, registers, the jeweler, and customers; outputs to external customers are services and sold merchandise. Inputs to a factory manufacturing blue jeans include denim, machines, the plant, workers, managers, and services provided by outside consultants; outputs are clothing and supporting services. The fundamental role of inputs, processes, and customer outputs holds true for processes at all organizations.

Figure 1.1 can represent a whole firm, a department or small group, or even a single individual. Each one has inputs and uses processes at various operations to provide outputs. The dashed lines represent two special types of input: participation by customers and information on performance from both internal and external sources. Participation by customers occurs not only when they receive outputs but also when they take an active part in the processes, such as when students participate in a class

process Any activity or group of activities that takes one or more inputs, transforms and adds value to them, and provides one or more outputs for its customers.

external customers A customer who is either an end user or an intermediary (such as manufacturers, wholesalers, or retailers) buying the firm's finished products and services.

internal customers One or more other employees who rely on inputs from earlier processes in order to perform processes in the next office, shop, or department.

FIGURE 1.1

Processes and Operations

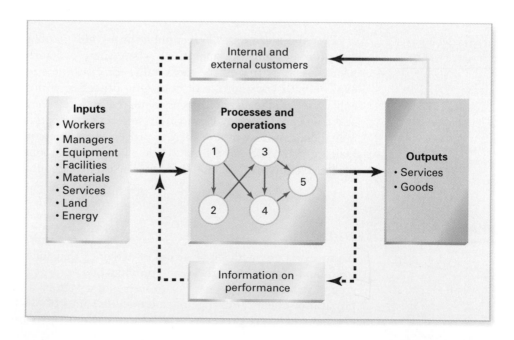

discussion. Information on performance includes internal reports on customer service or inventory levels and external information from market research, government reports, or telephone calls from suppliers. Managers need all types of information to manage processes most effectively.

NESTED PROCESSES. Processes can be broken down into subprocesses, which can in turn be broken down into still more subprocesses. We refer to this concept of a process within a process as a **"nested process."** One part of a process can be separated from another for several reasons. One person or one department may be unable to do all parts of the process, or different segments in the process may require different skills. Some parts of the process may be standardized for all customers, making high-volume operations possible. Other parts of the process may be customized, requiring processes best suited to flexible, low-volume operations.

nested process The concept of a process within a process.

As Figure 1.2 illustrates, a large bank has thousands of nested processes. *Retail* processes represent one of several parts of its business. The others include operations (such as cash management, loan operations, and trading operations), products (such as auto finance, cards, and mortgages), and wholesale (such as trading, loan administration, and leasing). In turn, there are four basic groupings of processes within retail processes—distribution, compliance, finance, and human resources. Distribution, for example, can be broken down into 15 nested processes, including processing teller line transactions, tracking and managing branch sales activity, and providing an ATM hotline. Processing teller line transactions then breaks down into 15 distinct processes, including processing deposits, cashing checks, and providing access to safe deposit boxes. Nested within processing deposits are still other steps. Nested processes sometimes are performed sequentially. Often they can be performed independently of each other, although all of the activities nested within a process must be performed to provide the full set of services.

FIGURE 1.2

Nested Processes at a Large Bank

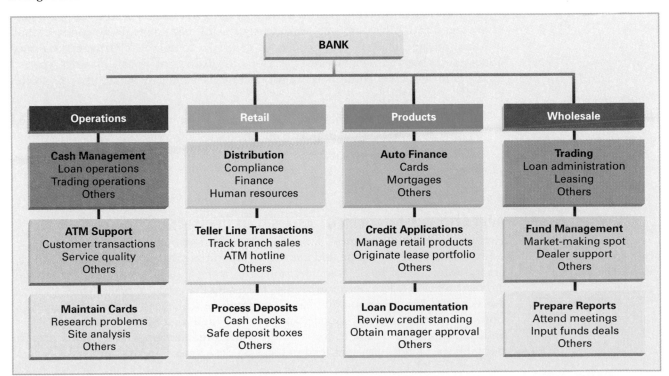

WHAT IS OPERATIONS MANAGEMENT?

operations management
The direction and control of the processes that transform inputs into products and services.

The term **operations management** refers to the direction and control of the processes that transform inputs into products and services. Broadly interpreted, operations management underlies all functional areas, because processes are found in all business activities. Narrowly interpreted, operations refers to a particular department (or more likely several departments). The operations area manages the processes that produce the primary services or products for the external customers but is closely involved with the other areas of a firm.

With either the broad or narrow view, managing operations is crucial to each area of an organization because only through successful management of people, capital, information, and materials can it meet its goals. As tomorrow's manager, you must understand the fundamentals of operations, regardless of your skill area, current major, or future career path. As you study operations management, keep two principles in mind:

1. Each part of an organization, not just the operations function, must design and operate processes and deal with quality, technology, and staffing issues.

2. Each part of an organization has its own identity and yet is connected with operations.

OPERATIONS MANAGEMENT AS A SET OF DECISIONS

What types of decisions are involved in managing operations?

Here, we preview the types of decisions that operations managers make. These decisions define both the scope and content of operations management (OM) and the organization of this book. Some decisions are strategic in nature; others are tactical. Strategic plans are developed further into the future than tactical plans. Thus, strategic decisions are less structured and have long-term consequences, whereas tactical decisions are more structured, routine, and repetitive and have short-term consequences. Strategic choices also tend to focus on the entire organization, cutting across departmental lines; tactical decisions tend to focus on departments, teams, and tasks.

TYPES OF OM DECISIONS

Decision making, both strategic and tactical, is an essential aspect of all management activity, including operations management. What sets operations managers apart, however, are the *types* of decisions that they make or participate in making. These types of decisions may be divided into five categories, each of which is a distinct part of this book. As we identify each category of decisions, we give the name of the chapter (in parentheses) in which we discuss it.

1. *Part 1: Strategic Choices.* We begin with the strategic decisions that affect a company's future direction. Operations managers help determine the company's global strategies and competitive priorities and how best to design processes that fit with its competitive priorities (*Operations Strategy*).

2. *Part 2: Process.* As Figure 1.1 illustrates, processes are fundamental to all activities that produce goods or services. For example, operations managers make process decisions about the types of work to be done in-house, the amount of automation to use, and methods of improving existing processes (*Process Management*); how to manage processes for one-time projects (*Managing Project Processes*); and the technologies to pursue and ways to provide leadership in technological change (*Managing Technology*).

3. *Part 3: Quality.* Quality issues underlie all processes and work activity. Operations managers help establish quality objectives and seek ways to improve the quality of the firm's products and services (*Total Quality Management*) and the use of inspection and statistical methods to monitor the quality produced by the various processes (*Statistical Process Control*).

4. *Part 4: Capacity, Location, and Layout.* The types of decisions in this category often require long-term commitments. Operations managers help determine the system's capacity (*Capacity*); the location of new facilities, including global operations (*Location*); and the organization of departments and a facility's physical layout (*Layout*).

5. *Part 5: Operating Decisions.* Operating decisions (sometimes called the *operations infrastructure*) deal with operating the facility after it has been built. At this stage, operations managers help coordinate the various parts of the internal and external supply chain (*Supply-Chain Management*), forecast demand (*Forecasting*), manage inventory (*Inventory Management*), and control output and staffing levels over time (*Aggregate Planning*). They also make decisions that synchronize internal processes with those of suppliers and that release new purchase or production orders (*Resource Planning*), whether to implement just-in-time techniques (*Lean Systems*), and which customers or jobs to give top priority (*Scheduling*).

THE ORIENTATION OF THE BOOK. To provide more in-depth coverage of techniques, we offer several supplements throughout the book (*Decision Making, Computer-Integrated Manufacturing, Waiting Line Models, Simulation, Special Inventory Models, Linear Programming,* and *Master Production Scheduling*). The first supplement provides a basic set of tools that assist in the decision-making process. The later supplements present and illustrate still more techniques. Many of the supplements apply to multiple chapters, not simply to the chapter that they follow. Even more supplements are accessible on the Student CD-ROM that came with your text (*Learning Curve Analysis, Measuring Output Rates, Acceptance Sampling Plans,* and *Financial Analysis*). The truth is that there is too much content in operations management to cover in one course. Thus, your instructor will assign some materials and not others. The sequencing of materials also depends on the orientation of your instructor and what topics have already been covered in your program. For example, we discuss long-range (or strategic) operations decisions first and then cover tactical decisions in later chapters. It may be more effective for your class to cover the tactical decisions first, perhaps after covering the first two chapters. We designed the book to be used flexibly, regardless of the orientation.

STRATEGIC AND TACTICAL THINKING. Although we discuss strategic decisions first, you should not underestimate the importance of tactical decisions. For example, scheduling, which requires detailed analysis and numerous interrelated decisions, can have a significant financial impact on a firm, with millions of dollars at stake in completing a power plant or a hotel on time.

Although the specifics of each situation vary, decision making generally involves the same basic steps: (1) recognize and clearly define the problem, (2) collect the information needed to analyze possible alternatives, and (3) choose the most attractive alternative and implement it. Managers must carefully link both strategic and tactical decisions for maximum effectiveness.

Linking Decisions. The operations manager's decisions should reflect corporate strategy (see the Operations Strategy chapter). In addition, plans, policies, and actions within operations should be linked and mutually supportive. For example, process, quality, capacity, and inventory decisions shouldn't be made independently. Even though individual choices may make sense on their own, collectively they might not achieve the best result.

Strategy and Analysis. A manager must deal with "big picture" issues as well as analytical issues. This book's subtitle, "Strategy *and* Analysis," emphasizes the point. A course in operations management isn't just about "concepts" or just about "numbers—it has both dimensions. Both strategy and analysis are necessary and should complement each other. Fortunately, operations managers have a variety of analytic techniques at their disposal. These techniques range from simple pencil-and-paper techniques to sophisticated computer techniques. The tutor and solver spreadsheets in OM Explorer, which are on the Student CD-ROM that was packaged with your text, help you learn and use these techniques.

OPERATIONS MANAGEMENT AS A FUNCTION

How does operations differ from other functions?

As a firm grows in size, different departments must be created that assume responsibility for certain clusters of processes. Often, these departments are organized around *functions* (sometimes called *functional areas*). Figure 1.3 shows that operations is one of several functions within an organization. Each function is specialized, having its own knowledge and skill areas, primary responsibilities, processes, and decision domains. Business school programs, for example, are traditionally organized around such functions, creating considerable knowledge bases and skills in various specialties. Regardless of how lines are drawn, departments and functions remain interrelated. Many processes are enterprisewide and cut across departmental boundaries. Thus, coordination and effective communication are essential to achieving organizational goals.

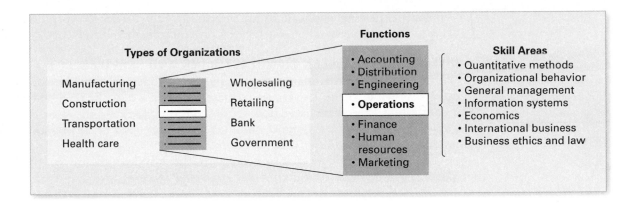

FIGURE 1.3

*Operations
Management as
a Function*

In large organizations, the *operations* (or *production) department* is usually responsible for the actual transformation of inputs into finished products or services. *Accounting* collects, summarizes, and interprets financial information. *Distribution* deals with the movement, storage, and handling of inputs and outputs. *Engineering* develops product and service designs and production methods. *Finance* secures and invests the company's capital assets. *Human resources* (or *personnel*) hires and trains employees. *Marketing* generates demand for the company's output.

Some organizations never need to perform certain functions. Other organizations may save money by contracting for a function, such as legal services or engineering, when they need it, rather than maintain an in-house department. In small businesses, the owners might manage one or more functions, such as marketing or operations.

As you can see from Figure 1.3, operations managers draw on many skill areas: quantitative analysis to solve problems; knowledge of information systems to manage vast quantities of data; concepts of organizational behavior to aid in designing jobs and managing the workforce; and an understanding of international business methods to gain useful ideas about facility location, technology, and inventory management.

Operations serves as an excellent career path to upper-management positions in many organizations. One survey of manufacturing firms showed over 45 percent of the chief executives appointed had operations background. In manufacturing firms, the head of operations usually holds the title vice-president of manufacturing (or production or operations). The corresponding title in a service organization might be vice-president (or director) of operations. Reporting to the vice-president are the managers of departments such as production and inventory control, industrial engineering, quality assurance, and plant supervision.

MANUFACTURING AND SERVICES: DIFFERENCES AND SIMILARITIES

 In the early history of operations management and until the middle of the twentieth century, the focus was on manufacturing organizations, and the field was thus called *industrial management* or *production management*. Service organizations, because they performed almost at handicraft levels, were largely ignored. Today's managers apply concepts of process analysis, quality, job design, capacity, facility location, layout, inventory, and scheduling to both manufacturing and the provision of services.

The benefits of these applications are improved quality, reduced costs, and increased value to the customers, all of which give a firm a competitive edge.

DIFFERENCES BETWEEN MANUFACTURING AND SERVICES

How do service operations differ from manufacturing operations?

The differences between manufacturing and service operations fall into the eight categories shown in Figure 1.4. However, these distinctions actually represent the ends of a continuum. The first distinction arises from the physical nature of the product. Manufactured goods are *physical, durable* products. Services are *intangible, perishable* products, often being ideas, concepts, or information.

The second distinction also relates to the physical nature of the product. Manufactured goods are outputs that can be produced, stored, and transported in anticipation of future demand. Creating *inventories* allows managers to cope with fluctuations in demand by smoothing output levels. By contrast, services can't be preproduced. Service operations don't have the luxury of using finished goods inventories as a cushion against erratic customer demand.

A third distinction is *customer contact*. Most customers for manufactured products have little or no contact with the production system. Primary customer contact is left to distributors and retailers. However, in many service organizations the customers themselves are inputs and active participants in the process. At a college, for example, the student studies, attends lectures, takes exams, and finally receives a diploma. Hospitals and entertainment centers are other places where the customer is present during the provision of most of the services. Some service operations have low customer contact at one level of the organization and high customer contact at other levels. For example, the branch offices of parcel delivery, banking, and insurance organizations deal with customers daily, but their central offices have little direct customer contact. Similarly, the backroom operations of a jewelry store require little customer contact, whereas sales-counter operations involve a high degree of contact.

A related distinction is *response time* to customer demand. While manufacturers generally have days or weeks to meet customer demand, many services must be offered within minutes of customer arrival. The purchaser of a forklift truck may be willing to wait 16 weeks for delivery. By contrast, a grocery store customer may grow impatient after waiting five minutes in a checkout line. Because customers for services usually

FIGURE 1.4

Continuum of Characteristics of Manufacturing and Service Operations

More like a manufacturing organization ← → More like a service organization

More like a manufacturing organization	More like a service organization
• Physical, durable product	• Intangible, perishable product
• Output that can be inventoried	• Output that cannot be inventoried
• Low customer contact	• High customer contact
• Long response time	• Short response time
• Regional, national, or international markets	• Local markets
• Large facilities	• Small facilities
• Capital intensive	• Labor intensive
• Quality easily measured	• Quality not easily measured

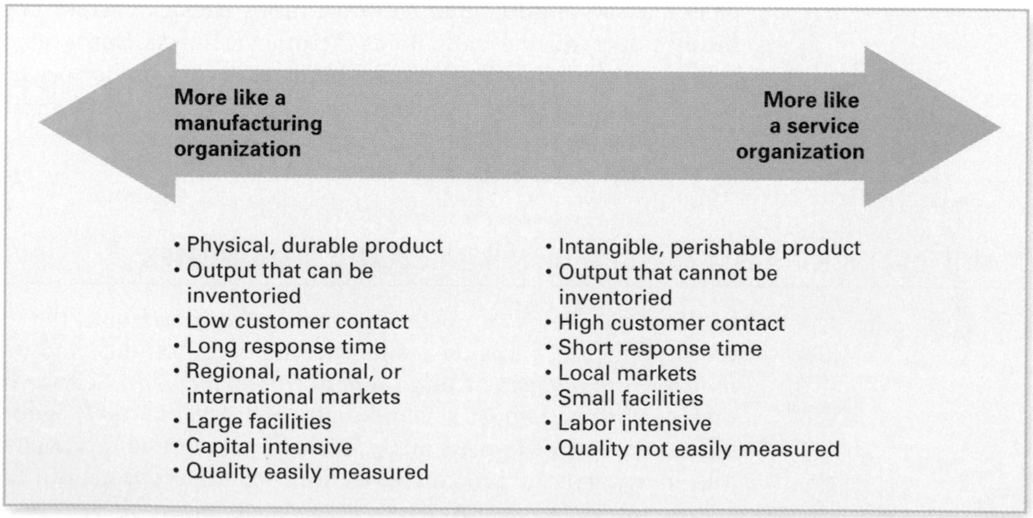

arrive at times of their choosing, service operations may have difficulty matching capacity with demand. Furthermore, arrival patterns may fluctuate daily or even hourly, creating even more short-term demand uncertainty.

Two other distinctions concern the *location* and *size* of an operation. Manufacturing facilities often serve regional, national, or even international markets and therefore generally require larger facilities, more automation, and greater capital investment. In general, services cannot be shipped to distant locations. For example, a hairstylist in Manhattan cannot give a haircut to someone in Topeka. Thus, service organizations requiring direct customer contact must locate relatively near their customers.

A final distinction is the measurement of *quality*. As manufacturing systems tend to have tangible products and less customer contact, quality is relatively easy to measure. The quality of service systems, which generally produce intangibles, is harder to measure. Moreover, individual preferences affect assessments of service quality, making objective measurement difficult. For example, one customer might value a friendly chat with the salesclerk during a purchase, whereas another might assess quality by the speed and efficiency of a transaction.

SIMILARITIES BETWEEN MANUFACTURING AND SERVICES

espite these distinctions, the similarities between manufacturing and service operations are compelling. Every organization has processes that must be designed and managed effectively. Some type of technology, be it manual or computerized, must be used in each process. Every organization is concerned about quality, productivity, and the timely response to customers. A service provider, like a manufacturer, must make choices about the capacity, location, and layout of its facilities. Every organization deals with suppliers of outside services and materials, as well as scheduling problems. Matching staffing levels and capacities with forecasted demands is a universal problem. Finally, the distinctions between manufacturing and service operations can get cloudy. Consider how the first three distinctions in Figure 1.4 can get blurred.

❑ Manufacturers do not just offer products, and service organizations do not just offer services. Both types of organizations normally provide a package of goods and services. Customers expect both good service and good food at a restaurant and both good service and quality goods from a retailer. Manufacturing firms offer many customer services, and a decreasing proportion of the value added by them directly involves the transformation of materials.

❑ Despite the fact that service providers cannot inventory their outputs, they must inventory the *inputs* for their products. These inputs must undergo further transformations during provision of the service. Hospitals, for example, must maintain an adequate supply of medications. As a result, wholesale and retail firms hold 48 percent of the U.S. economy's inventory. In addition, manufacturing firms that make customized products or limited-shelf-life products cannot inventory their outputs.

❑ As for customer contact, many service operations have little outside customer contact, such as the backroom operations of a bank or the baggage handling area at an airport. However, everyone in an organization has some customers—outside customers or inside customers—whether in services or in manufacturing.

Clearly, operations management is relevant to both manufacturing and service operations. You need to know about operations management, regardless of the type of organization you work in or the function that most interests you.

MANAGERIAL PRACTICE 1.1
Manufacturers Do Not Just Offer Products

Despite the high marks that U.S. manufacturers achieved in productivity increases during the 1990s and despite thriving economic expansion, the growth in sales for many manufacturing sectors has stagnated. For example, the annual growth in sales of industrial machinery dropped from 5.2 percent in the 1960s to 2 percent in the 1990s. Thanks to past purchases and longer product life spans, the installed base of products has been expanding over the years. Today, the number of U.S. autos in service is 200 million, while new sales have been flat at 15 million vehicles a year. This pattern is repeated across many manufacturing sectors. Revenues from downstream service-based activities now represent 10 to 30 times the annual dollar volume of underlying product sales. In corporate computing, the average company puts 20 percent of its annual personal-computer budget into purchasing the equipment itself; the rest goes to technical support, administration, and other maintenance activities. New distribution channels, such as the Internet, have also emerged to threaten manufacturers. Dozens of companies like Amazon.com, Autobytel.com, and eBay are becoming electronic intermediaries with powerful advantages, putting new pressure on manufacturers and traditional channels.

The upshot is that smart manufacturers are getting increasingly involved with downstream services. Product sales are seen as a way to open the door to providing future services. Four basic models for moving downstream are proving successful for some companies. Honeywell (www.honeywell.com), using the *embedded services* model, builds traditional services into its product with new digital technologies. Its Airplane Information Management System (AIMS) ties airplane systems together with a microprocessor and software. AIMS performs a variety of tasks that used to be performed manually by Honeywell's customers, reducing the need for expensive flight engineers and allowing Honeywell to charge a premium for its products. GE (www.ge.com) uses the *comprehensive services* model. In the locomotive market, for example, it provides financing, supplies parts, provides boxcar-scheduling and routing services and helps manage maintenance facilities. The Finnish company Nokia (www.nokia.com/

Autobytel.com offers a wide variety of services to customers. Visitors to its web site can buy or sell cars, obtain insurance, finance a car loan, or get useful shopping information.

main.html) uses the *integrated services* model, which combines products and services into a seamless customer offering. It seeks to address all of the equipment and service needs of its customers—cellular carriers. Its products include handsets, transmission equipment, and switches for the carriers. Its services include managing customer networks, meeting zoning requirements for new transmission towers, and providing technical support. The fourth approach is the *distribution control* model. Coca-Cola (www.coke.com/gateway.html) is a good example. It has gained control over lucrative distribution activities. Today, it controls 70 percent of its U.S. bottling and distribution, and it is expanding its control overseas.

Such models blur the line between manufacturers and service providers, because these manufacturers do not just offer products.

Source: Wise, Richard and Peter Baumgartner. "Go Downstream: The New Profit Imperative in Manufacturing," *Harvard Business Review* (September–October 1999), pp. 133–141.

TRENDS IN OPERATIONS MANAGEMENT

Several business trends are currently having a great impact on operations management: the growth of the service sector; productivity changes; global competitiveness; quality, time, and technological change; and environmental, ethical, and diversity issues. In this section, we look at these trends and their implications for operations managers.

FIGURE 1.5

Percentage of Jobs in the U.S. Service Sector

Source: Economic Report of the President, 2000.

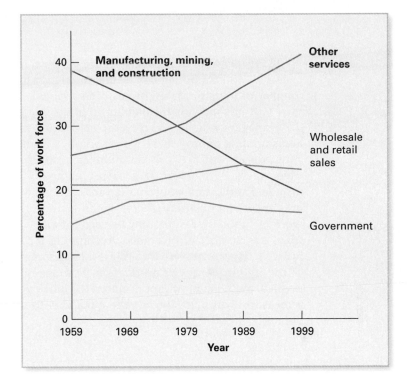

SERVICE SECTOR GROWTH

What are the implications of recent employment and productivity trends in the service sector?

The service sector of the economy is significant. As Figure 1.5 shows, services may be divided into three main groups:

1. government (local, state, and federal);
2. wholesale and retail sales; and
3. other services (transportation, public utilities, communication, health, financial services, real estate, insurance, repair services, business services, and personal service).

Between 1955 and 1999, the number of U.S. jobs in service-producing industries rose from 60 to 80 percent of total nonfarm jobs. Manufacturing and other goods-producing industries currently account for the remaining 20 percent. Thus, although the absolute number of manufacturing jobs has increased (from 20.5 to 25.2 million), the percent of manufacturing jobs in the total economy has declined. Similar increases in the percent of the workforce in service jobs are taking place in the other industrial countries. For example, the share of the workforce in service jobs is well above 60 percent in Britain, Canada, France, and Japan.

Nonetheless, manufacturing remains a significant part of the U.S. economy. Moreover, the service and manufacturing sectors of the economy are complementary. For example, the output of many firms is purchased by other firms as inputs. More than 25 percent of these intermediate outputs, such as express mail and consulting services, are classified as services while going to companies in the nonservice sector.

productivity The value of outputs (goods and services) produced divided by the values of input resources (wages, costs of equipment, and the like).

PRODUCTIVITY CHANGES

Productivity is the value of outputs (goods and services) produced divided by the values of input resources (wages, cost of equipment, and the like) used:

$$\text{Productivity} = \frac{\text{Output}}{\text{Input}}$$

Many measures of productivity are possible, and all are rough approximations. For example, value of output can be measured by what the customer pays or simply by the number of units produced or customers served. The value of inputs can be judged by their cost or simply by the number of hours worked.

Managers usually pick several reasonable measures and monitor trends to spot areas needing improvement. For example, a manager at an insurance firm might measure office productivity as the number of insurance policies processed per employee each week. A manager at a carpet company might measure the productivity of installers as the number of square yards of carpet installed per hour. Both of these measures reflect *labor productivity*, which is an index of the output per person or hour worked. Similar measures may be used for *machine productivity*, where the denominator is the number of machines. Accounting for several inputs simultaneously is also possible. *Multifactor productivity* is an index of the output provided by more than one of the resources used in production. For example, it may be the value of the output divided by the sum of labor, materials, and overhead costs. When developing such a measure, you must convert the quantities to a common unit of measure, typically dollars.

| EXAMPLE 1.1 | *Productivity Calculations* |

**TUTOR
1.1**

Calculate the productivity for the following operations:

   a. Three employees process 600 insurance policies in a week. They work 8 hours per day, 5 days per week.

   b. A team of workers make 400 units of a product, which is valued by its standard cost of $10 each (before markups for other expenses and profit). The accounting department reports that for this job the actual costs are $400 for labor, $1,000 for materials, and $300 for overhead.

SOLUTION

a. Labor productivity $= \dfrac{\text{Policies processed}}{\text{Employee hours}}$

$$= \frac{600 \text{ policies}}{(3 \text{ employees})(40 \text{ hours/employee})} = 5 \text{ policies/hour}$$

b. Multifactor productivity $= \dfrac{\text{Quantity at standard cost}}{\text{Labor cost} + \text{Materials cost} + \text{Overhead cost}}$

$$= \frac{(400 \text{ units})(\$10/\text{unit})}{\$400 + \$1,000 + \$300} = \frac{\$4,000}{\$1,700} = 2.35$$

Decision Point These measures must be compared with both performance levels in prior periods and with future goals. If they are not living up to expectations, the process should be investigated for improvement opportunities. ❑

The way processes are managed plays a key role in productivity improvement. The challenge is to increase the value of output relative to the cost of input. If processes can generate more output or output of better quality using the same amount of input, productivity increases. If they can maintain the same level of output while reducing the use of resources, productivity also increases.

USE MULTIPLE MEASURES. Although labor and multifactor productivity measures can be informative, they also can be deceptive when applied to the firm or process levels. For example, a firm can decide to transfer some of its work to outside suppliers and lay off some of its own workforce. Labor productivity will increase considerably, because the value of the firm's total sales (the numerator) remains unchanged while the number of employees (the denominator) drops. In this case, the multifactor productivity measure would be more informative than labor productivity, because the increased cost of purchased materials and services would appear in the denominator of the ratio. Both

FIGURE 1.6a

Using Tutors in OM Explorer
The icon next to Example 1.1 means that there is a *tutor* spreadsheet in OM Explorer, software that was packaged on the Student CD-ROM that came with your text. Open up the Tutor menu for Chapter 1 and select *Tutor 1.1: Productivity.* You will be presented with three worksheets for this Tutor. The Introduction describes an entirely new example. The Inputs requires you to enter your inputs and answers in the areas shaded in yellow, and the Results gives the correct answers in the areas shaded in green. There are 66 such tutors throughout the book. Most of them are for more complex techniques than demonstrated here. Use them when you are not sure about an example, when you want to test your understanding, or when you want to do some "what-if" analysis on a different problem.

Introduction

OM Explorer

Tutor 1.1 - Productivity Measures

The state ferry service charges $18 per ticket, plus a $3 surcharge to fund planned equipment upgrades. It expects to sell 4,700 tickets during the eight-week summer season. During that period, the ferry service will experience $110,000 in labor costs. Materials required for each passage sold (tickets, a tourist-information sheet, and the like) cost $1.30. Overhead during the period comes to $79,000.

a. What is the *multifactor* productivity ratio?
b. If ferry-support staff work an average of 310 person-hours per week for the 8 weeks of the summer season, what is the *labor* productivity ratio? Calculate labor productivity here on an hourly basis.

Click here to continue.

FIGURE 1.6b   Inputs

Tutor 1.1 - Productivity Measures

Enter data in yellow-shaded areas.

a. Multifactor productivity is the ratio of the value of output to the value of input.

Step 1. Enter the number of tickets sold during a season, the price per ticket, and the surcharge per ticket. To compute value of output, multiply tickets sold by the sum of price and surcharge.

Tickets sold: Value of output:
Price:
Surcharge:

Step 2. Enter labor costs, materials costs per passenger, and overhead cost. For value of input, add labor costs, materials costs times number of passengers, and overhead costs.

Labor costs: Materials costs: Overhead:

                          Value of input:

Step 3. To calculate multifactor productivity, divide value of output by value of input.

                    Multifactor productivity:

b. Labor productivity is the ratio of the value of output to labor hours. The value of output is computed in part a, step 1.

Step 1. Enter person-hours per week and the number of weeks in the season; multiply the two together to calculate labor hours of input.

Hours per week: Weeks:

                          Labor hours of input:

Step 2. To calculate labor productivity, divide value of output by labor hours of input.

                          Labor productivity:

Click here to view the Results sheet.

FIGURE 1.6c

Results

Tutor 1.1 - Productivity Measures

a. Multifactor productivity is the ratio of the value of output to the value of input.

Step 1. Enter the number of tickets sold during a season, the price per ticket, and the surcharge per ticket. To compute value of output, multiply tickets sold by the sum of price and surcharge.

Tickets sold:	4,700	Value of output:	$98,700
Price:	$18		
Surcharge:	$3		

Step 2. Enter labor costs, materials costs per passenger, and overhead cost. For value of input, add labor costs, materials costs times number of passengers, and overhead costs.

Labor costs:	$110,000	Materials costs:	$1.30	Overhead:	$79,000
				Value of input:	$195,110

Step 3. To calculate multifactor productivity, divide value of output by value of input.

Multifactor productivity: 0.51

b. Labor productivity is the ratio of the value of output to labor hours. The value of output is computed in part a, step 1.

Step 1. Enter person-hours per week and the number of weeks in the season; multiply the two together to calculate labor hours of input.

Hours per week:	310	Weeks:	8	
			Labor hours of input:	2,480

Step 2. To calculate labor productivity, divide value of output by labor hours of input.

Labor productivity: $39.80

---

productivity measures are often insufficient, however, when tracking performance at the department and individual process level. Customers of many processes are internal customers, making it difficult to assign a dollar value to the value of process output. Just as important, managers must monitor performance measures on quality, inventory levels, capacity utilization, on-time delivery, employee satisfaction, customer satisfaction, and the like. The smart manager monitors *multiple* measures of performance, setting goals for the future and seeking better ways to design and operate processes.

PRODUCTIVITY AND STANDARD OF LIVING. Improving processes pays off because it links directly to the rewards for individuals, work teams, and even a country's whole economy. At the national level, productivity typically is measured as the *dollar value of output per unit of labor*. This measure depends on the quality of the products and services generated in a nation and on the efficiency with which they are produced. Productivity is the prime determinant of a nation's standard of living. If the value of output per work hour goes up, the nation benefits from higher overall income levels, because the productivity of human resources determines employee wages. Conversely, lagging or declining productivity lowers the standard of living. Wage or price increases not accompanied by productivity increases lead to inflationary pressures rather than real increases in the standard of living.

Figure 1.7 is a report card on U.S. and worldwide productivity growth. The 1990s was an encouraging decade for U.S. productivity after a downward trend over the two prior decades. (The graph reflects manufacturing and services combined but excludes farms, which represent less than 5 percent of U.S. output and employment.) Productivity is measured as the dollar value of output per hour worked, and percent changes are shown. As you can see, the annual productivity increase during the 1950s averaged 2.8 percent, but dropped below 2 by the 1980s and 1990.

Is productivity increasing faster in manufacturing or in services?

It is interesting and even surprising to break out productivity improvements between the manufacturing and services sectors. Although employment in the U.S. service sector has grown rapidly, productivity gains have been much lower. The sector's lagging productivity slows overall growth. Major trading partners such as Japan and Germany have experienced the same problem. There are signs of improvement. The surge of investment across national boundaries can stimulate productivity gains by exposing service firms to greater competition and providing the motivation to increase productivity. Perhaps the investment in information technology also will begin to pay off for service providers, as workers and managers begin to use new technologies for competitive advantage. However, productivity improvement is a particular concern in services. If productivity growth stagnates, so does the overall standard of living.

Productivity gains expressed as a percent, as shown in Figure 1.7(a), don't tell the whole story. The original base from which the percentages are calculated must also be considered. For example, although U.S. productivity gains since the 1970s have been smaller than in earlier periods. U.S. workers are still more productive than their counterparts in other developed economies. Figure 1.7(b) shows that the average value added per hour worked in the United States is well above the productivity achieved elsewhere (in the whole economy and particularly in manufacturing). Even in manufacturing, Japanese productivity is 20 percent less than that in the United States. However, the differences between the United States and these countries is smaller now than several decades ago, as global competition increases.

GLOBAL COMPETITION

Today, businesses accept the fact that, to prosper, they must view customers, suppliers, facility locations, and competitors in global terms. Most products today are global composites of materials and services from throughout the world. Your Gap polo shirt is sewn in Honduras from cloth cut in the United States. Sitting in the theater, you

FIGURE 1.7

U.S. and Worldwide Productivity Growth

Sources: Major Sector Productivity and Costs Index (Series ID: PRS85006092), Bureau of Labor Statistics, (May 2, 2000). "International Comparisons Data," *Monthly Labor Review* (June 1993).

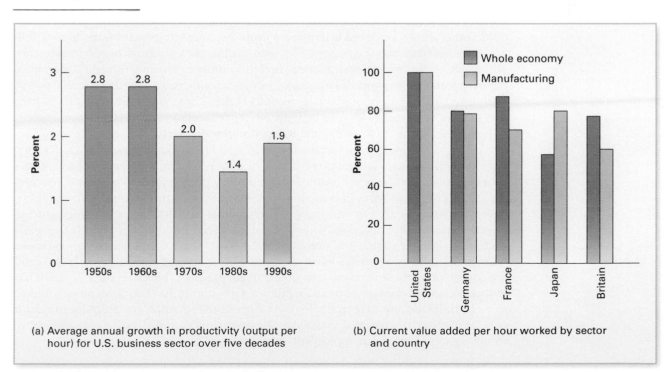

(a) Average annual growth in productivity (output per hour) for U.S. business sector over five decades

(b) Current value added per hour worked by sector and country

munch a Nestlé's Crunch bar (Swiss) while watching a Columbia Pictures movie (Japanese) at a Cineplex theater (Canadian).

Strong global competition affects industries everywhere. For example, U.S. manufacturers have experienced declining shares of the domestic and international markets in steel, appliances and household durable goods, machinery, and chemicals. Even so, in globally competitive manufacturing industries, the United States attracts 37 percent of sales, Japan 32 percent, and Europe 31 percent. In fact, the United States garners 48 percent of corporate profits in these industries, particularly in energy equipment, aerospace, data processing and software, electronic components, beverages and tobacco, and health and personal care products.

With the value of world trade in services now at more than $1.5 trillion per year, banking, law, data processing, airlines, and consulting services operations are beginning to face many of the same international pressures as U.S. manufacturers. And regional trading blocks such as the European Union (EU) and North American Free Trade Agreement (NAFTA) further change the competitive landscape in both services and manufacturing.

COMPETITION BASED ON QUALITY, TIME, AND TECHNOLOGY

What can be done to compete better in terms of quality, time, and technology?

Another trend in managing processes has been an increasing emphasis on competing on the basis of quality, time, and technological advantage. Part of the success of foreign competitors has been their ability to provide products and services of high quality at reasonable prices. During the 1970s and 1980s, customers grew more attuned to the *quality* of the good or service being purchased. Without quality products or services, a firm loses its ability to compete in the marketplace, and its cost structure can also become uncompetitive (because of scrap, rework, and warranty costs). Operations managers, in conjunction with the managers of other functional departments, are giving more attention to quality than ever. Total quality management is a way of involving everyone in the organization in continuously improving quality (see the Total Quality Management chapter). Statistical process control is a set of useful statistical tools for monitoring quality performance (see the Statistical Process Control chapter).

Another important trend is that more firms are competing on the basis of *time*: filling orders earlier than the competition, introducing new products or services quickly, and reaching the market first. Honda used this ability to thwart Yamaha's attempt to replace Honda as the world's largest motorcycle manufacturer. Honda's strategy was to introduce a wide variety of products so quickly that Yamaha would be unable to keep up. Within 18 months, Honda introduced or replaced 113 models of motorcycles. Yamaha was unable to keep up, and its sales all but dried up.

Another increasingly important factor in operations management is accelerating *technological change*. It affects the design of new products and services and a firm's processes themselves (see the Managing Technology chapter). Many new opportunities are coming from advances in computer technology. Robots and various forms of information technology are but two examples. E-commerce is dramatically changing many sales and purchasing processes. U.S. firms alone spend hundreds of billions of dollars each year on information technology. The *Internet*—part of the telecommunications "information highway"—has emerged as a vital tool linking firms internally and linking firms externally with customers and strategic partners. This computer network has global e-mail and data exchange capabilities, with almost 200 countries already linked to it. Introducing any new technology involves risk, and employee attitudes toward it depend on how the change is managed. The right choices and effective management of technology can give a firm a competitive advantage.

ETHICAL, WORKFORCE DIVERSITY, AND ENVIRONMENTAL ISSUES

How do ethics and the environment affect operations?

Businesses face more ethical quandaries than ever before, intensified by an increasing global presence and rapid technological change. Companies are locating new operations, and have more suppliers and customers, in other countries. Potential ethical dilemmas arise when business can be conducted by different rules. Some countries are more sensitive than others about lavish entertainment, conflicts of interest, bribery, discrimination against minorities and women, poverty, minimum-wage levels, unsafe workplaces, and workers' rights. Managers must decide in such cases whether or not to design and operate processes that do more than just meet local standards that are lower than those back home. In addition, technological change brings debates about data protection and customer privacy, such as on the Internet. In an electronic world, businesses are geographically far from their customers, and a reputation of trust may become even more important.

Recognizing such issues, studies culminating in the Porter-McKibbin Report and the Graduate Management Admission Council Report have encouraged both U.S. and European business schools to train managers versed in basic concerns about ethics, workforce diversity, and the environment. Such reports decried the fact that too many business students, both undergraduates and graduates, are unprepared to face the difficult "soft" issues in the fast-changing global marketplace.

One expert suggests a more ethical approach to business in which firms

❐ have responsibilities that go beyond producing goods and services at a profit,

❐ help solve important social problems,

❐ respond to a broader constituency than shareholders alone,

❐ have impacts beyond simple marketplace transactions, and

❐ serve a range of human values that go beyond the merely economic.

Environmental issues, such as toxic wastes, poisoned drinking water, poverty, air quality, and global warming are getting more emphasis. In the past, many people viewed environmental problems as quality-of-life issues; in the 2000s, many people see them as survival issues. Interest in a clean, healthy environment is increasing. Industrial

Leading companies have found that workforce diversity can provide a forum for unique perspectives and solutions.

nations have a particular burden because their combined populations, representing only 25 percent of the total global population, consume 70 percent of all resources. Just seven nations, including the United States and Japan, produce almost half of all greenhouse gases. The United States and some European nations now spend 2 percent of their gross domestic products on environmental protection, a level that environmentalists believe should be increased.

The message is clear: consideration of ethics, workforce diversity, and the environment are becoming part of every manager's job. When designing and operating processes, they should consider integrity, respect for the individual, and respecting the customer along with more conventional performance measures such as productivity, quality, cost, and profit.

OPERATIONS MANAGEMENT ACROSS THE ORGANIZATION

We have described operations management as designing and operating processes in both manufacturing and services, as a set of decisions, and as one of several functional areas within an organization. In this final section, we describe operations management as an interfunctional imperative and a competitive weapon for organizations.

OPERATIONS MANAGEMENT AS AN INTERFUNCTIONAL IMPERATIVE

Operations managers need to build and maintain solid relationships both interorganizationally and intraorganizationally. We discuss interorganizational relationships, such as those with suppliers, later in the book (see the Supply-Chain Management chapter). Here, our focus is on intraorganizational relationships, which call for cross-functional coordination.

Too often managers allow artificial barriers to be erected between functional areas and departments. In these situations, jobs or tasks move sequentially from marketing to engineering to operations. The result is often slow or poor decision making because each department bases its decisions solely on its own limited perspective, not the organization's overall perspective. A new approach being tried by many organizations is to replace sequential decision making with more cross-functional coordination and flatter organizational structures. For example, Hallmark Cards formed cross-functional teams and cut its product development time by 50 percent.

CROSS-FUNCTIONAL COORDINATION. Cross-functional coordination is essential to effective operations management. For example, consider how other functional areas interact with operations. Perhaps the strongest connection is with the marketing function, which determines the need for new products and services and the demand for existing ones. Operations managers must bring together human and capital resources to handle demand effectively. The operations manager must consider facility locations and relocations to serve new markets, and the design of layouts for service organizations must match the image that marketing seeks to convey to the customer. Marketing and sales make delivery promises to customers, which must be related to current operations capabilities. Marketing demand forecasts guide the operations manager in planning output rates and capacities.

The operations manager also needs feedback from the accounting function to understand current performance. Financial measures help the operations manager assess labor costs, the long-term benefits of new technologies, and quality improvements. Accounting can help the operations manager monitor the production system's vital signs by developing multiple tracking methods. The operations manager can then identify problems and prescribe remedies. Accounting also has an impact on the operations function because of the order-fulfillment cycle, which begins when the customer places an order and is completed when operations hands it off to accounting for billing.

In securing and investing the company's capital assets, finance influences operations' decisions about investments in new technology, layout redesign, capacity expansion, and even inventory levels. Similarly, human resources interacts with operations to hire and train workers and aids in changeovers related to new process and job designs. Human resources can help make promotions and transfers into and out of operations easier, thereby encouraging cross-functional understanding. Engineering can also have a big impact on operations. In designing new products, engineering needs to consider technical trade-offs. It must ensure that product designs do not create costly specifications or exceed operations capabilities.

ACHIEVING CROSS-FUNCTIONAL COORDINATION. Several approaches may be used to achieve cross-functional coordination. Each organization should select some blend of them to get everyone pulling in the same direction.

How can coordination be achieved with other functional areas?

❏ A unified strategy should be developed by management as a starting point, giving each department a vision of what it must do to help fulfill the overall organizational strategy.

❏ The organizational structure and management hierarchy can be redesigned to promote cross-functional coordination. Drawing departmental lines around areas of specialization may work against integration by creating insular views and "turf battles." Another option is to organize around major product lines or processes.

❏ The goal-setting process and reward systems can encourage cross-functional coordination. So can bringing people together from different functional areas—through task forces or committees—to make decisions and solve problems.

❏ Improvements to information systems also can boost coordination. Information must in part be tailored to the needs of each functional manager. However, sharing information helps harmonize the efforts of managers from different parts of the organization and enables them to make decisions consistent with organizational goals.

❏ Informal social systems are another device that can be used to encourage better understanding across functional lines. Joint cafeteria facilities, exercise rooms, and social events can help build a sense of camaraderie, as can corporate training and development programs.

❏ Employee selection and promotion also can help foster more cross-functional coordination by encouraging broad perspectives and common goals. Of course, employees must first be competent in their own skill areas.

The best mix of approaches depends on the organization. Some organizations need more coordination than others. The need is greatest when functions are dispersed (owing to organizational structure or geographical distance), organizations are large, and many products or services are customized. The need is also crucial in service organizations that have high customer contact and provide services directly to the customer.

OPERATIONS MANAGEMENT AS A COMPETITIVE WEAPON

In the global era, business and government leaders are increasingly recognizing the importance of involving the whole organization in making strategic decisions. Because the organization usually commits the bulk of its human and financial assets to operations, operations is an important function in meeting global competition. More than 30 years ago, Wickham Skinner suggested that operations could be either a competitive weapon or a millstone (see Skinner, 1969). He concluded that, all too often, operations policies covering inventory levels, schedules, and capacity reflect incorrect assumptions about corporate strategy and may work against a firm's strategic goals. This lack of understanding can waste a firm's resources for years.

Largely because of foreign competition and the explosion of new technologies, recognition is growing that a firm competes not only by offering new products and services, creative marketing, and skillful finance but also with unique competencies in operations. The organization that can offer superior products and services at lower prices is a formidable competitor.

To conclude this chapter, Managerial Practice 1.2 demonstrates what four companies are doing to improve quality and productivity and how management can use operations as a competitive weapon. These examples offer insight into the role that operations managers play in an organization.

The steps taken by these companies cover almost every type of decision (shown in parentheses) in operations management. Note that each decision category in operations management plays a vital role in gaining competitive advantage. These descriptions indicate that there are many ways to succeed with operations, not one single magic formula.

What are companies doing to make operations a competitive weapon?

MANAGERIAL PRACTICE 1.2
Meeting the Competitive Challenge

Continental Airlines

In 1994, Continental Airlines (www.continental.com) was in poor financial condition, quickly running out of customers and cash. Over 40,000 jobs were at stake. Today, Continental is flying high, thanks to what it has done to better design and operate its processes. The key in the turnaround was to get many things done fast in a coordinated fashion, so that everyone pulled together (*managing project processes*). After years of a low-cost approach (*operations strategy*), quality and customer-response policies were improved dramatically. Continental revised its processes to focus on adding customer value rather than on cutting costs. The hard part was figuring out how to improve the customer's experience so that revenues increased faster than costs (*operations as a competitive weapon*). The airline set up a toll-free hotline to handle employee suggestions on how to improve operations, such as speeding up the reservation process (*process management*). Management sought to change the customer's experience (*total quality management*) by selecting places where people want to go, at the times they wanted to go, and in clean, attractive airplanes.

It also chose 15 or so key measures to track and compare against competitors (*statistical quality control*), including on-time arrivals, baggage handling, and customer complaints. Maintenance was improved, providing better capacity utilization (*capacity management*). Planes were fixed so that they were not breaking down when they needed to be flying. In one year, the maintenance budget dropped from $777 million to $395 million,

Baggage handling at the new Denver International airport. Baggage handling is one of 15 key measures that Continental tracks and compares against competitors.

and the airline jumped from worst to first in the industry in dispatch reliability. It decided to build up its Houston, Newark, and Cleveland hubs (*location*). Finally, to improve reliability, it fostered better cross-functional communication between the people who made the flight schedule (*scheduling*) and the operating departments who controlled the mechanics, crews, and parts inventory (*inventory management*).

GTE Corporation

GTE's operation (www.gte.com) in Florida's Tampa–Sarasota region is typical of companies that are doing more with less. Over the past five years, although the area's population and telephone system have grown by about 7 percent annually, GTE still employs the same number of service people, about 250. Laptop computers (*managing technology*) let repair crews plan their daily schedules (*scheduling*) and give customers more accurate times of arrival. The support staff (*process management*) has dropped from 45 to 11, as software-driven "expert" systems (*managing technology*) take customer requests and arrange them in the most efficient order.

Merlin Metalworks, Inc.

Merlin Metalworks (www.merlinbike.com) began as a three-person company in 1986, and it keeps growing. Sales for 2000 are expected to exceed $4 million. Its manufacturing facility now covers more than 12,000 square feet (*capacity*) in a new plant in Cambridge, Massachusetts (*location*). The heart of its business is bike frames, which are made from titanium to make them tough, durable, and rustproof (*process management*). The Merlin process, praised by reviews in *Bicycle Guide* and *Bicycling*, stresses precision and attention to detail during manufacturing (*total quality management*). Welding is critical to the process and carefully monitored (*statistical process control*). The company invested $100,000 in one machine just to cut the bottom bracket threads exactly straight and uses a proprietary butting technology (*managing technology*). Merlin uses almost 50 different tube sizes in its frame and makes all its frames (*process management*). Merlin makes about 100 style and size combinations. It plans to sell 3,000 this year (*forecasting*); 20 percent will be custom-built (*operations strategy*). Half of this year's sales should be models introduced since 1998. Merlin's growing size as a

titanium customer allows it to dictate precisely the types of titanium tubing that it will buy for use in its frames (*supply-chain management*).

Sharp Corporation

Sharp Corporation (www.sharp-world.com), a $14 billion consumer-electronic giant, was once regarded as a second-tier competitor by its Japanese rivals. Today, however, its consistent pursuit of technological creativity, particularly in the area of specialized optoelectronics, is giving it a competitive advantage (*managing technology*). Each year, nearly one-third of Sharp's R&D budget is spent on 10 to 15 Gold Badge projects (*managing project processes*). Such projects cut across product groups. All project members are vested with the authority of the company president and wear gold-colored badges so that they can call on people throughout Sharp for assistance. Sharp is organized around functional lines so that applied research and manufacturing occur in a single unit where economies of scale (*capacity*) can be exploited. To assure cross-functional coordination, product managers are given the responsibility—but not the authority—for coordinating the entire set of value-chain processes (*supply-chain management*).

Sources: "The Mechanic Who Fired Continental." *Fortune* (December 20, 1999); "Right Away and All at Once: How We Saved Continental." *Harvard Business Review* (September–October 1998), pp. 162–175; "Riding High." *Business Week* (October 9, 1995), "Boston Becoming a Hub to High-End Bike Industry, *The Boston Globe* (July 28, 1999); and "Creating Corporate Advantage." *Harvard Business Review* (May–June 1998), pp. 71–84.

FORMULA REVIEW

1. Productivity is the ratio of output to input, or

$$\text{Productivity} = \frac{\text{Output}}{\text{Input}}$$

CHAPTER HIGHLIGHTS

❒ Every organization must manage processes and the operations by which these processes are performed. Processes are the fundamental activity that organizations use to do work and achieve their goals. Value is added for the customer by transforming inputs into outputs for customers. Inputs include human resources (workers and managers), capital resources (equipment and facilities), purchased materials and services, land, and energy. Outputs are goods and services.

❒ The concept of processes applies not just to an entire organization but also to the work of each department and individual. Each has work processes and customers (whether internal or external).

❒ A process can be broken down into subprocesses, which in turn can be broken down still more. A process within a process is known as a *nested process*.

❏ Types of decisions with which operations managers are involved include *strategic choices* (operations strategy); *process* (process management, project processes, managing technology); *quality* (total quality management and statistical process control); *capacity, location,* and *layout;* and *operating decisions* (supply-chain management, forecasting, inventory management, aggregate planning, resource planning, lean systems, and scheduling).

❏ Decisions within operations should be linked. For example, quality, process, capacity and inventory decisions affect one another and should not be made independently. Strategy (long-range plans) and tactical analysis (for short-range decision making) should complement each other.

❏ Operations require utilization of a variety of skills and technologies. They play a key role in determining productivity, which is the prime determinant of profitability and, in the aggregate, a nation's standard of living.

❏ Manufacturers produce physical, durable products. These products can be stored to create inventories that allow smoothing output levels when demand fluctuates. Most customers for manufactured goods have little, if any, contact with the production system.

❏ In contrast, service providers tend to have intangible products that cannot be stocked as inventory, more direct contact with the customer, shorter response times, local markets, smaller facilities, labor-intensive operations, and less measurable quality. Although there are differences between manufacturing and service operations, the concepts of productivity, quality, process management, capacity, facility location, layout, inventory, scheduling, and the use of technology apply to both.

❏ Smart managers use multiple performance measures to monitor and improve performance.

❏ Several trends are at work in operations management: Service sector employment is growing; productivity is a concern, particularly in the service sector; and global competition is intensifying. The pursuit of better quality, competition based on time, and rapid technological change are also important trends. Awareness in business education of environmental, ethical, and workforce diversity concerns is increasing.

❏ Operations managers must deal with both intra-organizational and interorganizational relationships. For operations to be used successfully as a competitive weapon, it must address interfunctional concerns. Tomorrow's managers in every functional area must understand operations.

KEY TERMS

external customers *4*	nested process *5*	process *4*
internal customers *4*	operations management *6*	productivity *13*

SOLVED PROBLEM 1

Student tuition at Boehring University is $100 per semester credit hour. The state supplements school revenue by matching student tuition, dollar for dollar. Average class size for a typical three-credit course is 50 students. Labor costs are $4,000 per class, materials costs are $20 per student per class, and overhead costs are $25,000 per class.

a. What is the *multifactor* productivity ratio?

b. If instructors work an average of 14 hours per week for 16 weeks for each three-credit class of 50 students, what is the *labor* productivity ratio?

SOLUTION

a. Multifactor productivity is the ratio of the value of output to the value of input resources.

$$\text{Value of output} = \left(\frac{50 \text{ students}}{\text{class}}\right)\left(\frac{3 \text{ credit hours}}{\text{student}}\right)\left(\frac{\$100 \text{ tuition} + \$100 \text{ state support}}{\text{credit hour}}\right)$$
$$= 30,000/\text{class}$$

$$\text{Value of input} = \text{Labor} + \text{Materials} + \text{Overhead}$$

$$= \frac{\$4,000 + (\$20/\text{student} \times 50 \text{ students}) + \$25,000}{\text{class}}$$

$$= \$30,000/\text{class}$$

$$\text{Multifactor productivity} = \frac{\text{Output}}{\text{Input}} = \frac{\$30,000/\text{class}}{\$30,000/\text{class}} = 1.00$$

b. Labor productivity is the ratio of the value of output to labor hours. The value of output is the same as in part (a), or $30,000/class, so

$$\text{Labor hours of input} = \left(\frac{14 \text{ hours}}{\text{week}}\right)\left(\frac{16 \text{ weeks}}{\text{class}}\right) = 224 \text{ hours/class}$$

$$\text{Labor productivity} = \frac{\text{Output}}{\text{Input}} = \frac{\$30,000/\text{class}}{224 \text{ hours/class}}$$

$$= \$133.93/\text{hour}$$

SOLVED PROBLEM 2

Natalie Attired makes fashionable garments. During a particular week employees worked 360 hours to produce a batch of 132 garments, of which 52 were "seconds" (meaning that they were flawed). Seconds are sold for $90 each at Attired's Factory Outlet Store. The remaining 80 garments are sold to retail distribution, at $200 each. What is the *labor* productivity ratio?

SOLUTION

$$\text{Value of Output} = (52 \text{ defective} \times \$90/\text{defective})$$
$$+ (80 \text{ garments} \times \$200/\text{garment})$$
$$= \$20,680$$

$$\text{Labor hours of input} = 360 \text{ hours}$$

$$\text{Labor productivity} = \frac{\text{Output}}{\text{Input}} = \frac{\$20,680}{360 \text{ hours}}$$

$$= \$57.44 \text{ in sales per hour}$$

OM EXPLORER AND INTERNET EXERCISES

Visit our Web site at www.prenhall.com/krajewski for OM Explorer Tutors, which explain quantitative techniques; Solvers, which help you apply mathematical models; and Internet Exercises, including Facility Tours, which expand on the topics in this chapter.

DISCUSSION QUESTIONS

1. Consider your last (or current) job.
   a. What activities did you perform?
   b. Who were your customers (internal and external), and how did you interact with them?
   c. How could you measure the customer value you were adding by performing your processes?
   d. Was your position in accounting, finance, human resources, management information systems, marketing, operations, or other? Explain.

2. Make a list of possible endings to this sentence: "The responsibility of a business is to _____" (for example, ". . . *make money*" or ". . . *provide health care for its employees*"). Make a list of the responsibilities that you would support and a list of those that you would not support. Form a small group, and compare your lists with those of the others in the group. Discuss the issues and try to arrive at a consensus. An alternative discussion question: "The responsibility of a student is to _____."

3. Multinational corporations are formed to meet global competition. Although they operate in several countries, workers do not have international unions. Some union leaders complain that multinationals are in a position to play off their own plants against each other to gain concessions from labor. What responsibilities do multinational corporations have to host countries? To employees? To customers? To shareholders? Would you support provisions of international trade treaties to address this problem? Form a small group, and compare your views with those of the others in the group. Discuss the issues and try to obtain a consensus.

PROBLEMS

An icon in the margin next to a problem identifies the software that can be helpful but is not mandatory. The software is available on the Student CD-ROM that is packaged with every new copy of the textbook.

1. **OM Explorer** (Refer to Solved Problem 1.) Under Coach Bjourn Toulouse, several football seasons for the Big Red Herrings have been disappointing. Only better recruiting will return the Big Red Herrings to winning form. Because of the current state of the program, Boehring University fans are unlikely to support increases in the $192 season ticket price. Improved recruitment will increase overhead costs to $30,000 per class section from the current $25,000 per class section. The University's budget plan is to cover recruitment costs by increasing the average class size to 75 students. Labor costs will increase to $6,500 per three-credit course. Material costs are about $25 per student for each three-credit course. Tuition will be $200 per semester credit, which is matched by state support of $100 per semester credit.

   a. What is the productivity ratio? Compared to the result obtained in Solved Problem 1, did productivity increase or decrease?

   b. If instructors work an average of 20 hours per week for 16 weeks for each three-credit class of 75 students, what is the *labor* productivity ratio?

2. Suds and Duds Laundry washed and pressed the following numbers of dress shirts per week.

WEEK	WORK CREW	HOURS	SHIRTS
1	Sud and Dud	24	68
2	Sud and Jud	46	130
3	Sud, Dud, and Jud	62	152
4	Sud, Dud, and Jud	51	125
5	Dud and Jud	45	131

   Calculate the *labor* productivity ratio for each week. Explain the labor productivity pattern exhibited by the data.

3. Compact disc players are produced on an automated assembly line. The standard cost of compact disc players is $150 per unit (labor, $30; materials, $70; and overhead, $50). The sales price is $300 per unit.

   a. To achieve a 10 percent multifactor productivity improvement by reducing materials costs only, by what percent must those costs be reduced?

   b. To achieve a 10 percent multifactor productivity improvement by reducing labor costs only, by what percent must those costs be reduced?

   c. To achieve a 10 percent multifactor productivity improvement by reducing overhead costs only, by what percent must those costs be reduced?

Advanced Problem

4. The Big Black Bird Company (BBBC) has a large order for special plastic-lined military uniforms to be used in an urgent Mideast operation. Working the normal two shifts of 40 hours, BBBC usually produces 2,500 uniforms per week at a standard cost of $120 each. Seventy employees work the first shift and 30 the second. The contract price is $200 per uniform. Because of the urgent need, BBBC is authorized to use around-the-clock production, six days per week. When each of the two shifts works 72 hours per week, production increases to 4,000 uniforms per week but at a cost of $144 each.

   a. Did the productivity ratio increase, decrease, or remain the same? If it changed, by what percent did it change?

   b. Did the labor productivity ratio increase, decrease, or remain the same? If it changed, by what percent did it change?

   c. Did weekly profits increase, decrease, or remain the same?

CASE **CHAD'S CREATIVE CONCEPTS**

Chad's Creative Concepts designs and manufactures wood furniture. Founded by Chad Thomas on the banks of Lake Erie in Sandusky, Ohio, the company began by producing custom-made wooden furniture for vacation cabins located along the coast of Lake Erie and on nearby Kelly's Island and Bass Island. Being an "outdoors" type himself, Chad Thomas originally wanted to bring "a bit of the outdoors" inside. Chad's Creative Concepts developed a solid reputation for creative designs and high-quality workmanship. Sales eventually encompassed the entire Great Lakes region. Along with growth came additional opportunities.

Traditionally, the company had focused entirely on custom-made furniture, with the customer specifying the kind of wood from which the piece would be made. As the company's reputation grew and sales increased, the sales force began selling some of the more popular pieces to retail furniture outlets. This move into retail outlets led Chad's Creative Concepts into the production of a more standard line of furniture. Buyers of this line were much more price sensitive and imposed more stringent delivery requirements than did clients for the custom line. Custom-designed furniture, however, continued to dominate sales, accounting for 60 percent of volume and 75 percent of dollar sales. Currently, the company operates a single manufacturing facility in Sandusky, where both custom and standard furniture is manufactured. The equipment is mainly general purpose in nature in order to provide the flexibility needed for producing custom pieces of furniture. The layout groups saws in one section of the facility, lathes in another, and so on. The quality of the finished product reflects the quality of the wood chosen and the craftsmanship of individual workers. Both custom and standard furniture compete for processing time on the same equipment by the same craftspeople.

During the past few months, sales of the standard line have steadily increased, leading to more regular scheduling of this line. However, when scheduling trade-offs had to be made, custom furniture was always given priority because of its higher sales and profit margins. Thus, scheduled lots of standard furniture pieces were left sitting around the plant in various stages of completion.

As he reviews the progress of Creative Concepts, Thomas is pleased to note that the company has grown. Sales of custom furniture remain strong, and sales of standard pieces are steadily increasing. However, finance and accounting have indicated that profits aren't what they should be. Costs associated with the standard line are rising. Dollars are being tied up in inventory, both of raw materials and work in process. Expensive public warehouse space has to be rented to accommodate the inventory volume. Thomas also is concerned with increased lead times for both custom and standard orders, which are causing longer promised delivery times. Capacity is being pushed, and no space is left in the plant for expansion. Thomas decides that the time has come to take a careful look at the overall impact that the new standard line is having on his operations.

Questions

1. What types of decisions must Chad Thomas make daily for his company's operations to run effectively? Over the long run?
2. How did sales and marketing affect operations when they began to sell standard pieces to retail outlets?
3. How has the move to producing standard furniture affected the company's financial structure?
4. What might Thomas have done differently to avoid some of the problems he now faces?

Source: This case was prepared by Dr. Brooke Saladin, Wake Forest University, as a basis for classroom discussion.

SELECTED REFERENCES

Bowen, David E., Richard B. Chase, Thomas G. Cummings, and Associates. *Service Management Effectiveness*. San Francisco: Jossey-Bass, 1990.

Buchholz, Rogene A. "Corporate Responsibility and the Good Society: From Economics to Ecology." *Business Horizons* (July–August 1991), pp. 19–31.

Cohen, Stephen S., and John Zysman. *Manufacturing Matters: The Myth of the Post-Industrial Economy*. New York: Basic Books, 1987.

Collier, David A. *Service Management: Operating Decisions*. Englewood Cliffs, NJ: Prentice-Hall, 1987.

Commission on Admission to Graduate Management Education. *Leadership for a Changing World: The Future Role of Graduate Management Education*. Los Angeles: Graduate Management Admission Council (GMAC), 1990, pp. 1–43.

Hayes, Robert H., and Gary P. Pisano. "Beyond World-Class: The New Manufacturing Strategy." *Harvard Business Review* (January–February 1994), pp. 77–86.

Heskett, James L., W. Earl Sasser, Jr., and Christopher Hart. *Service Breakthroughs: Changing the Rules of the Game*. New York: Free Press, 1990.

Heyl, Jeff E., Jon L. Bushnell, and Linda A. Stone. *Cases in Operations Management*. Reading, MA: Addison-Wesley, 1994.

"The Horizontal Corporation." *Business Week* (December 20, 1993), pp. 76–81.

Kaplan, Robert S., and David P. Norton. *Balanced Scoreboard*. Boston, MA: Harvard Business School Press, 1997.

"Management Education." *The Economist* (March 2, 1991), pp. 2–26.

Parker, Glenn. *Cross-Functional Teams*. San Francisco: Jossey-Bass, 1994.

Porter, Lyman W., and Lawrence E. McKibbin. *Management Education and Development: Drift or Thrust into 21st Century?* New York: McGraw-Hill, 1988.

Post, James E. "Managing As If the Earth Mattered." *Business Horizons* (July–August 1991), pp. 32–38.

Roach, Stephen S. "Services Under Siege—The Restructuring Imperative." *Harvard Business Review* (September–October 1991), pp. 82–91.

Schmenner, Roger W. *Service Operations Management*. Englewood Cliffs, NJ: Prentice-Hall, 1995.

"Service Exports and the U.S. Economy." *International Trade Association*. U.S. Government. www.ita.doc.gov/industry/osi/se.html.

Skinner, Wickham. "Manufacturing—Missing Link in Corporate Strategy." *Harvard Business Review* (May–June 1969), pp. 136–145.

"Time for a Reality Check in Asia." *Business Week* (December 2, 1996), pp. 58–66.

"Under Pressure, Business Schools Devise Changes." *Wall Street Journal* (April 23, 1991), p. 15.

van Biema, Michael, and Bruce Greenwald, "Managing Our Way to Higher Service-Sector Productivity." *Harvard Business Review* (July–August 1997), pp. 87–95.

Wheelwright, Steven C. "Manufacturing Strategy: Defining the Missing Link." *Strategic Management Journal,* vol. 5 (1984), pp. 71–91.

Womack, James P., Daniel T. Jones, and Daniel Roos. *The Machine That Changed the World*. New York: HarperPerennial, 1991.

CHAPTER 2

Operations Strategy

Across the Organization

Operations strategy is important to . . .

- ❏ **engineering,** which must design the products and the processes needed to produce them.
- ❏ **finance,** which performs the financial analyses of alternative product or service designs.
- ❏ **management information systems,** which designs the systems that provide market data and competitor information in a global environment.
- ❏ **marketing,** which determines the products and services the firm has the capability to produce.
- ❏ **operations,** which must determine the best operations strategies and manage the processes that produce the products or services to achieve the firm's market strategy.

Learning Goals

After reading this chapter, you will be able to . . .

1. describe the role of operations strategy as a source of competitive strength in a global marketplace.
2. explain how to link marketing strategy to operations strategy through the use of competitive priorities.
3. provide examples of how firms use competitive priorities for competitive advantage.
4. distinguish between the make-to-stock, standardized-services, assemble-to-order, make-to-order, and customized-services strategies and show how they relate to competitive priorities.
5. explain how operations strategy is a pattern of decisions directed at processes, systems, and procedures in order to achieve certain competitive priorities.

FedEx (www.fedex.com) is a $17 billion-a-year delivery service company that thrives on speed and reliability. FedEx delivers 4.5 million packages a day—25 percent of the world's package delivery business. Because 70 percent of the packages that FedEx delivers go by plane, it can charge premium prices for the service. For the past 25 years, companies have used FedEx delivery services when they suddenly realized that they were short of critical parts or that they were low on goods demanded by customers. Companies have traditionally chosen FedEx because of its technological superiority in tracking packages. The Internet, however, has changed the way business is conducted. Many businesses are now using complex Web-based systems designed to eliminate much of the unpredictability in their operations by communicating directly with customers and suppliers. E-mail reliably delivers documents instantaneously, and low-cost truck lines, discount air carriers, and even ocean vessels can now track shipments via the Internet.

While these technological advances have been an advantage to some firms, they have cut into the demand for FedEx's traditional services. The growth potential now is in ground transportation services,

An employee of FedEx Home Delivery division drops off a delivery at a residence. Emphasizing low-cost operations and dependable deliveries, FedEx changed its operations strategy to reflect technological changes.

presently dominated by United Parcel Service. This demand is fueled by Internet companies such as Amazon.com who rely heavily on ground transportation services to deliver packages directly to the customer's door and by the vast business-to-business supply networks energized by Web-based purchasing systems. To remain competitive in this changing environment, FedEx is changing its operations strategy. In particular, it is creating two new divisions: FedEx Ground and FedEx Home Delivery. FedEx Ground focuses on business-to-business deliveries via a recently procured trucking company; FedEx Home Delivery specializes in deliveries to residences. Both divisions will strive for low-cost operations and dependable deliveries—a change from the goals of present operations, which stress speed. In addition, FedEx will rely on its core competency in technology. It is investing $100 million in processes that will coordinate the flow of goods from a company such as Cisco with shipments from suppliers of major components, all to be delivered to a customer within a short window of time for assembly of the final product. FedEx is relying on its operations to compete successfully in a dynamic environment being reshaped by the Internet.

THE CHANGES AT FEDEX provide one example of a customer-driven operations strategy in action. Major processes must be created for the new ground delivery businesses that satisfy the needs of customers. The new delivery system will involve the coordination of processes from all functional areas of the firm. Operations management plays a major role in the design of the processes and systems needed to support the new initiatives.

Developing a customer-driven operations strategy begins with *corporate strategy,* which coordinates the firm's overall goals with its core competencies. It determines which customers the firm will serve, which new products or services it will produce, which responses it will take to changes in its business and socioeconomic environment, and which strategy it will employ in international markets. Based on the corporate strategy, a *market analysis* categorizes the firm's customers, identifies their needs, and assesses competitor's strengths. This information is used to develop **competitive priorities**, which are the operating advantages that the firm's processes must possess to outperform its competitors. The competitive priorities and the directives from corporate strategy provide input for the *functional strategies*, or the goals and long-term plans of each functional area. Through its strategic planning process, each functional area is responsible for identifying ways to develop the capabilities it will need to carry out functional strategies and achieve corporate goals. This input, along with the current status and capability of each area, is fed back into the corporate strategic planning process to indicate whether corporate strategy should be modified. Figure 2.1 shows how corporate strategy, market analysis, competitive priorities, and functional strategies are linked.

In this chapter, we focus on **operations strategy**, which specifies the means by which operations implements the firm's corporate strategy. Basically, operations strategy links long- and short-term operations decisions to corporate strategy. Continuous cross-functional interaction must occur in implementing operations strategy. For example, operations needs feedback from marketing to determine how much capacity to allocate to various product lines, and operations must work with finance regarding the timing and funding of increased capacity. Thus, in identifying the operational capabilities needed for the future, the operations manager must work closely with the managers of

competitive priorities
Operating advantages that a firm's processes must possess to outperform its competitors.

operations strategy The means by which operations implements the firm's corporate strategy.

FIGURE 2.1

*Competitive Priorities:
Link Between
Corporate Strategy and
Functional Area
Strategies*

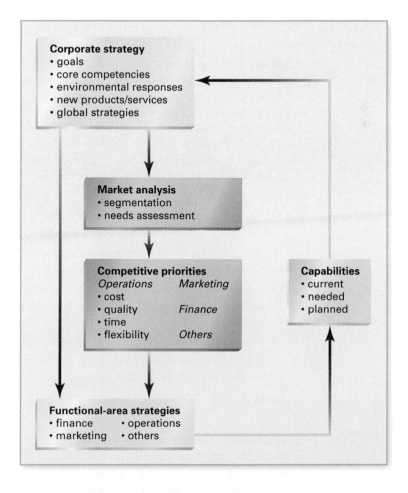

other functional areas. In this chapter, we describe the linking of corporate strategy and operations strategy and the types of feedback needed during the development of these strategies.

CORPORATE STRATEGY

Whatever the type of firm, top management's responsibility is to plan the organization's long-term future. Corporate strategy specifies the business(es) that the company will pursue, isolates new opportunities and threats in the environment, and identifies the growth objectives that it should achieve. Also addressed is business strategy, or how a firm can differentiate itself from the competition. Choices could include producing standardized products versus customized products or competing on the basis of cost advantage versus responsive delivery. Corporate strategy provides an overall direction that serves as the framework for carrying out all the organization's functions. In this section, we discuss the considerations involved in corporate strategy and how global markets affect strategic planning.

STRATEGIC CONSIDERATIONS

Corporate strategy specifies the direction of the organization over the long term and determines the goals that must be achieved for the firm to be successful. Developing a corporate strategy involves three considerations: responding to pressures for flexibility, monitoring and adjusting to changes in the business environment, and identifying and developing the firm's core competencies.

FLEXIBILITY. E-commerce companies as well as traditional Rust Belt companies have found that they must frequently revise corporate strategies to remain competitive, even on a weekly or quarterly basis. Low economic barriers to entry in such businesses as retailing or finance have caused tremendous competition and the need to reevaluate strategies on a short-term basis. In addition, the Internet has put companies in close touch with their customers, both through direct sales and by soliciting feedback. Customers tell companies what they want, and companies must respond or lose out. Such conditions call for flexibility in the strategic planning process. There are five ways companies can respond to the need for flexibility:

- ❐ *Scenario Building*. Strategists plan several different outcomes for each initiative, thus permitting quick responses to competitive threats.
- ❐ *Reality Checks*. Key decision makers meet regularly at short intervals to assess ways that rivals might make inroads in the marketplace.
- ❐ *Communication*. To get everyone thinking of the effects of the change on their operations, executives announce strategy shifts to employees within hours of a decision.
- ❐ *Hires*. Employers fill jobs with people who thrive on change and ambiguity.
- ❐ *Shortening the Budget Cycle*. To ensure that individual and departmental goals are properly revised, managers link the budget review to strategy review.

From a strategic perspective, the message is clear: develop a capability for change.

ENVIRONMENT. The external business environment in which a firm competes changes continually, and an organization needs to adapt to those changes. Adaptation begins

How can management identify and deal with environmental change when formulating corporate strategy?

with *environmental scanning,* the process by which managers monitor trends in the socioeconomic environment, including the industry, the marketplace, and society, for potential opportunities or threats. A crucial reason for environmental scanning is to stay ahead of the competition. Competitors may be gaining an edge by broadening product lines, improving quality, or lowering costs. New entrants into the market or competitors who offer substitutes for a firm's product or service may threaten continued profitability. Other important environmental concerns include economic trends, technological changes, political conditions, social changes (such as attitudes toward work), the availability of vital resources, and the collective power of customers or suppliers.

Environmental changes may cause a company to reconsider its current strategies. A case in point is Xerox, which was faced with the problem of what to do with old machines accepted as trade-ins or coming off lease. Ecological concerns and governmental regulations precluded merely dumping unusable machines or parts in landfills. Rather than viewing the ecology as a constraint, Xerox saw an opportunity to make profits. The company started with simple recycling to recover materials that could be melted down. The next step in the plan was to refurbish recovered parts and reuse them in new machines. That step, however, was thwarted because most of the parts were not designed for reuse. Xerox assigned a team of managers and engineers to examine ways to make a machine totally recyclable and remanufacturable. It took years for Xerox to reorient itself, drastically changing the way it procures parts and raw materials, designs products, and runs production. Today, when Xerox designs a machine, it simultaneously develops processes for both "new-build" manufacturing and remanufacturing. The effort has paid off: The $19.5 billion-a-year company enjoys $250 million in annual savings.

core competencies The unique resources and strengths that an organization's management considers when formulating strategy.

CORE COMPETENCIES. Good managerial skill alone can't overcome environmental changes. Rather, corporate strategy must address them. Firms succeed by taking advantage of what they do particularly well—that is, the organization's unique strengths. **Core competencies** are the unique resources and strengths that an organization's management considers when formulating strategy. They reflect the collective learning of the organization, especially in how to coordinate diverse processes and integrate multiple technologies. These competencies include the following.

Assembling a copier at the Xerox's flagship factory complex in Webster, New York. The plant is a model on environmental awareness, where over the past ten years bad air emissions have been curtailed by 80 percent. With its approach to "green manufacturing," it takes back copiers previously owned or leased by customers, stripping out parts that can be reused or refurbished, and puts them in remanufactured machines that perform like new.

1. *Workforce.* A well-trained and flexible workforce allows organizations to respond to market needs in a timely fashion. This competency is particularly important in service organizations, where the customer comes in direct contact with the employees.

2. *Facilities.* Having well-located facilities—offices, stores, and plants—is a primary advantage because of the long lead time needed to build new ones. Expansion into new products or services may be accomplished quickly. In addition, flexible facilities that can handle a variety of products or services at different levels of volume provide a competitive advantage.

3. *Market and Financial Know-How.* An organization that can easily attract capital from stock sales, market and distribute its products, or differentiate its products from similar products on the market has a competitive edge.

4. *Systems and Technology.* Organizations with expertise in information systems will have an edge in industries that are data—and information—intensive, such as banking. Particularly advantageous is expertise in Internet technologies and applications, such as business-to-consumer and business-to-business systems. Having the patents on a new technology is also a big advantage.

A study by Porter (1990) showed that companies achieving international leadership employed strategies that took advantage of their core competencies. They achieved competitive advantage by designing new products, installing new production technologies, adapting training programs, using quality control techniques, and improving supplier relationships. The same is true today except that the Internet has caused many companies to reevaluate their core competencies. Upstart companies can reach customers faster and for a fraction of the cost of stores and salespeople. Suddenly, bricks-and-mortar assets, capital equipment, salespeople and other assets that once determined many a competitive advantage have become potential liabilities. A typical response of companies in this position is to divest themselves of processes and assets that they no longer think enhance their competitiveness—a tactic that is enhanced by the Internet. The Internet allows companies to find other companies with expertise in various processes, such as transportation, accounting, or manufacturing, and work with these suppliers as if they were extensions of their own businesses. We will have more to say about outsourcing in the Process Management and Supply-Chain Management chapters.

The flexibility of the Internet, however, emphasizes the need for companies to evaluate carefully what their core competencies really are. In the process, some companies have actually redefined themselves. Hewlett-Packard, for example, is hoping to use the Internet to remake one of its divisions from a manufacturer of large computers to an e-services company that will provide computing power over the Internet. It has always been true that competitors will eventually overtake a company that stops innovating and upgrading. The Internet, however, has shortened the grace period that companies once enjoyed.

GLOBAL STRATEGIES

What role does operations play in entering international markets?

Identifying opportunities and threats today requires a global perspective. A global strategy may include buying foreign parts or services, combating threats from foreign competitors, or planning ways to enter markets beyond traditional national boundaries. Although warding off threats from global competitors is necessary, firms should also actively seek to penetrate foreign markets. Two effective global strategies are strategic alliances and locating abroad.

STRATEGIC ALLIANCES. One way for a firm to open foreign markets is to create a *strategic alliance.* A strategic alliance is an agreement with another firm that may take one of three forms:

1. collaborative effort,
2. joint venture, or
3. technology licensing.

Collaborative Effort. A *collaborative effort* often arises when one firm has core competencies that another needs but is unwilling (or unable) to duplicate. The two companies agree to work together to their mutual benefit. Such arrangements are common in buyer–supplier relationships, as when a U.S. firm supplies parts to a foreign manufacturer, but also may be used in nontraditional ways. For example, Kodak entered into agreements with IBM, Businessland, and DEC to handle all its information systems, thereby relieving Kodak of the need for an information systems department. In such an arrangement, procedures for maintaining data confidentiality must be carefully specified.

Joint Venture. In a *joint venture,* two firms agree to produce a product or service jointly. This approach often is used by firms to gain access to foreign markets. For example, a firm wanting to do business in Singapore might set up a joint venture with a firm there. The outside firm normally supplies technology and expertise, and the local firm supplies the resources for the operation, including local workers and knowledge of labor practices. Often this type of technology transfer is necessary for doing business in the Far East. For example, companies such as Motorola, Xerox, Ericsson, and Rockwell International are actively involved in joint ventures in China but must pay a steep price. Beijing is getting multinationals to subsidize large R&D efforts, modernize university curriculums, and promise to use China as an export base.

Technology Licensing. *Technology licensing* is a form of strategic alliance in which one company licenses its production or service methods to another. Licenses may be used to gain access to foreign markets. For example, a large percent of all laser printers sold today use print-engine technology licensed by Canon of Japan.

LOCATING ABROAD. Another way to enter global markets is to locate operations in a foreign country. However, managers must recognize that what works well in their home country might not work well elsewhere. The economic and political environment or customers' needs may be very different. For example, McDonald's is known for the consistency of its products—a Big Mac tastes the same anywhere in the world. However, a family-owned chain, Jollibee Foods Corporation, has become the dominant fast-food chain in the Philippines. Jollibee caters to a local preference for sweet-and-spicy flavors, which it incorporates into its fried chicken, spaghetti, and burgers. Jollibee's strength is its understanding of local tastes and claims that its burger is similar to the one a Filipino would cook at home. McDonald's responded by introducing its own Filipino-style spicy burger, but competition is stiff. McDonald's experience demonstrates that, to be successful, corporate strategies must recognize customs, preferences, and economic conditions in other countries.

MARKET ANALYSIS

One key to success in formulating a customer-driven operations strategy for both manufacturing and service firms is understanding what the customer wants and how to provide it better than the competition does. *Market analysis* first divides the firm's customers into market segments and then identifies the needs of each segment. In this section, we define and discuss the concepts of market segmentation and needs assessment.

MARKET SEGMENTATION

Market segmentation is the process of identifying groups of customers with enough in common to warrant the design and provision of products or services that the larger group wants and needs. For instance, The Gap, Inc., a major provider of casual clothes, has targeted teenagers and young adults and, for its GapKids stores, the parents or guardians of infants through 12-year-olds. Chaparral Steel has three market segments—standard steel customers, special bar-quality steel customers, and mixed steel customers—each with different product needs. In general, to identify market segments, the analyst must determine the characteristics that clearly differentiate each segment. A sound marketing program can then be devised and an effective operating strategy developed to support it.

Once the firm has identified a market segment, it can incorporate the needs of customers into the design of the product or service and the processes for its production. The following characteristics are among those that can be used to determine market segments.

1. *Demographic Factors.* Age, income, educational level, occupation, and location can differentiate markets.

2. *Psychological Factors.* Factors such as pleasure, fear, innovativeness, and boredom can serve to segment markets. For example, people with a fear of crime constitute a market segment that has prompted a flood of new products and services for protection.

3. *Industry Factors.* Customers may utilize specific technologies (e.g., electronics, robotics, or microwave telecommunications), use certain materials (e.g., rubber, oil, or wood), or participate in a particular industry (e.g., banking, health care, or automotive). These factors are used for market segmentation when the firm's customers use its goods or services to produce other goods or services.

At one time, managers thought of customers as a homogeneous mass market. Managers now realize that two customers may use the same product for very different reasons. Identifying the key factors in each market segment is the starting point in devising a customer-driven operations strategy.

NEEDS ASSESSMENT

The second step in market analysis is to make a *needs assessment,* which identifies the needs of each segment and assesses how well competitors are addressing those needs. Once it has made this assessment, the firm can differentiate itself from its competitors. The needs assessment should include both the tangible and the intangible product attributes and features that a customer desires. These attributes and features, known as the *customer benefit package* (Collier, 1994), consist of a core product or service and a set of peripheral products or services. The customer views the customer benefit package as a whole. For example, when you purchase an automobile, the core product is the car itself—its features and qualities. However, the peripheral services offered by the dealer play a key role in whether you will buy the car. They include the manner in which you are treated by the salesperson, the availability of financing, and the quality of postsale service at the dealership. Thus, the customer benefit package is the automobile plus the services provided by the dealership. Customers won't be completely satisfied unless they receive the entire customer benefit package.

Understanding the customer benefit package for a market segment enables management to identify ways to gain competitive advantage. Each market segment has market needs that can be related to product/service, process, or demand attributes. Market needs may be grouped as follows:

- ☐ *Product* or *Service Needs*. Attributes of the product or service, such as price, quality, and degree of customization desired.
- ☐ *Delivery System Needs*. Attributes of the processes and the supporting systems and resources needed to deliver the customer benefit package, such as availability, convenience, courtesy, safety, accuracy, reliability, delivery speed, and delivery dependability.
- ☐ *Volume Needs*. Attributes of the demand for the product or service, such as high or low volume, degree of variability in volume, and degree of predictability in volume.
- ☐ *Other Needs*. Other attributes, such as reputation and number of years in business, after-sale technical support, ability to invest in international financial markets, competent legal services, and product or service design capability.

COMPETITIVE PRIORITIES

What are the key capabilities that operations must develop to compete successfully in a market segment?

A customer-driven operations strategy reflects a clear understanding of the firm's long-term goals as embodied in its corporate strategy. It also requires a cross-functional effort by marketing and operations to understand the needs of each market segment and to specify the operating advantages that the firm needs to outperform competitors. Operating advantages must be related to each of the firm's processes. We call these operating advantages *competitive priorities*. In this text, we focus on competitive priorities for processes that relate to the product or service itself, to its delivery system, and to related volume factors. There are eight possible competitive priorities for processes, which fall into four groups:

Cost	1. Low-cost operations
Quality	2. High-performance design
	3. Consistent quality
Time	4. Fast delivery time
	5. On-time delivery
	6. Development speed
Flexibility	7. Customization
	8. Volume flexibility

A firm is composed of many processes that must be coordinated to provide the overall desirable outcome for the customer. Most customers view a business as an aggregate process that accepts orders for products or services and finally delivers them in a fashion that satisfies their needs. However, a business consists of many *nested* processes, each one performing operations needed to serve the firm's customers. For example, a manufacturing firm has an accounting process, a marketing process, an order-fulfillment process, a treasury-management process, and many other processes. These processes can be broken down still further. The accounting process has a billing process and a financial statement process. The marketing process has a pricing process and a sales-realization process. The order-fulfillment process has an order-entry process,

MANAGERIAL PRACTICE 2.1
Using Operations for Profit at Costco

Looking for bargains on items ranging from watermelons to symphonic baby grand pianos? One company addressing those needs is Costco (www.costco.com), a wholesale club with 347 stores that generate $31 billion in annual revenue and $542 million in annual profits. Its closest competitor is Wal-Mart's Sam's Club, whose 200 more stores generate $1 billion less in annual revenue. Individual and business customers pay Costco from $45 to $100 a year for a membership and the privilege of buying staple items in bulk quantities and other select items at big discounts.

What makes Costco so successful? It has linked the needs of its customers to its operations by developing a customer-driven operations strategy that supports its retailing concept. Costco's competitive priorities are low-cost operations, quality, and flexibility. A visit to one of Costco's stores will show how these competitive priorities manifest themselves.

Low-Cost Operations
Customers come to Costco because of low prices, which are possible because processes are designed for efficiency. The store is actually a warehouse where products are stacked on pallets with little signage. New products can replace old products efficiently. In addition, Costco managers are tough price negotiators with suppliers because they buy in high volumes. Suppliers are expected to change factory runs to produce specially built packages that are bigger but cheaper per unit. Costco's profit margins are low, but annual profits are high because of the volume.

Quality
Customers are not looking for high levels of customer service, but they are looking for high value. In addition to low prices, Costco backs everything it sells with a return-anything-at-any-time guarantee. Customers trust Costco, which has generated an 86 per-

Shoppers checking out the bargains that they found at one of Costco's wholesale clubs. Costco operates member-centered discount warehouse outlets in North America and Asia.

cent membership renewal rate—the highest in the industry. To support the need for high value, operations must ensure that products are of high quality and undamaged when placed in the store.

Flexibility
One of the key aspects of Costco's operations is the fact that it carries only 4,000 carefully selected items in a typical store, while a Wal-Mart Superstore carries 125,000 items. However, items change frequently to provide return customers with a "surprise" aspect to the shopping experience. Processes must be flexible to accommodate a dynamic store layout. In addition, the supply chain must be carefully managed because the products are constantly changing.

Source: "Inside the Cult of Costco." *Fortune* (September 6, 1999), pp. 184–190.

a manufacturing process, and a delivery process. The treasury-management process has a capital budgeting process and an investment process. Many of a firm's processes may even serve more than one market segment. The challenge for management is to assign the appropriate competitive priorities to each process so as to support the needs of the firm's customers.

COST

Lowering prices can increase demand for products or services, but it also reduces profit margins if the product or service cannot be produced at lower cost. To compete based on cost, operations managers must address labor, materials, scrap, overhead, and other costs to design a system that lowers the cost per unit of the product or service. Often, lowering costs requires additional investment in automated facilities and equipment. Managerial Practice 2.1 shows how Costco uses operations strategy to lower costs and increase margins.

QUALITY

Quality is a dimension of a product or service that is defined by the customer. Today, more than ever, quality has important market implications. As for operations, two competitive priorities deal with quality: high-performance design and consistent quality.

high-performance design Determination of the level of operations performance required in making a product or performing a service.

HIGH-PERFORMANCE DESIGN. The first, **high-performance design,** may include superior features, close tolerances, and greater durability; helpfulness, courteousness, and availability of service employees; convenience of access to service locations; and safety of products or services. High-performance design determines the level of operations performance required in making a product or performing a service. The operations system for Club Med, the all-inclusive resorts with entertaining, dining, recreation, and hotel facilities, has much more demanding requirements for customer service than does a no-frills motel. Managerial Practice 2.2 shows how high-performance design can be profitable for a ready-to-wear clothing manufacturer.

consistent quality Measurement of the frequency with which the product or service meets design specifications.

CONSISTENT QUALITY. The second quality priority, **consistent quality,** measures the frequency with which the product or service meets design specifications. Customers want products or services that consistently meet the specifications they contracted for, have come to expect, or saw advertised. For example, customers of a foundry expect castings to meet specific tolerances for length, diameter, and surface finish. Similarly, bank customers expect that the bank will not make errors when recording transactions. To compete on the basis of consistent quality, managers need to design and monitor operations to reduce errors. Although consistent quality is as important now as it has ever been, it is increasingly expected by customers. A firm that does not have consistent quality does not last long in a competitive global marketplace.

TIME

As the saying goes, "time is money." Some companies do business at "Internet speed," while others thrive on consistently meeting delivery promises. Three competitive priorities deal with time: fast delivery time, on-time delivery, and development speed.

fast delivery time The elapsed time between receiving a customer's order and filling it.

lead time The way industrial buyers often refer to fast delivery time.

FAST DELIVERY TIME. The first, **fast delivery time,** is the elapsed time between receiving a customer's order and filling it. Industrial buyers often call it **lead time.** An acceptable delivery time can be a year for a complex, customized machine, several weeks for scheduling elective surgery, and minutes for an ambulance. Manufacturers can shorten delivery times by storing inventory; manufacturers and service providers can do so by having excess capacity.

on-time delivery Measurement of the frequency with which delivery-time promises are met.

ON-TIME DELIVERY. The second time priority, **on-time delivery,** measures the frequency with which delivery-time promises are met. Manufacturers measure on-time delivery as the percent of customer orders shipped when promised, with 95 percent often considered the goal. A service provider, such as a supermarket, might measure on-time delivery as the percent of customers who wait in the checkout line for less than three minutes.

development speed Measurement of how quickly a new product or service is introduced, covering the elapsed time from idea generation through final design and production.

DEVELOPMENT SPEED. The third time priority, **development speed,** measures how quickly a new product or service is introduced, covering the elapsed time from idea generation through final design and production. Getting the new product or service to market first

MANAGERIAL PRACTICE 2.2
High Performance Design in the Clothing Industry

In Naples, Italy, you will find a marble-lined factory that looks more like a pallazzo than a plant for hand-tailoring clothing for men and women. Kiton (www.kiton.com) employs 250 master tailors and produces approximately 18,000 garments a year. The United States is the company's largest customer, with Germany and Italy close behind. The ready-to-wear price tags reflect the quality built into the products: Men's suits range from $2,800 to $5,200, a woman's cashmere overcoat retails for $4,500, and hand-sewn men's shirts from $375 to $550. Eighty percent of Kiton's business is ready-to-wear, although the 20 percent devoted to custom work is steadily growing with prices ranging from $8,000 to $25,000 for a suit made from 13.2 Micron Wool.

Operations supports this business in three ways: in designing the manufacturing process, in managing the employees, and in procuring the materials. The manufacturing process is highly labor-intensive, with painstaking attention to quality. Because fabric stretches when it is cut, Kiton stores it in an air-conditioned vault for two weeks before it is hand-sewn. Seams, linings, collars, and pockets are also sewn expertly to create a garment that "hangs well." Pocket cutters specialize in matching the pattern of the fabric exactly, while other technicians focus on fitting breast pockets into jackets to follow the curve of a chest. Embroidery experts use silk thread to add the touch of elegance to hand-sewn buttonholes.

Keeping highly skilled employees satisfied is as important as the tailoring of a quality product. The factory has marble floors and tall windows that shed considerable natural light to make the workplace light and airy. There is an on-site nursery for childcare and lavish daily lunches of fresh fish and pasta. Workers are even sent home early after a favorite soccer team loses so that their disappointment does not cause poor workmanship.

Kiton features high performance design in the production of its clothing, which is supported by labor intensive processes involving highly skilled employees. Here a master tailor manually cuts the fabric of a suit made to specific customer requirements.

Fabric is an essential ingredient of the final product. Kiton has most of its fabrics specially manufactured. For example, Kiton was the first company to offer a 13.4 Micron super 180 wool suit, made of the softest, downiest wool available. Only one herd of Australian merino sheep produces such wool, and Kiton was the first to find a supplier to separate it out.

A customer-driven operations strategy focusing on the manufacturing process, on employees, and on materials has enabled Kiton to grow at the rate of 20 percent per year since 1993.

Source: "The Sweetest Suit Money Can Buy." *Fortune* (September 27, 1999), pp. 330–332.

---

time-based competition
The process by which managers define the steps and time needed to deliver a product or service, and then critically analyze each step to determine whether they can save time without hurting quality.

gives the firm an edge on the competition that is difficult to overcome in a rapidly changing business environment. Development speed is especially important in the fashion apparel industry. The Limited, for example, can design a new garment, transmit the design to Hong Kong, produce the garment, ship it to the United States, and put it on store shelves in less than 25 weeks.

TIME-BASED COMPETITION. Many companies focus on the competitive priorities of development speed and fast delivery time. With **time-based competition,** managers carefully define the steps and time needed to deliver a product or service and then critically analyze each step to determine whether they can save time without hurting quality. In

concurrent engineering
A process during which design engineers, manufacturing specialists, marketers, buyers, and quality specialists work jointly to design a product or service and select the production process.

a process called **concurrent engineering**, design engineers, manufacturing specialists, marketers, buyers, and quality specialists work jointly to design a product or service and select the production process. Ford Motor Company, for example, gives full responsibility for each new product to a program manager who forms a product team representing every revelant part of the organization. In such a system, each department can raise concerns or anticipate problems while there is still time to alter the product. Changes are much simpler and less costly at this step than after the product or service has been introduced to the market.

FLEXIBILITY

Flexibility is a characteristic of a firm's operations that enables it to react to customer needs quickly and efficiently. Some firms give top priority to two types of flexibility: customization and volume flexibility.

customization The ability to satisfy the unique needs of each customer by changing product or service designs.

CUSTOMIZATION. Customization is the ability to satisfy the unique needs of each customer by changing product or service designs. However, products or services tailored to individual preferences may not have long lives. A hairdresser works with the customer to design a hairstyle that may be unique to the individual, but the life of that service may be no longer than a week. In contrast, a customized plastic bottle design for a shampoo manufacturer may last for years. Customization typically implies that the operating system must be flexible to handle specific customer needs and changes in designs. Managerial Practice 2.3 shows how customization and the Internet can be combined to competitive advantage.

volume flexibility The ability to accelerate or decelerate the rate of production quickly to handle large fluctuations in demand.

VOLUME FLEXIBILITY. Volume flexibility is the ability to accelerate or decelerate the rate of production quickly to handle large fluctuations in demand. Volume flexibility is an important operating capability that often supports the achievement of other competitive priorities (e.g., development speed or fast delivery times). The time between peaks may be years, as with cycles in the home-building industry or political campaigns. It may be months, as with ski resorts or the manufacture of lawn fertilizers. It may even be hours, as with the systematic swings in demand at a large postal facility where mail is received, sorted, and dispatched.

RELATING COMPETITIVE PRIORITIES TO MARKET SEGMENTS

To illustrate how competitive priorities relate to market segments, let us consider American Airlines and two market segments: first-class passengers and coach passengers. The core services in the customer benefit packages for both market segments are identical: transportation to the customer's destination. However, the peripheral services are quite different. A needs assessment would reveal that, relative to coach passengers, first-class passengers require more comfortable seats, better meals and beverages, more frequent service from cabin attendants, and priority in boarding. In addition, personalized service (cabin attendants who refer to customers by name), courtesy, and low volumes characterize the needs of this segment. Both first-class and coach passengers require dependability, but coach passengers are satisfied with standardized services (no surprises), courteous cabin attendants, and low prices. In addition, this market segment has high volumes. Consequently, we can say that the competitive priorities for the first-class market segment are *high-performance design, customization,* and *on-time delivery,* whereas the competitive priorities for the coach market segment are *low-cost operations, consistent quality,* and *on-time delivery.*

MANAGERIAL PRACTICE 2.3
Marshfield Door Systems Uses E-Commerce to Make Door Customization Profitable

Located in Marshfield, Wisconsin, the Marshfield Door Systems plant (www.marshfielddoors.com), formerly the door division of Weyerhaeuser, cuts, glues, drills, and shapes custom doors according to each buyer's needs. Two million configurations are possible—from size, style, and color to the veneer and hardware options. Individual order sizes are small, averaging six or seven doors. In 1995, however, the Marshfield plant shipped only 40 percent of its orders on time and held only 12 percent of the custom-door market. Plagued by bloated costs, lagging sales, and poor morale, significant changes to operations had to be made if the plant was to survive.

Key competitive priorities for this business are high-performance design, on-time delivery, delivery speed, and customization flexibility. Marshfield management decided to reengineer several processes by using an Intranet-based system called Door-Builder™. The system links customers to company operations, thereby avoiding the mountain of paperwork normally associated with the complex business of custom-door manufacturing. The system focused on the following key processes:

❏ *Order-Entry Process.*   Before reengineering, packages of customized doors were configured manually. The process took months, with time spent haggling with suppliers, distributors, and buyers. With DoorBuilder, customers assemble their own orders through a "virtual distributor" Web site. They can get instant packaging and pricing information. Orders get placed in minutes, with fewer errors and faster delivery times, which have shrunk by three weeks or more.

❏ *Pricing Process.*   Pricing was done on hunches with preference to certain customers, suppliers, and distributors. Now a computerized cost-tracking system lets managers know the cost of manufacturing a particular configuration. The system bases prices on this cost as well as on the creditworthiness of the customer and volumes ordered

Marshfield Door Systems produces more than 2 million custom door configurations such as the one shown here. High-performance design, on-time delivery, delivery speed, and customization flexibility are key competitive priorities for its processes.

in the past. The plant no longer produces unprofitable doors.

❏ *Order-Tracking Process.*   Handwritten notes on orders were often lost and generally incomplete or inaccurate. A computer system now tracks progress in real time and does not allow the customer to make changes once the order has been accepted. This capability permits better scheduling, more precise inventory control, and faster delivery.

❏ *Delivery Process.*   The tracking and scheduling software has enabled Marshfield to deliver complete orders 97 to 100 percent of the time. Marshfield gets paid faster when performance is faster and more consistent.

Source: "How an Intranet Opened Up the Door to Profits." *Business Week* (July 26, 1999), pp. EB32–EB38.

SELECTING COMPETITIVE PRIORITIES

You might wonder why firms have to choose among competitive priorities. Why not compete in all areas at once and dramatically improve your competitive position? In certain situations, firms *can* improve on all competitive priorities simultaneously. For example, in a manufacturing firm, scrap from mistakes in operations and the need to rework defective parts and products sometimes account for 20 to 30 percent of a product's cost. By reducing defects and improving quality, the firm can reduce costs, improve productivity, and cut delivery time—all at the same time.

At some point, though, further improvements in one area may require a trade-off with one or more of the others. A survey of manufacturers indicated that raising the degree of customization or producing high-performance design products may lead to both higher costs and higher prices.[1] Therefore, firms must choose a select set of competitive priorities to emphasize. For example, Rolls-Royce produces cars with top-of-the-line specifications, making premium prices necessary. However, delivery lead times of six months are slower than those of other car manufacturers because of the painstaking hand-assembly process.

Sometimes trade-offs are not possible because a competitive priority has become a requirement for doing business in a particular market segment.[2] Such a requirement is called an *order qualifier*. In such situations, customers will not place orders for products or services unless a certain level of performance can be demonstrated. Fulfilling the order qualifier will not ensure competitive success in a market; it will only position the firm to compete. For example, in the market for TV sets, one measure of quality is product reliability. Customers expect to purchase a set that will not require repairs for many years. Products that do not live up to that level of quality do not last long in the market. In the electronics industry in general, product reliability is rapidly becoming an order qualifier. In the automobile-repair industry, because quality has not yet become an order qualifier in all segments, trade-offs between low-cost operations and quality can still be used to gain an advantage.

SERVICE STRATEGIES

Competitive priorities provide a basis for the design of processes. Standardized services, assemble-to-order, and customized-services strategies are used for processes devoted to the delivery of services.

STANDARDIZED-SERVICES STRATEGY

standardized-services strategy The service strategy utilized by processes that provide services with little variety in high volumes.

Processes that provide services with little variety in high volumes tend to use the **standardized-services strategy.** Typical competitive priorities are consistent quality, on-time delivery, and low cost. Because of the high volume, processes providing the primary service can be organized so that the flow of customers follows a linear pattern in the facility. For example, the U.S. Postal Service uses standardized-service strategies for the letter mail process and the parcel process. The millions of letters and parcels that arrive daily for processing are sorted by destination and loaded into trucks according to customers' priorities. Parcel processing is separate from letter processing because of the different market segments and because of the nature of the automated sorting equipment required for each type of item. The tasks required of the employees and equipment are repetitive and routine, ideal for the standardized-services strategy. FedEx and UPS use a standardized-services strategy for the same reasons.

ASSEMBLE-TO-ORDER STRATEGY

assemble-to-order services strategy The service strategy that designs operations to include processes that produce a set of standardized services and processes that are devoted to assembling standardized offerings for a specific customer's needs.

The **assemble-to-order services strategy** amounts to designing operations to include processes devoted to producing a set of standardized services and processes devoted to assembling standardized offerings for a specific customer's needs. The assembly processes must be flexible so that the correct package can be assembled for the customer. Typical competitive priorities are customization and fast delivery time. For example, long-distance telephone service providers offer customized service packages to retain customers in a highly competitive industry. Internet access, cellular phone

[1]Safizadeh, H. M., L. P. Ritzman, D. Sharma, and C. Wood. "An Empirical Analysis of the Product–Process Matrix," *Management Science*, vol. 42, no. 11 (1996), pp. 1576–1591.
[2]Hill, Terry. *Manufacturing Strategy: Text and Cases,* 3d ed. Homewood, Ill.: Irwin, 2000.

The parcel process at the U.S. Postal Service is high volume, and follows a linear pattern. Here a worker processes, with the push of a button, one of many packages to come through her line.

service, credit cards, satellite broadcast service, personal 800 numbers, and cable TV are among the list of options. The assembly process could be automated, as on a web page, or personalized through telemarketing. Companies such as AT&T, MCI, and Sprint work with the customer to assemble the appropriate mix of services and provide a billing service that combines all charges on one itemized bill.

CUSTOMIZED-SERVICES STRATEGY

customized-services strategy A service strategy designed to provide individualized services.

Processes designed to provide individualized services tend to use a **customized-services strategy.** Typical competitive priorities include high-performance design and customization. Volume, in terms of service requirements per customer, is low. Nested processes tend to be grouped by the function they perform, and customers are routed from process to process until the service is completed. This strategy enables the production of a high variety of customized services while providing reasonable utilization of the processes. For example, Figure 2.2 shows the flow pattern of patients through a health clinic process. Although there are five processes providing services, any one customer may not need all of them. The customers may have to compete for the resources: Note that all patients must see the doctor. Many different routing patterns

FIGURE 2.2

Health Clinic Process

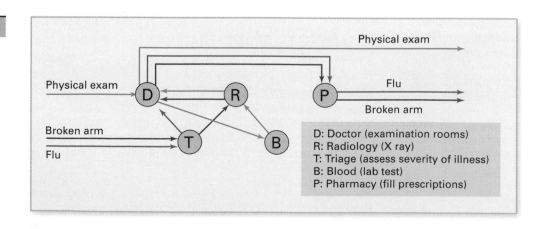

may exist in a facility employing a customized-services strategy. Barber shops and beauty salons, appliance repair shops, and interior decorating services are also suited for a customized-services strategy.

MANUFACTURING STRATEGIES

Manufacturing strategies differ from those in services because of the ability to use inventories. Make-to-stock, assemble-to-order, and make-to-order strategies address the competitive priorities of processes devoted to manufacturing.

MAKE-TO-STOCK STRATEGY

make-to-stock strategy
A manufacturing strategy that involves holding items in stock for immediate delivery, thereby minimizing customer delivery times.

Manufacturing firms that hold items in stock for immediate delivery, thereby minimizing customer delivery times, use a **make-to-stock strategy.** This strategy is feasible for standardized products with high volumes and reasonably accurate forecasts. For example, in Figure 2.3, which depicts a final automobile assembly process, both the midsize 6-cylinder and the compact 4-cylinder models are assembled on the same line. Collectively, the volume of the two models is sufficient to warrant a make-to-stock strategy for the facility. The routing pattern for the two products is straightforward, with four processes devoted to the two products.

A: Front-end body-to-chassis assembly
H: Hood attachment
F: Fluid filling
S: Start-up and testing

This strategy is also applicable to situations in which the firm is producing a unique product for a specific customer if the volumes are high enough. For example, a company producing a sensor for the transmission of the Ford Explorer would have enough volume to operate a production line specifically for that sensor and carry a stock of the finished product for scheduled shipments to the factory. Other examples of products produced with a make-to-stock strategy include garden tools, electronic components, soft drinks, and chemicals.

mass production The approach used by firms that employ a make-to-stock strategy.

The term **mass production** is often used to define firms using a make-to-stock strategy. Because their environment is stable and predictable, mass production firms typically have a bureaucratic organization, and workers repeat narrowly defined tasks. The competitive priorities for these companies typically are consistent quality and low costs.

ASSEMBLE-TO-ORDER STRATEGY

assemble-to-order manufacturing strategy
An approach to producing customized products from relatively few assemblies and components after customer orders are received.

The **assemble-to-order manufacturing strategy** is an approach to producing customized products from relatively few assemblies and components, after customer orders are received. Typical competitive priorities are customization and fast delivery time. The assemble-to-order strategy involves assembly processes and fabrication processes. Because they are devoted to manufacturing standardized components and assemblies in

An employee for a stuffed furniture manufacturer, using an assemble-to-order strategy, applies different fabrics to sofa cushions.

high volumes, the fabrication processes focus on creating appropriate amounts of inventories for the assembly processes. Once the specific order from the customer is received, the assembly processes create the product from the standardized components and assemblies produced by the fabrication processes. The fabrication processes should be efficient to keep costs low, while the assembly processes should be flexible to produce the varied products demanded by the customers.

Stocking finished products would be economically prohibitive because the numerous possible options make forecasting relatively inaccurate. For example, a manufacturer of upscale upholstered furniture can produce hundreds of a particular style of sofa, no two alike, to meet customers' selections of fabric and wood. Other examples include paint (any color can be produced at the paint store by mixing standard pigments) and prefabricated homes for which the customer chooses among color and trim options.

MAKE-TO-ORDER STRATEGY

make-to-order strategy
A strategy used by manufacturers that make products to customer specifications in low volumes.

Manufacturers that make products to customer specifications in low volumes tend to use a **make-to-order strategy.** With this strategy, a firm is viewed as a set of processes that can be used in many different ways to satisfy the unique needs of customers. This strategy provides a high degree of customization, which is a major competitive priority for these manufacturers. Because most products, components, and assemblies are custom-made, the manufacturing process must be flexible to accommodate the variety. Specialized medical equipment, castings, and expensive homes are suited to the make-to-order strategy.

MASS CUSTOMIZATION

At one extreme of the assemble-to-order strategy is **mass customization,** whereby a firm's flexible processes generate customized products or services in high volumes at reasonably low costs. Mass customizers attempt to provide the variety inherent in an assemble-to-order strategy but often focus on relatively high-volume markets. A key to being a successful mass customizer is postponing the task of differentiating a product or service for a specific customer until the latest possible moment. Doing so allows

mass customization An example of the assemble-to-order strategy, whereby a firm's flexible processes generate customized products or services in high volumes at reasonably low costs.

What are the operations implications of being a mass customizer?

the greatest application of standard modules of the product or service before specific customization. The Hewlett-Packard Company provides a good example of mass customization. HP postpones assembly of the printer with the country-specific power supply and packaging of the appropriate manuals until the last link in the process—the distributor in the region where the printer is being delivered. Being a successful mass customizer such as HP may require redesign of products or services and processes. We will have more to say about postponement in the Supply-Chain Management chapter.

PRODUCT OR SERVICE IMPLICATIONS

A product or service should be designed so that it consists of independent modules that can be assembled into different forms easily and inexpensively. For example, the Ritz-Carlton, an upscale chain of hotels, records the preferences expressed by customers during their stay and uses them to tailor the services that customers receive on their next visit. Requests for items such as hypoallergenic pillows, additional towels, or even chocolate chip cookies are recorded for future use so that personalized goods and services can be added to a standard Ritz-Carlton room for repeat customers.

PROCESS IMPLICATIONS

Processes should be designed so that they can be used to meet a wide variety of needs. We discuss process management in more detail in the Process Management chapter; however, one key to supporting mass customization is to design processes as independent modules that can be arranged to provide customization at the latest possible moment, as HP did with its printers. Another example is paint retail stores, which can produce any color the customer wants by using a chromatograph to analyze the customer's paint sample to determine paint and pigment mixture. The store stocks the base colors and pigments separately, mixing them as needed, thereby supplying an unlimited variety of colors without maintaining the inventory required to match each customer's particular color needs. The key is separating the paint-production process from the paint-mixing process. Benetton did a similar thing in its sweater manufacturing process. Rather than dyeing the yarn before manufacturing the sweater, Benetton reversed the dyeing and knitting processes so that sweaters were dyed after the customer had placed an order or the color preferences of consumers for the upcoming

A couple checking in at the Ritz-Carlton, where services are customized to individual preferences.

season had been determined. By rearranging the processes, Benetton saved millions of dollars in write-offs for obsolete inventory.

INTERNET IMPLICATIONS

The Internet has been a valuable technology for mass-customization strategies. Web pages can be designed to attract customers and allow them to configure their own products or services easily and quickly. Customers to Amazon.com fill baskets of goods from a vast array of possibilities, each one different from the next customer's. Dell sells computers through a web page that allows consumers to configure their own computers from a large variety of options. Fleet Corporation, a large bank, offers investment services along with its banking services for its Internet customers. Ford and GM are building systems to permit customers to configure their own automobiles over the Internet. Each of these ventures provides customers an enormous amount of choice in the products or services they buy, but they also put a lot of pressure on the processes that must produce them. Flexibility and short response times are prized qualities for mass-customization processes.

OPERATIONS STRATEGY AS A PATTERN OF DECISIONS

Operations strategy translates service or product plans and competitive priorities for each market segment into decisions affecting the processes that support those market segments. Figure 2.4 shows how corporate strategy provides the umbrella for key operations

FIGURE 2.4

Connection Between Corporate Strategy and Key Operations Management Decisions

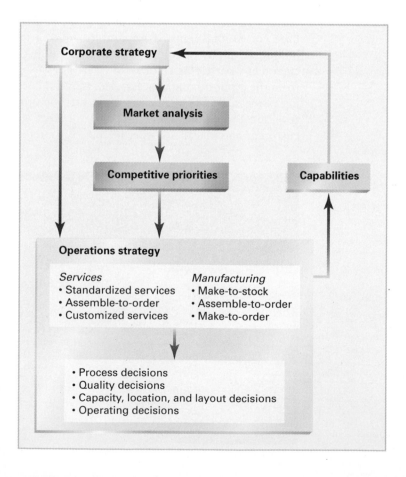

management decisions. The operations manager must select a service or manufacturing strategy for each process. This strategy determines how the firm's processes are organized to handle the volume and variety of products or services for each specific market segment. This initial choice sets in motion a series of other decisions that govern the design of the processes, systems, and procedures that support the operations strategy. These decisions are not static; they must be constantly reevaluated according to the dynamics of the marketplace. We cover these decisions in detail throughout this text. Nonetheless, from a strategic perspective, operations managers are responsible for making the decisions that ensure the firm has the capability to address the competitive priorities of new and existing market segments as they evolve. Furthermore, the pattern of decisions for one organization may be different from that of another, even if they are both in the same industry, because of differences in core competencies, market segments served, and degree of Web integration. Each process must be analyzed from the perspective of the customers it serves, be they external or internal.

In the remainder of this chapter, we show how two firms, one in services and one in manufacturing, chose their strategies and linked their processes to them. Visit the Student CD-ROM for more details on how other decisions were linked for these firms.

TOURING A SERVICE FACILITY: LOWER FLORIDA KEYS HEALTH SYSTEM[3]

The Lower Florida Keys Health System (LFKHS), a full-service acute care community hospital, serves residents from Marathon to Key West, Florida. Some services, such as chemical dependency and eating disorders, draw from a larger area. Although the patient population seems fairly stable, with no significant growth, the population may be shifting north because of the cost of living in Key West. The Florida Keys have a normal population of about 75,000, of which about 30,000 are in the LFKHS service area.

The hospital is typical of relatively small facilities, with 550 employees, 420 of them full-time. This total doesn't include the 55 doctors who practice at the hospital but aren't hospital employees. The emergency room (ER) typically sees 50 to 60 people per day. Inpatients stay in the hospital an average of 5.4 days. LFKHS's annual gross revenue is about $34 million, which generates a surplus of $0.7 million.

SERVICE STRATEGY AND COMPETITIVE PRIORITIES

This general-purpose hospital offers a broad range of services, from treating cuts in the emergency room to obstetrics to major surgery. Its service capabilities stop just short of full trauma care. Because of its small size and low volumes, it cannot offer standardized services at cut-rate prices. The services and procedures given to a patient tend to be "customized." Because of considerable shifts in volume, administrators give high priority to ease of changing staffing levels to match daily workload requirements. Insufficient staffing jeopardizes service quality, whereas excessive staffing hurts the hospital's financial performance. For these reasons, a customized-services strategy is appropriate.

Management also emphasizes high-performance design as a competitive priority. Quality is everyone's responsibility, but a quality assurance (QA) coordinator designs, develops, and implements policies and procedures that enhance quality performance. Accreditation and third-party payers (insurance) are requiring increasingly sophisticated quality assurance programs. A *utilization review* is done for every patient when

---

[3]We are indebted to Jeff E. Heyl and Linda Stone for background information on this tour.

service is completed. All charts and records are reviewed to be sure that hospital personnel did what they were supposed to do.

THE BIG PICTURE: Layout and Customer Flow at LFKHS

The Big Picture illustration on page 52 shows the layout of LFKHS's main hospital facility. Activities are grouped according to function typical of a customized-service strategy. Volumes are too low and unpredictable to set aside many human and capital resources exclusively for a particular type of patient—except for maternity patients. The first floor houses the emergency room, labs, administrative offices, radiology, materials receiving, and operating rooms. The second floor has three wards devoted to patient care, including maternity. The third floor has four more wards, as well as the intensive-care unit. Nurses' stations are centrally located on each patient-care floor.

The customized services provided to each patient cause jumbled patient flows, with lots of individual handling. The number of stops that patients make during their stay varies greatly. Some patients make only 3 or 4 stops, but others may require 20 or more. For simplicity, only one patient's path is shown in the illustration.

PROCESSES
The BIG PICTURE of LFKHS depicts a firm that has undertaken a customized-services strategy. The collection of services provided by LFKHS requires a number of nested processes. For example, it offers emergency care, intensive care, and maternity care. Each of these major processes requires certain other processes from those available at LFKHS, including laboratory, radiology, surgery, and physical therapy. Purchasing, library, cafeteria, and admissions tend to serve all the major processes. Each process must be designed to support the overall goals of the firm.

Owing to its small size, LFKHS acquires certain services—such as pharmacy services—by contracting with others rather than performing them in-house. Contractors handle all orders and obtain the supplies and materials needed to provide their services. In contrast, larger hospitals have sufficiently high volumes to justify performing these services in-house.

Some processes, such as the emergency care process, insist that employees have broad education and experience, giving them the greatest possible flexibility in meeting patient needs. Accreditation standards require at least one registered nurse (RN) on duty at all times on each floor. Employee cross-training is a hospitalwide approach, even for areas where services are more standardized. Salaries and wages are comparable to those in the Miami area, where nurses are paid $15 to $16 per hour. Within classes of employment, wages generally don't vary much, although experience and merit do affect wages within job classifications.

The procedures performed throughout the hospital are rigidly specified by traditional health care approaches, with little employee involvement in methods improvement. A patient's "routing" through the hospital is highly individualized; and few patients have exactly the same routing. Scheduled admissions follow a predetermined routing upon arrival, depending on the reason for the patient's hospitalization. Different surgical procedures involve slightly different routings. Patients admitted from the emergency room have less well-defined routings because there has been no advance planning for their treatment. As actual services are performed on the patient, cost data are collected. Employee hours are recorded in less detail, but time and task linkage are noted.

Because of the advanced technology that is now available and expected by patients, hospitals can be quite capital intensive. For example, a CT scan machine can cost $2 million, and intensive-care monitoring equipment $250,000. LFKHS's investment in equipment and facilities is $12 million, or $28,571 per full-time employee. This total may seem high, but it is less than the total investment of some larger hospitals with higher patient volumes.

TOURING A MANUFACTURING FACILITY: CHAPARRAL STEEL[4]

Chaparral Steel started in 1973 as a joint venture between Texas Industries, Inc. (TXI), of Dallas, Texas, and Co-Steel, Inc., of Toronto, Canada, and is now a wholly owned subsidiary of TXI. Groundbreaking in Midlothian, just outside Dallas, took place in the fall of 1973. The first heat (batch of steel) was melted in May, 1975. The rolling mill started running three months later.

Chaparral Steel fosters innovation and strives to keep on the leading edge of technology. Chaparral is clearly an international producer and marketer, having received Japanese Industrial Standard certification in 1989, which allows the company to sell steel in Japan. In 1996, some 4 percent of Chaparral's shipments were exports. Canada and Mexico are included in the company's home (domestic) market. Within the United States, most sales are to Sun Belt customers.

Chaparral's facilities and operating philosophy reflect the latest advances in worldwide steel making. A customer orientation runs throughout the organization, a team concept blurs the lines between marketing and the other functional areas, and decision making is pushed down to the lowest levels of the organization, with an emphasis on action rather than on bureaucratic procedures. For instance, production workers often are included in the selection, purchase, and installation of major pieces of production equipment.

Chaparral's customers are large steel buyers, who are evaluated by the sales department before the company takes on new business. For example, a customer should have the potential to buy at least 600 tons per year to qualify as a purchaser from the mill. This restriction ensures continuity and stable demand for Chaparral's high-volume operation.

MANUFACTURING STRATEGY AND COMPETITIVE PRIORITIES

Chaparral prides itself on providing good prices, fast delivery, and consistent quality. As for "customer orientation," Chaparral intends to be the easiest company from which to buy steel. Initially, the Midlothian plant was able to produce 250,000 tons of steel per year; now it can produce 2 million. With the exception of certain specialty steels, it is a high-volume producer of standardized products. For these reasons, a make-to-stock strategy is appropriate. The finished inventories allow for fast delivery, and the standardization of processes enables low-cost operations.

The three rolling mills at Chaparral—the Bar Mill, the Medium Section Mill, and the Large Section Mill—determine the range of hot-rolled products the mill can produce. Customers can order standard products in different lengths and sizes; standard products are made to stock and can be cut to length as needed.

Quality assurance is maintained throughout the manufacturing process. Chaparral has a policy of building quality into its products at each step of manufacturing, rather than depending on inspections at the end of the process. The quality control department trains all employees to recognize and remove questionable products as soon as they are discovered. The quality control lab will do any necessary chemical testing to identify quality problems and explain how to fix them. During the process, a front and a back sample are drawn from each heat (batch). For construction materials, the lab tests only for tensile strength. For customized, special bar quality (SBQ) steel, the lab may

---

[4]We are indebted to Jeff E. Heyl and Linda Stone for background information on this tour.

THE BIG PICTURE LOWER FLORIDA KEYS HOSPITAL

Larry is a typical emergency room admission, who has twisted his ankle while jogging on the beach. He hobbles into the emergency room (ER) entrance (1) and sits down to fill out a patient history while he waits (2). Soon a nurse escorts him to an ER triage room (3), where she checks the severity of his injury. He returns to a seat in the waiting room (4), until an ER bed (5) opens up for him.

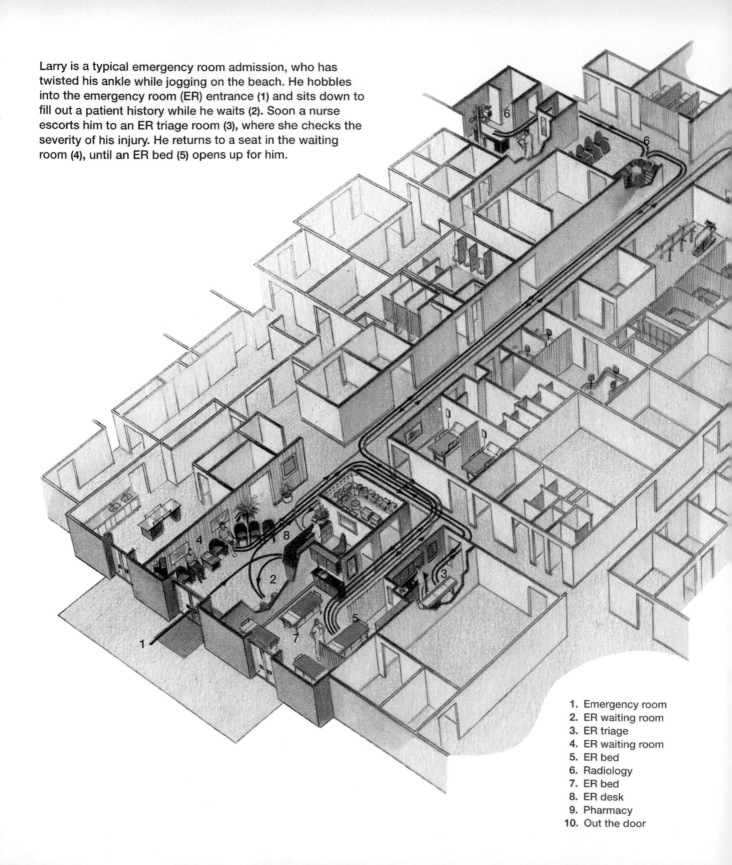

1. Emergency room
2. ER waiting room
3. ER triage
4. ER waiting room
5. ER bed
6. Radiology
7. ER bed
8. ER desk
9. Pharmacy
10. Out the door

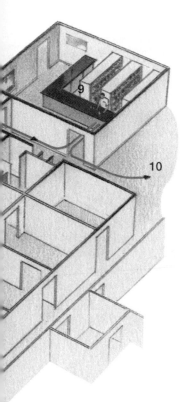

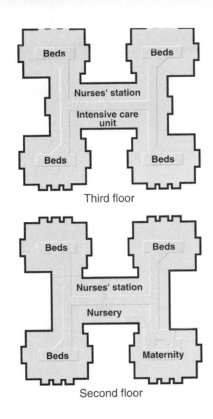

There a nurse and doctor palpate the ankle and question Larry about the level and type of pain he's experiencing. The doctor determines that X rays will be necessary, and Larry is wheeled to the Radiology Department (6), where the radiologist takes the X rays. Larry then returns to his bed in the ER (7). Shortly, the doctor returns to tell him that he has a simple strain; suggests ice, compression, and elevation; and prescribes a muscle relaxant. Larry checks out at the ER desk (8) and picks up his prescription at the hospital pharmacy (9) on his way out the door (10).

Third floor

Second floor

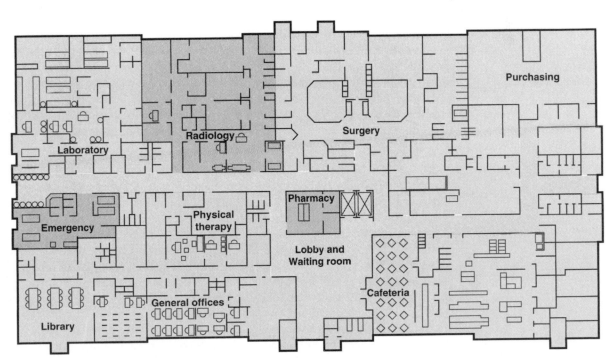

First floor

perform a variety of tests, depending on the customer's specifications. In addition, SBQ material is hot bed–inspected (on the cooling bed after rolling) for seams and cracks.

PROCESSES

Chaparral Steel is very capital intensive and innovative in its choice of technologies. High volumes are necessary to fully utilize expensive equipment. Chaparral does what it can to exceed customer expectations by making it easy to place orders, delivering orders quickly, and providing consistent quality at low prices. The order-fulfillment process is facilitated by a new Web page that allows customers to place orders online, check on the status of their shipment, and download current plant schedules. The Web page also allows customers to access account information, thereby improving the accuracy of the billing process. Manufacturing processes are organized so that the general flow of products is uniform. Although products follow the same general sequence of processes, most of the processes are tailored to specific products. The major manufacturing processes at Chaparral are melting, casting, milling, and shearing.

MELTING PROCESS. Melting is done in computer-assisted, high-powered electric arc furnaces. The melt charge, or raw material, consists exclusively of scrap metal, rather than the iron ore used in most steel-making operations. Chaparral's automobile shredder alone supplies more than 700,000 tons of prepared scrap per year. The shredder has both ferrous and nonferrous separators, as well as a wet scrubber, to ensure that the charge is of acceptable quality. A furnace can melt a batch of metal in two hours, called the charge-to-tap time.

CASTING PROCESS. Continuous casting converts the molten metal into long steel bars called billets. Continuous casting eliminates several steps in the traditional steel-making process of pouring ingots. Chaparral has casters for each of its rolling mills. The four-strand curved mold caster supplies billets up to 49 feet in length to the Bar Mill, the smallest of the rolling mills. The five-strand caster supplies somewhat wider and shorter billets to the Medium Section Mill. The average yield of both these casters is more than 90 percent. The newest mill, the Large Section Mill, was built to utilize an internally developed "near net shape" caster. Instead of casting a rectangular billet, it casts one that is closer to the desired end shape of the beam. The casters have been carefully analyzed to improve quality. For example, electromagnetic stirring goes on within the molds, giving the billets superior surface and interior quality characteristics.

MILLING PROCESS. The billets go next to one of the *rolling* mills, where they must be heated to 2,200° Fahrenheit in gas-fired reheat furnaces. At this temperature, the billet becomes pliable and can be easily deformed. The heated billets are fed into a vertical reducing unit by a set of pinch rolls. The hot steel then moves untouched through 16 in-line stands, which progressively roll it into the desired product shape. In the Large Section Mill, the product has to be rolled fewer times to get the desired end shape. An old-style mill might call for 50 passes through rollers to accomplish what the Large Section Mill can do in 8 to 12. The result is considerable savings in processing costs across the board. Energy costs were cut by about 55 percent, and labor costs also are down, with only 0.25 labor hour per ton required in this mill.

The rolling mills have a sophisticated computerized control system assisting production personnel in maintaining precise roll speed at each stand. The computer automatically prints out metal bundle tags, which include the heat number, theoretical weight, and piece count.

SHEARING PROCESS. The formed bars next travel to an automatic cooling bed. The cooled bars are then transferred to the cold shear, where they are cut to standard lengths of 20 to 60 feet. The sheared bars are automatically collected, strapped in bundles of 2 to 5 tons each, and tagged. Finally, they are moved to the warehouse for storage or to the shipping yard to await distribution. Angle and channel products are processed slightly differently. They are bulk-bundled, stored in the yard, and then restraightened off-line at the Bar Mill Straightener.

THE BIG PICTURE: Bar Mill Process at Chaparral Steel

The Big Picture illustration on the next spread shows that the material flows are linear in the Bar Mill. Products follow a one-directional route from the reheat furnace to storage of the finished product. An overhead crane is used to change the mill rolls on the line. At the end of the process, electromagnetic cranes and forklifts move material off the mill to storage. With these exceptions, materials handling tends to be automated and to follow fixed paths. For example, the steel flows down through the rolling mills automatically. Compare this linear, high-volume flow with the jumbled, customized flows at Lower Florida Keys Health System.

In terms of performance measures for the manufacturing processes, Chaparral monitors production per hour, yield, alloys used per ton, electricity per ton, and tons per hour per employee. But tons shipped (produced) is the number that matters the most. A sign at the plant entrance shows yesterday's tonnage. As at any similar type of facility, running at nearly full capacity is the best way for Chaparral to make money.

DIFFERENCES BETWEEN LFKHS AND CHAPARRAL STEEL

What impact does flow strategy have on other operating decisions?

The sharp contrast between LFKHS and Chaparral Steel, summarized in Table 2.1, gives a sense of how decisions in operations must mesh. Clearly, the two firms utilize different strategies. Competitive priorities on which these strategies are based also differ. LFKHS has a customized-services strategy. The hospital's strategy calls for low-volume, customized services. Chaparral Steel has a make-to-stock strategy. The product volumes at Chaparral are huge: 2 million tons of steel per year, most of which is for standardized products. Its dominant competitive priorities are low cost, fast delivery, and consistent quality. The opposite is true at LFKHS, where competitive priorities cover a broad range of services customized to individual patients. LFKHS also has considerable volume flexibility, as it can adjust its capacity with overtime and part-time help to match staffing requirements with patient census and acuity.

Although LFKHS has advanced and expensive technologies in certain areas, its operation is labor intensive. Its financial health depends heavily on its being able to manage its labor costs. Chaparral Steel is quite different. To be cost competitive, it must use automation and technology to the fullest. Clearly, these two organizations have linked their processes to their respective operations strategies.

TABLE 2.1	Decision Area	LFKHS	Chaparral
Operations Strategies at LFKHS and Chaparral	Business strategy	Low-volume, customized services	High-volume, standardized products made to stock
	Competitive priorities	Customized services, consistent quality, and volume flexibility	Low cost, fast delivery, and consistent quality
	Process design	Labor intensive	Capital intensive

THE BIG PICTURE CHAPARRAL STEEL

The Chaparral Steel plant covers some 75 acres which includes the Bar Mill, the Medium Section Mill, the Large Section Mill, and the melt shop and continuous caster. The entire process is continuous in design, with a sophisticated computerized control system assisting personnel. The floor plan of the Bar Mill is illustrated with an expanded cutaway on the opposite page, highlighting the linear flow of the steel as it passes through operations.

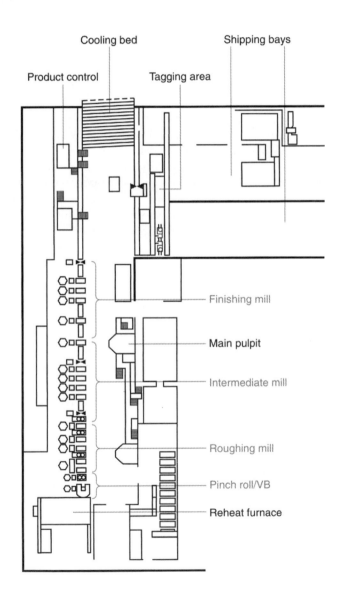

A truncated (for space reasons) version of the Bar Mill, used for the plant's small hot-rolled products. A four-strand mold caster supplies billets to the Bar Mill, where they are heated in the reheat furnace (1). The heat-softened billets then pass through the pinch rolls and VB (2) and move in a linear path (bottom to top) through the 16 in-line stands (3), which roll them into the desired shape. The mill is equipped with a computerized control system. From the main control pulpit (4), an operator can read out status and maintain precise roll speed at each stand. The off-line machine shop (5) machines and stores the massive mill rolls, which workers can move into place with overhead cranes (6), to set up the line for each new product. The formed bars travel to the cooling bed (7). From there they come back to the cold shear station, where they are cut, bundled, and tagged for storage or shipment (8).

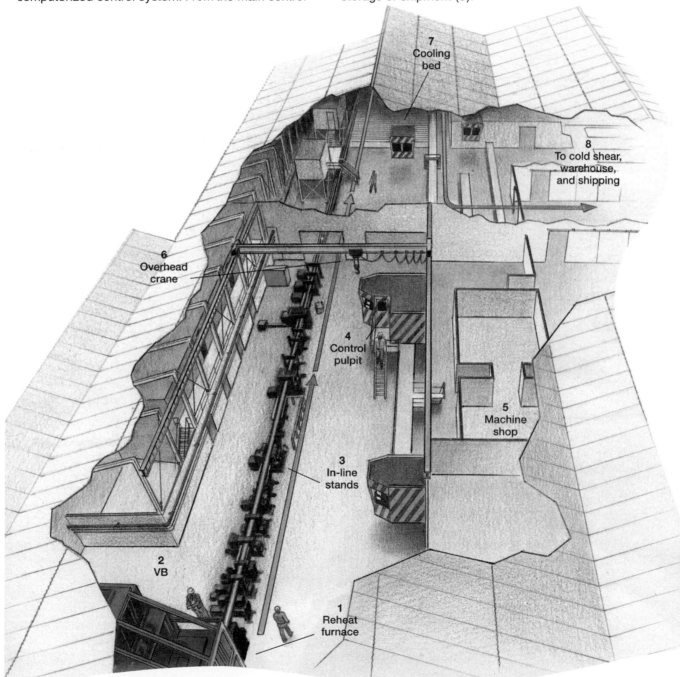

7
Cooling bed

8
To cold shear, warehouse, and shipping

6
Overhead crane

4
Control pulpit

5
Machine shop

3
In-line stands

2
VB

1
Reheat furnace

OPERATIONS STRATEGY ACROSS THE ORGANIZATION

Corporate strategy affects every functional area of a firm. It views the organization as a system of interconnected parts, or functional areas, each working in concert with the others to achieve desired goals. Operations strategy, which supports corporate strategy, also requires a close connection among the functional areas. A key area is *management information systems*, which designs the systems that provide market data and competitor information in a global environment. However, this connectivity transcends information flows and extends to full collaboration on decisions. As we have indicated, operations strategy specifies the overall service or manufacturing strategy and involves a pattern of decisions that affect the processes, systems, and procedures of the firm. Consequently, when *marketing* wants to add a new product or service, it should coordinate with *operations* to ensure that the firm has the ability to support the new endeavor. Adding new products or services without the ability to produce them can lead to poor performance.

Often, new investments are required to support new endeavors or to improve existing operations. An operations strategy may require investments in new equipment and other financial support for improvements, both of which must be coordinated with *finance*. In addition, finance is interested in the operations strategy because it affects the ability of the firm to generate revenues, which contribute to its financial performance.

Invariably, operations strategies involve the design of new processes or the redesign of existing ones. *Engineering* works with operations to arrive at the designs that achieve the appropriate competitive priorities. Engineering also is heavily involved in the design of new products and services and must do so in light of the ability of the firm to produce them.

CHAPTER HIGHLIGHTS

❐ Corporate strategy involves monitoring and adjusting to changes in the external environment and exploiting core competencies. The Internet has caused firms to reevaluate their strategic planning process. Firms taking a global view may form strategic alliances through collaborative efforts, joint ventures, or licensing of technology.

❐ Market analysis is key to formulating a customer-driven operations strategy. Market segmentation and needs assessment are methods of pinpointing elements of a product or service that satisfy customers.

❐ Customer-driven operations strategy requires translating market needs into desirable capabilities for the operations function, called competitive priorities. There are eight priorities: low-cost operations, high-performance design, consistent quality, fast delivery time, on-time delivery, development speed, customization, and volume flexibility. Trade-offs among them are sometimes necessary. Management must decide on which dimensions the firm's processes should excel.

❐ With time-based competition, managers seek to save time on the various steps taken to deliver a product or service.

❐ Concurrent engineering during product and service planning involves operations and other functions early in the development and testing of a new product or service.

❐ Processes devoted to producing services choose one of the following three operations strategies: standardized services, which facilitates low-cost operations, consistent quality, and on-time delivery; assemble-to-order services, which facilitates customization and fast delivery time; and customized services, which facilitates high-performance design and customization.

❐ Processes devoted to manufacturing choose one of the following three operations strategies: make-to-stock, which facilitates low costs, consistent quality, and fast delivery time; manufacturing assemble-to-order, which facilitates fast delivery time and customization; and make-to-order, which facilitates customization and low volumes.

❐ Mass customization is a form of the assemble-to-order strategy, whereby a firm uses both flexible and standard processes to produce customized products or services in high volumes at reasonable costs.

❐ Operations strategy is a pattern of decisions, starting with a choice of service or manufacturing strategy and addressing the many processes that support it.

KEY TERMS

assemble-to-order manufacturing strategy *45*
assemble-to-order services strategy *43*
competitive priorities *31*
concurrent engineering *41*
consistent quality *39*
core competencies *33*
customization *41*

customized-services strategy *44*
development speed *39*
fast delivery time *39*
high-performance design *39*
lead time *39*
make-to-order strategy *46*
make-to-stock strategy *45*
mass customization *47*

mass production *45*
on-time delivery *39*
operations strategy *31*
standardized-services strategy *43*
time-based competition *40*
volume flexibility *41*

OM EXPLORER AND INTERNET EXERCISES

Visit our Web site at www.prenhall.com/krajewski for OM Explorer Tutors, which explain quantitative techniques; Solvers, which help you apply mathematical models; and Internet Exercises, including Facility Tours, which expand on the topics in this chapter.

DISCUSSION QUESTIONS

1. The onset of exponential growth in the development of information technologies has encouraged the birth of many "dot-com" companies. The Internet has enabled these companies to reach customers in very effective ways. Consider Amazon.com, whose Web site enjoys millions of "hits" each day and puts customers in touch with more than 18 million products and services. What are Amazon.com's competitive priorities and what should its operations strategy focus on?

2. In its mission statement, a local hospital declares that it is committed to provide *care* to patients arriving at the emergency unit in less than 15 minutes and that it will never turn away patients who need to be hospitalized for further medical care. What implications does this mission have for strategic operations management decisions (e.g., decisions relating to capacity and workforce)?

3. FedEx has built its business on quick, dependable delivery of items being shipped by air from one business to another. Its early advantages included global tracking of shipments using Web technology. The advancement of Internet technology has enabled competitors to become much more sophisticated in order tracking. In addition, the

advent of dot-com business has put pressure on increased ground transportation deliveries. Explain how this change in the environment could affect FedEx's operations strategy, especially relative to UPS, which has a stronghold on the business-to-consumer ground delivery business.

4. Understanding the customer benefit package enables management to identify ways to gain competitive advantage in the marketplace. What do you consider to be the components of the customer benefit package in the provision of

   a. an automobile insurance policy.
   b. dental work to install a crown.
   c. an airline flight.

5. Suppose that you were conducting a market analysis for a new textbook about technology management. What would you need to know to identify a market segment? How would you make a needs assessment? What would be the customer benefit package?

6. Although all eight of the competitive priorities discussed in the chapter are relevant to a company's success in the marketplace, explain why a company should not necessarily try to excel in all of them. What determines the

choice of the competitive priorities that a company should emphasize?

7. A local fast-food restaurant processes several customer orders at once. Service clerks cross paths, sometimes nearly colliding, while they trace different paths to fill customer orders. If customers order a special combination of toppings on their hamburgers, they must wait quite some time while the special order is cooked. How would you modify the restaurant's operations to achieve competitive advantage? Because demand surges at lunchtime, volume flexibility is a competitive priority in the fast-food business. How would you achieve volume flexibility?

8. Kathryn Shoemaker established Grandmother's Chicken Restaurant in Middlesburg five years ago. It features a unique recipe for chicken, "just like grandmother used to make." The facility is homey, with relaxed and friendly service. Business has been good during the past two years, for both lunch and dinner. Customers normally wait about 15 minutes to be served, although complaints about service delays have increased. Shoemaker is currently considering whether to expand the current facility or open a similar restaurant in neighboring Uniontown, which has been growing rapidly.

   a. What types of strategic plans must Shoemaker make?
   b. What environmental forces could be at work in Middlesburg and Uniontown that Shoemaker should consider?
   c. What are the possible distinctive competencies of Grandmother's?

9. For 20 years, Russell's Pharmacy has been located on the town square of River City, the only town for 20 miles in any direction. River City's economy is dominated by agriculture and generally rises and falls with the price of corn. But Russell's Pharmacy enjoys a steady business. Jim Russell is on a first-name basis with the entire town. He provides friendly, accurate service, listens patiently to health complaints, and knows the family health history of everyone. He keeps an inventory of the medicines required by regular customers but sometimes has a one-day delay to fill new prescriptions. However, he cannot obtain drugs at the same low price as the large pharmacy chains can. There's trouble right here in River City. Several buildings around the town square are now abandoned or used as storerooms for old cars. The town is showing signs of dying off right along with the family farm. Twenty miles upstream, situated on a large island in the river, is the growing town of Large Island. Russell is considering a move to the Conestoga Mall in Large Island.

   a. What types of strategic plans must Russell make?
   b. What environmental forces could be at work that Russell should consider?
   c. What are the possible core competencies of Russell's Pharmacy?

10. Wild West, Inc., is a regional telephone company that inherited nearly 100,000 employees and 50,000 retirees from AT&T. Wild West has a new mission: to diversify. It calls for a 10-year effort to enter the financial services, real estate, cable TV, home shopping, entertainment, and cellular communication services markets—and to compete with other telephone companies. Wild West plans to provide cellular and fiber-optic communication services in markets with established competitors, such as the United Kingdom, and in markets with essentially no competition, such as Russia and former Eastern Bloc countries.

   a. What types of strategic plans must Wild West make? Is the "do-nothing" option viable? If Wild West's mission appears too broad, which businesses would you trim first?
   b. What environmental forces could be at work that Wild West should consider?
   c. What are the possible core competencies of Wild West? What weaknesses should it avoid or mitigate?

11. You are in the process of choosing a bank to open a checking with interest account. Several banks in your community offer competitive checking services with the same interest payment. Identify the order qualifiers that would guide your choice.

12. You are designing a grocery delivery business. Via the Internet, your company will offer staple and frozen foods in a large metropolitan area and then deliver them within a customer-defined window of time. You plan to partner with two major food stores in the area. What should be your competitive priorities and what capabilities do you want to develop in your operations?

13. Volume flexibility can be a competitive advantage. Under what conditions would the benefits of volume flexibility be significant in a particular type of operation? Specifically, which facility—LFKHS or Chaparral Steel—would have a greater need for volume flexibility, based on the information given in the Plant Tours? Why?

14. Based on your reading of the Chaparral Steel's plant tour, what are the core competencies of Chaparral Steel? How has the company utilized these core competencies with respect to the competitive priorities that it emphasizes?

CASE BSB, INC.: THE PIZZA WARS COME TO CAMPUS

Renee Kershaw, manager of food services at a medium-sized private university in the Southeast, has just had the wind taken out of her sails. She had decided that, owing to the success of her year-old pizza service, the time had come to expand pizza-making operations on campus. However, yesterday the university president announced plans to begin construction of a student center on campus that would house, among other facilities, a new food court. In a departure from past university policy, this new facility would permit and accommodate food-service operations from three private organizations: Dunkin' Donuts, Taco Bell, and Pizza Hut. Until now, all food service on campus had been contracted out to BSB, Inc.

CAMPUS FOOD SERVICE

BSB, Inc., is a large, nationally operated food-services company serving client organizations. The level of service provided varies, depending on the type of market being served and the particular contract specifications. The company is organized into three market-oriented divisions: corporate, airline, and university or college. Kershaw, of course, is employed in the university or college division.

At this particular university, BSB, Inc., is under contract to provide food services for the entire campus of 6,000 students and 3,000 faculty, staff, and support personnel. Located in a city of approximately 200,000 people, the campus was built on land donated by a wealthy industrialist. Because the campus is somewhat isolated from the rest of the town, students wanting to shop or dine off campus have to drive into town.

The campus itself is a "walking" campus, with dormitories, classrooms, and supporting amenities such as a bookstore, sundry shop, barber shop, branch bank, and food-service facilities—all within close proximity. Access to the campus by car is limited, with peripheral parking lots provided. The university also provides space, at a nominal rent, for three food-service facilities. The primary facility, a large cafeteria housed on the ground floor of the main administration building, is located in the center of campus. This cafeteria is open for breakfast, lunch, and dinner daily. A second location, called the Dogwood Room, on the second floor of the administration building, serves an upscale luncheon buffet on weekdays only. The third facility is a small grill located in the corner of a recreational building near the dormitories. The grill is open from 11 A.M. to 10 P.M. daily and until midnight on Friday and Saturday nights. Kershaw is responsible for all three operations.

THE PIZZA DECISION

BSB, Inc., has been operating the campus food services for the past 10 years—ever since the university decided that its mission and core competencies should focus on education, not on food service. Kershaw has been at this university for 18 months. Previously, she had been assistant manager of food services at a small university in the Northeast. After 3 to 4 months of getting oriented to the new position, she had begun to conduct surveys to determine customer needs and market trends.

An analysis of the survey data indicated that students were not as satisfied with the food service as Kershaw had hoped. A large amount of the food being consumed by students, broken down as follows, was not being purchased at the BSB facilities:

Percent of food prepared in dorm rooms	20
Percent of food delivered from off campus	36
Percent of food consumed off campus	44

The reasons most commonly given by students were (1) lack of variety in food offerings and (2) tight, erratic schedules that didn't always fit with cafeteria serving hours. Three other findings from the survey were of concern to Kershaw: (1) the large percentage of students with cars, (2) the large percentage of students with refrigerators and microwave ovens in their rooms, and (3) the number of times students ordered food delivered from off campus.

Percent of students with cars on campus	84
Percent of students having refrigerators or microwaves in their rooms	62
Percent of food that students consume outside BSB, Inc., facilities	43

In response to the market survey, Kershaw decided to expand the menu at the grill to include pizza. Along with expanding the menu, she also started a delivery service that covered the entire campus. Now students would have not only greater variety but also the convenience of having food delivered quickly to their rooms. To accommodate these changes, a pizza oven was installed in the grill and space was allocated to store pizza ingredients, to make cut-and-box pizzas, and to stage premade pizzas that were ready to cook. Existing personnel were trained to make pizzas, and additional personnel were hired to deliver them by bicycle. In an attempt to keep costs down and provide fast delivery, Kershaw limited the combinations of toppings available. That way a limited number of "standard pizzas" could be preassembled and ready to cook as soon as an order was received.

continued

continued

THE SUCCESS

Kershaw believed that her decision to offer pizza service in the grill was the right one. Sales over the past 10 months had steadily increased, along with profits. Follow-up customer surveys indicated a high level of satisfaction with the reasonably priced and speedily delivered pizzas. However, Kershaw realized that success brought with it other challenges.

The demand for pizzas had put a strain on the grill's facilities. Initially, space was taken from other grill activities to accommodate the pizza oven, preparation, and staging areas. As the demand for pizzas grew, so did the need for space and equipment. The capacities of existing equipment and space allocated for making and cooking pizzas now were insufficient to meet demand, and deliveries were being delayed. To add to the problem, groups were beginning to order pizzas in volume for various on-campus functions.

Finally, a closer look at the sales data showed that pizza sales were beginning to level off. Kershaw wondered whether the capacity problem and resulting increase in delivery times were the reasons. However, something else had been bothering her. In a recent conversation, Mack Kenzie, the grill's supervisor, had told Kershaw that over the past couple of months requests for pizza toppings and combinations not on the menu had steadily increased. She wondered whether her on-campus market was being affected by the "pizza wars" off campus and the proliferation of specialty pizzas.

THE NEW CHALLENGE

As she sat in her office, Kershaw thought about yesterday's announcement concerning the new food court. It would increase competition from other types of snack foods (Dunkin' Donuts) and fast foods (Taco Bell). Of more concern, Pizza Hut was going to put in a facility offering a limited menu and providing a limited selection of pizzas on a "walk-up-and-order" basis. Phone orders would not be accepted nor would delivery service be available.

Kershaw pondered several crucial questions: Why had demand for pizzas leveled off? What impact would the new food court have on her operations? Should she expand her pizza operations? If so, how?

Questions

1. How would you describe the mission of BSB, Inc., on this campus? Does BSB, Inc., enjoy any competitive advantages or core competencies?
2. Initially, how did Renee Kershaw choose to use her pizza operations to compete with off-campus eateries? What were her competitive priorities?
3. What impact will the new food court have on Kershaw's pizza operations? What competitive priorities might she choose to focus on now?
4. If she were to change the competitive priorities for the pizza operation, how might that affect her operating processes and capacity decisions?
5. What would be a good flow strategy for Kershaw's operations on campus to meet the food court competition?

Source: This case was prepared by Dr. Brooke Saladin, Wake Forest University, as a basis for classroom discussion.

EXPERIENTIAL LEARNING MIN-YO GARMENT COMPANY

The Min-Yo Garment Company is a small firm in Taiwan that produces sportswear for sale in the wholesale and retail markets. Min-Yo's garments are unique because they offer fine embroidery and fabrics with a variety of striped and solid patterns. Over the 20 years of its existence, the Min-Yo Garment Company has become known as a quality producer of sports shirts with dependable deliveries. However, during that same period, the nature of the apparel industry was undergoing change. In the past, firms could be successful producing standardized shirts in high volumes with few pattern or color choices and long production lead times. Currently, with the advent of regionalized merchandising and intense competition at the retail level, buyers of the shirts are looking for shorter lead times and much more variety in patterns and colors. Consequently, many more business opportunities are available today than ever before to a respected company such as Min-Yo.

Even though the opportunity for business success seemed bright, the management meeting last week was gloomy. Mr. Min-Yo Lee, president and owner of Min-Yo Garment, expressed concerns over the performance of the company: "We are facing strong competition for our products. Large apparel firms are driving prices down on high-volume licensed brands. Each day more firms enter the customized shirt business. Our profits are lower than expected, and delivery performance is deteriorating. We must reexamine our capabilities and decide what we can do best."

PRODUCTS

Min-Yo has divided its product line into three categories: licensed brands, subcontracted brands, and special garments.

Licensed Brands. Licensed brands are brands that are owned by one company but, through a licensing agreement, are produced by another firm that also markets the brand in a specific geographic region. The licenser may have licensees all over the world. The licensee pays the licenser a fee for the privilege of marketing the brand in its region, and the licenser agrees to provide some advertising for the product, typically through media outlets that have international exposure. A key aspect of the licensing agreement is that the licensee must agree to provide sufficient quantities of product at the retail level. Running out of stock hurts the image of the brand name.

Presently, only one licensed brand is manufactured by Min-Yo. The brand, called the Muscle Shirt, is owned by a large "virtual corporation" in Italy that has no manufacturing facilities of its own. Min-Yo has been licensed to manufacture Muscle Shirts and sell them to large retail chains in Taiwan. The retail chains require prompt shipments at the end of each week. Because of competitive pressures from other licensed brands, low prices are important. Min-Yo sells each Muscle Shirt to retail chains for $6.

The demand for Muscle Shirts averages 900 shirts per week. The following demand for Muscle Shirts has been forecasted for the next 12 weeks.

WEEK	DEMAND	WEEK	DEMAND
1*	700	7	1,100
2	800	8	1,100
3	900	9	900
4	900	10	900
5	1,000	11	800
6	1,100	12	700

*In other words, the company expects to sell 700 Muscle Shirts at the end of week 1.

Min-Yo has found that its forecasts of Muscle Shirts are accurate to within ±200 shirts per week. If demand exceeds supply in any week, the excess demand is lost. No backorders are taken, and there is no cost penalty to Min-Yo for lost sales.

Subcontracted Brands. Manufacturers in the apparel industry often face uncertain demand. To maintain level production at their plants, many manufacturers seek subcontractors to produce their brands. Min-Yo is often considered as a subcontractor because of its reputation in the industry. Although price is a consideration, the owners of subcontracted brands emphasize dependable delivery and the ability of the subcontractor to adjust order quantities on short notice.

Currently, Min-Yo manufactures only one subcontracted brand, called the Thunder Shirt because of its bright colors. Thunder Shirts are manufactured to order for a company in Singapore. Min-Yo's price to this company is $7 per shirt. When orders are placed, usually twice a month, the customer specifies the delivery of certain quantities in each of the next two weeks. The last order the customer placed is overdue, forcing Min-Yo to pay a penalty charge. To avoid another penalty, 200 shirts must be shipped in week 1. The company is expected to specify the quantities it requires for weeks 2 and 3 at the beginning of week 1. The delivery schedule containing the orders for weeks 4 and 5 is expected to arrive at the beginning of week 3, and so on. The customer has estimated its average weekly needs for the year to be 200 shirts per week, although its estimates are frequently inaccurate.

Because of the importance of this large customer to Min-Yo and the lengthy negotiations of the sales department to get the business, management always tries to satisfy its needs. Management believes that, if Min-Yo Garment ever refuses to accept an order from this company, Min-Yo will lose its business. Under the terms of the sales contract, Min-Yo agreed to pay this customer $1 for every shirt not shipped on time for each week the shipment of the shirt is delinquent. *Delinquent shipments must be made up.*

Special Garments. Special garments are made only to customer order because of their low volume and specialized nature. Customers come to Min-Yo Garment to manufacture shirts for special promotions or special company occasions. Min-Yo's special garments are known as Dragon Shirts because of the elaborate embroidery and oriental flair of the designs. Because each shirt is made to a particular customer's specifications and requires a separate setup, special garments cannot be produced in advance of a firm customer order.

Although price is not a major concern for the customers of special garments, Min-Yo sells Dragon Shirts for $8 a shirt to ward off other companies seeking to enter the custom shirt market. Its customers come to Min-Yo because the company can produce almost any design with high quality and deliver an entire order on time. When placing an order for a Dragon Shirt, a customer specifies the design of the shirt (or chooses from Min-Yo's catalog), supplies specific designs for logos, and specifies the quantity of the order and the delivery date. In the past, management checked to see if such an order could be fitted into the schedule and either accepted or rejected it on that basis. If Min-Yo accepts an order for delivery at the *end* of a certain week and fails to meet this commitment, it pays a penalty of $2 per shirt for each week delivery is delayed. This penalty is incurred weekly until the delinquent order

continued

continued

continued

TABLE 2.2   *Min-Yo Open-Order File**
(as of the end of week 0)

WEEK OF DELIVERY	PRODUCT TYPE	QUANTITY
1	Thunder	200 (past due)

*All orders are to be delivered at the *end* of the week indicated, after production for the week has been completed and before the next week's production is started.

is delivered. The company tried to forecast demand for specific designs of Dragon Shirts but has given up.

Table 2.2, Min-Yo's current open-order file, shows a past-due order of Thunder Shirts that has already been promised for delivery. Orders for Dragon Shirts (none shown here) are specified by order number to emphasize that each order quantity is unique.

MANUFACTURING

Process. Min-Yo Garment has the latest process technology in the industry—a machine, called a garment maker, which is run by one operator on each of three shifts. This single machine process can make every garment Min-Yo produces; however, the changeover times consume a substantial amount of capacity. Company policy is to run the machine three shifts a day, five days a week. If there is insufficient business to keep the machine busy, the worker(s) are idle because Min-Yo has made a definite commitment to never fire or lay off a worker. By the same token, the firm

has a policy of never working on weekends. Thus, the capacity of the process is 5 days × 24 hours = 120 hours per week. The hourly wage is $10 per hour, so the firm is committed to a fixed labor cost of $10 × 120 = $1,200 per week. Once the machine has been set up to make a particular type of garment, it can produce them at the rate of 10 garments per hour, regardless of type. The cost of the material in each garment, regardless of type, is $4. Raw materials are never a problem and can be obtained overnight.

Scheduling the Garment Maker. Scheduling at Min-Yo Garment is done once each week, after production for the week has been completed and shipped, after new orders from customers have arrived, and before production for the next week has started. Scheduling results in two documents. The first is a profit and loss (P&L) statement for the week that factors in sales and production costs, including penalty charges and inventory carrying costs, as shown in Table 2.3. The inventory carrying cost for *any type of product* is $0.10 per shirt per week left in inventory after shipments for the week have been made.

The second document, a production schedule, is shown in Table 2.4. The schedule shows what management wants the garment maker process to produce for each week in the future. Because the schedule loses validity (owing to uncertainty) the farther into the future that it is projected, it is reformulated each week. Note that the schedule specifies two things that are important in the "action" bucket (the next period for which definite, *irrevocable* commitments

TABLE 2.3   *P&L Statement (week 0)*

(1) PRODUCT	(2) PRICE	(3) BEGINNING INVENTORY	(4) PRODUCTION	(5) AVAILABLE[2]	(6) DEMAND	(7) SALES[3]	(8) ENDING INVENTORY[1] (PAST DUE)	(9) INVENTORY/PAST-DUE COST[4]
Muscle	$6	550	800	1,350	750	$4,500	600	$ 60
Thunder	7	—	200	200	400	1,400	(200)	200
Dragon	8	—	—	—	—	—	—	—
Totals			1,000			$5,900		$260

Sales (total of column 7) $5,900
Costs:
  Labor $1,200
  Materials (total of column 4 × $4)   4,000
  Inventory/past due (total of column 9)   260
    Total cost $5,460
  Contribution to profit $ 440   ($5,900 − $5,460)
  Cumulative contribution $ 440   (add to next period's contribution)

[1] Past due refers to the quantity of shirts not shipped as promised.

[2] Available = column 3 + column 4.

[3] Sales = column 6 × column 2 when demand < available; column 5 × column 2, otherwise.

[4] Inventory cost = 0.10 times number of shirts in ending inventory. Past-due cost equals number of shirts not shipped when promised times the penalty ($1 for Thunder Shirts; $2 for the Dragon Shirts).

TABLE 2.4 *Production Schedule (week 0)*											
Week—Product	0	1	2	3	4	5	6	7	8	9	10
Muscle	800 ①										
Hours	88										
Thunder	200 ②										
Hours	30										
Dragon											
Hours											
Total hours scheduled	118										

must be made). The first is the number of hours (setup + run) that are allocated to each product to be produced. The garment maker can produce 10 shirts per hour, so the hours required to produce a particular product is calculated by adding the setup time to the production quantity divided by 10. For example, in Table 2.4 the setup times for Muscle Shirts and Thunder Shirts are 8 and 10 hours, respectively. The time spent on Muscle Shirts is $8 + 800/10 = 88$ hours. For Thunder Shirts, it is $10 + 200/10 = 30$ hours. The total time spent by the garment maker process on all products in a week *cannot exceed 120 hours.*

The second important piece of information is a circled number indicating the sequence in which products are to be produced. This information is important because, at the end of a week, the garment maker process will be set up for the last product produced. If the same product is to be produced first the following week, no new setup will be required (as indicated by this number sequence). The only exception to this rule is Dragon Shirts. As each order is unique, a new setup is required for each Dragon Shirt order. Table 2.4 shows that in week 0 the sequence was Muscle Shirts followed by Thunder Shirts.

THE SIMULATION

At Min-Yo Garment Company, the executive committee meets weekly to discuss the new order possibilities and the load on the garment maker process. The executive committee consists of top management representatives from finance, marketing, and operations. You will be asked to participate on a team and play the role of a member of the executive committee in class. During this exercise, you must decide how far into the future to plan. Some decisions, such as the markets you want to exploit, are long-term in nature. Before class, you may want to think about the markets and their implications for manufacturing. Other decisions are short-term and have an impact on the firm's ability to meet its commitments. The instructor will give each team the latest company data, including the setup times for each product, before the simulation begins. In class, the simulation will proceed as follows.

1. You will start by specifying the production schedule for week 1, based on the forecasts for week 1 in the case narrative for Muscle Shirts and additional information on new and existing orders for the customized shirts. This decision is to be made in collaboration with your executive committee colleagues in class.

2. When all the teams have finalized their production plans for week 1, the instructor will supply the *actual* demands for Muscle Shirts in week 1. At this point, one of the members of the executive committee is to complete the P&L statement for week 1, assuming that the production schedule for week 1 has been completed. Blank copies of Table 2.3 will be provided.

3. While the P&L statement for week 1 is being completed, the instructor will announce the new order requests for Thunder Shirts and Dragon Shirts to be shipped in week 2 and the weeks beyond.

4. You should look at your order requests, accept those that you want, and reject the rest. Add those that you accept for delivery in future periods to your open-order file (blank copies will be provided). You are then irrevocably committed to them and their consequences.

continued

continued

5. You should then make out a new production schedule, specifying at least what you want your garment maker process to do in the next week (it will be for week 2 at that time).

6. The instructor will impose a time limit for each period of the simulation. When the time limit for one period has been reached, the simulation will proceed to the next week.

SELECTED REFERENCES

Berry, W. L., C. Bozarth, T. Hill, and J. E. Klompmaker. "Factory Focus: Segmenting Markets from an Operations Perspective." *Journal of Operations Management,* vol. 10, no. 3 (1991), pp. 363–387.

Blackburn, Joseph. *Time-Based Competition: The Next Battle-ground in American Manufacturing.* Homewood, Ill.: Business One–Irwin, 1991.

Collier, David A. *The Service Quality Solution.* Milwaukee: ASQC Quality Press, and Burr Ridge, Ill.: Irwin Professional Publishing, 1994.

Feitzinger, Edward, and Hau L. Lee. "Mass Customization at Hewlett-Packard: The Power of Postponement." *Harvard Business Review,* vol. 75, no. 1 (1997), pp. 116–121.

Ferdows, Kasra, and Arnoud De Meyer. "Lasting Improvements in Manufacturing Performance: In Search of a New Theory." *Journal of Operations Management*, vol. 9, no. 2 (1990), pp. 168–184.

Fitzsimmons, James A., and Mona Fitzsimmons. *Service Management for Competitive Advantage.* New York: McGraw-Hill, 1994.

Gilmore, James H., and B. Joseph Pine II. "The Four Faces of Mass Customization." *Harvard Business Review,* vol. 75, no. 1 (1997), pp. 91–101.

Hammer, Michael, and Steven Stanton. "How Process Enterprises Really Work." *Harvard Business Review* (November–December 1999), pp. 108–120.

Hayes, Robert H., and G. P. Pisano. "Manufacturing Strategy: At the Intersection of Two Paradigm Shifts." *Production and Operations Management*, vol. 5, no. 1 (1996), pp. 25–41.

Heskett, James L., and Leonard A. Schlesenger. "The Service-Driven Service Company." *Harvard Business Review* (September–October 1991), pp. 71–81.

Hill, Terry. *Manufacturing Strategy: Text and Cases,* 3d ed. Homewood, Ill.: Irwin/MaGraw-Hill, 2000.

Leong, G. K., D. L. Snyder, and P. T. Ward. "Research in the Process and Content of Manufacturing Strategy." *OMEGA*, vol. 18, no. 2 (1990), pp. 109–122.

O'Reilly, Brian. "They've Got Mail!" *Fortune* (February 7, 2000), pp. 101–112.

Pine, B. Joseph II, Bart Victor, and Andrew C. Boynton. "Making Mass Customization Work." *Harvard Business Review* (September–October 1993), pp. 108–119.

Porter, Michael E. "The Competitive Advantage of Nations." *Harvard Business Review* (March–April 1990), pp. 73–93.

Prahalad, C. K., and Venkatram Ramaswamy. "Co-opting Customer Competence." *Harvard Business Review* (January–February 2000), pp. 79–87.

Roth, Aleda V., and Marjolijn van der Velde. "Operations as Marketing: A Competitive Service Strategy." *Journal of Operations Management,* vol. 10, no. 3 (1993), pp. 303–328.

Safizadeh, H. M., L. P. Ritzman, D. Sharma, and C. Wood. "An Empirical Analysis of the Product–Process Matrix." *Management Science,* vol. 42, no. 11 (1996), pp. 1576–1591.

Schmenner, Roger W. *Plant Tours and Service Tours in Operations Management,* 3d ed. New York: Macmillan, 1991.

Skinner, Wickham. "Manufacturing Strategy on the 'S' Curve." *Production and Operations Management,* vol. 5, no. 1 (1996), pp. 3–14.

Stalk, George, Jr., P. Evans, and P. E. Schulman. "Competing on Capabilities: The New Rules of Corporate Strategy," *Harvard Business Review* (March–April 1992), pp. 57–69.

Vickery, S. K., C. Droge, and R. R. Markland. "Production Competence and Business Strategy: Do They Affect Business Performance?" *Decision Sciences,* vol. 24, no. 2 (1993), pp. 435–456.

Ward, Peter T., Deborah J. Bickford, and G. Keong Leong. "Configurations of Manufacturing Strategy, Business Strategy, Environment and Structure." *Journal of Management,* vol. 22, no. 4 (1996), pp. 597–626.

Wheelwright, Steven C., and H. Kent Bowen. "The Challenge of Manufacturing Advantage." *Production and Operations Management,* vol. 5, no. 1 (1996), pp. 59–77.

Womack, J. P., D. T. Jones, and D. Roos. *The Machine That Changed the World.* New York: Rawson Associates, 1990.

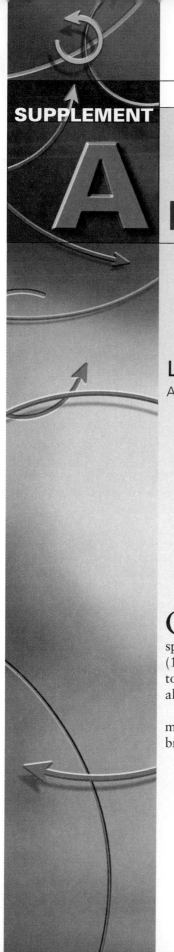

Decision Making

Learning Goals

After reading this supplement, you will be able to . . .

1. apply break-even analysis, using both the graphic and algebraic approaches, to evaluate new products and services and different process methods.
2. evaluate decision alternatives with a preference matrix for multiple criteria.
3. construct a payoff table and then select the best alternative by using a decision rule such as maximin, maximax, Laplace, minimax regret, or expected value.
4. calculate the value of perfect information.
5. draw and analyze a decision tree.

O PERATIONS MANAGERS MAKE MANY choices as they deal with various decision areas (see the Operations as a Competitive Weapon chapter). Although the specifics of each situation vary, decision making generally involves the same basic steps: (1) recognize and clearly define the problem, (2) collect the information needed to analyze possible alternatives, and (3) choose and implement the most feasible alternative.

Sometimes hard thinking in a quiet room is sufficient. At other times reliance on more formal procedures is needed. Here, we present four such formal procedures: break-even analysis, the preference matrix, decision theory, and the decision tree.

❑ Break-even analysis helps the manager identify how much change in volume or demand is necessary before a second alternative becomes better than the first one.

❑ The preference matrix helps a manager deal with multiple criteria that cannot be evaluated with a single measure of merit, such as total profit or cost.

❑ Decision theory helps the manager choose the best alternative when outcomes are uncertain.

❑ A decision tree helps the manager when decisions are made sequentially—when today's best decision depends on tomorrow's decisions and events.

BREAK-EVEN ANALYSIS

break-even point The volume at which total revenues equal total costs.

break-even analysis The use of the break-even point; can be used to compare production methods by finding the volume at which two different processes have equal costs.

To evaluate an idea for a new product or service or to assess the performance of an existing one, determining the volume of sales at which the product or service breaks even is useful. The **break-even point** is the volume at which total revenues equal total costs. Use of this technique is known as **break-even analysis**. Break-even analysis can also be used to compare production methods by finding the volume at which two different processes have equal total costs.

EVALUATING PRODUCTS OR SERVICES

We begin with the first purpose: to evaluate the profit potential of a new or existing product or service. This technique helps the manager answer questions such as the following:

- ❏ Is the predicted sales volume of the product or service sufficient to break even (neither earning a profit nor sustaining a loss)?
- ❏ How low must the variable cost per unit be to break even, based on current prices and sales forecasts?
- ❏ How low must the fixed cost be to break even?
- ❏ How do price levels affect the break-even volume?

Break-even analysis is based on the assumption that all costs related to the production of a specific product or service can be divided into two categories: variable costs and fixed costs.

variable cost The portion of the total cost that varies directly with volume of output.

fixed cost The portion of the total cost that remains constant regardless of changes in levels of output.

The **variable cost**, c, is the portion of the total cost that varies directly with volume of output: costs per unit for materials, labor, and usually some fraction of overhead. If we let Q equal the number of units produced and sold per year, total variable cost $= cQ$. The **fixed cost**, F, is the portion of the total cost that remains constant regardless of changes in levels of output: the annual cost of renting or buying new equipment and facilities (including depreciation, interest, taxes, and insurance), salaries, utilities, and portions of the sales or advertising budget. Thus, the total cost of producing a good or service equals fixed costs plus variable costs times volume, or

$$\text{Total cost} = F + cQ$$

The variable cost per unit is assumed to be the same no matter how many units Q are sold, and thus total cost is linear. If we assume that all units produced are sold, total annual revenues equal revenue per unit sold, p, times the quantity sold, or

$$\text{Total revenue} = pQ$$

If we set total revenue equal to total cost, we get the break-even point as

$$pQ = F + cQ$$
$$(p - c)Q = F$$
$$Q = \frac{F}{p - c}$$

We can also find this break-even quantity graphically. Because both costs and revenues are linear relationships, the break-even point is where the total revenue line crosses the total cost line.

EXAMPLE A.1

Finding the Break-Even Quantity

A hospital is considering a new procedure to be offered at $200 per patient. The fixed cost per year would be $100,000, with total variable costs of $100 per patient. What is the break-even quantity for this service? Use both algebraic and graphic approaches to get the answer.

**TUTOR
A.1**

SOLUTION

The formula for the break-even quantity yields

$$Q = \frac{F}{p - c} = \frac{100,000}{200 - 100} = 1,000 \text{ patients}$$

To solve graphically we plot two lines—one for costs and one for revenues. Two points determine a line, so we begin by calculating costs and revenues for two different output levels. The following table shows the results for $Q = 0$ and $Q = 2,000$. We selected zero as the first point because of the ease of plotting total revenue (0) and total cost (F). However, we could have used any two reasonably spaced output levels.

QUANTITY (PATIENTS) (Q)	TOTAL ANNUAL COST ($) ($100,000 + 100Q$)	TOTAL ANNUAL REVENUE ($) ($200Q$)
0	100,000	0
2,000	300,000	400,000

We can now draw the cost line through points (0, 100,000) and (2,000, 300,000). The revenue line goes between (0, 0) and (2,000, 400,000). As Figure. A.1 indicates, these two lines intersect at 1,000 patients, the break-even quantity.

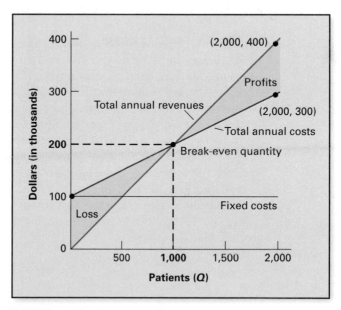

FIGURE A.1 • Graphic Approach to Break-Even Analysis

Decision Point Management expects the number of patients needing the new procedure will exceed the 1,000-patient break-even point but first wants to learn how sensitive the decision is to demand levels before making a final choice. ◻

sensitivity analysis
A technique for systematically changing parameters in a model to determine the effects of such changes.

Break-even analysis cannot tell a manager whether to pursue a new product or service idea or drop an existing line. The technique can only show what is likely to happen for various forecasts of costs and sales volumes. To evaluate a variety of "what-if" questions, we use an approach called **sensitivity analysis,** a technique for systematically changing parameters in a model to determine the effects of such changes. The concept can be applied later to other techniques, such as linear programming (see the Linear Programming supplement). Here we assess the sensitivity of total profit to different pricing strategies, sales volume forecasts, or cost estimates.

| EXAMPLE A.2 | *Sensitivity Analysis of Sales Forecasts* |

If the most pessimistic sales forecast for the proposed service in Figure A.1 were 1,500 patients, what would be the procedure's total contribution to profit and overhead per year?

SOLUTION

The graph shows that even the pessimistic forecast lies above the break-even volume, which is encouraging. The product's total contribution, found by subtracting total costs from total revenues, is

$$pQ - (F + cQ) = 200(1,500) - [100,000 + 100(1,500)]$$
$$= \$50,000$$

Decision Point Even with the pessimistic forecast, the new procedure contributes \$50,000 per year. After having the proposal evaluated by the present value method (see the Financial Analysis Supplement on the Student CD-ROM), management added the new procedure to the hospital's services. ☐

EVALUATING PROCESSES

Often, choices must be made between two processes or between an internal process and buying services or materials on the outside (see the Process Management chapter). In such cases, we assume that the decision does not affect revenues. The operations manager must study all the costs and advantages of each approach. Rather than find the quantity at which total costs equal total revenues, the analyst finds the quantity for which the total costs for two alternatives are equal. For the make-or-buy decision, it is the quantity for which the total "buy" cost equals the total "make" cost. Let F_b equal the fixed cost (per year) of the buy option, F_m equal the fixed cost of the make option, c_b equal the variable cost (per unit) of the buy option, and c_m the variable cost of the make option. Thus, the total cost to buy is $F_b + c_bQ$, and the total cost to make is $F_m + c_mQ$. To find the break-even quantity, we set the two cost functions equal and solve for Q:

$$F_b + c_bQ = F_m + c_mQ$$
$$Q = \frac{F_m - F_b}{c_b - c_m}$$

The make option should be considered, ignoring qualitative factors, only if its variable costs are lower than those of the buy option. The reason is that the fixed costs for making the product or service are typically higher than the fixed costs for buying. Under these circumstances, the buy option is best if production volumes are less than the break-even quantity. Beyond that quantity, the make option becomes best.

| EXAMPLE A.3 | *Break-Even Analysis for Make-or-Buy Decisions* |

**TUTOR
A.2**

The manager of a fast-food restaurant featuring hamburgers is adding salads to the menu. There are two options, and the price to the customer will be the same for each. The make option is to install a salad bar stocked with vegetables, fruits, and toppings and let the customer assemble the salad. The salad bar would have to be leased and a part-time employee hired. The manager estimates the fixed costs at $12,000 and variable costs totaling $1.50 per salad. The buy option is to have pre-assembled salads available for sale. They would be purchased from a local supplier at $2.00 per salad. Offering preassembled salads would require installation and operation of additional refrigeration, with an annual fixed cost of $2,400. The manager expects to sell 25,000 salads per year.

What is the break-even quantity?

SOLUTION

The formula for the break-even quantity yields

$$Q = \frac{F_m - F_b}{c_b - c_m}$$

$$= \frac{12,000 - 2,400}{2.0 - 1.5} = 19,200 \text{ salads}$$

Figure A.2 shows the solution from OM Explorer's *Break-Even Analysis* Solver.

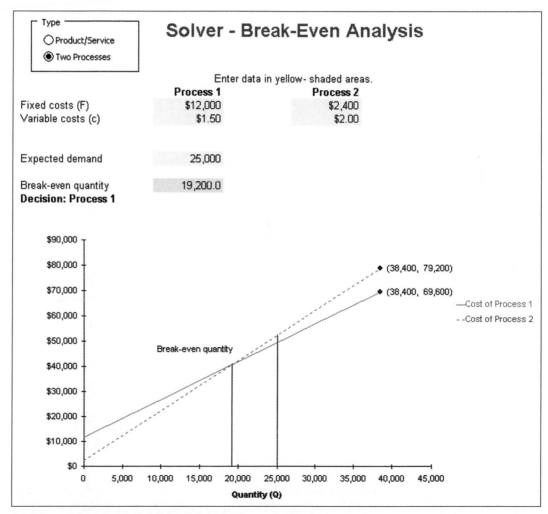

FIGURE A.2 • Break-Even Analysis Solver for Example A.3

The break-even quantity is 19,200 salads. As the 25,000-salad sales forecast exceeds this amount, the make option is preferred. Only if the restaurant expected to sell fewer than 19,200 salads would the buy option be better.

Decision Point Management chose the make option, after considering other qualitative factors such as customer preferences and demand uncertainty. A deciding factor was that the 25,000-salad sales forecast is well above the 19,200-salad break-even point. ☐

PREFERENCE MATRIX

preference matrix A table that allows the manager to rate an alternative according to several performance criteria.

Decisions often must be made in situations where multiple criteria cannot be naturally merged into a single measure (such as dollars). For example, a manager deciding in which of two cities to locate a new plant would have to consider such unquantifiable factors as quality of life, worker attitudes toward work, and community reception in the two cities. These important factors cannot be ignored. A **preference matrix** is a table that allows the manager to rate an alternative according to several performance criteria. The criteria can be scored on any scale, such as from 1 (worst possible) to 10 (best possible) or from 0 to 1, as long as the same scale is applied to all the alternatives being compared. Each score is weighted according to its perceived importance, with the total of these weights typically equaling 100. The total score is the sum of the weighted scores (weight times score) for all the criteria. The manager can compare the scores for alternatives against one another or against a predetermined threshold.

EXAMPLE A.4

TUTOR A.3

Evaluating an Alternative with a Preference Matrix

The following table shows the performance criteria, weights, and scores (1 = worst, 10 = best) for a new product: a thermal storage air conditioner. If management wants to introduce just one new product and the highest total score of any of the other product ideas is 800, should the firm pursue making the air conditioner?

PERFORMANCE CRITERION	WEIGHT (A)	SCORE (B)	WEIGHTED SCORE (A × B)
Market potential	30	8	240
Unit profit margin	20	10	200
Operations compatibility	20	6	120
Competitive advantage	15	10	150
Investment requirement	10	2	20
Project risk	5	4	20
		Weighted score =	750

SOLUTION

Because the sum of the weighted scores is 750, it falls short of the score of 800 for another product. This result is confirmed by the output from OM Explorer's *Preference Matrix* Solver in Figure A.3.

Solver - Preference Matrix

Replace the labels Criterion 1, Criterion 2, etc. with descriptions of your own criteria. Use the buttons above the list if you want to insert a criterion (between existing ones), add a criterion (at the end of the list), or remove a criterion. (You will not be able to reduce the number of criteria below two).

Enter the relative weights for the criteria. Remember that the weights must add up to 100. Enter the score for each criterion. Formulas in the weighted score column do the rest. The Final Weighted Score is the overall score for the product, procedure, or strategy you're considering.

Insert a Criterion	Add a Criterion	Remove a Criterion

	Weight (A)	Score (B)	Weighted Score (A x B)
Market potential	30	8	240
Unit profit margin	20	10	200
Operations compatability	20	6	120
Competitive advantage	15	10	150
Investment requirement	10	2	20
Project risk	5	4	20
		Final Weighted Score	750

FIGURE A.3 • Preference Matrix Solver for Example A.4

Decision Point Management should drop the thermal storage air conditioner idea. Another new product idea is better, considering the multiple criteria, and management only wanted to introduce just one new product at the time. ⌐

Not all managers are comfortable with the preference matrix technique. It requires the manager to state criteria weights before examining the alternatives, although the proper weights may not be readily apparent. Perhaps only after seeing the scores for several alternatives can the manager decide what is important and what is not. Because a low score on one criterion can be compensated for or overridden by high scores on others, the preference matrix method also may cause managers to ignore important signals. In Example A.4, the investment required for the thermal storage air conditioner might exceed the firm's financial capability. In that case, the manager should not even be considering the alternative, no matter how high its score.

DECISION THEORY

decision theory A general approach to decision making when the outcomes associated with alternatives are often in doubt.

Decision theory is a general approach to decision making when the outcomes associated with alternatives are often in doubt. It helps operations managers with decisions on process, capacity, location, and inventory because such decisions are about an uncertain future. Decision theory can also be used by managers in other functional areas. With decision theory, a manager makes choices using the following process.

1. List the feasible *alternatives*. One alternative that should always be considered as a basis for reference is to do nothing. A basic assumption is that the number of alternatives is finite. For example, in deciding where to locate a new retail store in a certain part of the city, a manager could theoretically consider every grid coordinate on the city's map. Realistically, however, the manager must narrow the number of choices to a reasonable number.

2. List the *events* (sometimes called *chance events* or *states of nature*) that have an impact on the outcome of the choice but are not under the manager's control. For example, the demand experienced by the new facility could be low or high, depending not only on whether the location is convenient to many customers but also on what the competition does and general retail trends. Then group events into reasonable categories. For example, suppose that the average number of sales per day could be anywhere from 1 to 500. Rather than have 500 events, the manager could represent demand with just 3 events: 100 sales/day, 300 sales/day, or 500 sales/day. The events must be mutually exclusive and exhaustive, meaning that they do not overlap and that they cover all eventualities.

payoff table A table that shows the amount for each alternative if each possible event occurs.

3. Calculate the *payoff* for each alternative in each event. Typically, the payoff is total profit or total cost. These payoffs can be entered into a **payoff table**, which shows the amount for each alternative if each event occurs. For 3 alternatives and 4 events, the table would have 12 payoffs (3 × 4). If significant distortions will occur if the time value of money is not recognized, the payoffs should be expressed as present values or internal rates of return (see the Financial Analysis supplement on the Student CD-ROM). For multiple criteria with important qualitative factors, use the weighted scores of a preference matrix approach as the payoffs.

4. Estimate the likelihood of each event, using past data, executive opinion, or other forecasting methods. Express it as a *probability*, making sure that the probabilities sum to 1.0. Develop probability estimates from past data if the past is considered a good indicator of the future.

5. Select a *decision rule* to evaluate the alternatives, such as choosing the alternative with the lowest expected cost. The rule chosen depends on the amount of information the manager has on the event probabilities and the manager's attitudes toward risk.

Using this process, we examine decisions under three different situations: certainty, uncertainty, and risk.

DECISION MAKING UNDER CERTAINTY

The simplest situation is when the manager knows which event will occur. Here the decision rule is to pick the alternative with the best payoff for the known event. The best alternative is the highest payoff if the payoffs are expressed as profits. If the payoffs are expressed as costs, the best alternative is the lowest payoff.

| EXAMPLE A.5 | *Decisions Under Certainty* |

A manager is deciding whether to build a small or a large facility. Much depends on the future demand that the facility must serve, and demand may be small or large. The manager knows with certainty the payoffs that will result under each alternative, shown in the following payoff table. The payoffs (in $000) are the present values (see the Financial Analysis supplement on the Student CD-ROM) of future revenues minus costs for each alternative in each event.

	POSSIBLE FUTURE DEMAND	
ALTERNATIVE	Low	High
Small facility	200	270
Large facility	160	800
Do nothing	0	0

What is the best choice if future demand will be low?

SOLUTION

In this example, the best choice is the one with the highest payoff. If the manager knows that future demand will be low, the company should build a small facility and enjoy a payoff of $200,000. The larger facility has a payoff of only $160,000. The "do nothing" alternative is dominated by the other alternatives; that is, the outcome of one alternative is no better than the outcome of another alternative for each event. Because the "do nothing" alternative is dominated, the manager doesn't consider it further.

Decision Point If management really knows future demand, it would build the small facility if demand will be low and the large facility if demand will be high. If demand is uncertain, it should consider other decision rules. ⌑

DECISION MAKING UNDER UNCERTAINTY

Here, we assume that the manager can list the possible events but cannot estimate their probabilities. Perhaps a lack of prior experience makes it difficult for the firm to estimate probabilities. In such a situation, the manager can use one of four decision rules.

1. *Maximin.* Choose the alternative that is the "best of the worst." This rule is for the *pessimist*, who anticipates the "worst case" for each alternative.

2. *Maximax.* Choose the alternative that is the "best of the best." This rule is for the *optimist* who has high expectations and prefers to "go for broke."

3. *Laplace.* Choose the alternative with the best *weighted payoff*. To find the weighted payoff, give equal importance (or, alternatively, equal probability) to each event. If there are n events, the importance (or probability) of each is $1/n$, so they add up to 1.0. This rule is for the *realist*.

4. *Minimax Regret.* Choose the alternative with the best "worst regret." Calculate a table of regrets (or opportunity losses), in which the rows represent the alternatives and the columns represent the events. A regret is the difference between a given payoff and the best payoff in the same column. For an event, it shows how much is lost by picking an alternative to the one that is best for this event. The regret can be lost profit or increased cost, depending on the situation.

EXAMPLE A.6   *Decisions Under Uncertainty*

**TUTOR
A.4**

Reconsider the payoff matrix in Example A.5. What is the best alternative for each decision rule?

SOLUTION

a. *Maximin.* An alternative's worst payoff is the *lowest* number in its row of the payoff matrix, because the payoffs are profits. The worst payoffs ($000) are

ALTERNATIVE	WORST PAYOFF
Small facility	200
Large facility	160

The best of these worst numbers is $200,000, so the pessimist would build a small facility.

b. *Maximax.* An alternative's best payoff ($000) is the *highest* number in its row of the payoff matrix, or

ALTERNATIVE	BEST PAYOFF
Small facility	270
Large facility	800

The best of these best numbers is $800,000, so the optimist would build a large facility.

c. *Laplace.* With two events, we assign each a probability of 0.5. Thus, the weighted payoffs ($000) are

ALTERNATIVE	WEIGHTED PAYOFF
Small facility	0.5(200) + 0.5(270) = **235**
Large facility	0.5(160) + 0.5(800) = **480**

The best of these weighted payoffs is $480,000, so the realist would build a large facility.

d. *Minimax Regret.* If demand turns out to be low, the best alternative is a small facility and its regret is 0 (or 200 − 200). If a large facility is built when demand turns out to be low, the regret is 40 (or 200 − 160).

	REGRET		
ALTERNATIVE	Low Demand	High Demand	MAXIMUM REGRET
Small facility	200 − 200 = **0**	800 − 270 = **530**	**530**
Large facility	200 − 160 = **40**	800 − 800 = **0**	**40**

The column on the right shows the worst regret for each alternative. To minimize the maximum regret, pick a large facility. The biggest regret is associated with having only a small facility and high demand.

Decision Point The pessimist would choose the small facility. The realist, optimist, and manager choosing to minimize the maximum regret would build the large facility. ❏

DECISION MAKING UNDER RISK

Here we assume that the manager can list the events and estimate their probabilities. The manager has less information than with decision making under certainty but more information than with decision making under uncertainty. For this intermediate situation, the *expected value* decision rule is widely used. The expected value for an alternative is found by weighting each payoff with its associated probability and then adding the weighted payoff scores. The alternative with the best expected value (highest for profits and lowest for costs) is chosen.

This rule is much like the Laplace decision rule, except that the events are no longer assumed to be equally likely (or equally important). The expected value is what the *average* payoff would be if the decision could be repeated time after time. Of course, the expected value decision rule can result in a bad outcome if the wrong event occurs. However, it gives the best results if applied consistently over a long period of time. The rule should not be used if the manager is inclined to avoid risk.

EXAMPLE A.7	*Decisions Under Risk*

Reconsider the payoff matrix in Example A.5. For the expected value decision rule, which is the best alternative if the probability of small demand is estimated to be 0.4 and the probability of large demand is estimated to be 0.6?

SOLUTION

The expected value for each alternative is

ALTERNATIVE	EXPECTED VALUE
Small facility	$0.4(200) + 0.6(270) =$ **242**
Large facility	$0.4(160) + 0.6(800) =$ **544**

Figure A.4 confirms this $544 expected value for the large facility, using **OM** Explorer's *Decision Theory* Solver. With the drop-down menu, it can also show the choices for the other four decision rules that we covered.

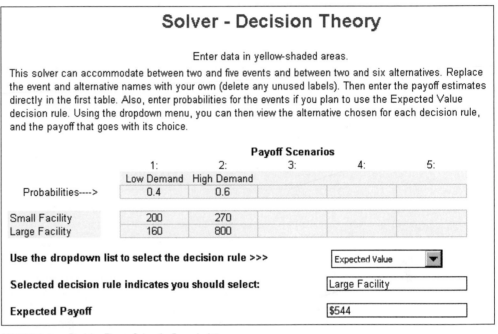

FIGURE A.4 • Decision Theory Solver for Example A.7

Decision Point Management would choose a large facility if it used this expected value decision rule, because it provides the best long-term results if consistently applied over time. ◻

VALUE OF PERFECT INFORMATION

value of perfect information The amount by which the expected payoff will improve if the manager knows which event will occur.

Suppose that a manager has a way of improving the forecasts—say, through more expensive market research or studying past trends. Assume that the manager, although unable to affect the probabilities of the events, can predict the future without error. The **value of perfect information** is the amount by which the expected payoff will improve if the manager knows which event will occur. It can be found with the following procedure:

1. Identify the best payoff for each event.
2. Calculate the expected value of these best payoffs by multiplying the best payoff for each event by the probability that the event will occur.

3. Subtract the expected value of the payoff without perfect information from the expected value of the payoff with perfect information. This difference is the value of perfect information.

EXAMPLE A.8

TUTOR
A.5

Value of Perfect Information

What is the value of perfect information to the manager in Example A.7?

SOLUTION

The best payoff for each event is the highest number in its column of the payoff matrix, or

EVENT	BEST PAYOFF
Low demand	200
High demand	800

The expected values, with and without perfect information, are

$$EV_{perfect} = 200(0.4) + 800(0.6) = 560$$
$$EV_{imperfect} = 160(0.4) + 800(0.6) = 544$$

Therefore, the value of perfect information is $560,000 − $544,000 = $16,000.

Decision Point Management will not pay more than $16,000 for any effort to improve forecast accuracy, even if it ensures a perfect forecast. ◻

DECISION TREES

decision tree
A schematic model of
alternatives available to
the decision maker, along
with their possible
consequences.

The decision tree method is a general approach to a wide range of OM decisions, such as product planning, process management, capacity, and location. It is particularly valuable for evaluating different capacity expansion alternatives when demand is uncertain and sequential decisions are involved. For example, a company may expand a facility in 2002 only to discover in 2006 that demand is much higher than forecasted. In that case, a second decision may be necessary to determine whether to expand again or build a second facility.

A **decision tree** is a schematic model of alternatives available to the decision maker, along with their possible consequences. The name derives from the tree-like appearance of the model. It consists of a number of square *nodes,* representing decision points, that are left by *branches* (which should be read from left to right), representing the alternatives. Branches leaving circular, or chance, nodes represent the events. The probability of each chance event, $P(E)$, is shown above each branch. The probabilities for all branches leaving a chance node must sum to 1.0. The conditional payoff, which is the payoff for each possible alternative–event combination, is shown at the end of each combination. Payoffs are given only at the outset, before the analysis begins, for the end points of each alternative–event combination. In Figure A.5, for example, payoff 1 is the financial outcome the manager expects if alternative 1 is chosen and then chance event 1 occurs. No payoff can be associated yet with any branches farther to the left, such as alternative 1 as a whole, because it is followed by a chance event and is not an end point. Payoffs often are expressed as the present value (see the Financial Analysis supplement in the Student CD-ROM) of net profits. If revenues are not affected by the decision, the payoff is expressed as net costs.

FIGURE A.5

A Decision Tree Model

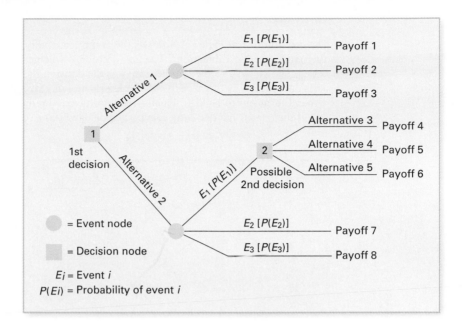

= Event node

= Decision node

E_i = Event *i*

$P(E_i)$ = Probability of event *i*

After drawing a decision tree, we solve it by working from right to left, calculating the *expected payoff* for each node as follows:

1. For an event node, we multiply the payoff of each event branch by the event's probability. We add these products to get the event node's expected payoff.

2. For a decision node, we pick the alternative that has the best expected payoff. If an alternative leads to an event node, its payoff is equal to that node's expected payoff (already calculated). We "saw off," or "prune," the other branches not chosen by marking two short lines through them. The decision node's expected payoff is the one associated with the single remaining unpruned branch.

We continue this process until the leftmost decision node is reached. The unpruned branch extending from it is the best alternative to pursue. If multistage decisions are involved, we must await subsequent events before deciding what to do next. If new probability or payoff estimates are obtained, we repeat the process.

EXAMPLE A.9

Analyzing a Decision Tree

A retailer must decide whether to build a small or a large facility at a new location. Demand at the location can be either small or large, with probabilities estimated to be 0.4 and 0.6, respectively. If a small facility is built and demand proves to be high, the manager may choose not to expand (payoff = $223,000) or to expand (payoff = $270,000). If a small facility is built and demand is low, there is no reason to expand and the payoff is $200,000. If a large facility is built and demand proves to be low, the choice is to do nothing ($40,000) or to stimulate demand through local advertising. The response to advertising may be either modest or sizable, with their probabilities estimated to be 0.3 and 0.7, respectively. If it is modest, the payoff is estimated to be only $20,000; the payoff grows to $220,000 if the response is sizable. Finally, if a large facility is built and demand turns out to be high, the payoff is $800,000.

Draw a decision tree. Then analyze it to determine the expected payoff for each decision and event node. Which alternative—building a small facility or building a large facility—has the higher expected payoff?

SOLUTION

The decision tree in Figure A.6 shows the event probability and the payoff for each of the seven alternative–event combinations. The first decision is whether to build a small or a large facility. Its node is shown first, to the left, because it is the decision the retailer must make now. The second decision node—whether to expand at a later date—is reached only if a small facility is built and demand turns out to be high. Finally, the third decision point—whether to advertise—is reached only if the retailer builds a large facility and demand turns out to be low.

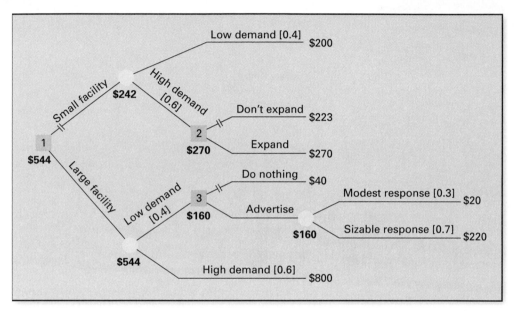

FIGURE A.6 • Decision Tree for Retailer

Analysis of the decision tree begins with calculation of the expected payoffs from right to left, shown on Figure A.6 beneath the appropriate event and decision nodes.

1. For the event node dealing with advertising, the expected payoff is 160, or the sum of each event's payoff weighted by its probability [0.3(20) + 0.7(220)].
2. The expected payoff for decision node 3 is 160 because *Advertise* (160) is better than *Do nothing* (40). Prune the *Do nothing* alternative.
3. The payoff for decision node 2 is 270 because *Expand* (270) is better than *Do not expand* (223). Prune *Do not expand*.
4. The expected payoff for the event node dealing with demand, assuming that a small facility is built, is 242 [or 0.4(200) + 0.6(270)].
5. The expected payoff for the event node dealing with demand, assuming that a large facility is built, is 544 [or 0.4(160) + 0.6(800)].
6. The expected payoff for decision node 1 is 544 because the large facility's expected payoff is largest. Prune *Small facility*.

Decision Point The retailer should build the large facility. This initial decision is the only one made now. Subsequent decisions are made after learning whether demand actually is low or high. ❑

FORMULA REVIEW

1. Break-even volume: $Q = \dfrac{F}{p - c}$

2. Evaluating processes, make-or-buy indifference quantity: $Q = \dfrac{F_m - F_b}{c_b - c_m}$

SUPPLEMENT HIGHLIGHTS

❒ Break-even analysis can be used to evaluate the profit potential of products and services. It can also be used to compare alternative production methods. Sensitivity analysis can be used to predict the effect of changing forecasts, costs, or prices.

❒ At times, decision alternatives cannot be evaluated in light of a single performance measure such as profit or cost. The preference matrix is a method of rating alternatives according to several objectives. The technique calls for important objectives to receive more weight in the decision, but determining in advance which objectives are important may be difficult.

❒ Applications of decision theory in operations management include decisions on process, capacity, location, and inventory. Decision theory is a general approach to decision making under conditions of certainty, uncertainty, or risk.

KEY TERMS

break-even analysis *68*
break-even point *68*
decision theory *73*
decision tree *78*

fixed cost *68*
payoff table *74*
preference matrix *72*
sensitivity analysis *70*

value of perfect information *77*
variable cost *68*

SOLVED PROBLEM 1

The owner of a small manufacturing business has patented a new device for washing dishes and cleaning dirty kitchen sinks. Before trying to commercialize the device and add it to her existing product line, she wants reasonable assurance of success. Variable costs are estimated at $7 per unit produced and sold. Fixed costs are about $56,000 per year.

a. If the selling price is set at $25, how many units must be produced and sold to break even? Use both algebraic and graphic approaches.

b. Forecasted sales for the first year are 10,000 units if the price is reduced to $15. With this pricing strategy, what would be the product's total contribution to profits in the first year?

SOLUTION

a. Beginning with the algebraic approach, we get

$$Q = \frac{F}{p - c} = \frac{56,000}{25 - 7}$$

$$= 3,111 \text{ units}$$

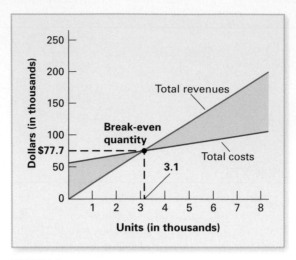

FIGURE A.7

Using the graphic approach, shown in Figure A.7, we first draw two lines:

$$\text{Total revenue} = 25Q$$
$$\text{Total cost} = 56{,}000 + 7Q$$

The two lines intersect at $Q = 3{,}111$ units, the break-even quantity.

b.

$$\text{Total profit contribution} = \text{Total revenue} - \text{Total cost}$$
$$= pQ - (F + cQ)$$
$$= 15(10{,}000) - [56{,}000 + 7(10{,}000)]$$
$$= \$124{,}000$$

SOLVED PROBLEM 2

Binford Tool Company is screening three new product ideas, A, B, and C. Resource constraints allow only one of them to be commercialized. The performance criteria and ratings, on a scale of 1 (worst) to 10 (best), are shown in the following table. The Binford managers give equal weights to the performance criteria. Which is the best alternative, as indicated by the preference matrix method?

| | RATING | | |
PERFORMANCE CRITERION	Product A	Product B	Product C
1. Demand uncertainty and project risk	3	9	2
2. Similarity to present products	7	8	6
3. Expected return on investment (ROI)	10	4	8
4. Compatibility with current manufacturing process	4	7	6
5. Competitive advantage	4	6	5

SOLUTION

Each of the five criteria receives a weight of 1/5 or 0.20.

PRODUCT	CALCULATION	TOTAL SCORE
A	$(0.20 \times 3) + (0.20 \times 7) + (0.20 \times 10) + (0.20 \times 4) + (0.20 \times 4)$	= 5.6
B	$(0.20 \times 9) + (0.20 \times 8) + (0.20 \times 4) + (0.20 \times 7) + (0.20 \times 6)$	= 6.8
C	$(0.20 \times 2) + (0.20 \times 6) + (0.20 \times 8) + (0.20 \times 6) + (0.20 \times 5)$	= 5.4

The best choice is product B. Products A and C are well behind in terms of total weighted score.

SOLVED PROBLEM 3

TUTOR A.6

Adele Weiss manages the campus flower shop. Flowers must be ordered three days in advance from her supplier in Mexico. Although Valentine's Day is fast approaching, sales are almost entirely last-minute, impulse purchases. Advance sales are so small that Weiss has no way to estimate the probability of low (25 dozen), medium (60 dozen), or high (130 dozen) demand for red roses on the big day. She buys roses for $15 per dozen and sells them for $40 per dozen. Construct a payoff table. Which decision is indicated by each of the following decision criteria?

a. Maximin

b. Maximax

c. Laplace

d. Minimax regret

SOLUTION

The payoff table for this problem is

	DEMAND FOR RED ROSES		
ALTERNATIVE	Low (25 dozen)	Medium (60 dozen)	High (130 dozen)
Order 25 dozen	$625	$625	$625
Order 60 dozen	$100	$1,500	$1,500
Order 130 dozen	($950)	$450	$3,250
Do nothing	$0	$0	$0

a. Under the maximin criteria, Weiss should order 25 dozen, because if demand is low, Weiss's profits are $625.

b. Under the maximax criteria, Weiss should order 130 dozen. The greatest possible payoff, $3,250, is associated with the largest order.

c. Under the Laplace criteria, Weiss should order 60 dozen. Equally weighted payoffs for ordering 25, 60, and 130 dozen are about $625, $1,033, and $917, respectively.

d. Under the minimax regret criteria, Weiss should order 130 dozen. The maximum regret of ordering 25 dozen occurs if demand is high: $3,250 − $625 = $2,625. The maximum regret of ordering 60 dozen occurs if demand is high: $3,250 − $1,500 = $1,750. The maximum regret of ordering 130 dozen occurs if demand is low: 625 − (−$950) = $1,575.

SOLVED PROBLEM 4

White Valley Ski Resort is planning the ski lift operation for its new ski resort. Management is trying to determine whether one or two lifts will be necessary; each lift can accommodate 250 people per day. Skiing normally occurs in the 14-week period from December to April, during which the lift will operate seven days per week. The first lift will operate at 90 percent capacity if economic conditions are bad, the probability of which is believed to be about a 0.3. During normal times the first lift will be utilized at 100 percent capacity, and the excess crowd will provide 50 percent utilization of the second lift. The probability of normal times is 0.5. Finally, if times are really good, the probability of which is 0.2, the utilization of the second lift will increase to 90 percent. The equivalent annual cost of installing a new lift, recognizing the time value of money and the lift's economic life, is $50,000. The annual cost of installing two lifts is only $90,000 if both are purchased at the same time. If used at all, each lift costs $200,000 to operate, no matter how low or high its utilization rate. Lift tickets cost $20 per customer per day.

a. Should the resort purchase one lift or two?

b. What is the value of perfect information?

SOLUTION

a. The decision tree is shown in Figure A.8. The payoff ($000) for each alternative−event branch is shown in the following table. The total revenues from one lift operating at 100 percent capacity are $490,000 (or 250 customers × 98 days × $20/customer-day).

ALTERNATIVE	ECONOMIC CONDITION	PAYOFF CALCULATION (REVENUE−COST)
One lift	Bad times	0.9(490) − (50 + 200) = 191
	Normal times	1.0(490) − (50 + 200) = 240
	Good times	1.0(490) − (50 + 200) = 240
Two lifts	Bad times	0.9(490) − (90 + 200) = 151
	Normal times	1.5(490) − (90 + 400) = 245
	Good times	1.9(490) − (90 + 400) = 441

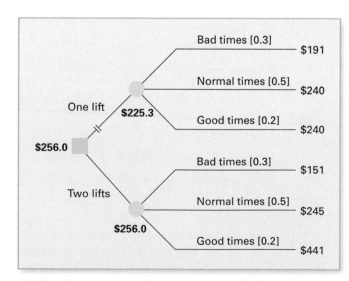

FIGURE A.8

b. The value of perfect information is

ECONOMIC CONDITION	BEST PAYOFF	PROBABILITY	WEIGHTED PAYOFF
Bad times	$191,000	0.3	$ 57,300
Normal times	$245,000	0.5	$122,500
Good times	$441,000	0.2	$ 88,200
	Expected value with perfect information		$268,000
	Without perfect information, part (a)		$256,000
	The value of perfect information is		$ 12,000

OM EXPLORER AND INTERNET EXERCISES

Visit our Web site at *www.prenhall.com/krajewski* for OM Explorer Tutors, which explain quantitative techniques; Solvers, which help you apply mathematical models; and Internet Exercises, including Facility Tours, which expand on the topics in this chapter.

PROBLEMS

An icon in the margin next to a problem identifies the software that can be helpful, but is not mandatory. The software is available on the Student CD-ROM that is packaged with every new copy of the textbook.

Problems 1–11 show a variety of applications for break-even analysis. Problems 1–4 apply break-even analysis to product or service planning decisions (discussed in the Operations Strategy chapter). Problems 12 and 13 demonstrate use of the preference matrix for product or service planning, and Problem 14 applies the preference matrix to location decisions. Decision theory Problems 15, 16, and 19–22 apply to capacity decisions (discussed in the Capacity chapter). Problems 17 and 18 involve the use of decision trees to evaluate fairly complex product or service planning decisions.

Break-Even Analysis

1. **OM Explorer** Mary Williams, owner of Williams Products, is evaluating whether to introduce a new product line. After thinking through the production process and the costs of raw materials and new equipment, Williams estimates the variable costs of each unit produced and sold at $6 and the fixed costs per year at $60,000.

   a. If the selling price is set at $18 each, how many units must be produced and sold for Williams to break even? Use both graphic and algebraic approaches to get your answer.

   b. Williams forecasts sales of 10,000 units for the first year if the selling price is set at $14.00 each. What would be the total contribution to profits from this new product during the first year?

   c. If the selling price is set at $12.50, Williams forecasts that first-year sales would increase to 15,000 units. Which pricing strategy ($14.00 or $12.50) would result in the greater total contribution to profits?

   d. What other considerations would be crucial to the final decision about making and marketing the new product?

2. **OM Explorer** A product at the Jennings Company has enjoyed reasonable sales volumes, but its contributions to profits have been disappointing. Last year, 17,500 units were produced and sold. The selling price is $22 per unit, *c* is $18, and *F* is $80,000.

   a. What is the break-even quantity for this product? Use both graphic and algebraic approaches to get your answer.

   b. Jennings is considering ways to either stimulate sales volumes or decrease variable costs. Management believes that sales can be increased by 30 percent or that *c* can be reduced to 85 percent of its current level. Which alternative leads to higher contributions to profits, assuming that each is equally costly to implement? (*Hint:* Calculate profits for both alternatives and identify the one having the greatest profits.)

   c. What is the percent change in the per-unit profit contribution generated by each alternative in part (b).

3. An interactive television service that costs $10 per month to provide can be sold on the information highway for $15 per client per month. If a service area includes a potential of 15,000 customers, what is the most a company could spend on annual fixed costs to acquire and maintain the equipment?

4. A restaurant is considering adding fresh brook trout to its menu. Customers would have the choice of catching their own trout from a simulated mountain stream or simply asking the waiter to net the trout for them. Operating the stream would require $10,600 in fixed costs per year. Variable costs are estimated to be $6.70 per trout. The firm wants to break even if 800 trout dinners are sold per year. What should be the price of the new item?

5. 🔵 **OM Explorer** Gabriel Manufacturing must implement a manufacturing process that reduces the amount of toxic by-products. Two processes have been identified that provide the same level of toxic by-product reduction. The first process would incur $300,000 of fixed costs and $600 per unit of variable costs. The second process has fixed costs of $120,000 and variable costs of $900 per unit.

   a. What is the break-even quantity beyond which the first process is more attractive?

   b. What is the difference in total cost if the quantity produced is 800 units?

6. 🔵 **OM Explorer** A news clipping service is considering modernization. Rather than manually clipping and photocopying articles of interest and mailing them to its clients, employees electronically input stories from most widely circulated publications into a database. Each new issue is searched for key words, such as a client's company name, competitors' names, type of business, and the company's products, services, and officers. When matches occur, affected clients are instantly notified via an on-line network. If the story is of interest, it is electronically transmitted, so the client often has the story and can prepare comments for follow-up interviews before the publication hits the street. The manual process has fixed costs of $400,000 per year and variable costs of $6.20 per clipping mailed. The price charged the client is $8.00 per clipping. The computerized process has fixed costs of $1,300,000 per year and variable costs of $2.25 per story electronically transmitted to the client.

   a. If the same price is charged for either process, what is the annual volume beyond which the automated process is more attractive?

   b. The present volume of business is 225,000 clippings per year. Many of the clippings sent with the current process are not of interest to the client or are multiple copies of the same story appearing in several publications. The news clipping service believes that by improving service and by lowering the price to $4.00 per story, modernization will increase volume to 900,000 stories transmitted per year. Should the clipping service modernize?

   c. If the forecasted increase in business is too optimistic, at what volume will the new process break even?

7. 🔵 **OM Explorer** Hahn Manufacturing has been purchasing a key component of one of its products from a local supplier. The current purchase price is $1,500 per unit. Efforts to standardize parts have succeeded to the point that this same component can now be used in five different products. Annual component usage should increase from 150 to 750 units. Management wonders whether it is time to make the component in-house, rather than to continue buying it from the supplier. Fixed costs would increase by about $40,000 per year for the new equipment and tooling needed. The cost of raw materials and variable overhead would be about $1,100 per unit, and labor costs would go up by another $300 per unit produced.

   a. Should Hahn make rather than buy?

   b. What is the break-even quantity?

   c. What other considerations might be important?

8. Techno Corporation is currently manufacturing an item at variable costs of $5.00 per unit. Annual fixed costs of manufacturing this item are $140,000. The current selling price of the item is $10.00 per unit, and the annual sales volume is 30,000 units.

   a. Techno can substantially improve the item's quality by installing new equipment at additional annual fixed costs of $60,000. Variable costs per unit would increase by $1.00, but, as more of the better-quality product could be sold, the annual volume would increase to 50,000 units. Should Techno buy the new equipment and maintain the current price of the item? Why or why not?

   b. Alternatively, Techno could increase the selling price to $11.00 per unit. However, the annual sales volume would be limited to 45,000 units. Should Techno buy the new equipment and raise the price of the item? Why or why not?

9. The Tri-County Generation and Transmission Association is a nonprofit cooperative organization that provides electrical service to rural customers. Based on a faulty long-range demand forecast, Tri-County overbuilt its generation and distribution system. Tri-County now has much more capacity than it needs to serve its customers. Fixed costs, mostly debt service on investment in plant and equipment, are $82.5 million per year. Variable costs, mostly fossil fuel costs, are $25 per megawatt-hour (MWh, or million watts of power used for one hour). The new person in charge of demand forecasting prepared a short-range forecast for use in next year's budgeting process. That forecast calls for Tri-County customers to consume 1 million MWh of energy next year.

a. How much will Tri-County need to charge its customers per MWh to break even next year?

b. The Tri-County customers balk at that price and conserve electrical energy. Only 95 percent of forecasted demand materializes. What is the resulting surplus or loss for this nonprofit organization?

10. 💿 **OM Explorer** Earthquake, drought, fire, economic famine, flood, and a pestilence of TV court reporters have caused an exodus from the City of Angels to Boulder, Colorado. The sudden increase in demand is straining the capacity of Boulder's electrical system. Boulder's alternatives have been reduced to buying 150,000 MWh of electric power from Tri-County G&T at a price of $75 per MWh, or refurbishing and recommissioning the abandoned Pearl Street Power Station in downtown Boulder. Fixed costs of that project are $10 million per year, and variable costs would be $35 per MWh. Should Boulder build or buy?

11. Tri-County G&T sells 150,000 MWh per year of electrical power to Boulder at $75 per MWh, has fixed costs of $82.5 million per year, and has variable costs of $25 per MWh. If Tri-County has 1,000,000 MWh of demand from its customers (other than Boulder) what will Tri-County have to charge to break even?

Preference Matrix

12. 💿 **OM Explorer** The Forsite Company is screening three ideas for new services. Resource constraints allow only one idea to be commercialized at the present time. The following estimates have been made for the five performance criteria that management believes to be most important.

	RATING		
PERFORMANCE CRITERION	**Service A**	**Service B**	**Service C**
Capital equipment investment required	0.6	0.8	0.3
Expected return on investment (ROI)	0.7	0.3	0.9
Compatibility with current workforce skills	0.4	0.7	0.5
Competitive advantage	1.0	0.4	0.6
Compatibility with EPA requirements	0.2	1.0	0.5

a. Calculate a total weighted score for each alternative. Use a preference matrix and assume equal weights for each performance criterion. Which alternative is best? Worst?

b. Suppose that the expected ROI is given twice the weight assigned to each of the remaining criteria.

(Sum of weights should remain the same as in part (a).) Does this modification affect the ranking of the three potential services?

13. 💿 **OM Explorer** You are in charge of analyzing five new product ideas and have been given the information shown in Table A.1 on page 88 (1 = worst, 10 = best). Management has decided that criteria 2 and 3 are equally important and that criteria 1 and 4 are each four times as important as criterion 2. Only two new products can be introduced, and a product can be introduced only if its score exceeds 70 percent of the maximum possible total points. Which product ideas do you recommend?

14. 💿 **OM Explorer** Soft-Brew, Inc., collected the following information on where to locate a brewery (1 = poor, 10 = excellent).

		LOCATION SCORE	
LOCATION FACTOR	**FACTOR WEIGHT**	**A**	**B**
Construction costs	10	8	5
Utilities available	10	7	7
Business services	10	4	7
Real estate cost	20	7	4
Quality of life	20	4	8
Transportation	30	7	6

a. Which location, A or B, should be chosen on the basis of the total weighted score?

b. If the factors were weighted equally, would the choice change?

Decision Theory

15. 💿 **OM Explorer** Build-Rite Construction has received favorable publicity from guest appearances on a public TV home improvement program. Public TV programming decisions seem to be unpredictable, so Build-Rite cannot estimate the probability of continued benefits from its relationship with the show. Demand for home improvements next year may be either low or high. But Build-Rite must decide now whether to hire more employees, do nothing, or develop subcontracts with other home improvement contractors. Build-Rite has developed the following payoff table.

	DEMAND FOR HOME IMPROVEMENTS		
ALTERNATIVE	**Low**	**Moderate**	**High**
Hire	($250,000)	$100,000	$625,000
Subcontract	$100,000	$150,000	$415,000
Do nothing	$ 50,000	$ 80,000	$300,000

TABLE A.1   *Analysis of New Product Ideas*

	RATING				
PERFORMANCE CRITERION	**Product A**	**Product B**	**Product C**	**Product D**	**Product E**
Compatibility with current manufacturing	8	7	3	6	9
Expected return on investment (ROI)	3	8	4	7	7
Compatibility with current workforce skills	9	5	7	6	5
Unit profit margin	7	6	9	2	7

Which alternative is best, according to each of the following decision criteria?

a. Maximin

b. Maximax

c. Laplace

d. Minimax regret

16.   🔵 **OM Explorer** Once upon a time in the Old West, Fletcher, Cooper, and Wainwright (the Firm) was deciding whether to make arrows, barrels, or Conestoga wagons. The Firm understood that demand for products would vary, depending on U.S. government policies concerning the development of travel routes to California. If land routes were chosen and treaties with Native Americans could not be negotiated, the demand for arrows would be great. Success in those negotiations would favor demand for Conestoga wagons. If the water route was chosen, the success of negotiations would be irrelevant. Instead, many barrels would be needed to contain goods during the long sea voyage around Cape Horn. Although the Firm was expert at forecasting the effect of policy on its business, it could not estimate the probability of the U.S. government favoring one policy over another. Based on the Firm's forecasted demand, which alternative is best, according to each of the following decision criteria?

a. Maximin

b. Maximax

c. Laplace

	FORECASTED DEMAND		
POLICY	**Arrows**	**Barrels**	**Conestoga Wagons**
Land, no treaty	9,000,000	300,000	5,000
Land with treaty	5,000,000	200,000	50,000
Sea	2,500,000	500,000	3,000

	PRODUCT		
PRICE AND COSTS	**Arrows**	**Barrels**	**Conestoga Wagons**
Fixed costs	$60,000	$80,000	$100,000
Variable costs per unit	$0.05	$1.50	$50
Price per unit	$0.15	$3.00	$75

17.   🔵 **SmartDraw** Returning to Problem 16, assume that Fletcher, Cooper, and Wainwright has contributed to the reelection campaign and legal defense fund for the Chairman of the House Ways and Means Committee. In return, the Firm learns that the probability of choosing the sea route is 0.2, the probability of developing the land route and successful treaty negotiations is 0.3, and the probability of developing the land route and unsuccessful negotiations is 0.5.

a. Draw a decision tree to analyze the problem. Calculate the expected value of each product alternative.

b. The Chairman informs Fletcher, Cooper and Wainwright that a more accurate forecast of events is available "for a price." What is the value of perfect information?

Decision Tree

18. Analyze the decision tree in Figure A.9. What is the expected payoff for the best alternative? First, be sure to infer the missing probabilities.

19.   🔵 **SmartDraw** A manager is trying to decide whether to buy one machine or two. If only one is purchased and demand proves to be excessive, the second machine can be purchased later. Some sales will be lost, however, because the lead time for producing this type of machine is six months. In addition, the cost per machine will be lower if both are purchased at the same time. The probability of low demand is estimated to be 0.20. The after-tax net present value of the benefits from purchasing the

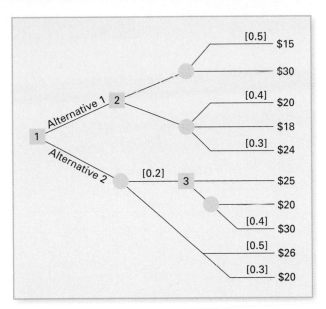

FIGURE A.9

two machines together is $90,000 if demand is low and $180,000 if demand is high.

If one machine is purchased and demand is low, the net present value is $120,000. If demand is high, the manager has three options. Doing nothing has a net present value of $120,000; subcontracting, $160,000; and buying the second machine, $140,000.

a. Draw a decision tree for this problem.

b. How many machines should the company buy initially? What is the expected payoff for this alternative?

20. ● **SmartDraw** A manager is trying to decide whether to build a small, medium, or large facility. Demand can be low, average, or high, with the estimated probabilities being 0.25, 0.40, and 0.35, respectively.

A small facility is expected to earn an after-tax net present value of just $18,000 if demand is low. If demand is average, the small facility is expected to earn $75,000; it can be increased to average size to earn a net present value of $60,000. If demand is high, the small facility is expected to earn $75,000 and can be expanded to average size to earn $60,000 or to large size to earn $125,000.

A medium-sized facility is expected to lose an estimated $25,000 if demand is low and earn $140,000 if demand is average. If demand is high, the medium-sized facility is expected to earn a net present value of $150,000; it can be expanded to a large size for a net payoff of $145,000.

If a large facility is built and demand is high, earnings are expected to be $220,000. If demand is average for the large facility, the present value is expected to be $125,000; if demand is low, the facility is expected to lose $60,000.

a. Draw a decision tree for this problem.

b. What should management do to achieve the highest expected payoff?

21. ● **SmartDraw** A manufacturing plant has reached full capacity. The company must build a second plant—either small or large—at a nearby location. The demand is likely to be high or low. The probability of low demand is 0.3. If demand is low, the large plant has a present value of $5 million and the small plant, $8 million. If demand is high, the large plant pays off with a present value of $18 million and the small plant with a present value of only $10 million. However, the small plant can be expanded later if demand proves to be high, for a present value of $14 million.

a. Draw a decision tree for this problem.

b. What should management do to achieve the highest expected payoff?

22. ● **SmartDraw** Benjamin Moses, chief engineer of Offshore Chemicals, Inc., must decide whether to build a new processing facility based on an experimental technology. If the new facility works, the company will realize a net profit of $20 million. If the new facility fails, the company will lose $10 million. Benjamin's best guess is that there is a 40 percent chance that the new facility will work.

a. What decision should Benjamin Moses make?

b. How much should he be willing to pay for perfect information?

SELECTED REFERENCES

Bonini, Charles P., Warren H. Hausman, and Harold Bierman, Jr. *Quantitative Analysis for Management.* Burr Ridge Parkway, Ill.: Irwin/McGraw-Hill, 1996.

Clemen, Robert T. *Making Hard Decisions: An Introduction to Decision Analysis.* Boston: PWS-Kent, 1991.

Taylor, Bernard W., III. *Introduction to Management Science.* Needham Heights, MA: Allyn & Bacon, 1990.

CHAPTER 3

Process Management

Across the Organization

Process management is important to . . .

- ☐ **accounting,** which seeks better ways to perform its work processes and provides cost analyses of process improvement proposals.
- ☐ **finance,** which seeks better processes to perform its work, does financial analyses of new process proposals, and looks for ways to raise funds to finance automation.
- ☐ **human resources,** which melds process and job design decisions into an effective whole.
- ☐ **management information systems,** which identifies how information technologies can support the exchange of information.
- ☐ **marketing,** which seeks better processes to perform its work and explores opportunities to expand market share by encouraging ongoing customer dialogue.
- ☐ **operations,** which designs and manages production processes in order to maximize customer value and enhance a firm's core competencies.

Learning Goals

After reading this chapter, you will be able to . . .

1. describe each of the main process decisions and how they must relate to volume.
2. explain when less vertical integration and more outsourcing are appropriate and how resource flexibility supports competitive priorities.
3. describe the different ways that customer contact can affect a process.
4. explain the meaning of automation and economies of scope.
5. discuss how service strategy, capital intensity, and customer involvement influence processes of service providers.
6. define job specialization and describe three ways to expand jobs.
7. explain the concept of focused factories and how it applies to service providers.
8. explain how to analyze a process, using such supporting tools as flow diagrams, process charts, and simulation.
9. describe the key elements of process reengineering and analyze a process for improvements, using flow diagrams, process charts, and a questioning attitude.

Duke Power (www.duke-energy.com) is a true pioneer of the enterprise process. The electric utility arm of Duke Energy, Duke Power serves nearly 2 million customers in North and South Carolina. In 1995, with deregulation looming, the company realized that its processes had to do a much better job of customer service. But the existing organizational structure of Customer Operations, the business unit responsible for delivering electricity to customers, was getting in the way of process improvements. The unit was divided into four regional profit centers, and regional vice-presidents had little time for wrestling with process improvements for customer service. And even if they had, there was no way to coordinate their efforts across regions.

To resolve the problem, Duke Power identified the five core processes that, together, encompassed the essential work of Customer Operations: developing market strategies, maintaining customers, providing reliability and integrity, delivering products and services, and calculating and collecting revenues. Each process was assigned an owner, and the five process owners, like the four existing regional vice-presidents, now report directly to the head of Customer Operations. Process owners are senior managers, with end-to-end responsibility for enterprise processes, and they embody the company's commitment to better process management.

The new structure proved to be highly successful. Virtually every activity involved in serving customers was redesigned from the ground up. For the deliver-products-and-services process, for example, the process owner worked with regional units, suppliers, and his own 10-person staff to improve the warehousing processes. Materials that will be required by installation crews, for example, are laid out the night before, so that crew is on the road the next morning in just 10 minutes, a frac-

The new structure at Duke Power requires collaboration between process managers and the regional VPs. Teamwork is essential in the design and operation of processes.

tion of the 70 minutes previously required. Because crews do more installations in a day, customer service is improved.

In another area, Duke was meeting only 30 to 50 percent of its commitments to building-contractor customers to lay cables by certain dates. The process was revamped with a new scheduling system that provides much more detailed information about the availability of field personnel and allows more accurate assignments. People were also designated to negotiate commitment dates with contractors and to keep them apprised of changes. Duke Power now meets 98 percent of its construction commitments.

With the new structure, regional vice-presidents continue to manage their own workforces—the process owners have only small staffs—but process owners have been given vast authority over the design and operation of the processes. They decide how work will proceed at every step. Then they establish performance targets and set budgets among regions. In other words, while regions have authority over people, they are evaluated on how well they meet goals set by process owners. This structure requires a new collaborative style of management, in which the process managers and regional VPs act as partners rather than rivals. Teams are composed of individuals with broad process knowledge and they are measured on performance. They take over most of the managerial responsibilities usually held by supervisors. Supervisors, in turn, become more like coaches. Because the same employees are often involved in several processes, sometimes simultaneously, processes overlap. Process owners promote process improvements and continually seek to add value to the customer.

Source: Stanton, Steven. "How Process Enterprises Really Work," *Harvard Business Review* (November–December 1999), pp. 108–117.

O NE ESSENTIAL ISSUE IN the design of processes is deciding how to make products or provide services. Deciding on processes involves many different choices in selecting human resources, equipment, and materials. Processes are involved in how marketing prepares a market analysis, how accounting bills customers, how a retail store provides services on the sales floor, and how a manufacturing plant performs its assembly operations. Process decisions can affect an organization's ability to compete over the long run.

Process decisions are also strategic in nature: as we saw in Chapter 2, they should further a company's long-term competitive goals. In making process decisions, managers focus on controlling such competitive priorities as quality, flexibility, time, and cost. For example, firms can improve their ability to compete on the basis of time by examining each step of their processes and finding ways to respond more quickly to their customers. Productivity (and therefore cost) is affected by choices made when processes are designed. Process management is an ongoing activity, with the same principles applying to both first-time and redesign choices. Thus, the processes at Duke Power are in constant change.

We begin by defining five basic process decisions: process choice, vertical integration, resource flexibility, customer involvement, and capital intensity. We discuss these decisions for both manufacturing and service processes, methods of focusing operations, and the impact of job design. We pay particular attention both to ways in which services strategy, capital intensity, and customer involvement affect service operations and to methods for focusing operations. We then present a systematic approach to designing processes, using flow diagrams, process charts, and simulation. We conclude with two basic philosophies of analyzing and modifying processes—reengineering and process improvement.

WHAT IS PROCESS MANAGEMENT?

A process involves the use of an organization's resources to provide something of value. No product can be made and no service provided without a process, and no process can exist without a product or service.

process management The selection of the inputs, operations, work flows, and methods that transform inputs into outputs.

Process management is the selection of the inputs, operations, work flows, and methods that transform inputs into outputs. Input selection begins by deciding which processes are to be done in-house and which processes are to be done outside and purchased as materials and services. Process decisions also deal with the proper mix of human skills and equipment and which parts of the processes are to be performed by each. Decisions about processes must be consistent with competitive priorities (see the Operations Strategy chapter) and the organization's ability to obtain the resources necessary to support them.

Process decisions must be made when

- ❏ a new or substantially modified product or service is being offered,
- ❏ quality must be improved,
- ❏ competitive priorities have changed,
- ❏ demand for a product or service is changing,
- ❏ current performance is inadequate,
- ❏ the cost or availability of inputs has changed,
- ❏ competitors are gaining by using a new process, or
- ❏ new technologies are available.

Not all such situations lead to changes in current processes. Process decisions must also take into account other choices, such as quality, capacity, layout, and inventory. Moreover, as Managerial Practice 3.1 shows, managers must consider advances in technology and changing competitor capabilities. The impact on the environment is another consideration. A good example is McDonald's. It made subtle changes in the processes used to package food, reducing waste by more than 30 percent since 1990 and becoming one of the country's leading buyers of recycled materials. The greening of McDonald's entailed replacing "clamshell" boxes with special light-weight paper, introducing shorter napkins, and relying less on plastics in straws, dining trays, and playground equipment. McDonald's is now looking at a plan to

MANAGERIAL PRACTICE 3.1
Changing the Product Design Process at Netscape

The advent of the World Wide Web opens up a whole new approach to the product development process. Traditionally, design implementation begins once a product's concept has been determined in its entirety. This approach still works well when technology, customer preferences, and competitive conditions are predictable and stable. However, when new technologies or competitors appear overnight, and when a company's customers can easily switch to new suppliers, a different development process is needed. The Internet makes possible a more flexible, more dynamic development process. Designers, for example, can continue shaping products even after implementation has begun. Companies can incorporate rapidly evolving customer requirements and changing technologies into their designs until the last possible moment before a product is introduced to the market.

A good example is in the Internet industry itself, where there is considerable turbulence in technology and competing products. Founded in 1994, Netscape (www.netscape.com) pioneered the easy-to-use Web browser—that is, a software interface that provides access to the World Wide Web. Navigator was designed and updated in a rapidly evolving industry in which fast-changing technology makes product development a project manager's nightmare. Even the most basic design decisions about a product must be continually revised as new information arises. Netscape thus introduced Navigator 2.0 in January of 1996 and immediately began to develop Navigator 3.0. The Netscape development group produced the first 3.0 prototype in just six weeks. This Beta 0 version was put on the company's internal project Web site for testing by the development staff. Although many of the product's functions were not yet available, the Beta 0 version captured enough of the essence of the new product to get meaningful feedback for change. Two weeks later, the development team issued an updated version, Beta 1, again for internal

Two designers at Netscape, where the use of the World Wide Web opened up a new way to develop Navigator.

development staff only. By early March, with major bugs worked out, the first public release, Beta 2, appeared on Netscape's Internet web site. Additional public refinements followed every few weeks until the official release date in August, with gradual refinements appearing in each beta iteration.

This iterative testing process was extremely useful to Netscape because the development team could react to user feedback and changes in customer preferences throughout the design process. It also allowed the development team to monitor competing products, such as Microsoft's Explorer. Microsoft has since adopted a similar process. For example, more than 650,000 customers tested a beta version of Microsoft's Windows 2000 and shared their ideas for changing product features. The beta tests also helped clear the glitches from early versions of the software.

Source: Iansiti, Marco, and Alan MacCormack. "Developing Products on Internet Time," *Harvard Business Review* (September–October, 1997), pp. 108–117.

turn waste into fertilizer, so that eating out could generate less waste than eating at many homes.

There are two principles concerning process management that are particularly important.

1. Processes underlie all work activity and are found in all organizations and in all functions of an organization. Accounting uses certain processes to do payroll, ledger control, and revenue accounting. Finance uses other processes to evaluate investment alternatives and project financial performance. Human resources uses various processes to administer benefits, recruit new employees, and conduct training programs. Marketing uses its own processes to do market research and communicate with external customers.

2. Processes are nested within other processes along an organization's supply chain. A firm's **supply chain** (sometimes called the *value chain*) is an interconnected set of linkages among suppliers of materials and services that spans the transformation processes that convert ideas and raw materials into finished goods and services. One key decision, which we cover here, is selecting the parts of the chain to provide internally and how best to perform these processes. An essential task is to coordinate process linkages. Whether processes are internal or external, management must pay particular attention to the interfaces between processes. Having to deal with these interfaces underscores the need for cross-functional coordination (see the Operations as a Competitive Weapon chapter) and coordination with suppliers and customers (see the Supply-Chain Management chapter).

supply chain An interconnected set of linkages among suppliers of materials and services that spans the transformation processes that convert ideas and raw materials into finished goods and services; also referred to as the value chain.

MAJOR PROCESS DECISIONS

Process decisions directly affect the process itself, and indirectly the products and services that it provides. Whether dealing with processes for offices, service providers, or manufacturers, operations managers must consider five common process decisions.

process choice A process decision that determines whether resources are organized around products or processes.

❏ **Process choice** determines whether resources are organized around products or processes. The process choice decision depends on volume and degree of customization to be provided. Understanding such relationships helps the process manager to identify possible misalignments in processes, paving the way for reengineering and process improvements.

vertical integration The degree to which a firm's own production system or service facility handles the entire supply chain.

❏ **Vertical integration** is the degree to which a firm's own production system or service facility handles the entire supply chain. The more that the processes are performed in-house rather than by suppliers or customers, the greater is the degree of vertical integration.

resource flexibility The ease with which employees and equipment can handle a wide variety of products, output levels, duties, and functions.

❏ **Resource flexibility** is the ease with which employees and equipment can handle a wide variety of products, output levels, duties, and functions.

❏ **Customer involvement** reflects the ways in which customers become part of the process and the extent of their participation.

customer involvement The ways in which customers become part of the process and the extent of their participation.

❏ **Capital intensity** is the mix of equipment and human skills in a process: The greater the relative cost of equipment, the greater is the capital intensity.

These five decisions are best understood at the process or subprocess level, rather than at the firm level. Process decisions act as building blocks that are used in different ways to implement operations strategy.

PROCESS CHOICE

capital intensity The mix
of equipment and human
skills in a process.

One of the first decisions a manager makes in designing a well-functioning process is to choose a process *type* that best achieves the relative importance placed on quality, time, flexibility, and cost. The importance comes in part from operations strategy and competitive priorities (see Operations Strategy chapter). However, what is emphasized for the overall facility or product line is not necessarily what should be emphasized for each of the processes or subprocesses that provide the product or service. The manager has five process types, which form a continuum, to choose from:

1. project,
2. job,
3. batch,
4. line, and
5. continuous.

Figure 3.1 shows that these types of processes are found in manufacturing and services organizations alike. In fact, some manufacturer's processes provide a service and do not involve manufacturing, as Figure 3.1a demonstrates with the project process examples. The fundamental message in Figure 3.1 is that the best choice for a process depends on the volume and degree of customization required of the process. A process choice might apply to an entire process or just one subprocess within it. For example, one of a service facility's processes might best be characterized as a job process and another process as a line process. Because our definition of a process in Chapter 1 provides a basic understanding of processes in general, we now concentrate on the differences among the five process choices.

PROJECT PROCESS. Examples of a project process are building a shopping center, forming a project team to do a task (such as a student team doing a course project), planning a major event, running a political campaign, putting together a comprehensive training program, constructing a new hospital, doing management consulting work, or developing

*The banking industry
has used technology
to get customers
involved in banking
processes. Here a
customer uses an
interactive banking
center at Citibank.*

FIGURE 3.1a

The Influence of Customization and Volume on Process Choice

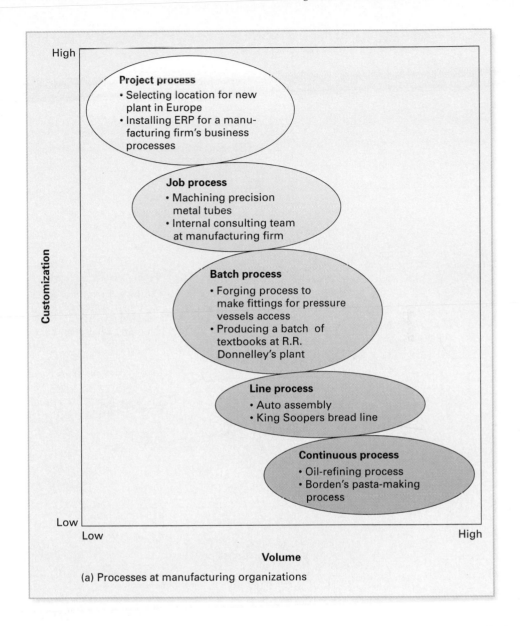

(a) Processes at manufacturing organizations

project process A process characterized by a high degree of job customization, the large scope of each project, and the release of substantial resources once a project is completed.

a new technology or product. A **project process** is characterized by a high degree of job customization, the large scope of each project, and the release of substantial resources once a project is completed. A project process lies at the high-customization, low-volume end of the process-choice continuum. The sequence of operations and the process involved in each are unique to the project, creating one-of-a-kind products or services made specifically to customer order. Although some projects may look similar, each is unique. Project processes are valued on the basis of their capabilities to do certain kinds of work, rather than their ability to produce specific products or services. Projects tend to be complex, take a long time, and be large. Many interrelated tasks must be completed, requiring close coordination (see the Managing Project Processes chapter). Resources needed for a project are assembled and then released for further use after the project is finished. Projects typically make heavy use of certain skills and resources at particular stages and then have little use for them the rest of the time. With a project process, work flows are redefined with each new project.

FIGURE 3.1b

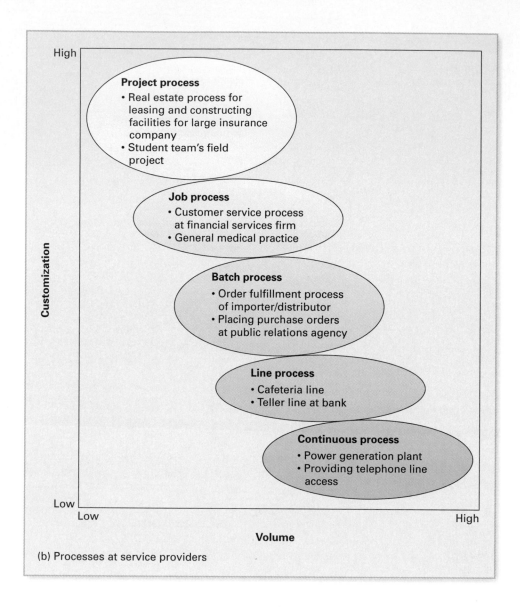

(b) Processes at service providers

JOB PROCESS. Next in the continuum of process choices is the job process. Examples are machining a metal casting for a customized order, providing emergency room care, handling special-delivery mail, or making customized cabinets. A **job process** creates the flexibility needed to produce a variety of products or services in significant quantities. Customization is relatively high and volume for any one product or service is low. However, volumes are not as low as for a project process, which by definition does not produce in quantity. The workforce and equipment are flexible and handle various tasks.

As with a project process, companies choosing a job process often bid for work. Typically, they make products to order and do not produce them ahead of time. The specific needs of the next customer are unknown, and the timing of repeat orders from the same customer is unpredictable. Each new order is handled as a single unit—as a job.

A job process primarily organizes all like resources around itself (rather than allocating them out to specific products and services); equipment and workers capable of certain types of work are located together. These resources process all jobs requiring that type of work. Because customization is high and most jobs have a different

job process A process with the flexibility needed to produce a variety of products or services in significant qualities.

line flow The linear movement of materials, information, or customers from one operation to the next according to a fixed sequence.

sequence of processing steps, this process choice creates *jumbled flows* through the operations rather than a line flow. A **line flow** means that materials, information, or customers move linearly from one operation to the next according to a fixed sequence. While there is considerable variability in the flows through a job process, there can be some line flows within it. Some subprocesses nested within the process can be identical for all jobs or customers. For example, the auto finance process at a bank is a job process, but subprocesses (such as handling retail loan payments) are batch or line processes. Also, some customers of a job process place repeat orders from time to time. These conditions create higher volumes, some line flows, and more make-to-stock and standardized-service possibilities than are found with a project process.

batch process A process that differs from the job process with respect to volume, variety, and quality.

BATCH PROCESS. Examples of a batch process are scheduling air travel for a group, making components that feed an assembly line, processing mortgage loans, and manufacturing capital equipment. A **batch process** differs from the job process with respect to volume, variety, and quantity. The primary difference is that volumes are higher because the same or similar products or services are provided repeatedly. Another difference is that a narrower range of products and services is provided. Variety is achieved more through an assemble-to-order strategy than the job process's make-to-order or customized-services strategies (see the Operations Strategy chapter).

Some of the components going into the final product or service may be processed in advance. A third difference is that production lots or customer groups are handled in larger quantities (or *batches*) than they are with job processes. A batch of one product or customer grouping is processed, and then production is switched to the next one. Eventually, the first product or service is produced again. A batch process has average or moderate volumes, but variety is still too great to warrant dedicating a separate process for each product or service. The flow pattern is jumbled, with no standard sequence of operations throughout the facility. However, more dominant paths emerge than at a job process, and some segments of the process have a line flow.

line process A process that lies between the batch and continuous processes on the continuum, volumes are high, and products or services are standardized, which allows resources to be organized around a product or service.

LINE PROCESS. Products created by a line process include automobiles, appliances, and toys. Services based on a line process are fast-food restaurants and cafeterias. A **line process** lies between the batch and continuous processes on the continuum, volumes are high, and products or services are standardized, which allows resources to be organized around a product or service. There are line flows, with little inventory held between operations. Each operation performs the same process over and over, with little variability in the products or services provided.

Production orders are not directly linked to customer orders, as is the case with project and job processes. Service providers with a line process follow a standardized-services strategy. Manufacturers with line processes often follow a make-to-stock strategy, with standard products held in inventory so that they are ready when a customer places an order. This use of a line process is sometimes called *mass production*, which is what the popular press commonly refers to as a manufacturing process. However, the assemble-to-order strategy and *mass customization* (see the Operations Strategy chapter) are other possibilities with line processes. Product variety is possible by careful control of the addition of standard options to the main product or service.

continuous process The extreme end of high-volume, standardized production with rigid line flows.

CONTINUOUS PROCESS. Examples are petroleum refineries, chemical plants, and plants making beer, steel, and food (such as Borden's huge pasta-making plant). Firms with such facilities are also referred to as the *process industry*. An electric generation plant represents one of the few continuous processes found in the service sector. A **continuous process** is the extreme end of high-volume, standardized production with rigid line

THE BIG PICTURE   KING SOOPERS BAKERY

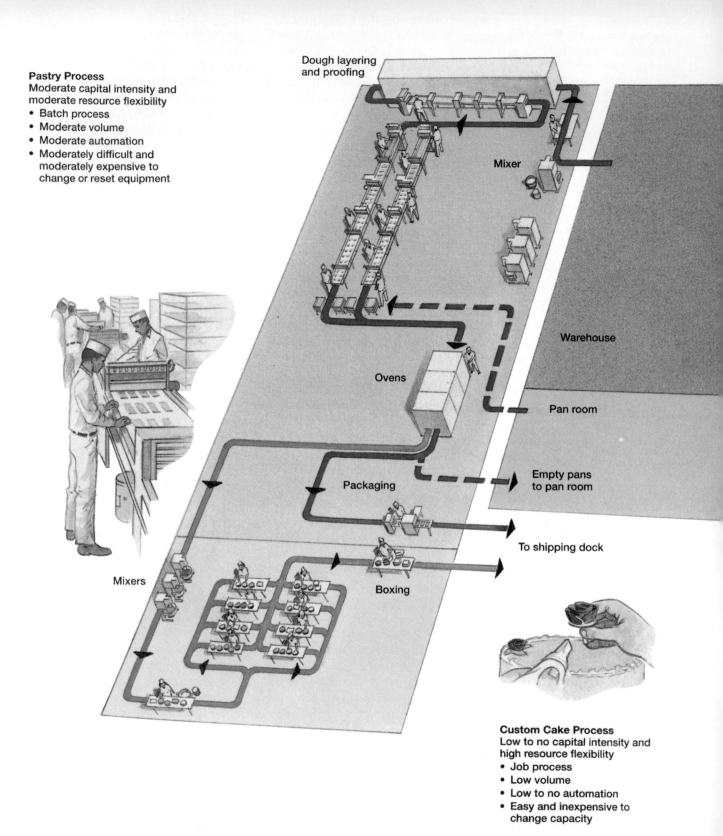

Pastry Process
Moderate capital intensity and moderate resource flexibility
- Batch process
- Moderate volume
- Moderate automation
- Moderately difficult and moderately expensive to change or reset equipment

Dough layering and proofing

Mixer

Warehouse

Ovens

Pan room

Packaging

Empty pans to pan room

To shipping dock

Boxing

Mixers

Custom Cake Process
Low to no capital intensity and high resource flexibility
- Job process
- Low volume
- Low to no automation
- Easy and inexpensive to change capacity

Bulk storage tanks

Holding tanks

Bread mixers

Cutting, rolling, and loading machines

Proofing oven

Bread oven

Cooling conveyor

Slicing and bagging

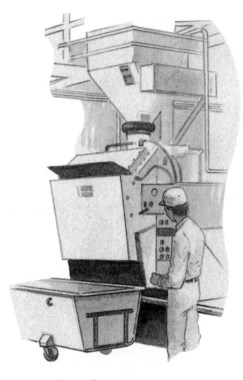

Bread Process
High capital intensity and low resource flexibility
- Line process
- High volume
- Difficult and expensive to change capacity

FIGURE 3.2

Volumes at King Soopers.

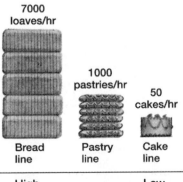

7000 loaves/hr

1000 pastries/hr

50 cakes/hr

Bread line

Pastry line

Cake line

High   Low

flows. Its name derives from the way materials move through the process. Usually, one primary material, such as a liquid, gas, or powder, moves without stopping through the facility. The processes seem more like separate entities than a series of connected operations. The process is often capital-intensive and operated round the clock to maximize utilization and to avoid expensive shutdowns and start-ups.

THE BIG PICTURE: Process Choice at King Soopers Bakery

In the Big Picture illustration on pages 100–101, we literally lifted the roof of the multi-product bakery King Soopers, a division of Kroger Company, in Denver, Colorado, to show process choice at work. King Soopers makes three types of baked goods—custom-decorated cakes, pastries, and bread—with widely varying volumes and degrees of customization. It uses three different production processes to meet varying demand.

As you can see from the bar graph of relative volumes to the right (Figure 3.2), the custom cake process is a low-volume process. It starts with basic cakes of the appropriate sizes, which are made from a batch process (not shown). From that point on, the product is highly customized and cakes are produced to order. The process choice is best described as a *job process*. Customers may choose some standard selections from a catalog but often request one-of-a-kind designs. Frosting colors and cake designs are limited only by the worker's imagination.

The pastry process has higher volumes but not high enough for each product to have dedicated resources. The process choice is best described as a *batch process*. Dough is mixed in relatively small batches and sent to the proofing room (not shown), where general-purpose equipment feeds the batch of dough through rollers. Special fixtures, each unique to the product being made, cut the dough into the desired shapes. A great deal of product variety is handled, with each batch comprising about 1,000 units before a change is made to the next type of pastry.

The bread line is a high-volume process, making 7,000 loaves per hour. The bread is a standardized product made to stock, and production is not keyed to specific customer orders. The process choice is a *line process*. Because of the rigid line flows, it is not a batch process, even though a batch of dough is made each day. Once the line starts, it must run until empty so that no dough is left in the mixers overnight and no bread is left in the oven. The line usually doesn't operate round the clock and, in this sense, is less like a continuous process.

VERTICAL INTEGRATION

Which services and products should be created in-house

outsourcing Allotting work to suppliers and distributors to provide needed services and materials and to perform those processes that the organization does not perform itself.

make-or-buy decisions Decisions that either involve more integration (a *make* decision) or more outsourcing (a *buy* decision).

All businesses buy at least some inputs to their processes, such as professional services, raw materials, or manufactured parts, from other producers. King Soopers is no exception and buys such materials as flour, sugar, butter, and water. Management decides the level of vertical integration by looking at all the processes performed between the acquisition of raw materials or outside services and the delivery of finished products or services. The more processes in the supply chain that the organization performs itself, the more vertically integrated it is. If it doesn't perform some processes itself, it must rely on **outsourcing**, or paying suppliers and distributors to perform those processes and provide needed services and materials. When managers opt for more vertical integration, there is by definition less outsourcing. These decisions are sometimes called **make-or-buy decisions,** with a *make* decision meaning more integration and a *buy* decision meaning more outsourcing. After deciding what to outsource and what to do in-house, management must find ways to coordinate and integrate the various processes and suppliers involved (see the Supply-Chain Management chapter).

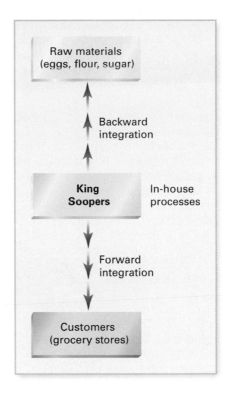

FIGURE 3.3

*Vertical Integration at
King Soopers*

backward integration A
firm's movement upstream
toward the sources of raw
materials and parts.

forward integration A
firm's movement
downstream by acquiring
more channels of
distribution, such as its
own distribution centers
(warehouses) and retail
sources.

BACKWARD AND FORWARD INTEGRATION. Vertical integration can be in two directions, as Figure 3.3 illustrates for King Soopers. **Backward integration** represents movement upstream toward the sources of raw materials and parts, such as a major grocery chain having its own plants to produce house brands of ice cream, frozen pizza dough, and peanut butter. **Forward integration** means that the firm acquires more channels of distribution, such as its own distribution centers (warehouses) and retail stores. It can also mean that the firm goes even further by acquiring its business customers. For example, King Soopers could acquire some of its own grocery stores that sell its products.

ADVANTAGES OF VERTICAL INTEGRATION AND OUTSOURCING. The advantages of vertical integration are the disadvantages of more outsourcing. Similarly, the advantages of more outsourcing are disadvantages of more vertical integration. Managers must study the options carefully before making choices. Break-even analysis (see the Decision Making supplement) and financial analysis (see the Financial Analysis CD supplement) are good starting points. However, the need for strategic fit is fundamental to all choices and must reflect qualitative as well as quantitative factors if analyses are to be complete.

Advantages of Vertical Integration. More vertical integration can sometimes improve market share and allow a firm to enter foreign markets more easily than it could otherwise. A firm can also achieve savings if it has the skills, volume, and resources to perform processes at lower cost and produce higher-quality goods and services than outsiders can. Doing the work in-house may mean better quality and more timely delivery—and taking better advantage of the firm's human resources, equipment, and space. Extensive vertical integration is generally attractive when input volumes are high because high volumes allow task specialization and greater efficiency. It is also

MANAGERIAL PRACTICE 3.2
Choosing the Right Amount of Vertical Integration

More Integration (Less Outsourcing)

The Citgo Petroleum Corporation's (www.citgo.com) triangular emblem is more visible at U.S. gas stations thanks to its addition of 14,000 new U.S. outlets, surpassing the number bearing the rival Texaco star. The red, white, and blue emblem is a symbol of a massive push into the United States by parent Petroleos de Venezuela (PDVA), the $22 billion Venezuelan state oil company. It also signals a drive by key producers in OPEC to lock up shares in global markets by investing heavily in "downstream" refining and retailing as the cartel loses its hold on crude supplies and prices. "We believe that the fundamentals of the oil business indicate that you should be as integrated as possible," says the PDVA president.

Tulsa-based Citgo, PDVA's $10 billion U.S. refining and marketing subsidiary, has been growing at double-digit rates. To add to its six refineries in the United States, it is discussing ventures with Phillips Petroleum Company, Mobil Corporation, and others that could add retailing strength. In Europe, it has a joint refining venture with Germany's Veba. PDVA's strategy of increased vertical integration is being embraced by other big OPEC members. Saudi Arabia and Kuwait, for example, are buying into refineries in markets such as the Philippines and India.

Less Integration (More Outsourcing)

Li & Fung (www.lifung.com), Hong Kong's largest export trading company, has a predominantly American and European customer base. This multinational firm outsources most of its manufacturing, using what is called "dispersed manufacturing" or "borderless manufacturing." It still performs the higher-value-added processes in Hong Kong, but outsources lower-value-added processes to the best possible locations around the world. Thus, it retains processes for designing products, buying and inspecting raw materials, managing factories and developing production schedules, and controlling quality. But it does not manage the workers, and it does not own the factories.

Suppose Li & Fung gets an order from a European retailer to produce 10,000 garments. It might decide to buy yarn from a Korean producer but have it woven and dyed in Taiwan. So it selects the yarn and ships it to Taiwan. The Japanese have the best zippers and buttons, but they manufacture them mostly in China. So Li & Fung orders the right zippers from YKK, a big Japanese zipper manufacturer, directly from the latter's Chinese plants. Because of quotas and labor constraints, the best place to make the garments might be Thailand. Thus, Li & Fung ships everything there. Because the customer needs quick delivery, it divides the order across five factories in Thailand. Five weeks after Li & Fung received the order, the 10,000 garments arrive on shelves in Europe, all looking as if they came from one factory, even though they are, of course, a truly global product.

Li & Fung's approach goes beyond outsourcing to suppliers and letting them worry about contracting for raw materials. Any single factory is small and does not have the buying power to demand fast deliveries and good prices. Li & Fung may know, for instance, that The Limited is going to order 100,000 garments but does not yet know the style or colors. The firm reserves undyed yarn from its yarn supplier and locks up capacity at supplier mills for weaving. Because this approach is more complicated, Li & Fung was forced to get smart about logistics and dissecting the value chain. It is an innovator in supply-chain management techniques, using a host of information-intensive service processes for product development, sourcing, shipping, handling, and logistics. For its enterprise process of executing and tracking orders, it has its own standardized, fully computerized operating system, and everybody in the company uses it. Essentially, therefore, Li & Fung manages information and the relationships among 350 customers and 7,500 suppliers and does so with a lot of phone calls, faxes, and on-site visits. In time, the firm will need a sophisticated information system with an open architecture that can handle work in Hong Kong and New York, as well as in places like Bangladesh, where you cannot always count on a good phone line.

Despite the coordination requirements and higher transportation costs, dispersed manufacturing is best for Li & Fung for several reasons. Starting in the 1990s, Hong Kong became an increasingly expensive and uncompetitive place to manufacture. Dispersed manufacturing not only reduces labor costs but also fits neatly with the additional competitive priorities of customization and delivery speed. For each step, the goal is to customize the value chain and meet the customer's specific needs. It pulls apart the value chain and optimizes each step—and does it globally.

The competitive priorities of customization and fast delivery usually do not match up well together, but Li & Fung achieves both by organizing around small, customer-focused units. One unit might be a theme-store division that serves a handful of customers such as Warner Brothers stores and Rainforest Café. Its retailing customers are in consumer-driven, fast-moving markets and face the problem of obsolete inventory with a vengeance. If a retailer shortens its buying cycle from three months to five weeks, it gains eight weeks to develop a better sense of where the market is heading. Forecasting accuracy improves, and there is less need for markdowns of obsolete inventory at the end of the selling season. Such payoffs to Li & Fung's customers make it a valued supplier. During the last decade, the focus was on supplier partnerships to improve cost and quality. In today's faster-paced markets, the focus has shifted to innovation, flexibility, and speed.

Sources: "Stepping on the Gas with Citgo," *Business Week* (March 11, 1996); "Fast, Global, and Entrepreneurial: Supply Chain Management, Hong Kong Style: An Interview with Victor Fung," *Harvard Business Review* (September–October 1998), pp. 103–115.

attractive if the firm has the relevant skills and views the processes that it is integrating as particularly important to its future success.

Management must identify, cultivate, and exploit its core competencies to prevail in global competition. Recall that core competencies are the collective learning of the firm, especially its ability for coordinating diverse processes and integrating multiple technologies (see the Operations Strategy chapter). They define the firm and provide its reason for existence. Management must look upstream toward its suppliers and downstream toward its customers and bring in-house those processes that give it the right core competencies—those that allow the firm to organize work and deliver value better than its competitors. Management should also realize that if the firm outsources a critical process, it may lose control over that area of its business—and perhaps the ability to bring the work in-house later.

Advantages of Outsourcing. Outsourcing offers several advantages to firms. It is particularly attractive to those that have low volumes. For example, LoanCity.com, an on-line mortgage company, set up shop in August, 1999. It started life with zero revenue but planned to serve more than a million customers in a few years. Any on-line operation of that size would require a sprawling computing center, which in turn would require a few million dollars of hardware, software licenses, and a staff of as many as 20 specialists. Instead, the company hired an application service provider, or ASP, to set up and run the various business-software packages needed to handle its sales, accounting, and human resource processes. It uses the Internet to connect to the applications needed on machines located at its ASP. Outsourcing can also provide better quality and cost savings. For example, foreign locations sometimes offer lower wages and yield higher productivity.

Firms are doing more outsourcing than ever before. The NCNB bank in Charlotte, North Carolina, outsourced the processing of card transactions and saved $5 million per year. Merrill Lynch, Sears Roebuck, and Texaco outsource their mailroom and photocopying operations to Pitney Bowes Management Services. Many firms do the same with payroll, security, cleaning, and other types of services, rather than employ personnel to provide these services. One recent survey showed that 35 percent of more than 1,000 large corporations have increased the amount of outsourcing they do.

Even Texas Instruments Inc., a company that can not only claim to have invented the microchip but has been long admired for the capabilities of its internally developed software, has turned to off-the-shelf software to address its supply-chain needs. It is investing millions of dollars and tens of thousands of work hours to buy and implement products from software vendors and consultants. The software will allow TI to streamline various aspects of its supply chain, so it can cut down on paperwork and cut lead times. Instead of the traditional approach, the software allows TI to show suppliers its inventory levels and manufacturing schedules, and lets the suppliers manage the supply process. TI reasons that developing this kind of software is not a core competency, in contrast to its semiconductor manufacturing. What will set it apart from the competition is not the information technology tools that it uses, but how its business processes use them.

Two factors are contributing to this trend: global competition and information technology. Globalization creates more supplier options, and advances in information technology make coordination with suppliers easier. IKEA, the largest retailer of home furnishings, has 30 buying offices around the world to seek out suppliers. Its Vienna-based business service department runs a computer database that helps suppliers locate raw materials and new business partners. Cash registers at its stores around the world relay sales data to the nearest warehouse and its operational headquarters in Älmhult, Sweden, where its information systems provide the data needed to control its shipping patterns worldwide.

virtual corporation
A situation in which competitors enter into short-term partnerships to respond to market opportunities.

network companies
Companies that contract with other firms for most of their production and for many of their other functions.

The Virtual Corporation. Information technology allows suppliers to come together as a virtual corporation. In a **virtual corporation,** competitors actually enter into short-term partnerships to respond to market opportunities. Teams in different organizations and at different locations collaborate on design, production, and marketing, with information going electronically from place to place. They disband when the project is completed. Virtual corporations allow firms to change their positions flexibly in response to quickly changing market demands.

An extreme case of outsourcing is **network companies,** which contract with other firms for most of their production—and for many of their other functions. Li & Fung, which we discussed in Managerial Practice 3.2, is a good example. The name comes from their employees spending most of their time on the telephone or at the computer, coordinating suppliers. If demand for the network company's products or services changes, its employees simply pass this message along to suppliers, who change their output levels. Network companies can move in and out of markets, riding the waves of fashion and technology. However, network companies are vulnerable to new competition because the investment barriers to enter their businesses are low and because they lose business if their suppliers integrate forward or their customers integrate backward. Moreover, the risk of losing business to suppliers or customers increases as product volumes increase and product life cycles lengthen.

The Own-or-Lease Option. When a firm decides to increase vertical integration, it must also decide whether to own or to lease the necessary facilities and equipment. The lease option is often favored for items affected by fairly rapid changes in technology, items that require frequent servicing, or items for which industry practices have made leasing the norm, as in the photocopier industry. Leasing is also common when a firm has a short-term need for equipment. For example, in the construction industry, where projects usually take months or years to complete, heavy equipment is often leased only as needed.

RESOURCE FLEXIBILITY

Is general-purpose or special-purpose equipment needed, and how flexible should the workforce be?

The choices that management makes concerning competitive priorities determine the degree of flexibility required of a company's resources—its employees, facilities, and equipment. For example, when a process handles products and services with short life cycles or high customization, employees need to perform a broad range of duties and equipment must be general purpose. Otherwise, resource utilization will be too low for economical operation.

flexible workforce
A workforce whose members are capable of doing many tasks, either at their own workstations or as they move from one workstation to another.

WORKFORCE. Operations managers must decide whether to have a **flexible workforce.** Members of a flexible workforce are capable of doing many tasks, either at their own workstations or as they move from one workstation to another. However, such flexibility often comes at a cost, requiring greater skills and thus more training and education. Nevertheless, benefits can be large: Worker flexibility can be one of the best ways to achieve reliable customer service and alleviate capacity bottlenecks. Resource flexibility helps to absorb the feast-or-famine workloads in individual operations that are caused by low-volume production, jumbled routings, and fluid scheduling.

The type of workforce required also depends on the need for volume flexibility. When conditions allow for a smooth, steady rate of output, the likely choice is a permanent workforce that expects regular full-time employment. If the process is subject to hourly, daily, or seasonal peaks and valleys in demand, the use of part-time or temporary employees to supplement a smaller core of full-time employees may be the best solution. However, this approach may not be practical if knowledge and skill requirements are too high for a temporary worker to grasp quickly. Controversy is growing over the practice of replacing full-time workers with temporary or part-time workers.

EQUIPMENT. When products or services have a short life cycle and a high degree of customization, low volumes mean that process managers should select flexible, general-purpose equipment. Figure 3.4 illustrates this relationship by showing the total cost lines for two different types of equipment that can be chosen for a process. Each line represents the total annual cost of the process at different volume levels. It is the sum of fixed costs and variable costs (see the Decision Making supplement). When volumes are low (because customization is high), process 1 is the best choice. It calls for inexpensive general-purpose equipment, which keeps investment in equipment low and makes fixed costs (F_1) small. Its variable unit cost is high, which gives its total cost line a relatively steep slope. Process 1 does the job but not at peak efficiency. However, volumes are not high enough for total variable costs to overcome the benefit of low fixed costs.

Conversely, process 2 is the best choice when volumes are high and customization is low. Its advantage is low variable unit cost, as reflected in the flatter total cost line. This efficiency is possible when customization is low because the equipment can be designed for a narrow range of products or tasks. Its disadvantage is high equipment investment and thus high fixed costs (F_2). When annual volume produced is high

FIGURE 3.4

Relationship between Process Costs and Product Volume

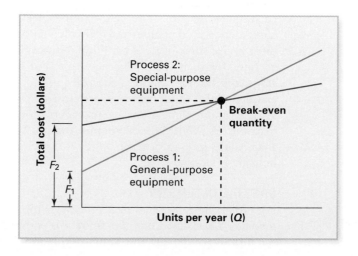

enough, spreading these fixed costs over more units produced, the advantage of low variable costs more than compensates for the high fixed costs.

The break-even quantity in Figure 3.4 is the quantity at which the total costs for the two alternatives are equal. At quantities beyond this point, the cost of process 1 exceeds that of process 2. Unless the firm expects to sell more than the break-even amount (which is unlikely with high customization and low volume), the capital investment of process 2 is not warranted.

TUTOR 3.1

How much should customers be involved in processes?

CUSTOMER INVOLVEMENT

The fourth significant process decision is the extent to which customers interact with the process. The amount of customer involvement may range from self-service to customization of product to deciding the time and place that the service is to be provided.

SELF-SERVICE. Self-service is the process decision of many retailers, particularly when price is a competitive priority. To save money, some customers prefer to do part of the process formerly performed by the manufacturer or dealer. Manufacturers of goods such as toys, bicycles, and furniture may also prefer to let the customer perform the final assembly because production, shipping, and inventory costs frequently are lower, as are losses from damage. The firms pass the savings on to customers as lower prices.

PRODUCT SELECTION. A business that competes on customization frequently allows customers to come up with their own product specifications or even become involved in designing the product. A good example of customer involvement is in custom-designed and -built homes: The customer is heavily involved in the design process and inspects the work in process at various times.

TIME AND LOCATION. When services cannot be provided in the customer's absence, customers may determine the time and location that the service is to be provided. If the service is delivered to the customer, client, or patient by appointment, decisions involving the location become part of process design. Will the customer be served only on the supplier's premises, will the supplier's employees go to the customer's premises, or will the service be provided at a third location? Although certified public accountants frequently work on their clients' premises, both the time and the place are likely to be known well in advance.

In a market where customers are technology-enabled, companies can now engage in an active dialogue with customers and make them partners in creating value. Customers are a new source of competence for an organization. To harness customer competencies, companies must involve customers in an ongoing dialogue. They also must revise some of their traditional processes, such as pricing and billing systems, to account for their customer's new role. For example, in business-to-business relationships, the Internet changes the roles that companies play with other businesses. For example, Ford's suppliers now are close collaborators in the process of developing new vehicles and no longer passive providers of materials and services. The same is true for distributors. Wal-Mart does more than just distribute Procter & Gamble's goods: It shares daily sales information and works with P&G in managing inventories and warehousing operations.

How much should a firm depend on machinery and automated processes?

CAPITAL INTENSITY

For either the design of a new process or the redesign of an existing one, an operations manager must determine the amount of capital intensity required. Capital intensity is the mix of equipment and human skills in the process; the greater the relative cost of

automation A system, process, or piece of equipment that is self-acting and self-regulating.

equipment, the greater is the capital intensity. As the capabilities of technology increase and its costs decrease, managers face an ever-widening range of choices, from operations utilizing very little automation to those requiring task-specific equipment and very little human intervention. **Automation** is a system, process, or piece of equipment that is self-acting and self-regulating. Although automation is often thought to be necessary to gain competitive advantage, it has both advantages and disadvantages. Thus, the automation decision requires careful examination.

One advantage of automation is that adding capital intensity can significantly increase productivity and improve quality. Gillette, for example, spent $750 million on the production lines and robotics that gave it a capacity to make 1.2 billion Mach3 razor cartridges a year. The equipment is complicated and expensive. Fortunately, sales of core blade and razor products has climbed 10 percent on a worldwide basis, thanks largely to high demand for the flagship Mach3 product. Only with such high volumes could this continuous process produce the product at a price low enough that consumers could afford to buy it.

One big disadvantage of capital intensity can be the prohibitive investment cost for low-volume operations. Look again at Figure 3.4. Process 1, which uses general-purpose equipment, is not capital-intensive and therefore has small fixed costs, F_1. Although its variable cost per unit produced is high, as indicated by the slope of the total cost line, process 1 is well below the break-even quantity if volumes are low. Generally, capital-intensive operations must have high utilization to be justifiable. Also, automation does not always align with a company's competitive priorities. If a firm offers a unique product or high-quality service, competitive priorities may indicate the need for skilled servers, hand labor, and individual attention rather than new technology.

fixed automation A manufacturing process that produces one type of part or product in a fixed sequence of simple operations.

FIXED AUTOMATION. Manufacturers use two types of automation: fixed and flexible (or programmable). Particularly appropriate for line and continuous process choices, **fixed automation** produces one type of part or product in a fixed sequence of simple operations. Until the mid-1980s, most U.S. automobile plants were dominated by fixed automation—and some still are. Chemical processing plants and oil refineries also utilize this type of automation.

Operations managers favor fixed automation when demand volumes are high, product designs are stable, and product life cycles are long. These conditions compensate for the process's two primary drawbacks: large initial investment cost and relative inflexibility. The investment cost is particularly high when a single, complex machine (called a *transfer machine*) must be capable of handling many operations. Because fixed automation is designed around a particular product, changing equipment to accommodate new products is difficult and costly. However, fixed automation maximizes efficiency and yields the lowest variable cost per unit if volumes are high.

flexible (or programmable) automation A manufacturing process that can be changed easily to handle various products.

FLEXIBLE AUTOMATION. Flexible (or **programmable**) **automation** can be changed easily to handle various products. The ability to reprogram machines is useful for both low-customization and high-customization processes. In the case of high customization, a machine that makes a variety of products in small batches can be programmed to alternate between products. When a machine has been dedicated to a particular product or family of products, as in the case of low customization and a line flow, and the product is at the end of its life cycle, the machine can simply be reprogrammed with a new sequence of operations for a new product.

Cummins Engine Company, a manufacturer of diesel engines based in Columbus, Indiana, utilizes such flexibility to handle frequent design modifications. For example, in the first 18 months after introducing new compression brakes for its engines, Cummins' engineers made 14 design changes to the brakes. If the brakes had been made on less-flexible machines, these improvements probably would have taken several years and millions of dollars to implement—and in fact might not have been made. Flexible automation cut time to the market by two years, reduced annual warranty expenses by an estimated $300,000, and reduced costs to the customer by more than 30 percent.

RELATIONSHIPS BETWEEN DECISIONS IN MANUFACTURING

How should decisions be coordinated for manufacturing processes?

The process manager should understand how these five process decisions usually tie together, so as to spot ways of improving poorly designed processes. The common denominator in this relationship is volume, which in turn comes from the manufacturing strategy (see Operations Strategy chapter). Figure 3.5 shows how process choice (represented as ovals within the graph) and the other key process decisions (shown on the left axis) are tied to volume. The vertical arrows within the graph reflect the link between volume and process choice, and the horizontal arrows represent the subsequent link between process choice and the other process decisions.

FIGURE 3.5

Volume and the Major Process Decisions

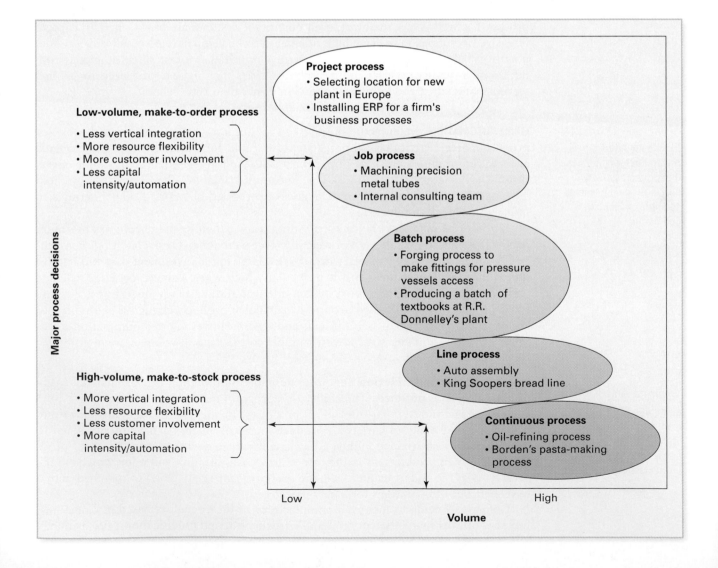

High volumes at a process typically mean all of the following:

1. *A Line or Continuous Process.* For example, the high volumes at King Soopers's bread line combined with a standard product, making possible a line process.

2. *More Vertical Integration.* High volumes create more opportunities for vertical integration.

3. *Less Resource Flexibility.* When volumes are high, there is no need for flexibility to utilize resources effectively, and specialization can lead to more efficient processes. King Soopers' bread line can make just one product—bread.

4. *Less Customer Involvement.* At high volumes, firms cannot meet the unpredictable demands required by customized orders.

5. *More Capital Intensity.* High volumes justify the large fixed costs of an efficient operation. The King Soopers bread line is capital-intensive. It is automated from dough mixing to placement of the product on shipping racks. Expanding this process would be very expensive.

Low volumes typically mean all of the following:

1. *A Project or Job Process.* For example, King Soopers uses a job process for its custom cake production and keys its cake production to specific customer orders.

2. *Less Vertical Integration.* Low volumes eliminate most opportunities for backward or forward vertical integration. An example of less backward integration is King Soopers, which outsources frosting coloring and prune filling. The volumes of customized cakes and pastries in which they are used are low.

3. *More Resource Flexibility.* When volumes are low, as in the custom cake process, workers are trained to handle all types of customer requests.

4. *More Customer Involvement.* King Soopers has more customer involvement with its custom cake process because customers often order one-of-a-kind decorations not found in the catalog.

5. *Less Capital Intensity.* The custom cake line is very labor-intensive and requires little investment to equip the workers.

Of course, these are general tendencies rather than rigid prescriptions. Exceptions can be found, but these relationships provide a way of understanding how process decisions can be linked coherently.

RELATIONSHIPS BETWEEN DECISIONS IN SERVICES

How should decisions be coordinated for service processes?

Figure 3.6 summarizes the relationships between volume and process decisions for service operations. It is similar to Figure 3.5, which summarizes manufacturing processes, except that particular attention must be given to the following two major process decisions:

1. customer involvement and
2. capital intensity and automation.

Processes must be designed around the service strategies selected for them. We singled out customer contact and capital intensity as key differences between typical manufacturing and service operations (see Figure 1.4). Thus, the manager must give particular attention to these strategies when designing a service process.

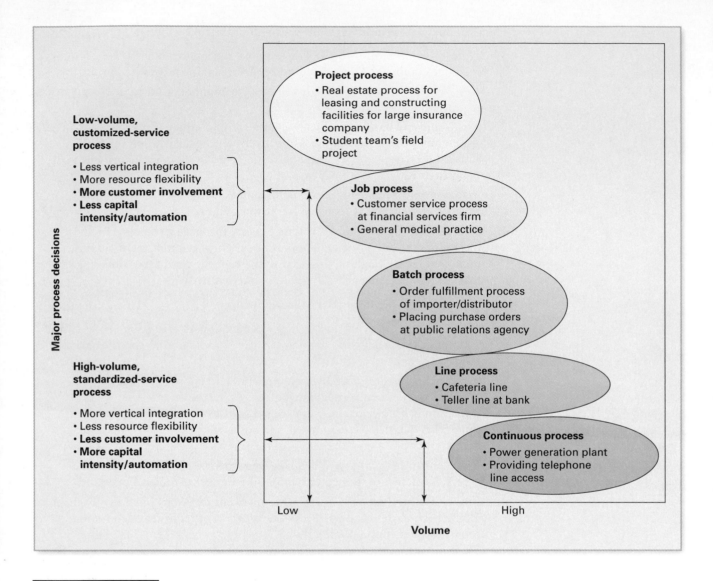

Major process decisions

Low-volume, customized-service process

- Less vertical integration
- More resource flexibility
- **More customer involvement**
- **Less capital intensity/automation**

High-volume, standardized-service process

- More vertical integration
- Less resource flexibility
- **Less customer involvement**
- **More capital intensity/automation**

Project process
- Real estate process for leasing and constructing facilities for large insurance company
- Student team's field project

Job process
- Customer service process at financial services firm
- General medical practice

Batch process
- Order fulfillment process of importer/distributor
- Placing purchase orders at public relations agency

Line process
- Cafeteria line
- Teller line at bank

Continuous process
- Power generation plant
- Providing telephone line access

Low ——————— High

Volume

FIGURE 3.6

Volume and the Major Process Decisions for Services

High volumes at a service process typically mean all of the following:

1. *A Line Process.* Line flows are preferred, with jobs or customers moving through a series of standardized steps. Each customer gets the same basic service, and service specifications are tightly controlled. Standardized services increase volumes and process repeatability. One example is the front-end process of a cafeteria line, where the customer moves from one station to the next, making food selections and then paying at the end of the line. Other examples include processes in public transportation; movie theatres; backroom processes in banking, insurance, and postal service; airport baggage handling; spectator sports; and large lecture halls.

2. *More Vertical Integration.* High volumes make it more likely that the service provider will keep the process in-house rather than outsourcing.

3. *Less Resource Flexibility.* High process volumes and repetition create less need for resource flexibility, which can be more expensive. Resources can be dedicated to each standardized service. Skill levels are not high, and jobs are more specialized.

4. *Less Customer Involvement.* Often, the customer is not present when the process is performed, as in the backroom operations of financial services institutions. The little contact that occurs between employees and customers is for standardized services. If the customer is involved in the process, it is in performing self-service activities to get lower prices or in selecting from standard service options rather than getting customized treatment.

5. *More Capital Intensity and Automation.* Because the customer is not involved with the process, automation possibilities increase. High process volumes and repetition also allow for more automation. Capital intensity is high, making labor intensity low. Of course, there can be exceptions to always automating high-volume standardized services. Examples are wholesalers, full-service retailers, and large university lecture halls. In such cases, capital intensity is low because the nature of the work being done makes it difficult to achieve automation for these processes.

Low volumes typically mean all of the following:

1. *A Project or Job Process.* Processes must be defined for each new project or job and change considerably from one to the next. Customized treatment means a low-volume process, and each customer requires different changes in the process itself. Examples are processes for management consultants, lawyers, physicians, gourmet restaurants, and corporate bankers. Each customer has individual needs that must be understood and accounted for in the process. Considerable attention is given to a customer's unique requirements and preferences.

2. *Less Vertical Integration.* Low volumes make it more likely that the service provider will seek to outsource many processes rather than keeping them in house.

3. *More Resource Flexibility.* Employees and equipment must be able to handle new or unique services on demand. Thus, they must be versatile and flexible and able to handle a wide array of customer requests. Skill levels are high and jobs enlarged.

4. *More Customer Involvement.* Employees interact frequently with customers, often on a one-to-one basis, to understand and diagnose each customer's individual needs. They must be able to relate well to their customers, not merely possess technical skills. Exercising judgment as they provide new or unique services and solutions is commonplace.

5. *Less Capital Intensity and Automation.* Because of the infinite variability of problems confronted, the mental and physical requirements of these services are difficult to automate. Capital intensity is low, which means high labor intensity; the high skill levels required are very expensive. Employees have a great deal of operating discretion and relatively loose superior–subordinate relationships. Exceptions do occur, such as certain processes at medical facilities in a smaller community. Some low-volume processes are capital-intensive, because certain expensive equipment is needed to perform services regardless of the volume.

Should jobs be specialized or enlarged?

specialization The degree to which a job involves a narrow range of tasks, a high degree of repetition, and, presumably, great efficiency and high quality.

JOB DESIGN CONSIDERATIONS

Process choice, resource flexibility, and capital intensity influence how a manager designs jobs that go into a process. In particular, the manager must decide how much the jobs should be specialized or enlarged. A job with a high degree of **specialization** involves a narrow range of tasks, a high degree of repetition, and, presumably, great efficiency and high quality. For example, an appliance repairperson specializing in refrigerators can quickly diagnose problems and make the correct repairs based on previous experience. Specialization results in such benefits as

❑ less training time per employee because methods and procedures are limited,

❑ faster work pace, leading to more output in less time, and

❑ lower wages because education and skill requirements are lower.

However, the arguments against job specialization suggest that narrowly defined jobs lead to

❑ Poor employee morale, high turnover, and lower quality because of the monotony and boredom of repetitive work;

❑ the need for more management attention because the total activity is broken into a large number of jobs for a large number of employees, all of whom have to be coordinated to produce the entire product or service; and

❑ less flexibility to handle changes or employee absences.

ALTERNATIVES TO SPECIALIZATION. Considerable process specialization is usually associated with competitive priorities of low costs and consistent quality, with little product variety; with line or continuous processes; with low resource flexibility; and with high capital intensity. A low degree of process specialization is typically associated with competitive priorities of customization, high-performance design, and volume flexibility; with project or job processes; with high resource flexibility; and with low capital intensity. However, there are notable exceptions. Some firms (e.g., Motorola and AT&T) are having success with less specialization, even with process characteristics that seem to call for more specialization, by using three alternative strategies: job enlargement, job rotation, and job enrichment.

job enlargement The horizontal expansion of a job, increasing the range of tasks at the same level.

Job Enlargement. The *horizontal* expansion of a job—that is, increasing the range of tasks at the same level—is called **job enlargement**. The employee completes a larger proportion of the total work required for the product or service. Typically, this approach requires that workers have various skills, and it is often accompanied by training programs and wage increases. Besides reducing boredom, job enlargement has the potential to increase employee satisfaction because the worker feels a greater sense of responsibility, pride, and accomplishment.

For example, the Capita Credit unit of AT&T Capital Credit Corporation, which leases telecommunications, computer, and other equipment, is organized so that teams of workers perform three major leasing functions for a customer: receiving applications and checking credit ratings, drawing up contracts, and collecting payments. Other financial institutions often devote three separate departments to these functions and design the jobs with a high degree of specialization. Employees at Capita Credit feel responsible for the quality of the service they provide and understand how their activities contribute to the success of the business as a whole. With this job design, Capita Credit processes up to 250 applications a day, more than double the number of a bank using the traditional job design processes.

job rotation A system whereby workers exchange jobs periodically, thus getting more diverse experience in task assignment.

Job Rotation. A system whereby workers exchange jobs periodically, thus getting more diverse experience in task assignment, is called **job rotation**. This approach is most effective when the jobs require an equal level of skill. For example, workers at a family restaurant may rotate duties from bussing tables to cooking meals to taking orders. Because workers learn many aspects of the job, job rotation increases the skills of the workforce, giving management the flexibility to replace absent workers or to move workers to different workstations as necessary. In addition, rotating jobs can give each worker a better appreciation of the production problems of others and the value of passing only good quality to the next person.

job enrichment A vertical expansion of job duties; workers have greater control and responsibility for an entire process, not just a specific skill or operation.

Job Enrichment. The most comprehensive approach to job design is **job enrichment**, which entails a *vertical* expansion of job duties. That is, workers have greater control and responsibility for an entire process, not just a specific skill or operation. This approach supports the development of *employee empowerment* and *self-managed teams*, whereby employees make basic decisions about their jobs. For example, a chef at an elegant restaurant may be given the responsibility of purchasing ingredients at the market and arranging her own work schedule. Job enrichment generally increases job satisfaction because it gives workers a sense of achievement in mastering many tasks, recognition and direct feedback from users of the output, and responsibility for the quality of the output.

ECONOMIES OF SCOPE

Should more economies of scope be sought?

Note that capital intensity and resource flexibility vary inversely in Figures 3.5 and 3.6. If capital intensity is high, resource flexibility is low. King Soopers produces a high-volume product (loaves of bread) efficiently on an automated (high-capital-intensity) bread line, with few people monitoring its operation, but the process has low resource flexibility. In contrast, the custom cake line produces a low volume of product because it requires high customization. To complete the unique customer orders, resources must be flexible, and because the process requires hand work, capital intensity is low.

economies of scope Economies that reflect the ability to produce multiple products more cheaply in combination than separately.

In certain types of manufacturing operations, such as machining and assembly, programmable automation breaks this inverse relationship between resource flexibility and capital intensity (see the Computer-Integrated Manufacturing supplement). It makes possible both high capital intensity and high resource flexibility, creating economies of scope. **Economies of scope** reflect the ability to produce multiple products more cheaply in combination than separately. In such situations, two conflicting competitive priorities—customization and low price—become more compatible. However, taking advantage of economies of scope requires that a family of parts or products have enough collective volume to utilize equipment fully. Adding a product to the family results in one-time programming (and sometimes fixture) costs. (*Fixtures* are reusable devices that maintain exact tolerances by holding the product firmly in position while it is processed.)

Economies of scope also apply to service processes. Consider, for example, Disney's approach to the Internet. When the company's managers entered the volatile Internet world, their businesses were only weakly tied together. They wanted plenty of freedom to evolve in and even shape emerging markets. They wanted flexibility and agility, not control, in these fast-moving markets. Disney's Infoseek business, in fact, was not even fully owned. However, once its Internet markets became more crystallized, managers at Disney moved to reap the benefits of economies of scope. They aggressively linked their Internet processes with one another and with other parts of Disney. They bought the rest of the Infoseek business, and then combined it with Internet businesses such as Disney Travel Online into a single business (Go.com). They made their content Web sites accessible from a single portal (Go Network) and created new links to established businesses like ESPN. A flexible technology that handles many services together can be less expensive than handling each one separately, particularly when the markets are not too volatile.

How can operations be focused?

GAINING FOCUS

Before 1970, many firms were willing to endure the additional complexity that went with size. New products or services were added to a facility in the name of better utilizing fixed costs and keeping everything under the same roof. The result was a jumble of competitive priorities, process choices, and technologies. In the effort to do everything, nothing was done well.

focused factories The result of a firm's splitting large plants that produced all the company's products into several specialized smaller plants.

FOCUSED FACTORIES. Hewlett-Packard, S. C. Johnson and Sons, Japan's Ricoh and Mitsubishi, and Britain's Imperial Chemical Industries PLC are some of the firms that have created **focused factories**, splitting large plants that produced all the company's products into several specialized smaller plants. The theory is that narrowing the range of demands on a facility will lead to better performance because management can concentrate on fewer tasks and lead a workforce toward a single goal. In some situations, a plant that used to produce all the components of a product and assemble them may split into one that produces the components and one that assembles them so that each can focus on its own individual process technology.

plants within plants (PWPs) Different operations within a facility with individual competitive priorities, processes, and workforces under the same roof.

FOCUS BY PROCESS SEGMENTS. A facility's process often can neither be characterized nor actually designed for one set of competitive priorities and one process choice. King Soopers had three processes under one roof, but management segmented them into three separate operations that were relatively autonomous. At a services facility, some parts of the process might seem like a job process and other parts like a line process. Such arrangements can be effective, provided that sufficient focus is given to each process. **Plants within plants (PWPs)** are different operations within a facility with individualized competitive priorities, processes, and workforces under the same roof. Boundaries for PWPs may be established by physically separating subunits or simply by revising organizational relationships. At each PWP, customization, capital intensity, volume, and other relationships are crucial and must be complementary. The advantages of PWPs are fewer layers of management, greater ability to rely on team problem solving, and shorter lines of communication between departments.

cell A group of two or more dissimilar workstations located close to each other that process a limited number of parts or models that have similar process requirements.

Another way of gaining focus is with the use of cells. A **cell** is a group of two or more dissimilar workstations located close to each other that process a limited number of parts or models that have similar process requirements. A cell has line flows, even though the operations around it may have flexible flows (see the Layout chapter). The small size of focused factories, PWPs, and cells offers a flexible, agile system that competes better on the basis of short lead times.

FOCUSED SERVICE OPERATIONS. Service industries also have implemented the concepts of focus, PWPs, and cells. Specialty retailers, such as Gap and The Limited, opened stores that have smaller, more accessible spaces. These focused facilities have generally chipped away at the business of large department stores. Using the same philosophy, some department stores are focusing on specific customers or products. Remodeled stores create the effect of many small boutiques under one roof.

DESIGNING PROCESSES

The five main process decisions represent broad, strategic issues. The next issue in process management is determining exactly how each process will be performed. We begin with a systematic approach to analyzing a process, spotting areas for improvement, developing ways to improve them, and implementing the desired changes. Three supporting techniques—flow diagrams, process charts, and simulation—can give good insights into both the current process and proposed changes. We conclude with two different but complementary philosophies for designing processes: process reengineering and process improvement. Both approaches are actually projects, which we discuss in the next chapter.

A SYSTEMATIC APPROACH

Managers or teams might use process reengineering or process improvement, but process analysis should follow a systematic procedure. Here is a six-step procedure that can pay off with improvements.

1. *Describe the More Strategic Dimensions of the Process.* What are the competitive priorities, operations strategy, process choice, and other major process decisions that apply? If it is an ongoing process, look for unexpected departures from the norms shown in Figures 3.5 and 3.6. If there are unexpected relationships, are they justified or are they symptoms that the process needs change?

2. *Identify the Inputs, Outputs, and Customers of the Process.* Make a comprehensive list so that the value-added capability of the process can be evaluated. Consider both internal and external customers.

3. *Identify the Important Performance Measures, Sometimes Called "Metrics," of the Process.* Possible performance measures could be multiple measures of quality, customer satisfaction, throughput time, cost, errors, safety, environmental measures, on-time delivery, flexibility, and the like.

4. *Document the Process.* Use "as is" for an ongoing process and "as proposed" for a process being designed for the first time. Be particularly alert for one or more of the following characteristics.

❐ Customers are dissatisfied with the value of the product or service that they receive from the process.

❐ The process introduces too many quality problems or errors.

❐ The process is slow in responding to customers.

❏ The process is costly.

❏ The process is often a bottleneck (see Capacity chapter), with work piling up waiting to go through it.

❏ The process creates disagreeable work, pollution, waste, or little value added.

Collect information on each part of the process and for each of the performance measures selected in step 3. Whenever possible, benchmark against similar processes within or external to the firm. Managerial Practice 3.3 demonstrates how benchmarking can expose areas of substandard performance.

MANAGERIAL PRACTICE 3.3
Benchmarking to Improve Marketing Process

Xerox (www.xerox.com) has an almost religious belief in benchmarking processes and sharing best practices. Benchmarking means identifying who is best at something (in your company, in your industry, or in the world), not by guesswork or reputation but by the numbers. Sharing best practices means identifying who is doing the process best and then adapting their ideas to your own operations. Xerox applies benchmarking not only to the cost side of the ledger but also to the revenue side. Headquartered in Dublin, Ireland, Xerox Europe, a 100 percent-owned subsidiary of Xerox Corporation, sells more than $5.3 billion worth of products and services annually, mostly in Europe. A team was formed, charged with learning where sales performance was best for different products and how these results were achieved. The team consisted of a couple of dozen people from the sales, service, and administrative staffs, of whom a third worked for Marlow and two-thirds for operating divisions across Europe, the Middle East, and Africa. Team members gathered all kinds of sales data, making country-by-country (division) comparisons. They needed just a couple of weeks to find eight cases in which one division dramatically outperformed the others. Somehow, France sold five times more color copiers than its sister divisions, Switzerland's sales of Xerox's top-of-the-line DocuPrint machines were ten times those of any other country, Austria suffered only a 4-percent attrition rate when service contracts came up for renewal, and so on. The team then found out how these benchmark results were achieved and what specific processes were used. Country managers were then told to pick three or four best practices to implement. They were given the ambitious goal of achieving 70 percent of the benchmark standard during the first year. In most cases, country managers visited benchmark divisions and installed their methods in a matter of weeks. The results were breathtaking. By copying France's practices in selling color copiers, chiefly by improving sales training and pushing color copiers through dealer channels as well as direct sales, Switzerland

Xerox has invested in excess of 400 million pounds to create 4,100 jobs in two new facilities in Ireland by 2003. Benchmarking has helped Xerox create state-of-the-art facilities. Here teams of technicians explore ways to improve products at the Electronics facility at the Xerox Technology Park in Dundalk.

increased its unit sales by 328 percent, Holland by 300 percent, and Norway by 152 percent.

Clearly, a lot more knowledge is lying around organizations than many managers are aware of, regardless of the functional area and type of process involved. Putting this knowledge to work improves both the process and the bottom line.

In 2000, the American Productivity and Quality Center named Xerox one of five global organizations that serve as models for implementing knowledge management successful. It said that Xerox changed the way the business world looks at benchmarking and knowledge sharing.

Source: "Beat the Budget and Astound your CFO," *Fortune* (October 28, 1996), p. 187

5. *Redesign or refine the process to achieve better performance.* In order to do so, the manager or team should ask six questions.

1. *What* is being done?
2. *When* is it being done?
3. *Who* is doing it?
4. *Where* is it being done?
5. *How* is it being done?
6. *How well* does it do on the various performance measures?

Answers to these questions are challenged by asking still another series of questions. *Why* is the process even being done? *Why* is it being done where it is being done? *Why* is it being done when it is being done? Such questioning often leads to creative answers and breakthroughs in process design. Once again, benchmarking against processes elsewhere, either inside or outside the organization, can pay off with new ideas and substantial improvements.

6. Evaluate the changes and implement those that appear to give the best payoffs on the various performance measures selected in step 3. Later on, after the process has been changed, check to see if the changes worked. Go back to step 1 as needed.

THREE TECHNIQUES

Three techniques are effective for documenting and evaluating processes: flow diagrams, process charts, and simulation. We fully describe the first two techniques, leaving a fuller treatment of simulation for the Simulation Analysis supplement. Later on, we also introduce more techniques for analyzing processes, that focus on quality improvement (see the Total Quality Management chapter). These techniques involve the systematic observation and recording of process details to allow better assessment. They also lend themselves to brainstorming the process for improvements, which is step 5. Finally, they are useful for performing step 6 because they should be reapplied to the newly proposed process, along with information on how performance measures are affected. Thus, they provide a "before" and "after" look at the process. Important inputs to these three techniques are time estimates of how long it takes to do various tasks. There are several ways to make these estimates, ranging from reasoned guesses to the more formal methods discussed in CD Supplements H and L (Learning Curve Analysis and Measuring Output Rates).

flow diagram A diagram that traces the flow of information, customers, employees, equipment, or materials through a process.

FLOW DIAGRAMS. A **flow diagram** traces the flow of information, customers, employees, equipment, or materials through a process. There is no precise format, and the diagram can be drawn simply with boxes, lines, and arrows. Figure 3.7 is a diagram of an automobile repair process, beginning with the customer's call for an appointment and ending with the customer's pickup of the car and departure. Various software packages are available to draw flow diagrams; this one was created using SmartDraw, which is available on the Student CD-ROM that was packaged with this book. In this figure, the dotted *line of visibility* divides activities that are directly visible to the customers from those that are invisible. Such information is particularly valuable for service operations involving considerable customer contact. Operations that are essential to success and where failure occurs most often are identified. Other formats are just as acceptable, and it is often helpful to show beside each box:

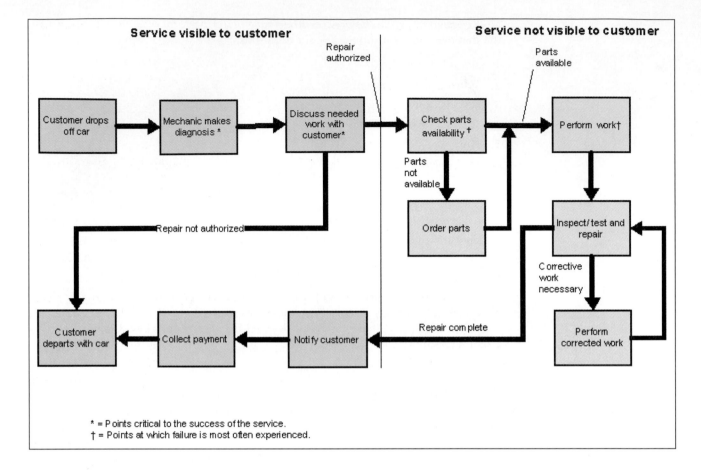

Service visible to customer   **Service not visible to customer**

* = Points critical to the success of the service.
† = Points at which failure is most often experienced.

FIGURE 3.7

Flow Diagram for Automobile Repair (Created with SmartDraw)

1. total elapsed time,
2. quality losses,
3. error frequency,
4. capacity, or
5. cost.

Sometimes flow diagrams are overlaid on a facility's layout. To make this special kind of flow diagram, the analyst first does a rough sketch of the area in which the process is performed. On a grid the analyst plots the path followed by the person, material, or equipment, using arrows to indicate the direction of movement or flow.

process chart An organized way of recording all the activities performed by a person, by a machine, at a workstation, with a customer, or on materials.

PROCESS CHARTS. A **process chart** is an organized way of recording all the activities performed by a person, by a machine, at a workstation, with a customer, or on materials. For our purposes we group these activities into five categories.

❑ *Operation.* Changes, creates, or adds something. Drilling a hole and serving a customer are examples of operations.

❑ *Transportation.* Moves the study's subject from one place to another (sometimes called *materials handling*). The subject can be a person, a material, a tool, or a piece of equipment. A customer walking from one end of a counter to the other, a crane hoisting a steel beam to a location, and a conveyor carrying a partially completed product from one workstation to the next are examples of transportation.

❑ *Inspection.* Checks or verifies something but does not change it. Checking for blemishes on a surface, weighing a product, and taking a temperature reading are examples of inspections.

❑ *Delay.* Occurs when the subject is held up awaiting further action. Time spent waiting for materials or equipment, cleanup time, and time that workers, machines, or workstations are idle because there is nothing for them to do are examples of delays.

❑ *Storage.* Occurs when something is put away until a later time. Supplies unloaded and placed in a storeroom as inventory, equipment put away after use, and papers put in a file cabinet are examples of storage.

Depending on the situation, other categories can be used. For example, subcontracting for outside services might be a category, or temporary storage and permanent storage might be two separate categories. Choosing the right category for each activity requires taking the perspective of the subject charted. A delay for the equipment could be inspection or transportation for the operator.

To complete a chart for a new process, the analyst must identify each step performed. If the process is an existing one, the analyst can actually observe the steps, categorizing each step according to the subject being studied. The analyst then records the distance traveled and the time taken to perform each step. After recording all the activities and steps, the analyst summarizes the number of steps, times, and distances data. Figure 3.8 shows a process chart prepared using OM Explorer's *Process Chart* solver. It is for a patient with a twisted ankle being treated at Lower Florida Keys Hospital (see the Big Picture in the Operations Strategy chapter). The process begins at the entrance and ends with the patient exiting after picking up the prescription.

After a process is charted, the analyst sometimes estimates the annual cost of the entire process. It becomes a benchmark against which other methods for performing the process can be evaluated. Annual labor cost can be estimated by finding the product of (1) time in hours to perform the process each time, (2) variable costs per hour, and (3) number of times the process is performed each year, or

$$\begin{pmatrix}\text{Annual} \\ \text{labor cost}\end{pmatrix} = \begin{pmatrix}\text{Time to perform} \\ \text{the process}\end{pmatrix}\begin{pmatrix}\text{Variable costs} \\ \text{per hour}\end{pmatrix}\begin{pmatrix}\text{Number of times process} \\ \text{performed per year}\end{pmatrix}$$

TUTOR 3.2

In the case of the patient at LFKH in Figure 3.8, this conversion wouldn't be necessary, with total patient time being sufficient. What is being tracked is the patient's time, not the time and costs of the service providers.

SIMULATION MODELS. A flow diagram is a simple but powerful tool for understanding each of the activities that make up a process and how they tie together. A process chart provides information similar to a table rather than a diagram but also provides time and cost information for the process. A simulation model goes one step further by showing how the process performs dynamically over time. **Simulation** is an act of reproducing the behavior of a process using a model that describes each step of the process. Once the current process is modeled, the analyst can make changes in the process to measure the impact on certain performance measures, such as response time, waiting lines, resource utilization, and the like. Example 3.1 demonstrates some of the capabilities of simulation using Extend, simulation software that is on the Student CD-ROM packaged with each new textbook. To learn more about how simulation works, see the Simulation Analysis supplement. To learn more specifically about Extend, see its tutorials and work through the simulation exercises at the end of this and several other chapters.

simulation The act of reproducing the behavior of a process using a model that describes each step of the process.

FIGURE 3.8

Process Chart for Emergency Room Admission (Created with OM Explorer)

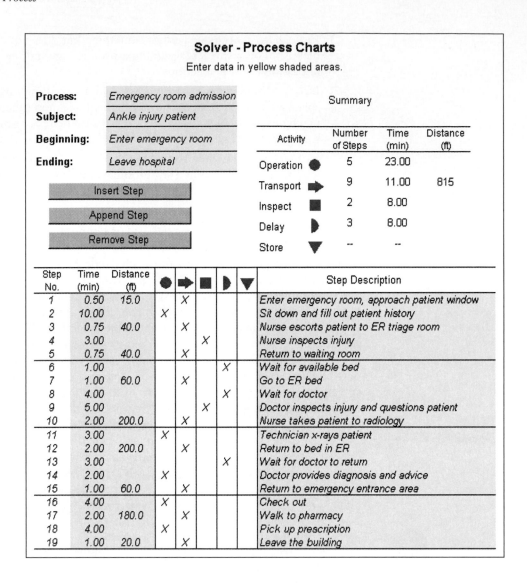

Solver - Process Charts

Enter data in yellow shaded areas.

Process:	Emergency room admission
Subject:	Ankle injury patient
Beginning:	Enter emergency room
Ending:	Leave hospital

Insert Step

Append Step

Remove Step

Summary

Activity		Number of Steps	Time (min)	Distance (ft)
Operation	●	5	23.00	
Transport	➡	9	11.00	815
Inspect	■	2	8.00	
Delay	▶	3	8.00	
Store	▼	--	--	

Step No.	Time (min)	Distance (ft)	●	➡	■	▶	▼	Step Description
1	0.50	15.0		X				Enter emergency room, approach patient window
2	10.00		X					Sit down and fill out patient history
3	0.75	40.0		X				Nurse escorts patient to ER triage room
4	3.00				X			Nurse inspects injury
5	0.75	40.0		X				Return to waiting room
6	1.00					X		Wait for available bed
7	1.00	60.0		X				Go to ER bed
8	4.00					X		Wait for doctor
9	5.00				X			Doctor inspects injury and questions patient
10	2.00	200.0		X				Nurse takes patient to radiology
11	3.00		X					Technician x-rays patient
12	2.00	200.0		X				Return to bed in ER
13	3.00					X		Wait for doctor to return
14	2.00		X					Doctor provides diagnosis and advice
15	1.00	60.0		X				Return to emergency entrance area
16	4.00		X					Check out
17	2.00	180.0		X				Walk to pharmacy
18	4.00		X					Pick up prescription
19	1.00	20.0		X				Leave the building

THE GOAL: PROCESS IMPROVEMENT. Flow diagrams, process charts, and simulation models are means to an end—continually improving the process. After a chart has been prepared, either for a new or for an existing process, it becomes the basis for brainstorming the process for improvement ideas. During this creative part of process analysis, the analyst asks the what, when, who, where, how long, and how questions, challenging each of the steps of the process charted. The summary of the process chart indicates which activities take the most time. To make a process more efficient, the analyst should question each delay and then analyze the operation, transportation, inspection, and storage activities to determine whether they can be combined, rearranged, or eliminated. There is always a better way, but someone must think of it. Improvements in productivity, quality, time, and flexibility can be significant.

EXAMPLE 3.1

Simulation of Stained-Glass Panel Process

The Artistic Glass Works produces stained-glass panels, which are collections of cut pieces of colored and textured glass arranged in attractive patterns and held in place by strips of lead or brass "came." Manufacturing these panels requires five basic process steps. First, the glass pieces are cut and ground according to a specific pattern. Next, the lead came segments are cut, again to match the required pattern. Third, the pieces of glass and came are assembled into a pattern with the came segments holding each piece of glass in position. Each joint then is individually soldered, a labor-intensive operation that requires the most skill. Following assembly, the entire glass panel is tempered in a "hot room," where the panel is gradually heated and cooled to improve its strength and durability. Finally, the finished panel is cleaned and packaged for customer delivery. The following table shows the five basic steps in the process, along with per-unit processing time information. For example, a worker spends an average of 2.2 hours cutting the glass for each panel. Glass is cut for six such panels before moving the "batch of six" to the next operation, where the came-cutting step is completed on the batch. All operations require the worker to be involved, except for the tempering operation, where the worker simply puts the panels in the hot room and then later removes them after the tempering is finished.

| | TIME TO PERFORM (HOURS) | |
OPERATION	Average	Standard Deviation
1. Cut glass	2.2	0.5
2. Cut came	1.1	0.3
3. Assemble panel	4.5	1.5
4. Temper	8.0	—
5. Clean and package	0.2	0.05

Two apprentices work at the process. It is a flexible workforce, because they perform all operations (except tempering) on the panels. Each worker performs the first three operations in sequence. To accommodate both people working at the same time, two stations have been set up for both glass cutting and assembly. Only one station is needed to accommodate both workers at the cut-came and clean-and-package operations. The last two operations are handled differently. After completing the first three operations for a particular batch, the worker checks whether there is a previous batch in the hot room that has finished tempering and is ready for packaging. If so, the worker leaves off the upstream batch for tempering and then works on the finished batch, cleaning and packaging it for immediate customer delivery. When done, the worker returns to the first operation and begins a new batch. If after completing the first three operations, the worker finds the hot room occupied with an unfinished batch, he leaves his current batch off for tempering and begins a new batch at the cut-glass operation. Management wants to know how well this low-volume batch process performs, assuming that customer demand is roughly equal to the production rate of the two workers.

  a. How many panels can be produced over the course of one year, or 2,000 working hours?

  b. What is the average *work-in-process inventory* (see Supply-Chain Management chapter), which is the unfinished inventory held somewhere along the process prior to being finished?

  c. What is the average *throughput time,* or the time elapse between when a batch is started and finished?

SOLUTION

The Extend software, packaged on the Student CD-ROM, is used to model and simulate Artistic Glass Works. Figure 3.9(a) shows the simulation model for the process. The five operations are shown as "stations" in the diagram. Other modules (such as count, merge, and release) are needed to model the process with Extend LT. There is also a data and calculations area (not shown), which inputs processing times and how they are distributed. Figure 3.9(b) has two sections, one for controls and one for graphical output. In the controls area, there is one resource pool and three slider controls. The analyst can establish the size of the workforce (currently set at two) and use the slider controls to vary the batch size, improvements in processing times, and reductions in process time variability. The graphical output section calls for graphs to be generated on the number of units produced over the simulated time (count), throughput time,

FIGURE 3.9

*Artistic Glass Works
Modeled with Extend*

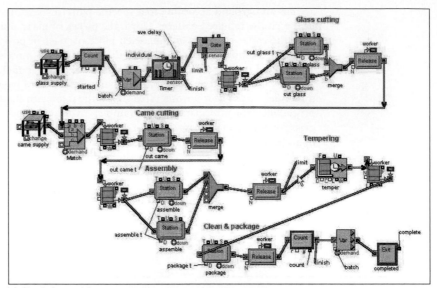

(a) Simulation model

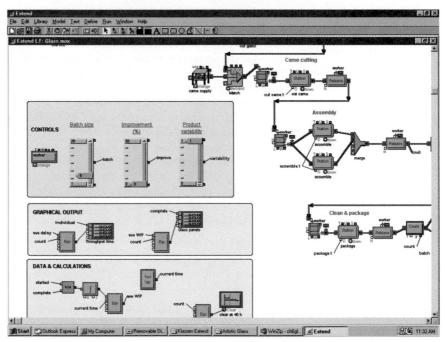

(b) Controls and graphical output

and work-in-process inventory (WIP). The simulation results are shown in two graphs. Figure 3.9(c) shows the production output (green line) and WIP inventory (blue line). The cumulative average for the WIP inventory begins to be plotted after the first 300 hours of experience, after the process has stabilized. The horizontal axis measures time over the course of a year, or 2,000 work hours. The simulation shows that 492 panels can be produced in a year, and the average WIP will be about 16.5 units. Figure 3.9(d) shows throughput times, both the individual throughput times (red dots) and cumulative average. The average throughput time averages just less than 62 hours per batch. If management seeks better performance on these three performance measures, options for improving the process should be evaluated by simulating revised models that reflect different improvement ideas.

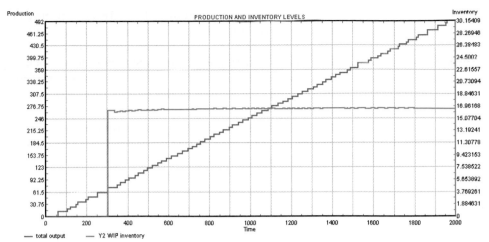

(c) Production and WIP inventory

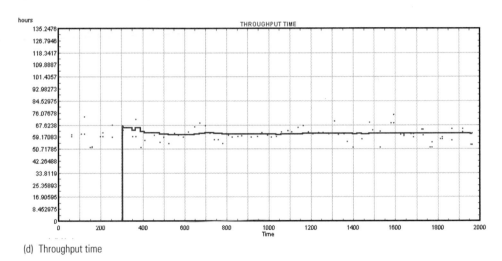

(d) Throughput time

Decision Point Demand is growing, and management expects demand to be well above 492 panels per year. It also is dissatisfied with the high throughput time and WIP. Management should explore ways of improving the process for glass panels, evaluating the improvement ideas with Extend. ◻

Source: This case and simulation experience was provided by Professor Robert Klassen, University of Western Ontario.

Do some of the organization's key processes need reengineering?

reengineering The fundamental rethinking and radical redesign of processes to improve performance dramatically in terms of cost, quality, service, and speed.

PROCESS REENGINEERING

Processes can be designed or redesigned using two different approaches: process reengineering and process improvement. We begin with process engineering, which is getting considerable attention today in management circles.

Reengineering is the fundamental rethinking and radical redesign of processes to improve performance dramatically in terms of cost, quality, service, and speed. Process reengineering is about reinvention, rather than incremental improvement. It is strong medicine and not always needed or successful. Pain, in the form of layoffs and large cash outflows for investments in information technology, almost always accompanies massive change. However, reengineering processes can have big payoffs. For example, Bell Atlantic reengineered its telephone business. After five years of effort, it cut the

MANAGERIAL PRACTICE 3.4
Process Improvement at Work

Process improvement helps the Freudenberg–NOK (www.freudenberg-nok.com) autoparts factory in Ligonier, Indiana, become more competitive. This plant makes 123,000 parts a month for Ford Motor Company's Aerostar vans and Ranger pickup trucks. A key element of the approach is quick-hit teams of plant workers, managers, and people from other functional areas who come up with ways to improve operations in different sections of the plant. These teams make *Kaizen,* a Japanese term for continuous improvement, pay off through productivity improvements. Other elements are worker cooperation (bolstered by a no-layoff pledge), strong management backing, measurable goals and results, continuity between teams so that unfinished "to-do" lists are passed on to the next team, and a bias for immediate action on many fronts, rather than costly, technological big fixes. The multiple, small changes add up. For example, a typical 12-member team worked between Monday and Thursday to propose and test ways to improve the engine-mount line of the factory. After a training session, the team members grabbed their stopwatches

and white lab coats and headed for the shop floor. They analyzed the current process, talked with the operators, and brainstormed ideas for improvement. Subteams were formed to attack different problems simultaneously. On Thursday, the team presented its results to plant management. It had cut work-in-process inventory by 50 percent and improved productivity by some 20 percent. It had also increased capacity somewhat, although it fell short of its 20 percent goal. In one year, 40 such teams move through this factory. "What we are doing today is what any company will have to do to survive a decade from now, says the chief executive of Freudenberg–NOK, a $420 million German–Japanese joint venture with 14 U.S. plants that make rubber seals, vibration dampers, and engine mounts. He expects kaizen teams to help the company more than double sales by 2000 without adding people or factory space.

Source: "Improving the Soul of an Old Machine," *Business Week* (October 25, 1993).

its four regions. The calculate and collect revenues process is most closely aligned with accounting, the deliver products and services process with operations, the develop market strategies process and maintain customers process with marketing, and the provide reliability and integrity process with quality assurance (see Total Quality Management chapter and Statistical Process Control chapter). Cross-functional coordination paid off in better performance. This payoff came in part by reorganizing to create process owners but also by creating a new collaborative style of management. The process owners and regional VPs acted as partners rather than rivals.

CHAPTER HIGHLIGHTS

❏ Process management deals with *how* to make a product or service. Many choices must be made concerning the best mix of human resources, equipment, and materials.

❏ Process management is of strategic importance and is closely linked to a firm's long-term success. It involves the selection of inputs, operations, work flows, and methods used to produce goods and services.

❏ Process decisions are made in the following circumstances: a new product is to be offered or an existing product modified, quality improvements are

necessary, competitive priorities are changed, demand levels change, current performance is inadequate, competitor capabilities change, new technology is available, or cost or availability of inputs changes.

❏ The five major process decisions are process choice, degree of capital intensity, resource flexibility, vertical integration, and customer involvement. Basic *process choices* are project, job, batch, line, and continuous. *Capital intensity* is the mix of capital equipment and human skills in a process. *Resource flexibility* is the degree to which equipment is general purpose and individuals can handle a wide variety of work. *Vertical integration* involves decisions about whether to outsource certain processes. *Customer involvement* is the extent to which customers are allowed to interact with the process. Self-service, product selection, and the timing and location of the interaction must all be considered.

❑ Fixed automation maximizes efficiency for high-volume products with long life cycles, but flexible (programmable) automation provides economies of scope. Flexibility is gained and setups are minimized because the machines can be reprogrammed to follow new instructions.

❑ The variable underlying the relationships among the five major process decisions is volume, which in turn is shaped by operations strategy. For example, high volume is associated with a line or continuous process, vertical integration, little resource flexibility, little customer involvement, and capital intensity.

❑ Service operations follow the same pattern and are best understood through the lens of service strategy, customer involvement, and automation.

❑ Job design and process decisions are related, particularly in determining the extent of specialization versus enlargement.

❑ Focusing operations avoids confusion among competitive priorities, process choices, and technologies. Focused facilities, plants within plants, and cells are ways to achieve focus in both manufacturing and service operations.

❑ Three basic techniques for analyzing process activities and flows are flow diagrams, process charts, and simulation. They are ways to organize the detailed study of process components.

❑ Process reengineering uses cross-functional teams to rethink the design of critical processes. Process improvement is a systematic analysis of activities and flows that occurs continuously.

KEY TERMS

automation *109*
backward integration *103*
batch process *99*
capital intensity *96*
cell *117*
continuous process *99*
customer involvement *95*
economies of scope *115*
fixed automation *109*
flexible (or programmable) automation *109*
flexible workforce *107*
flow diagram *119*

focused factories *116*
forward integration *103*
job enlargement *114*
job enrichment *115*
job process *98*
job rotation *114*
line flow *99*
line process *99*
make-or-buy decisions *102*
network companies *106*
outsourcing *102*
plants within plants (PWPs) *116*

process chart *120*
process choice *95*
process improvement *127*
process management *93*
project process *97*
reengineering *125*
resource flexibility *95*
simulation *121*
specialization *113*
supply chain *95*
vertical integration *95*
virtual corporation *106*

SOLVED PROBLEM 1

An automobile service is having difficulty providing oil changes in the 29 minutes or less mentioned in its advertising. You are to analyze the process of changing automobile engine oil. The subject of the study is the service mechanic. The process begins when the mechanic directs the customer's arrival and ends when the customer pays for the services.

SOLUTION

Figure 3.10 shows the completed process chart. The process is broken into 21 steps. A summary of the times and distances traveled is shown in the upper right-hand corner of the process chart.

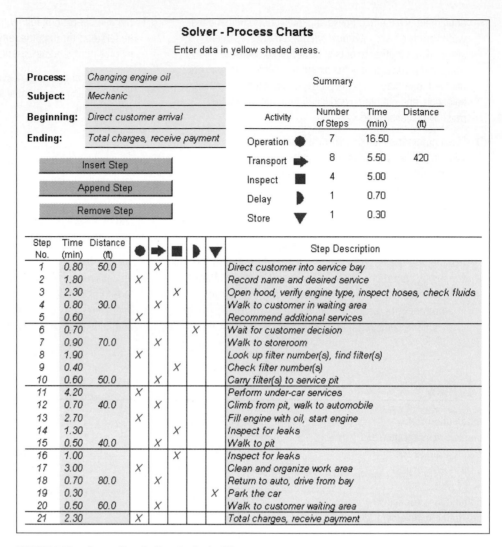

FIGURE 3.10 • Process Chart for Changing Engine Oil

The times add up to 28 minutes, which does not allow much room for error if the 29-minute guarantee is to be met and the mechanic travels a total of 420 feet.

SOLVED PROBLEM 2

What improvement can you make in the process shown in Figure 3.10?

SOLUTION

Your analysis should verify the following three ideas for improvement. You may also be able to come up with others.

1. *Move Step 17 to Step 21.* Customers shouldn't have to wait while the mechanic cleans the work area.

2. *Store Small Inventories of Frequently Used Filters in the Pit.* Steps 7 and 10 involve travel to the storeroom. If the filters are moved to the pit, a copy of the reference material must also be placed in the pit. The pit will have to be organized and well lighted.

3. *Use Two Mechanics.* Steps 10, 12, 15, and 17 involve running up and down the steps to the pit. Much of this travel could be eliminated. The service time could be shortened by having one mechanic in the pit working simultaneously with another working under the hood.

DISCUSSION QUESTIONS

1. To give utilities an incentive to spend money on new pollution-control technology, the EPA proposes that flue gas emission limits be changed to require slightly cleaner stacks than the older technology is capable of producing. To comply, some utilities will install the new technology. Some will not. Utilities that reduce emissions below the new requirements will receive "credits," which they can sell to utilities that choose not to install the pollution-control technology. These utilities can then continue business as usual, so long as they have purchased enough credits to account for the extra pollution they create. The price of the credits will be determined by the free market.

   Form sides and discuss the ethical, environmental, and political issues and trade-offs associated with this proposition.

2. The Hydro-Electric Company (HEC) has three sources of power. A small amount of hydroelectric power is generated by damming wild and scenic rivers; a second source of power comes from burning coal, with emissions that create acid rain and contribute to global warming; the third source of power comes from nuclear fission. HEC's coal-fired plants use obsolete pollution-control technology, and an investment of several hun-

dred million dollars would be required to update it. Environmentalists urge HEC to promote conservation and purchase power from suppliers that use the cleanest fuels and technology.

   However, HEC is already suffering from declining sales, which have resulted in billions of dollars invested in idle equipment. Its large customers are taking advantage of laws that permit them to buy power from low-cost suppliers. HEC must cover the fixed costs of idle capacity by raising rates charged to its remaining customers or face defaulting on bonds (bankruptcy). The increased rates motivate even more customers to seek low-cost suppliers, the start of a death spiral for HEC. To prevent additional rate increases, HEC implements a cost-cutting program and puts its plans to update pollution controls on hold.

   Form sides, and discuss the ethical, environmental, and political issues and trade-offs associated with HEC's strategy.

3. The Dewpoint Chemical Company is deciding where to locate a fertilizer plant near the Rio Grande. What are the ethical, environmental, and political issues and trade-offs associated with locating a fertilizer plant on the north bank versus the south bank of the Rio Grande?

OM EXPLORER AND INTERNET EXERCISES

Visit our Web site at www.prenhall.com/krajewski for OM Explorer Tutors, which explain quantitative techniques; Solvers, which help you apply mathematical models; and Internet Exercises, including Facility Tours, which expand on the topics in this chapter.

PROBLEMS

An icon in the margin next to a problem identifies the software that can be helpful, but not mandatory. The software is available on the Student CD-ROM that is packaged with every new copy of the textbook. Problems 9 and 10 apply break-even analysis (discussed in the Decision Making supplement) to process decisions.

1. 🔵 **OM Explorer** Your class has volunteered to work for Referendum #13 on the November ballot, which calls for free tuition and books for all college courses except operations management. Support for the referendum includes assembling 10,000 yard signs (preprinted

water-resistant paper signs to be glued and stapled to a wooden stake) on a fall Saturday. Construct a flow diagram and a process chart for yard sign assembly. What inputs in terms of materials, human effort, and equipment are involved? Estimate the amount of volunteers, staples, glue, equipment, lawn and garage space, and pizza required.

2. 🔵 **SmartDraw** Prepare a flow diagram for the three processes at King Soopers.

3. 🔵 **OM Explorer** Suppose that you are in charge of a large mailing to the alumni of your college inviting them to contribute to a scholarship fund. The letters and envelopes have been individually addressed (mailing labels were not used). The letters are to be folded and stuffed into the correct envelopes, the envelopes are to be sealed, and a large commemorative stamp is to be placed in the upper right-hand corner of each envelope. Make a process chart for this activity, assuming that it is a one-person operation. Estimate how long it will take to stuff, seal, and stamp 2,000 envelopes. Assume that the person doing this work is paid $8.00 per hour. How much will it cost to process 2,000 letters, based on your time estimate? Consider how each of the following changes individually would affect the process:

- Each letter has the greeting "Dear Alumnus or Alumna," instead of the person's name.
- Mailing labels are used and have to be put on the envelopes.
- Prestamped envelopes are used.

- Envelopes are stamped by a postage meter.
- Window envelopes are used.
- A preaddressed envelope is included with each letter for contributions.

a. Which of these changes would reduce the time and cost of the process?

b. Would any of these changes be likely to reduce the effectiveness of the mailing? If so, which ones? Why?

c. Would the changes that increase time and cost be likely to increase the effectiveness of the mailing? Why or why not?

d. What other factors need to be considered for this project?

4. Diagrams of two self-service gasoline stations, both located on corners, are shown in Figures. 3.11(a) and (b). Both have two rows of four pumps and a booth at which an attendant receives payment for the gasoline. At neither station is it necessary for the customer to pay in advance. The exits and entrances are marked on the diagrams. Analyze the flows of cars and people through each station.

a. Which station has the more efficient flows from the standpoint of the customer?

b. Which station is likely to lose more potential customers who cannot gain access to the pumps because another car is headed in the other direction?

c. At which station can a customer pay without getting out of the car?

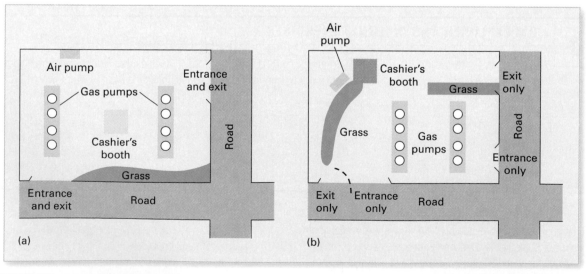

FIGURE 3.11

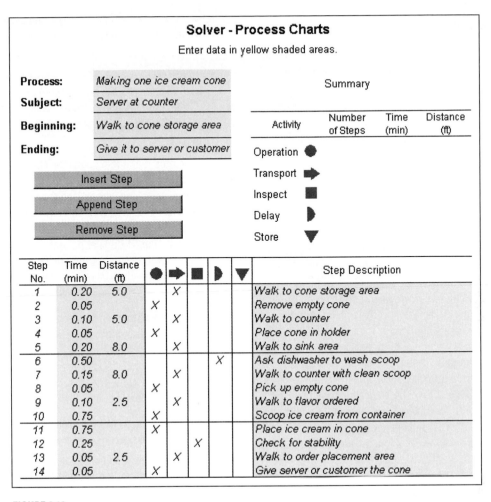

Solver - Process Charts
Enter data in yellow shaded areas.

Process:	Making one ice cream cone
Subject:	Server at counter
Beginning:	Walk to cone storage area
Ending:	Give it to server or customer

Insert Step

Append Step

Remove Step

Summary

Activity		Number of Steps	Time (min)	Distance (ft)
Operation	●			
Transport	➡			
Inspect	■			
Delay	◗			
Store	▼			

Step No.	Time (min)	Distance (ft)	●	➡	■	◗	▼	Step Description
1	0.20	5.0		X				Walk to cone storage area
2	0.05		X					Remove empty cone
3	0.10	5.0		X				Walk to counter
4	0.05		X					Place cone in holder
5	0.20	8.0		X				Walk to sink area
6	0.50					X		Ask dishwasher to wash scoop
7	0.15	8.0		X				Walk to counter with clean scoop
8	0.05		X					Pick up empty cone
9	0.10	2.5		X				Walk to flavor ordered
10	0.75		X					Scoop ice cream from container
11	0.75		X					Place ice cream in cone
12	0.25				X			Check for stability
13	0.05	2.5		X				Walk to order placement area
14	0.05		X					Give server or customer the cone

FIGURE 3.12

5. 🌐 **OM Explorer** The management of the Just Like Home restaurant has asked you to analyze some of its processes. One of these processes is making a single-scoop ice cream cone. Cones can be ordered by a server (for table service) or by a customer (for takeout). Figure 3.12 illustrates the process chart for this operation.
   - The ice cream counter server earns $10 per hour (including variable fringe benefits).
   - The process is performed 10 times per hour (on average).
   - The restaurant is open 363 days a year, 10 hours a day.
   a. Complete the summary (top-right) portion of the chart.
   b. What is the total labor cost associated with the process?
   c. How can this operation be made more efficient? Draw a process chart of the improved process. What are the annual labor savings if this new process is implemented?

6. As a graduate assistant, your duties include grading and keeping records for operations management course homework assignments. Five sections for 40 students each are offered each semester. A few graduate students attend sections 3 and 4. Graduate students must complete some extra work to higher standards for each assignment. Every student delivers (or is supposed to deliver) directly to (under) the door of your office one homework assignment every Tuesday. Your job is to correct the homework, record grades, sort the papers by class section, sort by student last name in alphabetical order, and return the homework papers to the appropriate instructors (not necessarily in that order). There are some complications. A fair majority of the students sign their names legibly, others identify their work with the correct I.D. number, and a few do neither. Rarely do students identify their section number or graduate status. Prepare a list of process chart steps and place them in an efficient sequence.

7. ● **OM Explorer** At the Department of Motor Vehicles, the process of getting license plates for your car begins when you enter the facility and take a number. You walk 50 feet to the waiting area. During your wait, you count about 30 customers waiting for service. You notice that many customers become discouraged and leave. When a number is called, if a customer stands, the ticket is checked by a uniformed person, and the customer is directed to the available clerk. If no one stands, several minutes are lost while the same number is called repeatedly. Eventually, the next number is called, and more often than not, that customer has left too. The DMV clerk has now been idle for several minutes but does not seem to mind.

   An unkempt man walks over to the ticket dispenser, picks up several tickets from the floor, and returns to his seat. A new arrival, carrying a stack of paper and looking like a car dealer, walks directly to the unkempt man. Some sort of transaction takes place. A few more numbers are called and it is the car dealer's number! After 4 hours, your number is called and checked by the uniformed person. You walk 60 feet to the clerk, and the process of paying city sales taxes is completed in 4 minutes. The clerk then directs you to the waiting area for paying state personal property tax, 80 feet away. With a sinking heart, you take a different number and sit down with some different customers who are just renewing licenses. You notice the same unkempt man. A 1-hour, 40-minute wait this time, and after a walk of 25 feet you pay property taxes in a process that takes 2 minutes. Now that you have paid taxes you're eligible to pay registration and license fees. That department is 50 feet away, beyond the employees' cafeteria. As you walk by the cafeteria, you notice the unkempt man having coffee with a uniformed person.

   The registration and license customers are called in the same order in which personal property taxes were paid. There is only a 10-minute wait and a 3-minute process. You receive your license plates, take a minute to abuse the license clerk, and leave exactly 6 hours after arriving.

   Make a process chart to depict this process, and suggest improvements.

8. Refer to the process chart for the automobile oil change in Solved Problem 1. Calculate the annual labor cost if
   - The mechanic earns $40 per hour (including variable fringe benefits),

- the process is performed twice per hour (on average), and
- the shop is open 300 days a year, 10 hours a day.

   a. What is the total labor cost associated with the process?

   b. If steps 7, 10, 12, and 15 were eliminated, estimate the annual labor savings associated with implementing this new process.

9. ● **OM Explorer** Dr. Gulakowicz is an orthodontist. She estimates that adding two new chairs will increase fixed costs by $150,000, including the annual equivalent cost of the capital investment and the salary of one more technician. Each new patient is expected to bring in $3,000 per year in additional revenue, with variable costs estimated at $1,000 per patient. The two new chairs will allow her to expand her practice by as many as 200 patients annually. How many patients would have to be added for the new process to break even?

10. ● **OM Explorer** Two different manufacturing processes are being considered for making a new product. The first process is less capital-intensive, with fixed costs of only $50,000 per year and variable costs of $700 per unit. The second process has fixed costs of $400,000 but variable costs of only $200 per unit.

    a. What is the break-even quantity, beyond which the second process becomes more attractive than the first?

    b. If the expected annual sales for the product is 800 units, which process would you choose?

Advanced Problem

This problem should be solved as a team exercise.

   Shaving is a process that most men perform each morning. Assume that the process begins at the bathroom sink with the shaver walking (say, 5 feet) to the cabinet (where his shaving supplies are stored) to pick up bowl, soap, brush, and razor. He walks back to the sink, runs the water until it gets warm, lathers his face, shaves, and inspects the results. Then, he rinses the razor, dries his face, walks over to the cabinet to return the bowl, soap, brush, and razor, and comes back to the sink to clean it up and complete the process.

   a. ● **OM Explorer** Develop a process chart for shaving. (Assume suitable values for the time required for the various activities involved in the process.)

   b. Brainstorm to generate ideas for improving the shaving process. (Do not try to evaluate the ideas until the group has compiled as complete a list as possible. Otherwise, judgment will block creativity).

SIMULATION EXERCISE

These simulation exercises require the use of the Extend LT and SimQuick simulation packages. Extend LT is on the Student CD-ROM that is packaged with every new copy of the textbook. SimQuick is an optional simulation package that your instructor may or may not have ordered.

1. Consider the process at the Artistic Glass Works, which is introduced as Example 3.1. Use the Extend LT simulator to evaluate the current process and other designs. See the full Artistic Glass Works case on the Student CD-ROM, along with the basic model and information on how to use it. Answer the various questions asked about the current and proposed process.

2. A manufacturing cell consists of 6 workstations. Raw materials are taken from inventory and proceed through the cell in a fixed route, starting with workstation 1 and ending with workstation 6. The finished product is then stored in an inventory. Management has the option of assigning 2, 3, or 6 workers to the cell. For example, if 2 workers are in the cell, one would be assigned to workstations 1, 2, and 3 while the other would be assigned to the other machines. The workers would be highly flexible in that they can do several different tasks. Use SimQuick to find the mean throughput for each option. See Example 13 in SimQuick: Process Simulation in Excel for details of this problem and additional exercises.

CASE **CUSTOM MOLDS, INC.**

Custom Molds, Inc., manufactures custom-designed molds for plastic parts and produces custom-made plastic connectors for the electronics industry. Located in Tucson, Arizona, Custom Molds was founded by the father and son team of Tom and Mason Miller in 1975. Tom Miller, a mechanical engineer, had more than 20 years of experience in the connector industry with AMP, Inc., a large multinational producer of electronic connectors. Mason Miller had graduated from the University of Arizona in 1974 with joint degrees in chemistry and chemical engineering.

The company was originally formed to provide manufacturers of electronic connectors with a source of high-quality, custom-designed molds for producing plastic parts. The market consisted mainly of the product design and development divisions of those manufacturers. Custom Molds worked closely with each customer to design and develop molds to be used in the customer's product development processes. Thus, virtually every mold had to meet exacting standards and was somewhat unique. Orders for multiple molds would arrive when customers moved from the design and pilot-run stage of development to large-scale production of newly designed parts.

As the years went by, Custom Molds' reputation grew as a designer and fabricator of precision molds. Building on this reputation, the Millers decided to expand into the limited manufacture of plastic parts. Ingredient-mixing facilities and injection-molding equipment were added, and by the mid-1980s Custom Molds developed its reputation to include being a supplier of high-quality plastic parts. Because of limited capacity, the company concentrated its

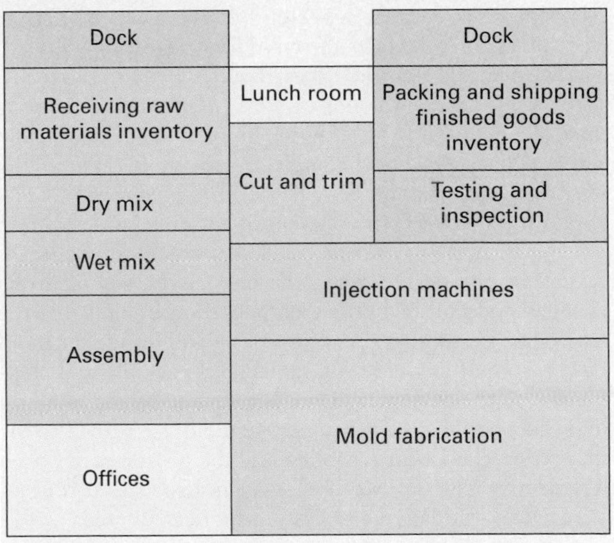

FIGURE 3.13 • Plant Layout

sales efforts on supplying parts that were used in limited quantities for research and development efforts and in pre-production pilot runs.

PRODUCTION PROCESSES

By 1985, operations at Custom Molds involved two distinct processes: one for fabricating molds and one for producing plastic parts. Although different, in many instances

continued

continued

these two processes were linked, as when a customer would have Custom Molds both fabricate a mold and produce the necessary parts to support the customer's R&D efforts. All fabrication and production operations were housed in a single facility. The layout was characteristic of a typical job shop, with like processes and similar equipment grouped in various places in the plant. Figure 3.13 shows a schematic of the plant floor. Multiple pieces of various types of high-precision machinery, including milling, turning, cutting, and drilling equipment, were located in the mold-fabrication area.

Fabricating molds is a skill-oriented, craftsman-driven process. When an order is received, a design team, comprising a design engineer and one of 13 master machinists, reviews the design specifications. Working closely with the customer, the team establishes the final specifications for the mold and gives them to the master machinist for fabrication. It is always the same machinist who was assigned to the design team. At the same time, the purchasing department is given a copy of the design specifications, from which it orders the appropriate raw materials and special tooling. The time needed to receive the ordered materials is usually three to four weeks. When the materials are received for a particular mold, the plant master scheduler reviews the workload of the assigned master machinist and schedules the mold for fabrication.

Fabricating a mold takes from two to four weeks, depending on the amount of work the machinist already has scheduled. The fabrication process itself takes only three to five days. Upon completion, the mold is sent to the testing and inspection area, where it is used to produce a small number of parts on one of the injection molding machines. If the parts meet the design specifications established by the design team, the mold is passed on to be cleaned and polished. It is then packed and shipped to the customer. One day is spent inspecting and testing the mold and a second day cleaning, polishing, packing, and shipping it to the customer. If the parts made by the mold do not meet design specifications, the mold is returned to the master machinist for retooling and the process starts over. Currently, Custom Molds has a published lead time of nine weeks for delivery of custom-fabricated molds.

The manufacturing process for plastic parts is somewhat different from that for mold fabrication. An order for parts may be received in conjunction with an order for a mold to be fabricated. In instances where Custom Molds has previously fabricated the mold and maintains it in inventory, an order may be just for parts. If the mold is already available, the order is reviewed by a design engineer, who verifies the part and raw material specifications. If the design engineer has any questions concerning the specifications, the customer is contacted and any revisions to specifications are mutually worked out and agreed upon.

Upon acceptance of the part and raw material specifications, raw material orders are placed and production is scheduled for the order. Chemicals and compounds that support plastic-parts manufacturing are typically ordered and received within one week. Upon receipt, the compounds are first dry-mixed and blended to achieve the correct composition. Then the mixture is wet-mixed to the desired consistency (called slurry) for injection into molding machines. When ready, the slurry is transferred to the injection molding area by an overhead pipeline and deposited in holding tanks adjacent to the injection machines. The entire mixing process takes only one day.

When the slurry is staged and ready, the proper molds are secured—from inventory or from the clean and polish operation if new molds were fabricated for the order—and the parts are manufactured. Although different parts require different temperature and pressure settings, the time to produce a part is relatively constant. Custom Molds has the capacity to produce 5,000 parts per day in the injection-molding department; historically, however, the lead time for handling orders in this department has averaged one week. Upon completion of molding, the parts are taken to the cut and trim operation, where they are disconnected and leftover flashing is removed. After being inspected, the parts may be taken to assembly or transferred to the packing and shipping area for shipment to the customer. If assembly of the final parts is not required, the parts can be on their way to the customer two days after being molded.

Sometimes the final product requires some assembly. Typically, this entails attaching metal leads to plastic connectors. If assembly is necessary, an additional three days is needed before the order can be shipped. Custom Molds is currently quoting a three-week lead time for parts not requiring fabricated molds.

THE CHANGING ENVIRONMENT

In early 1991, Tom and Mason Miller began to realize that the electronics industry they supplied, along with their own business, was changing. Electronics manufacturers had traditionally used vertical integration into component-parts manufacturing to reduce costs and ensure a timely supply of parts. By the late 1980s, this trend had changed. Manufacturers were developing strategic partnerships with parts suppliers to ensure the timely delivery of high-quality, cost-effective parts. This approach allowed funds to be diverted to other uses that could provide a larger return on investment.

The impact on Custom Molds could be seen in sales figures over the past three years. The sales mix was changing. Although the number of orders per year for mold fabrication remained virtually constant, orders for multiple, molds were declining, as shown in the following table:

ORDER SIZE	NUMBER OF ORDERS		
	Molds 1988	Molds 1989	Molds 1990
1	80	74	72
2	60	70	75
3	40	51	55
4	5	6	5
5	3	5	4
6	4	8	5
7	2	0	1
8	10	6	4
9	11	8	5
10	15	10	5
Total orders	230	238	231

The reverse was true for plastic parts, for which the number of orders per year had declined but for which the order sizes were becoming larger, as illustrated in the following table:

ORDER SIZE	NUMBER OF ORDERS		
	Parts 1988	Parts 1989	Parts 1990
50	100	93	70
100	70	72	65
150	40	30	35
200	36	34	38
250	25	27	25
500	10	12	14
750	1	3	5
1,000	2	2	8
3,000	1	4	9
5,000	1	3	8
Total orders	286	280	277

During this same period Custom Molds began having delivery problems. Customers were complaining that parts orders were taking four to five weeks instead of the stated three weeks and that the delays were disrupting production schedules. When asked about the situation, the master scheduler said that determining when a particular order could be promised for delivery was very difficult. Bottlenecks were occurring during the production process, but where or when they would occur could not be predicted. They always seemed to be moving from one operation to another.

Tom Miller thought that he had excess labor capacity in the mold-fabrication area. So, to help push through those orders that were behind schedule, he assigned one of the master machinists the job of identifying and expediting those late orders. However, that tactic did not seem to help much. Complaints about late deliveries were still being received. To add to the problems, two orders had been returned recently because of the number of defective parts. The Millers knew that something had to be done. The question was "What?"

Questions

1. What are the major issues facing Tom and Mason Miller?
2. Identify the individual processes on a flow diagram. What are the competitive priorities for these processes and the changing nature of the industry?
3. What alternatives might the Millers pursue? What key factors should they consider as they evaluate these alternatives?

Source: This case was prepared by Dr. Brooke Saladin, Wake Forest University, as a basis for classroom discussion.

SELECTED REFERENCES

Alster, Norm. "What Flexible Workers Can Do." *Fortune* (February 13, 1989), pp. 62–66.

Brown, Donna. "Outsourcing: How Corporations Take Their Business Elsewhere." *Management Review* (February 1992), pp. 16–19.

Byrne, John A. "The Virtual Corporation." *Business Week* (February 8, 1993), pp. 98–102.

Collier, David A. *Service Management: The Automation of Services.* Reston, VA: Reston, 1985.

Dixon, J. Robb, Peter Arnold, Janelle Heineke, Jay S. Kim, and Paul Mulligan. "Business Process Reengineering: Improving in New Strategic Directions." *California Management Review* (Summer 1994), pp. 1–17.

Ellis, Christian M., and Lea A. P. Tonkin. "Mature Teams Rewards and the High-Performance Workplace: Change and Opportunity." *Target*, vol. 11, no. 6 (1995).

Gephart, Martha A. "The Road to High Performance." *Training and Development,* vol. 49 (June 1995), pp. 29–44.

Goldhat, J. D., and Mariann Jelinek. "Plan for Economies of Scope." *Harvard Business Review* (November–December 1983), pp. 141–148.

Grover, Varun, and Manoj K. Malhotra, P. S. "Business Process Reengineering: A Tutorial on the Concept, Evolution, Method, Technology and Application." *Journal of Operations Management,* vol. 15, no. 3 (1997), pp. 194–213.

Hall, Gene, Jim Rosenthal, and Judy Wade. "How to Make Reengineering Really Work." *Harvard Business Review* (November–December 1993), pp. 119–131.

Hammer, M. "Reengineering Work: Don't Automate, Obliterate." *Harvard Business Review*, vol. 68, no. 4 (1990), pp. 104–112.

Hammer, M. *Beyond Reengineering.* New York: HarperBusiness, 1996.

Hammer, Michael, and James Champy. *Reengineering the Corporation: A Manifesto for Business Revolution.* New York: HarperBusiness, 1993.

Harrigan, K. R. *Strategies for Vertical Integration.* Lexington, MA: D. C. Heath, 1983.

Katzenbach, Jon R., and Douglas K. Smith. "The Discipline of Teams." *Harvard Business Review* (March–April 1993), pp. 111–120.

Leibs, Scott. "A Little Help from Their Friends." *Industry Week,* February 2, 1998.

"Making it by the Billions." *The Boston Globe*, August 9, 1998.

Malhotra, Manoj K., and Larry P. Ritzman. "Resource Flexibility Issues in Multistage Manufacturing." *Decision Sciences,* vol. 21, no. 4 (1990), pp. 673–690.

Normann, Richard, and Rafael Ramirez. "From Value Chain to Value Constellation: Designing Interactive Strategy." *Harvard Business Review* (July–August 1993), pp. 65–77.

Port, Otis. "The Responsive Factory." *Business Week,* Enterprise 1993, pp. 48–51.

Porter, Michael E. "The Competitive Advantage of Nations." *Harvard Business Review* (March–April 1990), pp. 73–93.

Prahalad, C. K., and Gary Hamel. "The Core Competence of the Corporation." *Harvard Business Review,* vol. 90, no. 3 (1990), pp. 79–91.

"Process, Process, Process." *Planning Review* (special issue), vol. 22, no. 3 (1993), pp. 1–56.

"Reengineering: The Hot New Managing Tool." *Fortune* (August 23, 1994), pp. 41–48.

Roth, Aleda V., and Marjolijn van der Velde. *The Future of Retail Banking Delivery Systems.* Rolling Meadows, Ill.: Bank Administration Institute, 1988.

Safizadeh, M. Hossen, Larry P. Ritzman, and Debasish Mallick, "Revisiting Alternative Theoretical Paradigms in Manufacturing." *Production and Operations Management,* vol. 9, no. 2 (2000), pp. 111–127.

Skinner, Wickham. "Operations Technology: Blind Spot in Strategic Management." *Interfaces,* vol. 14 (January–February 1984), pp. 116–125.

"Somebody Else's Problem." *The Wall Street Journal,* November 15, 1999.

Tonkin, Lea A. P. "Outsourcing: A Tool, Not a Solution." *Target,* vol. 15, no. 2 (1999), pp. 44–45.

Wheelwright, Steven C., and Robert H. Hayes. "Competing Through Manufacturing." *Harvard Business Review* (January–February 1985), pp. 99–109.

"When the Going Gets Rough, Boeing Gets Touchy-Feely." *Business Week* (January 17, 1994), pp. 65–67.

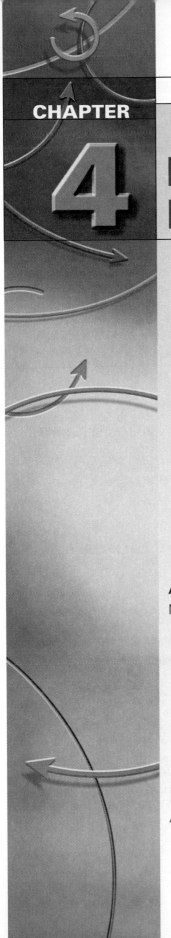

4

Managing Project Processes

Across the Organization

Managing project processes is important to . . .

- ❏ **finance,** which uses project processes for financing new business acquisitions.
- ❏ **human resources,** which uses project processes for initiating new training and development programs.
- ❏ **management information systems,** which uses project processes for designing new information systems to support reengineered processes.
- ❏ **marketing,** which uses project processes to design and execute new product advertising campaigns.
- ❏ **operations,** which uses project processes to manage the introduction of new technologies for the production of goods and services.

Learning Goals

After reading this chapter, you will be able to . . .

1. identify the three major activities associated with successful project processes.
2. diagram the network of interrelated activities in a project.
3. identify the sequence of critical activities that determine the duration of a project.
4. compute the probability of completing a project on time.
5. determine the minimum-cost project schedule.

Bechtel Group, Inc. (www.bechtel.com), is a 102-year-old, $12.6 billion-a-year construction contractor that specializes in large projects. The venerable company built Hoover Dam early in the twentieth century and has built scores of rail systems, refineries, airports, and power plants since then. Bechtel led the rebuilding of Kuwait after Desert Storm and became the first U.S. company to be granted a construction license in China. Bechtel's traditional bricks-and-mortar customers chose the company because of its ability to deliver projects on time. However, Bechtel's new customers include fleet-footed Internet companies that thrive on speed. They have chosen Bechtel because of another of its capabilities—the ability to deliver projects quickly. For example, Webvan Group, Inc., wanted to build 26 distribution centers in two years, each with 330,000 square feet of space. Equinix, Inc., contracted for 30 high-security data centers worldwide in four years, each filled with security gadgetry such as doors that open only when a handprint is verified by computer. iMotors.com, a company that sells refurbished autos on-line, wanted Bechtel to build 30 plants over a two-year period. Web-based companies such as these typically want to set up facilities nationwide or around the world with short lead times and do not have the time to deal with a multitude of local contractors. Bechtel satisfies their needs.

Bechtel must set up a project process for each major project it undertakes with on-time delivery and short delivery lead times in mind. Because of the complexity of many ongoing projects with diverse needs, processes must also be flexible enough to respond to changes in schedules or requirements. Communication is a major issue; it takes an average of five days to get a piece of paper from Bechtel's Singapore office to a project in Thailand. Paperwork ranging from routine requests for information to detailed architectural drawings can suffer unnecessary delays when it must be copied and faxed or sent by mail, thereby delaying decisions and lengthening a project. Bechtel has thus initiated a Web-based communications system that provides access to project information electronically. Members of the project team can access schedules, progress reports, drawings, and messages at one web site without having to rely on faxes. Decisions on various issues can be made quickly, thereby reinforcing Bechtel's competitive priorities.

Bechtel Group Inc. was the construction contractor for the Hoover Dam, the highest dam in the Western Hemisphere. On the Colorado River, it has a power capacity of 1,345 megawatts.

project An interrelated set of activities that have a definite starting and ending point and that result in a unique outcome for a specific allocation of resources.

COMPANIES SUCH AS BECHTEL are experts at managing projects. They have mastered the ability to schedule activities and monitor progress within strict time, cost, and performance guidelines. A **project** is an interrelated set of activities that has a definite starting and ending point and that results in a unique outcome for a specific allocation of resources. Typical competitive priorities for such processes include on-time delivery and customization (see the Process Management chapter). A project process is the mechanism for completing a project.

Project processes can be complex and challenging to manage. Projects often cut across organizational lines because they need the skills of multiple professions and organizations. Furthermore, each project is unique, even if it is routine, requiring new combinations of skills and resources in the project process. Uncertainties, such as the advent of new technologies or the activities of competitors, can change the character of projects and require responsive countermeasures. Finally, project processes themselves are temporary because personnel, materials, and facilities are organized to complete a project within a specified time frame and then disbanded.

Projects are common in everyday life as well as in business. Planning weddings, remodeling bathrooms, writing term papers, and organizing surprise parties are examples of small projects in everyday life. Conducting company audits, planning mergers, creating advertising campaigns, reengineering processes, developing new products or services, and establishing a strategic alliance are examples of large projects in business. In this chapter, we discuss three major activities associated with managing project processes: defining and organizing projects, planning projects, and monitoring and controlling projects.

DEFINING AND ORGANIZING PROJECTS

Successful projects begin with a clear definition of scope, objectives, and tasks. However, a successful project *process* begins with a clear understanding of its organization and how personnel are going to work together to complete the project. In this section, we will address three important activities in this initial phase of managing projects: selecting the project manager and team, defining scope and objectives, and planning the format for meetings and communication.

SELECTING THE PROJECT MANAGER AND TEAM

Project managers should be good motivators, teachers, and communicators. They should be able to organize a set of disparate activities and work with personnel from a variety of disciplines. These qualities are important because project managers have the responsibility to see that their projects are completed successfully. The project manager is responsible for establishing the project goals and providing the means to achieve them. The project manager must also specify how the work will be done and ensure that any necessary training is conducted. Finally, the project manager evaluates progress and takes appropriate action when schedules are in jeopardy.

The project team is a group of people led by the project manager. Members of the project team may represent entities internal to the firm, such as marketing, finance, accounting, or operations, or entities external to the firm, such as customers or suppliers. A clear definition of who is on the team is essential, as is a clear understanding of their specific roles and responsibilities, such as helping to create the project plan, performing specific tasks, and reporting progress and problems. Everyone performing work for the project should be a part of the project team. Consequently, the size and makeup of the team may fluctuate during the life of the project.

EFFICIENCY AND ORGANIZATIONAL STRUCTURE. The efficiency of a project team is often influenced by the firm's organizational structure. The traditional structure is the *functional* organization, whereby the project is housed in a specific functional area, presumably the one with the most interest in it. Assistance from personnel in other functional areas must be negotiated by the project manager. Under this structure, the project manager has minimal control over the timing of the project, but resource duplication across functional areas is minimized. At the other extreme is the *pure project* structure, whereby the team members work exclusively for the project manager on a particular project. Although this structure simplifies the lines of authority for the project manager, it could result in significant duplication of resources across functional areas. A compromise is the *matrix* structure, whereby each functional area maintains authority over who will work on the project and the technology to be used. In some cases, functional area managers also maintain the authority to prioritize the project work performed within their areas. Resource duplication is reduced relative to the pure project structure, but the project manager may lose some control over the project because team members have two bosses.

DEFINING THE SCOPE AND OBJECTIVES

A thorough statement of project scope, time frame, and allocated resources is essential to managing the project process. The scope captures the essence of the desired project outcomes in the form of major deliverables, which are concrete outcomes of the project process. These deliverables become the focus of management attention during the life of the project. For example, suppose a firm wants to reengineer its billing process. Major deliverables for the project might include a list of all affected processes in both the firm and entities exterior to the firm, revision of the billing process and a new process flowchart, an implementation plan, a staffing plan; and a new, fully operational billing process.

The time frame for a project should be as specific as possible. For example, "by the first quarter, 2003," is too vague for most purposes. Some people could interpret it as the beginning and others the end. Even though it should be considered only as a target at this early stage of the project plan, the time frame should be much more specific, as in "the billing process reengineering project should be completed by January 1, 2003."

Although specifying an allocation of resources to a project may be difficult at the early stages of planning, it is important for managing the project process. The allocation could be expressed as a dollar figure or as full-time equivalents of personnel time. For example, in the billing process reengineering project, the allocated resources might be $250,000. Avoid statements such as "with available resources" because they are too vague and imply that there are sufficient resources to complete the project when there may not be. A specific statement of allocated resources makes it possible to make adjustments to the scope of the project as it proceeds.

Each of the deliverables requires activities to achieve it; therefore, it is important to avoid many changes to the scope of the project once it is underway. Changes to the scope of a project inevitably increase costs and delay completion. For example, adding a requirement to recommend an e-commerce software solution to the reengineering project after it has started might require a reanalysis of the recommended changes to the existing internal processes and a consultant to recommend a software package. Such a change will not only delay the completion of a project but will add to the needed resources to complete it. Collectively, changes to scope are called *scope creep* and, in sufficient quantity, are primary causes of failed projects.

PLANNING THE PROJECT FORMAT

A key activity for any project process is making decisions. The managers of successful project processes specify the format for how the team will make decisions and who will make them. Such a format sets down guidelines for meetings, for resolving issues, and for communication among team members.

MEETINGS. One of the quickest ways to undermine morale in a project team is to hold too many meetings. The project manager should specify a standard meeting time and an attendance policy. An agenda should be provided in advance, and at the meeting the issues should be discussed and meted out for further resolution if necessary.

RESOLVING ISSUES. The project manager should specify in advance how decisions will be made (by consensus, majority, or project manager). Invariably, team members will raise issues at each meeting. These issues should be logged and someone given the responsibility, with a deadline, to resolve them. Sometimes an issue will need to be resolved by a senior manager not on the team.

COMMUNICATION. It will typically save a lot of time on large projects if the method of communication is thought out in advance. For example, team members can communicate by e-mail for most issues that do not require immediate responses and voice mail for issues with more immediacy. In addition, the question of who should get what information is an important operating issue, if not a political one. The project manager needs to determine the nature of the interim information that senior managers need and when they should get it.

PLANNING PROJECTS

Once the project has been defined and the project process organized, the team must formulate a plan that identifies the specific tasks to be accomplished and a schedule for their completion. Planning projects involves five steps:

1. defining the work breakdown structure,
2. diagramming the network,
3. developing the schedule,
4. analyzing cost–time trade-offs, and
5. assessing risks.

DEFINING THE WORK BREAKDOWN STRUCTURE

work breakdown structure (WBS) A statement of all work that has to be completed.

The **work breakdown structure (WBS)** is a statement of all work that has to be completed. Perhaps the single most important contributor to delay is the omission of work that is germane to the successful completion of the project. The project manager must work closely with the team to identify all work tasks. Typically, in the process of accumulating work tasks, the team generates a hierarchy to the work breakdown. Major work components are broken down to smaller tasks by the project team. Care must be taken to include all important tasks in the WBS, otherwise project delays are possible. For example, a project for improving the delivery of groceries directly to consumers might have as a major activity "build a warehouse," which might be further refined to a host of construction-related tasks that include "pour a foundation" and "wire for electrical service." Easily overlooked, however, are tasks such as "getting final approval for the warehouse" or "preparing final reports," which can take considerable time and can affect the completion date of the project.

activity The smallest unit of work effort consuming both time and resources that the project manager can schedule and control.

An **activity** is the smallest unit of work effort consuming both time and resources that the project manager can schedule and control. Each activity in the work breakdown structure must have an "owner" who is responsible for doing the work. *Task ownership* avoids confusion in the execution of activities and assigns responsibility for timely completion. The team should have a defined procedure for assigning tasks to team members, which can be democratic (consensus of the team) or autocratic (project manager).

What tools are available for scheduling and controlling projects?

DIAGRAMMING THE NETWORK

network diagram A network planning method, designed to depict the relationships between activities, that consists of nodes (circles) and arcs (arrows).

Network planning methods can help managers monitor and control projects. These methods treat a project as a set of interrelated activities that can be visually displayed in a **network diagram,** which consists of nodes (circles) and arcs (arrows) that depict

program evaluation and review technique (PERT) A network planning method created for the U.S. Navy's Polaris missile project in the 1950s, which involved 3,000 separate contractors and suppliers.

critical path method (CPM) A network planning method developed in the 1950s by J. F. Kelly of Remington-Rand and M. R. Walker of Du Pont as a means of scheduling maintenance shutdowns at chemical-processing plants.

precedence relationship A relationship that determines a sequence for undertaking activities; it specifies that one activity cannot start until a preceding activity has been completed.

activity-on-arc (AOA) network An approach used to create a network diagram that uses arcs to represent activities and nodes to represent events.

event The point at which one or more activities are to be completed and one or more other activities are to begin.

activity-on-node (AON) network An approach used to create a network diagram, in which nodes represent activities and arcs represent the precedence relationships between them.

the relationships between activities. Two network planning methods were developed in the 1950s. The **program evaluation and review technique (PERT)** was created for the U.S. Navy's Polaris missile project, which involved 3,000 separate contractors and suppliers. The **critical path method (CPM)** was developed as a means of scheduling maintenance shutdowns at chemical-processing plants. Although early versions of PERT and CPM differed in their treatment of activity–time estimates, today the differences between PERT and CPM are minor. For purposes of our discussion, we refer to them collectively as PERT/CPM. These methods offer several benefits to project managers, including the following.

1. Considering projects as networks forces project teams to identify and organize the data required and to identify the interrelationships between activities. This process also provides a forum for managers of different functional areas to discuss the nature of the various activities and their resource requirements.

2. Networks enable project managers to estimate the completion time of projects, an advantage that can be useful in planning other events and in conducting contractual negotiations with customers and suppliers.

3. Reports highlight the activities that are crucial to completing projects on schedule. They also highlight the activities that may be delayed without affecting completion dates, thereby freeing up resources for other, more critical activities.

4. Network methods enable project managers to analyze the time and cost implications of resource trade-offs.

ESTABLISHING PRECEDENCE RELATIONSHIPS. Diagramming the project as a network requires establishing the precedence relationships between activities. A **precedence relationship** determines a sequence for undertaking activities; it specifies that one activity cannot start until a preceding activity has been completed. For example, brochures announcing a conference for executives must first be designed by the program committee (activity A) before they can be printed (activity B). In other words, activity A must *precede* activity B. For large projects, this task is essential because incorrect or omitted precedence relationships will result in costly delays. The precedence relationships are represented by a network diagram.

SELECTING A NETWORK DIAGRAM APPROACH. Two different approaches may be used to create a network diagram. The first approach, the **activity-on-arc (AOA) network,** uses arcs to represent activities and nodes to represent events. An **event** is the point at which one or more activities are to be completed and one or more other activities are to begin. An event consumes neither time nor resources. Because the AOA approach emphasizes activity connection points, we say that it is *event oriented*. Here, the precedence relationships require that an event not occur until all preceding activities have been completed. Conventionally, AOA networks number events sequentially from left to right.

The second approach is the **activity-on-node (AON) network,** in which nodes represent activities and arcs the precedence relationships between them. This approach is *activity oriented*. Here, precedence relationships require that an activity not begin until all preceding activities have been completed. In AON networks, when there are multiple activities with no predecessors, it is usual to show them emanating from a common node called Start. When there are multiple activities with no successors, it is usual to show them connected to a node called Finish. We will use AON networks later to describe assembly lines (see the Layout chapter).

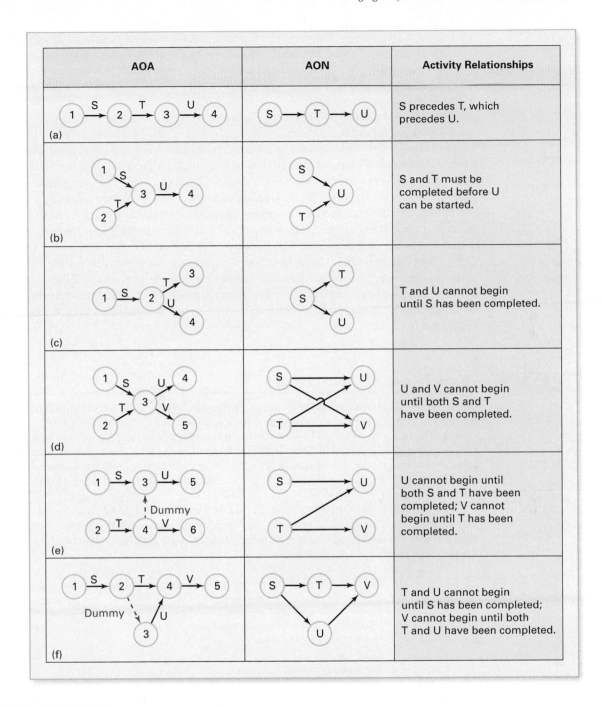

	AOA	AON	Activity Relationships

FIGURE 4.1

AOA and AON Approaches to Activity Relationships

Figure 4.1 shows the AOA and AON approaches for several commonly encountered activity relationships. In Figure 4.1(a), activity S must be completed before activity T, which in turn must be completed before activity U can be started. For example, in the AOA diagram, event 1 might be "the start of the project" and event 2 "the completion of activity S." The arrows in the AOA diagram denote both precedence and the activity itself. The arrow for activity S starts from event 1 and ends at event 2, indicating that the sequence of events is from 1 to 2. In the AON diagram, the arrows represent precedence relationships only. The direction of the arrows indicates the sequence of activities, from S to T to U.

Figure 4.1(b) shows that activities S and T can be worked simultaneously, but both must be completed before activity U can begin. In Figure 4.1(c), neither activity T nor U can begin until activity S has been completed. Multiple dependencies also can be identified. For example, Figure 4.1(d) shows that U and V cannot begin until both S and T have been completed.

Sometimes the AOA approach requires the addition of a *dummy activity* to clarify the precedence relationships between two activities. Figure 4.1(e) shows an example of this situation. Activity U cannot begin until both S and T have been completed; however, V depends only on the completion of T. A dummy activity, which has an activity time of zero and requires no resources, must be used to clarify the precedence between T and V and between S and T and U. A dummy activity also is used when two activities have the same starting and ending nodes. For example, in Figure 4.1(f), both activities T and U cannot begin until S has been completed, and activity V can't begin until both T and U have been completed. The dummy activity enables activities T and U to have unique beginning nodes. This distinction is important for computer programs because activities often are identified by their beginning and ending nodes. Without dummy activities, the computer could not differentiate activities having identical beginning and ending nodes from each other, which is essential when the activities have different time requirements.

EXAMPLE 4.1   *Diagramming a Hospital Project*

In the interest of better serving the public in Benjamin County, St. Adolf's Hospital has decided to relocate from Christofer to Northville, a large suburb that at present has no primary medical facility. The move to Northville will involve constructing a new hospital and making it operational. Judy Kramer, executive director of the board of St. Adolf's, must prepare for a hearing, scheduled for next week, before the Central Ohio Hospital Board (COHB) on the proposed project. The hearing will address the specifics of the total project, including time and cost estimates for its completion.

With the help of her team, Kramer has developed a work breakdown structure consisting of 11 major project activities. The team also has specified the immediate predecessors (those activities that must be completed before a particular activity can begin) for each activity, as shown in the following table.

ACTIVITY	DESCRIPTION	IMMEDIATE PREDECESSOR(S)
A	Select administrative and medical staff.	—
B	Select site and do site survey.	—
C	Select equipment.	A
D	Prepare final construction plans and layout.	B
E	Bring utilities to the site.	B
F	Interview applicants and fill positions in nursing, support staff, maintenance, and security.	A
G	Purchase and take delivery of equipment.	C
H	Construct the hospital.	D
I	Develop an information system.	A
J	Install the equipment.	E, G, H
K	Train nurses and support staff.	F, I, J

a. Draw the AON network diagram.

b. Draw the AOA network diagram.

SOLUTION

a. The AON network for the hospital project, based on Kramer's 11 activities and their precedence relationships, is shown in Figure 4.2. It depicts activities as circles, with arrows indicating the sequence in which they are to be performed. Activities A and B emanate from a *start* node because they have no immediate predecessors. The arrows connecting activity A to activities C, F, and I indicate that all three require completion of activity A before they can begin. Similarly, activity B must be completed before activities D and E can begin, and so on. Activity K connects to a *finish* node because no activities follow it. The start and finish nodes do not actually represent activities. They merely provide beginning and ending points for the network.

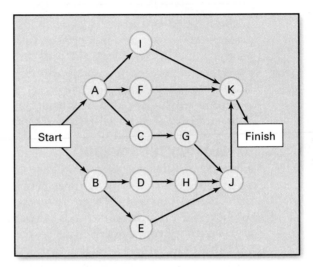

FIGURE 4.2 • AON Network for the St. Adolf's Hospital Project

b. The AOA diagram is shown in Figure 4.3. Event 1 is the start of the project. Activities A and B have no immediate predecessors; therefore, the arrows representing those activities both have event 1 as their base. Event 2 signals the completion of activity A. Because activities C, F, and I all require the completion of A, the arrows representing these activities leave the node representing event 2. Similarly, the arrows for activities D and E leave the node for event 4, which signals the completion of activity B. The arrow for activity G leaves event 3, and event

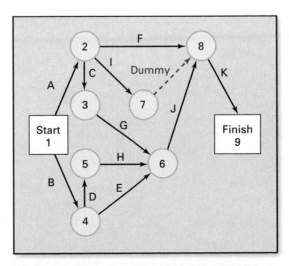

FIGURE 4.3 • AOA Network for the St. Adolf's Hospital Project

6 is needed to tie activities G, H, and E together because they must be completed before activity J can begin.

Properly representing the relationship for activity K requires the use of a dummy activity. Activities I and F both emanate from event 2, and both must be completed before K can begin. Activities I and F will have the same beginning and ending nodes unless a dummy activity is used. Thus, event 7 signals the end of activity I and event 8 the end of activity F, with a dummy activity joining them. Now all activities are uniquely defined, and the network shows that activities F, I, and J must be completed before activity K can begin. Event 9 indicates the completion of the project. ❑

Both the AON and the AOA methods can accurately represent all the activities and precedence relationships in a project. Regardless of the method used, modeling a large project as a network forces the project team to identify the necessary activities and recognize the precedence relationships. If this preplanning is skipped, unexpected delays often occur.

In the remainder of our discussion of PERT/CPM, we use the AON convention, although AOA diagrams also can be applied to all procedures.

DEVELOPING THE SCHEDULE

Which activities determine the duration of an entire project?

Next, the project team must make time estimates for activities. When the same type of activity has been done many times before, time estimates are apt to have a relatively high degree of certainty. There are several ways to get time estimates in such an environment. First, statistical methods can be used if the project team has access to data on actual activity times experienced in the past (see Measuring Output Rates in the Student CD-ROM). Second, if activity times improve with the number of replications, the times can be estimated using learning curve models (see Learning Curves in the Student CD-ROM). Finally, the times for first-time activities are often estimated using managerial opinions based on similar prior experiences (see the Forecasting chapter). If there is a high degree of uncertainty in the estimates, probability distributions for activity times can be used. We discuss two approaches for incorporating uncertainty in project networks when we address risk assessment later. For now, we assume that the activity times are known with certainty. Figure 4.4 shows the estimated time for each activity of the St. Adolf's project.

FIGURE 4.4

Network for St. Adolf's Hospital Project, Showing Activity Times

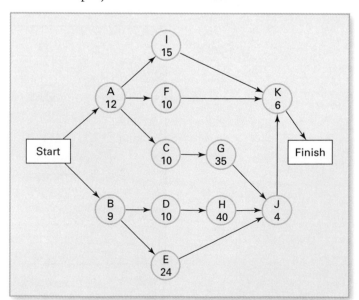

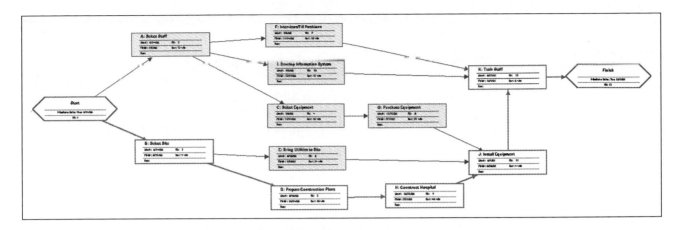

FIGURE 4.5

MS Project Network Diagram for the Hospital Project, with the Critical Path Shown in Red

path The sequence of activities between a project's start and finish.

critical path The sequence of activities between a project's start and finish that takes the longest time to complete.

A crucial aspect of project management is estimating the time of completion. If each activity in relocating the hospital were done in sequence, with work proceeding on only one activity at a time, the time of completion would equal the sum of the times for all the activities, or 175 weeks. However, Figure 4.4 indicates that some activities can be carried on simultaneously given adequate resources. We call each sequence of activities between the project's start and finish a **path.** The network describing the hospital relocation project has five paths: A–I–K, A–F–K, A–C–G–J–K, B–D–H–J–K, and B–E–J–K. The **critical path** is the sequence of activities between a project's start and finish that takes the longest time to complete. Thus, the activities along the critical path determine the completion time of the project; that is, if one of the activities on the critical path is delayed, the entire project will be delayed. The estimated times for the paths in the hospital project network are

Path	Estimated Time (wk)
A–F–K	28
A–I–K	33
A–C–G–J–K	67
B–D–H–J–K	69
B–E–J–K	43

The activity string B–D–H–J–K is estimated to take 69 weeks to complete. As the longest, it constitutes the critical path and is shown in red in Figure 4.5.

Because the critical path defines the completion time of the project, Judy Kramer and the project team should focus on these activities. However, projects can have more than one critical path. If activity A, C, or G were to fall behind by two weeks, the string A–C–G–J–K would become a second critical path. Consequently, the team should be aware that delays in activities not on the critical path could cause delays in the entire project.

Manually finding the critical path in this way is easy for small projects; however, computers must be used for large projects. Computers calculate activity slack and prepare periodic reports, enabling managers to monitor progress. **Activity slack** is the maximum length of time that an activity can be delayed without delaying the entire project. Activities on the critical path have zero slack. Constantly monitoring the progress of activities with little or no slack enables managers to identify activities that need to be expedited to keep the project on schedule. Activity slack is calculated from four times for each activity: earliest start time, earliest finish time, latest start time, and latest finish time.

activity slack The maximum length of time that an activity can be delayed without delaying the entire project.

earliest finish time (EF) An activity's earliest start time plus its estimated duration, *t*, or EF = ES + *t*.

earliest start time (ES) The earliest finish time of the immediately preceding activity.

EARLIEST START AND EARLIEST FINISH TIMES. The earliest start and earliest finish times are obtained as follows.

The **earliest finish time (EF)** of an activity equals its earliest start time plus its estimated duration, *t*, or EF = ES + *t*.

The **earliest start time (ES)** for an activity is the earliest finish time of the immediately preceding activity. For activities with more than one preceding activity, ES is the latest of the earliest finish times of the preceding activities.

To calculate the duration of the entire project, we determine the EF for the last activity on the critical path.

EXAMPLE 4.2   *Calculating Earliest Start and Earliest Finish Times*

Calculate the earliest start and finish times for the activities in the hospital project. Figure 4.5 contains the activity times.

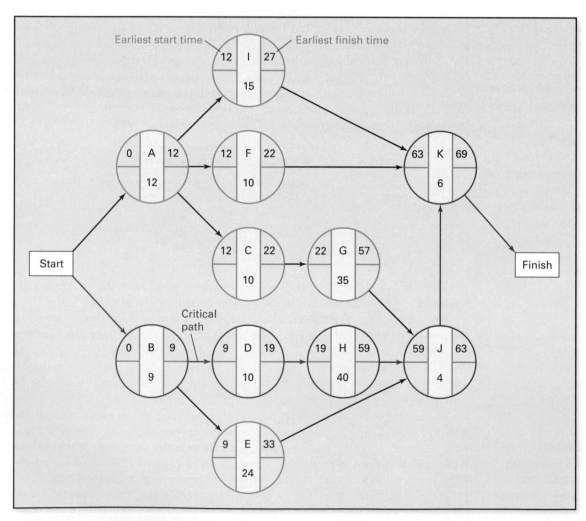

FIGURE 4.6 • Network for the Hospital Project, Showing Earliest Start and Earliest Finish Times

SOLUTION

We begin at the start node at time zero. Because activities A and B have no predecessors, the earliest start times for these activities are also zero. The earliest finish times for these activities are

$$EF_A = 0 + 12 = 12 \quad \text{and} \quad EF_B = 0 + 9 = 9$$

Because the earliest start time for activities I, F, and C is the earliest finish time of activity A,

$$ES_I = 12, \quad ES_F = 12, \quad \text{and} \quad ES_C = 12$$

Similarly,

$$ES_D = 9 \quad \text{and} \quad ES_E = 9$$

After placing these ES values on the network diagram as shown in Figure 4.6, we determine the EF times for activities I, F, C, D, and E:

$$EF_I = 12 + 15 = 27, \quad EF_F = 12 + 10 = 22, \quad EF_C = 12 + 10 = 22$$

$$EF_D = 9 + 10 = 19, \quad \text{and} \quad EF_E = 9 + 24 = 33$$

The earliest start time for activity G is the latest EF time of all immediately preceding activities. Thus,

$$\begin{array}{cc} ES_G = EF_C & ES_H = EF_D \\ = 22 & = 19 \\ EF_G = ES_G + t & EF_H = ES_H + t \\ = 22 + 35 & = 19 + 40 \\ = 57 & = 59 \end{array}$$

Decision Point The project team can now determine the earliest time any activity can be started. Because activity J has several predecessors, the earliest time that activity J can begin is the latest of the EF times of any of its preceding activities: EF_G, EF_H, EF_E. Thus, $EF_J = 59 + 4 = 63$. Similarly, $ES_K = 63$ and $EF_K = 63 + 6 = 69$. Because activity K is the last activity on the critical path, the earliest the project can be completed is week 69. The earliest start and finish times for all activities are shown in Figure 4.6. ❐

latest finish time (LF) The latest start time of the activity immediately following.

LATEST START AND LATEST FINISH TIMES. To obtain the latest start and latest finish times, we must work backward from the finish node. We start by setting the latest finish time of the project equal to the earliest finish time of the last activity on the critical path.

The **latest finish time (LF)** for an activity is the latest start time of the activity immediately following it. For activities with more than one activity immediately following, LF is the earliest of the latest start times of those activities.

latest start time (LS) The latest finish time of an activity minus its estimated duration, *t,* or LS = LF − *t.*

The **latest start time (LS)** for an activity equals its latest finish time minus its estimated duration, *t,* or LS = LF − *t.*

| EXAMPLE 4.3 | *Calculating Latest Start and Latest Finish Times* |

For the hospital project, which activity should Kramer start immediately? In addition, calculate the latest start and latest finish times for each activity from Figure 4.6.

SOLUTION

We begin by setting the latest finish activity time of activity K at week 69, its earliest finish time as determined in Example 4.2. Thus, the latest start time for activity K is

$$LS_K = LF_K - t = 69 - 6 = 63$$

If activity K is to start no later than week 63, all its predecessors must finish no later than that time. Consequently,

$$LF_I = 63, \qquad LE_F = 63, \qquad \text{and} \qquad LF_j = 63$$

The latest start times for these activities are shown in Figure 4.7 as

$$LS_I = 63 - 15 = 48, \qquad LS_F = 63 - 10 = 53, \qquad \text{and} \qquad LS_J = 63 - 4 = 59$$

After obtaining LS_J, we can calculate the latest start times for the immediate predecessors of activity J:

$$LS_G = 59 - 35 = 24, \qquad LS_H = 59 - 40 = 19, \qquad \text{and} \qquad LS_E = 59 - 24 = 35$$

Similarly, we can now calculate latest start times for activities C and D:

$$LS_C = 24 - 10 = 14 \qquad \text{and} \qquad LS_D = 19 - 10 = 9$$

Activity A has more than one immediately following activity: I, F, and C. The earliest of the latest start times is 14 for activity C. Thus,

$$LS_A = 14 - 12 = 2$$

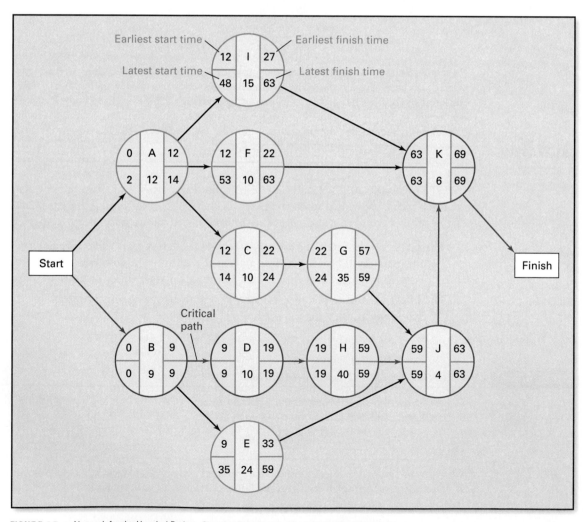

FIGURE 4.7 • Network for the Hospital Project, Showing Data Needed for Activity Slack Calculation

Similarly, activity B has two immediate followers, D and E. Because the earliest of the latest start times of these activities is 9,

$$LS_B = 9 \quad 9 - 0$$

Decision Point   The earliest or latest start dates can be used for developing a project schedule. For example, Kramer should start activity B immediately because the latest start date is 0; otherwise, the project will not be completed by week 69. When the LS is greater than the ES for an activity, that activity could be scheduled for any date between ES and LS. Such is the case for activity E, which could be scheduled to start anytime between week 9 and week 35, depending on the availability of resources. The earliest start and earliest finish times and the latest start and latest finish times for all activities are shown in Figure 4.7. ⊐

PROJECT SCHEDULE. The project manager, often with the assistance of computer software, creates the project schedule by superimposing project activities, with their precedence relationships and estimated duration times, on a time line. The resulting diagram is called a **Gantt Chart.** Figure 4.8 shows a Gantt chart for the hospital project created with Microsoft Project 2000, a popular software package for project management that is included with OM Explorer. The critical path is shown in red. The chart clearly

Gantt Chart A project schedule, usually created by the project manager using computer software, that superimposes project activities, with their precedence relationships and estimated duration times, on a time line.

MS Project Gantt Chart for the Hospital Project Schedule

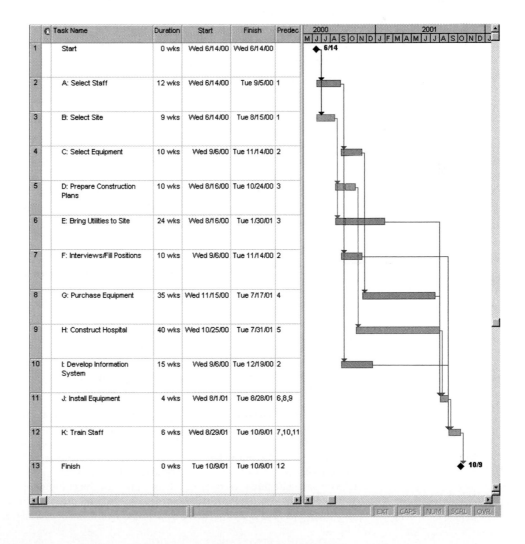

shows which activities can be undertaken simultaneously and when they should be started. In this example, the schedule calls for all activities to begin at their earliest start times. Gantt charts are popular because they are intuitive and easy to construct.

ACTIVITY SLACK. Information on slack can be useful because it highlights activities that need close attention. In this regard, activity slack is the amount of schedule slippage that can be tolerated for an activity before the entire project will be delayed. Activities on the critical path have zero slack. Slack at an activity is reduced when the estimated time duration of an activity is exceeded or when the scheduled start time for the activity must be delayed because of resource considerations. For example, activity G in the hospital project is estimated to have 2 weeks of slack. Suppose that the orders for the new equipment are placed in week 22, the activity's earliest start date. If the supplier informs the project team that it will have a two-week delay in the normal delivery time, the activity time becomes 37 weeks, consuming all the slack and making activity G critical. Management must carefully monitor the delivery of the equipment to avoid delaying the entire project.

Sometimes managers can manipulate slack to overcome scheduling problems. Slack information helps the project team make decisions regarding the reallocation of resources. When resources can be used on several different activities in a project, they can be taken from activities with slack and given to activities that are behind schedule until the slack is used up.

total slack Slack shared by other activities; calculated as LS-ES or LF-EF.

There are two types of activity slack. **Total slack** for an activity is a function of the performance of activities leading to it. It can be calculated in one of two ways for any activity:

$$S = LS - ES \qquad \text{or} \qquad S = LF - EF$$

free slack The amount of time that an activity's earliest finish time can be delayed without delaying the earliest start time of any activity immediately following it.

Free slack is the amount of time that an activity's earliest finish time can be delayed without delaying the earliest start time of any activity immediately following it. The distinction between the two types of slack is important for making resource-allocation decisions. If an activity has total slack but no free slack, any slippage in its start date will affect the slack of other activities. However, the start date for an activity with free slack can be delayed without affecting the schedules of other activities.

EXAMPLE 4.4

Calculating Activity Slack

Calculate the slack for the activities in the hospital project. Use the data in Figure 4.7.

SOLUTION

The following table from Microsoft Project 2000 shows the total slack and free slack for each activity. Figure 4.9 shows activities B, D, H, J and K are on the critical path because they have zero slack.

Decision Point The total slack at an activity depends on the performance of activities leading to it. If the project team decides to schedule activity A to begin in week 2 instead of immediately, the total slack for activities C and G would be zero. Thus, total slack is shared among all activities on a particular path. The table also shows that several activities have free slack. For example, activity G has two weeks of free slack. If the schedule goes as planned to week 22 when activity G is scheduled to start, and the supplier for the equipment asks for a two-week extension on the delivery date, the project team knows that the delay will not affect the schedule for the other activities. Nonetheless, activity G would be on the critical path.

	Task Name	Start	Finish	Late Start	Late Finish	Free Slack	Total Slack
1	Start	Wed 6/14/00	Wed 6/14/00	Wed 6/14/00	Wed 6/14/00	0 wks	0 wks
2	A: Select Staff	Wed 6/14/00	Tue 9/5/00	Wed 6/20/00	Tue 9/19/00	0 wks	2 wks
3	B: Select Site	Wed 6/14/00	Tue 8/15/00	Wed 6/14/00	Tue 8/15/00	0 wks	0 wks
4	C: Select Equipment	Wed 9/6/00	Tue 11/14/00	Wed 9/20/00	Tue 11/28/00	0 wks	2 wks
5	D: Prepare Constructi	Wed 8/16/00	Tue 10/24/00	Wed 8/16/00	Tue 10/24/00	0 wks	0 wks
6	E: Bring Utilities to Site	Wed 8/16/00	Tue 1/30/01	Wed 2/14/01	Tue 7/31/01	26 wks	26 wks
7	F: Interviews/Fill Posit	Wed 9/6/00	Tue 11/14/00	Wed 6/20/01	Tue 8/28/01	41 wks	41 wks
8	G: Purchase Equipme	Wed 11/15/00	Tue 7/17/01	Wed 11/29/00	Tue 7/31/01	2 wks	2 wks
9	H: Construct Hospital	Wed 10/25/00	Tue 7/31/01	Wed 10/25/00	Tue 7/31/01	0 wks	0 wks
10	I: Develop Information	Wed 9/6/00	Tue 12/19/00	Wed 5/16/01	Tue 8/28/01	36 wks	36 wks
11	J: Install Equipment	Wed 8/1/01	Tue 8/28/01	Wed 8/1/01	Tue 8/28/01	0 wks	0 wks
12	K: Train Staff	Wed 8/29/01	Tue 10/9/01	Wed 8/29/01	Tue 10/9/01	0 wks	0 wks
13	Finish	Tue 10/9/01	Tue 10/9/01	Tue 10/9/01	Tue 10/9/01	0 wks	0 wks

FIGURE 4.9 • Schedule Table Showing Activity Slacks for the Hospital Project

ANALYZING COST–TIME TRADE-OFFS

How do project planning methods increase the potential to control costs and provide better customer service?

Keeping costs at acceptable levels is almost always as important as meeting schedule dates. In this section, we discuss the use of PERT/CPM methods to obtain minimum-cost schedules.

The reality of project management is that there are always time–cost trade-offs. For example, a project can often be completed earlier than scheduled by hiring more workers or running extra shifts. Such actions could be advantageous if savings or additional revenues accrue from completing the project early. *Total project costs* are the sum of direct costs, indirect costs, and penalty costs. These costs are dependent either on activity times or on project completion time. *Direct costs* include labor, materials, and any other costs directly related to project activities. Managers can shorten individual activity times by using additional direct resources such as over-time, personnel, or equipment. *Indirect costs* include administration, depreciation, financial, and other variable overhead costs that can be avoided by reducing total project time: The shorter the duration of the project, the lower the indirect costs will be. Finally, a project may incur penalty costs if it extends beyond some specific date, whereas a bonus may be provided for early completion. Thus, a project manager may consider *crashing,* or expediting, some activities to reduce overall project completion time and total project costs. Managerial Practice 4.1 shows how substantial project penalty costs can be.

normal time (NT) The time necessary to complete an activity under normal conditions.

normal cost (NC) The activity cost associated with the normal time.

crash time (CT) The shortest possible time to complete the activity.

crash cost (CC) The activity cost associated with the crash time.

COST TO CRASH. To assess the benefit of crashing certain activities—from either a cost or a schedule perspective—the project manager needs to know the following times and costs:

1. The **normal time (NT)** is the time to complete the activity under normal conditions.
2. The **normal cost (NC)** is the activity cost associated with the normal time.
3. The **crash time (CT)** is the shortest possible time to complete the activity.
4. The **crash cost (CC)** is the activity cost associated with the crash time.

Our cost analysis is based on the assumption that direct costs increase linearly as activity time is reduced from its normal time. This assumption implies that for every week the activity time is reduced, direct costs increase by a proportional amount. For example, suppose that the normal time for activity C in the hospital project is 10 weeks and is associated with a direct cost of $4,000. If, by crashing activity C, we can reduce its time to only 5 weeks at a crash cost of $7,000, the net time reduction is 5 weeks at

MANAGERIAL PRACTICE 4.1
Project Delays Are Costly for Amtrak and Its Suppliers

Amtrak (www.amtrak.com), also known as the National Railroad Passenger Corporation, is a $1.84 billion-a-year federally funded corporation whose mandate is to provide passenger rail service to major cities. Competition in the transportation industry is fierce; passengers can use airplanes, busses, cars, and trains to get to their destinations. To gain a larger share of transportation services in the Northeast, Amtrak initiated the Acela Regional project in 1996, with a goal of providing high-speed electric rail service between Boston and Washington, DC, by December, 1999. The project included enhancements to existing rail infrastructure, particularly the 156-mile stretch between New Haven and Boston. Amtrak and its contractors erected 12,200 catenary poles, strung 1,550 miles of electrical wire across three states, and built 25 power stations. In addition, Amtrak installed 115 miles of continuous welded rail, laid 455,000 concrete ties, and poured 500,000 tons of ballast to allow for the faster acceleration and higher top speeds than could be achieved with existing diesel technology.

A key deliverable in the project was the Acela Express train, which is capable of 150 mile-per-hour speeds and includes such amenities as modem jacks at every seat and microbrews on tap. Each train has two locomotives, a business-class car, six coach-class cars, and a café car. In September 1999, Amtrak, though on schedule with the electrification part of the project, discovered that the delivery of 20 locomotives was going to be delayed. The development of the locomotives, which were designed and manufactured by a consortium of two companies, began in 1996 and was on schedule until it was discovered during testing that the wheels underwent excessive wear. Additional design and testing would add several months to the promised delivery date. Without the locomotives, Amtrak could not test the rails and electrification improvements on schedule. The inaugural of the new service would have to be delayed, causing Amtrak to lose some needed revenue.

The Acela Express, North America's first high-speed passenger train, leaves New York on November 16, 2000 enroute to Boston on its inaugural run. The train, which started its trip in Washington, D.C., reached New York in two hours and twentysix minutes. Regular passenger service began in December, 2000.

The contract between Amtrak and the consortium specified penalties for late delivery of the locomotives. The fines started at $1,000 per day per train and went as high as $13,500 per day per train as delays continued. The fines were over and above compensation for certain other damages to Amtrak caused by nonperformance of the consortium. The Acela Regional service has been a success for Amtrak, outperforming the revenues generated by the old trains by 55 to 65 percent.

Sources: "Fast Train to Nowhere?" *Business Week* (September 27, 1999), p. 56.

a net cost increase of $3,000. We assume that crashing activity C costs $3,000/5 = $600 per week—an assumption of linear marginal costs that is illustrated in Figure 4.10. Thus, if activity C were expedited by 2 weeks (i.e., its time reduced from 10 weeks to 8 weeks), the estimated direct costs would be $4,000 + 2($600) = $5,200. For any activity, the cost to crash an activity by 1 week is

$$\text{Cost to crash per week} = \frac{\text{CC} - \text{NC}}{\text{NT} - \text{CT}}$$

Table 4.1 contains direct cost and time data and the costs of crashing per week for the activities in the hospital project.

FIGURE 4.10

Cost–Time Relationships in Cost Analysis

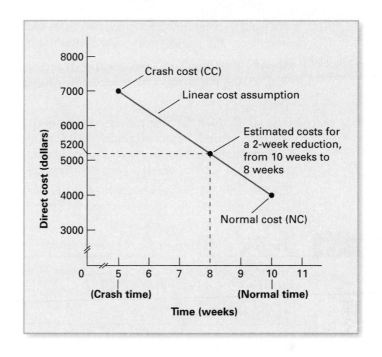

TABLE 4.1

Direct Cost and Time Data for the Hospital Project

Activity	Normal Time (NT)	Normal Cost (NC)	Crash Time (CT)	Crash Cost (CC)	Maximum Time Reduction (wk)	Cost of Crashing per Week
A	12	$ 12,000	11	$ 13,000	1	$ 1,000
B	9	50,000	7	64,000	2	7,000
C	10	4,000	5	7,000	5	600
D	10	16,000	8	20,000	2	2,000
E	24	120,000	14	200,000	10	8,000
F	10	10,000	6	16,000	4	1,500
G	35	500,000	25	530,000	10	3,000
H	40	1,200,000	35	1,260,000	5	12,000
I	15	40,000	10	52,500	5	2,500
J	4	10,000	1	13,000	3	1,000
K	6	30,000	5	34,000	1	4,000
	Totals	$1,992,000		$ 2,209,500		

minimum-cost schedule A schedule determined by starting with the normal time schedule and crashing activities along the critical path, in such a way that the costs of crashing do not exceed the savings in indirect and penalty costs.

MINIMIZING COSTS. The objective of cost analysis is to determine the project schedule that minimizes total project costs. Suppose that project indirect costs are $8,000 per week. Suppose also that, after week 65, the Central Ohio Hospital Board imposes on St. Adolf's a penalty cost of $20,000 per week if the hospital is not fully operational. With a critical path completion time of 69 weeks, the hospital faces potentially large penalty costs unless the schedule is changed. For every week that the project is short-ened—to week 65—the hospital saves one week of penalty *and* indirect costs, or $28,000. For reductions beyond week 65, the savings are only the weekly indirect costs of $8,000.

In determining the **minimum-cost schedule**, we start with the normal time schedule and crash activities along the critical path, whose length equals the length of the project.

We want to determine how much we can add in crash costs without exceeding the savings in indirect and penalty costs. The procedure involves the following steps:

Step 1. Determine the project's critical path(s).

Step 2. Find the activity or activities on the critical path(s) with the lowest cost of crashing per week.

Step 3. Reduce the time for this activity until (a) it cannot be further reduced, (b) another path becomes critical, or (c) the increase in direct costs exceeds the savings that result from shortening the project. If more than one path is critical, the time for an activity on each path may have to be reduced simultaneously.

Step 4. Repeat this procedure until the increase in direct costs is larger than the savings generated by shortening the project.

| EXAMPLE 4.5 | *Finding a Minimum Cost Schedule* |

Determine the minimum-cost schedule for the St. Adolf's Hospital project. Use the information in Table 4.1 and Figure 4.7.

SOLUTION

The projected completion time of the project is 69 weeks. The project costs for that schedule are $1,992,000 in direct costs, 69($8,000) = $552,000 in indirect costs, and (69 − 65)($20,000) = $80,000 in penalty costs, for total project costs of $2,624,000. The five paths in the network have the following normal times.

A–I–K:	33 weeks	B–D–H–J–K:	69 weeks
A–F–K:	28 weeks	B–E–J–K:	43 weeks
A–C–G–J–K:	67 weeks		

It will simplify our analysis if we can eliminate some paths from further consideration. If all activities on A–C–G–J–K were crashed, the path duration would be 47 weeks. Crashing all activities on B–D–H–J–K results in a duration of 56 weeks. Because the *normal* times of A–I–K, A–F–K, and B–E–J–K are less than the minimum times of the other two paths, we can disregard those three paths; they will never become critical regardless of the crashing we may do.

Stage 1

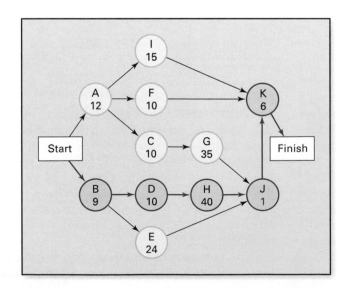

Step 1. The critical path is B–D–H–J–K.

Step 2. The cheapest activity to crash per week is J at $1,000, which is much less than the savings in indirect and penalty costs of $28,000 per week.

Step 3. Crash activity J by its limit of 3 weeks because the critical path remains unchanged. The new expected path times are

A–C–G–J–K: 64 weeks   B–D–H–J–K: 66 weeks

The net savings are 3($28,000) − 3($1,000) = $81,000. The total project costs are now $2,624,000 − $81,000 = $2,543,000.

Stage 2

Step 1. The critical path is still B–D–H–J–K.

Step 2. The cheapest activity to crash per week now is D at $2,000.

Step 3. Crash D by two weeks. The first week of reduction in activity D saves $28,000 because it eliminates a week of penalty costs, as well as indirect costs. Crashing D by a second week saves only $8,000 in indirect costs because, after week 65, there are no more penalty costs. These savings still exceed the cost of crashing D by 2 weeks. Updated path times are

A–C–G–J–K: 64 weeks   B–D–H–J–K: 64 weeks

The net savings are $28,000 + $8,000 − 2($2,000) = $32,000. Total project costs are now $2,543,000 − $32,000 = $2,511,000.

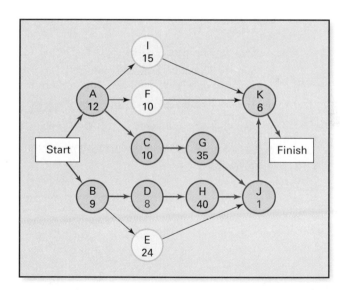

Stage 3

Step 1. After crashing D, we now have two critical paths. *Both* critical paths must now be shortened to realize any savings in indirect project costs. If one is shortened and the other is not, the length of the project remains unchanged.

Step 2. Our alternatives are to crash one of the following combinations of activities—(A, B), (A, H), (C, B), (C, H), (G, B), (G, H)—or to crash activity K, which is on both critical paths (J has already been crashed). We consider only those alternatives for which the cost of crashing is less than the potential savings of $8,000 per week. The only viable alternatives are (C, B) at a cost of $7,600 per week and K at $4,000 per week. We choose activity K to crash.

Step 3. We crash activity K to the greatest extent possible—a reduction of 1 week—because it is on both critical paths. Updated path times are

A–C–G–J–K: 63 weeks   B–D–H–J–K: 63 weeks

The net savings are $8,000 − $4,000 = $4,000. Total project costs are $2,511,000 − $4,000 = $2,507,000.

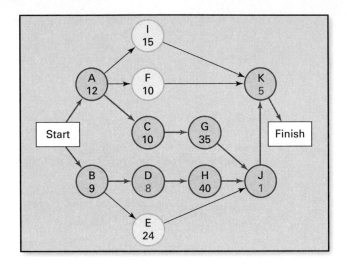

Stage 4

Step 1. The critical paths are B–D–H–J–K and A–C–G–J–K.

Step 2. The only viable alternative at this stage is to crash activities B and C simultaneously at a cost of $7,600 per week. This amount is still less than the savings of $8,000 per week.

Step 3. Crash activities B and C by 2 weeks, the limit for activity B. Updated path times are

A–C–G–J–K: 61 weeks   B–D–H–J–K: 61 weeks

Net savings are 2($8,000) − 2($7,600) = $800. Total project costs are $2,507,000 − $800 = $2,506,200.

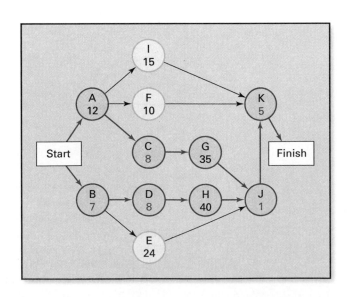

Decision Point Because the crash costs exceed weekly indirect costs, any other combination of activities will result in a net increase in total project costs. The minimum-cost schedule is 61 weeks, with a total cost of $2,506,200. To obtain this schedule, the project team must crash activities B, D, J, and K to their limits and activity C to 8 weeks. The other activities remain at their normal times. This schedule costs $117,800 less than the normal-time schedule. ▢

ASSESSING RISKS

Risk is a measure of the probability and consequence of not reaching a defined project goal. Risk involves the notion of uncertainty as it relates to project timing and costs. Often, project teams must deal with uncertainty caused by labor shortages, weather, supply delays, or the outcomes of critical tests. A major responsibility of the project manager at the start of a project is to develop a *risk-management plan*. Team members should have an opportunity to describe the key risks to the project's success and prescribe ways to circumvent them, either by redefining key activities or by developing contingency plans in the event problems occur. A good risk-management plan will quantify the risks and predict their impact on the project. For each risk, the outcome is either acceptable or unacceptable, depending on the project manager's tolerance level for risk.

The following Big Picture describes some of the uncertainties in activity times that may affect a major project.

THE BIG PICTURE: Coors Field Baseball Stadium Project

Play ball! is a familiar call in the spring, and the people of Denver, Colorado, wanted to hear those words directed at their own National League baseball team. The Denver Metropolitan Major League Baseball Stadium District, a political subdivision of the state, was created by the Colorado Legislature in June 1989. It was given the authority and responsibility to promote the acquisition of a major league franchise and develop a baseball stadium. A key requirement of the National League for granting a franchise is that the community either have a state-of-the-art ballpark dedicated to baseball or commit to building one. One of the first challenges, then, was to secure from the community a financial commitment to build a new stadium.

The district prepared a financial plan and recommended using a sales tax levy contingent on the awarding of a baseball franchise. After the sales tax had been approved by the voters, the district entered into an agreement with the Colorado Baseball Partnership (team ownership group), which provided for building a state-of-the-art ballpark if the partnership succeeded in procuring a franchise. The partnership then proceeded with the application for the franchise. At the same time, the district proceeded with site selection.

On July 5, 1991, the National League approved the partnership's application for the Colorado Rockies baseball franchise, allowing the district to initiate the tax levy, purchase the land, and proceed with the development of Coors Field. The Big Picture illustration on the next two-page spread shows the layout of the Stadium Complex. The Colorado Rockies began competition in April 1993, initially playing their games in Denver's Mile High Stadium. On such a complex project, it is normal to develop a schedule of milestones at the beginning of the project to provide a framework for managing it. As the project proceeded and additional tasks become known, more detailed schedules were developed. Scheduling techniques such as CPM were important tools

THE BIG PICTURE   COORS FIELD

Construction of the ballpark required 57,000 cubic yards of concrete, 700,000 masonry blocks, 1,400,000 bricks, and 9000 tons of steel. Before construction could begin, quantities of these materials had to be estimated, suppliers selected, and delivery schedules determined. Quantities and schedules then had to be changed when the seating capacity was increased. Construction started in October 1992 and was completed in March 1995.

Seating (A). From the start in 1993, attendance figures at the Colorado Rockies games at Mile High Stadium consistently surpassed expectations, with average crowds of over 57,000 fans per game exceeding the seating capacity of 43,000 planned for Coors Field. The seating capacity was increased by 500, then by 1500, and finally by another 5000 one year after construction began on the stadium, resulting in a total of over 50,000 seats. The final design called for 18,300 seats in the main concourse, 3200 in left field, 2300 in center field, 2600 in right field, 18,500 in the upper deck, 4400 in the club mezzanine, and 700 in the suites. Included in these figures are 500 wheelchair seats with 500 companion seats and 500 seats without arms for disabled fans.

The Playing Field (B). Creating the playing field involved a number of sequential steps. Once the site had been excavated, 10,000 feet of drainage pipes were positioned throughout the site and 3000 tons of pea gravel spread on top to improve drainage. The pipes can drain 5 inches of rain an hour. The 3-acre playing field was made from 6000 tons of sand in an organic peat growing mixture. Forty-five miles of wire were installed beneath the surface to lengthen the growing season of the turf. The sod, a bluegrass/ryegrass blend, was planted at a turf farm in June 1993 and transplanted to Coors Field in October 1994.

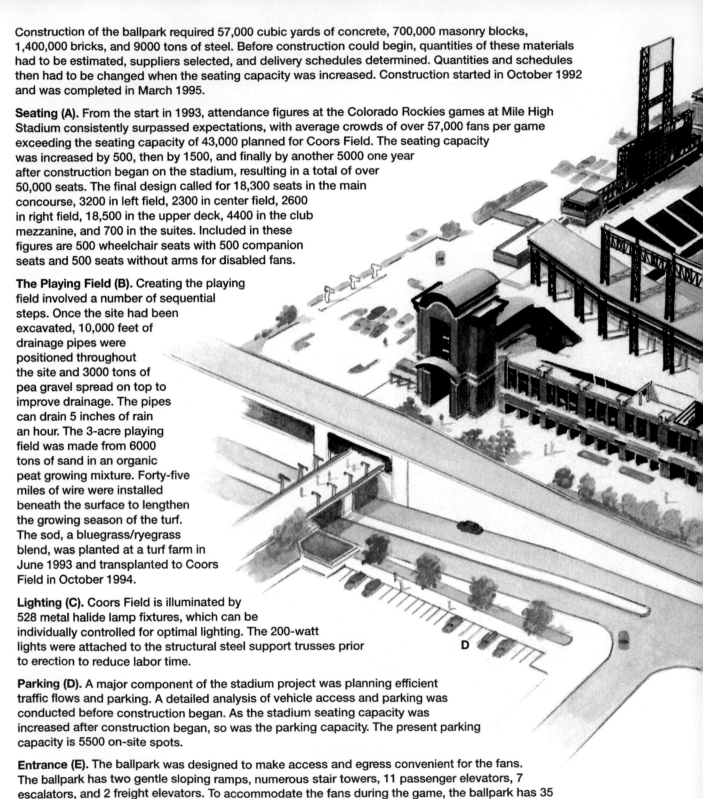

Lighting (C). Coors Field is illuminated by 528 metal halide lamp fixtures, which can be individually controlled for optimal lighting. The 200-watt lights were attached to the structural steel support trusses prior to erection to reduce labor time.

Parking (D). A major component of the stadium project was planning efficient traffic flows and parking. A detailed analysis of vehicle access and parking was conducted before construction began. As the stadium seating capacity was increased after construction began, so was the parking capacity. The present parking capacity is 5500 on-site spots.

Entrance (E). The ballpark was designed to make access and egress convenient for the fans. The ballpark has two gentle sloping ramps, numerous stair towers, 11 passenger elevators, 7 escalators, and 2 freight elevators. To accommodate the fans during the game, the ballpark has 35 separate concession stands, numerous portable stands, 35 women's restrooms, 31 men's restrooms, and 8 family restrooms.

used by the project team to manage change. Following is a list of the major milestones in the project:

June 2, 1989	District legislation becomes effective
May 10, 1990	Architect selected
May 15, 1990	Request for proposals for site selection
July 11, 1990	Plan for finance prepared
August 14, 1990	Sales tax election—voters approve tax
September 1, 1990	National League deadline for franchise applications
September 18, 1990	Colorado delegation presentation to National League in New York
March 13, 1991	Lower downtown site selected
March 26, 1991	National League selection committee visit to Denver
July 5, 1991	National League awards franchise to Colorado Baseball Partnership, 1993, Ltd.
December 31, 1991	Largest portion of land purchased
February 13, 1992	Final lease negotiations start
April 1, 1992	Schematic design of ballpark starts
April 21, 1992	Contractor selected
October 8, 1992	Architect presents exterior elevations of ballpark to the public
October 16, 1992	Constructions starts
November 11, 1992	Satellite site location of home plate
November 30, 1992	Mass excavation commences
February 2, 1993	Agreement on final terms of lease
February 15, 1993	Caissons and foundation start
June 8, 1993	Playing field turf planted at a farm in northeastern Colorado
July 14, 1993	Last parcel of land purchased
September 24, 1993	First steel raised
October 6, 1993	Final seating capacity set
March 11, 1994	First bricks placed
September 19, 1994	Scoreboard installed
October 25, 1994	Sod transplanted to playing field
February 27, 1995	Sports lighting turned on at night
March 31, 1995	Field ready for opening day

Construction of the stadium started on October 16, 1992. One of the techniques the contractor used to help manage the progress of the thousands of construction activities was the critical path method (CPM). However, planned start times and the durations of many construction activities had to be altered because of nonconstruction-related occurrences. For example, land acquisition took longer than anticipated because one property owner refused to sell a parcel of land on the site slated to become the home-plate entrance to the stadium. Consequently, construction had to begin out of sequence in order to maintain construction progress and avoid changing the scheduled completion date. In addition, owing to the enthusiastic response of baseball fans to the Colorado Rockies, the district altered its estimates of needed seating capacity three times before finally settling on 50,000. Each change required a design modification, which then caused a change in construction activities. Eventually, the stadium took 29 months to construct and cost more than $215.5 million.

To ensure community input on key components of project design, District Executive Director John Lehigh and his team held regular meetings with six different citizen advisory committees representing traffic and transportation, stadium design, handicapped person accessibility, ballpark operations, environmental concerns, art and decorations, media access, and neighborhood interests and concerns. These meetings generated numerous recommendations, to which the project design team responded during the project. For example, neighborhood residents' concerns about the stadium location prompted extensive parking and traffic studies, resulting in a traffic-management plan that helped mitigate concerns. The results were good. On April 26, 1995, the citizens of Denver watched the Colorado Rockies beat the New York Mets in what has been billed as the finest ballpark in the major leagues.

PERT/CPM networks can be used to quantify risks associated with project timing. Often, the uncertainty associated with an activity can be reflected in the activity's time duration. For example, an activity in a new product development project might be developing the enabling technology to manufacture it, an activity that may take from eight months to a year. To incorporate uncertainty into the network model, probability distributions of activity times can be used. There are two approaches: computer simulation and statistical analysis. With simulation, the time for each activity is randomly chosen from its probability distribution (see the Simulation supplement). The critical path of the network is determined and the completion date of the project computed. The procedure is repeated many times, which results in a probability distribution for the completion date. See the Simulation Exercises section at the end of this chapter for examples of how simulation can be used to incorporate uncertainty in a project network.

The statistical analysis approach requires that activity times be stated in terms of three reasonable time estimates:

1. The **optimistic time** (a) is the shortest time in which the activity can be completed, if all goes exceptionally well.
2. The **most likely time** (m) is the probable time required to perform the activity.
3. The **pessimistic time** (b) is the longest estimated time required to perform the activity.

In the remainder of this section, we will discuss how to calculate activity statistics using these three time estimates and how to analyze project risk using probabilities.

CALCULATING TIME STATISTICS. With three time estimates—the optimistic, most likely, and pessimistic—the project manager has enough information to estimate the probability that an activity will be completed on schedule. To do so, the project manager must first calculate the mean and variance of a probability distribution for each activity. In PERT/CPM, each activity time is treated as though it were a random variable derived from a beta probability distribution. This distribution can have various shapes, allowing the most likely time estimate (m) to fall anywhere between the pessimistic (b) and optimistic (a) time estimates. The most likely time estimate is the *mode* of the beta distribution, or the time with the highest probability of occurrence. This condition is not possible with the normal distribution, which is symmetrical, because the normal distribution requires the mode to be equidistant from the end points of the distribution. Figure 4.11 shows the difference between the two distributions.

(margin notes)

How can uncertainty in time estimates be incorporated into project planning?

optimistic time The shortest time in which an activity can be completed, if all goes exceptionally well.

most likely time The probable time required to perform an activity.

pessimistic time The longest estimated time required to perform an activity.

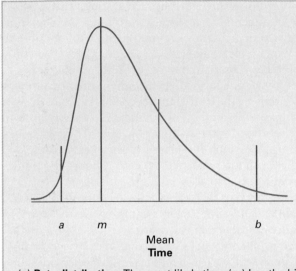

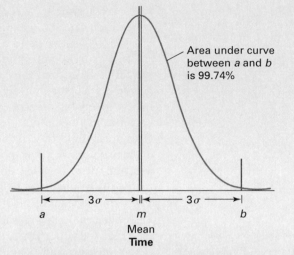

Area under curve
between *a* and *b*
is 99.74%

(a) **Beta distribution:** The most likely time (*m*) has the highest probability and can be placed anywhere between the optimistic (*a*) and pessimistic (*b*) times.

(b) **Normal distribution:** The mean and most likely times must be the same. If *a* and *b* are chosen to be 6σ apart, there is a 99.74 percent chance that the actual activity time will fall between them.

FIGURE 4.11

Differences Between Beta and Normal Distributions for Project Analysis

Two other key assumptions are required. First, we assume that *a*, *m*, and *b* can be estimated accurately. The estimates might best be considered values that define a reasonable time range for the activity duration negotiated between the project manager and the team members responsible for the activities. Second, we assume that the standard deviation, σ, of the activity time is one-sixth the range $b - a$. Thus, the chance that actual activity times will fall between *a* and *b* is high. Why does this assumption make sense? If the activity time followed the normal distribution, six standard deviations would span approximately 99.74 percent of the normal distribution.

Even with these assumptions, derivation of the mean and variance of each activity's probability distribution is complex. These derivations show that the mean of the beta distribution can be estimated by using the following weighted average of the three time estimates:

$$t_e = \frac{a + 4m + b}{6}$$

Note that the most likely time has four times the weight of the pessimistic and optimistic estimates.

The variance of the beta distribution for each activity is

$$\sigma^2 = \left(\frac{b - a}{6} \right)^2$$

The variance, which is the standard deviation squared, increases as the difference between *b* and *a* increases. This result implies that the less certain a person is in estimating the actual time for an activity, the greater will be the variance.

EXAMPLE 4.6   *Calculating Means and Variances*

Suppose that the project team has arrived at the following time estimates for activity B (site selection and survey) of the hospital project:

$a = 7$ weeks, $m = 8$ weeks,   and $b = 15$ weeks

a. Calculate the expected time for activity B and the variance.

b. Calculate the expected time and variance for the other activities in the project.

SOLUTION

a. The expected time for activity B is

$$t_e = \frac{7 + 4(8) + 15}{6} = \frac{54}{6} = 9 \text{ weeks}$$

Note that the expected time (9 weeks) does not equal the most likely time (8 weeks) for this activity. These times will be the same only when the most likely time is equidistant from the optimistic and pessimistic times. We calculate the variance for activity B as

$$\sigma^2 = \left(\frac{15 - 7}{6}\right)^2 = \left(\frac{8}{6}\right)^2 = 1.78$$

b. The following table shows expected activity times and variances for the activities listed in the project description.

ACTIVITY	TIME ESTIMATES (wk)			ACTIVITY STATISTICS	
	Optimistic (a)	Most Likely (m)	Pessimistic (b)	Expected Time (t_e)	Variance (σ^2)
A	11	12	13	12	0.11
B	7	8	15	9	1.78
C	5	10	15	10	2.78
D	8	9	16	10	1.78
E	14	25	30	24	7.11
F	6	9	18	10	4.00
G	25	36	41	35	7.11
H	35	40	45	40	2.78
I	10	13	28	15	9.00
J	1	2	15	4	5.44
K	5	6	7	6	0.11

Decision Point The project team should notice that the greatest uncertainty lies in the time estimate for activity I, followed by the estimates for activities E and G. These activities should be analyzed for the source of the uncertainties and actions should be taken to reduce the variance in the time estimates. For example, activity I, developing an information system, may entail the use of a consulting firm. The availability of the consulting firm for the time period scheduled for activity I may be in doubt because of the firm's other commitments. To reduce the risk of delay in the project, the project team could explore the availability of other reputable firms or scale down the requirements for the information system and undertake much of that activity themselves. ▢

ANALYZING PROBABILITIES. Because time estimates for activities involve uncertainty, project managers are interested in determining the probability of meeting project completion deadlines. To develop the probability distribution for project completion time, we assume that the duration time of one activity does not depend on that of any other activity. This assumption enables us to estimate the mean and variance of the probability distribution of the time duration of the entire project by summing the duration times and variances of the activities along the critical path. However, if one work crew is assigned two activities that can be done at the same time, the activity times will be interdependent. In addition, if other paths in the network have small amounts of slack, one of them might become the critical path before the project is completed. In such a case, we should calculate a probability distribution for those paths.

Because of the assumption that the activity duration times are independent random variables, we can make use of the central limit theorem, which states that the sum of a group of independent, identically distributed random variables approaches a normal distribution as the number of random variables increases. The mean of the normal distribution is the sum of the expected activity times on the path. In the case of the critical path, it is the earliest expected finish time for the project:

$$T_E = \Sigma \text{ (Activity times on the critical path)} = \text{Mean of normal distribution}$$

Similarly, because of the assumption of activity time independence, we use the sum of the variances of the activities along the path as the variance of the time distribution for that path. That is,

$$\sigma^2 = \Sigma \text{ (Variances of activities on the critical path)}$$

To analyze probabilities of completing a project by a certain date using the normal distribution, we use the *z*-transformation formula:

$$z = \frac{T - T_E}{\sqrt{\sigma^2}}$$

where

$$T = \text{due date for the project}$$

$$T_E = \text{earliest expected completion date for the project}$$

The procedure for assessing the probability of completing any activity in a project by a specific date is similar to the one just discussed. However, instead of the critical path, we would use the longest time path of activities from the start node to the activity node in question.

EXAMPLE 4.7 | *Calculating the Probability of Completing a Project by a Given Date*

Calculate the probability that St. Adolf's Hospital will become operational in 72 weeks, using (a) the critical path and (b) path A–C–G–J–K.

SOLUTION

a. The critical path B–D–H–J–K has a length of 69 weeks. From the table in Example 4.6, we obtain the variance of path B–D–H–J–K: $\sigma^2 = 1.78 + 1.78 + 2.78 + 5.44 + 0.11 = 11.89$. Next, we calculate the *z*-value:

$$z = \frac{72 - 69}{\sqrt{11.89}} = \frac{3}{3.45} = 0.87$$

Using the Normal Distribution appendix, we find that the probability is about 0.81 that the length of path B–D–H–J–K will be no greater than 72 weeks. Because this path is the critical path, there is a 19-percent probability that the project will take longer than 72 weeks. This probability is shown graphically in Figure 4.12.

b. From the table in Example 4.6 (p. 167), we determine that the sum of the activity times on path A–C–G–J–K is 67 weeks and that $\sigma^2 = 0.11 + 2.78 + 7.11 + 5.44 + 0.11 = 15.55$. The *z*-value is

$$z = \frac{72 - 67}{\sqrt{15.55}} = \frac{5}{3.94} = 1.27$$

The probability is about 0.90 that the length of path A–C–G–J–K will be no greater than 72 weeks.

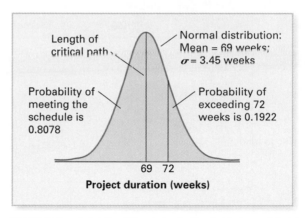

FIGURE 4.12 • Probability of Completing the Hospital Project on Schedule

Decision Point The project team should be aware that there is a 10-percent chance that path A–C–G–J–K will cause a delay in the project. Although the probability is not high for that path, activities A, C, and G bear watching during the first 57 weeks of the project to make sure that there is no more than 2 weeks of slippage in their schedules. This is especially true for activity G, which has a high time variance. ◻

MONITORING AND CONTROLLING PROJECTS

Once project planning is over, the challenge becomes keeping the project on schedule within the budget of allocated resources. In this section, we discuss how to monitor project status and resource usage. In addition, we identify the features of project management software useful for monitoring and controlling projects.

MONITORING PROJECT STATUS

A good tracking system will help the project team accomplish its project goals. Often, the very task of monitoring project progress motivates the team as it sees the benefits of its planning efforts come to fruition. It also focuses attention on the decisions that must be made as the project unfolds. Effective tracking systems collect information on three topics: open issues, risks, and schedule status.

OPEN ISSUES AND RISKS. One of the duties of the project manager is to make sure that issues that have been raised during the project actually get resolved in a timely fashion. The tracking system should remind the project manager of due dates for open issues and who was responsible for seeing that they are resolved. Likewise, it should provide the status of each risk to project delays specified in the risk-management plan so that the team can review them at each meeting. The project manager should also enter new issues or risks into the system as they arise. To be effective, the tracking system requires team members periodically to update information regarding their respective responsibilities. Although the tracking system can be computerized, it can also be as simple as using e-mail, voice mail, or meetings to convey the necessary information.

SCHEDULE STATUS. Even the best laid project plans can go awry. Monitoring slack time in the project schedule can help the project manager control activities along the critical

TABLE 4.2	Activity	Duration	Earliest Start	Latest Start	Slack
	C	10	16	14	−2
Slack Calculations After	G	35	26	24	−2
Activities A and B Have	J	4	61	59	−2
Been Completed	K	6	65	63	−2
	D	10	10	9	−1
	H	40	20	19	−1
	E	24	10	35	25
	I	15	16	48	32
	F	10	16	53	37

path. Suppose in the hospital project that activity A is completed in 16 weeks rather than the anticipated 12 weeks and that activity B takes 10 weeks instead of the expected 9 weeks. Table 4.2 shows how these delays affect slack times as of the sixteenth week of the project. Activities A and B are not shown because they have already been completed.

Negative slack occurs when the assumptions used to compute planned slack are invalid. Activities C, G, J, and K, which depend on the timely completion of activities A and B, show negative slack because they have been pushed beyond their planned latest start dates. The activities at the top of Table 4.2 are more critical than those at the bottom because they are the furthest behind schedule and affect the completion time of the entire project. To meet the original completion target of week 69, the project manager must try to make up two weeks of time somewhere along path C–G–J–K. Moreover, one week will have to be made up along path D–H. If that time is made up, there will be two critical paths: C–G–J–K and D–H–J–K. Many project managers work with computer scheduling programs that generate slack reports like the one shown in Table 4.2.

MONITORING PROJECT RESOURCES

The resources allocated to a project are consumed at an uneven rate that is a function of the timing of the schedules for the project's activities. Projects have a *life cycle* that consists of four major phases: definition and organization, planning, execution, and close out. Figure 4.13 shows that each of the four phases requires different resource commitments.

We have already discussed the activities associated with the project definition and organization and project planning phases. The phase that takes the most resources is the *execution phase,* during which managers focus on activities pertaining to deliverables. The project schedule becomes very important because it shows when each resource devoted to a given activity will be required. Monitoring the progress of activities throughout the project is important in order to avoid potential overloading of resources. Problems arise when a specific resource, such as a construction crew or staff specialist, is required on several activities with overlapping schedules. Project managers have several options to alleviate resource problems, including:

❐ *Resource leveling,* which is an attempt to reduce the peaks and valleys in resource needs by shifting the schedules of conflicting activities within their earliest and latest start dates. If an activity must be delayed beyond its latest start date, the completion date of the total project will be delayed unless activities on the critical path can be reduced to compensate. The crashing techniques we discussed in the cost–time trade-off section of this chapter might

FIGURE 4.13

Project Life Cycle

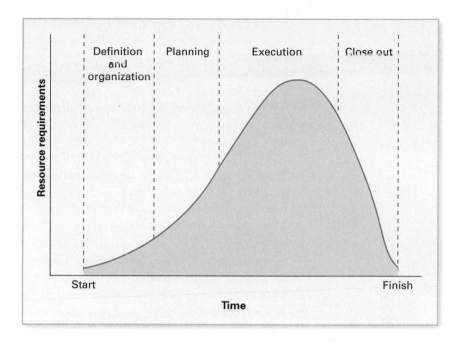

help to bring the schedule back on track, but there is the possibility of added costs to consider.

❑ *Resource allocation,* which is an attempt to shift resources from activities with slack to those on the critical path where resources are overloaded. A slack report such as the one in Table 4.2 identifies potential candidates for resource shifting. However, efficiency can be compromised if shifted employees do not have all the skills required for their new assignments.

❑ *Resource acquisition,* which simply adds more of an overloaded resource to maintain the schedule of an activity.

The project *close out* is an activity that many project managers forget to include in their consideration of resource usage. The purpose of this final phase in the project life cycle is to write final reports and complete remaining deliverables. A very important aspect of this phase, however, is compiling the team's recommendations for improving the project process of which they were a part. Many team members will be assigned to other projects where they can apply what they learned.

PROJECT MANAGEMENT SOFTWARE

Project management software is accessible to most organizations and is being used extensively in government, services, and manufacturing. Ford Motor Company used computerized network planning for retooling assembly lines, and Chrysler Corporation used it for building a new assembly plant. Other users include the San Francisco Opera Association, the Walt Disney Company, and Procter & Gamble.

Bechtel Group, Inc., had to purchase a sophisticated software package because of the complexity of its scheduling problems. However, with the advent of personal computers, "off-the-shelf" project management software has become accessible to many companies. Large as well as small projects are routinely managed with the assistance of standard computerized scheduling packages. Software costs have come down, and user–computer interfaces are friendly. Standard software programs may differ in terms of their output reports and may include one or more of the following capabilities:

❐ *Gantt Charts and PERT/CPM Diagrams.*   The graphics capabilities of software packages allow for visual displays of project progress on Gantt charts and PERT/CPM network diagrams. Most packages allow the user to display portions of the network on the video monitor to analyze specific problems.

❐ *Project Status and Summary Reports.*   These reports include budget variance reports that compare planned to actual expenses at any stage in the project, resource histograms that graphically display the usage of a particular resource over time, status reports for each worker by task performed, and summary reports that indicate project progress to top management.

❐ *Tracking Reports.*   These reports identify areas of concern such as the percent of activity completion with respect to time, budget, or labor resources. Most software packages allow multiple projects to be tracked at the same time. This feature is important when resources must be shared jointly by several projects.

❐ *Project Calendar.*   This feature allows the project manager to lay out calendars based on actual workdays, weekends, and vacations and enables the software to present all schedules and reports in terms of the project calendar.

❐ *What-If Analysis.*   Some packages allow the project manager to enter proposed changes to activity times, precedence relationships, or start dates in order to see what effect the changes might have on the project completion date.

Today there are more than 200 software packages, most of which are user friendly and available for the PC.

MANAGING PROJECT PROCESSES ACROSS THE ORGANIZATION

Projects are big and small. They are contained within a single department or cut across several departments. Many organizations have several projects ongoing at any one time, addressing issues of concern to finance, marketing, accounting, human resources, information systems, or operations. Regardless of the scope, projects are completed with the use of a project process. The size of the project team may be small, and the need for project management software marginal, but successful projects will use the principles we discussed in this chapter regardless of the discipline the project addresses.

The applicability of project processes is pervasive across all types of organizations and disciplines. Managers often find themselves working with counterparts from other departments. For example, consider a project to develop a corporate database at a bank. Because no department knows exactly what services a customer is receiving from the other departments, the project will consolidate information about corporate customers from many areas of the bank into one corporate database. From this information corporate banking services could be designed not only to better serve the corporate customers but to provide a basis for evaluating the prices that the bank charges. Marketing is interested in knowing all the services a customer is receiving so that it can package and sell other services that the customer may not be aware of. Finance is interested in how "profitable" a customer is to the bank and whether provided services are appropriately priced. The project team should consist of representatives from marketing, the finance departments with a direct interest in corporate clients, and management information systems. Projects such as this one are becoming more common as companies take advantage of the Internet to provide services and products directly to the customer.

FORMULA REVIEW

1. Start and finish times:

   ES = max [EF times of all activities immediately preceding activity]
   EF = ES + t
   LS = LF − t
   LF = min [LS times of all activities immediately following activity]

2. Activity slack:

   S = LS − ES   or S = LF − EF

3. Project costs:

   $$\text{Crash cost per unit of time} = \frac{\text{Crash cost} - \text{Normal cost}}{\text{Normal time} - \text{Crash time}} = \frac{\text{CC} - \text{NC}}{\text{NT} - \text{CT}}$$

4. Activity time statistics:

   $$t_e = \frac{a + 4m + b}{6} \quad \text{(expected activity time)}$$

   $$\sigma^2 = \left(\frac{b - a}{6}\right)^2 \quad \text{(variance)}$$

5. z-transformation formula:

   $$z = \frac{T - T_E}{\sqrt{\sigma^2}}$$

   where

   T = due date for the project
   $T_E = \Sigma$ (expected activity times on the critical path)
      = mean of normal distribution
   $\sigma^2 = \Sigma$ (variances of activities on the critical path)

CHAPTER HIGHLIGHTS

❐ A project is an interrelated set of activities that often transcends functional boundaries. A project process is the organization and management of the resources dedicated to completing a project. Managing project processes involves defining and organizing, planning, and monitoring and controlling the project.

❐ Project planning involves defining the work breakdown structure, diagramming the network, developing a schedule, analyzing cost–time trade-offs, and assessing risks.

❐ Project planning and scheduling focuses on the critical path: the sequence of activities requiring the greatest cumulative amount of time for completion. Delay in critical activities will delay the entire project.

❐ Risks associated with the completion of activities on schedule can be incorporated in project networks by recognizing three time estimates for each activity and then calculating expected activity times and variances. The probability of completing the schedule by a certain date can be computed with this information.

❐ Cost–time trade-offs can be analyzed with network planning methods such as PERT/CPM under the assumption of linear marginal costs.

❐ Monitoring and controlling the project involves the use of activity-time slack reports and reports on actual resource usage. Overloads on certain resources can be rectified by resource leveling, allocation, or acquisition.

KEY TERMS

activity 143
activity-on-arc (AOA) network 144
activity-on-node (AON) network 144
activity slack 149
crash cost (CC) 155
crash time (CT) 155
critical path 149
critical path method (CPM) 144
earliest finish time (EF) 150
earliest start time (ES) 150

event 144
free slack 154
Gantt Chart 153
latest finish time (LF) 151
latest start time (LS) 151
minimum-cost schedule 157
most likely time (m) 165
network diagram 143
normal cost (NC) 155
normal time (NT) 155

optimistic time (a) 165
path 149
pessimistic time (b) 165
precedence relationship 144
program evaluation and review
    technique (PERT) 144
project 140
total slack 154
work breakdown structure (WBS) 143

SOLVED PROBLEM 1

Your company has just received an order from a good customer for a specially designed electric motor. The contract states that, starting on the thirteenth day from now, your firm will experience a penalty of $100 per day until the job is completed. Indirect project costs amount to $200 per day. The data on direct costs and activity precedence relationships are given in Table 4.3.

						TABLE 4.3 *Electric Motor Project Data*				
ACTIVITY	NORMAL TIME (DAYS)	NORMAL COST ($)	CRASH TIME (DAYS)	CRASH COST ($)	IMMEDIATE PREDECESSOR(S)
A	4	1,000	3	1,300	None
B	7	1,400	4	2,000	None
C	5	2,000	4	2,700	None
D	6	1,200	5	1,400	A
E	3	900	2	1,100	B
F	11	2,500	6	3,750	C
G	4	800	3	1,450	D, E
H	3	300	1	500	F, G

a. Draw the project network diagram.

b. What completion date would you recommend?

SOLUTION

a. The AON network diagram, including normal activity times, for this procedure is shown in Figure 4.14. Keep the following points in mind while constructing a network diagram.

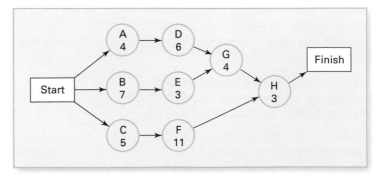

FIGURE 4.14 • AON Diagram for the Electric Motor Project

❑ Always have start and finish nodes.
❑ Try to avoid crossing paths to keep the diagram simple.
❑ Use only one arrow to directly connect any two nodes.
❑ Put the activities with no predecessors at the left and point the arrows from left to right.
❑ Use scratch paper and be prepared to revise the diagram several times before you come up with a correct and uncluttered diagram.

b. With these activity durations, the project will be completed in 19 days and incur a $700 penalty. Determining a good completion date requires the use of the minimum-cost schedule procedure. Using the data in Table 4.3; you can determine the maximum crash-time reduction and crash cost per day for each activity. For example, for activity A:

$$\text{Maximum crash time} = \text{Normal time} - \text{Crash time} = 4 \text{ days} - 3 \text{ days} = 1 \text{ day}$$

$$\frac{\text{Crash cost}}{\text{per day}} = \frac{\text{Crash cost} - \text{Normal cost}}{\text{Normal time} - \text{Crash time}} = \frac{CC - NC}{NT - CT} = \frac{\$1,300 - \$1,000}{4 \text{ days} - 3 \text{ days}} = \$300$$

ACTIVITY	CRASH COST PER DAY ($)	MAXIMUM TIME REDUCTION (DAYS)
A	300	1
B	200	3
C	700	1
D	200	1
E	200	1
F	250	5
G	650	1
H	100	2

Table 4.4 summarizes the analysis and the resultant project duration and total cost. The critical path is C–F–H at 19 days—the longest path in the network. The cheapest of these activities to crash is H, which costs only an extra $100 per day to crash. Doing so saves $200 + $100 = $300 per day in indirect and penalty costs. If you crash this activity two days (the maximum), the lengths of the paths are now

A–D–G–H: 15 days   B–E–G–H: 15 days   C–F–H: 17 days

The critical path is still C–F–H. The next cheapest critical activity to crash is F at $250 per day. You can crash F only two days because at that point you will have three critical paths. Further reductions in project duration will require simultaneous crashing of more than one activity (D, E, and F). The cost to do so, $650, exceeds the savings, $300. Consequently, you should stop. Note that every activity is critical. The project costs are minimized when the completion date is day 15. However, there may be some goodwill costs associated with disappointing a customer who wants delivery in 12 days.

TABLE 4.4 *Project Cost Analysis*

STAGE	CRASH ACTIVITY	RESULTING CRITICAL PATH(S)	TIME REDUCTION (DAYS)	PROJECT DURATION (DAYS)	PROJECT DIRECT COSTS, LAST TRIAL	CRASH COST ADDED	TOTAL INDIRECT COSTS	TOTAL PENALTY COSTS	TOTAL PROJECT COSTS
0	—	C–F–H	—	19	$10,100	—	$3,800	$700	$14,600
1	H	C–F–H	2	17	$10,100	$200	$3,400	$500	$14,200
2	F	A–D–G–H B–E–G–H C–F–H	2	15	$10,300	$500	$3,000	$300	$14,100

SOLVED PROBLEM 2

An advertising project manager has developed the network diagrams shown in Figure 4.15 for a new advertising campaign. In addition, the manager has gathered the time information for each activity, as shown in the accompanying table.

ACTIVITY	TIME ESTIMATES (wk)			IMMEDIATE PREDECESSOR(S)
	Optimistic	Most Likely	Pessimistic	
A	1	4	7	—
B	2	6	7	—
C	3	3	6	B
D	6	13	14	A
E	3	6	12	A, C
F	6	8	16	B
G	1	5	6	E, F

a. Calculate the expected time and variance for each activity.

b. Calculate the activity slacks and determine the critical path using the expected activity times.

c. What is the probability of completing the project within 23 weeks?

SOLUTION

a. The expected time for each activity is calculated as follows:

$$t_e = \frac{a + 4m + b}{6}$$

ACTIVITY	EXPECTED TIME (wk)	VARIANCE
A	4.0	1.00
B	5.5	0.69
C	3.5	0.25
D	12.0	1.78
E	6.5	2.25
F	9.0	2.78
G	4.5	0.69

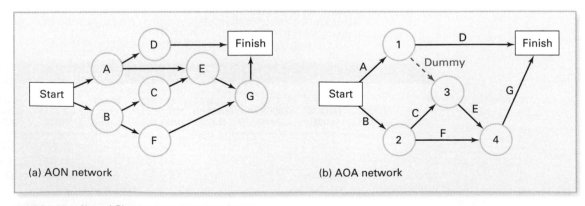

(a) AON network

(b) AOA network

FIGURE 4.15 • Network Diagrams for an Advertising Program

b. We need to calculate the earliest start, latest start, earliest finish, and latest finish times for each activity. Starting with activities A and B, we proceed from the beginning of the network and move to the end, calculating the earliest start and finish times:

ACTIVITY	EARLIEST START (wk)	EARLIEST FINISH (wk)
A	0	0 + 4.0 = 4.0
B	0	0 + 5.5 = 5.5
C	5.5	5.5 + 3.5 = 9.0
D	4.0	4.0 + 12.0 = 16.0
E	9.0	9.0 + 6.5 = 15.5
F	5.5	5.5 + 9.0 = 14.5
G	15.5	15.5 + 4.5 = 20.0

Based on expected times, the earliest finish for the project is week 20, when activity G has been completed. Using that as a target date, we can work backward through the network, calculating the latest start and finish times (shown graphically in Figure 4.16):

ACTIVITY	LATEST START (wk)	LATEST FINISH (wk)
G	15.5	20.0
F	6.5	15.5
E	9.0	15.5
D	8.0	20.0
C	5.5	9.0
B	0.0	5.5
A	8.0	12.0

We now calculate the activity slacks and determine which activities are on the critical path:

ACTIVITY	START		FINISH		ACTIVITY SLACK	CRITICAL PATH
	Earliest	Latest	Earliest	Latest		
A	0.0	4.0	4.0	8.0	4.0	No
B	0.0	0.0	5.5	5.5	0.0	Yes
C	5.5	5.5	9.0	9.0	0.0	Yes
D	4.0	8.0	16.0	20.0	4.0	No
E	9.0	9.0	15.5	15.5	0.0	Yes
F	5.5	6.5	14.5	15.5	1.0	No
G	15.5	15.5	20.0	20.0	0.0	Yes

The paths, and their total expected times and variances, are

PATH	TOTAL EXPECTED TIME (wk)	TOTAL VARIANCE
A–D	4 + 12 = 16	1.00 + 1.78 = 2.78
A–E–G	4 + 6.5 + 4.5 = 15	1.00 + 2.25 + 0.69 = 3.94
B–C–E–G	5.5 + 3.5 + 6.5 + 4.5 = 20	0.69 + 0.25 + 2.25 + 0.69 = 3.88
B–F–G	5.5 + 9 + 4.5 = 19	0.69 + 2.78 + 0.69 = 4.16

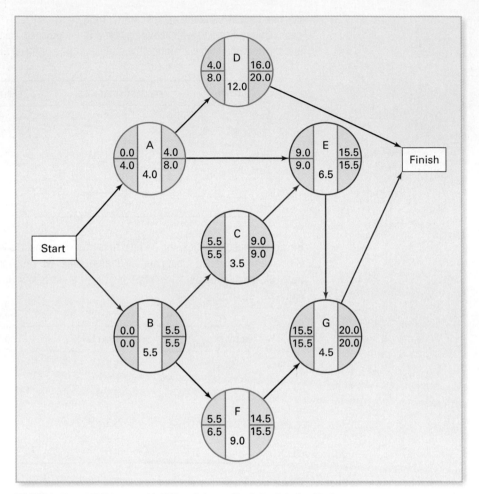

FIGURE 4.16 • AON Diagram with All Time Estimates Needed to Calculate Slack

The critical path is B–C–E–G, with a total expected time of 20 weeks. However, path B–F–G is 19 weeks and has a large variance. In this solution, we used the AON notation, showing the start and finish times within the node circles. The same results can be obtained with the AOA notation, except that times are typically shown in a box drawn near the arc (arrow). For example:

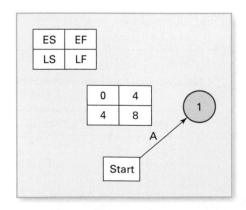

c. We first calculate the z-value:

$$z = \frac{T - T_E}{\sqrt{\sigma^2}} = \frac{23 - 20}{\sqrt{3.88}} = 1.52$$

Using the Normal Distribution appendix, we find that the probability of completing the project in 23 weeks or less is 0.9357. Because the length of path B–F–G is very close to that of the critical path and has a large variance, it might well become the critical path during the project.

OM EXPLORER AND INTERNET EXERCISES

Visit our Web site at www.prenhall.com/krajewski for OM Explorer Tutors, which explain quantitative techniques; Solvers, which help you apply mathematical models; and Internet Exercises, including Facility Tours, which expand on the topics in this chapter.

DISCUSSION QUESTIONS

1. One of your colleagues comments that software is the ultimate key to project management success. How would you respond?

2. When a large project is mismanaged, it makes news. Form a discussion group and identify penalties associated with a mismanaged project in your experience or in recent headlines. Identify the cause of the problem, such as inaccurate time estimates, changed scope, unplanned or improperly sequenced activities, inadequate resources, or poor management–labor relations.

3. Describe a project in which you participated. What activities were involved and how were they interrelated? How would you rate the project manager? What is the basis of your evaluation?

PROBLEMS

In the following problems, network diagrams can be drawn in the AOA or AON format. Your instructor will indicate which is preferred. An icon in the margin next to a problem identifies the software that can be helpful, but not mandatory. The software is available on the Student CD–ROM that is packaged with every new copy of the textbook.

1.   **MS Project** Consider the following data for a project.

ACTIVITY	ACTIVITY TIME (DAYS)	IMMEDIATE PREDECESSOR(S)
A	2	—
B	4	A
C	5	A
D	2	B
E	1	B
F	8	B, C
G	3	D, E
H	5	F
I	4	F
J	7	G, H, I

a. Draw the network diagram.

b. Calculate the critical path for this project.

c. How much total slack is in activities G, H, and I?

2. **MS Project** The following information is known about a project.

a. Draw the network diagram for this project.

b. Determine the critical path and project duration.

ACTIVITY	ACTIVITY TIME (DAYS)	IMMEDIATE PREDECESSOR(S)
A	7	—
B	2	A
C	4	A
D	4	B, C
E	4	D
F	3	E
G	5	E

3. **MS Project** A project has the following precedence relationships and activity times.

ACTIVITY	ACTIVITY TIME (wks)	IMMEDIATE PREDECESSOR(S)
A	4	—
B	10	—
C	5	A
D	15	B, C
E	12	B
F	4	D
G	8	E
H	7	F, G

a. Draw the network diagram.

b. Calculate the total slack for each activity. Which activities are on the critical path?

4. **MS Project** The following information is available about a project.

ACTIVITY	ACTIVITY TIME (DAYS)	IMMEDIATE PREDECESSOR(S)
A	3	—
B	4	—
C	5	—
D	4	—
E	7	A
F	2	B, C, D
G	4	E, F
H	6	F
I	4	G
J	3	G
K	3	H

a. Draw the network diagram.

b. Find the critical path.

5. **MS Project** The following information has been gathered for a project.

ACTIVITY	ACTIVITY TIME (wk)	IMMEDIATE PREDECESSOR(S)
A	4	—
B	7	A
C	9	B
D	3	B
E	14	D
F	10	C, D
G	11	F, E

a. Draw the network diagram.

b. Calculate the total slack for each activity and determine the critical path. How long will the project take?

6. **MS Project** Consider the following project information.

ACTIVITY	ACTIVITY TIME (wk)	IMMEDIATE PREDECESSOR(S)
A	4	—
B	3	—
C	5	—
D	3	A, B
E	6	B
F	4	D, C
G	8	E, C
H	12	F, G

a. Draw the network diagram for this project.

b. Specify the critical path.

c. Calculate the total slack for activities A and D.

d. What happens to the slack for D if A takes five days?

7. **MS Project** Barbara Gordon, the project manager for Web Ventures, Inc., compiled a table showing time estimates for each of the company's manufacturing activities of a project, including optimistic, most likely, and pessimistic.

a. Calculate the expected time, t_e for each activity.

b. Calculate the variance, σ^2, for each activity.

ACTIVITY	OPTIMISTIC (*a*)	MOST LIKELY (*m*)	PESSIMISTIC (*b*)
A	3	8	19
B	12	15	18
C	2	6	16
D	4	9	20
E	1	4	7

8. **MS Project** Recently, you were assigned to manage a project for your company. You have constructed a network diagram depicting the various activities in the project (Fig. 4.17). In addition, you have asked your team to

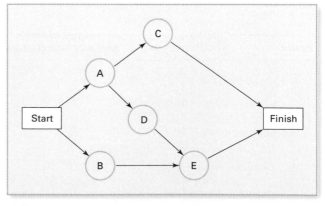

FIGURE 4.17 • AON Project Diagram

estimate the amount of time that they would expect each of the activities to take. Their responses are shown in the following table.

ACTIVITY	TIME ESTIMATES (DAYS)		
	Optimistic	Most Likely	Pessimistic
A	5	8	11
B	4	8	11
C	5	6	7
D	2	4	6
E	4	7	10

a. What is the expected completion time of the project?

b. What is the probability of completing the project in 21 days?

c. What is the probability of completing the project in 17 days?

9. In Solved Problem 2, estimate the probability that the noncritical path B–F–G will take more than 20 weeks. *Hint:* Subtract from 1 the probability that B–F–G will take 20 weeks or less.

10. **MS Project** Consider the following data for a project never before attempted by your company.

ACTIVITY	EXPECTED TIME, T_e (wk)	IMMEDIATE PREDECESSOR(S)
A	5	—
B	3	—
C	2	A
D	5	B
E	4	C, D
F	7	D

a. Draw the network diagram for this project.

b. Identify the critical path and estimate the project's duration.

c. Calculate the total slack for each activity.

11. **MS Project** The director of continuing education at Bluebird University has just approved the planning for a sales-training seminar. Her administrative assistant has identified the various activities that must be done and their relationships to each other, as shown in Table 4.5.

Because of the uncertainty in planning the new course, the assistant also has supplied the following time estimates for each activity.

TABLE 4.5 *Activities for the Sales-Training Seminar*

ACTIVITY	DESCRIPTION	IMMEDIATE PREDECESSOR(S)
A	Design brochure and course announcement.	—
B	Identify prospective teachers.	—
C	Prepare detailed outline of course.	—
D	Send brochure and student applications.	A
E	Send teacher applications.	B
F	Select teacher for course.	C, E
G	Accept students.	D
H	Select text for course.	F
I	Order and receive texts.	G, H
J	Prepare room for class.	G

ACTIVITY	TIME ESTIMATES (DAYS)		
	Optimistic	Most Likely	Pessimistic
A	5	7	8
B	6	8	12
C	3	4	5
D	11	17	25
E	8	10	12
F	3	4	5
G	4	8	9
H	5	7	9
I	8	11	17
J	4	4	4

The director wants to conduct the seminar 47 working days from now. What is the probability that everything will be ready in time?

12. Table 4.6 contains information about a project. Shorten the project three weeks by finding the minimum-cost schedule. Assume that project indirect costs and penalty costs are negligible. Identify activities to crash while minimizing the additional crash costs.

TABLE 4.6 *Project Activity and Cost Data*

ACTIVITY	NORMAL TIME (DAYS)	CRASH TIME (DAYS)	COST TO CRASH ($ PER DAY)	IMMEDIATE PREDECESSOR(S)
A	7	6	200	None
B	12	9	250	None
C	7	6	250	A
D	6	5	300	A
E	1	1	—	B
F	1	1	—	C, D
G	3	1	200	D, E
H	3	2	350	F
I	2	2	—	G

13. Information concerning a project is given in Table 4.7. Indirect project costs amount to $250 per day. The company will incur a $100 per day penalty for each day the project lasts beyond day 14.

    a. What is the project's duration if only normal times are used?

    b. What is the minimum-cost schedule?

    c. What is the critical path for the minimum-cost schedule?

TABLE 4.7 *Project Activity and Cost Data*

ACTIVITY	NORMAL TIME (DAYS)	NORMAL COST ($)	CRASH TIME (DAYS)	CRASH COST ($)	IMMEDIATE PREDECESSOR(S)
A	5	1,000	4	1,200	None
B	5	800	3	2,000	None
C	2	600	1	900	A, B
D	3	1,500	2	2,000	B
E	5	900	3	1,200	C, D
F	2	1,300	1	1,400	E
G	3	900	3	900	E
H	5	500	3	900	G

14. Jason Ritz, district manager for Gumfull Foods, Inc., is in charge of opening a new fast-food outlet in the college town of Clarity. His major concern is the hiring of a manager and a cadre of hamburger cooks, assemblers, and dispensers. He has also to coordinate the renovation of a building that was previously owned by a pet-supplies retailer. He has gathered the data shown in Table 4.8.

    Top management has told Ritz that the new outlet is to be opened as soon as possible. Every week that the project can be shortened will save the firm $1,200 in lease costs. Ritz thought about how to save time during the project and came up with two possibilities. One was to employ Arctic, Inc., a local employment agency, to locate some good prospects for the manager's job. This approach would save three weeks in activity A and cost Gumfull Foods $2,500. The other was to add a few workers to shorten the time for activity B by two weeks at an additional cost of $2,700.

    Help Jason Ritz by answering the following questions.

    a. How long is the project expected to take?

    b. Suppose that Ritz has a personal goal of completing the project in 14 weeks. What is the probability that this will happen?

    c. What additional expenditures should be made to reduce the project's duration? Use the expected time for each activity as though it were certain.

15. The diagram in Figure 4.18 was developed for a project that you are managing. Suppose that you are interested in finding ways to speed up the project at minimal additional cost. Determine the schedule for completing the project in 25 days at minimum cost. Penalty and project-overhead costs are negligible. Alternative time and cost data for each activity are shown in Table 4.9.

TABLE 4.9 *Project Activity and Cost Data*

ACTIVITY	ALTERNATIVE 1 Time (days)	ALTERNATIVE 1 Cost ($)	ALTERNATIVE 2 Time (days)	ALTERNATIVE 2 Cost ($)
A	12	1,300	11	1,900
B	13	1,050	9	1,500
C	18	3,000	16	4,500
D	9	2,000	5	3,000
E	12	650	10	1,100
F	8	700	7	1,050
G	8	1,550	6	1,950
H	2	600	1	800
I	4	2,200	2	4,000

TABLE 4.8 *Data for the Fast-Food Outlet Project*

ACTIVITY	DESCRIPTION	IMMEDIATE PREDECESSOR(S)	TIME (wk) *a*	TIME (wk) *m*	TIME (wk) *b*
A	Interview at college for new manager.	—	2	4	6
B	Renovate building.	—	5	8	11
C	Place ad for employees and interview applicants.	—	7	9	17
D	Have new-manager prospects visit.	A	1	2	3
E	Purchase equipment for new outlet and install.	B	2	4	12
F	Check employee applicant references and make final selection.	C	4	4	4
G	Check references for new manager and make final selection.	D	1	1	1
H	Hold orientation meetings and do payroll paperwork.	E, F, G	2	2	2

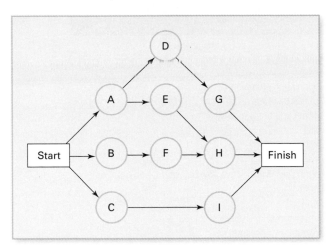

FIGURE 4.18 • AON Network Diagram

16. 💿 **MS Project** Paul Silver, owner of Sculptures International, just initiated a new art project. The following data are available for the project.

ACTIVITY	ACTIVITY TIME (DAYS)	IMMEDIATE PREDECESSOR(S)
A	4	—
B	1	—
C	3	A
D	2	B
E	3	C, D

   a. Draw the network diagram for the project.

   b. Determine the project's critical path and duration.

   c. What is the total slack for each activity?

17. 💿 **MS Project** Reliable Garage is completing production of the J2000 kit car. The following data are available for the project.

ACTIVITY	ACTIVITY TIME (DAYS)	IMMEDIATE PREDECESSOR(S)
A	2	—
B	6	A
C	4	B
D	5	C
E	7	C
F	5	C
G	5	F
H	3	D, E, G

   a. Draw the network diagram for the project.

   b. Determine the project's critical path and duration.

   c. What is the total slack for each activity?

18. 💿 **MS Project** The following information concerns a new project your company is undertaking.

ACTIVITY	ACTIVITY TIME (DAYS)	IMMEDIATE PREDECESSOR(S)
A	10	—
B	11	—
C	9	A, B
D	5	A, B
E	8	A, B
F	13	C, E
G	5	C, D
H	10	G
I	6	F, G
J	9	E, H
K	11	I, J

   a. Draw the network diagram for this project.

   b. Determine the critical path and project completion time.

Advanced Problems

19. The project manager of Good Public Relations has gathered the data shown in Table 4.10 for a new advertising campaign.

   a. How long is the project likely to take?

   b. What is the probability that the project will take more than 38 weeks?

   c. Consider the path A–E–G–H–J. What is the probability that this path will exceed the expected project duration?

TABLE 4.10 *Activity Data for Advertising Project*

| | TIME ESTIMATES (DAYS) | | | |
ACTIVITY	Optimistic	Most Likely	Pessimistic	IMMEDIATE PREDECESSOR(S)
A	8	10	12	—
B	5	8	17	—
C	7	8	9	—
D	1	2	3	B
E	8	10	12	A, C
F	5	6	7	D, E
G	1	3	5	D, E
H	2	5	8	F, G
I	2	4	6	G
J	4	5	8	H
K	2	2	2	H

TABLE 4.11 *Michaelson Construction-Building Activities*

ACTIVITY	DESCRIPTION	ACTIVITY	DESCRIPTION
Start			
A	Appliance installation	M	Roughing-in plumbing
B	Building permit	N	Outside painting
C	Carpets and flooring	O	Interior painting
D	Dry wall	P	Roof
E	Electrical wiring	Q	Siding
F	Foundation	R	Final wood trim
G	Framing	S	Pouring sidewalks, driveway, basement, and garage floors
H	Heating and air conditioning	T	Doors
I	Insulation	U	Windows
J	Kitchen and bath cabinets	V	Bath fixtures
K	Lighting fixtures	W	Lawn sprinkler system
L	Moving in	X	Landscaping

20. 💿 **MS Project** Michaelson Construction builds houses. Create a network showing the precedence relationships for the activities listed in Table 4.11.

21. 💿 **MS Project** Fronc is a wedding coordinator. Beatrice Wright and William Bach have asked Fronc to help them organize their wedding. Create a network showing the precedence relationships for the activities listed in Table 4.12.

22. The information in Table 4.13 is available about a large project.

a. Determine the critical path and the expected completion time of the project.

b. Plot the total project cost, starting from day 1 to the expected completion date of the project, assuming the earliest start times for each activity. Compare that

TABLE 4.12 *Will & Bea Wright-Bach Wedding Activities*

ACTIVITY	DESCRIPTION	ACTIVITY	DESCRIPTION
Start	Accept proposal	O	Order cake, mints, cashews
A	Select and print announcements	P	Photographer
B	Blood tests	Q	Reserve reception hall
C	Color theme selection	R	Rings
D1	Wedding dress	S	Bachelor party
D2	Bridesmaids' dresses	T	Tuxedo rental
D3	Bride's mother's dress	U	Ushers
D4	Groom's mother's dress	V	Reserve church
E	Establish budget and net worth of parents	W	Wedding ceremony
F	Flowers	X	Select groomsmen, ring bearer
G	Gifts for wedding party	Y	Select bridesmaids, flower girls
H	Honeymoon planning	Z	Rehearsal and prenuptial dinner
I	Mailed invitations	AA	Prenuptial agreement
J	Guest list	BB	Groom's nervous breakdown
K	Caterer	CC	Register for china, flatware, gifts
L	Marriage license	DD	Dance band
M	Menu for reception	EE	Thank you notes
N	Newspaper picture, society page announcement	FF	Finish

	TABLE 4.13 *Activity and Cost Data*		
ACTIVITY	**ACTIVITY TIME (DAYS)**	**ACTIVITY COST**	**IMMEDIATE PREDECESSOR(S)**
A	3	100	—
B	4	150	—
C	2	125	A
D	5	175	B
E	3	150	B
F	4	200	C, D
G	6	75	C
H	2	50	C, D, E
I	1	100	E
J	4	75	D, E
K	3	150	F, G
L	3	150	G, H, I
M	2	100	I, J
N	4	175	K, M
O	1	200	H, M
P	5	150	N, L, O

result to a similar plot for the latest start times. What implication does the time differential have for cash flows and project scheduling?

SIMULATION EXERCISES

These simulation exercises require the use of the Extend and SimQuick simulation packages. Extend is on the Student CD-ROM that is packaged with every new copy of the textbook. SimQuick is an optional simulation package that your instructor may or may not have ordered.

1. ⬤ **Extend** Connect Telecom is a rapidly growing international supplier of consumer-oriented telecommunications products, including wireless telephones and digital answering machines. Senior management plans to introduce approximately 10 new products over the next two years. The director of marketing wants to establish more formal project plans for this new wave of product introductions. Many tasks are involved, such as selecting marketing personnel for training, preparing a separate media plan, reviewing TV commercials, and the like. The project team has a list of activities and time estimates (most likely, pessimistic, and optimistic). Use the Extend simulator and PERT/CPM methods to analyze their project. See the New Product Introduction at Connect Telecom case on the Student CD-ROM, which includes the basic model and how to use it. Answer the various questions asked about the project, recognizing the uncertainty in activity times.

2. Ⓢ Management is concerned about the completion time of a software development project. There are eight major tasks with highly uncertain duration times. Use SimQuick to determine the minimum, average, and maximum time duration of this project. See Example 19 in SimQuick: Process Simulation in Excel for details of this problem and additional exercises.

CASE **THE PERT STUDEBAKER**

The new director of service operations for Roberts's Auto Sales and Service (RASAS) started work at the beginning of the year. It is now mid-February. RASAS consists of three car dealerships that sell and service several makes of American and Japanese cars, two auto parts stores, a large body shop and car painting business, and an auto salvage yard. Vikky Roberts, owner of RASAS, went into the car business when she inherited a Studebaker dealership from her father. The Studebaker Corporation was on the wane when she obtained the business, but she was able to capitalize on her knowledge and experience to build her business into the diversified and successful "mini-empire" it is today. Her motto, "Sell 'em today, repair 'em tomorrow!" reflects a strategy that she refers to in private as "Get 'em coming and going."

Roberts has always retained a soft spot in her heart for Studebaker automobiles. They were manufactured in South Bend, Indiana, from 1919 to 1966, and many are still operable today because of a vast number of collectors and loyal fans. Roberts has just acquired a 1963 Studebaker Avanti that needs a lot of restoration. She has also noted the public's growing interest in the restoration of vintage automobiles.

Roberts is thinking of expanding into the vintage car restoration business and needs help in assessing the feasibility of such a move. She also wants to restore her 1963 Avanti to mint condition, or as close to mint condition as possible. If she decides to go into the car restoring business, she can use the Avanti as an exhibit in sales and advertising and take it to auto shows to attract business for the new shop.

Roberts believes that many people want the thrill of restoring an old car themselves but don't have time to run down all the old parts. Still others just want to own a vintage auto because it is different, and many of them have plenty of money to pay someone to restore an auto for them.

Roberts wants the new business to appeal to both types of people. For the first group, she envisions serving as a parts broker for NOS ("new old stock"), new parts that were manufactured many years ago and still packaged in their original cartons. It can be a time-consuming process to find the right part. RASAS could also machine new parts to replicate those that are hard to find or no longer exist.

In addition, RASAS could assemble a library of parts and body manuals for old cars to serve as an information resource for do-it-yourself restorers. The do-it-yourselfers could come to RASAS for help in compiling parts lists, and RASAS could acquire the parts for them. For others, RASAS would take charge of the entire restoration.

Roberts asks the new director of service operations to take a good look at her Avanti and determine what needs to be done to restore it to the condition it was in when it came from the factory more than 30 years ago. She wants to restore it in time to exhibit it at the National Studebaker Meet in Springfield, Missouri. If the car wins first prize in its category, it will be a real public relations coup for RASAS—especially if Roberts decides to enter this new venture. Even if she doesn't, the car will be a showpiece for the rest of the business.

Roberts asks the director of service operations to prepare a report about what is involved in restoring the car and whether it can be done in time for the Springfield meet in 45 working days using PERT/CPM. The parts manager, the body shop manager, and the chief mechanic have provided the following estimates of times and tasks that need to be done, as well as cost estimates.

- ❒ Order all needed material and parts (upholstery, wind-shield, carburetor, and oil pump). Time: 2 days. Cost (phone calls and labor): $100.
- ❒ Receive upholstery material for seat covers. Can't do until order is placed. Time: 30 days. Cost: $250.
- ❒ Receive windshield. Can't do until order is placed. Time: 10 days. Cost: $130.
- ❒ Receive carburetor and oil pump. Can't do until order is placed. Time: 7 days. Cost: $180.
- ❒ Remove chrome from body. Can do immediately. Time: 1 day. Cost: $50.
- ❒ Remove body (doors, hood, trunk, and fenders) from frame. Can't do until chrome is removed. Time: 1 day. Cost: $150.
- ❒ Have fenders repaired by body shop. Can't do until body is removed from frame. Time: 4 days. Cost: $200.
- ❒ Repair doors, trunk, and hood. Can't do until body is removed from frame. Time: 6 days. Cost: $300.
- ❒ Pull engine from chassis. Do after body is removed from frame. Time: 1 day. Cost: $50.
- ❒ Remove rust from frame. Do after the engine has been pulled from the chassis. Time: 3 days. Cost: $300.
- ❒ Regrind engine valves. Have to pull engine from chassis first. Time: 5 days. Cost: $500.
- ❒ Replace carburetor and oil pump. Do after engine has been pulled from chassis and after carburetor and oil pump have been received. Time: 1 day. Cost: $50.

❒ Rechrome the chrome parts. Chrome must have been removed from the body first. Time: 3 days. Cost: $150.

❒ Reinstall engine. Do after valves are reground and carburetor and oil pump have been installed. Time: 1 day. Cost: $150.

❒ Put doors, hood, and trunk back on frame. The doors, hood, and trunk must have been repaired. The frame also has to have had its rust removed. Time: 1 day. Cost: $80.

❒ Rebuild transmission and replace brakes. Do so after the engine has been reinstalled and the doors, hood, and trunk are back on the frame. Time: 4 days. Cost: $700.

❒ Replace windshield. Windshield must have been received. Time: 1 day. Cost: $70.

❒ Put fenders back on. The fenders must already have been repaired and the transmission rebuilt and the brakes replaced. Time: 1 day. Cost: $60.

❒ Paint car. Can't do until the fenders are back on and windshield replaced. Time: 4 days. Cost: $1,700.

❒ Reupholster interior of car. Must have first received upholstery material. Car must also have been painted. Time: 7 days. Cost: $1,200.

❒ Put chrome parts back on. Car has to have been painted and chrome parts rechromed. Time: 1 day. Cost: $50.

❒ Pull car to Studebaker show in Springfield, Missouri. Must have completed reupholstery of interior and have put the chrome parts back on. Time: 2 days. Cost: $500.

Roberts wants to limit expenditures on this project to what could be recovered by selling the restored car. She has already spent $1,500 to acquire the car.

In addition, she wants a brief report on some of the aspects of the proposed business, such as how it fits in with RASAS's other businesses and what RASAS's operations task should be with regard to cost, quality, customer service, and flexibility.

According to *Turning Wheels,* a publication for owners and drivers of Studebakers, and other books on car restoration, there are various categories of restoration. A basic restoration gets the car looking great and running,

but a mint condition restoration puts the car back in original condition—as it was "when it rolled off the line." When restored cars compete, a car in mint condition has an advantage over one that is just a basic restoration. As cars are restored, they can also be customized. That is, something is put on the car that couldn't have been on the original. Customized cars compete in a separate class. Roberts wants a mint condition restoration, without customization. (The proposed new business would accept any kind of restoration a customer wanted.)

The total budget can't exceed $8,500 including the $1,500 Roberts has already spent. In addition, Roberts cannot spend more than $1,700 in any week given her present financial position. Even though much of the work will be done by Roberts's own employees, labor and materials costs must be considered. All relevant costs have been included in the cost estimates.

Questions

1. 💿 **MS Project** Using the information provided, prepare the report that Roberts requested, assuming that the project will begin immediately. Assume 45 working days are available to complete the project, including transporting the car to Springfield before the meet begins. Your report should briefly discuss the aspects of the proposed new business, such as the competitive priorities (see the Operations Strategy chapter), that Roberts asked about.

2. 💿 **MS Project** Construct a table containing the project activities, with a letter assigned to each activity, the time estimates, and the precedence relationships from which you will assemble the network diagram.

3. 💿 **MS Project** Draw an AON network diagram of the project similar to Figure 4.4: Determine the activities on the critical path and the estimated slack for each activity.

4. 💿 **MS Project** Prepare a project budget showing the cost of each activity and the total for the project. Can the project be completed within the budget? Are there any cash-flow problems? If so, how might Roberts overcome them?

Source: This case was prepared by and is used by courtesy of Professor Sue Perrott Siferd, Arizona State University.

SELECTED REFERENCES

Bloom, R. "Software for Project Management." *Transportation & Distribution,* vol. 34, 1993, pp. 33–34.

Branston, Lisa. "Construction Firms View the Web as a Way to Get Out From Under a Mountain of Paper." *The Wall Street Journal* (November 15, 1999).

Celand, D. I. *Project Management: Strategic Design and Implementation.* New York: McGraw-Hill, 1994.

Day, P. J. *Microsoft Project 4.0 for Windows and the Macintosh: Setting Project Management Standards.* New York: Van Nostrand Reinhold, 1995.

Denzler, David R. "A Review of CA-SuperProject." *APICS—The Performance Advantage* (September 1991), pp. 40–41.

IPS Associates. *Project Management Manual.* Boston: Harvard Business School Publishing, 1996.

Kerzner, Harold. *Applied Project Management: Best Practices on Implementation.* New York: John Wiley & Sons, 2000.

Kerzner, Harold. *Project Management: A Systems Approach to Planning, Scheduling and Controlling,* 6th ed. New York: John Wiley & Sons, 1998.

Littlefield, T. K., and P. H. Randolph. "PERT Duration Times: Mathematical or MBO." *Interfaces,* vol. 21, no. 6 (1991), pp. 92–95.

Meredith, Jack R., and Samuel J. Mantel. *Project Management: A Managerial Approach,* 4th ed. New York: John Wiley & Sons, 2000.

Nichols, John M. *Managing Business and Engineering Projects.* Englewood Cliffs, NJ: Prentice-Hall, 1990.

"Project Management Software Buyer's Guide." *Industrial Engineering* (March 1995), pp. 36–37.

Smith-Daniels, Dwight E., and Nicholas J. Aquilano. "Constrained Resource Project Scheduling." *Journal of Operations Management,* vol. 4, no. 4 (1984), pp. 369–387.

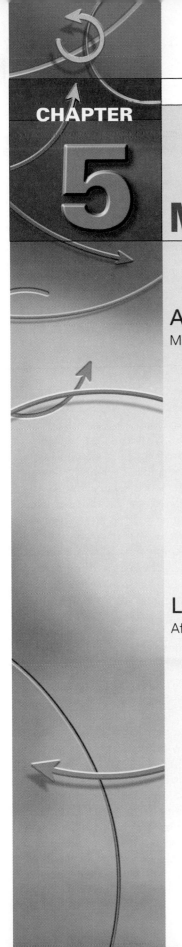

Managing Technology

Across the Organization

Management of technology is important to . . .

- ☐ **accounting,** which can use new technologies to perform its work better and provide important information on new product and process proposals.
- ☐ **engineering,** which designs products and processes that use new technologies.
- ☐ **finance,** which seeks better ways to perform its work, provides input to top management on the financial advisability of new products and process changes, and looks for ways to finance technological change.
- ☐ **human resources,** which needs to anticipate and manage the impact that technological change has on the workforce.
- ☐ **management information systems,** which helps identify new information technologies and implements them when approved.
- ☐ **marketing,** which seeks better technologies for its processes and how new product and service possibilities can better meet customer needs.
- ☐ **operations,** which needs new technologies to produce products and services more effectively, provide better value to customers, and enhance the firm's core competencies.

Learning Goals

After reading this chapter, you will be able to . . .

1. define the meaning of technology and describe how best to manage it.
2. demonstrate the importance of technology to the firm's supply chain and within each functional area and discuss real examples of its impact in manufacturing and service industries.
3. describe the fundamental role of the computer and information technology in reshaping an organization's processes.
4. describe how the Internet, electronic commerce, and enterprise resource planning are changing business processes.
5. discuss the stages of the research and development process and how firms use R&D to create and apply new technology.
6. identify the factors that managers must consider when making technological choices.
7. describe the ways a firm can acquire new technology and evaluate when each way is best.
8. discuss the close connections between technology and human resources and how teams can help integrate the R&D process.
9. describe the different, sometimes conflicting, roles that the operations manager must play with regard to technological change and innovation.

Technology needs to be managed, like any other aspect of processes. Such is the case at Seven-Eleven Japan (www.sej.co.jp), which has invested aggressively in information technology over the years. Since Seven-Eleven Japan began in the early 1970s, founder Toshifumi Suzuki has sought the upgrade processes that better satisfy customers' demand for convenience, quality, and service. Achieving these competitive priorities has led to the continual application of information technology. The company's information system rivals any in the West for just-in-time logistics excellence and deep knowledge of customers. It allows stores to be very responsive to consumers' shifting tastes. If a particular type of *bento* (take-out lunch box) sells out by midday, extra stock can be in the stores by early afternoon. If it's raining and *bentos* will not be in high demand, deliveries are reduced. However, the information system reminds operators to put umbrellas on sale next to the cash register.

Seven Eleven Japan uses technology to expand its services to customers. Here a customer picks up a book she purchased from an online bookseller. The book has been delivered to the Seven Eleven for pickup.

This responsiveness to customer needs is made possible by a sophisticated point-of-sale data-collection system and an electronic ordering system that link individual stores to a central distribution area. Because Japanese customers place a high premium on freshness, the company makes multiple daily deliveries. Now stores receive four batches of fresh inventory each day, and fresh food turns over entirely three times a day—a fact that allows managers to change the physical layout throughout the day, as the flow of customers shifts from housewives to students to workers.

Seven-Eleven Japan's early investments in such systems, and its constant additions to them, have paid off. The company is now the largest and most profitable retailer in Japan. It has continually increased the number of stores, each store's average profit margin, and average daily sales, while reducing the average turnover time of its stock. Seven-Eleven Japan has been so successful that it took over its troubled parent, the Southland Corporation, owner of the U.S. Seven-Eleven chain.

Several lessons can be learned from Seven-Eleven Japan on the task of managing technology. Its managers see IT as just one competitive lever among many and, as such, a way to improve processes. They choose technology, whether old or new, that helps them achieve process performance goals. Investments are chosen to add customer value to processes and to help managers learn how to understand their customers better. IT projects are not assessed primarily by financial metrics and "value for money" thinking. Instead, performance-improvement goals drive investments. Rather than seeking "technology solutions" and "technology for technology's sake," Seven-Eleven Japan executives prefer "appropriate technology" to "first-mover" advantages. They identify the tasks to be done and desired performance levels. Then they pick a technology that suits the people doing the work. This approach avoids new IT that is difficult to use, counterintuitive, and annoying—a problem that plagues many firms. The goal is enhancing the contribution of people rather than boasting the latest technological solution. Seven-Eleven Japan also makes a substantial investment in training and supporting front-line workers in the use of its systems. As Chairman Suzuki says: "It is not enough to exchange information. The information has no value unless it is understood and properly integrated by the franchises and allows them to work better."

The company is also expanding its e-commerce initiatives, both in the United States and Japan. The process is envisioned somewhat differently in Japan, where there is a widespread preference for cash payments and money transfers instead of credit cards. The shopper in Tokyo would browse on the Web and place the order electronically, just as in the United States. The difference is that, a few days later, the shopper will traipse to his or her local Seven-Eleven, fork over some yen to the clerk, and receive his or her purchases.

Despite such an exemplary IT user, some Japanese managers perceive weaknesses in their use of information technology, particularly in white collar settings where computer use in offices is patchy. Economic and competitive pressures are focusing management attention on white-collar productivity. Technology is beginning to replace people in some aspects of information processing. Despite a cultural preference for face-to-face discussions, electronic networks are being used more to share information more efficiently, to send and receive documents and proposals, to schedule meetings, and to vote on proposals.

Sources: Earl, Michael, and M. M. Bensaou. "The Right Mind-Set for Managing Information Technology." *Harvard Business Review* (September–October 1998), pp. 119–129; "E-Commerce Japanese Style." *Wired* (June 1999), www.wired.com/news/business/0,1367,20061,00.html.

TECHNOLOGICAL CHANGE IS A major factor in gaining competitive advantage. It can create whole new industries and dramatically alter the landscape in existing industries. The development and innovative use of technology can give a firm a distinctive competence that is difficult to match, as with Seven-Eleven Japan. Competitive advantage comes not just from creating new technology but also by applying and integrating existing technologies. Advances in technology spawn new products and services and reshape processes. Thus, technology takes many forms, beginning with ideas, knowledge, and experience, and then uses them to create new and better ways of doing things.

In this chapter, we explore how technology can create a competitive advantage. We begin with a general definition of technology and then apply it specifically to products, processes, and information. We single out for more discussion three high-growth information technologies: the Internet, e-commerce, and enterprise resource planning. We then examine the various stages of technological development from its creation to its application to products and processes. Finally, we examine the management of technology, offering guidelines on choosing new technologies and implementing them successfully.

THE MEANING AND ROLE OF TECHNOLOGY

What are the key aspects of technology and its management?

technology The know-how, physical equipment, and procedures used to produce products and services.

support network A network comprised of the physical, informational, and organizational relationships that make a technology complete and allow it to function as intended.

We define **technology** as the know-how, physical equipment, and procedures used to produce products and services. Know-how is the knowledge and judgment of how, when, and why to employ equipment and procedures. Craftsmanship and experience are embodied in this knowledge and often cannot be written into manuals or routines. Equipment consists of such tools as computers, scanners, ATMs, or robots. Procedures are the rules and techniques for operating equipment and performing the work. All three components work together, as illustrated by air-travel technology. Knowledge is reflected in scheduling, routing, and pricing decisions. The airplane is the equipment, consisting of many components and assemblies. The procedures are rules and manuals on aircraft maintenance and how to operate the airplane under many different conditions. Technologies do not occur in a vacuum but are embedded in support networks. A **support network** comprises the physical, informational, and organizational relationships that make a technology complete and allow it to function as intended. Thus, the support network for air-travel technology includes the infrastructure of airports, baggage-handling facilities, travel agencies, air traffic control operations, and the communication systems connecting them.

THREE PRIMARY AREAS OF TECHNOLOGY

Within an organization, technologies reflect what people are working on and what they are using to do that work. The most widespread view of technology is that of *product technology*, which a firm's engineering and research groups develop when creating new products and services. Another view is that of *process technology*, which a firm's employees use to do their work. A third area, which is becoming increasingly important, is *information technology*, which a firm's employees use to acquire, process, and communicate information. The way in which a specific technology is classified depends on its application. As Managerial Practice 5.1 demonstrates, a product technology to one firm (PixelVision's flat-panel monitor) may be part of the process technology of another (NYSE's trading process). The monitor and DOT system information technologies at the NYSE in turn are part of its full set of process technologies.

MANAGERIAL PRACTICE 5.1
Product, Process, and Information Technologies at the New York Stock Exchange

The operations of the New York Stock Exchange (NYSE) illustrate many of the ways in which technology can create new products, reshape processes, and manage information (www.nyse.com). PixelVision (www.pixelvision.com), for example, is a fast-growing company in a young and competitive industry. Using active-matrix liquid crystal display technology, it developed new flat-screen computer monitors that offer superior readability. The striking features of this product are its thinness—just 3 in. deep—and its "plug-and-play" interface technology. Its monitors can replace any CRT without hardware or software modification. They also take up less space, display more information, and consume less energy. For these reasons, PixelVision's *product* technology is now part of the *process* technologies used on the NYSE training floor.

The NYSE uses such computer and telecommunications technologies, key components of *information technology*, to receive buy and sell orders, make share exchanges, report transactions and quotes, inform the initiating party of the results, and report to the clearinghouse. These technologies help satisfy multiple independent parties, make transactions more or less instantaneously, and set prices fairly and quickly. Volume variation is large: Capacity requirements may exceed 600 million shares one day and only 140 million the next. Orders arrive at electronic speed on stock specialists' computer terminals.

The NYSE's automated trading process uses new hardware *and* new software. One important part of the process is the *designated order turnaround* (DOT) *system*, which helps report a transaction. With this software, a specialist on the trading floor reports the trade by feeding a card into an optical reader for

The Pixel-Vision blue flat screens are much in evidence on the trading floor of the New York Stock Exchange. Computer and telecom-munications technologies are an essential part of the trading process. Over a billion shares changed hands on October 28, 1997 for the first time ever, soon after the plunge in the Hong Kong markets.

computer entry. The specialist need not repeat any fixed information on the order, but merely stroke a "turnaround number" to summon the information from the computer's databank. The DOT "bunching" feature built into the software allows individual orders to be aggregated, according to parameters set by floor officials on-line, during volume surges. This process reduces the number of transactions to be handled.

Operations managers are interested in all three aspects of technology. Product technology is important because a firm's processes must be designed to produce products and services spawned by technological advances. Process technology is important because it can improve methods currently used in the production system. Information technology is important because it can improve the way information is used to operate the firm's processes.

product technology Ideas that are developed within the organization and translated into new products and services.

PRODUCT TECHNOLOGY. Developed within the organization, **product technology** translates ideas into new products and services. Product technology is developed primarily by engineers and researchers. They develop new knowledge and ways of doing things, merge them with and extend conventional capabilities, and translate them into specific products and services with features that customers value. Developing new product technologies requires close cooperation with marketing to find out what customers really want and with operations to determine how goods or services can be produced effectively.

In this chapter, we cover product technology in several ways. We give numerous examples of new types of product technology. The discussion of creating and applying technology, including the R&D stages, is directly related to product technology. The discussion of technology strategy and what technologies to pursue are highly relevant to product technology.

What process technologies are used in a supply chain?

process technology The methods by which an organization does things.

PROCESS TECHNOLOGY. The methods by which an organization does things rely on the application of **process technology.** Some of the large number of process technologies used by an organization are unique to a functional area; others are used more universally. Of interest are the many technologies used in a firm's supply chain (see the Process Management chapter and the Supply-Chain Management chapter).

Figure 5.1 shows how technologies support the processes in the supply chain for both service providers and manufacturers. Each technology can be further broken into still more technologies. For example, Table 5.1 shows in greater detail the *basic processes* category for service and manufacturing operations.

The Computer-Integrated Manufacturing supplement at the end of this chapter, which describes a new family of manufacturing technologies, will give you a sense of the widening array of possibilities. All functional areas, not just those areas directly involved with the supply chain, rely on process technologies. Figure 5.2 identifies the process technologies commonly used in these other functional areas.

Developments in process technology for each area can be dramatic. Consider sales processes that use vending machines to distribute products. This process technology is shedding its low-tech image. New electronic vending machines are loaded with circuit boards and microprocessors rather than gears and chains. They determine how much product is left, audit coin boxes, and make sure that the mechanisms work properly. These capabilities simplify product ordering and inventory control processes.

With more sophisticated versions, vending machine communication may even allow companies at distant locations to change product prices, reset thermostats, and verify credit cards. Hand-held computers have also caught on, and some drivers tending vending machines use them to "read" the status of certain machines in just seconds. When the data are processed, the computers prepare restocking lists for route drivers. Now that replenishments can be made more quickly and accurately, some customers are reporting inventory reductions of 20 percent with no loss in service—a reduction that amounts to a significant savings in addition to the time savings for the drivers.

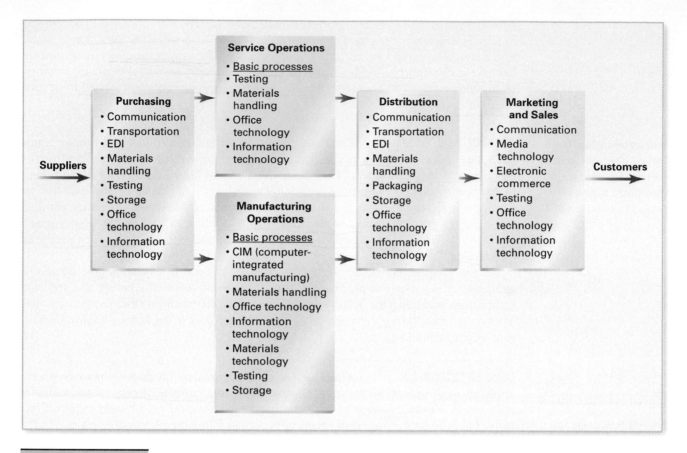

FIGURE 5.1

Process Technologies Along the Supply Chain

TABLE 5.1

Basic Processes

In Services	
Process Technology	**Industry Type**
Electronic funds transfer and encoded check processors	Banking
Autopilots and ship navigation systems	Transportation
CAT scanners and dentist chair systems	Health care
Electronic library cataloguing and language translation computers	Education
Computerized meter reading and optical mail scanners	Utilities and government
Vending machines and point-of-sale electronic terminals	Wholesale and retail trade
Electronic reservation systems and electronic key-and-lock systems	Hotels
In Manufacturing	
Process Technology	**Process Type**
Chemical reactions and refining	Changing the physical property of materials
Casting and shearing	Changing the shape of physical materials
Sawing and optical lasers	Machining to fixed dimensions
Painting and polishing	Obtaining a surface finish
Soldering and screw fastening	Joining parts or materials

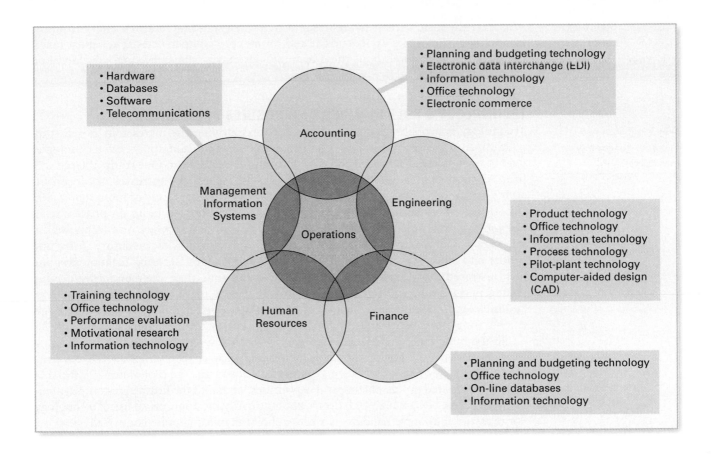

- Hardware
- Databases
- Software
- Telecommunications

- Planning and budgeting technology
- Electronic data interchange (EDI)
- Information technology
- Office technology
- Electronic commerce

Accounting

Management Information Systems

Engineering

Operations

- Product technology
- Office technology
- Information technology
- Process technology
- Pilot-plant technology
- Computer-aided design (CAD)

- Training technology
- Office technology
- Performance evaluation
- Motivational research
- Information technology

Human Resources

Finance

- Planning and budgeting technology
- Office technology
- On-line databases
- Information technology

FIGURE 5.2

Technologies for Other Functional Areas

information technology
Technology used to acquire, process, and transmit information with which to make more effective decisions.

management of technology The joining together of R&D, engineering, and management in the processes of planning, developing, and implementing technological capabilities that can carry out corporate and operations strategies.

INFORMATION TECHNOLOGY. Managers use **information technology** to acquire, process, and transmit information with which to make more effective decisions. Information technology pervades every functional area in the workplace (see Figs. 5.1 and 5.2). Nowhere is it more revolutionary than in offices, whether main offices, branch offices, back offices, front offices, sales offices, or functional area offices. Office technologies include various types of telecommunication systems, word processing, computer spreadsheets, computer graphics, e-mail, on-line databases, the Internet, and the intranet.

MANAGEMENT OF TECHNOLOGY

Management of technology links R&D, engineering, and management in the processes of planning, developing, and implementing new technological capabilities that can carry out corporate and operations strategies. It means identifying technological possibilities that should be pursued through R&D, choosing from both internal and external sources the technologies to implement and then following through their successful implementation as products, processes, and services. We discuss these management issues in sections that follow.

The number of different technologies is mind-boggling, and yet managers must be knowledgeable about the technologies used in their operations. This paradox raises the question: What does a manager need to know about technology? One view is that the manager merely needs to understand what a technology can do, including its cost and performance possibilities. An alternative view is that such understanding isn't enough: The effective manager must also understand how the technology works and what goes on in the technological "black box." Our view is somewhere between these positions.

What do managers need to
know about specific
technologies?

Whatever the firm, managers are less effective when standing at arm's length from the technologies that make up its current and future core competencies. They must invest the time to learn more about these technologies and at the same time develop good sources of technical advice within the firm.

TECHNOLOGY'S ROLE IN IMPROVING BUSINESS PERFORMANCE

Why is technology so
important to operations
managers?

Technology is probably the most important force driving the increase in global competition. As various studies show, companies that invest in and apply new technologies tend to have stronger financial positions than those that do not. One study of large U.S. firms showed that, as the investment in R&D for technology increases, so do profitability and new product introductions (Steel, 1988). Another study of more than 1,300 manufacturers in Europe, Japan, and North America focused more on process technologies and revealed a strong link between financial performance and technological innovation. Companies with stellar performance in annual sales, inventory turns, and profits had more experience with multiple advanced manufacturing technologies and demonstrated more leadership in technological change than their underperforming counterparts (Roth, 1996). Even small firms that have more technological know-how and use computer-based information and manufacturing technologies more intensively enjoy stronger competitive positions (Lefebvre, Langley, Harvey, and Lefebvre, 1992).

At the same time, the relationship between technology and competitive advantage is often misunderstood. High technology and technological change for its own sake are not always best. They might not create a competitive advantage, be economically justifiable, fit with the desired profile of competitive priorities, or add to the firm's core competencies. In other words, being a high-tech firm is not necessarily the appropriate use of technology. For many jobs, a simple handsaw is a better choice than a computer-controlled laser.

INFORMATION TECHNOLOGY

Information technology is crucial to operations everywhere along the supply chain and to every functional area (see Figs. 5.1 and 5.2). Computers are spawning a huge proportion of current technological changes and innovations, either directly or indirectly. Computer-based information technology, in particular, has greatly influenced how operations are managed and how offices work. Office workers can now do things that were not even possible a short time ago, such as accessing information simultaneously from several locations and diverse functional areas. Information technology makes cross-functional coordination easier and links a firm's basic processes. In a manufacturing plant, information technologies can link people with the work centers, databases, and computers.

Let us first examine the four basic building blocks of information technology. Then we can show how they are being used in two of the fastest-growing areas of information technology: e-commerce and enterprise resource planning.

COMPONENTS OF INFORMATION TECHNOLOGY

What are the components
of information technology?

Information technology is made up of four subtechnologies:

1. hardware,
2. software,
3. databases, and
4. telecommunications.

HARDWARE. A computer and the devices connected to it, which can include (among other things) an Intel semiconductor or a PixelVision flat-panel monitor, are called **hardware**. Improved hardware memory, processing capability, and speed have, in large part, driven recent technological change. Scientists and engineers at computer and telecommunications companies and academics are the primary sources of these advances.

hardware A computer and the devices connected to it.

SOFTWARE. The computer programs that make hardware work and carry out different application tasks are called **software**. It has become such an important technology that people often get the mistaken impression that software is the sum total of information systems. Application software, such as that provided by Microsoft, Sun, and others, is what computer users work with. It allows information to be recorded, manipulated, and presented as output that is invaluable in performing work and managing operations. Information systems specialists, both inside and outside a firm, work with the managers who ultimately must decide what the firm's systems should do, who should have access to them, and how the information should be used.

software The computer programs that make hardware work and carry out different application tasks.

Software is available for use with almost all the decision tools described in this book, including flow diagramming, statistical process control techniques, learning curves, simulation, queuing models, location and layout techniques, forecasting models, linear programming, production and inventory control systems, and scheduling techniques. Software is essential to many manufacturing capabilities, such as computer-aided design and manufacturing, robots, automated materials handling, computerized numerically controlled machines, automated guided vehicles, and flexible manufacturing systems (see the Computer-Integrated Manufacturing supplement at the end of this chapter). Software also provides various executive support systems, including management information systems and decision support systems. These software tools allow managers to evaluate business issues quickly and effectively.

DATABASES. A **database** is a collection of interrelated data or information stored on a data storage device such as a computer hard drive, a floppy disk, or tape. A database can be a firm's inventory records, time standards for different kinds of processes, cost data, or customer demand information. For example, a database helps the New York Police Department target its assault on neighborhood drug trafficking by keeping track of drug-selling locations and activity. Thousands of on-line databases are also available commercially. Some are organized according to numbers: economic indicators, stock market prices, and the like. Others are built on collections of key subjects or words: weather data, ski conditions, and full texts of major newspapers and journals around the world, to name a few.

database A collection of interrelated data or information stored on a data storage device such as a computer hard drive, a floppy disk, or tape.

American Express uses its database of some 30 million cardholders to offer an innovative marketing program called CustomExtras. Marketing information contains customers' purchase records and other information. Using proprietary software with this database allows American Express to add personalized offers and messages to the invoices of selected customers. The database tracks customer reactions to these offers and eligibility for reward programs and redemptions. This one-to-one marketing process is based on the notion that different customers should be treated differently and that the best customers should get the most attention. This approach has relevance for airlines, mutual fund companies, mass-customization manufacturers, and many other types of business.

telecommunications The final component of information technology that makes electronic networks possible.

TELECOMMUNICATIONS. The final component of information technology, which many believe might be the most important, is **telecommunications**. Fiber optics, telephones, modems, fax machines, and their related components make electronic networks possible. Such networks, and the use of compatible software, allow computer users at one location to communicate directly with computer users at another location and can pay big dividends. Sun Microsystems, Inc., used to need almost a month to close its financial books after each quarter ended. Now, all transactions are made on one network of Sun computers, permitting the quarterly accounting process to be completed in only 24 hours. Sun also has cut in half the time it required to receive payment after an order is delivered. General Electric has set up a new corporate **intranet**—an internal Internet network, surrounded by a "firewall" for security purposes—that connects the organization's various electronic systems. An employee at GE's motors business division in Indiana, for example, can use the intranet to find out how buyers in other divisions rate a potential supplier. To help draw employees into using the system, the company's home page displays a particularly popular piece of data: GE's current stock price.

Connecting different organizations by computer has also paid dividends. Wal-Mart Stores, Inc., revolutionized retailing during the past decade by linking its computers with those of its suppliers. Its pioneering use of computer networks to conduct business electronically squeezed cost and time from its supply chains (see the Supply-Chain Management chapter). Such private networks are now about to move to the wide-open Internet as components of the information superhighway.

intranet An internal Internet network surrounded by a "firewall" for security purposes.

E-COMMERCE

Global access to the Internet gives organizations unprecedented market and process information. The Web has a huge impact on how firms interact with their suppliers, customers, employees, and investors. **Electronic commerce (e-commerce)** is the application of information and communication technology anywhere along the entire supply chain of business processes. Both whole processes and subprocesses nested within them can be conducted as e-commerce. E-commerce encompasses business-to-business as well as business-to-consumer and consumer-to-business transactions. It is the sharing of business information, maintaining business relationships, and conducting business transactions by means of telecommunications networks. It is, however, more than simply buying and selling goods electronically and includes the use of network communications technology to perform processes up and down the supply chain, both within and outside the organization. E-commerce—the paperless exchange of business information—allows firms to improve their processes that give competitive advantage by cutting costs, improving quality, and increasing the speed of service delivery.

electronic commerce (e-commerce) The application of information and communication technology anywhere along the entire supply chain of business processes.

THE INTERNET

What is the Internet?

Internet A network of networks; a medium to exchange all forms of digital data, including text, graphics, audio, video, programs, and faxes.

E-commerce is not limited to the Internet and Web-based systems to perform transactions, because it includes proprietary services such as EDI (see the Supply-Chain Management chapter). However, the Internet is the fundamental enabling technology for e-commerce, and so we begin our discussion with it. The **Internet** is a network of networks—thousands of interconnected communications networks and millions of users. It is a medium to exchange all forms of digital data, including text, graphics, audio, video, programs, and faxes. It is also an infrastructure for providing various services, such as e-mail, electronic data exchange (EDI), FTP (file transfer protocol), UserNet News, and the World Wide Web. It works because Internet software is designed according to a common set of protocols (TCP/IP) for routing and transporting data. This protocol suite sets standards by which computers communicate with each other.

WORLD WIDE WEB

World Wide Web An Internet service that consists of software called *Web servers* running on thousands of independently owned computers and computer networks that work together.

One of the most popular Internet services is the World Wide Web, which emerged in 1993. The World Wide Web consists of software called *Web servers* running on thousands of independently owned computers and computer networks that work together as part of this Internet service. All information on the Web originates within computers dedicated to the role of serving every imaginable type of data and information. Users request information from the Web using software called Web browsers. Web browsers, such as Microsoft's Internet Explorer and Netscape's Navigator, are software that allow users to view documents at Web sites. The Web is user-friendly because the user has several tools from which to select Web sites. *Search engines* are navigational services that allow users to search the Web. Most search engines have developed into *portals*—Web sites that provide a variety of services in addition to search, including chat, free e-mail, bulletin boards, news, stock quotes, and games. Yahoo! (www.yahoo.com/) is a good example of a widely used portal, with 50 million visitors to its site each month. Each visitor is counted only once, regardless of how many times he or she visits the site. The open protocols of the Net allow anyone with an Internet connection to share data with other users, regardless of the type of access device employed. Of course, some sites might prohibit unauthorized access or transmission.

Web browsers Software that allows users to view documents at Web sites.

How does the Internet work?

Internet service providers (ISPs) Companies that connect a user to the network.

HOW THE INTERNET WORKS. A user connects with the Internet through an Internet service provider. **Internet service providers (ISPs)**, such as America Online and MSN Internet Access, are companies that connect the user to the network, usually for a fee. They are much like on-ramps that put drivers on the Internet "superhighway." The highway itself is owned and leased by a small number of **network service providers (NSPs)**, including AT&T, MCI, WorldCom, Sprint Corp., GTE, and PSINet Inc. Sometimes called "backbone providers," NSPs own the long-haul fiber-optic cables spanning large regions. They pick up and deliver traffic to and from many smaller ISPs. Backbone providers constitute a system, much like the highway system, over which most high-volume Internet freight travels. For local travel, they use the fast T1 technology that transfers 1.544 megabits per second using wider bandwidth. For long-distance transmissions, backbone providers typically use ultrafast T3 technology, which transfers data at 44.736 megabits per second. In fact, AT&T and Cable & Wireless both use lines that are even faster, at roughly 10 Gbps.

network service providers (NSPs) Also called "backbone providers"; companies that own the long-haul fiber-optic cables spanning large regions.

Home and LAN Connections. At home, individuals typically connect through their personal computers using analog modems. Transmissions usually connect to the Internet over regular telephone lines of copper wire. Home users suffer slow access speeds because of the limited speeds of analog modems—a disadvantage sometimes known as the "last-mile problem": A network is only as fast as its slowest link, and this last mile to a user's home is typically the slowest. At the office, desktop or laptop computers are probably part of a **local area network (LAN)**. Instead of an analog modem, each PC probably has a network interface card that provides a dedicated, high-speed digital connection. The LAN provides faster service and, in turn, connects to the Internet not by a modem but by a high-speed leased line from the local phone company.

local area network (LAN) A computer connected to the Internet not by a modem but by a high-speed leased line from the local phone company.

Transmission Technologies. Other connections are rapidly becoming available that help solve the last-mile problem—DSL, cable modems, and wireless. *Digital subscriber line (DSL)* technology, now available in many market areas, gives high-speed Internet access to residential users, small and midsize businesses, and branch offices of larger corporations. Transmission still requires copper phone lines but takes advantage of special transmitting and receiving equipment. The *cable modem* is a broadband technology gaining popularity. Access speeds approach T1 territory, although realistic speeds are in the neighborhood of 400 Kbits to 1.330 megabits per second. A cable modem is not actually a modem at all, but rather a network interface that works in conjunction with the customer's PC standard ethernet card. The result is a permanent, always-on connection to a high-speed LAN that operates over the neighborhood's digital cable TV wiring. *Wireless connections*, both terrestrial and satellite, are becoming available. They give customers any-place, any-time access to the Internet. Midpoint distribution service (MMDS), for example, is a little-known but fast-growing wireless technology that uses microwaves to beam data at about 800 Kbps to small receivers at subscriber locations. Direct broadcast satellite (DBS) uses a relatively small dish antenna to receive data broadcast from a satellite. Certainly the most popular wireless technology to date is the cellular phone, which is equipped with special software that can now connect with the Internet and which allows users to surf the Web and send e-mail. Nearly 9 million Japanese and Europeans already have a taste of this technology. In the United States, there is a smaller number of such cell-phone users. Access speeds are currently slow, screens difficult to read, and messages tough to enter. However, wireless technologies are developing at a dramatic rate, particularly outside the United States.

Access Devices. Computers, phones, set-top boxes, Internet appliances, personal digital assistants, and video games offer many options to access the Internet. *Television set-top boxes* for cable television networks allow users to surf the Internet using television sets without the need of an expensive computer. Do not confuse set-top boxes with cable modems. Because cable can provide a high-speed connection regardless of access device, customers can use cable modems on home PCs without accessing the Internet from the TV. *Internet appliances* are low-cost, special-purpose computers designed specifically to do nothing more than access the Web and e-mail. The premise behind them is that today's PCs are too complicated and costly for beginners or people who just want to use the Internet. *Personal digital assistant (PDA)* technologies, such

The DoCoMo I-mode cellular phone is a handheld Internet device. This Japanese product is equipped with special software, so that it can access Web sites, I-mode mail, and other on-line services.

as Palm and Pocket PC, are hand-held computers that access the Internet to provide e-mail, web content, and messaging services. Even some *video games*, such as Dreamcast, Playstation 2, and Microsoft X-Box, can be hooked up to a modem. Matsushita, Sony, and Philips envision eventually that cell phones will be linked up with hundreds of gadgets just like clocks and radios.

GLOBAL IMPACT OF THE INTERNET. The Internet moves information back and forth between users in almost 200 countries. Internet usage is heading for the half-billion mark around the globe, with 300 million already on the Internet in 1999, and up to 490 million projected for 2002. That means there are 79 people with Internet access per 1,000 people worldwide. Over half of them are in the United States and Canada. In the United States, 61 percent of home users go on-line at least once every day and a half. Reasons for high usage include the flat-rate pricing structures of local residential telephone calls, the flat per-month fees of Internet service providers, and the availability of broadband access. Europe has seen big gains in usage, particularly in Germany and the United Kingdom. Internet usage in Europe ranges from 58 percent of the population in Sweden to only 16 percent in France. The Asia or Pacific region is another Internet growth area, followed by Latin America. The Middle East and Africa have much less Internet usage. By 2004, it is expected that half of all on-line sales will be made outside the United States. The English language still dominates the Web, but one-third of all pages are not in English.

HOW E-COMMERCE AFFECTS PROCESSES

How does electronic commerce affect business processes?

It is no secret that e-commerce is growing and changing at breathtaking speed. For example, it took Sam Walton 12 years to reach $150 million in sales at Wal-Mart, but Amazon.com did it in 3. GE was the first firm to do $1 billion of business on the Internet, and Intel sold its first billion in goods on-line in less than a week. Relative to the size of the whole economy, the dollar value of e-commerce transactions is still small, but both the new Internet-based companies (the so-called dot-coms) and the traditional producers of goods and services are increasingly turning to the Web. E-commerce cuts costs because it links companies to their customers and suppliers, improves inventory management, automates fax-and-phone procurement processes, and provides inexpensive sales, marketing, and customer support channels. Managerial Practice 5.2 describes a major e-commerce initiative in the financial services industry.

BUSINESS-TO-CONSUMERS (B2C) COMMERCE

Many of the advantages of e-commerce were first exploited by retail "e-businesses," such as Amazon.com, E*Trade, and Auto-by-tel. These three companies created Internet versions of traditional bookstores, brokerage firms, and auto dealerships. Business-to-consumer commerce, sometimes called "B2C e-commerce," offers individual consumers a new buying alternative. The Internet is changing operations, processes, and cost structures for many retailers, and the overall growth in usage has been dramatic. On-line business sales to individual customers reached over $30 billion in 2000, more than double the total for the previous year. The growth of B2C commerce is accelerating and there is no sign that it will let up. Some experts predict $1.6 trillion in on-line purchases by 2003.

However, the mix of companies using B2C e-commerce is shifting. It is no longer limited to the original dot-com retailers, because their emergence forced their "brick-and-mortar" competitors to reconsider their own e-commerce options. Now many of these more established companies are operating their own on-line stores and putting pressure on dot-com retailers. A shakeout is expected for those on-line retailers that

MANAGERIAL PRACTICE 5.2
Web-Based Financial Services with Clicks and Mortar

Boston-based Fleet, the eighth-largest U.S. bank (www.fleet.com/), earlier spent $40 million on a computerized *data warehouse* that collects and sorts details about customers. More recently, it applied that same tailored marketing strategy, known as *data mining*, to on-line customers. The idea is to pitch products so that middle-aged customers will not be offered student loans and college students will not be bombarded with home-equity refinancing plans.

Fleet's latest leap into cyberspace is what it calls its biggest technology bet ever. Fleet will spend up to $100 million over the next two years to launch a comprehensive Web-based financial service that will place banking, stock trading, mutual funds, credit cards, mortgages, financial news, bill payment, and incentives all on one Web site for 8 million household customers in the northeast United States. Among the planned cyber offerings: real-time account data, mortgage application-taking, portfolio calculators, corporate research, investment advice from high-end financial publishers, and even reduced monthly fees from Microsoft Network, the Internet service provider. The project will be rolled out in stages and would be the newest entrant in the fast-shifting world of Web finance. It has already linked its basic Web bank services with Quick & Reilly, its discount stock brokerage, so customers can now bank and trade stocks in one place. Fleet sees Quick & Reilly, a national franchise that it acquired in 1997, as its secret weapon. Fleet believes that the best financial product on the Web is the brokerage product. High-yield certificates of deposit and checking accounts that are the staple offerings of Internet-only banks do not give Fleet a competitive advantage.

Fleet's bet is about more than technology. It is a bet that the future of on-line banking is inseparable from the future of on-line investing, a trend that has taken off in recent years. Still, Fleet's move is a leap into uncertainty, and some executives decline to say how much the on-line business could add to Fleet's bottom line. The payoffs from the project are not yet clear. "We're not at this point thinking of going national with a broad Internet product," says Charles Gifford, Fleet president and former BankBoston head. "I'm not sure how you make money on it." While many banks have Web outputs and a few, like Fleet, own brokerages, Fleet will be one of a tiny group to offer bank products and stock trading in one place. Fleet's efforts reflect a dilemma faced by banks now grappling with an investing revolution that has lured legions on-line and left banks in the dust. To date, most institutions have experienced the Internet as a money-losing proposition, but everybody still wants to be out there with an Internet presence. Given these uncertainties, Fleet is hedging its bet. Its basic strategy is to stick with old-fashioned bricks-and-mortar branches and automated teller machines while developing a major virtual presence—an idea known as "clicks and mortar."

Source: "Fleet Poised to Place Bet on Net Finance." *The Boston Globe* (October 27, 1999).

face slim profit margins, too little product differentiation, and not enough size to control their own order-fulfillment processes and guarantee customer satisfaction. Anyone with an Internet connection can open a store in cyberspace, but delivering the goods to consumers has proven to be a much more complicated task.

B2C e-commerce offers a new "distribution channel," and consumers can avoid shopping at crowded department stores, with their checkout lines and parking-space shortages. A business can publish information using hypertext markup language (HTML) not only on the World Wide Web but also on major on-line services. Many leading retailers and catalog companies have opened Web "stores" where consumers can browse thousands of virtual aisles and millions of items. Such methods allow customers to do much more "shopping" in an hour than they could possibly do in person at a traditional retail outlet. Browsers can find intriguing products at exotic sites, such as an authentic turn-of-the-century rocking horse from a London antiques broker, a gift pack of 7-ounce portions of beef Wellington, and a personalized Louisville Slugger baseball bat. The most popular on-line purchases are books, travel arrangements, CDs, computer software, health and beauty products, and clothing. Banking and financial services are further down the line but are growing (as the example of Fleet Bank demonstrates). E-commerce is particularly attractive for products that the consumer does not have to look at carefully or touch. The Internet has an advantage with higher-value branded convenience goods over the in-store experience.

The Internet also has potential in "greening" the environment. There is less need for building retail space, warehouse space, and commercial office space. Energy saved means less pollution from power plants, which release greenhouse gases into the atmosphere. Furthermore, fewer trips to malls and stores would mean savings on gasoline. Less reliance on catalogs would save millions of tons of paper.

The question of security, primarily involving credit card numbers, continues to make many people reluctant to buy over the Internet. However, a card number follows a prescribed path and is encrypted the moment it leaves the computer. **Encryption** is the process of coding customer information and sending it over the Internet in "scrambled" form. Although no credit card transaction is entirely secure, the risk of fraud on the Internet is no higher than giving a credit card number over the phone or handing a credit card to a salesclerk.

encryption The process of coding customer information and sending it over the Internet in "scrambled" form.

BUSINESS-TO-BUSINESS (B2B) COMMERCE

Many of the same advantages that arise from B2C e-commerce hold for business-to-business (B2B) commerce. E-commerce helps businesses enhance the services they offer to customers. Business-to-business transactions continue to outpace business-to-consumer transactions in e-commerce. Because trade between businesses makes up more than 70 percent of the regular economy, it is no surprise that B2B e-commerce also dwarfs the B2C variety. In 2000, B2B e-commerce was $335 billion and represented only 3 percent of the total U.S. nonservice market. But growth is expected to be very rapid, reaching $6 trillion, or 45 percent of the total market, by 2005. That is 10 times the amount expected for B2C trade.

Consider Fruit of the Loom, Inc., an apparel maker that depends on its wholesalers to ship products to various retailer customers. It put its wholesalers on the Web and gave each one a complete computer system that displays colorful catalogs, processes electronic orders round the clock, and manages inventories. If one of its distributors is out of stock, the company's central warehouse is notified to ship replacement stock directly to the customer. Building such an integrated e-commerce system took only a few months, using software from Connect, Inc., called OneServer, and a catalog program from Snickleways Interactive to get online. The firm's retailer customers need only an Internet connection and some Web-browsing software. Milacron, Inc., a producer of consumable products for metalworking, is another example. It launched a Web site to give more than 100,000 smaller U.S. metalworking businesses an easy-to-use and secure way of selecting, purchasing, and applying more than 50,000 Milacron metalworking products.

Electronic commerce can transform almost all B2B processes, not just their sales processes, as Managerial Practice 5.3 demonstrates. Even more impressive is how the Web is streamlining the supply-chain process. It can dramatically reduce a firm's purchasing costs, as transactions move away from the numbing pace of paper to the lightning speed of electronics. By eliminating paper forms, firms spend less time and money rekeying information into different computers and correcting the inevitable errors. Electronic commerce previously operated primarily on private links. However, software and security measures now allow the Web to become the global infrastructure for e-commerce. Moving from private networks to the Internet allows a company to reach thousands of new businesses around the world.

MANAGERIAL PRACTICE 5.3
Internet Builder Cisco Uses Internet to Buy, Sell, and Hire

Cisco Systems, Inc. (www.cisco.com/) prospers by building the Internet. The name *Cisco* is synonymous with the Internet. It supplies Internet service providers with 80 percent of their routers and switches—the equipment that directs data to the right destination on the Net. It is also the biggest supplier of Internet plumbing, including the equipment that directs data around big corporate networks and corporate data-networking equipment for small and medium business. Cisco's revenues have exploded from $1.3 billion in 1994 to $17 billion in 2000.

Less well known is how Cisco uses the Internet in almost every phase of its own processes—an approach known in the tech industry as "eating its own dog food." With the company's state-of-the-art Internet programs, every employee, customer, and supplier can use browsers for instant access to Cisco's vast storehouses of data. All told, the typical employee taps Cisco's internal Web site more than 30 times per day. Most human resources functions, from expense reports to benefit changes and employee evaluations, are handled on-line. Cisco encourages job aspirants to apply on-line, and 85 percent do. Most new-hire orientation and 80 percent of all sales training are now conducted on-line. Managers can pull up staff records and information on competitors.

Cisco also gets over 80 percent of its sales orders over the Net. Its Web site is chock-full of information and free software, and most customer service issues are handled electronically, shaving millions off product support costs. Cisco's on-line system uses software that dramatically reduces the cost of configuring the product, because each sales order is a potentially customized product. Within a year, Cisco aims to become the first company in the world that can "virtually" close its books any day of the quarter to gauge financial results.

Finally, the Net is woven deeply into Cisco's manufacturing operations. Orders from the Internet are fed directly into the software programs that run Cisco's business—scheduling products to be built, ordering parts, and arranging shipments. The company outsources most of its production to manufacturers like Flextronics, Inc., and half of all customer orders placed on Cisco's Web site flow directly to contractors who ship to customers. For those orders, no Cisco employee ever touches a piece of paper until a check arrives in the mail to pay for the goods. Soon, with e-payment, even the check could become a thing of the past. Flextronics's computers are so closely tied to Cisco that Flextronics, the supplier, often can build and ship a product faster than a customer can obtain the same model from a distributor's shelf. By building products assemble-to-order rather than to stock, Flextronics lowers inventory costs. By revamping its operations around Net technologies, Cisco created a blueprint by which other companies can do the same.

Source: "Meet Mr. Internet." *Business Week* (September 13, 1999), pp. 129–140.

Currently, e-commerce is dominated by the model of one seller to many buyers, as is the case with Fruit of the Loom and Milacron. However, e-commerce is beginning to take place in *virtual marketplaces*. These trading posts allow buyers and sellers who may not know each other to meet electronically and trade products and services without the aid or cost of traditional agents and brokers. Web marketplaces are growing for B2B trade. Analogies in the B2C world include eBay and Priceline.com, although the B2B customers are companies. For example, Ford, GM, and DaimlerChrysler are putting together a marketplace to procure parts from suppliers. Similar marketplaces are forming around the buying and selling of paper, plastic, steel, bandwidth, chemicals, and the like.

E-COMMERCE AND SMALL BUSINESSES

Electronic commerce is not just for big businesses. Small businesses are increasingly purchasing on-line, although few are selling yet on-line. In the United States, 40 percent of small businesses have their own Web sites and 70 percent have Internet access. The activity that is growing most rapidly is the purchase of goods and services for business. Small business owners are proceeding cautiously into the realm of B2C commerce. Only 38 percent of those with Web sites transacted business with customers over their sites. When they do, it is often just as a communication channel for introducing products and services to potential customers.

ENTERPRISE RESOURCE PLANNING

What is ERP?

enterprise resource planning (ERP) A large, integrated information system that supports many enterprise processes and data-storage needs.

enterprise process A companywide process that cuts across functional areas, business units, geographic regions, and product lines.

Enterprise resource planning (ERP) refers to a large, integrated information system that supports many enterprise processes and data storage needs. An **enterprise process** is a companywide process that cuts across functional areas, business units, geographic regions, and product lines. Also known as an *enterprise system*, ERP is essentially a collection of compatible software modules, possibly interfacing to existing (sometimes called "legacy") information systems, that allow a company to have one comprehensive, fully integrated information system.

We cover different aspects of ERP in several places throughout this book. For example, we describe the process decisions about how work is to be performed in the Process Management chapter. Designing an ERP system requires that a company carefully define its major processes so that appropriate decisions about the coordination of legacy systems and new software modules can be made. Processes to be used by ERP applications must also be fully specified. In many cases, a company's processes must be reengineered before the company can enjoy the benefits of an integrated information system. In the Supply-Chain Management chapter, we describe how ERP systems help coordinate relations among customers, internal operations, and suppliers. In the Resource Planning chapter, we examine ERP from the perspective of what it has to offer by way of resource planning, both in manufacturing and service organizations. Finally, we discuss the enabling of advanced planning and scheduling systems by Internet technologies and integrated with ERP systems in the Scheduling chapter.

WHAT ERP DOES

By integrating functional areas, ERP systems allow a firm to concentrate on enterprise processes rather than functional boundaries. For example, suppose that a U.S. manufacturer of telecommunication products has an ERP system and that an Athens-based sales representative wants to prepare a customer quote. When the salesperson enters information about the customer's needs into a laptop computer, the ERP system automatically generates a formal contract, in Greek, giving the product's specifications, delivery date, and price. After the customer accepts it, the salesperson makes an entry, whereupon ERP verifies the customer's credit limit and records the order. The next application takes over to schedule shipment using the best routing. Backing up from the delivery date, it reserves the necessary materials from inventory and determines when to release production orders to its factories and purchase orders to its suppliers. Another application updates the sales and production forecasts, while still another credits the sales representative's payroll account the appropriate commission, in drachma. The accounting application calculates the actual product cost and profitability, in U.S. dollars, and reflects the transaction in the accounts payable and accounts receivable ledgers. Divisional and corporate balance sheets are updated, as are cash levels. In short, the system supports all of the enterprise processes that are activated as a result of the sale.

ERP APPLICATIONS

ERP revolves around a single comprehensive database that can be made available across the entire organization (or enterprise). Of course, security locks are possible and highly recommended in order to protect sensitive data from accidental or malicious damage. It provides visibility to relevant data enterprisewide, for all products, at all locations, and at all times. The database collects data from and feeds it into the various modular applications (or "suites") of the software system. As new information is entered as a *transaction* in one application, related information is automatically updated in the other applications, including (but not limited to) financial and accounting information, human resource and payroll information, supply-chain information, and customer information. ERP streamlines data flows throughout the organization and allows management direct access to a wealth of real-time operating information. It seamlessly connects information among different enterprise processes and can eliminate many of the cross-functional coordination problems that existed under prior poorly integrated and noninterfaced legacy systems. Figure 5.2 shows some of the typical applications, with a few subprocesses nested within each one. Some of the applications are for back-office operations such as manufacturing and payroll, while others are for front-office operations such as customer service and employee self-service.

ERP is used by both service providers and manufacturers. Amazon.com is a value-added reseller who uses ERP. The supply-chain application is of particular importance because it allows Amazon.com to link customer orders to warehouse shipments and, ultimately, to supplier-replenishment orders. Universities put particular emphasis on the human resources and accounting and finance applications, and manufacturers have an interest in almost every application suite. Not all applications in Figure 5.3 need be integrated into an ERP system, but those left out will not share their information in the corporate database.

FIGURE 5.3

ERP Application Modules

Source: Scalle, Cedric X., and Mark J. Cotteleer. *Enterprise Resource Planning (ERP)*. Boston, MA: Harvard Business School Publishing, No. 9-699-020, 1999.

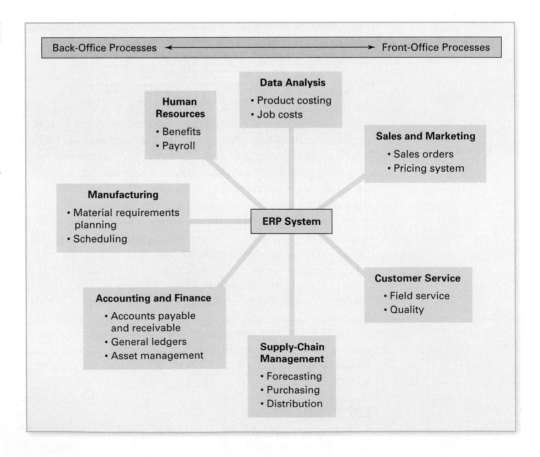

HOW TO USE ERP

Most ERP systems today use a graphical user interface, although the older keyboard-driven, text-based systems are still very popular because of their dependability and technical simplicity. Users navigate through various screens and menus. When they are trained, such as during ERP implementation, the focus is on these screens and how to use them to get their jobs done. The biggest supplier of these off-the-shelf commercial ERP packages is Germany's SAP AG (www.sap.com), followed by Oracle (www.oracle.com), PeopleSoft (www.peoplesoft.com), J.D. Edwards (www.jdedwards.com), and Baan (www.baan.com). Figure 5.4 shows screen shots of the J.D. Edwards ERP software, called OneWorld. Part (a) shows the menu for the various

FIGURE 5.4A

J.D. Edwards ERP Package—Menu for Various Applications

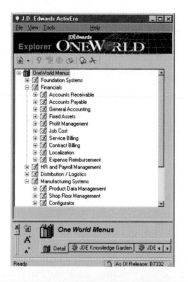

FIGURE 5.4B

J.D. Edwards ERP Package—Entering a Sales Order

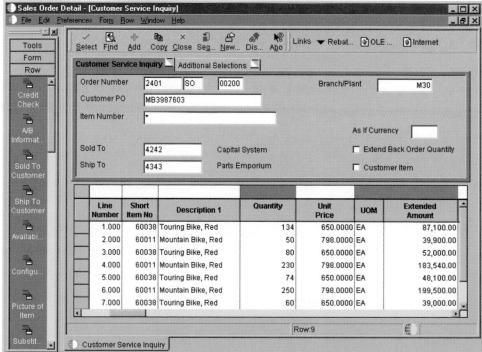

applications. Within the Distribution suite, for example, a user may select the Sales Order Entry process. Part (b) shows the screen for entering a Sales Order.

interoperability The ability of one piece of software to interact with others.

INTEROPERABILITY. ERP has changed a good deal over the last five years. One important direction is **interoperability**—the ability of one piece of software to interact with others. Electronic Data Interchange, a system that allows data interchange between companies on a batch basis (see the Supply-Chain Management chapter), has been a major workhorse over the years. However, there is increasing interest in moving to the "new economy" of e-commerce. Thus, considerable attention is now being given to XML (eXtensible Markup Language), IBM's *Message Queue* (MQ Series), and Microsoft's MSMQ as vehicles for this new approach. XML, for example, lets companies structure and exchange information without rewriting existing systems or adding large amounts of heavyweight middleware. These enablers of collaborative commerce are shaping the ways in which previously disparate and possibly competing pieces of software are working together to add value and reduce costs. The goal of all such methods is to automate, in almost real time, the sharing of information across enterprise boundaries.

IMPLEMENTATION CONSIDERATIONS

Should a firm implement ERP?

ERP is a complex information technology that often requires the reengineering of many enterprise processes. Although it offers substantial advantages, it also presents some problems.

ADVANTAGES. By one estimate, businesses around the globe are spending $10 billion per year on ERP, and that figure probably doubles when consulting service fees are included. Despite these costs, and while the Internet and e-commerce get the most media attention, ERP surely is the most important IT development for business during the last decade. ERP is attractive because it solves a major problem in many large businesses—the fragmentation of information. A large business gathers, analyzes, and stores vast quantities of data, and it does so in many geographic locations, functional areas, departments, and computer systems. Maintaining different systems, rekeying and reformatting redundant data, creating ways to transfer data from one place to another, and updating obsolete code can be a heavy drag on productivity.

Even more troublesome are hidden costs. If people working with the sales and ordering process cannot communicate with people in production and inventory control, then demands placed on production will be unrealistic and customer service will suffer. If marketing and financial systems do not interface, then managers will make important decisions by instinct rather than through a detailed analysis of operations. An ERP package can replace incompatible information systems and inconsistent processes, eliminating many of these costs and customer service problems. The results can be dramatic. Before ERP, Autodesk, which makes computer-aided design software, took two weeks to deliver an order. With its ERP system in place, it ships 98 percent of its orders within two days. IBM's Storage Systems division reduced the time to perform a credit check from 20 minutes to 3 seconds.

PROBLEMS. ERP certainly is not for every company. The installation cost of complex off-the-shelf packages is high, perhaps $2 million, with another $10 million for implementation. Software and installation costs for very large companies can skyrocket to $50 to $500 million, primarily from the cost of implementing ERP into highly complex business processes. Implementing the accounting and financial applications could take two months; the manufacturing application two years. It is not unusual for the full implementation to take four or five years.

Smaller packages are now being made available with the basic features needed by midmarket companies (say those under $1 billion in annual sales), but companies with revenues less than $25 to $50 million are unlikely ERP candidates. Not only can installation costs be excessive, the benefits are smaller. In smaller organizations, of course, the problem of fragmented information is of less concern.

However, concerns about whether ERP will succeed for a particular company are not limited to small companies. There have been some notable failures among large firms. FoxMeyer points to ERP as a major cause of its bankruptcy. Mobile Europe's expenditure of millions of dollars was in vain because its merger partner did not want ERP. Other failures, although temporary, resulted in painful losses. Hershey lost $140 million in sales because its ERP-driven ordering and distribution system failed to deliver candy to major distributors in time for Halloween. Glitches in Whirlpool's ERP system resulted in extended shipping delays that prompted Home Depot to switch to Maytag and General Electric. Keep in mind, however, that ERP systems are complex—glitches in implementation should be expected. Also, the software is not always the culprit.

Implementing an ERP system not only pushes a company toward full integration but offers it an opportunity to examine its processes, culture, and strategy. Some packaged ERP systems require that generic processes supplant customized processes in all business units. Processes within the same firm can differ widely on volume, customization, customer involvement, necessary flexibility, and the like (see the Process Management chapter). For example, a company that has one business unit producing a standard product and another producing a customized product could have two very different purchasing and customer-order-placement processes. Imposing one standard approach on both purchasing and customer-order-placement processes in the organization may ignore different needs and can eliminate sources of competitive advantage. In such a situation, the company would have to revise or completely overhaul its processes to fit the ERP system's logic requirements, rather than vice versa. Then the task becomes one of process reengineering rather than process improvement. In addition, the inherent complexity of ERP makes major code modifications difficult.

Finally, not all software packages use the same architecture and some are more flexible that others. For example, SAP AG's R/3 system is known to have the widest array of applications, but it is not as flexible as the J.D. Edwards, Oracle, and PeopleSoft systems. Because they allow more tailoring of processes for any given organization, new applications or product lines can be added more quickly.

Companies must decide what is best for them. Some processes might continue to be supported with legacy systems, which might be doing an excellent job, especially if the fragmentation problem is minor. Some modules can be written in-house to better fit the customized requirements of a process—flexibility that would otherwise be lost with off-the-shelf software. For example, Compaq Computer wrote its own proprietary software for its forecasting and order-management processes. These processes gave it a competitive advantage with its newly adopted build-to-order operations strategy. Management believed that this advantage outweighed the considerably higher cost of developing its own applications and of losing some integration. The differences in ERP packages provide a basis for selection for a given company. Those with diverse operations requiring flexibility might opt for ERP systems that are more amenable to decentralized applications. Companies more focused on standardized operations might prefer systems requiring uniformity in organizationwide processes. While these

MANAGERIAL PRACTICE 5.4
Implementing ERP at ATOFINA Chemicals, Inc.

Sometimes, implementing ERP is almost mandatory, as in the chemical industry. So thoroughly do companies share information electronically throughout the supply chain that it is difficult to do business without it. ATOFINA Chemicals (www.atofinachemicals.com/newelf/company) is a $2 billion regional chemicals subsidiary of the French company Total Fino Elf. ATOFINA Chemicals had a highly fragmented information system among its 12 different business units. Ordering was not integrated with production, and sales forecasting was not tied to budgeting systems or financial systems. Each unit tracked its own financial data independently.

The company decided to implement SAP's R/3 system for ERP but did not regard ERP as simply a technology solution. Rather, it seized an opportunity to reconfigure itself and its corporate strategy. It saw its problem not just as fragmentation of its information system but fragmentation of the organization as a whole. Customers perceived up to 12 different businesses, each managed independently. To place an order, a customer would frequently have to call many different businesses and process many different invoices. Even inside a given business unit, numerous handoffs were needed to process an order, and response time was slow.

ATOFINA Chemicals chose to implement modules for four key processes: materials management, production planning, order management, and financial reporting. These processes cut across many units, were the most fragmented, and had the biggest impact on good customer relations. At the same time, organizational structure was revised. In the financial area, the accounts receivable and credit departments were combined as a single companywide function. Thus, all customer orders would be handled as one account and with a single invoice. Another change was to create a "demand manager" responsible for integrating

A team of three employees at ATOFINA Chemicals, Inc. keep things under control using various computer technologies after implementing ERP. Previously it took many more people, more handoffs between people, and more time delays to get an order processed.

the sales process with the production planning process. Implementation was overseen by a 60-person project team, consisting of business analysts, IT specialists, and software users from different functions. This broadly representative team installed ERP one business unit at a time, and the same set of procedures for the four selected processes were implemented for all.

Once implemented at 9 of the company's 12 units, the benefits of ERP were already apparent. Customer satisfaction was up dramatically, now that most customer orders were completed with just one call. Inventory levels, receivables, and production and distribution costs were down, saving millions of dollars each year.

Source: Davenport, Thomas H. "Putting the Enterprise into the Enterprise System." *Harvard Business Review* (July–August 1998), pp. 121–131.

differences in packages are present today, it is likely that the ability to accommodate diversity in processes will be an attribute of most major software packages in the future.

In deciding whether to implement ERP and which modules to implement, each company must weigh long-term advantages against costs and risks. The choice may be to stay with legacy systems or even to reduce the number of computerized processes. Managerial Practice 5.4 describes how Elf Atochem made its choices implementing ERP.

CREATING AND APPLYING TECHNOLOGY

research and development (R&D) A firm's way of generating new knowledge of materials and technologies and then applying it to the creation and introduction of new products, processes, and services.

Applying new technologies is an ongoing challenge at all firms. In this section, we cover the creation and application of both product and process technologies. Understanding product and process technologies first requires an understanding of the innovation process. Figure 5.5 presents an overview of this process, which is aimed at creating and applying technology to improve a firm's products, processes, and services. The innovation process focuses technical and scientific efforts on better ways to meet market needs. One way for a firm to acquire new technology is to do its own **research and development (R&D)**, which generates new knowledge of materials and technologies and then applies it to the creation and introduction of new products, processes, and services. An example of innovation is 3M's removable adhesive, which the firm then used to create Post-it Notes. By translating ideas into something of commercial value, R&D helps firms avoid technological obsolescence.

RESEARCH AND DEVELOPMENT STAGES

In what ways should a firm get involved in R&D?

Innovation and R&D projects go through the stages shown in Figure 5.5. Stages 1 and 2 are *research* stages, and stage 3 is the *development* stage. In the United States, nearly 2 percent of the gross domestic product (GDP) is devoted to industrial expenditures for R&D. About one-fourth of those expenditures are for research and the remaining three-fourths are for development. Companies doing *basic research* attempt to generate original ideas and inventions that advance knowledge and technology and may have applications in the future. Companies doing *applied research* attempt to solve the practical problems involved in turning an idea or invention into a commercially feasible product, process, or service. Companies adopting and perfecting technologies already developed by others usually do so at the development stage. As we show later in the section on acquiring new technologies, few firms are involved in both research and development.

BASIC RESEARCH. Work that explores the potential of narrowly defined technological possibilities, such as electromagnetic theory and quantum mechanics, seeking to generate

FIGURE 5.5

Research and Development Stages

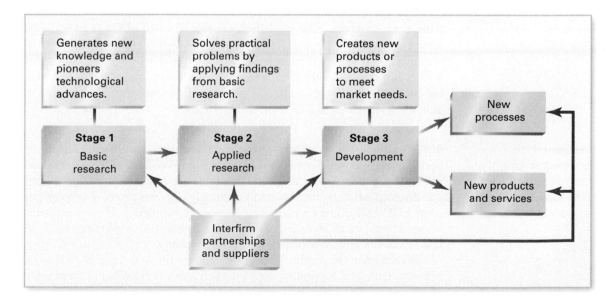

basic research Work that explores the potential of narrowly defined technological possibilities seeking to generate new knowledge and pioneer technological advances.

new knowledge and pioneer technological advances, is called **basic research**. Basic research seeks fundamental truths, such as the knowledge that ultimately made possible the Mars Rover vehicle. It is generally nondirective research that isn't targeted for a particular product or process. Basic research is often science-based, as with computer and biotechnology technologies, but not always. Success may come from an inventive mind or a flash of genius. More often, basic research implies a purposeful and systematic search using experimental-scale equipment. Basic research is performed in labs by government agencies (such as NASA or the Department of Defense), some large firms (such as telecommunications and computer companies), and universities. In the United States, the giants in basic research include Lucent Technologies (formerly Bell Labs), Boeing, DuPont, Ford, IBM, 3M, Motorola, Raychem, Raytheon, Texas Instruments, and Xerox.

applied research Work geared toward solving practical problems.

APPLIED RESEARCH. Work geared toward solving practical problems is called **applied research**. It tends to be done mostly by large firms and is more directed than basic research, and its results are more likely to lead to actual improvements in products, processes, and services. For example, a group of scientists and engineers might be formed to build a small-scale pilot plant to test and refine ideas coming from basic research efforts.

A good example of applied research and how it differs from basic research is the famous case of innovation in the glass industry by Pilkington. In 1952, the company was the preeminent glass manufacturer in the United Kingdom. Until then, transparent glass was manufactured either by drawing glass upward as a ribbon from a bath of molten glass or by rolling cooling glass horizontally between rollers. The first method created considerable optical distortion, and the second method was costly. Alastair Pilkington, a cousin of the firm's owning family and a production manager in the plant, began thinking of alternative ways of producing plate glass. He conceived the idea of floating molten glass onto a bed of molten metal. He settled on tin as a metal because it had a low-enough melting point to remain molten even as the glass solidified on it. Moreover, the tin could be kept oxide free if the atmosphere were controlled. He took the results of this basic research to the company's board. The board saw the potential in the idea and committed the firm to doing applied research. A three-person team was created and built a small pilot plant. The team found, by accident, that when the glass cooled on the molten tin, it happened to be precisely 7 millimeters thick. Most flat-glass sales were for 6-millimeter-thick glass, which could be obtained by a little stretching. Following these discoveries, a large team was formed and began the development stage. The team solved many problems, such as preventing the tin's oxidation, in a larger pilot plant and eventually were able to produce salable glass.

development The activities that turn a specified set of technologies into detailed designs and processes.

DEVELOPMENT. The activities that turn a specified set of technologies into detailed designs and processes are called **development**. Product and process designs are developed with an eye to both marketability and ease of production. Development is not just the domain of large firms—small firms also get involved. For example, PixelVision used LCD technology to develop computer monitors. However, studies show that many development ideas begin with the recognition of market and production needs, rather than from a new technological opportunity.

Development of product technology moves through several phases—concept development, technical feasibility, detailed product or service design, and process design.

Let us take a more detailed look at each of these steps.

1. During the *concept development* phase, the product idea is conceived. For example, developing a computer requires a decision about whether the central processing unit (CPU) and the monitor can be combined or must be separate.

2. During the *technical feasibility* phase, tests are conducted to determine whether the concept will work. Options are thoroughly pretested, a step that often involves considerable engineering effort. For the computer example, tests may show that because quality is lost by putting both the CPU and monitor in the same box, they must be separated.

3. During the detailed *product design* phase, prototypes of the product features may be built, tested, and analyzed. For the computer, decisions are made about the actual shape and size of the box holding the CPU. Detailed design goes beyond engineering, with operations and marketing getting involved in assessing the design for its manufacturability and marketability. Details of product characteristics are thought through, often by using lists of specifications, process formulas, and drawings. Marketing uses trial tests in limited markets or with customer panels to help gauge market reactions to specific product features or packaging. Test results may lead to changes in the product or the way it is presented before it is actually produced and marketed. These tests provide reasonable assurance that the product is technically feasible, can be produced in quantity at the desired quality level, and has customer appeal.

4. During the final development phase, *process design*, final decisions are made regarding the inputs, operations, work flows, and methods to be used to make the product (see the Process Management chapter). Large pilot plants, or even full-scale plants, are built—or existing plants modified—to refine the production processes.

How does R&D apply to service providers?

Developing Service Products. The R&D stages apply equally well to service providers, although stages 1 and 2 are far less formal and extensive than they are for manufacturers. When developing new services, service providers still must define their *customer benefit packages* (see the Operations Strategy chapter), which is an important part of the development stage. At a restaurant, for example, core products are food and drink. Peripheral products are tables, chairs, and tableware. Services include courtesy, speed, quality, and the less tangible characteristics of taste, atmosphere, perceptions of status, comfort, and a general sense of well-being. In developing the customer benefit package for its Olive Garden restaurants, General Mills opened its prototype facility in a failed steakhouse in Orlando, Florida, in 1982. It canvassed 1,000 restaurants for recipes, interviewed 5,000 consumers, and tried more than 80 pots of spaghetti sauce. During the process design phase, the company developed videotapes showing how each job was to be done for employee training. Even singing waiters' lyrics were carefully crafted.

Development, Competitiveness, and Profitability. The development stage is particularly important to a firm's future profitability. Historically, many technology and resource-rich firms failed to develop and compete with new technologies that they helped create. The Swiss watch consortium, SSIH, is a good example. It dominated worldwide markets through the 1970s. It had even developed the quartz movements that would allow it to re-create its market. However, organizational complacency held back this technology leader, and nimble competitors that actually had fewer resources outmaneuvered it. For example, Seiko made the bold decision to substitute the quartz watch for its existing mechanical watches. When SSIH did not move on to quartz technology, its market share suddenly dropped and it eventually went under. Xerox is another example. It may have invented the office as it is known today and will be known in the future. It pioneered work in laser printing, networking, icon-based computing, and the laptop computer. However, it failed to develop innovations into products and services, thus creating no substantial new businesses other than its copier core.

TECHNOLOGY FUSION

Knowledge-based innovation often demands not just one type of knowledge but many. The computer, for example, is based on at least six separate strands of knowledge. Binary arithmetic, Charles Babbage's concept for the calculating machine, and the punch card were known before 1900. Yet they were not combined with the other three strands (an electronic switch called the audion tube, symbolic logic, and the concepts of programming and feedback) to make an operational computer until 1946.

technology fusion The process of combining several *existing* technologies and scientific disciplines to create a hybrid technology.

Technology fusion refers to the process of combining several *existing* technologies and scientific disciplines to create a hybrid technology. Only a fraction of all product and process innovations come from a breakthrough in knowledge. Most are the creative applications of technologies that are already available. Moreover, adding one technology to another can produce something greater than the sum of the parts. For example, marrying electronics and optics gave birth to fiber-optics communication systems. And fusing electronics and mechanical technologies transformed the machine-tool industry. Thus, the advantage in the competitive game often goes to the firms that make the right choices among a vast array of technological options, not necessarily to the firms that create those options. Firms haven't stopped conducting basic research, but they have shifted much of their focus to applied research and development.

Some of the strongest proponents of technology fusion are the leading high-tech manufacturers in Japan. Fanuc, Nissan, NEC, and Sharp have developed their own versions of technology fusion and linked them to their R&D strategy. Fanuc, for example, fused electronic, mechanical, and material technologies to develop an affordable numerical controller (see the Computer-Integrated Manufacturing supplement), a cabinet-sized system that controls the movements of industrial machine tools. It is now the world market leader in computerized numerically controlled (CNC) machines. It added one technology to another, combining rather than replacing existing technologies.

Two important principles guide successful technology fusion. First, the market should drive the R&D process, not the other way around. If the customer wants a cheaper and smaller numerical controller, that is the starting point for development. Second, companies need intelligence-gathering abilities to monitor technological developments both inside and outside the industry. All employees, from senior managers to front-line workers, should be part of this surveillance process. A firm must not only look at its immediate competitors but also at invisible competitors outside the industry that have the technological capability to enter it sometime in the future.

TECHNOLOGY STRATEGY

Which technologies should be pursued and when?

Because technology is changing so rapidly and because of the many technologies available, operations managers must more than ever make intelligent, informed decisions about new product and process technologies. The stakes are high because such choices affect the human as well as the technical aspects of operations. Here we examine how technologies should be chosen and how these choices link with strategy to create a competitive advantage. An appropriate technology is one that fits corporate and operations strategies and gives the firm a sustainable advantage. Several tests of a potential technological change should be made. If the change being considered fails these tests, it shouldn't be pursued even if it represents an impressive technological accomplishment. Tests leading to *technological choice* are valid for both manufacturers and service providers.

Technology strategy deals with more than just technological choice. It also determines whether an organization should be a leader or follower in technological change and aids in evaluating radically new technologies when conventional financial analyses won't do the job.

TECHNOLOGY AS A COMPETITIVE ADVANTAGE

A new technology should create some kind of competitive advantage. *Competitive advantage* is created by increasing the value of a product to a customer or reducing the costs of bringing the product to market. The potential for increasing value and reducing costs from a new technology are vast. The most obvious cost-reduction strategy is that of reducing the *direct costs* of labor and materials. Labor savings are still used to justify most automation projects, but labor is a shrinking component—only 10 to 15 percent—of total costs. Therefore, to understand a new technology's true value, a manager should assess factors other than cost savings.

For example, *sales* can increase, as MCI Communications found when it spent $300 million to update its computer systems and offer innovative residential calling services. *Quality* can improve, as illustrated by the new magnetic resonance imaging (MRI) machines that can diagnose heart and liver diseases without using X rays and radioactive materials. With MRIs, scanning times are reduced from about 45 to 20 minutes, thus increasing the number of patients who can be served, reducing costs per patient, and increasing patient comfort. In manufacturing, Giddings & Lewis makes groups of machine tools by using automated materials handling equipment and computer control. These systems reduce human error and thus improve product quality. In addition, they yield *quicker delivery times* by reducing processing times. These reductions in turn allow for *smaller inventories*, with less inventory held on the shop floor.

The *environment* might even improve: CSX Corporation replaced the mufflers on some of its unloading machinery with a noise-cancellation system that eliminates engine noise completely. The system, consisting of tiny speakers, a microphone, and a small signal processor, analyzes noise and instantly generates identical waves that are 180° out of phase with the sound waves. The new technology eliminates the need for ear protection in a workplace that used to produce a noise level equivalent to that of a commercial jet during takeoff. Managerial Practice 5.5 gives another example of how technology's impact on the environment can be an important consideration in its selection.

Of course, new technology also can have its downside. Investment in new technology can be forbidding, particularly for complex and expensive projects that require new facilities or extensive facility overhaul. The investment also can be risky because of uncertainties in demand and in per-unit benefits. Finally, technology may have hidden costs, requiring different employee knowledge and skills to maintain and operate the new equipment. Such requirements may generate employee resistance and lower morale and increase turnover. Thus, the operations manager must sort out the many benefits and costs of different technological choices.

FIT WITH COMPETITIVE PRIORITIES

Another important test is how technological change will help a firm achieve the competitive priorities of cost, quality, time, and flexibility. Such a change should have a positive impact on one or more of these priorities, particularly on those that are

MANAGERIAL PRACTICE 5.5
Technological Choice and the Environment

The chemical industry's record on the environment has been bad, and its production processes still account for almost half of all toxic pollution produced in the United States. Things are changing, however, Chemical companies are beginning to view waste produced by their processes as a measure of efficiency. The more unusable by-products a process creates, the less efficient it is. Some companies plan to cut air emissions and waste sharply by using recycling and less toxic materials, with an ultimate goal of "closed-loop" manufacturing that emits no discharges. Similarly, a new ethylene plant of Dow Chemical Company (www.dow.com) in Fort Saskatchewan, Alberta, will release just 10 gallons of cleaned-up wastewater per minute into the North Saskatchewan River, down from the current plant's 360 gallons per minute.

There is growing global interest in supporting technologies that cut emissions of carbon dioxide and other so-called greenhouse gases, one of the culprits behind global warming. One possibility is an international agreement that commits companies to reducing emissions. The basic idea is to impose an overall cap on emissions but maintain flexibility with a credit-trading system. Some companies, such as BP-Amoco PLC (www.bpamoco.com) and Royal Dutch/Shell Group, are already doing this internally. When BP's Western Gas business unit slashed its emissions by 1.4 million metric tons of carbon dioxide yearly, it more than met the company's cap and was thus able to sell 40,000 tons of extra emissions to other BP units that could not make cuts so cheaply. The World Bank launched a "venture capital" fund, with companies and governments chipping in to pay for technology projects that cut emissions and then divvying up shares of whatever reductions are achieved.

Source: Carey, John. "A Free-Market Cure for Global Warming." *Business Week* (May 15, 2000), pp. 167–170.

emphasized for the product or service in question and on determining whether this advantage can be protected from imitation. For example, FedEx promises fast delivery time (overnight delivery) and that parcels will be "absolutely, positively" delivered on time. FedEx chose bar code technology to give it an early ability to track packages throughout the handling cycle—a capability possessed by none of its competitors at the time. Combining this technology with its own fleet of airplanes allowed its operations to support its strategic orientation and gave FedEx a large market share. Its competitors could not easily match FedEx's differentiation strategy on the basis of time.

CORE COMPETENCIES

Which technologies will add to the firm's core competencies?

strategic fit The degree to which technologies chosen and decisions made help achieve current corporate and operations strategies.

core competencies Capabilities that form the basis for new strategies, leading down a long-term patch to improvement.

Achieving **strategic fit**, whereby chosen technologies help achieve current corporate and operations strategies, isn't enough. New technologies can build new production capabilities that form the basis for new strategies, leading down a long-term path to improvement. Thus, management must not merely preserve the past but create the firm's future with new operating capabilities. It does so by developing a set of **core competencies** and technologies that enable the firm to adapt quickly to changing opportunities. These capabilities allow coordination of diverse production skills and integration of multiple streams of technologies. Unlike facilities and equipment, these competencies and technologies do not deteriorate as they are used, but instead grow and get stronger. They give rise to new generations of products and processes that cannot be obtained by outsourcing and original-equipment-manufacturer (OEM) supply relationships.

The core competencies and technologies of 3M in substrates, coatings, and adhesives allowed it to dream up such diverse products as Post-it Notes, magnetic tape, photographic film, pressure-sensitive tapes, and coated abrasives. This wide-ranging set of capabilities comes from just a few core competencies with sticky tape. Honda's core competencies in engines and power trains gives it a competitive advantage in the automobile, lawn mower, motorcycle, and generator businesses. The need for core competencies is just as strong in services. Citicorp moved ahead of others by investing in an operating system that allowed it to participate in world markets 24 hours a day. Its competence in systems provided the means for Citicorp to differentiate itself from many of its financial services competitors.

core technologies
Technologies that are developed internally and used along a company's supply chain to give it the strongest competitive advantage.

CORE TECHNOLOGIES. Management must identify a firm's **core technologies**, which are crucial to the firm's success and should be developed internally. Core technologies generally can't be easily bought on the market or quickly plugged into the production system. Generally, the broader a firm's set of core technologies, the less vulnerable it is to new entrants into its industry. Resource constraints, however, limit the number of technologies that can be developed internally. Thus, management must analyze the technologies used along its supply chain to identify those that will give it the strongest competitive advantage (see the Supply-Chain Management Chapter).

FIRST-MOVER CONSIDERATIONS

Should the firm be a technology leader or follower?

This strategic consideration deals with *when* to adopt a new technology rather than which technology to choose. Being the first to market with a new technology offers a firm numerous advantages that can outweigh the financial investment needed. Technological leaders lay down the competitive rules that others will follow with regard to a new product or process. A "first-mover" may be able to gain an early large market share that creates an entry barrier for other firms. Even if competitors are able to match the new technology, the first-mover's initial advantage in the market can endure. Being first can give a firm the reputation that emulators will find difficult to overcome. A first-mover strategy may lead to at least temporary advantage with suppliers of outside materials and services and with contracts negotiated earlier than those of its competitors that follow suit. Technology leadership might also allow the firm to get patents that discourage imitation.

Of course, a company that pursues a first-mover strategy faces risks that can jeopardize its financial and market position. First, pioneering costs can be high, with R&D costs exceeding the firm's financial capabilities. Second, market demand for a new technology is speculative, and estimates of future financial gains may be overstated. Third, a new product or process technology may well become outdated quickly because of new technological breakthroughs. In the global market, government regulations in foreign countries might require local firms to be licensed with the new technology first so that some first-mover advantages are lost. Thus, managers must carefully analyze these risks and benefits before deciding which technologies to pursue.

ECONOMIC JUSTIFICATION

Managers should make every effort to translate considerations of sources of competitive advantages, fit with competitive priorities, existence of core competencies, and first-mover strategy into a financial analysis to estimate whether investment in a new technology is economically justified. Operations managers should state precisely what they expect from a new technology and then quantify costs and performance goals. They should determine whether the expected after-tax cash flows resulting from the investment are likely to outweigh the costs, after accounting for the time value of money. Traditional techniques such as the net present value method, internal rate of return method, and the payback method can be used to estimate financial impact (see CD supplement on Financial Analysis).

However, uncertainties and intangibles must also be considered, even though they cannot be easily measured. For example, there may be uncertainty about whether a new technology can be successfully developed. If it is a known technology, uncertainty may exist about how well it can be adapted to current processes or vice versa. Certain downstream benefits may be hard to quantify. For example, flexible automation might be of value for products that will be introduced well into the future, long after the life of the product for which it was first implemented. For these reasons, financial analyses should be augmented by qualitative judgments.

Operations managers must look beyond the direct costs of a new technology to its impact on customer service, delivery times, inventories, and resource flexibility. These are often the most important considerations. Quantifying such intangible goals as the ability to move quickly into a new market may be difficult. However, a firm that fails to make technological changes along with its competitors can quickly lose its competitive advantage and face declining revenues and layoffs. Justification should begin with financial analyses recognizing all quantifiable factors that can be translated into dollar values. The resulting financial measures should then be merged with an evaluation of the qualitative factors and intangibles involved. The manager can then estimate the risks associated with uncertain cost and revenue estimates. Decision-making tools such as the preference matrix approach, decision theory, and decision trees can help the manager make a final decision (see the Decision Making supplement).

DISRUPTIVE TECHNOLOGIES

What is a disruptive technology and how can it be dealt with?

Many companies have invested aggressively and successfully in technologies to retain current customers and to improve current processes. They have done all the right things in terms of seeking a competitive advantage and funding the technology projects that should lead to the highest profit margins and largest market share, relative to their *current* customers. They have pursued new process technologies that address the next-generation performance requirements of their customers. And yet, paradoxically, what seems like good business practice may be devastating and prevent many firms from investing in the technologies that *future* customers will want and need.

This paradox is likely to occur because of disruptive technologies, which occur infrequently and are nearly impossible to justify on the basis of rational, analytical investment techniques. A **disruptive technology** is one that

disruptive technology A technology that has performance attributes that are not valued yet by *existing* customers or for current products, or performs much worse on some performance attributes that existing or future customers value but will quickly surpass existing technologies on such attributes when it is refined.

1. has performance attributes that are not valued yet by *existing* customers or for current products, or
2. performs much worse on some performance attributes that existing or future customers value but will quickly surpass existing technologies on such attributes when it is refined.

The hard-disk–drive industry demonstrates the danger of staying too close to current customers. Between 1976 and 1992, disk-drive performance improved at a stunning rate. The size of a 100-megabyte (MB) system shrank from 5,400 to 8 cubic in., and the cost per MB dropped from $560 to $5. With each wave of disruptive technology, companies that had developed the mainstream *sustaining* technologies demanded by their customers had to drop out of the race. In fact, none of the independent disk-drive makers from 1976 survive today. In 1976, the sustaining technology was the 14-in. drive, which then shrank to 8 in., then to 5.25 in., and finally to 3.5 in. Each of these new architectures initially offered the market substantially less storage capacity than the typical user in the established market required. For example, the 8-in. drive offered only 20 MB when it was introduced, with the primary market for disk drives at the time (mainframes) needing at least 200 MB. Not surprisingly, the leading computer manufacturers rejected the 8-in. architecture at first. As a result, their suppliers, whose mainstream products were for 14-in. drives with more than 200 MG of capacity, did not pursue aggressively the disruptive technology. The pattern was repeated when the 5.25-in. and 3.5-in. drives came out. The computer makers rejected them as inadequate and thus their suppliers ignored them. For example, the capacity of the 5.25-in. drive initially was only 5 MB in 1980, which was only a fraction of the capacity that the minicomputer market needed. However, it became fully competitive in the minicomputer market by 1986 and in the mainframe market by 1991. Although the disruptive technologies offered less capacity, they had other performance attributes, such as small size and low power consumption, that created the new markets for minicomputers, desktop PCs, and portable computers.

COUNTERING DISRUPTIVE TECHNOLOGIES. How can a company deal with the paradox of disruptive technology? The first step is to recognize that it is a disruptive rather than a sustaining technology. One indicator could be internal disagreement over the advisability of producing the new technology. Marketing and financial managers will rarely support a disruptive technology, but technical personnel may argue forcibly that a new technology market can be achieved. A second indicator is to compare the likely slope of performance improvement of the technology with market demand. If its performance trajectory, as judged by knowledgeable analysts, is much faster than market expectations, it might be a disruptive technology that could become strategically crucial. It might best meet future market needs even though it is currently an inferior product.

Managers must be willing to undertake major and rapid change with disruptive technologies that are strategically crucial, even if doing so means initially serving emerging markets and realizing low profit margins. When both technology and customers change rapidly, as at many high-tech firms, one of two conflicting methods can be used to manage disruptive technologies. One method is to develop these technologies in a different part of the organization, with one part of the firm pursuing innovation and the other parts pursuing efficiency and continual improvement of technologies for existing customer bases. A team, sometimes referred to as a *skunk works*, can be formed to develop the new technology without disrupting normal operations. Such teams often work in close quarters, without many amenities, but band together in almost missionary zeal.

The other method is to use different methods of management at different times in the course of technological development. Firms can alternate periods of consolidation and continuity with sharp reorientation, interspersing periods of action and change with periods of evaluation and efficiency. With either method, the operations manager must seek ways to improve continually the existing technologies driving the production system, while being alert for radical innovations and discontinuities that can make technologies obsolete.

IMPLEMENTATION GUIDELINES

Managing technology means more than choosing the right process and equipment. It also means supporting selected technology throughout its implementation. Job satisfaction and positive employee attitudes can be maintained only if technological change is managed well. Although there are no guarantees of success, several useful implementation guidelines have emerged; they relate to technology acquisition, technology integration, the human side, and leadership.

TECHNOLOGY ACQUISITION

What is the best way for a firm to acquire new technology?

technology acquisition
Decisions on how far back in the R&D stream a firm gets involved (basic research, applied research, or development) to secure new technologies and which options it uses to do so.

Technology acquisition deals with how far back in the R&D stream a firm gets involved (basic research, applied research, or development) to secure new technologies and which options it uses to do so. Large firms are more likely to enter the early stages of the R&D stream, whereas small firms are more likely to enter later, at the development stage. There are three main options for acquiring new technology: internal sources, interfirm relationships, and purchasing from suppliers.

INTERNAL SOURCES. A firm might rely on internal sources for acquiring technology. The firm might do its own R&D or, as is more likely, some part of it. It can also look to its engineering department to refine product and process designs during the development stage or to other departments that have successfully applied new technologies. Even the largest organizations cannot rely exclusively on this option, particularly for the earliest research stages of the R&D process. For example, DuPont gets more than 50 percent of its major innovations from external sources.

INTERFIRM RELATIONSHIPS. To acquire technology, a firm might build cooperative *interfirm relationships*. Firms now look to outside sources more than ever for new technologies. Many firms, including most small companies, do not have their own R&D and engineering departments. Their challenge is to choose and refine the best mix of available technologies that others have created. They might even simply wait until information about a new technology comes into the public domain.

However, this passive option can mean long delays and incomplete information. Thus, a continuum of more aggressive options is available, with varying levels of commitment required of the firm.

1. Firms may outsource research to universities or laboratories by giving research grants. This option requires the least commitment by the firm but probably minimizes the transfer of knowledge to the firm. For example, Cyrix and Hewlett-Packard subcontract most of their R&D and high-volume microprocessor manufacturing to either Intel or IBM.

2. A firm may obtain a *license* for the technology from another organization, gaining the legal right to use it in its processes or products. A good example is Sun's licensing of Java to IBM. One drawback is that the licensing company can place constraints on the technology's use that can limit the licensee's flexibility.

3. Two or more firms may enter into a *joint venture* or *alliance*. In a joint venture, the firms agree to jointly produce a product or service (see the Operations Strategy chapter). In an alliance, the firms share the costs and benefits of R&D, as do the Electric Power Institute consortium in the United States and the more than 75 research associations in Japan. This option requires a greater commitment but establishes more of a market presence than the first two options. NEC, a well-known Japanese company, entered into more than 100 alliances in the 1980s. The company found that, from an investment standpoint, using foreign technology was quicker and cheaper than developing its own. NEC built new competencies in this way, and its strategy paid off. The company emerged as a world leader in semiconductors and a first-tier player in telecommunication products and computers.

4. A firm can *buy out* another firm which has the desired technological know-how. This option requires the greatest commitment to exploiting the new technology and can lead to market dominance.

A good example of the various technology acquisition options is provided by the actions of 3M. In the 1970s, it was the dominant producer of copper connectors that connect one strand of copper to another. However, fiber-optic technology began to emerge as a potential breakthrough that could undermine 3M's core competence in copper connectors. The company began to do basic research on fiber optics and then moved to applied research. Other companies were developing the technology so rapidly that 3M bought Dorran Photonics to gain immediate access to the new technology. Using what it learned from Dorran Photonics, 3M developed *fiber-splice* technology, which joins two cables by mechanical means. Through its acquisition of technology, 3M gained substantial access to both the connector and splice markets in fiber optics.

SUPPLIERS. Firms can gain new technology from outside *suppliers*. Suppliers can be the source of parts for a firm's own technology products (such as the LCD displays that PixelVision gets from Japanese manufacturers), or they can be the source of new innovative equipment or services that the firm uses in its processes. Operations managers must be alert to new technologies available from suppliers that will raise productivity, improve product quality, shorten lead times, or increase product variety. Outsourcing gives a firm access to the latest technology that has been developed throughout the world. Sometimes a firm can acquire new technology off-the-shelf from a supplier, but some development work is likely to be needed to adapt the technology to the firm's requirements. For example, before a firm can utilize computerized process control equipment that it might buy from a supplier software must be developed for the firm's specific application.

TECHNOLOGY INTEGRATION

During the 1960s and 1970s, the approach to technology improvement in the United States was for companies such as IBM and AT&T to make breakthroughs in their R&D laboratories and then develop these inventions and discoveries into radically new products. The R&D process was sequential, with isolated research groups exploring new technologies and choosing which should be passed on to the development segment of the organization. Engineers and scientists would then refine the technologies and develop new products and processes. Their outputs were then passed on to production experts to remove the final bugs. The result was a good deal of *fragmentation* in efforts to be innovative and push technological change.

concurrent engineering
The act of bringing design engineers, manufacturing engineers, buyers, quality specialists, information technology specialists, and others together to bridge the gaps between research and development and between development and manufacturing.

CONCURRENT ENGINEERING. Today, cross-functional teams are responsible for implementing new technology. These teams bridge the gaps between research and development and between development and manufacturing. Bringing design engineers, manufacturing engineers, buyers, quality specialists, information technology specialists, and others together at this stage is called **concurrent engineering**. It can significantly shorten the time to market and allow the firm to meet time-based and quality competition better (see the Operations Strategy chapter). These teams are charged to take a broad, systemic outlook in choosing technologies to pursue. Team members are knowledgeable about various technologies and able to integrate technological choices. In doing so, they test a relatively small number of possible technologies simultaneously with a number of carefully selected experiments. This new approach to R&D is credited with helping the U.S. electronics industry make an almost miraculous comeback in the 1990s in the production and marketing of semiconductors, personal computers, servers, and laptops. Intel and Microsoft consolidated their leadership in microprocessors and software. IBM introduced a variety of impressive new products with its improved development process and manufacturing capabilities.

THE HUMAN SIDE

How do technology and
human resources issues
relate?

The jobs that people actually perform are largely determined by technology. When technology changes, so do jobs. New technology affects jobs at all levels—eliminating some, upgrading some, and downgrading others. Even when technological change is small, people related issues may become large. The operations manager must anticipate and prepare for such changes.

Education and employee involvement help a firm identify new technological possibilities and then prepare employees for the jobs modified or created when the new technologies are implemented. When Ford revamped its plant to make the Aerostar minivan, management reviewed proposed methods with workers directly responsible for specific operations. Employees made 434 suggestions, about 60 percent of which were adopted. Both the number and the percent were considered quite good. Before Chrysler opened its automated plant in Sterling Heights, Michigan, it put its employees through 900,000 labor hours of training collectively.

Chaparral Steel (see our "tour" in the Operations Strategy chapter) emphasizes education and employee involvement as it continually seeks technological improvements. Loyalty and commitment to the firm increase when employees know that the firm is helping them continually upgrade their skills. Such investment in human resources means longterm employment and minimal resistance to change for fear of job loss. Chaparral Steel recognizes that all employees, from senior managers to front-line workers, should be part of the surveillance process, searching for technological improvements from both inside and outside the company. Thus, employees become an essential way for the firm to create the future rather than preserve the past. Everyone in the organization recognizes the need for Chaparral Steel to get there first—and for less. Such an emphasis on highly skilled workers is not unique to Chaparral Steel. During the mid-1980s, innovative companies such as Corning and Motorola began to boost their investment in employee training and education, helping raise their technical competence and enabling them to add more value to their products and services. This approach has become much more widespread.

LEADERSHIP

Managers must play several, often conflicting, roles in managing technology. They must be *good stewards* and hold to tight budgets and schedules. Implementation speed to keep up with technological changes requires good project manager skills (see the Managing Project Processes chapter). Managers must continually monitor program targets and completion dates. They must also be *realists* in assessing the risks, costs, and benefits of a new technology. As *visionaries*, they need to have a technical vision of a goal and relentlessly pursue it. As *advocates*, they must make a commitment to the project and stand behind it. Finally, as *gatekeepers*, they have to keep everyone focused.

When new technologies are being developed or implemented, the operations manager should assemble a team representing all affected departments to lead and coordinate the work. A *project champion* who promotes the project at every opportunity and who has contagious enthusiasm should be in charge. This leader should be respected by all team members and reflect management's support of the team throughout the project. Everyone should know that the operations manager is knowledgeable about the project, stands behind it, and will give it the resources it needs to succeed.

MANAGING TECHNOLOGY ACROSS THE ORGANIZATION

Technologies are embedded in processes throughout an organization (see Fig. 5.2, p. 195). In each of their functional areas and business units, both service providers and manufacturers use many technologies. For example, Seven-Eleven Japan uses point-of-sale technology to assess customers' needs (*marketing*) and to control inventory in its supply chain (*operations*). Technology also creates special needs for training and supporting employees (*human resources*). The New York Stock Exchange uses computer equipment and software (*management information systems*) to streamline trading processes (*finance*). *Engineering* is heavily involved in R&D, creating new products and services and applying them to the organization's processes. Fleet Bank's new Web services show how B2B e-commerce has an increasingly important role in the marketing of financial services, and Cisco shows how the Internet can establish connections throughout the whole organization and to its suppliers. The very essence of enterprise resource planning illustrates many of the ways in which this chapter's topic, management of technology, is important to all business areas. ERP makes connections among applications in sales and marketing, customer service, supply-chain management, accounting and finance, manufacturing, and human resources.

CHAPTER HIGHLIGHTS

❐ Technology consists of physical equipment, procedures, know-how, and the support network used at operations to produce products and services. Managers must make informed decisions about which technological possibilities to pursue and how best to implement those chosen.

❐ Innovation and technological change is a primary source of productivity improvement and a driver of global competition. Organizations more experienced at adapting to changing technologies tend to enjoy stronger competitive positions worldwide.

❐ Technologies are involved in all the processes along a firm's supply chain and in each of the firm's functional areas. Office and information technologies are pervasive. Managers need to invest the time to learn about the technologies that are used or could be used at their organizations.

❐ Information technology deals with how managers use and communicate information to make decisions effectively. Hardware, software, databases, and telecommunications are the main components that make up information technology.

❐ The Internet is a network of networks, allowing the exchange of text, graphics, video, programs, and faxes. It is connected to almost 200 countries and will soon have half a billion users around the globe.

❐ Electronic commerce, both B2C and B2B, is creating totally new ways for a firm to relate to customers, suppliers, employees, and investors.

❐ Enterprise resource planning is a large, integrated information system. Its applications cut across many processes, functional areas, business units, regions,

and products. In deciding whether or not to implement ERP, instead of continuing on with legacy systems, managers must carefully weigh its advantages and disadvantages.

❐ Research and development (R&D) creates and applies new technologies, leading to better products, services, and processes. The R&D stages apply to both manufacturers and service providers. Basic research is performed more in labs by government agencies, some large firms, and universities. Applied research, and particularly development, are performed by many firms—even small ones. Many firms also utilize technology fusion to combine several existing technologies in innovative ways.

❐ High-tech options are not necessarily appropriate solutions to operations problems. Tests of the advisability of technological change include competitive advantages measured in terms of costs, sales, quality, delivery times, inventory, and the environment; financial analyses; first-mover or follower considerations; identifying disruptive technologies; fit with competitive priorities; and core competencies.

❐ How technology is acquired is an important implementation issue. Instead of performing the R&D itself, a firm might best gain access to new technology from others through research grants, licenses, alliances, outside suppliers, or the acquisition of another firm.

❐ Managers are using team approaches and concurrent engineering to avoid the fragmentation of efforts between different parts of the organization and cut development times.

❑ Human resources issues are closely tied to technology. Successful implementation is more likely if the manager deals with people-related issues on an ongoing basis. Many firms devote considerable resources to education and training, fostering employee involvement in

technological change and ensuring more commitment to the firm. Education raises the technical expertise of the employees and makes them even more valuable assets.

❑ Managers play several roles in managing technology. They must be good stewards, realists, visionaries, advocates, and gatekeepers. Creating a team led by a project champion helps ensure implementation success.

KEY TERMS

applied research *212*
basic research *212*
concurrent engineering *221*
core competencies *216*
core technologies *217*
database *197*
development *212*
disruptive technology *218*
electronic commerce
    (e-commerce) *198*
encryption *203*
enterprise process *205*

enterprise resource planning
    (ERP) *205*
hardware *197*
information technology *194*
Internet *198*
interoperability *208*
Internet service providers (ISPs) *199*
intranet *198*
local area network (LAN) *199*
management of technology *194*
network service providers
    (NSPs) *199*

process technology *193*
product technology *193*
research and development (R&D) *211*
software *197*
strategic fit *216*
support network *191*
technology *191*
technology acquisition *220*
technology fusion *214*
telecommunications *197*
Web browsers *199*
World Wide Web *199*

DISCUSSION QUESTIONS

1. Why are traditional financial analysis techniques criticized when they are used to justify new technologies? Must such projects just be accepted as a leap of faith and an act of hope? Explain.

2. Chip "Hacker" Snerdly works for the sales department of Farr and Wyde, an office equipment supplier in a cutthroat competitive market. Farr and Wyde's competitors use voice mailboxes to receive messages while calling on other customers. Snerdly discovers that a surprising number of voice-mailbox occupants do not bother to use passwords and that others rarely change their passwords. So he listens to, copies, and deletes messages left for his competitors by their customers. Snerdly calls on those customers himself, knowing that

they are in the market for office equipment. What are the ethical issues here? What policies are necessary to foil Snerdly?

3. Discuss how increased Internet use of business-to-business interactions would affect customer–supplier relationships.

4. For an organization of your choice, such as where you previously worked, discuss how an ERP system could be used and whether it would increase process effectiveness.

5. How does an on-line retailer such as Amazon.com make use of datamining to boost their revenues?

PROBLEMS

Advanced Problems

An icon in the margin next to a problem identifies the software that can be helpful, but not mandatory. The software is available on the Student CD-ROM that is packaged with every new copy of the textbook. Problems 1–4 require reading the Decision Making supplement. Problems 6–8 require reading CD Supplement K

on financial analysis. Problem 9 should be solved as a team exercise.

1. **OM Explorer** You have been asked to analyze four new advanced manufacturing technologies and recommend the best one for adoption by your company. Management has rated these technologies with respect

to seven criteria, using a 0–100 scale (0 = worst; 100 = best). Management has given the performance criteria different weights. Table 5.2 summarizes the relevant information. Which technology would you recommend?

TABLE 5.2 *Analysis of New Technologies*

CRITERION	WEIGHT	TECHNOLOGY RATING			
		A	B	C	D
Financial measures	25	60	70	10	100
Volume flexibility	15	90	25	60	80
Quality of output	20	70	90	75	90
Required facility space	5	60	20	40	50
Market share	10	60	70	90	90
Product mix flexibility	20	90	80	30	90
Required labor skills	5	80	40	20	10

2. 💿 **OM Explorer** Hitech Manufacturing Company, Inc., must select a process technology for one of its new products from among three different alternatives. The following cost data have been obtained for the three process technologies.

COST	PROCESS A	PROCESS B	PROCESS C
Fixed costs per year	$20,000	$40,000	$100,000
Variable costs per unit	$15	$10	$6

a. Find the range for the annual production volume in which each process will be preferred.

b. If the expected annual production volume is 12,000 units, which process should be selected?

3. 💿 **OM Explorer** Technology Enterprises Company is evaluating three different manufacturing technologies to choose the best one for manufacturing its new product line. The payoffs from the technologies will depend on market conditions for the new product line, which is uncertain but could be buoyant, moderate, or dismal. Although management is unable to estimate the probabilities for these market conditions because of the nature of the new products, it has developed the following payoff table.

ALTERNATIVE	MARKET CONDITION		
	Buoyant	Moderate	Dismal
Technology A	$500,000	$150,000	($200,000)
Technology B	$200,000	$50,000	$20,000
Technology C	$900,000	$25,000	($300,000)

Which alternative would you recommend for each of the following decision criteria?

a. Maximin

b. Maximax

c. Laplace

d. Minimax regret

4. 💿 **SmartDraw** Super Innovators, Inc., is faced with the decision of switching its production facilities to new (promising, but not yet completely tried) processing technology. The technology may be implemented in one or two steps, with the option to stop after the initial step. Because the benefits from the new technology (cost savings and productivity improvements) are subject to uncertainty, the firm is considering two options. The first option is to make the full switchover in one step to take advantage of economies of scale in investment and opportunities to gain a larger market share. For this choice the investment cost is $5 million. The expected present value of the cash flows is $20 million if the new processing technology works as well as expected and $6 million if it does not work as well as expected. The second option is to implement part of the system as a first step and then extend the system to full capability. If the technology does not work as well as expected and the firm had decided to go for the full switchover, the total investment cost could be higher (because of diseconomies of scale) and the payoff could be lower. The investment cost for the initial step is $2 million, and the present value of the combined investment in two steps will be $6 million. If both steps are implemented, the expected present value of the cash flows is $15 million if the new processing technology works as well as expected and $8 million otherwise. If only the first step is implemented, the expected present value of the cash flows is $4 million if the new processing technology works as well as expected and $2 million otherwise. The firm estimates that there is a 40 percent chance that the new technology will work as well as expected.

a. Draw a decision tree to solve this problem.

b. What should the firm do to achieve the highest expected payoff?

5. The GSX Company is considering an automated manufacturing system to replace its current system. At present, the monthly cost of goods sold is $1 million. Direct labor accounts for 40 percent of this cost. Scrap and rework costs are $200,000. Working capital (primarily inventories) required for the smooth operation of the

current system averages four months' cost of goods sold. The anticipated benefits of the proposed automated system are (i) reduction of 25 percent in direct labor and 75 percent in scrap and rework costs and (ii) a 50 percent reduction in the working capital investment resulting from a one-time reduction in work-in-process inventories.

a. Estimate the annual savings from the automated system in dollars per year.

b. What is the reduction in the dollar amount invested in working capital?

6. 💿 **OM Explorer** Riverbend Hospital is considering two different computerized information systems to improve pharmacy productivity. The first alternative is a portable computer system that will require a one-time investment of $80,000 for the computer hardware, software, and necessary employee training. After-tax cash flows attributable to the investment are expected to be $20,000 per year for the next eight years. Savings would accrue from increased pharmacist productivity and the value of having timely and accurate information. The second alternative is to install a mainframe computer linked to bedside terminals that would allow doctors to prescribe treatments directly to the pharmacy from patients' rooms. This system would require an investment of $170,000, but is expected to generate after-tax cash flows of $40,000 per year for eight years. The hospital seeks to earn 16 percent on its investments. Assume that both systems will have no salvage value at the end of eight years.

a. Calculate the net present value, internal rate of return (IRR), and payback period for each alternative.

b. Based on your financial analysis, what do you recommend?

c. Are there any valid considerations other than financial? If so, what are they?

7. 💿 **OM Explorer** First State Bank is considering installing a new automatic teller machine (ATM) at either of two new locations: inside a supermarket or inside the bank itself. An initial investment of $60,000 is required for the ATM regardless of location. The operating costs of the ATM at the supermarket would be $15,000 per year and of the ATM inside the bank $10,000 per year. The higher costs of the supermarket ATM reflect the additional cost of leasing supermarket space and transportation. Revenue generated from new accounts because of the installation of each ATM should also differ, with the supermarket ATM generating $55,000 per year and

the bank ATM $52,000 per year. Assume a tax rate of 30 percent and a desired rate of return of 18 percent on investment. The ATMs have an expected life of eight years, with no salvage value at the end of that time. Use MACRS depreciation allowances, noting that the ATMs may be considered as assets in the five-year class.

a. Calculate the net present value for each alternative.

b. Based on your analysis, which location do you recommend?

8. 💿 **OM Explorer** New England Power and Electric, a supplier of electric power to the northeast United States, is considering the purchase of a robot to repair welds in nuclear reactors. Two types of vision-system robots are being considered: a "smart" robot, whose actions in the reactor would be controlled by what it "sees", and a different kind of robot, whose actions in the reactor would be controlled by an external operator. The "smart" robot requires an initial investment of $300,000, and the operator-controlled robot requires an initial investment of $200,000. Both robots have an expected life of five years and no salvage value at the end of that time. Welds are currently repaired by a human welder. The job is hazardous, so the welder's annual pay and fringe benefits total $150,000. Buying either robot eliminates the need for the human welder, but the operator-controlled robot requires an operator whose annual salary (and benefits) would be $50,000. The "smart" robot requires an extra $15,000 in technical support. New England Power and Electric seeks at least 18 percent on its investments, and its tax rate is 50 percent. As these robots are specially designed tools, treat them as assets in the three-year class and use MACRS depreciation allowances.

a. Calculate the net present value for each alternative.

b. Based on your financial analysis, which do you recommend?

9. Imagine that you are a member of the operations management team in a firm that manufactures flashlights. Your firm is faced with the problem of choosing the equipment and process technology for manufacturing the casings for the flashlights. After an evaluation of several alternative technologies, the choice has been narrowed to two technologies: (i) deep drawing of metal bars on a press using a die, and (ii) injection molding of a variety of plastic materials. Compare the two technologies in terms of how each one will influence various elements of the operating system.

a. First, make a list of the various elements (e.g., equipment, raw materials, building, operators, safety, etc.) and then indicate how the two technologies influence each element.

b. For which of these elements is the contrast between the influences of the two technologies most striking?

CASE BILL'S HARDWARE

It had been a very busy week at Bill Murton's hardware store. A storm had blown through early in the week, and sales of tools and repair parts had been brisk. This morning was relatively quiet, however, so Murton was using it as an opportunity to look over his shelves to get an idea of inventory levels. Some items had sold much less than he would have expected; others had sold out completely.

I sure wish I could predict what will be sold each week, he mused. It seems like I always have too much of some things and not enough of others. I wonder if the POS system that our cooperative is considering would help me deal with this uncertainty.

Bill's Hardware is a member of a hardware store cooperative, a group of more than 300 independently owned hardware stores that banded together for greater buying power and better merchandise distribution. Many of the items carried by a typical hardware store are similar. By buying these items as a group and storing them at a few centrally located distribution centers, individual stores can achieve economies of scale, allowing them to compete better with large nationwide chains. The cooperative is member owned. An annual membership fee and a service charge are applied to the cost of the items that a store purchases through the cooperative. Any revenues generated beyond the cooperative's operating costs are returned to members as a dividend.

Typically, a member store reviews inventory once a week and places orders that will bring stock back up to a target level. That level is the quantity of an item that, based on the time of year, the storeowner wants to have on the shelf. Owners place orders by using a PC-based software program and a modem over a dial-up telephone connection to the cooperative's computer. The cooperative leases a fleet of trucks to deliver goods weekly to member stores from one of three distribution centers. Each geographic area receives shipments on a designated day. Surges in demand, if detected, can be met by midcycle orders shipped via UPS.

Target inventory levels are based on forecasts made from historical information kept in the store's inventory database. These forecasts are adjusted by the owner's past experience and information gleaned from trade journals

and listening to customers. Additionally, the cooperative makes aggregate sales data from member stores available, along with projected demand trends. The challenge for the storeowner is to project weekly requirements accurately and detect unusual demand for items that exceed inventory in time to avoid stockouts.

THE POS SYSTEM

The cooperative's directors have formulated a plan to obtain and install point-of-sale (POS) technology in members' stores. The motivation is to take advantage of technology that can allow the distribution center to know, in real time, what items are being sold in various stores. Armed with this information, the cooperative can improve its product forecasting, make better purchasing decisions, and reduce the chance that an item will be out of stock at distribution centers. Although the original plan was to make installation of the system mandatory, the cooperative's directors decided that such a requirement could place an excessive burden on some of the smaller or less profitable stores. Consequently, installation will be optional.

The POS system is to comprise a scanning device attached to a cash register that operates with a microprocessor. This cash register will be networked to a PC so that an item's current price can be obtained for checkout and a perpetual inventory maintained. Each night, the distribution center will telephone the store's computer, which will answer and download the day's sales. At the end of the business day, the storeowner can also review the day's sales and determine current inventory levels. The system will be designed to detect any items likely to sell out. The owner can tag any item, permitting an order to be placed that night (when the distribution center calls) for midcycle delivery.

The cost of the POS system will be borne by individual stores but, because of combined purchasing power, systems can be obtained for 40 percent less than list price. The cooperative's directors propose that each distribution center contract with an installer to do on-site equipment installation at individual stores. However, individual storeowners would be allowed to have local technicians do the installation. The cost of system installation at the distribution

continued

continued

center will be borne by a one-time assessment of all member stores, whether or not they install and use the system.

A two-day training session will be conducted at distribution centers whenever five or more storeowners have installed the system and are ready to learn how to use it. Optionally, store owners can travel to the POS vendor's home office in Atlanta at their own expense for a two-day training session, which is to be offered once a month.

A vote has been scheduled prior to the cooperative's annual members' meeting. Members are asked to vote "yes" or "no" on the proposal, and a majority of those voting will determine the outcome.

As Bill Murton completes his shelf scan and returns to his office, he thinks to himself: Since the new POS system will automatically track inventory, I wonder if I will still be able to get a gut feel for what is selling and what is not. There is nothing like examining the shelves like I just did

and talking to customers to understand what I should be stocking. And, I wonder how much it will cost to run the system once it is installed?

Questions

1. How will a POS system enhance the operations of Bill's Hardware? The operations of the cooperative?
2. What strategic advantages will the system confer on Bill's Hardware? What strategic advantages will accrue to the cooperative?
3. What criteria should be considered when assessing the benefits of the POS technology? What costs should be included?
4. How should Bill Murton vote?

Source: This case was prepared by Larry Meile, Boston College, as a basis for classroom discussion.

SELECTED REFERENCES

Alsop, Stewart. "Sun's Java: What's Hype and What's Real." *Fortune* (July 7, 1997); pp. 191–192.

"AT&T IP Backbone Network," www.ipservices.att.com/backbone/.

Betz, Frederick. *Managing Technology: Competing Through New Ventures, Innovation, and Corporate Research*. Englewood Cliffs, NJ: Prentice-Hall, 1987.

Bower, Joseph L., and Clayton M. Christensen. "Disruptive Technologies: Catching the Wave." *Harvard Business Review* (January–February 1995), pp. 43–53.

Burgelman, Robert A., Modesto A. Maidique, and Steven C. Wheelwright. *Strategic Management of Technology and Innovation*. Chicago: Irwin, 1996.

Cohen, Morris A., and Uday M. Apte. *Manufacturing Automation*. Chicago: Irwin, 1997.

Collier, David A. *Service Management: The Automation of Services*. Reston, VA: Reston, 1985.

Davenport, Thomas H. "Putting the Enterprise into the Enterprise System." *Harvard Business Review* (July–August 1998), pp. 121–131.

Earl, Michael, and M. M. Bensaou. "The Right Mind-Set for Managing Information Technology." *Harvard Business Review* (September–October 1998), pp. 119–129.

"The Emerging Digital Economy II," 1999. (www.ecommerce.gov/ede/).

How the Internet Works, *Internet World*, vol. 8, no. 10 (1996). www.internetworld.com/print/monthly /1996/10/howitworks.html.

How the Internet Works: All You Really Need to Know, *Business Week* (July 20, 1998). www.businessweek.com/1998/29/b3587123.htm.

Iansiti, Marco, and Jonathan West. "Technology Integration: Turning Great Research into Great Products." *Harvard Business Review* (May–June 1997), pp. 69–79.

Jacobs, F. Robert, and D. Clay Whybark. *Why ERP?* New York: Irwin McGraw-Hill, 2000.

Kodama, Fumio, "Technological Fusion and the New R&D." *Harvard Business Review* (May–June 1992), pp. 70–91.

Lefebvre, Louis A., Ann Langley, Jean Harvey, and Elisabeth Lefebvre. "Exploring the Strategy–Technology Connection in Small Manufacturing Firms." *Production and Operations Management*, vol. 1, no. 3 (1992), pp. 269–285.

National Research Council. *Management of Technology: The Hidden Competitive Advantage*. Washington, DC: National Academic Press, 1987.

Noori, Hamid. *Managing the Dynamics of New Technology*. Englewood Cliffs, NJ: Prentice-Hall, 1990.

Noori, Hamid, and Russell W. Radford. *Readings and Cases in the Management of New Technology*. Englewood Cliffs, NJ: Prentice-Hall, 1990.

Pisano, Gary P., and Steven C. Wheelwright. "High-Tech R&D." *Harvard Business Review* (September–October 1995), pp. 93–105.

Porter, Michael P. *Competitive Advantage*. New York: Free Press, 1985.

Prahalad, C. K., and Gary Hamel. "The Core Competence of the Corporation." *Harvard Business Review* (May–June 1990), pp. 79–91.

Quinn, James B., and Penny C. Paquette. "Technology in Services: Creating Organizational Revolutions." *Sloan Management Review* (Winter 1990), pp. 67–78.

Roth, Aleda V. "Neo-Operations Strategy: Linking Capabilities-Based Competition to Technology." In *Handbook of Technology Management*, G. H. Gaynor (ed.). New York: McGraw-Hill, 1996, pp. 38.1–38.44.

Scalle, Cedric X., and Mark J. Cotteleer. *Enterprise Resource Planning (ERP)*. Boston, MA: Harvard Business School Publishing, No. 9–699–020, 1999.

Skinner, Wickham. "Operations Technology: Blind Spot in Strategic Management." *Interfaces*, vol. 14 (January–February 1984), pp. 116–125.

Steele, Lowell W. *Managing Technology: The Strategic View*. New York: McGraw-Hill, 1988.

Swamidass, Paul M. "Manufacturing Flexibility." *OMA* Monograph 2 (January 1988).

"Wireless in Cyberspace," *Business Week Online* (May 22, 2000). www.businessweek.com/common_frames/bws.htm?http://www.businessweek.com/2000/00_21/b3682029.htm.

B Computer-Integrated Manufacturing

Learning Goals

After reading this supplement, you will be able to . . .

1. describe several types of technologies that comprise computer-integrated manufacturing.
2. discuss the advantages of these different technologies.

T HE POPULAR PRESS OFTEN writes about the factory of the future: a fully automated factory that manufactures a wide variety of products without human intervention. Although some "peopleless" factories do exist and others will be built, the major advances being made today occur in manufacturing operations where computers are being integrated into the process to help workers create high-quality products.

Computer-integrated manufacturing (CIM) is an umbrella term for the total integration of product design and engineering, process planning, and manufacturing by means of complex computer systems. Less comprehensive computerized systems for production planning, inventory control, or scheduling are often considered part of CIM. By using these powerful computer systems to integrate all phases of manufacturing, from initial customer order to final shipment, firms hope to increase productivity, improve quality, meet customer needs faster, and offer more flexibility. For example, McDonnell Douglas spent $10 million to introduce CIM in its Florida factory. The computer systems automatically schedule manufacturing tasks, keep track of labor, and send instructions to computer screens at workstations along the assembly line. Eliminating paperwork led to an increase of 30 percent in worker productivity. Less than 1 percent of U.S. manufacturing companies have approached full-scale use of CIM, but more than 40 percent are using one or more elements of CIM technology.

A recent study asked managers how much their companies invest in several of the technologies that comprise CIM (Boyer, Ward, and Leong, 1996). The study focused on firms in the metal-working industry (i.e., primary metal, fabricated metal, machinery, electronic equipment, and transportation equipment), in which the use of CIM is believed to be most widespread. The study measured investment on a 7-point scale (1 = no investment and 7 = heavy investment). Computer-aided design received the highest average score (5.2), followed by numerically controlled machines (4.8), computer-aided manufacturing (4.0), flexible manufacturing systems (2.5), automated materials handling (2.3), and robots (2.1). Another study across all industries found company expectations for future investments to have the same rank ordering of CIM components (Kim and Miller, 1990). Thus, CIM is an important aspect of technology in manufacturing, but it is just one set of tools that helps many manufacturing firms, even those with high wages, remain competitive in the global marketplace. In the following sections, we describe these tools and their potential benefits.

COMPUTER-AIDED DESIGN AND MANUFACTURING

computer-integrated manufacturing (CIM) The total integration of product design and engineering, process planning, and manufacturing by means of complex computer systems.

computer-aided design (CAD) An electronic system for designing new parts or products or altering existing ones, replacing drafting traditionally done by hand.

computer-aided manufacturing (CAM) The component of CIM that deals directly with manufacturing operations.

Computer-aided design (CAD) is an electronic system for designing new parts or products or altering existing ones, replacing drafting traditionally done by hand. The heart of CAD is a powerful desktop computer and graphics software that allow a designer to manipulate geometric shapes. The designer can create drawings and view them from any angle on a display monitor. The computer can also simulate the reaction of a part to strength and stress tests. Using the design data stored in the computer's memory, manufacturing engineers and other users can quickly obtain printouts of plans and specifications for a part or product. CAD cuts the cost of product development and sharply reduces the time to market for new products. It is revolutionizing in-house design departments, from IBM to Rubbermaid and AT&T to Steelcase. CAD literacy is now a prerequisite for designers, and investments in it are growing rapidly. Many company budgets for CAD are three times what they were in 1990. The largest sums are going for software, with Pro-Engineer clearly approaching a national standard in the United States.

Analysts can use CAD to store, retrieve, and classify data about various parts. This information is useful in creating families of parts to be manufactured by the same group of machines. Computer-aided design saves time by enabling designers to access and modify old designs quickly, rather than start from scratch.

The component of CIM that deals directly with manufacturing operations is called **computer-aided manufacturing (CAM)**. CAM systems are used to design production processes and to control machine tools and materials flow through programmable automation. For example, researchers at the Technology/Clothing Technology Corporation are developing a concept to enable clothing manufacturers to create "custom"

A computer artist demonstrates the functions of a Hong-Kong-developed computer-aided design and manufacturing system specifically designed for the textile and apparel industry. CAD/CAM systems are being used extensively in the industry to produce customized clothing.

clothing. The concept involves using a computer scan of a customer's body and a computer-driven machine to cut the fabric to fit the customer perfectly. Automated custom clothing goes against established apparel industry procedures, whereby companies cut dozens of layers of cloth at the same time to hold down labor costs. However, labor costs account for only 11 percent of the cost of the garment delivered to the customer. Nonvalue-added handling (including inventory costs) after manufacture accounts for 27 percent, which is the cost category that this technology can reduce. It also has the advantage of fostering customization and speedy delivery as competitive priorities. For example, Levi Strauss is already using similar, although more cumbersome, technology for women's jeans, and its customers are willing to pay a $15 premium.

A *CAD/CAM system* integrates the design and manufacturing function by translating final design specifications into detailed machine instructions for manufacturing an item. CAD/CAM is quicker, less error prone than humans, and eliminates duplication between engineering and manufacturing. CAD/CAM systems allow engineers to see how the various parts of a design interact with each other without having to build a prototype. One of the more recent and stunning examples is the ability of Boeing to design and build its 777 widebody airframe without *any* prototype work at all. The first physical version was the actual plane that test pilots flew in 1994. Boeing's engineers used Dassault Systemes' software called CATIA, short for Computer Assisted Three-Dimensional Interactive Analysis. This French company is one of the most prominent of dozens of software suppliers. Another example is the K2 Corporation, the largest U.S. manufacturer of Alpine skis, which must continually redesign its products to meet changing customer needs. It produces about 20 different models in 12 different lengths. Its CAD and CAM workstations allow designers to convert the numerical descriptions for a new ski shape into drawings and tooling designs and to create machining instructions that can be used directly by the milling machines.

NUMERICALLY CONTROLLED MACHINES

numerically controlled (NC) machines Large machine tools programmed to produce small- to medium-sized batches of intricate parts.

Numerically controlled (NC) machines are large machine tools programmed to produce small- to medium-sized batches of intricate parts. Following a preprogrammed sequence of instructions, NC machines drill, turn, bore, or mill many different parts in various sizes and shapes. The technology was developed in the early 1950s at the Massachusetts Institute of Technology to find more efficient methods of manufacturing jet aircraft for the U.S. Air Force.

computerized numerically controlled (CNC) machines Stand-alone pieces of equipment, each controlled by its own microcomputer.

Currently, NC machines are the most commonly used form of flexible (programmable) automation. Early models received their instructions from a punched tape or card. **Computerized numerically controlled (CNC) machines** are usually stand-alone pieces of equipment, each controlled by its own microcomputer. Since the early 1980s, Japanese industry has spent twice as much money as North American or European industry on factory equipment, more than half of which went for CNC machines. NC and CNC machines rank just after CAD in terms of the most popular CIM technologies.

INDUSTRIAL ROBOTS

industrial robots Versatile, computer-controlled machines programmed to perform various tasks.

Robots are more glamorous than NC workhorses. The first industrial robot joined the GM production line in 1961. **Industrial robots** are versatile, computer-controlled machines programmed to perform various tasks. These "steel-collar" workers operate independently of human control. Most are stationary and mounted on the floor, with an arm that can reach into difficult locations. Figure B.1 shows the six standard movements of a robot's arm. Not all robots have every movement.

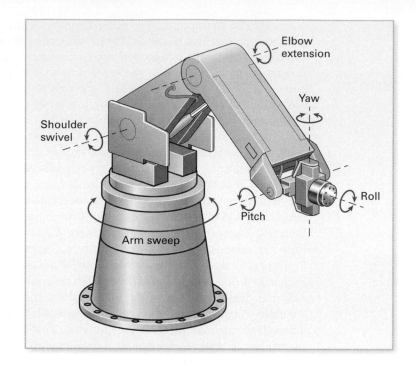

The robot's "hand," sometimes called an *end effector* or *tool*, actually does the work. The hand (not shown) can be changed to perform different tasks, including materials handling, spot welding, spray painting, assembly, and inspection and testing. Second-generation robots equipped with sensors that simulate touch and sight have spawned new applications. For example, robots can wash windows, pick fruit from trees, mix chemicals in laboratories, and handle radioactive materials.

An army of robots (in orange) at work in an automobile assembly plant. Each robot has been programmed to perform a different spot welding task along the process, producing showers of sparks. Such repetitive, precision work is ideally suited to robots. They can perform a great variety of tasks tirelessly round the clock for maximum line utilization.

The initial cost of a robot depends on its size and function. Other potential costs include modifying both product and process to accommodate the robot, preparing the worksite, installing and debugging the robot, and retraining and relocating workers. Benefits from robot installation include less waste materials, more consistent quality, and labor savings. Robots are the drudges of the workforce, performing highly repetitive tasks without tiring, taking a lunch break, or complaining.

By the late 1980s, there were more than 20,000 robots in North America, 28,000 in Europe, and 80,000 in Japan. The conversion of U.S. industry to robots has fallen short of expectations: Less than 30 percent of manufacturers have even moderate experience with robots. One possible reason is that U.S. employers have not faced a labor shortage, whereas in Japan a limited supply of workers led the government to subsidize robots. Cincinnati Milacron, the last big U.S. robot maker, recently left the robot business and returned to making basic machine tools. Robotics is but one of many possible technologies that can be used to gain a competitive advantage.

AUTOMATED MATERIALS HANDLING

materials handling The processes of moving, packaging, and storing a product.

In both manufacturing and service industries, the choice of how, when, and by whom materials are handled is an important technological decision. **Materials handling** covers the processes of moving, packaging, and storing a product. Moving, handling, and storing materials costs time and money but adds no value to the product. Therefore, operations managers are always looking for ways to reduce costs by automating the flow of materials to and from an operation.

Whether materials handling automation is justifiable depends on the process. When the process experiences low volumes and must provide a high degree of customization, job paths vary and there is little repeatability in materials handling. Such variability means that workers must move materials and equipment in open-top containers, carts, or lift trucks. However, when the process experiences high volumes, line flows, and high repeatability, handling can be automated. In addition, other types of flexible automation are now available for processes that fall between these two extremes. Let's look at two such technologies: automated guided vehicles and automated storage and retrieval systems.

AGVs

automated guided vehicle (AGV) A small, driverless, battery-driven truck that moves materials between operations, following instructions from either an on-board or a central computer.

An **automated guided vehicle (AGV)** is a small, driverless, battery-driven truck that moves materials between operations, following instructions from either an onboard or a central computer. Most older models follow a cable installed below the floor, but the newest generation follows optical paths and can go anywhere with aisle space and a relatively smooth floor.

The AGV's ability to route around problems such as production bottlenecks and transportation blockages helps production avoid expensive, unpredictable shutdowns. Furthermore, AGVs enable operations managers to deliver parts as they are needed, thus reducing stockpiles of expensive inventories throughout the plant. The automotive industry now uses AGVs in some plants as mobile assembly stands, primarily for heavy loads. Workers prefer them to inflexible conveyors because the AGVs do not leave until the workers have done the job correctly at their own pace. NCR Corporation installed a $100,000 AGV system in one of its electronics fabrication facilities. Machines run along a 3,000-foot guidepath at 1.5 miles per hour, ferrying parts between the stockroom, assembly stations, and the automated storage and retrieval system.

AS/RS

automated storage and retrieval system (AS/RS)
A computer-controlled method of storing and retrieving materials and tools using racks, bins, and stackers.

An **automated storage and retrieval system (AS/RS)** is a computer-controlled method of storing and retrieving materials and tools using racks, bins, and stackers. With support from AGVs, an AS/RS can receive and deliver materials without the aid of human hands. For example, IBM's new distribution center in Mechanicsburg, Pennsylvania, ships 105,000 spare computer parts and related publications each day—a staggering volume—using an AS/RS and 13 AGVs. Computer control assigns newly arrived materials to one of 37,240 storage locations. If optical sensors confirm that the materials will fit, the automated system moves them along to the proper location. Production at this highly automated facility has increased 20 percent, and accuracy of filled orders has reached 99.8 percent.

FLEXIBLE MANUFACTURING SYSTEM

flexible manufacturing system (FMS)
A configuration of computer-controlled, semi-independent workstations where materials are automatically handled and machine loaded.

A **flexible manufacturing system (FMS)** is a configuration of computer-controlled, semi-independent workstations where materials are automatically handled and machine loaded. An FMS is a type of flexible automation system that builds on the programmable automation of NC and CNC machines. Programs and tooling setups can be changed with almost no loss of production time for moving from production of one product to the next. Such systems require a large initial investment ($5 to $20 million) but little direct labor to operate. An FMS system has three key components:

1. several computer-controlled workstations, such as CNC machines or robots, that perform a series of operations;

2. a computer-controlled transport system for moving materials and parts from one machine to another and in and out of the system; and

3. loading and unloading stations.

Workers bring raw materials for a part family to the loading points, where the FMS takes over. Computer-controlled transporters deliver the materials to various workstations where they pass through a specific sequence of operations unique to each part.

FIGURE B.2

A Flexible Manufacturing System

Source: Courtesy of Vincent Mabert. Reprinted by permission.

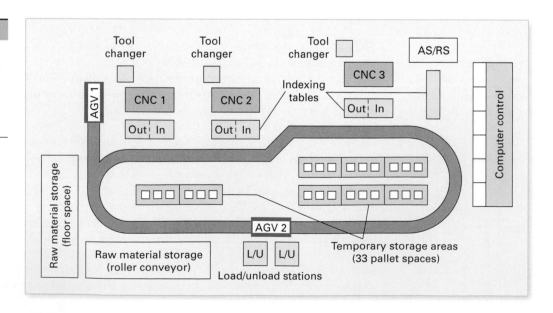

The route is determined by the central computer. The goal of using FMS systems is to synchronize activities and maximize the system's utilization. Because automation makes it possible to switch tools quickly, setup times for machines are short. This flexibility often allows one machine to perform an operation when another is down for maintenance and avoids bottlenecks by routing parts to another machine when one is busy.

Figure B.2 shows the layout of a typical FMS, which produces turning and machining centers.[1] Specific characteristics of this FMS include the following:

❒ The computer control room (right) houses the main computer, which controls the transporter and sequence of operations.

❒ Three CNC machines, each with its own microprocessor, control the details of the machining process.

❒ Two AGVs, which travel around a 200-foot-long oval track, move materials on pallets to and from the CNCs. When the AGVs' batteries run low, the central computer directs them to certain spots on the track for recharging.

❒ Indexing tables lie between each CNC and the track. Inbound pallets from an AGV are automatically transferred to the right side of the table, and out-bound pallets holding finished parts are transferred to the left side for pickup.

❒ A tool changer located behind each CNC loads and unloads tool magazines. Each magazine holds an assortment of tools. A machine automatically selects tools for the next specific operation. Changing from one tool to another takes only 2 minutes.

❒ Two load and unload stations are manually loaded by workers; loading takes 10 to 20 minutes.

❒ An automatic AS/RS (upper right) stores finished parts. The AGV transfers parts on its pallet to an indexing table, which then transfers them to the AS/RS. The process is reversed when parts are needed for assembly into finished products elsewhere in the plant.

This particular system fits processes involving medium-level variety (5 to 100 parts) and volume (annual production rates of 40 to 2,000 units per part). The system can simultaneously handle small batches of many products. In addition, an FMS can be used a second way: At any given time, an FMS can produce low-variety, high-volume products in much the same way that fixed manufacturing systems do. However, when these products reach the end of their life cycles, the FMS can be reprogrammed to accommodate a different product. This flexibility makes FMS very appealing, especially to operations where life cycles are short.

Since the first FMS was introduced in the mid-1960s, the number installed worldwide has grown to almost 500, with about half of them either in Japan or the United States and the other half in Europe. A much more popular version of flexible automation is the **flexible manufacturing cell (FMC)**, which is a scaled-down version of FMS that consists of one or a very small group of NC machines that may or may not be linked to a materials handling mechanism. The FMC doesn't have a materials handling system controlled by a computer, which moves parts to the appropriate machines, as does the more sophisticated FMS.

flexible manufacturing cell (FMC) A scaled-down version of FMS that consists of one or a very small group of NC machines that may or may not be linked to a materials handling mechanism.

---

[1] We are indebted to Vincent Mabert for much of the information about this FMS, including Figure B.2.

SUPPLEMENT HIGHLIGHTS

❐ The concept of automation goes beyond the labor savings of displacing humans with machines. By totally integrating product design, engineering, process planning, and manufacturing through complex computer systems, computer-integrated manufacturing (CIM) allows companies to compete on the basis of time and flexibility while creating higher-paying jobs. Computer-aided manufacturing (CAM) is the part of CIM that deals directly with manufacturing.

❐ A CAD/CAM system links computerized product design and production. It's the first step toward a paperless factory.

❐ Numerically controlled (NC) machines follow preprogrammed instructions to perform a variety of machining operations on parts having different sizes and shapes. Computerized numerically controlled (CNC) machines are distinguished by the use of a dedicated microcomputer for control. Industrial robots also are capable of a variety of tasks. However, their costs increase with size, the number of axes of rotation, and travel and

sensory (sight, proximity) capability. These machines are used for flexibility, but not for high volume. Fixed automation is used for high-volume, standardized production.

❐ Two relatively new methods used to automate materials handling systems are the automated guided vehicle (AGV) and the automated storage and retrieval system (AS/RS).

❐ Flexible automation includes flexible manufacturing systems (FMSs), which consist of several computer-controlled workstations, an interconnecting transport system, and areas for loading and unloading. An FMS is very expensive to acquire but is flexible enough to accommodate new product families.

❐ A flexible manufacturing cell is a stripped-down version of an FMS but is a much more widely used technology. It consists of one or a few numerically controlled machines that may or may not be linked to a materials handling mechanism.

KEY TERMS

automated guided vehicle (AGV) *235*
automated storage and retrieval system
   (AS/RS) *236*
computer-aided design (CAD) *232*
computer-aided manufacturing
   (CAM) *232*

computer-integrated manufacturing
   (CIM) *232*
computerized numerically controlled
   (CNC) machines *233*
flexible manufacturing cell (FMC) *237*
flexible manufacturing system (FMS) *236*

industrial robots *233*
materials handling *235*
numerically controlled (NC)
   machines *233*

DISCUSSION QUESTIONS

1. Through widespread use of robots, an automobile manufacturer improved its global competitiveness and economic success. Much of the savings resulted from reducing its workforce from 138,000 to 72,000. There was a human cost of displaced workers, however, and displaced employees had a difficult time finding new jobs. Was the automation decision defensible on ethical grounds? What steps can a firm take to be a responsible and ethical employer when cutbacks are necessary?

2. "The central problem of America's economic future is that the nation is not moving quickly enough out of high-volume, standardized production. The extraordinary success of the half-century of the management era has left the United States a legacy of economic

inflexibility. Thus, our institutional heritage now imperils our future."

This quote from Robert Reich, an economist later appointed Secretary of Labor by President Clinton, suggests that U.S. managers were not moving rapidly enough away from high-volume mass production. If so, into what type of production or other type of business should they have been moving? Keep in mind that the U.S. economy was already dominated by services and that people could not all sell one another insurance. What is the relationship between high-volume standardized production and economic inflexibility? What characterized the corporate investment decisions of the 1980s? Were those investments generally guided by a desire to increase economic flexibility?

SELECTED REFERENCES

Adler, P. S. "Managing Flexible Automation." *California Management Review,* vol. 30, no. 3 (1988), pp. 34–56.

Ayers, Robert U., and Duane C. Butcher. "The Flexible Factory Revisited." *American Scientist,* vol. 81 (September–October 1993), pp. 448–459.

Boyer, Kenneth K., Peter T. Ward, and G. Keong Leong. "Approaches to the Factory of the Future: An Empirical Taxonomy." *Journal of Operations Management,* vol. 14 (1996), pp. 297–313.

Cohen, Morris A., and Uday M. Apte. *Manufacturing Automation.* Chicago: Irwin, 1997.

Foston, A., C. Smith, and T. Au. *Fundamentals of Computer Integrated Manufacturing.* Englewood Cliffs, NJ: Prentice-Hall, 1991.

Gerwin, Donald. "Do's and Don'ts of Computerized Manufacturing." *Harvard Business Review* (March–April 1982), pp. 107–116.

Gold, Bela. "CAM Sets New Rules for Production." *Harvard Business Review* (November–December 1982), pp. 88–94.

Groover, Mikell P., and E. W. Zimmers, Jr. CAD/CAM: *Computer-Aided Design and Manufacturing.* Englewood Cliffs, NJ: Prentice-Hall, 1984.

Holusha, John. "Can Computers Guarantee Perfectly Fitted Clothes?" *Cyber Times* (February 19, 1996).

Jaikumar, Jay. "The Boundaries of Business: The Impact of Technology." *Harvard Business Review* (September–October 1991), pp. 100–101.

Kim, Jay S., and Jeffrey G. Miller. "The Manufacturing Futures Factbook: 1990 U.S. Manufacturing Futures Survey." Boston University, 1990.

Melnyk, S. A., and R. Narasimhan. *Computer Integrated Manufacturing: Guidelines and Applications from Industrial Leaders.* Homewood, Ill.: Business One–Irwin, 1992.

Nemetz, P. L., and L. W. Fry. "Flexible Manufacturing Organizations: Implications for Strategy Formulation and Organization Design." *Academy of Management Review,* vol. 13, no. 4 (1988), pp. 627–638.

Noori, Hamid. *Managing the Dynamics of New Technology: Issues in Manufacturing Management.* Englewood Cliffs, NJ: Prentice-Hall, 1990.

Rosenthal, Stephen. "Progress Toward the Factory of the Future." *Journal of Operations Management,* vol. 4, no. 3 (1984), pp. 203–229.

Stecke, Kathryn E., and James J. Solberg. "Loading and Control Policies for a Flexible Manufacturing System." *International Journal of Production Research,* vol. 19, no. 5 (1981), pp. 481–490.

Venkatesan, Ravi. "Cummins Engine Flexes Its Factory." *Harvard Business Review,* vol. 68 (March–April 1990), pp. 120–127.

6

Part Three Quality

Total Quality Management

Across the Organization

Total quality management is important to . . .

- ❑ **accounting,** which must measure and estimate the costs of poor quality and provide error-free data to its internal customers.
- ❑ **finance,** which must assess the cash flow implications of TQM programs and provide defect-free financial reports to its internal customers.
- ❑ **human resources,** which recruits employees who value quality work and motivates and trains them.
- ❑ **management information systems,** which designs the systems for tracking productivity and quality performance.
- ❑ **marketing,** which uses quality and performance data for promotional purposes.
- ❑ **operations,** which designs and implements TQM programs.

Learning Goals

After reading this chapter, you should be able to . . .

1. define *quality* from the customer's perspective.
2. describe the principles of a TQM program and how the elements fit together to make improvements in quality and productivity.
3. identify the four major costs of poor quality.
4. discuss how TQM programs improve quality through benchmarking, product and service design, quality function deployment, and quality-conscious purchasing.
5. distinguish among the various tools for improving quality and explain how each should be used.
6. discuss the nature and benefits of the Malcolm Baldrige National Quality Award and international documentation standards for quality programs and environmental management programs.

The Parkroyal Christchurch, a luxury hotel in Christchurch, New Zealand, has 297 guest rooms, three restaurants, three lounges, and 338 employees to serve 2,250 guests each week who purchase an average of 2,450 meals. Even though the operation is complex, service quality gets top priority at the Parkroyal because customers demand it. Customers have many opportunities to evaluate the quality of service they are receiving. For example, prior to the guest's arrival, the reservation staff has gathered a considerable amount of information about the guest's particular likes and dislikes. This information (e.g., preference for firm pillows or extra towels) is distributed to housekeeping and other hotel operations and is used to customize the service that each guest receives. Upon arrival, a guest is greeted by a porter who opens the car door and unloads the luggage. Then the guest is escorted to the receptionist who registers the guest and assigns the room. Finally, when the guest goes to dinner, servers and cooks must also live up to the high standard of quality that distinguishes the Parkroyal from its competitors.

The Parkroyal Christchurch offers the utmost in quality for its guests. The Café offers a wide variety of dishes that must live up to the reputation of the hotel.

How can such a level of quality be sustained? The Parkroyal has empowered employees to take preventive and, if necessary, corrective action without management approval. Also, management and employees use line charts, histograms, and other graphs to track performance and identify areas needing improvement. In the restaurants, photos of finished dishes remind employees of presentation and content. Finally, in this service business with high customer contact, employee recruiting, training, and motivation are essential for achieving and sustaining high levels of service quality.

Source: Operations Management in Action video.

THE CHALLENGE FOR BUSINESS today is to produce quality products or services efficiently. The Parkroyal Christchurch is but one example of a company that has met the challenge and is using quality as a competitive weapon. This chapter is the first of two in which we address the topic of quality. Here, we explore the competitive implications of quality, focusing on the philosophy of total quality management, which many firms have embraced. **Total quality management** (TQM) stresses three principles: customer satisfaction, employee involvement, and continuous improvements in quality. As Figure 6.1 indicates, TQM also involves benchmarking, product and service design, process design, purchasing, and problem-solving tools. Later, we address statistical process control, which consists of techniques useful for appraising and monitoring quality in operating systems (see the Statistical Process Control chapter).

total quality management (TQM) A philosophy that stresses three principles: customer satisfaction, employee involvement, and continuous improvements in quality.

QUALITY: A MANAGEMENT PHILOSOPHY

Anyone born in 1970 or later probably takes for granted consumer demand for high-quality products and services and the need for firms to improve their operations to make quality a competitive priority. However, quality was not always a top priority. In international markets, the quality of products coming out of Japan in the 1950s

FIGURE 6.1

TQM Wheel

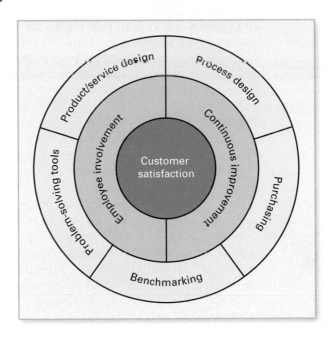

and 1960s was very poor, owing to the destruction of Japanese industry by Allied bombing during World War II. Following the war, Japan had to rebuild its industrial base completely. Starting in the 1970s, Japanese manufacturers, with the help of American consultants such as W. Edwards Deming and Joseph M. Juran, began making quality a competitive priority. Deming's philosophy was that quality is the responsibility of management, not the worker, and that management must foster an environment for detecting and solving quality problems. Juran believed that continuous improvement, hands-on management, and training are fundamental to achieving excellence in quality. At the time, U.S. automobile manufacturers scoffed at the ability of the small, fuel-efficient Japanese cars to compete against their large luxury sedans. However, the energy crisis in the mid-1970s created a demand for fuel efficiency and, coupled with the consumers' belief that Japanese cars were of better quality than U.S.-built cars, opened the door for Japanese manufacturers to gain an advantage in the marketplace. The quality practices used in the automobile industry spilled over into other Japanese industries. By the 1980s, U.S. car manufacturers realized that they needed to listen to the customer or lose market share. In a short 30 years, Japanese manufacturers turned quality levels once considered a joke into global standards of excellence. Today, the gap in quality between Japanese automobiles and those produced by others has narrowed dramatically. Nonetheless, the lesson learned by firms worldwide is clear: The global economy of the 2000s and beyond dictates that companies provide the customer with an ever-widening array of products and services having high levels of quality.

We've previously identified two competitive priorities that deal with quality: high-performance design and consistent quality (see the Operations Strategy chapter). These priorities characterize an organization's competitive thrust. Strategic plans that recognize quality as an essential competitive priority must be based on some operational definition of quality. In this section, we discuss various definitions of quality and emphasize the importance of bridging the gap between consumer expectations of quality and operating capabilities.

CUSTOMER-DRIVEN DEFINITIONS OF QUALITY

How do customers perceive
the quality of services?

quality The ability of a firm
to meet or exceed the
expectations of the
customer.

Customers define **quality** in various ways. In a general sense, quality may be defined as meeting or exceeding the expectations of the customer. For practical purposes, it is necessary to be more specific. Quality has multiple dimensions in the mind of the customer, and one or more of the following definitions may apply at any one time.

CONFORMANCE TO SPECIFICATIONS. Customers expect the products or services they buy to meet or exceed certain advertised levels of performance. For example, Seagate, a disk drive manufacturer, advertises that its high-performance Cheetah disk drives have a "mean time between failures" of 1.2 million hours. All the components of the disk drive must conform to their individual specifications to achieve the desired performance of the complete product. Customers will measure quality by the performance of the complete product and the length of time between failures.

In service systems also, conformance to specifications is important, even though tangible outputs are not produced. Specifications for a service operation may relate to on-time delivery or response time. Bell Canada measures the performance of its operators in Ontario by the length of time to process a call (called "handle time"). If the group average time exceeds the standard of 23 seconds, managers work with the operators to reduce it.

VALUE. Another way customers define quality is through value, or how well the product or service serves its intended purpose at a price customers are willing to pay. How much value a product or service has in the mind of the customer depends on the customer's expectations before purchasing it. For example, if you spent $2.00 for a plastic ballpoint pen and it served you well for six months, you might feel that the purchase was worth the price. Your expectations for the product were met or exceeded. However, if the pen lasted only two days, you might be disappointed and feel that the value was not there.

FITNESS FOR USE. In assessing fitness for use, or how well the product or service performs its intended purpose, the customer may consider the mechanical features of a product or the convenience of a service. Other aspects of fitness for use include appearance, style, durability, reliability, craftsmanship, and serviceability. For example, you may judge your dentist's quality of service on the basis of the age of her equipment because new dental technology greatly reduces the discomfort associated with visits to the dentist. Or you may define the quality of the entertainment center you purchased on the basis of how easy it was to assemble and how well it housed your equipment.

SUPPORT. Often the product or service support provided by the company is as important to customers as the quality of the product or service itself. Customers get upset with a company if financial statements are incorrect, responses to warranty claims are delayed, or advertising is misleading. Good product support can reduce the consequences of quality failures in other areas. For example, if you just had a brake job done, you would be upset if the brakes began squealing again a week later. If the manager of the brake shop offers to redo the work at no additional charge, the company's intent to satisfy the customer is clear.

PSYCHOLOGICAL IMPRESSIONS. People often evaluate the quality of a product or service on the basis of psychological impressions: atmosphere, image, or aesthetics. In the provision of services, where the customer is in close contact with the provider, the appearance and actions of the provider are very important. Nicely dressed, courteous, friendly, and sympathetic employees can affect the customer's perception of service quality. For example, rumpled, discourteous, or grumpy waiters can undermine a restaurant's best efforts to provide high-quality service. In manufacturing, product quality often is judged on the basis of the knowledge and personality of salespeople, as well as the product image presented in advertisements.

 These consumer-driven definitions of quality are applicable to traditional bricks-and-mortar businesses as well as Internet businesses, which use business-to-consumer (B2C) systems to sell merchandise ranging from textbooks to groceries directly to consumers (see the Technology Management and Supply-Chain Management chapters). How does the customer in such situations define quality service? The following factors influence a customer's perception of service on the Internet:

❏ *Web Page.* A good Web site is easy to navigate and convenient to use and place orders (*fitness for use; psychological impressions*). It also provides ample information about the product or service that the customer wants to purchase and information about other similar or related items the customer may be interested in (*value*). Billing is accurate (*support*).

❏ *Product Availability.* Having a wide variety of selections and having the specific product the customer wants to purchase ready to ship are keys to good service marks (*value*).

❏ *Delivery Performance.* Often, delivery is promised within a certain time frame (*conformance to specifications*) and the faster, the better (*value*). Deliveries are made at a time and location convenient to the customer, such as a home residence between the hours of 4 and 6 P.M. (*fitness for use; value; conformance to specifications*).

❏ *Personal Contact.* The opportunity to talk to a live person is often comforting to a customer who is doubtful of the right choice (*psychological impressions*).

With nearly an estimated $4 billion in on-line revenues lost annually because of poor service quality, it is clear that factors such as these are very important for the success of Internet companies.

In automobile manufacturing, processes must be designed to reduce the potential for product failures once customers have taken delivery. Here a mechanic uses a computer to make sure the suspension assembly of a new car meets its design specifications.

QUALITY AS A COMPETITIVE WEAPON

Attaining quality in all areas of a business is a difficult task. To make things even more difficult, consumers change their perceptions of quality. For instance, changes in lifestyles and economic conditions have drastically altered consumer perceptions of automobile quality. When the oil crisis hit in the mid-1970s, consumer preferences shifted from power and styling to fuel economy. To consumers' preferences in the 1980s for quality of design and performance has been added a demand for greater safety in the 1990s and 2000s. By failing to identify these trends and respond to them quickly in the 1970s and 1980s, U.S. automakers lost opportunities to maintain or increase their market shares relative to foreign competition. Today, U.S. automakers are more aware that the customer has a choice and are doing a better job of anticipating customer preferences.

In general, a business's success depends on the accuracy of its perceptions of consumer expectations and its ability to bridge the gap between those expectations and operating capabilities. Consumers are much more quality-minded now than in the past. A survey of 2,000 business units conducted by the Strategic Planning Institute of Cambridge, Massachusetts, indicated that a high-quality product has a better chance of gaining market share than does a low-quality product. In another survey by *Industry Week* magazine, 85 percent of the firms responding believed that their TQM programs were moderately or highly successful in retaining customers and building satisfaction. Moreover, perception plays as important a role as performance: A product or service that is *perceived* by customers to be of higher quality stands a much better chance of gaining market share than does one *perceived* to be of low quality, even if the actual levels of quality are the same. However, perceptions are based on information, and accurate measures of service quality may be difficult to quantify. Managerial Practice 6.1 shows that this is the case for medical care.

Good quality can also pay off in higher profits. High-quality products and services can be priced higher than comparable lower-quality ones and yield a greater return for the same sales dollar. Poor quality erodes the firm's ability to compete in the marketplace and increases the costs of producing its product or service. For example, by improving conformance to specifications, a firm can increase its market share *and* reduce the cost of its products or services, which in turn increases profits. Management is better able to compete on both price and quality.

THE COSTS OF POOR QUALITY

What are the costs of poor quality?

Most experts on the costs of poor quality estimate losses in the range of 20 to 30 percent of gross sales for defective or unsatisfactory products. For example, "dirty" electric power supplied by utility companies to manufacturers can be very costly. Tiny power surges, sags, and outages, often less than a millisecond long, rarely faze old manufacturing equipment but wreak havoc on new equipment that relies heavily on delicate computer chips. In one instance, General Motors' computer-run robots on its minivan assembly line in Baltimore kept shutting down. Finally, the problem was traced to the local utility's faulty underground wiring: Current surges and outages were shutting down the robot's computers. Such blackouts can cost a manufacturer as much as $500,000 per hour.

Four major categories of costs are associated with quality management: prevention, appraisal, internal failure, and external failure.

prevention costs Costs associated with preventing defects before they happen.

PREVENTION COSTS

Prevention costs are associated with preventing defects before they happen. They include the costs of redesigning the process to remove the causes of poor quality,

MANAGERIAL PRACTICE 6.1
Measurers of Quality in Medical Care Are Difficult to Quantify

A cut? A fishhook in your finger? No problem—go to the nearest medical clinic. What if the situation was more serious, such as a stroke or esophageal cancer? Which hospital would you choose? Your choice could have profound repercussions. A study in Pennsylvania found that the death rates of comparably ill stroke patients ranged from 0 to 36.8 percent, depending on the hospital. Further, a national study revealed that death rates for esophageal cancer surgery varied by hospital from 0 to 26 percent. Obviously, your choices in any situation would be those hospitals you can get access to that have the lowest (or zero) death rates. But how would you know which ones? That was the question a number of leading corporations in the Cleveland area had. The companies wanted to provide the best health care available to their employees, over 130,000 in number, and at the best cost. There was a bigger question: How can such information be gathered?

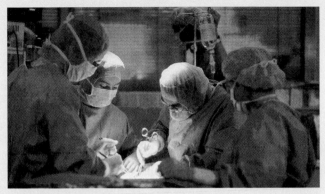

Extreme care must be taken by surgery teams to ensure the high quality of their services. Here a surgery team works in a sterile operating "theater" specially equipped for the procedures they must perform.

The companies formed in 1993 the Cleveland Health Quality Choice program, which intended to create a marketplace for the selection of health care providers in the Cleveland area. It published public reports twice annually with customer satisfaction levels and death rates for a range of illnesses and procedures performed by area hospitals. The Cleveland area hospitals were eager to provide the mountains of information the program required because of the economic clout the participating companies had. For some hospitals, the program improved the quality of health care by forcing then to think about their medical practices once they found out they had above-average death rates. For example, after Lakewood Hospital found out its death rate from heart attack and congestive heart failure was too high, it modified its application of certain drugs and focused its attention on the practices of those doctors who had too many patients die. Also, when doctors at Allen Memorial Hospital found out that they had a higher-than-expected death rate of 16.8 percent for pneumonia patients, they made changes in their use of antibiotics, which reduced the death rate to 3 percent.

While death rate is a very important quality measure in ranking hospital performance, comparing hospitals in this way is fraught with difficulties. To be fair, a hospital's rating should accurately reflect the risk factors the hospital faces for each illness. The mix of patients the hospital gets may determine the death rate. For example, factors such as the family history of heart disease, electrocardiogram results, and smoking have been shown to have a statistical link to the death rates of heart attack patients. For each of these factors, statistical experts compute expected percentages of cases that would result in death. However, hospitals ranked low in a particular category often debate as to whether additional factors should be considered in their situation. For instance, one hospital complained that the number of patients awaiting heart transplants, the number of patients specifically transported to the hospital because of the dire status of their condition, and a key lung-function measure were not considered in the ranking of its performance. It is critical to recognize all the relevant factors if quality measures are to be used to compare performance across a wide variety of hospitals.

In the end, the Cleveland Health Quality Choice program failed, not because it was a bad idea, but because of economics and the lack of a solid basis for measurement. A major motivation of the companies was to reduce the cost of health care programs for their employees. By 1997, the growth in health care costs was only 0.2 percent and, although the costs increased 6.1 percent in 1998, the pressure to reduce costs—rampant in the late 1980s— was off. Health maintenance organizations and managed care programs had a lot to do with that. In addition, the cost to gather the information was high. Beyond the economics, the program was not able to provide a universally agreeable set of measures for the severity of illnesses. Death is a very infrequent outcome of hospitalization, and large numbers of hospitalized patients are required to develop statistical significance in comparing death rates at different hospitals for patients with specific diagnoses.

Source: Burton, Thomas. "Operation That Rated Hospitals Was Success, but the Patience Died." *Wall Street Journal* (August 23, 1999).

re-designing the product to make it simpler to produce, training employees in the methods of continuous improvement, and working with suppliers to increase the quality of purchased items or contracted services. In order to improve quality, firms have to invest additional time, effort, and money. We explore these costs further later in this chapter.

APPRAISAL COSTS

appraisal costs Costs incurred in assessing the level of quality attained by the operating system.

Appraisal costs are incurred in assessing the level of quality attained by the operating system. Appraisal helps management identify quality problems. As preventive measures improve quality, appraisal costs decrease, because fewer resources are needed for quality inspections and the subsequent search for causes of any problems that are detected. We discuss appraisal costs for quality audits and statistical quality control programs in more detail later (see the Statistical Process Control chapter).

INTERNAL FAILURE COSTS

internal failure costs Costs resulting from defects that are discovered during the production of a product or service.

Internal failure costs result from defects that are discovered during the production of a product or service. They fall into two major cost categories: *yield losses,* which are incurred if a defective item must be scrapped, and *rework costs,* which are incurred if the item is rerouted to some previous operation(s) to correct the defect or if the service must be performed again. For example, if the final inspector at an automobile paint shop discovers that the paint on a car has a poor finish, the car may have to be completely resanded and repainted. The additional time spent correcting such a mistake results in lower productivity for the sanding and painting departments. In addition, the car may not be finished by the date on which the customer is expecting it. Such activities are great candidates for continuous improvement projects.

EXTERNAL FAILURE COSTS

external failure costs Costs that arise when a defect is discovered after the customer has received the product or service.

External failure costs arise when a defect is discovered after the customer has received the product or service. For instance, suppose that you have the oil changed in your car and that the oil filter is improperly installed, causing the oil to drain onto your garage floor. You might insist that the company pay for the car to be towed and restore the oil and filter immediately. External failure costs to the company include the towing and additional oil and filter costs, as well as the loss of future revenue because you decide never to take your car back there for service. Dissatisfied customers talk about bad service or products to their friends, who in turn tell others. If the problem is bad enough, consumer protection groups alert the media. The potential impact on future profits is difficult to assess, but without doubt external failure costs erode market share and profits.

warranty A written guarantee that the producer will replace or repair defective parts or perform the service to the customer's satisfaction.

External failure costs also include warranty service and litigation costs. A **warranty** is a written guarantee that the producer will replace or repair defective parts or perform the service to the customer's satisfaction. Usually, a warranty is given for some specified period. For example, television repairs are usually guaranteed for 90 days and new automobiles for five years or 50,000 miles, whichever comes first. Warranty costs must be considered in the design of new products or services, particularly as they relate to reliability (discussed later in this chapter).

Encountering defects and correcting them after the product is in the customer's hands is costly. As Figure 6.2 shows, the closer a product is to its finished state, the costlier it is to find and correct defects. When the product has been shipped to the customer, the cost to fix a defect skyrockets. For example, sending a customer engineer from IBM to a remote computer installation to find out what is wrong and fix it is far more expensive than finding and correcting the defect in the factory before the computer is shipped. An extreme example is provided by the Hubble space telescope.

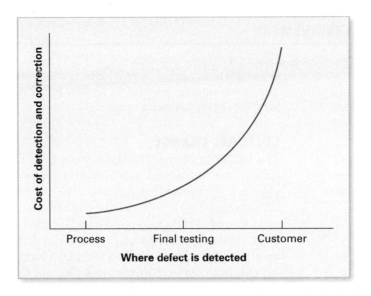

FIGURE 6.2

The Costs of Detecting and Fixing a Defect

Placed in orbit from a space shuttle in 1990, the telescope proved to have blurred vision resulting from an improperly ground lens. A test costing a few hundred thousand dollars could have detected the problem while the telescope was still on earth. Instead, NASA had to send a team of astronauts on a shuttle mission to correct the defect at a cost of more than $600 million.

 Of course, you do not have to go into space to incur heavy costs to repair defects once the product has left the final assembly line. In 1999, GE had to recall 3.1 million dishwashers manufactured between April 1983 and January 1989 to resolve a defective energy switch that allegedly caused seven fires. The cost of the repairs to the machines would be greater than the value of the machines themselves, according to company officials. Service providers are not immune to external failure costs, except that a recall is not always possible. In Tacoma, Washington, a two-year-old child died from food poisoning after eating a meal at a Jack-in-the-Box restaurant. As many as 300 people were infected with the same *E. coli* bacteria that killed the boy. Sales at Jack-in-the-Box restaurants dropped 20 percent after the poisonings, and many managers and employees had to be laid off. Since then, management has corrected the problems in the supply chain and the food preparation processes. Nonetheless, external failure costs can rock a company to its core.

Defective products can injure and even kill consumers who purchase them. An increasing number of states are adopting strict product liability laws that force companies to pay damages—often large amounts—to injured plaintiffs or heirs, even when they have not proved that the manufacturer was negligent in designing the product. All that needs to be shown is that a product was defective and that it caused the injury or death. For example, the Ford Motor Company, whose 23 million automatic transmissions manufactured from 1968 to 1980 were alleged to slip from park into reverse if the engine was left running, at one time faced more than 1,000 lawsuits exceeding $500 million in claims for injuries and deaths supposedly caused by the transmissions.

Litigation costs include not only legal fees but also the time and effort of employees who must appear for the company in court. In addition, there is the cost of bad publicity. For instance, Procter & Gamble's Rely tampon, allegedly a cause of toxic shock syndrome, and Merrell-Dow Pharmaceuticals' Bendectin, allegedly a cause of birth defects, eventually were taken off the market by their manufacturers because of media reports. Regardless of whether a company is ultimately judged to be at fault in a court of law, the cost of litigation is enormous and the negative publicity can be devastating.

EMPLOYEE INVOLVEMENT

One of the important elements of TQM is employee involvement as shown in Figure 6.1. A complete program in employee involvement includes changing organizational culture, encouraging teamwork, fostering individual development through training, and establishing awards and incentives.

CULTURAL CHANGE

How can employees be included in the quality improvement process?

The challenge of quality management is to instill an awareness of the importance of quality in all employees and to motivate them to improve product quality. With TQM, everyone is expected to contribute to the overall improvement of quality—from the administrator who finds cost-saving measures to the salesperson who learns of a new customer need to the engineer who designs a product with fewer parts to the manager who communicates clearly with other department heads. In other words, TQM involves all the functions that relate to a product or service.

One of the main challenges in developing the proper culture for TQM is to define *customer* for each employee. In general, customers are internal or external (see the Introduction chapter). External customers are the people or firms who buy the product or service. In this sense, the entire firm is a single unit that must do its best to satisfy external customers. However, communicating customers' concerns to everyone in the organization is difficult. Some employees, especially those having little contact with external customers, may have difficulty seeing how their jobs contribute to the whole effort. However, each employee also has one or more internal customers—employees in the firm who rely on the output of other employees. For example, a machinist who drills holes in a component and passes it on to a welder has the welder as her customer. Even though the welder is not an external customer, he will have many of the same definitions of quality as an external customer, except that they will relate to the component instead of a complete product. All employees must do a good job of serving their internal customers if external customers ultimately are to be satisfied. The concept of internal customers works if each internal customer demands only value-added activities of their internal suppliers: that is, activities that the external customer will recognize and pay for. The notion of internal cus-

At Kawasaki's plant in Lincoln, Nebraska, employees are trained to spot quality problems and correct them before passing the unit to the next work station.

tomers applies to all parts of a firm and enhances cross-functional coordination. For example, accounting must prepare accurate and timely reports for management, and purchasing must provide high-quality materials on time for operations.

In TQM, everyone in the organization must share the view that quality control is an end in itself. Errors or defects should be caught and corrected at the source, not passed along to an internal customer. This philosophy is called *quality at the source.* In addition, firms should avoid trying to "inspect quality into the product" by using inspectors to weed out defective products or unsatisfactory services after all operations have been performed. In some manufacturing firms, workers have the authority to stop a production line if they spot quality problems. At Kawasaki's U.S. plant, some of the assembly lines have lights of different colors strung along them to indicate the severity of the quality problem detected. Workers activate a yellow light to indicate that a problem has been detected and a red light when the problem is serious enough to stop the line. If the line is stopped, the problem must be resolved quickly, because each lost minute results in less output and costs money. However, in TQM, quality consistency has a higher priority than the level of output.

TEAMS

How can a company develop teams?

Employee involvement is a key tactic for improving competitiveness. One way to achieve employee involvement is by the use of **teams,** which are small groups of people who have a common purpose, set their own performance goals and approaches, and hold themselves accountable for success. Teams differ from the more typical "working group" because

teams Small groups of people who have a common purpose, set their own performance goals and approaches, and hold themselves accountable for success.

- ❏ the members have a common commitment to an overarching purpose that all believe in and that transcends individual priorities;
- ❏ the leadership roles are shared rather than held by a single, strong leader;
- ❏ performance is judged not only by individual contributions but also by collective "work products" that reflect the joint efforts of all the members;
- ❏ open-ended discussion, rather than a managerially defined agenda, is prized at meetings; and
- ❏ the members of the team do real work together, rather than delegating to subordinates.

Teamwork is never more important than it is in car racing. Driver Jeff Burton gets service from his crew at the North Carolina Speedway near Rockingham, N.C., Saturday, October 21, 2000, during the 34th Annual Pit Crew Competition. Burton's crew won the competition with a pit stop of 18.355 seconds.

Management plays an important role in determining whether teams are successful. Survey results suggest that the following approaches lead to more successful teams (Katzenbach and Smith, 1993):

1. The team's project should be meaningful, with well-defined performance standards and direction.
2. Particular attention should be paid to creating a positive environment at the first few meetings.
3. Team members should create clear rules regarding attendance, openness, constructive confrontation, and commitment to the team.
4. To foster a sense of accomplishment, the team should set a few immediate performance-oriented tasks and goals that will allow it to achieve some early successes.
5. People outside the team should be consulted for fresh ideas and information.
6. If possible, team members should spend lots of time together to foster creative insights and personal bonding.
7. Managers should look for ways beyond direct compensation to give the *team* positive reinforcement.

The three approaches to teamwork most often used are problem-solving teams, special-purpose teams, and self-managing teams. All three use some amount of **employee empowerment,** which moves responsibility for decisions farther down the organizational chart—to the level of the employee actually doing the job.

employee empowerment An approach to teamwork that moves responsibility for decisions farther down the organizational chart—to the level of the employee actually doing the job.

PROBLEM-SOLVING TEAMS. First introduced in the 1920s, problem-solving teams, also called **quality circles,** became more popular in the late 1970s after the Japanese had used them successfully. Problem-solving teams are small groups of supervisors and employees who meet to identify, analyze, and solve production and quality problems. The philosophy behind this approach is that the people who are directly responsible for making the product or providing the service will be best able to consider ways to solve a problem. Also, employees take more pride and interest in their work if they are allowed to help shape it. The teams typically consist of 5 to 12 volunteers, drawn from different areas of a department or from a group of employees assigned to a particular task, such as automobile assembly or credit application processing. The teams meet several hours a week to work on quality and productivity problems and make suggestions to management. Such teams are used extensively by Japanese-managed firms in the United States. The Japanese philosophy is to encourage employee inputs while maintaining close control over their job activities. Although problem-solving teams can successfully reduce costs and improve quality, they die if management fails to implement many of the suggestions generated.

quality circles Another name for problem-solving teams; small groups of supervisors and employees who meet to identify, analyze, and solve production and quality problems.

The Wilson Sporting Goods Company plant in Humboldt, Tennessee, has used problem-solving teams to rebound from a dismal market share of 2 percent in the golf ball business to 17 percent in seven years. Problem-solving teams focused on achieving better customer service and reducing costs of production. For example, employees in the injection molding area, where Du Pont Surlyn covers are applied in the production of two-piece balls, found ways to reduce the defect rate from 15 percent to only 1.4 percent. Plantwide, the employees working in problem-solving teams helped reduce defective workmanship by 67 percent and generated annual savings of $9.5 million.

special-purpose teams Groups that address issues of paramount concern to management, labor, or both.

SPECIAL-PURPOSE TEAMS. An outgrowth of the problem-solving teams, **special-purpose teams** address issues of paramount concern to management, labor, or both. For example, management may form a special-purpose team to design and introduce new work policies or new technologies or to address customer service problems. Essentially, this approach gives workers a voice in high-level decisions, Special-purpose teams, which first appeared in the United States in the early 1980s, are becoming more popular.

 Special-purpose teams usually consist of representatives from several different departments or functions. Such was the case at Victory Memorial Hospital in Waukegan, Illinois, where a cross-functional team was assembled to address complaints of lengthy delays in treating patients. The predominance of complaints came from level-two patients—patients who were not in immediate danger but were in pain. A team of representatives from diagnostic services, admitting, emergency, patient accounts, medical laboratory, quality assurance, and telemetry found that the three most likely causes for the lengthy delays were (1) waiting for a sample from patients suspected of urinary tract infections, (2) waiting for lab test results, and (3) waiting for a physical exam. The team recommended various solutions, including having the admitting nurse start the patient specimen process as soon as the ailment has been assessed, drawing an extra tube of blood at the time the initial sample is taken to reduce delays when the doctor asks for additional tests, and adding another emergency treatment room with an examining table. The team effort at Victory Memorial reduced the average length of stay from 9.1 to 6.7 days, reduced receivables from 73.6 to 59.3 days, reduced inventory investment from $270,000 to $200,000, improved patient satisfaction by 30 percent, and improved employee satisfaction generally.

self-managing teams A small group of employees who work together to produce a major portion, or sometimes all, of a product or service.

SELF-MANAGING TEAMS. The **self-managing teams** approach takes worker participation to its highest level: A small group of employees work together to produce a major portion, or sometimes all, of a product or service. Members learn all the tasks involved in the operation, rotate from job to job, and take over managerial duties such as work and vacation scheduling, ordering supplies, and hiring. In some cases, team members design the process and have a high degree of latitude as to how it takes shape. Self-managing teams essentially change the way work is organized because employees have control over their jobs. Only recently have self-managing teams begun to catch on in the United States, but some have increased productivity by 30 percent or more in their firms.

Developing self-managed work teams faces certain challenges. In a recent survey by the Association for Manufacturing Excellence, the most common challenges mentioned by firms included (1) difficulty in defining roles and responsibilities and transferring control from first-line supervisors to the team; (2) lack of necessary skill development, owing to the lack of training and other resources; and (3) difficulty in accepting an increased level of responsibility and coping with substantial change. The common remedies for these challenges included (1) training, coaching, and continuous support; and (2) perseverance, patience, and time.

INDIVIDUAL DEVELOPMENT

On-the-job training programs can help improve quality. Teaching new work methods to experienced workers or training new employees in current practices can increase productivity and reduce the number of product defects. Some companies train workers to perform related jobs to help them understand how quality problems in their own work can cause problems for other workers. Honda of America, Inc., gives more than 100,000 hours of classroom instruction each year (taught by Honda associates to other Honda associates) in the Anna and Marysville, Ohio, plants.

Managers too need to develop new skills—not only those directly relating to their own duties but also those needed to teach their subordinates. Many companies are putting their managers through "train-the-trainer" programs that give managers the skills to train others in quality improvement practices.

AWARDS AND INCENTIVES

The prospect of merit pay and bonuses can give employees some incentive for improving quality. Companies may tie monetary incentives directly to quality improvements. For example, at Honda of America, Inc., an employee incentive program gives monetary awards to associates whose suggestions for improvements in equipment or procedures have paid off. Associates are responsible for assembling all the necessary information and implementing the suggestion if it is approved. One year, Honda associates received approximately $190,000 in cash awards and five Honda Civic automobiles as part of this program.

Nonmonetary awards, such as recognition in front of co-workers, also can motivate quality improvements. Each month some companies select an employee who has demonstrated quality workmanship and give that person special recognition, such as a privileged parking spot, a dinner at a fine restaurant, or a plaque. Typically, the event is reported in the company newsletter.

CONTINUOUS IMPROVEMENT

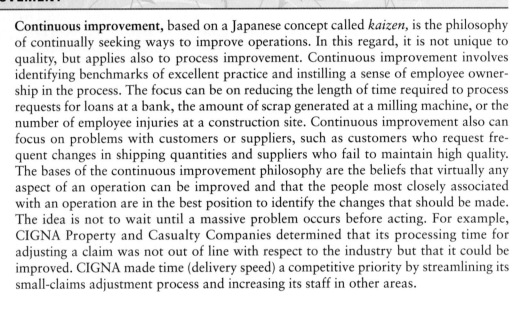

continuous improvement
The philosophy of continually seeking ways to improve operations, based on a Japanese concept called *kaizen*.

Continuous improvement, based on a Japanese concept called *kaizen,* is the philosophy of continually seeking ways to improve operations. In this regard, it is not unique to quality, but applies also to process improvement. Continuous improvement involves identifying benchmarks of excellent practice and instilling a sense of employee ownership in the process. The focus can be on reducing the length of time required to process requests for loans at a bank, the amount of scrap generated at a milling machine, or the number of employee injuries at a construction site. Continuous improvement also can focus on problems with customers or suppliers, such as customers who request frequent changes in shipping quantities and suppliers who fail to maintain high quality. The bases of the continuous improvement philosophy are the beliefs that virtually any aspect of an operation can be improved and that the people most closely associated with an operation are in the best position to identify the changes that should be made. The idea is not to wait until a massive problem occurs before acting. For example, CIGNA Property and Casualty Companies determined that its processing time for adjusting a claim was not out of line with respect to the industry but that it could be improved. CIGNA made time (delivery speed) a competitive priority by streamlining its small-claims adjustment process and increasing its staff in other areas.

GETTING STARTED WITH CONTINUOUS IMPROVEMENT

Instilling a philosophy of continuous improvement in an organization may be a lengthy process, and several steps are essential to its eventual success.

1. Train employees in the methods of statistical process control (SPC) and other tools for improving quality and performance.
2. Make SPC methods a normal aspect of daily operations.
3. Build work teams and employee involvement.
4. Utilize problem-solving tools within the work teams.
5. Develop a sense of operator ownership in the process.

Note that employee involvement is central to the philosophy of continuous improvement. However, the last two steps are crucial if the philosophy is to become part of everyday operations. Problem solving addresses the aspects of operations that need improvement and evaluates alternatives for achieving improvements. A sense of operator ownership emerges when employees feel as though they own the processes and

FIGURE 6.3

*Plan–Do–Check–Act
Cycle*

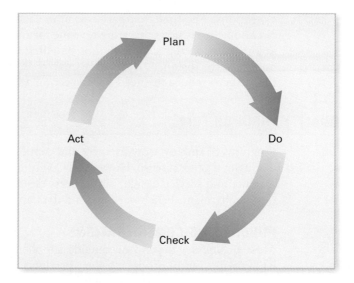

FIGURE 6.3

*Plan–Do–Check–Act
Cycle*

methods they use and take pride in the quality of the product or service they produce. It comes from participation on work teams and in problem-solving activities, which instill in employees a feeling that they have some control over their workplace and tasks.

PROBLEM-SOLVING PROCESS

plan–do–check–act cycle
A cycle, also called the Deming Wheel, used by firms actively engaged in continuous improvement to train their work teams in problem solving.

Most firms actively engaged in continuous improvement train their work teams to use the **plan–do–check–act cycle** for problem solving. Another name for this approach is the Deming Wheel. Figure 6.3 shows this cycle, which lies at the heart of the continuous improvement philosophy. The cycle comprises the following steps.

1. *Plan.* The team selects a process (e.g., activity, method, machine, or policy) that needs improvement. The team then documents the selected process, usually by analyzing data (using the tools we discuss later in the chapter); sets qualitative goals for improvement; and discusses various ways to achieve the goals. After assessing the benefits and costs of the alternatives, the team develops a plan with quantifiable measures for improvement.

2. *Do.* The team implements the plan and monitors progress. Data are collected continuously to measure the improvements in the process. Any changes in the process are documented, and further revisions are made as needed.

3. *Check.* The team analyzes the data collected during the *do* step to find out how closely the results correspond to the goals set in the *plan* step. If major shortcomings exist, the team may have to reevaluate the plan or stop the project.

4. *Act.* If the results are successful, the team documents the revised process so that it becomes the standard procedure for all who may use it. The team may then instruct other employees in the use of the revised process.

Problem-solving projects often focus on those aspects of operations that do not add value to the product or service. Value is added during operations such as machining a part or serving a customer on a Web page. No value is added in activities such as inspecting parts for quality defects or routing requests for loan approvals to several different departments. The idea of continuous improvement is to reduce or eliminate activities that do not add value and thus are wasteful. For example, suppose that a firm has identified three non-value-added activities in the manufacture of its products: inspection of each part, repair of defects, and handling of materials between operations. The time that parts spend in each activity is not adding value to the product and hence is not generating revenue for the firm. Continuous improvement projects might focus on reducing materials handling time by rearranging machine locations to minimize the distances traveled by materials, or improving the methods for producing the parts to reduce the need for inspection and rework.

IMPROVING QUALITY THROUGH TQM

What factors in the operations system are causing major quality problems?

Programs of employee involvement and continuous improvement are aimed at improving quality in a general sense. However, TQM often focuses on processes such as purchasing, product and service design, and process design, and utilizes tools such as quality function deployment, benchmarking, and data analysis.

PURCHASING CONSIDERATIONS

Most businesses depend on outside suppliers for some of the materials, services, or equipment used in producing their products and services. Large companies have hundreds and even thousands of suppliers, some of which supply the same types of parts. The quality of these inputs can affect the quality of the firm's work, and purchased parts of poor quality can have a devastating effect. For example, the Ford Motor Company was forced to halt Tempo and Topaz production at its Kansas City, Missouri, and Oakville, Ontario, plants when a faulty engine part purchased from an outside supplier caused some gears in the engine to lose a few teeth during a test run. Approximately 5,500 hourly workers were temporarily laid off. In addition, Ford lost about 2,000 cars each day that production was stopped.

Both the buyer's approach and specification management are keys to controlling supplier quality. The firm's buyer must emphasize not only the cost and speed of delivery to the supplier but also the quality of the product. A competent buyer will identify suppliers that offer high-quality products or services at a reasonable cost. After identifying these suppliers, the buyer should work with them to obtain essentially defect-free parts. To do so may require examining and evaluating trade-offs between receiving off-specification materials and seeking corrective action.

The specifications for purchased parts and materials must be clear and *realistic*. As a check on specifications, buyers in some companies initiate *process capability studies* for important products (see the Statistical Process Control chapter). These studies amount to trial runs of small product samples to ensure that all components, including the raw materials and purchased parts, work together to form a product that has the desired quality level at a reasonable cost. Analysis of study results may identify unrealistic specifications and the need for changes.

Management needs to allow sufficient time for the purchasing department to identify several low-cost, qualified suppliers and to analyze the information they submit. An unrealistic deadline can lead to poor selection based on incomplete information about supplier qualifications. In addition, improved communication between purchasing and other departments, such as engineering and quality control, is needed when those departments must provide information to assess supplier qualifications and the supplier's manufacturing process. We cover additional purchasing considerations later (see the Supply-Chain Management chapter).

PRODUCT AND SERVICE DESIGN

Because design changes often require changes in methods, materials, or specifications, they can increase defect rates. Change invariably increases the risk of making mistakes, so stable product and service designs can help reduce internal quality problems.

However, stable designs may not be possible when a product or service is sold in markets globally. Although changed designs have the potential to increase market share, management must be aware of possible quality problems resulting from the changes. If a firm needs to make design changes to remain competitive, it should carefully test new designs and redesign the product or service and the process with a focus on the market.

Implementing both strategies involves a trade-off: Higher quality and increased competitiveness are exchanged for added time and cost. Ashton-Tate, producer of dBase software, suffered the penalties of inadequate planning and testing when it introduced its dBase IV in 1985. The program had bugs that caused it to crash even when doing simple routines, and it was issued to customers long after it had been promised. As a result, the product's U.S. market share plunged from 68 percent in 1985 to 48 percent in 1988. The loss in sales resulting from coding errors and delays could have been avoided by more thorough planning and checking during the design and testing stages. Between 1988 and 1991, dBase product developers performed extensive testing of 45,000 functions to weed out glitches. Nonetheless, profits plummeted, and in 1991 Borland International acquired Ashton-Tate.

reliability The probability that a product will be functional when used.

Another dimension of quality related to product design is **reliability,** which refers to the probability that the product will be functional when used. Products often consist of a number of components that all must be operative for the product to perform as intended. Sometimes products can be designed with extra components (or subsystems) so that if one component fails another can be activated.

Suppose that a product has n subsystems, each with its own reliability measure (the probability that it will operate when called upon). The reliability of each subsystem contributes to the quality of the total system; that is, the reliability of the complete product equals the product of all the reliabilities of the subsystems, or

$$r_s = (r_1)(r_2)\cdots(r_n)$$

where

$$r_s = \text{reliability of the complete product}$$
$$n = \text{number of subsystems}$$
$$r_n = \text{reliability of the subsystem or component } n$$

This measure of reliability is based on the assumption that the reliability of each component or subsystem is independent of the others.

TUTOR 6.1

Suppose that a small portable radio designed for joggers has three components: a motherboard with a reliability of 0.99, a housing assembly with a reliability of 0.90, and a headphone set with a reliability of 0.85. The reliabilities are the probabilities that each subsystem will still be operating two years from now. The reliability of the portable radio is

$$r_s = (0.99)(0.90)(0.85) = 0.76$$

The poor headsets and housings hurt the reliability of this product. Suppose that new designs resulted in a reliability of 0.95 for the housing and 0.90 for the headsets. Product reliability would improve to

$$r_s = (0.99)(0.95)(0.90) = 0.85$$

Manufacturers must be concerned about the quality of every component, because the product fails when any one of them fails.

PROCESS DESIGN

The design of the process used to produce a product or service greatly affects its quality. Managers at the First National Bank of Chicago noticed that customers' requests for a letter-of-credit took four days to go through dozens of steps involving nine employees before a letter of credit would be issued. To improve the process and shorten the waiting time for customers, the bank trained letter-of-credit issuers to do all the required tasks so that the customer could deal with just one person. In addition, customers were given the same employee each time they requested a letter. First Chicago now issues letters of credit in less than a day.

The purchase of new machinery can help prevent or overcome quality problems. Suppose that the design specification for the distance between two holes in a metal plate is 3.000 ± 0.0005 in. Suppose also that too many plates are defective; that is, the space between holes falls outside the design specification. One way to reduce the percentage of defective parts produced by the process would be to purchase new machinery with the capability of producing metal plates with holes 3.000 ± 0.0003 in. apart. The cost of the new machinery is the trade-off for reducing the percentage of defective parts and their cost.

One of the keys to obtaining high quality is concurrent engineering (see the Operations Strategy chapter), in which operations managers and designers work closely together in the initial phases of product or service design to ensure that production requirements and process capabilities are synchronized. The result is much better quality and shorter development time. NCR, an Atlanta company that makes terminals for checkout counters, used concurrent engineering to develop a new model in 22 months, or half the usual time. The terminal had 85 percent fewer parts and could be assembled in only two minutes. Quality rejects and engineering changes dropped significantly. The National Institute of Standards and Technology estimates that manufacturing firms using concurrent engineering need 30 to 70 percent less development time, require 20 to 90 percent less time to market, and produce 200 to 600 percent better quality. Managerial Practice 6.2 tells how Teradyne implemented concurrent engineering.

QUALITY FUNCTION DEPLOYMENT

quality function deployment (QFD) A means of translating customer requirements into the appropriate technical requirements for each stage of product or service development and production.

A key to improving quality through TQM is linking the design of products or services to the processes that produce them. **Quality function deployment (QFD)** is a means of translating customer requirements into the appropriate technical requirements for each stage of product or service development and production. Bridgestone Tire and Mitsubishi Heavy Industries originated QFD in the late 1960s and early 1970s when they used quality charts that take customer requirements into account in the product design process. In 1978, Yoji Akao and Shigeru Mizuno published the first work on this subject, showing how design considerations could be "deployed" to every element of competition. Since then, more than 200 U.S. companies have used the approach, including Digital Equipment, Texas Instruments, Hewlett-Packard, AT&T, ITT, Ford, Chrysler, General Motors, Procter & Gamble, Polaroid, and Deere & Company.

This approach seeks answers to the following six questions.

1. *Voice of the Customer.*   What do our customers need and want?
2. *Competitive Analysis.*   In terms of our customers, how well are we doing relative to our competitors?
3. *Voice of the Engineer.*   What technical measures relate to our customers' needs?
4. *Correlations.*   What are the relationships between the voice of the customer and the voice of the engineer?
5. *Technical Comparison.*   How does our product or service performance compare to that of our competition?
6. *Trade-Offs.*   What are the potential technical trade-offs?

MANAGERIAL PRACTICE 6.2
TQM and Concurrent Engineering at Teradyne

Teradyne (www.teradyne.com), a $1.5 billion-a-year company with assembly plants in California, Massachusetts, New Hampshire, Illinois, Ireland, and Japan, produces testing systems for newly made chips, printed circuit boards and modules, computerized phone systems, and even software. Its newest product, called the Catalyst, has 250,000 parts and costs between $1.5 and $2 million. Teradyne produces the Catalyst in a plant with only 69 assemblers and 51 test workers, mostly in teams of 14 divided into shifts that work around the clock to put together a single machine in as little as two weeks. Catalyst has become the leading product in its field, and Teradyne has become a favorite of Wall Street because it has not had a losing quarter since 1991, while its major competitors have had a much rockier road.

Teradyne management attributes much of its success to the installation of TQM. Key aspects of the implementation of TQM were total involvement of management and employees and concurrent engineering. Although the company had already tried quality programs in the past, Alexander d'Arbelof, cofounder and CEO, decided to get personally involved by studying TQM and leading the implementation effort. He used three quality improvement teams to address three goals: increase market share, reduce costs, and reduce cycle time. The teams, composed of managers who were scientists and engineers, used their background and training to analyze the issues needing attention. Their common sense along with the TQM problem-solving approach generated solutions that improved operations. For example, Teradyne had been purchasing circuit boards from suppliers based on their capacities, rather than on who could do the job best. Changing their approach resulted in savings of $6 million a year, with an increase in quality. To maintain top management involvement, a top executive serves as a companywide TQM director on a rotating basis, and each division has its own TQM chief. Finally, employees were rewarded for company success through new profit sharing, stock option, and stock purchase plans.

A second key aspect of the implementation was the realization of design engineers and manufacturing assemblers that they

Concurrent engineering, a key to the successful implementation of TQM, has contributed to the success of Teradyne through improved process and product designs. To ensure the best in quality, great care goes into assembling the Catalyst's test head, which contains 700 cable connections.

would be much better off working together—using concurrent engineering. Before TQM, engineers would literally send prototypes down elevators from their upstairs laboratories to assemblers who had to figure out how to deal with design problems or send the prototype back with complaints. For example, assemblers would wonder why they must use 20 different types of screws and six different tools to fasten them. After TQM, assemblers had an equal voice with design engineers and, for the first time, the design engineers were required to work on the factory floor as a team with the assemblers to iron out design problems on the prototype models. As a result, the prototypes were built in 2.5 as opposed to 4 weeks, and with far fewer types of screws.

Source: Gene Bylinsky. "America's Elite Factories." *Fortune* (August 16, 1999), pp. 136P–136T.

The competitive analysis provides a place to start looking for ways to gain a competitive advantage. Then the relationships between customer needs and engineering attributes need to be specified. Finally, the fact that improving one performance measure may detract from another must be recognized.

The QFD approach provides a way to set targets and debate their effects on product quality. Engineering uses the data to focus on significant product design features. Marketing uses this input for determining marketing strategies. Operations uses the information to identify the processes that are crucial to improving product quality as perceived by the customer. As a result, QFD encourages interfunctional communication for the purpose of improving the quality of products and services.

BENCHMARKING

How good is the company's quality relative to that of competitors?

benchmarking A continuous, systematic procedure that measures a firm's products, services, and processes against those of industry leaders.

Benchmarking is a continuous, systematic procedure that measures a firm's products, services, and processes against those of industry leaders. Companies use benchmarking to understand better how outstanding companies do things so that they can improve their own operations. Typical measures used in benchmarking include cost per unit, service upsets (breakdowns) per customer, processing time per unit, customer retention rates, revenue per unit, return on investment, and customer satisfaction levels. Those involved in continuous improvement efforts rely on benchmarking to formulate goals and targets for performance. Benchmarking consists of four basic steps.

1. *Planning.* Identify the product, service, or process to be benchmarked and the firm(s) to be used for comparison, determine the measures of performance for analysis, and collect the data.
2. *Analysis.* Determine the gap between the firm's current performance and that of the benchmark firm(s) and identify the causes of significant gaps.
3. *Integration.* Establish goals and obtain the support of managers who must provide the resources for accomplishing the goals.
4. *Action.* Develop cross-functional teams of those most affected by the changes, develop action plans and team assignments, implement the plans, monitor progress, and recalibrate benchmarks as improvements are made.

The benchmarking process is similar to the plan–do–check–act cycle in continuous improvement, but benchmarking focuses on setting quantitative goals for continuous improvement. *Competitive* benchmarking is based on comparisons with a direct industry competitor. *Functional* benchmarking compares areas such as administration, customer service, and sales operations with those of outstanding firms in any industry. For instance, Xerox benchmarked its distribution function against L. L. Bean's because Bean is renowned as a leading retailer in distribution efficiency and customer service.

Internal benchmarking involves using an organizational unit with superior performance as the benchmark for other units. This form of benchmarking can be advantageous for firms that have several business units or divisions. All forms of benchmarking are best applied in situations where a long-term program of continuous improvement is needed.

DATA ANALYSIS TOOLS

How can areas for quality improvement be identified?

checklist A form used to record the frequency of occurrence of certain product or service characteristics related to quality.

The first step in improving the quality of an operation is data collection. Data can help uncover operations requiring improvement and the extent of remedial action needed. There are nine tools for organizing and presenting data to identify areas for quality and performance improvement: flow diagrams, process charts, checklists, histograms and bar charts, Pareto charts, scatter diagrams, cause-and-effect diagrams, graphs, and control charts. We have already discussed flow diagrams and process charts in the Process Management chapter, and we discuss control charts later (see the Statistical Process Control chapter). In this section we demonstrate the use of the other six methods to emphasize the breadth of applications possible. We conclude this section with an example showing how several of the approaches can be used together to focus on causes and remedies for a specific quality problem.

CHECKLISTS. Data collection through the use of a checklist is often the first step in the analysis of quality problems. A **checklist** is a form used to record the frequency of

histogram A summarization of data measured on a continuous scale, showing the frequency distribution of some quality characteristic (in statistical terms, the central tendency and dispersion of the data).

bar chart A series of bars representing the frequency of occurrence of data characteristics measured on a yes-or-no basis.

Pareto chart A bar chart on which the factors are plotted in decreasing order of frequency along the horizontal axis.

TUTOR 6.2

occurrence of certain product or service characteristics related to quality. The characteristics may be measurable on a continuous scale (e.g., weight, diameter, time, or length) or on a yes-or-no basis (e.g., paint discoloration, odors, rude servers, or too much grease).

HISTOGRAMS AND BAR CHARTS. The data from a checklist often can be presented succinctly and clearly with histograms or bar charts. A **histogram** summarizes data measured on a continuous scale, showing the frequency distribution of some quality characteristic (in statistical terms, the central tendency and dispersion of the data). Often the mean of the data is indicated on the histogram. A **bar chart** is a series of bars representing the frequency of occurrence of data characteristics measured on a yes-or-no basis. The bar height indicates the number of times a particular quality characteristic was observed.

PARETO CHARTS. When managers discover several quality problems that need to be addressed, they have to decide which should be attacked first. Vilfredo Pareto, a nineteenth-century Italian scientist whose statistical work focused on inequalities in data, proposed that most of an "activity" is caused by relatively few of its factors. In a restaurant quality problem, the activity could be customer complaints and the factor could be "discourteous waiter." For a manufacturer, the activity could be product defects and a factor could be "missing part." Pareto's concept, called the 80–20 rule, is that 80 percent of the activity is caused by 20 percent of the factors. By concentrating on the 20 percent of the factors (the "vital few"), managers can attack 80 percent of the quality problems.

The few vital factors can be identified with a **Pareto chart,** a bar chart on which the factors are plotted in decreasing order of frequency along the horizontal axis. The chart has two vertical axes, the one on the left showing frequency (as in a histogram) and the one on the right showing the cumulative percentage of frequency. The cumulative frequency curve identifies the few vital factors that warrant immediate managerial attention.

EXAMPLE 6.1 *Pareto Chart for a Restaurant*

The manager of a neighborhood restaurant is concerned about the smaller numbers of customers patronizing his eatery. The number of complaints have been rising, and he would like some means of finding out what issues to address and of presenting the findings in a way his employees can understand them.

SOLUTION

The manager surveyed his customers over several weeks and collected the following data:

COMPLAINT	FREQUENCY
Discourteous server	12
Slow service	42
Cold dinner	5
Cramped tables	20
Smoky air	10

Figure 6.4 is a bar chart and Figure 6.5 is Pareto chart, both developed by OM6 using Solver-TQM Charts. They present the data in a way that shows which complaints are the most prevalent (the vital few).

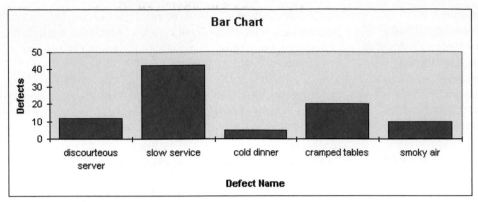

FIGURE 6.4 • Bar Chart

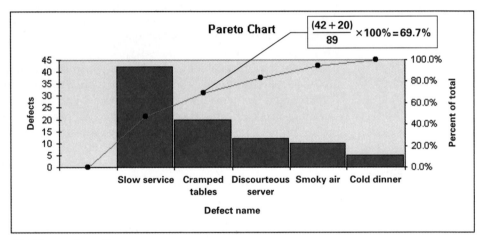

FIGURE 6.5 • Pareto Chart

Decision Point It was clear to the manager and all employees which complaints, if rectified, would cover most of the quality problems in the restaurant. First, slow service will be addressed by training the existing staff, adding another server, and improving the food preparation process. Removing some decorative, but otherwise unnecessary, furniture from the dining area and spacing the tables better will solve the problem with cramped tables. The Pareto chart shows that these two problems, if rectified, will account for almost 70 percent of the complaints. ◻

scatter diagram A plot of two variables showing whether they are related.

SCATTER DIAGRAMS. Sometimes managers suspect but are not sure that a certain factor is causing a particular quality problem. A **scatter diagram**, which is a plot of two variables showing whether they are related, can be used to verify or negate the suspicion. Each point on the scatter diagram represents one data observation. For example, the manager of a castings shop may suspect that casting defects are a function of the diameter of the casting. A scatter diagram could be constructed by plotting the number of defective castings found for each diameter of casting produced. After the diagram is completed, any relationship between diameter and number of defects could be observed.

CAUSE-AND-EFFECT DIAGRAMS. An important aspect of TQM is linking each aspect of quality prized by the customer to the inputs, methods, and process steps that build a particular attribute into the product. One way to identify a design problem that needs

cause-and-effect diagram
A diagram that relates a key quality problem to its potential causes.

to be corrected is to develop a **cause-and-effect diagram** that relates a key quality problem to its potential causes. First developed by Kaoru Ishikawa, the diagram helps management trace customer complaints directly to the operations involved. Operations that have no bearing on a particular defect aren't shown on the diagram for that defect.

The cause-and-effect diagram sometimes is called a *fishbone diagram*. The main quality problem is labeled as the fish's "head," the major categories of potential causes as structural "bones," and the likely specific causes as "ribs." When constructing and using a cause-and-effect diagram, an analyst identifies all the major categories of potential causes for the quality problem. For example, these might be personnel, machines, materials, and processes. For each major category, the analyst lists all the likely causes of the quality problem. For example, under personnel might be listed "lack of training," "poor communication," and "absenteeism." Brainstorming helps the analyst identify and properly classify all suspected causes. The analyst then systematically investigates the causes listed on the diagram for each major category, updating the chart as new causes become apparent. The process of constructing a cause-and-effect diagram calls management and worker attention to the primary factors affecting product or service quality. Example 6.2 demonstrates the use of a cause-and-effect diagram by an airline.

| EXAMPLE 6.2 | *Analysis of Flight Departure Delays* |

The operations manager for Checker Board Airlines at Port Columbus International Airport noticed an increase in the number of delayed flight departures.

SOLUTION

To analyze all the possible causes of that problem, he constructed a cause-and-effect diagram, shown in Figure 6.6. The main problem, delayed flight departures, is the "head" of the diagram. He brainstormed all possible causes with his staff, and together they identified several major

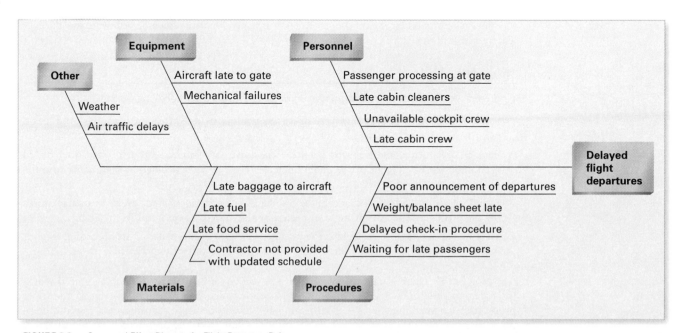

FIGURE 6.6 • Cause-and-Effect Diagram for Flight Departure Delays

categories: equipment, personnel, materials, procedures, and "other factors," which are beyond managerial control. Several suspected causes were identified for each major category.

Decision Point The operations manager suspected that most of the flight delays were caused by problems with materials. Consequently, he had food service, fueling, and baggage-handling operations examined. He learned that there were not enough tow trucks for the baggage-transfer operations and that planes were delayed waiting for baggage from connecting flights. ◻

---

graphs Representations of data in a variety of pictorial forms, such as line graphs and pie charts.

GRAPHS. Graphs represent data in a variety of pictorial formats, such as line graphs and pie charts. *Line graphs* represent data sequentially with data points connected by line segments to highlight trends in the data. Line graphs are used in control charts (see the Statistical Process Control chapter) and forecasting (see the Forecasting chapter). Pie charts represent quality factors as slices of a pie; the size of each slice is in proportion to the number of occurrences of the factor. Pie charts are useful for showing data from a group of factors that can be represented as percentages totaling 100 percent.

DATA SNOOPING

Each of the tools for improving quality may be used independently, but their power is greatest when they are used together. In solving a quality problem, managers often must act as detectives, sifting data to clarify the issues involved and deducing the causes. We call this process *data snooping*. Example 6.3 demonstrates how the tools for improving quality can be used for data snooping.

EXAMPLE 6.3   *Identifying Causes of Poor Headliner Quality*

The Wellington Fiber Board Company produces headliners, the fiberglass components that form the inner roof of passenger cars. Management wanted to identify which defects were most prevalent and to find the cause.

SOLUTION

Figure 6.7 shows the sequential application of several tools for improving quality.

Step 1. A checklist of different types of defects was constructed from last month's production records.

Step 2. A Pareto chart prepared from the checklist data indicated that broken fiber board accounted for 72 percent of the quality defects. The manager decided to dig further into the problem of broken fiber board.

Step 3. A cause-and-effect diagram for broken fiber board identified several potential causes for the problem. The one strongly suspected by the manager was employee training.

Step 4. The manager reorganized the production reports into a bar chart according to shift because the personnel on the three shifts had varied amounts of experience.

Decision Point The bar chart indicated that the second shift, with the least experienced workforce, had most of the defects. Further investigation revealed that workers were not using proper procedures for stacking the fiber boards after the press operation, causing cracking and chipping. The manager initiated additional training sessions focused on board handling after the press operation. Although the second shift was not responsible for all the defects, finding the source of many defects enabled the manager to improve the quality of her operations. ◻

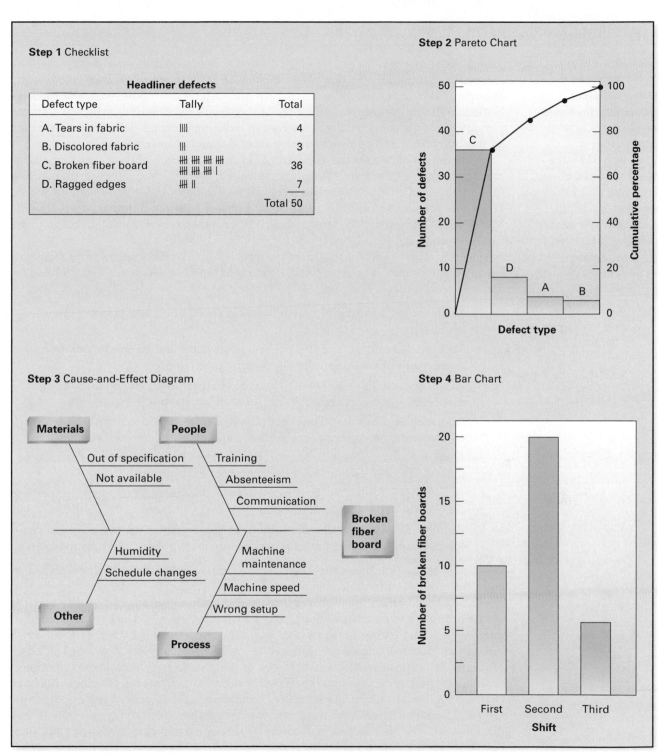

Step 1 Checklist

Step 2 Pareto Chart

Step 3 Cause-and-Effect Diagram

Step 4 Bar Chart

FIGURE 6.7 • Application of the Tools for Improving Quality

MALCOLM BALDRIGE NATIONAL QUALITY AWARD

Malcolm Baldrige National Quality Award
An award named for the late secretary of commerce, who was a strong proponent of enhancing quality as a means of reducing the trade deficit; the award promotes, recognizes, and publicizes quality strategies and achievements.

All organizations have to produce high-quality products and services if they are to be competitive. To emphasize that point, in August 1987, Congress signed into law the Malcolm Baldrige National Quality Improvement Act, creating the **Malcolm Baldrige National Quality Award.** Named for the late secretary of commerce, who was a strong proponent of enhancing quality as a means of reducing the trade deficit, the award promotes, recognizes, and publicizes quality strategies and achievements.

A maximum of two awards can be made each year in each of three categories: large manufacturers, large service companies, and small businesses in either manufacturing or services. As of 1999, 39 sites had received this prestigious award: 19 manufacturers, 10 service providers, and 10 small businesses. The more familiar firms include Motorola, IBM, Xerox, 3M, Selectron, AT&T, Federal Express, Merrill Lynch, and the Ritz-Carlton Hotel.

The application and four-stage review process for the Baldrige award is rigorous, but often the process helps companies define what quality means for them. The seven major criteria for the award are

1. *Leadership.*   Leadership system, values, expectations, and public responsibilities;
2. *Strategic Planning.*   The effectiveness of strategic and business planning and deployment of plans, focusing on performance requirements;
3. *Customer and Market Focus.*   How the company determines customer and market requirements and achieves customer satisfaction;
4. *Information Analysis.*   The effectiveness of information systems to support customer-driven performance excellence and marketplace success;
5. *Human Resource Focus.*   The success of efforts to realize the full potential of the workforce to create a high-performance organization;
6. *Process Management.*   The effectiveness of systems and processes for assuring the quality of products and services;
7. *Business Results.*   Performance results and competitive benchmarking in customer satisfaction, financials, human resources, suppliers, and operations.

Customer satisfaction underpins these seven criteria. Criterion 7, business results, is given the most weight in selecting winners.

The Baldrige award has focused attention on the importance of quality and the operations factors that must be improved to achieve excellence. The efforts required to implement a quality program usually pay off. The 16 award winners from 1988 through 1995 outperformed the Standard & Poor's 500 stock index by 3 to 1 in terms of return on investment. Millions of copies of the criteria have been mailed to organizations that have no intention of applying for the award. However, the guidelines have changed the thinking of many managers, who then have improved their operations. Organizations that applied for the award found that they received benefits even if they did not win. The 48 companies from 1990 through 1995 that made it to the final round of judging, but did not win, bested the S&P 500 by 2 to 1. The main benefit is that they learned about their organization's strengths and weaknesses—and came up with ways to improve operations. Further testimony to the impact of this award is that 11 states and several foreign countries have used its guidelines as a model for their own awards. The Malcolm Baldrige National Quality Award is an important step in promoting the cause of quality in the United States and raising the awareness of good quality practice in the eyes of the public.

INTERNATIONAL QUALITY DOCUMENTATION STANDARDS

From a quality perspective, how can an organization prepare to do business in foreign markets?

If each country had its own set of standards, companies selling in international markets would have difficulty complying with quality documentation standards in the countries where they did business. To overcome this problem, the International Organization for Standardization devised a set of standards called ISO 9000 for companies doing business in the European Union. Subsequently, a new set of documentation standards, ISO 14000, were devised for environmental management systems.

THE ISO 9000 DOCUMENTATION STANDARDS

ISO 9000 A set of standards governing documentation of a quality program.

ISO 9000 is a set of standards governing documentation of a quality program. Companies become certified by proving to a qualified external examiner that they have complied with all the requirements. Once certified, companies are listed in a directory so that potential customers can see which companies have been certified and to what level. Compliance with ISO 9000 standards says *nothing* about the actual quality of a product. Rather, it indicates to customers that companies can provide documentation to support whatever claims they make about quality.

ISO 9000 actually consists of five documents: ISO 9000–9004. ISO 9000 is an overview document, which provides guidelines for selection and use of the other standards. ISO 9001 is a standard that focuses on 20 aspects of a quality program for companies that design, produce, install, and service products. These aspects include management responsibility, quality system documentation, purchasing, product design, inspection, training, and corrective action. It is the most comprehensive and difficult standard to attain. ISO 9002 covers the same areas as ISO 9001 for companies that produce to the customer's designs or have their design and service activities at another location. ISO 9003 is the most limited in scope and addresses only the production process. ISO 9004 contains guidelines for interpreting the other standards.

ISO 14000—AN ENVIRONMENTAL MANAGEMENT SYSTEM

ISO 14000 Documentation standards that require participating companies to keep track of their raw materials use and their generation, treatment, and disposal of hazardous waste.

The **ISO 14000** documentation standards require participating companies to keep track of their raw materials use and their generation, treatment, and disposal of hazardous wastes. Although not specifying what each company is allowed to emit, the standards require companies to prepare a plan for ongoing improvement in their environmental performance. ISO 14000 is a series of five standards that cover a number of areas, including the following:

- ❑ *Environmental Management System.*   Requires a plan to improve performance in resource use and pollutant output.
- ❑ *Environmental Performance Evaluation.*   Specifies guidelines for the certification of companies.
- ❑ *Environmental Labeling.*   Defines terms such as *recyclable, energy efficient,* and *safe for the ozone layer.*
- ❑ *Life-Cycle Assessment.*   Evaluates the lifetime environmental impact from the manufacture, use, and disposal of a product.

To maintain their certification, companies must be inspected by outside, private auditors on a regular basis.

BENEFITS OF ISO CERTIFICATION

Completing the certification process can take as long as 18 months and involve many hours of management and employee time. For example, ABB Process Automation, Inc., a manufacturer of control systems for pulp, paper, and chemical producers, spent

25,000 labor hours over 9 months and $1.2 million, including a $200,000 audit fee, to achieve ISO 9001 certification. As much as one-third of the time necessary to establish an ISO 9000–based system is devoted to developing and creating the required documentation, which includes flow charts, computer programs, videotapes, and pages of written information. Like ISO 9000, ISO 14000 certification is not cheap. A manufacturing firm of 3,000 employees might expend $200,000 just in employee time. Consequently, most of the companies considering ISO 14000 certification are large global manufacturers, such as Lucent, Hewlett-Packard, and IBM.

Despite the expense and commitment involved in ISO certification, it bestows significant external and internal benefits. The external benefits come from the potential sales advantage that companies in compliance have. Companies looking for a supplier will more likely select a company that has demonstrated compliance with ISO documentation standards, all other factors being equal. Registered companies report an average of 48 percent increased profitability and 76 percent improvement in marketing. Consequently, more and more firms are seeking certification to gain a competitive advantage. Hundreds of thousands of manufacturing sites worldwide are ISO 9000 certified.

Internal benefits relate directly to the firm's TQM program. The British Standards Institute, a leading third-party auditor, estimates that most ISO 9000–registered companies experience a 10 percent reduction in the cost of producing a product because of the quality improvements they make while striving to meet the documentation requirements. Certification in ISO 9000 requires a company to analyze and document its procedures, which is necessary in any event for implementing continuous improvement, employee involvement, and similar programs. The internal benefits can be significant. DuPont, which has 160 ISO 9000 registrations worldwide, realized significant benefits, including

- ❐ a $3 million reduction in costs at an electronics site;
- ❐ an increase in on-time delivery from 70 to 90 percent;
- ❐ a decrease in outgoing nonconformances to specifications from 500 parts-per-million (ppm) to 150 ppm;
- ❐ a reduction in the number of test methods from 3,200 to 1,100;
- ❐ a drop in the product cycle time from 15 to 1.5 days;
- ❐ a lowering of operational costs by $750 million at one site by eliminating unnecessary tasks, overtime reductions, and job clarifications; and
- ❐ an increase in first-pass yields from 72 to 92 percent.

As demonstrated by the DuPont experience, the guidelines and requirements of the ISO documentation standards provide companies with a jump start in pursuing TQM programs.

TQM ACROSS THE ORGANIZATION

Total quality management is a philosophy that must permeate the entire organization if it is to be successful. The payoffs can be great; however, everyone must be involved. TQM has value for manufacturing as well as service companies. For example, Merrill Lynch Credit Corporation (MLCC), a winner of the Malcolm Baldrige National Quality Award, found out that focusing on quality management and performance excellence throughout the organization has significant rewards. MLCC, which originates over $4 billion in loans a year and manages a portfolio of nearly $10 billion, has 8 core and 10 support processes, involving 830 employees, that need to be coordinated. Communication from top to bottom in the organization is critical. Each year senior managers translate the company's strategic imperatives into a few critical objectives, which are accompanied by specific targets and measures. These objectives become the basis for determining employee performance plans, which in turn facilitate the communication loop between top management and the employees. Employees are empowered to take initiative and responsibility, especially in being flexible in responding rapidly to customer needs and in individual development. Employees receive an average of 74 hours of training a year, emphasizing the need to keep abreast of changes in technology to better serve customers.

A key element of MLCC's quality initiative is the "voice of the client" process, which identifies customer satisfaction drivers for each market segment and credit category. These priority customer requirements provide the basis for key performance measures for the eight core processes. In addition, data snooping is used to analyze customer satisfaction data to detect trends. Negative trends and recurring problems trigger process improvement teams to develop countermeasures and to prevent recurrences. Clients receive feedback on the resolution of the problem within five working days. MLCC's complete organizational commitment is exemplary of the pervasiveness of TQM, and it has paid off. In the two years after the initiation of the TQM philosophy, net income rose 100 percent, return on equity increased 74 percent, and return on assets improved 36 percent.

FORMULA REVIEW

1. The reliability of a product: $r_s = (r_1)(r_2) \cdots (r_n)$

CHAPTER HIGHLIGHTS

❐ Total quality management stresses three principles: a customer-driven focus, employee involvement, and continuous improvements in quality.

❐ The consumer's view of quality may be defined in a variety of ways. The customer may make a quantitative judgment about whether a product or service meets specified design characteristics. In other situations, qualitative judgments about value, fitness for the customer's intended use, product or service support, and aesthetics may take on greater importance. One TQM responsibility of marketing is to listen to customers and report their changing perceptions of quality.

❐ Quality can be used as a competitive weapon. High-performance design and consistent quality are competitive priorities associated with quality. World-class competition requires businesses to produce quality products or services efficiently.

❐ Responsibility for quality is shared by all employees in the organization. Employee involvement programs include leadership in changing organizational culture, individual development, awards and incentives, and teamwork.

❐ Managers need to develop skills for teaching their subordinates. The best improvement projects are those that emanate from the employees themselves. Employee-related strategies for improving quality include employee training, adequate monetary incentives, and quality circles.

❐ Continuous improvement involves identifying benchmarks of excellent practice and instilling a sense of ownership in employees so that they will continually identify product, services, and process improvements that should be made.

❐ Quality management is important because of its impact on market share, price, and profits and because of the costs of poor quality. The four main categories of costs associated with quality management are prevention, appraisal, internal failure, and external failure. If quality is to be improved, prevention costs must increase. Appraisal, internal failure, and external failure costs all decline as quality is improved through preventive measures.

❐ Benchmarking is a comparative measure. It is used to establish goals for continuous improvement. Forms of benchmarking include competitive, functional, and internal.

❑ Concurrent engineering improves the match between product design and production process capabilities. The higher quality and shorter product-development times associated with concurrent engineering are competitive advantages.

❑ Quality improvement requires close cooperation among functions (design, operations, marketing, purchasing, and others). Quality function deployment (QFD) encourages interfunctional planning and communication.

❑ Keys to controlling supplier quality are the buyer's approach and specification management. The buyer must consider quality, delivery, and cost. Specifications must be clear and realistic. Improved communication between purchasing and other departments is needed.

❑ Approaches to organizing and presenting quality improvement data include checklists, histograms and bar charts, Pareto charts, scatter diagrams, cause-and-effect diagrams, graphs, and control charts.

❑ The Malcolm Baldrige National Quality Award promotes, recognizes, and publicizes the quality strategies and achievements of outstanding American manufacturers, service providers, and small businesses.

❑ ISO 9000 is a set of standards governing the documentation of quality programs. ISO 14000 standards require participating companies to keep track of their raw materials use and their generation, treatment, and disposal of hazardous wastes.

KEY TERMS

appraisal costs *248*
bar chart *261*
benchmarking *260*
cause-and-effect diagram *263*
checklist *260*
continuous improvement *254*
employee empowerment *252*
external failure costs *248*
graphs *264*
histogram *261*

internal failure costs *248*
ISO 9000 *267*
ISO 14000 *267*
Malcolm Baldrige National Quality
    Award *266*
Pareto chart *261*
plan–do–check–act cycle *255*
prevention costs *246*
quality *244*
quality circles *252*

quality function deployment (QFD) *258*
reliability *257*
scatter diagram *262*
self-managing teams *253*
special purpose teams *252*
teams *251*
total quality management (TQM) *242*
warranty *248*

SOLVED PROBLEM 1

Kathryn Chou is experiencing high repair costs for her snack vending machines. She suspects that the machines are being vandalized by customers who are irate because of low vending machine reliability. For the machines to work properly, all of the following must occur:

SUBSYSTEM	RELIABILITY
Vending machine plugged in to power supply	0.97
Coins and bills read accurately	0.92
Customer pushes button matching selection	0.98
Vending machine is properly filled	0.98
Machine actually releases the product	0.85

What is the reliability of the vending operation?

SOLUTION

The reliability of the system is the simultaneous occurrence of independent events expressed by the formula

$$r_s = (r_1)(r_2) \cdots (r_n)$$

Substituting $r_1 = 0.97$, $r_2 = 0.92$, ..., yields

$$r_s = (0.97)(0.92)(0.98)(0.98)(0.85)$$
$$= 0.7285, \quad \text{or} \quad \text{about 73\% reliability}$$

SOLVED PROBLEM 2

Vera Johnson and Merris Williams manufacture vanishing cream. The following are the operations and reliabilities of their packaging operation. The reliabilities are the probabilities that each operation will be performed to the desired specifications.

OPERATION	RELIABILITY
Mix	0.99
Fill	0.98
Cap	0.99
Label	0.97

Johnson and Williams ask their spouses to keep track of and analyze reported defects. They find the following.

DEFECT	FREQUENCY
Lumps of unmixed product	7
Over- or underfilled jars	18
Jar lids did not seal	6
Labels rumpled or missing	29
Total	60

a. What is the reliability of the packaging operation?

b. Draw a Pareto chart to identify the vital defects.

SOLUTION

a. The formula is

$$r_s = (r_1)(r_2) \cdots (r_n)$$

Substituting $r_1 = 0.99$, $r_2 = 0.98$, ..., gives

$$r_s = (0.99)(0.98)(0.99)(0.97)$$
$$= 0.9317, \text{ or about 93\% reliability}$$

b. Defective labels account for 48.33% of the total number of defects:

$$\frac{29}{60} \times 100\% = 48.33\%$$

Improperly filled jars account for 30% of the total number of defects:

$$\frac{18}{60} \times 100\% = 30.00\%$$

The cumulative percent for the two most frequent defects is

$$48.33\% + 30.00\% = 78.33\%$$

Lumps represent $\dfrac{7}{60} \times 100\% = 11.67\%$ of defects; the cumulative percentage is

$$78.33\% + 11.67\% = 90.00\%$$

Defective seals represent $\dfrac{6}{60} \times 100\% = 10\%$ of defects; the cumulative percentage is

$$10\% + 90\% = 100.00\%$$

The Pareto chart is shown in Figure 6.8.

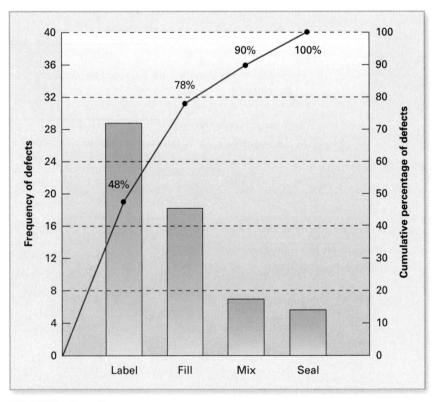

FIGURE 6.8 • Pareto Chart

OM EXPLORER AND INTERNET EXERCISES

Visit our Web site at www.prenhall.com/krajewski for OM Explorer Tutors, which explain quantitative techniques; Solvers, which help you apply mathematical models; and Internet Exercises, including Facility Tours, which expand on the topics in this chapter.

DISCUSSION QUESTIONS

1. Considerable success has been achieved by companies practicing TQM. What are the major hurdles to continuing quality improvements that manufacturers and service providers face?

2. Recently, the Polish General Corporation, well-known for manufacturing appliances and automobile parts, initiated a $13 billion project to produce automobiles. A great deal of learning on the part of management and employees was required. While pressure was mounting to get a new product to market in early 2000, the production manager of the newly formed automobile division insisted on almost a year of trial runs before sales started because workers have to do their jobs 60 to 100 times before they can memorize the right sequence. The launch date was set for early 2001. What are the consequences of using this approach to entering the market with a new product?

3. Continuous improvement recognizes that many small improvements add up to sizable benefits. Will continuous improvement take a company at the bottom of an industry to the top? Explain.

PROBLEMS

An icon next to a problem identifies the software that can be helpful, but not mandatory. The software is available on the Student CD-ROM that is packaged with every new copy of the textbook.

1. **OM Explorer** Contented Airlines (CA) is reluctant to begin service at the new Delayed Indefinitely Airport (DIA) until the automated baggage-handling system can transport luggage to the correct location with at least 99 percent reliability for any given flight. Lower reliability will result in damage to CA's reputation for quality service. The baggage system will not deliver to the right location if any of its subsystems fail. The subsystems and their reliability for satisfactory performance during operation for any given flight are shown in the following table.

SUBSYSTEM	RELIABILITY
Power supply	70.0% surge free
Scanner reading	99.8% accurate
Computer software	98.2% glitch free
Mechanical systems	97.5% jam free
Operators	96.0% error free

a. What is the reliability of the luggage system for any given flight?

b. When the passenger shuttle system operates, power surges trip the motors on the baggage system. Each of the luggage system motors must then be manually reset. Installing surge protectors increases power supply reliability to 99.9 percent. What is the reliability of the luggage system?

c. What could be done to improve the reliability of the luggage system?

2. **OM Explorer** A semiconductor has three components in series. Component 1 has a reliability of 0.98; component 2, 0.95; and component 3, 0.99. What is the reliability of the semiconductor?

3. A space launch vehicle has 100 subsystems that must all check out "A-okay" before the rocket can be launched. If each of the subsystems has a reliability of 99.9%, what is the probability that the rocket will launch on schedule?

4. **OM Explorer** Each semester at Copernicus University begins in chaos. Long lines of confused students form outside departmental offices. Students are not getting into the right class at the right place at the right time.

PROBLEM	PROBABILITY
Students register for wrong course	0.06
Classroom assignment conflict	0.05
Class roster error occurs	0.01
Error in published class schedule	0.005

On average, each student registers for five courses. What is the reliability of the registration process? In other words, what are the chances that a student will show up at the right place at the right time for the right class for all five courses?

5. **OM Explorer** The manager of Perrotti's Pizza collects data concerning customer complaints about delivery. Pizza is arriving late, or the wrong pizza is being delivered.

PROBLEM	FREQUENCY
Topping stuck to box lid	17
Pizza is late	35
Wrong topping or combination	9
Wrong style of crust	6
Wrong size	4
Pizza is partially eaten	3
Pizza never showed up	6

   a. Use a Pareto chart to identify the "few vital" delivery problems.

   b. Use a cause-and-effect diagram to identify potential causes of late pizza delivery.

6. **OM Explorer** Smith, Schroeder, and Torn (SST) is a short-haul household furniture moving company. SST's labor force, selected from the local community college football team, is temporary and part-time. SST is concerned with recent complaints, as tabulated on the following tally sheet.

COMPLAINT	TALLY
Broken glass	///// ///// ///
Delivered to wrong address	///// ////
Furniture rubbed together while on truck	///// ///// ///// /////
Late delivery	/////
Late arrival for pickup	///// ///// ///// ///
Missing items	///// ///// ///// ///// ///// /
Nicks and scratches from rough handling	///// /////
Soiled upholstery	///// ///

   a. Draw a bar chart and a Pareto chart to identify the most serious moving problems.

   b. Use a cause-and-effect diagram to identify potential causes of complaints.

7. **OM Explorer** Rick DeNeefe, manager of the Golden Valley Bank credit authorization department, recently noticed that a major competitor was advertising that applications for equity loans could be approved within two working days. As fast credit approval was a competitive priority, DeNeefe wanted to see how well his department was doing relative to the competitor's. Golden Valley stamps each application with the date and time it is received and again when a decision is made. A total of 104 applications were received in March. The time required for each decision, rounded to the nearest hour, is

shown in the following table. Golden Valley's employees work 8 hours per day.

DECISION PROCESS TIME	FREQUENCY
7–9 hours	8
10–12 hours	19
13–15 hours	28
16–18 hours	10
19–21 hours	25
22–24 hours	4
25–27 hours	10
Total	104

   a. Draw a bar chart for these data.

   b. Analyze the data. How is Golden Valley Bank doing with regard to this competitive priority?

8. **OM Explorer** Last year, the manager of the service department at East Woods Lincoln–Mercury instituted a customer opinion program to find out how to improve service.

One week after service on a vehicle was performed, his assistant would call the customer to find out whether the work had been done satisfactorily and how service could be improved. After a year of gathering data, the assistant discovered that the complaints could be grouped into the following five categories.

COMPLAINT	FREQUENCY
Unfriendly atmosphere	5
Long wait for service	17
Price too high	20
Incorrect bill	8
Need to return to correct problem	50
Total	100

   a. Draw a bar chart and a Pareto chart to identify the significant service problems.

   b. Use a cause-and-effect diagram to identify potential causes of complaints.

9. Oregon Fiber Board makes roof liners for the automotive industry. The manufacturing manager is concerned about product quality. She suspects that one particular defect, tears in the fabric, is related to production-run size. An assistant gathers the following data from production records.

RUN	SIZE	DEFECTS (%)	RUN	SIZE	DEFECTS (%)
1	1,000	3.5	11	6,500	1.5
2	4,100	3.8	12	1,000	5.5
3	2,000	5.5	13	7,000	1.0
4	6,000	1.9	14	3,000	4.5
5	6,800	2.0	15	2,200	4.2
6	3,000	3.2	16	1,800	6.0
7	2,000	3.8	17	5,400	2.0
8	1,200	4.2	18	5,800	2.0
9	5,000	3.8	19	1,000	6.2
10	3,800	3.0	20	1,500	7.0

a. Draw a scatter diagram for these data.

b. Does there appear to be a relationship between run size and percent defects? What implications does this have for Wellington's business?

10. Grindwell, Inc., a manufacturer of grinding tools, is concerned about the durability of its products, which depends on the permeability of the sinter mixtures used in production. Suspecting that the carbon content might be the source of the problem, the plant manager collected the following data.

CARBON CONTENT (%)	PERMEABILITY INDEX
5.5	16
3.0	31
4.5	21
4.8	19
4.2	16
4.7	23
5.1	20
4.4	11
3.6	20

a. Draw a scatter plot for these data.

b. Is there a relationship between permeability and carbon content?

c. If low permeability is desirable, what does the scatter plot suggest with regard to the carbon content?

11. **SmartDraw** The operations manager for Superfast Airlines at Port Columbus International Airport noticed an increase in the number of delayed flight departures. She brain-stormed possible causes with her staff:
 - Aircraft late to gate
 - Acceptance of late passengers
 - Passengers arrive late at gate
 - Passenger processing delays at gate
 - Late baggage to aircraft
 - Other late personnel or unavailable items
 - Mechanical failures

Draw a cause-and-effect diagram to organize the possible causes of delayed flight departures into the following major categories: equipment, personnel, material, procedures, and "other factors" beyond managerial control. Provide a detailed set of causes for each major cause identified by the operations manager, and incorporate them in your cause-and-effect diagram.

12. **OM Explorer** Plastomer, Inc., specializes in the manufacture of high-grade plastic film used to wrap food products. Film is rejected and scrapped for a variety of reasons (e.g., opacity, high carbon content, incorrect thickness or gauge, scratches, etc.). During the past month, management collected data on the types of rejects and the amount of scrap generated by each type. The following table presents the results.

TYPE OF DEFECT	AMOUNT OF SCRAP (LB)
Air bubbles	500
Bubble breaks	19,650
Carbon content	150
Unevenness	3,810
Thickness or gauge	27,600
Opacity	450
Scratches	3,840
Trim	500
Wrinkles	10,650

Draw a Pareto chart to identify which type of defect management should attempt to eliminate first.

13. Management of a shampoo bottling company introduced a new 13.5-ounce pack and used an existing machine, with some modifications, to fill it. To measure filling consistency by the modified machine (set to fill 13.85 ounces), an analyst collected the following data (volume in ounces) for a random sample of 100 bottles.

13.0	13.3	13.6	13.2	14.0	12.9	14.2	12.9	14.5	13.5
14.1	14.0	13.7	13.4	14.4	14.3	14.8	13.9	13.5	14.3
14.2	14.1	14.0	13.9	13.9	14.0	14.5	13.6	13.3	12.9
12.8	13.1	13.6	14.5	14.6	12.9	13.1	14.4	14.0	14.4
13.1	14.1	14.2	12.9	13.3	14.0	14.1	13.1	13.6	13.7
14.0	13.6	13.2	13.4	13.9	14.5	14.0	14.4	13.9	14.6
12.9	14.3	14.0	12.9	14.2	14.8	14.5	13.1	12.7	13.9
13.6	14.4	13.1	14.5	13.5	13.3	14.0	13.6	13.5	14.3
13.2	13.8	13.7	12.8	13.4	13.8	13.3	13.7	14.1	13.7
13.7	13.8	13.4	13.7	14.1	12.8	13.7	13.8	14.1	14.3

a. Draw a histogram for these data.

b. Bottles with less than 12.85 ounces or more than 14.85 ounces are considered to be out of specification. Based on the sample data, what percent of the bottles filled by the machine will be out of specification?

Advanced Problem

14. 💿 **OM Explorer** At Conner Company, a custom manufacturer of printed circuit boards, the finished boards are subjected to a final inspection prior to shipment to its customers. As Conner's quality assurance manager, you are responsible for making a presentation to management on quality problems at the beginning of each month. Your assistant has analyzed the reject memos for all the circuit boards that were rejected during the past month. He has given you a summary statement listing the reference number of the circuit board and the reason for rejection from one of the following categories:

A = Poor electrolyte coverage

B = Improper lamination

C = Low copper plating

D = Plating separation

E = Improper etching

For 50 circuit boards that had been rejected last month, the summary statement showed the following:

CBCCDECCBADACCCBCACDCACCB
ACACBCCACAACCDACCCECCABAC

a. Prepare a tally sheet (or checklist) of the different reasons for rejection.

b. Develop a Pareto chart to identify the more significant types of rejection.

c. Examine the causes of the most significant type of defect, using a cause-and-effect diagram.

CASE CRANSTON NISSAN

Steve Jackson, General Manager of Cranston Nissan, slowly sifted through his usual Monday morning stack of mail. The following letter was one he would not soon forget.

Dear Mr. Jackson:

I am writing this letter so that you will be aware of a nightmare I experienced recently regarding the repair of my 300ZX in your body shop and subsequently in your service department. I will detail the events in chronological order.

AUGUST 28

I dropped the car off for repair of rust damage in the following areas:

Roof—along the top of the windshield area
Left rocker panel—under driver's door
Left quarter panel—near end of bumper
Rear body panel—under license plate

I was told it would take three or four days.

SEPTEMBER 1

I called to inquire about the status of the car, since this was the fifth day the car was in the shop. I was told that I could pick up the car anytime after 2 P.M. My wife and I arrived

at 5 P.M. The car was still not ready. In the meantime, I paid the bill of $443.17 and waited. At 6 P.M. the car was driven up dripping wet (presumably from a wash to make it look good). I got into the car and noticed the courtesy light in the driver's door would not turn off when the door was closed. I asked for help, and Jim Boyd, body shop manager, could not figure out what was wrong. His solution was to remove the bulb and have me return after the Labor Day holiday to have the mechanic look at it. I agreed and began to drive off. However, the voice warning, "Left door is open," repeatedly sounded. Without leaving the premises I returned to Mr. Boyd, advising him to retain the car until it was fixed—there was no way I could drive the car with that repeated recording. Mr. Boyd then suggested I call back the next day (Saturday) to see if the mechanic could find the problem. I must emphasize, I brought the car to the body shop on August 28 in perfect mechanical working condition—the repair work was for body rust. This point will become important as the story unfolds.

SEPTEMBER 2

I called Jim Boyd at 10:30 A.M. and was told that the car had not been looked at yet. He promised to call back before the shop closed for the holiday, but he never did. I later learned that he did not call because "there was nothing to report." The car sat in the shop Saturday, Sunday, and Monday.

SEPTEMBER 5

I called Jim Boyd to check on the status of the car. It was 4 P.M., and Mr. Boyd told me nothing had been done, but that it should be ready by the next day. At this point it was becoming obvious that my car did not have priority in the service department.

SEPTEMBER 6

I called Jim Boyd again (about 4 P.M.) and was told that work had halted on the car because the service department needed authorization and they did not know how much it would run. At the hint that I would have to pay for this mess I became very upset and demanded that the car be brought immediately to the mechanical condition it was in when it was dropped off on August 28. At this point Ted Simon, service department manager, was summoned, and he assured me that if the problem was caused by some action of the body shop, I would not be financially responsible. I had not driven the car since I dropped it off, and I could not fathom the evidence anyone could produce to prove otherwise.

SEPTEMBER 7

Again late in the day, I called Mr. Simon, who said that Larry (in the service department) knew about the problem and switched me over to him. Larry said that they had narrowed it down to a wire that passed several spots where body work was performed. He said the work was very time-consuming and that the car should be ready sometime tomorrow.

SEPTEMBER 8

I called Mr. Simon to check on the status of the car once more. He told me that the wiring problem was fixed, but now the speedometer did not work. The short in the wires was caused by the body work. Larry got on the phone and said I could pick up the car, but they would send the car out to a subcontractor on Monday to repair the speedometer. He said that when the mechanic test-drove the car he noticed the speedometer pinned itself at the top end, and Larry thought that someone must have done something while searching for the other problem. I asked him if there would be charges for this and he said there would not. My wife and I arrived to pick up the car at 5 P.M. I clarified the next steps with Larry and was again assured that the speedometer would be repaired at no charge to me.

The car was brought to me, and as I walked up to it I noticed that the rubber molding beneath the driver's door was hanging down. I asked for some help, and Mr. Simon

came out to look at it. He said it must have been left that way after the search process for the bad wire. He took the car back into the shop to screw it on. When it finally came out again, he said that he would replace the molding because it was actually damaged.

When I arrived home, I discovered that the antitheft light on the dash would not stop blinking when the doors were closed. Attempting to activate the security system did not help. The only way I could get the light to stop flashing was to remove the fuse. In other words, now my security system was damaged. Needless to say, I was very upset.

SEPTEMBER 11

On Sunday evening I dropped off the car and left a note with my keys in the "early bird" slot. The note listed the two items that needed to be done from the agreement of last Friday—the molding and the speedometer. In addition, I mentioned the security system problem and suggested that "somebody must have forgotten to hook something back up while looking for the wire problem." On Monday I received a call from someone in the service department (I think his name was John), who said that the problem in the security system was in two places—the hatchback lock and "some wires in the driver's door." The lock would cost me $76, and the cost for the rest was unknown. The verbal estimate was for a total of $110. I asked him why he did not consider this problem a derivative of the other problems. He said that both the body shop and the mechanic who worked on the wire problem said they could see no way that they could have caused this to happen.

I told the fellow on the phone to forget fixing the security system because I was not going to pay for it. At this point, I just wanted the car back home, thinking I could address the problem later with someone such as yourself. I told him to have the speedometer fixed and again asked about charges for it. I was assured there would be none.

SEPTEMBER 13

The service department called to say I could pick up the car anytime before 8 P.M. He also said that the molding had to be ordered because it was not in stock. The need for the part was known on September 8, and NOW the part must be ordered. This will cause me another trip to the shop.

When I went to the service department to pick up the car, I was presented a bill for $126. I asked what the bill was for, and I was shown an itemized list that included speedometer repair and searching for the security problem. I said my understanding was that there would be no charges. Somebody at the service desk was apprised of the problem and released the car to me with the understanding that the service manager would review the situation the next day.

My car was brought around to me by the same person who brought it to me September 8. As I got into the

continued

continued

driver's seat, I noticed there was no rearview mirror—it was lying in the passenger's seat, broken off from its mounting. I was too shocked to even get mad. I got out of the car and asked how something like this could happen without anyone noticing. Jim Boyd said someone probably did not want to own up to it. He requisitioned a part and repaired the mirror mounting.

Mr. Jackson, I realize this is a long letter, but I have been so frustrated and upset over the past three weeks that I had to be sure that you understood the basis for that frustration. I am hoping you can look into this matter and let me know what you think.
Sincerely,
Sam Monahan
555 South Main, Turnerville

Questions

Answer the following questions from the perspective of TQM.
1. Categorize the quality problems in this case.
2. What are the probable causes of so many mishaps?
3. Prepare a cause-and-effect chart for "failure to remedy repair problem to customer satisfaction."
4. What specific actions should Jackson take immediately? What should some of his longer-term goals be?

CASE JOSÉ'S AUTHENTIC MEXICAN RESTAURANT

"Two bean tacos, a chicken burrito grande, and a side order of Spanish rice, please," Ivan Karetski called his table's order into the kitchen as he prepared the beverage orders. Business was brisk. Karetski liked it that way. Lots of customers meant lots of tips and, as a struggling graduate student, the extra income was greatly appreciated. Lately, however, his tips had been declining.

José's is a small, 58-seat restaurant that offers a reasonably broad range of Mexican food prepared and presented in a traditional Mexican style. It is located in New England in a mature business district on the edge of a large metropolitan area. The site is adjacent to a central artery and offers limited free off-street parking. The restaurant's interior decoration promotes the Mexican theme: The walls appear to be made of adobe and are draped with serapes, the furniture is Spanish–Mexican style, and flamenco guitar and mariachi alternate as background music.

Patrons enter the restaurant through a small vestibule that opens directly into the dining area; there is no separate waiting area. Upon arrival, patrons are greeted by a hostess and either seated directly or apprised of the expected wait, Seating at José's is usually immediate except for Friday and Saturday nights when waits of as long as 45 minutes can be encountered. Because space inside for waiting is very limited, patrons must remain outside until their party is called. José's does not take reservations.

After seating patrons, the hostess distributes menus and fills glasses with water. If standards are being met, the waiter assigned to the table greets the patrons within one minute of their being seated. (Being a traditional Mexican restaurant, all its waitstaff are male.) The waiter introduces himself, announces the daily specials, and takes the beverage orders. After delivering the beverages, the waiter takes the meal orders.

The menu consists of 23 main entrees which are assembled from eight basic stocks (chicken, beef, beans, rice, corn tortillas, flour tortillas, tomatoes, and lettuce) and a variety of other ingredients (fruits, vegetables, sauces, herbs, and spices). Before the dining hours begin, the cook prepares the basic stocks so that they can be quickly combined and finished off to complete the requested meals. The typical amount of time needed to complete a meal once it has been ordered is 12 minutes. A good portion of this time is for final cooking, so several meals may be in preparation at the same time. As can be imagined, one of the skills a good cook needs is to be able to schedule production of the various meals ordered at a table so that they are ready at approximately the same time. Once all the meals and any side dishes have been completed by the cook, the waiter checks to see that all meals are correct and pleasing to the eye, corrects any mistakes, and adds any finishing touches. When everything is in order, he assembles them on a tray and delivers them to the table. From this point on, the waiter keeps an eye on the table to detect when any additional service or assistance is needed.

When the diners at the table appear to be substantially finished with their main meal, the waiter approaches, asks if he can clear away any dishes, and takes any requests for dessert or coffee. When the entire meal has been completed, the waiter presents the bill and shortly thereafter collects payment. José's accepts cash or major credit card but no checks.

Karetski feels that his relationship with the cook is important. As the cook largely controls the quality of the food, Karetski wants to stay on good terms with him. He treats the cook with respect, tries to place the items on his order slip in the sequence of longest preparation time, and makes sure to write clearly so that the orders are easy to read. Although it is not his job, he helps out by fetching food stocks from the refrigerator or the storage area when the cook is busy and by doing some of the food preparation himself. The cook has been irritable lately, complaining of the poor quality of some of the ingredients that have been delivered. Last week, for example, he received lettuce that appeared wilted and chicken that was tough and more bone than meat. During peak times, it can take more than 20 minutes to get good meals delivered to the table.

Karetski had been shown the results of a customer survey that management conducted last Friday and Saturday during the evening mealtime. The following table shows a summary of the responses.

CUSTOMER SURVEY RESULTS				
Were you seated promptly?	Yes	70	No	13
Was your waiter satisfactory?	Yes	73	No	10
Were you served in a reasonable time?	Yes	58	No	25
Was your food enjoyable?	Yes	72	No	11
Was your dining experience worth the cost?	Yes	67	No	16

As Karetski carried the tray of drinks to the table, he wondered whether the recent falloff in tips was due to anything that he could control.

Questions

1. How should quality be defined at this restaurant?
2. What are the restaurant's costs of poor quality?
3. Use some of the tools for improving quality to assess the situation at José's.

Source: This case was prepared by Larry Meile, Boston College, as a basis for classroom discussion.

SELECTED REFERENCES

Benson, Tracy E. "TQM: A Child Takes a Few Faltering Steps." *Industry Week* (April 5, 1993), pp. 16–17.

Brown, Ed. "The Best Business Hotels." *Fortune* (March 17, 1997), pp. 204–205.

Collier, David A., *The Service Quality Solution.* New York: Irwin Professional Publishing; Milwaukee: ASQC Quality Press, 1994.

Crosby, Phillip B. *Quality Is Free.* New York: McGraw-Hill, 1979.

Davis, Deborah. "Victory Memorial Solves Operations Problems with TQM." *Target*, vol. 9, no. 6 (1993), pp. 14–19.

Deming, W. Edwards. "Improvement of Quality and Productivity Through Action by Management." *National Productivity Review*, vol. 1, no. 1 (Winter 1981–1982), pp. 12–22.

Deming, W. Edwards. *Out of the Crisis.* Cambridge, Mass.: Massachusetts Institute of Technology Center for Advanced Engineering Study, 1986.

Feigenbaum, A. V. *Total Quality Control: Engineering and Management,* 3d ed. New York: McGraw-Hill, 1983.

Garvin, David A. "How the Baldrige Award Really Works." *Harvard Business Review* (November–December 1991), pp. 80–93.

Garvin, David A. "Quality on the Line." *Harvard Business Review* (September–October 1983), pp. 65–75.

Hauser, John R., and Don Clausing. "The House of Quality." *Harvard Business Review* (May–June 1988), pp. 63–73.

Heskett, James L., W. Earl Sasser, Jr., and Christopher W. L. Hart. *Service Breakthroughs: Changing the Rules of the Game.* New York: Free Press, 1990.

Juran, J. M., and Frank Gryna, Jr. *Quality Planning and Analysis,* 2d ed. New York: McGraw-Hill, 1980.

Kalinosky, Ian S., "The Total Quality System—Going Beyond ISO 9000." *Quality Progress* (June 1990), pp. 50–53.

Miller, Bill. "ISO 9000 and the Small Company: Can I Afford It?" *APICS—The Performance Advantage* (September 1994), pp. 45–46.

Nakhai, Benham, and Joao S. Neves. "The Deming, Baldrige, and European Quality Awards." *Quality Progress* (April 1994), pp. 33–37.

Neves, Joao S., and Benham Nakhai. "The Evolution of the Baldrige Award." *Quality Progress* (June 1994), pp. 65–70.

Prahalad, C. K., and M. S. Krishnan. "The New Meaning of Quality in the Information Age." *Harvard Business Review* (September–October 1999), pp. 109–118.

Rabbitt, John T., and Peter A. Bergh. *The ISO 9000 Book.* White Plains, NY: Quality Resources, 1993.

Roth, Daniel. "Motorola Lives!" *Fortune* (September 27, 1999), pp. 305–306.

Rust, Roland T., Timothy Keiningham, Stephen Clemens, and Anthony Zahorik. "Return on Quality at Chase Manhattan Bank," *Interfaces*, vol. 29, no. 2 (March–April 1999), pp. 62–72.

Sanchez, S. M., J. S. Ramberg, J. Fiero, and J. J. Pignatiello, Jr. "Quality by Design." *Concurrent Engineering*, Chapter 10, A. Kusiak (ed). New York: John Wiley & Sons, 1994.

Sanders, Lisa. "Going Green with Less Red Tape." *Business Week* (September 23, 1996), pp. 75–76.

"Want EC Business? You Have Two Choices." *Business Week* (October 19, 1992), pp. 58–59.

"Why Online Browsers Don't Become Buyers" *Computerworld* (November 29, 1999), p. 14.

Statistical Process Control

Across the Organization

Statistical process control is important to . . .

- ☐ **accounting,** which audits the performance measures of processes.
- ☐ **engineering,** which designs, maintains, and repairs the machines that produce the products or services.
- ☐ **management information systems,** which designs statistical process control software.
- ☐ **marketing,** which introduces new products or services that require certain process capabilities.
- ☐ **operations,** which is responsible for ensuring process capability.

Learning Goals

After reading this chapter, you will be able to . . .

1. describe the differences between common causes and assignable causes of variation in process performance and why that distinction is important.
2. distinguish between variable measures and attribute measures of quality and apply the appropriate control charting approach for each measure.
3. discuss how control charts are developed and used.
4. construct $\bar{x}$, R, p, and c charts and use them to determine whether a process is out of statistical control.
5. explain the implications of choosing the spread between control limits on a control chart.
6. determine whether a process is capable of producing a product or service to specifications.

ADM Cocoa produces chocolate drops and other chocolate products for a wide variety of customers in the confectionery, dairy, and baking industries. The production process for chocolate drops is highly automated and has a product focus. Some 500,000 pounds of cocoa beans are unloaded, cleaned, and roasted each day. The roasted beans are ground into a liquid, called *liquor,* which is then blended with other ingredients according to a particular recipe for a given product to form a paste. The paste is heated to a specified temperature and then is pumped to a depositing machine that forms the paste into drops and controls their cooling. The drops then are packaged for delivery.

ADM utilizes total quality management (TQM) techniques with statistical process control (SPC) as the backbone component. The characteristics of agricultural commodities used for raw materials in the production of chocolate differ. For example, the fat content of cocoa beans varies according to the conditions under which the beans were grown. Fat content is crucial to determining the proper amount of each additive for blending into a specific product. ADM samples each batch of liquor just before the blending operation to measure fat content. If the sample is unacceptable, the liquor is reprocessed until it has the proper fat content.

Heated chocolate is poured from a holding tank into the depositing machine that forms the chocolate drops.

Because the fat content is standardized, the blending operation also can be standardized from batch to batch.

ADM's customers depend on receiving consistent quantities of chocolate drops. Customers have specifications such as $4,000 \pm 200$ drops per pound and gear their production processes accordingly. An essential step in production of the drops is the operation of the depositing machine. Every hour, a random sample of 100 drops is taken from the production line, the total weight is recorded, and the average number of drops per pound is estimated. If the result is unacceptable, the operator of the machine explores the possible reasons for the problem (e.g., the temperature of the paste entering the depositing machine or the setting of the aperture that forms the drops). Adjustments require 15 minutes to take effect because of the amount of time needed to clear the defective products. Operators must be well trained in both statistical process control techniques and machine operations because a mistake in the adjustment means that at least 30 minutes of production will be lost.

Source: Krajewski, David. Archer Daniels Midland Company, 2000; www.admworld.com.

WE HAVE PREVIOUSLY EXPLORED THE philosophy of total quality management (TQM) and defined five customer-driven characteristics of quality: conformance to specifications, value, fitness for use, support, and psychological impressions (see the Total Quality Management chapter). Many organizations attempt to design quality into their processes through continuous improvement methods (see the Total Quality Management and the Process Management chapters). Quality improvement relies on continual monitoring of the inputs and outputs of the processes producing goods or services. When inputs and outputs can be measured or compared, TQM statistical tools, such as control charts, can be useful to evaluate the degree of conformance to specifications.

statistical process control (SPC) The application of statistical techniques to determine whether the output of a process conforms to the product or service design.

Statistical process control (SPC) is the application of statistical techniques to determine whether the output of a process conforms to the product or service design. In SPC, tools called control charts are used primarily to detect production of defective products or services or to indicate that the production process has changed and that products or services will deviate from their design specifications unless something is done to correct the situation. SPC can also be used to inform management of process changes that have changed the output of the process for the better. Some examples of process changes that can be detected by SPC are

- ❏ a sudden increase in the proportion of defective gear boxes,
- ❏ a decrease in the average number of complaints per day at a hotel,
- ❏ a consistently low measurement in the diameter of a crankshaft,
- ❏ a decline in the number of scrapped units at a milling machine, and
- ❏ an increase in the number of claimants receiving late payment from an insurance company.

Let us consider the last situation. Suppose that the manager of the accounts payable department of an insurance company notices that the proportion of claimants receiving late payment has risen from an average of 0.01 to 0.03. The first question is whether the rise is a cause for alarm or just a random occurrence. Statistical process control can help the manager decide whether further action should be taken. If the rise in the proportion is large, the manager should not conclude that it was just a random occurrence and should seek other explanations of the poor performance. Perhaps the number of claims significantly increased, causing an overload on the employees in the department. The decision might be to hire more personnel. Or perhaps the procedures being used are ineffective or the training of employees is inadequate.

acceptance sampling The application of statistical techniques to determine whether a quantity of material should be accepted or rejected based on the inspection or test of a sample.

Another approach to quality management, **acceptance sampling,** is the application of statistical techniques to determine whether a quantity of material should be accepted or rejected, based on the inspection or test of a sample (see the Acceptance Sampling supplement in the Student CD-ROM). In addition, statistical charts, graphs, and diagrams can be used to judge the quality of products or services (see the Total Quality Management chapter). In this chapter, we explore the techniques of statistical process control to understand better the role they play in decision making.

SOURCES OF VARIATION
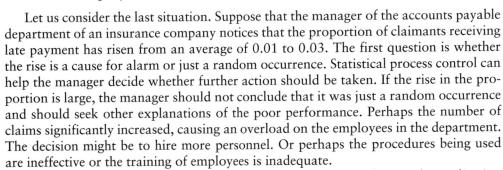

No two products or services are exactly alike because the processes used to produce them contain many sources of variation, even if the processes are working as intended. For example, the diameter of two crankshafts may vary because of differences in tool wear, material hardness, operator skill, or temperature during the period in which they were produced. Similarly, the time required to process a credit card application varies because of the load on the credit department, the financial background of the applicant, and the skills and attitudes of the employees. Nothing can be done to eliminate variation in process output completely, but management can investigate the *causes* of variation to minimize it.

common causes of variation The purely random, unidentifiable sources of variation that are unavoidable with the current process.

COMMON CAUSES

There are two basic categories of variation in output: common causes and assignable causes. **Common causes of variation** are the purely random, unidentifiable sources of variation that are unavoidable with the current process. For example, a machine that fills cereal boxes will not put exactly the same amount of cereal in each box. If you weighed a large number of boxes filled by the machine and plotted the results in a scatter diagram, the data would tend to form a pattern that can be described as a *distribution*. Such a distribution may be characterized by its mean, spread, and shape.

1. The *mean* is the sum of the observations divided by the total number of observations:

$$\bar{x} = \frac{\sum_{i=1}^{n} x_i}{n}$$

where

x_i = observation of a quality characteristic (such as weight)

n = total number of observations

$\bar{x}$ = mean

2. The *spread* is a measure of the dispersion of observations about the mean. Two measures commonly used in practice are the range and the standard deviation. The *range* is the difference between the largest observation in a sample and the smallest. The *standard deviation* is the square root of the variance of a distribution. An estimate of the population standard deviation based on a sample is given by

$$\sigma = \sqrt{\frac{\sum(x_i - \bar{x})^2}{n-1}} \qquad \text{or} \qquad \sigma = \sqrt{\frac{\sum x_i^2 - \frac{(\sum x_i)^2}{n}}{n-1}}$$

where

σ = standard deviation of a sample

n = total number of observations in the sample

$\bar{x}$ = mean

x_i = observation of a quality characteristic

Relatively small values for the range or the standard deviation imply that the observations are clustered near the mean.

3. Two common *shapes* of process distributions are symmetric and skewed. A *symmetric* distribution has the same number of observations above and below the mean. A *skewed* distribution has a preponderance of observations either above or below the mean.

Process Distribution for the Box-Filling Machine When Only Common Causes of Variation Are Present

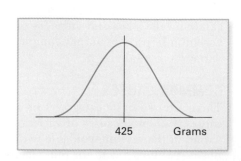

425   Grams

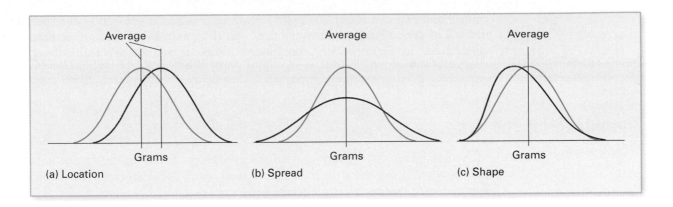

FIGURE 7.2

Effects of Assignable Causes on the Process Distribution for the Box-Filling Machine

If process variability comes solely from common causes of variation, a typical assumption is that the distribution is symmetric, with most observations near the center. Figure 7.1 shows the distribution for the box-filling machine when only common causes of variation are present. The mean weight is 425 grams, and the distribution is symmetric relative to the mean.

ASSIGNABLE CAUSES

assignable causes of variation Any variation-causing factors that can be identified and eliminated.

The second category of variation, **assignable causes of variation,** also known as *special causes,* includes any variation-causing factors that can be identified and eliminated. Assignable causes of variation include an employee needing training or a machine needing repair. Let us return to the example of the box-filling machine. Figure 7.2 shows how assignable causes can change the distribution of output for the box-filling machine. The green curve is the process distribution when only common causes of variation are present. The purple lines depict a change in the distribution because of assignable causes. In Figure 7.2(a), the purple line indicates that the machine put more cereal than planned in all the boxes, thereby increasing the average weight of each box. In Figure 7.2(b), an increase in the variability of the weight of cereal in each box affected the spread of the distribution. Finally, in Figure 7.2(c), the purple line indicates that the machine produced more lighter than heavier boxes. Such a distribution is skewed—that is, it is no longer symmetric to the average value.

A process is said to be in statistical control when the location, spread, or shape of its distribution does not change over time. After the process is in statistical control, managers use SPC procedures to detect the onset of assignable causes so that they can be eliminated. Figure 7.3 shows the differences between a process that is in statistical

FIGURE 7.3

Effects of Assignable Causes on Process Control

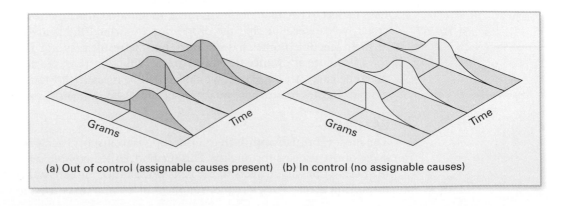

(a) Out of control (assignable causes present)   (b) In control (no assignable causes)

control and one that is not. In Figure 7.3(a), the machine is generating different distributions of cereal box weight over time, indicating assignable causes that need to be eliminated. In Figure 7.3(b), the distributions of weight are stable over time. Consequently, the process is in statistical control. Later, we discuss how SPC techniques can be used in continuous improvement projects to reduce process variability.

THE INSPECTION PROCESS

Many companies use quality inspection improperly, merely trying—often unsuccessfully—to weed out the defectives before they reach the customer. This approach is doomed to failure because of internal and external failure costs (see the Total Quality Management chapter). In contrast, world-class companies combine early inspection with SPC to monitor quality and detect and correct abnormalities. Important decisions in implementing such a program include how to measure quality characteristics, what size sample to collect, and at which stage in the process to conduct inspections.

QUALITY MEASUREMENTS

What trade-offs are involved in using attribute measurements instead of variable measurements of quality?

variables Product or service characteristics, such as weight, length, volume, or time, that can be measured.

attributes Product or service characteristics that can be quickly counted for acceptable quality.

To detect abnormal variations in output, inspectors must be able to measure quality characteristics. Quality can be evaluated in two ways. One way is to measure **variables**—that is, product or service characteristics, such as weight, length, volume, or time, that can be *measured*. For example, inspectors at Harley-Davidson measure the diameter of a piston to determine whether the product adheres to the specifications (within the allowable tolerance) and identify differences in diameter over time. Similarly, United Parcel Service managers monitor the length of time drivers spend delivering packages. The advantage of measuring a quality characteristic is that if a product or service misses its quality specifications, the inspector knows by how much. The disadvantage is that such measurements typically involve special equipment, employee skills, exacting procedures, and time and effort.

Another way to evaluate quality is to measure **attributes**—that is, product or service characteristics that can be quickly *counted* for acceptable quality. The method allows inspectors to make a simple yes–no decision about whether a product or service meets the specifications. Attributes often are used when quality specifications are complex and measuring by variables is difficult or costly. Some examples of attributes that can be counted are the number of insurance forms containing errors that cause underpayments or overpayments, the proportion of radios inoperative at the final test, the proportion of airline flights arriving within 15 minutes of scheduled times, and the number of stove-top assemblies with spotted paint. The advantage of attribute counts is that less effort and fewer resources are needed than for measuring variables. The disadvantage is that, even though attribute counts can reveal that quality of performance has changed, they may not be of much use in indicating by how much. For example, a count may determine that the proportion of airline flights arriving within 15 minutes of their scheduled times has declined, but the result may not show how much beyond the 15-minute allowance the flights are arriving. For that, the actual deviation from the scheduled arrival, a variable, would have to be measured. Managerial Practice 7.1 provides examples of attribute quality measures used in health care services.

SAMPLING

The most thorough approach to inspection is to inspect each product or service at each stage of the process for quality. This method, called *complete inspection,* is used when the costs of passing defects to the next workstation or external customer outweigh the inspection costs. For example, suppliers of components for the space shuttles check

MANAGERIAL PRACTICE 7.1
Quality Measures In Health Care Services

Unisys, a major provider of computers and computer services, is expanding into the fast-growing computerized health care services business. In addition to health insurance claims processing for government employees, which it has been doing for a long time, Unisys secured a contract to run Florida's state employee health insurance business, which required organizing a network of doctors and hospitals. To secure the contract, Unisys had to beat out Blue Cross/Blue Shield of Florida, Inc., which appealed the decision and lost. Nonetheless the delay reduced the amount of time Unisys had to get the system up and running. Things did not run smoothly, and the Florida Department of Management Services fined Unisys for not meeting performance standards.

What quality measures did the State of Florida use to make its case? The number of incidences of conflicting information given to customers by Unisys and its subcontractors and several deficiencies in the process that compromised the security of confidential customer information both played a role. However, failure to meet two measures of quality significantly influenced the state's decision to levy the fines.

❐ *Percentage of Claims Processed in Error.* This is an attribute measure because a claim is either processed correctly, or it is not. A simple count of the number of incorrectly processed claims in a sample divided by the total number of claims in the sample, multiplied by 100, will produce this quality measure. A Coopers & Lybrand audit found that Unisys made errors in 8.5 percent of the claims it processed, as opposed to an industry standard of 3.5 percent.

❐ *Percent of Claims Processed Within a Given Time Limit* This is also an attribute measure. A claim is "defective" if

Office workers are processing claims for an insurance company. Processing claims without errors, and doing so in a timely fashion, are important quality measures.

processing time is longer than the contractual time limit. In the contract with Unisys, at most 5 percent of the claims could take longer than 30 days to process. In one month's sample, 13 percent of the claims exceeded the 30-day limit.

Both of these quality measures can be tracked by using the statistical process control techniques presented in this chapter. Since that incident, Unisys has corrected the problems and has expanded its health care services business.

Source: "Unisys: Nobody Said Diversifying Was Easy." *Business Week* (July 15, 1996), p. 32; www.unisys.com, 2000.

---

sampling plan A plan that specifies a sample size, the time between successive samples, and decision rules that determine when action should be taken.

sample size A quantity of randomly selected observations of process outputs.

each component many times before shipping it to a contractor. In such a situation, the cost of failure—injury, death, and the destruction of highly expensive equipment—greatly exceeds the cost of inspection. Complete inspection virtually guarantees that defective units do not pass to the next operation or to the customer, a policy consistent with TQM. Nonetheless, when human inspectors are involved, even complete inspection may not uncover all defects. Inspector fatigue or imperfect testing methods may allow some defects to pass unnoticed. Firms can overcome these failings by using automated inspection equipment that can record, summarize, and display data. Many companies have found that automated inspection equipment can pay for itself in a reasonably short time.

A well-conceived **sampling plan** can approach the same degree of protection as complete inspection. A sampling plan specifies a **sample size**, which is a quantity of

*Relationship Between
the Distribution of
Sample Means and the
Process Distribution*

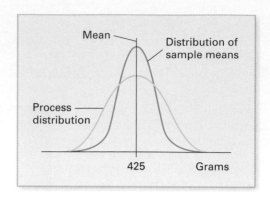

randomly selected observations of process outputs; the time between successive samples; and decision rules that determine when action should be taken. Sampling is appropriate when inspection costs are high because of the special knowledge, skills, procedures, or expensive equipment required to perform the inspections. For example, accounting firms use sampling plans when conducting an audit.

SAMPLING DISTRIBUTIONS. The purpose of sampling is to calculate a variable or attribute measure for some quality characteristic of the sample. That measure is then used to assess the performance of the process itself. For example, in the cereal box-filling example, an important quality dimension is the weight of the product in each box. Suppose that management wants the machine to produce boxes so that the average weight is 425 grams. That is, it wants the process distribution to have a mean of 425 grams. An inspector periodically taking a sample of five boxes filled by the machine and calculating the sample mean (a variable measure) could use it to determine how well the machine is doing.

Plotting a large number of these means would show that they have their own distribution, with a mean centered on 425 grams, as did the process distribution, but with much less variability. The reason is that means offset the highs and lows of the individual box weights. Figure 7.4 shows the relationship between the sampling distribution and the process distribution for the box weights.

Some sampling distributions (e.g., for means with sample sizes of 4 or more and proportions with sample sizes of 20 or more) can be approximated by the *normal* distribution, allowing the use of the normal tables (see the Normal Distribution appendix). Figure 7.5 shows the percent of values within certain ranges of the normal distribution. For example, 68.26 percent of the sample will have values within ± 1 standard deviation of the distribution mean. We can determine the probability that any particular sample result will fall outside certain limits. For example, there is a 2.28 percent chance, or $(100 - 95.44)/2$, that a sample mean will be more than 2 standard deviations *greater* than the mean. The ability to assign probabilities to sample results is important for the construction and use of control charts.

CONTROL CHARTS. To determine whether observed variations are abnormal, we can measure and plot the quality characteristic taken from the sample on a time-ordered diagram called a **control chart**. A control chart has a nominal value, or central line, which typically is a target that managers would like the process to achieve, and two control limits based on the sampling distribution of the quality measure. The control limits are used to judge whether action is required. The larger value represents the *upper control limit* (UCL), and the smaller value represents the *lower control limit*

control chart A time-ordered diagram that is used to determine whether observed variations are abnormal.

FIGURE 7.5

*The Normal
Distribution*

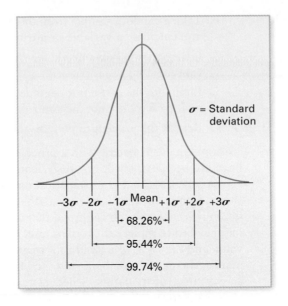

σ = Standard
deviation

−3σ −2σ −1σ Mean +1σ +2σ +3σ

68.26%

95.44%

99.74%

(LCL). Figure 7.6 shows how the control limits relate to the sampling distribution. A sample statistic that falls between the UCL and the LCL indicates that the process is exhibiting common causes of variation; a statistic that falls outside the control limits indicates that the process is exhibiting assignable causes of variation.

Observations falling outside the control limits do not always mean poor quality. For example, in Figure 7.6 the assignable cause may be a new billing process introduced to reduce the number of incorrect bills sent to customers. If the proportion of incorrect bills, the quality statistic from a sample of bills, falls *below* the LCL of the control chart, the new procedure has likely changed the billing process for the better and a new control chart should be constructed.

Managers or employees responsible for monitoring a process can use control charts in the following ways:

FIGURE 7.6

*Relationship of Control
Limits to Sampling
Distribution and
Observations from
Three Samples*

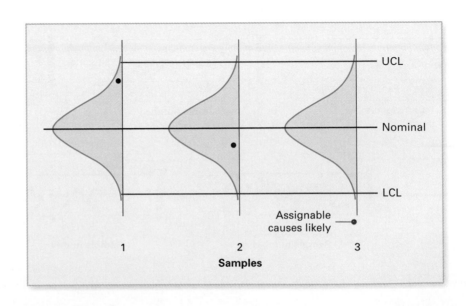

UCL

Nominal

LCL

Assignable
causes likely

1   2   3

Samples

1. Take a random sample from the process, measure the quality characteristic, and calculate a variable or attribute measure.

2. If the statistic falls outside the chart's control limits, look for an assignable cause.

3. Eliminate the cause if it degrades quality; incorporate the cause if it improves quality. Reconstruct the control chart with new data.

4. Repeat the procedure periodically.

Sometimes, problems with a process can be detected even though the control limits have not been exceeded. Figure 7.7 contains five examples of control charts. Chart (a) shows a process that is in statistical control. No action is needed. However, chart (b) shows a pattern called a *run,* or a sequence of observations with a certain characteristic. In this case, the run is a trend that could be the result of gradual tool wear, indicating the need to replace the tool or reset the machine to some value between the nominal value and the UCL to extend tool wear. For an airline concerned with on-time performance, the cause may be a slow buildup of air traffic at an airport at the scheduled arrival times of its flights. Schedule changes may be in order. A typical rule is to take remedial action when there is a trend of five or more observations, even if the points have not yet exceeded the control limits.

Chart (c) shows that the process has taken a sudden change from its normal pattern. The last four observations are unusual: three rising toward the UCL and the fourth remaining above the nominal value. A manager should be concerned with such sudden changes even though the control limits have not been exceeded. Chart (d) demonstrates another situation where action is needed even though the limits haven't been exceeded. Whenever a run of five or more observations above or below the nominal value occurs, the operator should look for a cause. The probability is very low that such a result could take place by chance. Finally, chart (e) indicates that the process went out of control twice because two sample results fell outside the control limits. The probability that the process distribution has changed is high. We discuss more implications of being out of statistical control when we discuss process capability later in this chapter.

FIGURE 7.7

Control Chart Examples

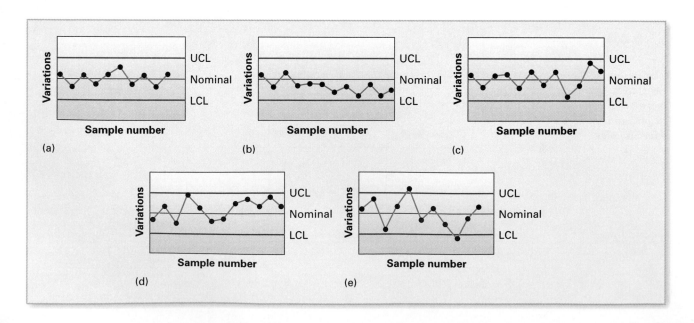

type I error An error that occurs when the employee concludes that the process is out of control based on a sample result that falls outside the control limits, when in fact it was due to pure randomness.

type II error An error that occurs when the employee concludes that the process is in control and only randomness is present, when actually the process is out of statistical control.

Control charts are not perfect tools for detecting shifts in the process distribution because they are based on sampling distributions. Two types of error are possible with the use of control charts. A **type I error** occurs when the employee concludes that the process is out of control based on a sample result that falls outside the control limits, when in fact it was due to pure randomness. A **type II error** occurs when the employee concludes that the process is in control and only randomness is present, when actually the process is out of statistical control.

Management can control these errors by the choice of control limits. The choice would depend on the costs of looking for assignable causes when none exist versus the cost of not detecting a shift in the process.

Figure 7.8 shows the consequences of these errors when the process average is the quality measure. In chart (a) the control limits for the sampling distribution were set for 3 standard deviations from the mean. We refer to these control limits as *three-sigma limits*. In this regard, "sigma" refers to the standard deviation of the *sampling distribution*, not the process distribution. In the leftmost curve, the shaded portion shows the probability of making a type I error. For three-sigma limits, that probability is quite small. In the rightmost curve, the process average has shifted. The shaded portion of

FIGURE 7.8

Relationship of Control Limit Spread to Type I and Type II Errors

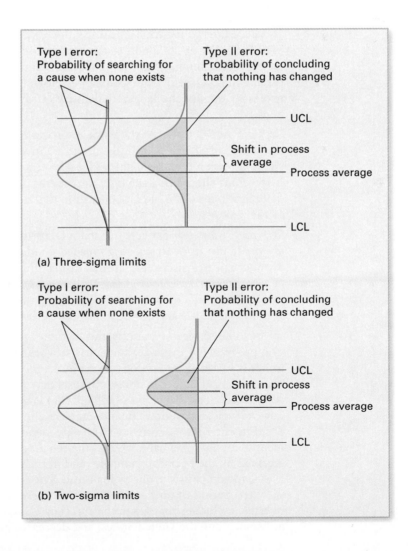

the curve now shows the probability of making a type II error, which is quite large. In chart (b), the control chart has only two-sigma control limits, a narrower spread than the three-sigma control chart. Now the probability of a type I error has increased, and the probability of a type II error has decreased. Thus, increasing the spread decreases type I errors while increasing type II errors.

A manager who uses three-sigma limits is implying that the cost of searching for assignable causes is large relative to the cost of not detecting a shift in the process average. Quite a few samples may have to be taken to generate a sample average that falls outside the control limits. Conversely, a manager who uses two-sigma limits is implying that the cost of not detecting a shift in the process average exceeds the cost of searching for assignable causes. With smaller control limits, more sample means will fall outside the limits, causing more searching for assignable causes. Often, no assignable causes will be found, but a shift in the process average will be detected sooner.

LOCATION OF INSPECTION PROCESSES

Where should inspection stations be put?

To decide at which stage of the process to make inspections, management must identify the aspects of quality important to the consumer and the key steps in the process that affect those characteristics. Inspection stations usually occur at three points in the total process:

❑ *Raw Material Inputs.*   The inspection of purchased materials ensures the proper quality of the inputs to the production process. At this stage, various acceptance-sampling plans (see the Acceptance Sampling supplement in the CD text.) could be used. Many companies, however, rely on their suppliers to do the necessary quality checks before delivery of raw materials or purchased components.

❑ *Work in Process.*   At the work-in-process stage, an inspection station could be located after each step in the process. However, this approach could be very costly if testing requires highly skilled inspectors and expensive technology. Inspections should be done *after* any operation that produces a large number of defective items or *before* any operation that adds high materials or labor costs to the product.

❑ *Final Product or Service.*   In manufacturing systems, final product inspections are made just prior to stocking finished goods or shipping them to the customer. Product failures discovered at final inspection are costly because they may result in (1) scrapping the defective items or batch, (2) routing the defective items or batch to a previous step for rework, or (3) routing the defective items or batch to a special area for diagnosis and correction of the defects.

In some service operations, the customer plays a major role in the final inspection process. For instance, a hair stylist works with the customer until the customer is satisfied, or a mechanic may take the customer for a test drive after repairing a car. In other situations, tests may be made before customers purchase the service. Such is the case of a bank that is introducing a new financial product. For example, a corporate finance employee in a U.S. bank might submit a proposal to enter into a currency swap agreement with a Mexican residential development company. The bank would take the monthly mortgage payments in pesos received by the Mexican company and in turn make the monthly payments on the Mexican company's property loan in U.S dollars. Because the agreement is for a specified period of time at fixed rates of interest, the bank is exposed to a number of risks, including changes in the currency exchange rates, changes in interest rates in Mexico and the United States, and decreases in the creditworthiness of the

Mexican company. The bank charges a fee for this service that reflects these risks. However, to judge the worthiness of the product, the bank can conduct a *stress test* where a computer program is used to simulate the potential effect of the new product on the bank's bottom line. The program simulates extreme conditions of currency and interest rate volatility and the ability of the Mexican company to repay the loan obligation if some of its customers default on their mortgages and creates a distribution of the profit-and-loss position of the bank under the agreement. If the risk exposure to the bank is too large, the proposal may be rejected and returned to the corporate finance department for further development.

In deciding on the number and location of inspection stations, the operations manager must remember that quality cannot be inspected into the product; inspection can only detect that the process is not operating according to specifications and identify the need for corrective action.

STATISTICAL PROCESS CONTROL METHODS

Statistical process control (SPC) methods are useful for both measuring the current quality of products or services and detecting whether the process itself has changed in a way that will affect quality. In this section, we first discuss mean and range charts for variable measures of quality and then consider control charts for product or service attributes.

CONTROL CHARTS FOR VARIABLES

Control charts for variables are used to monitor the mean and the variability of the process distribution.

R-chart A chart used to monitor process variability.

R-CHARTS. A range chart, or **R-chart**, is used to monitor process variability. To calculate the range of a set of sample data, the analyst subtracts the smallest from the largest measurement in each sample. If any of the data fall outside the control limits, the process variability is not in control.

The control limits for the R-chart are

$$\text{UCL}_R = D_4\overline{R} \qquad \text{and} \qquad \text{LCL}_R = D_3\overline{R}$$

where

$\overline{R}$ = average of several past R values and the central line of the control chart

D_3, D_4 = constants that provide 3 standard deviation (three-sigma) limits for a given sample size

Values for D_3 and D_4 are contained in Table 7.1 and change as a function of the sample size. Note that the spread between the control limits narrows as the sample size increases. This change is a consequence of having more information on which to base an estimate for the process range.

x̄-chart A chart used to measure the mean.

x̄-CHARTS. An $\overline{x}$-chart (read "x-bar chart") is used to measure the mean. When the assignable causes of process variability have been identified and the process variability is in statistical control, the analyst can construct an $\overline{x}$-chart to control the process average. The control limits for the $\overline{x}$-chart are

$$\text{UCL}_{\overline{x}} = \overline{\overline{x}} + A_2\overline{R} \qquad \text{and} \qquad \text{LCL}_{\overline{x}} = \overline{\overline{x}} - A_2\overline{R}$$

TABLE 7.1

Factors for Calculating Three-Sigma Limits for the x̄-Chart and R-Chart

Source: 1950 *ASTM Manual on Quality Control of Materials*, copyright © American Society for Testing Materials. Reprinted with permission.

Size of Sample (n)	Factor for UCL and LCL for x̄-Charts (A_2)	Factor for LCL for R-Charts (D_3)	Factor for UCL for R-Charts (D_4)
2	1.880	0	3.267
3	1.023	0	2.575
4	0.729	0	2.282
5	0.577	0	2.115
6	0.483	0	2.004
7	0.419	0.076	1.924
8	0.373	0.136	1.864
9	0.337	0.184	1.816
10	0.308	0.223	1.777

where

$\bar{\bar{x}}$ = central line of the chart and either the average of past sample means or a target value set for the process

A_2 = constant to provide three-sigma limits for the sample mean

The values for A_2 are contained in Table 7.1. Note that the control limits use the value of $\bar{R}$; therefore, the x̄-chart must be constructed *after* the process variability is in control.

Analysts can develop and use x̄- and R-charts in the following way:

Step 1. Collect data on the variable quality measurement (such as weight, diameter, or time) and organize the data by sample number. Preferably, at least 20 samples should be taken for use in constructing a control chart.

Step 2. Compute the range for each sample and the average range, $\bar{R}$, for the set of samples.

Step 3. Use Table 7.1 to determine the upper and lower control limits of the R-chart.

Step 4. Plot the sample ranges. If all are in control, proceed to step 5. Otherwise, find the assignable causes, correct them, and return to step 1.

Step 5. Calculate x̄ for each sample and the central line of the chart, $\bar{\bar{x}}$.

Step 6. Use Table 7.1 to determine the parameters for $UCL_{\bar{x}}$ and $LCL_{\bar{x}}$ and construct the x̄-chart.

Step 7. Plot the sample means. If all are in control, the process is in statistical control in terms of the process average and process variability. Continue to take samples and monitor the process. If any are out of control, find the assignable causes, correct them, and return to step 1. If no assignable causes are found after a diligent search, assume that the out-of-control points represent common causes of variation and continue to monitor the process.

EXAMPLE 7.1

Using x̄- and R-Charts to Monitor a Process

The management of West Allis Industries is concerned about the production of a special metal screw used by several of the company's largest customers. The diameter of the screw is critical. Data from five samples are shown in the accompanying table. The sample size is 4. Is the process in control?

SOLUTION

Step 1. For simplicity we have taken only five samples. In practice, more than 20 samples would be desirable. The data are shown in the following table.

Data for the $\bar{x}$- and R-Charts: Observations of Screw Diameter (in.)

SAMPLE NUMBER	OBSERVATION				R	$\bar{x}$
	1	2	3	4		
1	0.5014	0.5022	0.5009	0.5027	0.0018	0.5018
2	0.5021	0.5041	0.5024	0.5020	0.0021	0.5027
3	0.5018	0.5026	0.5035	0.5023	0.0017	0.5026
4	0.5008	0.5034	0.5024	0.5015	0.0026	0.5020
5	0.5041	0.5056	0.5034	0.5047	0.0022	0.5045
				Average	0.0021	0.5027

Step 2. Compute the range for each sample by subtracting the lowest value from the highest value. For example, in sample 1 the range is $0.5027 - 0.5009 = 0.0018$ in. Similarly, the ranges for samples 2, 3, 4, and 5 are 0.0021, 0.0017, 0.0026, and 0.0022 in., respectively. As shown in the table, $\bar{R} = 0.0021$.

Step 3. To construct the R-chart, select the appropriate constants from Table 7.1 for a sample size of 4. The control limits are

$$\text{UCL}_R = D_4\bar{R} = 2.282(0.0021) = 0.00479 \text{ in.}$$

$$\text{LCL}_R = D_3\bar{R} = 0(0.0021) = 0 \text{ in.}$$

Step 4. Plot the ranges on the R-chart, as shown in Figure 7.9. None of the sample ranges falls outside the control limits. Consequently, the process variability is in statistical control. If any of the sample ranges had fallen outside of the limits, or an unusual pattern had appeared (see Figure 7.7), we would have had to search for the causes of the excessive variability, correct them, and repeat step 1.

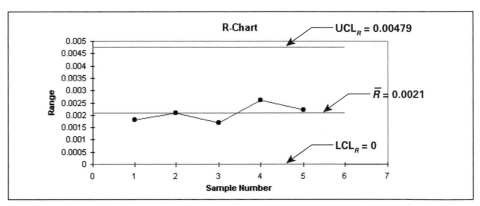

FIGURE 7.9 • Range Chart from the OM Explorer $\bar{x}$- and R-Chart Solver for the Metal Screw, Showing That the Process Variability Is in Control

Step 5. Compute the mean for each sample. For example, the mean for sample 1 is

$$\frac{0.5014 + 0.5022 + 0.5009 + 0.5027}{4} = 0.5018 \text{ in.}$$

Similarly, the means of samples 2, 3, 4, and 5 are 0.5027, 0.5026, 0.5020, and 0.5045 in., respectively. As shown in the table, $\bar{\bar{x}} = 0.5027$.

Step 6. Now construct the $\bar{x}$-chart for the process average. The average screw diameter is 0.5027 in. and the average range is 0.0021 in., so use $\bar{\bar{x}} = 0.5027$, $\overline{R} = 0.0021$, and A_2 from Table 7.1 for a sample size of 4 to construct the control limits:

$$\text{UCL}_{\bar{x}} = \bar{\bar{x}} + A_2\overline{R} = 0.5027 + 0.729(0.0021) = 0.5042 \text{ in.}$$
$$\text{LCL}_{\bar{x}} = \bar{\bar{x}} - A_2\overline{R} = 0.5027 - 0.729(0.0021) = 0.5012 \text{ in.}$$

Step 7. Plot the sample means on the control chart, as shown in Figure 7.10.

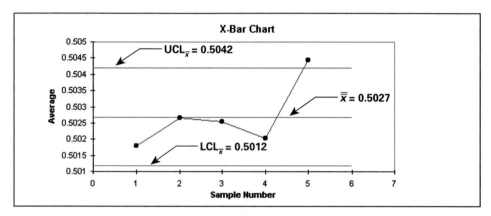

FIGURE 7.10 • The $\bar{x}$-Chart from the OM Explorer $\bar{x}$- and R-Chart Solver for the Metal Screw, Showing That Sample 5 Is Out of Control

The mean of sample 5 falls above the upper control limit, indicating that the process average is out of control and that assignable causes must be explored, perhaps using a cause-and-effect diagram (see the Total Quality Management chapter).

Decision Point A new employee operated the lathe machine that makes the screw on the day the sample was taken. Management initiated a training session for the employee. Subsequent samples showed that the process was back in statistical control. ❑

If the standard deviation of the process distribution is known, another form of the $\bar{x}$-chart may be used:

$$\text{UCL}_{\bar{x}} = \bar{\bar{x}} + z\sigma_{\bar{x}} \qquad \text{and} \qquad \text{LCL}_{\bar{x}} = \bar{\bar{x}} - z\sigma_{\bar{x}}$$

where

$\sigma_{\bar{x}} = \sigma/\sqrt{n} =$ standard deviation of sample means

$\sigma =$ standard deviation of the process distribution

$n =$ sample size

$\bar{\bar{x}} =$ average of sample means or a target value set for the process

$z =$ normal deviate

The analyst can use an R-chart to be sure that the process variability is in control before constructing the $\bar{x}$-chart. The advantage of using this form of the $\bar{x}$-chart is that the analyst can adjust the spread of the control limits by changing the value of z. This approach can be useful for balancing the effects of type I and type II errors.

| EXAMPLE 7.2 | *Designing an $\bar{x}$-Chart Using the Process Standard Deviation* |

The Sunny Dale Bank monitors the time required to serve customers at the drive-by window because it is an important quality factor in competing with other banks in the city. After analyzing the data gathered in an extensive study of the window operation, bank management determined that the mean time to process a customer at the peak demand period has been five minutes, with a standard deviation of 1.5 minutes. Management wants to monitor the mean time to process a customer by using a sample size of six customers. Assume that the process variability is in statistical control. Design an $\bar{x}$-chart that has a type I error of 5 percent. After several weeks of sampling, two successive samples came in at 3.70 and 3.68 minutes, respectively. Is the customer service process in statistical control?

SOLUTION

$$\bar{\bar{x}} = 5.0 \text{ minutes}$$
$$\sigma = 1.5 \text{ minutes}$$
$$n = 6 \text{ customers}$$
$$z = 1.96$$

The process variability is in statistical control, so we proceed directly to the $\bar{x}$-chart. The control limits are

$$\text{UCL}_{\bar{x}} = \bar{\bar{x}} + z\sigma/\sqrt{n} = 5.0 + 1.96(1.5)/\sqrt{6} = 6.20 \text{ minutes}$$

$$\text{LCL}_{\bar{x}} = \bar{\bar{x}} - z\sigma/\sqrt{n} = 5.0 - 1.96(1.5)/\sqrt{6} = 3.80 \text{ minutes}$$

The value for z can be obtained in the following way. The normal distribution table (see the Normal Distribution appendix) gives the proportion of the total area under the normal curve from $-\infty$ to z. We want a type I error of 5 percent, or 2.5 percent of the curve above the upper control limit and 2.5 percent below the lower control limit. Consequently, we need to find the z value in the table that leaves only 2.5 percent in the upper portion of the normal curve (or 0.9750 in the table). That value is 1.96. The two new samples are below the LCL of the chart, implying that the average time to serve a customer has dropped. Assignable causes should be explored to see what caused the improvement.

Decision Point Management studied the time period over which the samples were taken and found that the supervisor of the process was experimenting with some new procedures. Management decided to make the new procedures a permanent part of the customer service process. After all employees were trained in the new procedures, new samples were taken and the control chart reconstructed. ◻

CONTROL CHARTS FOR ATTRIBUTES

Two charts commonly used for quality measures based on product or service attributes are the *p*- and *c*-chart. The *p*-chart is used for controlling the proportion of defective products or services generated by the process. The *c*-chart is used for controlling the number of defects when more than one defect can be present in a product or service.

p-**CHARTS.** The *p*-chart is a commonly used control chart for attributes. The quality characteristic is counted rather than measured, and the entire item or service can be declared good or defective. For example, in the banking industry, the attributes counted might be the number of nonendorsed deposits or the number of incorrect

Of the alternative attribute process charts available, which one can best be used in a given situation?

p-chart A chart used for controlling the proportion of defective products or services generated by the process.

financial statements sent. The method involves selecting a random sample, inspecting each item in it, and calculating the sample proportion defective, *p*, which is the number of defective units divided by the sample size.

Sampling for a *p*-chart involves a yes–no decision: The item or service either is or is not defective. The underlying statistical distribution is based on the binomial distribution. However, for large sample sizes, the normal distribution provides a good approximation to it. The standard deviation of the distribution of proportion defective, σ_p, is

$$\sigma_p = \sqrt{\bar{p}(1 - \bar{p})/n}$$

where

n = sample size

$\bar{p}$ = historical average population proportion defective or target value and

central line on the chart

The central line on the *p*-chart may be the average of past sample proportion defective or a target that management has set for the process. We can use σ_p to arrive at the upper and lower control limits for a *p*-chart:

$$\text{UCL}_p = \bar{p} + z\sigma_p \qquad \text{and} \qquad \text{LCL}_p = \bar{p} - z\sigma_p$$

where

z = normal deviate (number of standard deviations from the average)

The chart is used in the following way. Periodically, a random sample of size *n* is taken, and the number of defective products or services is counted. The number of defectives is divided by the sample size to get a sample proportion defective, *p*, which is plotted on the chart. When a sample proportion defective falls outside the control limits, the analyst assumes that the proportion defective generated by the process has changed and searches for the assignable cause. Observations falling below the LCL_p indicate that the process may actually have improved. The analyst may find no assignable cause because there is always a small chance that an "out-of-control" proportion will have occurred randomly. However, if the analyst discovers assignable causes, those sample data should not be used to calculate the control limits for the chart.

| EXAMPLE 7.3 | *Using a p-Chart to Monitor a Process* |

TUTOR
7.2

The operations manager of the booking services department of Hometown Bank is concerned about the number of wrong customer account numbers recorded by Hometown personnel. Each week a random sample of 2,500 deposits is taken, and the number of incorrect account numbers is recorded. The results for the past 12 weeks are shown in the following table. Is the process out of control? Use three-sigma control limits.

SAMPLE NUMBER	WRONG ACCOUNT NUMBERS	SAMPLE NUMBER	WRONG ACCOUNT NUMBERS
1	15	7	24
2	12	8	7
3	19	9	10
4	2	10	17
5	19	11	15
6	4	12	3
		Total	147

SOLUTION

Step 1. Construct the *p*-chart, using past data to calculate $\bar{p}$.

$$\bar{p} = \frac{\text{Total defectives}}{\text{Total number of observations}} = \frac{147}{12(2,500)} = 0.0049$$

$$\sigma_p = \sqrt{\bar{p}(1 - \bar{p})/n} = \sqrt{0.0049(1 - 0.0049)/2,500} = 0.0014$$

$$\text{UCL}_p = \bar{p} + z\sigma_p = 0.0049 + 3(0.0014) = 0.0091$$

$$\text{LCL}_p = \bar{p} - z\sigma_p = 0.0049 - 3(0.0014) = 0.0007$$

Step 2. Calculate the sample proportion defective. For sample 1, the proportion of defectives is 15/2,500 = 0.0060.

Step 3. Plot each sample proportion defective on the chart, as shown in Figure 7.11.

Solver - p-Charts

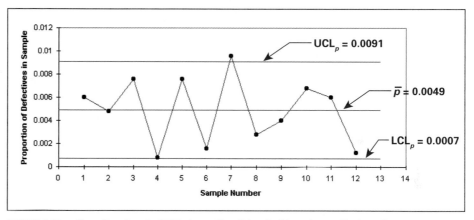

FIGURE 7.11 • The *p*-Chart from the OM Explorer *p*-Chart Solver for Wrong Account Numbers, Showing That Sample 7 Is Out of Control

Sample 7 exceeds the upper control limit; thus, the process is out of control and the reasons for the poor performance that week should be determined.

Decision Point Management explored the circumstances when sample 7 was taken. The encoding machine used to print the account numbers on the checks was defective that week. The following week the machine was repaired; however, the recommended preventive maintenance was not performed for months prior to the failure. Management reviewed the performance of the maintenance department and instituted changes to the maintenance procedures for the encoding machine. After the problem was corrected, the quality analyst recalculated the control limits using the data without sample 7. Subsequent weeks were sampled and the process was determined to be in statistical control. Consequently, the *p*-chart provides a tool to indicate when a process needs adjustment. ❑

***c*-CHARTS.** Sometimes products have more than one defect per unit. For example, a roll of carpeting may have several defects, such as tufted or discolored fibers or stains from the production process. Other situations in which more than one defect may occur include defects in a television picture tube face panel, accidents at a particular intersection,

c-chart A chart used for controlling the number of defects when more than one defect can be present in a product or service.

and complaints at a hotel. When management is interested in reducing the number of defects per unit, another type of control chart, the **c-chart**, is useful.

The underlying sampling distribution for a *c*-chart is the Poisson distribution. It is based on the assumption that defects occur over a continuous region and that the probability of two or more defects at any one location is negligible. The mean of the distribution is $\bar{c}$ and the standard deviation is $\sqrt{\bar{c}}$. A useful tactic is to use the normal approximation to the Poisson so that the central line of the chart is $\bar{c}$ and the control limits are

$$\text{UCL}_c = \bar{c} + z\sqrt{\bar{c}} \quad \text{and} \quad \text{LCL}_c = \bar{c} - z\sqrt{\bar{c}}$$

| EXAMPLE 7.4 | *Using a c-Chart to Monitor Defects per Unit* |

The Woodland Paper Company produces paper for the newspaper industry. As a final step in the process, the paper passes through a machine that measures various quality characteristics. When the process is in control, it averages 20 defects per roll.

**TUTOR
7.3**

a. Set up a control chart for the number of defects per roll. For this example, use two-sigma control limits.

b. Five rolls had the following number of defects: 16, 21, 17, 22, and 24, respectively. The sixth roll, using pulp from a different supplier, had 5 defects. Is the process in control?

SOLUTION

a. The average number of defects per roll is 20. Therefore

$$\text{UCL}_c = \bar{c} + z\sqrt{\bar{c}} = 20 + 2(\sqrt{20}) = 28.94$$
$$\text{LCL}_c = \bar{c} - z\sqrt{\bar{c}} = 20 - 2(\sqrt{20}) = 11.06$$

The control chart is shown in Figure 7.12.

Solver - c-Charts

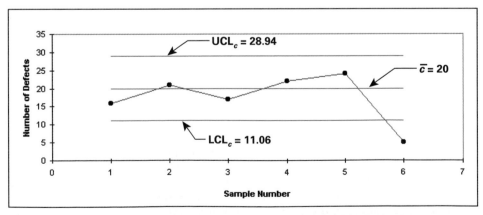

FIGURE 7.12 • The *c*-Chart from the OM Explorer *c*-Chart Solver for Defects per Roll of Paper

b. Because the first roll had only 16 defects, or less than the upper control limit, the process is still in control. Five defects, however, is less than the lower control limit, and therefore, the process is technically "out of control." The control chart indicates that something good has happened.

Decision Point The supplier for the first 5 samples has been used by Woodland Paper for many years. The supplier for the sixth sample is new to the company. Management decided to continue using the new supplier for a while, monitoring the number of defects to see if it stays low. If the number remains below the LCL for 20 consecutive samples, management will make the switch permanent and recalculate the control chart parameters. ⊐

What information technologies are available for improving process performance?

TECHNOLOGY IN STATISTICAL PROCESS CONTROL

Recent advances in information technologies have provided managers with the opportunity to gather tremendous amounts of data for monitoring and improving process performance (see the Managing Technology chapter). Managers can get up-to-the-minute data from the factory floor and have it analyzed and summarized by the computer in scatterplots, histograms, pie charts, Pareto charts, or bar charts (see the Total Quality Management chapter). Users can define the type and appearance of the charts they get and can specify the control limits for control charts or allow the program to compute the limits, using a historical database. In addition, employee training modules have been put on CD-ROMs, which contain video clips, animation, and interactive exercises to show employees how to use SPC techniques in their jobs and motivate them to do so.

For some companies, particularly those in the process industries, machine-specific monitors may be less costly than general-purpose PC-network options and provide more data right at the machine site. These monitors are connected to a specific machine and track its performance. For example, a plastics injection-molding machine has critical parameters such as cycle time, pressure, and temperature. These parameters are monitored and compared to upper and lower control limits during each cycle. Alarms alert personnel when outputs do not meet specifications. In addition, $\bar{x}$- and R-charts can be constructed for as many as 100 machine parameters and displayed at the machine site. Such equipment can also be used to measure process capabilities, which we discuss next.

PROCESS CAPABILITY

What determines whether a process is capable of producing the products or services that customers demand?

process capability The ability of the process to meet the design specifications for a product or service.

nominal value A target for design specifications.

tolerance An allowance above or below the nominal value.

Statistical process control techniques help managers achieve and maintain a process distribution that does not change in terms of its mean and variance. The control limits on the control charts signal when the mean or variability of the process changes. However, a process that is in statistical control may not be producing products or services according to their design specifications because the control limits are based on the mean and variability of the *sampling distribution*, not the design specifications. **Process capability** refers to the ability of the process to meet the design specifications for a product or service. Design specifications often are expressed as a **nominal value,** or target, and a **tolerance,** or allowance above or below the nominal value. For example, design specifications for the useful life of a light bulb might have a nominal value of 1,000 hours and a tolerance of ±200 hours. This tolerance gives an *upper specification* of 1,200 hours and a *lower specification* of 800 hours. The process producing the bulbs must be capable of doing so within these design specifications; otherwise, it will produce a certain proportion of defective bulbs. Management also is interested in detecting occurrences of light-bulb life exceeding 1,200 hours because something might be learned that can be built into the process in the future.

DEFINING PROCESS CAPABILITY

Figure 7.13 shows the relationship between a process distribution and the upper and lower specifications for the process producing light bulbs under two conditions. In Figure 7.13(a), the process is capable because the extremes of the process distribution

FIGURE 7.13

*Relationship Between
Process Distribution
and Specifications*

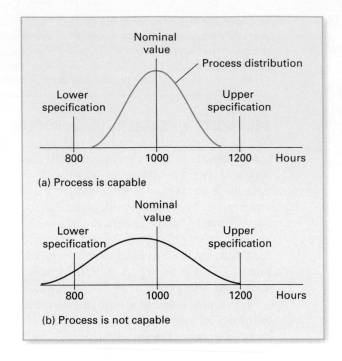

fall within the upper and lower specifications. In Figure 7.13(b) the process is not capable because it produces too many bulbs with short lives.

Figure 7.13 shows clearly why managers are so concerned with reducing process variability. The less variability—represented by lower standard deviations—the less frequently bad output is produced. Figure 7.14 shows what reducing variability means for a process distribution that is a normal probability distribution. The firm with two-sigma quality (the tolerance limits equal the process distribution mean ± 2 standard deviations) produces 4.56 percent defective parts, or 45,600 defective parts per million. The firm with four-sigma quality produces only 0.0063 percent defectives,

FIGURE 7.14

*Effects of Reducing
Variability on Process
Capability*

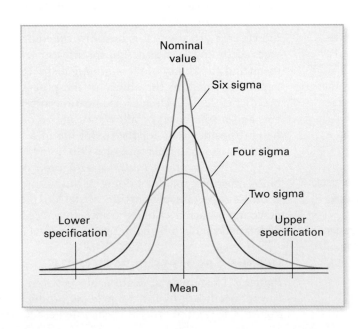

or 63 defective parts per million. Finally, the firm with six-sigma quality produces only 0.0000002 percent defectives, or 0.002 defective parts per million.

How can a manager determine quantitatively whether a process is capable? Two measures commonly are used in practice to assess the capability of a process: process capability ratio and process capability index.

process capability ratio, C_p The tolerance width divided by 6 standard deviations (process variability).

PROCESS CAPABILITY RATIO. A process is *capable* if it has a process distribution whose extreme values fall within the upper and lower specifications for a product or service. As a general rule, most values of a process distribution fall within ± 3 standard deviations of the mean. In other words, the range of values of the quality measure generated by the process is approximately 6 standard deviations. Hence, if a process is capable, the difference between the upper and lower specification, called the *tolerance width*, must be greater than 6 standard deviations (process variability). The **process capability ratio, C_p**, is defined as

$$C_p = \frac{\text{Upper specification} - \text{Lower specification}}{6\sigma}$$

where

σ = standard deviation of the process distribution

If C_p is greater than 1.0, the tolerance range is greater than the range of actual process outputs. If C_p is less than 1.0, the process will produce products or services outside their allowable tolerance. Firms often choose an arbitrary critical value for the process capability ratio, such as 1.33, to establish a target for reducing process variability. The value is greater than 1.0 to allow for some change in the process distribution before bad output is generated.

PROCESS CAPABILITY INDEX. The process is capable only when the capability ratio is greater than the critical value (e.g., 1.33) and the process distribution is centered on the nominal value of the design specifications. For example, the bulb-producing process may have a process capability ratio greater than 1.33. However, if the mean of the distribution of process output, $\bar{\bar{x}}$, is closer to the lower specification, defective bulbs may still be generated. Likewise, if $\bar{\bar{x}}$ is closer to the upper specification, very good bulbs may be generated. Thus, we need to compute a capability index that measures the potential for the process to generate outputs relative to either upper or lower specifications.

process capability index, C_{pk} An index that measures the potential for a process to generate defective outputs relative to either upper or lower specifications.

The **process capability index, C_{pk}**, is defined as

$$C_{pk} = \text{Minimum of} \left[\frac{\bar{\bar{x}} - \text{Lower specification}}{3\sigma}, \frac{\text{Upper specification} - \bar{\bar{x}}}{3\sigma} \right]$$

We take the minimum of the two ratios because it gives the *worst-case* situation. If C_{pk} is greater than a critical value greater than 1.0 (say, 1.33) and the process capability ratio is greater than its critical value, we can finally say the process is capable. If C_{pk} is less than 1.0, the process average is close to one of the tolerance limits and is generating defective output.

The capability index will always be less than or equal to the capability ratio. When C_{pk} equals the process capability ratio, the process is centered between the upper and lower specifications and hence the mean of the process distribution is centered on the nominal value of the design specifications.

| EXAMPLE 7.5 | *Assessing the Process Capability of the Light-Bulb Production Process* |

The light-bulb production process yields bulbs with an average life of 900 hours and a standard deviation of 48 hours. The nominal value of the tolerance range is 1,000 hours, with an upper specification of 1,200 hours and a lower specification of 800 hours. The operations manager wants to determine whether the process is capable of producing the bulbs to specification.

**TUTOR
7.4**

SOLUTION

To assess process capability, we calculate the process capability ratio and the process capability index:

$$C_p = \frac{1,200 - 800}{6(48)} = 1.39$$

Lower specification calculation: $\dfrac{900 - 800}{3(48)} = 0.69$

Upper specification calculation: $\dfrac{1,200 - 900}{3(48)} = 2.08$

$$C_{pk} = \text{Minimum of } [0.69, 2.08] = 0.69$$

The process capability ratio of 1.39 tells us that the machine's variability is acceptable relative to the range of the tolerance limits. However, the process capability index tells us that the distribution of output is too close to the lower specification and that short-lived bulbs will be produced.

Decision Point The operations manager searched for the causes of the off-center production. In conjunction with product design engineers, he determined that the filament materials used in the light bulb were not capable of achieving the nominal 1,000-hour life. New materials were selected for the filaments, and the process began producing high-quality light bulbs. ◻

USING CONTINUOUS IMPROVEMENT TO DETERMINE THE CAPABILITY OF A PROCESS

To determine the capability of a process to produce within the tolerances, use the following steps.

Step 1. Collect data on the process output, and calculate the mean and the standard deviation of the process output distribution.

Step 2. Use the data from the process distribution to compute process control charts, such as an $\bar{x}$- or an R-chart.

Step 3. Take a series of random samples from the process, and plot the results on the control charts. If at least 20 consecutive samples are within the control limits of the charts, the process is in statistical control. If the process is not in statistical control, look for assignable causes and eliminate them. Recalculate the mean and standard deviation of the process distribution and the control limits for the charts. Continue until the process is in statistical control.

Step 4. Calculate the process capability ratio and the process capability index. If the results are acceptable, document any changes made to the process and continue to monitor the output by using the control charts. If the results are unacceptable, further explore assignable causes for reducing the variance in the output. As changes are

MANAGERIAL PRACTICE 7.2
Process Capability Study At Ross Products

Ross Products (www.rosslabs.com), a division of Abbott Laboratories, produces a variety of pediatric and adult nutritional products under the brand names Similac, Isomil, and Ensure. Management wanted to assess the process capability of the 32-ounce-can filling line, which comprised several machines and conveyors. A critical quality measure is the weight of the cans after filling. The standard calls for specifications of 974 ± 14 grams.

Initial Capability Study

Initial capability of the multistation filling line was determined by measuring the output of the line and calculating the mean weight (or process average, $\bar{x}$) and standard deviation, σ, of the process distribution. Using these data, an $\bar{x}$- and an R-chart were developed for the process. The sample size was 6 cans. After 35 consecutive samples (a total of 210 cans) were in statistical control (i.e., the means and ranges of the samples fell within the control limits and no runs were present), the mean and standard deviation of the process distribution (all 210 cans) were recalculated. In addition, the process capability ratio and the process capability index were calculated:

$\bar{\bar{x}} = 975.7$ grams

$\sigma = 4.7581$ grams

$C_p = 0.9808$

$C_{pk} = 0.8617$

The overall variability of the filling line was unacceptable because the process was centered too close to the upper specification.

Attacking Assignable Causes

The capability study team brainstormed possible assignable causes for variation in the filling-line process:

1. changeover procedures from product to product,
2. product splash when moving from filler to conveyor,
3. worn parts,
4. valve stems too long, too short, or not in appropriate location,
5. bowl level not constant during fill cycle,
6. foaming in filler bowl,
7. cylinder walls out of round, and
8. variation in dimensions of cans.

The team systematically addressed the likely assignable causes and collected data to determine the amount of improvement. First, they changed all wearable parts on the filling machines. Then they addressed the operator-controlled sources of variation, such as valve stems in the wrong location. They also worked with the maintenance department to install new piston cylinders and to reduce splash at the point where the can moves from the filler to the conveyor. During this period, the team continuously monitored output and evaluated it weekly.

Final Capability Analysis

After it had eliminated all known assignable causes, the team again used output data to compute control limits for $\bar{x}$- and R-charts. Forty-six consecutive in-control samples yielded:

$\bar{\bar{x}} = 976.1$ grams

$\sigma = 2.891$ grams

$C_p = 1.61$

$C_{pk} = 1.37$

The team concluded that the changes it had made ensured long-term process capability for the design specifications currently in use.

---

quality engineering An approach originated by Genichi Taguchi that involves combining engineering and statistical methods to reduce costs and improve quality by optimizing product design and manufacturing processes.

made, recalculate the mean and standard deviation of the process distribution and the control limits for the charts and repeat step 3.

Managerial Practice 7.2 shows how a manufacturer of infant formula achieved process capability on a filling line by using continuous improvement.

QUALITY ENGINEERING

Originated by Genichi Taguchi, **quality engineering** is an approach that involves combining engineering and statistical methods to reduce costs and improve quality by optimizing product design and manufacturing processes. Taguchi believes that

Taguchi's Quality Loss Function

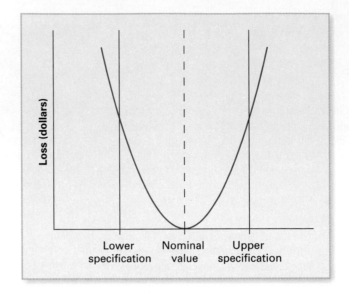

How can quality engineering help improve the quality of products and services?

quality loss function The rationale that a product or service that barely conforms to the specifications is more like a defective product or service than a perfect one.

unwelcome costs are associated with *any* deviation from a quality characteristic's target value. Taguchi's view is that there is a **quality loss function** of zero when the quality characteristic of the product or service is exactly on the target value and that the value rises exponentially as the quality characteristic gets closer to the tolerance limits. The rationale is that a product or service that barely conforms to the specifications is more like a defective product or service than a perfect one. Figure 7.15 shows Taguchi's quality loss function schematically. Taguchi concluded that managers should continually search for ways to reduce *all* variability from the target value in the production process and not be content with merely adhering to specification limits.

STATISTICAL PROCESS CONTROL ACROSS THE ORGANIZATION

As we have been saying in the previous chapters, every employee in an organization is an integral part of one or more processes that cut across traditional functional boundaries. Managing these processes requires a means such as statistical process control to measure its outputs so that corrective actions can be taken when necessary. SPC organizes data so that a manager can determine when a process performance has changed—for better or worse. SPC is used extensively to determine if a change to a process has indeed improved operations. That is the way Ross Products used it in Managerial Practice 7.2. Variation in the filling-line process was the culprit that caused overfilled cans of Similac, and a project team suggested changes to work methods and maintenance procedures at the filling-line process. SPC was used to determine if the new procedures worked, which they did. However, in this chapter, we also showed how SPC can be used in activities other than manufacturing. Drive-by window processes, bank account-posting processes, billing processes, delivery service processes, airline transportation processes, and insurance payment processes can all be analyzed using statistical process control methods. Of course, there are many more that we could demonstrate in this chapter. Nonetheless, it is clear that SPC is a methodology that has application across the organization.

FORMULA REVIEW

1. Mean: $\bar{x} = \dfrac{\sum\limits_{i=1}^{n} x_i}{n}$

2. Standard deviation of a sample: $\sigma = \sqrt{\dfrac{\sum(x_i - \bar{x})^2}{n-1}}$ or $\sigma = \sqrt{\dfrac{\sum x^2 - \dfrac{(\sum x_i)^2}{n}}{n-1}}$

3. Control limits for variable process control charts

   a. *R*-chart, range of sample:

   Upper control limit $= \text{UCL}_R = D_4 \bar{R}$
   Lower control limit $= \text{LCL}_R = D_3 \bar{R}$

   b. $\bar{x}$-chart, sample mean:

   Upper control limit $= \text{UCL}_{\bar{x}} = \bar{\bar{x}} + A_2 \bar{R}$
   Lower control limit $= \text{LCL}_{\bar{x}} = \bar{\bar{x}} - A_2 \bar{R}$

   c. When the standard deviation of the process distribution, σ, is known:

   Upper control limit $= \text{UCL}_x = \bar{\bar{x}} + z\sigma_x$
   Lower control limit $= \text{LCL}_x = \bar{\bar{x}} - z\sigma_x$

   where

   $\sigma_{\bar{x}} = \dfrac{\sigma}{\sqrt{n}}$

4. Control limits for attribute process control charts

   a. *p*-chart, proportion defective:

   Upper control limit $= \text{UCL}_p = \bar{p} + z\sigma_p$
   Lower control limit $= \text{LCL}_p = \bar{p} - z\sigma_p$

   where

   $\sigma_p = \sqrt{\bar{p}(1 - \bar{p})/n}$

   b. *c*-chart, number of defects:

   Upper control limit $= \text{UCL}_c = \bar{c} + z\sqrt{\bar{c}}$
   Lower control limit $= \text{LCL}_c = \bar{c} - z\sqrt{\bar{c}}$

5. Process capability ratio: $C_p = \dfrac{\text{Upper specification} - \text{Lower specification}}{6\sigma}$

6. Process capability index:

   $C_{pk} = \text{Minimum of} \left[\dfrac{\bar{\bar{x}} - \text{Lower specification}}{3\sigma}, \dfrac{\text{Upper specification} - \bar{\bar{x}}}{3\sigma} \right]$

CHAPTER HIGHLIGHTS

❑ A key to meeting design specifications in a product or service is to reduce output variability. When a process is in a state of statistical control, outputs subject to common causes of variation follow a stable probability distribution. When assignable causes of variation are present, the process is out of statistical control. Statistical process control (SPC) methods are used to detect the presence of assignable causes of variation.

❑ Inspection stations may be located at three points in the process: where incoming materials are received, at selected points in the process, and at the end of the process. Inspection identifies whether processes need corrective action.

❑ Statistical process control charts are useful for measuring the current quality generated by the process and for detecting whether the process has changed to the detriment of quality. Thus, R-charts are used to monitor process variability, $\bar{x}$- and p-charts identify abnormal variations in the process average, and c-charts are used for controlling the number of defects when a product or service process could result in multiple defects per unit

of output. The presence of abnormal variation triggers a search for assignable causes.

❑ Process variability should be in control before process average control charts are constructed. The reason is that the average range is used in the calculation of control limits for process average control charts. Crucial decisions in the design of control charts are sample size and control limits.

❑ The central line of a control chart can be the average of past averages of the quality measurement or a management target related to product or service specifications. The spread in control limits affects the chances of detecting a shift in the process average or range, as well as the chances of searching for assignable causes when none exist.

❑ A process can be in statistical control but still not be capable of producing all of its output within design specifications. The process capability ratio and the process capability index are quantitative measures used to assess the capability of a process.

KEY TERMS

acceptance sampling *283*
assignable causes of variation *285*
attributes *286*
c-chart *300*
common causes of variation *283*
control chart *288*
nominal value *301*
p-chart *297*

process capability *301*
process capability index (C_{pk}) *303*
process capability ratio (C_p) *303*
quality engineering *305*
quality loss function *306*
R-chart *293*
sample size *287*
sampling plan *287*

statistical process control (SPC) *283*
tolerance *301*
type I error *291*
type II error *291*
variables *286*
$\bar{x}$-chart *293*

SOLVED PROBLEM 1

The Watson Electric Company produces incandescent light bulbs. The following data on the number of lumens for 40-watt light bulbs were collected when the process was in control.

SAMPLE	OBSERVATION			
	1	2	3	4
1	604	612	588	600
2	597	601	607	603
3	581	570	585	592
4	620	605	595	588
5	590	614	608	604

a. Calculate control limits for an *R*-chart and an $\bar{x}$-chart.

b. Since these data were collected, some new employees were hired. A new sample obtained the following readings: 570, 603, 623, and 583. Is the process still in control?

SOLUTION

a. To calculate $\bar{x}$, compute the mean for each sample. To calculate *R*, subtract the lowest value in the sample from the highest value in the sample. For example, for sample 1,

$$\bar{x} = \frac{604 + 612 + 588 + 600}{4} = 601$$

$$R = 612 - 588 = 24$$

SAMPLE	$\bar{X}$	*R*
1	601	24
2	602	10
3	582	22
4	602	32
5	604	24
Total	2,991	112
Average	$\bar{\bar{x}} = 598.2$	$\bar{R} = 22.4$

The *R*-chart control limits are

$$\text{UCL}_R = D_4\bar{R} = 2.282(22.4) = 51.12$$
$$\text{LCL}_R = D_3\bar{R} = 0(22.4) = 0$$

The $\bar{x}$-chart control limits are

$$\text{UCL}_x = \bar{\bar{x}} + A_2\bar{R} = 598.2 + 0.729(22.4) = 614.53$$
$$\text{LCL}_x = \bar{\bar{x}} - A_2\bar{R} = 598.2 - 0.729(22.4) = 581.87$$

b. First check to see whether the variability is still in control based on the new data. The range is 53 (or 623−570), which is outside the upper control limit for the *R*-chart. Even though the sample mean, 594.75, is within the control limits for the process average, process variability is not in control. A search for assignable causes must be conducted.

SOLVED PROBLEM 2

The data processing department of the Arizona Bank has five data entry clerks. Each day their supervisor verifies the accuracy of a random sample of 250 records. A record containing one or more errors is considered defective and must be redone. The results of the last 30 samples are shown in the table. All were checked to make sure that none were out of control.

SAMPLE	NUMBER OF DEFECTIVE RECORDS	SAMPLE	NUMBER OF DEFECTIVE RECORDS	SAMPLE	NUMBER OF DEFECTIVE RECORDS
1	7	11	18	21	17
2	5	12	5	22	12
3	19	13	16	23	6
4	10	14	4	24	7
5	11	15	11	25	13
6	8	16	8	26	10
7	12	17	12	27	14
8	9	18	4	28	6
9	6	19	6	29	11
10	13	20	11	30	9
				Total	300

a. Based on these historical data, set up a *p*-chart using $z = 3$.

b. Samples for the next four days showed the following:

SAMPLE	NUMBER OF DEFECTIVE RECORDS
31	17
32	15
33	22
34	21

What is the supervisor's assessment of the data-entry process likely to be?

SOLUTION

a. From the table, the supervisor knows that the total number of defective records is 300 out of a total sample of 7,500 [or 30(250)]. Therefore, the central line of the chart is

$$\bar{p} = \frac{300}{7,500} = 0.04$$

The control limits are

$$UCL_p = \bar{p} + z \sqrt{\frac{\bar{p}(1 - \bar{p})}{n}} = 0.04 + 3\sqrt{\frac{0.04(0.96)}{250}} = 0.077$$

$$LCL_p = \bar{p} - z \sqrt{\frac{\bar{p}(1 - \bar{p})}{n}} = 0.04 - 3\sqrt{\frac{0.04(0.96)}{250}} = 0.003$$

b. Samples for the next four days showed the following:

SAMPLE	NUMBER OF DEFECTIVE RECORDS	PROPORTION
31	17	0.068
32	15	0.060
33	22	0.088
34	21	0.084

Samples 33 and 34 are out of control. The supervisor should look for the problem and, upon identifying it, take corrective action.

SOLVED PROBLEM 3

The Minnow County Highway Safety Department monitors accidents at the intersection of Routes 123 and 14. Accidents at the intersection have averaged three per month.

a. Which type of control chart should be used? Construct a control chart with three-sigma control limits.

b. Last month seven accidents occurred at the intersection. Is this sufficient evidence to justify a claim that something has changed at the intersection?

SOLUTION

a. The safety department cannot determine the number of accidents that did *not* occur, so it has no way to compute a proportion defective at the intersection. Therefore, the administrators must use a *c*-chart for which

$$UCL_c = \bar{c} + z\sqrt{\bar{c}} = 3 + 3\sqrt{3} = 8.20$$
$$LCL_c = \bar{c} - z\sqrt{\bar{c}} = 3 - 3\sqrt{3} = -2.196$$

There cannot be a negative number of accidents, so the lower control limit in this case is adjusted to zero.

b. The number of accidents last month falls within the upper and lower control limits of the chart. We conclude that no assignable causes are present and that the increase in accidents was due to chance.

SOLVED PROBLEM 4

Pioneer Chicken advertises "lite" chicken with 30 percent fewer calories. (The pieces are 33 percent smaller.) The process average distribution for "lite" chicken breasts is 420 calories, with a standard deviation of the population of 25 calories. Pioneer randomly takes samples of six chicken breasts to measure calorie content.

a. Design an $\bar{x}$-chart, using the process standard deviation.

b. The product design calls for the average chicken breast to contain 400 ± 100 calories. Calculate the process capability ratio (target $= 1.33$) and the process capability index. Interpret the results.

SOLUTION

a. For the process standard deviation of 25 calories, the standard deviation of the sample mean is

$$\sigma_{\bar{x}} = \frac{\sigma}{\sqrt{n}} = \frac{25}{\sqrt{6}} = 10.2 \text{ calories}$$

$$\text{UCL}_{\bar{x}} = \bar{\bar{x}} + z\sigma_{\bar{x}} = 420 + 3(10.2) = 450.6 \text{ calories}$$

$$\text{LCL}_{\bar{x}} = \bar{\bar{x}} - z\sigma_{\bar{x}} = 420 - 3(10.2) = 389.4 \text{ calories}$$

b. The process capability ratio is

$$C_p = \frac{\text{Upper specification} - \text{Lower specification}}{6\sigma} = \frac{500 \text{ calories} - 300 \text{ calories}}{6(25)} = 1.333$$

The process capability index is

$$C_{pk} = \text{Minimum of} \left[\frac{\bar{\bar{x}} - \text{Lower specification}}{3\sigma}, \frac{\text{Upper specification} - \bar{\bar{x}}}{3\sigma} \right]$$

$$= \text{Minimum of} \left[\frac{420 - 300}{3(25)} = 1.60, \frac{500 - 420}{3(25)} = 1.07 \right] = 1.07$$

Because the process capability ratio is greater than 1.33, the process should be able to produce the product reliably within specifications. The process capability index is 1.07, so the current process is capable.

DISCUSSION QUESTIONS

1. Form a group and choose a manufacturer or service provider and a functional area, such as accounting, finance, or marketing. Define a process important to that functional area (see the Process Management chapter) and then identify a key quality measure for that process. How can SPC be used to manage that process?

2. Is the concept of process capability transferable to non-manufacturing processes? Explain.

OM EXPLORER AND INTERNET EXERCISES

Visit our Web site at www.prenhall.com/krajewski for OM Explorer Tutors, which explain quantitative techniques; Solvers, which help you apply mathematical models; and Internet Exercises, including Facility Tours, which expand on the topics in this chapter.

PROBLEMS

An icon next to a problem identifies the software that can be helpful, but not mandatory. The software is available on the Student CD-ROM that is packaged with every new copy of the textbook.

1. 💿 **OM Explorer** At Green Owl Potato Chips, the filling process is set so that the average weight is 390 grams per bag. The average range for sample sizes of 9 bags is 10 grams. Use Table 7.1 to establish control limits for sample means and ranges for the filling process.

2. 💿 **OM Explorer** At Isogen Pharmaceuticals the filling process for its asthma inhaler is set to dispense 150 milliliters (mL) of steroid solution per container. The average range for a sample of 4 containers is 3 mL. Use Table 7.1 to establish control limits for sample means and ranges for the filling process.

3. 💿 **OM Explorer** Garcia's Garage desires to create some colorful charts and graphs to illustrate how reliably its mechanics "get under the hood and fix the problem." Garcia's goal for the proportion of customers that return for the same repair within the 30-day warranty period is 0.10. Each month, Garcia tracks 100 customers to see whether they return for warranty repairs. The results are plotted as a proportion to report progress toward the goal. If the control limits are to be set at 2 standard deviations on either side of the goal, determine the control limits for this chart. In March, 8 of the 100 customers in the sample group returned for warranty repairs. Is the repair process in control?

4. 💿 **OM Explorer** The Canine Gourmet Company produces delicious dog treats for canines with discriminating tastes. Management wants the box-filling line to be set so that the process average weight per packet is 45 grams. To make sure that the process is in control, an inspector at the end of the filling line periodically selects a random box of ten packets and weighs each packet. When the process is in control, the range in the weight of each sample has averaged 6 grams.

   a. Design an R- and an $\bar{x}$-chart for this process.

   b. The results from the last five samples of eight packets are

SAMPLE	$\bar{X}$	R
1	44	9
2	40	2
3	46	5
4	39	8
5	48	3

   Is the process in control? Explain.

5. 💿 **OM Explorer** The Marlin Company produces plastic bottles to customer order. The quality inspector randomly selects four bottles from the bottle machine and measures the outside diameter of the bottle neck, a critical quality dimension that determines whether the bottle cap will fit properly. The dimensions (in.) from the last six samples are

	BOTTLE			
SAMPLE	1	2	3	4
1	0.604	0.612	0.588	0.600
2	0.597	0.601	0.607	0.603
3	0.581	0.570	0.585	0.592
4	0.620	0.605	0.595	0.588
5	0.590	0.614	0.608	0.604
6	0.585	0.583	0.617	0.579

   a. Assume that only these six samples are sufficient and use the data to determine control limits for an R- and an $\bar{x}$-chart.

   b. Suppose that the specification for the bottle neck diameter is 0.600 ± 0.050 in. If the population standard deviation is 0.012 in, is the process capable of producing the bottle?

6. In an attempt to judge and monitor the quality of instruction, the administration of Mega-Byte Academy devised an examination to test students on the basic concepts that all should have learned. Each year, a random sample of 10 graduating students is selected for the test. The average score is used to track the quality of the educational process. Test results for the past 10 years are shown in Table 7.2 on page 314.

   Use these data to estimate the center and standard deviation for this distribution. Then calculate the two-sigma control limits for the process average. What comments would you make to the administration of the Mega-Byte Academy?

7. 💿 **OM Explorer** As a hospital administrator of a large hospital you are concerned with the absenteeism among nurse's aides. The issue has been raised by registered nurses, who feel they often have to perform work normally done by their aides. To get the facts, absenteeism data were gathered for the last two weeks, which is considered a representative period for future conditions. After taking random samples of 64 personnel files each day, the following data were produced:

					STUDENT						
TABLE 7.2					*Test Scores on Exit Exam*						
Year	1	2	3	4	5	6	7	8	9	10	Average
1	63	57	92	87	70	61	75	58	63	71	69.7
2	90	77	59	88	48	83	63	94	72	70	74.4
3	67	81	93	55	71	71	86	98	60	90	77.2
4	62	67	78	61	89	93	71	59	93	84	75.7
5	85	88	77	69	58	90	97	72	64	60	76.0
6	60	57	79	83	64	94	86	64	92	74	75.3
7	94	85	56	77	89	72	71	61	92	97	79.4
8	97	86	83	88	65	87	76	84	81	71	81.8
9	94	90	76	88	65	93	86	87	94	63	83.6
10	88	91	71	89	97	79	93	87	69	85	84.9

DAY	AIDES ABSENT	DAY	AIDES ABSENT
1	4	9	7
2	3	10	2
3	2	11	3
4	4	12	2
5	2	13	1
6	5	14	3
7	3	15	4
8	4		

Since your assessment of absenteeism is likely to come under careful scrutiny, you would like a type I error of only 1 percent. You want to be sure to identify any instances of unusual absences. If some are present, you will have to explore them on behalf of the registered nurses.

a. Design a *p*-chart.

b. Based on your *p*-chart and the data from the last two weeks, what can you conclude about the absenteeism of nurses' aides?

8. **OM Explorer** A textile manufacturer wants to set up a control chart for irregularities (e.g., oil stains, shop soil, loose threads, and tears) per 100 square yards of carpet. The following data were collected from a sample of twenty 100-square-yard pieces of carpet.

Sample	1	2	3	4	5	6	7	8	9	10
Irregularities	11	8	9	12	4	16	5	8	17	10

Sample	11	12	13	14	15	16	17	18	19	20
Irregularities	11	5	7	12	13	8	19	11	9	10

a. Using these data, set up a *c*-chart with $z = 3$.

b. Suppose that the next five samples had 15, 18, 12, 22, and 21 irregularities. What do you conclude?

9. **OM Explorer** The IRS is concerned with improving the accuracy of tax information given by its representatives over the telephone. Previous studies involved asking a set of 25 questions of a large number of IRS telephone representatives to determine the proportion of correct responses. Historically, the average proportion of correct responses has been 70 percent. Recently, IRS representatives have been receiving more training. On April 1, the set of 25 tax questions were again asked of 20 randomly selected IRS telephone representatives. The proportions of correct answers were 0.88, 0.76, 0.64, 1.00, 0.76, 0.76, 0.72, 0.88, 0.50, 0.50, 0.40, 1.00, 0.88, 1.00, 0.64, 0.76, 0.76, 0.88, 0.40, and 0.76. Interpret the results of that study.

10. **OM Explorer** A travel agency is concerned with the accuracy and appearance of itineraries prepared for its clients. Defects can include errors in times, airlines, flight numbers, prices, car rental information, lodging, charge card numbers, and reservation numbers, as well as typographical errors. As the possible number of errors is nearly infinite, the agency measures the number of errors that do occur. The current process results in an average of three errors per itinerary.

a. What are the two-sigma control limits for these defects?

b. A client scheduled a trip to Dallas. Her itinerary contained six errors. Interpret this information.

11. **OM Explorer** Jim's Outfitters, Inc., makes custom fancy shirts for cowboys. The shirts could be flawed in various ways, including flaws in the weave or color of the fabric, loose buttons or decorations, wrong dimensions, and uneven stitches. Jim randomly examined 10 shirts, with the following results:

SHIRT	DEFECTS
1	8
2	U
3	7
4	12
5	5
6	10
7	2
8	4
9	6
10	6

a. Assuming that 10 observations are adequate for these purposes, determine the three-sigma control limits for defects per shirt.

b. Suppose that the next shirt has 13 flaws. What can you say about the process now?

12. ● **OM Explorer** The Big Black Bird Company produces fiberglass camper tops. The process for producing the tops must be controlled so as to keep the number of dimples low. When the process was in control, the following defects were found in randomly selected sheets over an extended period of time.

TOP	DIMPLES
1	7
2	9
3	14
4	11
5	3
6	12
7	8
8	4
9	7
10	6

a. Assuming 10 observations are adequate for these purposes, determine the three-sigma control limits for dimples per camper top.

b. Suppose that the next camper top has 15 dimples. What can you say about the process now?

13. ● **OM Explorer** The production manager at Sunny Soda, Inc., is interested in tracking the quality of the company's 12-ounce bottle filling line. The bottles must be filled within the tolerances set for this product because the dietary information on the label shows 12 ounces as the serving size. The design standard for the product calls for a fill level of 12.00 ± 0.10 ounces. The manager collected the following sample data (in fluid ounces per bottle) on the production process:

SAMPLE	OBSERVATION			
	1	2	3	4
1	12.00	11.97	12.10	12.08
2	11.91	11.94	12.10	11.96
3	11.89	12.02	11.97	11.99
4	12.10	12.09	12.05	11.95
5	12.08	11.92	12.12	12.05
6	11.94	11.98	12.06	12.08
7	12.09	12.00	12.00	12.03
8	12.01	12.04	11.99	11.95
9	12.00	11.96	11.97	12.03
10	11.92	11.94	12.09	12.00
11	11.91	11.99	12.05	12.10
12	12.01	12.00	12.06	11.97
13	11.98	11.99	12.06	12.03
14	12.02	12.00	12.05	11.95
15	12.00	12.05	12.01	11.97

a. Are the process average and range in statistical control?

b. Is the process capable of meeting the design standard? Explain.

14. ● **OM Explorer** In a bearing production shop, control charts were set up to monitor the bearing sleeve production process. Fifteen samples of five sleeves each were taken during a period when the process was believed to be under control. The eccentricities (i.e., out-of-roundness) of the sleeves were measured. The means and ranges of the eccentricities of these samples, measured in thousandths of an inch, are as follows.

Sample	1	2	3	4	5	6	7	8	9	10	11	12	13	14	15
Mean	17	14	8	17	12	13	15	16	13	14	16	9	11	9	12
Range	6	11	4	8	9	14	12	15	10	10	11	6	9	11	13

Subsequently, samples of size 5 were taken from the production line every hour for the next 10 hours. The eccentricities were measured and the following results obtained.

Sample	16	17	18	19	20	21	22	23	24	25
Mean	11	14	9	15	17	19	13	22	20	18
Range	7	11	6	4	12	14	11	10	8	6

a. Construct the control charts for the mean and the range, using the original 15 samples. Were these samples sufficient for developing the control chart? Explain your answer.

b. On the control charts, plot the sample values subsequently obtained and comment on whether the process is in control.

c. In part b if you concluded that the process was out of control, would you attribute it to a drift in the mean, or an increase in the variability, or both? Explain your answer.

15. 💿 **OM Explorer** The bearing production shop of Problem 14 made some changes to the process and undertook a process capability study. The following data were obtained for 15 samples of size five. Based on the individual observations, management estimated the process standard deviation to be 4.21 (in thousandths of an inch) for use in the process capability analysis. The lower and upper specification limits (in thousandths of an inch) for the eccentricity of the bearing sleeves were 5 and 25.

Sample	1	2	3	4	5	6	7	8	9	10	11	12	13	14	15
Mean	11	12	8	16	13	12	17	16	13	14	17	9	15	14	9
Range	9	13	4	11	10	9	8	15	14	11	6	6	12	10	11

a. Calculate the process capability ratio and the process capability index values.

b. What conclusions is management likely to draw from the capability analysis? Can valid conclusions about the process be drawn from the analysis?

c. What remedial actions, if any, do you suggest that management take?

16. 💿 **OM Explorer** Webster Chemical Company produces mastics and caulking for the construction industry. The product is blended in large mixers and then pumped into tubes and capped. Management is concerned about whether the filling process for tubes of caulking is in statistical control. The process should be centered on eight ounces per tube. Several samples of eight tubes were taken, each tube was weighed, and the weights in Table 7.3 were obtained.

a. Assume that only six samples are sufficient and develop the control charts for the mean and the range.

b. Plot the observations on the control chart and comment on your findings.

17. 💿 **OM Explorer** Management at Webster in Problem 16 is now concerned as to whether caulking tubes are being properly capped. If a significant proportion of the tubes are not being sealed, Webster is placing its customers in a messy situation. Tubes are packaged in large boxes of 144. Several boxes are inspected, and the following numbers of leaking tubes are found:

SAMPLE	TUBES	SAMPLE	TUBES	SAMPLE	TUBES
1	3	8	6	15	5
2	5	9	4	16	0
3	3	10	9	17	2
4	4	11	2	18	6
5	2	12	6	19	2
6	4	13	5	20	1
7	2	14	1	Total	72

Calculate *p*-chart three-sigma control limits to assess whether the capping process is in statistical control.

18. 💿 **OM Explorer** At Webster Chemical Company, lumps in the caulking compound could cause difficulties in dispensing a smooth bead from the tube. Even when the process is in control, an average of four lumps per tube of caulk will remain. Testing for the presence of lumps destroys the product, so an analyst takes random samples. The following results are obtained.

TUBE NO.	LUMPS	TUBE NO.	LUMPS	TUBE NO.	LUMPS
1	6	5	6	9	5
2	5	6	4	10	0
3	0	7	1	11	9
4	4	8	6	12	2

Determine the *c*-chart two-sigma upper and lower control limits for this process.

19. 💿 **OM Explorer** A critical dimension of a certain part is its length. Periodically, random samples of three units are measured for length. The results of the last four samples are in the table on the facing page.

TABLE 7.3	*Ounces of Caulking per Tube*						
	TUBE NUMBER						
SAMPLE	**1**	**2**	**3**	**4**	**5**	**6**	**7**	**8**
1	7.98	8.34	8.02	7.94	8.44	7.68	7.81	8.11
2	8.33	8.22	8.08	8.51	8.41	8.28	8.09	8.16
3	7.89	7.77	7.91	8.04	8.00	7.89	7.93	8.09
4	8.24	8.18	7.83	8.05	7.90	8.16	7.97	8.07
5	7.87	8.13	7.92	7.99	8.10	7.81	8.14	7.88
6	8.13	8.14	8.11	8.13	8.14	8.12	8.13	8.14

TABLE 7.4 *Sample Data for Precision Machining Company*											
MINUTES					**DIAMETER**						
1–12	15	16	18	14	16	17	15	14	14	13	16	17
13–24	15	16	17	16	14	14	13	14	15	16	15	17
25–36	14	13	15	17	18	15	16	15	14	15	16	17
37–48	18	16	15	16	16	14	17	18	19	15	16	15
49–60	12	17	16	14	15	17	14	16	15	17	18	14
61–72	15	16	17	18	13	15	14	14	16	15	17	18
73–80	16	16	17	18	16	15	14	17				

SAMPLE	LENGTH (MM)		
1	495	501	498
2	512	508	504
3	505	497	501
4	496	503	492

a. Assuming that management is willing to use three-sigma limits, and using only the historical information contained in the four samples, show that the process producing the part is in statistical control.

b. Suppose that the standard deviation of the process distribution is 5.77. If the specifications for the length of the part are 500 ± 18 mm, is the process capable? Why or why not?

20. 💿 **OM Explorer** An automatic lathe produces rollers for roller bearings, and the process is monitored by statistical process control charts. The central line of the chart for the sample means is set at 8.50 and for the mean range at 0.31 mm. The process is in control, as established by samples of size 5. The upper and lower specifications for the diameter of the rollers are $(8.50 + 0.25)$ and $(8.50 - 0.25)$ mm, respectively.

a. Calculate the control limits for the mean and range charts.

b. If the standard deviation of the process distribution is estimated to be 0.13 mm, is the process capable of meeting specifications?

c. If the process is not capable, what percent of the output will fall outside the specification limits? (*Hint*: Use the normal distribution.)

Advanced Problems

21. 💿 **OM Explorer** Canine Gourmet Super Breath dog treats are sold in boxes labeled with a net weight of 12 ounces (340 grams) per box. Each box contains eight individual $\frac{1}{2}$-ounce packets. To reduce the chances of shorting the customer, product design specifications call for the packet-filling process average to be set at 43.5 grams so that the average net weight per box will be 348 grams. Tolerances are set for the box to weigh 348 ± 12 grams. The standard deviation for the *packet-filling* process is 3.52 grams. The target process capability ratio is 1.33. One day, the packet-filling process average weight drifts down to 43.0 grams. Is the packaging process capable? Is an adjustment needed?

22. 💿 **OM Explorer** The Precision Machining Company makes hand-held tools on an assembly line that produces one product every minute. On one of the products, the critical quality dimension is the diameter (measured in thousandths of an inch) of a hole bored in one of the assemblies. Management wants to detect any shift in the process average diameter from 0.015 in. Management considers the variance in the process to be in control. Historically, the average range has been 0.002 in., regardless of the process average. Design an *x*-chart to control this process, with a center line at 0.015 in. and the control limits set at three sigmas from the center line.

Management has provided the results of 80 minutes of output from the production line, as shown in Table 7.4. During this 80 minutes, the process average changed once. All measurements are in thousandths of an inch.

a. Set up an $\bar{x}$-chart with $n = 4$. The frequency should be sample four, then skip four. Thus, your first sample would be for minutes 1–4, the second would be for minutes 9–12, and so on. When would you stop the process to check for a change in the process average?

b. Set up an $\bar{x}$-chart with $n = 8$. The frequency should be sample eight, then skip four. When would you stop the process now? What can you say about the desirability of large samples on a frequent sampling interval?

23. 💿 **OM Explorer** Using the data from Problem 22, continue your analysis of sample size and frequency by trying the following plans.

a. Using the $\bar{x}$-chart for $n = 4$, try the frequency sample four, then skip eight. When would you stop the process in this case?

TABLE 7.5   *Sample Data for Northern Pines Brewery*

SAMPLES	NUMBER OF REJECTED BOTTLES IN SAMPLE OF 250									
1–10	4	9	6	12	8	2	13	10	1	9
11–20	4	6	8	10	12	4	3	10	14	5
21–30	13	11	7	3	2	8	11	6	9	5

b. Using the $\bar{x}$-chart for $n = 8$, try the frequency sample eight, then skip eight. When would you consider the process to be out of control?

c. Using your results from parts a and b, determine what trade-offs you would consider in choosing between them.

24. **● OM Explorer** The plant manager at Northern Pines Brewery decided to gather data on the number of defective bottles generated on the line. Every day a random sample of 250 bottles was inspected for fill level, cracked bottles, bad labels, and poor seals. Any bottle failing to meet the standard for any of these criteria was counted as a reject. The study lasted 30 days and yielded the data in Table 7.5. Based on the data, what can you tell the manager about the quality of the bottling line? Do you see any nonrandom behavior in the bottling process? If so, what might cause this behavior?

25. **● OM Explorer** Red Baron Airlines serves hundreds of cities each day, but competition is increasing from smaller companies affiliated with major carriers. One of the key competitive priorities is on-time arrivals and departures. Red baron defines *on time* as any arrival or departure that takes place within 15 minutes of the scheduled time. To stay on top of the market, management has set the high standard of 98 percent on-time performance. The operations department was put in charge of monitoring the performance of the airline. Each week, a random sample of 300 flight arrivals and departures was checked for schedule performance. Table 7.6 contains the numbers of arrivals and departures over the last 30 weeks that did not meet Red Baron's definition of on-time service. What can you tell management about the quality of service? Can you identify any nonrandom behavior in the process? If so, what might cause the behavior?

26. **● OM Explorer** Beaver Brothers, Inc., is conducting a study to assess the capability of its 150-gram bar soap production line. A critical quality measure is the weight of the soap bars after stamping. The upper and lower specification limits are 162 and 170 grams, respectively. As a part of an initial capability study, 25 samples of size 5 were collected by the quality assurance group and the observations in Table 7.7 were recorded.

After analyzing the data by using statistical control charts, the quality assurance group calculated the process capability ratio, C_p, and the process capability index, C_{pk}. It then decided to improve the stamping process, especially the feeder mechanism. After making all the changes that were deemed necessary, 18 additional samples were collected. The summary data for these samples are

$$\bar{\bar{x}} = 163 \text{ grams},$$
$$\bar{R} = 2.326 \text{ grams}$$
$$\sigma = 1 \text{ gram}$$

All sample observations were within the control chart limits. With the new data, the quality assurance group recalculated the process capability measures. It was pleased with the improved C_p but felt that the process should be centered at 166 grams to ensure that everything was in order. Its decision concluded the study.

a. Draw the control charts for the data obtained in the initial study and verify that the process was in statistical control.

b. What were the values obtained by the group for C_p and C_{pk} for the initial capability study? Comment on your findings and explain why further improvements were necessary.

TABLE 7.6   *Sample Data for Red Baron Airlines*

SAMPLES	NUMBER OF LATE PLANES IN SAMPLE OF 300 ARRIVALS AND DEPARTURES									
1–10	3	8	5	11	7	2	12	9	1	8
11–20	3	5	7	9	12	5	4	9	13	4
21–30	12	10	6	2	1	8	4	5	8	2

			TABLE 7.7 *Sample Data for Beaver Brothers, Inc.*		
SAMPLE	**OBS. 1**	**OBS. 2**	**OBS. 3**	**OBS. 4**	**OBS. 5**
1	167.0	159.6	161.6	164.0	165.3
2	156.2	159.5	161.7	164.0	165.3
3	167.0	162.9	162.9	164.0	165.4
4	167.0	159.6	163.7	164.1	165.4
5	156.3	160.0	162.9	164.1	165.5
6	164.0	164.2	163.0	164.2	163.9
7	161.3	163.0	164.2	157.0	160.6
8	163.1	164.2	156.9	160.1	163.1
9	164.3	157.0	161.2	163.2	164.4
10	156.9	161.0	163.2	164.3	157.3
11	161.0	163.3	164.4	157.6	160.6
12	163.3	164.5	158.4	160.1	163.3
13	158.2	161.3	163.5	164.6	158.7
14	161.5	163.5	164.7	158.6	162.5
15	163.6	164.8	158.0	162.4	163.6
16	164.5	158.5	160.3	163.4	164.6
17	164.9	157.9	162.3	163.7	165.1
18	155.0	162.2	163.7	164.8	159.6
19	162.1	163.9	165.1	159.3	162.0
20	165.2	159.1	161.6	163.9	165.2
21	164.9	165.1	159.9	162.0	163.7
22	167.6	165.6	165.6	156.7	165.7
23	167.7	165.8	165.9	156.9	165.9
24	166.0	166.0	165.6	165.6	165.5
25	163.7	163.7	165.6	165.6	166.2

c. What are the C_p and C_{pk} after the improvements? Comment on your findings, indicating why the group decided to change the centering of the process.

d. What are the C_p and C_{pk} at the conclusion of the study? Comment on your findings.

SIMULATION EXERCISES

These simulation exercises require the use of the Extend and SimQuick simulation packages. Extend is on the Student CD-ROM that is packaged with every new copy of the textbook. SimQuick is an optional simulation package that your instructor may or may not have ordered.

1. ⊙ **Extend** Best Burger is a small regional fast-food chain in an industry that has become increasingly competitive. An increasing number of complaints are being made about its slow service, particularly in the drive-through operations. A management team has been formed to improve this process and is using statistical process control methods to monitor service times and track the effects of changes. Use the Extend simulator and control chart techniques to analyze their process. See the *Service Quality at Best Burger* case on the Student CD-ROM, which includes the basic model and how to use it. Answer

the various questions asked about the process and improvements made to it.

2. **SimQuick** Management is evaluating the advantages of replacing a machine in a printed circuit board process. The boards are passed, one at a time, to a workstation where a worker installs a few components. Each board is then passed to a quality control station where the installation is tested. Ninety percent of the boards pass this test and are then put into finished goods inventory. Those that fail are returned to the worker to be immediately reworked and retested. Management would like to know the advantages of investing in a new machine that would have 95 percent of its output pass the test. Use SimQuick to determine the additional throughput of the process with a new machine. See Example 17 in *SimQuick: Process Simulation in Excel* for details of this problem and additional exercises.

EXPERIENTIAL LEARNING STATISTICAL PROCESS CONTROL WITH A COIN CATAPULT

EXERCISE A: CONTROL CHARTS FOR VARIABLES

Materials

    1 ruler
    1 pen or pencil
    1 coin (a quarter will do nicely)
    1 yardstick
    An exercise worksheet
    Access to a calculator

Tasks

    Divide into teams of two to four. If four people are on
       a team,
    one person holds the yardstick and observes the
       action,
    one person adjusts the catapult and launches the coin,
    one person observes the maximum height for each
       trial, and
    one person records the results.

If teams of less than four are formed, provide a support for
the yardstick and combine the other tasks as appropriate.

Practice

To catapult the coin, put a pen or pencil under the 6-in.
mark of the ruler. Put the coin over the 11-in. mark. Press
both ends of the ruler down as far as they will go. Let the
end that holds the coin snap up, catapulting the coin into
the air. The person holding the yardstick should place the
stick so that it is adjacent to, but does not interfere with,
the trajectory of the coin. To observe the maximum height
reached by the coin, the observer should stand back with
his or her eye at about the same level as the top of the
coin's trajectory. Practice until each person is comfortable
with his or her role. The person operating the catapult
should be sure that the pen or pencil fulcrum has not
moved between shots and that the launch is done as consistently as possible.

Step 1

Gather data. Take four samples of five observations
(launches) each. Record the maximum height reached by
the coin in the first data table on the worksheet. When you
have finished, determine the mean and range for each sample, and compute the mean of the means $\bar{\bar{x}}$ and the mean of
the ranges $\bar{R}$.

Step 2

Develop an R-chart. Using the data gathered and the
appropriate D_3 and D_4 values, compute the upper and
lower three-sigma control limits for the range. Enter these
values and plot the range for each of the four samples on

the range chart on the worksheet. Be sure to indicate an
appropriate scale for range on the y axis.

Step 3

Develop an $\bar{x}$ chart. Now, using the data gathered and the
appropriate value for A_2, compute the upper and lower
three-sigma control limits for the sample means. Enter
these values and plot the mean for each of the four samples
on the $\bar{x}$ chart on the worksheet. Again, indicate an appropriate scale for the y axis.

Step 4

Observe the process. Once a control chart has been established for a process, it is used to monitor the process and
to identify when it isn't running "normally." Collect two
more samples of five trials each, as you did to collect the
first set of data. Plot the range and the sample mean on the
charts you constructed on the worksheet each time you
collect a sample. What have you observed that affects the
process? Does the chart indicate that the process is operating the way it did when you first collected data?

Step 5

Observe a changed process. Now change something (for
instance, move the pencil out to the 8-in. mark). Collect
data for Samples 7 and 8. Plot the range and the sample
mean on the charts you constructed on the worksheet as
you complete each sample. Can you detect a change in the
process from your control chart? If the process has
changed, how sure are you that this change is real and not
just due to the particular sample you chose?

EXERCISE B: CONTROL CHARTS FOR ATTRIBUTES

Materials

    1 ruler
    1 pen or pencil
    1 coin (a quarter will do nicely)
    1 paper or plastic cup (with a 4-in. mouth)
    An exercise worksheet
    Access to a calculator

Tasks

    Divide into teams of two or three. If three people are
       on a team,
    one person adjusts the catapult and launches the coin,
    one person observes the results and fetches the coin,
       and
    one person records the results.

If teams of two are formed, combine the tasks as appropriate.

Practice
The object is to flip a coin into a cup using a ruler. To catapult the coin, put a pen or pencil under the 6-in. mark of the ruler. Put a coin over the 11-in. mark and let its weight hold that end of the ruler on the tabletop. Strike the raised end of the ruler with your hand to flip the coin into the air. Position a cup at the place where the coin lands so that on the next flip, the coin will land inside. You will have to practice several times until you find out how hard to hit the ruler and the best position for the cup. Be sure that the pen or pencil fulcrum has not moved between shots and that the launch is done as consistently as possible.

Step 1
Gather data. Try to catapult the coin into the cup 10 times for each sample. Record each trial in the data table on the worksheet as a hit (H) when the coin lands inside or a miss (M) when it does not. The proportion of misses will be the number of misses divided by the sample size, n—in this case, 10. A miss is a "defect," so the proportion of misses is the proportion defective, p.

Step 2
Develop a p-chart. Compute the upper and lower three-sigma control limits for the average fraction defective. Plot these values and the mean for each of the four samples on the *p*-chart on the worksheet.

Step 3
Observe the process. Once a chart has been established for a process, it is used to monitor the process and to identify abnormal behavior. Exchange tasks so that someone else is catapulting the coin. After several practice launches, take four more samples of 10. Plot the proportion defective for this person's output. Is the process still in control? If it is not, how sure are you that it is out of control? Can you determine the control limits for a 95 percent confidence level? With these limits, was your revised process still in control?

Source: The basis for Exercise A was written by J. Christopher Sandvig, Western Washington University, as a variation of the "Catapulting Coins" exercise from *Games and Exercises for Operations Management* by Janelle Heinke and Larry Meile (Prentice-Hall, 1995). Given these foundations, Larry Meile of Boston College wrote Exercise A. He also wrote Exercise B as a new extension.

SELECTED REFERENCES

Barnard, William, and Thomas F. Wallace. *The Innovation Edge.* Essex Junction, VT: Oliver Wight Publications, Inc., 1994.

Besterfield, Dale. *Quality Control,* 6th ed. Upper Saddle River, NJ: Prentice-Hall, 2001.

Charbonneau, Harvey C., and Gordon L. Webster. *Industrial Quality Control.* Englewood Cliffs, NJ: Prentice-Hall, 1978.

Crosby, Philip B. *Quality Is Free: The Art of Making Quality Certain.* New York: McGraw-Hill, 1979.

Deming, W. Edwards. *Out of the Crisis.* Cambridge, MA: MIT Center for Advanced Engineering Study, 1986.

Denton, D. Keith. "Lessons on Competitiveness: Motorola's Approach." *Production and Inventory Management Journal* (Third Quarter 1991), pp. 22–25.

Duncan, Acheson J. *Quality Control and Industrial Statistics,* 5th ed. Homewood, Ill.: Irwin, 1986.

Gitlow, Howard S., Shelly Gitlow, Alan Oppenheim, and Rosa Oppenheim. *Tools for the Improvement of Quality.* Homewood, Ill.: Irwin, 1989.

Juran, J. M., and F. M. Gryna, Jr. *Quality Planning and Analysis,* 2d ed. New York: McGraw-Hill, 1980.

Mitra, Amitava. *Fundamentals of Quality Control and Improvement,* 2nd ed. Upper Saddle River, NJ: Prentice-Hall, 1998.

Sullivan, Lawrence P. "The Power of Taguchi Methods." *Quality Progress,* vol. 20, no. 6 (1987), pp. 76–79.

Tiffany, Susan. "Grace Cocoa Unveils Engineering Marvel." *Candy Industry* (April 1993), pp. 22–29.

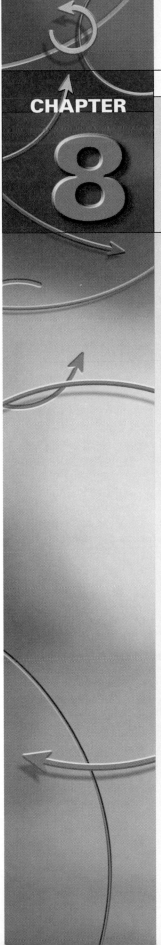

Capacity

Across the Organization

Capacity is important to . . .

- ☐ **accounting,** which prepares the cost accounting information needed to evaluate capacity expansion decisions.
- ☐ **finance,** which performs the financial analysis of proposed capacity expansion investments and raises funds to support them.
- ☐ **human resources,** which must hire and train employees to support capacity plans.
- ☐ **management information systems,** which designs databases used in determining work standards that help in calculating capacity gaps.
- ☐ **marketing,** which provides demand forecasts needed to identify capacity gaps.
- ☐ **operations,** which must select capacity strategies that provide the capacity levels to meet future demand most effectively.
- ☐ **purchasing,** which obtains outside capacity that is outsourced.

Learning Goals

After reading this chapter, you will be able to . . .

1. describe different ways to measure capacity, establish maximum capacity, and calculate capacity utilization.
2. discuss long- and short-term strategies to ease bottlenecks and the concept of the theory-of-constraints approach.
3. explain the reasons for economies and diseconomies of scale.
4. discuss strategic issues such as capacity cushions, timing and sizing options, and linkages with other decisions.
5. calculate capacity gaps and then evaluate plans for filling them.
6. describe how waiting-line models, simulation, and decision trees can assist capacity decisions.

In 1995, the Chemical Banking Corporation and the venerable Chase Manhattan Corporation, the bank of the Rockefellers, merged. With combined assets of $297 billion, the new Chase (www.chase.com) dwarfed even Citicorp, the largest U.S. bank until this merger. Combining two operations that competed directly in two markets, the new Chase Bank had more than $163 billion in overall deposits and some 4 million consumer accounts. One primary motivation for increasing its capacity was cost savings. Chase expected to cut 12,000 employees and $1.5 billion in annual expenses by the first quarter of 1999. Back in 1991, Chemical itself had merged with Manufacturers Hanover Corporation, which cut 6,200 jobs and $750 million in annual costs. By late 1999, Chase expanded its capacity again when Chase Global Investor Services acquired Morgan Stanley's Trust Company. By January, 2001, it had acquired J.P. Morgan and considerable expertise in investment banking, becoming J.P. Morgan Chase & Co. (www.jpmorganchase.com). The Morgan Stanley acquisition, for example, gave $400 billion of assets in trust to Chase to manage. In addition to economies-of-scale benefits, the acquisition added almost 330 highly trained professional staff to its firm. In the investment banking industry where it is often said that "the assets go home at night," management estimates that it costs about $250,000 per person to recruit, train, and retain such professionals.

A doubling of capacity is by no means unique, as the banking industry is in the biggest wave of consolidation in its history. In part, consolidation is a sensible response to excess capacity. Banking is also becoming a technology-driven business. More than ever, financial products and services, from loans to credit cards, are marketed through computers and telephones instead of through bank branches. Banks able to make large investments in technology gain an unparalleled ability to reach customers nationwide. Unprecedented capital investments create the need to spread costs over a broader customer base. The electronic revolution also undermines a bank's traditional role of intermediaries between borrowers and savers, making it easier for both kinds of customers to get together directly. Lower profit margins in retail banking encourage moves into wholesale business, such as investment banking, where size and large capacity can, to some extent, be equated with strength. The trend toward megabanks has been obvious in North America but now has gripped France, Germany, and even Japan—though banks there are moving toward union at a typically sedate pace. Dealing with a product—money—that moves across borders electronically, banks are quick to feel the forces of globalization and technological change.

Although these reasons for large size can be impressive, there can also be qualms about capacity getting too big. When that happens, customers may withdraw their accounts and turn to smaller banks that meet a variety of personal and business banking needs. To protect revenue, large banks must offer the same exceptional service that small banks offer. Small banks almost have it easier than big banks because they're accustomed to giving a high degree of personalized service. A large bank must try to provide the same level and type of service, which customers want.

The headquarters of Chase Manhattan Bank in New York, just before the merger with J.P. Morgan. Consolidation of operations not only can lead to cost savings, but provide economies-of-scale benefits in an increasingly technology-driven industry.

Source: "The Bank-Merger Splurge," *The Economist* (August 28, 1999).

A FTER DECIDING WHAT PRODUCTS or services should be offered and how they should be made, management must plan the capacity of its processes. The new J.P. Morgan Chase's experience demonstrates how important capacity plans are to an organization's future. **Capacity** is the maximum rate of output for a process. The operations manager must provide the capacity to meet current and future demand; otherwise, the organization will miss opportunities for growth and profits.

capacity The maximum rate of output for a process.

Capacity plans are made at two levels. Long-term capacity plans, which we describe in this chapter, deal with investments in new facilities and equipment. These plans cover at least two years into the future, but construction lead times alone can force much longer time horizons. Currently, U.S. firms invest more than $600 billion annually in *new* plant and equipment. Service industries account for more than 68 percent of the total. Such sizable investments require top-management participation and approval because they are not easily reversed. Short-term capacity plans focus on workforce size, overtime budgets, inventories, and other types of decisions that we explore in later chapters.

CAPACITY PLANNING

Capacity planning is central to the long-term success of an organization. Too much capacity can be as agonizing as too little, as Managerial Practice 8.1 demonstrates. When choosing a capacity strategy, managers have to consider questions such as the following: How much of a cushion is needed to handle variable, uncertain demand? Should we expand capacity before the demand is there or wait until demand is more certain? A systematic approach is needed to answer these and similar questions and to develop a capacity strategy appropriate for each situation.

MEASURES OF CAPACITY

How should the maximum rate of output be measured?

No single capacity measure is applicable to all types of situations. A retailer measures capacity as annual sales dollars generated per square foot; an airline measures capacity as available seat-miles (ASMs) per month; a theater measures capacity as number of seats; and a job shop measures capacity as number of machine hours. In general, capacity can be expressed in one of two ways: output measures or input measures.

Output measures are the usual choice for high-volume processes. Nissan Motor Company states capacity at its Tennessee plant to be 450,000 vehicles per year. That plant produces only one type of vehicle, making capacity easy to measure. However, many organizations produce more than one product or service. For example, a restaurant may be able to handle 100 take-out customers *or* 50 sit-down customers per hour. It might also handle 50 take-out *and* 25 sit-down customers or many other combinations of the two types of customers. As the amount of customization and variety in the product mix becomes excessive, output-based capacity measures become less useful. Output measures are best utilized when the firm provides a relatively small number of standardized products and services, or when applied to individual processes within the overall firm. For example, a bank would have one capacity measure for processes that serve customers with B2C e-commerce and another measure for customers served with traditional "brick-and-mortar" facilities (see Managing Technology chapter).

Input measures are the usual choice for low-volume, flexible processes. For example, in a photocopy shop, capacity can be measured in machine hours or number of machines. Just as product mix can complicate output capacity measures, so too can demand complicate input measures. Demand, which invariably is expressed as an output rate, must be converted to an input measure. Only after making the conversion can a manager compare demand requirements and capacity on an equivalent basis. For

MANAGERIAL PRACTICE 8.1
The Agony of Too Much—and Too Little—Capacity

Carnival Cruise Line (www.carnivalcorp.com) has a fleet of cruise ships that ply the waters off Florida. The capacity of these ships is huge. The *Destiny* is its largest, which displaces 100,000 tons and can carry over 3,100 passengers. But Carnival has been sailing in choppy seas during the last year, plagued by three onboard fires and technical problems. The most pressing problem, however, is the glut of new ships being added throughout the industry. Carnival alone is bringing in a cadre of 15 new amenity-filled ships, boosting its fleet to 61. With other cruise lines also adding to their fleets, the number of available beds jumped by 12 percent in 2000. But historically, passenger volume has grown at only about 8 percent annually. Carnival argues that with the baby boomers now approaching their peak cruise-vacation years, the industry has lots of room to grow beyond the 6.5 million people who will book a cruise this year. "What is important to us is that we're building over the next five years $6.5 billion worth of new ships," says COO Frank. "We're going to continue to grow our business, and we're going to grow it profitably." Not everyone is convinced. Some experts worry about the overcapacity issue and Carnival's decreasing return on investment. During 2000, the company's share prices plunged by more than 50 percent. For now, Carnival is filling its berths by slashing prices. After years of rising prices in this industry, the capacity glut is causing the steep discounts. For a seven-day cruise, the cheapest fare has dropped from $599 to $549, and discounted tickets have gone as low as $359. Carnival is also adding a variety of shorter and cheaper voyages as a way to expand the market, because high utilization is a key to success when its resources are so capital-intensive.

The aircraft industry experienced the opposite problem in the late 1980s—not enough capacity. The world's airlines reequipped their fleets to carry more passengers on existing planes and vied to buy a record number of new commercial passenger jets. Orders received by Boeing (boeing.com), Airbus (www.airbus.com), and

Passengers on the sun deck of a cruise liner enjoying the sun. Such ships have a huge capacity and investments costs are steep, making high utilization a key factor for success.

McDonnell Douglas surged to more than 2,600 planes. McDonnell Douglas alone had a backlog of some $18 billion in firm orders for its MD-80 and new MD-11 widebody—enough to keep its plant fully utilized for more than three years. Despite the number of orders, Douglas's commercial aircraft division announced a startling loss, Airbus struggled to make money, and even mighty Boeing fought to improve subpar margins. Capacity shortage caused many problems for McDonnell Douglas: Its suppliers were unable to keep pace, its doubled workforce was inexperienced and less productive, and considerable work had to be subcontracted to other plants. The result was that costs skyrocketed and profits plummeted. In 1997, Boeing acquired McDonnell Douglas.

Sources: "Carnival Isn't Shipshape These Days," *Business Week* (April 24, 2000); "Floating Fantasy," *The Economist* (January 10, 1998).

example, the manager of a copy center must convert its annual demand for copies from different clients to the number of machines required.

utilization The degree to which equipment, space, or labor is currently being used.

UTILIZATION. Capacity planning requires a knowledge of the current capacity of a process and its utilization. **Utilization,** or the degree to which equipment, space, or labor is currently being used, is expressed as a percent:

$$\text{Utilization} = \frac{\text{Average output rate}}{\text{Maximum capacity}} \times 100\%$$

The average output rate and the capacity must be measured in the same terms—that is, time, customers, units, or dollars. The utilization rate indicates the need for adding extra capacity or eliminating unneeded capacity. The greatest difficulty in calculating utilization lies in defining *maximum capacity,* the denominator in the ratio. Two definitions of maximum capacity are useful: peak capacity and effective capacity.

peak capacity The maximum output that a process or facility can achieve under ideal conditions.

PEAK CAPACITY. The maximum output that a process or facility can achieve under ideal conditions is called **peak capacity.** When capacity is measured relative to equipment alone, the appropriate measure is **rated capacity:** an engineering assessment of maximum annual output, assuming continuous operation except for an allowance for normal maintenance and repair downtime. Peak capacity can be sustained for only a short time, such as a few hours in a day or a few days in a month. A process reaches it by using marginal methods of production, such as excessive overtime, extra shifts, temporarily reduced maintenance activities, overstaffing, and subcontracting. Although they can help with temporary peaks, these options cannot be sustained for long. Employees do not want to work excessive overtime for extended periods, overtime and night-shift premiums drive up costs, and quality drops.

rated capacity An engineering assessment of maximum annual output, assuming continuous operation except for an allowance for normal maintenance and repair downtime.

effective capacity The maximum output that a process or firm can economically sustain under normal conditions.

EFFECTIVE CAPACITY. The maximum output that a process or firm can economically sustain under normal conditions is its **effective capacity.** In some organizations, effective capacity implies a one-shift operation; in others, it implies a three-shift operation. For this reason, Census Bureau surveys define *capacity* as the greatest level of output the firm can *reasonably sustain* by using realistic employee work schedules and the equipment currently in place.

When operating close to peak capacity, a firm can make minimal profits or even lose money despite high sales levels. Such was the case with the aircraft manufacturers mentioned in Managerial Practice 8.1. Similarly, Cummins Engine Company reacted a few years ago to an unexpected demand surge caused by the weakened dollar by working at peak capacity: The plant operated three shifts, often seven days a week. Overtime soared and exhausted workers dragged down productivity. Productivity also suffered when Cummins called back less-skilled workers, laid off during an earlier

A bus powered by a Cummins natural gas engine is running a route in the north San Diego area. Several years ago, Cummins Engine experienced a $6.2 million loss in one quarter despite record high sales because inadequate production capacity required the company to operate at peak capacity.

slump. These factors together caused Cummins to report a quarterly loss of $6.2 million, even as sales jumped.

| EXAMPLE 8.1 | *Calculating Utilization* |

**TUTOR
8.1**

If operated around the clock under ideal conditions, the fabrication department of an engine manufacturer can make 100 engines per day. Management believes that a maximum output rate of only 45 engines per day can be sustained economically over a long period of time. Currently, the department is producing an average of 50 engines per day. What is the utilization of the department relative to peak capacity? Effective capacity?

SOLUTION

The two utilization measures are

$$\text{Utilization}_{\text{peak}} = \frac{\text{Average output rate}}{\text{Peak capacity}} = \frac{50}{100} \times 100\% = 50\%$$

$$\text{Utilization}_{\text{effective}} = \frac{\text{Average output rate}}{\text{Effective capacity}} = \frac{50}{45} \times 100\% = 111\%$$

Tutor 8.1 in OM Explorer confirms these calculations, as Figure 8.1 shows.

Tutor 8.1 - Capacity Utilization

Move the cell pointer to green cells to compare the formulas with your own.

Both kinds of capacity-utilization measures require the operation's current average output rate:

Average Output Rate   50

a. To compute design (or peak) utilization, then divide the output rate by the capacity:

Peak Capacity   100   Peak Utilization   50.0%

b. To compute effective utilization, enter the design capacity, then divide the output rate by this second capacity value:

Effective Capacity   45   Effective Utilization   111.1%

FIGURE 8.1 • Analyzing the Fabrication Department with Tutor 8.1

Decision Point Even though the fabrication department falls well short of the peak capacity, it is well beyond the output rate judged to be the most economical. Its operation could be sustained at that level only through the use of considerable overtime. Capacity expansion options should be evaluated. ☐

---

bottleneck An operation that has the lowest effective capacity of any operation in the process and thus limits the system's output.

INCREASING MAXIMUM CAPACITY. Most processes involve multiple operations, and often their effective capacities are not identical. A **bottleneck** is an operation that has the lowest effective capacity of any operation in the process and thus limits the system's output. Figure 8.2(a) shows a process where operation 2 is a bottleneck that limits the output to 50 units per hour. In effect, the process can produce only as fast as the slowest operation. Figure 8.2(b) shows the process when the capacities are perfectly balanced, making every operation a bottleneck. True expansion of a process's capacity occurs only when bottleneck capacity is increased. In Figure 8.2(a), initially adding capacity at operation 2 (and not operation 1 or 3) will increase system capacity. However, when operation 2's capacity reaches 200 units per hour, as in Figure 8.2(b), all three operations must be expanded simultaneously to increase capacity further.

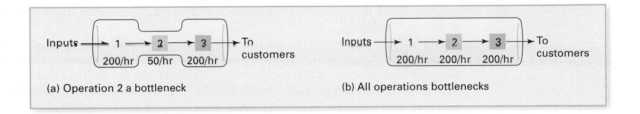

Inputs → 1 → 2 → 3 → To customers
200/hr 50/hr 200/hr

(a) Operation 2 a bottleneck

Inputs → 1 → 2 → 3 → To customers
200/hr 200/hr 200/hr

(b) All operations bottlenecks

FIGURE 8.2

Capacity Bottlenecks at a Three-Operation Facility

A project or job process does not enjoy the simple line flows shown in Figure 8.2. Its operations may process many different items, and the demands on any one operation could vary considerably from one day to the next. Bottlenecks can still be identified by computing the average utilization of each operation. However, the variability in workload also creates *floating bottlenecks*. One week the mix of work may make operation 1 a bottleneck, and the next week it may make operation 3 the constraint. This type of variability increases the complexity of day-to-day scheduling. In this situation, management prefers lower utilization rates, which allow greater slack to absorb unexpected surges in demand.

The long-term capacity of bottleneck operations can be expanded in various ways. Investments can be made in new equipment and in brick-and-mortar facility expansions. The bottleneck's capacity also can be expanded by operating it more hours per week, such as going from a one-shift operation to multiple shifts, or going from five workdays per week to six or seven workdays per week. Managers also might relieve the bottleneck by redesigning the process, either through process reengineering or process improvement (see Process Management chapter).

THEORY OF CONSTRAINTS

Long-term capacity expansions are not the only way to ease bottlenecks. Overtime, temporary or part-time employees, or temporarily outsourcing during peak periods are short-term options. Managers should also explore ways to increase the effective capacity utilization at bottlenecks, without experiencing the higher costs and poor customer service usually associated with maintaining output rates at peak capacity. The key is to carefully monitor short-term schedules (see Scheduling chapter), keeping bottleneck resources as busy as practical. They should minimize the idle time lost at bottlenecks because jobs or customers are delayed at upstream operations in the process, or because the necessary materials or tools are temporarily unavailable. They should also minimize the time spent unproductively for setups, which is changing over from one product or service to another. When a changeover is made at a bottleneck operation, the number of units or customers processed before the next changeover should be large, compared to the number processed at less critical operations. Maximizing the number processed per setup means that there will be fewer setups per year and thus less total time lost to setups.

Developing schedules that focus on bottlenecks has great potential for improving a firm's financial performance. The **theory of constraints (TOC)**, sometimes referred to as the **drum–buffer–rope method,** is an approach to management that focuses on whatever impedes progress toward the goal of maximizing the flow of total value-added funds or sales less sales discounts and variable costs. The impediments, or bottlenecks, might be overloaded processes such as order entry, new product development, or a manufacturing operation. The fundamental idea is to focus on the bottlenecks to increase their throughput, thereby increasing the flow of total value-added funds. In

theory of constraints (TOC) An approach to management that focuses on whatever impedes progress toward the goal of maximizing the flow of total value-added funds or sales less discounts and variable costs. **Also referred to as drum–buffer–rope method.**

drum–buffer–rope method See Theory of constraints.

terms of TOC, the key to the performance of the overall system lies in how the bottlenecks are scheduled.

With TOC, the bottlenecks are scheduled to maximize their throughput of products or services while adhering to promised completion dates. For example, manufacturing garden rakes involves the attachment of a bow to the head. Rake heads must be processed on the blanking press, welded to the bow, cleaned, and attached to the handle to make the rake, which is packaged and finally shipped to Sears, Kmart or Wal-Mart according to a specific delivery schedule. Suppose that the delivery commitments for all styles of rakes for the next month indicate that the welder is loaded at 105 percent of its capacity but that the other processes will be used at only 75 percent of their capacities. According to TOC, the welder is a bottleneck resource, whereas the blanking, cleaning, handle attaching, packaging, and shipping processes are nonbottleneck resources. Any idle time on the welder is a lost opportunity to generate total value-added funds. To maximize throughput of the rake manufacturing system, managers should focus on the welder schedule.

Application of TOC involves the following steps.

1. *Identify the System Bottleneck(s).*   For the rake example, the bottleneck is the welder because it is restricting the firm's ability to meet the shipping schedule and hence total value-added funds.

2. *Exploit the Bottleneck(s).*   Create schedules that maximize the throughput of the bottleneck(s). For the rake example, schedule the welder to maximize its utilization while meeting the shipping commitments to the extent possible.

3. *Subordinate All Other Decisions To Step 2.*   Nonbottleneck resources should be scheduled to support the schedule of the bottleneck and not produce more than it can handle. That is, the blanking press should not produce more than the welder can handle, and the activities of the cleaning and subsequent operations should be based on the output rate of the welder.

4. *Elevate the Bottleneck(s).*   After the scheduling improvements in steps 1–3 have been exhausted and the bottleneck is still a constraint to throughput, management should consider increasing the capacity of the bottleneck. For example, if welding is still a constraint after exhausting schedule improvements, consider increasing its capacity by adding another shift or another welding machine.

5. *Do Not Let Inertia Set In.*   Actions taken in steps 3 and 4 will improve the welder throughput and may alter the loads on other processes. Consequently, the system constraint(s) may have shifted.

Details on the scheduling method used in TOC can be found in Simons and Simpson III (1997).

Large corporations have applied the principles of the theory of constraints. These corporations include Delta Airlines, National Semiconductor, ITT, Dresser Industries, Allied-Signal, Bethlehem Steel, United Airlines, Johnson Controls, and Rockwell Automotive. Smaller companies can also use TOC, as Managerial Practice 8.2 shows.

What is the maximum reasonable size for a facility?

economies of scale
A concept that states that the average unit cost of a good or service can be reduced by increasing its output rate.

ECONOMIES OF SCALE

Historically, organizations have accepted a concept known as **economies of scale**, which states that the average unit cost of a good or service can be reduced by increasing its output rate. There are four principal reasons why economies of scale can drive costs down when output increases: Fixed costs are spread over more units, construction costs are reduced, costs of purchased materials are cut, and process advantages are found.

MANAGERIAL PRACTICE 8.2
Use of the Theory of Constraints at Dixie Iron Works

Dixie Iron Works (www.endyn.com/comp4.htm) is a machining shop with annual sales of $8 million that serves the oil field industry. Oil rigs operate 24 hours a day, seven days a week, and their operators demand speedy and on-time delivery from suppliers. Dixie specializes in gas compressor and engine components and produces its own line of oil field plug valves. It also creates new specialty parts and replacements for broken parts. Even though it could command premium prices, in 1993 Dixie was barely breaking even with a 3 percent operating profit. Inventory turns were a disappointing two per year.

What was wrong? Dixie management undertook a problem analysis and discovered that due date performance was poor: Only one of every 20 jobs was being completed on time. In addition, the company was taking on any and all work, even though some jobs were small and tied up valuable machine time, causing delays for larger orders. Management decided that the present scheduling system was inadequate. A system was needed that recognized the capacities of the machines and provided a way to estimate what would happen if a particular order were accepted. Management decided on a system that applies TOC principles.

Dixie began by applying TOC principles manually. Management eventually purchased software that could generate the schedules more quickly and offered other useful capabilities. The advantage of the TOC software is apparent when a customer brings in a large order with a tight deadline. In the past, Dixie would have accepted the order, but the other orders in the shop would have been delayed. Customers who have their orders delayed may never return. Now, a new order is entered into the program to determine the implications for the existing orders in the shop. If the total order cannot be completed on time, the customer may be able to get by with a smaller quantity now and accept the rest later.

Use of the TOC software improved Dixie's financial performance. Inventory turns are now 12 per year and operating profit is 12 percent of sales. Due date performance has increased to 65 percent on-time delivery, a dramatic improvement in only three years.

Source: Danos, Gerard. "Dixie Reengineers Scheduling." *APICS—The Performance Advantage* (March 1996), pp. 28–31.

SPREADING FIXED COSTS. In the short term, certain costs do not vary with changes in the output rate. These fixed costs include heating costs, debt service, and management salaries. Depreciation of plant and equipment already owned is also a fixed cost in the accounting sense. When the output rate—and, therefore, the facility's utilization rate—increases, the average unit cost drops because fixed costs are spread over more units. As increments of capacity often are rather large, a firm initially might have to buy more capacity than it needs. However, demand increases in subsequent years can then be absorbed without additional fixed costs.

REDUCING CONSTRUCTION COSTS. Certain activities and expenses are required in building small and large facilities alike: building permits, architects' fees, rental of building equipment, and the like. Doubling the size of the facility usually does not double construction costs. The construction cost of equipment or a facility often increases relative to its surface area, whereas its capacity increases in proportion to its cubic volume. For example, the cost of steel to build an oil tanker increases more slowly than the tanker's capacity increases. Industries such as breweries and oil refineries benefit from strong economies of scale because of this phenomenon.

 CUTTING COSTS OF PURCHASED MATERIALS. Higher volumes can reduce the costs of purchased materials and services. They give the purchaser a better bargaining position and the opportunity to take advantage of quantity discounts. Retailers such as Wal-Mart

Stores and Toys " Я " Us reap significant economies of scale because their national and international stores sell huge volumes of each item. Producers who rely on a vast network of suppliers (e.g., Toyota) and food processors (e.g., Kraft General Foods) also can buy inputs for less because of the quantity they order. In the personal computer business, large firms can negotiate volume discounts on the components that determine up to 80 percent of a PC's costs. Thus, Compaq can sell its base model for just $100 more than it costs a smaller firm, making only 200 to 500 units a month, for materials alone.

MANAGERIAL PRACTICE 8.3
Economies of Scale at Work

Hospitals

Hospital bills in Kalamazoo, a metropolitan area of only 200,000, are the second highest in Michigan and among the highest in the nation. The reason is that the two archrival hospitals in Kalamazoo are not getting the full benefit from economies of scale. Borgess Medical Center (www.healthdirection.com/borgess/Default.html) and Bronson Methodist Hospital (www.csmgroup.com/bronson_methodist_2.htm) each has its own heart programs, maternity wards, state-of-the-art emergency rooms, and radiology services. They even each have their own helicopter ambulances—two of only 90 in the entire country. Operating both helicopter units costs a total of $5 million a year, and combining their operations would save at least $1 million, even if both choppers were kept running. In general, hospital costs in two-hospital towns like Kalamazoo are 30 percent higher than in one-hospital communities, where consolidated volumes allow the hospital to enjoy greater economies of scale.

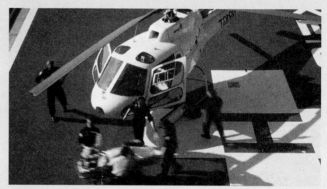

A hospital emergency helicopter delivers a patient to the rooftop of a hospital. The high cost of such rescue helicopters make capacity utilization a key to cost control.

South American Airlines

In the mid-1990s, many of the airlines in the Latin America region expanded their capacity, expecting demand to rise. But it shrank in the wake of Brazil's devaluation crisis in early 1999 at the same time as the airlines were facing ever more competition from airlines in the United States, which enjoy bigger economies of scale. Brazil's domestic flights in the first quarter of 2000 showed only 58 percent of seats were taken, much below the 65 percent occupation that is the industry's typical break-even point. Without enough volume over which to spread fixed costs, the results were inevitable. A rescue plan for Aerolineas Argentinas (www.aerolineas.com.ar) announced big cuts in domestic and international services. TAM (www.tam.com.br) and Transbrasil (www.transbrasil.com.br), two of Brazil's four big airlines, were discussing an "operational partnership" to cut the overlap between their flights, a step widely seen as leading to an even-

tual merger and significant cuts. Vasp (www.vasp.com.br), another of Brazil's big four, announced the suspension of its flights to North America and Europe after Boeing had demanded some of its airplanes back because Vasp was not keeping up its lease payments. The president of the Brazilian Development Bank suggested that there might be room for only one large local airline in Brazil, pointing to Canada and Mexico where in each case two big local airlines have merged. Fortunately, the Latin America region's economy is now back on track for growth and the U.S. Federal Aviation Authority says that the world's fastest growth rates are likely to be in Latin America. Such increasing volumes will give the remaining airlines strong economies-of-scale benefits.

Sources: "Rival Operations," *Wall Street Journal* (June 6, 1990); "South American Airlines," *The Economist* (May 6, 2000).

FINDING PROCESS ADVANTAGES. High-volume production provides many opportunities for cost reduction. At a higher output rate, the process shifts toward a line process, with resources dedicated to individual products. Firms may be able to justify the expense of more efficient technology or more specialized equipment. The benefits from dedicating resources to individual products or services may include speeding up the learning effect, lowering inventory, improving process and job designs, and reducing the number of changeovers. For example, higher volumes allow James River Corporation, a paper manufacturer, to achieve greater efficiency than manufacturers producing a wide variety of products in small volumes, because the mill can set up its machines for one long run of a certain grade of paper and not have to make as many adjustments for different grades.

Managerial Practice 8.3 gives examples of economies of scale in health care and airline organizations. The economies of scale come from all four sources—spreading fixed costs, reducing construction costs, cutting purchasing costs, and finding process advantages.

DISECONOMIES OF SCALE

diseconomies of scale
When the average cost per unit increases as the facility's size increases.

At some point a facility can become so large that **diseconomies of scale** set in; that is, the average cost per unit increases as the facility's size increases. The reason is that excessive size can bring complexity, loss of focus, and inefficiencies that raise the average unit cost of a product or service. There may be too many layers of employees and bureaucracy, and management loses touch with employees and customers. The organization is less agile and loses the flexibility needed to respond to changing demand. Many large companies become so involved in analysis and planning that they innovate less and avoid risks. The result is that small companies outperform corporate giants in numerous industries.

Figure 8.3 illustrates the transition from economies of scale to diseconomies of scale. The 500-bed hospital shows economies of scale because the average unit cost at its *best operating level*, represented by the blue dot, is less than that of the 250-bed hospital. However, further expansion to a 750-bed hospital leads to higher average unit costs and diseconomies of scale. One reason the 500-bed hospital enjoys greater economies of scale than the 250-bed hospital is that the cost of building and equipping it is less than twice the cost for the smaller hospital. The 750-bed facility would enjoy similar savings. Its higher average unit costs can be explained only by diseconomies of scale, which outweigh the savings realized in construction costs.

Figure 8.3 does not mean that the optimal size for all hospitals is 500 beds. Optimal size depends on the number of patients per week to be served. On the one

FIGURE 8.3

Economies and Diseconomies of Scale

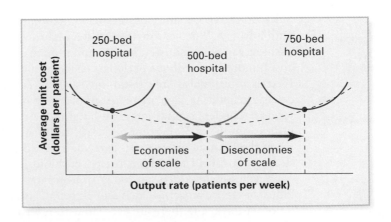

hand, a hospital serving a small community would have lower costs by choosing a 250-bed capacity rather than the 500-bed capacity. On the other hand, assuming the same cost structure, a large community will be served more efficiently by two 500-bed hospitals than by one 1,000-bed facility.

Economies of scale vary by industry, which affects plant size. Thus, managers often set policies regarding the maximum size for any one facility. Plant size ceilings of 300 employees are common for industries such as metal working. For example, Dana Corporation, a $5 billion supplier of steel to United States, European, and Japanese automakers, has a cap of 200 employees at all but a few of its 120 plants. When a division gets too big, it simply gets split in half (see *focused factories* in the Process Management chapter). For industries such as transportation equipment or electronics, where economies of scale are particularly strong, the limits are as large as 6,000 employees. The real challenge in setting such limits is predicting how costs and revenues will change for different output rates and facility sizes.

An example of going too far could be the Incredible Universe superstores of Tandy Corporation. This Fort Worth–based electronics retailer opened its first superstore in 1992. The average store packed some 85,000 products into 185,000 square feet, or more than four times the average at rival Circuit City Stores. The superstores never were profitable, and by 1996, were expected to lose $90 million per year. Tandy opted to sell all 17 Incredible Universe stores at bargain-basement prices, and focus on Radio Shack. The lack of focus and huge size of the superstores made it impossible to generate enough sales per square foot to make the stores profitable.

CAPACITY STRATEGIES

How much capacity cushion is best for various processes?

Operations managers must examine three dimensions of capacity strategy before making capacity decisions: sizing capacity cushions, timing and sizing expansion, and linking capacity and other operating decisions.

SIZING CAPACITY CUSHIONS. Average utilization rates should not get too close to 100 percent. When they do, that usually is a signal to increase capacity or decrease order acceptance so as to avoid declining productivity. The **capacity cushion** is the amount of reserve capacity that a firm maintains to handle sudden increases in demand or temporary losses of production capacity; it measures the amount by which the average utilization (in terms of *effective* capacity) falls below 100 percent. Specifically,

capacity cushion The amount of reserve capacity that a firm maintains to handle sudden increases in demand or temporary losses of production capacity; it measures the amount by which the average utilization (in terms of *effective* capacity) falls below 100 percent.

$$\text{Capacity cushion} = 100\% - \text{Utilization rate (\%)}$$

Since 1948, U.S. manufacturers have maintained an average cushion of 18 percent, with a low of 9 percent in 1966 and a high of 27 percent. The appropriate size of the cushion varies by industry. In the capital-intensive paper industry, where machines can cost hundreds of millions of dollars each, cushions well under 10 percent are preferred. Electric utilities also are capital-intensive but consider cushions of 15 to 20 percent in electric generating capacity to be optimal to avoid brownouts and loss of service to customers. The less capital-intensive hotel industry breaks even with a 60 to 70 percent utilization (40 to 30 percent cushion), and begins to suffer customer-service problems when the cushion drops to 20 percent. The more capital-intensive cruiseship industry, such as Carnival Cruise Line, prefers cushions as small as 5 percent.

Businesses find large cushions appropriate when demand varies. In certain service industries (e.g., groceries), demand on some days of the week is predictably higher than on other days, and there are even hour-to-hour patterns. Long customer waiting times are not acceptable because customers grow impatient if they have to wait in a super-market checkout line for more than a few minutes. Prompt customer service requires supermarkets to maintain a capacity cushion large enough to handle peak demand.

Large cushions also are necessary when future demand is uncertain, particularly if resource flexibility is low. One large bank operated its computer for six months at an average 77 percent load on the central processing unit (CPU) during peak demand. Top management believed that the capacity cushion was more than ample and rejected a proposal to expand capacity. During the next six months, however, the average CPU utilization during peaks unexpectedly surged to 83 percent, causing a dramatic decline in customer service. The 17 percent capacity cushion proved to be too small to meet the bank's customer-service objectives. Waiting-line analysis and simulation (see the Waiting-Lines supplement and the Simulation supplement) can help managers antici-pate better the relationship between capacity cushion and customer service.

Another type of demand uncertainty occurs with a changing product mix. Though total demand might remain stable, the load can shift unpredictably from one work cen-ter to another as the mix changes. High customization also leads to uncertainty. An example is a municipal court system, where the capacity in courtroom hours varies with the nature of the trials and whether a jury is needed. The mix varies from week to week and month to month.

Supply uncertainty also favors large capacity cushions. Capacity often comes in large increments, so expanding even by the minimum amount possible may create a large cushion. Firms also need to build in excess capacity to allow for employee absen-teeism, vacations, holidays, and any other delays. Penalty costs for overtime and sub-contracting can create the need for further increases in capacity cushions.

The argument in favor of small cushions is simple: Unused capacity costs money. For capital-intensive firms, minimizing the capacity cushion is vital. Since the mid-1970s, airlines have expanded capacity by cramming about 20 percent more seats into the same-size aircraft. Some airlines have recently removed some seats to decrease cus-tomer dissatisfaction with tight quarters, but high utilization still remains essential. Studies indicate that businesses with high capital intensity achieve a low return on investment when the capacity cushion is high. This strong correlation does not exist for labor-intensive firms, however. Their return on investment is about the same because the lower investment in equipment makes high utilization less critical. Small cushions have other advantages; they reveal inefficiencies that may be masked by capacity excesses—problems with absenteeism, for example, or unreliable suppliers. Once man-agers and workers have identified such problems, they often can find ways to correct them.

Should an expanionist or a wait-and-see strategy be followed?

TIMING AND SIZING EXPANSION. The second issue of capacity strategy is when to expand and by how much. Figure 8.4 illustrates two extreme strategies: the *expansionist strat-egy*, which involves large, infrequent jumps in capacity, and the *wait-and-see strategy*, which involves smaller, more frequent jumps.

During an industrywide slump in the late 1980s, The Limited, a firm with seven specialty apparel store divisions, opted for an expansionist strategy by aggressively opening new outlets and expanding existing ones. As a result of the store expansions and clustering of stores from its seven divisions, The Limited became one of the largest specialty store tenants in hundreds of malls. In a shopping center in Columbus, Ohio, The Limited divisions account for 125,000 square feet, or 25 percent of the total. That amount of space earns concessions such as prime locations, cheaper rents, and even money from developers to help with construction costs. By 1990, The Limited's hold-ings had grown by 27 percent, to 3,419 stores, and its sales by 68 percent, to $5.2

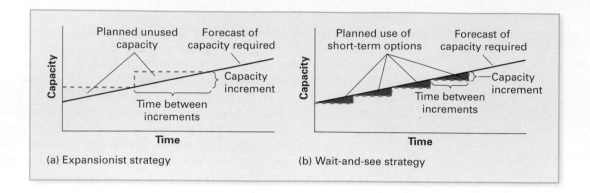

FIGURE 8.4

*Two Capacity
Strategies*

billion. The best strategy for a firm can change over time. American Airlines followed an expansionist strategy in the 1980s, when it aggressively pursued overseas routes. After several setbacks, including lack of proper equipment and rising fuel costs because of the Persian Gulf War, American adopted a less risky wait-and-see strategy.

The timing and sizing of expansion are related; that is, if demand is increasing and the time between increments increases, the size of the increments must also increase. The expansionist strategy, which stays ahead of demand, minimizes the chance of sales lost to insufficient capacity. The wait-and-see strategy lags behind demand, relying on short-term options such as use of overtime, temporary workers, subcontractors, stock-outs, and postponement of preventive maintenance to meet any shortfalls. However, these options have their drawbacks. For example, overtime requires payment of time-and-a-half wages for some employees and may result in lower productivity or quality during overtime hours; union agreements may even limit the amount of allowable overtime. Nonetheless, some mix of short-term options might make the wait-and-see strategy best in certain situations.

Several factors favor the expansionist strategy. Expansion may result in economies of scale and a faster rate of learning, thus helping a firm reduce its costs and compete on price. This strategy might increase the firm's market share or act as a form of pre-emptive marketing. By making a large capacity expansion or announcing that one is imminent, the firm uses capacity to preempt expansion by other firms. These other firms must sacrifice some of their market share or risk burdening the industry with overcapacity. To be successful, however, the preempting firm must have the credibility to convince the competition that it will carry out its plans—and must signal its plans before the competition can act.

The conservative wait-and-see strategy is to expand in smaller increments, such as by renovating existing facilities rather than building new ones. Because the wait-and-see strategy follows demand, it reduces the risks of overexpansion based on overly optimistic demand forecasts, obsolete technology, or inaccurate assumptions regarding the competition. American Honda Company's new plant in Lincoln, Alabama, which will make Odyssey minivans and engines, is a good example. The total investment is only $400 million, compared with a typical $1 billion spent by rivals on similar products. Honda's factories are very expandable; they start small and grow with demand for the products. Honda is likely to run some equipment round the clock to reduce the number of expensive machines it needs. Their wait-and-see strategy is a far cry from Detroit's expansionist approach, which operates with too much capacity and force-feeds the market with incentives.

However, this strategy has its own risks, such as being preempted by a competitor or being unable to respond if demand is unexpectedly high. The wait-and-see strategy has been criticized as a short-term strategy typical of some U.S. management styles. Managers on the fast track to corporate advancement tend to take fewer risks. They earn promotions by avoiding the big mistake and maximizing short-term profits and return on investment. The wait-and-see strategy fits this short-term outlook but can erode market share over the long run.

Management may choose one of these two strategies or one of the many between these extremes. With strategies in the more moderate middle, firms may expand more frequently (on a smaller scale) than with the expansionist strategy but do not always lag behind demand as with the wait-and-see strategy. An intermediate strategy could be to *follow-the-leader*, expanding when others do. If others are right, so are you, and nobody gains a competitive advantage. If they make a mistake and overexpand, so have you, but everyone shares in the agony of overcapacity.

How should capacity and competitive priorities be linked? Capacity and other types of decisions?

LINKING CAPACITY AND OTHER DECISIONS. Capacity decisions should be closely linked to strategies and processes throughout the organization. When managers make decisions about location, resource flexibility, and inventory, they must consider the impact on capacity cushions. Capacity cushions buffer the organization against uncertainty, as do resource flexibility, inventory, and longer customer lead times. If a system is well balanced and a change is made in some other decision area, then the capacity cushion may need change to compensate. Examples of such links with capacity include the following.

- ❑ *Competitive Priorities.* A change in competitive priorities that emphasizes faster deliveries for a process requires a larger capacity cushion to allow for quick response and uneven demand, if holding finished goods inventory is infeasible or uneconomical.

- ❑ *Quality Management.* A drive that has obtained higher levels of quality allows for a smaller capacity cushion because there will be less uncertainty caused by yield losses.

- ❑ *Capital Intensity.* An investment in expensive new technologies makes a process more capital-intensive and increases pressure to have a smaller capacity cushion to get an acceptable return on the investment.

- ❑ *Resource Flexibility.* A change to less worker flexibility requires a larger capacity cushion to compensate for the operation overloads that are more likely to occur with a less-flexible workforce.

- ❑ *Inventory.* A change to less reliance on inventory in order to smooth the output rate requires a larger capacity cushion to meet increased demands during peak periods.

- ❑ *Scheduling.* A change to a more stable environment allows a smaller cushion because products or services can be scheduled with more assurance.

Another crucial linkage is between capacity and location decisions. A firm that is expanding eventually must add new facilities and find suitable locations for them, whereas a multisite firm that is downsizing often must identify which locations to eliminate. During the past decade, General Motors cut back its capacity by shutting down several factories to stop large losses in its North American automobile operation. It faced tough choices between closing older factories with cooperative and productive workforces and abandoning expensive, modern plants where labor relations were poor. The UAW contract made closing a facility quite costly, so some plants that otherwise should have been closed remained open.

A SYSTEMATIC APPROACH TO CAPACITY DECISIONS

How can capacity plans be systematically developed?

Although each situation is somewhat different, a four-step procedure generally can help managers make sound capacity decisions. In describing this procedure, we assume that management has already performed the preliminary step of determining existing capacity.

1. Estimate future capacity requirements.
2. Identify gaps by comparing requirements with available capacity.
3. Develop alternative plans for filling the gaps.
4. Evaluate each alternative, both qualitatively and quantitatively, and make a final choice.

STEP 1: ESTIMATE CAPACITY REQUIREMENTS

The foundation for estimating long-term capacity needs is forecasts of demand, productivity, competition, and technological changes that extend well into the future. Unfortunately, the farther ahead you look, the more chance you have of making an inaccurate forecast (see the Forecasting chapter).

The demand forecast has to be converted to a number that can be compared directly with the capacity measure being used. Suppose that capacity is expressed as the number of available machines at an operation. When just one product (service) is being processed, the number of machines required, M, is

$$\text{Number of machines required} = \frac{\text{Processing hours required for year's demand}}{\substack{\text{Hours available from one machine per year,} \\ \text{after deducting desired cushion}}}$$

$$M = \frac{Dp}{N[1 - (C/100)]}$$

where

$\quad D$ = number of units (customers) forecast per year

$\quad p$ = processing time (in hours per unit or customers)

$\quad N$ = total number of hours per year during which the process operates

$\quad C$ = desired capacity cushion

The processing time, p, in the numerator depends on the process and methods selected to do the work (see the Process Management chapter). Estimates of p come from established work standards (see the CD supplement on Measuring Output Rates). The denominator is the total number of hours, N, available for the year, multiplied by a proportion that accounts for the desired capacity cushion, C. The proportion is simply $1.0 - C$, where C is converted from a percent to a proportion by dividing by 100.

If multiple products or services are involved, extra time is needed to change over from one product or service to the next. **Setup time** is the time required to change a machine from making one product or service to making another. Setup time is derived from process decisions, as is processing time (see the Process Management chapter). The total setup time is found by dividing the number of units forecast per year, D, by the number of units made in each lot, which gives the number of setups per year, and then multiplying by the time per setup. For example, if the annual demand is 1,200 units and the average lot size is 100, there are $1,200/100 = 12$ setups per year. Accounting for both processing and setup time when there are multiple products (services), we get

setup time The time required to change a machine from making one product or service to making another.

$$\text{Number of machines required} = \frac{\text{Processing } and \text{ setup hours required for year's demand, summed over all products}}{\text{Hours available from one machine per year, after deducting desired cushion}}$$

$$M = \frac{[Dp + (D/Q)s]_{\text{product 1}} + [Dp + (D/Q)s]_{\text{product 2}} + \cdots + [Dp + (D/Q)s]_{\text{product } n}}{N[1 - (C/100)]}$$

where

$$Q = \text{number of units in each lot}$$
$$s = \text{setup time (in hours) per lot}$$

Always round up the fractional part unless it is cost efficient to use short-term options such as overtime or stockouts to cover any shortfalls.

EXAMPLE 8.2

TUTOR 8.2

Estimating Requirements

A copy center in an office building prepares bound reports for two clients. The center makes multiple copies (the lot size) of each report. The processing time to run, collate, and bind each copy depends on, among other factors, the number of pages. The center operates 250 days per year, with one eight-hour shift. Management believes that a capacity cushion of 15 percent (beyond the allowance built into time standards) is best. It currently has three copy machines. Based on the following table of information, determine how many machines are needed at the copy center.

ITEM	CLIENT X	CLIENT Y
Annual demand forecast (copies)	2,000	6,000
Standard processing time (hour/copy)	0.5	0.7
Average lot size (copies per report)	20	30
Standard setup time (hours)	0.25	0.40

SOLUTION

$$M = \frac{[Dp + (D/Q)s]_{\text{product 1}} + [Dp + (D/Q)s]_{\text{product 2}} + \cdots + [Dp + (D/Q)s]_{\text{product } n}}{N[1 - (C/100)]}$$

$$= \frac{[2{,}000(0.5) + (2{,}000/20)(0.25)]_{\text{client X}} + [6{,}000(0.7) + (6{,}000/30)(0.40)]_{\text{client Y}}}{[(250 \text{ days/year})(1 \text{ shift/day})(8 \text{ hours/shift})](1.0 - 15/100)}$$

$$= \frac{5{,}305}{1{,}700} = 3.12$$

Rounding up to the next integer gives a requirement of four machines.

Decision Point The copy center's capacity is being stretched and no longer has the desired 15 percent capacity cushion. Not wanting customer service to suffer, management decided to use overtime as a short-term solution to handle past-due orders. If demand continues at the current level or grows, it will acquire a fourth machine. ❏

STEP 2: IDENTIFY GAPS

capacity gap Any difference (positive or negative) between projected demand and current capacity.

A **capacity gap** is any difference (positive or negative) between projected demand and current capacity. Identifying gaps requires use of the correct capacity measure. Complications arise when multiple operations and several resource inputs are involved. For example, in the early 1970s, airline executives incorrectly concluded that airlines having the larger share of seats flown attract a larger share of total passengers. In other words, fly more seats to get more passengers. Many airlines responded by buying more jumbo jets, but competitors flying smaller planes were more successful. The correct measure of capacity was the number of departures rather than the number of seats. Thus, several airlines had to adjust the capacity imbalance between small and large planes by buying smaller planes and discontinuing use of some jumbo jets. Expanding the capacity of some operations may increase overall capacity. However, if one operation is a bottleneck, capacity can be expanded only if the capacity of the bottleneck operation is expanded.

| EXAMPLE 8.3 | *Identifying Capacity Gaps* |

Grandmother's Chicken Restaurant is experiencing a boom in business. The owner expects to serve a total of 80,000 meals this year. Although the kitchen is operating at 100 percent capacity, the dining room can handle a total of 105,000 diners per year. Forecasted demand for the next five years is as follows:

Year 1:   90,000 meals
Year 2:   100,000 meals
Year 3:   110,000 meals
Year 4:   120,000 meals
Year 5:   130,000 meals

What are the capacity gaps in Grandmother's kitchen and dining room through year 5?

SOLUTION

The kitchen is currently the bottleneck at a capacity of 80,000 meals per year. Based on the demand forecast, the capacity gap for the kitchen is

Year 1: $90,000 - 80,000 = 10,000$
Year 2: $100,000 - 80,000 = 20,000$
Year 3: $110,000 - 80,000 = 30,000$
Year 4: $120,000 - 80,000 = 40,000$
Year 5: $130,000 - 80,000 = 50,000$

Before year 3, the capacity of the dining room (105,000) is greater than demand. In year 3 and subsequently, there are capacity gaps for the dining room:

Year 3: $110,000 - 105,000 =   5,000$
Year 4: $120,000 - 105,000 = 15,000$
Year 5: $130,000 - 105,000 = 25,000$

Decision Point Management decided to act now by developing and evaluating several alternatives for expanding capacity, because operating at 100 percent capacity is already creating some customer dissatisfaction and because the capacity gaps are projected to increase. ☐

STEP 3: DEVELOP ALTERNATIVES

base case The act of doing nothing and losing orders from any demand that exceeds current capacity.

The next step is to develop alternative plans to cope with projected gaps. One alternative, called the **base case,** is to do nothing and simply lose orders from any demand that exceeds current capacity. Other alternatives are various timing and sizing options for adding new capacity, including the expansionist and wait-and-see strategies illustrated in Figure. 8.4. For example, BMW expanded its facility in Spartanburg, South Carolina in two stages when, in 1995, it added the Z-3 roadster production line to its already existing 325 line. Additional possibilities include expanding at a different location and using short-term options such as overtime, temporary workers, and subcontracting.

STEP 4: EVALUATE THE ALTERNATIVES

In this final step, the manager evaluates each alternative, both quantitatively and qualitatively.

QUALITATIVE CONCERNS. Qualitatively, the manager has to look at how each alternative fits the overall capacity strategy and other aspects of the business not covered by the financial analysis. Of particular concern might be uncertainties about demand, competitive reaction, technological change, and cost estimates. Some of these factors cannot be quantified and have to be assessed on the basis of judgment and experience. Others can be quantified, and the manager can analyze each alternative by using different assumptions about the future. One set of assumptions could represent a worst case, where demand is less, competition is greater, and construction costs are higher than expected. Another set of assumptions could represent the most optimistic view of the future. This type of "what-if" analysis allows the manager to get an idea of each alternative's implications before making a final choice.

cash flow The difference between the flows of funds into and out of an organization over a period of time, including revenues, costs, and changes in assets and liabilities.

QUANTITATIVE CONCERNS. Quantitatively, the manager estimates the change in cash flows for each alternative over the forecast time horizon compared to the base case. **Cash flow** is the difference between the flows of funds into and out of an organization over a period of time, including revenues, costs, and changes in assets and liabilities. The manager is concerned here only with calculating the cash flows attributable to the project.

A good example of capacity's impact on revenues is a steakhouse restaurant in Lexington, Kentucky. Customers liked the neon signs that dotted the wall, the blaring jukebox, and the way they could throw peanut shells on the floor. However, they had to wait as long as two hours to be seated, and the choice of items on the menu was limited. The restaurant expanded capacity by adding more seats and enlarging the kitchen to handle larger volumes and offer more choices. Within months, the restaurant started to bring in $80,000 a week, a 60 percent increase. This facility became the prototype for Logan's Roadhouse, Inc., the Nashville-based dining chain that was one of the fastest-growing companies in 1996. Logan's has since opened 10 restaurants in Indiana, Kentucky, and Tennessee. Each one costs $2.2 million to build, but high volume yields a sales average of some $3.8 million a year.

EXAMPLE 8.4

**TUTOR
8.3**

Evaluating the Alternatives

One alternative for Grandmother's Chicken Restaurant is to expand both the kitchen and the dining room now, bringing their capacities up to 130,000 meals per year. The initial investment would be $200,000, made at the end of this year (year 0). The average meal is priced at $10, and the before-tax profit margin is 20 percent. The 20 percent figure was arrived at by determining that, for each $10 meal, $6 covers variable costs and $2 goes toward fixed costs (other than depreciation). The remaining $2 goes to pretax profit.

What are the pretax cash flows from this project for the next five years compared to those of the base case of doing nothing?

SOLUTION

Recall that the base case of doing nothing results in losing all potential sales beyond 80,000 meals. With the new capacity, the cash flow would equal the extra meals served by having a 130,000-meal capacity, multiplied by a profit of $2 per meal. In year 0, the only cash flow is

−$200,000 for the initial investment. In year 1, the 90,000-meal demand will be completely satisfied by the expanded capacity, so the incremental cash flow is $(90,000 − 80,000)(2) = \$20,000$. For subsequent years, the figures are as follows:

Year 2:	Demand = 100,000; Cash flow = (100,000 − 80,000)2 = $40,000
Year 3:	Demand = 110,000; Cash flow = (110,000 − 80,000)2 = $60,000
Year 4:	Demand = 120,000; Cash flow = (120,000 − 80,000)2 = $80,000
Year 5:	Demand = 130,000; Cash flow = (130,000 − 80,000)2 = $100,000

Because the owner is evaluating an alternative that provides enough capacity to meet all demand through year 5, the added meals served are identical to the capacity gaps in Example 8.3. That would not be true if the new capacity were smaller than the expected demand in any year. To find the added meals in that case, we would subtract the base case capacity from the new capacity (rather than the demand). The result would be smaller than the capacity gap.

Tutor 8.3 in OM Explorer confirms these calculations, as Figure 8.5 shows.

Tutor 8.3 - Projecting Cash Flows

Position cell pointer on green-tinted cells to examine formulas.

Start by entering the capacity (measured as customers or clients per year) before the expansion, the cost of the expansion, the postexpansion capacity, and the average profit per customer served.

Preexpansion capacity	80,000
Cost of expansion	$200,000
Postexpansion capacity	130,000
Profit per customer	$2

Enter the expected demand (number of customers) in each year. Then calculate cash flows. In year 0, cash flow is the negative of the cost of expanding. For each subsequent year, subtract preexpansion capacity from that year's demand or from the postexpansion capacity, whichever is less. If this difference is negative, cash flow is zero. Otherwise, multiply the difference by the per-customer profit to get the cash flow.

Year	Expected Demand	Cash Flow
0	80,000	($200,000)
1	90,000	$20,000
2	100,000	$40,000
3	110,000	$60,000
4	120,000	$80,000
5	130,000	$100,000

FIGURE 8.5 • Analyzing Cash Flows with Tutor 8.3

Decision Point Before deciding on this capacity alternative, the owner should account for the time value of money, applying such techniques as the present value or internal rate of return methods (see CD supplement on Financial Analysis). The owner should also examine the qualitative concerns. For example, the homey atmosphere that the restaurant has projected may be lost with expansion. Furthermore, other alternatives should be considered, such as the one in Solved Problem 2 at the end of this chapter. ❐

TOOLS FOR CAPACITY PLANNING

What tools can help in planning capacities?

Long-term capacity planning requires demand forecasts for an extended period of time. Unfortunately, forecast accuracy declines as the forecasting horizon lengthens. In addition, anticipating what competitors will do increases the uncertainty of demand forecasts. Finally, demand during any period of time is not evenly distributed; peaks and valleys of demand may (and often do) occur within the time period. These realities necessitate the use of capacity cushions. In this section, we introduce three tools that deal more formally with demand uncertainty and variability: waiting-line models, simulation, and decision trees. Waiting-line models and simulation account for the random, independent behavior of many customers, in terms of both their time of arrival and their processing needs. Decision trees allow anticipation of events such as competitors' actions.

WAITING-LINE MODELS

Waiting-line models often are useful in capacity planning. Waiting lines tend to develop in front of a work center, such as an airport ticket counter, a machine center, or a central computer. The reason is that the arrival time between jobs or customers varies and the processing time may vary from one customer to the next. Waiting-line models use probability distributions to provide estimates of average customer delay time, average length of waiting lines, and utilization of the work center. Managers can use this information to choose the most cost-effective capacity, balancing customer service and the cost of adding capacity.

The Waiting Lines supplement provides a fuller treatment of waiting lines. It introduces formulas for estimating important characteristics of a waiting line, such as average customer waiting time and average facility utilization, for different facility designs. For example, a facility might be designed to have one or multiple lines at each operation and to route customers through one or multiple operations. Given the estimating capability of these formulas and cost estimates for waiting and idle time, managers can select cost-effective designs and capacity levels that also provide the desired level of customer service.

SIMULATION

More complex waiting-line problems must be analyzed with simulation (see the Simulation supplement). It can identify the process's bottlenecks and appropriate capacity cushions, even for complex processes with random demand patterns with predictable surges in demand during a typical day. Example 8.5 demonstrates some of these capabilities using the Extend software. To learn more specifically about Extend, see its tutorials and work through the simulation exercises at the end of this and several other chapters.

| EXAMPLE 8.5 | *Provincial Automobile License Renewals* |

The department of motor vehicles in Toronto, Ontario, is conducting an assessment of its driver's license renewal process. There are six basic steps to its process.

	TIME TO PERFORM (SECONDS)	
OPERATION	Average	Standard Deviation
1. Review renewal application for correctness	15	3
2. Check file for violations and restrictions	60	15
3. Process and record payment	25	6
4. Conduct eye test	35	10
5. Photograph applicant	20	5
6. Issue temporary license	30	5

Each customer should pass through all the steps, although approximately 10 percent of the customers did not complete the application correctly and have to have it reviewed again (they will get higher priority to process than new arrivals when their application is corrected). Operation 1 should be performed before any other step could be taken. Similarly, operation 6 could not be performed until all the other steps were completed.

Operations 1–4 are handled by three clerks who were each paid $10 per hour. Operation 5 is assigned to a photographer paid $12 per hour. Operation 6, issuing temporary licenses, must be handled by a uniformed motor vehicle officer paid $15 per hour. During slack times, the officer could be assigned to any job except photography. Customer demand is uneven and tends to peak when the office opens in the morning and over the lunch hour.

TIME	AVERAGE CUSTOMER ARRIVAL (PEOPLE PER MINUTE)
8:00 A.M.–9:00 A.M.	1.25
9:00 A.M.–12:00 P.M.	0.75
12:00 P.M.–1:00 P.M.	2.00
1:00 P.M.–4:00 P.M.	0.75

a. What are the bottleneck(s) ahead of which long lines can form?

b. How long will the lines be over the lunch hour?

c. What is the average utilization (and capacity cushions) for the six operations?

SOLUTION

The Extend software, packaged on the Student CD-ROM, is used to model and simulate this process. Figure 8.6(a) shows the simulation model for the process, with stations for the three clerks, photographer, and officer. Figure 8.6(b) shows the waiting-line lengths that develop over the course of three simulated days. The system can work only as fast as the slowest station,

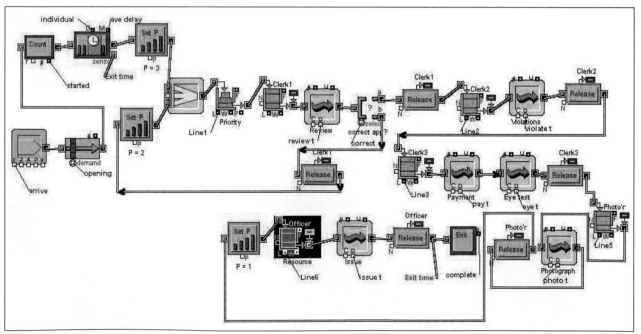

(a) Simulation model

FIGURE 8.6 • Extend Model for Automobile License Renewals

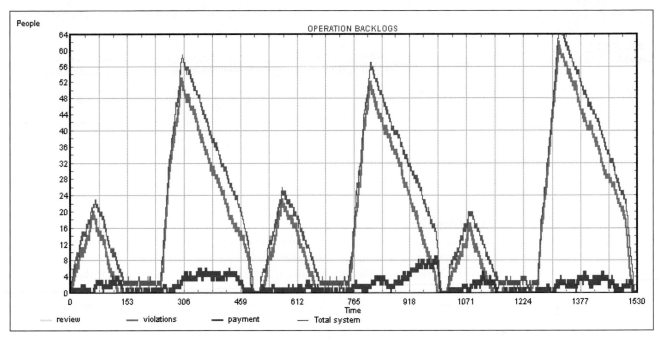

(b) Waiting lines for three simulated days

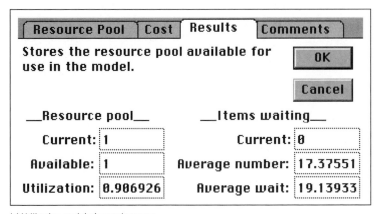

(c) Utilization at violations subprocess

which clearly is the violations subprocess, where lines of over 50 customers develop over the three lunch hours. Customer wait times (not shown) for the whole process are over 55 minutes during the peaks, even though the average is about 20 minutes over the course of the three days. Figure 8.6(c) shows that the utilization statistics for clerk 2, who handles the violations subprocess, is 90.6 percent, meaning the capacity cushion is less than 10 percent. An average of 17.4 customers are waiting in front of this subprocess, and the average wait time here alone is 19.1 minutes. This operation is the bottleneck. With the exception of clerk 2 (whose utilization is over 90 percent), the other operations are not bottlenecks. Increasing their capacity will not materially affect customer service.

Decision Point Management must make some changes, such as providing more resources during peak times, reallocating tasks between the employees, adding another clerk, or improving the process with a particular attention to the subprocess performed by clerk 2.

Source: This case and simulation experience was provided by Professor Robert Klassen, University of Western Ontario. □

FIGURE 8.7

A Decision Tree for Capacity Expansion (Payoffs in Thousands of Dollars)

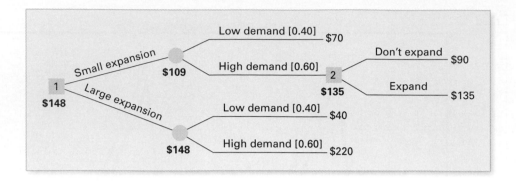

DECISION TREES

A decision tree can be particularly valuable for evaluating different capacity expansion alternatives when demand is uncertain and sequential decisions are involved (see the Decision Making supplement). For example, the owner of Grandmother's Chicken Restaurant (see Example 8.4) may expand the restaurant now, only to discover in year 4 that demand growth is much higher than forecasted. In that case, she needs to decide whether to expand further. In terms of construction costs and down time, expanding twice is likely to be much more expensive than building a large facility from the outset. However, making a large expansion now when demand growth is low means poor facility utilization. Much depends on the demand.

Figure 8.7 shows a decision tree for this view of the problem, with new information provided. Demand growth can be either low or high, with probabilities of 0.4 and 0.6, respectively. The initial expansion in year 1 (square node 1) can either be small or large. The second decision node (square node 2), whether to expand at a later date, is reached only if the initial expansion is small and demand turns out to be high. If demand is high and if the initial expansion was small, a decision must be made about a second expansion in year 4. Payoffs for each branch of the tree are estimated. For example, if the initial expansion is large, the financial benefit is either $40,000 or $220,000, depending on whether demand is low or high. Weighting these payoffs by the probabilities yields an expected value of $148,000. This expected payoff is higher than the $109,000 payoff for the small initial expansion, so the best choice is to make a large expansion in year 1.

MANAGING CAPACITY ACROSS THE ORGANIZATION

Managers make capacity choices at the organization level, as illustrated by J.P. Morgan Chase & Co. in our chapter opener. They also must make capacity decisions at the individual-process level in accounting, finance, human resources, information technology, marketing, and operations. Capacity issues can cut across departmental lines, because relieving a bottleneck in one part of an organization does not have the desirable effect unless a bottleneck in another part of the organization is also addressed. Managers everywhere must understand capacity measures, economies and diseconomies of scale, capacity cushions, timing-and-sizing strategies, capacity cushions, and trade-offs between customer service and capacity utilization. They also must understand how such capacity decisions link with other decisions that have to be made about their processes.

FORMULA REVIEW

1. Utilization, expressed as a percent:

$$\text{Utilization} = \frac{\text{Average output rate}}{\text{Maximum capacity}} \times 100\%$$

2. Capacity cushion, C, expressed as a percent:

$$C = 100\% - \text{Utilization (\%)}$$

3. a. Capacity requirement for one product:

$$M = \frac{Dp}{N[1 - (C/100)]}$$

   b. Capacity requirement for multiple products:

$$M = \frac{[Dp + (D/Q)s]_{\text{product 1}} + [Dp + (D/Q)s]_{\text{product 2}} + \cdots + [Dp + (D/Q)s]_{\text{product } n}}{N[1 - (C/100)]}$$

CHAPTER HIGHLIGHTS

❏ Operations managers plan for timely acquisition, use, and disposition of capacity.

❏ Long-term capacity planning is crucial to an organization's success because it often involves large investments in facilities and equipment and because such decisions are not easily reversed.

❏ Capacity can be stated in terms of either input or output measures. Output measures giving the number of products or services completed in a time period are useful when a firm provides *standardized* products or services. However, a statement of the number of *customized* products or services completed in a time period is meaningless, because the work content per unit varies. Demand for customized products and services must be translated into input measures, such as labor hours, machine hours, and material requirements.

❏ Operating at peak capacity calls for extraordinary effort, using marginal production methods, that usually is not sustainable. Maximum output under normal conditions is called effective capacity. The operation having the lowest effective capacity is called a bottleneck and limits the capacity of the entire system. Variable work loads and changing product mix complicate measuring capacity and can cause different operations to become bottlenecks under varying circumstances. Such floating bottlenecks make determining a firm's effective capacity difficult.

❏ Focusing capacity and scheduling decisions on bottleneck resources can help maximize the flow of total value-added funds.

❏ Economies of scale derive from spreading fixed costs, reducing construction costs, reducing purchased materials costs, and obtaining process advantages. Diseconomies of scale cause some firms to focus their operations and move to smaller, rather than larger, facilities.

❏ The desirable amount of capacity cushion varies, depending on competitive priorities, cost of unused capacity, resource flexibility, supply uncertainties, shelf life, variability and uncertainty of demand, and other factors.

❏ Three capacity strategies are expansionist, wait-and-see, and follow-the-leader. The expansionist strategy is attractive when there are economies of scale, learning effects, and a chance for preemptive marketing. The wait-and-see strategy minimizes risk by relying more on short-term options. The follow-the-leader strategy maintains the current balance between competitors.

❏ Capacity choices must be linked to other operations management decisions.

❏ The four steps in capacity planning are (1) estimate capacity requirements, (2) identify gaps, (3) develop alternatives, and (4) evaluate the alternatives.

❏ Waiting-line models help the manager choose the capacity level that best balances customer service and the cost of adding more capacity. As waiting-line problems involve more servers, mathematical models quickly become very complex. Simulation is used to analyze most multiple- server waiting-line situations. Decision trees are schematic models that can be helpful in evaluating different capacity-expansion alternatives when demand is uncertain and sequential decisions are involved.

KEY TERMS

base case *340*	cash flow *341*	peak capacity *327*
bottleneck *328*	diseconomies of scale *333*	rated capacity *327*
capacity *325*	drum–buffer–rope method *329*	setup time *338*
capacity cushion *334*	economies of scale *330*	theory of constraints (TOC) *329*
capacity gap *339*	effective capacity *327*	utilization *326*

SOLVED PROBLEM 1

You have been asked to put together a capacity plan for a critical bottleneck operation at the Surefoot Sandal Company. Your capacity measure is number of machines. Three products (men's, women's, and children's sandals) are manufactured. The time standards (processing and setup), lot sizes, and demand forecasts are given in the following table. The firm operates two 8-hour shifts, 5 days per week, 50 weeks per year. Experience shows that a capacity cushion of 5 percent is sufficient.

PRODUCT	TIME STANDARDS		LOT SIZE (pairs/lot)	DEMAND FORECAST (pairs/yr)
	Processing (hr/pair)	Setup (hr/lot)		
Men's sandals	0.05	0.5	240	80,000
Women's sandals	0.10	2.2	180	60,000
Children's sandals	0.02	3.8	360	120,000

a. How many machines are needed?

b. If the operation currently has two machines, what is the capacity gap?

SOLUTION

a. The number of hours of operation per year, N, is

$$N = \text{(2 shifts/day) (8 hours/shift) (250 days/machine-year)}$$

$$= 4{,}000 \text{ hours/machine-year}$$

The number of machines required, M, is the sum of machine-hour requirements for all three products divided by the number of productive hours available for one machine:

$$M = \frac{[Dp + (D/Q)s]_{\text{men}} + [Dp + (D/Q)s]_{\text{women}} + [Dp + (D/Q)s]_{\text{children}}}{N[1 - (C/100)]}$$

$$= \frac{[80{,}000(0.05) + (80{,}000/240)0.5] + [60{,}000(0.10) + (60{,}000/180)2.2]}{4{,}000[1 - (5/100)]}$$

$$= \frac{14{,}567 \text{ hours/year}}{3{,}800 \text{ hours/machine-year}} = 3.83 \quad \text{or} \quad 4 \text{ machines}$$

Solver - Capacity Requirements

Enter data in yellow-shaded areas.

Shifts/Day	2		Components	3		
Hours/Shift	8					
Days/Week	5		↑ More Components			
Weeks/Year	50		↓ Fewer Components			
Cushion (as %)	5%					
Current capacity	2					

Components	Processing (hr/unit)	Setup (hr/lot)	Lot Size (units/lot)	Demand Forecasts Pessimistic	Expected	Optimistic
Men's sandals	0.05	0.5	240		80,000	
Women's sandals	0.10	2.2	180		60,000	
Children's sandals	0.02	3.8	360		120,000	

Productive hours from one capacity unit for a year   3,800

	Pessimistic		Expected		Optimistic	
	Process	Setup	Process	Setup	Process	Setup
Men's sandals	0	0.0	4,000	166.7	0	0.0
Women's sandals	0	0.0	6,000	733.3	0	0.0
Children's sandals	0	0.0	2,400	1,266.7	0	0.0
	0	0.0	12,400	2,166.7	0	0.0
Total hours required		0.0		14,566.7		0.0

Total capacity requirements (M)	0.00	3.83	0.00
Rounded	0	4	0

Scenarios that can be met with current systems/capacity: **Pessimistic, Optimistic**

If capacity increased by	0%	
Expanded current capacity	3,800	

Total capacity requirements (M)	0.00	3.83	0.00
Rounded	0	4	0

Scenarios that can be met with expanded current capacity: **Pessimistic, Optimistic**

FIGURE 8.8 • Using the *Capacity Requirements Solver* for Solved Problem 1

b. The capacity gap is 1.83 machines (3.83 − 2). Two more machines should be purchased, unless management decides to use short-term options to fill the gap.

The *Capacity Requirements Solver* in OM Explorer confirms these calculations, as Figure 8.8 shows, using only the "Expected" scenario for the demand forecasts.

SOLVED PROBLEM 2

The base case for Grandmother's Chicken Restaurant (see Example 8.3) is to do nothing. The capacity of the kitchen in the base case is 80,000 meals per year. A capacity alternative for Grandmother's Chicken Restaurant is a two-stage expansion. This alternative expands the kitchen at the end of year 0, raising its capacity from 80,000 meals per year to that of the dining area (105,000 meals per year). If sales in year 1 and 2 live up to expectations, the capacities of both the kitchen and the dining room will be expanded at the *end* of year 3 to 130,000 meals per year. The initial investment would be $80,000 at the end of year 0 and an additional investment of $170,000 at the end of year 3. The pretax profit is $2 per meal. What are the pretax cash flows for this alternative through year 5, compared with the base case?

SOLUTION

Table 8.1 shows the cash inflows and outflows. The year 3 cash flow is unusual in two respects. First, the cash inflow from sales is $50,000 rather than $60,000. The increase in sales over the base is 25,000 meals (105,000 − 80,000) instead of 30,000 meals (110,000 − 80,000) because the restaurant's capacity falls somewhat short of demand. Second, a cash outflow of $170,000 occurs at the end of year 3, when the second-stage expansion occurs. The net cash flow for year 3 is $50,000 − $170,000 = −$120,000.

TABLE 8.1 *Cash Flows for Two-Stage Expansion at Grandmother's Chicken Restaurant*

YEAR	PROJECTED DEMAND (meals/yr)	PROJECTED CAPACITY (meals/yr)	CALCULATION OF INCREMENTAL CASH FLOW COMPARED TO BASE CASE (80,000 meals/yr)	CASH INFLOW (Outflow)
0	80,000	80,000	Increase kitchen capacity to 105,000 meals =	($80,000)
1	90,000	105,000	90,000 − 80,000 = (10,000 meals)($2/meal) =	$20,000
2	100,000	105,000	100,000 − 80,000 = (20,000 meals)($2/meal) =	$40,000
3	110,000	105,000	105,000 − 80,000 = (25,000 meals)($2/meal) =	$50,000
			Increase total capacity to 130,000 meals =	($170,000)
				($120,000)
4	120,000	130,000	120,000 − 80,000 = (40,000 meals)($2/meal) =	$80,000
5	130,000	130,000	130,000 − 80,000 = (50,000 meals)($2/meal) =	$100,000

SOLVED PROBLEM 3

Penelope and Peter Legume own a small accounting service and one personal computer. If their customers keep organized records, either of the owners can use the computer to prepare one tax return per hour, on average. During the first two weeks of April, both Legumes work seven 12-hour shifts. This allows them to use their computer around the clock.

a. What is the peak capacity, measured in tax returns per week?

b. The Legumes normally operate from 9 A.M. to 7 P.M., five days per week. What is their effective capacity, measured in tax returns per week?

c. During the third week of January, the Legumes processed 40 tax returns. What is their utilization, as a percent of effective capacity?

SOLUTION

a.   Peak capacity = (12 hours/shift) (2 shifts/day) (7 days/week) (1 return/hour)

= 168 returns/week

b. Although both Legumes may be present in the shop, the capacity is limited by the number of hours their one computer is available:

Effective capacity = (10 hours/day) (5 days/week) (1 return/hour)

= 50 returns/week

c. Utilization is the ratio of output to effective capacity:

$$\text{Utilization} = \frac{40 \text{ returns/week}}{50 \text{ returns/week}} \times 100\%$$

= 80%

DISCUSSION QUESTIONS

1. What are the economies of scale in operations management class size? As class size increases, what symptoms of diseconomies of scale appear?

2. A young boy has set up a lemonade stand on the corner of College Street and Air Park Boulevard. Temperatures in the area climb to 100° during the summer. The intersection is near a major university and a large construction site. Explain to this young entrepreneur how his business might benefit from economies of scale. Explain also some conditions that might lead to diseconomies of scale.

3. John B. Galipault, president of the Aviation Safety Institute, said: "Airlines since the mid-1970s have stuffed 20 percent more seats in the same-size aircraft." The standard first-class and coach configuration of an MD-11 holds about 300 passengers. With narrower, more upright seats and coach seating throughout, an MD-11 will seat about 410 passengers. Some 747s presently fly with 568 passengers. Double-deck airplanes are being designed to carry even more passengers. What are the trade-offs between safety and capacity utilization? What other facility changes are associated with increasing the number of passengers per plane?

4. Consider the Lower Florida Keys Health System and the Chaparral Steel tours in the Operations Strategy chapter and the Virtual Text on the Student CD-ROM. The organizations are quite different in terms of customization as a competitive priority, size of markets served, capital intensity, ability to use inventory to smooth output rates, and degree of certainty in future demands. What are the likely differences between these two organizations on whether output or input capacity measures are used, on desired capacity cushions, and on the need to exploit economies of scale? Explain.

OM EXPLORER AND INTERNET EXERCISES

Visit our Web site at www.prenhall.com/krajewski for OM Explorer Tutors, which explain quantitative techniques; Solvers, which help you apply mathematical models; and Internet Exercises, including Facility Tours, which expand on the topics in this chapter.

PROBLEMS

An icon next to a problem identifies the software that can be helpful, but not mandatory. The software is available on the Student CD-ROM that is packaged with every new copy of the textbook.

1. **OM Explorer** Bob Greer operates Bob's Garage and Manhole Cover Recycling Center at the corner of Lookout Highway and Ruff Road. Bob's Garage has one bay dedicated to wheel alignments. Although the recycling center is open at night, the garage normally is open only on weekdays from 7 A.M. to 7 P.M. and on Saturdays from 8 A.M. to noon. An alignment takes an average of 60 minutes to complete, although Bob charges customers for two hours according to a nationally published mechanic's labor-standard manual. During March, the height of pothole season, Bob's Garage is open from 6 A.M. to 10 P.M. on weekdays and from 6 A.M. to 6 P.M. on Saturdays.

   a. What are the garage's peak and effective capacities, in alignments per week?

   b. During the second week in March, Bob's Garage completed 90 alignments. What is the utilization as a percent of effective capacity? As a percent of peak capacity?

2. **OM Explorer** Sterling Motors is a telephone or mail-order dealer in British auto parts. Sterling has six telephones for receiving orders. Order takers answer the telephones, check inventory availability, and prepare picking tickets for the warehouse stockpickers. One order may consist of several lines, with a different part or multiple of a part ordered on each line. Each order taker can prepare picking tickets at a rate of one line every three minutes. The telephones are normally answered weekdays from 6 A.M. to 4 P.M., Pacific Time. Stock-pickers can fill and package parts at a rate of one line every five minutes. Sterling employs eight stock pickers, who normally work weekdays from 8 A.M. to 5 P.M. (except for lunch hours).

TABLE 8.2 *Capacity Information for Automotive Brake Supplier*

	TIME STANDARD			DEMAND FORECAST		
COMPONENT	Processing (hr/unit)	Setup (hr/lot)	LOT SIZE (units/lot)	Pessimistic	Expected	Optimistic
A	0.05	1.0	60	15,000	18,000	25,000
B	0.20	4.5	80	10,000	13,000	17,000
C	0.05	8.2	120	17,000	25,000	40,000

a. What is the effective capacity of order taking, in lines per week? Stockpicking?

b. For three weeks after the spring catalog is mailed in May, the eight warehouse employees work 10 hours per day between 7 A.M. and 6 P.M., six days per week. What is the peak capacity of the system, in lines per week?

c. During the second week of May, Sterling filled 5,000 order lines. What is the utilization as a percent of effective capacity? As a percent of peak capacity?

3. ● **OM Explorer** The Dahlia Medical Center has 30 labor rooms, 15 combination labor and delivery rooms, 3 delivery rooms, and 1 special delivery room reserved for complicated births. All of these facilities operate around the clock. Time spent in labor rooms varies from hours to days, with an average of about a day. The average uncomplicated delivery requires about one hour in a delivery room.

During an exceptionally busy three-day period, 115 healthy babies were born at or received by Dahlia Medical Center. Sixty babies were born in separate labor and delivery rooms, 45 were born in combined labor and delivery rooms, 6 were born en route to the hospital, and only 4 babies required a labor room and the complicated-delivery room. Which of the facilities (labor rooms, labor and delivery rooms, or delivery rooms) had the greatest utilization rate?

4. ● **OM Explorer** The Clip Joint operates four barber's chairs in the student center. During the week before semester break and the week before graduation, The Clip Joint experiences peak demands. Military-style haircuts take 5 minutes each, and other styles require 20 minutes each. Operating from 9 A.M. to 6 P.M. on the six days before semester break, The Clip Joint completes 500 military-style haircuts and 400 other haircuts. During a comparable six-day week before graduation, The Clip Joint completes 700 military haircuts and 300 other haircuts. In which week is utilization higher?

5. ● **OM Explorer** An automobile brake supplier operates on two eight-hour shifts, five days per week, 52 weeks per year. Table 8.2 shows the time standards, lot sizes, and demand forecasts for three components. Because of demand uncertainties, the operations manager obtained three demand forecasts (pessimistic, expected, and optimistic). The manager believes that a 20 percent capacity cushion is best.

a. What is the minimum number of machines needed? The expected number? The maximum number?

b. If the operation currently has three machines and the manager is willing to expand capacity by 20 percent through short-term options in the event that the optimistic demand occurs, what is the capacity gap?

6. ● **OM Explorer** Up, Up, and Away is a producer of kites and wind-socks. Relevant data on a bottleneck operation in the shop for the upcoming fiscal year are given in the following table:

ITEM	KITES	WINDSOCKS
Demand forecast	30,000 units/year	12,000 units/year
Lot size	20 units	70 units
Standard processing time	0.3 hour/unit	1.0 hour/unit
Standard setup time	3.0 hours/lot	4.0 hours/lot

The shop works two shifts per day, eight hours per shift, 200 days per year. There currently are four machines, and a 25 percent capacity cushion is desired. How many machines should be purchased to meet the upcoming year's demand without resorting to any short-term capacity solutions?

7. ● **OM Explorer** Tuff-Rider, Inc., manufactures touring bikes and mountain bikes in a variety of frame sizes, colors, and component combinations. Identical bicycles are produced in lots of 100. The projected demand, lot size, and time standards are shown in the following table:

ITEM	TOURING	MOUNTAIN
Demand forecast	5,000 units/year	10,000 units/year
Lot size	100 units	100 units
Standard processing time	1/4 hour/unit	1/2 hour/unit
Standard setup time	2 hour/lot	3 hour/lot

The shop currently works eight hours a day, five days a week, 50 weeks a year. It has five workstations, each producing one bicycle in the time shown in the table. The shop maintains a 15 percent capacity cushion. How many workstations will be required next year to meet expected demand without using overtime and without decreasing the firm's current capacity cushion?

8. 🔘 **OM Explorer** Accumold, Inc., supplies a molded part to several large automobile manufacturers. Its molding department works eight hours a day, five days a week, and has 10 machines. Under ideal operating conditions, each machine is capable of producing 50 parts per hour. The molding department produced 350,000 parts during the past six months (i.e., 25 working weeks), and management believes that this output can be sustained economically over long periods of time. To meet the current level of demand, each machine is producing at the rate of 40 parts per hour.

   a. What is the peak capacity of the department in parts per day? Currently, what is the utilization of the department relative to its peak capacity?

   b. What is the effective capacity of the department in parts per day? Currently, what is the utilization of the department relative to its effective capacity?

   c. What is the current capacity cushion in the molding department?

9. 🔘 **OM Explorer** Worcester Athletic Club is considering expanding its facility to include two adjacent suites. The owner will remodel the suites in consideration of a seven-year lease. Expenditures for rent, insurance, utilities, and exercise equipment leasing would increase by $45,000 per year. This expansion would increase Worcester's lunchtime rush hour capacity from the present 150 members to 225 members. A maximum of 30 percent of the total membership attends the Athletic Club during any one lunch hour. Therefore, Worcester's facility can presently serve a total membership of 500. Membership fees are $40 per month. Based on the following membership forecasts, determine what before-tax cash flows the expansion will produce for the next several years:

YEAR	1	2	3	4	5	6	7
MEMBERSHIP	450	480	510	515	530	550	600

10. Arabelle is considering expanding the floor area of her high-fashion import clothing store, The French Prints of Arabelle, by increasing her leased space in the upscale Cherry Creek Mall from 2,000 square feet to 3,000 square feet. The Cherry Creek Mall boasts one of the country's highest ratios of sales value per square foot. Rents (including utilities, security, and similar costs) are $110 per square foot per year. Salary increases related to French Prints' expansion are shown in the following table, along with projections of sales per square foot. The purchase cost of goods sold averages 70 percent of the sales price. Sales are seasonal, with an important peak during the year-end holiday season.

YEAR	QUARTER	SALES (per sq ft)	INCREMENTAL SALARIES
1	1	$ 90	$12,000
	2	60	8,000
	3	110	12,000
	4	240	24,000
2	1	99	12,000
	2	66	8,000
	3	121	12,000
	4	264	24,000

   a. If Arabelle expands French Prints at the end of year 0, what will her quarterly pretax cash flows be through year 2?

   b. Project the quarterly pretax cash flows assuming that the sales pattern (10 percent annually compounded increase) continues through year 3.

11. The Astro World amusement park has the opportunity to expand its size now (the end of year 0) by purchasing adjacent property for $250,000 and adding attractions at a cost of $550,000. This expansion is expected to increase attendance by 30 percent over projected attendance without expansion. The price of admission is $30, with a $5 increase planned for the beginning of year 3. Additional operating costs are expected to be $100,000 per year. Estimated attendance for the next five years, *without expansion*, follows:

YEAR	1	2	3	4	5
ATTENDANCE	30,000	34,000	36,250	38,500	41,000

a. What are the pretax combined cash flows for years 0 through 5 that are attributable to the park's expansion?

b. Ignoring tax, depreciation, and the time value of money, determine how long it will take to recover (pay back) the investment.

12. Kim Epson operates a full-service car wash, which operates from 8 A.M. to 8 P.M., seven days a week. The car wash has two stations: an automatic washing and drying station and a manual interior cleaning station. The automatic washing and drying station can handle 30 cars per hour. The interior cleaning station can handle 200 cars per day. Based on a recent year-end review of operations, Kim estimates that future demand for the interior cleaning station for the seven days of the week, expressed in average number of cars per day, would be as follows:

DAY	Mon.	Tues.	Wed.	Thurs.	Fri.	Sat.	Sun.
CARS	160	180	150	140	280	300	250

By installing additional equipment (at a cost of $50,000) Kim can increase the capacity of the interior cleaning station to 300 cars per day. Each car wash generates a pretax contribution of $4.00. Should Kim install the additional equipment if she expects a pretax payback period of three years or less?

13. Roche Brothers is considering a capacity expansion of its supermarket. The landowner will build the addition to suit in return for $200,000 upon completion and a five-year lease. The increase in rent for the addition is $10,000 per month. The annual sales projected through year 5 follow. The current effective capacity is equivalent to 500,000 customers per year. Assume a 2 percent pretax profit on sales.

YEAR	1	2	3	4	5
CUSTOMERS	560,000	600,000	685,000	700,000	715,000
AVERAGE SALES PER CUSTOMER	$50.00	$53.00	$56.00	$60.00	$64.00

a. If Roche expands its capacity to serve 700,000 customers per year now (end of year 0), what are the projected annual incremental pretax cash flows attributable to this expansion?

b. If Roche expands its capacity to serve 700,000 customers per year at the end of year 2, the landowner will build the same addition for $240,000 and a

three-year lease at $12,000 per month. What are the projected annual incremental pretax cash flows attributable to this expansion alternative?

Advanced Problems

Problems 14, 17, and 18 require reading of the Decision Making supplement. Problems 15 and 18 require reading of CD supplement on Financial Analysis.

14. **SmartDraw** A manager is trying to decide whether to buy one machine or two. If only one machine is purchased and demand proves to be excessive, the second machine can be purchased later. Some sales would be lost, however, because the lead time for delivery of this type of machine is six months. In addition, the cost per machine will be lower if both machines are purchased at the same time. The probability of low demand is estimated to be 0.30 and that of high demand, 0.70. The after-tax net present value of the benefits (NPV) from purchasing two machines together is $90,000 if demand is low and $170,000 if demand is high.

If one machine is purchased and demand is low, the NPV is $120,000. If demand is high, the manager has three options. Doing nothing, which has an NPV of $120,000; subcontracting, with an NPV of $140,000; and buying the second machine, with an NPV of $130,000.

a. Draw a decision tree for this problem.

b. What is the best decision and what is its expected payoff?

15. **OM Explorer** Several years ago, River City built a water purification plant to remove toxins and filter the city's drinking water. Because of population growth, the demand for water next year will be more than the plant's capacity of 120 million gallons per year. Therefore, the city must expand the facility. The estimated demand over the next 20 years is given in Table 8.3.

TABLE 8.3 *Water Demand*					
YEAR	CAPACITY	YEAR	CAPACITY	YEAR	CAPACITY
0	120	7	148	14	176
1	124	8	152	15	180
2	128	9	156	16	184
3	132	10	160	17	188
4	136	11	164	18	192
5	140	12	168	19	196
6	144	13	172	20	200

The city planning commission is considering three alternatives.

- *Alternative 1.* Expand enough at the end of year 0 to last 20 years. This means an 80 million gallon increase (200–120).
- *Alternative 2.* Expand at the end of year 0 and at the end of year 10.
- *Alternative 3.* Expand at the end of years 0, 5, 10, and 15.

Each alternative would provide the needed 200 million gallons per year at the end of 20 years, when the value of the plant would be the same regardless of the alternative chosen. There are significant economies of scale in construction costs: A 20 million gallon expansion would cost $18 million; a 40 million gallon expansion, $30 million; and an 80 million gallon expansion, only $50 million. The level of future interest rates is uncertain, leading to uncertainty about the hurdle rate. The city believes that it could be as low as 12 percent and as high as 16 percent (see the Decision Making supplement).

a. Compute the cash flows for each alternative, compared to a base case of doing nothing. (*Note*: As a municipal utility, the operation pays no taxes.)

b. Which alternative minimizes the present value of construction costs over the next 20 years if the discount rate is 12 percent? 16 percent?

c. Because the decision involves public policy and compromise, what political considerations does the planning commission face?

16. Two new alternatives have come up for expanding Grandmother's Chicken Restaurant (see Solved Problem 2). They involve more automation in the kitchen and feature a special cooking process that retains the original-recipe taste of the chicken. Although the process is more capital-intensive, it would drive down labor costs, so the pretax profit for *all* sales (not just the sales from the capacity added) would go up from 20 to 22 percent. This gain would increase the pretax profit by 2 percent of each sales dollar through $800,000 (80,000 meals × $10) and by 22 percent of each sales dollar between $800,000 and the new capacity limit. Otherwise, the new alternatives are much the same as those in Example 8.4 and Solved Problem 2.

Alternative 1. Expand both the kitchen and the dining area now (at the end of year 0), raising the capacity to 130,000 meals per year. The cost of construction, including the new automation, would be $336,000 (rather than the earlier $200,000).

Alternative 2. Expand only the kitchen now, raising its capacity to 105,000 meals per year. At the end of year 3, expand both the kitchen and the dining area to the 130,000 meals-per-year volume. Construction and equipment costs would be $424,000, with $220,000 at the end of year 0 and the remainder at the end of year 3. As with alternative 1, the contribution margin would go up to 22 percent.

With both new alternatives, the salvage value would be negligible. Compare the cash flows of all alternatives. Should Grandmother's Chicken Restaurant expand with the new or the old technology? Should it expand now or later?

17. ● **SmartDraw** Acme Steel Fabricators has experienced booming business for the past five years. The company fabricates a wide range of steel products, such as railings, ladders, and light structural steel framing. The current manual method of materials handling is causing excessive inventories and congestion. Acme is considering the purchase of an overhead rail-mounted hoist system or a forklift truck to increase capacity and improve manufacturing efficiency.

The annual pretax payoff from the system depends on future demand. If demand stays at the current level, the probability of which is 0.50, annual savings from the overhead hoist will be $10,000. If demand rises, the hoist will save $25,000 annually because of operating efficiencies in addition to new sales. Finally, if demand falls, the hoist will result in an estimated annual loss of $65,000. The probability is estimated to be 0.30 for higher demand and 0.20 for lower demand.

If the forklift is purchased, annual payoffs will be $5,000 if demand is unchanged, $10,000 if demand rises, and –$25,000 if demand falls.

a. Draw a decision tree for this problem, and compute the expected value of the payoff for each alternative.

b. Which is the best alternative, based on the expected values?

18. ● **SmartDraw** The vice-president of operations at Dintell Corporation, a major supplier of passenger-side automotive air bags, is considering a $50 million expansion at the firm's Fort Worth production complex. The most recent economic projections indicate a 0.60 probability that the overall market will be $400 million per year over the next five years and a 0.40 probability that the market will be only $200 million per year during the same period. The marketing department estimates that Dintell has a 0.50 probability of capturing 40 percent of the market and an equal probability of obtaining only 30 percent of the market. The cost of goods sold is estimated to be 70 percent of sales. For planning purposes, the company currently uses a 12 percent discount rate, a 40 percent

tax rate, and the MACRS depreciation schedule (see CD supplement on Financial Analysis). The criteria for investment decisions at Dintell are (1) the net expected present value must be greater than zero; (2) there must be at least a 70 percent chance that the net present value will be positive; and (3) there must be no more than a 10 percent chance that the firm will lose more than 20 percent of the initial value.

a. Based on the stated criteria, determine whether Dintell should fund the project.

b. What effect will a probability of 0.70 of capturing 40 percent of the market have on the decision?

c. What effect will an increase in the discount rate of 15 percent have on the decision? A decrease of 10 percent?

d. What effect will the need for another $10 million in the third year have on the decision?

SIMULATION EXERCISES

These simulation exercises require the use of the Extend and SimQuick simulation packages. Extend is on the Student CD-ROM that is packaged with every new copy of the textbook. SimQuick is an optional simulation package that your instructor may or may not have ordered.

1. Consider the process at the Canadian provincial department of motor vehicles, which is introduced as Example 8.5. Use the Extend simulator to identify bottlenecks, capacity cushions, and ways of improving the effectiveness of the process. See the full *Provincial Automobile License Renewals* case on the Student CD-ROM, along with the basic model and information on how to use it. Answer the various questions asked about the capacity of the process.

2. A jewelry box is made from the following parts: two identical square pieces (the top and bottom), four identical rectangular pieces (the sides), and a hinge.

At the beginning of the process is a pile of sheets of wood. One sheet at a time is taken to the cutter, which cuts four square pieces and eight rectangular pieces. The four square pieces are sent to a buffer inventory, which feeds the TB finishing machine that makes them into tops and bottoms. The parts are then taken to a buffer inventory. The eight rectangular pieces are also sent to a buffer inventory, which feeds the S finishing machine that makes them into sides. After this operation, the sides are taken to another buffer inventory. The final workstation is the box assembly, which assembles the top, bottom, and sides to make a finished jewelry box. Management knows that the S finishing machine is a bottleneck. Use SimQuick to determine the increase in throughput if the S finishing machine is replaced with a faster one. See Example 14 in SimQuick, *Process Simulation in Excel*, for details about this problem and additional exercises.

CASE FITNESS PLUS, PART A

Fitness Plus, Part B, explores alternatives to expanding a new downtown facility and is included in the Instructor's Manual. *If you're interested in this topic, ask your instructor for a preview.*

Fitness Plus is a full-service health and sports club in Greensboro, North Carolina. The club provides a range of facilities and services to support three primary activities: fitness, recreation, and relaxation. Fitness activities generally take place in four areas of the club: the aerobics room, which can accommodate 35 people per class; a room equipped with free weights; a workout room with 24 pieces of Nautilus equipment; and a large workout room containing 29 pieces of cardiovascular equipment. This equipment includes nine stairsteppers, six treadmills, six life-cycle bikes, three airdyne bikes, two cross-aerobics machines, two rowing machines, and one climber. Recreational facilities comprise eight racquetball courts, six tennis courts, and a large outdoor pool. Fitness Plus also sponsors softball, volleyball, and swim teams in city recreation leagues. Relaxation is accomplished through yoga classes held twice a week in the aerobics room, whirlpool tubs located in each locker room, and a trained massage therapist.

Situated in a large suburban office park, Fitness Plus opened its doors in 1991. During the first two years, membership was small and use of the facilities was light. By 1992, membership had grown as fitness began to play a large role in more and more people's lives. Along with this growth came increased use of club facilities. Records indicate that, in 1995, an average of 15 members per hour checked into the club during a typical day. Of course, the actual number of members per hour varied by both day and time. On some days during a slow period, only six to eight members would check in per hour. At a peak time, such as Mondays from 4:00 P.M. to 7:00 P.M., the number would be as high as 40 per hour.

The club was open from 6:30 A.M. to 11:00 P.M. Monday through Thursday. On Friday and Saturday, the club closed at 8:00 P.M., and on Sunday the hours were 12:00 noon to 8:00 P.M.

As the popularity of health and fitness continued to grow, so did Fitness Plus. By May 2000, the average number of members arriving per hour during a typical day had increased to 25. The lowest period had a rate of 10 members per hour; during peak periods, 80 members per hour checked in to use the facilities. This growth brought complaints from members about overcrowding and unavailability of equipment. Most of these complaints centered on the Nautilus, cardiovascular, and aerobics fitness areas. The owners began to wonder whether the club was indeed too small for its membership. Past research had indicated

that individuals work out an average of 60 minutes per visit. Data collected from member surveys showed the following facilities usage pattern: 30 percent of the members do aerobics, 40 percent use the cardiovascular equipment, 25 percent use the Nautilus machines, 20 percent use the free weights, 15 percent use the racquetball courts, and 10 percent use the tennis courts. The owners wondered whether they could use this information to estimate how well existing capacity was being utilized.

If capacity levels were being stretched, now was the time to decide what to do. It was already May, and any expansion of the existing facility would take at least four months. The owners knew that January was always a peak membership enrollment month and that any new capacity needed to be ready by then. However, other factors had to be considered. The area was growing both in terms of population and geographically. The downtown area had just received a major facelift, and many new offices and businesses were moving back to it, causing a resurgence in activity.

With this growth came increased competition. A new YMCA was offering a full range of services at a low cost. Two new health and fitness facilities had opened within the past year in locations 10 to 15 minutes from Fitness Plus. The first, called the Oasis, catered to the young adult crowd and restricted the access of children under 16 years old. The other facility, Gold's Gym, provided excellent weight and cardiovascular training only.

As the owners thought about the situation, they had many questions: Were the capacities of the existing facilities constrained, and if so, where? If capacity expansion was necessary, should the existing facility be expanded? Because of the limited amount of land at the present site, expansion of some services might require reducing the capacity of others. Finally, owing to increased competition and growth downtown, was now the time to open a facility to serve that market? A new facility would take six months to renovate, and the financial resources were not available to do both.

Questions

1. What method would you use to measure the capacity of Fitness Plus? Has Fitness Plus reached its capacity?
2. Which capacity strategy would be appropriate for Fitness Plus? Justify your answer.
3. How would you link the capacity decision being made by Fitness Plus to other types of operating decisions?

SELECTED REFERENCES

"Avoiding Plant Failures Grows More Difficult for Many Industries." *Wall Street Journal* (January 8, 1981).

Bakke, Nils Arne, and Ronald Hellberg. "The Challenges of Capacity Planning." *International Journal of Production Economics,* 31–30 (1993), pp. 243–264.

Bowman, Edward H. "Scale of Operations—An Empirical Study." *Operations Research* (June 1958), pp. 320–328.

Goldratt, E. Y., and J. Cox. *The Goal.* New York: North River, 1984.

Hammesfahr, R. D., Jack, James A. Pope, and Alireza Ardalan. "Strategic Planning for Production Capacity." *International Journal of Operations and Production Management,* vol. 13, no. 5 (1993), pp. 41–53.

"How Goliaths Can Act Like Davids." *Business Week/Enterprise* (1993), pp. 192–200.

"Logan's Roadhouse." *Business Week* (May 27, 1996), p. 113.

Ritzman, Larry P., and M. Hossein Safizadeh. "Linking Process Choice with Plant-Level Decisions about Capital and Human Resources." *Production and Operations Management,* vol. 8, no. 4 (1999), pp. 374–392.

Sassar, W. Earl. "Match Supply and Demand in Service Industries." *Harvard Business Review* (November–December 1976), pp. 133–140.

Simons, Jacob, Jr., and Wendell P. Simpson III. "An Exposition of Multiple Constraint Scheduling as Implemented in the Goal System (Formerly Disaster™)." *Production and Operations Management,* vol. 6, no. 1 (Spring 1997), pp. 3–22.

Skinner, Wickham. "The Focused Factory." *Harvard Business Review* (May–June 1974), pp. 113–121.

"Wow! That's Some Bank." *Business Week* (September 11, 1995), pp. 36–39.

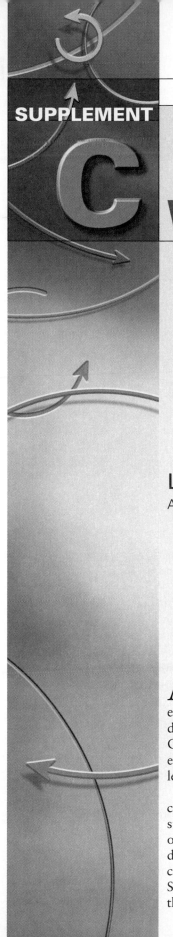

Waiting Lines

Learning Goals

After reading this supplement, you will be able to . . .

1. recognize the elements of a waiting-line problem in a real situation.
2. use waiting-line models to estimate the operating characteristics of a system.
3. know when to use the single-server, multiple-server, and finite-source models.
4. describe how waiting-line models can be used to make managerial decisions.

A NYONE WHO HAS HAD to wait at a stoplight, at McDonald's, or at the registrar's office has experienced the dynamics of waiting lines. Perhaps one of the best examples of effective management of waiting lines is that of Walt Disney World. One day there may be only 25,000 customers, but on another day there may be 90,000. Careful analysis of process flows, technology for people-mover (materials handling) equipment, capacity, and layout keeps the waiting times for attractions to acceptable levels.

The analysis of waiting lines is of concern to managers because it affects design, capacity planning, layout planning, inventory management, and scheduling. In this supplement we discuss why waiting lines form, the uses of waiting-line models in operations management, and the structure of waiting-line models. We also discuss the decisions managers address with the models. Waiting lines can also be analyzed using computer simulation. Software such as Extend, included in the Student CD-ROM, or SimQuick, an optional simulation package, can be used to analyze the problems in this supplement (see the Simulation supplement for more details).

WHY WAITING LINES FORM

waiting line One or more "customers" waiting for service.

A **waiting line** is one or more "customers" waiting for service. The customers can be people or inanimate objects such as machines requiring maintenance, sales orders waiting for shipping, or inventory items waiting to be used. A waiting line forms because of a temporary imbalance between the demand for service and the capacity of the system to provide the service. In most real-life waiting-line problems, the demand rate varies; that is, customers arrive at unpredictable intervals. Most often, the rate of producing the service also varies, depending on customer needs. Suppose that bank customers arrive at an average rate of 15 per hour throughout the day and that the bank can process an average of 20 customers per hour. Why would a waiting line ever develop? The answers are that the customer arrival rate varies throughout the day and the time required to process a customer can vary. During the noon hour, 30 customers may arrive at the bank. Some of them may have complicated transactions, requiring above-average process times. The waiting line may grow to 15 customers for a period of time before it eventually disappears. Even though the bank manager provided for more than enough capacity on average, waiting lines can still develop.

Waiting lines can develop even if the time to process a customer is constant. For example, a subway train is computer controlled to arrive at stations along its route. Each train is programmed to arrive at a station, say, every 15 minutes. Even with the constant service time, waiting lines develop while riders wait for the next train or can not get on a train because of the size of the crowd at a busy time of the day. Consequently, variability in the rate of demand determines the sizes of the waiting lines in this case. In general, if there is no variability in the demand or service rates and enough capacity has been provided, no waiting lines form.

USES OF WAITING-LINE THEORY

Waiting-line theory applies to service as well as manufacturing firms, relating customer arrival and service-system processing characteristics to service-system output characteristics. In our discussion, we use the term *service* broadly—the act of doing work for a customer. The service system might be hair cutting at a hair salon, satisfying customer complaints, or processing a production order of parts on a certain machine. Other examples of customers and services include lines of theatergoers waiting to purchase tickets, trucks waiting to be unloaded at a warehouse, machines waiting to be repaired by a maintenance crew, and patients waiting to be examined by a physician. Regardless of the situation, waiting-line problems have several common elements.

STRUCTURE OF WAITING-LINE PROBLEMS

customer population An input that generates potential customers.

service facility A person (or crew), a machine (or group of machines), or both necessary to perform the service for the customer.

Analyzing waiting-line problems begins with a description of the situation's basic elements. Each specific situation will have different characteristics, but four elements are common to all situations:

1. an input, or **customer population**, that generates potential customers;
2. a waiting line of customers;
3. the **service facility**, consisting of a person (or crew), a machine (or group of machines), or both necessary to perform the service for the customer; and
4. a **priority rule**, which selects the next customer to be served by the service facility.

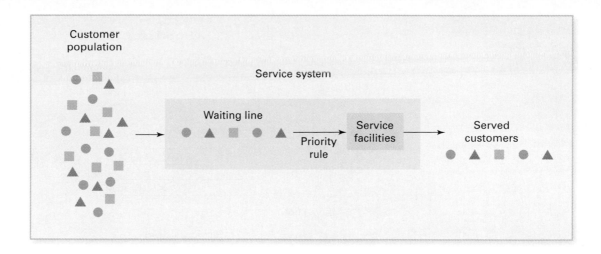

FIGURE C.1

Basic Elements of Waiting-Line Models

priority rule A rule that selects the next customer to be served at the service facility.

service system The number of lines and the arrangement of the facilities.

Figure C.1 shows these basic elements. The **service system** describes the number of lines and the arrangement of the facilities. After the service has been performed, the served customers leave the system.

CUSTOMER POPULATION

A customer population is the source of input to the **service system.** If the potential number of new customers for the service system is appreciably affected by the number of customers already in the system, the input source is said to be *finite*. For example, suppose that a maintenance crew is assigned responsibility for the repair of 10 machines. The customer population for the maintenance crew is 10 machines in working order. The population generates customers for the maintenance crew as a function of the failure rates for the machines. As more machines fail and enter the service system, either waiting for service or being repaired, the customer population becomes smaller and the rate at which it can generate another customer falls. Consequently, the customer population is said to be finite.

Alternatively, an *infinite* customer population is one in which the number of customers in the system does not affect the rate at which the population generates new customers. For example, consider a mail-order operation for which the customer population consists of shoppers who have received a catalog of products sold by the company. Because the customer population is so large and only a small fraction of the shoppers place orders at any one time, the number of new orders it generates is not appreciably affected by the number of orders waiting for service or being processed by the service system. In this case, the customer population is said to be infinite.

Customers in waiting lines may be *patient* or *impatient*, which has nothing to do with the colorful language a customer may use while waiting in line for a long time on a hot day. In the context of waiting-line problems, a patient customer is one who enters the system and remains there until being served; an impatient customer is one who either decides not to enter the system (balks) or leaves the system before being served (reneges). For the methods used in this supplement, we make the simplifying assumption that all customers are patient.

THE SERVICE SYSTEM

The service system may be described by the number of lines and the arrangement of facilities.

FIGURE C.2

*Waiting-Line
Arrangements*

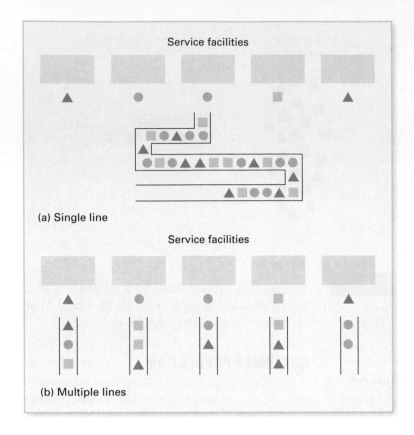

(a) Single line

(b) Multiple lines

NUMBER OF LINES. Waiting lines may be designed to be a *single line* or *multiple lines*. Figure C.2 shows an example of each arrangement. Generally, single lines are utilized at airline counters, inside banks, and at some fast-food restaurants, whereas multiple lines are utilized in grocery stores, at drive-in bank operations, and in discount stores. When multiple servers are available and each one can handle general transactions, the single-line arrangement keeps servers uniformly busy and gives customers a sense of fairness. Customers believe that they are being served on the basis of when they arrived, not how well they guessed their waiting time when selecting a particular line. The multiple-line design is best when some of the servers provide a limited set of services. In this arrangement, customers select the services they need and wait in the line where that service is provided, such as at a grocery store where there are special lines for customers paying with cash or having fewer than 10 items.

Sometimes, queues are not organized neatly into "lines." Machines that need repair on the production floor of a factory may be left in place, and the maintenance crew comes to them. Nonetheless, we can think of such machines as forming a single line or multiple lines, depending on the number of repair crews and their specialties. Likewise, passengers who telephone for a taxi also form a line even though they may wait at different locations.

ARRANGEMENT OF SERVICE FACILITIES. Service facilities consist of the personnel and equipment necessary to perform the service for the customer. Figure C.3 shows examples of the five basic types of service facility arrangements. Managers should choose an arrangement based on customer volume and the nature of services performed. Some services require a single step, also called a **phase**, whereas others require a sequence of steps.

phase A single step in providing a service.

Weary tourists wait to check in at a hotel registration desk.

In the *single-channel, single-phase* system, all services demanded by a customer can be performed by a single-server facility. Customers form a single line and go through the service facility one at a time. Examples are a drive-through car wash and a machine that must process several batches of parts.

The *single-channel, multiple-phase* arrangement is used when the services are best performed in sequence by more than one facility, yet customer volume or other constraints limit the design to one channel. Customers form a single line and proceed sequentially from one service facility to the next. An example of this arrangement is a McDonald's drive-through, where the first facility takes the order, the second takes the money, and the third provides the food.

FIGURE C.3

Examples of Service Facility Arrangements

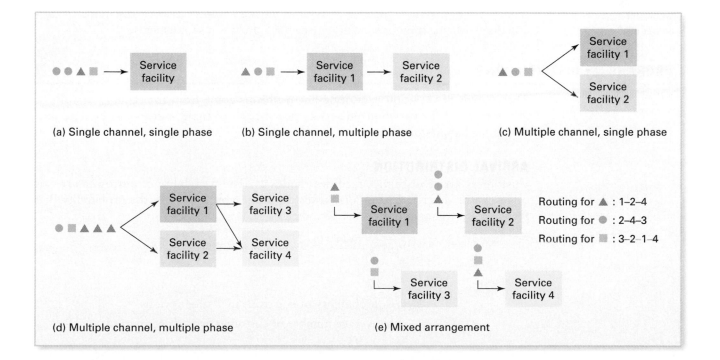

The *multiple-channel, single-phase* arrangement is used when demand is large enough to warrant providing the same service at more than one facility or when the services offered by the facilities are different. Customers form one or more lines, depending on the design. In the single-line design, customers are served by the first available server, as in the lobby of a bank. If each channel has its own waiting line, customers wait until the server for their line can serve them, as at a bank's drive-through facilities.

The *multiple-channel, multiple-phase* arrangement occurs when customers can be served by one of the first-phase facilities but then require service from a second-phase facility, and so on. In some cases, customers cannot switch channels after service has begun; in others they can. An example of this arrangement is a laundromat. Washing machines are the first-phase facilities, and dryers are the second-phase facilities. Some of the washing machines and dryers may be designed for extra-large loads, thereby providing the customer a choice of channels.

The most complex waiting-line problem involves customers who have unique sequences of required services; consequently, service can not be described neatly in phases. A *mixed* arrangement is used in such a case. In the mixed arrangement, waiting lines can develop in front of each facility, as in a job shop, where each customized job may require the use of various machines and different routings.

PRIORITY RULE

The priority rule determines which customer to serve next. Most service systems that you encounter use the first-come, first-served (FCFS) rule. The customer at the head of the waiting line has the highest priority, and the customer who arrived last has the lowest priority. Other priority disciplines might take the customer with the earliest promised due date (EDD) or the customer with the shortest expected processing time (SPT). We focus on FCFS in this supplement and discuss EDD and SPT elsewhere (see the Scheduling chapter).

preemptive discipline A rule that allows a customer of higher priority to interrupt the service of another customer.

A **preemptive discipline** is a rule that allows a customer of higher priority to interrupt the service of another customer. For example, in a hospital emergency room, patients with the most life-threatening injuries receive treatment first, regardless of their order of arrival. Modeling of systems having complex priority disciplines is usually done using computer simulation (see the Simulation supplement).

PROBABILITY DISTRIBUTIONS

The sources of variation in waiting-line problems come from the random arrivals of customers and the variations in service times. Each of these sources can be described with a probability distribution.

ARRIVAL DISTRIBUTION

Customers arrive at service facilities randomly. The variability of customer arrivals often can be described by a Poisson distribution, which specifies the probability that n customers will arrive in T time periods:

$$P(n) = \frac{(\lambda T)^n}{n!} e^{-\lambda T} \qquad \text{for } n = 0, 1, 2, \ldots$$

where

$$P(n) = \text{probability of } n \text{ arrivals in } T \text{ time periods}$$
$$\lambda = \text{average number of customer arrivals per period}$$
$$e = 2.7183$$

The mean of the Poisson distribution is λT, and the variance also is λT. The Poisson distribution is a discrete distribution; that is, the probabilities are for a specific number of arrivals per unit of time.

| EXAMPLE C.1 | *Calculating the Probability of Customer Arrivals* |

Management is redesigning the customer service process in a large department store. Accommodating four customers is important. Customers arrive at the desk at the rate of two customers per hour. What is the probability that four customers will arrive during any hour?

SOLUTION

In this case $\lambda = 2$ customers per hour, $T = 1$ hour, and $n = 4$ customers. The probability that four customers will arrive in any hour is

$$P(4) = \frac{[2(1)]^4}{4!} e^{-2(1)} = \frac{16}{24} e^{-2} = 0.090$$

Decision Point The manager of the customer service desk can use this information to determine the space requirements for the desk and waiting area. There is a relatively small probability that four customers will arrive in any hour. Consequently, seating capacity for two or three customers should be more than adequate unless the time to service each customer is lengthy. Further analysis on service times is warranted. ⊐

interarrival times The time between customer arrivals.

Another way to specify the arrival distribution is to do it in terms of customer **interarrival times**—that is, the time between customer arrivals. If the customer population generates customers according to a Poisson distribution, the *exponential distribution* describes the probability that the next customer will arrive in the next T time periods. As the exponential distribution also describes service times, we discuss the details of this distribution in the next section.

SERVICE TIME DISTRIBUTION

The exponential distribution describes the probability that the service time of the customer at a particular facility will be no more than T time periods. The probability can be calculated by using the formula

$$P(t \leq T) = 1 - e^{-\mu T}$$

where

μ = mean number of customers completing service per period

t = service time of the customer

T = target service time

The mean of the service time distribution is $1/\mu$, and the variance is $(1/\mu)^2$. As T increases, the probability that the customer's service time will be less than T approaches 1.0.

For simplicity, let us look at a single-channel, single-phase arrangement.

| EXAMPLE C.2 | *Calculating the Service Time Probability* |

The management of the large department store in Example C.1 must determine if more training is needed for the customer service clerk. The clerk at the customer service desk can serve an average of three customers per hour. What is the probability that a customer will require less than 10 minutes of service?

SOLUTION

We must have all the data in the same time units. Because $\mu = 3$ customers per *hour*, we convert minutes of time to hours, or $T = 10$ minutes $= 10/60$ hour $= 0.167$ hour. Then

$$P(t \leq T) = 1 - e^{-\mu T}$$
$$P(t \leq 0.167 \text{ hour}) = 1 - e^{-3(0.167)} = 1 - 0.61 = 0.39$$

Decision Point The probability that the clerk will require only 10 minutes or less is not very high, which leaves the possibility that customers may experience lengthy delays. Management should consider additional training for the clerk so as to reduce the time it takes to process a customer request. ❐

Some characteristics of the exponential distribution do not always conform to an actual situation. The exponential distribution model is based on the assumption that each service time is independent of those that preceded it. In real life, however, productivity may improve as human servers learn about the work. Another assumption underlying the model is that very small, as well as very large, service times are possible. However, real-life situations often require a fixed-length start-up time, some cutoff on total service time, or nearly constant service time.

USING WAITING-LINE MODELS TO ANALYZE OPERATIONS

Operations managers can use waiting-line models to balance the gains that might be made by increasing the efficiency of the service system against the costs of doing so. In addition, managers should consider the costs of *not* making improvements to the system: Long waiting lines or long waiting times may cause customers to balk or renege. Managers should therefore be concerned about the following operating characteristics of the system.

1. *Line Length.* The number of customers in the waiting line reflects one of two conditions. Short queues could mean either good customer service or too much capacity. Similarly, long queues could indicate either low server efficiency or the need to increase capacity.

2. *Number of Customers in System.* The number of customers in queue and being served also relates to service efficiency and capacity. A large number of customers in the system causes congestion and may result in customer dissatisfaction, unless more capacity is added.

3. *Waiting Time in Line.* Long lines do not always mean long waiting times. If the service rate is fast, a long line can be served efficiently. However, when waiting time seems long, customers perceive the quality of service to be poor. Managers may try to change the arrival rate of customers or design the system to make long wait times seem shorter than they really are. For example, at Walt Disney World customers in line for an attraction are entertained by videos and also are informed about expected waiting times, which seems to help them endure the wait.

4. *Total Time in System.* The total elapsed time from entry into the system until exit from the system may indicate problems with customers, server efficiency, or capacity. If some customers are spending too much time in the service system, there may be a need to change the priority discipline, increase productivity, or adjust capacity in some way.

5. *Service Facility Utilization.* The collective utilization of service facilities reflects the percentage of time that they are busy. Management's goal is to

maintain high utilization and profitability without adversely affecting the other operating characteristics.

The best method for analyzing a waiting-line problem is to relate the five operating characteristics and their alternatives to dollars. However, placing a dollar figure on certain characteristics (such as the waiting time of a shopper in a grocery store) is difficult. In such cases, an analyst must weigh the cost of implementing the alternative under consideration against a subjective assessment of the cost of *not* making the change.

We now present three models and some examples showing how waiting-line models can help operations managers make decisions. We analyze problems requiring the single-server, multiple-server, and finite-source models, all of which are single phase. References to more advanced models are cited at the end of this supplement.

SINGLE-SERVER MODEL

The simplest waiting-line model involves a single server and a single line of customers. To further specify the model, we make the following assumptions:

1. The customer population is infinite and all customers are patient.
2. The customers arrive according to a Poisson distribution, with a mean arrival rate of λ.
3. The service distribution is exponential, with a mean service rate of μ.
4. Customers are served on a first come, first served basis.
5. The length of the waiting line is unlimited.

With these assumptions we can apply various formulas to describe the operating characteristics of the system:

$$\rho = \text{average utilization of the system}$$
$$= \frac{\lambda}{\mu}$$

$$P_n = \text{probability that } n \text{ customers are in the system}$$
$$= (1 - \rho)\rho^n$$

$$L = \text{average number of customers in the service system}$$
$$= \frac{\lambda}{\mu - \lambda}$$

$$L_q = \text{average number of customers in the waiting line}$$
$$= \rho L$$

$$W = \text{average time spent in the system, including service}$$
$$= \frac{1}{\mu - \lambda}$$

$$W_q = \text{average waiting time in line}$$
$$= \rho W$$

EXAMPLE C.3

Calculating the Operating Characteristics of a Single-Channel, Single-Phase System

The manager of a grocery store in the retirement community of Sunnyville is interested in providing good service to the senior citizens who shop in his store. Presently, the store has a separate checkout counter for senior citizens. On average, 30 senior citizens per hour arrive at the counter, according to a Poisson distribution, and are served at an average rate of 35 customers per hour, with exponential service times. Find the following operating characteristics:

  a. Probability of zero customers in the system
  b. Utilization of the checkout clerk
  c. Number of customers in the system
  d. Number of customers in line
  e. Time spent in the system
  f. Waiting time in line

SOLUTION

The checkout counter can be modeled as a single-channel, single-phase system. Figure C.4 shows the results from the *Waiting-Lines* Solver from OM Explorer. Manual calculations of the equations for the *single-server model* are demonstrated in Solved Problem 1 at the end of the supplement.

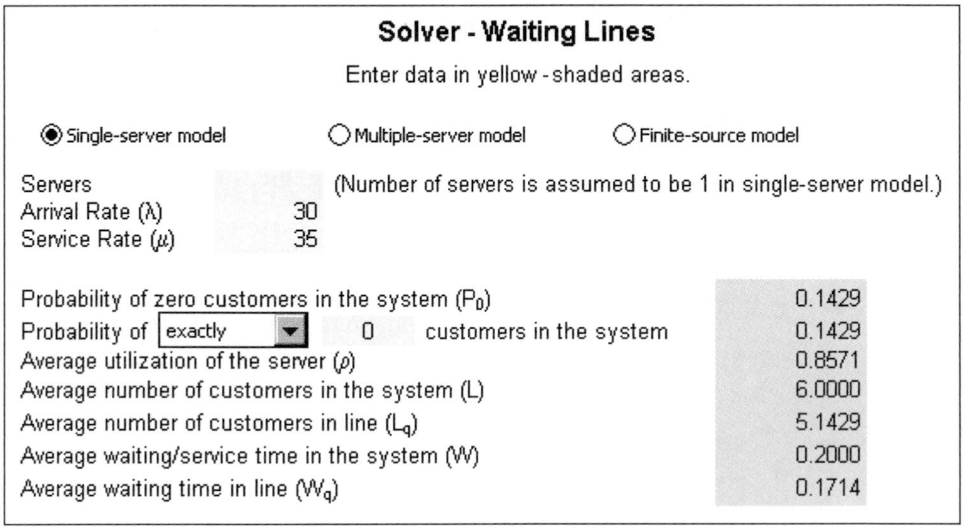

Solver - Waiting Lines

Enter data in yellow-shaded areas.

◉ Single-server model   ○ Multiple-server model   ○ Finite-source model

Servers   (Number of servers is assumed to be 1 in single-server model.)
Arrival Rate (λ)   30
Service Rate (μ)   35

Probability of zero customers in the system (P_0)	0.1429
Probability of [exactly ▼] 0 customers in the system	0.1429
Average utilization of the server (ρ)	0.8571
Average number of customers in the system (L)	6.0000
Average number of customers in line (L_q)	5.1429
Average waiting/service time in the system (W)	0.2000
Average waiting time in line (W_q)	0.1714

FIGURE C.4

Both the average waiting time in the system (W) and the average time spent waiting in line (W_q) are expressed in hours. To convert the results to minutes, simply multiply by 60 minutes/hour. For example, $W = 0.20(60) = 12.00$ minutes, and $W_q = 0.1714(60) = 10.28$ minutes. ◻

EXAMPLE C.4

Analyzing Service Rates with the Single-Server Model

The manager of the Sunnyville grocery in Example C.3 wants answers to the following questions:

  a. What service rate would be required to have customers average only eight minutes in the system?
  b. For that service rate, what is the probability of having more than four customers in the system?
  c. What service rate would be required to have only a 10 percent chance of exceeding four customers in the system?

TUTOR C.1

SOLUTION

The *Waiting-Lines* Solver from OM Explorer could be used iteratively to answer the questions. Here we show how to solve the problem manually.

a. We use the equation for the average time in the system and solve for μ.

$$W = \frac{1}{\mu - \lambda}$$

$$8 \text{ minutes} = 0.133 \text{ hour} = \frac{1}{\mu - 30}$$

$$0.133\,\mu - 0.133(30) = 1$$

$$\mu = 37.52 \text{ customers/hour}$$

b. The probability that there will be more than four customers in the system equals 1 minus the probability that there are four or fewer customers in the system.

$$P = 1 - \sum_{n=0}^{4} P_n$$

$$= 1 - \sum_{n=0}^{4} (1 - \rho)\rho^n$$

and

$$\rho = \frac{30}{37.52} = 0.80$$

Then,

$$P = 1 - 0.2(1 + 0.8 + 0.8^2 + 0.8^3 + 0.8^4)$$

$$= 1 - 0.672 = 0.328$$

Therefore, there is a nearly 33 percent chance that more than four customers will be in the system.

c. We use the same logic as in part (b), except that μ is now a decision variable. The easiest way to proceed is to find the correct average utilization first and then solve for the service rate.

$$P = 1 - (1 - \rho)(1 + \rho + \rho^2 + \rho^3 + \rho^4)$$

$$= 1 - (1 + \rho + \rho^2 + \rho^3 + \rho^4) + \rho(1 + \rho + \rho^2 + \rho^3 + \rho^4)$$

$$= 1 - 1 - \rho - \rho^2 - \rho^3 - \rho^4 + \rho + \rho^2 + \rho^3 + \rho^4 + \rho^5$$

$$= \rho^5$$

or

$$\rho = P^{1/5}$$

If $P = 0.10$,

$$\rho = (0.10)^{1/5} = 0.63$$

Therefore, for a utilization rate of 63 percent, the probability of more than four customers in the system is 10 percent. For $\lambda = 30$, the mean service rate must be

$$\frac{30}{\mu} = 0.63$$

$$\mu = 47.62 \text{ customers/hour}$$

Decision Point The service rate would only have to modestly increase to achieve the eight-minute target. However, the probability of having more than four customers in the system is too high. The manager must now find a way to increase the service rate from 35 per hour to approximately 48 per hour. She can increase the service rate in several different ways, ranging from employing a high school student to help bag the groceries to installing electronic point-of-sale equipment that reads the prices from bar-coded information on each item. ◻

MULTIPLE-SERVER MODEL

With the multiple-server model, customers form a single line and choose one of s servers when one is available. The service system has only one phase. We make the following assumption in addition to those for the single-server model: There are s identical servers, and the service distribution for each server is exponential, with a mean service time of $1/\mu$.

With these assumptions, we can apply several formulas to describe the operating characteristics of the service system:

ρ = average utilization of the system

$$= \frac{\lambda}{s\mu}$$

P_0 = probability that zero customers are in the system

$$= \left[\sum_{n=0}^{s-1} \frac{(\lambda/\mu)^n}{n!} + \frac{(\lambda/\mu)^s}{s!}\left(\frac{1}{1-\rho}\right) \right]^{-1}$$

P_n = probability that n customers are in the system

$$= \begin{cases} \dfrac{(\lambda/\mu)^n}{n!}\,P_0, & 0 < n < s \\[2ex] \dfrac{(\lambda/\mu)^n}{s!s^{n-s}}\,P_0, & n \geq s \end{cases}$$

L_q = average number of customers in line

$$= \frac{P_0(\lambda/\mu)^s\rho}{s!(1-\rho)^2}$$

W_q = average waiting time of customers in line

$$= \frac{L_q}{\lambda}$$

W = average time spent in the system, including service

$$= W_q + \frac{1}{\mu}$$

L = average number of customers in the service system

$$= \lambda W$$

A U.S. Postal Service
worker loads a
delivery van.

| EXAMPLE C.5 |

Estimating Idle Time and Hourly Operating Costs with the *Multiple-Server Model*

The management of the American Parcel Service terminal in Verona, Wisconsin, is concerned about the amount of time the company's trucks are idle, waiting to be unloaded. The terminal operates with four unloading bays. Each bay requires a crew of two employees, and each crew costs $30 per hour. The estimated cost of an idle truck is $50 per hour. Trucks arrive at an average rate of three per hour, according to a Poisson distribution. On average, a crew can unload a semitrailer rig in one hour, with exponential service times. What is the total hourly cost of operating the system?

**TUTOR
C.2**

SOLUTION

The *multiple-server model* is appropriate. To find the total cost of labor and idle trucks, we must calculate the average number of trucks in the system.

Figure C.5 shows the results for the American Parcel Service problem using the *Waiting-Lines* Solver from OM Explorer. Manual calculations using the equations for the *multiple-server model* are demonstrated in Solved Problem 2 at the end of this supplement. The results show that the four-bay design will be utilized 75 percent of the time and that the average number of trucks either being serviced or waiting in line is 4.53 trucks. We can now calculate the hourly costs of labor and idle trucks:

Labor cost:	$30(s) = $30(4)	= $120.00
Idle truck cost:	$50(L) = $50(4.53)	= 226.50
	Total hourly cost	= $346.50

Decision Point Management must now assess whether $346.50 per day for this operation is acceptable. Attempting to reduce costs by eliminating crews will only increase the waiting time

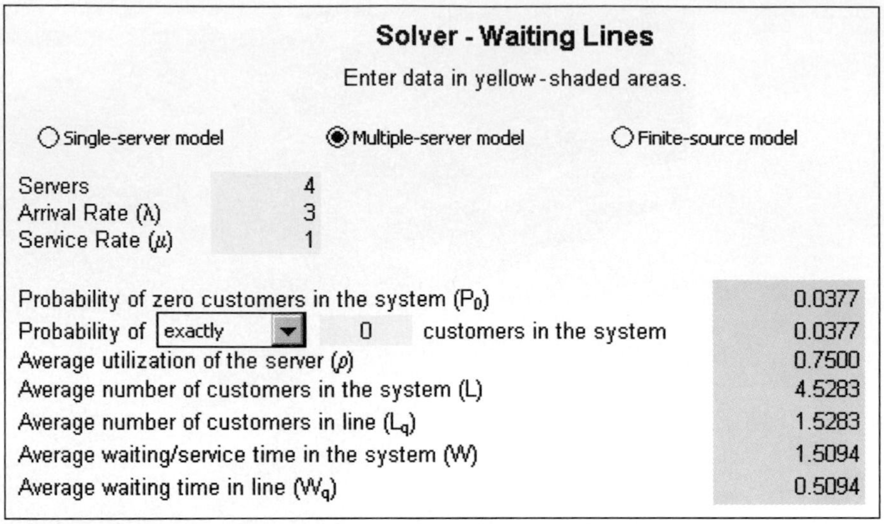

Solver - Waiting Lines

Enter data in yellow-shaded areas.

○ Single-server model   ◉ Multiple-server model   ○ Finite-source model

Servers	4
Arrival Rate (λ)	3
Service Rate (μ)	1

Probability of zero customers in the system (P_0)	0.0377
Probability of [exactly ▼] 0 customers in the system	0.0377
Average utilization of the server (ρ)	0.7500
Average number of customers in the system (L)	4.5283
Average number of customers in line (L_q)	1.5283
Average waiting/service time in the system (W)	1.5094
Average waiting time in line (W_q)	0.5094

FIGURE C.5

of the trucks, which is more expensive per hour than the crews. However, if the service rate can be increased through better work methods, for example, L can be reduced and daily operating costs will be less. ☐

FINITE-SOURCE MODEL

We now consider a situation in which all but one of the assumptions of the single-server model are appropriate. In this case, the customer population is finite, having only N potential customers. If N is greater than 30 customers, the single-server model with the assumption of an infinite customer population is adequate. Otherwise, the finite-source model is the one to use. The formulas used to calculate the operating characteristics of this service system are

P_0 = probability that zero customers are in the system

$$= \left[\sum_{n=0}^{N} \frac{N!}{(N-n)!} \left(\frac{\lambda}{\mu} \right)^n \right]^{-1}$$

ρ = average utilization of the server

$$= 1 - P_0$$

L_q = average number of customers in line

$$= N - \frac{\lambda + \mu}{\lambda} (1 - P_0)$$

L = average number of customers in the system

$$= N - \frac{\mu}{\lambda} (1 - P_0)$$

W_q = average waiting time in line

$$= L_q [(N - L)\lambda]^{-1}$$

W = average time in the system

$$= L[(N - L)\lambda]^{-1}$$

EXAMPLE C.6   *Analyzing Maintenance Costs with the Finite-Source Model*

The Worthington Gear Company installed a bank of 10 robots about three years ago. The robots greatly increased the firm's labor productivity, but recently attention has focused on maintenance. The firm does no preventive maintenance on the robots because of the variability in the breakdown distribution. Each machine has an exponential breakdown (or interarrival) distribution with an average time between failures of 200 hours. Each machine hour lost to downtime costs $30, which means that the firm has to react quickly to machine failure. The firm employs one maintenance person, who needs 10 hours on average to fix a robot. Actual maintenance times are exponentially distributed. The wage rate is $10 per hour for the maintenance person, who can be put to work productively elsewhere when not fixing robots. Determine the daily cost of labor and robot downtime.

SOLUTION

The *finite-source model* is appropriate for this analysis because there are only 10 machines in the customer population and the other assumptions are satisfied. Here, λ = 1/200, or 0.005 breakdown per hour, and μ = 1/10 = 0.10 robot per hour. To calculate the cost of labor and robot downtime, we need to estimate the average utilization of the maintenance person and L, the average number of robots in the maintenance system. Figure C.6 shows the results for the Worthington Gear Problem using the *Waiting-Lines* Solver from OM Explorer. Manual computations using the equations for the *finite-source model* are demonstrated in Solved Problem 3 at the end of this supplement. The results show that the maintenance person is utilized only 46.2 percent of the time and the average number of robots waiting in line or being repaired is 0.76 robot. However, a failed robot will spend an average of 16.43 hours in the repair system, of which 6.43 hours of that time is spent waiting for service.

The daily cost of labor and robot downtime is

Labor cost:	($10/hour)(8 hours/day)(0.462 utilization) =	$ 36.96
Idle robot cost:	(0.76 robot)($30/robot hour)(8 hours/day) =	182.40
	Total daily cost =	$219.36

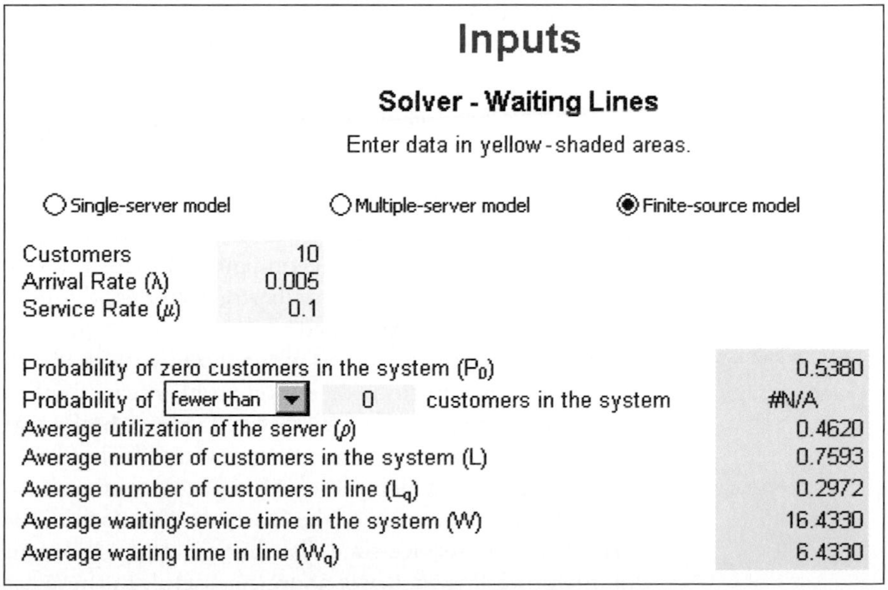

Inputs

Solver - Waiting Lines

Enter data in yellow-shaded areas.

○ Single-server model   ○ Multiple-server model   ◉ Finite-source model

Customers	10
Arrival Rate (λ)	0.005
Service Rate (μ)	0.1

Probability of zero customers in the system (P_0)	0.5380
Probability of [fewer than ▼] 0 customers in the system	#N/A
Average utilization of the server (ρ)	0.4620
Average number of customers in the system (L)	0.7593
Average number of customers in line (L_q)	0.2972
Average waiting/service time in the system (W)	16.4330
Average waiting time in line (W_q)	6.4330

FIGURE C.6

Decision Point The labor cost for robot repair is only 20 percent of the idle cost of the robots. Management might consider having a second repair person on call in the event two or more robots are waiting for repair at the same time. ◻

DECISION AREAS FOR MANAGEMENT

After analyzing a waiting-line problem, management can improve the service system by making changes in one or more of the following areas.

1. *Arrival Rates.* Management often can affect the rate of customer arrivals, λ, through advertising, special promotions, or differential pricing. For example, a telephone company uses differential pricing to shift residential long-distance calls from daytime hours to evening hours.

2. *Number of Service Facilities.* By increasing the number of service facilities, such as tool cribs, toll booths, or bank tellers, or by dedicating some facilities in a phase to a unique set of services, management can increase system capacity.

3. *Number of Phases.* Managers can decide to allocate service tasks to sequential phases if they determine that two sequential service facilities may be more efficient than one. For instance, in the assembly-line problem discussed in the Layout chapter, the decision concerns the number of phases needed along the assembly line. Determining the number of workers needed on the line also involves assigning a certain set of work elements to each one. Changing the facility arrangement can increase the service rate, μ, of each facility and the capacity of the system.

4. *Number of Servers per Facility.* Managers can influence the service rate by assigning more than one person to a service facility.

5. *Server Efficiency.* By adjusting the capital-to-labor ratio, devising improved work methods, or instituting incentive programs, management can increase the efficiency of servers assigned to a service facility. Such changes are reflected in μ.

6. *Priority Rule.* Managers set the priority rule to be used, decide whether to have a different priority rule for each service facility, and decide whether to allow preemption (and, if so, under what conditions). Such decisions affect the waiting times of the customers and the utilization of the servers.

7. *Line Arrangement.* Managers can influence customer waiting times and server utilization by deciding whether to have a single line or a line for each facility in a given phase of service.

Obviously, these factors are interrelated. An adjustment in the customer arrival rate, λ, might have to be accompanied by an increase in the service rate, μ, in some way. Decisions about the number of facilities, the number of phases, and waiting-line arrangements also are related.

For each of the problems we analyzed with the waiting-line models, the arrivals had a Poisson distribution (or exponential interarrival times), the service times had an exponential distribution, the service facilities had a simple arrangement, and the priority discipline was first come, first served. Waiting-line theory has been used to develop other models in which these criteria are not met, but these models are very complex. Many times, the nature of the customer population, the constraints on the line, the priority rule, the service-time distribution, and the arrangement of the facilities are such that waiting-line theory is no longer useful. In these cases, simulation often is used (see the Simulation supplement).

FORMULA REVIEW

1. Customer arrival Poisson distribution: $P_n = \dfrac{(\lambda T)^n}{n!} e^{-\lambda T}$

2. Service-time exponential distribution: $P(t \le T) = 1 - e^{-\mu T}$

	SINGLE-SERVER MODEL	MULTIPLE-SERVER MODEL	FINITE-SOURCE MODEL
Average utilization of the system	$\rho = \dfrac{\lambda}{\mu}$	$\rho = \dfrac{\lambda}{s\mu}$	$\rho = 1 - P_0$
Probability that n customers are in the system	$P_n = (1 - \rho)\rho^n$	$P_n = \begin{cases} \dfrac{(\lambda/\mu)^n}{n!} P_0, & 0 < n < s \\[2mm] \dfrac{(\lambda/\mu)^n}{s!\,s^{n-s}} P_0, & n \ge s \end{cases}$	
Probability that zero customers are in the system	$P_0 = 1 - \rho$	$P_0 = \left[\displaystyle\sum_{n=0}^{s-1} \dfrac{(\lambda/\mu)^n}{n!} + \dfrac{(\lambda/\mu)^s}{s!} \left(\dfrac{1}{1-\rho} \right) \right]^{-1}$	$P_0 = \left[\displaystyle\sum_{n=0}^{N} \dfrac{N!}{(N-n)!} \left(\dfrac{\lambda}{\mu} \right)^n \right]^{-1}$
Average number of customers in the service system	$L = \dfrac{\lambda}{\mu - \lambda}$	$L = \lambda W$	$L = N - \dfrac{\mu}{\lambda} (1 - P_0)$
Average number of customers in the waiting line	$L_q = \rho L$	$L_q = \dfrac{P_0(\lambda/\mu)^s \rho}{s!(1-\rho)^2}$	$L_q = N - \dfrac{\lambda + \mu}{\lambda} (1 - P_0)$
Average time spent in the system, including service	$W = \dfrac{1}{\mu - \lambda}$	$W = W_q + \dfrac{1}{\mu}$	$W = L[(N - L)\lambda]^{-1}$
Average waiting time in line	$W_q = \rho W$	$W_q = \dfrac{L_q}{\lambda}$	$W_q = L_q [(N - L)\lambda]^{-1}$

SUPPLEMENT HIGHLIGHTS

❏ Waiting lines form when customers arrive at a faster rate than they are being served. Because customer arrival rates vary, long waiting lines may occur even when the system's designed service rate is substantially higher than the average customer arrival rate.

❏ Four elements are common to all waiting-line problems: a customer population, a waiting line, a service system, and a priority rule for determining which customer is to be served next.

❏ Waiting-line models have been developed for use in analyzing service systems. If the assumptions made in creating a waiting-line model are consistent with an actual situation, the model's formulas can be solved to predict the performance of the system with respect to server utilization, average customer waiting time, and the average number of customers in the system.

KEY TERMS

customer population *360*
interarrival times *365*
phase *362*

preemptive discipline *364*
priority rule *361*
service facility *360*

service system *361*
waiting line *360*

SOLVED PROBLEM 1

A photographer at the post office takes passport pictures at an average rate of 20 pictures per hour. The photographer must wait until the customer blinks or scowls, so the time to take a picture is exponentially distributed. Customers arrive at a Poisson-distributed average rate of 19 customers per hour.

a. What is the utilization of the photographer?

b. How much time will the average customer spend at the photograph step of the passport issuing process?

SOLUTION

a. The assumptions in the problem statement are consistent with a single-server model. Utilization is

$$\rho = \frac{\lambda}{\mu} = \frac{19}{20} = 0.95$$

b. The average customer time spent at the photographer's station is

$$W = \frac{1}{\mu - \lambda} = \frac{1}{20 - 19} = 1 \text{ hour}$$

SOLVED PROBLEM 2

The Mega Multiplex Movie Theater has three concession clerks serving customers on a first-come, first-served basis. The service time per customer is exponentially distributed with an average of 2 minutes per customer. Concession customers wait in a single line in a large lobby, and arrivals are Poisson distributed with an average of 81 customers per hour. Previews run for 10 minutes before the start of each show. If the average time in the concession area exceeds 10 minutes, customers become dissatisfied.

a. What is the average utilization of the concession clerks?

b. What is the average time spent in the concession area?

SOLUTION

a. The problem statement is consistent with the multiple-server model, and the average utilization rate is

$$\rho = \frac{\lambda}{s\mu} = \frac{81 \text{ customers/hour}}{(3 \text{ servers}) \left(\dfrac{60 \text{ minutes/server hour}}{2 \text{ minutes/customer}} \right)} = 0.90$$

The concession clerks are busy 90 percent of the time.

b. The average time spent in the system, W, is

$$W = W_q + \frac{1}{\mu}$$

Here,

$$W_q = \frac{L_q}{\lambda}, \qquad L_q = \frac{P_0(\lambda/\mu)^s\rho}{s!(1-\rho)^2}, \qquad \text{and} \qquad P_0 = \left[\sum_{n=0}^{s-1}\frac{(\lambda/\mu)^n}{n!} + \frac{(\lambda/\mu)^s}{s!}\left(\frac{1}{1-\rho}\right)\right]^{-1}$$

We must solve for P_0, L_q, and W_q, in that order, before we can solve for W:

$$P_0 = \left[\sum_{n=0}^{s-1}\frac{(\lambda/\mu)^n}{n!} + \frac{(\lambda/\mu)^s}{s!}\left(\frac{1}{1-\rho}\right)\right]^{-1}$$

$$= \frac{1}{1 + \dfrac{(81/30)}{1} + \dfrac{(2.7)^2}{2} + \left[\dfrac{(2.7)^3}{6}\left(\dfrac{1}{1-0.9}\right)\right]}$$

$$= \frac{1}{1 + 2.7 + 3.645 + 32.805} = \frac{1}{40.15} = 0.0249$$

$$L_q = \frac{P_0(\lambda/\mu)^s\rho}{s!(1-\rho)^2} = \frac{0.0249\,(81/30)^3(0.9)}{3!(1-0.9)^2} = \frac{0.4411}{6(0.01)} = 7.352 \text{ customers}$$

$$W_q = \frac{L_q}{\lambda} = \frac{7.352 \text{ customers}}{81 \text{ customers/hour}} = 0.0908 \text{ hour}$$

$$W = W_q + \frac{1}{\mu} = 0.0908 \text{ hour} + \frac{1}{30} \text{ hour} = (0.1241 \text{ hour})\left(\frac{60 \text{ minutes}}{\text{hour}}\right)$$
$$= 7.45 \text{ minutes}$$

With three concession clerks, customers will spend an average of 7.45 minutes in the concession area.

SOLVED PROBLEM 3

The Severance Coal Mine serves six trains having exponentially distributed interarrival times averaging 30 hours. The time required to fill a train with coal varies with the number of cars, weather-related delays, and equipment breakdowns. The time to fill a train can be approximated by a negative exponential distribution with a mean of 6 hours 40 minutes. The railroad requires the coal mine to pay very large demurrage charges in the event that a train spends more than 24 hours at the mine. What is the average time a train will spend at the mine?

SOLUTION

The problem statement describes a finite-source model, with $N = 6$. The average time spent at the mine is $W = L\,[(N - L)\lambda]^{-1}$, with $1/\lambda = 30$ hours/train, $\lambda = 0.8$ train/day, and $\mu = 3.6$ trains/day. In this case,

$$P_0 = \left[\sum_{n=0}^{N} \frac{N!}{(N-n)!} \left(\frac{\lambda}{\mu} \right)^n \right]^{-1} = \frac{1}{\displaystyle\sum_{n=0}^{6} \frac{6!}{(6-n)!} \left(\frac{0.8}{3.6} \right)^n}$$

$$= \frac{1}{\left[\frac{6!}{6!} \left(\frac{0.8}{3.6} \right)^0 \right] + \left[\frac{6!}{5!} \left(\frac{0.8}{3.6} \right)^1 \right] + \left[\frac{6!}{4!} \left(\frac{0.8}{3.6} \right)^2 \right] + \left[\frac{6!}{3!} \left(\frac{0.8}{3.6} \right)^3 \right] + \left[\frac{6!}{2!} \left(\frac{0.8}{3.6} \right)^4 \right] + \left[\frac{6!}{1!} \left(\frac{0.8}{3.6} \right)^5 \right] + \left[\frac{6!}{0!} \left(\frac{0.8}{3.6} \right)^6 \right]}$$

$$= \frac{1}{1 + 1.33 + 1.48 + 1.32 + 0.88 + 0.39 + 0.09} = \frac{1}{6.49} = 0.1541$$

$$L = N - \frac{\mu}{\lambda}(1 - P_0) = 6 - \left[\frac{3.6}{0.8}(1 - 0.1541) \right] = 2.193 \text{ trains}$$

$$W = L[(N-L)\lambda]^{-1} = \frac{2.193}{(3.807)0.8} = 0.72 \text{ day}$$

Arriving trains will spend an average of 0.72 day at the coal mine.

OM EXPLORER AND INTERNET EXERCISES

Visit our Web site at www.prenhall.com/krajewski for OM Explorer Tutors, which explain quantitative techniques; Solvers, which help you apply mathematical models; and Internet Exercises, including Facility Tours, which expand on the topics in this chapter.

PROBLEMS

An icon next to a problem identifies the software that can be helpful, but not mandatory. The software is available on the Student CD-ROM that is packaged with every new copy of the textbook.

1. **OM Explorer** The Solomon, Smith, and Samson law firm produces many legal documents that must be typed for clients and the firm. Requests average 8 pages of documents per hour, and they arrive according to a Poisson distribution. The secretary can type 10 pages per hour on average according to an exponential distribution.

   a. What is the average utilization rate of the secretary?

   b. What is the probability that more than 4 pages are waiting or being typed?

   c. What is the average number of pages waiting to be typed?

2. **OM Explorer** Benny's Arcade has six video game machines. The average time between machine failures is 50 hours. Jimmy, the maintenance engineer, can repair a machine in 15 hours on the average. The machines have an exponential failure distribution, and Jimmy has an exponential service-time distribution.

   a. What is Jimmy's utilization?

   b. What is the average number of machines out of service, that is, waiting to be repaired or being repaired?

   c. What is the average time a machine is out of service?

3. **OM Explorer** Moore, Aiken, and Payne is a dental clinic serving the needs of the general public on a first-come, first-served basis. The clinic has three dental chairs, each staffed by a dentist. Patients arrive at the rate of five per hour, according to a Poisson distribution, and do not balk or renege. The average time required for a dental checkup is 30 minutes, according to an exponential distribution.

   a. What is the probability that no patients are in the clinic?

   b. What is the probability that six or more patients are in the clinic?

   c. What is the average number of patients waiting?

   d. What is the average total time that a patient spends in the clinic?

4. **OM Explorer** Fantastic Styling Salon is run by two stylists, Jenny Perez and Jill Sloan, each capable of serving five customers per hour, on average. Eight customers, on average, arrive at the salon each hour.

   a. If all arriving customers wait in a common line for the next available stylist, how long would a customer wait in line, on average, before being served?

   b. Suppose that 50 percent of the arriving customers want to be served only by Perez and that the other 50 percent want only Sloan. How long would a customer wait in line, on average, before being served by Perez? By Sloan? What is the average customer waiting time in the line?

   c. Do you observe a difference in the answers to parts (a) and (b)? If so, why? Explain.

5. **OM Explorer** You are the manager of a local bank where three tellers provide services to customers. On average, each teller takes three minutes to serve a customer. Customers arrive, on average, at a rate of 50 per hour. Having recently received complaints from some customers that they have had to wait for a long time before being served, your boss asks you to evaluate the service system. Specifically, you must provide answers to the following questions:

   a. What is the average utilization of the three-teller service system?

   b. What is the probability that no customers are being served by a teller or are waiting in line?

   c. What is the average number of customers waiting in line?

   d. On average, how long does a customer wait in line before being served?

   e. On average, how many customers would be at a teller's station and in line?

6. **OM Explorer** Jake Tweet hosts a psychology talk show on WTPG radio. Jake's advice averages 8 minutes per caller but varies according to an exponential distribution. The average time between calls is 20 minutes, exponentially distributed. Generating calls in this local market is difficult, so Jake doesn't want to lose any calls to busy signals. The radio station has only three telephone lines. What is the probability that a caller receives a busy signal?

7. **OM Explorer** The supervisor at the Precision Machine Shop wants to determine the staffing policy that minimizes total operating costs. The average arrival rate at the tool crib, where tools are dispensed to the workers, is 8 machinists per hour. Each machinist's pay is $20 per hour. The supervisor can staff the crib either with a junior attendant who is paid $5 per hour and can process 10 arrivals per hour or with a senior attendant who is paid $12 per hour and can process 16 arrivals per hour. Which attendant should be selected, and what would be the total estimated hourly cost?

8. **OM Explorer** The daughter of the owner of a local hamburger restaurant is preparing to open a new fast-food restaurant called Hasty Burgers. Based on the arrival rates at her father's outlets, she expects customers to arrive at the drive-in window according to a Poisson distribution, with a mean of 20 customers per hour. The service rate is flexible; however, the service times are expected to follow an exponential distribution. The drive-in window is a single-server operation.

   a. What service rate is needed to keep the average number of customers in the service system (waiting line and being served) to 4?

   b. For the service rate in part (a), what is the probability that more than 4 customers are in line and being served?

   c. For the service rate in part (a), what is the average waiting time in line for each customer? Does this average seem satisfactory for a fast-food business?

Advanced Problems

9. **OM Explorer** Three employees in the maintenance department are responsible for repairing the video games at Pinball Wizard, a video arcade. A maintenance worker can fix one video game machine every 8 hours on average, with an exponential distribution. An average of one video game machine fails every three hours, according to a Poisson distribution. Each down machine costs the

Wizard $10 per hour in lost income. A new maintenance worker would cost $8 per hour.

Should the manager hire any new personnel? If so, how many? What would you recommend to the manager, based on your analysis?

10. 💿 **OM Explorer** The College of Business and Public Administration at Benton University has a copy machine on each floor for faculty use. Heavy use of the five copy machines causes frequent failures. Maintenance records show that a machine fails every 2.5 days (or $\lambda = 0.40$ failure/day). The college has a maintenance contract with the authorized dealer of the copy machines. Because the copy machines fail so frequently, the dealer has assigned one person to the college to repair them. This person can repair an average of 2.5 machines per day. Using the finite-source model, answer the following questions:

   a. What is the average utilization of the maintenance person?

   b. On average, how many copy machines are being repaired or waiting to be repaired?

   c. What is the average time spent by a copy machine in the repair system (waiting and being repaired)?

11. 💿 **OM Explorer** You are in charge of a quarry that supplies sand and stone aggregates to your company's construction sites. Empty trucks from construction sites arrive at the quarry's huge piles of sand and stone aggregates and wait in line to enter the station, which can load either sand or aggregate. At the station, they are filled with material, weighed, checked out, and proceed to a construction site. Currently, nine empty trucks arrive per hour, on average. Once a truck has entered a loading station, it takes six minutes for it to be filled, weighed, and checked out. Concerned that trucks are spending too much time waiting and being filled, you are evaluating two alternatives to reduce the average time the trucks spend in the system. The first alternative is to add side boards to the trucks (so that more material could be loaded) and to add a helper at the loading station (so that filling time could be reduced) at a total cost of $50,000. The arrival rate of trucks would change to six per hour, and the filling time would be reduced to four minutes. The second alternative is to add another loading station at a cost of $80,000. The trucks would wait in a common line and the truck at the front of the line would move to the next available station.

Which alternative would you recommend if you want to reduce the current average waiting time in the system?

SELECTED REFERENCES

Cooper, Robert B. *Introduction to Queuing Theory,* 2d ed. New York: Elsevier–North Holland, 1980.

Hillier, F. S., and G. S. Lieberman. *Introduction to Operations Research,* 2d ed. San Francisco: Holden-Day, 1975.

Moore, P. M. *Queues, Inventories and Maintenance.* New York: John Wiley & Sons, 1958.

Saaty, T. L. *Elements of Queuing Theory with Applications.* New York: McGraw-Hill, 1961.

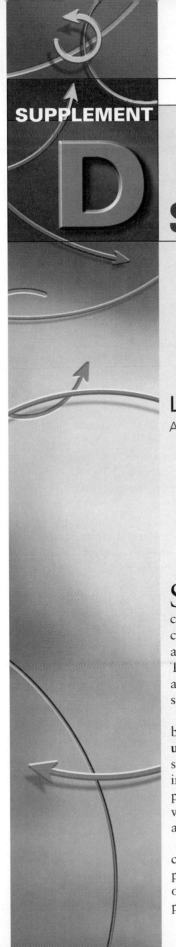

D

Simulation

Learning Goals

After reading this supplement, you will be able to . . .

1. recognize the problems best suited for the use of simulation models.
2. describe the Monte Carlo simulation process.
3. design a simple simulation model and use it to help make a decision.

S IMULATION IS THE ACT of reproducing the behavior of a system using a model that describes the processes of the system. Once the model has been developed, the analyst can manipulate certain variables to measure the effects of changes on the operating characteristics of interest. A simulation model cannot prescribe what should be done about a problem. Instead, it can be used to study alternative solutions to the problem. The alternatives are systematically used in the model, and the relevant operating characteristics are recorded. After all the alternatives have been tried, the best one is selected.

Waiting-line models (see the Waiting Lines supplement) are not simulation models because they describe the operating characteristics with known equations. With **simulation,** the equations describing the operating characteristics are unknown. Using a simulation model, the analyst actually generates customer arrivals, puts customers into waiting lines, selects the next customer to be served by using some priority discipline, serves that customer, and so on. The model keeps track of the number in line, waiting time, and the like during the simulation and calculates the averages and variances at the end.

Simulation also may be used in other ways. For example, pilots are tested periodically on flight simulators. The cockpit of the simulator is identical to that of a real plane, but it is inside a large building. Through the use of computer graphics and other visual and mechanical effects, a pilot seems to be actually flying a plane. The pilot's reactions to various unexpected situations are measured and evaluated.

REASONS FOR USING SIMULATION

simulation The act of reproducing the behavior of a system using a model that describes the processes of the system.

Simulation is useful when waiting-line models become too complex. There are other reasons for using simulation for analyzing processes. First, when the relationship between the variables is nonlinear or when there are too many variables or constraints to handle with optimizing approaches, simulation models can be used to estimate operating characteristics or objective function values and analyze a problem.

Second, simulation models can be used to conduct experiments without disrupting real systems. Experimenting with a real system can be very costly. For example, a simulation model can be used to estimate the benefits of purchasing and installing a new flexible manufacturing system without first installing such a system. Also, the model could be used to evaluate different configurations or processing decision rules without disrupting production schedules.

time compression The feature of simulation models that allows them to obtain operating characteristic estimates in much less time than is required to gather the same operating data from a real system.

Third, simulation models can be used to obtain operating characteristic estimates in much less time than is required to gather the same operating data from a real system. This feature of simulation is called **time compression**. For example, a simulation model of airport operations can generate statistics on airplane arrivals, landing delays, and terminal delays for a year in a matter of minutes on a computer. Alternative airport designs can be analyzed and decisions made quickly.

Finally, simulation is useful in sharpening managerial decision-making skills through gaming. A descriptive model that relates managerial decisions to important operating characteristics (e.g., profits, market share, and the like) can be developed. From a set of starting conditions, the participants make periodic decisions with the intention of improving one or more operating characteristics. In such an exercise a few hours' "play" can simulate a year's time. Gaming also enables managers to experiment with new ideas without disrupting normal operations.

Although simulation is used extensively, many analysts still think of it as the method of last resort. Mathematical analysis is preferred because it yields the optimal solution to a problem, whereas simulation requires the analyst to try various alternatives and possibly obtain a suboptimal solution. In addition, simulation modeling usually is very expensive because of the detail required in the computer model. Spending thousands of hours on programming and debugging complex models is not uncommon. Optimizing approaches, if they apply, usually are less expensive.

THE SIMULATION PROCESS

Monte Carlo simulation A simulation process that uses random numbers to generate simulation events.

The simulation process includes data collection, random-number assignment, model formulation, and analysis. This process is known as **Monte Carlo simulation**, after the European gambling capital, because of the random numbers used to generate the simulation events.

DATA COLLECTION

Simulation requires extensive data gathering on costs, productivities, capacities, and probability distributions. Typically, one of two approaches to data collection is used. Statistical sampling procedures are used when the data are not readily available from published sources or when the cost of searching for and collecting the data is high. Historical search is used when the data are available in company records, governmental and industry reports, professional and scientific journals, or newspapers.

| EXAMPLE D.1 | *Data Collection for a Simulation* |

The Specialty Steel Products Company produces items such as machine tools, gears, automobile parts, and other specialty items in small quantities to customer order. Because the products are so diverse, demand is measured in machine-hours. Orders for products are translated into required machine-hours, based on time standards for each operation. Management is concerned about capacity in the lathe department. Assemble the data necessary to analyze the addition of one more lathe machine and operator.

SOLUTION

Historical records indicate that lathe department demand varies from week to week as follows.

WEEKLY PRODUCTION REQUIREMENTS (hr)	RELATIVE FREQUENCY
200	0.05
250	0.06
300	0.17
350	0.05
400	0.30
450	0.15
500	0.06
550	0.14
600	0.02
Total	1.00

To gather these data, all weeks with requirements of 175.00–224.99 hours were grouped in the 200-hour category, all weeks with 225.00–274.99 hours in the 250-hour category, and so on. The average weekly production requirements for the lathe department are

$$200(0.05) + 250(0.06) + 300(0.17) + \cdots + 600(0.02) = 400 \text{ hours}$$

Employees in the lathe department work 40 hours per week on 10 machines. However, the number of machines actually operating during any week may be less than 10. Machines may need repair, or a worker may not show up for work. Historical records indicate that actual machine-hours were distributed as follows:

REGULAR CAPACITY (hr)	RELATIVE FREQUENCY
320 (8 machines)	0.30
360 (9 machines)	0.40
400 (10 machines)	0.30

The average number of operating machine-hours in a week is

$$320(0.30) + 360(0.40) + 400(0.30) = 360 \text{ hours}$$

The company has a policy of completing each week's workload on schedule, using overtime and subcontracting if necessary. The maximum amount of overtime authorized in any week is 100 hours, and requirements in excess of 100 hours are subcontracted to a small machine shop in town. Lathe operators receive $10 per hour for regular time. However, management estimates that the cost for overtime work is $25 per hour per employee, which includes premium-wage, variable-overhead, and supervision costs. Subcontracting costs $35 per hour, exclusive of materials costs.

To justify adding another machine and worker to the lathe department, weekly savings in overtime and subcontracting costs should be at least $650. These savings would cover the cost of the additional worker and provide for a reasonable return on machine investment. Management estimates from prior experience that with 11 machines the distribution of weekly capacity machine-hours would be

REGULAR CAPACITY (hour)	RELATIVE FREQUENCY
360 (9 machines)	0.30
400 (10 machines)	0.40
440 (11 machines)	0.30

RANDOM-NUMBER ASSIGNMENT

Before we can begin to analyze this problem with simulation, we must specify a way to generate demand and capacity each week. Suppose that we want to simulate 100 weeks of lathe operations with 10 machines. We would expect that 5 percent of the time (5 weeks of the 100) we would have a demand for 200 hours. Similarly, we would expect that 30 percent of the time (30 weeks of the 100) we would have 320 hours of capacity. However, we cannot use these averages of demand in our simulation because a real system does not operate that way. Demand may be 200 hours one week but 550 hours the next.

random number A number that has the same probability of being selected as any other number.

We can obtain the effect we want by using a random-number table to determine the amount of demand and capacity each week. A **random number** is a number that has the same probability of being selected as any other number (see the Table of Random Numbers in Appendix 2 for five-digit random numbers).

The events in a simulation can be generated in an unbiased way if random numbers are assigned to the events in the same proportion as their probability of occurrence. We expect a demand of 200 hours 5 percent of the time. If we have 100 random numbers (00–99), we can assign 5 numbers (or 5 percent of them) to the event "200 hours demanded." Thus, we can assign the numbers 00–04 to that event. If we randomly choose numbers in the range of 00–99 enough times, 5 percent of the time they will fall in the range of 00–04. Similarly, we can assign the numbers 05–10, or 6 percent of the numbers, to the event "250 hours demanded." In Table D.1, we show the allocation of the 100 random numbers to the demand events in the same proportion as their probability of occurrence. We similarly assigned random numbers to the *capacity* events for 10 machines. The capacity events for the 11-machine simulation would have the same random-number assignments, except that the events would be 360, 400, and 440 hours, respectively.

TABLE D.1

Random-Number Assignments to Simulation Events

Event: Weekly Demand (hour)	Probability	Random Numbers	Event: Existing Weekly Capacity (hour)	Probability	Random Numbers
200	0.05	00–04	320	0.30	00–29
250	0.06	05–10	360	0.40	30–69
300	0.17	11–27	400	0.30	70–99
350	0.05	28–32			
400	0.30	33–62			
450	0.15	63–77			
500	0.06	78–83			
550	0.14	84–97			
600	0.02	98–99			

MODEL FORMULATION

Formulating a simulation model entails specifying the relationships among the variables. Simulation models consist of decision variables, uncontrollable variables, and dependent variables. **Decision variables** are controlled by the decision maker and will change from one run to the next as different events are simulated. For example, the number of lathe machines is the decision variable in the Specialty Steel Products problem in Example D.1. **Uncontrollable variables,** however, are random events that the decision maker cannot control. At Specialty Steel Products, the weekly production requirements and the *actual* number of machine-hours available are uncontrollable variables for the simulation analysis. Dependent variables reflect the values of the decision variables and the uncontrollable variables. At Specialty Steel Products, operating characteristics such as idle time, overtime, and subcontracting hours are dependent variables.

The relationships among the variables are expressed in mathematical terms so that the dependent variables can be computed for any values of the decision variables and uncontrollable variables. For example, in the simulation model for Specialty Steel Products, the methods of determining weekly production requirements and actual capacity availability must be specified first. Then the methods of computing idle-time hours, overtime hours, and subcontracting hours for the values of production requirements and capacity hours can be specified.

decision variables
Variables that are controlled by the decision maker and will change from one run to the next as different events are simulated.

uncontrollable variables
Random events that the decision maker cannot control.

Formulating a Simulation Model

Formulate a simulation model for Specialty Steel Products that will estimate idle-time hours, overtime hours, and subcontracting hours for a specified number of lathes. Design the simulation model to terminate after 20 weeks of simulated lathe department operations.

SOLUTION

Let us use the first two rows of random numbers in the random number table for the demand events and the third and fourth rows for the capacity events (see the Table of Random Numbers in Appendix 2). Because they are five-digit numbers, we use only the first two digits of each number for our random numbers. The choice of the rows in the random-number table was arbitrary. The important point is that we must be consistent in drawing random numbers and should not repeat the use of numbers in any one simulation.

To simulate a particular capacity level, we proceed as follows:

1. Draw a random number from the first two rows of the table. Start with the first number in the first row, then go to the second number in the first row, and so on.
2. Find the random-number interval for production requirements associated with the random number.
3. Record the production hours (PROD) required for the current week.
4. Draw another random number from row 3 or 4 of the table. Start with the first number in row 3, then go to the second number in row 3, and so on.
5. Find the random-number interval for capacity (CAP) associated with the random number.
6. Record the capacity hours available for the current week.
7. If CAP ≥ PROD, then IDLE HR = CAP − PROD.
8. If CAP < PROD, then SHORT = PROD − CAP.
   If SHORT ≤ 100, then OVERTIME HR = SHORT
   and SUBCONTRACT HR = 0.

If SHORT > 100, then OVERTIME HR = 100
and SUBCONTRACT HR = SHORT − 100.

9. Repeat steps 1–8 until you have simulated 20 weeks. □

ANALYSIS

Table D.2 contains the simulations for the two capacity alternatives at Specialty Steel Products. We used a unique random-number sequence for weekly production requirements for each capacity alternative and another sequence for the existing weekly capacity to make a direct comparison between the capacity alternatives.

Based on the 20-week simulations, we would expect average weekly overtime hours (highlighted in red) to be reduced by 41.5 − 29.5 = 12 hours and subcontracting hours (highlighted in gray) to be reduced by 18 − 10 = 8 hours per week. The average weekly savings would be

Overtime:	(12 hours)($25/hour) = $300
Subcontracting:	(8 hours)($35/hour) = __280
	Total savings per week = $580

This amount falls short of the minimum required savings of $650 per week. Does that mean that we should not add the machine and worker? Before answering, let us look at Table D.3, which shows the results of a *1,000-week* simulation for each alternative. The costs (highlighted in blue) are quite different from those of the 20-week

TABLE D.2

20-Week Simulations of Alternatives

				10 Machines				11 Machines			
Week	Demand Random Number	Weekly Production (hr)	Capacity Random Number	Existing Weekly Capacity (hr)	Idle Hours	Overtime Hours	Sub-contract Hours	Existing Weekly Capacity (hr)	Idle Hours	Overtime Hours	Sub-contract Hours
1	71	450	50	360		90		400		50	
2	68	450	54	360		90		400		50	
3	48	400	11	320		80		360		40	
4	99	600	36	360		100	140	400		100	100
5	64	450	82	400		50		440		10	
6	13	300	87	400	100			440	140		
7	36	400	41	360		40		400			
8	58	400	71	400				440	40		
9	13	300	00	320	20			360	60		
10	93	550	60	360		100	90	400		100	50
11	21	300	47	360	60			400	100		
12	30	350	76	400	50			440	90		
13	23	300	09	320	20			360	60		
14	89	550	54	360		100	90	400		100	50
15	58	400	87	400				440	40		
16	46	400	82	400				440	40		
17	00	200	17	320	120			360	160		
18	82	500	52	360		100	40	400		100	
19	02	200	17	320	120			360	160		
20	37	400	19	320		80		360		40	
			Total		490	830	360		890	590	200
			Weekly average		24.5	41.5	18.0		44.5	29.5	10.0

	10 Machines	11 Machines
Idle hours	26.0	42.2
Overtime hours	48.3	34.2
Subcontract hours	18.4	8.7
Cost	$1,851.50	$1,159.50

simulations. Now the savings are estimated to be $1,851.50 − $1,159.50 = $692 and exceed the minimum required savings for the additional investment. This result emphasizes the importance of selecting the proper run length for a simulation analysis. We can use statistical tests to check for the proper run length.

Simulation analysis can be viewed as a form of hypothesis testing, whereby the results of a simulation run provide sample data that can be analyzed statistically. Data can be recorded and compared with the results from other simulation runs. Statistical tests also can be made to determine whether differences in the alternative operating characteristics are statistically significant. Commonly used statistical methods include *analysis of variance, t-tests,* and *regression analysis.* These techniques require replication of each simulation experiment. For example, if we wanted to test the null hypothesis that the difference between total weekly costs is zero, we would have to run the simulation model several times for each capacity alternative. Each time, we would use a different set of random numbers to generate weekly production requirements and weekly existing capacity. The number of replications is analogous to the sample size in statistical terminology. If we can show that the weekly cost for 11 machines is significantly different (in a statistical sense) from the weekly cost for 10 machines, we can be more confident of the estimate of the difference between the two.

Even though a difference between simulation experiments may be statistically significant, it may not be *managerially* significant. For example, suppose that we developed a simulation model of a car-wash operation. We may find, by changing the speed of the car wash from 3 to 2.75 minutes per car, that we can reduce the average waiting time per customer by 0.20 minute. Even though this may be a statistically significant difference in the average waiting time, the difference is so small that customers may not even notice it. What is managerially significant often is a judgment decision.

COMPUTER SIMULATION

The manual simulation of the lathe process in Examples D.1 and D.2 demonstrates the basics of simulation. However, there is only one step in the process, two uncontrollable variables (weekly production requirements and the actual number of machine-hours available), and 20 time periods in the simulation. It is important to simulate a process long enough to achieve **steady state**, so that the simulation is repeated over enough time that the average results for performance measures remain constant. In Figure 3.9, achieving steady state explains why the simulation was continued over 2,000 hours and the averages were not plotted in the graph until after the first 300 hours. Visually plotting the averages shows that steady state was achieved. Manual simulations can be excessively time consuming, particularly if there are many subprocesses, many products or services with unique flow patterns, many uncontrollable variables, complex logic for releasing new jobs and assigning work, and the like.

Simulating these more complex, real-world situations requires a computer. Simulation programming can be done in a variety of computer languages, including general-purpose programming languages such as VISUAL BASIC, FORTRAN, or

steady state The state that occurs when the simulation is repeated over enough time that the average results for performance measures remain constant.

C^{++}. The advantage of general-purpose programming languages is that they are available on most computer systems. Special simulation languages, such as GPSS, SIMSCRIPT, and SLAM, are also available. These languages simplify programming because they have macroinstructions for the commonly used elements of simulation models. These macroinstructions automatically contain the computer instructions needed to generate arrivals, keep track of waiting lines, and calculate the statistics on the operating characteristics of a system.

Simulation is also possible with PC-based packages. Simple simulation models can be developed using Excel, where random numbers between 0 and 1 can be generated by entering a formula, = RAND( ), in a cell. With random numbers—and adding formulas elsewhere in the worksheet to specify relationships between demand, production, inventory, and output—the Monte Carlo simulation approach can be modeled. Even more computer power comes from commercial, prewritten simulation software. The SimQuick package, for example, is an easy-to-use package that has some macroinstructions to create simulation models for a variety of simple processes such as waiting lines, inventory control, and projects. The Extend software, which is packaged on the Student CD-ROM with this textbook, is another example. Going one step further than SimQuick, its graphical interface helps users create models and then use them to answer a variety of "what-if" questions. The output graphs on performance measures actually show what is occurring as the simulation takes place. An animation option can be clicked on to show customers or jobs working their way from one subprocess to the next subprocess over the whole simulation horizon. The user must invest time to fully understand the Extend modeling features because of its large range of capabilities. Its versatility also means that it can be applied to most issues about processes. We provide end-of-chapter simulation exercises as cases for most topics—process management, project processes, statistical process control, capacity, supply-chain management, inventory management, aggregate planning, lean systems, and scheduling. Example D.3 demonstrates some of its capabilities for a layout problem. To learn more about Extend, work through the end-of-chapter simulation exercises. These cases are accompanied with prebuilt Extend models that can evaluate the current process, as well as proposed changes in the process and key decision variables.

EXAMPLE D.3

Security Inspection at the Sharpville Plant

The chief of security at the Sharpville plant of a large defense contractor is concerned. The security inspection at the plant entrance is creating delays. Currently, there is one main security gate and all employees are required to show identification and allow a visual search of their vehicle when entering the plant. Each day, approximately 800 salaried and hourly workers enter the plant prior to the 8:00 A.M. shift. As Figure D.1 shows, arriving vehicles enter one of two lanes to be inspected on a first-come, first-served basis. The plant allocates space for approximately 40 cars in each lane on the plant's property ahead of the gate.

Employees commute to work by personal vehicle (cars), vanpools, or bus. Approximately 300 vehicles are inspected each morning between 7:00 and 8:00 A.M., with the peak occurring just after 7:30. Figure D.2 gives the arrival rates based on data collected over several days. Approximately 10 percent of the entering vehicles are vans, each carrying about 10 people. The Sharpville plant sponsors seven buses from areas with very high concentrations of workers. Unlike the cars and vans, buses are formally scheduled to arrive at 7:30, although in reality they arrive up to five minutes either early or late. Given the relatively large number of people in each bus, management decided to give the buses priority. One inspection lane was designated as an "express" lane for buses (Lane 1). Visitors to the plant also used this lane. All other employee vehicles (cars and vanpools) use the second lane (Lane 0). This lane has up to three checkpoint positions; the number in use depends on the availability of guards. Usually, two guards were available for morning inspections, and one guard performed inspections at Checkpoint 1, while

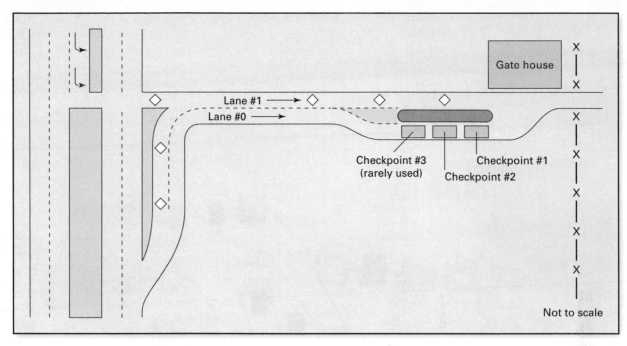

FIGURE D.1 • Security Inspection Layout

another inspected at Checkpoint 2. When the buses begin to arrive, the second guard shifts to the express lane (Lane 1), leaving only one guard in Lane 0. Inspection times are as follows:

	INSPECTION TIME (sec)	
VEHICLE	Average	Standard Deviation
Cars	10	3
Vanpools	30	9
Buses	50	10

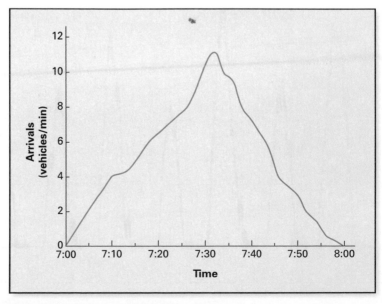

FIGURE D.2 • Vehicle Arrival Pattern

a. During the 7:00 to 8:00 A.M. interval, what is the average time to service each type of vehicle?

b. What is the average line length in each lane? Maximum?

c. What is the guard utilization?

SOLUTION

The Extend software, packaged on the Student CD-ROM, is used to model and simulate this process during the 7:00 to 8:00 A.M. arrival hour over the course of 10 days. Figure D.3(a) shows

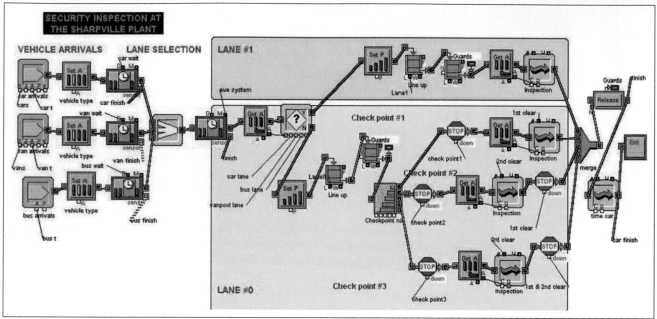

(a) Simulation model

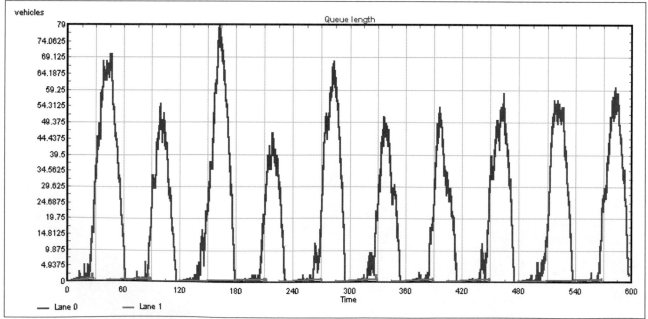

(b) Waiting lines for ten simulated arrival periods

FIGURE D.3 · Extend Model for Security Inspection Process

(c) Performance measures

the simulation model for this inspection process, with the three types of vehicles arriving and going into one of two lanes for inspection. Figure D.3(b) shows how the length of the lines behaves. Every day the number of vehicles in the waiting lines exceeds 40, which means that some vehicles must wait in line on the highway. Figure D.3(c) reports additional performance measures. The average service time (waiting and inspection) is 4.018 minutes but is particularly high for vans. Lane 0, where cars and vans are inspected, is the critical bottleneck, with the maximum wait time reaching 11.2 minutes and the maximum waiting line reaching 79 vehicles.

Decision Point Management must make some changes, such as adding capacity, redesigning the process, changing the priority rules, or spreading out the arrival-time pattern. The current process is causing significant employee frustration and is creating a potentially dangerous traffic problem.

Source: This case and simulation experience was provided by Professor Robert Klassen, University of Western Ontario. ❐

SUPPLEMENT HIGHLIGHTS

❐ Simulation is used to model the important operating characteristics of complex waiting-line situations. Information that is not attainable through the use of waiting-line formulas, such as the maximum number in line and the effect of disruptions to steady-state operations, also can be collected.

❐ Simulation models consist of decision variables (e.g., number of servers), uncontrollable variables (e.g., incidence of machine breakdowns), and dependent variables (e.g., utilization or the maximum number in line). Dependent variables reflect the behavior of the system defined by the decision variables as it is affected by uncontrollable variables. For example, simulation of three machines (decision variable) may show that when one machine breaks down for two hours (uncontrollable variable), the maximum number in line grows to seven customers (dependent variable).

❏ Computer support is required for most real simulation problems, so as to handle more complex situations and ensure steady state. Both general-purpose and special-purpose programming languages are available. PC-based packages are also, such as SimQuick and Extend. Extend is a prewritten simulator with a graphical interface that has the versatility for modeling many of the decision areas that operations managers face.

KEY TERMS

decision variables *385*	simulation *382*	uncontrollable variables *385*
Monte Carlo simulation *382*	steady state *387*	
random number *384*	time compression *382*	

SOLVED PROBLEM

A manager is considering production of several products in an automated facility. The manager would purchase a combination of two robots. The two robots (named Mel and Danny) in series are capable of doing all the required operations. Every batch of work will contain 10 units. A waiting line of several batches will be maintained in front of Mel. When Mel completes his portion of the work, the batch will then be transferred directly to Danny.

Each robot incurs a setup before it can begin processing a batch. Each unit in the batch has equal run time. The distributions of the setup times and run times for Mel and Danny are identical. But, as Mel and Danny will be performing different operations, simulation of each batch requires four random numbers from the table. The first random number determines Mel's setup time, the second determines Mel's run time per unit, and the third and fourth random numbers determine Danny's setup and run times, respectively.

SETUP TIME (min)	PROBABILITY	RUN TIME PER UNIT (sec)	PROBABILITY
1	0.10	5	0.10
2	0.20	6	0.20
3	0.40	7	0.30
4	0.20	8	0.25
5	0.10	9	0.15

Estimate how many units will be produced in an hour. Then use the first column of random numbers to simulate 60 minutes of operation for Mel and Danny.

SOLUTION

Except for the time required for Mel to set up and run the first batch, we assume that the two robots run simultaneously. The expected average setup time per batch is

$$[(0.1 \times 1 \text{ min}) + (0.2 \times 2 \text{ min}) + (0.4 \times 3 \text{ min}) + (0.2 \times 4 \text{ min}) + (0.1 \times 5 \text{ min})]$$
$$= 3 \text{ minutes,} \quad \text{or} \quad 180 \text{ seconds per batch}$$

The expected average run time per batch (of 10 units) is

$$[(0.1 \times 5 \text{ sec}) + (0.2 \times 6 \text{ sec}) + (0.3 \times 7 \text{ sec}) + (0.25 \times 8 \text{ sec}) + (0.15 \times 9 \text{ sec})]$$
$$= 7.15 \text{ seconds/unit} \times 10 \text{ units/batch} = 71.5 \text{ seconds per batch}$$

Thus, the total of average setup and run times per batch is 251.5 seconds. In an hour's time we might expect to complete about 14 batches (3,600/251.5 seconds = 14.3). However, this estimate is probably too high.

Keep in mind that Mel and Danny operate in sequence and that Danny cannot begin to do work until it has been completed by Mel (see batch 2 of Table D.4). Nor can Mel start a new batch until Danny is ready to accept the previous one. Refer to batch 6, where Mel completes this batch at time 25:50 but cannot begin the seventh batch until Danny is ready to accept the sixth batch at time 28:00.

Mel and Danny completed only 12 batches in one hour. Even though the robots used the same probability distributions and therefore have perfectly balanced production capacities, Mel and Danny did not produce the expected capacity of 14 batches because Danny was sometimes idle while waiting for Mel (see batch 2) and Mel was sometimes idle while waiting for Danny (see batch 6). This loss-of-throughput phenomenon occurs whenever variable processes are closely linked, whether those processes are mechanical, such as Mel's and Danny's, or functional, such as production and marketing. The simulation shows the need to place between the two robots sufficient space to store several batches to absorb the variations in process times. Subsequent simulations could be run to show how many batches are needed.

TABLE D.4 *Simulation Results for Mel and Danny*

	MEL						DANNY					
BATCH NO.	START TIME	RANDOM NO.	SETUP	RANDOM NO.	PROCESS	COMPLETION TIME	START TIME	RANDOM NO.	SETUP	RANDOM NO.	PROCESS	COMPLETION TIME
1	0:00	71	4 min	50	7 sec	5 min 10 sec	5:10	21	2 min	94	9 sec	8 min 40 sec
2	5:10	50	3 min	63	8 sec	9 min 30 sec	9:30	47	3 min	83	8 sec	13 min 50 sec
3	9:30	31	3 min	73	8 sec	13 min 50 sec	13:50	04	1 min	17	6 sec	15 min 50 sec
4	13:50	96	5 min	98	9 sec	20 min 20 sec	20:20	21	2 min	82	8 sec	23 min 40 sec
5	20:20	25	2 min	92	9 sec	23 min 50 sec	23:50	32	3 min	53	7 sec	28 min 0 sec
6	23:50	00	1 min	15	6 sec	25 min 50 sec	28:00	66	3 min	57	7 sec	32 min 10 sec
7	28:00	00	1 min	99	9 sec	30 min 30 sec	32:10	55	3 min	11	6 sec	36 min 10 sec
8	32:10	10	2 min	61	8 sec	35 min 30 sec	36:10	31	3 min	35	7 sec	40 min 20 sec
9	36:10	09	1 min	73	8 sec	38 min 30 sec	40:20	24	2 min	70	8 sec	43 min 40 sec
10	40:20	79	4 min	95	9 sec	45 min 50 sec	45:50	66	3 min	61	8 sec	50 min 10 sec
11	45:50	01	1 min	41	7 sec	48 min 00 sec	50:10	88	4 min	23	6 sec	55 min 10 sec
12	50:10	57	3 min	45	7 sec	54 min 20 sec	55:10	21	2 min	61	8 sec	58 min 30 sec
13	54:20	26	2 min	46	7 sec	57 min 30 sec	58:30	97	5 min	31	7 sec	64 min 40 sec

PROBLEMS

1. Comet Dry Cleaners specializes in same-day dry cleaning. Customers drop off their garments early in the morning and expect them to be ready for pickup on their way home from work. There is a risk, however, that the work needed on a garment cannot be done that day, depending on the type of cleaning required. Historically, an average of 20 garments have had to be held over to the next day. The outlet's manager is contemplating expanding to reduce or eliminate that backlog. A simulation model was developed with the following distribution for garments per day:

NUMBER	PROBABILITY	RANDOM NUMBERS
50	0.10	00–09
60	0.25	10–34
70	0.30	35–64
80	0.25	65–89
90	0.10	90–99

With expansion, the maximum number of garments that could be dry-cleaned per day is

NUMBER	PROBABILITY	RANDOM NUMBERS
60	0.30	00–29
70	0.40	30–69
80	0.30	70–99

In the simulation for a specific day, the number of garments needing cleaning (NGNC) is determined first. Next, the maximum number of garments that could be dry-cleaned (MNGD) is determined. If MNGD ≥ NGNC, all garments are dry-cleaned for that day. If MNGD < NGNC, then (NGNC – MNGD) garments must be added to the number of garments arriving the next day to obtain the NGNC for the next day. The simulation continues in this manner.

a. Assuming that the store is empty at the start, simulate 15 days of operation. Use the following random numbers, the first determining the number of arrivals and the second setting the capacity:

   (49, 77), (27, 53), (65, 08), (83, 12), (04, 82),
   (58, 44), (53, 83), (57, 72), (32, 53), (60, 79),
   (79, 30), (41, 48), (97, 86), (30, 25), (80, 73)

   Determine the average daily number of garments held overnight, based on your simulation.

b. If the cost associated with garments being held over is $25 per garment per day and the added cost of expansion is $200 per day, is expansion a good idea?

2. The Precision Manufacturing Company is considering the purchase of an NC machine and has narrowed the possible choices to two models. The company produces several products, and batches of work arrive at the NC machine every six minutes. The number of units in the batch has the following discrete distribution:

NUMBER OF UNITS IN BATCH	PROBABILITY
3	0.1
6	0.2
8	0.3
14	0.2
18	0.2

The distributions of the setup times and processing times for the two NC models follow. Assume that the work in a batch shares a single setup and that each unit in the batch has equal processing time. Simulate two hours (or

10 batch arrivals) of operation for the two NC machines. Use the following random numbers, the first one for the number of units in a batch, the second one for setup times, and the third one for run times:

(71, 21, 50), (50, 94, 63), (96, 93, 95), (83, 09, 49),
(10, 20, 68), (48, 23, 11), (21, 28, 40), (39, 78, 93),
(99, 95, 61), (28, 14, 48)

Which one would you recommend if both machines cost the same to purchase, operate, and maintain?

NC Machine 1

SETUP TIME (min)	PROBABILITY	RUN TIME PER UNIT (sec)	PROBABILITY
1	0.10	5	0.10
2	0.20	6	0.20
3	0.40	7	0.30
4	0.20	8	0.25
5	0.10	9	0.15

NC Machine 2

SETUP TIME (min)	PROBABILITY	RUN TIME PER UNIT (sec)	PROBABILITY
1	0.05	3	0.20
2	0.15	4	0.25
3	0.25	5	0.30
4	0.45	6	0.15
5	0.10	7	0.10

3. In Problem 2, what factors would you consider if the initial cost of NC Machine 1 was $4,000 less than that of NC Machine 2?

4. The 30 management professors at Omega University (ΩU) find out that telephone calls made to their offices are not being picked up. A call-forwarding system redirects calls to the management office after the fourth ring. A department office assistant answers the telephone and takes messages. An average of 90 telephone calls per hour are placed to the management faculty, and each telephone call consumes about one minute of the assistant's time. The calls arrive according to a Poisson distribution, with an average of 1.5 calls per minute, as shown in Figure D.4(a). Because the professors spend much of their time in class and in conferences, there is only a 40 percent chance that they will pick up a call themselves, as shown in Figure D.4(b). If two or more telephone calls are forwarded to the office during the same minute, only the first call will be answered.

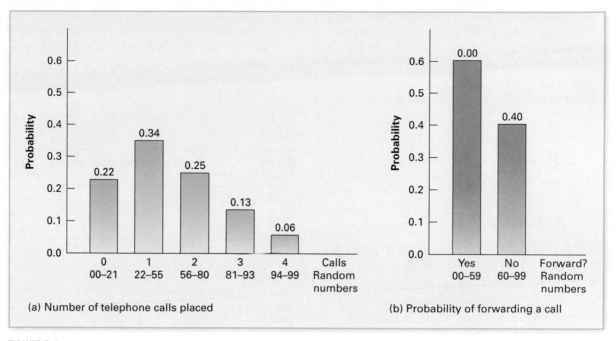

FIGURE D.4

a. Without using simulation, make a preliminary guess of what proportion of the time the assistant will be on the telephone and what proportion of the telephone calls will not be answered.

b. Now use random numbers to simulate the situation for one hour starting at 10:00 A.M. Table D.5 will get you started.

c. What proportion of the time is the office assistant on the telephone? What proportion of the telephone calls are not answered? Are these proportions close to what you expected?

5. The management chair at ΩU is considering installing a voice-mail system. Monthly operating costs are $25 per voice-mailbox, but the system will reduce the amount of time the office assistant spends answering the telephone by 60 percent. The department has 32 telephones. Use the results of your simulation in Problem 4 to estimate the proportion of the assistant's time presently spent answering the telephone. The office assistant's salary (and overhead) is $3,000 per month. Should the management chair order the voice-mail system?

TABLE D.5 *Office Assistant Simulation*												
TIME	RN	NUMBER OF CALLS MADE	RN	1st CALL FORWARDED? (Yes/No)	RN	2d CALL FORWARDED? (Yes/No)	RN	3d CALL FORWARDED? (Yes/No)	RN	4th CALL FORWARDED? (Yes/No)	NUMBER OF CALLS NOT ANSWERED	ASSISTANT IDLE (✓)
10:00	68	2	30	Yes	54	Yes					1	
10:01	76	2	36	Yes	32	Yes					1	
10:02	68	2	04	Yes	07	Yes					1	
10:03	98	4	08	Yes	21	Yes	28	Yes	79	No	2	
10:04	25	1	77	No							0	✓
10:05	51	1	23	Yes							0	
10:06	67	2	22	Yes	27	Yes					1	
10:07	80	2	87	No	06	Yes					0	
10:08	03	0									0	✓
10:09	03	0									0	✓
10:10	33	1	78	No							0	✓

6. Weekly demand at a local E-Z Mart convenience store for 1-gallon jugs of low-fat milk for the last 50 weeks has varied between 60 and 65 jugs, as shown in the following table. Demand in excess of stock cannot be backordered.

DEMAND (jugs)	NUMBER OF WEEKS
60	5
61	7
62	17
63	11
64	6
65	4
	Total 50

a. Assign random numbers between 00 and 99 to simulate the demand probability distribution.

b. E-Z Mart orders 62 jugs every week. Simulate the demand for this item for 10 weeks, using the random numbers 97, 2, 80, 66, 99, 56, 54, 28, 64, and 47. Determine the shortage or excess stock for each week.

c. What is the average shortage and the average excess stock for the 10 weeks?

7. The Brakes-Only Service Shop promises its customers same-day service by working overtime if necessary. The shop's two mechanics can handle a total of 12 brake jobs a day during regular hours. Over the past 100 days, the number of brake jobs at the shop varied between 10 and 14, as shown in the following table:

DEMAND (jobs)	NUMBER OF DAYS
10	10
11	30
12	30
13	20
14	10
	Total 100

a. Assign random numbers between 00 and 99 to simulate the demand probability distribution for brake jobs.

b. Simulate the demand for the next 10 days, using the random numbers 28, 83, 73, 7, 4, 63, 37, 38, 50, and 92.

c. On how many days will overtime work be necessary? On how many days will the mechanics be underutilized?

d. What percent of days, on average, will overtime work be necessary?

8. A machine center handles four types of clients: A, B, C, and D. The manager wants to assess the number of machines required to produce goods for these clients. Setup times for changeover from one client to another are negligible. Annual demand and processing times are uncertain; demand may be low, normal, or high. The probabilities for these three events are shown in the following tables:

Client A

DEMAND (units/yr)	PROBABILITY	PROCESSING TIME (hr/unit)	PROBABILITY
3,000	0.10	10	0.35
3,500	0.60	20	0.45
4,200	0.30	30	0.20

Client B

DEMAND (units/yr)	PROBABILITY	PROCESSING TIME (hr/unit)	PROBABILITY
500	0.30	60	0.25
800	0.50	90	0.50
900	0.20	100	0.25

Client C

DEMAND (units/yr)	PROBABILITY	PROCESSING TIME (hr/unit)	PROBABILITY
1,500	0.10	12	0.25
3,000	0.50	15	0.60
4,500	0.40	20	0.15

Client D

DEMAND (units/yr)	PROBABILITY	PROCESSING TIME (hr/unit)	PROBABILITY
600	0.40	60	0.30
650	0.50	70	0.65
700	0.10	80	0.05

a. Explain how simulation could be used to generate a probability distribution for the total number of machine hours required per year to serve the clients.

b. Simulate one year, using the following random numbers. For example, use random number 88 for client A's demand and 24 for client A's processing time.

88, 24, 33, 29, 52, 84, 37, 92

SIMULATION EXERCISE

These simulation exercises require the use of the Extend and SimQuick simulation packages. Extend is on the Student CD-ROM that is packaged with every new copy of the textbook. SimQuick is an optional simulation package that your instructor may or may not have ordered.

1. Consider the inspection process at the Sharpville plant, which is introduced as Example D.3. Use the Extend simulator to evaluate the basic process, and then analyze the impact of various changes in the process such as increased staffing, changing the flow pattern, reconfiguring the inspection checkpoints, and changing the mix of vehicles requiring inspection. For the full case and its requirements, see the *Security Inspection at the Sharpville Plant* case on the Student CD-ROM, which includes the basic model and how to use it.

2. The management of a grocery store is concerned about the waiting time of customers between the hours of 5 and 8 P.M. on week nights. Three checkout lanes are typically open; each register clerk can handle customers with any number of items, and there is a bagger always available. The checkout times are normally distributed, with a mean of 3 minutes per customer and a standard deviation of 0.5 minutes. The time between customer arrivals is exponentially distributed, with a mean of 1 minute and a standard deviation of 1 minute. The owner of the store is considering the purchase of a new barcode scanner that would reduce the mean checkout time to 2.6 minutes with a standard deviation of 0.5 minutes. Use SimQuick to assess the effect the new scanner would have on the mean number of customers in the system and the mean waiting time per customer. See Example 2 in *SimQuick: Process Simulation in Excel* (Hartvigsen, 2001) for more details about this problem and additional exercises.

SELECTED REFERENCES

Abdou, G., and S. P. Dutta. "A Systematic Simulation Approach for the Design of JIT Manufacturing Systems." *Journal of Operations Management,* vol. 11, no. 3 (1993), pp. 25–38.

Brennan, J. E., B. L. Golden, and H. K. Rappoport. "Go with the Flow: Improving Red Cross Bloodmobiles Using Simulation Analysis." *Interfaces,* vol. 22, no. 5 (1992), p. 1.

Christy, D. P., and H. J. Watson. "The Application of Simulation: A Survey of Industry Practice." *Interfaces,* vol. 13, no. 5 (October 1983), pp. 47–52.

Conway, R., W. L. Maxwell, J. D. McClain, and S. L. Worona. *XCELL & Factory Modeling System Release 4.0.* San Francisco: Scientific Press, 1990.

Ernshoff, J. R., and R. L. Serson. *Design and Use of Computer Simulation Models.* New York: Macmillan, 1970.

Hartvigsen, David. *SimQuick: Process Simulation in Excel.* Upper Saddle River, NJ: Prentice-Hall, 2001.

Imagine That! (www.imaginethatinc.com). *Extend Simulation Package.* San Jose, CA.

Law, A. M., and W. D. Kelton. *Simulation Modeling and Analysis,* 2d ed. New York: McGraw-Hill, 1991.

Meier, R. C., W. T. Newell, and H. L. Pazer. *Simulation in Business and Economics.* Englewood Cliffs, NJ: Prentice-Hall, 1969.

MicroAnalysis and Design Software Inc. "Hospital Overcrowding Solutions Are Found with Simulation." *Industrial Engineering* (December 1993), p. 557.

Naylor, T. H., et al. *Computer Simulation Techniques.* New York: John Wiley & Sons, 1966.

Pritsker, A. A. B., C. E. Sigal, and R. D. Hammesfahr. *SLAM II: Network Models for Decision Support.* Upper Saddle River, NJ: Prentice-Hall, 1989.

Solomon, S. L. *Simulation of Waiting Lines.* Englewood Cliffs, NJ: Prentice-Hall, 1983.

Swedish, Julian. "Simulation Brings Productivity Enhancements to the Social Security Administration." *Industrial Engineering* (May 1993), pp. 28–30.

Winston, Wayne L. "Simulation Modeling Using @RISK." Belmont, CA: Wadsworth Publishing Company, 1996.

Location

Across the Organization

Location is important to . . .

- ❑ **accounting,** which prepares cost estimates for operating at new locations.
- ❑ **finance,** which performs the financial analysis for investments in facilities at new locations and raises funds to support them.
- ❑ **human resources,** which hires and trains employees to support new or relocated operations.
- ❑ **management information systems,** which provides information technologies that link operations at different locations.
- ❑ **marketing,** which assesses how new locations will appeal to customers and possibly open up entirely new markets.
- ❑ **operations,** which locates its facilities where they can meet current customer demand most effectively.

Learning Goals

After reading this chapter, you will be able to . . .

1. describe the factors leading to globalization.
2. identify the hot spots in global economic activity.
3. discuss the managerial challenges in global operations.
4. describe the factors affecting location choices, both in manufacturing and services.
5. apply the load–distance method and break-even analysis to single-site location problems and the transportation method to locating a facility within a network of facilities.

Commuters hurrying to work from subway and rail line stations in Boston can't avoid walking past an Au Bon Pain cafe. This fast-growing chain is known for its gourmet sandwiches, freshly baked French bread, and croissants. It embraced the unconventional strategy of locating retail outlets close together. Au Bon Pain (www.aubonpain.com) clustered 16 cafes in the downtown area alone, with many less than 100 yards apart. Although putting too many outlets close together can hurt individual store sales in some cases, the advantages can outweigh the drawbacks. Clustering shops can reduce advertising expenses, make for easier supervision, and attract customers from the competition. This saturation approach won't work in suburban or residential areas because Au Bon Pain is not a "destination restaurant" that people drive to.

Au Bon Pain has grown beyond Boston. It purchased the St. Louis Bread company, now called Panera (www.panera.com), in 1993. This up-and-

One of the Au Bon Pain cafes in Santiago, Chile, as part of its international expansion.

coming bread cafe company grew from 19 Missouri cafes to 216 outlets by 2000. While Panera focuses on locations in the Midwest, Au Bon Pain concentrates more on the east coast and international locations. In 2000, Au Bon Pain had 145 company stores and 72 domestic franchises located in some of the most visible urban centers and crossroads, in transportation centers, hotels, regional shopping malls, hospitals, and universities. Its international expansion began in 1993 with new cafes in South America. Today, it has 65 international franchises in Canada, the UK, Singapore, Indonesia, the Philippines, Thailand, Brazil, and Chile. The company has made some mistakes on where to locate its cafes. For example, nine cafes were closed in 1996 because revenues weren't enough to sustain a profitable operations. Making the right location decisions, either domestically or internationally, is crucial to this company's future.

I N A TYPICAL YEAR in the United States, manufacturers build more than 3,000 new plants and expand 7,500 others. Service providers build and remodel innumerable stores, office buildings, warehouses, and other facilities. Choosing where to locate new manufacturing facilities, service outlets, or branch offices is a strategic decision. The location of a business's facilities has a significant impact on the company's operating costs, the prices it charges for goods and services, and its ability to compete in the marketplace.

Analyzing location patterns to discover a firm's underlying strategy is fascinating. For example, why does White Castle often locate restaurants near manufacturing plants? Why do competing new-car sales showrooms cluster near one another? White Castle's strategy is to cater to blue-collar workers. As a result, it tends to locate near the target population and away from competitors such as Wendy's and McDonald's. In contrast, managers of new-car showrooms deliberately locate near one another because customers prefer to do their comparison shopping in one area. In each case, management's location decision reflects a particular strategy.

Recognizing the strategic impact of location decisions, we first examine the most important trend in location patterns: the globalization of operations. We then consider qualitative factors that influence location choices. We end by presenting some analytic techniques for making single- or multiple-facility location decisions.

THE GLOBALIZATION AND GEOGRAPHIC DISPERSION OF OPERATIONS

Should facilities be opened overseas?

In the past, industries tended to concentrate in specific areas—for example, fabricated metals manufacturers in the industrial belt of the United States and international banking firms in London and New York City. Today, this tendency to concentrate in certain geographic regions is lessening. Although electric machinery and electronics remain key industries in New England, and sports shoes in Korea, these industries and many others have become more geographically diversified. Geography and distance are becoming increasingly irrelevant in location decisions, owing to improved communication technologies such as e-mail, faxes, video conferencing, and overnight delivery. An important exception is manufacturing firms that utilize just-in-time systems (see the Lean Systems chapter), which rely on supplier proximity. The trend of separating operations and putting thousands of miles between them applies to large corporations, medium-sized companies, and small businesses alike. For example, a high-fashion designer may choose to locate its headquarters in New York City because it is the center of fashion, its warehouses in Ohio because it is centrally located, customer service toll-free numbers in Des Moines because Iowans speak with an all-American accent, and manufacturing facilities in Hong Kong because people in Asia are skilled in textile work and receive lower wages.

globalization The description of a business's deployment of facilities and operations around the world.

The term **globalization** describes businesses' deployment of facilities and operations around the world. Worldwide exports now account for more than 30 percent of worldwide gross national product, up from 12 percent in 1962. For years, U.S. firms have built production facilities overseas. That trend continues, and foreign businesses have begun building facilities in this country. Total foreign investment in U.S. service and manufacturing industries exceeds $630 billion. Europe accounts for 65 percent of the total, with the United Kingdom leading the way at 23 percent. Japanese firms account for another 19 percent.

Globalization also results in more exports to and imports from other countries, often called *offshore* sales and imports. Offshore sales and purchases by U.S. manufacturers have increased to 14 percent of total sales and 10 percent of total purchases. The volume of corporate voice, data, and teleconferencing traffic between countries is growing at an annual rate of 15 to 20 percent—about double the corporate domestic rate—indicating how businesses are increasingly bridging national boundaries.

Globalization of services is also widespread. The value of world trade in services is roughly 20 percent of total world trade. Banking, law, information services, airlines, education, consulting, and restaurant services are particularly active globally. For example, McDonald's opened a record 220 restaurants in foreign countries in just one year. Wal-Mart Stores, the world's largest retailer, paid $10.8 billion in 1999 for the United Kingdom's Asda Group PLC, whose large stores and selection of goods closely mirrors its own. The purchase is part of Wal-Mart's push to expand across Europe. Small companies also are beginning to export their services. The Tokyo city government awarded a $50 million contract to a New York architect to design and build a $1 billion International Forum complex in downtown Tokyo. India's Steel Authority hired a Silver Spring, Maryland, consulting firm to design and implement quality systems for its five major steel plants.

REASONS FOR GLOBALIZATION

Four developments have spurred the trend toward globalization: improved transportation and communication technologies, loosened regulations on financial institutions, increased demand for imported goods, and lowered international trade barriers.

IMPROVED TRANSPORTATION AND COMMUNICATION TECHNOLOGIES. Improvements in communications technology and transportation are breaking down the barriers of time and space between countries. For example, air transportation can move goods quickly from, say, Kansas City to New York or even from Osaka, Japan, to Kansas City. Telecommunications (voice and data) technology—including electronic mail, facsimile machines, the Internet, and sophisticated toll-free telephone arrangements—allows facilities to serve larger market areas and allows firms to centralize some operations and provide support to branches located near their customers. It also permits managers around the world to communicate quickly, increasing the opportunities for cooperation and coordination.

OPENED FINANCIAL SYSTEMS. During the 1980s, U.S. banking regulators removed interest rate ceilings, which allowed banks to attract more foreign investors by offering higher rates. At the same time, foreign banks removed barriers to entry. As a result, the world's financial systems have become more open, making it easier for firms to locate where capital, supplies, and resources are cheapest.

INCREASED DEMAND FOR IMPORTS. Import penetration of the major economies is increasing, as political barriers to international trade have crumbled. Imported goods and services now are the equivalent of about 13 percent of total output in the United States and 14 percent in Japan, up considerably from earlier decades. Penetration has been increased by locating production facilities in foreign countries because a local presence reduces customer aversion to buying imports. For example, Elasticos Selectos, a Mexico City–based elastics concern, built a plant in the United States primarily to gain customers who demand a Made-in-the-U.S.A. label.

REDUCED IMPORT QUOTAS AND OTHER TRADE BARRIERS. Producing goods or services in the country where the customers live also circumvents import quotas and other trade barriers, such as India's restrictions on certain imports. During the 1980s, Japanese automakers located production facilities in the United States to avoid import quotas and negative public opinion. The recent development of regional trading blocks, such as the European Union (EU) and the North American Free Trade Agreement (NAFTA), also make trade between countries easier. So does the General Agreement on Tariffs and Trade (GATT), a tariff-cutting world trade agreement, and the U.S.–China Trade Relations Act of 2000 that helps restore normal trade relations with China. Japanese and Chinese markets are far more open to foreign entrants than in the past, creating an explosion of partnership opportunities that were unthinkable just a decade ago. Lastly, the World Trade Organization (WTO) facilitates free trade. Created in 1995 after massive negotiations over new trade rules among 123 nations, it has powers to hear trade disputes and to issue binding rulings. WTO's goals are free trade, open markets, and an unrestricted flow of capital.

Free trade is not without critics, however. Some unions and environmentalists argue that it is unfair for a low-wage country to suppress unions and thus keep wages artificially low, to undercut environmental laws, or to have factories using child labor. Free trade, they argue, should not make such practices part of a country's natural competitive advantage.

DISADVANTAGES TO GLOBALIZATION

Of course, operations in other countries can have disadvantages. A firm may have to relinquish proprietary technology if it turns over some of its component manufacturing to offshore suppliers or if suppliers need the firm's technology to achieve desired quality and cost goals.

There may be political risks. Each nation can exercise its sovereignty over the people and property within its borders. The extreme case is nationalization, in which a government may take over a firm's assets without paying compensation. Also, a firm may alienate customers back home if jobs are lost to offshore operations.

Employee skills may be lower in foreign countries, requiring additional training time. Korean firms moved much of their sports shoe production to low-wage Indonesia and China, but they still manufacture hiking shoes and in-line roller skates in Korea because of the greater skills required.

When a firm's operations are scattered, customer response times can be longer. Effective cross-functional connections also may be more difficult if face-to-face discussions are needed.

Where is global economic activity particularly visible?

HOT SPOTS OF GLOBAL ECONOMIC ACTIVITY

Globalization fosters an increasingly interdependent world economy. The economic slump and financial crisis in East Asian economies make forecasts uncertain, Figure 9.1 shows several areas where the trend toward globalization should be particularly

FIGURE 9.1

Global Hot Spots

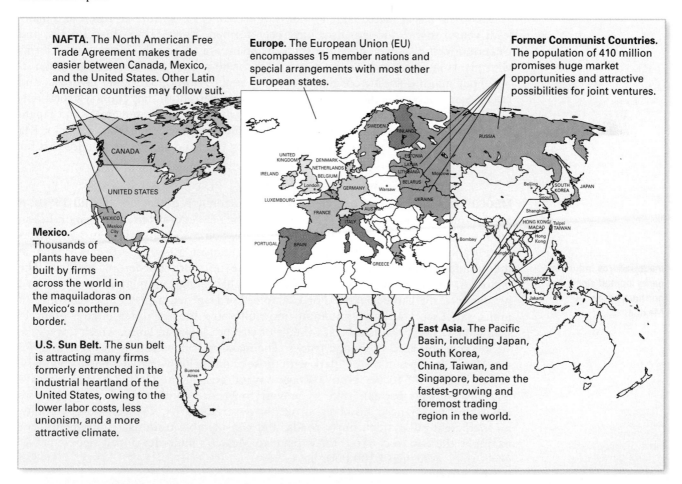

NAFTA. The North American Free Trade Agreement makes trade easier between Canada, Mexico, and the United States. Other Latin American countries may follow suit.

Europe. The European Union (EU) encompasses 15 member nations and special arrangements with most other European states.

Former Communist Countries. The population of 410 million promises huge market opportunities and attractive possibilities for joint ventures.

Mexico. Thousands of plants have been built by firms across the world in the maquiladoras on Mexico's northern border.

U.S. Sun Belt. The sun belt is attracting many firms formerly entrenched in the industrial heartland of the United States, owing to the lower labor costs, less unionism, and a more attractive climate.

East Asia. The Pacific Basin, including Japan, South Korea, China, Taiwan, and Singapore, became the fastest-growing and foremost trading region in the world.

visible. One recent survey of U.S. corporate real estate executives puts China at the top as a foreign target for future U.S. investment, followed by Mexico. Asia in general is the favorite regional target, with more than half of those surveyed planning to expand or open a facility somewhere in Asia. Nine of the top 14 cities named were in Asia: Singapore ranked first, followed by Mexico City, London, Shanghai, Hong Kong, Beijing, Seoul, Buenos Aires, Warsaw, Taipei, Moscow, Jakarta, Bombay, and Bangkok. The former East Bloc countries are another important target, with 40 percent of the respondents planning to begin operations in Russia within three years.

EAST ASIA. Business and government attention, which had long focused on Japan because of its manufacturing capacity, is now also focused on Korea, Taiwan, Singapore, and parts of China. They are rapidly industrializing areas with growing economic strength, and their economies depend heavily on the export of their manufactured goods. Korea could well become the first country to establish itself as an advanced industrial power since Japan's emergence. Taiwan exports 70 percent of its total output, including garments, electronics, software, and steel; it makes 20 percent of the world's personal computers. Hong Kong, which reverted in 1997 to the People's Republic of China, exports 90 percent of its manufacturing output, although its rising costs caused much of its manufacturing base to shift to the rest of China. The island state of Singapore has built itself into one of Asia's favorite manufacturing hubs for electronics, although low-cost competition from its neighbors (e.g., Malaysia, the Philippines, and Thailand) is increasingly stiff.

East Asia has attracted large amounts of investment from foreign firms, and many joint ventures with foreign firms have been formed. Apple, Texas Instruments, and General Electric, as well as Matsushita of Japan, are among the many foreign firms with plants in Singapore that are responsible for 60 percent of all manufacturing output. Four major domestic conglomerates in Korea (Daewoo, Samsung, Hyundai, and Lucky-Star), known as the *chaebol,* account for 40 percent of that country's total output. Korea attracts foreign investment, particularly from the United States and Japan. Daewoo has a joint venture with Suzuki to build Japanese minicars and trucks. Kia Motors, another Korean firm, is partly owned by Ford and Mazda and builds cars for the U.S. market.

maquiladoras Industrial parks located along the northern border of Mexico.

MEXICO. Although Mexico experienced some economic problems in the mid-1990s, it has rebounded and is seen as a top location for new operations. Its strength lies in labor-intensive operations. American, Japanese, South Korean, and European firms have opened nearly 2,000 plants employing almost 500,000 workers, many in **maquiladoras,** or industrial parks, along the northern border of Mexico. The *maquilas,* or plants in the maquiladoras, assemble foreign parts and export finished products to the United States. For example, Ford opened a plant in Hermosillo to make the Escort and is expanding its multivalve four-cylinder engine plant in Chihuahua. These plants take advantage of cheaper Mexican labor, which lowers the sticker price on Ford's cars and trucks. The massive devaluation of the peso in 1982 put Mexico's wages in the ballpark with those of newly industrialized Asian countries. A firm facing a $10 per hour average payroll cost in the United States can save $15,000 annually per employee by moving to Mexico. The incentive of inexpensive labor must be balanced, however, against lower productivity, less work-force stability, an inefficient rail system, dusty roads, and considerable training requirements. For example, the cost to connect a new plant to Mexico's underdeveloped electric power grid can be as high as $200,000.

EUROPEAN UNION. The EU has dropped most internal trade barriers, and significant economic expansion is expected in Western Europe over the next two decades. During the late 1980s, multinational firms positioned themselves to be treated as *EU corporations*, with the ability to trade freely within the EU and avoid import quotas or duties by locating production facilities in Europe. For a company to qualify, it must manufacture a product's core parts within the EU. The 1990s brought a new wave of investment as the European business climate became less regulated, triggering price wars and placing a premium on service. This trend encouraged U.S. companies to open European operations in finance, retailing, and technology. United Parcel Service unveiled its improved overnight delivery services in Europe as part of a $1.1 billion investment. In financial services, U.S. companies are eyeing opportunities in banks, insurance companies, and brokerages. Gap, Inc., the clothing retailer, has opened 78 European stores since 1987. Its inventory tracking methods allow it to feed new designs into stores three times faster than European retailers can.

The latest EU development is the *euro*—the new common European currency introduced in 1999. Although its exchange rate weakened by 2000, it should rebound; the lower euro makes Europe's exports cheaper, fueling sales and growth rates on the continent. The new euro, and the EU in general, pose dangers and present opportunities that no business can afford to ignore. Unifying the continent would make it easier for European companies to relocate production and distribution centers to gain competitive advantage. Newly energized European businesses are likely to prove tough competitors in other global markets. Meanwhile, corporations doing business in Europe must become euro-compliant. Compliance issues touch every corner of the business—from audit to risk management and from managing the supply chain to connecting with customers.

The vision of a totally united European economy is not easily achieved. Some nations, such as Britain, Denmark, and Sweden, have not joined the common currency of the euro. Some EU states are bickering over how to adapt its decision-making processes and institutions to encompass as many as 30 countries in the next decade, including a dozen new democracies in Central and Eastern Europe wishing to join the EU.

EASTERN EUROPE AND THE FORMER SOVIET UNION. With the political collapse of the former communist countries in Eastern Europe and the former Soviet Union, the region is beginning to post vibrant growth rates. Many firms began looking increasingly to those markets as a source of new customers, suppliers, and partners. Although the pace of growth may be less certain there than in other regions because of continuing political and economic turmoil, the region's population of 410 million promises huge market opportunities. Foreign companies are establishing joint ventures in local manufacturing at an accelerating pace. In the computer business, IBM is setting up joint ventures in Russia, the Czech Republic, and the former East Germany (now part of Germany).

In the razor-blade industry, Gillette entered a joint venture with the Leninets Concern in St. Petersburg, a local company that made a razor blade known as the Sputnik. After studying Russian consumer habits and importing some of its own brands, Gillette built a new $40 million factory of its own in 2000. At the time, Russia was its fastest-growing market worldwide, up 40 percent from 1999. Russian sales now exceed $200 million. The St. Petersburg plant is a beachhead, the latest installment in its strategy to win over consumers worldwide. Only 40 percent of Gillette's 1999 sales came from purchases made by U.S. consumers. Its exposure to global markets has been both a liability and an asset. After years of strong profit increases, fluctuations in foreign currency rates have lowered Gillette's momentum. On the upside, foreign markets mean big growth opportunities.

MANAGING GLOBAL OPERATIONS

How should global operations be managed, and what are their biggest challenges?

All the concepts and techniques described in this book apply to operations throughout the world. However, location decisions involve added complexities when a firm sets up facilities abroad. One study (see Klassen and Whybark, 1994) revealed that the most important barrier to effective global manufacturing operations is that many firms do not take a global view of their market opportunities and competitors. Global markets impose new standards on quality and time. Managers should not think about domestic markets first and then global markets later, if at all. Also, they must have a good understanding of their competitors, which requires greater appraisal capabilities when the competitors are global rather than domestic. Other important challenges of managing multinational operations include other languages and customs, different management styles, unfamiliar laws and regulations, and different costs. Radissan Slavjanskaya faced all these challenges, as Managerial Practice 9.1 illustrates.

OTHER LANGUAGES. The ability to communicate effectively is important to all organizations. Most U.S. managers are fluent only in English and thus are at a disadvantage when dealing with managers in Europe or Asia who are fluent in several languages. For example, despite the vast potential for trade with Russia, few U.S. students and managers are studying Russian.

DIFFERENT NORMS AND CUSTOMS. Several U.S. franchisers, such as Century 21 Real Estate, Levi Strauss, and Quality Inns International, found that even when the same language is spoken, different countries have unique norms and customs that shape their business values. The goals, attitudes toward work, customer expectations, desire for risk taking, and other business values can vary dramatically from one part of the world to another. For example, a survey showed that more than two-thirds of Japanese managers believed that business should take an active role in environmental protection, whereas only 25 percent of Mexican managers agreed.

WORKFORCE MANAGEMENT. Employees in different countries prefer different management styles. Managers moving to operations in another country often must reevaluate their on-the-job behaviors (e.g., superior–subordinate relationships), assumptions about workers' attitudes, and hiring and promotion practices. Practices that work well in one country may be ineffective in another.

UNFAMILIAR LAWS AND REGULATIONS. Managers in charge of overseas plants must deal with unfamiliar labor laws, tax laws, and regulatory requirements. The after-tax consequences of an automation project, for instance, can be quite different from country to country because of different tax laws. Legal systems also differ. Some policies and practices that are illegal in one country might be acceptable or even mandated elsewhere in the world.

UNEXPECTED COST MIX. Firms may shift some of their operations to another country because of lower inventory, labor, materials, and real estate costs. However, these same differences may mean that policies that worked well in one economic environment—such as automating a process—might be a mistake in the new environment.

In dealing with global operations, managers must decide how much of the firm's operations to shift overseas and how much control the home office should retain. At one extreme, firms can rely on their home offices for strategic direction and are highly centralized. At the other extreme, firms can have a worldwide vision but allow each subsidiary to operate independently. Here, the manager must be able to manage highly

The Radisson Hotels International, with headquarters in Minneapolis, Minnesota, had become by 1995 one of the world's fastest-growing upscale hotel companies. Its global expansion program was adding one new location every 10 days, on average. In 1991, it opened the four-star Radisson Slavjanskaya Hotel in Moscow, which has become a very successful hospitality oasis for Western business travelers. However, opening the Slavjanskaya forced Radisson to weather many storms and deal with every conceivable managerial challenge.

Multiple Languages
There is great diversity in the language of the hotel's managers, employees, suppliers, and customers. Most of the managers are expatriates, and most of the employees are Russians. The customer mix is American (55 percent), Western European (20 percent), Eastern European (15 percent), Asian (5 percent), and Russian (5 percent).

Different Norms and Customs
Russian standards of service quality were much lower than those expected by management. To attain and maintain top service quality, employees had to participate in intensive training. Employee attitudes toward work and ethical norms also were different. For example, employees often missed work because of sick leaves, maternal leaves, and vacations. Russian laws allow 24-day vacations and sick leaves of up to four months with pay, which can be renewed by returning to work for only a few days. Security requirements were demanding, with theft being commonplace. Once, the entire payroll was "lost" in a Russian bank. On another occasion, about 500 of the 600 champagne glasses were missing. The nearby train station was said to be controlled by gangs who offered "protection" to the vendors. Some 70 security guards were employed, many more than at a typical Radisson hotel.

Workforce Management
Staffing and training issues arose unexpectedly. For example, the Russian employees were offended by being rotated through various jobs to gain wider experience, viewing rotation as a lack of confidence in their abilities. They believed that Americans were too quick to punish and too slow to understand cultural differences. An important hiring requirement was that the applicant had smiled sometime during the interview and had expressed a willingness to reject bribes. The notion of linking pay and bonuses with performance was a radically new idea to Russian employees.

Unfamiliar Laws and Regulations
Communist-era "job-for-life" laws were still in effect, and firing an employee was difficult. The housekeeping people were paid for 8 1/2 hours per day, regardless of the actual hours worked. Tax laws were extremely complicated and sometimes were changed retroactively. Russian employees were paid in rubles at a time when inflation was 18 percent per month.

Radisson Hotels International's decision to open the upscale Radisson Slavjanskaya, the first American-managed hotel in Moscow, underscores the range of challenges that can be encountered in managing global operations.

Unexpected Cost Mix
Labor productivity was low relative to a comparable Western hotel, but salary rates were even lower. The net result was a savings because salaries accounted for only 13.5 percent of total costs, in contrast to the 35 percent in the United States. However, local suppliers were unreliable and procurement costs were quite high. About 93 percent of all products were imported from the West—shipped to Helsinki or St. Petersburg and then trucked to Moscow. This importing process was slowed by problems with customs, Russian fuel, truck breakdowns, and the need for "expediting payments." These uncertainties and delays created unusually large inventories. The infrastructure, including mail, telephone, banking, and city services, also was inadequate. For example, hot water came from city-run water-heating plants. Because this source wasn't always reliable, Slavjanskaya had to pay for the construction of a second hot water pipe to guarantee both heat and hot water.

Sources: "The Radisson Slavjanskaya Hotel and Business Center." International Institute for Management Development (IMD), Lausanne, Switzerland, 1996, distributed by ECCH at Babson, Ltd., Case 696-007-1; and "Murder in Moscow." *Fortune* (March 3, 1997), p. 128.

decentralized organizations that have a complex mix of product strategies, cultures, and consumer needs.

FACTORS AFFECTING LOCATION DECISIONS

Which factors are dominant in picking a new location? Secondary?

facility location The process of determining a geographic site for a firm's operations.

Facility location is the process of determining a geographic site for a firm's operations. Managers of both service and manufacturing organizations must weigh many factors when assessing the desirability of a particular site, including proximity to customers and suppliers, labor costs, and transportation costs. Managers generally can disregard factors that fail to meet at least one of the following two conditions.

1. The factor must be sensitive to location. That is, managers shouldn't consider a factor that is not affected by the location decision. For example, if community attitudes are uniformly good at all the locations under consideration, community attitudes shouldn't be considered as a factor.

2. The factor must have a high impact on the company's ability to meet its goals. For example, although different locations will be at different distances from suppliers, if shipments and communication can take place by overnight delivery, faxing, and other means, distance to suppliers shouldn't be considered as a factor.

Managers can divide location factors into dominant and secondary factors. Dominant factors are those derived from competitive priorities (cost, quality, time, and flexibility) and have a particularly strong impact on sales or costs. For example, a favorable labor climate and monetary incentives are dominant factors when locating call centers in Texas, as Managerial Practice 9.2 demonstrates. Secondary factors also are important, but management may downplay or even ignore some of them if other factors are more important. Thus, for GM's Saturn plant, which makes many parts on site, inbound transportation costs were considered to be a secondary factor.

DOMINANT FACTORS IN MANUFACTURING

Six groups of factors dominate location decisions for new manufacturing plants. Listed in order of importance, they are

1. favorable labor climate,
2. proximity to markets,
3. quality of life,
4. proximity to suppliers and resources,
5. proximity to the parent company's facilities, and
6. utilities, taxes, and real estate costs.

FAVORABLE LABOR CLIMATE. A favorable labor climate may be the most important factor in location decisions for labor-intensive firms in industries such as textiles, furniture, and consumer electronics. Labor climate is a function of wage rates, training requirements, attitudes toward work, worker productivity, and union strength. Many executives perceive weak unions or a low probability of union organizing efforts as a distinct advantage. One indicator of this attitude is that, although 50 percent of U.S. manufacturing plants are unionized, only 20 percent of new plants being opened have unions.

Having a favorable climate applies not just to the workforce already on site but in the case of relocation decisions to the employees that a firm hopes will transfer or will be attracted there. A good example is MCI Communications Corporations's decision

MANAGERIAL PRACTICE 9.2
Location Factors for Call Centers

Call centers are frequently mistaken for telemarketing operations, when in fact they are not. Most are "inbound" facilities that take reservations and orders or provide customer service. The industry has boomed during the last decade as more firms decided to outsource such customer service processes. Texas leads the United States in the number of new centers over the past decade—its number of call centers doubled in the last decade. By one estimate, 113 centers located there in the 1990s, compared with 81 in Florida, the runner-up. In the past, the vast majority of call centers went to the state's large metropolitan areas, but now smaller cities such as Big Spring, McAllen, and Brownsville are getting in on the act.

Two dominant factors favoring small Texan cities are their ample supply of inexpensive labor and the incentives that they are tossing in to land the companies. Before Denver-based StarTek opened a call center in Big Spring, a West Texas town of 23,000 where unemployment had been about 6 percent, a job fair attracted 1,200 applicants. Employees started at $6.50 per hour, far less than what would be paid in a bigger city. To seal the deal, Big Springs gave StarTek $2.3 million in interest-free loans. Smaller cities are more likely to get state funds for this type of economic development because the call centers are such an economic-development bonanza for them. In larger cities, companies usually do not qualify for incentives unless they make a substantial capital invest-

ment—and many do not, choosing to lease office space. The smaller cities need the jobs more. Call centers employ several hundred people, bringing jobs and a level of technical training and giving smaller cities a foot in the door to the new high-tech economy. Particularly if labor stays in short supply, call centers could be the first step for smaller cities to draw other burgeoning business, such as the distribution centers for e-commerce companies.

Other factors that favor Texas are the central time zone (making it convenient to reach markets on both coasts), the availability of advanced telecommunications structures (such as fiber-optic lines and digital switching systems), and the favorable regulatory climate. It is a one-party-consent state, meaning customers do not need to be notified if their conversations are being recorded; getting permission slows down the calling process. And the state also does not levy excise or sales taxes on out-of-state long-distance calls, as some states do. Border cities also offer a supply of bilingual workers—to take calls from Spanish-speaking customers. This advantage is particularly important as more companies expand their markets into Latin America.

Source: "Call Centers are Booming in Small Cities," *Wall Street Journal* (March 3, 2000).

to relocate its Systems Engineering division from its Washington, D.C. headquarters to Colorado Springs. This 4,000-employee division was MCI's brain trust that had created numerous breakthrough products. Management reasoned that this location would inspire the workers and that the mountains, low crime rate, healthy climate, and rock-bottom real estate prices would surely attract the best and brightest computer software engineers. The results were quite different than expected. Numerous executives and engineers and hundreds of the division's 51 percent minority population said "no" to the transfer or fled MCI soon after relocating. Colorado Springs' isolated and politically conservative setting repelled many employees who were used to living in larger, ethnically diverse urban areas. The relocated engineers also felt isolated from both top management and the marketing staff. That prevented the daily, informal contact that had spawned many successful innovations. Whereas Colorado Springs seemed destined to become a major center for MCI, it ended up being just a branch. After these disappointing results, the executive who made the location decision was relegated to managing a small R&D group at MCI.

PROXIMITY TO MARKETS. After determining where the demand for goods and services is greatest, management must select a location for the facility that will supply that demand. Locating near markets is particularly important when the final goods are bulky or heavy and *outbound* transportation rates are high. For example, manufacturers of products such as plastic pipe and heavy metals all emphasize proximity to their markets.

QUALITY OF LIFE. Good schools, recreational facilities, cultural events, and an attractive lifestyle contribute to **quality of life.** This factor is relatively unimportant on its own, but it can make the difference in location decisions. In the United States during the past two decades, more than 50 percent of new industrial jobs went to nonurban regions. A similar shift is taking place in Japan and Europe. Reasons for this movement include high costs of living, high crime rates, and general decline in the quality of life in many large cities.

quality of life A factor that can sometimes make the difference in location decisions; good schools, recreational facilities, cultural events, and an attractive life-style are all taken into consideration when determining quality of life.

PROXIMITY TO SUPPLIERS AND RESOURCES. Firms dependent on inputs of bulky, perishable, or heavy raw materials emphasize proximity to suppliers and resources. In such cases, *inbound* transportation costs become a dominant factor, encouraging such firms to locate facilities near suppliers. For example, locating paper mills near forests, and food processing facilities near farms is practical. Another advantage of locating near suppliers is the ability to maintain lower inventories.

PROXIMITY TO THE PARENT COMPANY'S FACILITIES. In many companies, plants supply parts to other facilities or rely on other facilities for management and staff support. These ties require frequent coordination and communication, which can become more difficult as distance increases.

UTILITIES, TAXES, AND REAL ESTATE COSTS. Other important factors that may emerge include utility costs (telephone, energy, and water), local and state taxes, financing incentives offered by local or state governments, relocation costs, and land costs. For example, MCI was attracted by being able to buy an abandoned 220,000 square foot IBM factory for its new Colorado Springs facility for just $13.5 million, a bargain by Washington standards. It was also able to wrangle $3.5 million in incentives from local governments. These strong attractions were much less important, in retrospect, than finding a favorable labor climate for its employees.

OTHER FACTORS. Still other factors may need to be considered, including room for expansion, construction costs, accessibility to multiple modes of transportation, the cost of shuffling people and materials between plants, insurance costs, competition from other firms for the workforce, local ordinances (such as pollution or noise control regulations), community attitudes, and many others. For global operations, firms are emphasizing local employee skills and education and the local infrastructure. Many firms are concluding that large, centralized manufacturing facilities in low-cost countries with poorly trained workers are not sustainable. Smaller, flexible facilities serving multiple markets allow the firm to deal with nontariff barriers such as sales-volume limitations, regional trading blocks, political risks, and exchange rates.

DOMINANT FACTORS IN SERVICES

How does the location decision for service facilities differ from that for manufacturing facilities?

The factors mentioned for manufacturers also apply to service providers, with one important addition: the impact that the location might have on sales and customer satisfaction. Customers usually care about how close a service facility is, particularly if the process requires considerable customer contact.

PROXIMITY TO CUSTOMERS. Location is a key factor in determining how conveniently customers can carry on business with a firm. For example, few people will patronize a remotely located dry cleaner or supermarket if another is more convenient. Thus, the influence of location on revenues tends to be the dominant factor. Managerial Practice 9.3 demonstrates that customer proximity is not enough—the key is proximity to customers who will patronize such a facility and seek its services.

TRANSPORTATION COSTS AND PROXIMITY TO MARKETS. For warehousing and distribution operations, transportation costs and proximity to markets are extremely important. With a warehouse nearby, many firms can hold inventory closer to the customer, thus reducing delivery time and promoting sales. For example, Invacare Corporation of Elyria, Ohio, gained a competitive edge in the distribution of home health care products by decentralizing inventory into 32 warehouses across the country. Invacare sells wheelchairs, hospital beds, and other patient aids, some of which it produces and some of which it buys from other firms, to small dealers who sell to consumers. Previously the dealers, often small mom-and-pop operations, had to wait three weeks for deliveries, which meant that a lot of their cash was tied up in excess inventory. With Invacare's new distribution network, the dealers get daily deliveries of products from one source. Invacare's location strategy shows how timely delivery can be a competitive advantage.

Should a firm be a leader or a follower in picking locations for new retail outlets?

critical mass A situation whereby several competing firms clustered in one location attract more customers than the total number who would shop at the same stores at scattered locations.

LOCATION OF COMPETITORS. One complication in estimating the sales potential at different locations is the impact of competitors. Management must not only consider the current location of competitors but also try to anticipate their reaction to the firm's new location. Avoiding areas where competitors are already well established often pays. However, in some industries, such as new-car sales showrooms and fast-food chains, locating near competitors is actually advantageous. The strategy is to create a **critical mass**, whereby several competing firms clustered in one location attract more customers than the total number who would shop at the same stores at scattered locations. Recognizing this effect, some firms use a follow-the-leader strategy when selecting new sites.

SITE-SPECIFIC FACTORS. Retailers also must consider the level of retail activity, residential density, traffic flow, and site visibility. Retail activity in the area is important, as shoppers often decide on impulse to go shopping or to eat in a restaurant. Traffic flows and visibility are important because businesses' customers arrive in cars. Management considers possible traffic tie-ups, traffic volume and direction by time of day, traffic signals, intersections, and the position of traffic medians. Visibility involves distance from the street and size of nearby buildings and signs. High residential density ensures nighttime and weekend business when the population in the area fits the firm's competitive priorities and target market segment.

LOCATING A SINGLE FACILITY

Having examined trends and important factors in location, we now consider more specifically how a firm can make location decisions. In this section, we consider the case of locating only one new facility. Where the facility is part of a firm's larger network of facilities, we assume that there is no interdependence; that is, a decision to open a restaurant in Tampa, Florida, is independent of whether the chain has a restaurant in Austin, Texas. Let's begin by considering how to decide whether a new location

MANAGERIAL PRACTICE 9.3
Marble Baths vs. Barbecue For Casino Locations

Mirage Resorts, Inc., reinvented Las Vegas with lush new casinos, including the $730 million Mirage, built in 1989, and the $1.8 billion Bellagio, which opened in 1998. In 1999, Mirage opened the Beau Rivage casino in Biloxi, Mississippi, as its first big casino located outside of Nevada. Management believed that the location would allow Mirage to join the nationwide expansion of casinos. The location scored high on many important location factors: The region offered low taxes, high population growth, state officials keen for investment, and an eager and plentiful workforce supply.

Aiming for high-paying customers as in Las Vegas, the goal was to build a high-end resort that would appeal to wealthy Southeasterners. Every detail sought perfection. Fifteen 75-year-old live-oak trees were painstakingly transplanted from a local farm to grace the drive of the casino. Seven pairs of live finches flutter in magnolia trees in the hotel's lobby, and 250 yards of fine silk line the spa's walls. The sushi bar is Rosso Verona marble. The resort invested in fine linens and marble bathrooms, and it promised nightly turn-down service and triple sheeting. Concrete ceilings were sanded to a perfect smoothness. The construction adapted offshore-oil-platform technology, floating the casino on five barges anchored by nine million pounds of structural steel. The projected costs metamorphosed when management added a $10-million, 31-slip floating marina built of Brazilian ipe hardwood. The resort claims that, per slip, it is the world's most expensive marina. Before the grand opening, Wall Street was enthusiastic: Upbeat analysts predicted annual returns of as much as 20 percent—well above industry averages.

But Beau Rivage failed spectacularly to draw the high-paying customers it sought and produced about half the cash flow that investors expected. The $1.6 billion property cost is at least double its original budget. Beau Rivage failed to comprehend several vital differences between Las Vegas and the Southeast region. Beau Rivage wasn't designed with Southerners in mind. The community on which it depends wants a good Southern buffet, friendly card dealers, and a sense of accessibility. Mirage did not understand the passions for barbecue, country-rock music, the value of valet parking, the high cost of flying in from surrounding areas, and the training needed for an inexperienced local workforce. Biloxi is a day-trippers market, where gamblers blow their $40 budgets before driving home. Biloxi customers, spiffed up for an evening on the town, place a high value on handing their car keys to a valet, but the resort was short on capacity and long

The location of the Beau Rivage casino in Biloxi, Mississippi, was selected because the region offered low taxes, high population growth, government officials keen on investment, and a plentiful workforce supply.

waiting lines developed. The resorts' creators proved right on one count—visitors flocked to Biloxi to gawk at the new place. But then they went elsewhere to gamble, where they were more comfortable. Casino revenues on the Gulf Coast rose 43 percent from the year before, but the increase was mainly enjoyed by the resort's rivals.

Changes have been made since the grand opening to correct many missteps. Costs have been slashed. Plans for "hands-free" luggage delivery to the airport, which cost $21 a customer, were cancelled. The night turn-down service was discontinued in standard rooms, saving $6 per room per customer. Soft rock replaced opera and Frank Sinatra elevator music. A second valet area was added, and the parking valets received scripts on greeting guests. Waiters were tutored in the pronunciation of foods such as foie gras. New restaurant managers made the crabcakes bigger, banned lobster crepes, and added an 11.5-ounce T-bone. There's prime rib on Mondays, and on Tuesdays, all-you-can-eat ribs. The improvements seem to be paying off, and Beau Rivage has enjoyed much stronger operating numbers in recent quarters. However, its occupancy rate in December is only 80 percent. Even though that rate is outstanding for Biloxi for that time of year, it is low in an industry that shoots for at least 95 percent capacity utilization.

Source: "Mississippi Gamble," *Wall Street Journal* (February 2, 2000).

is needed, and then examine a systematic selection process aided by the load–distance method to deal with proximity.

SELECTING ON-SITE EXPANSION, NEW LOCATION, OR RELOCATION

Should a firm expand on site, add a new facility, or relocate the existing facility?

Management must first decide whether to expand on site, build another facility, or relocate to another site. A survey of Fortune 500 firms showed that 45 percent of expansions were on site, 43 percent were in new plants at new locations, and only 12 percent were relocations of all facilities. On-site expansion has the advantage of keeping management together, reducing construction time and costs, and avoiding splitting up operations. However, a firm may overexpand a facility, at which point diseconomies of scale set in (see the Capacity chapter). Poor materials handling, increasingly complex production control, and simple lack of space all are reasons for building a new plant or relocating the existing one.

The advantages of building a new plant or moving to a new retail or office space are that the firm does not have to rely on production from a single plant, can hire new and possibly more productive labor, can modernize with new technology, and can reduce transportation costs. Most firms that choose to relocate are small (less than 10 employees). They tend to be single-location companies cramped for space and needing to redesign their production processes and layouts. More than 80 percent of all relocations are within 20 miles of the first location, which enables the firm to retain its current workforce.

COMPARING SEVERAL SITES

A systematic selection process begins after there is a perception or evidence that opening a retail outlet, warehouse, office, or plant in a new location will increase profits. A team may be responsible for the selection decision in a large corporation, or an individual may make the decision in a small company. The process of selecting a new facility location involves a series of steps.

1. Identify the important location factors and categorize them as dominant or secondary.

2. Consider alternative regions; then narrow the choices to alternative communities and finally to specific sites.

3. Collect data on the alternatives from location consultants, state development agencies, city and county planning departments, chambers of commerce, land developers, electric power companies, banks, and on-site visits. Governmental data provide a statistical mother lode. For example, the U.S. Census Bureau has a minutely detailed computerized map of the entire United States—the so-called Tiger file. Its formal name is the Topologically Integrated Geographic Encoding and Reference file (tiger.census.gov). It lists in digital form every highway, street, bridge, and tunnel in the 50 states. When combined with a database, such as the results of the 1990 census or a company's own customer files, Tiger gives desktop computer users the ability to ask various "what-if" questions about different location alternatives. The Internet also has Web sites (see maps.yahoo.com/yahoo, www.mapquest.com, and www.expediamaps.com) that provide maps, distances and travel time, and routes between any two locations, such as between Toronto, Ontario, and San Diego, California.

4. Analyze the data collected, beginning with the *quantitative* factors—factors that can be measured in dollars, such as annual transportation costs or taxes. These dollar values may be broken into separate cost categories (e.g., inbound and outbound transportation, labor, construction, and utilities) and separate revenue

sources (e.g., sales, stock or bond issues, and interest income). These financial factors can then be converted to a single measure of financial merit and used to compare two or more sites.

5. Bring the qualitative factors pertaining to each site into the evaluation. A *qualitative* factor is one that cannot be evaluated in dollar terms, such as community attitudes or quality of life. To merge quantitative and qualitative factors, some managers review the expected performance of each factor, while others assign each factor a weight of relative importance and calculate a weighted score for each site, using a preference matrix. What is important in one situation may be unimportant or less important in another. The site with the highest weighted score is best.

After thoroughly evaluating between 5 and 15 sites, those making the study prepare a final report containing site recommendations, along with a summary of the data and analyses on which they are based. An audiovisual presentation of the key findings usually is delivered to top management in large firms.

| EXAMPLE 9.1 | *Calculating Weighted Scores in a Preference Matrix* |

**TUTOR
9.1**

A new medical facility, Health-Watch, is to be located in Erie, Pennsylvania. The following table shows the location factors, weights, and scores (1 = poor, 5 = excellent) for one potential site. The weights in this case add up to 100 percent. A weighted score will be calculated for each site. What is the weighted score for this site?

LOCATION FACTOR	WEIGHT	SCORE
Total patient miles per month	25	4
Facility utilization	20	3
Average time per emergency trip	20	3
Expressway accessibility	15	4
Land and construction costs	10	1
Employee preferences	10	5

SOLUTION

The weighted score (WS) for this particular site is calculated by multiplying each factor's weight by its score and adding the results:

$$WS = (25 \times 4) + (20 \times 3) + (20 \times 3) + (15 \times 4) + (10 \times 1) + (10 \times 5)$$
$$= 100 + 60 + 60 + 60 + 10 + 50$$
$$= 340$$

The total weighted score of 340 can be compared with the total weighted scores for other sites being evaluated. ☐

Should a firm locate near its suppliers, workforce, or customers?

---

load–distance method
A mathematical model used to evaluate locations based on proximity factors.

APPLYING THE LOAD–DISTANCE METHOD

In the systematic selection process, the analyst must identify attractive candidate locations and compare them on the basis of quantitative factors. The load–distance method can facilitate this step. Several location factors relate directly to distance: proximity to markets, average distance to target customers, proximity to suppliers and resources, and proximity to other company facilities. The **load–distance method** is a mathematical model used to evaluate locations based on proximity factors. The objective is to select a location that minimizes the total weighted loads moving into and out of the facility. The distance between two points is expressed by assigning the points to grid coordinates on a map. (See the Layout chapter for the use of a similar approach in layout planning.) An alternative approach is to use time rather than distance.

DISTANCE MEASURES. Suppose that a new warehouse is to be located to serve Pennsylvania. It will receive inbound shipments from several suppliers, including one in Erie. If the new warehouse were located at State College, what would be the distance between the two facilities? If shipments travel by truck, the distance depends on the highway system and the specific route taken. Computer software is available for calculating the actual mileage between any two locations in the same country. However, for a rough calculation, which is all that is needed for the load–distance method, either a Euclidean or rectilinear distance measure may be used.

Euclidean distance is the straight-line distance, or shortest possible path, between two points. To calculate this distance, we create a graph. We place point *A* on the grid to represent the supplier's location in Erie. Then we place point *B* on the grid to represent the possible warehouse location at State College. In Figure 9.2, the distance between points *A* and *B* is the length of the hypotenuse of a right triangle, or

> **Euclidean distance** The straight-line distance, or shortest possible path, between two points.

$$d_{AB} = \sqrt{(x_A - x_B)^2 + (y_A - y_B)^2}$$

where

$$d_{AB} = \text{distance between points } A \text{ and } B$$
$$x_A = x\text{-coordinate of point } A$$
$$y_A = y\text{-coordinate of point } A$$
$$x_B = x\text{-coordinate of point } B$$
$$y_B = y\text{-coordinate of point } B$$

> **rectilinear distance** The distance between two points with a series of 90-degree turns, as along city blocks.

Rectilinear distance measures distance between two points with a series of 90° turns, as along city blocks. Essentially, this distance is the sum of the two dashed lines representing the base and side of the triangle in Figure 9.2. The distance traveled in the *x*-direction is the absolute value of the difference in *x*-coordinates. Adding this result to the absolute value of the difference in the *y*-coordinates gives

$$d_{AB} = |x_A - x_B| + |y_A - y_B|$$

FIGURE 9.2

Distance Between Erie (Point A) and State College (Point B)

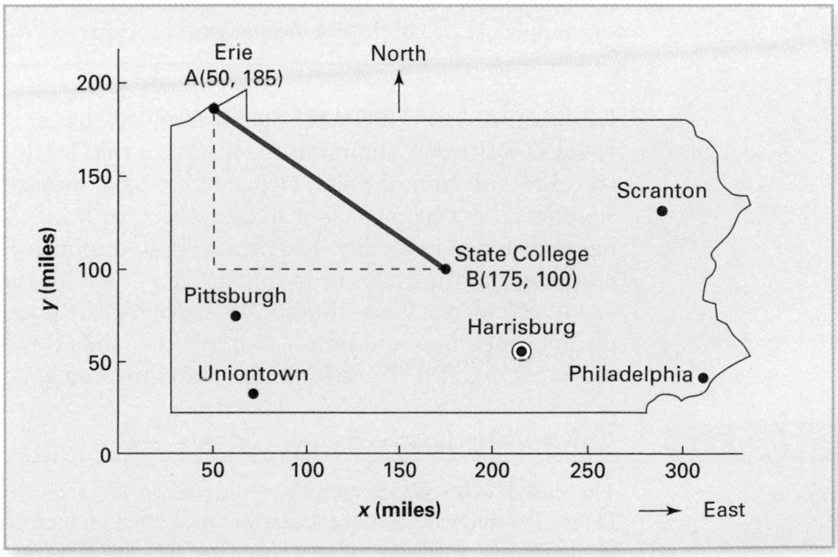

| EXAMPLE 9.2 | *Calculating Distances* |

What is the Euclidean distance between points *A* and *B* in Figure 9.2? The rectilinear distance?

**TUTOR
9.2**

SOLUTION

Calculating the Euclidean distance, we get

$$d_{AB} = \sqrt{(50 - 175)^2 + (185 - 100)^2}$$
$$= 151.2 \text{ miles}$$

The rectilinear distance,

$$d_{AB} = |50 - 175| + |185 - 100|$$
$$= 210 \text{ miles}$$

is longer. OM Explorer confirms these calculations (Figure 9.3).

Tutor 9.2 - Distance Measures

Enter the *x* and *y* coordinates of the two towns:

	x	*y*
Erie (Point A)	50	185
State College (Point B)	175	100

To find the Euclidean distance, subtract the second town's *x* value from that of the first town, and square the result. Do the same with the two *y* values. Then add the two and compute the square root.

(Erie *x* - State College *x*)²	15,625	Euclidean distance	151.16
(Erie *y* - State College *y*)²	7,225		

To find the rectilinear distance, get the absolute value of the result of subtracting the second town's *x* from the first town's. Do the same with *y*. Then add the absolute differences together:

(Erie *x* - State College *x*)	125	Rectilinear distance	210
(Erie *y* - State College *y*)	85		

FIGURE 9.3 • Distance Calculations Using Tutor 9.2

Decision Point The two measures give quite different numbers: 151.16 versus 210 miles. However, managers are interested in the relative performance of different locations. Hence, they can simply use one of the distance measures consistently throughout the calculations. ❑

CALCULATING A LOAD–DISTANCE SCORE. Suppose that a firm planning a new location wants to select a site that minimizes the distances that loads, particularly the larger ones, must travel to and from the site. Depending on the industry, a *load* may be shipments from suppliers, between plants, or to customers, or it may be customers or employees traveling to or from the facility. The firm seeks to minimize its load–distance, or *ld*, score, generally by choosing a location so that large loads go short distances.

To calculate a load–distance, *ld*, score for any potential location, we use either of the distance measures and simply multiply the loads flowing to and from the facility by the distances traveled. These loads may be expressed as tons or number of trips per week.

| EXAMPLE 9.3 | *Calculating Load–Distance Scores* |

The new Health-Watch facility is targeted to serve seven census tracts in Erie, Pennsylvania. Figure 9.4 shows the coordinates for the center of each census tract, along with the projected populations, measured in thousands. Customers will travel from the seven census tract centers to

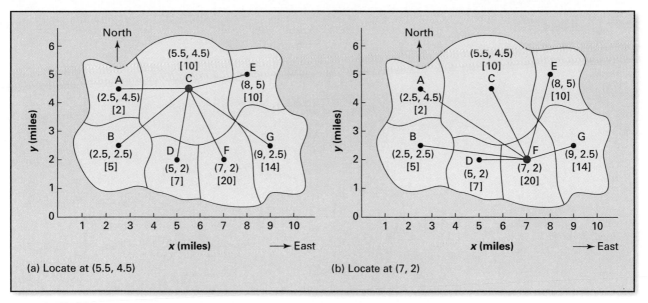

FIGURE 9.4 • Calculating Load–Distance Scores for Two Possible Locations.
Note: The numbers in parentheses are census tract coordinates; the numbers in brackets are the populations of the census tracts in thousands.

the new facility when they need health care. Two locations being considered for the new facility are at (5.5, 4.5) and (7, 2), which are the centers of census tracts C and F. If we use the population as the loads and use rectilinear distance, which location is better in terms of its total *ld* score?

SOLUTION

We want to calculate the *ld* score for each location. The distance between census tract A at (2.5, 4.5) and the first alternative location at (5.5, 4.5) is 3 miles in the east–west direction plus 0 miles in the north–south direction, or 3 miles. The *ld* score equals the distance multiplied by the population (measured in thousands), or 6. Using the coordinates from Figure. 9.4, we calculate the *ld* score for each tract.

CENSUS TRACT	(x, y)	POPULATION (*l*)	LOCATE AT (5.5, 4.5) DISTANCE (*d*)	*ld*	LOCATE AT (7, 2) DISTANCE (*d*)	*ld*
A	(2.5, 4.5)	2	3 + 0 = 3	6	4.5 + 2.5 = 7	14
B	(2.5, 2.5)	5	3 + 2 = 5	25	4.5 + 0.5 = 5	25
C	(5.5, 4.5)	10	0 + 0 = 0	0	1.5 + 2.5 = 4	40
D	(5, 2)	7	0.5 + 2.5 = 3	21	2 + 0 = 2	14
E	(8, 5)	10	2.5 + 0.5 = 3	30	1 + 3 = 4	40
F	(7, 2)	20	1.5 + 2.5 = 4	80	0 + 0 = 0	0
G	(9, 2.5)	14	3.5 + 2 = 5.5	77	2 + 0.5 = 2.5	35
			Total	239	Total	168

Decision Point Summing the scores for all tracts gives a total *ld* score of 239 when the facility is located at (5.5, 4.5) versus an *ld* score of 168 at location (7, 2). Therefore, the location in census tract F is a better location. However, before settling on census tract F, management wanted to evaluate still other candidate locations. ❑

FIGURE 9.5

*Load–Distance Scores
for Several Alternative
Locations*

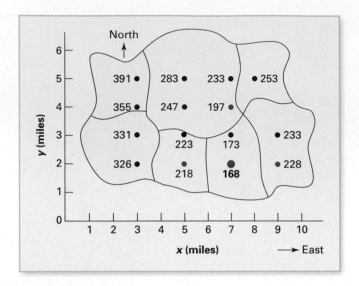

We should evaluate still other candidate locations before making a decision. Figure 9.5 gives *ld* scores for several alternative locations (shown as dots). The best location appears to be at about (7, 2), at least on the basis of *ld* scores. Should an acceptable medical facility site not be available in the immediate area, the grid shows the implications of selecting a location elsewhere. For example, a two-mile deviation directly north to (7, 4) increases the score to only 197, which is less of a penalty than the same deviation to the east or west.

We could solve directly for the optimal location in Example 9.3.[1] However, practical considerations rarely allow managers to select this exact location. For example, land may not be available there at a reasonable price, or other location factors may make the site undesirable. Further, the rectilinear distance measure may be unrealistic. For such reasons, an analysis such as the one shown in Figure 9.5 is particularly useful. Any distance measure can be used with these procedures.

CENTER OF GRAVITY. Testing different locations with the load–distance model is relatively simple if some systematic search process is followed. A good starting point is the **center of gravity** of the target area. The center of gravity's *x*-coordinate, denoted x^*, is found by multiplying each point's *x*-coordinate (x_i) by its load (l_i), summing these products ($\Sigma\, l_i x_i$), and then dividing by the sum of the loads ($\Sigma\, l_i$). The *y*-coordinate, denoted y^*, is found the same way, with the *y*-coordinates used in the numerator. The formulas are

center of gravity A good starting point in evaluating locations is with the load–distance model; the center of gravity's *x*-coordinate is found by multiplying each point's *x*-coordinate by its load (*l*), summing these products, and then dividing by the sum of the loads.

$$x^* = \frac{\sum_i l_i x_i}{\sum_i l_i} \quad \text{and} \quad y^* = \frac{\sum_i l_i y_i}{\sum_i l_i}$$

This location usually is not the optimal one for the Euclidean or rectilinear distance measures, but it still is an excellent starting point. Calculate the load–distance scores for locations in its vicinity until you're satisfied that your solution is near optimal.

---

[1]As long as rectilinear distance is assumed, the optimal site can be found by using the *cross-median* technique. See Fitzsimmons and Fitzsimmons (1998) and Problem 18 at the end of this chapter.

| EXAMPLE 9.4 | *Finding the Center of Gravity* |

TUTOR
9.3

What is the target area's center of gravity for the Health-Watch medical facility in Example 9.3?

SOLUTION

To calculate the center of gravity, we begin with the information in the following table, where population is given in thousands:

CENSUS TRACT	(x, y)	POPULATION (*l*)	*lx*	*ly*
A	(2.5, 4.5)	2	5	9
B	(2.5, 2.5)	5	12.5	12.5
C	(5.5, 4.5)	10	55	45
D	(5, 2)	7	35	14
E	(8, 5)	10	80	50
F	(7, 2)	20	140	40
G	(9, 2.5)	14	126	35
	Totals	68	453.5	205.5

Next we solve for x^* and y^*.

$$x^* = \frac{453.5}{68} = 6.67$$

$$y^* = \frac{205.5}{68} = 3.02$$

OM Explorer confirms these calculations (Figure 9.6).

Solver - Center of Gravity

Enter data in yellow - shaded areas.

Enter the names of the towns and the coordinates (*x* and *y*) and population (or load, *l*) of each town.

| Add A Town | Remove A Town |

City/Town Name	x	y	l	lx	ly
A	2.5	4.5	2	5	9
B	2.5	2.5	5	12.5	12.5
C	5.5	4.5	10	55	45
D	5	2	7	35	14
E	8	5	10	80	50
F	7	2	20	140	40
G	9	2.5	14	126	35
			68	453.5	205.5

| Center-of-Gravity Coordinates | x* | 6.67 |
| | y* | 3.02 |

FIGURE 9.6 • Location Analysis with Center-of-Gravity Solver

Decision Point The center of gravity is (6.67, 3.02), which is not necessarily optimal. It is in the general vicinity of location (7, 2), which was found best from the grid search in Figure 9.5. Using the center of gravity as a starting point, managers can now search in its vicinity for the optimal location. ☐

USING BREAK-EVEN ANALYSIS

How does the expected output level of the facility affect location choice?

Break-even analysis (see the Decision Making supplement) can help a manager compare location alternatives on the basis of quantitative factors that can be expressed in terms of total cost. It is particularly useful when the manager wants to define the ranges over which each alternative is best. The basic steps for graphic and algebraic solutions are as follows.

1. Determine the variable costs and fixed costs for each site. Recall that *variable costs* are the portion of the total cost that varies directly with the volume of output. Recall that *fixed costs* are the portion of the total cost that remains constant regardless of output levels.
2. Plot the total cost lines—the sum of variable and fixed costs—for all the sites on a single graph.
3. Identify the approximate ranges for which each location has the lowest cost.
4. Solve algebraically for the break-even points over the relevant ranges.

EXAMPLE 9.5

Break-Even Analysis for Location

TUTOR 9.4

An operations manager has narrowed the search for a new facility location to four communities. The annual fixed costs (land, property taxes, insurance, equipment, and buildings) and the variable costs (labor, materials, transportation, and variable overhead) are

COMMUNITY	FIXED COSTS PER YEAR	VARIABLE COSTS PER UNIT
A	$150,000	$62
B	$300,000	$38
C	$500,000	$24
D	$600,000	$30

a. Plot the total cost curves for all the communities on a single graph. Identify on the graph the approximate range over which each community provides the lowest cost.

b. Using break-even analysis, calculate the break-even quantities over the relevant ranges.

c. If the expected demand is 15,000 units per year, what is the best location?

SOLUTION

a. To plot a community's total cost line, let us first compute the total cost for two output levels: $Q = 0$ and $Q = 20,000$ units per year. For the $Q = 0$ level, the total cost is simply the fixed costs. For the $Q = 20,000$ level, the total cost (fixed plus variable costs) is

COMMUNITY	FIXED COSTS	VARIABLE COSTS (COST PER UNIT)(NO. OF UNITS)	TOTAL COST (FIXED + VARIABLE)
A	$150,000	$62(20,000) = $1,240,000	$1,390,000
B	$300,000	$38(20,000) = $ 760,000	$1,060,000
C	$500,000	$24(20,000) = $ 480,000	$ 980,000
D	$600,000	$30(20,000) = $ 600,000	$1,200,000

Figure 9.7 shows the graph of the total cost lines. The line for community A goes from (0, 150) to (20, 1,390). The graph indicates that community A is best for low volumes, B for intermediate volumes, and C for high volumes. We should no longer consider community D, as both its fixed *and* its variable costs are higher than community C's.

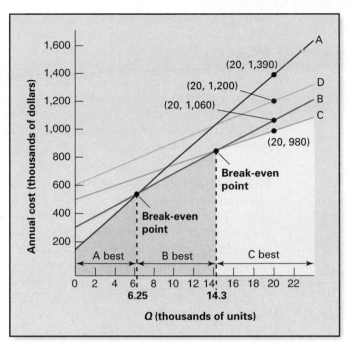

FIGURE 9.7 • Break-Even Analysis of Four Candidate Locations

b. The break-even quantity between A and B lies at the end of the first range, where A is best, and the beginning of the second range, where B is best. We find it by setting their total cost equations equal to each other and solving:

$$\begin{matrix} (A) & (B) \end{matrix}$$

$$\$150{,}000 + \$62Q = \$300{,}000 + \$38Q$$

$$Q = 6{,}250 \text{ units}$$

The break-even quantity between B and C lies at the end of the range over which B is best and the beginning of the final range where C is best. It is

$$\begin{matrix} (B) & (C) \end{matrix}$$

$$\$300{,}000 + \$38Q = \$500{,}000 + \$24Q$$

$$Q = 14{,}286 \text{ units}$$

No other break-even quantities are needed. The break-even point between A and C lies above the shaded area, which does not mark either the start or the end of one of the three relevant ranges.

Decision Point Management located the new facility at Community C, because the 15,000 units-per-year demand forecast lies in the high-volume range. ❑

LOCATING A FACILITY WITHIN A NETWORK OF FACILITIES

When a firm with a network of existing facilities plans a new facility, one of two conditions exists: Either the facilities operate independently (e.g., a chain of restaurants, health clinics, banks, or retail establishments) or the facilities interact (e.g., component manufacturing plants, assembly plants, and warehouses). Independently operating units can be located by treating each as a separate single facility, as described in the preceding section. Locating interacting facilities introduces new issues, such as how to allocate work between the facilities and how to determine the best capacity for each. Changing work allocations in turn affects the size (or capacity utilization) of the facilities. Thus, the multiple-facility location problem has three dimensions—location, allocation, and capacity—that must be solved simultaneously. In many cases, the analyst can identify a workable solution merely by looking for patterns in the cost, demand, and capacity data and using trial-and-error calculations. In other cases, more formal approaches are needed.

THE TRANSPORTATION METHOD

What is the best way to partition work among various facilities?

transportation method
A quantitative approach that can help solve multiple-facility location problems.

The **transportation method** is a quantitative approach that can help solve multiple-facility location problems. We use it here to determine the allocation pattern that minimizes the cost of shipping products from two or more plants, or *sources of supply*, to two or more warehouses, or *destinations*.[2] We focus on the setup and interpretation of the problem, leaving the rest of the solution process to a software package on a computer. The transportation method is based on linear programming (see the Linear Programming supplement). More efficient algorithms for solving this problem can be found in textbooks covering quantitative methods and management science.

The transportation method does not solve *all* facets of the multiple-facility location problem. It only finds the *best* shipping pattern between plants and warehouses for a particular set of plant locations, each with a given capacity. The analyst must try a variety of location–capacity combinations and use the transportation method to find the optimal distribution for each one. Distribution costs (variable shipping and possibly variable production costs) are but one important input in evaluating a particular location–allocation combination. Investment costs and other fixed costs also must be considered, along with various qualitative factors. This complete analysis must be made for each reasonable location–capacity combination. Because of the importance of making a good decision, this extra effort is well worth its cost.

SETTING UP THE INITIAL TABLEAU. The first step in solving a transportation problem is to format it in a standard matrix, sometimes called a *tableau*. The basic steps in setting up an initial tableau are as follows:

1. Create a row for each plant (existing or new) being considered and a column for each warehouse.

2. Add a column for plant capacities and a row for warehouse demands, and then insert their specific numerical values.

3. Each cell not in the requirements row or capacity column represents a shipping route from a plant to a warehouse. Insert the unit costs in the upper right-hand corner of each of these cells.

The Sunbelt Pool Company is considering building a new 500-unit plant, because business is booming. One possible location is Atlanta. Figure 9.8 shows a tableau with its plant capacity, warehouse requirements, and shipping costs. The tableau shows, for example, that shipping one unit from the existing Phoenix plant to warehouse 1 costs $5.00. Costs are assumed to increase linearly with the size of the shipment; that is, the cost is the same *per unit* regardless of the size of the total shipment.

---

[2] It can also be used to determine an optimal production plan (see the Aggregate Planning chapter) or an optimal allocation of service accounts to service centers.

FIGURE 9.8

Initial Tableau

Plant	Warehouse			Capacity
	1	2	3	
Phoenix	5.0	6.0	5.4	400
Atlanta	7.0	4.6	6.6	500
Requirements	200	400	300	900 / 900

In the transportation method, the sum of the shipments in a row must equal the corresponding plant's capacity. For example, in Figure 9.8, the total shipments from the Atlanta plant to warehouses 1, 2, and 3 must add up to 500. Similarly, the sum of shipments to a column must equal the corresponding warehouse's demand requirements. Thus, shipments to warehouse 1 from Phoenix and Atlanta must total 200 units.

DUMMY PLANTS OR WAREHOUSES. The transportation method also requires that the sum of capacities equal the sum of demands, which happens to be the case at 900 units (see Figure 9.8). In many real problems, total capacity may exceed requirements, or vice versa. If capacity exceeds requirements by *r* units, we add an extra column (a *dummy warehouse*) with a demand of *r* units and make the shipping costs in the newly created cells $0. Shipments are not actually made, so they represent unused plant capacity. Similarly, if requirements exceed capacity by *r* units, we add an extra row (a *dummy plant*) with a capacity of *r* units. We assign shipping costs equal to the stockout costs of the new cells. If stockout costs are unknown or are the same for all warehouses, we simply assign shipping costs of $0 per unit to each cell in the dummy row. The optimal solution will not be affected because the shortage of *r* units is required in all cases. Adding a dummy warehouse or dummy plant ensures that the sum of capacities equals the sum of demands. Some software packages automatically add them when we make the data inputs.

FINDING A SOLUTION. After the initial tableau has been set up, the goal is to find the least-cost allocation pattern that satisfies all demands and exhausts all capacities. This pattern can be found by using the transportation method, which guarantees the optimal solution. The initial tableau is filled in with a feasible solution that satisfies all warehouse demands and exhausts all plant capacities. Then a new tableau is created, defining a new solution that has a lower total cost. This iterative process continues until no improvements can be made in the current solution, signaling that the optimal solution has been found. When using a computer package, all that you have to input is the information for the initial tableau.

Another procedure is the simplex method (see the Linear Programming supplement), although more inputs are required. The transportation problem is actually a special case of linear programming, which can be modeled with a decision variable for each cell in the tableau, a constraint for each row in the tableau (requiring that each plant's capacity be fully utilized), and a constraint for each column in the tableau (requiring that each warehouse's demand be satisfied).

Whichever method is used, the number of nonzero shipments in the optimal solution will never exceed the sum of the numbers of plants and warehouses minus 1. The Sunbelt Pool Company has 2 plants and 3 warehouses, so there need not be more than 4 (or $3 + 2 - 1$) shipments in the optimal solution.

EXAMPLE 9.6

Interpreting the Optimal Solution

The printout in Figure 9.9 from OM Explorer is for the Sunbelt Pool Company. Tutor 9.5 is set up to handle up to three sources and four destinations (for larger problems, use the *Transportation Method* Solver). With only two sources, we make the third row a "dummy" with a capacity of 0, and the fourth warehouse a "dummy" with a demand of 0. The bold numbers show the optimal shipments. Verify that each plant's capacity is exhausted and that each warehouse's demand is filled. Also confirm that the total transportation cost of the solution is $4,580.

Inputs

Tutor 9.5 - Transportation Method

Enter data in yellow shaded areas.

Solve

Sources	Destinations				Capacity
	Warehouse 1	Warehouse 2	Warehouse 3	Dummy	
Phoenix	5 **200**	6	5.4 **200**	0	400
Atlanta	7	4.6 **400**	6.6 **100**	0	500
Dummy	0	0	0	0	0
					900
Requirements	200	400	300	0	900	900

Costs	$1,000	$1,840	$1,740	$0	
Total Cost					$4,580

FIGURE 9.9 • Optimal Tableau for Sun Belt Pool Using Tutor 9.5

SOLUTION

Phoenix ships 200 units to warehouse 1 and 200 units to warehouse 3, exhausting its 400-unit capacity. Atlanta ships 400 units of its 500-unit capacity to warehouse 2 and the remaining 100 units to warehouse 3. All warehouse demand is satisfied: Warehouse 1 is fully supplied by Phoenix and warehouse 2 by Atlanta. Warehouse 3 receives 200 units from Phoenix and 100 units from Atlanta, satisfying its 300-unit demand. The total transportation cost is $200(\$5.00) + 200(\$5.40) + 400(\$4.60) + 100(\$6.60) = \$4,580$.

Decision Point Management must evaluate other plant locations before deciding on the best one. The optimal solution does not necessarily mean that the best choice is to open an Atlanta plant. It just means that the best allocation pattern for the current choices on the other two dimensions of this multiple-facility location problem (i.e., a capacity of 400 units at Phoenix and the new plant's location at Atlanta) results in total *transportation* costs of $4,580. □

THE LARGER SOLUTION PROCESS. Other costs and various qualitative factors also must be considered as additional parts of a complete evaluation. For example, the annual profits earned from the expansion must be balanced against the land and construction costs of a new plant in Atlanta. Thus, management might use the preference matrix approach (see Example 9.1) to account for the full set of location factors.

The analyst should also evaluate other capacity and location combinations. For example, one possibility is to expand at Phoenix and build a smaller plant at Atlanta. Alternatively, a new plant could be built at another location, or several new plants could be built. The analyst must repeat the analysis for each such likely location strategy.

OTHER METHODS OF LOCATION ANALYSIS

Many location analysis problems are even more complex than those discussed so far. Consider the complexity that a medium-sized manufacturer faces when distributing products through warehouses, or *distribution centers,* to various demand centers. The problem is to determine the number, size, allocation pattern, and location of the warehouses. There could be thousands of demand centers, hundreds of potential warehouse locations, several plants, and multiple product lines. Transportation rates depend on the direction of shipment, product, quantity, rate breaks, and geographic area.

Such complexity requires use of a computer for a comprehensive evaluation. Three basic types of computer models have been developed for this purpose: heuristic, simulation, and optimization.

heuristics Solution guidelines, or rules of thumb, that find feasible—but not necessarily the best—solutions to problems.

HEURISTICS. Solution guidelines, or rules of thumb, that find feasible—but not necessarily the best—solutions to problems are called **heuristics.** Their advantages include efficiency and an ability to handle general views of a problem. The systematic search procedure utilizing a target area's center of gravity described earlier for single-facility location problems is a typical heuristic procedure. One of the first heuristics to be computerized for location problems was proposed more than three decades ago to handle several hundred potential warehouse sites and several thousand demand centers (Kuehn and Hamburger, 1963). Many other heuristic models are available today for analyzing a variety of situations.

simulation A modeling technique that reproduces the behavior of a system.

SIMULATION. A modeling technique that reproduces the behavior of a system is called **simulation.** Simulation allows manipulation of certain variables and shows the effect on selected operating characteristics (see the Simulation supplement). Simulation models allow the analyst to evaluate different location alternatives by trial and error. It is up to the analyst to propose the most reasonable alternatives. Simulation handles more realistic views of a problem and involves the analyst in the solution process itself. For each run, the analyst inputs the facilities to be opened, and the simulator typically makes the allocation decisions based on some reasonable assumptions that have been written into the computer program. The Ralston-Purina Company used simulation to assist in locating warehouses to serve 137 demand centers, 5 field warehouses, and 4 plants. Random demand at each demand center by product type was simulated over a period of time. Demand was met by the closest warehouse having available inventory. Data were produced by simulating inventory levels, transportation costs, warehouse operating costs, and backorders. Ralston-Purina implemented the result of the simulation, which showed that the least-cost alternative would be to consolidate the five field warehouses into only three.

optimization A procedure used to determine the "best" solution; generally utilizes simplified and less realistic views of a problem.

OPTIMIZATION. The transportation method was one of the first optimization procedures for solving one part (the allocation pattern) of multiple-facility location problems. In contrast to heuristics and simulation, **optimization** involves procedures to determine the "best" solution. Even though this approach might appear to be preferable, it has a limitation: Optimization procedures generally utilize simplified and less realistic views of a problem. However, the payoffs can be substantial. Hunt-Wesson Foods applied optimization techniques to the company's network. As a result of the analysis, five changes were made, reportedly saving millions of dollars.

MANAGING LOCATION ACROSS THE ORGANIZATION

Location decisions affect processes and departments throughout the organization. When locating new retail facilities, such as Au Bon Pain cafes, marketing must carefully assess how the location will appeal to customers and possibly open up new markets. Relocating the whole or part of an organization can significantly affect workforce attitudes and ability to operate effectively across department lines, as MCI's move of its Systems Engineering division from its Washington, D.C. headquarters to Colorado Springs. Locating new facilities or relocating existing ones can involve significant investment requirements, which must be carefully evaluated by accounting and finance people. Human resources must be attuned to the hiring and training needs, such as at StarTek's call center in Texas. Finally, operations also has an important stake in location decisions. The choices can significantly affect supply-chain effectiveness, workforce productivity, and the ability to provide quality products and services. International operations, such as at the Radisson Slavjanskaya hotel, introduce a new set of challenges and opportunities.

FORMULA REVIEW

1. Euclidean distance: $d_{AB} = \sqrt{(x_A - x_B)^2 + (y_A - y_B)^2}$

2. Rectilinear distance: $d_{AB} = |x_A - x_B| + |y_A - y_B|$

3. Load–distance score: $ld = \sum_i l_i d_i$

4. Center of gravity: $x^* = \dfrac{\sum_i l_i x_i}{\sum_i l_i}$ and $y^* = \dfrac{\sum_i l_i y_i}{\sum_i l_i}$

CHAPTER HIGHLIGHTS

❑ The globalization of operations affects both manufacturing and service industries. More facilities are being located in other countries, and offshore sales (and imports) are increasing. Four factors that spur globalization are improved transportation and communications technologies, opened financial systems, increased demand for imports, and fewer import quotas and other trade barriers. Offsetting the advantages of global operations are differences in language, regulations, and culture that create new management problems.

❑ Location decisions depend on many factors. For any situation some factors may be disregarded entirely; the remainder may be divided into dominant and secondary factors.

❑ Favorable labor climate, proximity to markets, quality of life, proximity to suppliers and resources, and proximity to other company facilities are important factors in most manufacturing plant location decisions. Proximity to markets, clients, or customers usually is the most important factor in service industry location decisions. Competition is a complicating factor in estimating the sales potential of a location. Having competitors' facilities nearby may be an asset or a liability, depending on the type of business.

One way of evaluating qualitative factors is to calculate a weighted score for each alternative location by using the preference matrix approach. The load–distance method brings together concerns of proximity (to markets, suppliers, resources, and other company facilities) during the early stages of location analysis. By making a full grid or patterned search of an area, an analyst identifies locations resulting in lower *ld* scores. The center of gravity of an area is a good starting point for making a patterned search. Break-even analysis can help compare location alternatives when location factors can be expressed in terms of variable and fixed costs.

Multiple-facility problems have three dimensions: location, allocation, and capacity. The transportation method is a basic tool for finding the best allocation pattern for a particular combination of location–capacity choices. Transportation costs are recalculated for each location–capacity combination under consideration. The transportation method's single criterion for determining the best shipping pattern is minimum transportation costs. To complete the location study, the analysis must be expanded to account for the full set of location factors.

Location analysis can become complex for multiple facilities. A variety of computerized heuristic, simulation, and optimization models have been developed over the last two decades to help analysts deal with this complexity.

KEY TERMS

SOLVED PROBLEM 1

An electronics manufacturer must expand by building a second facility. The search has been narrowed to four locations, all acceptable to management in terms of dominant factors. Assessment of these sites in terms of seven location factors is shown in Table 9.1. For example, location A has a factor score of 5 (excellent) for labor climate; the weight for this factor (20) is the highest of any.

TABLE 9.1 *Factor Information for Electronics Manufacturer*

LOCATION FACTOR	FACTOR WEIGHT	A	B	C	D
1. Labor climate	20	5	4	4	5
2. Quality of life	16	2	3	4	1
3. Transportation system	16	3	4	3	2
4. Proximity to markets	14	5	3	4	4
5. Proximity to materials	12	2	3	3	4
6. Taxes	12	2	5	5	4
7. Utilities	10	5	4	3	3

Calculate the weighted score for each location. Which location should be recommended?

SOLUTION

Based on the weighted scores in Table 9.2, location C is the preferred site, although location B is a close second.

TABLE 9.2 *Calculating Weighted Scores for Electronics Manufacturer*

LOCATION FACTOR	FACTOR WEIGHT	WEIGHTED SCORE FOR EACH LOCATION			
		A	B	C	D
1. Labor climate	20	100	80	80	100
2. Quality of life	16	32	48	64	16
3. Transportation system	16	48	64	48	32
4. Proximity to markets	14	70	42	56	56
5. Proximity to materials	12	24	36	36	48
6. Taxes	12	24	60	60	48
7. Utilities	10	50	40	30	30
Totals	100	348	370	374	330

SOLVED PROBLEM 2

The operations manager for Mile-High Beer has narrowed the search for a new facility location to seven communities. Annual fixed costs (land, property taxes, insurance, equipment, and buildings) and variable costs (labor, materials, transportation, and variable overhead) are shown in Table 9.3.

TABLE 9.3 *Fixed and Variable Costs for Mile-High Beer*

COMMUNITY	FIXED COSTS PER YEAR	VARIABLE COSTS PER BARREL
Aurora	$1,600,000	$17.00
Boulder	$2,000,000	$12.00
Colorado Springs	$1,500,000	$16.00
Denver	$3,000,000	$10.00
Englewood	$1,800,000	$15.00
Fort Collins	$1,200,000	$15.00
Golden	$1,700,000	$14.00

a. Which of the communities can be eliminated from further consideration because they are dominated (both variable and fixed costs are higher) by another community?

b. Plot the total cost curves for all remaining communities on a single graph. Identify on the graph the approximate range over which each community provides the lowest cost.

c. Using break-even analysis (see the Decision Making supplement), calculate the break-even quantities to determine the range over which each community provides the lowest cost.

SOLUTION

a. Aurora and Colorado Springs are dominated by Fort Collins, as both fixed and variable costs are higher for those communities than for Fort Collins. Englewood is dominated by Golden.

b. Figure 9.10 shows that Fort Collins is best for low volumes. Boulder for intermediate volumes, and Denver for high volumes. Although Golden is not dominated by any community, it is the second or third choice over the entire range. Golden does not become the lowest cost choice at any volume.

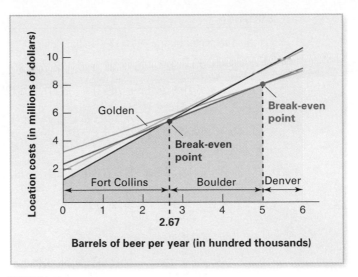

FIGURE 9.10

c. The break-even point between Fort Collins and Boulder is

$$\$1,200,000 + \$15Q = \$2,000,000 + \$12Q$$
$$Q = 266,667 \text{ barrels per year}$$

The break-even point between Denver and Boulder is

$$\$3,000,000 + \$10Q = \$2,000,000 + \$12Q$$
$$Q = 500,000 \text{ barrels per year}$$

SOLVED PROBLEM 3

A supplier to the electric utility industry has a heavy product, and transportation costs are high. One market area includes the lower part of the Great Lakes region and the upper portion of the Southeastern region. More than 600,000 tons are to be shipped to eight major customer locations, as shown in Table 9.4.

TABLE 9.4 *Markets for Electric Utilities Supplier*

CUSTOMER LOCATION	TONS SHIPPED	*XY*-COORDINATES
Three Rivers, Mich.	5,000	(7, 13)
Fort Wayne, Ind.	92,000	(8, 12)
Columbus, Ohio	70,000	(11, 10)
Ashland, Ky.	35,000	(11, 7)
Kingsport, Tenn.	9,000	(12, 4)
Akron, Ohio	227,000	(13, 11)
Wheeling, W.V.	16,000	(14, 10)
Roanoke, Va.	153,000	(15, 5)

a. Calculate the center of gravity, rounding distance to the nearest tenth.

b. Calculate the load–distance score for this location, using rectilinear distance.

SOLUTION

a. The center of gravity is (12.4, 9.2).

$$\sum_i l_i = 5 + 92 + 70 + 35 + 9 + 227 + 16 + 153 = 607$$

$$\sum_i l_i x_i = 5(7) + 92(8) + 70(11) + 35(11) + 9(12) + 227(13) + 16(14) + 153(15)$$
$$= 7{,}504$$

$$x^* = \frac{\sum_i l_i y_i}{\sum_i l_i} = \frac{7{,}504}{607} = 12.4$$

$$\sum_i l_i y_i = 5(13) + 92(12) + 70(10) + 35(7) + 9(4) + 227(11) + 16(10) + 153(5) = 5{,}572$$

$$y^* = \frac{\sum_i l_i y_i}{\sum_i l_i} = \frac{5{,}572}{607} = 9.2$$

b. The load–distance score is

$$ld = \sum_i l_i d_i = 5(5.4 + 3.8) + 92(4.4 + 2.8) + 70(1.4 + 0.8) + 35(1.4 + 2.2)$$
$$+ 9(0.4 + 5.2) + 227(0.6 + 1.8) + 16(1.6 + 0.8) + 153(2.6 + 4.2)$$
$$= 2{,}662.4$$

where $d_i = |x_i - x^*| + |y_i - y^*|$

SOLVED PROBLEM 4

The Arid Company makes canoe paddles to serve distribution centers in Worchester, Rochester, and Dorchester from existing plants in Battle Creek and Cherry Creek. Annual demand is expected to increase as projected in the bottom row of the tableau shown in Figure 9.11. Arid is considering locating a plant near the headwaters of Dee Creek. Annual capacity for each plant is shown in the right-hand column of the tableau. Transportation costs per paddle are shown in the tableau in the small boxes. For example, the cost to ship one paddle from Battle Creek to Worchester is $4.37. The optimal allocations are also shown. For example, Battle Creek ships 12,000 units to Rochester. What are the estimated transportation costs associated with this allocation pattern?

Source	Destination			Capacity
	Worchester	Rochester	Dorchester	
Battle Creek	$4.37	$4.25 **12,000**	$4.89	12,000
Cherry Creek	$4.00 **6,000**	$5.00 **4,000**	$5.27	10,000
Dee Creek	$4.13	$4.50 **6,000**	$3.75 **12,000**	18,000
Demand	6,000	22,000	12,000	40,000

FIGURE 9.11

SOLUTION

The total cost is $167,000.

Ship 12,000 units from Battle Creek to Rochester @ $4.25.	Cost = $51,000
Ship 6,000 units from Cherry Creek to Worchester @ $4.00.	Cost = $24,000
Ship 4,000 units from Cherry Creek to Rochester @ $5.00.	Cost = $20,000
Ship 6,000 units from Dee Creek to Rochester @ $4.50.	Cost = $27,000
Ship 12,000 units from Dee Creek to Dorchester @ $3.75.	Cost = $45,000
	Total	$167,000

DISCUSSION QUESTIONS

1. Break into teams. Select two organizations, one in services and one in manufacturing, that are known to some of your team members. What are the key factors that each organization would consider in locating a new facility? What data would you want to collect before evaluating the location options, and how would you collect it? Would additional factors or data be needed if some of the location options were in another country? Explain.

2. The owner of a major league baseball team is considering moving his team from its current city in the Rust Belt to a city in the Sun Belt. The Sun Belt city offers a larger television market and a new stadium and holds the potential for greater fan support. What ethical obligations, if any, does the owner have to the city in which the team is presently located?

3. Some observers say that maquiladoras allow U.S. companies to shift their unskilled jobs across the border while preserving the jobs of their skilled and knowledgeable workers in the United States. What ethical issues, if any, are involved with this use of maquiladoras?

OM EXPLORER AND INTERNET EXERCISES

Visit our Web site at www.prenhall.com/krajewski for OM Explorer Tutors, which explain quantitative techniques; Solvers, which help you apply mathematical models; and Internet Exercises, including Facility Tours, which expand on the topics in this chapter.

PROBLEMS

An icon next to a problem identifies the software that can be helpful, but not mandatory. The software is available on the Student CD-ROM that is packaged with every new copy of the textbook.

1. **OM Explorer** Calculate the weighted score for each location (A, B, C, and D) shown in Table 9.5. Which location would you recommend?

2. **OM Explorer** John and Jane Darling are newly-weds trying to decide among several available rentals. Alternatives were scored on a scale of 1 to 5 (5 = best) against weighted performance criteria, as shown in Table 9.6. The criteria included rent, proximity to work and

TABLE 9.5 *Factors for Locations A–D*

LOCATION FACTOR	FACTOR WEIGHT	FACTOR SCORE FOR EACH LOCATION			
		A	B	C	D
1. Labor climate	5	5	4	3	5
2. Quality of life	30	2	3	5	1
3. Transportation system	5	3	4	3	5
4. Proximity to markets	25	5	3	4	4
5. Proximity to materials	5	3	2	3	5
6. Taxes	15	2	5	5	4
7. Utilities	15	5	4	2	1
Total	100				

recreational opportunities, security, and other neighborhood characteristics associated with the couple's values and lifestyle. Alternative A is an apartment, B is a bungalow, C is a condo, and D is a downstairs apartment in Jane's parents' home.

TABLE 9.6   *Factors for Newlyweds*

| LOCATION FACTOR | FACTOR WEIGHT | FACTOR SCORE FOR EACH LOCATION | | | |
		A	B	C	D
1. Rent	25	3	1	2	5
2. Quality of life	20	2	5	5	4
3. Schools	5	3	5	3	1
4. Proximity to work	10	5	3	4	3
5. Proximity to recreation	15	4	4	5	2
6. Neighborhood security	15	2	4	4	4
7. Utilities	10	4	2	3	5
Total	100				

Which location is indicated by the preference matrix? What qualitative factors might cause this preference to change?

3. **OM Explorer** Two alternative locations are under consideration for a new plant: Jackson, Mississippi, and Dayton, Ohio. The Jackson location is superior in terms of costs. However, management believes that sales volume would decline if this location were chosen because it is farther from the market, and the firm's customers prefer local suppliers. The selling price of the product is $250 per unit in either case. Use the following information to determine which location yields the higher total profit contribution per year.

LOCATION	ANNUAL FIXED COST	VARIABLE COST PER UNIT	FORECAST DEMAND PER YEAR
Jackson	$1,500,000	$50	30,000 units
Dayton	$2,800,000	$85	40,000 units

4. **OM Explorer** Fall-Line, Inc., is a Great Falls, Montana, manufacturer of a variety of downhill skis. Fall-Line is considering four locations for a new plant: Aspen, Colorado; Medicine Lodge, Kansas; Broken Bow, Nebraska; and Wounded Knee, South Dakota. Annual fixed costs and variable costs per pair of skis are shown in the following table:

LOCATION	ANNUAL FIXED COSTS	VARIABLE COSTS PER PAIR
Aspen	$8,000,000	$250
Medicine Lodge	$2,400,000	$130
Broken Bow	$3,400,000	$ 90
Wounded Knee	$4,500,000	$ 65

a. Plot the total cost curves for all the communities on a single graph (see Solved Problem 2). Identify on the graph the range in volume over which each location would be best.

b. What break-even quantity defines each range?

Although Aspen's fixed and variable costs are dominated by those of the other communities, Fall-Line believes that both the demand and the price would be higher for skis made in Aspen than for skis made in the other locations. The following table shows those projections:

LOCATION	PRICE PER PAIR	FORECAST DEMAND PER YEAR
Aspen	$500	60,000 pairs
Medicine Lodge	$350	45,000 pairs
Broken Bow	$350	43,000 pairs
Wounded Knee	$350	40,000 pairs

c. Determine which location yields the highest total profit contribution per year.

d. Is this location decision sensitive to forecast accuracy? At what minimum sales volume does Aspen become the location of choice?

5. **OM Explorer** Wiebe Trucking, Inc., is planning a new warehouse to serve the West. Denver, Santa Fe, and Salt Lake City are under consideration. For each location, annual fixed costs (rent, equipment, and insurance) and average variable costs per shipment (labor, transportation, and utilities) are listed in the following table. Sales projections range from 550,000 to 600,000 shipments per year.

LOCATION	ANNUAL FIXED COSTS	VARIABLE COSTS PER SHIPMENT
Denver	$5,000,000	$4.65
Santa Fe	$4,200,000	$6.25
Salt Lake City	$3,500,000	$7.25

a. Plot the total cost curves for all the locations on a single graph.

b. Which city provides the lowest overall costs?

6. The operations manager for Hot House Roses has narrowed the search for a new facility location to seven communities. Annual fixed costs (land, property taxes, insurance, equipment, and buildings) and variable costs (labor, materials, transportation, and variable overhead) are shown in the following table:

COMMUNITY	FIXED COSTS PER YEAR	VARIABLE COSTS PER DOZEN
Aurora, Colo.	$210,000	$7.20
Flora, Ill.	$200,000	$7.00
Garden City, Kan.	$150,000	$9.00
Greensboro, N.C.	$280,000	$6.20
Roseland, La.	$260,000	$6.00
Sunnyvale, Calif.	$420,000	$5.00
Watertown, Mass.	$370,000	$8.00

a. Which of the communities can be eliminated from further consideration because they are dominated (both variable and fixed costs are higher) by another community?

b. Plot the total cost curves for the remaining communities on a single graph. Identify on the graph the approximate range over which each community provides the lowest cost.

c. Using break-even analysis (see the Decision Making supplement), calculate the break-even quantities to determine the range over which each community provides the lowest cost.

7. **OM Explorer** Ethel and Earl Griese narrowed their choice for a new oil refinery to three locations. Fixed and variable costs are as follows.

LOCATION	FIXED COSTS PER YEAR	VARIABLE COSTS PER UNIT
Albany	$ 350,000	$980
Baltimore	$1,500,500	$240
Chattanooga	$1,100,000	$500

a. Plot the total cost curves for all the communities on a single graph. Identify on the graph the range in volume over which each location would be best.

b. What break-even quantities define each range?

8. Sam Bagelstein is planning to operate a specialty bagel-sandwich kiosk but is undecided about whether to locate in the downtown shopping plaza or in a suburban shopping mall. Based on the following data, which location would you recommend?

LOCATION	DOWNTOWN	SUBURBAN
Annual rent including utilities	$12,000	$8,000
Expected annual demand (sandwiches)	30,000	25,000
Average variable costs per sandwich	$1.50	$1.00
Average selling price per sandwich	$3.25	$2.85

9. **OM Explorer** The following three points are the locations of important facilities in a transportation network: (20, 20), (30, 60), and (60, 0). The coordinates are in miles.

a. Calculate the Euclidean distances (in miles) between each of the three pairs of facilities.

b. Calculate these distances using rectilinear distances.

10. **OM Explorer** The following three points are the locations of important facilities in a transportation network: (20, 20), (50, 10), and (50, 60). The coordinates are in miles.

a. Calculate the Euclidean distances (in miles) between each of the three pairs of facilities.

b. Calculate these distances using rectilinear distances.

11. **OM Explorer** Centura High School is to be located at the population center of gravity of three communities: Boelus, population 228; Cairo, population 737; and Dannebrog, population 356. The coordinates (on a grid of square miles) for the communities are provided in Figure 9.12. Where should Centura High School be located? (Round to 0.1 mile.) What factors may result in locating at the site indicated by this technique?

12. **OM Explorer** Val's Pizza is looking for a single central location to make pizza for delivery only. This college town is arranged on a grid with arterial streets, as shown in Figure 9.13. The main campus (A), located at 14th and R streets, is the source of 4,000 pizza orders per week. Three smaller campuses (B, C, and D) are located at 52nd and V, at 67th and Z, and at 70th and South. Orders from the smaller campuses average 1,000 pizzas a week. In addition, the State Patrol headquarters (E) at 10th and A orders 500 pizzas per week.

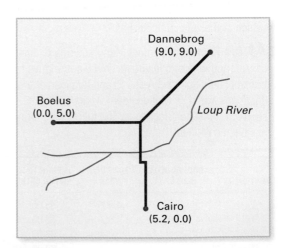

FIGURE 9.12

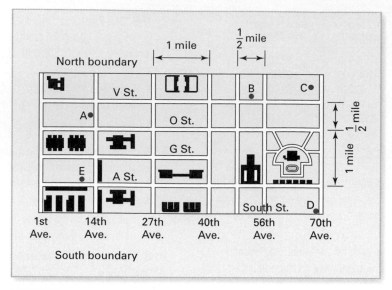

FIGURE 9.13

a. At about what intersection should Val start looking for a suitable site? (Estimate coordinates for the major demands accurate to the nearest 1/4 mile, and then find the center of gravity.)

b. What is the rectilinear weekly load–distance score for this location?

c. If the delivery person can travel 1 mile in two minutes on arterial streets and 1/4 mile per minute on residential streets, going from the center of gravity location to the farthest demand location will take how long?

13. The best location found manually so far for Figure 9.5 was (7, 2), with a load–distance score of 168. Search in the neighborhood of this point for a better solution. Using rectilinear distances, try (6.5, 2), (7, 2.5), and (7, 1.5). Which of these locations is best?

14. 🌐 **OM Explorer** Oakmont Manufacturing Company is considering where to locate its new plant relative to its two suppliers (in cities A and B) and two market areas (locations X and Y). Management wants to limit its search to these four locations. The following information has been collected:

LOCATION	*xy*-COORDINATES (MILES)	TONS PER YEAR	FREIGHT RATE ($/TON-MILE)
A	(200, 500)	4,000	$3.00
B	(400, 300)	2,000	$3.00
C	(300, 200)	5,000	$2.00
D	(600, 400)	3,000	$2.00

a. Which of these four locations gives the lowest total cost based on Euclidean distances? [*Hint*: The annual cost of inbound shipments from supplier A to the new plant is $20,000 per mile traveled (5,000 tons per year × $4.00 per ton-mile)].

b. Which location is best, based on rectilinear distances?

c. What are the coordinates of the center of gravity of the four locations?

15. 💿 **OM Explorer** A larger and more modern main post office is to be constructed at a new location in Davis, California. Growing suburbs have shifted the population density from where it was 40 years ago, when the current facility was built. Annette Werk, the postmaster, asked her assistants to draw a grid map of the seven points where mail is picked up and delivered in bulk. The coordinates and trips per day to and from the seven mail source points and the current main post office, M, are shown in the following table. M will continue to act as a mail source point after relocation.

MAIL SOURCE POINT	ROUND TRIPS PER DAY (*l*)	*xy*-COORDINATES (MILES)
1	6	(2, 8)
2	3	(6, 1)
3	3	(8, 5)
4	3	(13, 3)
5	2	(15, 10)
6	7	(6, 14)
7	5	(18, 1)
M	3	(10, 3)

a. Calculate the center of gravity as a possible location for the new facility (round to the nearest whole number).

b. Compare the load–distance scores for the location in part (a) and the current location, using rectilinear distance.

16. 🌐 **OM Explorer** Paramount Manufacturing is investigating which location would best position its new plant relative to two suppliers (located in cities A and B) and one market area (represented by city C). Management has limited the search for this plant to those three locations. The following information has been collected:

LOCATION	xy-COORDINATES (MILES)	TONS PER YEAR	FREIGHT RATE ($/TON-MILE)
A	(100, 200)	4,000	3
B	(400, 100)	3,000	1
C	(100, 100)	4,000	3

a. Which of the three locations gives the lowest total cost, based on Euclidean distances? [*Hint*: The annual cost of inbound shipments from supplier A to the new plant is $12,000 per mile (4,000 tons per year × $3 per ton-mile)].

b. Which location is best, based on rectilinear distances?

c. What are the coordinates of the center of gravity?

17. A personal computer manufacturer plans to locate its assembly plant in Taiwan and to ship its computers back to the United States through either Los Angeles or San Francisco. It has distribution centers in Atlanta, New York, and Chicago and will ship to them from whichever city is chosen as the port of entry on the West Coast. Overall transportation cost is the only criterion for choosing the port. Use the load–distance model and the information in Table 9.7 to select the more cost-effective city.

Advanced Problems

18. Continuing to assume rectilinear distance, use the cross-median technique (see the footnote on page 418) to find the optimal location for the problem in Example 9.3.

a. First calculate the median value, which is one-half the sum of the loads to all facilities.

b. Order the facilities by *x*-coordinate, starting with the facility having the smallest and ending with the one having the largest. Maintaining this order, add the facility loads until the total reaches or exceeds the median value calculated in part (a). Identify the facility that corresponds to the last load that entered the sum. Its *x*-coordinate is optimal for the new facility.

c. Repeat part (b), except order the facilities by *y*-coordinate, from smallest to largest. The *y*-coordinate of the facility corresponding to the last load entering the sum is optimal for the new facility.

d. How does the optimal solution compare with the best location shown in Figure 9.5 in terms of the load–distance score?

19. 🌐 **OM Explorer** Fire Brand makes picante sauce in El Paso and New York City. Distribution centers are located in Atlanta, Omaha, and Seattle. For the capacities, locations, and shipment costs per case shown in Figure 9.14, determine the shipping pattern that will minimize transportation costs. What are the estimated transportation costs associated with this optimal allocation pattern?

20. 🌐 **OM Explorer** The Pelican Company has four distribution centers (A, B, C, and D) that require 40,000, 60,000, 30,000, and 50,000 gallons of diesel fuel, respectively, per month for their long-haul trucks. Three fuel wholesalers (1, 2, and 3) have indicated their willingness to supply as many as 50,000, 70,000, and 60,000 gallons of fuel, respectively. The total cost (shipping plus price) of

TABLE 9.7 *Distances and Costs for PC Manufacturer*

		DISTRIBUTION CENTER (UNITS/YEAR)		
		CHICAGO (10,000)	ATLANTA (7,500)	NEW YORK (12,500)
Port of Entry	**Los Angeles**			
	Distance (miles)	1,800	2,600	3,200
	Shipping cost ($/unit)	0.0017/mile	0.0017/mile	0.0017/mile
	San Francisco			
	Distance (miles)	1,700	2,800	3,000
	Shipping cost ($/unit)	0.0020/mile	0.0020/mile	0.0020/mile

Source	Destination			Capacity
	Atlanta	Omaha	Seattle	
El Paso	$4	$5	$6	12,000
New York City	$3	$7	$9	10,000
Demand	8,000	10,000	4,000	22,000

FIGURE 9.14

delivering 1,000 gallons of fuel from each wholesaler to each distribution center is shown in the following table:

WHOLESALER	DISTRIBUTION CENTER			
	A	B	C	D
1	1.30	1.40	1.80	1.60
2	1.30	1.50	1.80	1.60
3	1.60	1.40	1.70	1.50

a. Determine the optimal solution. Show that all capacities have been exhausted and that all demands can be met with this solution.

b. What is the total cost of the solution?

21. 💿 **OM Explorer** The Acme Company has four factories that ship products to five warehouses. The shipping costs, requirements, capacities, and optimal allocations are shown in Figure 9.15. What is the total cost of the optimal solution?

22. 💿 **OM Explorer** The Giant Farmer Company processes food for sale in discount food stores. It has two plants: one in Chicago and one in Houston. The company also operates warehouses in Miami, Denver, Lincoln, and Jackson. Forecasts indicate that demand soon will exceed supply and that a new plant with a capacity of 8,000 cases per week is needed. The question is where to locate the new plant. Two potential sites are Buffalo

Factory	Shipping Cost per Case to Warehouse					Capacity
	W1	W2	W3	W4	W5	
F1	$1 — 60,000	$3 — 20,000	$4	$5	$6	80,000
F2	$2	$2	$1 — 50,000	$4 — 10,000	$5	60,000
F3	$1	$5	$1	$3 — 20,000	$1 — 40,000	60,000
F4	$5	$2 — 50,000	$4	$5	$4	50,000
Demand	60,000	70,000	50,000	30,000	40,000	250,000

FIGURE 9.15

and Atlanta. The following data on capacities, forecasted demand, and shipping costs have been gathered:

PLANT	CAPACITY (cases per week)	WAREHOUSE	DEMAND (cases per week)
Chicago	10,000	Miami	7,000
Houston	7,500	Denver	9,000
New plant	8,000	Lincoln	4,500
Total	25,500	Jackson	5,000
		Total	25,500

	SHIPPING COST TO WAREHOUSE (per case)			
PLANT	Miami	Denver	Lincoln	Jackson
Chicago	$7	$2	$4	$5
Houston	$3	$1	$5	$2
Buffalo (alternative 1)	$6	$9	$7	$4
Atlanta (alternative 2)	$2	$10	$8	$3

For each alternative new plant location, determine the shipping pattern that will minimize total transportation costs. Where should the new plant be located?

23. **OM Explorer** Pucchi, Inc., makes designer dog collars in Chihuahua, Mexico; Saint Bernard, Ohio; and Yorkshire, New York. Distribution centers are located in Baustin, Vegas, Nawlns, and New Yawk. The shipping costs, requirements, and capacities are shown in Figure 9.16. Use the transportation method to find the shipping schedule that minimizes shipping cost.

24. **OM Explorer** The Ajax International Company has four factories that ship products to five warehouses. The shipping costs, requirements, and capacities are shown in Figure 9.17. Use the transportation method to find the shipping schedule that minimizes shipping cost.

25. **OM Explorer** Consider further the Ajax International Company situation described in Problem 24. Ajax has decided to close F3 because of high operating costs. In addition, the company has decided to add 50,000 units of capacity to F4. The logistics manager is worried about the effect of this move on transportation costs. Presently, F3 is shipping 30,000 units to W4 and 50,000 units to W5 at a cost of $140,000 [or 30,000(3) + 50,000(1)]. If these warehouses were to be served by F4, the cost would increase to $350,000 [or 30,000(5) + 50,000(4)]. As a result, the Ajax logistics manager has requested a budget increase of $210,000 (or $350,000 − $140,000).

   a. Should the logistics manager get the budget increase?

   b. If not, how much would you budget for the increase in shipping costs?

26. **OM Explorer** Consider the facility location problem at the Giant Farmer Company described in Problem 22. Management is considering a third site, at Memphis. The shipping costs per case from Memphis are $3 to Miami, $11 to Denver, $6 to Lincoln, and $5 to Jackson. Find the minimum-cost plan for an alternative plant in Memphis. Would this result change the decision in Problem 22?

27. **OM Explorer** The Bright Paint Company has four factories (A, B, C, and D) that require 30,000, 20,000, 10,000, and 20,000 paint cans, respectively, per month. Three paint-can suppliers (1, 2, and 3) have indicated

Factory	Shipping Cost per Collar to Distribution Centers					Capacity
	Baustin	Vegas	Nawlns	New Yawk	Dummy	
Chihuahua	$8	$5	$4	$9	$0	12,000
Saint Bernard	$4	$6	$3	$3	$0	7,000
Yorkshire	$2	$8	$6	$1	$0	4,000
Demand	4,000	6,000	3,000	8,000	2,000	23,000

FIGURE 9.16

Factory	Shipping Cost per Case to Warehouse						Capacity
	W1	W2	W3	W4	W5	Dummy	
F1	$1	$3	$3	$5	$6	$0	50,000
F2	$2	$2	$1	$4	$5	$0	80,000
F3	$1	$5	$1	$3	$1	$0	80,000
F4	$5	$2	$4	$5	$4	$0	40,000
Demand	45,000	30,000	30,000	35,000	50,000	60,000	250,000

FIGURE 9.17

their willingness to supply as many as 40,000, 30,000, and 20,000 cans per month, respectively. The shipping costs per 100 cans are shown in Figure 9.18, along with capacity and demand quantities in hundreds of cans.

Currently supplier 1 is shipping 20,000 cans to plant B and 20,000 cans to D. Supplier 2 is shipping 30,000 cans to A, and supplier 3 is shipping 10,000 gallons to C. Does the present delivery arrangement minimize the total cost to the Bright Paint Company? If not, find a plan that does so.

28. 💿 **OM Explorer** The Chambers Corporation produces and markets an automotive theft-deterrent product, which it stocks in various warehouses throughout the country. Recently, its market research group compiled a forecast indicating that a significant increase in demand will occur in the near future, after which demand will level off for the foreseeable future. The company has decided to satisfy this demand by constructing new plant capacity. Chambers already has plants in Baltimore and Milwaukee

Supplier	Shipping Cost per 100 Cans to Plant					Capacity
	A	B	C	D	Dummy	
S1	$54	$48	$50	$46		400
S2	$52	$50	$54	$48		300
S3	$46	$48	$50	$52		200
Demand	300	200	100	200	100	900

FIGURE 9.18

and has no desire to relocate those facilities. Each plant is capable of producing 600,000 units per year.

After a thorough search, the company developed three site and capacity alternatives. *Alternative 1* is to build a 600,000-unit plant in Portland. *Alternative 2* is to build a 600,000-unit plant in San Antonio. *Alternative 3* is to build a 300,000-unit plant in Portland and a 300,000-unit plant in San Antonio. The company has four warehouses that distribute the product to retailers. The market research study provided the following data:

WAREHOUSE	EXPECTED ANNUAL DEMAND
Atlanta (AT)	500,000
Columbus (CO)	300,000
Los Angeles (LA)	600,000
Seattle (SE)	400,000

The logistics department compiled the following cost table that specified the cost per unit to ship the product from each plant to each warehouse in the most economical manner, subject to the reliability of the various carriers involved:

	WAREHOUSE			
PLANT	AT	CO	LA	SE
Baltimore	$0.35	$0.20	$0.85	$0.75
Milwaukee	$0.55	$0.15	$0.70	$0.65
Portland	$0.85	$0.60	$0.30	$0.10
San Antonio	$0.55	$0.40	$0.40	$0.55

As one part of the location–capacity decision, management wants an estimate of the total distribution cost for each alternative. Use the transportation method to calculate these estimates.

CASE **IMAGINATIVE TOYS**

When Gerald Kramb arrived at the company offices early on Monday, July 1, 1991, to review the end-of-the-year sales and operating figures, several pressing matters commanded his attention. Sales had been much stronger than projected in 1990 to 1991, and existing production capacity had been fully utilized, with excessive overtime, to meet demand. Sales forecasts for the coming year indicated further rapid growth in demand, and Kramb knew that added capacity was needed. Several alternatives were available to the company, and he wanted to be sure that all the key factors were considered in making the decision.

Imaginative Toys was founded in Seattle, Washington, in 1975. When he founded the company, Gerald Kramb envisioned that Imaginative Toys would develop and produce toys that "reach children's imagination and bring out their creativity." He liked to call these toys "learning toys." Two product lines quickly emerged as the mainstays of the company: construction toys that were similar to Lincoln Logs and Legos and maze and mind toys that focused on solving puzzles and developing hand–eye coordination. The toys were quickly accepted in the marketplace and became a popular choice for day care centers, preschool facilities, and elementary schools, as well as for parents.

Keys to success in this market were continual development of innovative products and a high level of product quality. Toys needed to be both creative and durable. Two other important factors were timing and availability. New products had to be ready to be introduced at the spring toy shows. Then, sufficient capacity was needed to fill retail orders by late summer in order to be ready for the Christmas buying season. Hence, Kramb knew that any capacity expansion decisions had to be made soon to meet next spring's production needs.

Because of the long-term nature of the decision, Kramb had asked Pat Namura, the marketing director, to prepare a four-year sales forecast. This forecast projected strong growth in sales during the four-year period for several reasons. First, the 1960s baby-boomers' children were reaching preschool and elementary school age, and child care facilities were rapidly expanding to accommodate these children, whose parents typically both worked. A second factor was the growth of international markets. Domestic sales remained strong, but international sales were growing at the rate of 25 percent per year. An important factor to consider was that, in a trendy business such as toys, the European market was one to two years behind the U.S. market. Namura attributed this lag to less developed television programming targeted toward children.

Finally, Imaginative Toys had just launched a new line of toys, and initial sales figures were very promising. The new line of toys was called Transformers. Much like a puzzle, each of the transformers could be rearranged and snapped together to form from two to four different toys. Designs were patterned after the robotic characters in children's Saturday morning cartoon shows. Namura was sure that this new line was just beginning to take off.

As Kramb reviewed the alternatives, he wished that expanding existing facilities were a viable option. Were the

continued

continued

necessary space available, adding to the Seattle facilities would put much less pressure on the company's already thin management structure. As it was, suitable space was nowhere to be found in the Seattle area. However, the processes used to manufacture the three product lines could be replicated easily at any location. All three line processes were labor intensive, with plastic parts molding being the only skilled position. The construction toys consisted of molded plastic parts that were assembled into kits and packaged for shipment. The maze and mind toys required some parts fabrication from wood and metal materials. Then these parts were assembled into toys that were packed for shipment. The transformers were made from molded plastic parts that were then assembled with various fasteners and packed for shipment. The operating costs breakdown across all three toy lines was estimated to be 30 percent materials, 30 percent labor, 20 percent overhead, and 20 percent transportation and distribution. Obtaining the raw materials used to manufacture the toys would not be a problem for any location.

Kramb and his staff had researched two alternative locations for expansion. One was in a maquiladora in Nogales, Mexico, across the border from Tucson, Arizona. The improving trade relations and projected relaxation of tariffs and duties made this an attractive alternative. Labor costs also could be substantially reduced. If skilled labor was not available to mold and fabricate the parts, these operations could be done in the United States and the parts could be shipped across the border to Nogales for assembly and packaging.

The second alternative was to locate in Europe. A plastic injection molding company outside Brussels had decided to close and was looking for a buyer. Labor costs would be comparable to those in Seattle, but transportation cost would be 10 to 15 percent higher on toys shipped back to the U.S. market. However, the Brussels location was attractive because of the European Community's projected single-market program. It was designed to bring free movement of people, goods, capital, and services to the EC by January 1, 1993. The 1988 Cecchini report developed for the European Commission forecasted an increase of 5 percent in the gross EC product from this program. By producing in Brussels, Imaginative Toys also could avoid the 6 percent tariff on goods entering the EC.

As Kramb prepared to meet with his staff, he wondered how the company would be affected by expanding to a multisite operation. Conceivably, the decision would be to expand into both Mexico and Europe. If the sales projections held, the demand would support a three-plant network.

Questions

1. In making the location decision, what factors would you consider to be dominant? Secondary?
2. What role, if any, do the competitive priorities of Imaginative Toys play in the location decision?

Source: This case was prepared by Dr. Brooke Saladin, Wake Forest University, as a basis for classroom discussion.

SELECTED REFERENCES

Andel, T. "Site Selection Tools Dig Data." *Transportation & Distribution*, vol. 37, no. 6 (1996), pp. 77–81.

Bartlett, Christopher, and Sumantra Ghoshal. *Managing Across Borders*. Boston: Harvard Business School Press, 1989.

Bartness, A. D. "The Plant Location Puzzle." *Harvard Business Review* (March–April, 1994), pp. 20–30.

"The Best Cities for Business." *Fortune* (November 4, 1991), pp. 52–84.

"The Boom Belt." *Business Week* (September 27, 1993), pp. 98–104.

Cook, Thomas M., and Robert A. Russell. *Introduction to Management Sciences*. Englewood Cliffs, NJ: Prentice-Hall, 1993.

DeForest, M. E. "Thinking of a Plant in Mexico?" *The Academy of Management Executive*, vol. 8, no. 1 (1994), pp. 33–40.

"Doing Well by Doing Good." *The Economist* (April 22, 2000) pp. 65–67.

Drezner, Z. *Facility Location: A Survey of Applications and Methods*. Secaucus, NJ: Springer-Verlag, 1995.

Ferdows, Kasra. "Making the Most of Foreign Factories." *Fortune* (March–April 1997), pp. 73–88.

Fitzsimmons, James A., and Mona J. Fitzsimmons. *Service Operations Management*. New York: McGraw-Hill, 1998.

Harris, Philip R., and Robert T. Moran. *Managing Cultural Differences*. Houston: Gulf, 1987.

"How Legend Lives Up to Its Name." *Business Week* (February 15, 1999), pp. 75–78.

Kanter, Rosabeth Moss. "Transcending Business Boundaries: 12,000 World Managers View Change." *Harvard Business Review* (May–June 1991), pp. 151–164.

"Korea." *Business Week* (July 31, 1995) pp. 56–64.

Khumawala, Basheer M., and D. Clay Whybark. "A Comparison of Some Recent Warehouse Location Techniques." *The Logistics Review*, vol. 7, no. 3 (1971), pp. 3–19.

Klassen, Robert D., and D. Clay Whybark. "Barriers to the Management of International Operations." *Journal of Operations Management*, vol. 11, no. 4 (1994), pp. 385–396.

Kuehn, Alfred A., and Michael J. Hamburger. "A Heuristic Program for Locating Warehouses." *Management Science*, vol. 9, no. 4 (1963), pp. 643–666.

"Long Distance: Innovative MCI Unit Finds Culture Shock in Colorado Springs." *Wall Street Journal* (June 25, 1996).

Love, Robert F., James G. Morris, and George O. Weslowsky. *Facilities Location: Models and Methods*. New York: North-Holland, 1988.

Markland, Robert E. "Analyzing Geographical Discrete Warehousing Networks by Computer Simulation." *Decision Sciences*, vol. 4, no. 2 (1973), pp. 216–236.

Markland, Robert E., and James R. Sweigart. *Quantitative Methods: Applications to Managerial Decision Making.* New York: John Wiley & Sons, 1987.

MacCormack, Alan D., Lawrence James Newman III, and David B. Rosenfield. "The New Dynamics of Global Manufacturing Site Location." *Sloan Management Review* (Summer 1994), pp. 69–77.

"Mexico: A Rough Road Back." *Business Week* (November 13, 1995), pp. 104–107.

Port Authority Bus Terminal: A Former Haven of Sleaze Is Now a Refuge of Retail." *New York Times* (March 17, 1996).

Porter, Michael E. "The Competitive Advantage of Nations." *Harvard Business Review* (March–April 1990), pp. 73–93.

Schmenner, Roger W. *Making Business Location Decisions.* Englewood Cliffs, NJ: Prentice-Hall, 1982.

"Spanning the Globe." *Wall Street Journal* (October 4, 1991).

Sugiura, Hideo. "How Honda Localizes Its Global Strategy." *Sloan Management Review* (Fall 1990), pp. 77–82.

Vargos, G. A., and T. W. Johnson. "An Analysis of Operational Experience in the U.S./Mexico Production Sharing (Maquiladora) Program." *Journal of Operations Management,* vol. 11, no. 1 (1993), pp. 17–34.

Layout

Across the Organization

Layout is important to . . .

- ❑ **accounting,** which seeks effective layouts for its operations and provides cost information on layout changes.
- ❑ **distribution,** which seeks warehouse layouts that make materials handing easier and make customer response times shorter.
- ❑ **engineering,** which considers the impact of product design choices on layout.
- ❑ **finance,** which performs the financial analysis on capital investments in new or revised layouts.
- ❑ **human resources,** which considers how layout designs affect employee attitudes and behavior.
- ❑ **management information systems,** which designs decision support systems for improving layout design.
- ❑ **marketing,** which uses layout as a tool to expand market share.
- ❑ **operations,** which seeks layouts of operations that best balance multiple performance criteria.

Learning Goals

After reading this chapter, you will be able to . . .

1. define the meaning of layout planning and the questions it addresses.
2. describe the four basic layout types and when each is best used.
3. identify the types of performance criteria that are important in evaluating layouts.
4. explain how cells can help create hybrid layouts.
5. recommend a step-by-step approach in designing process layouts.
6. calculate load–distance scores for a process layout and explain how this capability helps managers find a good solution.
7. discuss different strategies in the layout of warehouses and offices.
8. describe how to balance lines in a product layout and evaluate different solutions.

A 35-year-old mother does not know it, but the Internet has made her trips to the mall a little easier. In 2000, RiverTown Crossings (rivertowncrossings.mallibu.com) opened its doors in Grandville, Michigan. Since then she rarely ventures beyond just one section of the mall—the one with Abercrombie Kids, Gap Kids, Gymboree, and other kids' clothing stores. She can shop in that wing and find almost everything she needs. In an effort to compete with the allure of on-line shopping, the mall owner, General Growth Properties, Inc. (www.generalgrowth.com), selected a layout that runs counter to decades of retailing wisdom: It clustered competing stores together. Shoppers were asking for such clusters long before Web retailing took off, and General Growth began experimenting with the idea three years ago. Now, all of its new malls will have clusters. S

Worried about a future when shoppers point and click instead of park and walk and wait in line, developers are finally trying to make it more convenient to shop in malls. Some owners are revising their existing layouts by removing large fixtures, such as planters and fountains, to clear sightlines to storefronts. Others are adding directories that are easier to understand than current mall maps. A few malls in the design stages are opting to put anchor department stores closer together—a layout that cuts down on walking. A few malls are trying to offer shoppers elements of the Web using high-tech directories. At the Dayton Mall, in Ohio, sleek electronic kiosks give shoppers e-mail access and let them search for names of stores carrying types of merchandise, such as

"sweaters." The kiosks, made by the iPort unit of Omnitech Corporate Solutions, Inc. (www.omnitech-us.com), of Englewood, N.J., also have printers that can spit out a map with a store's location highlighted.

Beneath the new layout designs is an old retailing secret: The traditional mall was designed to be difficult. This planned inconvenience made customers who wanted to comparison-shop walk from one end of the mall to the other, so that they had every chance to make impulse purchases in between. Many developers left little to chance in directing the traffic flow to their advantage, using plants, carpeting, and other fixtures to set winding routes past stores.

Revising the layout of existing malls to make them more convenient is costly. Most of them are jungles of escalators, fountains, and play areas—and those are the easy obstacles. The tougher problem is figuring out how to rearrange similar stores that are probably operating on long leases. After all, a mall developer cannot simply order four shoe store tenants to pick up and move. And many retailers still prefer to keep their distance from competitors. RiverTown's Hallmark Gold Crown store is located on the first level on the north end of the mall, while an American Greetings store is on the second level on the south end. Hallmark Cards' location strategy calls for space between its stores and competitors.

The Internet has revolutionized the way traditional businesses design their processes, even to the point of layout design. RiverTown Crossings Mall has clustered company stores to improve comparison shopping, a convenience that Web retailing already offers online customers.

Source: "Making Malls (Gasp!) Convenient." *Wall Street Journal* (February 8, 2000).

FACILITY LAYOUT DECISIONS TRANSLATE the broader decisions about a firm's competitive priorities, process, and capacity into actual physical arrangements of people, equipment, and space. In this chapter, we examine layout in a variety of settings, along with techniques of layout analysis.

WHAT IS LAYOUT PLANNING?

What are some key layout questions that need to be addressed?

layout planning Planning that involves decisions about the physical arrangement of economic activity centers within a facility.

economic activity center Anything that consumes space; for example, a person or a group of people, a teller window, a machine, a workbench or workstation, a department, a stairway or an aisle, a timecard rack, a cafeteria or a storage room.

Layout planning involves decisions about the physical arrangement of economic activity centers within a facility. An **economic activity center** can be anything that consumes space: a person or group of people, a teller window, a machine, a workbench or workstation, a department, a stairway or an aisle, a timecard rack, a cafeteria or storage room, and so on. The goal of layout planning is to allow workers and equipment to operate most effectively. Before a manager can make decisions regarding physical arrangement, four questions must be addressed.

1. *What Centers Should the Layout Include?* Centers should reflect process decisions and maximize productivity. For example, a central storage area for tools is most efficient for certain processes, but keeping tools at individual workstations makes more sense for other processes.

2. *How Much Space and Capacity Does Each Center Need?* Inadequate space can reduce productivity, deprive employees of privacy, and even create health and safety hazards. However, excessive space is wasteful, can reduce productivity, and can isolate employees unnecessarily.

3. *How Should Each Center's Space Be Configured?* The amount of space, its shape, and the elements in a center are interrelated. For example, placement of a desk and chair relative to the other furniture is determined by the size and shape of the office, as well as the activities performed there. Providing a pleasing atmosphere also should be considered as part of the layout configuration decisions, especially in retail outlets and offices.

4. *Where Should Each Center Be Located?* Location can significantly affect productivity. For example, employees who must frequently interact with one another face to face should be placed in a central location rather than in separate, remote locations to reduce time lost traveling back and forth.

The location of a center has two dimensions: (1) *relative location,* or the placement of a center relative to other centers, and (2) *absolute location,* or the particular space that the center occupies within the facility. Both affect a center's performance. Look at the grocery store layout in Figure 10.1(a). It shows the location of five departments, with the dry groceries department allocated twice the space of each of the others. The location of frozen foods relative to bread is the same as the location of meats relative to vegetables,

Identical Relative Locations and Different Absolute Locations

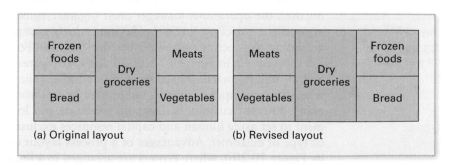

(a) Original layout   (b) Revised layout

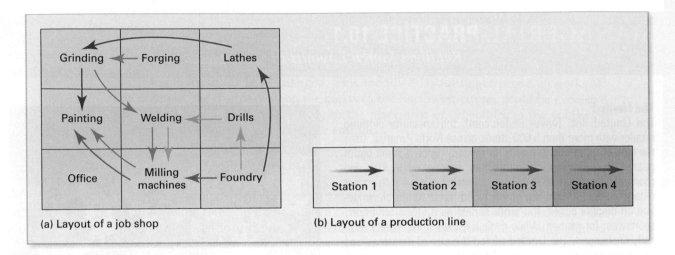

(a) Layout of a job shop

(b) Layout of a production line

FIGURE 10.2

Two Layout Types

1. Resources are relatively general purpose and less capital-intensive.

2. The process layout is less vulnerable to changes in product mix or new marketing strategies and is therefore more flexible.

3. Equipment utilization is higher. When volumes are low, dedicating resources to each product or service (as is done with a product layout) would require more equipment than pooling the requirements for all products does.[1]

4. Employee supervision can be more specialized, an important factor when job content requires a good deal of technical knowledge.

A job process, with the accompanying process layout, has its disadvantages.

1. Processing rates tend to be slower.

2. Productive time is lost in changing from one product or service to another.

3. More space and capital are tied up in inventory, which helps workstations to work independently despite their variable output rates.

4. The time lags between job starts and end points are relatively long.

5. Materials handling tends to be costly.

6. Diversity in routings and jumbled flows necessitate the use of variable path devices, such as carts rather than conveyors.

7. Production planning and control is more difficult.

A major challenge in designing a process layout is to locate centers so that they bring some order to the apparent chaos of the flexible flow operation.

product layout A layout in which workstations or departments are arranged in a linear path.

PRODUCT LAYOUT. With line or continuous processes, which are best for repetitive or continuous production, the operations manager dedicates resources to individual products or tasks. This strategy is achieved by a **product layout,** illustrated by Figure 10.2(b), in which workstations or departments are arranged in a linear path. As in an automated car wash, the product or customer moves along in a smooth, continuous flow. Resources are arranged around the product's route, rather than shared across many products. (Later, we demonstrate that some product layouts, called *mixed-model lines,* can handle several products as long as their processing requirements are similar.)

---

[1]However, management won't allow utilization to get too high. A larger capacity cushion with process layouts absorbs the more unpredictable demands of customized products and services.

Product layouts are common in high-volume types of operations. Although product layouts often follow a straight line, a straight line is not always best, and layouts may take an L, O, S, or U shape. A product layout often is called a *production line* or an *assembly line.* The difference between the two is that an assembly line is limited to assembly processes, whereas a production line can be used to perform other processes such as machining.

Product layouts often rely heavily on specialized, capital-intensive resources. When volumes are high, the advantages of product layouts over process layouts include

1. faster processing rates,
2. lower inventories, and
3. less unproductive time lost to changeovers and materials handling.

There is less need to decouple one operation from the next, allowing management to cut inventories. The Japanese refer to a line process as *overlapped operations,* whereby materials move directly from one operation to the next without waiting in queues. The disadvantages of product layouts include

1. greater risk of layout redesign for products or services with short or uncertain lives,
2. less flexibility, and
3. low resource utilization for low-volume products or services.

For product layouts, deciding where to locate centers is easy because operations must occur in a prescribed order. For example, in a car wash, the routing of the car must proceed from *washing* to *rinsing* to *drying;* rinsing and drying should be placed next to each other in the layout. This arrangement, which simply follows the product's routing, ensures that all interacting pairs of centers are as close together as possible or have a common boundary. The challenge of product layout is to group activities into workstations and achieve the desired output rate with the least resources. The composition and number of workstations are crucial decisions, which we explore later in the chapter.

hybrid layout A layout in which some portions of the facility are arranged in a process layout and others are arranged in a product layout.

HYBRID LAYOUT. More often than not, the process combines elements of both a product and a process focus. This intermediate strategy calls for a **hybrid layout,** in which some portions of the facility are arranged in a process layout and others are arranged in a product layout. Hybrid layouts are used in facilities having both fabrication and assembly operations, as would be the case if both types of layout shown in Figure 10.2 were in the same building. Fabrication operations—in which components are made from raw materials—have a jumbled flow, whereas assembly operations—in which components are assembled into finished products—have a line flow. Operations managers also create hybrid layouts when introducing cells and flexible automation, such as a flexible manufacturing system (FMS). A *cell* is two or more dissimilar workstations located close together through which a limited number of parts or models are processed with line flows (see the Process Management chapter). We cover two special types of cells—group technology (GT) cells and one-worker, multiple-machines (OWMM) cells—later in this chapter. An *FMS* is a group of computer-controlled workstations at which materials are automatically handled and machine loaded (see the Computer-Integrated Manufacturing supplement). These technologies help achieve repeatability, even when product volumes are too low to justify dedicating a single line to one product, by bringing together all resources needed to make a family of parts in one center. The rest of the facility represents a process layout.

A retail store is an example of a hybrid layout in a nonmanufacturing setting. The manager may group similar merchandise, enabling customers to find desired items easily (a process layout). At the same time, the layout often leads customers along predetermined paths, such as up and down aisles (a product layout). The intent is to maximize exposure to the full array of goods, thereby stimulating sales.

fixed-position layout An arrangement in which the product is fixed in place; workers, along with their tools and equipment, come to the product to work on it.

FIXED-POSITION LAYOUT. The fourth basic type of layout is the **fixed-position layout.** In this arrangement, the product is fixed in place; workers, along with their tools and equipment, come to the product to work on it. Many project processes have this arrangement. This type of layout makes sense when the product is particularly massive or difficult to move, as in shipbuilding, assembling locomotives, making huge pressure vessels, building dams, or repairing home furnaces. A fixed-position layout minimizes the number of times that the product must be moved and often is the only feasible solution.

PERFORMANCE CRITERIA

What performance criteria should be emphasized?

Other fundamental choices facing the layout planner concern *performance criteria*, which may include one or more of the following factors:

❏ level of capital investment
❏ requirements for materials handling

This aerial view of the Hyundi shipyard in Korea, which is Asia's major ship builder, shows a ship being built. The shipyard provides an example of a fixed-position layout, because the ship stays in place and the workers bring their tools to it to construct the ship and do repairs.

- ❏ ease of stockpicking
- ❏ work environment and "atmosphere"
- ❏ ease of equipment maintenance
- ❏ employee attitudes
- ❏ amount of flexibility needed
- ❏ customer convenience and level of sales

Managers must decide early in the process which factors to emphasize in order to come up with a good layout solution. In most cases, multiple criteria are used. For example, a warehouse manager may emphasize ease in stockpicking, flexibility, and amount of space needed (capital investment), whereas a retail store manager may emphasize flexibility, atmosphere, customer convenience, and sales. Sales are particularly important to retailers, which place items with high profitability per cubic foot of shelf space in the most prominent display areas and impulse-buy items near the entrance or checkout counter.

CAPITAL INVESTMENT. Floor space, equipment needs, and inventory levels are assets that the firm buys or leases. These expenditures are an important criterion in all settings. If an office layout is to have partitions to increase privacy, the cost rises. Even increasing space for filing cabinets can add up. A four-drawer lateral file occupies about nine square feet, including the space needed to open it. At $25 per square foot, that translates into a floor space "rental" of $225 a year. Renovation costs also can be significant. Several years ago, remodeling at JCPenney, Sears, and Kmart stores had a total price tag of almost $5 billion.

MATERIALS HANDLING. Relative locations of centers should restrict large flows to short distances. Centers between which frequent trips or interactions are required should be placed close to one another. In a manufacturing plant, this approach minimizes materials handling costs. In a warehouse, stockpicking costs are reduced by storing items typically needed for the same order next to one another. In a retail store, customer convenience improves if items are grouped predictably to minimize customer search and travel time. In an office, communication and cooperation often improve when people or departments that must interact frequently are located near one another, because telephone calls and memos can be poor substitutes for face-to-face communication. Spatial separation is one big reason why cross-functional coordination between departments can be challenging.

layout flexibility The property of a facility to be desirable after significant changes occur, or to be easily and inexpensively adapted in response to changes.

FLEXIBILITY. A flexible layout allows a firm to adapt quickly to changing customer needs and preferences and is best for many situations. **Layout flexibility** means either that the facility remains desirable after significant changes occur or that it can be easily and inexpensively adapted in response to changes. The changes can be in the mix of customers served by a store, goods made at a plant, space requirements in a warehouse, or organizational structure in an office. Using modular furniture and partitions, rather than permanent load-bearing walls, is one way to minimize the cost of office layout changes. So can having wide bays (fewer columns), heavy-duty floors, and extra electrical connections in a plant.

For retailers, the height of flexibility is the kiosks that display a variety of novelties and specialty items on sale in the center aisle of the malls. They have an ever-changing array of merchandise that transform once-utilitarian passageways into retailing hot spots. They are right where the customers have to walk and create a stream of impulse purchases. Unlike large retailers who are often locked into product up to a year in advance, kiosk operations are better able to follow trends, such as Pokemon. If the fad lasts only a few months, that is fine for a temporary retailer. Over the past 15 years, seasonal and temporary carts, kiosks, and stores have ballooned into a $10 billion business.

OTHER CRITERIA. Other criteria that may be important include labor productivity, machine maintenance, work environment, and organizational structure. Labor productivity can be affected if certain workstations can be operated by common personnel in some layouts but not in others. Downtime spent waiting for materials can be caused by materials handling difficulties resulting from poor layout. Equipment maintenance can be made difficult by inadequate space or poor access. The work environment, including temperature, noise level, and safety, can be layout related; its counterpart in an office or store is the atmosphere created by the layout. Office layouts can reinforce the organizational structure by grouping all members of the same department in the same area, or they can encourage interfunctional cooperation by grouping people by project rather than by function. Some warehouse layouts facilitate stockpicking on a FIFO (first-in, first-out) basis, minimizing loss from spoilage or limited shelf life. Finally, employee attitudes may depend on whether the layout allows workers to socialize, reflects equitably the employees' levels of responsibility, or puts workers under the watchful eyes of a supervisor.

CREATING HYBRID LAYOUTS

Can some miniature product layouts be created in a facility?

When volumes are not high enough to justify dedicating a single line of multiple workers to a single product, managers still may be able to derive the benefits of product layout—line flows, simpler materials handling, low setups, and reduced labor costs—by creating product layouts in some portions of the facility. Two techniques for creating hybrid layouts are one-worker, multiple-machines (OWMM) cells and group technology (GT) cells. They are special types of cells, which we described earlier as a way to focus operations (see the Process Management chapter). Flexible automation is still another way to achieve the benefits of high-volume production when volumes for individual items are low.

ONE WORKER, MULTIPLE MACHINES

one-worker, multiple-machines (OWMM) cell
A one-person cell in which a worker operates several different machines simultaneously to achieve a line flow.

If volumes are not sufficient to keep several workers busy on one production line, the manager might set up a line small enough to keep one worker busy. A one-person cell is the theory behind the **one-worker, multiple-machines (OWMM) cell,** in which a worker operates several different machines simultaneously to achieve a line flow. Having one worker operate several identical machines is not unusual. For example, in the semiconductor industry one worker operates several saws that cut silicon bars into slices for computer chips. However, with an OWMM cell, several different machines are in the line.

Figure 10.3 illustrates a five-machine OWMM cell that is being used to produce a flanged metal part, with the machines encircling one operator in the center. (A U shape also is common.) The operator moves around the circle, performing tasks (typically loading and unloading) that have not been automated. Different products or parts can be produced in an OWMM cell by changing the machine setups. If the setup on one machine is especially time-consuming for one part, management can add a duplicate machine to the cell for use whenever that part is being produced.

An OWMM arrangement reduces both inventory and labor requirements. Inventory is cut because, rather than piling up in queues, materials move directly into the next operation. Labor is cut because more work is automated. The addition of several

One-Worker, Multiple-Machines (OWMM) Cell

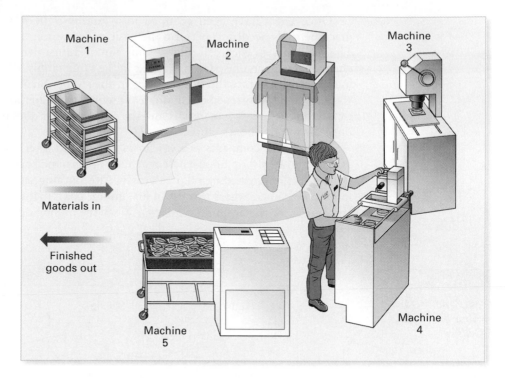

low-cost automated devices can maximize the number of machines included in an OWMM arrangement: automatic tool changers, loaders and unloaders, start and stop devices, and fail-safe devices that detect defective parts or products. Japanese manufacturers are applying the OWMM concept widely because of their desire to achieve low inventories.

GROUP TECHNOLOGY

group technology (GT)
An option for achieving product layouts with low-volume processes; creates cells not limited to just one worker and has a unique way of selecting work to be done by the cell.

A second option for achieving product layouts with low-volume processes is **group technology (GT)**. This manufacturing technique creates cells not limited to just one worker and has a unique way of selecting work to be done by the cell. The GT method groups parts or products with similar characteristics into *families* and sets aside groups of machines for their production. Families may be based on size, shape, manufacturing or routing requirements, or demand. The goal is to identify a set of products with similar processing requirements and minimize machine changeover or setup. For example, all bolts might be assigned to the same family because they all require the same basic processing steps regardless of size or shape. Figure 10.4 shows 13 parts that belong to the same family.

FIGURE 10.4

Thirteen Parts Belonging to the Same Family

Source: Mikell P. Groover. *Automation, Production Systems, and Computer-Aided Manufacturing.* Englewood Cliffs, NJ: Prentice-Hall, 1980, p. 540. Reprinted by permission.

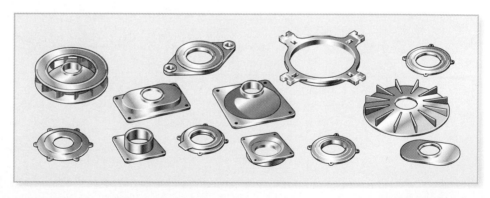

Once parts have been grouped into families, the next step is to organize the machine tools needed to perform the basic processes on these parts into separate cells. The machines in each cell require only minor adjustments to accommodate product changeovers from one part to the next in the same family. By simplifying product routings, GT cells reduce the time a job is in the shop. Queues of materials waiting to be worked on are shortened or eliminated. Frequently, materials handling is automated so that, after loading raw materials into the cell, a worker does not handle machined parts until the job has been completed.

Figure 10.5 compares process flows before and after creation of GT cells. Figure 10.5(a) shows a shop floor where machines are grouped according to function: lathing, milling, drilling, grinding, and assembly. After lathing, a part is moved to one of the milling machines, where it waits in line until it has a higher priority than any other job competing for the machine's capacity. When the milling operation on the part has been

FIGURE 10.5

Process Flows Before and After the Use of GT Cells

Source: Mikell P. Groover. *Automation, Production Systems, and Computer-Aided Manufacturing*. Englewood Cliffs, NJ: Prentice-Hall, 1980, pp. 540–541. Reprinted by permission.

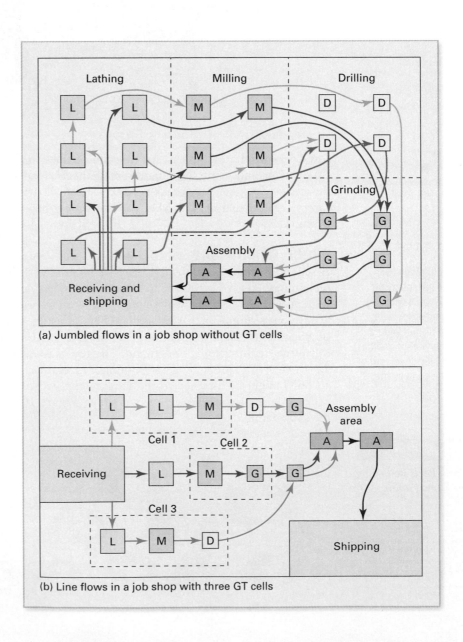

(a) Jumbled flows in a job shop without GT cells

(b) Line flows in a job shop with three GT cells

finished, the part is moved to a drilling machine, and so on. The queues can be long, creating significant time delays. Flows of materials are very jumbled because the part being processed in any one area of the shop have so many different routings.

By contrast, the manager of the shop shown in Figure 10.5(b) has identified three product families that account for a majority of the firm's production. One family always requires two lathing operations followed by one operation at the milling machines. The second family always requires a milling operation followed by a grinding operation. The third family requires the use of a lathe, milling machine, and drill press. For simplicity, only the flows of parts assigned to these three families are shown. The remaining parts are produced at machines outside the cells and still have jumbled routings. Some equipment might have to be duplicated, as when a machine is required for one or more cells and for operations outside the cells. However, by creating three GT cells, the manager has definitely created more line flows and simplified routings.

DESIGNING PROCESS LAYOUTS

How can a better process layout be found for a facility?

The approach to designing a layout depends on whether a process layout or a product layout has been chosen. A fixed-position format basically eliminates the layout problem, whereas the design of the hybrid layout partially uses process-layout principles and partially uses product layout principles.

Process layout involves three basic steps, whether the design is for a new layout or for revising an existing one: (1) gather information, (2) develop a block plan, and (3) design a detailed layout.

STEP 1: GATHER INFORMATION

Longhorn Machine is a machine shop that produces a variety of small metal parts on general-purpose equipment. A full shift of 26 workers and a second shift of 6 workers operate its 32 machines. Three types of information are needed to begin designing a revised layout for Longhorn Machine: space requirements by center, available space, and closeness factors.

SPACE REQUIREMENTS BY CENTER. Longhorn has grouped its processes into six different departments: burr and grind, NC equipment, shipping and receiving, lathes and drills, tool crib, and inspection. The exact space requirements of each department, in square feet, are as follows:

Department	Area Needed (ft²)
1. Burr and grind	1,000
2. NC equipment	950
3. Shipping and receiving	750
4. Lathes and drills	1,200
5. Tool crib	800
6. Inspection	700
Total	5,400

The layout designer must tie space requirements to capacity plans, calculate the specific equipment and space needs for each center, and allow circulation space such as aisles and the like.

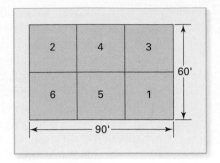

FIGURE 10.6

Current Block Plan for Longhorn Machine

block plan A plan that allocates space and indicates placement of each department.

AVAILABLE SPACE. A **block plan** allocates space and indicates placement of each department. To describe a new facility layout, the plan need only provide the facility's dimensions and space allocations. When an existing facility layout is being modified, the current block plan also is needed. Longhorn's available space is 90 feet by 60 feet, or 5,400 square feet. The designer could begin the design by dividing the total amount of space into six equal blocks (900 square feet each), even though inspection needs only 700 square feet and lathes and drills needs 1,200 square feet. The equal-space approximation shown in Figure 10.6 is sufficient until the detailed layout stage, when larger departments (such as lathes and drills) are assigned more block spaces than smaller departments.

CLOSENESS FACTORS. The layout designer must also know which centers need to be located close to one another. Location is based on the number of trips between centers and qualitative factors.

trip matrix A matrix that gives the number of trips (or some other measure of materials movement) between each pair of departments per day.

The following table shows Longhorn's **trip matrix,** which gives the number of trips (or some other measure of materials movement) between each pair of departments per day. The designer estimates the number of trips between centers by using routings and ordering frequencies for typical items made at the plant, by carrying out statistical sampling, or by polling supervisors and materials handlers. Only the right-hand portion of the matrix, which shows the number of trips in *both* directions, is used. For example, there are 75 trips per day between departments 2 (NC equipment) and 5 (tool crib). Showing the merged flow totals eliminates the need to add the flow in one direction to the flow in the other direction. The totals give clues as to which departments should be located close together. For example, the largest number of trips is between departments 3 and 6 (at 90 trips), with 1 and 6 close behind (at 80 trips). Thus, the designer should locate department 6 near both 1 and 3, which is not the arrangement in the current layout.

Trip Matrix

Department	Trips Between Departments					
	1	2	3	4	5	6
1. Burr and grind	—	20		20		80
2. NC equipment		—	10		75	
3. Shipping and receiving			—	15		90
4. Lathes and drills				—	70	
5. Tool crib					—	
6. Inspection						—

REL Chart

Department	\multicolumn{6}{c}{**Closeness Rating Between Departments**}	\multicolumn{2}{c}{**Closeness Ratings**}
	1	2	3	4	5	6	**Rating**	**Definition**
1. Burr and grind	—	E (3, 1)	U	I (2, 1)	U	A (1)	A E I O U X	Absolutely necessary Especially important Important Ordinary closeness Unimportant Undesirable
2. NC equipment		—	O (1)	U	E (1)	I (6)	\multicolumn{2}{c}{**Explanation Codes**}
3. Shipping and receiving			—	O (1)	U	A (1)	**Code**	**Meaning**
4. Lathes and drills				—	E (1)	X (5)	1 2 3 4 5 6	Materials handling Shared personnel Ease of supervision Space utilization Noise Employee attitudes
5. Tool crib					—	U		
6. Inspection						—		

REL chart A chart that reflects the qualitative judgments of managers and employees and that can be used in place of a trip matrix.

A **REL chart** (REL is short for *relationships*), which reflects the qualitative judgments of managers and employees, can be used in place of a trip matrix. Following is a REL chart for Longhorn Machine. An A rating represents the judgment that locating two particular departments close to each other is absolutely necessary; E is for especially important, I for important, O for ordinary closeness, U for unimportant, and X for undesirable. The A rating is higher than the E, but as the assessment is qualitative, the designer does not know by how much. One advantage of a REL chart is that the manager can account for multiple performance criteria when selecting closeness ratings, whereas a trip matrix focuses solely on materials handling or stockpicking costs. For example, the desired closeness between departments 1 and 2 is rated E because of two considerations: ease of supervision and materials handling.

OTHER CONSIDERATIONS. Finally, the information gathered for Longhorn includes performance criteria that depend on the *absolute* location of a department. Longhorn has two criteria based on absolute location:

1. Shipping and receiving (department 3) should remain where it is because it is next to the dock.
2. Lathes and drills (department 4) should remain where it is because relocation costs would be prohibitive.

Noise levels and management preference are other potential sources of performance criteria that depend on absolute location. A REL chart or trip matrix cannot reflect these criteria, because it reflects only *relative* location considerations. The layout designer must list them separately.

STEP 2: DEVELOP A BLOCK PLAN

The second step in layout design is to develop a block plan that best satisfies performance criteria and area requirements. The most elementary way to do so is by trial and error. Because success depends on the designer's ability to spot patterns in the data, this approach does not guarantee the selection of the best or even a nearly best solution. When supplemented by the use of a computer to evaluate solutions, however, such an approach often compares quite favorably with more sophisticated computerized techniques.

| EXAMPLE 10.1 | *Developing a Block Plan* |

Develop an acceptable block plan for Longhorn, using trial and error. The goal is to minimize materials handling costs.

SOLUTION

A good place to start is with the largest closeness ratings in the trip matrix (say, 70 and above). Beginning with the largest number of trips and working down the list, you might plan to locate departments as follows:

Departments 3 and 6 close together   Departments 2 and 5 close together

Departments 1 and 6 close together   Departments 4 and 5 close together

Departments 3 and 4 should remain at their current locations because of the "other considerations."

If after several attempts you cannot meet all five requirements, drop one or more and try again. If you can meet all five easily, add more (such as for interactions below 70).

The block plan in Figure 10.7 shows a trial-and-error solution that satisfies all five requirements. We started by keeping departments 3 and 4 in their original locations. As the first requirement is to locate departments 3 and 6 close to each other, we put 6 in the southeast corner of the layout. The second requirement is to have departments 1 and 6 close together, so we placed 1 in the space just to the left of 6, and so on.

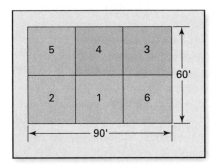

FIGURE 10.7 • Proposed Block Plan

Decision Point This solution fell into place easily for this particular problem, but it might not be the best layout. Management wants to consider several alternative layouts before making a final choice and needs some measure of effectiveness with which to compare them. ⊐

When *relative* locations are a primary concern, such as for effective materials handling, stockpicking, and communication, the load–distance method can be used to compare alternative block plans. Recall that we find the total load–distance, or *ld,* score by multiplying each load by the distance traveled and then summing over all of the loads (see the Location chapter). Here, the loads are just the numbers in the trip matrix. Each load goes between two centers (each represented by a row and a column in the matrix). The distance (actual, Euclidean, or rectilinear) between them is calculated from the block plan being evaluated. Of course, the loads need not be trips; any numerical closeness measure related to distance will do.

| EXAMPLE 10.2 | *Calculating the Total Desirability Score* |

How much better, in terms of the *ld* score, is the proposed block plan? Use the rectilinear distance measure.

SOLUTION

The accompanying table lists each pair of departments that has a nonzero closeness factor in the trip matrix. For the third column, calculate the rectilinear distances between the departments in the current layout. For example, in Figure 10.6, departments 1 and 2 are in the southeast and northwest blocks of the plant, respectively. The distance between the centers of these blocks is 3 units (two horizontally and one vertically). For the fourth column, we multiply the loads by the distances and then add the results for a total *ld* score of 785 for the current plan. Similar calculations for the proposed plan in Figure 10.7 produce an *ld* score of only 400. For example, between departments 1 and 2 is just 1 unit of distance (one horizontally and none vertically).

		CURRENT PLAN		PROPOSED PLAN	
DEPARTMENT PAIR	CLOSENESS FACTOR, *l*	DISTANCE *d*	LOAD–DISTANCE SCORE, *ld*	DISTANCE *d*	LOAD–DISTANCE SCORE, *ld*
1, 2	20	3	60	1	20
1, 4	20	2	40	1	20
1, 6	80	2	160	1	80
2, 3	10	2	20	3	30
2, 5	75	2	150	1	75
3, 4	15	1	15	1	15
3, 6	90	3	270	1	90
4, 5	70	1	70	1	70
			$ld = 785$		$ld = 400$

To be exact, we could multiply the two *ld* total scores by 30 because each unit of distance represents 30 feet. However, the relative difference between the two totals remains unchanged.

Decision Point Although the *ld* score for the proposed layout represents an almost 50 percent improvement, management is not sure the improvement outweighs the cost of relocating four of the six departments (all but 3 and 4). ❐

Although the *ld* score in Example 10.2 for the proposed layout represents an almost 50 percent improvement, the designer may be able to do better. However, the designer must first determine whether the revised layout is worth the cost of relocating four of the six departments (all but 3 and 4). If relocation costs are too high, a less-expensive proposal must be found.

OM Explorer can help identify some less-expensive proposals. The output in Figure 10.8 shows the *ld* score for the original layout and offers some clues about a better layout.

FIGURE 10.8

Original Block Plan with Process Layout Solver

Solver - Process Layout

Build Table ◉ Rectilinear Distances ○ Euclidean Distances

Department Pair	Closeness Factor	Distance	Score
3, 6	90	3	270
1, 6	80	2	160
2, 5	75	2	150
4, 5	70	1	70
1, 2	20	3	60
1, 4	20	2	40
3, 4	15	1	15
2, 3	10	2	20
		Total	785

2	4	3
6	5	1

Solver - Process Layout

Department Pair	Closeness Factor	Distance	Score
3, 6	90	2	180
1, 6	80	1	80
2, 5	75	1	75
4, 5	70	2	140
1, 2	20	3	60
1, 4	20	2	40
3, 4	15	1	15
2, 3	10	2	20
		Total	610

Much of the 785 score comes from trips between departments 3 and 6 (270) and between departments 1 and 6 (160). One option is to switch the locations of departments 5 and 6, putting department 6 closer to both departments 1 and 3. The output in Figure 10.9 indicates that the *ld* score for this revised plan drops to 610 and that only two departments have to be relocated. Perhaps this compromise is the best solution.

STEP 3: DESIGN A DETAILED LAYOUT

After finding a satisfactory block plan, the layout designer translates it into a detailed representation, showing the exact size and shape of each center, the arrangement of elements (e.g., desks, machines, and storage areas), and the location of aisles, stairways, and other service space. These visual representations can be two-dimensional drawings, three-dimensional models, or computer-aided graphics. This step helps decision makers discuss the proposal and problems that might otherwise be overlooked.

AIDS FOR PROCESS LAYOUT DECISIONS

Finding an acceptable block plan actually is a complex process. A company with 20 departments has 2.43×10^{18} possible layouts if each of the 20 departments can be assigned to any of the 20 locations. Fortunately, several computationally feasible aids are now available for helping managers make process layout decisions.

The **automated layout design program (ALDEP)** is a computer software package that uses REL chart information to construct a good layout. Being a heuristic method, it generally provides good—but not necessarily the best—solutions. ALDEP constructs a layout from scratch, adding one department at a time. The program picks the first department randomly. The second department must have a strong REL rating with the first (say, A or E), the third must have a strong rating with the second, and so on. When no department has a strong rating with the department just added, the system again randomly selects the next department. The program computes a score (somewhat different from the *ld* score used earlier) for each solution generated and prints out the layouts having the best scores for the manager's consideration.

Another powerful computer software package, the **computerized relative allocation of facilities technique (CRAFT)**, is a heuristic method that uses a trip matrix, including materials flow rates, transportation costs, and an initial block layout. Working from an initial block plan (or starting solution), CRAFT evaluates all possible paired exchanges of departments. The exchange that causes the greatest reduction in the total *ld* score is incorporated into a new starting solution. This process continues until no other

automated layout design program (ALDEP)
A computer software package that uses REL chart information to construct a good layout, starting from scratch and adding one department at a time.

computerized relative allocation of facilities technique (CRAFT)
A heuristic method that uses a trip matrix, including materials flow rates, transportation costs, and an initial block layout, and makes a series of paired exchanges of departments to find a better block plan.

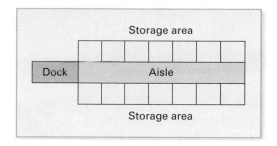

exchanges can be found to reduce the *ld* score. The starting solution at this point is also the final solution and is printed out with the *ld* score.

WAREHOUSE LAYOUTS

Warehouses are one of the invisible nerve centers of e-commerce, as Managerial Practice 10.2 demonstrates. Warehouses are similar to manufacturing plants in that materials are moved between activity centers. Much of the preceding discussion on manufacturing layouts applies to warehouses. However, warehouses are a special case because a warehouse's central process is one of storage, rather than physical or chemical change. Figure 10.10 illustrates the simplest type of warehousing layout. The A-1 Distribution Systems warehouse receives items at the dock and moves them to a storage area. Later, stockpickers withdraw inventory to fill individual customer orders. For example, the following table shows that 280 trips per week are made between the dock and the storage area for toasters.

Department	Trips to and from Dock	Area Needed (blocks)
1. Toasters	280	1
2. Air conditioners	160	2
3. Microwaves	360	1
4. Stereos	375	3
5. TVs	800	4
6. Radios	150	1
7. Bulk storage	100	2

A LAYOUT SOLUTION. We could find a layout solution by the method used in Examples 10.1 and 10.2. However, because all travel takes place between the dock and individual departments and there is no travel between departments, we can use an even simpler method, which is guaranteed to minimize the *ld* score. The decision rule is as follows:

1. *Equal Areas.* If all departments require the same space, simply place the one generating the most trips closest to the dock, the one generating the next-largest number of trips next closest to the dock, and so on.

2. *Unequal Areas.* If some departments need more space than others, give the location closest to the dock to the department with the largest ratio of trip frequency to block space. The department with the second-highest ratio gets the next-closest location, and so on.

MANAGERIAL PRACTICE 10.2
Warehouse Layouts and E-Commerce

There is a sprawling warehouse ringed by soybean and dairy farms in St. Cloud, Minnesota, that is one of the nerve centers of the Web-retailing revolution. Hundreds of employees whiz through the warehouse aisles on forklifts and cargo haulers, filling orders for the Web sites of Wal-Mart (www.walmartstores.com), Fingerhut (www.fingerhut.com), and other on-line retailers. The workers snatch goods off thousands of shelves and deliver them to an army of packers, who box the orders and drop them on conveyer belts. Every item has a special code to speed up the packing. A 27-in. television takes an X1, indicating the item is heavy and must be shipped by itself. Lighter-weight valuable items, like VCRs, take a 200 code. That means it requires an additional layer of wrapping paper to help disguise it on a customer's doorstep. Red lights scan each package as it zips by on the conveyer belt. If the weight of the box does not match the specifications on the label, the package is automatically shunted aside so a human inspector can make sure items weren't incorrectly added or omitted. The result is a high-tech process that has become one of the Internet's biggest and most admired distribution centers. The crew can process as many as 30,000 items an hour, and as many as 100 trailer loads of goods arrive each day at the warehouse.

Fingerhut has learned a lot on warehousing processes and layouts. One floor manager, for instance, noticed that employees who pick goods off the shelf would be more efficient if they did not have to travel from one end of the warehouse to the other to fill an order.

Fingerhut wrote a computer program to group customer orders for similar products, so that whenever possible, one employee could fill a bundle of orders without leaving a particular aisle. Each item's location in the warehouse layout is precisely charted. Green-and-white checkered pillow shams, for instance, recently occupied bin YH959 on the second shelf of aisle 52 in building 23A. Computers scan each customer's order, checking the dimensions of every item on the list to calculate the smallest possible box that can be used for shipping. Packages that pass inspection are then routed to one of 38 bays at the shipping dock, where trucks await to haul the goods away for mailing points all over the United States. A dedicated fleet of trucks departs daily to local post offices in points as far away as Seattle or Jacksonville, Florida. By paying local postage fees, Fingerhut saves a bundle on shipping costs.

At the Fingerhut warehouse in St. Cloud, Minnesota, a computer program is used to route the order pickers efficiently. Multiple orders of similar products can be filled without having to travel long distance. The program helps to reduce the load-distance score for Fingerhut's layout.

Fingerhut's warehouse illustrates a fact of life on the Internet: While anyone with a computer and an Internet connection can open up a "store" in cyberspace, delivering the goods to consumers has proven to be a much more complicated task. Major retailers, from traditional brick-and-mortar chains such as Macy's (www.federated-fds.com/divisions/mae_1_3.asp) to Web powerhouse Amazon.com Inc., learned that lesson the hard way during the Christmas of 1998, when an unexpected surge of on-line orders left thousands of irritated customers who did not get their gifts in time for the holidays. Since that time, Fingerhut's expertise has helped it score some of the biggest coups. It now ships all the on-line orders for mammoth Wal-Mart Stores, Inc., along with Fingerhut's own vast mail-order and on-line operations. Federated Department Stores, Inc. (www.federated-fds.com), gave it an even bigger vote of confidence in 1999 by spending $1.7 billion to buy Fingerhut, which now is handling orders for Macy's, Bloomingdale's, and Federated's other chains.

Source: "Retailing: Behind Doors of a Warehouse: Heavy Lifting of E-Commerce." *Wall Street Journal* (September 3, 1999).

| EXAMPLE 10.3 | *Determining a Warehouse Layout* |

Determine a new layout for the A-1 Distribution Systems warehouse that minimizes the *ld* score.

SOLUTION

Because the departments have different area requirements, we must first obtain the ratio of trips to block spaces.

DEPARTMENT	RATIO	RANK
1. Toasters	280/1 = 280	2
2. Air conditioners	160/2 = 80	6
3. Microwaves	360/1 = 360	1
4. Stereos	375/3 = 125	5
5. TVs	800/4 = 200	3
6. Radios	150/1 = 150	4
7. Bulk storage	100/2 = 50	7

Department 3 (microwaves) has the highest ratio and, therefore, ranks first. Although 360 trips per week are involved, the department occupies only one block of space. Ranking the remaining departments by their ratios, we get 1, 5, 6, 4, 2, and 7. Figure 10.11 shows the layout derived from this ranking. Department 3 had first choice and could have been placed in either of the two locations nearest the dock. We chose the north one and assigned the south one to department 1.

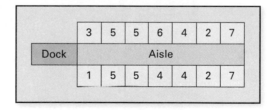

FIGURE 10.11 • Best Block Plan for A-1 Distribution Systems Warehouse

Decision Point Management implemented this layout, although it is changed from time to time because demand is seasonal. Thus radios are placed closer to the dock for Christmas, and air conditioning moved near the dock during the summer. ⌐

What type of layout pattern makes sense for a warehouse?

ADDITIONAL LAYOUT OPTIONS. Although one advantage of the layout just proposed is its simplicity, other options might be more effective. First, various ways of utilizing space offer additional layout options. For example, an 82,000-square-foot, 32-foot-high, racked warehouse can handle the same volume as a 107,000-square-foot, low-ceilinged warehouse, with the higher stockpicking productivity of the high-ceilinged warehouse offsetting the added rack and equipment costs. Another space-saving design assigns all incoming materials to the nearest available space, rather than to a predetermined area where all like items are clustered. A computer system tracks the location of each item. When it is time to retrieve an item, the system prints its location on the shipping bill and identifies the shortest route for the stockpicker. Canadiana Outdoor Products, in Brampton, Ontario, introduced a computer system with terminals mounted on lift trucks. This arrangement allows drivers to track the exact location and contents of each storage bin in the warehouse. With this new system, Canadiana can handle quadrupled sales with less storage space.

Three views of the layout at a modern warehouse that holds about 16 million books in inventory and processes between 2,000 and 5,000 orders per day.

Cases of the fastest-selling titles are stacked outside the flow racks in the "golden zone," where the 80 fastest-selling titles are stored. These titles comprise about 50 percent of all shipments. Whole cases are picked here in response to specific orders.

A floor-level conveyor transports boxes of books to the packaging area. There the boxes pass over a computerized weight-in-motion scale, which compares the total weight of the package to the sum of weights of individual titles.

Returned books are temporarily sorted in the 5,400 locations in the returns staging carousel. The number of returns is surprisingly large, comprising about 12.5 percent of the overall volume. Returns from schools and college occur when bookstores order more books than they actually sell to students.

Second, different layout patterns offer still more layout options. The warehouse depicted in Figure 10.10 has an *out-and-back pattern,* where items are picked one at a time, but there are other options. In a *route collection system,* the stockpicker selects a variety of items to be shipped to a customer. In a *batch picking system,* the stockpicker gathers the quantity of an item required to satisfy a group of customer orders to be shipped in the same truck or rail car. Finally, in the *zone system,* the stockpicker gathers all needed items in her assigned zone and places them on a powered conveyor line. Figure 10.12 illustrates the zone system for a warehouse. The conveyor line consists of five feeder lines and one trunk line. When the merchandise arrives at the control

Zone System for a Warehouse

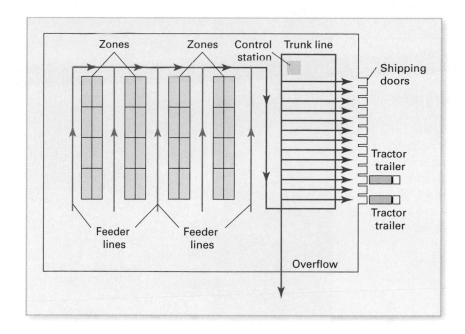

station, an operator directs it to the correct tractor trailer for outbound shipment. The advantage of the zone system is that pickers need not travel throughout the warehouse to fill orders; they are responsible only for their own zones.

OFFICE LAYOUTS

What is the best trade-off between proximity and privacy for an office layout?

More than 40 percent of the U.S. workforce is employed in offices, and office layout can affect both productivity and the quality of work life. In a recent survey, three-fourths of 1,400 employees polled said that productivity could be raised by improvements in their work environments.

PROXIMITY. Accessibility to co-workers and supervisors can enhance communication and develop mutual interest. Conversations tend to become more formal as individuals are placed farther apart. The famous Hawthorne study in 1939 showed that the physical work setting influences group formation. In the study, management used spatial language to tell workers in the experimental group that they were important. Management changed both absolute and relative locations of the workers by moving them to a separate room and away from the watchful eyes of a supervisor. The revised layout facilitated contact between workers and the setting of group norms. More recent studies confirm that proximity to others can help clarify what is expected of an employee on the job and in other ways.

Most formal procedures for designing office layouts try to maximize the proximity of workers whose jobs require frequent interaction. Data collected on the frequency and importance of interactions can be used in a REL chart or a trip matrix. Certain procedures can be used to identify natural clusters of workers to be treated as a center in a block plan. The goal of such approaches is to design layouts around work flows and communication patterns.

PRIVACY. Another key factor in office design—and one that is somewhat culturally dependent—is privacy. Outside disruptions and crowding can hurt a worker's performance. At Sperry Rand's and McDonald's world headquarters, employee reactions to open offices were favorable. However, when a newspaper company tried to increase

Office space at Microsoft's Redman, Washington, facility is designed to support the variety of needs of its employees. Software developers need private, quiet space while marketing personnel need open spaces conducive to face-face interactions.

worker proximity by going from private work spaces to an open-plan office, the results were disappointing. Employees felt as if they were in a fishbowl and that they had little control over their environment. Studies at several state government departments revealed a strong link between privacy and satisfaction with the supervisor and the job.

OPTIONS IN OFFICE LAYOUT. Providing both proximity and privacy for employees poses a dilemma for management. Proximity is gained by opening up the work area. Privacy is gained by more liberal space standards, baffled ceilings, doors, partitions, and thick carpeting that absorbs noise—expensive features that reduce layout flexibility. Thus, management must generally arrive at a compromise between proximity and privacy. No single type of space fits all workers. For example, Microsoft in Redmond, Washington, has found that software developers do their best work in private, quiet space. But its sales and marketing people work in a mixture of private and open spaces; the emphasis is on facilitating interactions among sales and marketing personnel and providing good spaces for meetings with customers. Its product support offices are about 90 percent open space.

Four different approaches are available: traditional layouts, office landscaping, activity settings, and electronic cottages. The choice requires an understanding of work requirements, the workforce itself, and top management's philosophy of work.

Traditional layouts call for closed offices for management and those employees whose work requires privacy and open areas (or bullpens) for all others. The resulting layout may be characterized by long hallways lined with closed doors, producing considerable isolation, and by open areas filled uniformly with rows of desks. In traditional layouts each person has a designated place. Its location, size, and furnishing signify the person's status in the organization.

An approach developed in Germany during the late 1950s puts everyone (including top management) in an open area. The headquarters of Johnson Wax is designed with open offices. So is Hewlett-Packard's Waltham, Massachusetts, plant. Shoulder-high dividers partition the space. The idea is to achieve closer cooperation among employees at *all* levels. However, the corporate nurse still keeps earplugs on hand for employees bothered by noise. An extension of this concept is called *office landscaping:* Attractive plants, screens, and portable partitions increase privacy and cluster or separate groups. Movable workstations and accessories help maintain flexibility. Because the workstations (or cubicles) are only semiprivate, employees might have trouble concentrating or might feel uncomfortable trying to hold sensitive discussions. Construction costs are as much as 40 percent less than for traditional layouts, and rearrangement costs are less still.

Activity settings represent a relatively new concept for achieving both proximity and privacy. The full range of work needs is covered by multiple workplaces, including a library, teleconferencing facility, reception area, conference room, special graphics area, and shared terminals. Employees move from one activity setting to the next as their work requires during the day. Each person also gets a small, personal office as a home base.

MANAGERIAL PRACTICE 10.3
Telecommuting At Pacific Bell and DKM Inc.

Pacific Bell

Pacific Bell (www.pacbell.com/), a subsidiary of Pacific Telesis Group, has a formal telecommuting policy. More than 1,000 of its managers work fairly regularly from sites other than their primary offices. The company opened two full-blown satellite offices four years ago, each able to accommodate 18 managers who communicate with co-workers and the outside world via personal computers, modems, facsimile machines, copying equipment, and laser printers.

One of the managers in sales support, for example, works at a neighborhood satellite just 15 minutes from his home. He used to make a 26 mile commute to the downtown Los Angeles office, which took an hour when everything went well and up to 2½ hours when it rained. Free from the time-consuming commute and the distractions of Pacific Telesis's main office, he feels that he is functioning more efficiently. He prefers working at an office to working at home, where there are distractions such as doing dishes, mowing the lawn, or seeing what's in the refrigerator. Like other satellite workers, he visits the main office from time to time.

DKM Inc.

DKM Inc. (www.netheaven.com/~dkm/dk) is a 25-person manufacturing consulting firm in the Los Angeles basin. The first thing a new employee receives is a notebook computer—a symbol of the firm's commitment to virtual work arrangements. Especially considering the Los Angeles traffic snarls, it does not make sense to have employees come to the office if the client is 10 minutes from home. The firm pays for a second phone line in each employee's home office and, if necessary, springs for a printer or scanner. As a result, DKM's consultants can meet at a manufacturer's plant in the morning and finish up their day's work at home

Virtual work arrangements are becoming popular in consulting firms. Here an employee at DKM receives her new laptop computer and instructions on how to use the firm's Web services.

in the afternoon. There are additional Web-based services that help bring together far-flung employees, such as free Web scheduling service SchedulePlus. Among other things, telecommuting employees use the site to reserve time in the office conference room and avoid scheduling conflicts. Others bounce their ideas around with others in real time using the free ICQ Internet chat service (www.placeware.com) or the Web conferencing service PlaceWare (www.placeware.com). For a fee of $400 annually per seat at the "virtual conference," you can present PowerPoint slides on a common Web page that all meeting participants can access. It also lets you receive answers to yes or no questions in real time to gauge the thoughts of others.

Source: "Tools of the Remote Trade." *Business Week* (March 27, 2000), p. F20.

Some futurists expect more and more employees to work at home or in neighborhood offices connected to the main office by computer. Called *telecommuting* or *electronic cottages,* this approach represents a modern-day version of the cottage industries that existed prior to the Industrial Revolution. Besides saving on commuting time, it offers flexibility in work schedules. Many working men and women with children, for example, prefer such flexibility. More than nine million Americans already have a taste of this arrangement, working at least part of the week at home. However, telecommuting can have drawbacks, such as lack of equipment, too many family disruptions, and too few opportunities for socialization and politicking. Some managers at Hartford Insurance complained that they couldn't supervise—much less get to know—employees they couldn't see. Managerial Practice 10.3 on the previous page discusses the telecommuting policy of two other companies, Pacific Bell and DKM, Inc.

DESIGNING PRODUCT LAYOUTS

How can a better product layout for a facility be determined?

Product layouts raise management issues entirely different from those of process layouts. Often called a production or assembly line, a product layout arranges workstations in sequence. The product moves from one station to the next until its completion at the end of the line. Typically, one worker operates each station, performing repetitive tasks. Little inventory is built up between stations, so stations cannot operate independently. Thus, the line is only as fast as its slowest workstation. In other words, if the slowest station takes 45 seconds per unit, the line's fastest possible output is one product every 45 seconds.

LINE BALANCING

line balancing The assignment of work to stations in a line so as to achieve the desired output rate with the smallest number of workstations.

Line balancing is the assignment of work to stations in a line so as to achieve the desired output rate with the smallest number of workstations. Normally, one worker is assigned to a station. Thus, the line that produces at the desired pace with the fewest workers is the most efficient one. Line balancing must be performed when a line is set up initially, when a line is rebalanced to change its hourly output rate, or when product or process changes. The goal is to obtain workstations with well-balanced workloads (e.g., every station takes roughly 45 seconds per unit produced).

Factory workers in Dong Guan, Guangdong Province, Peoples' Republic of China, assemble electronic boards. Each worker performs the same set of tasks at her station on each Electronic board that is assembled.

work elements The smallest units of work that can be performed independently.

immediate predecessors Work elements that must be done before the next element can begin.

The analyst begins by separating the work into **work elements,** the smallest units of work that can be performed independently. The analyst then obtains the labor standard (see CD Supplement I on *Measuring Output Rates*) for each element and identifies the work elements, called **immediate predecessors,** that must be done before the next can begin.

PRECEDENCE DIAGRAM. Most lines must satisfy some technological precedence requirements—that is, certain work elements must be done before the next can begin. However, most lines also allow for some latitude and more than one sequence of operations. To help you visualize immediate predecessors better, let us run through the construction of a **precedence diagram.**[2] We denote the work elements by circles, with the time required to perform the work shown below each circle. Arrows lead from immediate predecessors to the next work element.

| EXAMPLE 10.4 | *Constructing a Precedence Diagram* |

precedence diagram A diagram that allows one to visualize immediate predecessors better; work elements are denoted by circles, with the time required to perform the work shown below each circle.

Green Grass, Inc., a manufacturer of lawn and garden equipment, is designing an assembly line to produce a new fertilizer spreader, the Big Broadcaster. Using the following information on the production process, construct a precedence diagram for the Big Broadcaster.

WORK ELEMENT	DESCRIPTION	TIME (sec)	IMMEDIATE PREDECESSOR(S)
A	Bolt leg frame to hopper	40	None
B	Insert impeller shaft	30	A
C	Attach axle	50	A
D	Attach agitator	40	B
E	Attach drive wheel	6	B
F	Attach free wheel	25	C
G	Mount lower post	15	C
H	Attach controls	20	D, E
I	Mount nameplate	18	F, G
		Total 244	

SOLUTION

Figure 10.13 shows the complete diagram. We begin with work element A, which has no immediate predecessors. Next, we add elements B and C, for which element A is the only immediate

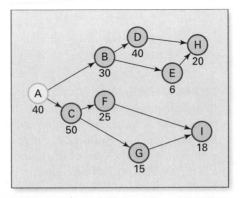

FIGURE 10.13 • Precedence Diagram for Assembling the Big Broadcaster

---

[2] Precedence relationships and precedence diagrams are important in the entirely different context of project scheduling (see the Managing Project Processes chapter).

predecessor. After entering labor standards and arrows showing precedence, we add elements D and E, and so on. The diagram simplifies interpretation. Work element F, for example, can be done anywhere on the line after element C is completed. However, element I must await completion of elements F and G.

Decision Point Management now has enough information to develop a layout which clusters work elements to form workstations, with a goal being to balance the workloads, and in the process minimize the number of workstations required. ◻

What should be a line's output rate?

DESIRED OUTPUT RATE. The goal of line balancing is to match the output rate to the production plan. For example, if the production plan calls for 4,000 units per week and the line operates 80 hours per week, the desired output rate ideally would be 50 units (4,000/80) per hour. Matching output to demand ensures on-time delivery and prevents buildup of unwanted inventory. However, managers should avoid rebalancing a line too frequently, because each time a line is rebalanced, many workers' jobs on the line must be redesigned, temporarily hurting productivity and sometimes even requiring a new detailed layout for some stations.

Some automobile plants avoid frequent changes by eliminating a shift entirely when demand falls and inventory becomes excessive, rather than gradually scaling back the output rate. Managers can also add shifts to increase equipment utilization, which is crucial for capital-intensive facilities. However, higher pay rates or low demand may make multiple shifts undesirable or unnecessary.

cycle time The maximum time allowed for work on a unit at each station.

CYCLE TIME. After determining the desired output rate for a line, the analyst can calculate the line's cycle time. A line's **cycle time** is the maximum time allowed for work on a unit at each station.[3] If the time required for work elements at a station exceeds the line's cycle time, the station will be a bottleneck, preventing the line from reaching its desired output rate. The target cycle time is the reciprocal of the desired hourly output rate:

$$c = \frac{1}{r}$$

where

c = cycle time in hours per unit

r = desired output rate in units per hour

For example, if the line's desired output rate is 60 units per hour, the cycle time is $c = 1/60$ hour per unit, or 1 minute.

THEORETICAL MINIMUM. To achieve the desired output rate, managers use line balancing to assign every work element to a station, making sure to satisfy all precedence requirements and to minimize the number of stations, n, formed. If each station is operated by a different worker, minimizing n also maximizes worker productivity. Perfect balance is achieved when the sum of the work-element times at each station equals the cycle time, c, and no station has any idle time. For example, if the sum of each station's work-element times is 1 minute, which is also the cycle time, there is perfect balance. Although perfect balance usually is unachievable in practice, owing to the unevenness

---

[3] Except in the context of line balancing, *cycle time* has a different meaning. It is the elapsed time between starting and completing a job. Some researchers and practitioners prefer the term *lead time*.

of work-element times and the inflexibility of precedence requirements, it sets a benchmark, or goal, for the smallest number of stations possible. The **theoretical minimum (TM)** for the number of stations is

$$\text{TM} = \frac{\Sigma t}{c}$$

where

Σt = total time required to assemble each unit (the sum of all work-element standard times)

c = cycle time

For example, if the sum of the work-element times is 15 minutes and the cycle time is 1 minute, TM = 15/1, or 15 stations. Any fractional values obtained for TM are rounded up because fractional stations are impossible.

IDLE TIME, EFFICIENCY, AND BALANCE DELAY. Minimizing n automatically ensures (1) minimal idle time, (2) maximal efficiency, and (3) minimal balance delay. Idle time is the total unproductive time for all stations in the assembly of each unit:

$$\text{Idle time} = nc - \Sigma t$$

where

n = number of stations

c = cycle time

Σt = total standard time required to assemble each unit

Efficiency is the ratio of productive time to total time, expressed as a percent:

$$\text{Efficiency(percent)} = \frac{\Sigma t}{nc}(100)$$

Balance delay is the amount by which efficiency falls short of 100 percent:

$$\text{Balance delay(percent)} = 100 - \text{Efficiency}$$

As long as c is fixed, we can optimize all three goals by minimizing n.

EXAMPLE 10.5   *Calculating the Cycle Time, Theoretical Minimum, and Efficiency*

TUTOR 10.1

Green Grass's plant manager has just received marketing's latest forecasts of Big Broadcaster sales for the next year. She wants its production line to be designed to make 2,400 spreaders per week for at least the next 3 months. The plant will operate 40 hours per week.

a. What should be the line's cycle time?

b. What is the smallest number of workstations that she could hope for in designing the line for this cycle time?

c. Suppose that she finds a solution that requires only five stations. What would be the line's efficiency?

SOLUTION

a. First convert the desired output rate (2,400 units per week) to an hourly rate by dividing the weekly output rate by 40 hours per week to get $r = 60$ units per hour. Then the cycle time is

$$c = \frac{1}{r} = \frac{1}{60} \text{ hour/unit} = 1 \text{ minute/unit}$$

b. Now calculate the theoretical minimum for the number of stations by dividing the total time, Σt, by the cycle time, $c = 1$ minute $= 60$ seconds. Assuming perfect balance, we have

$$\text{TM} = \frac{\Sigma t}{c} = \frac{244 \text{ seconds}}{60 \text{ seconds}} = 4.067, \quad \text{or} \quad 5 \text{ stations}$$

c. Now calculate the efficiency of a five-station solution, assuming for now that one can be found:

$$\text{Efficiency(percent)} = \frac{\Sigma t}{nc}(100) = \frac{244}{5(60)}(100) = 81.3\%$$

The OM Explorer output confirms these calculations (Figure 10.14).

Tutor 10.1 - Line Balancing

1. Enter the time required to assemble one unit (in seconds) and the desired production rate in units per hour. The formula below the inputs converts total production time (time to perform all work elements) from seconds to hours.

Overall production time	244	(seconds)
Desired output rate (r)	60	(units/hr)
Converted production time	0.0678	(hrs/unit)

2. Calculate cycle time by dividing 1 by the desired output.

Cycle time (c)	0.016666667	(hrs/unit)

3. To find the theoretical minimum number of workstations needed to achieve the desired output rate, divide the converted production time by cycle time. Round this up to the next whole number:

Theoretical minimum workstations	4.0667
Rounded up	5

4. To compute efficiency (if a solution can be found with just this minimum number of workstations), divide the production time by the result of multiplying number of machines by cycle time:

Theoretical maximum efficiency	81.3%

FIGURE 10.14 • Analyzing Product Layouts with Tutor 10.1

Decision Point Thus, if the manager finds a solution with five stations, that is the minimum number of stations possible. However, the efficiency (sometimes called the *theoretical maximum efficiency*) will be only 81.3 percent. Perhaps the line should be operated less than 40 hours per week and the employees transferred to other kinds of work when the line does not operate. ☐

FINDING A SOLUTION. Often, many assembly-line solutions are possible, even for such simple problems as Green Grass's. As for process layouts, computer assistance is available. For example, one software package considers every feasible combination of work elements that does not violate precedence or cycle-time requirements. The combination that minimizes the station's idle time is selected. If any work elements remain unassigned, a second station is formed, and so on.

The approach that we use here is even simpler. We select a work element from a list of candidates and assign it to a station. We repeat this process until all stations have been formed, using k as a counter for the station being formed.

Step 1. Start with station $k = 1$. Make a list of candidate work elements to assign to station k. Each candidate must satisfy three conditions:

   a. It has not yet been assigned to this or any previous station.
   b. All its predecessors have been assigned to this or a previous station.
   c. Its time does not exceed the station's idle time, which accounts for all work elements already assigned. If no work elements have been assigned, the station's idle time equals the cycle time.

If no such candidates can be found, go to step 4.

Step 2. Pick a candidate. Two decision rules are commonly used for selecting from the candidate list.

   a. Pick the candidate with the *longest work-element time.* This heuristic rule assigns as quickly as possible those work elements most difficult to fit into a station and saves work elements having shorter times for fine tuning the solution.
   b. Pick the candidate having the *largest number of followers.* Figure 10.13 shows, for example, that work element C has three followers and E has one follower. This rule helps keep options open for forming subsequent stations. Otherwise, precedence requirements may leave only a few possible sequences of work elements, all causing an unnecessary amount of station idle time as a result.

Assign the candidate chosen to station k. If two or more candidates are tied, arbitrarily choose one of them.

Step 3. Calculate the cumulative time of all tasks assigned so far to station k. Subtract this total from the cycle time to find the station's idle time. Go to step 1, and generate a new list of candidates.

Step 4. If some work elements are still unassigned, but none are candidates for station k, create a new station, station $k + 1$, and go to step 1. Otherwise, you have a complete solution.

EXAMPLE 10.6   *Finding a Solution*

Find a line-balancing solution for the Green Grass, Inc., problem. Use the manual solution procedure, the longest work-element time rule to pick candidates, and a cycle time of 1 minute.

SOLUTION

The following worksheet shows how to proceed, and the first few iterations reveal the pattern. Beginning with the first station, S1 ($k = 1$), the precedence diagram shows that only element A can be a candidate. It is the only one with all immediate predecessors (none, in this case) already assigned. With element A assigned, station S1 has an idle time of 20 seconds (60 − 40). Elements B and C cannot now become candidates for station S1, because their times exceed 20 seconds, and so S1 is complete. For the second station ($k = 2$), elements B and C are candidates, and we choose C because it has the larger work-element time. With station S2 now consisting of element C, its idle time equals 10 seconds (60 − 50). No candidates remain because adding the time of element B, F, or G brings the work content of S2 over the cycle time ($c = 60$). We continue through the procedure until we have assigned all work elements. The final solution calls for

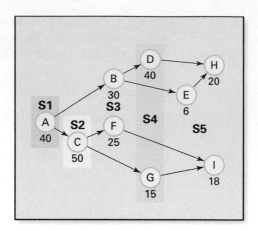

FIGURE 10.15 • Big Broadcaster Precedence Diagram Solution Using Longest Work-Element Time Rule

only five stations, as shown in Figure 10.15. As $n = TM = 5$, we can do no better than this with a 60-second cycle time.

Worksheet

STATION (Step 1)	CANDIDATE (Step 2)	CHOICE (Step 3)	CUMULATIVE TIME (sec) (Step 4)	IDLE TIME ($c = 60$ sec) (Step 4)
S1	A	A	40	20
S2	B, C	C	50	10
S3	B, F, G	B	30	30
	E, F, G	F	55	5
S4	D, E, G	D	40	20
	E, G	G	55	5
S5	E, I	I	18	42
	E	E	24	36
	H	H	44	16

When implementing this solution, we must observe precedence requirements within each station. For example, the worker at station S5 can do element I at any time but cannot start element H until element E is finished. ☐

OTHER CONSIDERATIONS

In addition to balancing a line for a given cycle time, managers must also consider four other options: pacing, behavioral factors, number of models produced, and cycle times.

PACING. The movement of product from one station to the next after the cycle time has elapsed is called **pacing**. Automated materials handling has a big advantage, but it also has a disadvantage. Capacity losses, difficulties in aligning components that are being assembled, or missing components mean that either the entire line must be slowed down or unfinished work must be pulled off the line to be completed later. *Paced lines* have no buffer inventory, making them particularly susceptible to capacity losses and variability in work-element times. *Unpaced lines* require that inventory storage areas be placed between stations. These storage areas make unexpected downtime at one station less likely to delay work downstream, but they increase space and inventory costs.

pacing The movement of product from one station to the next after the cycle time has elapsed.

BEHAVIORAL FACTORS. The most controversial aspect of product layouts is behavioral response. Studies have shown that installing production lines increases absenteeism, turnover, and grievances. Paced production and high specialization (say, cycle times of less than two minutes) lower job satisfaction. Workers generally favor inventory buffers as a means of avoiding mechanical pacing. One study even showed that productivity increased on unpaced lines.

Many companies are exploring job enlargement and rotation to increase job variety and reduce excessive specialization. For example, New York Life has redesigned the jobs of workers who process and evaluate claims applications. Instead of using a production line approach with several workers doing specialized tasks, New York Life has made each worker solely responsible for an entire application. This approach increased worker responsibility and raised morale. In manufacturing, at its plant in Kohda, Japan, Sony Corporation dismantled the conveyor belts on which as many as 50 people assembled camcorders. It set up tables for workers to assemble an entire camera themselves, doing everything from soldering to testing. Output per worker is up 10 percent, because the approach frees efficient assemblers to make more product instead of limiting them to a conveyor belt's speed. And if something goes wrong, only a small section of the plant is affected. This approach also allows the line to match actual demand better and avoid frequent shutdowns because of inventory buildups.

Such efforts are not always as successful because some workers react unfavorably to enlarged jobs. The new format, sometimes called a *craft line* because the workers are jacks-of-all-trades, usually is less efficient at making heavy, high-volume goods, such as automobiles. In fact, AB Volvo closed its much-publicized craft lines at two auto factories in Sweden.

NUMBER OF MODELS PRODUCED. A **mixed-model line** produces several items belonging to the same family, such as the Cadillac de Ville and Oldsmobile 98 models. In contrast, a single-model line produces one model with no variations. Mixed-model production enables a plant to achieve both high-volume production *and* product variety. However, it complicates scheduling and increases the need for good communication about the specific parts to be produced at each station. Care must be taken to alternate models so as not to overload some stations for too long. Despite these difficulties, the mixed-model line may be the only reasonable choice when product plans call for many customer options, as volumes may not be high enough to justify a separate line for each model.

CYCLE TIMES. A line's cycle time depends on the desired output rate (or sometimes on the maximum number of workstations allowed). In turn, the maximum line efficiency varies considerably with the cycle time selected. Thus, exploring a range of cycle times makes sense. A manager might go with a particularly efficient solution even if it does not match the output rate. The manager can compensate for the mismatch by varying the number of hours the line operates through overtime, extending shifts, or adding shifts. Multiple lines might even be the answer.

Another possibility is to let finished-goods inventory build up for some time and then rebalance the line at a lower output rate to deplete the excess. Use of this strategy should be weighed against the costs of rebalancing. Japanese automobile manufacturing strategy calls for rebalancing lines about 12 times a year. In the United States, the overall average is only about 3 times per year. The Japanese strategy minimizes inventories and balance delay. The primary disadvantage of the Japanese approach is that it disrupts production during the changeover from one line configuration to another. Greater worker flexibility, cross-training, and job rotation, which are additional elements of the Japanese approach, can minimize such disruptions.

What can be done to humanize product layouts?

Should a mixed-model line be considered?

mixed-model line
A product line that produces several items belonging to the same family.

MANAGING LAYOUT ACROSS THE ORGANIZATION

Layouts are found in every area of a business because every facility has a layout. Good layouts can improve coordination across departmental lines and functional area boundaries. Each process in a facility has a layout that should be carefully designed. The layouts of retail operations, such as the RiverTown Crossings mall or one of the stores at The Limited, can affect customer attitudes and therefore sales. How a manufacturing or warehousing process is laid out affects materials handling costs, throughput times, and worker productivity. Redesigning layouts can require significant capital investments, which need to be analyzed from an accounting and financial perspective. Layouts also affect employee attitudes, whether on a production line or in an office.

FORMULA REVIEW

1. Cycle time (in seconds): $c = \dfrac{1}{r}$ (3,600 seconds/hour)

2. Theoretical minimum number of workstations: $TM = \dfrac{\Sigma t}{c}$

3. Idle time (in seconds): $nc - \Sigma t$

4. Efficiency (percent): $\dfrac{\Sigma t}{nc}(100)$

5. Balance delay (percent): $100 - $ Efficiency

CHAPTER HIGHLIGHTS

❑ Layout decisions go beyond placement of economic activity centers. Equally important are which centers to include, how much space they need, and how to configure their space.

❑ There are four layout types: process, product, hybrid, and fixed position. Management's choice should reflect process choice. Flexible flows call for a process layout, whereas line flows call for a product layout. Hybrid layouts include OWMM, GT cells, and FMS.

❑ Capital investment, materials handling cost, and flexibility are important criteria in judging most layouts. Entirely different criteria, such as encouraging sales or communication, might be emphasized for stores or offices.

❑ If product volumes are too low to justify dedicating a production line to a single product, obtaining overlapped operations may still be possible. In such cases, the one-worker, multiple-machines (OWMM) concept or group technology (GT) cells, where machines are arranged to produce families of parts, may be feasible.

❑ Designing a process layout involves gathering the necessary information, developing an acceptable block plan, and translating the block plan into a detailed layout. Information needed for process layouts includes space requirements by center, available space, the block plan for existing layouts, closeness ratings, and performance criteria relating to absolute location concerns. Closeness ratings can be tabulated on either a trip matrix or a REL chart. A manual approach to finding a block plan begins with listing key requirements, which may be based on high closeness ratings or on other considerations. Trial and error is then used to find a block plan that satisfies most of the requirements. A load–distance score is helpful in evaluating the plan for relative location concerns. Several computer-based models, such as ALDEP and CRAFT, are now available to aid layout decision making.

❑ The simplest warehouse situation is the out-and-back pattern. Departmental proximity to the dock depends on the ratio of trip frequency to space needs. Other patterns are the route collection, batch picking, and the zone systems.

The effect of a layout on people is particularly apparent in offices. Layout affects productivity and the quality of work life. Four approaches to proximity–privacy trade-offs are traditional layouts, office landscaping, activity settings, and electronic cottages.

In product layouts, workstations are arranged in a somewhat naturally occurring, commonsense sequence as required for high-volume production of only one product or a family of products. Because the physical arrangement is determined by the product's design, management concerns become line balance, pacing, behavior, number of models, and cycle times.

In line balancing, tasks are assigned to stations so as to satisfy all precedence and cycle-time constraints while minimizing the number of stations required. Balancing minimizes idle time, maximizes efficiency, and minimizes delay. The desired output rate from a line depends not only on demand forecasts but also on frequency of rebalancing, capacity utilization, and job specialization. One approach to line balancing is to create one station at a time. A work element selected from a list of candidates is added to a station at each iteration. Two commonly used decision rules for making this choice are the longest work-element time and largest number of followers rules.

KEY TERMS

automated layout design program (ALDEP) *460*

balance delay *471*

block plan *456*

computerized relative allocation of facilities technique (CRAFT) *460*

cycle time *470*

economic activity center *445*

fixed-position layout *450*

group technology (GT) *453*

hybrid layout *449*

immediate predecessors *469*

layout flexibility *451*

layout planning *445*

line balancing *468*

mixed-model line *475*

one-worker, multiple-machines (OWMM) cell *452*

pacing *474*

precedence diagram *469*

process layout *446*

product layout *448*

REL chart *457*

theoretical minimum (TM) *471*

trip matrix *456*

work elements *469*

SOLVED PROBLEM 1

A defense contractor is evaluating its machine shop's current process layout. Figure 10.16 shows the current layout, and the table shows the trip matrix for the facility. Safety and health regulations require departments E and F to remain at their current locations.

	TRIPS BETWEEN DEPARTMENTS					
DEPARTMENT	A	B	C	D	E	F
A	—	8	3		9	5
B		—		3		
C			—		8	9
D				—		3
E					—	3
F						—

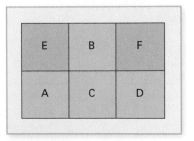

FIGURE 10.16 •   Current Layout

a. Use trial and error to find a better layout.

b. How much better is your layout than the current one, in terms of the *ld* score? Use rectilinear distance.

SOLUTION

a. In addition to keeping departments E and F at their current locations, a good plan would locate the following department pairs close to each other: A and E, C and F, A and B, and C and E. Figure 10.17 was worked out by trial and error and satisfies all these requirements. Start by placing E and F at their current locations. Then, because C must be as close as possible to both E and F, put C between them. Place A directly south of E, and B next to A. All of the heavy traffic concerns have now been accommodated. Department D is located in the remaining space.

DEPARTMENT PAIR	NUMBER OF TRIPS (1)	CURRENT PLAN		PROPOSED PLAN	
		DISTANCE (2)	LOAD × DISTANCE (1) × (2)	DISTANCE (3)	LOAD × DISTANCE (1) × (3)
A, B	8	2	16	1	8
A, C	3	1	3	2	6
A, E	9	1	9	1	9
A, F	5	3	15	3	15
B, D	3	2	6	1	3
C, E	8	2	16	1	8
C, F	9	2	18	1	9
D, F	3	1	3	1	3
E, F	3	2	6	2	6
			ld = $\overline{92}$		*ld* = $\overline{67}$

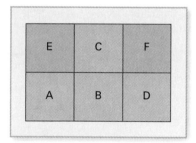

FIGURE 10.17 • Proposed Layout

b. The table reveals that the *ld* score drops from 92 for the current plan to 67 for the revised plan, a 27 percent reduction.

SOLVED PROBLEM 2

Using rectilinear distances, develop a layout for the warehouse docking area shown in Figure 10.18. Each of seven departments (A–G) requires one block space—except C, which needs two spaces. The daily trips to and from the dock are 390 for A, 180 for B, 220 for C, 250 for D, 160 for E, 120 for F, and 220 for G.

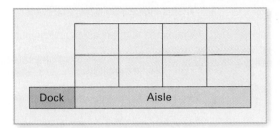

FIGURE 10.18

SOLUTION

Sequencing departments by the ratio of trips per block space, we get A, D, G, B, E, F, and C, as shown in the table. Giving preference to those higher in the sequence produces the layout shown in Figure 10.19. There are other optimal solutions because some locations are equidistant from the dock.

DEPARTMENT	TRIPS	BLOCK SPACE	TRIPS PER BLOCK SPACE
A	390	1	390
D	250	1	250
G	220	1	220
B	180	1	180
E	160	1	160
F	120	1	120
C	220	2	110

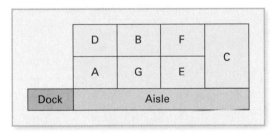

FIGURE 10.19

SOLVED PROBLEM 3

A company is setting up an assembly line to produce 192 units per eight-hour shift. The following table identifies the work elements, times, and immediate predecessors.

WORK ELEMENT	TIME (sec)	IMMEDIATE PREDECESSOR(S)
A	40	None
B	80	A
C	30	D, E, F
D	25	B
E	20	B
F	15	B
G	120	A
H	145	G
I	130	H
J	115	C, I
Total	720	

a. What is the desired cycle time?

b. What is the theoretical minimum number of stations?

c. Use the largest work-element time rule to work out a solution, and show your solution on a precedence diagram.

d. What are the efficiency and balance delay of the solution found?

SOLUTION

a. Substituting in the cycle-time formula, we get

$$c = \frac{1}{r} = \frac{8 \text{ hours}}{192 \text{ units}}(3{,}600 \text{ seconds/hour}) = 150 \text{ seconds/unit}$$

b. The sum of the work-element times is 720 seconds, so

$$TM = \frac{\Sigma t}{c} = \frac{720 \text{ seconds/unit}}{150 \text{ seconds/unit-station}} = 4.8, \qquad \text{or} \qquad 5 \text{ stations}$$

which may not be achievable.

c. The precedence diagram is shown in Figure 10.20. Each row in the following table represents one iteration of application of the largest work-element time rule in assigning work elements to workstations.

STATION	CANDIDATE(S)	CHOICE	WORK-ELEMENT TIME (sec)	CUMULATIVE TIME TIME (sec)	IDLE TIME (C = 150 sec)
S1	A	A	40	40	110
	B	B	80	120	30
	D, E, F	D	25	145	5
S2	E, F, G	G	120	120	30
	E, F	E	20	140	10
S3	F, H	H	145	145	5
S4	F, I	I	130	130	20
	F	F	15	145	5
S5	C	C	30	30	120
	J	J	115	145	5

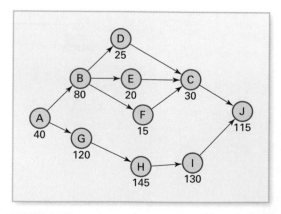

FIGURE 10.20

d. Calculating the efficiency, we get

$$\text{Efficiency} = \frac{\Sigma t}{nc}(100) = \frac{720 \text{ seconds/unit}}{5(150 \text{ seconds/unit})}(100)$$

$$= 96\%$$

Thus, the balance delay is only 4 percent (100 − 96).

DISCUSSION QUESTIONS

1. Identify the types of layout performance criteria that might be most important in the following settings.

   a. Airport
   b. Bank
   c. Classroom
   d. Office of product designers
   e. Law firm
   f. Fabrication of sheet-metal components
   g. Parking lot
   h. Human resources department

2. An office of 120 employees must be redesigned to accommodate 30 new employees. At the same time, it should be made as effective as possible. You want to improve communication, find space for everyone, create a good work environment, and minimize adverse reactions to space reductions and relocation.

   a. What information would you gather? How?
   b. How would you analyze this information?
   c. How much employee involvement would you recommend? Why?

3. Consider the Lower Florida Keys Health System and the Chaparral Steel tours in the Operations Strategy chapter and the Virtual Text on the Student CD-ROM. The organizations are quite different in terms of facility layout. Which one has a process layout? Product layout? How do these layout designs relate to process choice? Explain.

OM EXPLORER AND INTERNET EXERCISES

Visit our Web site at www.prenhall.com/krajewski for OM Explorer Tutors, which explain quantitative techniques; Solvers, which help you apply mathematical models; and Internet Exercises, including Facility Tours, which expand on the topics in this chapter.

PROBLEMS

An icon next to a problem identifies the software that can be helpful, but not mandatory. The software is available on the Student CD-ROM that is packaged with every new copy of the textbook.

1. 🌐 **OM Explorer** Baker Machine Company is a job shop specializing in precision parts for firms in the aerospace industry. Figure 10.21 shows the current block plan for the key manufacturing centers of the 75,000-square-foot facility. Referring to the trip matrix below the figure, use rectilinear distance (the current distance from inspection to shipping and receiving is 3 units) to calculate the change in the load–distance, *ld*, score if Baker exchanges the locations of the tool crib and inspection.

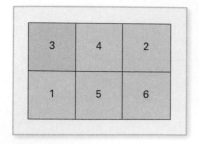

FIGURE 10.21

Trip Matrix

	TRIPS BETWEEN DEPARTMENTS					
DEPARTMENT	1	2	3	4	5	6
1. Burr and grind	—	8	3		9	5
2. NC equipment		—		3		
3. Shipping and receiving			—		8	9
4. Lathes and drills				—		3
5. Tool crib					—	3
6. Inspection						—

2. 💿 **OM Explorer** Use trial and error to find a particularly good block plan for Baker Machine (see Problem 1). Because of excessive relocation costs, shipping and receiving (department 3) must remain at its current location. Compare *ld* scores to evaluate your new layout, again assuming rectilinear distance.

3. 💿 **OM Explorer** The head of the information systems group at Conway Consulting must assign six new analysts to offices. The following trip matrix shows the expected frequency of contact between analysts. The block plan in Figure 10.22 shows the available office locations (1–6) for the six analysts (A–F). Assume equal-sized offices and rectilinear distance. Owing to their tasks, analyst A must be assigned to location 4 and analyst D to location 3. What are the best locations for the other four analysts? What is the *ld* score for your layout?

Trip Matrix

	CONTACTS BETWEEN ANALYSTS					
ANALYST	A	B	C	D	E	F
Analyst A	—		6			
Analyst B		—		12		
Analyst C			—	2	7	
Analyst D				—		4
Analyst E					—	
Analyst F						—

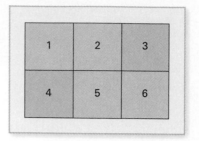

FIGURE 10.22 • Proposed Layout

4. 💿 **OM Explorer** Richard Garber is the head designer for Matthews and Novak Design Company. Garber has been called in to design the layout for a newly constructed office building. From statistical samplings over the past three months, Garber developed the trip matrix shown for daily trips between the department's offices.

Trip Matrix

	TRIPS BETWEEN DEPARTMENTS					
DEPARTMENT	A	B	C	D	E	F
A	—	25	90			165
B		—			105	
C			—		125	125
D				—	25	
E					—	105
F						—

a. If other factors are equal, which two offices should be located closest together?

b. Figure 10.23 shows an alternative layout for the department. What is the total load–distance score for this plan, based on rectilinear distance and assuming that offices A and B are 3 units of distance apart?

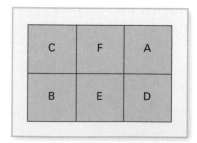

FIGURE 10.23

c. Switching which two departments will most improve the total load–distance score?

5. 💿 **OM Explorer** A firm with four departments has the following trip matrix and the current block plan shown in Figure 10.24.

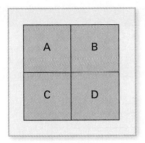

FIGURE 10.24 • Current Block Plan

a. What is the load–distance score for the current layout (assume rectilinear distance)?

Trip Matrix

| | \multicolumn{4}{c}{TRIPS BETWEEN DEPARTMENTS} |
DEPARTMENT	A	B	C	D
A	—	12	10	8
B		—	20	6
C			—	0
D				—

b. Develop a better layout. What is its total load–distance score?

6. 💿 **OM Explorer** The department of engineering at a university in New Jersey must assign six faculty members to their new offices. The trip matrix shown indicates the expected number of contacts per day between professors. The available office spaces (1–6) for the six faculty members are shown in Figure 10.25. Assume equal-sized offices. The distance between offices 1 and 2 (and between offices 1 and 3) is 1 unit.

Trip Matrix

| | \multicolumn{6}{c}{CONTACTS BETWEEN PROFESSORS} |
PROFESSOR	A	B	C	D	E	F
A	—		4			
B		—		12		10
C			—	2	7	
D				—		4
E					—	
F						—

a. Because of their academic positions, professor A must be assigned to office 1, professor C must be assigned to office 2, and professor D must be assigned to office 6. Which faculty members should be assigned to offices 3, 4, and 5, respectively, to minimize the

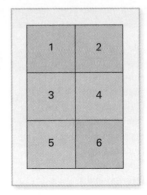

FIGURE 10.25 • Available Space

total load–distance score (assume rectilinear distance)?

b. What is the load–distance score of your solution?

7. As director of the Office of Budget Management for New Mexico's state government, Mike Rogers manages a department of 120 employees assigned to eight different sections. Because of budget cuts, 30 employees from another department have been transferred and must be placed somewhere within the existing space. While changing the layout, Rogers wants to improve communication and create a good work environment. One special consideration is that the state controlling board (section 2) should occupy the northeast location. The trip matrix shown in Table 10.1 on page 484 was developed from questionnaires sent to each of the 120 current employees. It contains section names, area requirements, and closeness ratings.

a. Develop a square block plan (4 rows and 4 columns) for Rogers.

b. What behavioral issues does Rogers need to address when revising the layout?

8. Figure 10.26 shows the block layout configuration for a warehouse docking area. Using the information in the following table, determine the best layout for an out-and-back pattern if each department must be assigned contiguous space on only one side of the aisle.

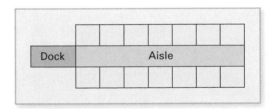

FIGURE 10.26 • Dock and Storage Space

TABLE 10.1   *Trip Matrix*

| SECTION | TRIPS BETWEEN SECTIONS | | | | | | | | AREA NEEDED (blocks) |
	1	2	3	4	5	6	7	8	
1. Administration	—	3	2	10		2	2		1
2. State controlling board		—		3		2	2		5
3. Program clearinghouse			—			2	2	6	1
4. Social services				—		5	3	2	2
5. Institutions					—	8			3
6. Accounting						—			2
7. Education							—		1
8. Internal audit								—	1

Trips and Space Requirements

DEPARTMENT	TRIPS TO AND FROM DOCK	AREA NEEDED (blocks)
A	250	2
B	180	1
C	390	3
D	320	4
E	100	1
F	190	2
G	220	1

9. The layout configuration for a warehouse docking area is shown in Figure 10.27. Using the information in the following table on travel frequencies and area requirements for departments A–G, determine the best layout for an out-and-back selection pattern.

Trips and Space Requirements

DEPARTMENTS	TRIPS TO AND FROM DOCK	AREA NEEDED (blocks)
A	360	3
B	240	1
C	310	2
D	520	4
E	375	1
F	60	1
G	190	2

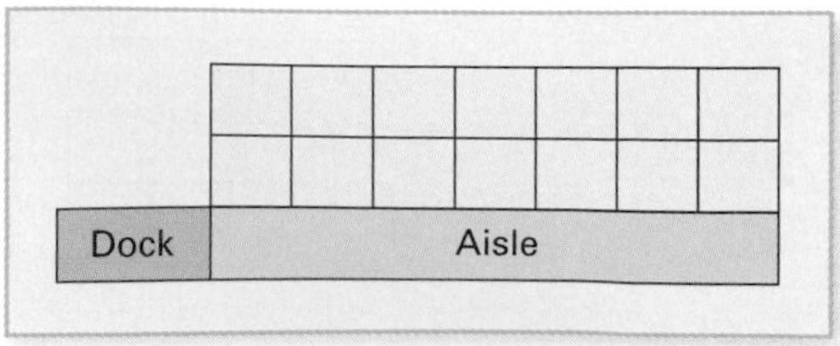

FIGURE 10.27 • Dock and Storage Space

10. King Biker plans to produce several new and larger motorcycle models at its New Hampshire manufacturing facility. Four major warehousing areas in the plant, divided into 12 equal sections, will be used to store the parts and components needed for the new models.

   Based on current inventory and output plans, the average number of trips per day between storage and the assembly line has been estimated for each of seven basic categories of parts. The number of storage sections needed for each category and the distance from each section to the assembly line have also been calculated (see the following tables). Assign each category of parts to one or more storage sections so as to provide the right amount of space for each. Find the assignment that minimizes travel from storage to the assembly line. Owing to size restrictions, part category G cannot be assigned to sections 1 and 2.

PART CATEGORY	TRIPS PER DAY	NUMBER OF SECTIONS NEEDED (blocks)
A	80	1
B	140	2
C	60	1
D	240	4
E	320	2
F	150	1
G	60	1

SECTION	DISTANCE TO ASSEMBLY LINE	SECTION	DISTANCE TO ASSEMBLY LINE
1	60	7	190
2	80	8	230
3	90	9	300
4	110	10	305
5	140	11	320
6	160	12	360

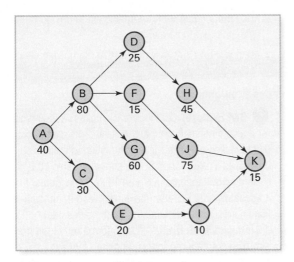

FIGURE 10.28

b. How many stations are required if the longest work-element time method is used?

c. How many stations are required if the largest number of followers method is used?

d. Suppose that a solution requiring five stations is obtained. What is its efficiency?

WORK ELEMENT	TIME (sec)	IMMEDIATE PREDECESSOR(S)
A	40	None
B	30	A
C	50	A
D	40	B
E	6	B
F	25	C
G	15	C
H	20	D, E
I	18	F, G
J	30	H, I
Total	274	

11. ● **OM Explorer** Use the longest work-element time rule to balance the assembly line described in the following table and Figure 10.28 so that it will produce 40 units per hour. Break ties using the largest number of followers rule.

   a. What is the cycle time?

   b. What is the theoretical minimum number of work-stations?

   c. Which work elements are assigned to each work-station?

   d. What are the resulting efficiency and balance delay percentages?

WORK ELEMENT	TIME (sec)	IMMEDIATE PREDECESSOR(S)
A	40	None
B	80	A
C	30	A
D	25	B
E	20	C
F	15	B
G	60	B
H	45	D
I	10	E, G
J	75	F
K	15	H, I, J
Total	415	

13. ● **OM Explorer** The Baxter Bicycle Company is installing a line to produce a new line of BMX bicycles, and you, as the operations manager, are responsible for designing the line. The line has to produce 576 units per day, and the company operates three 8-hour shifts each day. The work elements, time requirements, and immediate predecessor(s) are as follows:

WORK ELEMENT	TIME (sec)	IMMEDIATE PREDECESSOR(S)
A	75	None
B	50	A
C	30	B
D	25	B
E	45	B
F	55	D
G	70	D
H	50	F, G
I	25	E
J	90	C, H, I

   a. What is the theoretical number of stations?

   b. If you balance the line using the longest work-element time rule, which elements are assigned to station 3?

12. ● **Om Explorer** Johnson Cogs wants to set up a line to produce 60 units per hour. The work elements and their precedence relationships are shown in the following table.

   a. What is the theoretical minimum number of stations?

14. ● **OM Explorer; Smart Draw** The *trim line* at PW is a small subassembly line that, along with other such lines, feeds into the final chassis line. The entire assembly line, which consists of more than 900 workstations, is to make PW's new E cars. The trim line itself involves

only 13 work elements and must handle 20 cars per hour. In addition to the usual precedence constraints, there are two *zoning constraints*. First, work elements 11 and 12 should be assigned to the same station; both use a common component, and assigning them to the same station conserves storage space. Second, work elements 8 and 10 cannot be performed at the same station. Work-element data are as follows:

WORK ELEMENT	TIME (sec)	IMMEDIATE PREDECESSOR(S)
A	1.8	None
B	0.4	None
C	1.6	None
D	1.5	A
E	0.7	A
F	0.5	E
G	0.8	B
H	1.4	C
I	1.4	D
J	1.4	F, G
K	0.5	H
L	1.0	J
M	0.8	I, K, L

a. Draw a precedence diagram.

b. What cycle time (in minutes) results in the desired output rate?

c. What is the theoretical minimum number of stations?

d. Using trial and error, balance the line as best you can.

e. What is the efficiency of your solution?

15. ● **OM Explorer; SmartDraw** An assembly line must produce 40 microwave ovens per hour. The following data give the necessary information:

WORK ELEMENT	TIME (sec)	IMMEDIATE PREDECESSOR(S)
A	20	None
B	55	A
C	25	B
D	40	B
E	5	B
F	35	A
G	14	D, E
H	40	C, F, G

a. Draw a precedence diagram.

b. What cycle time (in seconds) ensures the desired output rate?

c. What is the theoretical minimum number of stations? the theoretical maximum efficiency?

d. Use the longest work-element rule to design the line. What is its efficiency?

e. Can you find any way to improve the line's balance? If so, explain how.

Advanced Problems

16. ● **OM Explorer** CCI Electronics makes various products for the communications industry. One of its manufacturing plants makes a device for sensing when telephone calls are placed. A from–to matrix is shown in Table 10.2; the current layout appears in Figure 10.29. Management is reasonably satisfied with the current layout, although it has heard some complaints about the placement of departments D, G, K, and L. Use information in the from–to matrix to create a trip matrix, and then find a revised block plan for moving only the four departments about which complaints have been made. Show that the load–distance score is improved. Assume rectilinear distance.

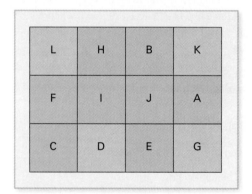

FIGURE 10.29 • Current Block Plan

17. A paced assembly line has been devised to manufacture calculators, as the following data show:

STATION	WORK ELEMENT ASSIGNED	WORK ELEMENT TIME (min)
S1	A	2.7
S2	D, E	0.6, 0.9
S3	C	3.0
S4	B, F, G	0.7, 0.7, 0.9
S5	H, I, J	0.7, 0.3, 1.2
S6	K	2.4

a. What is the maximum hourly output rate from this line? (*Hint*: The line can go only as fast as its slowest workstation.)

b. What cycle time corresponds to this maximum output rate?

TABLE 10.2 *From–To Matrix*

		TRIPS BETWEEN DEPARTMENTS											
DEPARTMENT	**A**	**B**	**C**	**D**	**E**	**F**	**G**	**H**	**I**	**J**	**K**	**L**
A. Network lead forming	—											80
B. Wire forming and subassembly		—							50	70		
C. Final assembly			—			120						
D. Inventory storage				—	40							
E. Presoldering			80		—						90	
F. Final testing						—	120					
G. Inventory storage		30					—	40	50			
H. Coil winding								—	80			
I. Coil assembly			70		40				—		60	
J. Network preparation	90									—		
K. Soldering			80								—	
L. Network insertion			60									—

c. If a worker is at each station and the line operates at this maximum output rate, how much idle time is lost during each 10-hour shift?

d. What is the line's efficiency?

18. Bronson Desk Company seeks a better layout for its plant. The table below shows the departments to be located on the first floor of the plant.

	DEPARTMENT	AREA NEEDED (square feet)
1	Materials storage	1,300
2	Forming	500
3	Machining	1,000
4	Painting	600
5	Assembly	1,400
6	Stamping	1,200
7	Saw	800
8	Inspection	700
82	Elevator	100
83	Stairs	200
84	Office	800
99	Aisle	2,200
	Total	10,800

Figure 10.30 divides the available space into 9 rows and 12 columns. Each block represents 100 square feet, which means that 13 blocks should be allocated to materials storage, 5 blocks to forming, and so on. Productive space is lost to the elevator, stairs, office, and aisle. Their positions, along with those for departments 1 and 6, must remain fixed. Table 10.3 on page 488 is a REL chart. The letters indicate the closeness score, whereas the numbers in parentheses explain the reason for the rating. For example, the forming department and the

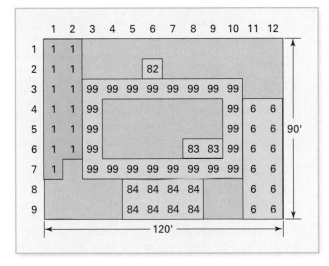

FIGURE 10.30 • Available Space

Note: Productive space lost to elevator, stairs, office, and aisle is shown in dark brown, as are required locations for department 1 and 6.

assembly department must be close to each other (rating = A) because personnel are shared and supervision is easier.

CLOSENESS RATINGS		EXPLANATION CODES	
RATING	**DEFINITION**	**CODE**	**MEANING**
A	Absolutely necessary	1	Materials handling
E	Especially important	2	Shared personnel
I	Important	3	Ease of supervision
O	Ordinary closeness	4	Space utilization
U	Unimportant	5	Noise
X	Undesirable	6	Employee attitudes

TABLE 10.3 *REL Chart*

CLOSENESS RATINGS BETWEEN DEPARTMENTS

DEPARTMENT	1	2	3	4	5	6	7	8
1. Materials storage	—	O (1)	O (1)	U	E (1)	U	O (1)	E (1)
2. Forming		—	E (1)	U	A (2, 3)	U	I (1)	O (1)
3. Machining			—	I (1)	O (1)	U (1)	I (1)	U
4. Painting				—	E (2, 3)	O	U (1)	E (4)
5. Assembly					—	X (5, 6)	I (1)	I (1)
6. Stamping						—	I (1)	O (1)
7. Saw							—	I (1)
8. Inspection								—

There are two additional considerations:

- Owing to noise factors and the need for special foundations, the stamping department should be put in the southeast corner.
- Materials storage should be on the northwest side, since this is where the shipping and receiving dock will be placed.

Develop an acceptable layout for Bronson, working the remaining departments around the prepositioned departments.

19. Calculate the ALDEP score for the solution found in Problem 18. The ALDEP score is computed differently from the *ld* score used earlier. First, the letter ratings are converted into numerical equivalents, as, for example, in the following table:

POINTS	REL LETTER	DESCRIPTION
6	A	Absolutely necessary
4	E	Especially important
3	I	Important
2	O	Ordinary closeness
0	U	Unimportant
5	X	Undesirable

(These numerical equivalents are arbitrary, and others could just as easily be used.) Second, these numerical

equivalents are added to the total ALDEP score whenever they belong to departments that touch somewhere along their borders—except in the case of X, where points are added when borders do not touch.

20. ● **OM Explorer; Smart Draw** The manager of Sugar Hams wants to organize the tasks involved in the preparation and delivery of hams. The manager plans to produce 60 hams per 10-hour workday. The table in the next column presents work-element times and precedence relationships.

WORK ELEMENT	TIME (min)	IMMEDIATE PREDECESSOR(S)
A	3	None
B	5	A
C	2	B
D	7	B
E	7	C, D
F	6	E
G	2	D, E
H	3	F
I	8	G
J	6	H
K	3	I, J
L	8	K

a. Construct a precedence diagram for this process.

b. What cycle time corresponds to the desired output rate?

c. Try to identify the best possible line-balancing solution. What work elements are assigned to each station?

d. What is the impact on your solution if the time for work element D increases by 3 minutes? Decreases by 3 minutes?

21. 🔘 **OM Explorer; Smart Draw** Green Grass, Inc., is expanding its product line to include a new fertilizer spreader called the Big Broadcaster. Operations plans to make the Big Broadcaster on a new assembly line, with most parts purchased from outside suppliers. The plant manager obtained the information shown in Table 10.4 concerning work elements, labor standards, and immediate predecessors for the Big Broadcaster.

a. Construct a precedence diagram for the Big Broadcaster.

b. Find a line-balancing solution using the longest work-element time rule so that the line will produce 2,400 Big Broadcasters per week with one shift of 40 hours.

c. Calculate the efficiency and balance delay of your solution.

22. 🔘 **OM Explorer** The table below has been partially completed from the information in Problem 21 for the Big Broadcaster.

a. Complete the table by filling in the last column.

b. Find a line-balancing solution using the largest number of followers rule. Break ties using the largest work-element time rule. If a tie remains, pick the work element with the highest numerical label.

c. Calculate the efficiency and balance delay of your solution.

WORK ELEMENT	NUMBER OF FOLLOWERS	WORK ELEMENT	NUMBER OF FOLLOWERS
A	23	M	
B	20	N	
C	19	O	
D	18	P	
E	19	Q	
F	18	R	
G	17	S	
H	8	T	
I	7	U	
J	6	V	
K	5	W	
L	8	X	

TABLE 10.4   *Big Broadcaster Assembly*

WORK ELEMENT	DESCRIPTION	TIME (sec)	IMMEDIATE PREDECESSOR(S)	WORK ELEMENT	DESCRIPTION	TIME (sec)	IMMEDIATE PREDECESSOR(S)
	Attach leg frame				*Attach free wheel*		
A	Bolt leg frame to hopper	51	None	L	Slip on free wheel	30	G
B	Insert impeller shaft into hopper	7	A	M	Place washer over axle	6	L
C	Attach agitator to shaft	24	B	N	Secure with cotter pin	15	M
D	Secure with cotter pin	10	C	O	Push on hub cap	9	N
	Attach axle				*Mount lower post*		
E	Insert bearings into housings	25	A	P	Bolt lower handle post to hopper	27	G
F	Slip axle through first bearing and shaft	40	E	Q	Seat post in square hole	13	P
G	Slip axle through second bearing	20	D, F	R	Secure leg to support strap	60	Q
	Attach drive wheel				*Attach controls*		
H	Slip on drive wheel	35	G	S	Insert control wire	28	K, O, R
I	Place washer over axle	6	H	T	Guide wire through slot	12	S
J	Secure with cotter pin	15	I	U	Slip T handle over lower post	21	T
K	Push on hub cap	9	J	V	Attach on-off control	26	U
				W	Attach level 58	V	
				X	Mount nameplate	29	R
						Total 576	

23. **OM Explorer** Green Grass's plant manager (see Problem 21) is willing to consider a line balance with an output rate of less than 60 units per hour if the gain in efficiency is sufficient. Operating the line longer (with either a second shift or overtime) and setting up two lines are ways to compensate for the lower rate.
    a. Calculate the theoretical maximum efficiency for output rates of 30, 35, 40, 45, 50, 55, and 60 units per hour. Is there any possible gain in efficiency when the output rate is reduced to as low as 30?
    b. Use the longest work-element time rule to explore solutions over the range of output rates for which efficiency gains might be achieved.

24. Miller Assemblies, Inc., manufactures customized wire harnesses for kitchen appliances, snowmobiles, farm machinery, and motorcycles. Table 10.5 shows the trip matrix and areas needed, and Figure 10.31 shows the current layout of the plant.
    a. Develop a better layout, but keep departments 2, 16, and 99 (dead space) at their current positions.
    b. Use ALDEP to calculate scores for both plants (see Problem 19). How much better is your plan?

	1	2	3	4	5	6
1	4	4	2	2	99	99
2	4	4	2	2	3	3
3	4	4	2	2	3	3
4	5	1	1	1	3	3
5	5	1	1	1	10	10
6	5	6	6	6	10	10
7	5	7	7	11	10	10
8	5	9	9	9	10	10
9	5	8	8	8	10	10
10	12	12	12	99	99	99
11	13	14	12	99	99	99
12	13	14	15	99	99	99
13	13	14	15	99	99	99
14	13	14	15	99	99	99
15	16	16	16	99	99	99

FIGURE 10.31

TABLE 10.5 *Trip Matrix*

DEPARTMENT	TRIPS BETWEEN DEPARTMENTS 1	2	3	4	5	6	7	8	9	10	11	12	13	14	15	16	99	AREA NEEDED (blocks)
1. Terminal storage	—	1		8	4		4											6
2. Shipping and receiving		—	1								2							6
3. Wire storage			—	8		5												6
4. Finished goods				—	11	16		1										6
5. Terminating					—	18	5			6			3	5	5			6
6. Cutting I						—	2											3
7. Cutting II							—	2		6			1	1	1			2
8. Painting								—		3								3
9. Processing									—									3
10. Work-in-process										—			3	2	3			10
11. Rest rooms											—							1
12. Supplies												—	2	2	1			4
13. Assembly I													—	2	2			4
14. Assembly II														—	1			4
15. Custom assembly															—			3
16. Offices																—		3
99. Dead space																	—	20

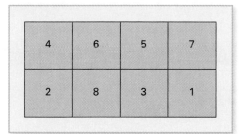

| 4 | 6 | 5 | 7 |
| 2 | 8 | 3 | 1 |

FIGURE 10.32 • Current Layout

25. The associate administrator at Getwell Hospital wants to evaluate the layout of the outpatient clinic. Table 10.6 shows the interdepartmental flows (patients/day) between departments; Figure 10.32 shows the current layout.

    a. Determine the effectiveness of the current layout, as measured by the total ld score, using rectilinear distances.

    b. Try to find the best possible layout based on the same effectiveness measure.

    c. What is the impact on your new solution if it must be revised to keep department 1 at its present location?

    d. How should the layout developed in part (c) be revised if the interdepartmental flow between the examining room and the X-ray department is increased by 50 percent? Decreased by 50 percent?

TABLE 10.6 *Trip Matrix*								
	TRIPS BETWEEN DEPARTMENTS							
DEPARTMENT	**1**	**2**	**3**	**4**	**5**	**6**	**7**	**8**
1. Reception	—	25	35	5	10	15		20
2. Business office		—	5	10	15			15
3. Examining room			—	20	30	20		10
4. X-ray				—	25	15		25
5. Laboratory					—	20		25
6. Surgery						—	40	
7. Postsurgery							—	15
8. Doctor's office								—

CASE **HIGHTEC, INC.**

"It's hard to believe," thought Glenn Moore as he walked into the employee lunch area, "that it has been only six years since I founded Hightec." He was not interested in lunch because it was only 9:30 A.M. His purpose was to inspect the new microcomputer, which had just been purchased to improve management of the company's inventory and accounting functions. The computer had to be housed at the rear of the employee lunch area, right next to the coffee, hot soup, and hot chocolate vending machines. There was absolutely no room for the computer elsewhere.

Hightec is a manufacturer of transducers, which convert gas or liquid pressure into an electrical signal. Another form of the device converts weight or force into an electrical signal. A typical customer order is for only 3 to 10 units. The firm currently rents a 12,000-square-foot, L-shaped building, housing four basic sections: the office area, an engineering area, a machine shop, and an assembly area. The 80 employees comprise machinists, engineers, assemblers, secretaries, and salespeople.

Although Moore concentrated on finance and marketing during the first two years of Hightec's existence, his activities now are more concerned with production costs, inventory, and capacity. Sales have been increasing about 30 percent per year, and this growth is expected to

continue. Specific symptoms of Hightec's problems include the following.

❏ Space limitations have delayed the purchase of a numerical control machine and a more efficient testing machine. Both promise greater capacity and higher productivity, and their costs are easily justified.

❏ The machine shop is so crowded that equipment not in constant use had to be moved into the inventory storage area.

❏ More machines are being operated on second and third shifts than would normally be justified. Productivity is falling, and quality is slipping.

❏ Approximately 10 percent of the workforce's time is spent moving materials to and from the inventory storage area, where inventory at all stages of production is kept. The chaotic supply room makes finding wanted parts difficult, and considerable time is lost searching.

❏ Approximately 1,000 square feet of storage space must be rented outside the plant.

❏ Lack of capacity has forced Moore to forgo bidding on several attractive jobs. One salesperson is

continued

continued

particularly disgruntled because she lost a potentially large commission.

❏ Several office workers have complained about the cramped quarters and lack of privacy. The quality of employee space also leaves an unfavorable impression on prospective customers who visit the plant.

❏ Additional help was just hired for the office. To make room for their desks, Moore had to discard his favorite tropical plant, which started as a cutting when Hightec was formed and had sentimental value.

THE OPTIONS

Glenn Moore has identified three options for increasing capacity at Hightec. The first is to renew the rental contract on the current facility for another five years and rent portable units to ease the cramped conditions. He discarded it as being inadequate for a growing problem. The second option is to purchase land and build a new 19,000-square-foot facility. The most attractive site would cost $100,000 for land, and the construction cost is estimated at $40 per square foot. His cost of capital is about 15 percent.

The third option is to renew the rental contract on the current building for another five years and rent an adjacent 7,000-square-foot building only 30 feet from the current one. The rental cost of both buildings would be $2,800 per month. Choice of this third option would necessitate building a $15,000 corridor connecting the buildings. However, Moore estimates the relocation costs (such as for moving and installing the machines and the loss of regular-time capacity) to be $20,000 less than with the second alternative.

THE LAYOUT

Regardless of which option Moore chooses, he must improve on the existing layout. It suffers in terms of materials handling costs and departmental coordination. When Moore initially designed it, he located the office first and then fit the other departments around it as best he could. The main consideration for the other departments was not to have the machine shop next to the cleaning room. Moore put together the information needed for planning the new layout, as shown in Table 10.7 and Figure 10.33.

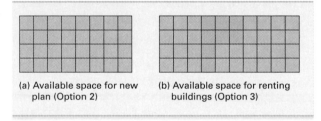

(a) Available space for new plan (Option 2)

(b) Available space for renting buildings (Option 3)

FIGURE 10.33

TABLE 10.7 *REL Chart*

| | CLOSENESS RATING BETWEEN DEPARTMENTS | | | | | | | | | | | | | | | AREA NEEDED |
DEPARTMENT	1	2	3	4	5	6	7	8	9	10	11	12	13	14	15	(blocks*)
1. Administrative office	—	I	A	E	U	A	E	O	O	O	O	I	E	O	U	3
2. Conference room		—	U	U	U	U	U	U	U	U	U	U	U	U	U	1
3. Engineering & mtls. mgt.			—	I	U	U	O	A	E	E	I	E	E	U	O	2
4. Production manager				—	U	A	A	A	A	A	I	I	E	O	A	1
5. Lunch room					—	U	U	U	U	U	U	U	U	U	U	2
6. Computer						—	A	X	U	U	U	O	I	U	U	1
7. Inventory storage							—	A	O	O	O	O	U	U	U	2
8. Machine shop								—	A	X	I	O	U	U	I	6
9. Assembly area									—	A	A	I	U	I	A	7
10. Cleaning										—	O	O	U	U	U	1
11. Welding											—	O	U	U	U	1
12. Electronic												—	E	U	U	1
13. Sales & accounting													—	O	U	2
14. Shipping & receiving														—	U	1
15. Load test															—	1

*Each block represents approximately 595 square feet.

The projected area requirements should be sufficient for the next five years. Both layouts provide for 19,000 square feet. The REL chart emphasizes materials handling and communication patterns.

Glenn Moore walked back to the office with a fresh cup of coffee in his hand. He hated hot chocolate, and it was too early for soup. He wondered what he should do next. Whatever the choice, he wanted a more attractive work environment for the engineering and materials-management staffs, currently located in a cramped, open-office setting. Attracting creative people in these areas had been difficult. He made a mental note that the adjacent building also is quite drab.

Questions

1. Which expansion option would you recommend to Glenn Moore? Justify your position.
2. Design an effective block plan and evaluate it. Cite any qualitative considerations that you believe make your design attractive.

CASE **THE PIZZA CONNECTION**

Dave Collier owns and operates the Pizza Connection in Worthington, Ohio. The restaurant is a franchise of a large, national chain of pizza restaurants; its product and operations are typical of the industry. As Figure 10.34 shows, the facility is divided into two areas: customer contact and pizza production. Customers enter the facility and

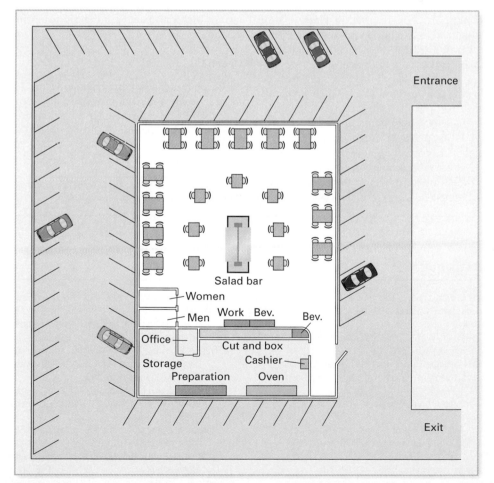

FIGURE 10.34

continued

continued

wait to be seated by a hostess. In the case of a carry-out order, the customer goes directly to the cashier at the front of the facility to place an order or to pick up a previously phoned-in order. Dine-in customers are served by waiters and waitresses; upon completion of their meal and receipt of the check from the server, they proceed to the cashier to pay their bill and leave. During peak hours at lunch and dinner, the cashier's area becomes quite crowded with customers waiting for carry-out orders and dine-in customers trying to pay their bills.

The pizza production area is somewhat of a hybrid layout. Major operations that comprise the pizza production process, such as the preparation tasks, baking, and the cut and box tasks, are grouped together. These individual work centers are arranged in a process flow pattern around the production area.

Historically, Collier's operation has been very successful, benefiting from the rise in popularity of pizza that swept across the country during the past few years. To help take advantage of this trend, the franchiser's home office provided coordinated national and regional marketing and advertising support. It also provided strong product development support. This resulted in a new line of specialty pizzas designed to expand pizza's market appeal.

Recently, however, Collier has noticed a decline in sales. Over the past few months the number of customers has been declining steadily. After doing some research, he came to the following conclusions, which he felt explained the decline in sales.

To begin with, customer demand had changed. Providing high-quality pizza at a reasonable price no longer was enough. The customers now demanded speed, convenience, and alternative dining options. If they were dine-in patrons, they wanted to be able to get in, eat, and get out quickly. Phoned-in, carry-out customers wanted

their orders ready when they arrived. Also, restaurant "parties" were a growing trend. Little league baseball teams, youth soccer teams, and birthdays all had been part of a growing demand for "party space" in restaurants. The busy, fast paced lifestyle of today's families was contributing to moving celebrations out of the home and into restaurants and activity centers such as Putt-Putt or the Discovery Zone.

Besides these changing market demands, Collier had seen competition for the consumer's dining dollar increase significantly in the geographic area his restaurant served. The number of dining establishments in the area had more than tripled during the last two years. They ranged from drive-through to dine-in options and covered the entire spectrum from Mexican to Chinese and chicken to burgers.

Collier wondered how he should respond to what he had learned about his market. He thought that a reconfiguration of the restaurant's layout would enable him to address some of these changing customer demands. He hoped that a change in facilities would also help with labor turnover problems. Collier was having difficulty keeping trained servers, which he knew was driving up labor costs and causing a deterioration in service to his customers.

Questions

1. Reconfigure the layout shown in Figure 10.34 to respond to customers' demands for speed and convenience.
2. Explain how your new layout addresses the issues that Dave Collier identified.
3. How can the effectiveness of this new layout be measured?

Source: This case was prepared by Dr. Brooke Saladin, Wake Forest University, as a basis for classroom discussion.

SELECTED REFERENCES

Ackerman, K. B., and B. J. LaLonde. "Making Warehousing More Efficient." *Harvard Business Review* (March–April 1980), pp. 94–102.

"Bank Branches May Go the Way of Dime Stores and Dinosaurs." *Wall Street Journal* (December 16, 1993).

Bitner, Mary Jo. "Servicescapes: The Impact of Physical Surroundings on Customers and Employees." *Journal of Marketing,* vol. 56 (April 1992), pp. 57–71.

"Bloomie's Tries Losing the Attitude." *Business Week* (November 13, 1995), p. 52.

Bozer, Y. A., and R. D. Meller. "A Reexamination of the Distance-Based Layout Problem." *IIE Transactions,* vol. 29, no. 7 (1997), pp. 549–560.

"Cool Offices." *Fortune* (December 9, 1996), pp. 204–210.

"Cummins Engine Flexes Its Factory." *Harvard Business Review* (March–April 1990), pp. 120–127.

"Deck the Malls with Kiosks." *Business Week* (December 13, 1999), p. 86.

Faaland, B. H., T. D. Klastorin, T. G. Schmitt, and A. Shtub. "Assembly Line Balancing with Resource Dependent Task Times." *Decision Sciences,* vol. 23, no. 2 (1992), pp. 343–364.

Francis, Richard L., Leon F. McGinnis, Jr., and John A. White. *Facility Layout and Location: An Analytical Approach,* 2d ed. Englewood Cliffs, NJ: Prentice-Hall, 1992.

Frazier, G. V., and M. T. Spriggs, "Achieving Competitive Advantage Through Group Technology," *Business Horizons,* vol. 39, no. 3 (1996), pp. 83–90.

Heragu, Sunderesh. *Facilities Design.* Boston, MA: PWS Publishing Company, 1997.

Hoffman, T. R. "Assembly Line Balancing with a Precedence Matrix." *Management Science,* vol. 9, no. 4 (1963), pp. 551–562.

Hyer, N. L., and K. H. Brown. "The Discipline of Real Cells." *Journal of Operations Management,* vol. 17, no. 5 (1999), pp. 557–574.

"Making Malls (Gasp!) Convenient." *Wall Street Journal* (February 8, 2000).

Oldham, G. R., and D. J. Brass. "Employee Reactions to an Open-Plan Office: A Naturally Occurring Quasi-Experiment." *Administrative Science Quarterly*, vol. 24 (1979), pp. 267–294.

Pesch, Michael J., Larry Jarvis, and Loren Troyer. "Turning Around the Rust Belt Factory: The $1.98 Solution." *Production and Inventory Management Journal* (Second Quarter 1993).

Pinto, Peter D., David Dannenbring, and Basheer Khumawala. "Assembly Line Balancing with Processing Alternatives." *Management Science*, vol. 29, no. 7 (1983), pp. 817–830.

"Retailing: Confronting the Challenges that Face Bricks-and-Mortar Stores." *Harvard Business Review* (July–August 1999), p. 159.

Schuler, Randall S., Larry P. Ritzman, and Vicki L. Davis. "Merging Prescriptive and Behavioral Approaches for Office Layout."

Journal of Operations Management, vol. 1, no. 3 (1981), pp. 131–142.

Stone, Philip J., and Robert Luchetti. "Your Office Is Where You Are." *Harvard Business Review* (March–April 1985), pp. 102–117.

Sule, D. R. *Manufacturing Facilities: Location, Planning, and Design.* Boston, MA: PWS Publishing Company, 1994.

Suresh, N. C., and J. M. Kay, eds. *Group Technology and Cellular Manufacturing: A State-of-the-Art Synthesis of Research and Practice.* Boston, MA: Kluwer Academic Publishers, 1997.

"Tools of the Remote Trade," *Business Week* (March 27, 2000), p. F20.

Winarchick, C., and R. D. Caldwell. "Physical Interactive Simulation: A Hands-On Approach to Facilities Improvements." *IIE Solutions,* vol. 29, no. 5 (1997), pp. 34–42.

"Will This Open Space Work?" *Harvard Business Review* (May–June 1999), p. 28.

Supply-Chain Management

Across the Organization

Supply-chain management is important to . . .

☐ **distribution,** which determines the best placement of finished goods inventories and selects the appropriate modes of transportation for serving the external supply chain.

☐ **finance** and **accounting,** which must understand how the performance of the supply chain affects key financial measures and how information flows into the billing process.

☐ **information systems,** which designs the information flows that are essential to effective supply-chain performance.

☐ **marketing,** which involves contact with the firm's customers and needs a supply chain that ensures responsive customer service.

☐ **operations,** which is responsible for managing effective supply chains.

☐ **purchasing,** which selects the suppliers for the supply chain.

Learning Goals

After reading this chapter, you will be able to . . .

1. define the nature of supply-chain management for both manufacturers and service providers.

2. describe the strategic importance of supply-chain management and give real examples of its application in manufacturing and service industries.

3. explain how the Internet has changed the ways companies are managing the customer and supplier interfaces.

4. discuss how critical operating measures of supply-chain performance are linked to key financial measures.

5. distinguish between efficient supply chains and responsive supply chains, and discuss the environments best suited for each one.

6. describe the causes of supply-chain dynamics and their effects.

The Dell Computer Corporation (www.dell.com), a mass customizer of personal computers, is experiencing phenomenal growth and profitability in an industry that traditionally has low profit margins. In 1996, Dell was selling laptops, desktops, and servers at the rate of $1 million a day. Today, Dell's Web site sells more than $30 million in products a day. This success has catapulted Dell into the number 1 position among PC makers, ahead of compaq, Apple Computer, and IBM. What is Dell's secret? In a single word—speed. A customer's order for a customized computer can be on a delivery truck in 36 hours. This capability allows Dell to keep parts costs and inventories low—16 days of sales—thereby enabling it to sell at prices 10 to 15 percent below those of competitors.

Employees at Dell's Austin, Texas, plant assemble, test, and package servers to customer order.

A primary factor in filling customers' orders is Dell's manufacturing operations and the performance of its suppliers. Dell's manufacturing process is flexible enough to postpone the ordering of components and the assembly of computers until an order is booked. In addition, Dell's warehousing plan calls for the bulk of its components to be warehoused within 15 minutes of its Austin (Texas), Limerick (Ireland), and Penang (Malaysia) plants. Dell's top 33 suppliers, which supply 90 percent of its goods, use a Web site for data on how they measure up to Dell's standards, what orders they've shipped, and the best way to ship. Dell plans to link the supplier Web site to its order placement Web site so that as customers place orders, the suppliers will know when to ship components such as motherboards or liquid-crystal displays. Dell's focus is on how fast the inventory moves, not on how much is there. At Austin, Dell does not actually have to order the components because the suppliers restock the warehouse and manage their own inventories. Dell uses the components as needed and is not billed for them until they leave the warehouse. This system of suppliers and manufacturing operations has proven to be a great advantage over competitors. For example, if Compaq suddenly needed a supply of components from its warehouse, 12 to 18 hours would be required to get them; at IBM or Gateway, two days would be needed. For Dell, only minutes are required.

Dell's efficient operations carry over to service providers, who also are used to lower costs and reduce lead time. For example, Dell might send an e-mail message to UPS requesting that a computer monitor from Sony be sent to a certain customer as part of a purchased computer system. UPS pulls a monitor from the monitor supplier's stocks and schedules it to arrive with the PC, saving Dell shipping and inventory costs.

Such careful management of the materials and services from the suppliers through production to the customer lets Dell operate more efficiently than any other computer company.

Sources: "The Power of Virtual Integration: An Interview with Dell Computer's Michael Dell." *Harvard Business Review* (March–April 1998), pp. 72–85; Roth, Daniel. "Dell's Big New Act." *Fortune* (December 6, 1999), pp. 152–156.

supply-chain management
The synchronization of a firm's processes and those of its suppliers to match the flow of materials, services, and information with customer demand.

SUPPLY-CHAIN MANAGEMENT SEEKS TO synchronize a firm's processes and those of its suppliers to match the flow of materials, services, and information with customer demand. Supply-chain management has strategic implications because the supply system can be used to achieve important competitive priorities, as with Dell Computer Corporation. It also involves the coordination of key processes in the firm such as order placement, order fulfillment, and purchasing, which are supported by marketing, finance, engineering, information systems, operations, and logistics. We begin by taking a bird's-eye view of supply-chain management, focusing on its implications for manufacturers and service providers. We then describe how companies manage their customer and supplier interfaces. Next, we discuss the important operating and financial measures of supply-chain performance, followed by a comparison of two supply-chain designs and their strategic implications. We conclude with discussions of the dynamics of supply chains and supply-chain software.

OVERVIEW OF SUPPLY-CHAIN MANAGEMENT

How is inventory created?

inventory A stock of materials used to satisfy customer demand or support the production of goods and services.

A basic purpose of supply-chain management is to control inventory by managing the flows of materials. **Inventory** is a stock of materials used to satisfy customer demand or support the production of goods or services. Figure 11.1 shows how inventories are created through the analogy of a water tank. The flow of water into the tank raises the water level. The inward flow of water represents input materials such as steel, component parts, office supplies, or a finished product. The water level represents the amount of inventory held at a plant, service facility, warehouse, or retail outlet. The flow of water from the tank lowers the water level in the tank. The outward flow of water represents the demand for materials in inventory, such as customer orders for a Huffy bicycle or requirements for supplies such as soap, food, or furnishings. Another possible outward flow is that of scrap, which also lowers the level of useable inventory. Together, the rates of the input and output flows determine the level of inventory. Inventories rise when more material flows into the tank than flows out; they fall when more flows out than flows in. Figure 11.1 also shows clearly why firms utilize total quality management (TQM) to reduce defective materials: the larger the scrap flows, the larger will be the input flow of materials required for a given level of output (see the Total Quality Management chapter).

raw materials (RM) The inventories that are needed for the production of goods and services.

work-in-process (WIP) Items such as components or assemblies needed for a final product in manufacturing.

Inventory exists in three aggregate categories, which are useful for accounting purposes. **Raw materials (RM)** are inventories needed for the production of goods or services. They are considered to be inputs to the transformation processes of the firm, whether they produce a product or a service. **Work-in-process (WIP)** consists of items such as components or assemblies needed for a final product in manufacturing. WIP is also present in some service operations, such as repair shops, restaurants, check

Creation of Inventory

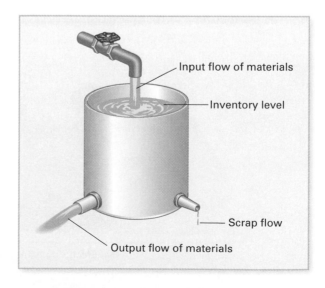

- Input flow of materials
- Inventory level
- Scrap flow
- Output flow of materials

finished goods (FG) The items in manufacturing plants, warehouses, and retail outlets that are sold to the firm's customers.

processing centers, and package delivery services. **Finished goods (FG)** in manufacturing plants, warehouses, and retail outlets are the items sold to the firm's customers. The finished goods of one firm may actually be the raw materials for another.

Figure 11.2 shows how inventory can be held in different forms and at various stocking points. In this example, raw materials—the finished goods of the supplier—are held both by the supplier and the manufacturer. Raw materials at the plant pass through one or more processes, which transform them into various levels of WIP inventory. Final processing of this inventory yields finished goods inventory. Finished goods can be held at the plant, the distribution center (which may be a warehouse owned by the manufacturer or the retailer), and retail locations.

Managing the flow of material is common to organizations in every segment of the economy: churches, governments, manufacturers, wholesalers, retailers, and universities. Manufacturers make products from materials and services they purchase from outside suppliers. Service providers use materials in the form of physical items purchased from suppliers. For example, churches buy envelopes, brochures, audiotapes, file folders, audio equipment, hymnals, and devotional readings. The typical U.S. manufacturer spends more than 60 percent of its total income from sales on purchased materials and services. A typical service provider might spend 30 to 40 percent of total revenues on purchased materials and services. Companies today are relying more than ever on suppliers from around the world. Because materials comprise such a large component of the sales dollar, companies can reap large profits with a small percentage reduction in the cost of materials. That is one reason why supply-chain management is a key competitive weapon.

SUPPLY CHAINS

Recall that the interconnected set of linkages between suppliers of materials and services that spans the transformation of raw materials into products and services and delivers them to a firm's customers is known as the supply chain (see the Process Management chapter). An important part of this process is provision of the information needed for planning and managing the supply chain. This information comes from internal and external sources and is disseminated to decision makers through ERP systems, which often contain supply-chain management modules.

The supply chain for a firm can be very complicated, as Figure 11.3 illustrates. However, the supply chain depicted is an oversimplification because many companies have hundreds, if not thousands, of suppliers. In this case, the firm owns its own distribution and transportation services. However, companies that engineer products

FIGURE 11.2

Inventory at Successive Stocking Points

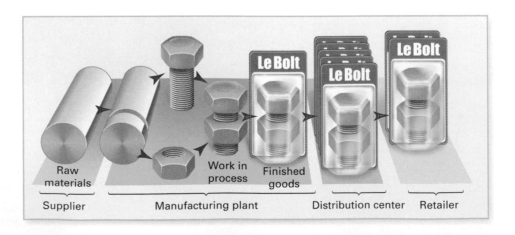

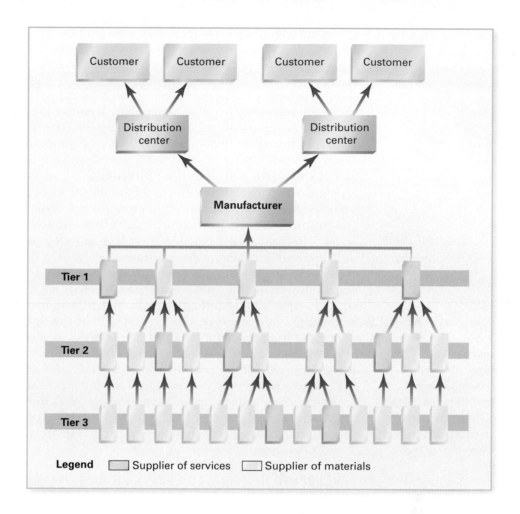

FIGURE 11.3

Supply Chain for a Manufacturing Firm

to customer specifications normally do not have distribution centers as part of their supply chains. Such companies often ship products directly to their customers. Suppliers are often identified by their position in the supply chain. Here, tier 1 suppliers provide materials or services that are used directly by the firm, tier 2 suppliers supply tier 1 suppliers, and so on.

The value of supply-chain management becomes apparent when the complexity of the supply chain is recognized. As we showed earlier, the flow of materials determines inventory levels. The performance of numerous suppliers determines the inward flow of materials. The performance of the firm's marketing, production, and distribution processes determines the outward flow of products.

What is the best way to control suppliers in a complex supply chain?

Imagine the chaos if all the firm's suppliers acted independently and never adjusted to changes in the firm's schedules. Hence, management of the flow of materials is crucial, but how much control does a firm have over its suppliers? One way to gain control is to buy controlling interest in the firm's major suppliers, which is called *backward integration* (see the Process Management chapter). The firm can then ensure its priority with the supplier and more forcefully lead efforts to improve efficiency and productivity. However, purchasing other companies takes a lot of capital, which reduces a firm's flexibility. Moreover, if demand drops, the firm cannot simply reduce the amount of materials purchased from the supplier to reduce costs because the supplier's fixed costs remain.

Another approach is to write agreements with the first-tier suppliers that hold them accountable for the performance of their own suppliers. For example, customers can provide a uniform set of guidelines to be followed throughout the supply chain. Companies such as Ford and Chrysler in the automotive industry have guidelines for quality, delivery, and reporting procedures to be followed by any company producing an item that ultimately becomes part of an automobile. First-tier suppliers then incorporate these guidelines in agreements with their own suppliers. This approach allows each first-tier supplier to manage its own suppliers without its customers having to do it for them.

SUPPLY CHAINS FOR SERVICE PROVIDERS

Supply-chain management is just as important for service providers as it is for manufacturers. Service providers must purchase the equipment, supplies, and services they need to produce their own services. An airline's supply chain provides soft drinks, peanuts, in-flight meals, and airsickness bags as well as maintenance and repair items such as engine parts and motor lubricants. Generally, a service provider's supply chain must be designed so that the right resources and tools are available to perform a service. In this regard, the service supply chain focuses on providing the appropriate supporting inventories, acquiring and scheduling the human and capital resources, and fulfilling the customer orders to satisfaction. For example, Figure 11.4 is a simplified diagram of a supply chain for an electric utility company that shows several types of first-tier suppliers. Utilities need to replace failed equipment in the field and may spend as much as one-half of their purchase expenditures for support services such as facilities maintenance, janitorial services, and computer programming.

purchasing The management of the acquisition process, which includes deciding which suppliers to use, negotiating contracts, and deciding whether to buy locally.

Supply-chain management offers service providers the opportunity to increase their competitiveness. Managerial Practice 11.1 shows how the Arizona Public Service company reduced costs and lowered prices with the help of an electronic purchasing system developed in conjunction with its suppliers.

What is the best approach for developing an integrated supply chain?

DEVELOPING INTEGRATED SUPPLY CHAINS

Successful supply-chain management requires a high degree of functional and organizational integration. Such integration does not happen overnight. Traditionally, organizations have divided the responsibility for managing the flow of materials and services among three departments: purchasing, production, and distribution. **Purchasing** is the

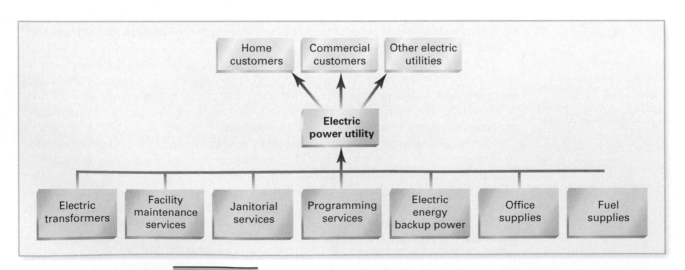

FIGURE 11.4 *Supply Chain for an Electric Power Utility, Showing Tier 1 Suppliers Only*

MANAGERIAL PRACTICE 11.1
Supply-Chain Management at Arizona Public Service

Arizona Public Service (APS), (aboutapsc.com) is the largest utility company in Arizona, serving 705,000 customers and generating $1.7 billion in revenues annually. The company has three diverse business units: Generation (fossil fuel and nuclear power), Transmission, and Cooperative Services, each with very different supply-chain requirements. Even though APS is a very successful utility company, it faces new challenges. The deregulation of the generation and cooperative services segments of the industry by Congress and the states has made the $200 billion industry fully competitive. Companies such as APS are preparing for added competition by driving down operating costs and improving customer services. For example, at APS, expenditures related to the procurement of equipment and services amounted to more than 33 percent of revenues. Because of the diversity of its business units, 20 percent of the items listed in the company's inventory catalog were duplicates. The costs of duplicate orders directly affected the profitability of the utility company.

APS decided to scrutinize its supply chain for ways to increase efficiency and invest in new technology to support the management of materials and provision of services. But first it had to overcome some old practices. For example, expensive line transformers were held in inventory in case a replacement was needed in the field. In addition, the company considered large inventories of replacement parts and other items needed to support the transmission of electric power and daily office operations to be a value-added aspect of doing business. Presumably, management believed that fast replacement of failed items was desirable and that stocking allowed buyers to get the best prices. Now management views these practices as expensive and time-consuming.

APS's solution was to develop an electronic system in accordance with prearranged price, quality, and delivery agreements with its suppliers. The system enables both buyers and other company personnel to buy products and services through the streamlined processes of three on-line software modules.

Materials Catalog. This module lists items kept on hand at various warehouse locations. Personnel needing materials from this catalog merely enter the items from their PC workstations. The system keeps track of the inventories and informs buyers when replenishment orders are required.

Description Buy. For items not listed in the materials catalog, users can determine whether the items have already been

Two Arizona Public Service employees are high above to repair some telephone lines in Flagstaff, Arizona.

ordered by other users. If so, another order may not be needed. Once a user has selected the needed items, a point-and-click action submits the on-line material and service request form, which is automatically routed to a company buyer.

Express Buy. For certain low-cost, high-volume items, APS maintains a list of approved suppliers who have entered into preestablished purchase agreements involving prices, payment terms, and delivery lead times. The module is linked to the suppliers' catalogs electronically and enables company personnel to order directly from the suppliers without involving a buyer.

The electronic system handles 50,000 to 80,000 transactions *daily*, or roughly one-half of the company's purchase orders. The time involved in obtaining materials and services has been drastically reduced to a few hours for items from the warehouse, 4 days (previously 22 days) for items ordered through the Description Buy module, and less than 48 hours for Express Buy items. The time spent on improving supply-chain performance was worthwhile. APS trimmed inventory by 20 percent, reduced materials management personnel by 25 percent, and reduced purchasing costs by 5 percent. In turn, APS reduced consumer electric rates by 5 percent.

Sources: Ettinger, Al. "Reinventing the Supply Chain: Bringing Materials Management to Light." *APICS—The Performance Advantage* (February 1997), pp. 42–45; Turdrick, James. "Supply-Chain Management: Not Just for Manufacturing Anymore." *APICS—The Performance Advantage* (December 1999), pp. 39–42.

production The
management of the
transformation process
devoted to producing the
product or service.

distribution The
management of the flow
of materials from
manufacturers to
customers and from
warehouses to retailers,
involving the storage and
transportation of products.

materials management The
decisions that are made
by a firm concerning the
purchase of materials and
services, inventories,
production levels, staffing
patterns, schedules, and
distribution.

management of the acquisition process, which includes deciding which suppliers to use, negotiating contracts, and deciding whether to buy locally. Purchasing is usually responsible for working with suppliers to ensure the desired flow of materials and services for both short and long terms. Purchasing may also be responsible for the levels of raw materials and maintenance and repair inventories. **Production** is the management of the transformation processes devoted to producing the product or service. It is responsible for determining production quantities and scheduling the machines and employees directly responsible for the production of the good or service. **Distribution** is the management of the flow of materials from manufacturers to customers and from warehouses to retailers, involving the storage and transportation of products. It may also be responsible for finished goods inventories and the selection of transportation service providers. Typically, firms willing to undergo the rigors of developing integrated supply chains progress through a series of phases, as Figure 11.5 shows. In phase 1, a starting point for most firms, external suppliers and customers are considered to be independent of the firm. Relations with these entities are formal, and there is little sharing of operating information and costs. Internally, purchasing, production, and distribution act independently, each optimizing its own activities without considering the other entities. Each external and internal entity in the supply chain controls its own inventories and often utilizes control systems and procedures that are incompatible with those of other entities. Because of organizational and functional boundaries, large amounts of inventory exist in the supply chain and the overall flow of materials and services is ineffective.

In phase 2, the firm initiates internal integration by creating a materials management department. **Materials management** is concerned with decisions about purchasing materials and services, inventories, production levels, staffing patterns, schedules, and distribution. Figure 11.6 shows the scope of materials management and the typical domains of responsibility for purchasing, production, and distribution for a manufacturer of cookies. The flow of materials begins with the purchase of raw materials (e.g., eggs, flour, and chocolate chips) and services (e.g., maintenance) from outside suppliers. Raw materials are stored and then converted into cookies by one or more transformation processes, which involves some short-term storage of work-in-process inventory. The

FIGURE 11.5

*Developing an
Integrated Supply
Chain*

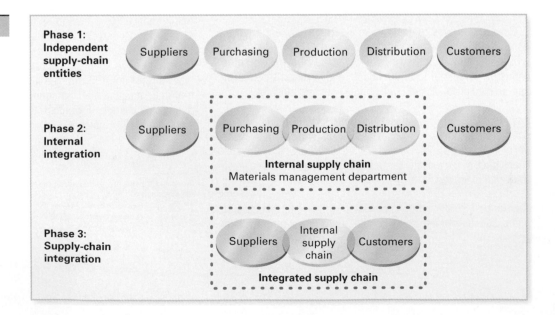

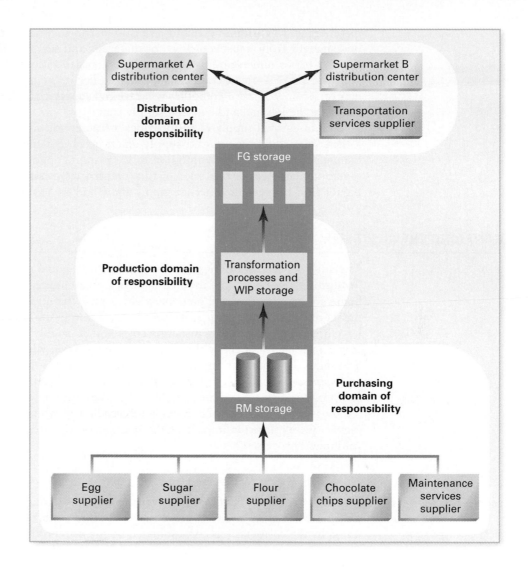

FIGURE 11.6

Materials Management for a Bakery and the Domains of Responsibility for Its Three Primary Processes

cookies are stored (briefly) as finished goods and then shipped by means of transportation services suppliers to large supermarket chains, which have their own distribution centers. This cycle repeats over and over, as the firm responds to customer demand.

The focus is on the integration of those aspects of the supply chain directly under the firm's control to create an *internal supply chain.* Firms in this phase utilize a seamless information and materials control system from distribution to purchasing, integrating marketing, finance, accounting, and operations. Efficiency and electronic linkages to customers and suppliers are emphasized. Nonetheless, the firm still considers its suppliers and customers to be independent entities and focuses on tactical, rather than strategic, issues.

Internal integration must precede phase 3, supply-chain integration. The internal supply chain is extended to embrace suppliers and customers, thereby linking it to the *external supply chain,* which is not under the direct control of the firm. The firm must change its focus from a product or service orientation to a customer orientation. This new focus means that the firm must identify the appropriate competitive priorities for each of its market segments. For its industrial customers, the firm must develop a better understanding of their products, culture, markets, and organization. Rather than merely react to customer demand, the firm strives to work with its customers so that both benefit from improved flows of materials and services. Similarly, the firm must develop better understanding of its suppliers' organizations, capacities, and strengths and weaknesses—and include its suppliers earlier in the design process for new products or services. Phase 3 embodies what we call supply-chain management and seeks to integrate the internal and external supply chains.

The integrated supply chain provides a framework for the operating decisions in a firm. Managing the internal supply chain involves issues of forecasting, inventory management, aggregate planning, resource planning, and scheduling, all topics in the remaining chapters of this text. In this chapter, we focus on the interfaces shown in Figure 11.5 between the internal supply chain and the customers and suppliers.

MANAGING THE CUSTOMER INTERFACE

The Internet has dramatically changed the way companies serve their customers. Traditional supply chains involve factories, warehouses, distributors, and retailers. Some companies, however, have been able to use the Internet to eliminate certain elements of their supply chains by substituting information for inventories. Other firms have used it to reduce the transaction costs in their supply chains. We use the term *customer* to refer to an entity the firm is trying to serve, which could be a consumer or a business. The popular literature has termed Internet systems dealing with consumers as *business-to-consumer systems,* or B2C. Systems dealing with businesses are called *business-to-business systems,* or B2B. (See the Technology Management chapter for a discussion of B2C and B2B systems.) Regardless of who the customer may be, in this section we explore the impact of the Internet on the order-placement and the order-fulfillment processes.

ORDER-PLACEMENT PROCESS

order-placement process
The activities required to register the need for a product or service and to confirm the acceptance of the order.

The **order-placement process** involves the activities required to register the need for a product or service and to confirm the acceptance of the order. These activities are initiated by the customer but consummated by the firm producing the product or service. Since it is the order-placement process that generates demand for the supply chain, it is to the firm's advantage to make it simple and fast. The Internet has enabled firms to reengineer their order-placement process to benefit both the customer and the firm. For example, a traveler may arrive at the Ritz-Carlton on Maui and request a room without an advance reservation. An employee at the hotel will take the appropriate information regarding the order, including the dates of stay, suite or other type of room, double or single occupancy, king-size bed or double beds, smoking or nonsmoking, and then check to see which rooms (if any) are available. This is a costly approach because of the time required of the employee, particularly at busy periods, not to mention the risk that the hotel will be unable to serve the customer. Alternatively, the traveler could use the hotel's Web site several weeks in advance, provide the same information, and get confirmation of the reservation. These two versions of the order-placement process for the hotel involve different amounts of employee time and provide different levels of service to the customer. The Internet provides the following advantages for a firm's order-placement process.

COST REDUCTION. Using the Internet can reduce the costs of processing orders because it allows for greater participation by the customer (see the Process Management chapter). Customers can select the products or services they want and place an order with the firm without actually talking to anyone. This approach reduces the need for call centers, which are labor intensive and often take longer to place orders.

REVENUE FLOW INCREASE. A firm's Web page can allow customers to enter credit card information or purchase-order numbers as part of the order-placement process. This approach reduces the time lags often associated with billing the customer or waiting for checks sent in the mail.

GLOBAL ACCESS. Another advantage the Internet has provided firms is the opportunity to accept orders 24 hours a day. Traditional bricks-and-mortar firms take standard orders during their normal business hours. Firms with Internet access can reduce the time it takes to satisfy a customer, thereby gaining a competitive advantage over bricks-and-mortar firms.

PRICING FLEXIBILITY. Firms with their products and services posted on the Web can easily change prices as the need arises, thereby avoiding the cost and delay of publishing new catalogs. Customers placing orders have current prices to consider when making their choices. From the perspective of supply chains, Dell Computer Corporation uses this capability to control for component shortages. Because of its direct-sales approach and promotional pricing, Dell can steer customers to certain configurations of computers for which ample supplies exist.

Reengineering the order-placement process in a traditional bricks-and-mortar company is not an easy task. Managerial Practice 11.2 reveals that behavioral issues should not be overlooked.

ORDER-FULFILLMENT PROCESS

order-fulfillment process
The activities required to deliver a product or service to a customer.

The **order-fulfillment process** involves the activities required to deliver a product or service to a customer. This process might be called upon to address any of the competitive priorities falling under the categories of cost, quality, time, or flexibility. We have separated the order-placement process from the order-fulfillment process in our discussion; however, in many instances, they occur simultaneously. For example, a customer at a Barnes and Noble store has in effect ordered a book, performing the work to actually find it in the inventory, and the store has delivered it when she checks out at the service desk. However, Barnes and Noble also has a Web page, where the order-placement and the order-fulfillment processes are separated. Customers doing business on its Web page must accept a delay in receiving their books, a delay Barnes and Noble seeks to minimize in its supply chain. Designing the order-fulfillment process can have competitive implications.

As we mentioned earlier, many activities of the order-fulfillment process associated with the internal supply chain are covered in the chapters to follow. In this section, we will focus on information sharing, the placement of inventories, and postponement.

INFORMATION SHARING. The Internet provides a quick and efficient means to share information along the supply chain. Within a firm, ERP systems facilitate the flow of information across functional areas, business units, geographic regions, and product lines. For a manufacturing firm, accurate information about its customer's operations, such as current inventory positions, future demands and production schedules, or expected orders for the firm's products, enables the firm's order-fulfillment process to better anticipate the future needs of its customers. The supply chain can better match supply with demand, thereby reducing inventory costs and decreasing the time to fulfill orders. For a service provider, accurate forecasts of its customers' demand enables the firm to derive its own forecasts of demand for its services. For example, UPS can better plan its delivery services when it has information about the demands faced by its major

MANAGERIAL PRACTICE 11.2
Behavioral Considerations in Designing the Order-Placement Process at Mercury Marine

Mercury Marine (www.mercurymarine.com), a $1.4 billion-a-year company, produces outboard, inboard, ski, and stern-drive engines. Mercury makes 200,000 outboard engines a year at its Fond du Lac, Wisconsin, plant, which accounts for about 40 percent of the U.S. outboard market. Even though it is a market leader, Mercury is facing stiff competition because of a change in government pollution regulations. The U.S. Environmental Protection Agency has ruled that emissions by new outboards must be reduced annually to a 78 percent overall reduction by 2006. Mercury has responded by producing a new four-stroke engine and offering a redesigned two-stroke engine that is low in emissions, both of which are much more costly to produce. However, some customers still want the old two-stroke engine, which forces Mercury to include three engine types, horsepower ratings from 2.5 to 250, and special versions for salt water in their catalog—a total of 400 variations.

The complexity of offering 400 variations of their product at competitive prices has caused Mercury to reengineer its order-placement process. To make it easier for its customers to do business with the company, Mercury is moving MercNet, an electronic system around since the mid-1980s, to the Internet. Dealers can access the site using a PC and a Web browser and order parts, get service notices for any engine, find ways to fix a certain problem with an engine, access forecast information from Mercury, and receive promotion information. However, the one thing they cannot do over the Internet is to buy outboard engines. Technology is not the issue—resistance by the sales department is. The sales staff wants a personal touch with customers, and they fear that electronic sales will eliminate up-selling or cross-selling—the ability of sales personnel to talk a customer into buying a more expensive engine or adding something else to an order. To overcome this hurdle, management is introducing a system enabling Mercury's *inboard* customers to buy engines over the Internet. The inboard sales personnel, located in Stillwater, Oklahoma, are willing to try the system; Mercury hopes that successes there will prove to the outboard people that up-selling and cross-selling will not be the problem they expect them to be. Cultural changes are necessary when companies tighten the supply chain through the use of technology.

Source: Siekman, Philip. "How a Tighter Supply Chain Extends the Enterprise." *Fortune* (November 8, 1999), pp. 272[A]–272[DD].

corporate customers. While electronic sharing of information can improve supply-chain operations, those firms that have successfully integrated the internal and external supply chains can only enjoy the advantage. Going on-line may require a significant investment in information systems and support.

INVENTORY PLACEMENT. A fundamental supply-chain decision is where to locate an inventory of finished goods. Placing inventories can have strategic implications, as in the case of international companies locating *distribution centers* (DC) in foreign countries to preempt local competition by reducing delivery times to its customers. However, the issue for any firm producing standardized products is where to position the inventory in the supply chain. At one extreme, the firm could keep all the finished-goods inventory at the manufacturing plant and ship directly to each of its customers. The advantage would come from what is referred to as **inventory pooling,** which is a reduction in inventory and safety stock because of the merging of variable demands from the customers. A higher-than-expected demand from one customer can be offset by a lower-than-expected demand from another. We discuss the methods for determining the amount of safety stock in the Inventory Management chapter. A disadvantage of placing inventory at the plant, however, is the added cost of shipping smaller, uneconomical quantities directly to the customers, typically over long distances.

Another approach is to use **forward placement,** which means locating stock closer to customers at a warehouse, DC, wholesaler, or retailer. Forward placement can have two advantages for the order-fulfillment process—faster delivery times and reduced

inventory pooling A reduction in inventory and safety stock because of the merging of variable demands from customers.

forward placement Locating stock closer to customers at a warehouse, DC, wholesaler, or retailer.

Should distribution centers be added to position inventory closer to the customer?

MANAGERIAL PRACTICE 11.3
Continuous Replenishment at the Campbell Soup Company

The Campbell Soup Company (www.campbellsoup.com) makes products that are very price sensitive. An important competitive priority for the company is low-cost operations, which extends to the entire supply chain. Campbell operates in an environment with a high degree of certainty. Only 5 percent of its products are new each year; the rest have been on the market for years, making forecasting demand easy. Even though Campbell already had high levels of customer service—98 percent of the time, Campbell's products were available in retailers' inventories—management believed that improvements in costs were possible. It scrutinized the entire supply chain to determine where performance could be improved.

The outcome was a program called *continuous replenishment*, which reduced the inventories of retailers from an average of 4 to 2 weeks' supply. This reduction amounts to savings on the order of 1 percent of retail sales. As the average retailer's profits are only 2 percent of sales, the result was a 50 percent increase in the average retailer's profits. Because of that increase in profitability, retailers purchased a broader line of Campbell products, thereby increasing Campbell's sales. The program works in the following way.

❑ Each morning Campbell uses Electronic Data Interchange to link with retailers.

❑ Retailers inform Campbell of demands for Campbell products and the current inventory levels in their distribution centers.

❑ Campbell determines which products need replenishment based on upper and lower inventory limits established with each retailer.

❑ Campbell makes daily deliveries of needed products.

Campbell must avoid actions that would disrupt the supply chain. For example, retailers on the continuous replenishment program

Forward buying poses problems for Campbell's high-volume, standardized, low-cost operations. Here, employees at the end of the automated can-making line inspect cans before they are filled with soup. Changing volumes is very difficult on such a process.

had to forgo forward buying, whereby retailers in the industry often buy excess stock at discounted prices so that they can offer price promotions. Forward buying causes ripples in the supply chain, increasing everyone's costs. That was the case with chicken soup. Campbell would offer deep discounts once a year and retailers would take advantage of them, sometimes buying an entire year's supply. Because of the bulge in demand, the chicken-boning plant would have to go on overtime. When that happened, costs in the entire supply chain increased—Campbell's production costs increased, and retailers had to pay for warehousing large stocks of chicken soup. With the continuous replenishment system, those extra costs are eliminated and everyone wins.

Source: Fisher, Marshall L. "What Is the Right Supply Chain for Your Product?" Harvard Business Review (March–April 1997), pp. 105–116.

---

vendor-managed inventories (VMI) An extreme application of the forward placement tactic, which involves locating the inventories at the customer.

transportation costs—that can stimulate sales. As inventory is placed closer to the customer, such as at a DC, the pooling effect of the inventories is reduced, but the time to get the product to the customer is also reduced. Consequently, service to the customer is quicker, and the firm can take advantage of larger, less costly shipments to the DCs. The extreme application of forward placement is to locate the inventories at the customer. This tactic is referred to as **vendor-managed inventories (VMI).** Some manufacturers, such as Dell Computer, have inventories of materials on consignment from their suppliers. Dell pays for the materials only when they are used. In deciding where to place inventories, firms must balance the inventory and transportation costs against the need to reduce the time to fulfill orders. Managerial Practice 11.3 explains a VMI

continuous replenishment
A VMI method in which the supplier monitors inventory levels at the customer and replenishes the stock as needed to avoid shortages.

postponement A tactic used by assemble-to-order and mass customization firms that refers to delaying the customizing of a product or service until the last possible moment.

channel assembly The process of using members of the distribution channel as if they were assembly stations in the factory.

method used by Campbell Soup called **continuous replenishment,** where the supplier monitors inventory levels at the customer and replenishes the stock as needed to avoid shortages. Manufacturing firms using a make-to-stock strategy, and traditional retailers using a standardized services strategy, often use forward placement.

POSTPONEMENT. Assemble-to-order and mass customization firms use a tactic called **postponement,** which refers to delaying the customizing of a product or service until the last possible moment. Mass customized products are assembled from a variety of standard components according to the specifications from a customer. When the order-placement process is separated from the order-fulfillment process, manufacturing and order fulfillment can take place after the customer has placed the order. The manufacturing process must be flexible to quickly respond to the customer's order. By forcing customization to the last possible moment, the manufacturing process spends more of its time on standardized components and assemblies, which are less costly to produce.

Postponement can be extended to the distribution channel. **Channel assembly** is the process of using members of the distribution channel as if they were assembly stations in the factory. Distributors might perform the final, customized assembly of a product for delivery to a particular customer. A special case of channel assembly is the organization and shipment of many disparate items for assembly at the customer's site. As we mentioned in the opener to the Operations Strategy chapter, FedEx is devising a system for Cisco that will transport as many as 100 different boxes destined for one of Cisco's customers from factories around the world and deliver them at the customer's door within hours of each other for final assembly. Such a system bypasses warehouses in the supply chain and reduces the cost and time required to fulfill an order.

MANAGING THE SUPPLIER INTERFACE

The application of ERP has forced firms to reengineer their enterprise processes to take advantage of large, integrated information systems. The Internet, however, has not only enabled firms to improve their processes for interfacing with customers, it has also changed the way firms deal with their suppliers. In this section, we will discuss electronic purchasing (e-purchasing), the considerations firms make when selecting suppliers or outsourcing internal processes, the implications for centralized buying, and the reasons why value analysis is important.

E-PURCHASING

The emergence of virtual marketplaces, enabled by Internet technologies, has provided firms with many opportunities to improve their purchasing processes. Not all e-purchasing opportunities, however, involve the Internet. In this section, we will discuss four approaches to e-purchasing: electronic data interchange, catalog hubs, exchanges, and auctions.

electronic data interchange (EDI) A technology that enables the transmission of routine business documents having a standard format from computer-to-computer over telephone or direct leased lines.

ELECTRONIC DATA INTERCHANGE. The most used form of e-purchasing today is **electronic data interchange (EDI),** a technology that enables the transmission of routine business documents having a standard format from computer to computer over telephone or direct leased lines. Special communications software translates documents into and out of a generic form, allowing organizations to exchange information even if they have different hardware and software components. Invoices, purchase orders, and payments are some of the routine documents that EDI can handle—it replaces the phone call or mailed document. An electronic purchasing system with EDI might work as follows. Buyers browse an electronic catalog and click on items to purchase from a supplier. A computer sends the order directly to the supplier. The supplier's computer checks the buyer's credit and determines that the items are available. The supplier's warehouse and shipping departments are notified electronically, and the items are readied for shipment. Finally, the supplier's accounting department bills the buyer electronically. For example, Chaparral Steel allows customers to have computer access to its sales database, to check inventory, and to place orders. EDI saves the cost of opening mail, directing it to the right department, checking the document for accuracy, and reentering the information in a computer system. It also improves accuracy, shortens response times, and can even reduce inventory. Savings (ranging from $5 to $125 per document) are considerable in light of the hundreds to thousands of documents many firms typically handle daily.

catalog hubs An approach to e-purchasing that is used to reduce the costs of placing orders to suppliers as well as the costs of the goods or services themselves.

CATALOG HUBS. **Catalog hubs** can be used to reduce the costs of placing orders to suppliers as well as the costs of the goods or services themselves. Suppliers post their catalog of items on the hub, and buyers select what they need and purchase them electronically. However, a buying firm can negotiate prices with specific suppliers for items such as office supplies, technical equipment, specialized items, services, or furniture. The catalog that the buying firm's employees see consists only of the approved items and their negotiated prices. Employees use their PCs to select the items they need, and the system generates the purchase orders, which are electronically dispatched to the suppliers. The hub connects the firm to potentially hundreds of suppliers through the Internet, saving the costs of EDI, which requires one-to-one connections to individual suppliers. Managerial Practice 11.4 explains why SwissAir developed a catalog hub for its diverse businesses.

exchange An electronic marketplace where buying firms and selling firms come together to do business.

EXCHANGES. An **exchange** is an electronic marketplace where buying and selling firms come together to do business. The exchange maintains relationships with buyers and sellers, making it easy to do business without the aspect of contract negotiations or other sorts of long-term conditions. Exchanges are often used for "spot" purchases, which are needed to satisfy an immediate need at the lowest possible cost. Commodity items such as oil, steel, or energy fit this category. However, exchanges can also be used for most any item. For example, Marriott International and Hyatt Corporation are forming an exchange for hotels. Hotels traditionally have bought supplies from thousands of firms, each focusing on selected items such as soap, food, and equipment, using faxes, telephones, and forms that were made in quadruplicate. Placing orders was expensive, and there was little opportunity to do comparison shopping. The new exchange will have one-stop shopping for hotels using the service.

auction An extension of the exchange in which firms place competitive bids to buy something.

AUCTIONS. An extension of the exchange is the **auction**, where firms place competitive bids to buy something. For example, a site may be formed for a particular industry at which firms with excess capacity or materials can offer them for sale to the highest bidder. Bids can either be closed or open to the competition. Industries where auctions have value include steel, chemicals, and the home mortgage industry, where financial institutions can bid for mortgages.

An approach that has received considerable attention is the so-called *reverse auction,* where suppliers bid for contracts with buyers. One such site is FreeMarkets, an electronic marketplace where Fortune 500 companies offer supply contracts for open bidding. Each bid is posted, so suppliers can see how much lower their next bid must be to remain in the running for the contract. Each contract has an electronic

MANAGERIAL PRACTICE 11.4
E-Purchasing at SAirGroup

SAirGroup (www.sairgroup.com), a $8.2 billion holding company, consists of 21 separate travel-related companies, including various maintenance, hotel, freight-handling, and catering units as well as the airline SwissAir. These units purchased many common items, ranging from motor oil to desk lamps. However, the purchasing of these items was haphazard, thereby bypassing significant quantity discounts. To increase efficiency in its purchases, SAirGroup created category managers who specialized in buying particular groups of products for all the business units. By decentralizing the purchasing process in this way, the company hoped to focus the expertise of the category managers and drive down the cost of procuring the common items. Although the managers secured good contracts, the result was less than stellar. The reason was poor communication: Employees unaware of the negotiated contracts were still buying products on the expensive open market from various suppliers.

To bring the purchasing process under control, SAirGroup is reducing the number of suppliers and creating a catalog hub for purchasing. The site automates and standardizes purchases made by the different business units by identifying a single supplier for each commodity line, the products available, and the negotiated prices for them. Employees can now access the site and make their own purchases from an approved list. The goal of the system is to con-

Customers are being served by SwissAir processes at the Zurich Airport. SwissAir streamlined how it purchases many common items throughout its business units, and created a catalog hub for purchasing supplies.

solidate the supplier base, pool the volumes to reduce costs, and enhance employee compliance with the negotiated contracts.

Source: Ferguson, Kevin. "How E-Purchasing Took Off at SAirGroup." *Business Week E.Biz* (November 1, 1999), pp. EB33–EB38.

prospectus that provides all the specifications, conditions, and other requirements that are nonnegotiable. The only thing left to determine is the cost to the buyer. Savings can be dramatic. For example, a company posted a contract for plastic parts with a benchmark starting price of $745,000, the most recent price for that contract. Twenty-five suppliers vied for the contract over a 20 minute bidding period. Within minutes of opening, the price was $738,000, then it plummeted to $612,000. With 30 seconds remaining in the auction, the price went to $585,000, then finally to $518,000 after 13 minutes of overtime bidding. In little more than a half-hour, the company saved about 31 percent. Driven by FreeMarkets' success, Ford, GM, and DaimlerChrysler have joined together to develop an auction site for the automotive industry.

Our discussion of these electronic approaches in purchasing should not leave the impression that cost is the only consideration in selecting a supplier. Exchanges and auctions are more useful for commodities, near-commodities, or infrequently needed items that require only short-term relationships with suppliers. The past two decades have taught us the lesson that suppliers should be thought of as partners when the needed supply is significant and steady over extended periods of time. Supplier involvement in product or service design and supply-chain performance improvement requires long-term relationships not found by competitive pricing on the Internet. We now turn to the considerations firms give to establishing long-term relationships with suppliers.

SUPPLIER SELECTION AND CERTIFICATION

Purchasing is the eyes and ears of the organization in the supplier marketplace, continuously seeking better buys and new materials from suppliers. Consequently, purchasing is in a good position to select suppliers for the supply chain and to conduct certification programs.

What criteria should be used to select suppliers and how should suppliers be certified?

SUPPLIER SELECTION. To make supplier selection decisions and to review the performance of current suppliers, management must review the market segments it wants to serve and relate their needs to the supply chain. Competitive priorities (see the Operations Strategy chapter) are a starting point in developing a list of performance criteria to be used. For example, food-service firms use on-time delivery and quality as the top two criteria for selecting suppliers. These criteria reflect the requirements that food-service supply chains need to meet.

Three criteria most often considered by firms selecting new suppliers are price, quality, and delivery. Because firms spend a large percentage of their total income on purchased items, finding suppliers that charge low *prices* is a key objective. However, the *quality* of a supplier's materials also is important. The hidden costs of poor quality can be high, particularly if defects are not detected until after considerable value has been added by subsequent operations (see the Total Quality Management and the Statistical Process Control chapters). For a retailer, poor merchandise quality can mean loss of customer goodwill and future sales. Finally, shorter lead times and on-time *delivery* help the buying firm maintain acceptable customer service with less inventory. For example, Maimonides Medical Center, a 700-bed hospital in Brooklyn, buys many of its materials from one supplier. The supplier offers very short lead times from a nearby warehouse, which allowed Maimonides to pare its inventory from about $1,200 to only $150 per bed.

The benefits of fast, on-time deliveries also apply to the manufacturing sector. Many manufacturers demand quick, dependable deliveries from their suppliers to minimize inventory levels. This constraint forces suppliers to have nearby plants or warehouses. Kasle Steel Corporation built a steel-processing plant adjacent to GM's Buick facility in Flint, Michigan, even though it already had two plants only 70 miles away. This new plant is part of a complex (called "Buick City") in which all parts are supplied to the GM facility by nearby plants. These clustered suppliers ship small quantities frequently to minimize the assembly plant's inventory. There is a 20-minute window during which a quantity of a particular part must be delivered; otherwise, the production line may have to be shut down. Kasle was selected as a supplier in part because of its willingness to provide quick, dependable deliveries.

A fourth criterion is becoming very important in the selection of suppliers—environmental impact. Many firms are engaging in **green purchasing,** which involves identifying, assessing, and managing the flow of environmental waste and finding ways to reduce it and minimize its impact on the environment. Suppliers are being asked to be environmentally conscious when designing and manufacturing their products, and claims such as *green, biodegradable, natural,* and *recycled* must be substantiated when bidding on a contract. In the not-too-distant future, this criterion could be one of the most important in the selection of suppliers.

green purchasing The process of identifying, assessing, and managing the flow of environmental waste and finding ways to reduce it and minimize its impact on the environment.

SUPPLIER CERTIFICATION. Supplier certification programs verify that potential suppliers have the capability to provide the materials or services the buying firm requires.

Certification typically involves site visits by a cross-functional team from the buying firm who do an in-depth evaluation of the supplier's capability to meet cost, quality, delivery, and flexibility targets from process and information system perspectives. The team may consist of members from operations, purchasing, engineering, information systems, and accounting. Every aspect of producing the materials or services is explored through observation of the processes in action and review of documentation for completeness and accuracy. Once certified, the supplier can be used by purchasing without its having to make background checks. Performance is monitored and performance records are kept. After a certain period of time, or if performance declines, the supplier may have to be recertified.

SUPPLIER RELATIONS

The nature of relations maintained with suppliers can affect the quality, timeliness, and price of a firm's products and services.

competitive orientation
A supplier relation that views negotiations between buyer and seller as a zero-sum game: Whatever one side loses, the other side gains; short-term advantages are prized over long-term commitments.

COMPETITIVE ORIENTATION. The **competitive orientation** to supplier relations views negotiations between buyer and seller as a zero-sum game: Whatever one side loses, the other side gains. Short-term advantages are prized over long-term commitments. The buyer may try to beat the supplier's price down to the lowest survival level or to push demand to high levels during boom times and order almost nothing during recessions. In contrast, the supplier presses for higher prices for specific levels of quality, customer service, and volume flexibility. Which party wins depends largely on who has the most clout.

How can purchasing power be used effectively in a supply chain?

Purchasing power determines the clout that a firm has. A firm has purchasing power when its purchasing volume represents a significant share of the supplier's sales or the purchased item or service is standardized and many substitutes are available. For example, Staples merged with Office Depot to create a chain of 1,100 office supply stores in the United States and Canada. The buying power of the new company is enormous. Clout is also used in the health care industry. Premier, Inc., a cooperative with 1,759 member hospitals, spends $10 billion a year on materials and services for its members. Suppliers are uneasy because they have to give Premier prices far lower than they do their other customers to keep its business, reflecting Premier's purchasing power. For example, Premier got a 30 percent savings in dye used in medical imaging and a 25 percent savings in the film for that process. Premier will buy from the lowest bidder without much loyalty to any supplier. Analysts estimate that Premier has helped reduce the cost of health care by $2 billion a year because of its efforts.

cooperative orientation
A supplier relation in which the buyer and seller are partners, each helping the other as much as possible.

COOPERATIVE ORIENTATION. With the **cooperative orientation** to supplier relations, the buyer and seller are partners, each helping the other as much as possible. A cooperative orientation means long-term commitment, joint work on quality, and support by the buyer of the supplier's managerial, technological, and capacity development. A cooperative orientation favors few suppliers of a particular item or service, with just one or two suppliers being the ideal number. As order volumes increase, the supplier gains repeatability, which helps movement toward high-volume operations at a low cost. When contracts are large and a long-term relationship is ensured, the supplier might even build a new facility and hire a new workforce, perhaps relocating close to the buyer's plant, as in the case of GM and Kasle Steel. Reducing the number of suppliers also can help the buyer, as suppliers become almost an extension of the buyer.

A cooperative orientation means that the buyer shares more information with the supplier on its future buying intentions. This forward visibility allows suppliers to make better, more reliable forecasts of future demand. The buyer visits suppliers' plants and cultivates cooperative attitudes. The buyer may even suggest ways to improve the suppliers' operations. This close cooperation with suppliers could even mean that the buyer does not need to inspect incoming materials. It also could mean giving the supplier more latitude in specifications, involving the supplier more in designing parts, implementing cost-reduction ideas, and sharing in savings.

A cooperative orientation has opened the door for innovative arrangements with suppliers. One extreme example of such an arrangement is the Volkswagen factory in Brazil. There, seven major suppliers make components on their own equipment. Then their own workers actually assemble the components into finished trucks and buses. Of 1,000 workers at the plant, only 200 are VW employees. This arrangement has several advantages. First, VW's capital investment is less: VW provides the building and the assembly-line conveyors, but suppliers install their own tools and fixtures. Second, if sales of trucks and buses go below the projected 30,000 annual capacity, all the partners take a hit, not just VW. Third, parts will arrive just before they are needed, so everyone's inventory costs will be low. Finally, improvements by suppliers in the assembly process will benefit all parties.

One advantage of reducing the number of suppliers in the supply chain is a reduction in the complexity of managing them. However, reducing the number of suppliers for an item or service may have the disadvantage of increased risk of an interruption in supply. Also, there is less opportunity to drive a good bargain in prices unless the buyer has a lot of clout. **Sole sourcing,** which is the awarding of a contract for an item or service to only one supplier, can amplify any problems with the supplier that may crop up.

Both the competitive and cooperative orientations have their advantages and disadvantages. The key is to use the approach that serves the firm's competitive priorities best. Some companies utilize a mixed strategy. A company can pursue a competitive orientation by seeking price reductions from its suppliers of common supplies and infrequently purchased items on an electronic marketplace, and also use a cooperative orientation with suppliers of higher volume, more continually used materials and services and negotiating long-term contracts with them. However, a cooperative orientation does not preclude the obligation to reduce costs. For example, automakers make long-term commitments to selected suppliers but require continuous improvement programs to gain annual price reductions from them (see the Total Quality Management chapter). Such commitments can give suppliers enough volume to invest in cost-saving equipment and new capacity.

OUTSOURCING

A special case of the cooperative orientation is *outsourcing* (see the Process Management chapter). The decision to outsource an activity, sometimes referred to as the *make-or-buy decision,* has implications for supply-chain management because it affects the number of activities under the direct control of the firm in its *internal supply chain*. This decision is not trivial because a firm must first have a clear understanding of its core competencies (see the Operations Strategy chapter) and retain them. Outsourcing has direct relevance for supply-chain management because of its implications for control and flexibility.

DEGREE OF SOURCING CONTROL. Sourcing control amounts to choosing the appropriate contract relationship with the supplier. These relationships range from full ownership and strategic alliances (see the Operations Strategy chapter) and long-term contracts, which provide high degrees of control, to short-term contracts, which provide low degrees of control. The more important the activity is for the achievement of the firm's competitive priorities, the greater the degree of control the firm will want.

FLEXIBILITY TO CHANGE THE SUPPLY CHAIN. A firm has a more flexible arrangement with a supplier if it has a short-term agreement with it. The firm can choose to renegotiate

sole sourcing The awarding of a contract for an item or service to only one supplier.

What are the implications for supply-chain management of outsourcing an activity?

the terms of the contract or change suppliers frequently. These options are not available if the firm enters into long-term arrangements with a supplier. If market needs change, or the supplier experiences business difficulties, the firm will have a more difficult time changing suppliers if it has a long-term commitment.

Consequently, supply-chain managers must balance the advantages of high degrees of control with those of flexibility to change. Long-term arrangements should be used only when the firm is confident that the supplier will fit into its long-term strategic plans.

CENTRALIZED VERSUS LOCALIZED BUYING

When an organization has several facilities (e.g., stores, hospitals, or plants), management must decide whether to buy locally or centrally. This decision has implications for the control of supply-chain flows.

Centralized buying has the advantage of increasing purchasing clout. Savings can be significant, often on the order of 10 percent or more. Increased buying power can mean getting better service, ensuring long-term supply availability, or developing new supplier capability. Companies with overseas suppliers favor centralization because of the specialized skills (e.g., understanding of foreign languages and cultures) needed to buy from foreign sources. Buyers also need to understand international commercial and contract law regarding the transfer of goods and services. Another trend that favors centralization is the growth of computer-based information systems and the Internet, which give specialists at headquarters access to data previously available only at the local level.

Probably the biggest disadvantage of centralized buying is loss of control at the local level. When plants or divisions are evaluated as profit or cost centers, centralized buying is undesirable for items unique to a particular facility. These items should be purchased locally whenever possible. The same holds for purchases that must be closely meshed with production schedules. Further, localized buying is an advantage when the firm has major facilities in foreign countries because the managers there, often foreign nationals, have a much better understanding of the culture than a staff would at the home office. Also, centralized purchasing often means longer lead times and another level in the firm's hierarchy. Perhaps the best solution is a compromise strategy, whereby both local autonomy and centralized buying are possible. For example, the corporate purchasing group at IBM negotiates contracts on a centralized basis only at the request of local plants. Then management at one of the facilities monitors the contract for all the participating plants.

VALUE ANALYSIS

A systematic effort to reduce the cost or improve the performance of products or services, either purchased or produced, is referred to as **value analysis.** It is an intensive examination of the materials, processes, information systems, and flows of material involved in the production of an item. Benefits include reduced production, materials, and distribution costs; improved profit margins; and increased customer satisfaction. Because teams involving purchasing, production, and engineering personnel from both the firm and its major suppliers play a key role in value analysis, another potential benefit is increased employee morale.

Value analysis encourages employees of the firm and its suppliers to address questions such as the following: What is the function of the item? Is the function necessary? Can a lower-cost standard part that serves the purpose be identified? Can the item be simplified, or its specifications relaxed, to achieve a lower price? Can the item be designed so that it can be produced more efficiently or more quickly? Can features that

value analysis A systematic effort to reduce the cost or improve the performace of products or services, either purchased or produced.

How can suppliers get involved in value analysis to benefit the supply chain?

early supplier involvement A program that includes suppliers in the design phase of a product or service.

presourcing In the automotive industry, a level of supplier involvement in which suppliers are selected early in a vehicle's concept development stage and are given significant, if not total, responsibility for the design of certain components or systems.

the customer values highly be added to the item? Value analysis should be part of a continual effort to improve the performance of the supply chain and increase the value of the item to the customer.

Value analysis can focus solely on the *internal* supply chain with some success, but its true potential lies in applying it to the *external* supply chain as well. An approach that many firms are using is called **early supplier involvement,** which is a program that includes suppliers in the design phase of a product or service. Suppliers provide suggestions for design changes and materials choices that will result in more efficient operations and higher quality. In the automotive industry, an even higher level of early supplier involvement is known as **presourcing,** whereby suppliers are selected early in a vehicle's concept development stage and are given significant, if not total, responsibility for the design of certain components or systems. Presourced suppliers also take responsibility for the cost, quality, and on-time delivery of the items they produce.

MEASURES OF SUPPLY-CHAIN PERFORMANCE

As we have shown, supply-chain management involves managing the flow of materials that create inventories in the supply chain. For this reason, managers closely monitor inventories to keep them at acceptable levels. The flow of materials also affects various financial measures of concern to the firm. In this section, we first define the typical inventory measures used to monitor supply-chain performance. We then present some process measures. Finally, we relate some commonly used supply-chain performance measures to several important financial measures.

INVENTORY MEASURES

What measures of inventory are important to supply-chain management?

average aggregate inventory value The total value of all items held in inventory for a firm.

All methods of measuring inventory begin with a physical count of units, volume, or weight. However, measures of inventories are reported in three basic ways: average aggregate inventory value, weeks of supply, and inventory turnover.

The **average aggregate inventory value** is the total value of all items held in inventory for a firm. We express all the dollar values in this inventory measure at cost because we can then sum the values of individual items in raw materials, work-in-process, and finished goods: Final sales dollars have meaning only for final products or services and cannot be used for all inventory items. It is an average because it usually represents the inventory investment over some period of time. Suppose that item A is a raw material that is transformed into a finished product, item B. One unit of item A may be worth only a few dollars, whereas one unit of item B may be valued in the hundreds of dollars because of the labor, technology, and other value-added operations performed in manufacturing the product. This measure for an inventory consisting of only items A and B is

$$\begin{aligned}\text{Average aggregate} \atop \text{inventory value} = &\left(\text{Number of units of item A} \atop \text{typically on hand}\right)\left(\text{Value of each} \atop \text{unit of item A}\right) \\ &+ \left(\text{Number of units of item B} \atop \text{typically on hand}\right)\left(\text{Value of each} \atop \text{unit of item B}\right)\end{aligned}$$

Summed over all items in an inventory, this total value tells managers how much of a firm's assets are tied up in inventory. Manufacturing firms typically have about 25 percent of their total assets in inventory, whereas wholesalers and retailers average about 75 percent.

weeks of supply An inventory measure obtained by dividing the average aggregate inventory value by sales per week at cost.

To some extent, managers can decide whether the aggregate inventory value is too low or too high by historical or industry comparison or by managerial judgment. However, a better performance measure would take demand into account. **Weeks of supply** is an inventory measure obtained by dividing the average aggregate inventory value by sales per week at cost. (In some low-inventory operations, days or even hours are a better unit of time for measuring inventory.) Firms in the automobile industry, for example, carry about two months' supply of finished goods. The amount varies from company to company, with Ford having the lowest target level among the Big Three and General Motors the highest. The formula (expressed in weeks) is

$$\text{Weeks of supply} = \frac{\text{Average aggregate inventory value}}{\text{Weekly sales (at cost)}}$$

Although the numerator includes the value of all items (raw materials, WIP, and finished goods), the denominator represents only the finished goods sold—at cost rather than the sale price after markups or discounts. This cost is referred to as the *cost of goods sold*.

inventory turnover An inventory measure obtained by dividing annual sales at cost by the average aggregate inventory value maintained during the year.

Inventory turnover (or *turns*) is an inventory measure obtained by dividing annual sales at cost by the average aggregate inventory value maintained during the year, or

$$\text{Inventory turnover} = \frac{\text{Annual sales (at cost)}}{\text{Average aggregate inventory value}}$$

The "best" inventory level, even when expressed as turnover, cannot be determined easily. Although six or seven turns per year is typical, the average high-tech firm settles for only about three turns. At the other extreme, some automobile firms report 40 turns per year for selected products.

| EXAMPLE 11.1 | *Calculating Inventory Measures* |

The Eagle Machine Company averaged $2 million in inventory last year, and the cost of goods sold was $10 million. Figure 11.7 shows the breakout of raw material, work-in-process, and finished goods inventories. The average inventory turnover in the company's industry is six turns per year. If the company has 52 business weeks per year, how many weeks of supply were held in inventory? What was the inventory turnover? What should the company do?

SOLUTION

TUTOR 11.1

The average aggregate inventory value of $2 million translates into 10.4 weeks of supply and five turns per year, calculated as follows:

$$\text{Weeks of supply} = \frac{\$2 \text{ million}}{(\$10 \text{ million})/(52 \text{ weeks})} = 10.4 \text{ weeks}$$

$$\text{Inventory turns} = \frac{\$10 \text{ million}}{\$2 \text{ million}} = 5 \text{ turns/year}$$

Decision Point The analysis indicates that management must improve the inventory turns by 20 percent. Management should improve its order-fulfillment process to reduce finished goods inventory assets through postponement, better placement of the inventories to increase the pooling effect, or improved information flows between the company and its customers. Internal supply-chain operations can be improved to reduce the need to have so much raw material and work-in-process inventory stock. It will take an inventory reduction of about 16 percent to achieve the target of six turns per year. However, inventories would not have to be reduced as much if there was an increase in sales. If the sales department targets an increase in sales of 8 percent ($10.8 million), inventories need only be reduced by 10 percent ($1.8 million) to get six turns a year. Management

```
                    Solver - Inventory Estimator
                    Enter data in yellow - shaded areas.


    Cost of Goods Sold      $10,000,000
    Weeks of Operation               52

                        Item Number   Average Level   Unit Value    Total Value
    Raw Materials                1         1,400         $50.00       $70,000
                                 2         1,000         $32.00       $32,000
                                 3           400         $60.00       $24,000
                                 4         2,400         $10.00       $24,000
                                 5           800         $15.00       $12,000
    Work in Progress             6           320        $700.00      $224,000
                                 7           160        $900.00      $144,000
                                 8           280        $750.00      $210,000
                                 9           240        $800.00      $192,000
                                10           400      $1,000.00      $400,000
    Finished Goods              11            60      $2,000.00      $120,000
                                12            40      $3,500.00      $140,000
                                13            50      $2,800.00      $140,000
                                14            20      $5,000.00      $100,000
                                15            40      $4,200.00      $168,000
    Total                                                          $2,000,000


    Average Weekly Sales at Cost        $192,308

    Weeks of Supply                         10.4

    Inventory Turnover                       5.0
```

FIGURE 11.7

can now do sensitivity analyses with OM Explorer to see what effect reductions in the inventory of specific items or increases in the annual sales have on weeks of supply or inventory turns. ▫

PROCESS MEASURES

We have discussed three major processes related to supply-chain management: order placement, order fulfillment, and purchasing. Supply-chain managers monitor performance by measuring costs, time, and quality. Table 11.1 contains examples of operating measures for the three processes.

Managers periodically collect data on measures such as these and track them to note changes in level or direction. Statistical process control charts can be used to determine if the changes are statistically significant, thereby prompting management's attention (see the Statistical Process Control chapter). The impact of improvements to the three processes can be monitored using control charts.

LINKS TO FINANCIAL MEASURES

How are operating measures of supply-chain performance related to a firm's typical financial measures?

Effective management of the supply chain has fundamental impact on the financial status of a firm. Inventory should be considered an investment because it is created for future use. However, it ties up funds that might be used more profitably in other operations. Managing the supply chain so as to reduce the aggregate inventory investment will reduce the *total assets* portion of the firm's balance sheet. An important financial

	Order Placement	Order Fulfillment	Purchasing
TABLE 11.1 *Supply-Chain Process Measures*	❑ Percent of orders taken accurately ❑ Time to complete the order-placement process ❑ Customer satisfaction with the order-placement process	❑ Percent of incomplete orders shipped ❑ Percent of orders shipped on time ❑ Time to fulfill the order ❑ Percent of returned items or botched services ❑ Cost to produce the item or service ❑ Customer satisfaction with the order-fulfillment process	❑ Percent of suppliers' deliveries on time ❑ Suppliers' lead times ❑ Percent defects in purchased materials and services ❑ Cost of purchased materials and services

measure is *return on assets* (ROA), which is net income divided by total assets. Consequently, reducing aggregate inventory investment will increase ROA. Nonetheless, the objective should be to have the proper amount of inventory, not the least amount of inventory.

Weeks of inventory and inventory turns are reflected in another financial measure, *working capital,* which is money used to finance ongoing operations. Increases in inventory investment require increased payments to suppliers, for example. Decreasing weeks of supply or increasing inventory turns reduces the pressure on working capital by reducing inventories. Increasing inventory turns can be accomplished by improving the order-placement, order-fulfillment, or purchasing processes. For example, reducing supplier lead times has the effect of reducing weeks of supply and increasing inventory turns: Matching the input and output flows of materials is easier because shorter-range, more reliable forecasts of demand can be used. Similarly, improvements in the other measures in Table 11.1 can be traced to improvements in working capital.

Managers can also reduce production and material costs through effective supply-chain management. Costs of materials are determined through the financial arrangements with suppliers, and production costs are a result of the design and execution of the internal supply chain. In addition, the percent of defects, experienced in the external as well as internal supply chains, also affects the costs of operation. Improvements in these measures are reflected in the *cost of goods sold* and ultimately in the *net income* of the firm. They also have an effect on *contribution margin,* which is the difference between price and variable costs to produce a good or service. Reducing production and material costs, and quality defect costs, increases the contribution margin, allowing for greater profits. Contribution margins are often used as inputs to decisions regarding the portfolio of products or services the firm offers.

Supply-chain performance measures related to time also have financial implications. Many manufacturers and service providers measure the percent of on-time deliveries of their product or services to their customers as well as materials and services from their suppliers. Increasing the percent of on-time deliveries to customers will increase *total revenue* because satisfied customers will buy more products and services from the firm. Increasing the percent of on-time deliveries from suppliers has the effect of reducing the costs of production and raw materials inventories, which has implications for the cost of goods sold and contribution margins.

The Internet has brought another financial measure related to time to the forefront: *cash-to-cash,* which is the time lag between paying for the materials and services needed to produce a product or service and receiving payment for it. The shorter the time lag, the better the *cash flow* position of the firm. There is less need for working capital; therefore, the firm can use the freed-up funds for projects or investments. Reengineering the order-placement process so that payment for the product or service is made at the time the order is placed can reduce the time lag. Billing the customer after the order is shipped or the service performed increases the need for working capital. The ultimate is to have a negative cash-to-cash situation, which is possible when the customer pays for the product before the firm has to pay for the materials needed to make it. In such a case, the firm must be using an assemble-to-order strategy and have supplier inventories on consignment, which allows the firm to pay for materials as it uses them. Dell Computer, in the chapter opener, is a prime example of a negative cash-to-cash situation.

SUPPLY-CHAIN LINKS TO OPERATIONS STRATEGY

What is the appropriate supply-chain design for a particular competitive environment?

Operations strategy seeks to link the design and use of a firm's infrastructure and processes to the competitive priorities of each of its products or services so as to maximize its potential in the marketplace. A supply chain is a network of firms. Thus, each firm in the chain should build its own supply chain to support the competitive priorities of its products or services. In this section, we discuss two distinct supply-chain designs and demonstrate how they can support the operations strategies of firms.

EFFICIENT VERSUS RESPONSIVE SUPPLY CHAINS

Even though extensive technologies such as EDI, the Internet, computer-assisted design, flexible manufacturing, and automated warehousing have been applied to all stages of the supply chain, the performance of many supply chains has been dismal. A recent study of the U.S. food industry estimated that poor coordination among supply-chain partners was wasting $30 billion annually. One possible cause for failures is that managers do not understand the nature of the demand for their products or services and therefore can't devise a supply chain that would best satisfy that demand. Two distinct designs used to competitive advantage are *efficient supply chains* and *responsive supply chains* (Fisher, 1997). The purpose of efficient supply chains is to coordinate the flow of materials and services so as to minimize inventories and maximize the efficiency of the manufacturers and service providers in the chain. Responsive supply chains are designed to react quickly to market demands by positioning inventories and capacities in order to hedge against uncertainties in demand. Table 11.2 shows the environments that best suit each design.

The nature of demand for the firm's products or services is a key factor in the best choice of supply-chain design. Efficient supply chains work best in environments where demand is highly predictable, such as demand for staple items purchased at grocery

TABLE 11.2

Environments Best Suited for Efficient and Responsive Supply Chains

Factor	Efficient Supply Chains	Responsive Supply Chains
Demand	Predictable; low forecast errors	Unpredictable; high forecast errors
Competitive priorities	Low cost; consistent quality; on-time delivery	Development speed; fast delivery times; customization; volume flexibility; high-performance design quality
New-product introduction	Infrequent	Frequent
Contribution margins	Low	High
Product variety	Low	High

stores or demand for a package delivery service. The focus of the supply chain is on the efficient flows of materials and services, that is, keeping inventories to a minimum. Because of the markets the firms serve, product or service designs last a long time, new introductions are infrequent, and variety is small. Such firms typically produce for markets in which price is crucial to winning an order; therefore, contribution margins are low and efficiency is important. Consequently, the firm's competitive priorities are low-cost operations, consistent quality, and on-time delivery.

Responsive supply chains work best when firms offer a great variety of products or services and demand predictability is low. The firms may not know what products or services they need to provide until customers place orders. In addition, demand may be short-lived, as in the case of fashion goods. The focus of responsive supply chains is reaction time so as to avoid keeping costly inventories that ultimately must be sold at deep discounts. Such is the operating environment of mass customizers or firms utilizing the assemble-to-order operations strategy (see the Operations Strategy chapter). To be competitive, such firms must frequently introduce new products or services. Nonetheless, because of the innovativeness of their products or services, these firms enjoy high contribution margins. Typical competitive priorities are development speed, fast delivery times, customization, volume flexibility, and high-performance design quality.

A firm may need to utilize both types of supply chain, especially when it focuses its operations on specific market segments (see the Process Management chapter) or when it uses postponement. For example, the supply chain for a standard product such as an oil tanker has different requirements than that for a customized product such as a luxury liner, even though both are ocean-going vessels and both may be manufactured by the same company. You might also see both types used in the same supply chain. For example, Gillette uses an efficient supply chain to manufacture its products so that it can utilize a capital-intensive manufacturing process and then postpones the packaging of the products until the very last moment to be responsive to the needs at the retail level. The packaging operation involves customization in the form of printing in different languages. Just as processes can be broken into parts, with different process choices for each (see the Process Management chapter), so can supply-chain processes be segmented to achieve optimal performance.

THE DESIGN OF EFFICIENT AND RESPONSIVE SUPPLY CHAINS

Table 11.3 contains the basic design features for efficient and responsive supply chains. The higher in an efficient supply chain that a firm is, the more likely it is to have a line flow strategy that supports high volumes of standardized products or services. Consequently, suppliers in efficient supply chains should have low capacity cushions

TABLE 11.3

Design Features for Efficient and Responsive Supply Chains

Factor	Efficient Supply Chains	Responsive Supply Chains
Operations strategy	Make-to-stock or standardized services; emphasize high-volume, standardized products, or services	Assemble-to-order, make-to-order, or customized services emphasize product or service variety
Capacity cushion	Low	High
Inventory investment	Low; enable high inventory turns	As needed to enable fast delivery time
Lead time	Shorten, but do not increase costs	Shorten aggressively
Supplier selection	Emphasize low prices; consistent quality; on-time delivery	Emphasize fast delivery time; customization; volume flexibility; high-performance design quality

because high utilization keeps the cost per unit low. High inventory turns are desired because inventory investment must be kept low to achieve low costs. Firms should work with their suppliers to shorten lead times, but care must be taken to use tactics that do not appreciably increase costs. For example, lead times for a supplier could be shortened by switching from rail to air transportation; however, the added cost may offset the savings obtained from the shorter lead times. Suppliers should be selected with emphasis on low prices, consistent quality, and on-time delivery. Because of low capacity cushions, disruptions in an efficient supply chain can be costly and must be avoided. Managerial Practice 11.5 shows how modular production can improve efficient supply-chain operations.

MANAGERIAL PRACTICE 11.5
Improving Efficient Supply Chains Through Modularization

In the automobile industry, a module is a major assembly in a vehicle, such as a dashboard, including all the electronics and wire harnesses. Often, modules are outsourced to suppliers who must deliver them to the automaker's assembly line in the sequence of production and just when production commences. To increase the efficiency of the supply chain, automakers are designing vehicles with even larger modules to be produced and delivered by specialist suppliers. For example, Dana Corporation (www.dana.com) built a plant in Curitiba, Brazil, to put together the biggest module to date in the automotive industry—a complete chassis for a Dakota pickup truck, including steering equipment, fuel tank, driveshaft, suspension, brakes, and wheels with inflated tires. The plant is just four miles from a new DaimlerChrysler plant where the Dakota trucks are assembled. Three of the chassis are delivered to the assembly plant every 42 minutes to support production. Production on a chassis at Dana begins 108 minutes before it is needed for a special vehicle to keep inventory costs at a minimum.

This "rolling chassis" is built by the Dana Corporation in Curitiba, Brazil, and then shipped to the nearby DaimlerChrysler plant where the Dakota pickup truck is assembled. It is the largest module built to date by auto industry suppliers.

There are several advantages for the automakers. First, using larger modules reduces the number of suppliers the automakers have to deal with. Second, the complexity of coordinating assembly of the vehicles is reduced. For example, Dana must undertake the task of procuring 207 parts made by 67 companies and two other Dana factories. Third, automakers get the advantage of using the supplier's expertise for the production of the modules, which may involve special methods. Finally, the automaker risks less of its own capital because the supplier must incur the costs of the factory space needed for the production of the modules.

Although the production of the large modules can be lucrative, suppliers have to make some considerations before signing the contract. The larger modules take longer to manufacture and, because

of their size, pose freight problems when they are completed. These concerns lead suppliers to locate near their customers to reduce logistical costs; however, such a move often implies that the new facility will be devoted to one customer. Consequently, the success of the venture in part depends on the success of the customer. Global companies, such as Delphi, cannot always locate a complete production facility near each of its customers. In such a case, Delphi might locate in an industrial park near the customer, a smaller facility that performs only the last few steps of production and then manages a long, possibly multinational supply chain to support it.

Source: Siekman, Philip. "Building 'Em Better in Brazil." *Fortune* (September 6, 1999), pp. 246[C]–246[V].

Because of the need for quick reactions and the high levels of product or service variety, firms in a responsive supply chain should have a flexible, or intermediate, flow strategy. Consequently, suppliers should have high capacity cushions. Inventories should be positioned in the chain to support delivery speed, but inventories of expensive finished goods should be avoided. Firms should aggressively work with their suppliers to shorten lead times because that allows firms to wait longer before committing to customer orders. Firms should select suppliers to support the competitive priorities of the products or services provided, which in this case would include the ability to provide quick deliveries, customize parts or components, adjust volumes quickly to match demand cycles in the market, and provide high-performance quality. Our discussion of the Dell Computer Company at the beginning of this chapter is an example of the use of a responsive supply chain for competitive advantage.

Poor supply-chain performance often is the result of using the wrong supply-chain design for the products or services provided. A common mistake is to use an efficient supply chain in an environment that calls for a responsive supply chain. Over time, a firm may add options to its basic product, or introduce variations of that product, so that the variety of products and options increases dramatically and demand predictability drops. Yet, the firm continues to measure the performance of its supply chain as it always has, emphasizing efficiency, even when contribution margins would allow a responsive supply-chain design. Clearly, effective alignment of supply-chain operations to its competitive priorities has strategic implications for a firm.

SUPPLY-CHAIN DYNAMICS

What causes the fluctuations in supply chains and what are the consequences?

Supply chains often involve linkages among many firms. Each firm depends on other firms for materials, services, and information needed to supply its immediate customer in the chain. Because firms typically are owned and managed independently, the actions of downstream members (toward the ultimate user of the product or service) of the supply chain can adversely affect the operations of upstream members (toward the lowest tier in the supply chain). Figure 11.8(a) shows a segment of a supply chain involving three firms. Firm A has two customers and is directly served by firm B, which is served by firm C. Information flows from A to B and from B to C, often with a considerable lag. A recent study by the Automotive Industry Action Group (AIAG) found that it takes four to six weeks for materials release information to filter down to the last tier in the automotive supply chain. Further, the information from firm A that does reach the bottom of the chain is often distorted by the ordering policies of firm B that are reflected in its materials purchases from firm C. As a result, firm C has to develop volume flexibility even when it is part of an efficient supply chain. Figure 11.8(b) shows that a relatively short-term increase in firm A's demand can lead to significant materials requirement swings for firm C. If firm B mistakenly thinks that the increase in requirements from firm A is long-term and orders a large quantity of material from firm C, it will reduce its order quantity next time because its inventory levels are too high, causing the swings for firm C. These dynamics are often referred to as the *bullwhip effect*.

What causes supply-chain dynamics? The causes are both external and internal.

EXTERNAL SUPPLY-CHAIN CAUSES

A firm has the least amount of control over the external supply chain. Consequently, it must design its operations with the understanding that it may have to respond to disruptions caused by suppliers or customers. Typical disruptions include the following.

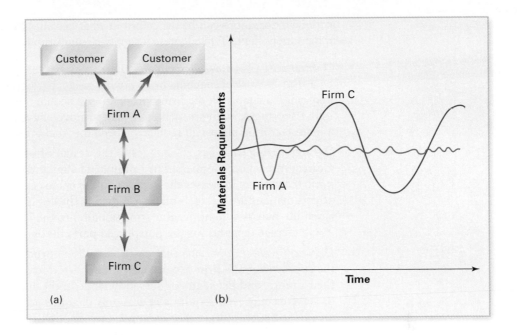

FIGURE 11.8

*Supply-Chain
Dynamics*

❏ *Volume Changes.*   Customers may change the quantity of the product or service they had ordered for a specific date or unexpectedly demand more of a standard product or service. If the market demands short lead times, the firm needs quick reactions from its suppliers. For example, an electric utility experiencing an unusually warm day may require immediate power backup from another utility to avoid a brownout in its region.

❏ *Product and Service Mix Changes.*   Customers may change the mix of items in an order and cause a ripple effect throughout the supply chain. For example, a major-appliance store chain may change the mix of washing machines in its orders from 60 percent Whirlpool brand and 40 percent Kitchen Aid brand to 40 percent Whirlpool and 60 percent Kitchen Aid. This decision changes the production schedule of the Whirlpool plant that makes both brands, causing imbalances in its inventories. Further, the company that makes the face plates for the washing machines must change its schedules, thereby affecting its suppliers.

❏ *Late Deliveries.*   Late deliveries of materials or delays in essential services can force a firm to switch its schedule from production of one product model to another. Firms that supply model-specific items may have their schedules disrupted. For example, the Whirlpool plant may find that a component supplier for its Model A washing machine could not supply the part on time. To avoid shutting down the assembly line, an expensive action, Whirlpool may decide to switch to Model B production. Suddenly there is a big demand on the suppliers for Model B-specific parts.

❏ *Underfilled Shipments.*   Suppliers that send partial shipments do so because of disruptions at their own plants. The effects of underfilled shipments are similar to those of late shipments unless there is enough to allow the firm to operate until the next shipment.

INTERNAL SUPPLY-CHAIN CAUSES

A famous line from a Pogo cartoon is "We have seen the enemy, and it is us!" Unfortunately, this statement is true for many firms when it comes to disruptions in the supply chain.

A firm's own operations can be the culprit in what becomes the source of constant dynamics in the supply chain. Typical internal supply-chain disruptions include the following.

❑ *Internally Generated Shortages.*   There may be a shortage of parts manufactured by a firm because of machine breakdowns or inexperienced workers. This shortage may cause a change in the firm's production schedule that will affect suppliers. Labor shortages, owing to strikes or high turnover, have a similar effect. A strike at a manufacturing plant will reduce the need for trucking services, for example.

❑ *Engineering Changes.*   Changes to the design of products or services can have a direct impact on suppliers. For example, changing cable TV feed lines to fiber-optic technology increases the benefits to the cable company's customers but affects demand for cable. Similarly, reducing the complexity of a dashboard assembly may not be noticeable (functionally) to the buyers of an automobile, but it will change demand for the outsourced parts that go into the dashboard.

❑ *New Product or Service Introductions.*   New products or services always affect the supply chain. A firm decides how many introductions there will be, as well as their timing, and hence introduces a dynamic in the supply chain. New products or services may even require a new supply chain or addition of new members to an existing supply chain. For example, introduction of a new refrigerated trucking service will have an impact on the suppliers of refrigerated trucks and the maintenance items for the new service.

❑ *Product or Service Promotions.*   A common practice of firms producing standardized products or services is to use price discounts to promote sales. This practice has the effect of creating a spike in demand that is felt throughout the supply chain. That is what the Campbell Soup Company found out when its annual deep-discount pricing program caused customers to buy large quantities of chicken soup, which had the effect of causing overtime production at its chicken-boning plant.

❑ *Information Errors.*   Demand forecast errors can cause a firm to order too many, or too few, materials and services. Also, forecast errors may cause expedited orders that force suppliers to react more quickly to avoid shortages in the supply chain. In addition, errors in the physical count of items in stock can cause shortages (panic purchases) or too much inventory (slowdown in purchases). Finally, communication links between buyers and suppliers can be faulty. For example, inaccurate order quantities and delays in information flows will affect supply-chain dynamics.

External and internal disruptions such as these impair the performance of any supply chain. However, they are particularly costly in an *efficient supply chain* because suppliers are less able to react to changes in schedules. Many disruptions are caused by ineffective coordination between external and internal supply chains or poorly executed internal supply-chain operations. Because supply chains involve so many firms and separate operations, it is unrealistic to think that all disruptions can be eliminated. Nonetheless, the challenge for supply-chain managers is to remove as many disruptions as possible and design a supply chain that minimizes the impact of those that they cannot eliminate.

SUPPLY-CHAIN SOFTWARE

Supply-chain software provides the capability to share information with suppliers and customers and make decisions affecting the internal and external supply chains. Supply-chain applications are often a part of enterprise resource planning (ERP) systems (see the Managing Technology chapter) or can be purchased independently from a variety of vendors. For example, Pepperidge Farm purchased a supply-chain management system to improve customer service, reduce costs in finished goods inventory, and gain efficiencies in materials purchasing. Pepperidge Farm produces fresh breads made-to-order as well as a number of other products that are made-to-stock. The system has the following modules:

- ❒ *Order Commitment.* Accepts customer orders, allocates resources to ensure that delivery is possible, and commits the firm to a specified delivery date.
- ❒ *Transportation Management.* Schedules freight movements, provides routing capability, allocates resources, and tracks shipments worldwide.
- ❒ *Purchasing Management.* Links to suppliers to share information and manage procurement contracts.
- ❒ *Demand Management.* Provides multiple forecasting algorithms and causal modeling to assist in estimating demands, allowing for management overrides to incorporate real-time customer information (see the Forecasting chapter).
- ❒ *Vendor-Managed Inventory.* Coordinates the replenishment of inventories stored at the customer's site.
- ❒ *Replenishment Planning.* Facilitates the order-fulfillment process by orchestrating the flow of inventory through the various stocking points in the distribution channel and allocates inventories among customers when shortages exist.
- ❒ *Configuration.* Enables the assemble-to-order strategy by checking for the availability of all components before accepting an order and facilitates the substitution of components or features based on availability.
- ❒ *Material Planning.* Determines the replenishment of components and assemblies to support the master schedule of finished products (see the Resource Planning chapter).
- ❒ *Scheduling.* Provides multisite schedules with the capability to reschedule as needed (see the Scheduling chapter).
- ❒ *Master Planning.* Offers optimization tools to allocate and coordinate limited resources across the distribution network based upon user strategies.
- ❒ *Strategic Planning.* Provides tools for designing global supply chains, which assist in deciding inventory levels and the appropriate product mix across the distribution network and the best production and storage locations subject to customer and resource constraints.

The Pepperidge Farm system is representative of the software packages available from a number of vendors. The supply-chain software business is booming—a recent survey by AMR Research Inc. indicated that software purchases of industrial enterprise applications, which includes ERP and supply-chain management systems, will increase at an annual compounded rate of 36 percent for the next several years. Most companies will purchase the software rather than create their own.

SUPPLY-CHAIN MANAGEMENT ACROSS THE ORGANIZATION

Supply chains permeate the entire organization. It is hard to envision a process in a firm that is not in some way affected by a supply chain. Supply chains must be managed to coordinate the inputs with the outputs in a firm so as to achieve the appropriate competitive priorities of the firm's enterprise processes. The Internet has offered firms an alternative to traditional methods for managing the supply chain. However, the firm must be committed to reengineering its information flows throughout the organization. The supply-chain processes most affected are the order-placement, order-fulfillment (including the internal supply chain), and purchasing processes. These processes intersect all of the traditional functional areas of the firm.

Supply-chain management is essential for manufacturing as well as service firms. In fact, service providers are beginning to realize the potential for organizational benefits through the reengineering of supply-chain processes. For example, hospitals have notoriously held to old-fashioned approaches for purchasing and materials management. Even with the advent of group purchasing organizations and centralized buying groups such as Premier, Inc., the materials management department in a typical hospital collects orders from throughout the hospital for medical supplies and equipment ranging from latex gloves to operating tables from a stack of often-outdated catalogs. Prices must be checked and the orders sent by phone or fax to literally thousands of distributors and suppliers. Can this process be improved? Columbia/HCA Healthcare Corporation and Tenet Healthcare Corporation think so. They are funding separate ventures that will create an electronic marketplace for placing orders on-line. The systems will include catalog hubs, which will contain several hundred-thousand medical and surgical supplies. Of course, to take full advantage of the marketplace, the hospitals will have to reengineer their processes to enable electronic ordering. The potential benefits to the health care industry for improved supply-chain practices are enormous. It is estimated that of the $83 billion hospitals spend annually on supplies, $11 billion could be eliminated by improved supply-chain management.

FORMULA REVIEW

1. Weeks of supply $= \dfrac{\text{Average aggregate inventory value}}{\text{Weekly sales (at cost)}}$

2. Inventory turnover $= \dfrac{\text{Annual sales (at cost)}}{\text{Average aggregate inventory value}}$

CHAPTER HIGHLIGHTS

❑ A basic purpose of supply-chain management is to control inventory by managing the flows of materials that create it. Three aggregate categories of inventories are raw materials, work-in-process, and finished goods. An important aspect of supply-chain management is materials management, which coordinates the firm's purchasing, production control, and distribution functions.

❑ A supply chain is a set of linkages among suppliers of materials and services that spans the transformation of raw materials into products and services and delivers them to a firm's customers. Supply chains can be very complicated, involving thousands of firms at various tiers in the chain. Both service providers and manufacturers have supply chains to manage.

❑ Firms that develop an integrated supply chain first link purchasing, production, and distribution to create an internal supply chain that is the responsibility of a materials management department. Then, they link suppliers and customers, an external supply chain, to the internal supply chain to form an integrated supply chain.

❏ The Internet has dramatically changed the way companies can manage their supply chains. The order-placement process can be reengineered to allow for more customer involvement and less employee involvement, to remain open for business 24 hours a day, and to enable the firm to use pricing as a means to control for material or product shortages. Designing the order-fulfillment process involves decisions regarding the postponement of customization until the last possible moment, forward placement of inventories, and final assembly of orders in the distribution channel.

❏ Electronic purchasing is changing the way that many firms are handling the purchasing function. Electronic data interchange (EDI) has been used since the 1970s. It is now more accessible through the Internet and will enable firms to include more suppliers in their supply chains. Catalog hubs, exchanges, and auctions are among the latest innovations brought on by the Internet.

❏ Buyers can take two approaches in dealing with their suppliers. The competitive orientation pits supplier against supplier in an effort to get the buyer's business. Price concessions are a major bargaining point, and the amount of clout that a buyer or supplier may have often determines the outcome of the negotiations. The cooperative orientation seeks to make long-term commitments to a small number of suppliers with advantages accruing to both parties. The ultimate form of a cooperative orientation is sole sourcing, whereby only one supplier is responsible for providing an item or service. The orientation utilized should be chosen so as to achieve the firm's competitive priorities.

❏ It is becoming more and more popular to award the supply of an item or service previously produced by the firm to another firm under a long-term arrangement. It is important for supply-chain management because it shifts an activity from direct control in an internal supply chain to less control in an external supply chain.

❏ Value analysis is used to reduce the cost or improve the performance of products or services either purchased or produced. It is an intensive examination of the materials, process, and information flows involved in the production of an item. Programs such as early supplier involvement and presourcing involve suppliers in the value analysis.

❏ Supply-chain performance is tracked with inventory measures such as aggregate inventory level, weeks of supply, and inventory turnover. Supply-chain process measures include production and materials costs, percent defects, percent on-time delivery, and supplier lead times. These measures are related to financial measures such as total assets, ROA, working capital, contribution margin, total revenue, and cash-to-cash.

❏ Efficient supply chains are designed to coordinate the flows of materials and services so as to minimize inventories and maximize the efficiency of the firms in the supply chain. Responsive supply chains are designed to react quickly to market demand through judicious use of inventories and capacities. A common error that firms make is to use an efficient supply-chain design when product variety is high and product demand is unpredictable.

❏ Because supply chains consist of many independent firms linked to other firms, disruptions at the top end can spread through the entire supply chain, causing firms lower in the supply chain to experience significant swings in demand. Such disruptions are caused by the dynamics of both external and internal supply chains.

KEY TERMS

auction *511*
average aggregate inventory value *517*
catalog hubs *511*
channel assembly *510*
competitive orientation *514*
continuous replenishment *510*
cooperative orientation *514*
distribution *504*
early supplier involvement *516*
electronic data interchange (EDI) *510*
exchange *511*

finished goods (FG) *500*
forward placement *508*
green purchasing *513*
inventory *499*
inventory pooling *508*
inventory turnover *518*
materials management *504*
order-placement process *506*
order-fulfillment process *507*
presourcing *517*
postponement *510*

production *504*
purchasing *502*
raw materials (RM) *499*
sole sourcing *515*
supply-chain management *498*
value analysis *516*
vendor-managed inventories (VMI) *509*
weeks of supply *518*
work-in-process (WIP) *499*

SOLVED PROBLEM 1

A firm's cost of goods sold last year was $3,410,000, and the firm operates 52 weeks per year. It carries seven items in inventory: three raw materials, two work-in-process items, and two finished goods. The following table contains last year's average inventory level for each item, along with its value.

a. What is the average aggregate inventory value?

b. What weeks of supply does the firm maintain?

c. What was the inventory turnover last year?

CATEGORY	PART NUMBER	AVERAGE LEVEL	UNIT VALUE
Raw materials	1	15,000	$ 3.00
	2	2,500	5.00
	3	3,000	1.00
Work-in-process	4	5,000	14.00
	5	4,000	18.00
Finished goods	6	2,000	48.00
	7	1,000	62.00

SOLUTION

a.

PART NUMBER	AVERAGE LEVEL	UNIT VALUE		TOTAL VALUE
1	15,000	× $ 3.00	=	$ 45,000
2	2,500	× $ 5.00	=	$ 12,500
3	3,000	× $ 1.00	=	$ 3,000
4	5,000	× $ 14.00	=	$ 70,000
5	4,000	× $ 18.00	=	$ 72,000
6	2,000	× $ 48.00	=	$ 96,000
7	1,000	× $ 62.00	=	$ 62,000
	Average aggregate inventory value		=	$360,500

b. Average weekly sales at cost = $3,410,000/52 weeks = $65,577/week

$$\text{Weeks of supply} = \frac{\text{Average aggregate inventory value}}{\text{Weekly sales (at cost)}} = \frac{\$360,500}{\$65,577} = 5.5 \text{ weeks}$$

c. $$\text{Inventory turnover} = \frac{\text{Annual sales (at cost)}}{\text{Average aggregate inventory value}} = \frac{\$3,410,000}{\$360,500} = 9.5 \text{ turns}$$

DISCUSSION QUESTIONS

1. Under the Defense Industry Initiative on Business Ethics and Conduct, 46 contractors agreed to establish internal codes of ethics, to conduct training sessions, and to report suspected abuses.

   a. Is this initiative an example of moving toward competitive or cooperative supplier relations?

   b. Suppose that you are a defense contracts manager. You have a friend in the military whom you have known for 20 years. As a gesture of friendship, she offers useful inside information about a competing contractor's bid. What would you do if your company were part of the industry's ethics project? If your company were not part of it?

c. To build a win–win relationship with its suppliers, the armed forces made agreements calling for suppliers to be reimbursed for the costs of supplier training and employee morale-building programs. According to that agreement, your company decided to hold a private party for employees to "build morale." Because the expenses were to be reimbursed, the party planners were not very careful in making the arrangements and got carried away. They rented the city auditorium and hired a nationally known music group to provide entertainment. Furthermore, the planners did not do a good job of contract negotiation and ended up paying five times the going rate for these services. The bill for the party now reaches your desk . . . $250,000! Under the terms of your agreement, your company is entitled to reimbursement of the entire amount. What should you do?

2. DaimlerChrysler and General Motors vigorously compete with each other in many automobile and truck markets. When Jose Ignacio Lopez was vice-president of purchasing for GM, he made it very clear that his buyers were not

to accept luncheon invitations from suppliers. Thomas Stalcamp, head of purchasing for Chrysler before the merger with Daimler, instructed his buyers to take suppliers to lunch. Rationalize these two directives in light of supply-chain design and management.

3. The Wal-Mart retail chain has great purchasing clout with its suppliers. The Limited retail chain owns Mast Industries, which is responsible for producing many of the fashion items sold in The Limited stores. The Limited boasts that it can go from the concept for a new garment to the store shelf in 1,000 hours. Compare and contrast the implications for supply-chain management for these two retail systems.

4. Consider the Lower Florida Keys Health System and the Chaparral Steel tours in the Operations Strategy chapter and the Virtual Text on the CD. Both organizations represent very different approaches to doing business in their respective industries. Compare and contrast the opportunities each organization has to engage in electronic purchasing. Also, compare them with respect to the nature of their relationships with suppliers.

OM EXPLORER AND INTERNET EXERCISES

Visit our Web site at www.prenhall.com/krajewski for OM Explorer Tutors, which explain quantitative techniques; Solvers, which help you apply mathematical models; and Internet Exercises, including Facility Tours, which expand on the topics in this chapter.

PROBLEMS

1. 🔵 **OM Explorer** Buzzrite company ended the current year with annual sales (at cost) of $48 million. During the year, the inventory turned over six times. For the next year, Buzzrite plans to increase annual sales (at cost) by 25 percent.

   a. What is the increase in the average aggregate inventory value required if Buzzrite maintains the same inventory turnover during the next year?

   b. What change in inventory turns must Buzzrite achieve if, through better supply-chain management, it wants to support next year's sales with no increase in the average aggregate inventory value?

2. 🔵 **OM Explorer** Jack Jones, the materials manager at Precision Enterprises, is beginning to look for ways to reduce inventories. A recent accounting statement shows the following inventory investment by category: raw materials $3,129,500; work-in-process $6,237,000; and finished goods $2,686,500. This year's cost of goods sold will be about $32.5 million. Assuming 52 business weeks per year, express total inventory as

   a. weeks of supply.

   b. inventory turns.

TABLE 11.4 *Supplier Performance Scores*

		RATING		
PERFORMANCE CRITERION	WEIGHT	Supplier A	Supplier B	Supplier C
1. Price	0.2	0.6	0.5	0.9
2. Quality	0.2	0.6	0.4	0.8
3. Delivery	0.3	0.6	0.3	0.8
4. Production facilities	0.1	0.5	0.9	0.6
5. Warranty and claims policy	0.1	0.7	0.8	0.6
6. Financial position	0.1	0.9	0.9	0.7

3. **OM Explorer** One product line has 10 turns per year and an annual sales volume (at cost) of $985,000. How much inventory is being held, on average?

4. **OM Explorer** The Bawl Corporation supplies alloy ball bearings to auto manufacturers in Detroit. Because of its specialized manufacturing process, considerable work-in-process and raw materials are needed. The current inventory levels are $2,470,000 and $1,566,000 respectively. In addition, finished goods inventory is $1,200,000 and sales (at cost) for the current year are expected to be about $48 million. Express total inventory as

a. weeks of supply.

b. inventory turns.

5. The following data have been collected for a firm:

Cost of goods sold	$3,500,000
Gross profit	$ 700,000
Operating costs	$ 500,000
Operating profit	$ 200,000
Total inventory	$1,200,000
Fixed assets	$ 750,000
Long-term debt	$ 300,000

Assuming 52 business weeks per year, express total inventory as

a. weeks of supply.

b. inventory turns.

Advanced Problems

Problems 6 and 7 require prior reading of the Decision Making supplement.

6. **OM Explorer** The Bennet Company purchases one of its essential raw materials from three suppliers. Bennet's current policy is to distribute purchases equally among the three. The owner's son, Benjamin Bennet, has

just graduated from business college. He proposes that these suppliers be rated (high numbers mean good performance) on six performance criteria weighted as shown in Table 11.4. A hurdle total score of 0.60 is proposed to screen suppliers. Purchasing policy would be revised to order raw materials from suppliers with performance scores greater than the hurdle total score, in proportion to their performance rating scores.

a. Use a preference matrix to calculate the total weighted score for each supplier.

b. Which supplier(s) survived the hurdle total score? Under the younger Bennet's proposed policy, what proportion of orders would each supplier receive?

c. What advantages does the proposed policy have over the current policy?

7. **OM Explorer** Beagle Company uses a weighted score for the evaluation and selection of its suppliers. Each supplier is rated on a 10-point scale (10 = highest) for four different criteria: price, quality, delivery, and flexibility (to accommodate changes in quantity and timing). Because of the volatility of the business in which Jennings operates, flexibility is given twice the weight of each of the other three criteria, which are equally weighted. Table 11.5 shows the scores for three potential suppliers for the four performance criteria. Based on the highest weighted score, which supplier should be selected?

TABLE 11.5 *Supplier Performance Scores*

CRITERIA	SUPPLIER A	SUPPLIER B	SUPPLIER C
Price	8	6	6
Quality	9	7	7
Delivery	7	9	6
Flexibility	5	8	9

8. 🔵 **OM Explorer** Sterling, Inc., operates 52 weeks per year, and its cost of goods sold last year was $6,500,000. The firm carries eight items in inventory: four raw materials, two work-in-process items, and two finished goods. Table 11.6 shows last year's average inventory levels for these items, along with their unit values.

   a. What is the average aggregate inventory value?

   b. How many weeks of supply does the firm have?

   c. What was the inventory turnover last year?

		TABLE 11.6 *Inventory Items*	
CATEGORY	**PART NUMBER**	**AVERAGE INVENTORY UNITS**	**VALUE PER UNIT**
Raw materials	RM-1	20,000	$ 1
	RM-2	5,000	5
	RM-3	3,000	6
	RM-4	1,000	8
Work-in-process	WIP-1	6,000	10
	WIP-2	8,000	12
Finished goods	FG-1	1,000	65
	FG-2	500	88

SIMULATION EXERCISES

These simulation exercises require the use of the Extend and SimQuick simulation packages. Extend is on the Student CD-ROM that is packaged with every new copy of the textbook. SimQuick is an optional simulation package that your instructor may or may not have ordered.

1. 🔵 **Extend** Like many producers of computer peripheral devices, Compware Peripherals subcontracts the manufacturing of its low-cost, high-volume products to firms in China for subsequent shipment to distribution centers in Asia, Europe, and North America. Management is exploring options to improve both the cost and timeliness of Compware's supply chain for a standard product, a basic inkjet printer. The supply chain is shown below.

   Competition on price and service has grown tremendously over the last few years. Use the Extend simulator to identify opportunities to improve the performance of Compware's supply chain. See the *Managing the Supply Chain at Compware Peripherals* case on the Student CD-ROM, which includes the basic model and how to use it. Answer the various questions asked about improving the supply chain.

2. **SimQuick** A company owns two retail stores that sell the same hand-held computer. Orders are placed to a regional warehouse, also owned by the company. The regional warehouse places orders to a manufacturer. The management of the company wants to determine the best ordering and inventory placement policies at the retail stores and the warehouse to achieve good customer service at minimum cost. Use SimQuick to determine the best policies to use. See Example 11 in SimQuick: *Process Simulation in Excel* for more details of this problem and additional exercises.

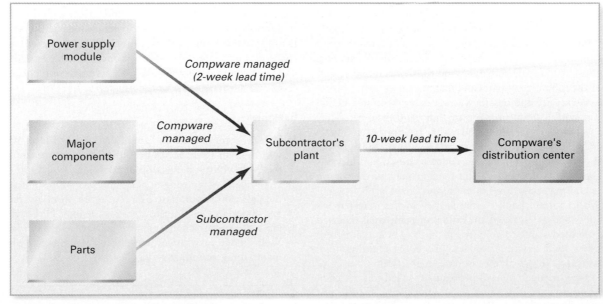

Simplified Supply Chain for Compware's Inkjet Printer

CASE **WOLF MOTORS**

John Wolf, president of Wolf Motors, had just returned to his office after visiting the company's newly acquired automotive dealership. It was the fourth Wolf Motors' dealership in a network that served a metropolitan area of 400,000 people. Beyond the metropolitan area, but within a 45-minute drive, were another 500,000 people. Each of the dealerships in the network marketed a different make of automobile and historically had operated autonomously.

Wolf was particularly excited about this new dealership because it was the first "auto supermarket" in the network. Auto supermarkets differ from traditional auto dealerships in that they sold multiple makes of automobiles at the same location. The new dealership sold a full line of Chevrolets, Nissans, and Volkswagens.

Starting 15 years ago with the purchase of a bankrupt Dodge dealership, Wolf Motors had grown steadily in size and in reputation. Wolf attributed this success to three highly interdependent factors. The first was volume. By maintaining a high volume of sales and turning over inventory rapidly, economies of scale could be achieved, which reduced costs and provided customers with a large selection. The second factor was a marketing approach called the "hassle-free buying experience." Listed on each automobile was the "one price–lowest price." Customers came in, browsed, and compared prices without being approached by pushy salespeople. If they had questions or were ready to buy, a walk to a customer service desk produced a knowledgeable salesperson to assist them. Finally, and Wolf thought perhaps most important, was the after-sale service. Wolf Motors had established a solid reputation for servicing, diagnosing, and repairing vehicles correctly and in a timely manner—the first time.

High-quality service after the sale depended on three essential components. First was the presence of a highly qualified, well-trained staff of service technicians. Second was the use of the latest tools and technologies to support diagnosis and repair activities. And third was the availability of the full range of parts and materials necessary to complete the service and repairs without delay. Wolf invested in training and equipment to ensure that the trained personnel and technology were provided. What he worried about, as Wolf Motors grew, was the continued availability of the right parts and materials. This concern caused him to focus on the purchasing process and management of the service parts and materials flows in the supply chain.

Wolf thought back on the stories in the newspaper's business pages describing the failure of companies that had not planned appropriately for growth. These companies outgrew their existing policies, procedures, and control systems. Lacking a plan to update their systems, the companies experienced myriad problems that led to inefficiencies and an inability to compete effectively. He did not want that to happen to Wolf Motors.

Each of the four dealerships purchased its own service parts and materials. Purchases were based on forecasts derived from historical demand data, which accounted for factors such as seasonality. Batteries and alternators had a high failure rate in the winter, and air-conditioner parts were in great demand during the summer. Similarly, coolant was needed in the spring to service air conditioners for the summer months, whereas antifreeze was needed in the fall to winterize automobiles. Forecasts also were adjusted for special vehicle sales and service promotions, which increased the need for materials used to prep new cars and service other cars.

One thing that made the purchase of service parts and materials so difficult was the tremendous number of different parts that had to be kept on hand. Some of these parts would be used to service customer automobiles, and others would be sold over the counter. Some had to be purchased from the automobile manufacturers or their certified wholesalers, and to support, for example, the "guaranteed GM parts" promotion. Still other parts and materials such as oils, lubricants, and fan belts could be purchased from any number of suppliers. The purchasing department had to remember that the success of the dealership depended on (1) lowering costs to support the hassle-free, one price–lowest price concept and (2) providing the right parts at the right time to support fast, reliable after-sale service.

As Wolf thought about the purchasing of parts and materials, two things kept going through his mind: the amount of space available for parts storage and the level of financial resources available to invest in parts and materials. The acquisition of the auto supermarket dealership put an increased strain on both finances and space, with the need to support three different automobile lines at the same facility. Investment dollars were becoming scarce, and space was at a premium. Wolf wondered what could be done in the purchasing area to address some of these concerns and alleviate some of the pressures.

Questions

1. What recommendations would you make to John Wolf with respect to structuring the purchasing process for the Wolf Motors dealership network?
2. How might purchasing policies and procedures differ as the dealerships purchase different types of service parts and materials (e.g., lubricants versus genuine GM parts)?
3. How can supply-chain management concepts help John Wolf reduce investment and space requirements while maintaining adequate service levels?

Source: This case was prepared by Dr. Brooke Saladin, Wake Forest University, as a basis for classroom discussion.

EXPERIENTIAL LEARNING **SONIC DISTRIBUTORS**

SCENARIO

Sonic Distributors produces and sells music CDs. The CDs are pressed at a single facility (factory), issued through the company's distribution center, and sold to the public from various retail stores. The goal is to operate the distribution chain at the lowest total cost.

Materials (available from instructor)

Retail and distributor purchase order forms

Factory work order forms

Factory and distributor materials delivery forms

Inventory position worksheets

A means of generating random demand (typically a pair of dice)

Setup

Each team is in the business of manufacturing music CDs and distributing them to retail stores where they are sold. Two or more people play the role of retail outlet buyers. Their task is to determine the demand for the CDs and order replenishment stock from the distributor. The distributor carries forward-placed stock obtained from the factory. The factory produces in lot sizes either to customer order or to stock.

Tasks

Divide into teams of four or five.

Two or three people operate the retail stores.

One person operates the distribution center.

One person schedules production at the factory.

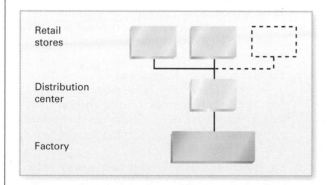

Every day, as play progresses, the participants at each level of the supply chain determine demand, fill customer orders, record inventory levels, and decide how much to order or produce and when to place orders with their supplier.

COSTS AND CONDITIONS

Unless your instructor indicates otherwise, the following costs and conditions hold.

Costs

Holding cost per unit per day:	Retail outlets: $1.00/CD/day Distribution Center: $0.50/CD/day Factory: $0.25/CD/day
Pipeline inventory cost:	Because plant space is no longer tied up, this cost is small and can be ignored (consider it zero).
Ordering cost (retailers and distributors):	$20/order
Factory setup cost (to run an order):	$50 (Note: cost is per order, not per day because even though successive orders from distributors are for the same item, the factory is busy fabricating other things between orders.)
Stockout (lost margin) cost:	Retail Store: $8 per CD sale lost in a period. $0 for back-orders for shortages from the factory or shipping new orders.
Shipping cost:	Since other products are already being distributed through this chain and because CDs are light and take up little volume, consider the cost to be zero.

Conditions

Starting inventory:	Retail stores each have 15 CDs Distribution center has 25 CDs Factory has 100 CDs
Lot sizing restrictions:	Retail outlets and distribution centers—no minimum order. Any amount may be stored. Factory production lot sizes and capacity—produce in minimum lots of 20. Maximum capacity, 200/day.
Outstanding orders:	None

continued

continued

Delays

Ordering Delay. One day to send an order from a retail store to the distributor and from the distributor to the factory (i.e., one day is lost between placing an order and acting on it).

There is no delay to start up production once an order has been received (but one day is needed for delivery of an order from the distributor to the factory).

Delivery Delay. One day shipping time between the distributor and a retail store and between the factory and the distributor (i.e., one day is lost between shipping an order and receiving it).

RUN THE EXERCISE

For simplicity sake, assume all transactions take place simultaneously at the middle of the day. For every simulated day, the sequence of play goes as follows.

Retailers

a. Each retailer receives any shipment due in from its distributor (one day after shipment) and places it in sales inventory (adds the quantity indicated on any incoming Material Delivery Form from the distributor—after its one-day delay—to the previous day's ending inventory level on the Retailer's Inventory Position Worksheet). (*Note*: for the first day of the exercise, no order will be coming in.)

b. The retailers each determine the day's retail demand (the quantity of CDs requested) by rolling a pair of dice. The roll determines the number demanded.

c. Retailers fill demand from available stock if possible. Demand is filled by subtracting it from the current inventory level to develop the ending inventory level which is recorded. If demand exceeds supply, sales are lost. Record all lost sales on the worksheet.

d. Retailers determine whether an order should be placed. If an order is required, the desired quantity of CDs is written on a Retail Store Purchase Order, which is forwarded to the distributor (who receives it after a one-day delay). If an order is made, it should be noted on the worksheet. Retailers may also desire to keep track of outstanding orders separately.

Distributor

a. The distributor receives any shipment due in from the factory and places the CDs in available inventory (adds the quantity indicated on any incoming Material Delivery Form from the factory—after its one-day delay—to the previous day's ending inventory level on the distributor's inventory position worksheet).

b. All outstanding backorders are filled (the quantity is subtracted from the current inventory level indicated on the worksheet) and prepared for shipment. CDs are shipped by filling out a Distribution Center Material Delivery Form indicating the quantity of CDs to be delivered.

c. The distributor uses the purchase orders received from the retail stores (after the designated one-day delay) to prepare shipments for delivery from available inventory. Quantities shipped are subtracted from the current level to develop the ending inventory level, which is recorded. If insufficient supply exists, backorders are generated.

d. The distributor determines whether a replenishment order should be placed. If an order is required, the quantity of CDs is written on a Distribution Center Purchase Order, which is forwarded to the factory (after a one-day delay). If an order is made, it should be noted on the worksheet. The distributor may also desire to keep track of outstanding orders separately.

Factory

a. The factory places any available new production into inventory (adds the items produced the previous day to the previous day's ending inventory level on the Factory Inventory Position Worksheet).

b. All outstanding backorders are filled (the quantity is subtracted from the current inventory level indicated on the worksheet) and prepared for shipment. CDs are shipped by filling out a Factory Material Delivery Form, indicating the quantity of CDs to be delivered.

c. The factory obtains the incoming distributor's purchase orders (after the designated one-day delay) and ships them from stock if it can. These amounts are subtracted from the current values on the inventory worksheet. Any unfilled orders become backorders for the next day.

d. The factory decides whether to issue a work order to produce CDs either to stock or to order. If production is required, a Factory Work Order is issued and the order is noted on the inventory worksheet. Remember that there is a setup cost for each *production* order. It is important to keep careful track of all production in process.

Remember that, once an order has been placed, it cannot be changed and no partial shipments can be made. For each day, record your ending inventory position, backorder or lost sales amount, and whether an order was made (or a production run initiated). When everyone has completed the transactions for the day, the sequence repeats (go to retailer step a). Your instructor will tell you how many simulated days to run the exercise.

When the play is stopped, find the cumulative amount of inventory and other costs. You can do so by summing up the numbers in each column, then multiplying these totals by the costs previously listed. Use the total of these costs to assess how well your team operated the distribution chain.

This exercise was developed by Larry Meile, Carroll School of Management, Boston College.

SELECTED REFERENCES

Bowersox, D. J., and D. J. Closs. *Logistical Management: The Integrated Supply Chain Process.* New York: McGraw-Hill, 1996.

Bridleman, Dan, and Jeff Herrmann. "Supply-Chain Management in a Make-to-Order World." *APICS—The Performance Advantage* (March 1997), pp. 32–38.

Chopra, Sunil, and Jan A. Van Mieghem. "Which E-Business Is Right for Your Supply Chain?" Working Paper, Northwestern University, Kellogg Graduate School of Management, 2000.

Dyer, Jeffrey H. "How Chrysler Created an American Keiretsu." *Harvard Business Review* (July–August 1996), pp. 42–56.

Fisher, Marshall L. "What Is the Right Supply Chain for Your Product?" *Harvard Business Review* (March–April 1997), pp. 105–116.

Gurusami, Senthil A. "Ford's Wrenching Decision." *OR/MS Today* (December 1998), pp. 36–39.

Harwick, Tom. "Optimal Decision Making for the Supply Chain." *APICS—The Performance Advantage* (January 1997), pp. 42–44.

Johnson, Eric, and Tom Davis. "Gaining an Edge with Supply-Chain Management." *APICS—The Performance Advantage* (December 1995), pp. 26–31.

Kaplan, Steven, and Mohanbir Sawhney. "E-Hubs: The New B2B Marketplaces." *Harvard Business Review* (May–June 2000), pp. 97–103.

Latamore, G. Benton. "Supply Chain Optimization at Internet Speed." *Apics—The Performance Advantage* (May, 2000), pp. 37–40.

Lee, Hau L., and Corey Billington. "Managing Supply Chain Inventory: Pitfalls and Opportunities." *Sloan Management Review* (Spring 1992), pp. 65–73.

Maloni, M., and W. C. Benton. "Power Influences in the Supply Chain." *Journal of Business Logistics*, vol. 21 (2000), pp. 49–73.

Melnyk, Steven A., and Robert Handfield. "Green Speak." *Purchasing Today*, vol. 7, no. 7 (1996), pp. 32–36.

Quinn, James Brian, and Frederick G. Hilmer. "Strategic Outsourcing." *Sloan Management Review* (Summer 1994), pp. 43–55.

Ross, David F. "Meeting the Challenge of Supply-Chain Management." *APICS—The Performance Advantage* (September 1996), pp. 38–63.

Stevens, Graham C. "Integrating the Supply Chain." *International Journal of Physical Distribution & Materials Management*, vol. 19, no. 8 (1989), pp. 3–8.

Tully, Shawn. "The B2B Tool That Really Is Changing the World." *Fortune* (March 20, 2000), pp. 132–145.

Venkatesan Ravi. "Strategic Sourcing: To Make or Not to Make." *Harvard Business Review* (November–December 1992), pp. 98–107.

Forecasting

Across the Organization

Forecasting is important to . . .

- ❏ **finance,** which uses long-term forecasts to project needs for capital.
- ❏ **human resources,** which uses forecasts to estimate the need for workers.
- ❏ **management information systems,** which design and implement forecasting systems.
- ❏ **marketing,** which develops sales forecasts that are used for medium and long-range plans.
- ❏ **operations,** which develops and uses forecasts for decisions such as scheduling workers, short-term inventory replenishment, and long-term planning for capacity.

Learning Goals

After reading this chapter, you will be able to . . .

1. identify the five basic demand patterns that combine to produce a demand time series.
2. choose the appropriate forecasting technique for a given decision problem.
3. describe the different types of judgmental forecasting approaches and when to apply them.
4. use the computer to produce a linear regression forecasting model.
5. compute forecasts, using the most common approaches for time series analysis.
6. explain the various measures of forecast errors and how to use them in monitoring and controlling forecast performance.

One of the critical drivers of supply-chain success is effective customer demand planning, which begins with accurate forecasts. Lucent Technologies (www.lucent.com), formed in 1995 when AT&T divided into three major businesses, is a leading supplier of data networking systems. Its other product lines include switching and access systems, wireless communications systems, optical networking systems, and fiber-optic systems. To improve its forecasting and planning, Lucent established a group called Customer Demand Planning (CDP), which is also a core business process. The CDP process is a business planning process enabling sales teams (and customers) to develop demand forecasts as input to inventory and production planning, revenue planning, and service planning processes. *Forecasting* is seen at Lucent as the process of developing the most probable view of what future demand will be, given a set of assumptions about technology, competitors, pricing, marketing expenditures, and sales efforts. *Planning*, on the other hand, is the process of making management decisions on how to deploy resources to best respond to the demand forecasts. Forecasts at Lucent precede plans: It is not possible to make decisions on production scheduling, purchasing, and inventory levels until forecasts are developed that give reasonably accurate views of demand over the forecasting horizon.

CDP is critical to the business because of the large number of "internal customers" that need accurate, credible forecasts. By 1999, there were over 2,000 different individuals from 33 countries using CDP forecasts. It generates over 16,000 monthly forecasts for over 2,000 product lines, using a single global schedule, data repository, and set of procedures. The CDP forecasting system forecasts in units, which can then be converted to revenue forecasts using historical average price data. Those who provide input to the CDP system have the ability to enter forecasts using a number of different forecast hierarchy levels, ranging from product families to individual products broken down by customer, project, or total application (a predefined combination of several different products). The normal time horizon for the CDP forecasting process is a rolling 12-month horizon. The CDP system is designed to be "user friendly" for those people in Lucent's sales organization who input information into the forecast. The user interface is designed to provide a "point-and-click" environment. In order to provide salespeople making inputs into the forecast with the most recent information, three years of global customer demand history, plus year-to-date customer demand, is provided by the system. This history is updated weekly. In addition, known future demand, which takes the form of long-term contract business for which there are not yet specific orders, is detailed for 12 months into the future. Also, order-level information is available for the previous three months and for all future-committed orders. The system also provides the capability for sales teams to enter subjective information, including the forecast risk and the significant upside or downside variables.

While the CDP forecasting process is well designed, it did not just happen. Accuracy measures were not originally at a level that the company felt was acceptable (75 to 85 percent accuracy across all major product lines and businesses), and this led Lucent to undertake a forecasting audit in a continuous improvement effort to evolve the CDP process. Performed by external experts, the audit has had a significant impact on the forecasting process itself, and the accuracy of the forecasts provided. Changes in the process include (1) more training of the forecasting group, on the role of forecasting, and use of statistical techniques to enhance their qualitative judgments, (2) a program of rewards and recognition directly linked to forecast performance, (3) software system enhancement to provide adequate measures of forecast errors and performance, and (4) a knowledge core group that uses statistical tools such as time-series techniques and regression to develop initial forecasts. These initial forecasts are then distributed to those knowledgeable individuals in the organization for their judgmental adjustments. By 1998, forecast accuracy improved to the 85 percent range, on-time delivery objectives were met, and inventory levels were more under control.

Source: Moon, Mark A., John T. Mentzer, and Dwight E. Thomas, Jr. "Customer Demand Planning at Lucent Technologies; A Case Study in Continuous Improvement Through Sales Forecast Auditing." *Industrial Marketing Management*, vol. 29, no. 1 (2000).

Why is forecasting important?

forecast A prediction of future events used for planning purposes.

$\mathbf{L}$ UCENT'S SUCCESS DEMONSTRATES THE value of forecasting. A **forecast** is a prediction of future events used for planning purposes. At Lucent, management needed accurate forecasts to ensure supply-chain success. Changing business conditions resulting from global competition, rapid technological change, and increasing environmental concerns exert pressure on a firm's capability to generate accurate forecasts. Forecasts are needed to aid in determining what resources are needed, scheduling existing resources, and acquiring additional resources. Accurate forecasts allow schedulers to use capacity efficiently, reduce customer response times, and cut inventories. The manager of a fast-food restaurant needs to forecast the number of customers at various times of the day, along with the products they will want, in order to schedule the correct number of cooks and counter clerks. Managers may need forecasts to anticipate changes in prices or costs or to prepare for new laws or regulations, competitors, resource shortages, or technologies.

Forecasting methods may be based on mathematical models using historical data available, qualitative methods drawing on managerial experience, or a combination of both. Variations of these methods are valuable in estimating future processing times and learning-curve effects (see CD Supplements on *Measuring Output Rates* and *Learning-Curve Analysis*). In this chapter, our focus is on demand forecasts. We will explore several forecasting methods commonly used today and their advantages and limitations. We also identify the decisions that managers should make in designing a forecasting system.

DEMAND CHARACTERISTICS

At the root of most business decisions is the challenge of forecasting customer demand. It is a difficult task because the demand for goods and services can vary greatly. For example, demand for lawn fertilizer predictably increases in the spring and summer months; however, the particular weekends when demand is heaviest may depend on uncontrollable factors such as the weather. Sometimes patterns are more predictable. Thus, weekly demand for haircuts at a local barbershop may be quite stable from week to week, with daily demand being heaviest on Saturday mornings and lightest on Mondays and Tuesdays. Forecasting demand in such situations requires uncovering the underlying patterns from available information. In this section, we first discuss the basic patterns of demand and then address the factors that affect demand in a particular situation.

PATTERNS OF DEMAND

time series The repeated observations of demand for a product or service in their order of occurrence.

The repeated observations of demand for a product or service in their order of occurrence form a pattern known as a **time series**. The five basic patterns of most demand time series are

1. *horizontal* or the fluctuation of data around a constant mean;
2. *trend,* or systematic increase or decrease in the mean of the series over time;
3. *seasonal,* or a repeatable pattern of increases or decreases in demand, depending on the time of day, week, month, or season;
4. *cyclical,* or less predictable gradual increases or decreases in demand over longer periods of time (years or decades); and
5. *random,* or unforecastable, variation in demand.

Cyclical patterns arise from two influences. The first is the business cycle, which includes factors that cause the economy to go from recession to expansion over a number of years. The other influence is the product or service life cycle, which reflects the stages of demand from development through decline. Business cycle movement is difficult to predict because it is affected by national or international events, such as presidential elections or political turmoil in other countries. Predicting the rate of demand buildup or decline in the life cycle also is difficult. Sometimes firms estimate demand for a new product by starting with the demand history for the product it is replacing. For example, the demand rate for digital audiotapes might emulate the demand buildup for stereo cassette tapes in the early stages of that product's life cycle. The ability to make intelligent long-range forecasts depends on accurate estimates of cyclical patterns.

Four of the patterns of demand—horizontal, trend, seasonal, and cyclical—combine in varying degrees to define the underlying time pattern of demand for a product or service. The fifth pattern, random variation, results from chance causes and thus cannot be predicted. Random variation is an aspect of demand that makes every forecast wrong. Figure 12.1 shows the first four patterns of a demand time series, all of which contain random variation. A time series may comprise any combination of these patterns.

FACTORS AFFECTING DEMAND

What factors cause changes in the demand for a particular product or service over time? Generally, such factors can be divided into two main categories: external and internal.

FIGURE 12.1

Patterns of Demand

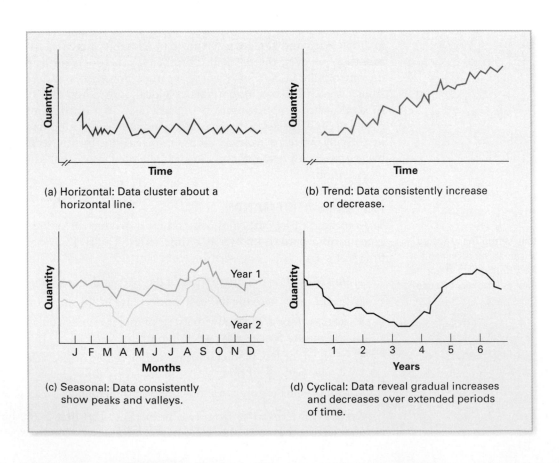

(a) Horizontal: Data cluster about a horizontal line.

(b) Trend: Data consistently increase or decrease.

(c) Seasonal: Data consistently show peaks and valleys.

(d) Cyclical: Data reveal gradual increases and decreases over extended periods of time.

EXTERNAL FACTORS. External factors that affect demand for a firm's products or services are beyond management's control. A booming economy may positively influence demand, although the effect may not be the same for all products and services. Furthermore, certain economic activities, such as changes in interest rates and government regulations, affect some products and services but not others. For example, a state law limiting the sulfur content of coal used in steam-powered electric generating plants reduces the demand for high-sulfur coal but does not affect the demand for electricity.

Certain government agencies and private firms compile statistics on general economic time series to help organizations predict the direction of change in demand for their products or services. Of prime importance is the *turning point*—that is, the period when the long-term rate of growth in demand for a firm's products or services will change. Although predicting the exact timing of turning points is impossible, some general economic time series have turning points that can be useful in estimating the timing of the turning points in a firm's demands.

Leading indicators, such as the rate of business failures, are external factors with turning points that typically precede the peaks and troughs of the general business cycle. For example, an upswing in residential building contracts might precede an increase in the demand for plywood by several weeks, for homeowners' insurance by several months, and for furniture by one year. This indicator gives some advance warning to plywood manufacturers, insurance companies, and furniture manufacturers about possible demand increases. **Coincident indicators,** such as unemployment figures, are time series with turning points that generally match those of the general business cycle. **Lagging indicators,** such as retail sales, follow those turning points, typically by several weeks or months. Knowing that a series is a lagging indicator can be useful. For example, a firm needing a business loan for expansion should realize that interest rates will drop to a low point several weeks after the business cycle reaches its trough.

Let us look briefly at other external factors that affect demand. Consumer tastes can change quickly, as they often do in clothing fashions. The consumer's image of a product can be another big factor in changing demand. For example, in the last decade sales of tobacco products in the United States have dropped significantly because many people believe that those products can be hazardous to their health. In addition, competitors' actions regarding prices, advertising promotions, and new products also affect sales. For example, a United Parcel Service commercial showing the speedy delivery of a parcel reduces the demand for the services of competitors, such as FedEx or DHL. Finally, the success of one product or service affects the demand for complementary products or services. The Milwaukee plant of Harley-Davidson stimulates the sales of many motorcycle parts and components locally. Future demand for parts and components there depends on Harley-Davidson's success in that area.

INTERNAL FACTORS. Internal decisions about product or service design, price and advertising promotions, packaging design, salesperson quotas or incentives, and expansion or contraction of geographic market target areas all contribute to changes in demand volume. The term **demand management** describes the process of influencing the timing and volume of demand or adapting to the undesirable effects of unchangeable demand patterns. For example, automobile manufacturers use rebates to boost car sales.

Management must carefully consider the timing of demand, an extremely important factor in efficiently utilizing resources and production capacity. Trying to produce for peak customer demand during the peak demand period can be very costly. To avoid this situation, firms often use price incentives or advertising promotions to encourage customers to make purchases before or after traditional times of peak demand. For

---

leading indicators
External factors with turning points that typically precede the peaks and troughs of the general business cycle.

coincident indicators
Time series with turning points that generally match those of the general business cycle.

lagging indicators An indicator that follows turning points typically by several weeks or months.

How can demand be influenced?

demand management The process of influencing the timing and volume of demand or adapting to the undesirable effects of unchangeable demand patterns.

example, telephone companies encourage customers to make long distance calls after normal business hours by offering lower evening and weekend rates. This practice helps spread demand more evenly over the day. Another tactic is to produce two products that have different heavy seasonal demand periods. A producer of engines for tractor lawn mowers, for instance, might also make engines for snowmobiles to even out resource and production requirements over the year. In this way costly changes in workforce level and inventory can be minimized.

Finally, some companies schedule delivery dates for products or services according to the current workload and capacity. Doctors, dentists, and other professionals use this approach by asking patients to make appointments for their services. Manufacturers of custom-built products also work to backlogs of demand.

DESIGNING THE FORECASTING SYSTEM

Before using forecasting techniques to analyze operations management problems, a manager must make three decisions: (1) what to forecast, (2) what type of forecasting technique to use, and (3) what type of computer hardware or software (or both) to use. We discuss each of these decisions before examining specific forecasting techniques.

DECIDING WHAT TO FORECAST

What makes a forecasting system best for any particular situation?

Although some sort of demand estimate is needed for the individual goods or services produced by a company, forecasting total demand for groups or clusters and then deriving individual product or service forecasts may be easiest. Also, selecting the correct unit of measurement (e.g., product or service units or machine-hours) for forecasting may be as important as choosing the best method.

LEVEL OF AGGREGATION. Few companies err by more than 5 percent when forecasting total demand for all their products. However, errors in forecasts for individual items may be much higher. By clustering several similar products or services in a process called **aggregation,** companies can obtain more accurate forecasts. Many companies utilize a two-tier forecasting system, first making forecasts for families of goods or services that have similar demand requirements and common processing, labor, and materials requirements and then deriving forecasts for individual items. For example, General Motors forecasts the demand for Saturn automobiles as a product family, then derives unit forecasts for the SL-1 and SL-2 models from the product family forecast. This approach maintains consistency between planning for the final stages of manufacturing (which requires the unit forecasts) and longer-term planning for sales, profit, and capacity (which requires the product family forecasts). We return to this point later (see the Aggregate Planning chapter).

aggregation The act of clustering several similar products or services so that companies can obtain more accurate forecasts.

UNITS OF MEASUREMENT. The most useful forecasts for planning and analyzing operations problems are those based on product or service units, such as Saturn SL-1s, express packages to deliver, or customers needing maintenance service or repairs for their cars, rather than dollars. Forecasts of sales revenue are not very helpful because prices often fluctuate. Thus, even though total sales in dollars might be the same from month to month, the actual number of units of demand could vary widely. Forecasting the number of units of demand—and then translating these estimates to sales revenue estimates by multiplying them by the price—often is the better method. If accurately forecasting the number of units of demand for a product or service is not possible, forecasting the standard labor or machine *hours* required of each of the critical resources, based on historical patterns, often is better. For companies producing goods or services to customer order, estimates of labor or machine hours are important to scheduling and capacity planning.

CHOOSING THE TYPE OF FORECASTING TECHNIQUE

The forecaster's objective is to develop a useful forecast from the information at hand with the technique appropriate for the different characteristics of demand. This choice sometimes involves a trade-off between forecast accuracy and costs, such as software purchases, the time required to develop a forecast, and personnel training. Two general types of forecasting techniques are used for demand forecasting: qualitative methods and quantitative methods. Lucent's CDP process uses a combination of both methods. Qualitative methods include **judgment methods,** which translate the opinions of managers, expert opinions, consumer surveys, and sales-force estimates into quantitative estimates. Quantitative methods include causal methods and time-series analysis. **Causal methods** use historical data on independent variables, such as promotional campaigns, economic conditions, and competitors' actions, to predict demand. **Time-series analysis** is a statistical approach that relies heavily on historical demand data to project the future size of demand and recognizes trends and seasonal patterns. We describe each technique in more detail later in this chapter. First, however, let us consider the conditions under which these techniques are likely to be applied.

A key factor in choosing the proper forecasting approach is the time horizon for the decision requiring forecasts. Forecasts can be made for the short term, medium term, and long term. Table 12.1 contains examples of demand-forecasting applications and the typical planning horizon for each.

SHORT TERM. In the short term (here, zero to three months in the future) managers typically are interested in forecasts of demand for individual products or services. There is little time to react to errors in demand forecasts, so forecasts need to be as accurate as possible for planning purposes. Time-series analysis is the method most often used for short-term forecasting. It is a relatively inexpensive and accurate way to generate the large number of forecasts required.

Although causal models can be used for short-term forecasts, they are not used extensively for this purpose because they are much more costly than time-series analysis

judgment methods A qualitative method that translates the opinions of managers, expert opinions, consumer surveys and sales-force estimates into quantitative estimates.

causal methods A quantitative method that uses historical data on independent variables, such as promotional campaigns, economic conditions, and competitors' actions to predict demand.

time-series analysis A statistical approach that relies heavily on historical demand data to project the future size of demand and recognizes trends and seasonal patterns.

When are time-series methods best and when are causal or judgment methods best?

TABLE 12.1

Demand Forecast Applications

Application	Time Horizon		
	Short Term (0–3 months)	Medium Term (3 months–2 years)	Long Term (more than 2 years)
Forecast quantity	Individual products or services	Total sales Groups or families of products or services	Total sales
Decision area	Inventory management Final assembly scheduling Workforce scheduling Master production scheduling	Staff planning Production planning Master production scheduling Purchasing Distribution	Facility location Capacity planning Process management
Forecasting technique	Time series Causal Judgment	Causal Judgment	Causal Judgment

and require more time to develop. In the short term, operations managers rarely can wait for development of causal models, even though they may be more accurate than time-series models. Finally, managers use judgment methods for short-term forecasts when historical data are not available for a specific item, such as a new product. However, these forecast techniques also are more expensive than forecasts generated from time-series analysis.

MEDIUM TERM. The time horizon for the medium term is three months to two years into the future. The need for medium-term forecasts relates to capacity planning. The level of forecast detail required is not as great as for the short term. Managers typically forecast total sales demand in dollars or in the number of units of a group (or family) of similar products or services. Causal models are commonly used for medium-term forecasts. These models typically do a good job of estimating the timing of turning points, as when slow sales growth will turn into rapid decline, which is useful to operations managers in both the medium and the long term.

Some judgment methods of forecasting also are helpful in identifying turning points. As we mentioned earlier, however, they are most often used when no historical data exist. Time-series analysis typically does not yield accurate results in the medium or long term primarily because it assumes that existing patterns will continue in the future. Although this assumption may be valid for the short term, it is less accurate over longer time horizons.

LONG TERM. For time horizons exceeding two years, forecasts usually are developed for total sales demand in dollars or some other common unit of measurement (e.g., barrels, pounds, or kilowatts). Accurate long-term forecasts of demand for individual products or services not only are very difficult to make but also are too detailed for long-range planning purposes. Three types of decisions—facility location, capacity planning, and process choice—require market demand estimates for an extended period into the future. Causal models and judgment methods are the primary techniques used for long-term forecasting. However, even mathematically derived causal-model forecasts have to be tempered by managerial experience and judgment because of the time horizon involved and the potential consequences of decisions based on them.

FORECASTING WITH COMPUTERS

In many short-term forecasting applications, computers are a necessity. Often, companies must prepare forecasts for hundreds or even thousands of products or services repeatedly. For example, a large network of health care facilities must calculate demand forecasts for each of its services for every department. This undertaking involves voluminous data that must be manipulated frequently. Analysts must examine the time series for each product or service and arrive at a forecast. However, as Managerial Practice 12.1 demonstrates, new software can ease the burden of coordinating forecasts between retailers and suppliers.

Many forecasting software packages are available for all sizes of computers and offer a wide variety of forecasting capabilities and report formats. As you will learn when we discuss forecasting techniques, the most arduous task associated with developing a good forecasting model is "fitting" it to the data. This task involves determining the values of certain model parameters so that the forecasts are as accurate as possible. Software packages provide varying degrees of assistance in this regard. The three categories of software packages (Yurkiewicz, 2000) are

1. *manual systems,* whereby the user chooses the forecasting technique and specifies the parameters needed for a specific forecasting model;

MANAGERIAL PRACTICE 12.1
Wal-Mart Uses the Internet to Improve Forecast Performance

Wal-Mart has long been known for its careful analysis of cash register receipts and working with suppliers to reduce inventories. However, like many other major retailers, it does not share its forecasts with its suppliers. The result is forecast errors as much as 60 percent of actual demand. Retailers order more than they need in order to avoid product shortages and lost sales, and suppliers produce more than they can sell. This behavior contributes to the costly effects of materials flow dynamics in supply chains (see the Supply-Chain Management chapter). ⓢ

To combat the ill effects of forecast errors on inventories, Benchmarking Partners, Inc., with funding from Wal-Mart, IBM, SAP, and Manugistics, has developed a software package called CFAR (pronounced "see far"), which stands for "collaborative forecasting and replenishment." A key benefit of the package is the capability of providing more reliable medium-term forecasts. The system allows manufacturers and merchants to work together on forecasts by using the Internet rather than fax or phone, which would be a heavy burden with the thousands of items stocked at each store requiring weekly forecasts.

The system works in the following way. A retailer and a manufacturer independently calculate the demand they expect for a product six months into the future, taking into consideration factors such as past sales trends and promotion plans. They then exchange their forecasts over the Internet. If the forecasts differ by more than a predetermined percent (such as 10 percent), the retailer and the manufacturer use the Internet to exchange written comments and supporting data. The parties go through as many cycles as it takes to converge on an acceptable forecast. This iterative process may take additional effort, but the potential payoff in working capital savings is great. For example, in the U.S. economy alone, such coordination could save as much as $179 billion in inventory investment.

Wal-Mart has initiated CFAR with Warner-Lambert, the manufacturer of Listerine. Procter & Gamble and some 20 other large companies will also use the system. Although CFAR is in its infancy and is still unproven, it warrants careful consideration because it represents an approach that will likely become more prevalent in the future.

Source: "Clearing the Cobwebs from the Stockroom." *Business Week* (October 21, 1996), p. 140.

2. *semiautomatic systems*, whereby the user specifies the forecasting technique but the software determines the parameters for the model so that the most accurate forecasts are provided; and

3. *automatic systems*, whereby the software examines the data and suggests not only the appropriate technique but also the best parameters for the model.

Software packages for forecasting typically can read data inputs from spreadsheet files, plot graphs of the data and the forecasts, and save forecast files for spreadsheet display of results. The prices of these programs range from $150 to more than $10,000, depending on the data analysis functions they provide. The design of these programs for personal computers and their relatively low price place these packages within the reach of any business.

Marketing and operations usually select a forecasting software package jointly. Typically, an implementation team consisting of marketing and operations staff is charged with selecting a package from the wide variety available. Team members may ask their departments for a "wish list" and then categorize the wishes as "musts" and "wants". Final selection is based on (1) how well the package satisfies the musts and wants, (2) the cost of buying or leasing the package, (3) the level of clerical support required, and (4) the amount of programmer maintenance required.

JUDGMENT METHODS

When adequate historical data are lacking, as when a new product is introduced or technology is expected to change, firms rely on managerial judgment and experience to generate forecasts. Judgment methods can also be used to modify forecasts generated by quantitative methods, as is done with Lucent's forecasting process. In this section, we discuss four of the more successful methods currently in use: sales-force estimates, executive opinion, market research, and the Delphi method.

SALES-FORCE ESTIMATES

Sometimes the best information about future demand comes from the people closest to the customer. **Sales-force estimates** are forecasts compiled from estimates of future demands made periodically by members of a company's sales force. This approach has several advantages.

> How can reasonable forecasts be obtained when no historical information is available?

sales-force estimates
The forecasts that are compiled from estimates of future demands made periodically by members of a company's sales force.

- ❏ The sales force is the group most likely to know which products or services customers will be buying in the near future, and in what quantities.
- ❏ Sales territories often are divided by district or region. Information broken down in this manner can be useful for inventory management, distribution, and sales-force staffing purposes.
- ❏ The forecasts of individual sales-force members can be combined easily to get regional or national sales.

But it also has several disadvantages.

- ❏ Individual biases of the salespeople may taint the forecast; moreover, some people are naturally optimistic, others more cautious.
- ❏ Salespeople may not always be able to detect the difference between what a customer "wants" (a wish list) and what a customer "needs" (a necessary purchase).
- ❏ If the firm uses individual sales as a performance measure, salespeople may underestimate their forecasts so that their performance will look good when they exceed their projections or may work hard only until they reach their required minimum sales.

EXECUTIVE OPINION

executive opinion A forecasting method in which the opinions, experience, and technical knowledge of one or more managers are summarized to arrive at a single forecast.

technological forecasting An application of executive opinion in light of the difficulties in keeping abreast of the latest advances in technology.

When a new product or service is contemplated, the sales force may not be able to make accurate demand estimates. **Executive opinion** is a forecasting method in which the opinions, experience, and technical knowledge of one or more managers are summarized to arrive at a single forecast. As we discuss later, executive opinion can be used to modify an existing sales forecast to account for unusual circumstances, such as a new sales promotion or unexpected international events. Executive opinion can also be used for **technological forecasting**. The quick pace of technological change makes keeping abreast of the latest advances difficult (see the Managing Technology chapter).

This method of forecasting has several disadvantages. Executive opinion can be costly because it takes valuable executive time. Although that may be warranted under certain circumstances, it sometimes gets out of control. In addition, if executives are allowed to modify a forecast without collectively agreeing to the changes, the resulting forecast will not be useful. For example, suppose that the marketing manager sees the sales-force estimates and, feeling a bit more optimistic than the sales force, increases the forecast to ensure the availability of enough product. After receiving the market forecasts, the manufacturing manager further increases the forecast to avoid being blamed for not meeting customer demand. When actual sales are much lower than the forecasts, everyone blames someone else for the extra inventory that was created. Hence, the key to effective use of executive opinion is to ensure that the forecast reflects not a series of independent modifications but consensus among executives on a single forecast.

MARKET RESEARCH

market research A systematic approach to determine consumer interest in a product or service by creating and testing hypotheses through data-gathering surveys.

Market research is a systematic approach to determine consumer interest in a product or service by creating and testing hypotheses through data-gathering surveys. Conducting a market research study includes

1. designing a questionnaire that requests economic and demographic information from each person interviewed and asks whether the interviewee would be interested in the product or service;
2. deciding how to administer the survey, whether by telephone polling, mailings, or personal interviews;
3. selecting a representative sample of households to survey, which should include a random selection within the market area of the proposed product or service; and
4. analyzing the information using judgment and statistical tools to interpret the responses, determine their adequacy, make allowance for economic or competitive factors not included in the questionnaire, and analyze whether the survey represents a random sample of the potential market.

Market research may be used to forecast demand for the short, medium, and long term. Accuracy is excellent for the short term, good for the medium term, and only fair for the long term. Although market research yields important information, one shortcoming is the numerous qualifications and hedges typically included in the findings. For example, a finding might be "The new diet burger product received good customer acceptance in our survey; however, we were unable to assess its longer-term acceptance once other competitor products make their appearance." Another is that the typical response rate for mailed questionnaires is poor (30 percent is often considered high). Yet another shortcoming is the possibility that the survey results do not reflect the opinions of the market. Finally, the survey might produce imitative, rather than innovative, ideas because the customer's reference point is often limited.

DELPHI METHOD

delphi method A process of gaining consensus from a group of experts while maintaining their anonymity.

The **Delphi method** is a process of gaining consensus from a group of experts while maintaining their anonymity. This form of forecasting is useful when there are no historical data from which to develop statistical models and when managers inside the firm have no experience on which to base informed projections. A coordinator sends questions to each member of the group of outside experts, who may not even know who else is participating. Anonymity is important when some members of the group tend to dominate discussion or command a high degree of respect in their fields. In an anonymous group, the members tend to respond to the questions and support their responses freely. The coordinator prepares a statistical summary of the responses along with a summary of arguments for particular responses. The report is sent to the same group for another round, and the participants may choose to modify their previous responses. These rounds continue until consensus is obtained.

The Delphi method can be used to develop long-range forecasts of product demand and new-product sales projections. It can also be used for technological forecasting. The Delphi method can be used to obtain a consensus from a panel of experts who can devote their attention to following scientific advances, changes in society, governmental regulations, and the competitive environment. The results can provide direction for a firm's research and development staff.

The Delphi method has some shortcomings, including the following major ones:

❏ The process can take a long time (sometimes a year or more). During that time, the panel of people considered to be experts may change, confounding the results or at least further lengthening the process.

❏ Responses may be less meaningful than if experts were accountable for their responses.

❏ There is little evidence that Delphi forecasts achieve high degrees of accuracy. However, they are known to be fair to good in identifying turning points in new-product demand.

❏ Poorly designed questionnaires will result in ambiguous or false conclusions.

These shortcomings should be carefully considered before the Delphi method is used.

GUIDELINES FOR USING JUDGMENT FORECASTS

Judgment forecasting is clearly needed when no quantitative data are available to use quantitative forecasting approaches. However, judgment approaches can be used in concert with quantitative approaches to improve forecast quality. Among the guidelines for the use of judgment to adjust the results of quantitative forecasts are the following (Sanders and Ritzman, 1992):

❏ *Adjust Quantitative Forecasts When Their Track Record Is Poor and the Decision Maker Has Important Contextual Knowledge.*   Contextual knowledge is knowledge that practitioners gain through experience, such as cause-and-effect relationships, environmental cues, and organizational information, that may have an effect on the variable being forecast. Often, these factors cannot be incorporated into quantitative forecasting approaches. The quality of forecasts generated by quantitative approaches also deteriorates as the variability of the data increases, particularly for time series. The more variable the data, the more likely it is that judgment forecasting will improve the forecasts. Consequently, the decision maker can bring valuable contextual information to the forecasting process when the quantitative approaches alone are inadequate.

❏ *Make Adjustments to Quantitative Forecasts to Compensate for Specific Events.*   Specific events such as advertising campaigns, the actions of competitors, or international developments often are not recognized in quantitative forecasting and should be acknowledged when a final forecast is being made.

In the remainder of this chapter, we focus on the commonly used quantitative forecasting approaches.

CAUSAL METHODS: LINEAR REGRESSION

Causal methods are used when historical data are available and the relationship between the factor to be forecasted and other external or internal factors (e.g., government actions or advertising promotions) can be identified. These relationships are expressed in mathematical terms and can be very complex. Causal methods provide the most sophisticated forecasting tools and are very good for predicting turning points in demand and preparing long-range forecasts. Although many causal methods are available, we focus here on linear regression, one of the best-known and most commonly used causal methods.

linear regression A causal method in which one variable (the dependent variable) is related to one or more independent variables by a linear equation.

In **linear regression,** one variable, called a **dependent variable,** is related to one or more **independent variables** by a linear equation. The dependent variable, such as demand for doorknobs, is the one the manager wants to forecast. The independent variables, such as advertising expenditures and new housing starts, are assumed to affect the dependent variable and thereby "cause" the results observed in the past. Figure 12.2 shows how a linear regression line relates to the data. In technical terms, the regression line minimizes the squared deviations from the actual data.

In the simplest linear regression models, the dependent variable is a function of only one independent variable, and therefore the theoretical relationship is a straight line:

$$Y = a + bX$$

dependent variable The variable that one wants to forecast.

where

Y = dependent variable

X = independent variable

a = Y-intercept of the line

b = slope of the line

independent variables Variables that are assumed to affect the dependent variable and thereby "cause" the results observed in the past.

The objective of linear regression analysis is to find values of a and b that minimize the sum of the squared deviations of the actual data points from the graphed line. Computer programs are used for this purpose. For any set of matched observations for Y and X, the program computes the values of a and b and provides measures of forecast accuracy. Three measures commonly reported are the sample correlation coefficient, the sample coefficient of determination, and the standard error of the estimate.

The *sample correlation coefficient, r,* measures the direction and strength of the relationship between the independent variable and the dependent variable. The value of r can range from -1.00 to $+1.00$. A correlation coefficient of $+1.00$ implies that period-by-period changes in direction (increases or decreases) of the independent variable are always accompanied by changes in the same direction by the dependent variable. An r of -1.00 means that decreases in the independent variable are always accompanied by increases in the dependent variable, and vice versa. A zero value of r

FIGURE 12.2

Linear Regression Line Relative to Actual Data

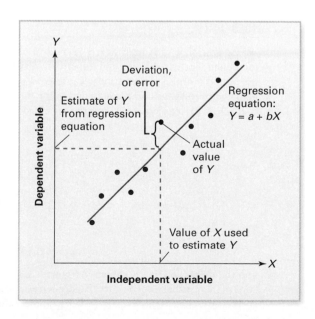

means that there is no relationship between the variables. The closer the value of r is to ± 1.00, the better the regression line fits the points.

The *sample coefficient of determination* measures the amount of variation in the dependent variable about its mean that is explained by the regression line. The coefficient of determination is the square of the correlation coefficient, or r^2. The value of r^2 ranges from 0.00 to 1.00. Regression equations with a value of r^2 close to 1.00 are desirable because the variations in the dependent variable and the forecast generated by the regression equation are closely related.

The *standard error of the estimate, s_{yx}*, measures how closely the data on the dependent variable cluster around the regression line. Although it is similar to the sample standard deviation, it measures the error from the dependent variable, Y, to the regression line, rather than to the mean. Thus, it is the standard deviation of the difference between the actual demand and the estimate provided by the regression equation. When determining which independent variable to include in the regression equation, you should choose the one with the smallest standard error of the estimate.

EXAMPLE 12.1   *Using Linear Regression to Forecast Product Demand*

The person in charge of production scheduling for a company must prepare forecasts of product demand in order to plan for appropriate production quantities. During a luncheon meeting, the marketing manager gives her information about the advertising budget for a brass door hinge. The following are sales and advertising data for the past five months:

MONTH	SALES (thousands of units)	ADVERTISING (thousands of $)
1	264	2.5
2	116	1.3
3	165	1.4
4	101	1.0
5	209	2.0

The marketing manager says that next month the company will spend $1,750 on advertising for the product. Use linear regression to develop an equation and a forecast for this product.

SOLUTION

We assume that sales are linearly related to advertising expenditures. In other words, sales are the dependent variable, Y, and advertising expenditures are the independent variable, X. Using the paired monthly observations of sales and advertising expenditures supplied by the marketing manager, we use the computer to determine the best values of a, b, the correlation coefficient, the coefficient of determination, and the standard error of the estimate.

$$a = -8.137$$
$$b = 109.230X$$
$$r = 0.980$$
$$r^2 = 0.960$$
$$s_{yx} = 15.603$$

The regression equation is

$$Y = -8.137 + 109.230X$$

and the regression line is shown in Figure 12.3.

Are advertising expenditures a good choice to use in forecasting sales? Note that the sample correlation coefficient, r, is 0.98. Because the value of r is very close to 1.00, we conclude that

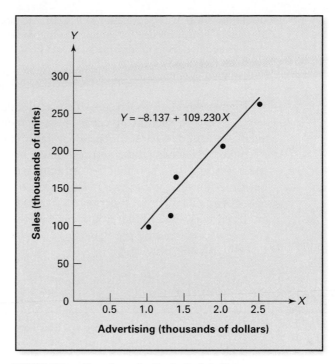

FIGURE 12.3 • Linear Regression Line for the Sales Data

there is a strong positive relationship between sales and advertising expenditures and that the choice was a good one.

Next, we examine the sample coefficient of determination, r^2, or 0.96. This value of r^2 implies that 96 percent of the variation in sales is explained by advertising expenditures. Most relationships between advertising and sales in practice are not this strong because other variables such as general economic conditions and the strategies of competitors often combine to affect sales.

As the advertising expenditure will be $1,750, the forecast for month 6 is

$$Y = -8.137 + 109.230(1.75)$$
$$= 183.016 \quad \text{or} \quad 183,016 \text{ units}$$

OM Explorer confirms these calculations and the forecast for month 6, as Figure 12.4 shows.

Solver - Regression Analysis

R-squared	0.960
R	0.980
Constant	-8.137
Standard Error of Estimate	15.603
Trial X1 Value	1.75

X1 Coefficient	109.230
Predicted Y Value	183.016

FIGURE 12.4

Decision Point The production scheduler can use this forecast to determine the quantity of brass door hinges needed for month 6. Suppose that she has 62,500 units in stock. The requirement to be filled from production is $183,015 - 62,500 = 120,015$ units, assuming that she does not want to lose any sales. □

Regression analysis can provide useful guidance for important operations management decisions, such as inventory management, capacity planning, and process management. Often, several independent variables may affect the dependent variable. For example, advertising expenditures, new corporation startups, and residential building contracts may be important for estimating the demand for door hinges. In such cases, *multiple regression analysis* is helpful in determining a forecasting equation for the dependent variable as a function of several independent variables. Such models can be analyzed with OM Explorer and can be quite useful for predicting turning points and solving many planning problems.

TIME-SERIES METHODS

Rather than using independent variables for the forecast as regression models do, time-series methods use historical information regarding only the dependent variable. These methods are based on the assumption that the dependent variable's past pattern will continue in the future. Time-series analysis identifies the underlying patterns of demand that combine to produce an observed historical pattern of the dependent variable and then develops a model to replicate it. In this section, we focus on time-series methods that address the horizontal, trend, and seasonal patterns of demand. Before we discuss statistical methods, let us take a look at the simplest time-series method for addressing all patterns of demand—the naive forecast.

NAIVE FORECAST

naive forecast A time-series method whereby the forecast for the next period equals the demand for the current period.

A method often used in practice is the **naive forecast,** whereby the forecast for the next period equals the demand for the current period. So, if the actual demand for Wednesday is 35 customers, the forecasted demand for Thursday is 35 customers. If the actual demand on Thursday is 42 customers, the forecasted demand for Friday is 42 customers.

The naive-forecast method may take into account a demand trend. The increase (or decrease) in demand observed between the last two periods is used to adjust the current demand to arrive at a forecast. Suppose that last week the demand was 120 units and the week before it was 108 units. Demand increased 12 units in one week, so the forecast for next week would be $120 + 12 = 132$ units. If the actual demand next week turned out to be 127 units, the next forecast would be $127 + 7 = 134$ units. The naive-forecast method also may be used to account for seasonal patterns. If the demand last July was 50,000 units, the forecast for this July is 50,000 units. Similarly, forecasts of demand for each month of the coming year may simply reflect actual demand in the same month last year.

The advantages of the naive-forecast method are its simplicity and low cost. The method works best when the horizontal, trend, or seasonal patterns are stable and random variation is small. If random variation is large, using last period's demand to estimate next period's demand can result in highly variable forecasts that are not useful for planning purposes. Nonetheless, if its level of accuracy is acceptable, the naive forecast is an attractive approach for time-series forecasting.

ESTIMATING THE AVERAGE

Every demand time series has at least two of the five patterns of demand: horizontal and random. It *may* have trend, seasonal, or cyclical patterns. We begin our discussion of statistical methods of time-series forecasting with demand that has no trend, seasonal, or cyclical patterns. The horizontal pattern in a time series is based on the mean of the demands, so we focus on forecasting methods that estimate the average of a time series of data. Consequently, for all the methods of forecasting we discuss in this section, the forecast of demand for *any* period in the future is the average of the time series computed in the current period. For example, if the average of past demand calculated on Tuesday is 65 customers, the forecasts for Wednesday, Thursday, and Friday are 65 customers each day.

Consider Figure 12.5, which shows patient arrivals at a medical clinic over the past 28 weeks. Assume that the demand pattern for patient arrivals has no trend, seasonal, or cyclical pattern. The time series has only a horizontal and random pattern. As no one can predict random error, we focus on estimating the average. The statistical techniques useful for forecasting such a time series are (1) simple moving averages, (2) weighted moving averages, and (3) exponential smoothing.

simple moving average method A time-series method used to estimate the average of a demand time series by averaging the demand for the *n* most recent time periods.

SIMPLE MOVING AVERAGES. The **simple moving average method** is used to estimate the average of a demand time series and thereby remove the effects of random fluctuation. It is most useful when demand has no pronounced trend or seasonal influences. Applying a moving average model simply involves calculating the average demand for the *n* most recent time periods and using it as the forecast for the next time period. For the next period, after the demand is known, the oldest demand from the previous average is replaced with the most recent demand and the average is recalculated. In this way, the *n* most recent demands are used, and the average "moves" from period to period.

Specifically, the forecast for period $t + 1$, can be calculated as

$$F_{t+1} = \frac{\text{Sum of last } n \text{ demands}}{n} = \frac{D_t + D_{t-1} + D_{t-2} + \cdots + D_{t-n+1}}{n}$$

where

$$D_t = \text{actual demand in period } t$$
$$n = \text{total number of periods in the average}$$
$$F_{t+1} = \text{forecast for period } t + 1$$

Weekly Patient Arrivals at a Medical Clinic

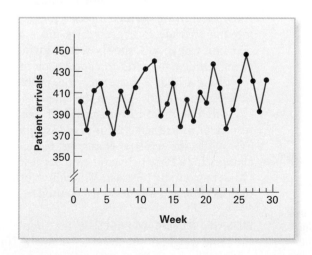

With the moving average method, the forecast of next period's demand equals the average calculated at the end of this period.

<table>
<tr><td>**EXAMPLE 12.2**</td><td>*Using the Moving Average Method to Estimate Average Demand*</td></tr>
</table>

**TUTOR
12.1**

a. Compute a *three-week* moving average forecast for the arrival of medical clinic patients in week 4. The numbers of arrivals for the past three weeks were

WEEK	PATIENT ARRIVALS
1	400
2	380
3	411

b. If the actual number of patient arrivals in week 4 is 415, what is the forecast for week 5?

SOLUTION

a. The moving average forecast at the end of week 3 is

$$F_4 = \frac{411 + 380 + 400}{3} = 397.0$$

b. The forecast for week 5 requires the actual arrivals from weeks 2–4, the three most recent weeks of data.

$$F_5 = \frac{415 + 411 + 380}{3} = 402.0$$

Decision Point Thus, the forecast at the end of week 3 would have been 397 patients for week 4. The forecast for week 5, made at the end of week 4, would have been 402 patients. In addition, at the end of week 4 the forecast for week 6 and beyond is also 402 patients. ◻

The moving average method may involve the use of as many periods of past demand as desired. The stability of the demand series generally determines how many periods to include (i.e., the value of n). Stable demand series are those for which the average (to be estimated by the forecasting method) only infrequently experiences changes. Large values of n should be used for demand series that are stable and small values of n for those that are susceptible to changes in the underlying average.

Consider Figure 12.6, which compares actual patient arrivals to a three-week and a six-week moving average forecast for the medical clinic data. Note that the three-week moving average forecast varies more and reacts more quickly to large swings in demand. Conversely, the six-week moving average forecast is more stable because large swings in demand tend to cancel each other. We defer discussion of which of the two forecast methods is better for this problem until we discuss the criteria for choosing time-series methods later in the chapter.

Including more historical data in the average by increasing the number of periods results in a forecast that is less susceptible to random variations. If the underlying average in the series is changing, however, the forecasts will tend to lag behind the changes for a longer time interval because of the additional time required to remove the old data from the forecast. We address other considerations in the choice of n when we discuss choosing a time-series method.

weighted moving average method A time-series method in which each historical demand in the average can have its own weight; the sum of the weights is equal to 1.0.

WEIGHTED MOVING AVERAGES. In the simple moving average method, each demand has the same weight in the average—namely, $1/n$. In the **weighted moving average method,**

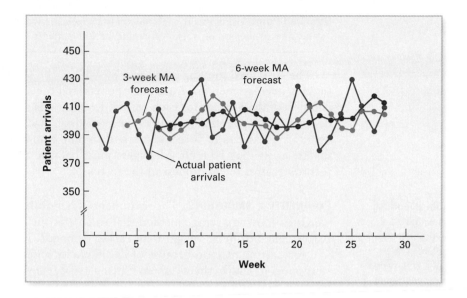

FIGURE 12.6

Comparison of Three- and Six-Week Moving Average Forecasts

each historical demand in the average can have its own weight. The sum of the weights equals 1.0. For example, in a *three-period* weighted moving average model, the most recent period might be assigned a weight of 0.50, the second most recent might be weighted 0.30, and the third most recent might be weighted 0.20. The average is obtained by multiplying the weight of each period by the value for that period and adding the products together:

$$F_{t+1} = 0.50D_t + 0.30D_{t-1} + 0.20D_{t-2}$$

The advantage of a weighted moving average method is that it allows you to emphasize recent demand over earlier demand. The forecast will be more responsive than the simple moving average forecast to changes in the underlying average of the demand series. Nonetheless, the weighted moving average forecast will still lag behind demand because it merely averages *past* demands. This lag is especially noticeable with a trend because the average of the time series is systematically increasing or decreasing.

EXAMPLE 12.3

Using the Weighted Moving Average Method to Estimate Average Demand

The analyst for the medical clinic has assigned weights of 0.70 to the most recent demand, 0.20 to the demand one week ago, and 0.10 to the demand two weeks ago. Use the data for the first three weeks from Example 12.2 to calculate the weighted moving average forecast for week 4.

SOLUTION

**TUTOR
12.2**

The average demand in week 3 is

$$F_4 = 0.70(411) + 0.20(380) + 0.10(400) = 403.7$$

Patients cannot be divided into fractions, so we round the answer to the nearest whole number. The forecast for week 4 therefore is 404 patients.

Now suppose that the actual demand for week 4 is 415 patients. The new average and the forecast for week 5 would be

$$F_5 = 0.70(415) + 0.20(411) + 0.10(380) = 410.7$$

Rounding up, the forecast for week 5 is 411 patients.

Decision Point Using this model, the analyst's forecast would have been 404 patients for week 4, and then at the end of week 4, it would be 411 patients for week 5 and beyond. ◻

The weighted moving average method has the same shortcomings as the simple moving average method: Data must be retained for n periods of demand to allow calculation of the average for each period. Keeping this amount of data is not a great burden in simple situations, such as the preceding three- and six-week examples. For a company that has to forecast many different demands, however, data storage and update costs may be high. Managers must balance the cost of keeping such detailed records against the usefulness of the forecasts.

exponential smoothing method A weighted moving average method that calculates the average of a time series by giving recent demands more weight than earlier demands.

EXPONENTIAL SMOOTHING. The **exponential smoothing method** is a sophisticated weighted moving average method that calculates the average of a time series by giving recent demands more weight than earlier demands. It is the most frequently used formal forecasting method because of its simplicity and the small amount of data needed to support it. Unlike the weighted moving average method, which requires n periods of past demand and n weights, exponential smoothing requires only three items of data: the last period's forecast; the demand for this period; and a smoothing parameter, alpha (α), which has a value between 0 and 1.0. To obtain an exponentially smoothed forecast we simply calculate a weighted average of the most recent demand and the forecast calculated last period. The equation for the forecast is

$$F_{t+1} = \alpha(\text{Demand this period}) + (1 - \alpha)(\text{Forecast calculated last period})$$
$$= \alpha D_t + (1 - \alpha)F_t$$

An equivalent equation is

$$F_{t+1} = F_t + \alpha(D_t - F_t)$$

This form of the equation shows that the forecast for the next period equals the forecast for the current period plus a proportion of the forecast error for the current period.

The emphasis given to the most recent demand levels can be adjusted by changing the smoothing parameter. Larger α values emphasize recent levels of demand and result in forecasts more responsive to changes in the underlying average. Smaller α values treat past demand more uniformly and result in more stable forecasts. This approach is analogous to adjusting the value of n in the moving average methods, except there smaller values of n emphasize recent demand and larger values give greater weight to past demand. In practice, various values of α are tried and the one producing the best forecasts is chosen. We discuss the choice of α further when we present the criteria for selecting time-series methods.

Exponential smoothing requires an initial forecast to get started. There are two ways to get this initial forecast: Either use last period's demand or, if some historical data are available, calculate the average of several recent periods of demand. The effect of the initial estimate of the average on successive estimates of the average diminishes over time because, with exponential smoothing, the weights given to successive historical demands used to calculate the average decay exponentially. We can illustrate this effect with an example. If we let $\alpha = 0.20$, the forecast for period $t + 1$ is

$$F_{t+1} = 0.20D_t + 0.80F_t$$

Using the equation for F_t, we expand the equation for F_{t+1}:

$$F_{t+1} = 0.20D_t + 0.80(0.20D_{t-1} + 0.80F_{t-1}) = 0.20D_t + 0.16D_{t-1} + 0.64F_{t-1}$$

Continuing to expand, we get

$$F_{t+1} = 0.20D_t + 0.16D_{t-1} + 0.128D_{t-2} + 0.1024D_{t-3} + \cdots$$

Eventually, the weights of demands many periods ago approach zero. As with the weighted moving average method, the sum of the weights must equal 1.0, which is implicit in the exponential smoothing equation.

EXAMPLE 12.4   *Using Exponential Smoothing to Estimate Average Demand*

Again consider the patient arrival data in Example 12.2. It is now the end of week 3. Using $\alpha = 0.10$, calculate the exponential smoothing forecast for week 4.

SOLUTION

TUTOR 12.3

The exponential smoothing method requires an initial forecast. Suppose that we take the demand data for the past two weeks and average them, obtaining $(400 + 380)/2 = 390$ as an initial forecast. To obtain the forecast for week 4, using exponential smoothing with $\alpha = 0.10$, we calculate the average at the end of week 3 as

$$F_4 = 0.10(411) + 0.90(390) = 392.1$$

Thus, the forecast for week 4 would be 392 patients. If the actual demand for week 4 proved to be 415, the new forecast for week 5 would be

$$F_5 = 0.10(415) + 0.90(392.1) = 394.4$$

or 394 patients. Note that we used F_4, not the integer-value forecast for week 4, in the computation for F_5. In general, we round off (when it is appropriate) only the final result to maintain as much accuracy as possible in the calculations.

Decision Point Using this exponential smoothing model, the analyst's forecasts would have been 392 patients for week 4 and then 394 patients for week 5 and beyond. As soon as the actual demand for week 5 is known, then the forecast for week 6 will be updated. ☐

Exponential smoothing has the advantages of simplicity and minimal data requirements. It is inexpensive to use and therefore very attractive to firms that make thousands of forecasts for each time period. However, its simplicity also is a disadvantage when the underlying average is changing, as in the case of a demand series with a trend. Like any method geared solely to the assumption of a stable average, exponential smoothing results will lag behind changes in the underlying average of demand. Higher α values may help reduce forecast errors when there is a change in the average of the time series; however, the lags will still be there if the average is changing systematically. Typically, if large α values (e.g., >0.50) are required for an exponential smoothing application, chances are good that a more sophisticated model is needed because of a significant trend or seasonal influence in the demand series.

INCLUDING A TREND

Let's now consider a demand time series that has a trend. Although several forecasting methods that recognize a trend are available, we focus on exponential smoothing because it is so widely used in practice.

A trend in a time series is a systematic increase or decrease in the average of the series over time. Where a trend is present, exponential smoothing approaches must be modified; otherwise, the forecasts always will be below or above the actual demand. For example, assume that actual demand is steadily increasing at 10 units per period. Forecasts using exponential smoothing with $\alpha = 0.3$ will lag severely behind the actual demand even if the first forecast is perfect, as the following table shows:

	ACTUAL DEMAND IN PERIOD T	FORECAST FOR PERIOD T
1	10	$F_1 = 10$
2	20	$F_2 = 0.30(10) + 0.70(10) = 10$
3	30	$F_3 = 0.30(20) + 0.70(10) = 13$
4	40	$F_4 = 0.30(30) + 0.70(13) = 18.1$

To improve the forecast we need to calculate an estimate of the trend. We start by calculating the *current* estimate of the trend, which is the difference between the average of the series computed in the current period and the average computed last period. To obtain an estimate of the long-term trend, you can average the current estimates. The method for estimating a trend is similar to that used for estimating the demand average with exponential smoothing.

The method for incorporating a trend in an exponentially smoothed forecast is called the **trend-adjusted exponential smoothing method**. With this approach the estimates for both the average and the trend are smoothed, requiring two smoothing constants. For each period, we calculate the average and the trend:

trend-adjusted exponential smoothing method The method for incorporating a trend in an exponentially smoothed forecast.

$$A_t = \alpha(\text{Demand this period}) + (1 - \alpha)(\text{Average} + \text{Trend estimate last period})$$
$$= \alpha D_t + (1 - \alpha)(A_{t-1} + T_{t-1})$$
$$T_t = \beta(\text{Average this period} - \text{Average last period})$$
$$+ (1 - \beta)(\text{Trend estimate last period})$$
$$= \beta(A_t - A_{t-1}) + (1 - \beta)T_{t-1}$$
$$F_{t+1} = A_t + T_t$$

where

A_t = exponentially smoothed average of the series in period t

T_t = exponentially smoothed average of the trend in period t

α = smoothing parameter for the average, with a value between 0 and 1

β = smoothing parameter for the trend, with a value between 0 and 1

F_{t+1} = forecast for period $t + 1$

Estimates for last period's average and trend needed for the first forecast can be derived from past data or based on an educated guess if no historical data exist. To find values for α and β, often an analyst systematically adjusts α and β until the forecast errors are lowest. This process can be carried out in an experimental setting with the model used to forecast historical demands.

EXAMPLE 12.5

Using Trend-Adjusted Exponential Smoothing to Forecast a Demand Series with a Trend

Medanalysis, Inc., provides medical laboratory services to patients of Health Providers, a group of 10 family-practice doctors associated with a new health maintenance program. Managers are interested in forecasting the number of patients requesting blood analysis per week. Supplies must be purchased and a decision made regarding the number of blood samples to be sent to another laboratory because of capacity limitations at the main laboratory. Recent

TUTOR
12.4

publicity about the damaging effects of cholesterol on the heart has caused a national increase in requests for standard blood tests. Medanalysis ran an average of 28 blood tests per week during the past four weeks. The trend over that period was 3 additional patients per week. This week's demand was for 27 blood tests. We use $\alpha = 0.20$ and $\beta = 0.20$ to calculate the forecast for next week.

SOLUTION

$$A_0 = 28 \text{ patients} \qquad \text{and} \qquad T_0 = 3 \text{ patients}$$

The forecast for week 2 (next week) is

$$A_1 = 0.20(27) + 0.80(28 + 3) = 30.2$$
$$T_1 = 0.20(30.2 - 28) + 0.80(3) = 2.8$$
$$F_2 = 30.2 + 2.8 = 33 \text{ blood tests}$$

If the actual number of blood tests requested in week 2 proved to be 44, the updated forecast for week 3 would be

$$A_2 = 0.20(44) + 0.80(30.2 + 2.8) = 35.2$$
$$T_2 = 0.2(35.2 - 30.2) + 0.80(2.8) = 3.2$$
$$F_3 = 35.2 + 3.2 = 38.4, \qquad \text{or} \qquad 38 \text{ blood tests}$$

Decision Point Using this trend-adjusted exponential smoothing model, the forecast for week 2 was 33 blood tests, and then 38 blood tests for week 3. If the analyst makes forecasts at the end of week 2 for periods beyond week 3, the forecast would be even greater because of the upward trend estimated to be 3.2 blood tests per week. ❐

Figure 12.7 shows the trend-adjusted forecast (the blue line) for Medanalysis for a period of 15 weeks. At the end of each week, we calculated a forecast for the next week, using the number of blood tests for the current week. Note that the forecasts (shown in the following tables) vary less than actual demand because of the smoothing effect of the procedure for calculating the estimates for the average and the trend. By adjusting α and β, we may be able to come up with a better forecast.

FIGURE 12.7

Trend-Adjusted Forecast for Medanalysis

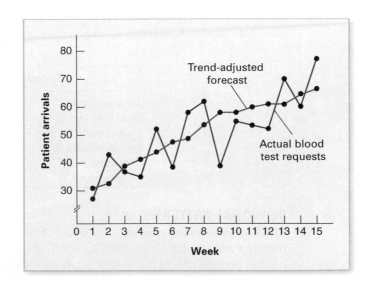

is 400/500 = 0.80, which indicates that March's demand is 20 percent below the average demand per month. Similarly, a seasonal index of 1.14 for April implies that April's demand is 14 percent greater than the average demand per month.

3. Calculate the average seasonal index for each season, using the results from step 2. Add the seasonal indices for a season and divide by the number of years of data. For example, suppose that we have calculated three seasonal indices for April: 1.14, 1.18, and 1.04. The average seasonal index for April is (1.14 + 1.18 + 1.04)/3 = 1.12. This is the index we will use for forecasting April's demand.

4. Calculate each season's forecast for next year. Begin by estimating the average demand per season for next year. Use the naive method, moving averages, exponential smoothing, trend-adjusted exponential smoothing, or linear regression to forecast annual demand. Divide annual demand by the number of seasons per year. Then obtain the seasonal forecast by multiplying the seasonal index by the average demand per season.

Using the Multiplicative Seasonal Method to Forecast the Number of Customers

EXAMPLE 12.6

The manager of the Stanley Steemer carpet cleaning company needs a quarterly forecast of the number of customers expected next year. The carpet cleaning business is seasonal, with a peak in the third quarter and a trough in the first quarter. Following are the quarterly demand data from the past four years:

QUARTER	YEAR 1	YEAR 2	YEAR 3	YEAR 4
1	45	70	100	100
2	335	370	585	725
3	520	590	830	1,160
4	100	170	285	215
Total	1,000	1,200	1,800	2,200

The manager wants to forecast customer demand for each quarter of year 5, based on her estimate of total year 5 demand of 2,600 customers.

SOLUTION

Step 1. The average number of customers per season is

Year 1: 1,000/4 = 250   Year 2: 1,200/4 = 300

Year 3: 1,800/4 = 450   Year 4: 2,200/4 = 550

Step 2. The seasonal indices are

QUARTER	YEAR 1	YEAR 2	YEAR 3	YEAR 4
1	45/250 = 0.18	70/300 = 0.23	100/450 = 0.22	100/550 = 0.18
2	335/250 = 1.34	370/300 = 1.23	585/450 = 1.30	725/550 = 1.32
3	520/250 = 2.08	590/300 = 1.97	830/450 = 1.84	1,160/550 = 2.11
4	100/250 = 0.40	170/300 = 0.57	285/450 = 0.63	215/550 = 0.39

Step 3. Note how the seasonal indices for each quarter fluctuate from year to year because of random effects. That is why the manager needs to compute the average seasonal index for each quarter.

QUARTER	AVERAGE SEASONAL INDEX
1	(0.18 + 0.23 + 0.22 + 0.18)/4 = 0.20
2	(1.34 + 1.23 + 1.30 + 1.32)/4 = 1.30
3	(2.08 + 1.97 + 1.84 + 2.11)/4 = 2.00
4	(0.40 + 0.57 + 0.63 + 0.39)/4 = 0.50

Step 4. Note that annual demand has been increasing by an average of 400 customers each year. The manager extends that trend and projects an annual demand in year 5 of 2,200 + 400 = 2,600 customers. Therefore, the estimated average demand per quarter is 2,600/4 = 650 customers in year 5. The manager then makes quarterly forecasts by multiplying the seasonal factors by the average demand per quarter.

QUARTER	FORECAST
1	650(0.20) = 130 customers
2	650(1.30) = 845 customers
3	650(2.00) = 1,300 customers
4	650(0.50) = 325 customers

Decision Point Using this seasonal method, the analyst makes a demand forecast as low as 130 customers in the first quarter and as high as 1,300 customers in the third quarter. The season of the year clearly makes a difference. ◻

At the end of each year, the average seasonal factor for each quarter can be updated. We calculate the average of all historical seasonal factors for that quarter or, if we want some control over the relevance of past demand patterns, we calculate a moving average or single exponentially smoothed average.

The multiplicative seasonal method gets its name from the way seasonal factors are calculated and used. Multiplying the seasonal factor by an estimate of the average period demand implies that the seasonal pattern depends on the level of demand. The peaks and valleys are more extreme when average demand is high, a situation faced most often by firms that produce goods and services having a seasonal demand. Figure 12.8(a) shows a time series with a multiplicative seasonal pattern. Note how the amplitude of the seasons increases, reflecting an upward trend in demand. The reverse occurs with a downward trend in demand. An alternative to the multiplicative seasonal method is the **additive seasonal method,** whereby seasonal forecasts are generated by adding a constant

additive seasonal method
A method in which seasonal forecasts are generated by adding a constant to the estimate of average demand per season.

FIGURE 12.8

Comparison of Seasonal Patterns

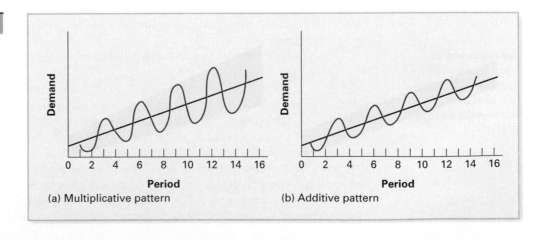

(a) Multiplicative pattern

(b) Additive pattern

(say, 50 units) to the estimate of average demand per season. This approach is based on the assumption that the seasonal pattern is constant, regardless of average demand. Figure 12.8(b) shows a time series with an additive seasonal pattern. Here, the amplitude of the seasons remains the same regardless of the level of demand.

CHOOSING A TIME-SERIES METHOD

We now turn to factors that managers must consider in selecting a method for time-series forecasting. One important consideration is forecast performance, as determined by forecast errors. Managers need to know how to measure forecast errors and how to detect when something is going wrong with the forecasting system. After examining forecast errors and their detection, we discuss criteria that managers can use to choose an appropriate time-series forecasting method.

FORECAST ERROR

Forecasts almost always contain errors. Forecast errors can be classified as either *bias errors* or *random errors*. Bias errors are the result of consistent mistakes—the forecast is always too high or too low. These errors often are the result of neglecting or not accurately estimating patterns of demand, such as a trend, seasonal, or cyclical pattern. For example, if the demand for playing time on a country club's tennis courts is steadily increasing and the club manager is using the naive forecasting method with the demand last year as the forecast for this year, the forecast will always be low because he did not take the trend into account.

The other type of forecast error, random error, results from unpredictable factors that cause the forecast to deviate from the actual demand. Forecasting analysts try to minimize the effects of bias and random errors by selecting appropriate forecasting models, but eliminating all forms of errors is impossible.

forecast error The difference found by subtracting the forecast from actual demand for a given period.

MEASURES OF FORECAST ERROR. Before they can think about minimizing forecast error, managers must have some way to measure it. **Forecast error** is simply the difference between the forecast and actual demand for a given period, or

$$E_t = D_t - F_t$$

where

$$E_t = \text{forecast error for period } t$$
$$D_t = \text{actual demand for period } t$$
$$F_t = \text{forecast for period } t$$

However, managers usually are more interested in measuring forecast error over a relatively long period of time.

The **cumulative sum of forecast errors (CFE)** measures the total forecast error:

cumulative sum of forecast errors (CFE) A measurement of the total forecast error that assesses the bias in a forecast.

$$\text{CFE} = \Sigma E_t$$

Large positive errors tend to be offset by large negative errors in the CFE measure. Nonetheless, CFE is useful in assessing bias in a forecast. For example, if a forecast is always lower than actual demand, the value of CFE will gradually get larger and larger. This increasingly large error indicates some systematic deficiency in the forecasting approach. Perhaps the analyst omitted a trend element or a cyclical pattern, or perhaps seasonal influences changed from their historical pattern. We explain later how to use CFE to develop a tracking signal to indicate when you should be concerned about forecast performance. Note that the average forecast error is simply

$$\overline{E} = \frac{\text{CFE}}{n}$$

mean squared error (MSE)
A measurement of the dispersion of forecast errors.

standard deviation (σ)
A measurement of the dispersion of forecast errors.

mean absolute deviation (MAD) A measurement of the dispersion of forecast errors.

The **mean squared error (MSE)**, standard deviation (σ), and mean absolute deviation (MAD) measure the dispersion of forecast errors:

$$\text{MSE} = \frac{\Sigma E_t^2}{n}$$

$$\sigma = \sqrt{\frac{\Sigma(E_t - \overline{E})^2}{n - 1}}$$

$$\text{MAD} = \frac{\Sigma |E_t|}{n}$$

The mathematical symbol | | is used to indicate the absolute value—that is, it tells you to disregard positive or negative signs. If MSE, σ, or MAD is small, the forecast is typically close to actual demand; a large value indicates the possibility of large forecast errors. The measures differ in the way they emphasize errors. Large errors get far more weight in MSE and σ because the errors are squared. MAD is a widely used measure of forecast error because managers can easily understand it; it is merely the mean of the forecast errors over a series of time periods, without regard to whether the error was an overestimate or an underestimate. MAD also is used in tracking signals and inventory control. Later, we discuss how MAD or σ can be used to determine safety stocks for inventory items (see the Inventory Management chapter).

mean absolute percent error (MAPE) A measurement that relates the forecast error to the level of demand and is useful for putting forecast performance in the proper perspective.

The **mean absolute percent error (MAPE)** relates the forecast error to the level of demand and is useful for putting forecast performance in the proper perspective:

$$\text{MAPE} = \frac{[\Sigma |E_t|/D_t]100}{n} \quad \text{(expressed as a percent)}$$

For example, an absolute forecast error of 100 results in a larger percentage error when the demand is 200 units than when the demand is 10,000 units.

EXAMPLE 12.7 *Calculating Forecast Error Measures*

The following table shows the actual sales of upholstered chairs for a furniture manufacturer and the forecasts made for each of the last eight months. Calculate CFE, MSE, σ, MAD, and MAPE for this product.

MONTH, t	DEMAND, D_t	FORECAST, F_t	ERROR, E_t	ERROR SQUARED, E_t^2	ABSOLUTE ERROR, $|E_t|$	ABSOLUTE PERCENT ERROR, $(|E_t|/D_t)(100)$
1	200	225	−25	625	25	12.5%
2	240	220	20	400	20	8.3
3	300	285	15	225	15	5.0
4	270	290	−20	400	20	7.4
5	230	250	−20	400	20	8.7
6	260	240	20	400	20	7.7
7	210	250	−40	1,600	40	19.0
8	275	240	35	1,225	35	12.7
		Total	−15	5,275	195	81.3%

SOLUTION

Using the formulas for the measures, we get

$$\text{Cumulative forecast error:} \qquad \text{CFE} = -15$$

$$\text{Average forecast error:} \qquad \overline{E} = \frac{\text{CFE}}{8} = -1.875$$

$$\text{Mean squared error:} \qquad \text{MSE} = \frac{\Sigma\, E_t^2}{n} = \frac{5{,}275}{8} = 659.4$$

$$\text{Standard deviation:} \qquad \sigma = \sqrt{\frac{\Sigma\,[E_t - (-1.875)]^2}{7}} = 27.4$$

$$\text{Mean absolute deviation:} \qquad \text{MAD} = \frac{\Sigma\,|E_t|}{n} = \frac{195}{8} = 24.4$$

$$\text{Mean absolute percent error:} \quad \text{MAPE} = \frac{[\Sigma\,|E_t|/D_t]\,100}{n} = \frac{81.3\%}{8} = 10.2\%$$

A CFE of -15 indicates that the forecast has a tendency to overestimate demand. The MSE, σ, and MAD statistics provide measures of forecast error variability. A MAD of 24.4 means that the average forecast error was 24.4 units in absolute value. The value of σ, 27.4, indicates that the sample distribution of forecast errors has a standard deviation of 27.4 units. A MAPE of 10.2 percent implies that, on average, the forecast error was about 10 percent of actual demand. These measures become more reliable as the number of periods of data increases.

Decision Point Although reasonably satisfied with these forecast performance results, the analyst decided to test out a few more forecasting methods before reaching a final forecasting method to use for the future. ☐

tracking signal A measure that indicates whether a method of forecasting is accurately predicting actual changes in demand.

TRACKING SIGNALS. A **tracking signal** is a measure that indicates whether a method of forecasting is accurately predicting actual changes in demand. The tracking signal measures the number of MADs represented by the cumulative sum of forecast errors, the CFE. The CFE tends to be 0 when a correct forecasting system is being used. At any time, however, random errors can cause the CFE to be a nonzero number. The tracking signal formula is

$$\text{Tracking signal} = \frac{\text{CFE}}{\text{MAD}}$$

What types of controls are needed for the forecasting system?

Each period, the CFE and MAD are updated to reflect current error, and the tracking signal is compared to some predetermined limits. The MAD can be calculated in one of two ways: (1) as the simple average of all absolute errors (as demonstrated in Example 12.7) or (2) as a weighted average determined by the exponential smoothing method:

$$\text{MAD}_t = \alpha|E_t| + (1 - \alpha)\text{MAD}_{t-1}$$

The latter approach has certain advantages. Less historical data have to be retained for each estimate. The value of α need not be the same as the value used for the forecasting model. Forecasters often use small values of α, about 0.1, to smooth the effects of recent errors relative to the past.

If forecast errors are normally distributed with a mean of 0, there is a simple relationship between σ and MAD:

$$\sigma = (\sqrt{\pi/2})(\text{MAD}) \cong 1.25(\text{MAD})$$
$$\text{MAD} = 0.7978\sigma \cong 0.8\sigma$$

where

$$\pi = 3.1416$$

This relationship allows use of the normal probability tables to specify limits for the tracking signal. If the tracking signal falls outside those limits, the forecasting model no longer is tracking demand adequately. A tracking system is useful when forecasting systems are computerized because it alerts analysts when forecasts are getting far from desirable limits. Table 12.2 shows the area of the normal probability distribution within the control limits of 1 to 4 MAD.

Figure 12.9 shows tracking signal results for 23 periods plotted in a *control chart*. The control chart is useful for determining whether any action needs to be taken to improve the forecasting model. In the example, the first 20 points cluster around 0, as we would expect if the forecasts are not biased. The CFE will tend toward 0. When the underlying characteristics of demand change but the forecasting model does not, the tracking signal eventually goes out of control. The steady increase after the 20th point in Figure 12.9 indicates that the process is going out of control. The 21st and 22nd points are acceptable, but the 23rd point is not.

Choosing the limits for the tracking signal involves a trade-off between the cost of poor forecasts and the cost of checking for a problem when none exists. For example, suppose that CFE = 180 and MAD = 100; the tracking signal would be +1.8. If we set the control limits of the tracking signal at ±1.5, as in Figure 12.9, a result of +1.8 would require a check of our forecasting method to see whether it needs to be revised because of changes in the demand pattern. Two modifications may be required: either a change in the model *form* (such as adding a trend estimate) or a change in the values of the smoothing parameters.

However, even when the forecasting method is correct for the situation, the tracking signal can exceed the control limits of the chart by chance. In fact, with a limit of ±1.5 MAD on the control chart, the probability is 0.115 (half the area outside the control limits) that we will get a value of the tracking signal greater than +1.5 as a result of random variation. The value of 1.8 exceeds the upper limit on the chart, but that could have happened by chance. As in statistical process control charts, the choice of control limits must recognize the costs of searching for problems when none exist and the costs of not detecting poor performance.

TABLE 12.2 *Percent of the Area of the Normal Probability Distribution Within the Control Limits of the Tracking Signal*	**Control Limit Spread (number of MAD)**	**Equivalent Number of σ***	**Percent of Area Within Control Limits†**
	±1.0	±0.80	57.62
	±1.5	±1.20	76.98
	±2.0	±1.60	89.04
	±2.5	±2.00	95.44
	±3.0	±2.40	98.36
	±3.5	±2.80	99.48
	±4.0	±3.20	99.86

*The equivalent number of standard deviations is found by using the approximation of MAD $\cong 0.8\sigma$.

†The area of the normal curve included within the control limits is found in Appendix 1. For example, the cumulative area from $-\infty$ to 0.80σ is 0.7881. The area between 0 and $+0.80\sigma$ is $0.7881 - 0.5000 = 0.2881$. Since the normal curve is symmetric, the area between -0.80σ and 0 is also 0.2881. Therefore, the area between $\pm0.80\sigma$ is $0.2881 + 0.2881 = 0.5762$.

FIGURE 12.9

Tracking Signal

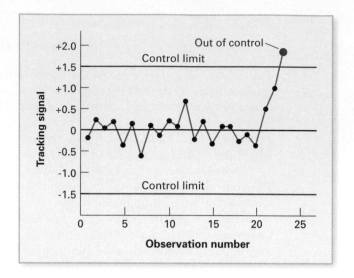

FORECAST ERROR RANGES. Calculating MAD can also provide additional information. Forecasts that are stated as a single value, such as 1,200 units or 26 customers, rarely are useful because they do not indicate the range of likely errors that the forecast typically generates. A far more useful approach is to provide the manager with a forecasted value and an error range. For example, suppose that the forecasted value for a product is 1,000 units, with a MAD of 20 units. Table 12.2 shows that there is about a 95 percent chance that actual demand will fall within ±2.5 MAD of the forecast; that is, for a forecast of 1,000 units, we can say with a 95 percent confidence level that actual demand will fall in the range of 950 to 1,050 units. This information gives the manager a better feel for the uncertainty in the forecast and allows better planning for inventories, staffing levels, and the like.

COMPUTER SUPPORT. Computer support, such as from *OM Explorer*, makes error calculations easy when evaluating how well forecasting models fit with past data. Figure 12.10 shows some of the information provided for the Medanalysis time-series data (see the plot in Figure 12.7). Four different time-series models are evaluated: moving averages ($n = 3$), weighted moving averages ($n = 3$), exponential smoothing ($\alpha = 0.10$), and trend-adjusted exponential smoothing ($\alpha = 0.20$, $\beta = 0.20$). The trend-adjusted exponential smoothing model performs best on the past data, as measured by CFE, MAD, and MSE. It is slightly worse than the weighted moving average model on MAPE (15.98 vs. 12.37 percent). Other versions of these models could be evaluated by testing other reasonable values for n, α, and β.

CRITERIA FOR SELECTING TIME-SERIES METHODS

What is involved in choosing the best time-series forecasting method?

Forecast error measures provide important information for choosing the best forecasting method for a product or service. They also guide managers in selecting the best values for the parameters needed for the method: n for the moving average method, the weights for the weighted moving average method, and α for the exponential smoothing method. The criteria to use in making forecast method and parameter choices include (1) minimizing bias, (2) minimizing MAD or MSE, (3) meeting managerial expectations of changes in the components of demand, and (4) minimizing the forecast error last period. The first two criteria relate to statistical measures based on historical performance, the third reflects expectations of the future that may not be rooted in the

FIGURE 12.10

Forecast Errors for Different Time-Series Models Using OM Explorer

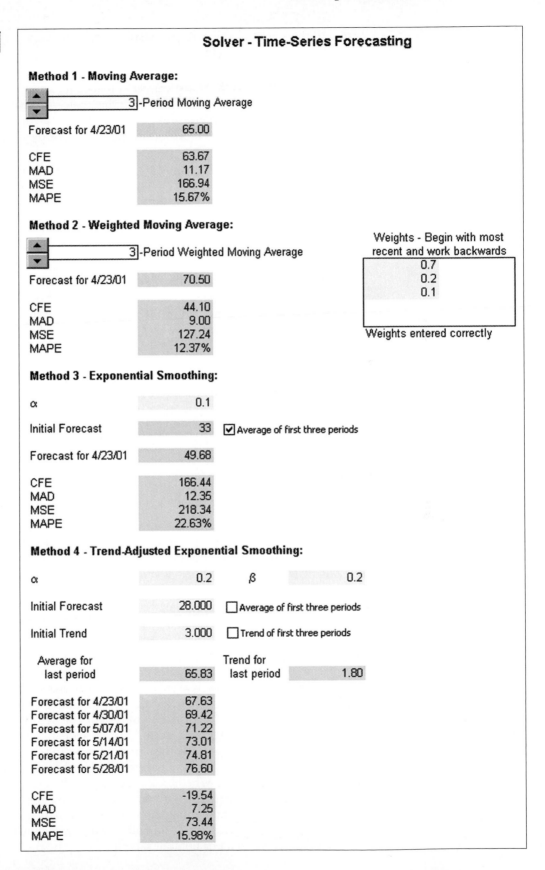

Solver - Time-Series Forecasting

Method 1 - Moving Average:

[3]-Period Moving Average

Forecast for 4/23/01	65.00
CFE	63.67
MAD	11.17
MSE	166.94
MAPE	15.67%

Method 2 - Weighted Moving Average:

[3]-Period Weighted Moving Average

Forecast for 4/23/01	70.50
CFE	44.10
MAD	9.00
MSE	127.24
MAPE	12.37%

Weights - Begin with most recent and work backwards
0.7
0.2
0.1

Weights entered correctly

Method 3 - Exponential Smoothing:

α	0.1
Initial Forecast	33

☑ Average of first three periods

Forecast for 4/23/01	49.68
CFE	166.44
MAD	12.35
MSE	218.34
MAPE	22.63%

Method 4 - Trend-Adjusted Exponential Smoothing:

α	0.2	β	0.2

Initial Forecast   28.000   ☐ Average of first three periods

Initial Trend   3.000   ☐ Trend of first three periods

Average for last period	65.83	Trend for last period	1.80

Forecast for 4/23/01	67.63
Forecast for 4/30/01	69.42
Forecast for 5/07/01	71.22
Forecast for 5/14/01	73.01
Forecast for 5/21/01	74.81
Forecast for 5/28/01	76.60
CFE	-19.54
MAD	7.25
MSE	73.44
MAPE	15.98%

past, and the fourth is a way to use whatever method seems to be working best at the time a forecast must be made.

USING STATISTICAL CRITERIA. Statistical performance measures can be used in the selection of a forecasting method. To illustrate the choice process and possible trade-offs involved, let us consider the results in Figure 12.10 for the four techniques. MAD, MSE, and MAPE are related measures for forecast error dispersion, and CFE is the single measure of bias.

Let us begin with the moving average methods. The *weighted moving average* is better than *simple moving average* on all counts in Figure 12.10—CFE, MAD, MSE, and MAPE. Two explanations are possible: a strong trend or strong seasonal pattern. Because no seasonal effects are apparent from inspection, we conclude that there is a trend at work. Under this condition, the weighted moving average performs better because it gives disproportionate weight to the most recent demand. Perhaps even better results could be obtained for both methods by decreasing n from 3 to 2 weeks. In fact, the naive model might perform surprisingly well. *Exponential smoothing*, with $\alpha = 0.10$, is the worst of the four models. Its performs poorly because it is always lagging behind the strong trend, but probably can be improved somewhat by increasing α. Clearly, the best single model, however, is *trend-adjusted exponential smoothing* with both α and β values set at the relatively high level of 0.20. Its good performance offers additional evidence that there is a strong upward trend. Figure 12.9 shows that there is *upward* movement, because the trend coefficient (1.80) is positive.

This example illustrates two guidelines when searching for the best time-series models:

1. For projections of more stable demand patterns, use lower α and β values or larger n values to emphasize historical experience.
2. For projections of more dynamic demand patterns, using the models covered in this chapter, try higher α and β values or smaller n values. When historical demand patterns are changing, recent history should be emphasized.

Often, the forecaster must make trade-offs between bias (CFE) and the measures of forecast error dispersion (MAD, MSE, and MAPE). For example, the weighted moving average performs slightly better than the trend-adjusted exponential smoothing model in terms of MAPE, although it has more bias as measured by CFE. A positive CFE value indicates that, on balance, the forecasts have been too low. This result can be detrimental to operations at Medanalysis, particularly if CFE is large and purchasing procedures and staffing schedules are based on the raw forecasts. However, the differences in MAPE for the Medanalysis data are modest (12.37 vs. 15.98), and the MAD and MSE measures actually favor the trend-adjusted exponential smoothing model. Considering only the four techniques in Figure 12.10, the trend-adjusted exponential smoothing model is the most reasonable choice for forecasting the future.

However, managers recognize that the best technique in explaining the past data is not necessarily the best to predict the future. For this reason, some analysts prefer to use a **holdout set** as a final test. To do so, they set aside some of the more recent periods from the time series, and use only the earlier time periods to develop and test different models. Once the final models have been selected in the first phase, then they are tested again with the holdout set. Whether this idea is used or not, managers should monitor future forecast errors, perhaps with tracking signals, and modify their forecasting approaches as needed. Maintaining data on forecast performance, such as is done by Lucent's forecasting process, is the ultimate test of forecasting power—rather than how well a model fits past data or holdout samples.

holdout set Actual demands from the more recent time periods in the time series, which are set aside to test different models developed from the earlier time periods.

USING MULTIPLE TECHNIQUES

We have described several individual forecasting methods and shown how to assess their forecast performance. However, there is no need to rely on only a single forecasting method. The forecasting process of Lucent's CDP group brings together several different forecasts when arriving at a final forecast. Initial statistical forecasts using several time-series methods and regression are distributed to knowledgeable individuals, such as marketing directors and sales teams, for their adjustments. They can account for current market and customer conditions that are not necessarily reflected in past data. Furthermore, there can be multiple forecasts from different sales teams, and some teams may have a better record on forecast errors than others. There are two approaches to using several forecasting techniques in unison—combination forecasts and focus forecasting.

COMBINATION FORECASTS

combination forecasts Forecasts that are produced by averaging independent forecasts based on different methods or different data, or both.

Research during the last two decades suggest that combining forecasts from multiple sources often produces more accurate forecasts. **Combination forecasts** are forecasts that are produced by averaging independent forecasts, based on different methods or different data or both. It is intriguing that combination forecasts often perform better over time than do even the *best* single forecasting procedure. For example, suppose that the forecast for next period is 100 units from technique #1 and 120 units from technique #2, and that technique #1 has provided more accurate forecasts to date. The combination forecast for next period, giving equal weight to each technique, is 110 units (or $0.5 \times 100 + 0.5 \times 120$). When this averaging technique is used consistently into the future, its combination forecasts often will be much more accurate than those of any single best forecasting technique (in this example, technique #1). Combining is most effective when the individual forecasts bring different kinds of information into the forecasting process. Forecasters have achieved excellent results by weighting forecasts equally, and this is a good starting point. However, unequal weights may provide better results under some conditions.

OM Explorer has solvers that allow you to evaluate several forecasting models, and then create combination forecasts from them. The models can be the ones evaluated separately in Figure 12.10, but can also include forecasts from regression, judgment, or the naive method. To evaluate the judgment method, the forecaster should be given actual demand just one period at a time, preferably as the actual events are happening, and then commit to a forecast for the next period.

FOCUS FORECASTING

Is the most sophisticated forecasting system always the best one to use?

focus forecasting A method of forecasting which selects the best forecast from a group of forecasts generated by simple techniques.

Does a more sophisticated forecasting model always produce a better forecast? Is there one best forecasting technique for all products or services? The answer to both questions is *no*. In 1984, Bernard Smith, an inventory manager at American Hardware Supply, recognized these realities of forecasting and developed what he called **focus forecasting**, which selects the best forecast from a group of forecasts generated by simple techniques.

Smith was responsible for an inventory of 100,000 different items purchased by the company's 21 buyers. Originally, the company used a basic exponential smoothing system with a sophisticated method for projecting seasonal patterns. The forecasts generated were supposed to be used to determine purchase quantities. However, the buyers altered 53 percent of the forecasted purchase quantities, mainly because they didn't understand exponential smoothing and consequently didn't trust the system. Their continual changes resulted in excessive purchases and inventory.

Smith decided to survey the buyers to find out how they arrived at their own forecasts. One buyer computed the percent increase in demand experienced during the last period and used it to project the increase in demand for the next period. Another buyer simply used the demand from the last period as the forecast for the next period. Other buyers used similar simple methods for forecasting demand. Each buyer was responsible for a different group of items, and Smith had no reason to believe that any one of the methods would work for all items.

Using methods suggested by the buyers and adding some statistical methods, including exponential smoothing, Smith selected seven forecast methods as the basis for his focus forecasting technique. Every period all seven methods are used to make forecasts for each item—with the aid of a computer. Using historical data as the starting point for each method, the computer generates forecasts for the current period. The forecasts are compared to actual demand, and the method that produces the forecast with the least error is used to make the forecast for the next period. The method used for each item may change from period to period.

Each period the computer prints out the forecast for each of the 100,000 items. Buyers can still override the computer forecast, although Smith claims that his system provides excellent short-term forecasts for American Hardware Supply. The system is used for expensive as well as inexpensive items and has much more credibility with the buyers than the previous system did.

FORECASTING ACROSS THE ORGANIZATION

The organizationwide forecasting process cuts across functional areas. Forecasting overall demand typically originates with marketing, but internal customers throughout the organization depend on forecasts to formulate and execute their plans. Forecasts are critical inputs to business plans, annual plans, and budgets. Finance needs forecasts to project cash flows and capital requirements. Human resources needs forecasts to anticipate hiring and training needs. Marketing is a primary source for sales forecast information, because they are closest to external customers. Operations needs forecasts to plan output levels, purchases of materials and services, workforce and output schedules, inventories, and long-term capacities.

Managers throughout the organization make forecasts on many variables other than future demand, such as competitor strategies, regulatory changes, technological change, processing times, supplier lead times, and quality losses. Tools for making these forecasts are basically the same ones covered here for demand: judgment, opinions of knowledgeable people, averages of past experience, regression, and time-series techniques. Using them, forecasting performance can be improved, as the Lucent example demonstrates. But forecasts are rarely perfect. As Mark Twain said in *Following the Equator,* "prophesy is a good line of business, but it is full of risks." Smart managers recognize this reality and find ways to update their plans when the inevitable forecast error or unexpected event occurs.

FORMULA REVIEW

1. Naive forecasting: Forecast $= D_t$

2. Simple moving average: $F_{t+1} = \dfrac{D_t + D_{t-1} + D_{t-2} + \cdots + D_{t-n+1}}{n}$

3. Weighted moving average:
$$F_{t+1} = \text{Weight}_1(D_t) + \text{Weight}_2(D_{t-1}) + \text{Weight}_3(D_{t-2}) + \cdots + \text{Weight}_n(D_{t-n+1})$$

4. Exponential smoothing: $F_{t+1} = \alpha D_t + (1 - \alpha)F_t$

5. Trend-adjusted exponential smoothing:
$$A_t = \alpha D_t + (1 - \alpha)(A_{t-1} + T_{t-1})$$
$$T_t - \beta(A_t - A_{t-1}) + (1 - \beta)T_{t-1}$$
$$F_{t+1} = A_t + T_t$$

6. Forecast error:
$$E_t = D_t - F_t$$
$$\text{CFE} = \sum E_t$$
$$\text{MSE} = \frac{\sum E_t^2}{n}$$
$$\bar{E} = \text{CFE}/n$$
$$\sigma = \sqrt{\frac{\sum (E_t - \bar{E})^2}{n - 1}}$$
$$\text{MAD} = \frac{\sum |E_t|}{n}$$
$$\text{MAPE} = \frac{[\sum |E_t|/D_t]100}{n}$$

7. Exponentially smoothed error: $\text{MAD}_t = \alpha|E_t| + (1 - \alpha)\text{MAD}_{t-1}$

8. Tracking signal: $\dfrac{\text{CFE}}{\text{MAD}}$, or $\dfrac{\text{CFE}}{\text{MAD}_t}$

CHAPTER HIGHLIGHTS

❑ The five basic patterns of demand are the horizontal, trend, seasonal, cyclical, and random variation. Demand can be affected by external factors that are beyond management's control. Indicators of changes in external factors can help predict changes in demand for goods and services. Decisions about product design, price, and advertising are examples of internal decisions that may influence demand.

❑ Designing a forecasting system involves determining what to forecast, which forecasting technique to use, and how computerized forecasting systems can assist managerial decision making.

❑ Level of data aggregation and units of measure are important considerations in managerial decisions about what to forecast. Two general types of demand forecasting are used: qualitative methods and quantitative methods. Qualitative methods include judgment methods, and quantitative methods include causal methods and time-series analysis.

❑ Judgment methods of forecasting are useful in situations where relevant historical data are lacking. Sales-force estimates, executive opinion, market research, and the Delphi method are judgment methods. Judgment methods require the most human interaction and so are the most costly of these methods. Facility location and capacity planning are examples of long-term decisions that justify the expense of generating a judgment forecast.

❑ Causal forecasting methods hypothesize a functional relationship between the factor to be forecasted and other internal or external factors. Causal methods identify turning points in demand patterns but require more extensive analysis to determine the appropriate relationships between the item to be forecast and the external and internal factors. Causal methods tend to be used in medium-term production planning for product families. Linear regression is one of the more popular causal forecasting methods.

- Time-series analysis is often used with computer systems to generate quickly the large number of short-term forecasts required for scheduling products or services. Simple moving averages, weighted moving averages, and exponential smoothing are used to estimate the average of a time series. The exponential smoothing technique has the advantage of requiring that only a minimal amount of data be kept for use in updating the forecast. Trend-adjusted exponential smoothing is a method for including a trend estimate in exponentially smoothed forecasts. Estimates for the series average and the trend are smoothed to provide the forecast.

- Although many techniques allow for seasonal influences, a simple approach is the multiplicative seasonal method, which is based on the assumption that the seasonal influence is proportional to the level of average demand.

- The cumulative sum of forecast errors (CFE), mean squared error (MSE), standard deviation of forecast errors (σ), mean absolute deviation (MAD), and mean absolute percent error (MAPE) are all measures of forecast error used in practice. The CFE and MAD are used to develop a tracking signal that determines when a forecasting method no longer is yielding acceptable forecasts. Forecast error measures also are used to select the best forecast methods from available alternatives.

- Combination forecasts produced by averaging two or more independent forecasts often provide more accurate forecasts.

KEY TERMS

additive seasonal method *565*
aggregation *544*
causal methods *545*
coincident indicators *543*
combination forecasts *573*
cumulative sum of forecast errors (CFE) *566*
Delphi method *549*
demand management *543*
dependent variable *551*
executive opinion *548*
exponential smoothing method *558*
focus forecasting *573*

forecast *541*
forecast error *566*
holdout set *572*
independent variables *551*
judgment methods *545*
lagging indicators *543*
leading indicators *543*
linear regression *551*
market research *549*
mean absolute deviation (MAD) *567*
mean absolute percent error (MAPE) *567*
mean squared error (MSE) *567*

multiplicative seasonal method *563*
naive forecast *554*
sales-force estimates *548*
simple moving average method *555*
standard deviation (σ) *567*
technological forecasting *548*
time series *541*
time-series analysis *545*
tracking signal *568*
trend-adjusted exponential smoothing method *560*
weighted moving average method *556*

SOLVED PROBLEM 1

Chicken Palace periodically offers carryout five-piece chicken dinners at special prices. Let Y be the number of dinners sold and X be the price. Based on the historical observations and calculations in the following table, determine the regression equation, correlation coefficient, and coefficient of determination. How many dinners can Chicken Palace expect to sell at $3.00 each?

OBSERVATION	PRICE, X	DINNERS SOLD, Y
1	$ 2.70	760
2	$ 3.50	510
3	$ 2.00	980
4	$ 4.20	250
5	$ 3.10	320
6	$ 4.05	480
Total	$19.55	3,300
Average	$ 3.258	550

SOLUTION

We use the computer to calculate the best values of *a, b*, the correlation coefficient, and the coefficient of determination.

$$a = 1,450.12$$
$$b = -276.28$$
$$r = -0.84$$
$$r^2 = 0.71$$

The regression line is

$$Y = a + bX = 1,450.12 - 276.28X$$

The correlation coefficient ($r = -0.84$) shows a negative correlation between the variables. The coefficient of determination ($r^2 = 0.71$) indicates that other variables (in addition to price) appreciably affect sales.

If the regression equation is satisfactory to the manager, estimated sales at a price of $3.00 per dinner may be calculated as follows:

$$Y = a + bX = 1,450.12 - 276.28(3.00)$$
$$= 621.28, \quad \text{or} \quad 621 \text{ dinners}$$

SOLVED PROBLEM 2

The Polish General's Pizza Parlor is a small restaurant catering to patrons with a taste for European pizza. One of its specialties is Polish Prize pizza. The manager must forecast weekly demand for these special pizzas so that he can order pizza shells weekly. Recently, demand has been as follows:

WEEK OF	PIZZAS	WEEK OF	PIZZAS
June 2	50	June 23	56
June 9	65	June 30	55
June 16	52	July 7	60

a. Forecast the demand for pizza for June 23 to July 14 by using the simple moving average method with $n = 3$. Then repeat the forecast by using the weighted moving average method with $n = 3$ and weights of 0.50, 0.30, and 0.20, with 0.50 applying to the most recent demand.

b. Calculate the MAD for each method.

SOLUTION

a. The simple moving average method and the weighted moving average method give the following results.

CURRENT WEEK	SIMPLE MOVING AVERAGE FORECAST FOR NEXT WEEK	WEIGHTED MOVING AVERAGE FORECAST FOR NEXT WEEK
June 16	$\dfrac{52 + 65 + 50}{3} = 55.7$, or 56	$[(0.5 \times 52) + (0.3 \times 65) + (0.2 \times 50)] = 55.5$, or 56
June 23	$\dfrac{56 + 52 + 65}{3} = 57.7$, or 58	$[(0.5 \times 56) + (0.3 \times 52) + (0.2 \times 65)] = 56.6$, or 57
June 30	$\dfrac{55 + 56 + 52}{3} = 54.3$, or 54	$[(0.5 \times 55) + (0.3 \times 56) + (0.2 \times 52)] = 54.7$, or 55
July 7	$\dfrac{60 + 55 + 56}{3} = 57$	$[(0.5 \times 60) + (0.3 \times 55) + (0.2 \times 56)] = 57.7$, or 58

b. The mean absolute deviation is calculated as follows:

		SIMPLE MOVING AVERAGE		WEIGHTED MOVING AVERAGE	
WEEK	ACTUAL DEMAND	Forecast	Absolute Errors, $\lvert E_t \rvert$	Forecast	Absolute Errors, $\lvert E_t \rvert$
June 23	56	56	$\lvert 56 - 56 \rvert = 0$	56	$\lvert 56 - 56 \rvert = 0$
June 30	55	58	$\lvert 55 - 58 \rvert = 3$	57	$\lvert 55 - 57 \rvert = 2$
July 7	60	54	$\lvert 60 - 54 \rvert = 6$	55	$\lvert 60 - 55 \rvert = 5$
			MAD $= \dfrac{0 + 3 + 6}{3} = 3$		MAD $= \dfrac{0 + 2 + 5}{3} = 2.3$

For this limited set of data, the weighted moving average method resulted in a slightly lower mean absolute deviation. However, final conclusions can be made only after analyzing much more data.

SOLVED PROBLEM 3

The monthly demand for units manufactured by the Acme Rocket Company has been as follows:

MONTH	UNITS	MONTH	UNITS
May	100	September	105
June	80	October	110
July	110	November	125
August	115	December	120

a. Use the exponential smoothing method to forecast the number of units for June to January. The initial forecast for May was 105 units; $\alpha = 0.2$.

b. Calculate the absolute percentage error for each month from June through December and the MAD and MAPE of forecast error as of the end of December.

c. Calculate the tracking signal as of the end of December. What can you say about the performance of your forecasting method?

SOLUTION

a.

CURRENT MONTH, t	$F_{t+1} = \alpha D_t + (1-\alpha)F_t$	FORECAST, MONTH $t+1$
May	$0.2(100) + 0.8(105) = 104.0$, or 104	June
June	$0.2(80) + 0.8(104.0) = 99.2$, or 99	July
July	$0.2(110) + 0.8(99.2) = 101.4$, or 101	August
August	$0.2(115) + 0.8(101.4) = 104.1$, or 104	September
September	$0.2(105) + 0.8(104.1) = 104.3$, or 104	October
October	$0.2(110) + 0.8(104.3) = 105.4$, or 105	November
November	$0.2(125) + 0.8(105.4) = 109.3$, or 109	December
December	$0.2(120) + 0.8(109.3) = 111.4$, or 111	January

b.

MONTH, t	ACTUAL DEMAND, D_t	FORECAST, F_t	ERROR, $E_t = D_t - F_t$	ABSOLUTE ERROR, $\lvert E_t\rvert$	ABSOLUTE PERCENTAGE ERROR, $(\lvert E_t\rvert/D_t)(100\%)$
June	80	104	−24	24	30.0%
July	110	99	11	11	10.0
August	115	101	14	14	12.2
September	105	104	1	1	0.9
October	110	104	6	6	5.4
November	125	105	20	20	16.0
December	120	109	11	11	9.2
Total	765		39	87	83.7%

$$\text{MAD} = \frac{\Sigma \lvert E_t\rvert}{n} = \frac{87}{7} = 12.4 \quad \text{and} \quad \text{MAPE} = \frac{\Sigma [\lvert E_t\rvert(100)]/D_t}{n} = \frac{83.7\%}{7} = 11.9$$

c. As of the end of December, the cumulative sum of forecast errors (CFE) is 39. Using the mean absolute deviation calculated in part (b), we calculate the tracking signal:

$$\text{Tracking signal} = \frac{\text{CFE}}{\text{MAD}} = \frac{39}{12.4} = 3.14$$

The probability that a tracking signal value of 3.14 could be generated completely by chance is very small. Consequently, we should revise our approach. The long string of forecasts lower than actual demand suggests use of a trend method.

SOLVED PROBLEM 4

The demand for Krispee Crunchies, a favorite breakfast cereal of people born in the 1940s, is experiencing a decline. The company wants to monitor demand for this product closely as it nears the end of its life cycle. The trend-adjusted exponential smoothing method is used with $\alpha = 0.1$ and $\beta = 0.2$. At the end of December, the January estimate for the average number of cases sold per month, A_t, was 900,000 and the trend, T_t, was −50,000 per month. The following table shows the actual sales history for January, February, and March. Generate forecasts for February, March, and April.

MONTH	SALES
January	890,000
February	800,000
March	825,000

SOLUTION

We know the initial condition at the end of December and actual demand for January, February, and March. We must now update the forecast method and prepare a forecast for April. All data are expressed in thousands of cases. Our equations for use with trend-adjusted exponential smoothing are

$$A_t = \alpha D_t + (1 - \alpha)(A_{t-1} + T_{t-1})$$
$$T_t = \beta(A_t - A_{t-1}) + (1 - \beta)T_{t-1}$$
$$F_{t+1} = A_t + T_t$$

For January, we have

$$A_{Jan} = 0.1(890,000) + 0.9(900,000 - 50,000)$$
$$= 854,000 \text{ cases}$$
$$T_{Jan} = 0.2(854,000 - 900,000) + 0.8(-50,000)$$
$$= -49,200 \text{ cases}$$
$$F_{Feb} = A_{Jan} + T_{Jan} = 854,000 - 49,200 = 804,800 \text{ cases}$$

For February, we have

$$A_{Feb} = 0.1(800,000) + 0.9(854,000 - 49,200)$$
$$= 804,320 \text{ cases}$$
$$T_{Feb} = 0.2(804,320 - 854,000) + 0.8(-49,200)$$
$$= -49,296 \text{ cases}$$
$$F_{Mar} = A_{Feb} + T_{Feb} = 804,320 - 49,296 = 755,024 \text{ cases}$$

For March, we have

$$A_{Mar} = 0.1(825,000) + 0.9(804,320 - 49,296)$$
$$= 762,021.6, \quad \text{or} \quad 762,022 \text{ cases}$$
$$T_{Mar} = 0.2(762,022 - 804,320) + 0.8(-49,296)$$
$$= -47,896.4, \quad \text{or} \quad -47,897 \text{ cases}$$
$$F_{Apr} = A_{Mar} + T_{Mar} = 762,022 - 47,897 = 714,125 \text{ cases}$$

SOLVED PROBLEM 5

The Northville Post Office experiences a seasonal pattern of daily mail volume every week. The following data for two representative weeks are expressed in thousands of pieces of mail:

DAY	WEEK 1	WEEK 2
Sunday	5	8
Monday	20	15
Tuesday	30	32
Wednesday	35	30
Thursday	49	45
Friday	70	70
Saturday	15	10
Total	224	210

a. Calculate a seasonal factor for each day of the week.

b. If the postmaster estimates that there will be 230,000 pieces of mail to sort next week, forecast the volume for each day of the week.

SOLUTION

a. Calculate the average daily mail volume for each week. Then for each day of the week divide the mail volume by the week's average to get the seasonal factor. Finally, for each day, add the two seasonal factors and divide by 2 to obtain the average seasonal factor to use in the forecast (see part (b)).

	WEEK 1		WEEK 2		AVERAGE SEASONAL FACTOR [(1) + (2)]/2
DAY	Mail Volume	Seasonal Factor (1)	Mail Volume	Seasonal Factor (2)	
Sunday	5	5/32 = 0.15625	8	8/30 = 0.26667	0.21146
Monday	20	20/32 = 0.62500	15	15/30 = 0.50000	0.56250
Tuesday	30	30/32 = 0.93750	32	32/30 = 1.06667	1.00209
Wednesday	35	35/32 = 1.09375	30	30/30 = 1.00000	1.04688
Thursday	49	49/32 = 1.53125	45	45/30 = 1.50000	1.51563
Friday	70	70/32 = 2.18750	70	70/30 = 2.33333	2.26042
Saturday	15	15/32 = 0.46875	10	10/30 = 0.33333	0.40104
Total	224		210		
Average	224/7 = 32		210/7 = 30		

b. The average daily mail volume is expected to be 230,000/7 = 32,857 pieces of mail. Using the average seasonal factors calculated in part (a), we obtain the following forecasts:

DAY	CALCULATION	FORECAST
Sunday	0.21146(32,857) =	6,948
Monday	0.56250(32,857) =	18,482
Tuesday	1.00209(32,857) =	32,926
Wednesday	1.04688(32,857) =	34,397
Thursday	1.51563(32,857) =	49,799
Friday	2.26042(32,857) =	74,271
Saturday	0.40104(32,857) =	13,177
	Total	230,000

DISCUSSION QUESTIONS

1. Figure 12.11 shows summer air visibility measurements for Denver. The acceptable visibility standard is 100, with readings above 100 indicating clean air and good visibility and readings below 100 indicating temperature inversions, forest fires, volcanic eruptions, or collisions with comets.

   a. Is there a trend in the data? Which time-series techniques might be appropriate for estimating the average of these data?

   b. A medical center for asthma and respiratory diseases located in Denver has great demand for its services when air quality is poor. If you were in charge of developing a short-term (say, 3-day) forecast of visibility, which causal factor(s) would you analyze? In other words, which external factors hold the potential to significantly affect visibility in the *short term*?

   c. Tourism, an important factor in Denver's economy, is affected by the city's image. Air quality, as measured by visibility, affects the city's image. If you were responsible for development of tourism, which causal factor(s) would you analyze to forecast visibility for the *medium term* (say, the next two summers)?

   d. The federal government threatens to withhold several hundred million dollars in Department of Transportation funds unless Denver meets visibility standards within eight years. How would you proceed to generate a *long-term* judgment forecast of technologies that will be available to improve visibility in the next 10 years?

2. Kay and Michael Passe publish *What's Happening?*—a biweekly newspaper to publicize local events. *What's Happening?* has few subscribers; it typically is sold at checkout stands. Much of the revenue comes from advertisers of garage sales and supermarket specials. In an effort to reduce costs associated with printing too many papers or delivering them to the wrong location, Michael implemented a computerized system to collect sales data. Sales-counter scanners accurately record sales data for each location. Since the system was implemented, total sales volume has steadily declined. Selling advertising space and maintaining shelf space at supermarkets are getting more difficult.

   Reduced revenue makes controlling costs all the more important. For each issue, Michael carefully makes a forecast based on sales data collected at each location. Then he orders papers to be printed and distributed in quantities matching the forecast. Michael's forecast reflects a downward trend, which *is* present in the sales data. Now only a few papers are left over at only a few locations. Although the sales forecast accurately predicts

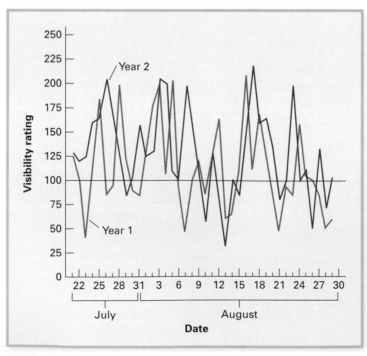

FIGURE 12.11

the actual sales at most locations, *What's Happening?* is spiraling toward oblivion. Kay suspects that Michael is doing something wrong in preparing the forecast but can find no mathematical errors. Tell her what's happening.

OM EXPLORER AND INTERNET EXERCISES

Visit our Web site at www.prenhall.com/krajewski for OM Explorer Tutors, which explain quantitative techniques; Solvers, which help you apply mathematical models; and Internet Exercises, including Facility Tours, which expand on the topics in this chapter.

PROBLEMS

An icon next to a problem identifies the software that can be helpful, but not mandatory. The software is available on the Student CD-ROM that is packaged with every new copy of the textbook.

Problems 7vi and 12–14 involve considerable computations. Use of regression software or a spreadsheet is recommended.

1. **OM Explorer** The owner of a computer store rents printers to some of her preferred customers. She is interested in arriving at a forecast of rentals so that she can order the correct quantities of supplies that go with the printers. Data for the last 10 weeks are shown here.

WEEK	RENTALS	WEEK	RENTALS
1	23	6	28
2	24	7	32
3	32	8	35
4	26	9	26
5	31	10	24

a. Prepare a forecast for weeks 6–10 by using a five-week moving average. What is the forecast for week 11?

b. Calculate the mean absolute deviation as of the end of week 10.

2. **OM Explorer** Sales for the past 12 months at Dalworth Company are given here.

MONTH	SALES ($ Millions)	MONTH	SALES ($ Millions)
January	20	July	53
February	24	August	62
March	27	September	54
April	31	October	36
May	37	November	32
June	47	December	29

a. Use a three-month moving average to forecast the sales for the months April through December.

b. Use a four-month moving average to forecast the sales for the months May through December.

c. Compare the performance of the two methods by using the mean absolute deviation as the performance criterion. Which method would you recommend?

d. Compare the performance of the two methods by using the mean absolute percent error as the performance criterion. Which method would you recommend?

e. Compare the performance of the two methods by using the mean squared error as the performance criterion. Which method would you recommend?

3. **OM Explorer** Karl's Copiers sells and repairs photocopy machines. The manager needs weekly forecasts of service calls so that he can schedule service personnel. The forecast for the week of July 3 was 24 calls. The manager uses exponential smoothing with $\alpha = 0.20$. Forecast the number of calls for the week of August 7, which is next week.

WEEK OF	ACTUAL SERVICE CALLS
July 3	24
July 10	32
July 17	36
July 24	23
July 31	25

4. **OM Explorer** Consider the sales data for Dalworth Company given in Problem 2.

a. Use a three-month weighted moving average to forecast the sales for the months April through December. Use weights of (3/6), (2/6), and (1/6), giving more weight to more recent data.

b. Use exponential smoothing with $\alpha = 0.6$ to forecast the sales for the months April through December. Assume that the initial forecast for January was $22 million.

c. Compare the performance of the two methods by using the mean absolute deviation as the performance criterion. Which method would you recommend?

d. Compare the performance of the two methods by using the mean absolute percent error as the performance criterion. Which method would you recommend?

e. Compare the performance of the two methods by using the mean squared error as the performance criterion. Which method would you recommend?

5. A convenience store recently started to carry a new brand of soft drink in its territory. Management is interested in estimating future sales volume to determine whether it should continue to carry the new brand or replace it with another brand. At the end of April, the average monthly sales volume of the new soft drink was 700 cans and the trend was +50 cans per month. The actual sales volume figures for May, June, and July are 760, 800, and 820, respectively. Use trend-adjusted exponential smoothing with $\alpha = 0.2$ and $\beta = 0.1$ to forecast usage for June, July, and August.

6. Dixie Bank in Dothan, Alabama, recently installed a new automatic teller machine to perform the standard banking services and handle loan applications and investment transactions. The new machine is a bit complicated to use, so management is interested in tracking its past use and projecting its future use. Additional machines may be needed if projected use is high enough.

   At the end of April, the average monthly use was 600 customers and the trend was +60 customers per month. The actual use figures for May, June, and July are 680, 710, and 790, respectively. Use trend-adjusted exponential smoothing with $\alpha = 0.3$ and $\beta = 0.2$ to forecast usage for June, July, and August.

7. 💿 **OM Explorer** The number of heart surgeries performed at Heartville General Hospital has increased steadily over the past years. The hospital's administration is seeking the best method to forecast the demand for such surgeries in year 6. The data for the past five years are shown. Six years ago, the forecast for year 1 was 41 surgeries, and the estimated trend was an increase of 2 per year.

YEAR	DEMAND
1	45
2	50
3	52
4	56
5	58

The hospital's administration is considering the following forecasting methods.
   i. Exponential smoothing with $\alpha = 0.6$.
   ii. Exponential smoothing with $\alpha = 0.9$.
   iii. Trend-adjusted exponential smoothing with $\alpha = 0.6$ and $\beta = 0.1$.
   iv. Three-year moving average.
   v. Three-year weighted moving average, using weights (3/6), (2/6), and (1/6), with more recent data given more weight.
   vi. Regression model, $Y = 42.6 + 3.2X$, where Y is the number of surgeries and X is the index for the year (e.g., $X = 1$ for year 1, $X = 2$ for year 2, etc.)

a. If MAD (mean absolute deviation) is the performance criterion chosen by the administration, which forecasting method should it choose?

b. If MSE (mean squared error) is the performance criterion chosen by the administration, which forecasting method should it choose?

c. If MAPE (mean absolute percent error) is the performance criterion chosen by the administration, which forecasting method should it choose?

8. The following data are for calculator sales in units at an electronics store over the past five weeks:

WEEK	SALES
1	46
2	49
3	43
4	50
5	53

Use trend-adjusted exponential smoothing with $\alpha = 0.2$ and $\beta = 0.2$ to forecast sales for weeks 3–6. Assume that the average of the time series was 45 units and that the average trend was +2 units per week just before week 1.

9. 💿 **OM Explorer** Forrest and Dan make boxes of chocolates for which the demand is uncertain. Forrest says, "That's life." But Dan believes that some demand patterns exist that could be useful for planning the purchase

of sugar, chocolate, and shrimp. Forrest insists on placing a surprise chocolate-covered shrimp in some boxes so that "You never know what you'll get." Quarterly demand (in boxes of chocolates) for the last three years follows:

QUARTER	YEAR 1	YEAR 2	YEAR 3
1	3,000	3,300	3,502
2	1,700	2,100	2,448
3	900	1,500	1,768
4	4,400	5,100	5,882
Total	10,000	12,000	13,600

a. Use intuition and judgment to estimate quarterly demand for the fourth year.

b. If the expected sales for chocolates are 14,800 cases for year 4, use the multiplicative seasonal method to prepare a forecast for each quarter of the year. Are any of the quarterly forecasts different from what you thought you'd get in part (a)?

10. **OM Explorer** The manager of Snyder's Garden Center must make her annual purchasing plans for rakes, gloves, and other gardening items. One of the items she stocks is Fast-Grow, a liquid fertilizer. The sales of this item are seasonal, with peaks in the spring, summer, and fall months. Quarterly demand (in cases) for the past two years follows:

QUARTER	YEAR 1	YEAR 2
1	40	60
2	350	440
3	290	320
4	210	280
Total	890	1,100

If the expected sales for Fast-Grow are 1,150 cases for year 3, use the multiplicative seasonal method to prepare a forecast for each quarter of the year.

11. **OM Explorer** The manager of a utility company in the Texas panhandle wants to develop quarterly forecasts of power loads for the next year. The power loads are seasonal, and the data on the quarterly loads in megawatts (MW) for the last four years are as follows:

YEAR	QUARTER 1	QUARTER 2	QUARTER 3	QUARTER 4
1	103.5	94.7	118.6	109.3
2	126.1	116.0	141.2	131.6
3	144.5	137.1	159.0	149.5
4	166.1	152.5	178.2	169.0

The manager has estimated the total demand for the next year at 780 MW. Use the multiplicative seasonal method to develop the forecast for each quarter.

12. **OM Explorer** Demand for oil changes at Garcia's Garage has been as follows:

MONTH	NUMBER OF OIL CHANGES
January	41
February	46
March	57
April	52
May	59
June	51
July	60
August	62

a. Use simple linear regression analysis to develop a forecasting model for monthly demand. In this application, the dependent variable, Y, is monthly demand and the independent variable, X, is the month. For January, let $X = 1$; for February, let $X = 2$; and so on.

b. Use the model to forecast demand for September, October, and November. Here, $X = 9$, 10, and 11, respectively.

13. **OM Explorer** At a hydrocarbon processing factory, process control involves periodic analysis of samples for a certain process quality parameter. The analytic procedure currently used is costly and time consuming. A faster and more economical alternative procedure has been proposed. However, the numbers for the quality parameter given by the alternative procedure are somewhat different from those given by the current procedure, not because of any inherent errors but because of changes in the nature of the chemical analysis. Management believes that, if the numbers from the new procedure can be used to forecast reliably the corresponding numbers from the current procedure, switching to the new procedure would be reasonable and cost effective. The following data were obtained for the quality parameter by analyzing samples using both procedures:

CURRENT, Y	PROPOSED, X	CURRENT, Y	PROPOSED, X
3.0	3.1	3.1	3.1
3.1	3.9	2.7	2.9
3.0	3.4	3.3	3.6
3.6	4.0	3.2	4.1
3.8	3.6	2.1	2.6
2.7	3.6	3.0	3.1
2.7	3.6	2.6	2.8

a. Use linear regression to find a relation to forecast Y, the quality parameter from the current procedure, using the values from the proposed procedure, X.

b. Is there a strong relationship between Y and X? Explain.

14. ● **OM Explorer** Ohio Swiss Milk Products manufactures and distributes ice cream in Ohio, Kentucky, and West Virginia. The company wants to expand operations by locating another plant in northern Ohio. The size of the new plant will be a function of the expected demand for ice cream within the area served by the plant. A market survey is currently under way to determine that demand.

Ohio Swiss wants to estimate the relationship between the manufacturing cost per gallon and the number of gallons sold in a year to determine the demand for ice cream and thus the size of the new plant. The following data have been collected:

PLANT	COST PER THOUSAND GALLONS, Y	THOUSANDS OF GALLONS SOLD, X
1	$1,015	416.9
2	973	472.5
3	1,046	250.0
4	1,006	372.1
5	1,058	238.1
6	1,068	258.6
7	967	597.0
8	997	414.0
9	1,044	263.2
10	1,008	372.0
Total	$10,182	3,654.4

a. Develop a regression equation to forecast the cost per gallon as a function of the number of gallons produced.

b. Compute the correlation coefficient and coefficient of determination. Comment on your regression equation in light of these measures.

c. Suppose that the market survey indicates a demand of 325,000 gallons in the Bucyrus, Ohio, area. Estimate the manufacturing cost per gallon for a plant producing 325,000 gallons per year.

Advanced Problems

15. ● **OM Explorer** The director of a large public library must schedule employees to reshelve books and periodicals checked out of the library. The number of items checked out will determine the labor requirements. The following data reflect the numbers of items checked out of the library for the past three years:

MONTH	YEAR 1	YEAR 2	YEAR 3
January	1,847	2,045	1,986
February	2,669	2,321	2,564
March	2,467	2,419	2,635
April	2,432	2,088	2,150
May	2,464	2,667	2,201
June	2,378	2,122	2,663
July	2,217	2,206	2,055
August	2,445	1,869	1,678
September	1,894	2,441	1,845
October	1,922	2,291	2,065
November	2,431	2,364	2,147
December	2,274	2,189	2,451

The director needs a time-series method for forecasting the number of items to be checked out during the next month. Find the best simple moving average forecast you can. Decide what is meant by "best" and justify your decision.

16. ● **OM Explorer** Using the data in Problem 15, find the best exponential smoothing solution you can. Justify your choice.

17. ● **OM Explorer** Using the data in Problem 15, find the best trend-adjusted exponential smoothing solution you can. Compare the performance of this method with those of the best moving average method and the exponential smoothing method. Which of the three would you choose?

18. ● **OM Explorer** Cannister, Inc., specializes in the manufacture of plastic containers. The data on the monthly sales of 10-ounce shampoo bottles for the last five years are as follows:

YEAR	1	2	3	4	5
January	742	741	896	951	1,030
February	697	700	793	861	1,032
March	776	774	885	938	1,126
April	898	932	1,055	1,109	1,285
May	1,030	1,099	1,204	1,274	1,468
June	1,107	1,223	1,326	1,422	1,637
July	1,165	1,290	1,303	1,486	1,611
August	1,216	1,349	1,436	1,555	1,608
September	1,208	1,341	1,473	1,604	1,528
October	1,131	1,296	1,453	1,600	1,420
November	971	1,066	1,170	1,403	1,119
December	783	901	1,023	1,209	1,013

a. Using the multiplicative seasonal method, calculate the monthly seasonal indices.

b. Develop a simple linear regression equation to forecast annual sales. For this regression, the dependent variable, Y, is the demand in each year and the independent variable, X, is the index for the year (i.e., $X = 1$ for year 1, $X = 2$ for year 2, and so on until $X = 5$ for year 5).

c. Forecast the annual sales for year 6 by using the regression model you developed in part (b).

d. Prepare the seasonal forecast for each month by using the monthly seasonal indices calculated in part (a).

19. **OM Explorer** The Midwest Computer Company serves a large number of businesses in the Great Lakes region. The company sells supplies and replacements and performs service on all computers sold through seven sales offices. Many items are stocked, so close inventory control is necessary to assure customers of efficient service. Recently, business has been increasing, and management is concerned about stockouts. A forecasting method is needed to estimate requirements several months in advance so that adequate replenishment quan-

tities can be purchased. An example of the sales growth experienced during the last 50 months is the growth in demand for item EP-37, a laser printer cartridge, shown in Table 12.3.

a. Develop a trend-adjusted exponential smoothing solution for forecasting demand. Find the "best" parameters and justify your choices. Forecast demand for months 51–53.

b. A consultant to Midwest's management suggested that new office building leases would be a good leading indicator for company sales. He quoted a recent university study finding that new office building leases precede office equipment and supply sales by three months. According to the study findings, leases in month 1 would affect sales in month 4; leases in month 2 would affect sales in month 5; and so on. Use linear regression to develop a forecasting model for sales, with leases as the independent variable. Forecast sales for months 51–53.

c. Which of the two models provides better forecasts? Explain.

20. **OM Explorer** A certain food item at P&Q Supermarkets has the demand pattern shown in the following table. Find the "best" forecast you can for month 25 and justify your methodology. You may use some of the data to find the best parameter value(s) for your method and the rest to test the forecast model. Your justification should include both quantitative and qualitative considerations.

TABLE 12.3 *EP-37 Sales and Lease Data*

MONTH	EP-37 SALES	LEASES	MONTH	EP-37 SALES	LEASES
1	80	32	26	1,296	281
2	132	29	27	1,199	298
3	143	32	28	1,267	314
4	180	54	29	1,300	323
5	200	53	30	1,370	309
6	168	89	31	1,489	343
7	212	74	32	1,499	357
8	254	93	33	1,669	353
9	397	120	34	1,716	360
10	385	113	35	1,603	370
11	472	147	36	1,812	386
12	397	126	37	1,817	389
13	476	138	38	1,798	399
14	699	145	39	1,873	409
15	545	160	40	1,923	410
16	837	196	41	2,028	413
17	743	180	42	2,049	439
18	722	197	43	2,084	454
19	735	203	44	2,083	441
20	838	223	45	2,121	470
21	1,057	247	46	2,072	469
22	930	242	47	2,262	490
23	1,085	234	48	2,371	496
24	1,090	254	49	2,309	509
25	1,218	271	50	2,422	522

MONTH	DEMAND	MONTH	DEMAND
1	33	13	37
2	37	14	43
3	31	15	56
4	39	16	41
5	54	17	36
6	38	18	39
7	42	19	41
8	40	20	58
9	41	21	42
10	54	22	45
11	43	23	41
12	39	24	38

21. **OM Explorer** The data for the visibility chart in Discussion Question 1 are shown in Table 12.4. The visibility standard is set at 100. Readings below 100 indicate that air pollution has reduced visibility, and readings above 100 indicate that the air is clearer.

TABLE 12.4 *Visibility Data*

DATE	YEAR 1	YEAR 2	DATE	YEAR 1	YEAR 2	DATE	YEAR 1	YEAR 2
July 22	125	130	Aug. 5	105	200	Aug. 19	170	160
23	100	120	6	205	110	20	125	165
24	40	125	7	90	100	21	85	135
25	100	160	8	45	200	22	45	80
26	185	165	9	100	160	23	95	100
27	85	205	10	120	100	24	85	200
28	95	165	11	85	55	25	160	100
29	200	125	12	125	130	26	105	110
30	125	85	13	165	75	27	100	50
31	90	105	14	60	30	28	95	135
Aug. 1	85	160	15	65	100	29	50	70
2	135	125	16	110	85	30	60	105
3	175	130	17	210	150			
4	200	205	18	110	220			

a. Use several methods to generate a visibility forecast for August 31 of the second year. Which method seems to produce the best forecast?

b. Use several methods to forecast the visibility index for the summer of the third year. Which method seems to produce the best forecast? Support your choice.

22. **OM Explorer** Tom Glass forecasts electrical demand for the Flatlands Public Power District (FPPD). The FPPD wants to take its Comstock power plant out of service for maintenance when demand is expected to be low. After shutdown, performing maintenance and getting the plant back on line takes two weeks. The utility has enough other generating capacity to satisfy 1,550 megawatts (MW) of demand while Comstock is out of service. Table 12.5 shows weekly peak demands (in MW) for the past several autumns. When next fall should the Comstock plant be scheduled for maintenance?

23. **OM Explorer** A manufacturing firm has developed a skills test, the scores from which can be used to predict workers' production rating factors. Data on the test scores of various workers and their subsequent production ratings are shown.

WORKER	TEST SCORE	PRODUCTION RATING	WORKER	TEST SCORE	PRODUCTION RATING
A	53	45	K	54	59
B	36	43	L	73	77
C	88	89	M	65	56
D	84	79	N	29	28
E	86	84	O	52	51
F	64	66	P	22	27
G	45	49	Q	76	76
H	48	48	R	32	34
I	39	43	S	51	60
J	67	76	T	37	32

a. Using linear regression, develop a relationship to forecast production ratings from test scores.

TABLE 12.5 *Weekly Peak Power Demands*

	AUGUST		SEPTEMBER				OCTOBER					NOVEMBER	
YEAR	1	2	3	4	5	6	7	8	9	10	11	12	13
1	2,050	1,925	1,825	1,525	1,050	1,300	1,200	1,175	1,350	1,525	1,725	1,575	1,925
2	2,000	2,075	2,225	1,800	1,175	1,050	1,250	1,025	1,300	1,425	1,625	1,950	1,950
3	1,950	1,800	2,150	1,725	1,575	1,275	1,325	1,100	1,500	1,550	1,375	1,825	2,000
4	2,100	2,400	1,975	1,675	1,350	1,525	1,500	1,150	1,350	1,225	1,225	1,475	1,850
5	2,275	2,300	2,150	1,525	1,350	1,475	1,475	1,175	1,375	1,400	1,425	1,550	1,900

b. If a worker's test score was 80, what would be your forecast of the worker's production rating?

c. Comment on the strength of the relationship between the test scores and production ratings.

24. ● **OM Explorer** The materials handling manager of a manufacturing company is trying to forecast the cost of maintenance for the company's fleet of over-the-road tractors. He believes that the cost of maintaining the tractors increases with their age. He has collected the following data:

AGE (years)	YEARLY MAINTENANCE COST ($)
4.5	619
4.5	1,049
4.5	1,033
4.0	495
4.0	723
4.0	681
5.0	890
5.0	1,522
5.5	987
5.0	1,194
0.5	163
0.5	182
6.0	764
6.0	1,373
1.0	978
1.0	466
1.0	549

a. Use linear regression to develop a relationship to forecast the yearly maintenance cost based on the age of a tractor.

b. If a section has 20 three-year-old tractors, what is the forecast for the annual maintenance cost?

CASE YANKEE FORK AND HOE COMPANY

The Yankee Fork and Hoe Company is a leading producer of garden tools ranging from wheelbarrows, mortar pans, and hand trucks to shovels, rakes, and trowels. The tools are sold in four different product lines ranging from the top-of-the-line Hercules products, which are rugged tools for the toughest jobs, to the Garden Helper products, which are economy tools for the occasional user. The market for garden tools is extremely competitive because of the simple design of the products and the large number of competing producers. In addition, more people are using power tools, such as lawn edgers, hedge trimmers, and thatchers, reducing demand for their manual counterparts. These factors compel Yankee to maintain low prices while retaining high quality and dependable delivery.

Garden tools represent a mature industry. Unless new manual products can be developed or there is a sudden resurgence in home gardening, the prospects for large increases in sales are not bright. Keeping ahead of the competition is a constant battle. No one knows this better than Alan Roberts, president of Yankee.

The types of tools sold today are, by and large, the same ones sold 30 years ago. The only way to generate new sales and retain old customers is to provide superior customer service and produce a product with high customer value. This approach puts pressure on the manufacturing system, which has been having difficulties lately. Recently, Roberts has been receiving calls from long-time customers, such as Sears and Tru-Value Hardware Stores, complaining about late shipments. These customers advertise promotions for garden tools and require on-time delivery.

Roberts knows that losing customers like Sears and Tru-Value would be disastrous. He decides to ask consultant Sharon Place to look into the matter and report to him in one week. Roberts suggests that she focus on the bow rake

continued

continued

as a case in point because it is a high-volume product and has been a major source of customer complaints of late.

PLANNING BOW RAKE PRODUCTION

A bow rake consists of a head with 12 teeth spaced one inch apart, a hardwood handle, a bow that attaches the head to the handle, and a metal ferrule that reinforces the area where the bow inserts into the handle. The bow is a metal strip that is welded to the ends of the rake head and bent in the middle to form a flat tab for insertion into the handle. The rake is about 64 in long.

Place decides to find out how Yankee plans bow rake production. She goes straight to Phil Stanton, who gives the following account:

> Planning is informal around here. To begin, marketing determines the forecast for bow rakes by month for the next year. Then they pass it along to me. Quite frankly, the forecasts are usually inflated—must be their big egos over there. I have to be careful because we enter into long-term purchasing agreements for steel, and having it just sitting around is expensive. So, I usually reduce the forecast by 10 percent or so. I use the modified forecast to generate a monthly final-assembly schedule, which determines what I need to have from the forging and woodworking areas. The system works well if the forecasts are good. But when marketing comes to me and says they are behind on customer orders, as they often do near the end of the year, it wreaks havoc with the schedules. Forging gets hit the hardest. For example, the presses that stamp the rake heads from blanks of steel can handle only 7,000 heads per day, and the bow rolling machine can do only 5,000 per day. Both operations are also required for many other products.

Because the marketing department provides crucial information to Stanton, Place decides to see the marketing manager, Ron Adams. Adams explains how he arrives at the bow rake forecasts.

> Things don't change much from year to year. Sure, sometimes we put on a sales promotion of some kind, but we try to give Phil enough warning before the demand kicks in—usually a month or so. I meet with several managers from the various sales regions to go over shipping data from last

year and discuss anticipated promotions, changes in the economy, and shortages we experienced last year. Based on these meetings I generate a monthly forecast for the next year. Even though we take a lot of time getting the forecast, it never seems to help us avoid customer problems.

THE PROBLEM

Place ponders the comments from Stanton and Adams. She understands Stanton's concerns about costs and keeping inventory low and Adams's concern about having enough rakes on hand to make timely shipments. Both are also somewhat concerned about capacity. Yet, she decides to check actual customer demand for the bow rake over the past four years (in Table 12.6) before making her final report to Roberts.

Questions

1. Comment on the forecasting system being used by Yankee. Suggest changes or improvements that you believe are justified.
2. Develop your own forecast for bow rakes for each month of the next year (year 5). Justify your forecast and the method you used.

TABLE 12.6 *Four-Year Demand History for the Bow Rake*

Month	Demand			
	Year 1	Year 2	Year 3	Year 4
1	55,220	39,875	32,180	62,377
2	57,350	64,128	38,600	66,501
3	15,445	47,653	25,020	31,404
4	27,776	43,050	51,300	36,504
5	21,408	39,359	31,790	16,888
6	17,118	10,317	32,100	18,909
7	18,028	45,194	59,832	35,500
8	19,883	46,530	30,740	51,250
9	15,796	22,105	47,800	34,443
10	53,665	41,350	73,890	68,088
11	83,269	46,024	60,202	68,175
12	72,991	41,856	55,200	61,100

Note: The demand figures shown in the table are the number of units promised for delivery each month. Actual delivery quantities differed because of capacity or shortages of materials.

SELECTED REFERENCES

Armstrong, J. S. *Long-range Forecasting: From Crystal Ball to Computer.* New York: John Wiley & Sons, 1995.

Armstrong, J. Scott, and F. Collopy. "Integration of Statistical Methods and Judgment for Time Series Forecasting: Principles from Empirical Research," in G. Wright and P. Goodwin (eds.), *Forecasting with Judgement,* New York: John Wiley and Sons, 1998.

Blattberg, R. C., and S. J. Hoch, "Database Models and Managerial Intuition: 50% Model + 50% Manager," *Management Science,* vol. 36 (1990), pp. 887–899.

Bowerman, Bruce L., and Richard T. O'Connell. *Forecasting and Time Series: An Applied Approach,* 3d ed., Belmont, CA: Duxbury Press, 1993.

Chambers, John C., Satinder K. Mullick, and Donald D. Smith. "How to Choose the Right Forecasting Technique." *Harvard Business Review* (July–August 1971), pp. 45–74.

Clemen, R. T. "Combining Forecasts: A Review and Annotated Bibliography." *International Journal of Forecasting,* vol. 5 (1989), pp. 559–583.

Gardner, Everette S., and David G. Dannenbring. "Forecasting with Exponential Smoothing: Some Guidelines for Model Selection." *Decision Sciences,* vol. 11, no. 2 (1980), pp. 370–383.

Hudson, William J. *Executive Economics: Forecasting and Planning for the Real World of Business.* New York: John Wiley & Sons, 1993.

Jenkins, Carolyn. "Accurate Forecasting Reduces Inventory and Increases Output at Henredon." *APICS—The Performance Advantage* (September 1992), pp. 37–39.

Kimes, Sheryl E., and James A. Fitzsimmons. "Selecting Profitable Hotel Sites at La Quinta Motor Inns." *Interfaces,* vol. 20, no. 2 (1990), pp. 12–20.

Li, X. "An Intelligent Business Forecaster for Strategic Business Planning." *Journal of Forecasting,* vol. 18, no. 3 (1999), pp. 181–205.

Lim, J. S., and M. O'Connor. "Judgmental Forecasting with Time Series and Causal Information." *International Journal of Forecasting,* vol. 12 (1996), pp. 139–153.

Melnyk, Steven. "1997 Forecasting Software Product Listing." *APICS—The Performance Advantage* (April 1997), pp. 62–65.

Moon, Mark A., John T. Mentzer, and Dwight E. Thomas Jr. "Customer Demand Planning at Lucent Technologies; A Case Study in Continuous Improvement Through Sales Forecast Auditing." *Industrial Marketing Management,* vol. 29, no. 1 (2000).

Principles of Forecasting: A Handbook for Researchers and Practitioners, J. Scott Armstrong (ed.). Norwell, MA: Kluwer Academic Publishers, 2001. Also visit (www-marketing.wharton.upenn.edu/ forecast) for valuable information on forecasting, including frequently asked questions, forecasting methodology tree, and dictionary.

Sanders, Nada R., and L. P. Ritzman. "Bringing Judgment into Combination Forecasts." *Journal of Operations Management,* vol. 13 (1995), pp. 311–321.

Sanders, Nada R., and K. B. Manrodt. "Forecasting Practices in U.S. Corporations: Survey Results." *Interfaces,* vol. 24 (1994), pp. 91–100.

Sanders, Nada R., and Larry P. Ritzman. "The Need for Contextual and Technical Knowledge in Judgmental Forecasting." *Journal of Behavioral Decision Making,* vol. 5, no. 1 (1992), pp. 39–52.

Smith, Bernard. *Focus Forecasting: Computer Techniques for Inventory Control.* Boston: CBI Publishing, 1984.

Stratton, William B. "How to Design a Viable Forecasting System." *Production and Inventory Management,* vol. 20, no. 1 (1979), pp. 17–27.

Yurkiewicz, Jack. "Forecasting 2000." *OR/MS Today,* vol. 27, no. 1 (2000), pp. 58–65.

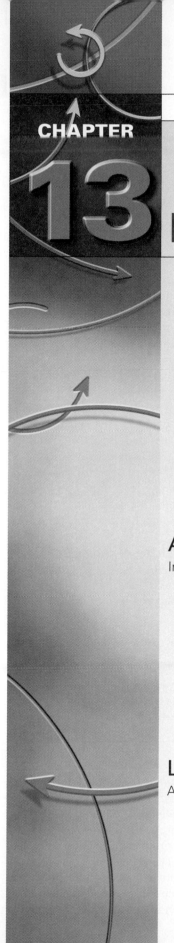

Inventory Management

Across the Organization

Inventory management is important to . . .

- ❏ **accounting,** which provides the cost estimates used in inventory control, pays suppliers, and bills customers.
- ❏ **finance,** which deals with the implications of interest or investment opportunity costs on inventory management and anticipates how best to finance inventory and the cash flows related to inventory.
- ❏ **management information systems,** which develops and maintains the systems for managing inventories.
- ❏ **marketing and sales,** which create the need for inventory systems and rely on inventories to satisfy customers.
- ❏ **operations,** which has the responsibility to control the firm's inventories.

Learning Goals

After reading this chapter, you will be able to . . .

1. describe the cost and service trade-offs involved in inventory decisions.
2. distinguish between the different types of inventory and know how to manage their quantities.
3. compute the economic order quantity and apply it in various situations.
4. develop policies for both the continuous review and the periodic review inventory control systems.
5. identify ways to maintain accurate inventory records.

The Internet has opened a realm of business opportunities not even dreamed about 10 years ago. Many Internet companies, however, were formed under the assumption that customers, retailers, manufacturers, distributors, and service providers can be linked electronically in a seamless network thereby eliminating the need for costly warehouses and retail stores. They thought that inventory management and distribution can be outsourced to someone else. If that assumption is true, then why have some major Internet companies gone against that conventional Internet wisdom? For example, Amazon.com (www.amazon.com) invested $300 million for 3 million square feet of warehouse space and Webvan (www.webvan.com) spent $1 billion to build giant warehouses in 26 cities.

Inventory management has become an important activity for many Internet companies. Customer delivery must be fast and contain exactly what the customer ordered. Here an employee packages an Amazon.com order for shipment.

The answer is that Internet companies are learning the lessons learned earlier by their bricks-and-mortar cousins—excellent customer service requires control over inventories. The Christmas of 1999 was a disaster for many "e-tailers." Etoys (www.etoys.com), while achieving on-time delivery for 96 percent of its orders, still got a black eye for shipping thousands of orders late. Now, Etoys must restore investor confidence by increasing total revenues and profitability. Its stock fell 90 percent in one year, placing its very existence in jeopardy.

Toysrus.com (www.toysrus.com) was unable to ship many orders on time, which prompted the Federal Trade Commission to impose a fine for not informing its customers of the delayed shipments. Low revenues from Internet operations caused Toysrus.com to seek an alliance with Amazon, whereby Amazon would manage the customer service, warehousing, and shipping and Toysrus.com would buy and manage the inventory of toys. The alliance builds on Toysrus' competence for managing toy inventories through traditional bricks-and-mortar operations that support its retail stores and Amazon's competence for customer service management. Even Amazon, however, had a difficult time. Most of its customers were happy, but it bought far too much inventory—including such things as a 50-week supply of Kermit the Frog telephones—leading to a major charge against earnings for unsold goods. Consequently, it is clear that inventory management is just as important now as it has ever been.

Source: Bannon, Lisa, and Joseph, Pereira. "Two Big Online Toy Sellers Fight over Delivery Speed and Exclusive Rights," *Wall Street Journal* (September 25, 2000), p. B1; Hof, Robert D. "What's With All the Warehouses?" *Business Week* (November 1, 1999), p. EB 88.

INVENTORY MANAGEMENT IS AN important concern for managers in all types of businesses. For companies that operate on relatively low profit margins, poor inventory management can seriously undermine the business. The challenge is not to pare inventories to the bone to reduce costs or to have plenty around to satisfy all demands, but to have the right amount to achieve the competitive priorities for the business most efficiently. In this chapter, we first introduce the basic concepts of inventory management for all types of businesses and then discuss inventory control systems appropriate for retail and distribution inventories. Later in the book, we focus on systems primarily used for manufacturing inventories (see the Resource Planning and Lean Systems chapters).

INVENTORY CONCEPTS

Inventory is created when the receipt of materials, parts, or finished goods exceeds their disbursement; it is depleted when their disbursement exceeds their receipt (see the Supply-Chain Management chapter). In this section, we identify the pressures for high and low inventories, define the different types of inventory, discuss tactics that can be used to reduce inventories when appropriate, identify the trade-offs involved in making manufacturing inventory placement decisions, and discuss how to identify the inventory items needing the most attention.

PRESSURES FOR LOW INVENTORIES

What are the costs for holding inventories?

inventory holding cost
The variable cost of keeping items on hand, including interest, storage and handling, taxes, insurance, and shrinkage.

An inventory manager's job is to balance the conflicting costs and pressures that argue for both low and high inventories and determine appropriate inventory levels. The primary reason for keeping inventories low is that inventory represents a temporary monetary investment in goods on which a firm must pay (rather than receive) interest. **Inventory holding** (or carrying) **cost** is the variable cost of keeping items on hand, including interest, storage and handling, taxes, insurance, and shrinkage. When these components change with inventory levels, so does the holding cost. Companies usually state an item's holding cost per period of time as a percent of its value. The annual cost to maintain one unit in inventory typically ranges from 20 to 40 percent of its value. Suppose that a firm's holding cost is 30 percent. If the average value of total inventory is 20 percent of sales, the average annual cost to hold inventory is 6 percent [0.30(0.20)] of total sales. This cost is sizable in terms of gross profit margins, which often are less than 10 percent. Thus, the components of holding cost create pressures for low inventories.

INTEREST OR OPPORTUNITY COST. To finance inventory, a company may obtain a loan or forgo the opportunity of an investment promising an attractive return. Interest or opportunity cost, whichever is greater, usually is the largest component of holding cost, often as high as 15 percent. For example, a car dealer may obtain a loan to finance an inventory of cars at an annual interest rate of 11 percent, or the dealer may pay cash and forgo the opportunity to invest the money in the stock market at an expected return of 13 percent.

STORAGE AND HANDLING COSTS. Inventory takes up space and must be moved into and out of storage. Storage and handling costs may be incurred when a firm rents space on either a long- or short-term basis. There also is an opportunity cost for storage when a firm could use storage space productively in some other way.

TAXES, INSURANCE, AND SHRINKAGE. More taxes are paid if end-of-year inventories are high, and insurance on assets increases when there is more to insure. Shrinkage takes three forms. Pilferage, or theft of inventory by customers or employees, is a significant percentage of sales for some businesses. Obsolescence occurs when inventory cannot be used or sold at full value, owing to model changes, engineering modifications, or unexpectedly low demand. Obsolescence is a big expense in retail clothing, where drastic discounts on seasonal clothing are offered at the end of a season. Deterioration through physical spoilage or damage results in lost value. Food and beverages, for example, lose value and might even have to be discarded when their shelf life is reached. When the rate of deterioration is high, building large inventories may be unwise.

PRESSURES FOR HIGH INVENTORIES

Why are inventories necessary?

The fact that inventory held in the U.S. economy exceeds the $1.3 trillion mark suggests that there are pressures for large inventories, despite the expense. Let us look briefly at each type of pressure.

CUSTOMER SERVICE. Creating inventory can speed delivery and improve on-time delivery. Inventory reduces the potential for stockouts and backorders, which are key concerns of wholesalers and retailers. A **stockout** occurs when an item that is typically stocked is not available to satisfy a demand the moment it occurs, resulting in loss of the sale. A **backorder** is a customer order that cannot be filled when promised or demanded but is filled later. Customers may be willing to wait for a backorder but next time may take their business elsewhere. Sometimes customers are given discounts for the inconvenience of waiting.

ORDERING COST. Each time a firm places a new order, it incurs an **ordering cost**, or the cost of preparing a purchase order for a supplier or a production order for the shop. For the same item, the ordering cost is the same, regardless of the order size: The purchasing agent must take the time to decide how much to order and, perhaps, select a supplier and negotiate terms. Time also is spent on paperwork, follow-up, and receiving. In the case of a production order for a manufactured item, a blueprint and routing instructions often must accompany the shop order. The Internet (see the Technology Management and the Supply-Chain Management chapters) can help streamline the order process and reduce the costs of placing orders.

SETUP COST. The cost involved in changing over a machine to produce a different component or item is the **setup cost.** It includes labor and time to make the changeover, cleaning, and new tools or fixtures. Scrap or rework costs can be substantially higher at the start of the run. Setup cost also is independent of order size, so there is pressure to order a large supply of the component and hold it in inventory.

LABOR AND EQUIPMENT UTILIZATION. By creating more inventory, management can increase workforce productivity and facility utilization in three ways. First, placing larger, less frequent production orders reduces the number of unproductive setups, which add no value to a product or service. Second, holding inventory reduces the chance of costly rescheduling of production orders because the components needed to make the product are not in inventory. Third, building inventories improves resource utilization by stabilizing the output rate for industries when demand is cyclical or seasonal. The firm uses inventory built during slack periods to handle extra demand in peak seasons and minimizes the need for extra shifts, hiring, layoffs, overtime, and additional equipment.

TRANSPORTATION COST. Sometimes, outbound transportation cost can be reduced by increasing inventory levels. Having inventory on hand allows more carload shipments and minimizes the need to expedite shipments by more expensive modes of transportation. Forward placement of inventory can also reduce outbound transportation cost, even though the pooling effect is lessened and more inventory is necessary (see the Supply-Chain Management chapter). Inbound transportation cost also may be reduced by creating more inventory. Sometimes, several items are ordered from the same supplier. Combining these orders and placing them at the same time may lead to rate discounts, thereby decreasing the costs of transportation and raw materials.

stockout The situation that occurs when an item that is typically stocked is not available to satisfy a demand the moment it occurs, resulting in loss of the sale.

backorder A customer order that cannot be filled when promised or demanded but is filled later.

ordering cost The cost of preparing a purchase order for a supplier or a production order for the shop.

setup cost The cost involved in changing over a machine to produce a different component or item.

PAYMENTS TO SUPPLIERS. A firm often can reduce total payments to suppliers if it can tolerate higher inventory levels. Suppose that a firm learns that a key supplier is about to increase prices. It might be cheaper for the firm to order a larger quantity than usual—in effect delaying the price increase—even though inventory will increase temporarily. Similarly, a firm can take advantage of quantity discounts. A **quantity discount,** whereby the price per unit drops when the order is sufficiently large, is an incentive to order larger quantities.

quantity discount A drop in the price per unit when the order is sufficiently large.

TYPES OF INVENTORY

Another perspective on inventory is to classify it by how it is created. In this context, there are four types of inventory for an item: cycle, safety, anticipation, and pipeline. They cannot be identified physically; that is, an inventory manager can't look at a pile of widgets and identify which ones are cycle inventory and which ones are pipeline inventory. However, conceptually, each of the four types comes into being in an entirely different way. Once you understand these differences, you can prescribe different ways to reduce inventory, which we discuss in the next section.

What types of inventory does a business own?

CYCLE INVENTORY. The portion of total inventory that varies directly with lot size is called **cycle inventory.** Determining how frequently to order, and in what quantity, is called **lot sizing.** Two principles apply.

cycle inventory The portion of total inventory that varies directly with lot size.

1. The lot size, Q, varies directly with the elapsed time (or cycle) between orders. If a lot is ordered every five weeks, the average lot size must equal five weeks' demand.

2. The longer the time between orders for a given item, the greater the cycle inventory must be.

lot sizing The determination of how frequently and in what quantity to order inventory.

At the beginning of the interval, the cycle inventory is at its maximum, or Q. At the end of the interval, just before a new lot arrives, cycle inventory drops to its minimum, or 0. The average cycle inventory is the average of these two extremes:

$$\text{Average cycle inventory} = \frac{Q + 0}{2} = \frac{Q}{2}$$

This formula is exact only when the demand rate is constant and uniform. However, it does provide a reasonably good estimate even when demand rates are not constant. Factors other than the demand rate (e.g., scrap losses) also may cause estimating errors when this simple formula is used.

SAFETY STOCK INVENTORY. To avoid customer service problems and the hidden costs of unavailable components, companies hold safety stock. **Safety stock inventory** protects against uncertainties in demand, lead time, and supply. Safety stocks are desirable when suppliers fail to deliver the desired quantity on the specified date with acceptable quality or when manufactured items have significant amounts of scrap or rework. Safety stock inventory ensures that operations are not disrupted when such problems occur, allowing subsequent operations to continue.

safety stock inventory Surplus inventory that a company holds to protect against uncertainties in demand, lead time, and supply.

To create safety stock, a firm places an order for delivery earlier than when the item is typically needed.[1] The replenishment order therefore arrives ahead of time, giving a cushion against uncertainty. For example, suppose that the average lead time from

---

[1] When orders are placed at fixed intervals, there is a second way. Each new order placed is larger than the quantity typically needed through the next delivery date.

MANAGERIAL PRACTICE 13.1
Improving Customer Service Through Inventory Management at Amazon.com

As alluded to in the chapter opener, Amazon.com (www.amazon.com) had a rough holiday season in 1999, owing primarily to mismanaged inventories and chaotic warehouse operations that resulted in major charges to earnings for unsold goods. Since then, Amazon has changed its ways. For example, it had housed items such as DVDs and DVD players in different states, which complicated collecting orders for a single customer. Now, the items are grouped together in its shipping facilities. Also, Amazon has started to forecast demands by areas of the country. Palm handheld computers are forecasted by ZIP code and the proper inventories are sent to the warehouse serving that area. This approach will reduce the time it takes to get a product to the customer, but it will increase the amount of inventory of the item in the distribution system (see the discussion of inventory pooling in the Supply-Chain Management chapter).

Jeffrey Wilke, vice-president and general manager of operations at Amazon, identified four things Amazon has done to improve customer service through inventory management:

❑ Increased warehouse capacity quickly. Three million square feet of warehouse capacity in less than a year, which enabled Amazon to develop the appropriate amount of cycle, safety stock, and anticipation inventories to service its customers.
❑ Introduced state-of-the-art automation and mechanization. The warehouses are efficient and flexible enough to move items in container sizes, pallet sizes, or lot sizes of one, thereby reducing handling costs.

❑ Linked order information to a customer archive through information technology. When a customer places an order for a particular basket of goods, the system captures the data and adds it to a database of past purchases from that customer. This capability enables Amazon to forecast future purchases and tailor the shopping experience the customer receives.
❑ Replicated the system across the distribution centers where possible. Linking capacity, automation, and information technology allows Amazon to expand in terms of product breadth and in terms of partnerships and alliances. Because the system can be replicated, Amazon has the capability to expand in modular fashion as new warehouses are added.

Amazon's approach is to control inventories themselves, rather than to delegate this important function to another company. While the use of the Internet is expanding at a blistering pace, the dream of a seamless interface between suppliers, retailers, and customers must still await the development of the enabling technology.

Sources: Wingsfield, Nick. "Amazon Vows to Avoid Mess of 1999 Christmas Rush: Too Many Kermit Phones," *Wall Street Journal* (September 25, 2000), p. B1; "Q&A With Jeffrey Wilke," *Business Week* (November 1, 1999), www.ebiz.businessweek.com.

a supplier is three weeks but a firm orders five weeks in advance just to be safe. This policy creates a safety stock equal to a two weeks' supply ($5 - 3$).

anticipation inventory
Inventory used to absorb uneven rates of demand or supply.

ANTICIPATION INVENTORY Inventory used to absorb uneven rates of demand or supply, which businesses often face, is referred to as **anticipation inventory**. Predictable, seasonal demand patterns lend themselves to the use of anticipation inventory. Manufacturers of air conditioners, for example, can experience 90 percent of their annual demand during just three months of a year. Such uneven demand may lead a manufacturer to stockpile anticipation inventory during periods of low demand so that output levels do not have to be increased much when demand peaks. Smoothing output rates with inventory can increase productivity because varying output rates and workforce size can be costly. Anticipation inventory also can help when supply, rather than demand, is uneven. A company may stock up on a certain purchased item if its suppliers are threatened with a strike or have severe capacity limitations.

pipeline inventory
Inventory moving from point to point in the materials flow system.

PIPELINE INVENTORY Inventory moving from point to point in the materials flow system is called **pipeline inventory**. Materials move from suppliers to a plant, from one operation to the next in the plant, from the plant to a distribution center or customer, and from the distribution center to a retailer. Pipeline inventory consists of orders that have been placed but not yet received. For example, NUMMI, the joint venture between General Motors and Toyota in California, uses parts produced in the Midwest. Shipments arrive daily at the plant, but the transportation lead time requires a pipeline inventory of parts in rail cars enroute from the Midwest at all times. Pipeline inventory between two points, for either transportation or production, can be measured as the average demand during lead time, $\overline{D}_L$, which is the average demand for the item per period (d) times the number of periods in the item's lead time (L) to move between the two points, or

$$\text{Pipeline inventory} = \overline{D}_L = dL$$

Note that the lot size does not directly affect the average level of the pipeline inventory. Increasing Q inflates the size of each order, so if an order has been placed but not received, there is more pipeline inventory for that lead time. But that increase is canceled by a proportionate decrease in the number of orders placed per year. The lot size can *indirectly* affect pipeline inventory, however, if increasing Q causes the lead time to increase. Here $\overline{D}_L$, and therefore pipeline inventory, will increase.

Managerial Practice 13.1 shows how Amazon.com has designed an inventory system to improve customer service.

EXAMPLE 13.1   *Estimating Inventory Levels*

**TUTOR
13.1**

A plant makes monthly shipments of electric drills to a wholesaler in average lot sizes of 280 drills. The wholesaler's average demand is 70 drills a week, and the lead time from the plant is three weeks. The wholesaler must pay for the inventory from the moment the plant makes a shipment. If the wholesaler is willing to increase its purchase quantity to 350 units, the plant will guarantee a lead time of two weeks. What is the effect on cycle and pipeline inventories?

SOLUTION

The current cycle and pipeline inventories are

$$\text{Cycle inventory} = \frac{Q}{2} = \frac{280}{2} = 140 \text{ drills}$$

$$\text{Pipeline inventory} = \overline{D}_L = dL = (70 \text{ drills/week})(3 \text{ weeks}) = 210 \text{ drills}$$

Figure 13.1 shows the cycle and pipeline inventories if the wholesaler accepts the new proposal.

Tutor 13.1 - Estimating Inventory Levels

Position the cell pointer on the green areas to see how formulas compare with your own.

1. Enter the average lot size, average demand during a period, and the number of periods of lead time:

Average lot size	350
Average demand	70
Lead time	2

2. To compute cycle inventory, simply divide average lot size by 2. To compute pipeline inventory, multipiy average demand by lead time:

Cycle inventory	175
Pipeline inventory	140

FIGURE 13.1

Decision Point The effect of the new proposal on cycle inventories is to increase them by 35 units, or 25 percent. The reduction in pipeline inventories, however, is 70 units, or 33 percent.

The proposal would reduce the total investment in cycle and pipeline inventories. Also, it is advantageous to have shorter lead times because the wholesaler only has to commit to purchases two weeks in advance, rather than three. ◻

INVENTORY REDUCTION TACTICS

What are the options for reducing inventory prudently?

Managers always are eager to find cost-effective ways to reduce inventory. Later in this chapter, we examine various ways for finding optimal lot sizes (see also the Special Inventory Models supplement). Here, we discuss something more fundamental—the basic tactics (which we call *levers*) for reducing inventory. A primary lever is one that must be activated if inventory is to be reduced. A secondary lever reduces the penalty cost of applying the primary lever and the need for having inventory in the first place.

CYCLE INVENTORY. The primary lever is simply to reduce the lot size. Methods of just-in-time production (see the Lean Systems chapter) use extremely small lots, compared to traditional lot sizes equaling several weeks' (or even months') supply. However, making such reductions in Q without making any other changes can be devastating. For example, setup costs can skyrocket, which leads to use of the two secondary levers.

1. Streamline methods for placing orders and making setups, which reduces ordering and setup costs and allows Q to be reduced.

repeatability The degree to which the same work can be done again.

2. Increase repeatability to eliminate the need for changeovers. **Repeatability** is the degree to which the same work can be done again. It can be increased through high product demand; use of specialization; devoting resources exclusively to a product; using the same part in many different products; flexible automation; the one-worker, multiple-machines concept; or group technology (see the Process Management and Layout chapters). Increased repeatability may justify new setup methods, reduce transportation costs, and allow quantity discounts from suppliers.

SAFETY STOCK INVENTORY. The primary lever for reducing safety stock inventory is to place orders closer to the time when they must be received. However, this approach can lead to unacceptable customer service—unless demand, supply, and delivery uncertainties can be minimized. Four secondary levers can be used.

1. Improve demand forecasts so that there are fewer surprises from customers. Perhaps customers can even be encouraged to order items before they need them.

2. Cut lead times of purchased or produced items to reduce demand uncertainty during lead time. For example, local suppliers with short lead times could be selected whenever possible.

3. Reduce supply uncertainties. Suppliers may be more reliable if production plans are shared with them, permitting them to make more realistic forecasts. Surprises from unexpected scrap or rework can be reduced by improving manufacturing processes. Preventive maintenance can minimize unexpected downtime caused by equipment failure.

4. Rely more on equipment and labor buffers, such as capacity cushions and cross-trained workers. These are the only buffers available to businesses in the service sector because they can't inventory their services.

ANTICIPATION INVENTORY. The primary lever for reducing anticipation inventory is simply to match demand rate with production rate. Secondary levers are used to level customer demand in one of the following ways:

1. Add new products with different demand cycles so that a peak in the demand for one product compensates for the seasonal low for another.
2. Provide off-season promotional campaigns.
3. Offer seasonal pricing plans.

PIPELINE INVENTORY. An operations manager has direct control over lead time but not demand rate. Because pipeline inventory is a function of demand during lead time, the primary lever is to reduce the lead time. Two secondary levers can help managers cut lead times.

1. Find more responsive suppliers and select new carriers for shipments between stocking locations or improve materials handling within the plant. Introducing a computer system could overcome information delays between a distribution center and retailer.
2. Decrease Q, at least in those cases where lead time depends on lot size. Smaller jobs generally require less time to complete.

PLACEMENT OF MANUFACTURING INVENTORIES

Just as distribution managers decide where to place finished goods inventory (see the Supply-Chain Management chapter), manufacturing managers make similar decisions for raw materials and work-in-process within the plant. In general, managers make inventory placement decisions by designating an item as either a special or a standard. A **special** is an item made to order, or if purchased, it is bought to order. Just enough are ordered to cover the latest customer request. A **standard** is an item that is made to stock and normally is available when needed. When a company makes more of its items as standards, particularly at the finished goods level, it places inventory closer to the customer.

Inventory held toward the finished goods level means short delivery times—but a higher dollar investment in inventory. Inventory placement at Shamrock Chemicals, a Newark, New Jersey, manufacturer of materials used in printing inks, illustrates this trade-off. Shamrock enjoys annual sales of more than $15 million because it can ship a product the same day a customer orders it. But because finished goods are treated as standards rather than specials, Shamrock is forced to maintain a large inventory. Holding inventory at the raw materials level would reduce the cost of carrying inventory—but at the expense of the quick customer response time that gives Shamrock its competitive advantage. R. R. Donnelley, a large manufacturer of books and other printed materials, chooses an opposite strategy by positioning inventory back at the raw materials, chooses an opposite strategy by positioning inventory back at the raw materials level (e.g., in rolled paper stock and ink). The reason is that the products Donnelley produces are made to order and therefore considered specials. Stocking them based on a forecast would be very expensive. Placing inventories closer to the raw materials level gives Donnelley great flexibility in meeting a variety of customer demands.

IDENTIFYING CRITICAL INVENTORY ITEMS WITH ABC ANALYSIS

Thousands of items are held in inventory by a typical organization, but only a small percentage of them deserve management's closest attention and tightest control. **ABC analysis** is the process of dividing items into three classes according to their dollar usage so that managers can focus on items that have the highest dollar value. This method is the equivalent of creating a Pareto chart (see the Total Quality Management chapter) except that it is applied to inventory rather than quality. As Figure 13.2 shows, class A items typically represent only about 20 percent of the items but account

Should most inventory be held at the raw materials, work-in-process, or finished goods level? Which items should be standards?

special An item made to order; if purchased, it is bought to order.

standard An item that is made to stock and normally is available when needed.

Which items demand the closest attention and control?

ABC analysis The process of dividing items into three classes according to their dollar useage so that managers can focus on items that have the highest dollar value.

*Typical Chart from
ABC Analysis*

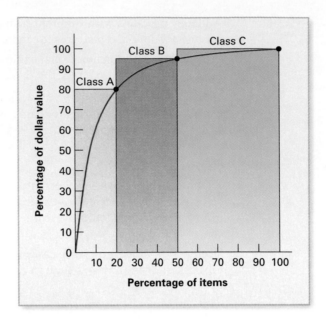

for 80 percent of the dollar usage. Class B items account for another 30 percent of the items but only 15 percent of the dollar usage. Finally, 50 percent of the items fall in class C, representing a mere 5 percent of the dollar usage.

The goal of ABC analysis is to identify the inventory levels of class A items and enable management to control them tightly by using the levers just discussed. The analyst begins by multiplying the annual demand rate for one item by the dollar value (cost) of one unit to determine its dollar usage. After ranking the items on the basis of dollar usage and creating the Pareto chart, the analyst looks for "natural" changes in slope. The dividing lines in Figure 13.2 between classes are inexact. Class A items could be somewhat higher or lower than 20 percent of all items, but normally account for the bulk of the dollar usage.

A manager can direct that class A items be reviewed frequently to reduce the average lot size and keep inventory records current. If the records show an on-hand balance of 100 units but the actual balance is 200 units, costly inventory is being carried needlessly. If a class A item is bought outside the firm, purchasing may be able to reduce its cost through centralized buying, switching suppliers, or more effective contract negotiation.

For class C items, much looser control is appropriate. A stockout of a class C item can be as crucial as for a class A item, but the inventory holding cost of class C items tends to be low. These features suggest that higher inventory levels can be tolerated and that more safety stock, larger lot sizes, and perhaps even a visual system, which we discuss later, may suffice for class C items.

ECONOMIC ORDER QUANTITY

**economic order quantity
(EOQ)** The lot size that
minimizes total annual
inventory holding and
ordering costs.

Recall that managers face conflicting pressures to keep inventories low enough to avoid excess inventory holding costs but high enough to reduce the frequency of orders and setups. A good starting point for balancing these conflicting pressures and determining the best cycle-inventory level for an item is finding the **economic order quantity** (EOQ), which is the lot size that minimizes total annual inventory holding and ordering costs. The approach to determining the EOQ is based on the following assumptions:

1. The demand rate for the item is constant (e.g., always 10 units per day) and known with certainty.

2. There are no constraints (e.g., truck capacity or materials handling limitations) on the size of each lot.

3. The only two relevant costs are the inventory holding cost and the fixed cost per lot for ordering or setup.

4. Decisions for one item can be made independently of decisions for other items (i.e., no advantage is gained in combining several orders going to the same supplier).

5. There is no uncertainty in lead time or supply. The lead time is constant (e.g., always 14 days) and known with certainty. The amount received is exactly what was ordered and it arrives all at once rather than piecemeal.

The economic order quantity will be optimal when the five assumptions are satisfied. In reality, few situations are so simple and well behaved. In fact, different lot-sizing approaches are needed to reflect quantity discounts, uneven demand rates, or interactions between items (see the Special Inventory Models supplement). However, the EOQ often is a reasonable first approximation of average lot sizes, even when one or more of the assumptions do not quite apply.

CALCULATING THE EOQ

How much should be ordered?

We begin by formulating the total cost for any lot size Q. Next, we derive the EOQ, which is the Q that minimizes total cost. Finally, we describe how to convert the EOQ into a companion measure, the elapsed time between orders.

When the EOQ assumptions are satisfied, cycle inventory behaves as shown in Figure 13.3. A cycle begins with Q units held in inventory, which happens when a new order is received. During the cycle, on-hand inventory is used at a constant rate and, because demand is known with certainty and the lead time is a constant, a new lot can be ordered so that inventory falls to 0 precisely when the new lot is received. Because inventory varies uniformly between Q and 0, the average cycle inventory equals half the lot size, Q.

The annual holding cost for this amount of inventory, which increases linearly with Q, as Figure 13.4(a) shows, is

$$\text{Annual holding cost} = (\text{Average cycle inventory})(\text{Unit holding cost})$$

FIGURE 13.3

Cycle-Inventory Levels

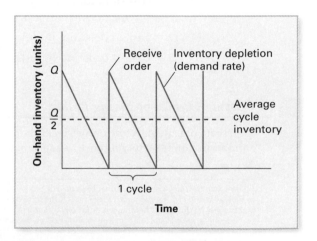

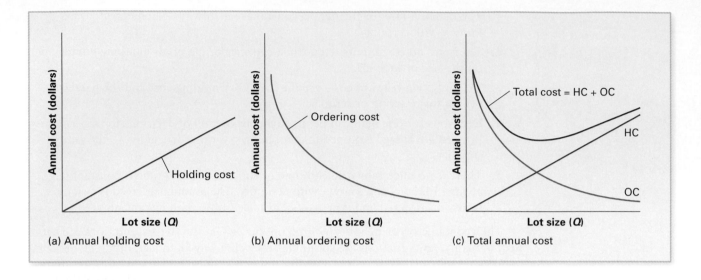

(a) Annual holding cost   (b) Annual ordering cost   (c) Total annual cost

FIGURE 13.4

*Graphs of Annual
Holding, Ordering, and
Total Costs*

The annual ordering cost is

Annual ordering cost = (Number of orders/year)(Ordering or setup cost)

The average number of orders per year equals annual demand divided by Q. For example, if 1,200 units must be ordered each year and the average lot size is 100 units, then 12 orders will be placed during the year. The annual ordering or setup cost decreases nonlinearly as Q increases, as shown in Figure 13.4(b), because fewer orders are placed.

The total annual cost,[2] as graphed in Figure 13.4(c), is the sum of the two cost components:

Total cost = Annual holding cost + Annual ordering or setup cost[3]

$$C = \frac{Q}{2}(H) + \frac{D}{Q}(S)$$

where

C = total cost per year

Q = lot size, in units

H = cost of holding one unit in inventory for a year,
   often calculated as a proportion of the item's value

D = annual demand, in units per year

S = cost of ordering or setting up one lot, in dollars per lot

EXAMPLE 13.2

Costing Out a Lot-Sizing Policy

A museum of natural history opened a gift shop two years ago. Managing inventories has become a problem. Low inventory turnover is squeezing profit margins and causing cash-flow problems.

---

[2] Expressing the total cost on an annual basis usually is convenient (though not necessary). Any time horizon can be selected, as long as D and H cover the same time period. If the total cost is calculated on a monthly basis, D must be monthly demand and H must be the cost of holding a unit for one month.

[3] The number of orders actually placed in any year is always a whole number, although the formula allows the use of fractional values. However, rounding is not needed because what is being calculated is an average for multiple years. Such averages often are nonintegers.

One of the top-selling items in the container group at the museum's gift shop is a birdfeeder. Sales are 18 units per week, and the supplier charges $60 per unit. The cost of placing an order with the supplier is $45. Annual holding cost is 25 percent of a feeder's value, and the museum operates 52 weeks per year. Management chose a 390 unit lot size so that new orders could be placed less frequently. What is the annual cost of the current policy of using a 390-unit lot size? Would a lot size of 468 be better?

SOLUTION

We begin by computing the annual demand and holding cost as

$$D = (18 \text{ units/week})(52 \text{ weeks/year}) = 936 \text{ units}$$
$$H = 0.25(\$60/\text{unit}) = \$15$$

The annual cost for the current policy is

$$C = \frac{Q}{2}(H) + \frac{D}{Q}(S)$$
$$= \frac{390}{2}(\$15) + \frac{936}{390}(\$45) = \$2{,}925 + \$108 = 3{,}033$$

The annual cost for the alternative lot size is

$$C = \frac{468}{2}(\$15) + \frac{936}{468}(\$45) = \$3{,}510 + \$90 = \$3{,}600$$

Decision Point The lot size of 468 units, which is a half-year supply, would be a more expensive option than the current policy. The savings in order costs are more than offset by the increase in holding costs. Management should use the total cost equation to explore other lot-size alternatives. ❑

Figure 13.5 displays the impact of using several Q values for the birdfeeder in Example 13.2. Eight different lot sizes were evaluated in addition to the current one. Both holding and ordering costs were plotted, but their sum—the total cost curve—is the important feature. The graph shows that the best lot size, or EOQ, is the lowest

FIGURE 13.5

Total Inventory Cost Function for Birdfeeder

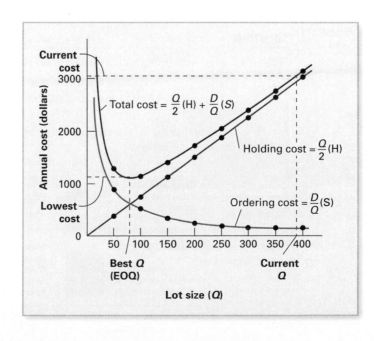

point on the total cost curve, or between 50 and 100 units. Obviously, reducing the current lot-size policy ($Q = 390$) can result in significant savings.

A more efficient approach is to use the EOQ formula:

$$EOQ = \sqrt{\frac{2DS}{H}}$$

We use calculus to obtain the EOQ formula from the total cost formula. We take the first derivative of the total cost function with respect to Q, set it equal to 0, and solve for Q. As Figure 13.5 indicates, the EOQ is the order quantity for which annual holding cost equals annual ordering cost. Using this insight, we can also obtain the EOQ formula by equating the formulas for annual ordering cost and annual holding cost and solving for Q. The graph in Figure 13.5 also reveals that, when the annual holding cost for any Q exceeds the annual ordering cost, as with the 390-unit order, we can immediately conclude that Q is too big. A smaller Q reduces holding cost and increases ordering cost, bringing them into balance. Similarly, if the annual ordering cost exceeds the annual holding cost, Q should be increased.

Sometimes inventory policies are based on the time between replenishment orders, rather than the number of units in the lot size. The **time between orders (TBO)** for a particular lot size is the average elapsed time between receiving (or placing) replenishment orders of Q units. Expressed as a fraction of a year, the TBO is simply Q divided by annual demand. When we use the EOQ and express time in terms of months, the TBO is

$$TBO_{EOQ} = \frac{EOQ}{D} \text{ (12 months/year)}$$

In Example 13.3, we show how to calculate TBO for years, months, weeks, and days.

time between orders (TBO) The average elapsed time between receiving (or placing) replenishment orders of Q units for a particular lot size.

EXAMPLE 13.3

TUTOR 13.2

Finding the EOQ, Total Cost and TBO

For the birdfeeders in Example 13.2, calculate the EOQ and its total cost. How frequently will orders be placed if the EOQ is used?

SOLUTION

Using the formulas for EOQ and annual cost, we get

$$EOQ = \sqrt{\frac{2DS}{H}} = \sqrt{\frac{2(936)(45)}{15}} = 74.94, \quad \text{or} \quad 75 \text{ units}$$

Figure 13.6 shows that the total annual cost is much less than the $3,033 cost of the current policy of placing 390-unit orders.

Parameters				
Current Lot Size (Q)	390		Economic Order Quantity	75
Demand (D)	936			
Order Cost (S)	$45			
Unit Holding Cost (H)	$15			
Annual Costs			**Annual Costs based on EOQ**	
Orders per Year	2.4		Orders per Year	12.48
Annual Ordering Cost	$108.00		Annual Ordering Cost	$561.60
Annual Holding Cost	$2,925.00		Annual Holding Cost	$562.50
Annual Inventory Cost	$3,033.00		Annual Inventory Cost	$1,124.10

FIGURE 13.6

When the EOQ is used, the time between orders (TBO) can be expressed in various ways for the same time period.

$$\text{TBO}_{EOQ} = \frac{\text{EOQ}}{D} = \frac{75}{936} = 0.080 \text{ year}$$

$$\text{TBO}_{EOQ} = \frac{\text{EOQ}}{D}(12 \text{ months/year}) = \frac{75}{936}(12) = 0.96 \text{ month}$$

$$\text{TBO}_{EOQ} = \frac{\text{EOQ}}{D}(52 \text{ weeks/year}) = \frac{75}{936}(52) = 4.17 \text{ weeks}$$

$$\text{TBO}_{EOQ} = \frac{\text{EOQ}}{D}(365 \text{ days/year}) = \frac{75}{936}(365) = 29.25 \text{ days}$$

Decision Point Using the EOQ, about 12 orders per year will be required. Using the current policy of 390 units per order, an average of 2.4 orders will be needed each year (every five months). The current policy saves on ordering costs but incurs a much larger cost for carrying the cycle inventory. While it is easy to see which option is best on the basis of total ordering and holding costs, other factors may affect the final decision. For example, if the supplier would reduce the price per unit for large orders, it may be better to order the larger quantity (see the Special Inventory Models supplement). ◻

UNDERSTANDING THE EFFECT OF CHANGES

How often should demand estimates, cost estimates, and lot sizes be updated?

Subjecting the EOQ formula to sensitivity analysis can yield valuable insights into the management of inventories. Sensitivity analysis is a technique for systematically changing crucial parameters to determine the effects of change (see the Decision Making supplement). Let us consider the effects on the EOQ when we substitute different values into the numerator or denominator of the formula.

A CHANGE IN THE DEMAND RATE. Because D is in the numerator, the EOQ (and, therefore, the best cycle-inventory level) increases in proportion to the square root of the annual demand. Therefore, when demand rises, the lot size also should rise, but more slowly than actual demand.

A CHANGE IN THE SETUP COSTS. Because S is in the numerator, increasing S increases the EOQ and, consequently, the average cycle inventory. Conversely, reducing S reduces the EOQ, allowing smaller lot sizes to be produced economically. This relationship explains why manufacturers are so concerned about cutting setup time and costs. When weeks of supply decline, inventory turns increase. When setup cost and setup time become trivial, a major impediment to small-lot production is removed.

A CHANGE IN THE HOLDING COSTS. Because H is in the denominator, the EOQ declines when H increases. Conversely, when H declines, the EOQ increases. Larger lot sizes are justified by lower holding costs.

ERRORS IN ESTIMATING *D, H,* AND *S*. Total cost is fairly insensitive to errors, even when the estimates are wrong by a large margin. The reasons are that errors tend to cancel each other out and that the square root reduces the effect of the error. Suppose that we incorrectly estimate the holding cost to be double its true value—that is, we calculate EOQ using $2H$, instead of H. For Example 13.3, this 100 percent error increases total cost by only 6 percent, from \$1,124 to \$1,192. Thus, the EOQ lies in a fairly large zone of acceptable lot sizes, allowing managers to deviate somewhat from the EOQ to accommodate supplier contracts or storage constraints.

INVENTORY CONTROL SYSTEMS

independent demand items Items for which demand is influenced by market conditions and is not related to the inventory decisions for any other item held in stock.

The EOQ and other lot-sizing methods (see the Special Inventory Models supplement) answer the important question: How much should we order? Another important question that needs an answer is: When should we place the order? An inventory control system responds to both questions. In selecting an inventory control system for a particular application, the nature of the demands imposed on the inventory items is crucial. An important distinction between types of inventory is whether an item is subject to dependent or independent demand. Retailers, such as JCPenney, and distributors must manage **independent demand items**—that is, items for which demand is influenced by market conditions and is not related to the inventory decisions for any other item held in stock. Independent demand inventory includes

1. wholesale and retail merchandise;
2. service industry inventory, such as stamps and mailing labels for post offices, office supplies for law firms, and laboratory supplies for research universities;
3. end-item and replacement-part distribution inventories; and
4. maintenance, repair, and operating (MRO) supplies—that is, items that don't become part of the final product or service, such as employee uniforms, fuel, paint, and machine repair parts.

How can inventory be controlled if fixing the lot-size quantity is advantageous?

Managing independent demand inventory can be tricky because demand is influenced by external factors. For example, the owner of a bookstore may not be sure how many copies of the latest best-seller customers will purchase during the coming month. As a result, she may decide to stock extra copies as a safeguard. Independent demand such as the demand for various book titles must be forecasted (see the Forecasting chapter).

In this chapter, we focus on inventory control systems for independent demand items, which is the type of demand the bookstore owner, other retailers, and distributors face. Even though demand from any one customer is difficult to predict, low demand from some customers often is offset by high demand from others. Thus, total demand for any independent demand item may follow a relatively smooth pattern, with some random fluctuations. *Dependent demand items* are those required as components or inputs to a product or service. Dependent demand exhibits a pattern very different from that of independent demand and must be managed with different techniques (see the Resource Planning chapter).

In this section, we discuss and compare two inventory control systems: the continuous review system, called a *Q* system, and the periodic review system, called a *P* system. We close with a look at hybrid systems, which incorporate features of both the *P* and *Q* systems.

continuous review (Q) system A system designed to track the remaining inventory of an item each time a withdrawal is made, to determine whether it is time to replenish.

reorder point (ROP) system See **Continuous reivew (Q) system.**

inventory position (IP) The measurement of an item's ability to satisfy future demand.

scheduled receipts (SR) Orders that have been placed but not yet received.

open orders See **Scheduled receipts (SR).**

CONTINUOUS REVIEW (Q) SYSTEM

A **continuous review (Q) system,** sometimes called a **reorder point (ROP) system** or fixed order-quantity system, tracks the remaining inventory of an item each time a withdrawal is made to determine whether it is time to reorder. In practice, these reviews are done frequently (e.g., daily) and often continuously (after each withdrawal). The advent of computers and electronic cash registers linked to inventory records has made continuous reviews easy. At each review a decision is made about an item's inventory position. If it is judged to be too low, the system triggers a new order. The **inventory position (IP)** measures the item's ability to satisfy future demand. It includes **scheduled receipts (SR)**, which are orders that have been placed but not yet received, plus on-hand inventory (OH) minus backorders (BO). Sometimes scheduled receipts are called **open orders.** More specifically,

$$\text{Inventory position} = \text{On-hand inventory} + \text{Scheduled receipts} - \text{Backorders}$$
$$\text{IP} = \text{OH} + \text{SR} - \text{BO}$$

reorder point (R) The predetermined minimum level that an inventory position must reach before a fixed quantity Q of the item is ordered.

When the inventory position reaches a predetermined minimum level, called the **reorder point (R)**, a fixed quantity Q of the item is ordered. In a continuous review system, although the order quantity Q is fixed, the time between orders can vary. Hence, Q can be based on the EOQ, a price break quantity (the minimum lot size that qualifies for a quantity discount), a container size (such as a truckload), or some other quantity selected by management.

SELECTING THE REORDER POINT WHEN DEMAND IS CERTAIN. To demonstrate the concept of a reorder point, suppose that the demand for feeders at the museum gift shop in Example 13.3 is always 18 per week, the lead time is a constant two weeks, and the supplier always ships on time the exact amount ordered. With both demand and lead time certain, the museum's buyer can wait until the inventory position drops to 36 units, or (18 units/week)(2 weeks), to place a new order. Thus, in this case, the reorder point, R, equals the *demand during lead time*, with no added allowance for safety stock.

Figure 13.7 shows how the system operates when demand and lead time are constant. The downward-sloping line represents the on-hand inventory, which is being depleted at a constant rate. When it reaches reorder point R (the horizontal line), a new order for Q units is placed. The on-hand inventory continues to drop throughout lead time L until the order is received. At that time, which marks the end of the lead time, on-hand inventory jumps by Q units. A new order arrives just when inventory drops to 0. The time between orders (TBO) is the same for each cycle.

The inventory position, IP, shown in Figure 13.7 corresponds to the on-hand inventory, except during the lead time. Just after a new order is placed, at the start of the lead time, IP increases by Q, as shown by the dashed line. The IP exceeds OH by this same margin throughout the lead time.[4] At the end of the lead time, when the scheduled receipts convert to on-hand inventory, IP = OH once again. The key point here is to compare IP, not OH, with R in deciding whether to reorder. A common error is to ignore scheduled receipts or backorders.

FIGURE 13.7

Q System When Demand and Lead Time Are Constant and Certain

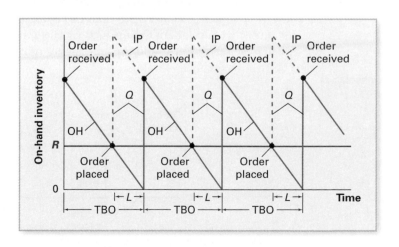

---

[4] A possible exception is the unlikely situation when more than one scheduled receipt is open at the same time because of long lead times.

| EXAMPLE 13.4 | *Determining Whether to Place an Order* |

Demand for chicken soup at a supermarket is 25 cases a day and the lead time is four days. The shelves were just restocked with chicken soup, leaving an on-hand inventory of only 10 cases. There are no backorders, but there is one open order for 200 cases. What is the inventory position? Should a new order be placed?

SOLUTION

$$R = \text{Average demand during lead time} = (25)(4) = 100 \text{ cases}$$
$$\text{IP} = \text{OH} + \text{SR} - \text{BO}$$
$$= 10 + 200 - 0 = 210 \text{ cases.}$$

Decision Point Because IP exceeds R (210 versus 100), do not reorder. Inventory is almost depleted, but there is no need to place a new order because the scheduled receipt is on the way. □

SELECTING THE REORDER POINT WHEN DEMAND IS UNCERTAIN. In reality, demand and lead times are not always predictable. For instance, the museum's buyer knows that *average* demand is 18 feeders per week and that the *average* lead time is two weeks. That is, a variable number of feeders may be purchased during the lead time, with an average demand during lead time of 36 feeders (assuming that each week's demand is identically distributed). This situation gives rise to the need for safety stocks. Suppose that she sets R at 46 units, thereby placing orders before they typically are needed. This approach will create a safety stock, or stock held in excess of expected demand, of 10 units (46 − 36) to buffer against uncertain demand. In general,

Reorder point = Average demand during lead time + Safety stock

Figure 13.8 shows how the Q system operates when demand is variable and uncertain. We assume that the variability in lead times is negligible and, therefore, can be treated as a constant, as we did in the development of the EOQ model. The wavy downward-sloping line indicates that demand varies from day to day. Its slope is steeper in the second cycle, which means that the demand rate is higher during this time period. The changing demand rate means that the time between orders changes, so $\text{TBO}_1 \neq \text{TBO}_2 \neq \text{TBO}_3$. Because of uncertain demand, sales during lead time are unpredictable, and safety stock is added to hedge against lost sales. This addition is why R is higher in Figure 13.8 than in Figure 13.7. It also explains why the on-hand inventory usually doesn't drop to 0 by the time a replenishment order arrives. The greater the safety stock, and thus the higher reorder point R, the less likely a stockout.

| FIGURE 13.8 |

Q System When Demand Is Uncertain

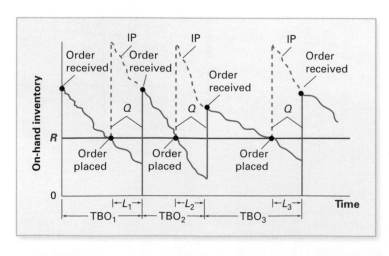

Because the average demand during lead time is variable and uncertain, the real decision to be made when selecting R concerns the safety stock level. Deciding on a small or large safety stock is a trade-off between customer service and inventory holding costs. Cost minimization models can be used to find the best safety stock, but they require estimates of stockout and backorder costs, which are usually difficult to make with any precision. The usual approach for determining R is for management—based on judgment—to set a reasonable service-level policy for the inventory and then determine the safety stock level that satisfies this policy.

CHOOSING AN APPROPRIATE SERVICE-LEVEL POLICY. Managers must weigh the benefits of holding safety stock against the cost of holding it. One way to determine the safety stock is to set a **service level**, or **cycle-service level**—the desired probability of not running out of stock in any one ordering cycle, which begins at the time an order is placed and ends when it arrives in stock. In a bookstore, the manager may select a 90 percent cycle-service level for a book. In other words, the probability is 90 percent that demand will not exceed the supply during the lead time. The probability of running short *during the lead time*, creating a stockout or backorder, is only 10 percent $(100 - 90)$. This stockout risk, which occurs only during the lead time in the Q system, is greater than the overall risk of stockout because the risk is nonexistent outside the ordering cycle.

To translate this policy into a specific safety stock level, we must know how demand during the lead time is distributed. If demand varies little around its average, safety stock can be small. Conversely, if demand during lead time varies greatly from one order cycle to the next, the safety stock must be large. Variability is measured with probability distributions, which are specified by a mean and a variance.

FINDING THE SAFETY STOCK. When selecting the safety stock, the inventory planner often assumes that demand during lead time is normally distributed, as shown in Figure 13.9. The average demand during the lead time is the centerline of the graph, with 50 percent of the area under the curve to the left and 50 percent to the right. Thus, if a cycle-service level of 50 percent were chosen, reorder point R would be the quantity represented by this centerline. As R equals demand during the lead time plus the safety stock, the safety stock is 0 when R equals this average demand. Demand is less than average 50 percent of the time, and thus having no safety stock will be sufficient only 50 percent of the time.

To provide a service level above 50 percent, the reorder point must be greater than average demand during the lead time. In Figure 13.9, that requires moving the reorder point to the right of the centerline so that more than 50 percent of the area under the curve is to the left of R. An 85 percent cycle-service level is achieved in Figure 13.9, with 85 percent of the area under the curve to the left of R (in blue) and only 15

service level The desired probability of not running out of stock in any one ordering cycle, which begins at the time an order is placed and ends when it arrives in stock.

cycle-service level See Service level.

FIGURE 13.9

Finding Safety Stock with a Normal Probability Distribution for an 85 Percent Cycle-Service Level

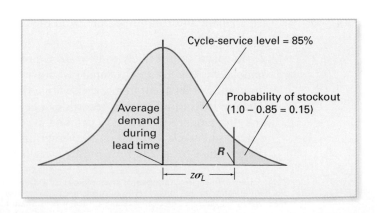

percent to the right (in pink). We compute the safety stock by multiplying the number of standard deviations from the mean needed to implement the cycle-service level, z, by the standard deviation of demand during lead time probability distribution, σ_L[5]:

$$\text{Safety stock} = z\sigma_L$$

The higher the value of z, the higher the safety stock and the cycle-service level should be. If $z = 0$, there is no safety stock, and stockouts will occur during 50 percent of the order cycles.

| EXAMPLE 13.5 | *Finding the Safety Stock and R* |

Records show that the demand for dishwasher detergent during the lead time is normally distributed, with an average of 250 boxes and $\sigma_L = 22$. What safety stock should be carried for a 99 percent cycle-service level? What is R?

SOLUTION

The first step is to find z, the number of standard deviations to the right of average demand during the lead time that places 99 percent of the area under the curve to the left of that point (0.9900 in the body of the table in the Normal Distribution appendix). The closest number in the table is 0.9901, which corresponds to 2.3 in the row heading and 0.03 in the column heading. Adding these values gives a z of 2.33. With this information, you can calculate the safety stock and reorder point:

$$\text{Safety stock} = z\sigma_L = 2.33(22) = 51.3, \quad \text{or} \quad 51 \text{ boxes}$$
$$\text{Reorder point} = \text{Average demand during lead time} + \text{Safety stock}$$
$$= 250 + 51 = 301 \text{ boxes}$$

We rounded the safety stock to the nearest whole number. In this case, the theoretical cycle-service level will be less than 99 percent. Raising the safety stock to 52 boxes will yield a cycle-service level greater than 99 percent.

Decision Point Management can control the quantity of safety stock by choosing a service level. Another approach to reducing safety stock is to reduce the standard deviation of demand during the lead time, which can be accomplished by closer coordination with major customers through information technology. ◻

Finding the appropriate reorder point and safety stock in practice requires estimating the demand distribution for the lead time. Sometimes average demand during the lead time and the standard deviation of demand during the lead time, σ_L, are not directly available and must be calculated by combining information on the demand rate with information on the lead time. There are two reasons for this additional calculation.

1. Developing estimates first for demand and then for the lead time, may be easier. Demand information comes from the customer, whereas lead times come from the supplier.

2. Records are not likely to be collected for a time interval that is exactly the same as the lead time. The same inventory control system may be used to manage thousands of different items, each with a different lead time. For example, if demand is reported *weekly*, records can be used directly to compute the average and the standard deviation of demand during the lead time if the lead time is exactly one week. However, the average and standard deviation of demand during the lead time for a lead time of three weeks are more difficult to determine.

---

[5] Some inventory planners using manual systems prefer to work with the mean absolute deviation (MAD) rather than the standard deviation because it is easier to calculate. Recall that to approximate the standard deviation you simply multiply the MAD by 1.25 (see the Forecasting chapter). Then, proceed to calculate the safety stock.

We can get at the more difficult case by making some reasonable assumptions. Suppose that the average demand, d, is known along with the standard deviation of demand, σ_t, over some time interval t (say, days or weeks), where t does not equal the lead time. Also, suppose that the probability distributions of demand for each time interval t are identical and independent of each other. For example, if the time interval is a week, the probability distributions of demand are the same each week (identical d and σ_t), and the total demand in one week does not affect the total demand in another week. Let L be the constant lead time, expressed as a multiple (or fraction) of t. If t represents a week and the lead time is three weeks, $L = 3$. Under these assumptions, average demand during the lead time will be the sum of the averages for each of the L identical and independent distributions of demand, or $d + d + d + \cdots = dL$. In addition, the variance of the demand distribution for the lead time will be the sum of the variances of the L identical and independent distributions of demand, or $\sigma_t^2 + \sigma_t^2 + \sigma_t^2 + \cdots = \sigma_t^2 L$. Finally, the standard deviation of the sum of two or more identically distributed independent random variables is the square root of the sum of their variances, or

$$\sigma_L = \sqrt{\sigma_t^2 L} = \sigma_t \sqrt{L}$$

Figure 13.10 shows how the demand distribution for the lead time is developed from the individual distributions of weekly demands, where $d = 75$, $\sigma_t = 15$, and $L = 3$ weeks. In this case, average demand during the lead time is $(75)(3) = 225$ units and $\sigma_L = 15\sqrt{3} = 25.98$, or 26. More complex formulas or simulation must be used when both demand and the lead time are variable or when the supply is uncertain. In such cases, the safety stock must be larger than otherwise.

CALCULATING TOTAL Q SYSTEM COSTS. Total costs for the continuous review (Q) system is the sum of three cost components:

Total cost = Annual cycle inventory holding cost + Annual ordering cost
                + Annual safety stock holding cost

$$C = \frac{Q}{2}(H) + \frac{D}{Q}(S) + Hz\sigma_L$$

The annual cycle inventory holding cost and annual ordering costs are the same equations we used for computing the annual cost in Examples 13.2 and 13.3. The annual cost of holding the safety stock is computed under the assumption that the safety stock is on hand all the time. Referring to Figure 13.8, in each order cycle, sometimes, we will have experienced a demand greater than the average demand during lead time, and

FIGURE 13.10

Development of Demand Distribution for the Lead Time

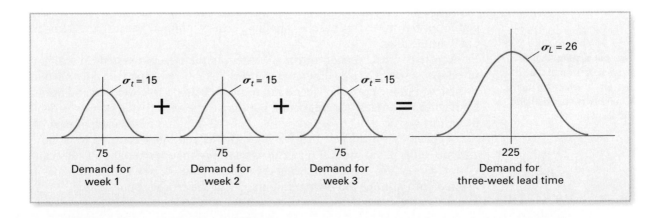

| 75 | 75 | 75 | 225 |
| Demand for week 1 | Demand for week 2 | Demand for week 3 | Demand for three-week lead time |

sometimes we will have experienced less. On average over the year, we can assume the safety stock will be on hand.

| EXAMPLE 13.6 | *Finding the Safety Stock and R When the Demand Distribution for the Lead Time Must Be Developed* |

TUTOR 13.3

Let's return to the birdfeeder example. Suppose that the average demand is 18 units per week with a standard deviation of 5 units. The lead time is constant at two weeks. Determine the safety stock and reorder point if management wants a 90 percent cycle-service level. What is the total cost of the Q system?

SOLUTION

In this case, $t = 1$ week, $d = 18$, and $L = 2$, so

$$\sigma_L = \sigma_t\sqrt{L} = 5\sqrt{2} = 7.1$$

Consult the body of the normal table for 0.9000, which corresponds to a 90 percent cycle-service level. The closest number is 0.8997, which corresponds to a z value of 1.28. With this information, we calculate the safety stock and reorder point as follows:

$$\text{Safety stock} = z\sigma_L = 1.28(7.1) = 9.1, \qquad \text{or} \qquad 9 \text{ units}$$

$$\text{Recorder point} = dL + \text{Safety stock}$$

$$= 2(18) + 9 = 45 \text{ units}$$

Hence, the Q system for the birdfeeder operates as follows: Whenever the inventory position reaches 45 units, order 75 units. The total Q system cost for the birdfeeder is

$$C = \frac{75}{2}(\$15) + \frac{936}{75}(\$45) + 9(\$15) = \$562.50 + \$561.60 + \$135 = \$1{,}259.10$$

Decision Point Various order quantities and safety stock levels can be used in the Q system. For example, management could specify a different order quantity (because of shipping constraints) or a different safety stock (because of storage limitations). The total costs of such systems can be calculated, and the trade-off between costs and service levels could be assessed. ☐

visual system A system that allows employees to place orders when inventory visibly reaches a certain marker.

TWO-BIN SYSTEM. The concept of a Q system can be incorporated in a **visual system**, that is, a system that allows employees to place orders when inventory visibly reaches a certain marker. Visual systems are easy to administer because records are not kept on the current inventory position. The historical usage rate can simply be reconstructed from past purchase orders. Visual systems are intended for use with low-value items that have a steady demand, such as nuts and bolts or office supplies. Overstocking is common, but the extra inventory holding cost is minimal because the items have relatively little value.

two-bin system A visual system version of the Q system, in which an item's inventory is stored at two different locations.

A visual system version of the Q system is the **two-bin system** in which an item's inventory is stored at two different locations. Inventory is first withdrawn from one bin. If the first bin is empty, the second bin provides backup to cover demand until a replenishment order arrives. An empty first bin signals the need to place a new order. Premade order forms placed near the bins let workers send one to purchasing or even directly to the supplier. When the new order arrives, the second bin is restored to its normal level and the rest is put in the first bin. The two-bin system operates like a Q system, with the normal level in the second bin being the reorder point R. The system also may be implemented with just one bin by marking the bin at the reorder point level.

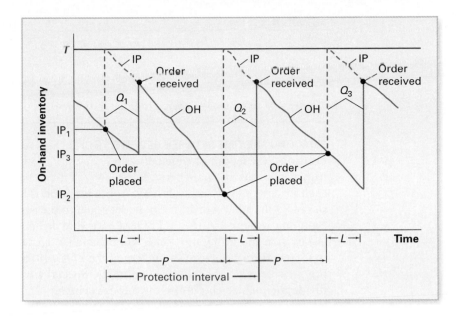

FIGURE 13.11

P System When Demand Is Uncertain

PERIODIC REVIEW (*P*) SYSTEM

How can inventories be controlled if the time between replenishment orders should be fixed?

periodic review (*P*) system A system in which an item's inventory position is reviewed periodically rather than continuously.

An alternative inventory control system is the **periodic review (*P*) system,** sometimes called a *fixed interval reorder system* or *periodic reorder system,* in which an item's inventory position is reviewed periodically rather than continuously. Such a system can simplify delivery scheduling because it establishes a routine. A new order is always placed at the end of each review, and the time between orders (TBO) is fixed at *P*. Demand is a random variable, so total demand between reviews varies. In a *P* system, the lot size, *Q*, may change from one order to the next, but the time between orders is fixed. An example of a periodic review system is that of a soft-drink supplier making weekly rounds of grocery stores. Each week, the supplier reviews the store's inventory of soft drinks and restocks the store with enough items to meet demand and safety stock requirements until the next week.

Four of the original EOQ assumptions are maintained: that there are no constraints on the size of the lot, that the relevant costs are holding and ordering costs, that decisions for one item are independent of decisions for other items, and that there is no uncertainty in lead times or supply. However, demand uncertainty is again allowed for. Figure 13.11 shows the periodic review system under these assumptions. The downward-sloping line again represents on-hand inventory. When the predetermined time, *P*, has elapsed since the last review, an order is placed to bring the inventory position, represented by the dashed line, up to the target inventory level, *T*. The lot size for the first review is Q_1, or the difference between inventory position IP_1 and *T*. As with the continuous review system, IP and OH differ only during the lead time. When the order arrives, at the end of the lead time, OH and IP again are identical. Figure 13.11 shows that lot sizes vary from one order cycle to the next. Because the inventory position is lower at the second review, a greater quantity is needed to achieve an inventory level of *T*.

EXAMPLE 13.7

Determining How Much to Reorder in a P System

There is a backorder of five 36-inch color TV sets at a distribution center. There is no on-hand inventory, and now is the time to review. How much should be reordered if *T* = 400 and there are no scheduled receipts?

SOLUTION

$$IP = OH + SR - BO$$
$$= 0 + 0 - 5 = -5 \text{ sets}$$
$$T - IP = 400 - (-5) = 405 \text{ sets}$$

That is, 405 sets must be ordered to bring the inventory position up to T sets. ⊐

SELECTING THE TIME BETWEEN REVIEWS. To run a P system, managers must make two decisions: the length of time between reviews, P, and the target inventory level, T. Let us first consider the time between reviews, P. It can be any convenient interval, such as each Friday or every other Friday. Another option is to base P on the cost trade-offs of the EOQ. In other words, P can be set equal to the average time between orders for the economic order quantity, or TBO_{EOQ}. Because demand is variable, some orders will be larger than the EOQ and some will be smaller. However, over an extended period of time, the average lot size should equal the EOQ. If other models are used to determine the lot size (e.g., those described in the Special Inventory Models supplement), we divide the lot size chosen by the annual demand, D, and use this ratio as P. It will be expressed as the fraction of a year between orders, which can be converted into months, weeks, or days as needed.

protection interval The time interval for which inventory must be planned when each new order is placed.

SELECTING THE TARGET INVENTORY LEVEL. Now let us consider how to calculate the target inventory level, T. Figure 13.11 reveals that an order must be large enough to make the inventory position, IP, last beyond the next review, which is P time periods away. The checker must wait P periods to revise, correct, and reestablish the inventory position. Then, a new order is placed, but it does not arrive until after the lead time, L. Therefore, as Figure 13.11 shows, a **protection interval** of $P + L$ periods is needed, or the time interval for which inventory must be planned when each new order is placed. A fundamental difference between the Q and P systems is the length of time needed for stockout protection. A Q system needs stockout protection only during the lead time because orders can be placed as soon as they are needed and will be received L periods later. A P system, however, needs stockout protection for the longer $P + L$ protection interval because orders are placed only at fixed intervals and the inventory isn't checked until the next designated review time.

As with the Q system, we need to develop the appropriate distribution of demand during the protection interval to specify the system fully. In a P system, we must develop the distribution of demand for $P + L$ time periods. The target inventory level T must equal the expected demand during the protection interval of $P + L$ periods, plus enough safety stock to protect against demand uncertainty over this same protection interval. We use the same statistical assumptions that we made for the Q system. Thus, the average demand during the protection interval is $d(P + L)$, or

$$T = d(P + L) + (\text{Safety stock for protection interval})$$

We compute safety stock for a P system much as we did for the Q system. However, the safety stock must cover demand uncertainty for a longer period of time. When using a normal probability distribution, we multiply the desired standard deviations to implement the cycle-service level, z, by the standard deviation of demand during the protection interval, σ_{P+L}. The value of z is the same as for a Q system with the same cycle-service level. Thus,

$$\text{Safety stock} = z\sigma_{P+L}$$

Based on our earlier logic for calculating σ_L, we know that the standard deviation of the distribution of demand during the protection interval is

$$\sigma_{P+L} = \sigma_t \sqrt{P + L}$$

Because a P system requires safety stock to cover demand uncertainty over a longer time period than a Q system, a P system requires more safety stock; that is, σ_{P+L} exceeds σ_L. Hence, to gain the convenience of a P system requires that overall inventory levels be somewhat higher than those for a Q system.

CALCULATING TOTAL *P* SYSTEM COSTS. The total costs for the P system are the sum of the same three cost elements as for the Q system. The differences are in the calculation of the order quantity and the safety stock. Referring to Figure 13.11, the average order quantity will be the average consumption of inventory during the P periods between orders. Consequently, $Q = dP$. Total costs for the P system are

$$C = \frac{dp}{2}(H) + \frac{D}{dp}(S) + Hz\sigma_{P+L}$$

Managerial Practice 13.2 shows how Hewlett-Packard implemented a periodic review system for many of their business units.

| EXAMPLE 13.8 | *Calculating P and T* |

**TUTOR
13.4**

Again, let us return to the birdfeeder example. Recall that demand for the birdfeeder is normally distributed with a mean of 18 units per week and a standard deviation in weekly demand of 5 units. The lead time is 2 weeks, and the business operates 52 weeks per year. The Q system developed in Example 13.6 called for an EOQ of 75 units and a safety stock of 9 units for a cycle-service level of 90 percent. What is the equivalent P system? What is the total cost? Answers are to be rounded to the nearest integer.

SOLUTION

We first define D and then P. Here, P is the time between reviews, expressed as a multiple (or fraction) of time interval t ($t = 1$ week because the data are expressed as demand *per week*):

$$D = (18 \text{ units/week})(52 \text{ weeks/year}) = 936 \text{ units}$$

$$P = \frac{EOQ}{D}(52) = \frac{75}{936}(52) = 4.2, \quad \text{or} \quad 4 \text{ weeks}$$

With $d = 18$ units per week, we can also calculate P by dividing the EOQ by d to get $75/18 = 4.2$, or 4 weeks. Hence, we would review the birdfeeder inventory every 4 weeks. We now find the standard deviation of demand over the protection interval ($P + L = 6$):

$$\sigma_{P+L} = \sigma_t\sqrt{P + L} = 5\sqrt{6} = 12 \text{ units}$$

Before calculating T, we also need a z value. For a 90 percent cycle-service level, $z = 1.28$ (see the Normal Distribution appendix). We now solve for T:

$$T = \text{Average demand during the protection interval} + \text{Safety stock}$$
$$= d(P + L) + z\sigma_{P+L}$$
$$= (18 \text{ units/week})(6 \text{ weeks}) + 1.28(12 \text{ units}) = 123 \text{ units}$$

Every 4 weeks we would order the number of units needed to bring inventory position IP (counting the new order) up to the target inventory level of 123 units. The safety stock for this P system is $1.28(12) = 15$ units.

The total P system cost for the birdfeeder is

$$C = \frac{4(18)}{2}(\$15) + \frac{936}{4(18)}(\$45) + 15(\$15) = \$540 + \$585 + \$225 = \$1,350$$

Decision Point The P system requires 15 units in safety stock, while the Q system only needs 9 units. If cost were the only criterion, the Q system would be the choice for the birdfeeder. As we discuss in the next section, there are other factors that may sway the decision in favor of the P system. ◻

single-bin system
A system of inventory control in which a maximum level is marked on the storage shelf or bin on a measuring rod, and the inventory is brought up to the mark periodically.

SINGLE-BIN SYSTEM. The concept of a P system can be translated into a simple visual system of inventory control. In the **single-bin system**, a maximum level is marked on the storage shelf or bin on a measuring rod, and the inventory is brought up to the mark periodically—say, once a week. The single bin may be, for example, a gasoline storage tank at a service station or a storage bin for small parts at a manufacturing plant.

MANAGERIAL PRACTICE 13.2
Implementing a Periodic Review Inventory System at Hewlett-Packard

Hewlett-Packard (www.hp.com) manufactures computers, accessories, and a wide variety of instrumentation devices in more than 100 separate businesses, each responsible for its own product designing, marketing, and manufacturing processes as well as the required inventories to service its customers. At most HP businesses, inventory-driven costs (which include currency devaluation, obsolescence, price protection, and financing) are now the biggest control lever that the manufacturing organization has on business performance, measured in terms of return on assets or economic value added. Inventory is a major cost driver and the most variable element on the balance sheet.

Most of HP's business units were inefficient, carrying more inventory than needed in order to achieve a desired level of product delivery performance. They often used simplified approaches such as ABC analysis to determine their safety stocks for independent demand items, ignoring supply or demand uncertainty, part commonality, desired part availability, or cost. The solution was to develop a periodic review system that used part availability targets and included as many uncertainties as possible. The system, although in principle similar to the P system discussed in this chapter, uses complex equations to determine the review interval and target inventory parameters. The complexity arises from considering uncertainties in supply as well as demand in the determination of the safety stocks.

Even though the system could be shown to reduce inventories and improve customer service, no benefits would be realized until the planning and procurement staff actually used it. Since each business unit had some unique characteristics, the results had to be easily understandable and credible, and the system had to be easily configurable to each situation. Consequently, HP developed a software wizard that allows the user to enter product data and costs in a friendly environment, develops the equations for the periodic review system, and then translates the results to the user's format requirements. The wizard is programmed in Excel, which allows users access to all of Excel's functionality for conducting their own analyses.

The periodic review system and the software wizard have been very successful. At HP's Integrated Circuit Manufacturing Division, for example, planners cut inventories by $1.6 million while simultaneously improving on-time delivery performance from 93 percent to 97 percent. Other benefits included less expediting, fewer disagreements about operating policy, and more control of the production system. The system is used across a wide variety of product lines and geographies worldwide. HP believes that, without exception, the product lines now have more efficient operations.

Source: Cargille, Brian, Steve Kakouros, and Robert Hall. "Part Tool, Part Process: Inventory Optimization at Hewlett-Packard Co." *OR/MS TODAY* (October 1999), pp. 18–24.

COMPARATIVE ADVANTAGES OF THE *Q* AND *P* SYSTEMS

Which type of system—
a *Q* or *P* system—should
be used to control
inventories?

Neither the *Q* nor *P* system is best for all situations. Three *P*-system advantages must be balanced against three *Q*-system advantages. The advantages of one system are implicitly disadvantages of the other one. The primary advantages of *P* systems are the following:

1. Administration of the system is convenient because replenishments are made at fixed intervals. Employees can regularly set aside a day or part of a day to concentrate on this particular task. Fixed replenishment intervals also allow for standardized pickup and delivery times.

2. Orders for multiple items from the same supplier may be combined into a single purchase order. This approach reduces ordering and transportation costs and may result in a price break from the supplier.

3. The inventory position, IP, needs to be known only when a review is made (not continuously, as in a *Q* system). However, this advantage is moot for firms using computerized record-keeping systems, in which a transaction is reported upon each receipt or withdrawal. When inventory records are always current, the system is called a **perpetual inventory system**.

perpetual inventory system A system of inventory control in which the inventory records are always current.

The primary advantages of *Q* systems are the following:

1. The review frequency of each item may be individualized. Tailoring the review frequency to the item can reduce total ordering and holding costs.

2. Fixed lot sizes, if large enough, may result in quantity discounts. Physical limitations such as truckload capacities, materials handling methods, and furnace capacities also may require a fixed lot size.

3. Lower safety stocks result in savings.

In conclusion, the choice between *Q* and *P* systems is not clear cut. Which one is better depends on the relative importance of its advantages in various situations. Management must weigh each alternative carefully in selecting the best system.

HYBRID SYSTEMS

What other types of
systems are possible?

Various hybrid inventory control systems merge some but not all the features of the *P* and *Q* systems. We briefly examine two such systems: optional replenishment and base stock.

optional replenishment system A system used to review the inventory position at fixed time intervals and, if the position has dropped to (or below) a predetermined level, to place a variable-sized order to cover expected needs.

OPTIONAL REPLENISHMENT SYSTEM. Sometimes called the optional review, min–max, or (*s*, *S*) system, the **optional replenishment system** is much like the *P* system. It is used to review the inventory position at fixed time intervals and, if the position has dropped to (or below) a predetermined level, to place a variable-sized order to cover expected needs. The new order is large enough to bring the inventory position up to a target inventory, similar to *T* for the *P* system. However, orders are not placed after a review unless the inventory position has dropped to the predetermined minimum level. The minimum level acts as reorder point *R* does in a *Q* system. If the target is 100 and the minimum level is 60, the minimum order size is 40 (or 100 − 60). The optional review system avoids continuous reviews and so is particularly attractive when both review and ordering costs are significant.

base-stock system An inventory control system that issues a replenishment order, *Q*, each time a withdrawal is made, for the same amount of the withdrawal.

BASE-STOCK SYSTEM. In its simplest form, the **base-stock system** issues a replenishment order, *Q*, each time a withdrawal is made, for the same amount as the withdrawal. This one-for-one replacement policy maintains the inventory position at a base-stock level equal to expected demand during the lead time plus safety stock. The base-stock level, therefore, is equivalent to the reorder point in a Q system. However, order quantities now vary to keep the inventory position at R at all times. Because this position is the lowest IP possible that will maintain a specified service level, the base-stock system may be used to minimize cycle inventory. More orders are placed, but each is smaller. This system is appropriate for very expensive items, such as replacement engines for jet airplanes. No more inventory is held than the maximum demand expected until a replacement order can be received. The base-stock system is used in just-in-time systems (see the Lean Systems chapter).

INVENTORY RECORD ACCURACY

Regardless of the inventory system in use, record accuracy is crucial to its success. One method of achieving and maintaining accuracy is to assign responsibility to specific employees for issuing and receiving materials and accurately reporting each transaction. A second method is to secure inventory behind locked doors or gates to prevent unauthorized or unreported withdrawals. This method also guards against storing new receipts in the wrong locations, where they can be lost for months. **Cycle counting** is a third method, whereby storeroom personnel physically count a small percentage of the total number of items each day, correcting errors that they find. Class A items are counted most frequently. A final method, for computerized systems, is to make logic error checks on each transaction reported and fully investigate any discrepancies. Discrepancies may include (1) actual receipts when there is no record of scheduled receipts, (2) disbursements that exceed the current on-hand balance, and (3) receipts with an inaccurate (nonexistent) part number.

These four methods can keep inventory record accuracy within acceptable bounds. Accuracy pays off mainly through better customer service, although some inventory reductions can be achieved by improving accuracy. A side benefit is that auditors may not require end-of-year counts if records prove to be sufficiently accurate.

cycle counting An inventory control method whereby storeroom personnel physically count a small percentage of the total number of items each day, correcting errors that they find.

INVENTORY MANAGEMENT ACROSS THE ORGANIZATION

Inventories are important to all types of organizations and their employees. Inventories affect everyday operations because they must be counted, paid for, used in operations, used to satisfy customers, and managed. Inventories require an investment of funds, as does the purchase of a new machine. Monies invested in inventory are not available for investment in other things; thus, they represent a drain on the cash flows of an organization. Carrying that notion to its extreme, one may conclude that inventories should be eliminated. Not only is that idea impossible, it is hazardous to the financial health of an organization.

We have focused on independent demand inventories in this chapter. These inventories are often found in retail and distribution operations. Consequently, independent demand inventories are often the last stocking point before the consumer. Companies concerned with customer service know that availability of products is a key selling point in many markets. Earlier, we discussed Internet retail companies that have discovered a competitive advantage by controlling their own inventories, rather than outsourcing that function to someone else. The consequences in Internet markets for lack of supply are dire—plummeting stock prices, financial restructuring, outsider acquisition, or bankruptcy.

Is inventory a boon or a bane? Certainly, profitability is reduced if there is too much inventory, and customer confidence is damaged if there is too little inventory.

The goal should not be to minimize inventory or to maximize customer service, but rather to have the right amount to support the competitive priorities of the company. The Internet has provided many alternatives for a successful business model. To date, we have seen pure Internet companies, combinations of Internet and bricks-and-mortar, and totally bricks-and-mortar.

Each of these models provides a different set of capabilities and opportunities to exploit different competitive priorities. Regardless of the model, inventory management will play a major role.

FORMULA REVIEW

1. Cycle inventory $= \dfrac{Q}{2}$

2. Pipeline inventory $= dL$

3. Total annual cost $=$ Annual holding cost $+$ Annual ordering or setup cost

$$C = \frac{Q}{2}\,(H) + \frac{D}{Q}\,(S)$$

4. Economic order quantity: $EOQ = \sqrt{\dfrac{2DS}{H}}$

5. Time between orders, expressed in weeks: $TBO_{EOQ} = \dfrac{EOQ}{D}\,(52 \text{ weeks/year})$

6. Inventory position $=$ On-hand inventory $+$ Scheduled receipts $-$ Backorders

$$IP = OH + SR - BO$$

7. Continuous review system:

   Reorder point $(R) =$ Average demand during the protection interval $+$ Safety stock
   $$= dL + z\sigma_L$$
   Protection interval $=$ Lead time (L)
   Standard deviation of demand during the lead time $= \sigma_L = \sigma_t\sqrt{L}$
   Order quantity $= EOQ$
   Replenishment rule: Order EOQ units when $IP \le R$.

   Total Q system cost: $C = \dfrac{Q}{2}\,(H) + \dfrac{D}{Q}\,(S) + Hz\sigma_L$

8. Periodic review system:

   Target inventory level $(T) =$ Average demand during the protection interval $+$ Safety stock
   $$= d(P + L) + z\sigma_{P+L}$$
   Protection interval $=$ Time between orders $+$ Lead time $= P + L$
   Review interval $=$ Time between orders $= P$
   Standard deviation of demand during the protection interval $= \sigma_{P+L} = \sigma_t\sqrt{P + L}$

Order quantity = Target inventory level − Inventory position = $T - $ IP

Replenishment rule: Every P time periods order $T - $ IP units.

Total P system cost: $C = \dfrac{dP}{2}(H) + \dfrac{D}{dP}(S) + Hz\sigma_{P+L}$

CHAPTER HIGHLIGHTS

❏ Inventory investment decisions involve trade-offs among the conflicting objectives of low inventory investment, good customer service, and high resource utilization. Benefits of good customer service and high resource utilization may be outweighed by the cost of carrying large inventories, including interest or opportunity costs, storage and handling costs, taxes, insurance, shrinkage, and obsolescence. Order quantity decisions are guided by a trade-off between the cost of holding inventories and the combined costs of ordering, setup, transportation, and purchased materials.

❏ Cycle, safety stock, anticipation, and pipeline inventories vary in size with order quantity, uncertainty, production rate flexibility, and lead time, respectively.

❏ Inventory placement at the plant level depends on whether an item is a standard or a special and on the trade-off between short customer response time and low inventory costs.

❏ ABC analysis helps managers focus on the few significant items that account for the bulk of investment in inventory. Class A items deserve the most attention, with less attention justified for class B and class C items.

❏ Independent demand inventory management methods are appropriate for wholesale and retail merchandise, service industry supplies, finished goods and service parts replenishment, and maintenance, repair, and operating supplies.

❏ A basic inventory management question is whether to order large quantities infrequently or to order small quantities frequently. The EOQ provides guidance for this choice by indicating the lot size that minimizes (subject to several assumptions) the sum of holding and ordering costs over some period of time, such as a year.

❏ In the continuous review (Q) system, the buyer places orders of a fixed lot size Q when the inventory position drops to the reorder point. In the periodic review (P) system, every P fixed time interval the buyer places an order to replenish the quantity consumed since the last order.

❏ The base-stock system minimizes cycle inventory by maintaining the inventory position at the base-stock level. Visual systems, such as single-bin and two-bin systems, are adaptations of the P and Q systems that eliminate the need for records.

KEY TERMS

ABC analysis *601*
anticipation inventory *598*
backorder *596*
base-stock system *619*
continuous review (Q) system *608*
cycle counting *620*
cycle inventory *597*
cycle-service level *611*
economic order quantity (EOQ) *602*
independent demand items *608*
inventory holding cost *595*
inventory position (IP) *608*

lot sizing *597*
open orders *608*
optional replenishment system *619*
ordering cost *596*
periodic review (P) system *615*
perpetual inventory system *619*
pipeline inventory *598*
protection interval *616*
quantity discount *597*
reorder point (R) *609*
reorder point (ROP) system *608*
repeatability *600*

safety stock inventory *597*
scheduled receipts (SR) *608*
service level *611*
setup cost *596*
single-bin system *618*
special *601*
standard *601*
stockout *596*
time between orders (TBO) *606*
two-bin system *614*
visual system *614*

SOLVED PROBLEM 1

A distribution center (DC) experiences an average weekly demand of 50 units for one of its items. The product is valued at $650 per unit. Average inbound shipments from the factory warehouse average 350 units. Average lead time (including ordering delays and transit time) is 2 weeks. The DC operates 52 weeks per year; it carries a 1-week supply of inventory as safety stock and no anticipation inventory. What is the average aggregate inventory being held by the DC?

SOLUTION

TYPE OF INVENTORY	CALCULATION OF AVERAGE INVENTORY QUANTITY	
Cycle	$\dfrac{Q}{2} = \dfrac{320}{2} =$	175 units
Safety stock	1-week supply =	50 units
Anticipation	None	
Pipeline	dL = (50 units/week)(2 weeks) =	100 units
	Average aggregate inventory	= 325 units

SOLVED PROBLEM 2

**TUTOR
13.5**

Booker's Book Bindery divides inventory items into three classes according to their dollar usage. Calculate the usage values of the following inventory items and determine which is most likely to be classified as an A item.

PART NUMBER	DESCRIPTION	QUANTITY USED PER YEAR	UNIT VALUE ($)
1	Boxes	500	3.00
2	Cardboard (square feet)	18,000	0.02
3	Cover stock	10,000	0.75
4	Glue (gallons)	75	40.00
5	Inside covers	20,000	0.05
6	Reinforcing tape (meters)	3,000	0.15
7	Signatures	150,000	0.45

SOLUTION

PART NUMBER	DESCRIPTION	QUANTITY USED PER YEAR		UNIT VALUE ($)		ANNUAL DOLLAR USAGE ($)
1	Boxes	500	×	3.00	=	1,500
2	Cardboard (square feet)	18,000	×	0.02	=	360
3	Cover stock	10,000	×	0.75	=	7,500
4	Glue (gallons)	75	×	40.00	=	3,000
5	Inside covers	20,000	×	0.05	=	1,000
6	Reinforcing tape (meters)	3,000	×	0.15	=	450
7	Signatures	150,000	×	0.45	=	67,500
					Total	81,310

The annual dollar usage for each item is determined by multiplying the annual usage quantity by the value per unit as shown in Figure 13.12. The items are sorted by annual dollar usage, in declining order. Finally, A–B and B–C class lines are drawn roughly according to the guidelines presented in the text. Here, class A includes only one item (signatures), which represents only 1/7, or 14 percent, of the items but accounts for 83 percent of annual dollar usage. Class B includes the

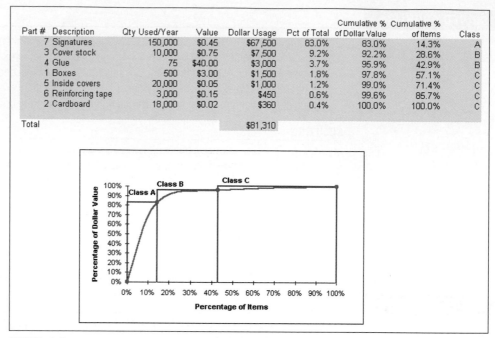

Part #	Description	Qty Used/Year	Value	Dollar Usage	Pct of Total	Cumulative % of Dollar Value	Cumulative % of Items	Class
7	Signatures	150,000	$0.45	$67,500	83.0%	83.0%	14.3%	A
3	Cover stock	10,000	$0.75	$7,500	9.2%	92.2%	28.6%	B
4	Glue	75	$40.00	$3,000	3.7%	95.9%	42.9%	B
1	Boxes	500	$3.00	$1,500	1.8%	97.8%	57.1%	C
5	Inside covers	20,000	$0.05	$1,000	1.2%	99.0%	71.4%	C
6	Reinforcing tape	3,000	$0.15	$450	0.6%	99.6%	85.7%	C
2	Cardboard	18,000	$0.02	$360	0.4%	100.0%	100.0%	C
Total				$81,310				

FIGURE 13.12

next two items, which taken together represent 28 percent of the items and account for 13 percent of annual dollar usage. The final four, class C, items represent over half the number of items but only 4 percent of total annual dollar usage.

SOLVED PROBLEM 3

In Example 13.3, the economic order quantity, EOQ, is 75 units when annual demand, D, is 936 units/year, setup cost, S, is $45, and holding cost, H, is $15/unit/year. Suppose that we mistakenly estimate inventory holding cost to be $30/unit/year.

a. What is the new order quantity, Q, if $D = 936$ units/year, $S = $45, and $H = $30/unit/year?

b. What is the change in order quantity, expressed as a percent of the economic order quantity (75 units)?

SOLUTION

a. The new order quantity is

$$EOQ = \sqrt{\frac{2DS}{H}} = \sqrt{\frac{2(936)(\$45)}{\$30}} = \sqrt{2,808} = 52.99, \quad \text{or} \quad 53 \text{ units}$$

b. The percent change is

$$\left(\frac{53 - 75}{75}\right)(100) = -29.33\%$$

The new order quantity (53) is about 29 percent smaller than the correct order quantity (75).

SOLVED PROBLEM 4

In Example 13.3, the total cost, C, is $1,124/year.

a. What is the annual total cost when $D = 936$ units/year, $S = \$45$, $H = \$15$/unit/year, and Q is the result from Solved Problem 3(a)?

b. What is the change in total cost, expressed as a percent of the total cost ($1,124)?

SOLUTION

a. With 53 as the order quantity, the annual cost is

$$C = \frac{Q}{2}(H) + \frac{D}{Q}(S) = \frac{53}{2}(\$15) + \frac{936}{53}(\$45) = \$397.50 + \$794.72$$

$$= \$1,192.22, \quad \text{or} \quad \text{about } \$1,192$$

b. The percent change is

$$\left(\frac{\$1,192 - \$1,124}{\$1,124}\right)(100) = 6.05\%, \quad \text{or} \quad \text{about } 6\%$$

A 100 percent error in estimating the holding cost caused the order quantity to be 29 percent too small, and that in turn increased annual costs by about 6 percent.

SOLVED PROBLEM 5

A regional warehouse purchases hand tools from various suppliers and then distributes them on demand to retailers in the region. The warehouse operates five days per week, 52 weeks per year. Only when it is open can orders be received. The following data are estimated for 3/8-inch hand drills with double insulation and variable speeds:

Average daily demand = 100 drills
Standard deviation of daily demand (σ_t) = 30 drills
Lead time (L) = 3 days
Holding cost (H) = $9.40/unit/year
Ordering cost (S) = $35/order
Cycle-service level = 92%

The warehouse uses a continuous review (Q) system.

a. What order quantity, Q, and reorder point, R, should be used?

b. If on-hand inventory is 40 units, there is one open order for 440 drills, and there are no backorders, should a new order be placed?

SOLUTION

a. Annual demand is

$$D = (5 \text{ days/week})(52 \text{ weeks/year})(100 \text{ drills/day}) = 26{,}000 \text{ drills/year}$$

The order quantity is

$$EOQ = \sqrt{\frac{2DS}{H}} = \sqrt{\frac{2(26{,}000)(\$35)}{\$9.40}} = \sqrt{193{,}167} = 440.02, \quad \text{or} \quad 440 \text{ drills}$$

and the standard deviation is

$$\sigma_L = \sigma_t\sqrt{L} = (30 \text{ drills}) \sqrt{3} = 51.96, \quad \text{or} \quad 52 \text{ drills}$$

A 92 percent cycle-service level corresponds to $z = 1.41$ (see the Normal Distribution appendix). Therefore,

$$\text{Safety stock} = z\sigma_L = 1.41(52 \text{ drills}) = 73.38, \quad \text{or} \quad 73 \text{ drills}$$
$$\text{Average demand during the lead time} = 100(3) = 300 \text{ drills}$$
$$\text{Reorder point} = \text{Average demand during the lead time} + \text{Safety stock}$$
$$= 300 \text{ drills} + 73 \text{ drills} = 373 \text{ drills}$$

With a continuous review system, $Q = 440$ and $R = 373$.

b. Inventory position = On-hand inventory + Scheduled receipts − Backorders

$$\text{IP} = \text{OH} + \text{SR} - \text{BO} = 40 + 440 - 0 = 480 \text{ drills}$$

Even though IP(480) exceeds R(373), do not place a new order.

SOLVED PROBLEM 6

Suppose that a periodic review (P) system is used at the warehouse, but otherwise the data are the same as in Solved Problem 5.

a. Calculate the P (in workdays, rounded to the nearest day) that gives approximately the same number of orders per year as the EOQ.

b. What is the value of the target inventory level, T? Compare the P system to the Q system in Solved Problem 6.

c. It is time to review the item. On-hand inventory is 40 drills; there is a scheduled receipt of 440 drills and no backorders. How much should be reordered?

SOLUTION

a. The time between orders is

$$P = \frac{\text{EOQ}}{D} (260 \text{ days/years}) = \frac{440}{26,000} (260) = 4.4, \quad \text{or} \quad 4 \text{ days}$$

b. Figure 13.13 shows that $T = 812$. The corresponding Q system for the hand drill requires less safety stock.

c. Inventory position is the amount on hand plus scheduled receipts minus backorders, or

$$\text{IP} = \text{OH} + \text{SR} - \text{BO} = 40 + 440 - 0 = 480 \text{ drills}$$

The order quantity is the target inventory level minus the inventory position, or

$$Q = T - \text{IP} = 812 \text{ drills} - 480 \text{ drills} = 332 \text{ drills}$$

In a periodic review system, the order quantity for this review period is 332 drills.

```
                          Solver - Inventory Systems


  Continuous Review (Q) System          Periodic Review (P) System

  z                          1.41        Time Between Reviews (P)        4.00  Days
                                                                       ☑ Enter manually
  Safety Stock                 73        Standard Deviation of Demand
                                            During Protection Interval    79.37
  Reorder Point               373
                                         Safety Stock                     112
  Annual Cost            $4,822.38
                                         Average Demand During
                                            Protection Interval           700

                                         Target Inventory Level (T)       812

                                         Annual Cost                 $5,207.80
```

FIGURE 13.13

DISCUSSION QUESTIONS

1. What is the relationship between inventory and the eight competitive priorities? (See the Operations Strategy chapter.) Suppose that two competing manufacturers, Company H and Company L, are similar except that Company H has much higher investments in raw materials, work-in-process, and finished goods inventory than Company L. In which of the eight competitive priorities will Company H have an advantage?

2. Form a discussion group in which each member represents a different functional area of a manufacturing business. Suppose that cycle inventories are to be reduced. Discuss the implications of that decision for each functional area.

3. Will organizations ever get to the point where they will no longer need inventories? Why or why not?

OM EXPLORER AND INTERNET EXERCISES

Visit our Web site at www.prenhall.com/krajewski for OM Explorer Tutors, which explain quantitative techniques; Solvers, which help you apply mathematical models; and Internet Exercises, including Facility Tours, which expand on the topics in this chapter.

PROBLEMS

1. **OM Explorer** A part is produced in lots of 1,000 units. It is assembled from two components worth $50 total. The value added in production (for labor and variable overhead) is $60 per unit, bringing total costs per completed unit to $110. The average lead time for the part is 6 weeks and annual demand is 3,800 units. There are 50 business weeks per year.

   a. How many units of the part are held, on average, in cycle inventory? What is the dollar value of this inventory?

   b. How many units of the part are held, on average, in pipeline inventory? What is the dollar value of this inventory? *Hint*. Assume that the typical part in pipeline inventory is 50 percent completed. Thus, half the labor and variable overhead costs has been added, bringing the unit cost to $80, or $50 + $60/2.

2. **OM Explorer** Prince electronics, a manufacturer of consumer electronic goods, has five distribution centers (DCs) in different regions of the country. For one of its products, a high-speed modem priced at $350 per unit, the

average weekly demand at *each* DC is 75 units. Average shipment size to each DC is 400 units, and average lead time for delivery is two weeks. Each DC carries two weeks' supply as safety stock but holds no anticipation inventory.

a. On average, how many dollars of pipeline inventory will be in transit to each DC?

b. How much total inventory (cycle, safety, and pipeline) does Prince hold for all five DCs?

3. **OM Explorer** Lockwood Industries is considering the use of ABC analysis to focus on the most critical items in its inventory. For a random sample of 8 items, the following table shows the annual dollar usage. Rank the items and assign them to the A, B, or C class.

ITEM	DOLLAR VALUE	ANNUAL USAGE
1	$0.01	1,200
2	$0.03	120,000
3	$0.45	100
4	$1.00	44,000
5	$4.50	900
6	$0.90	350
7	$0.30	70,000
8	$1.50	200

4. **OM Explorer** Terminator, Inc., manufactures a motorcycle part in lots of 250 units. The raw materials cost for the part is $150, and the value added in manufacturing one unit from its components is $300, for a total cost per completed unit of $450. The lead time to make the part is 3 weeks, and the annual demand is 4,000 units. Assume 50 working weeks per year.

a. How many units of the part are held, on average, as cycle inventory? What is its value?

b. How many units of the part are held, on average, as pipeline inventory? What is its value?

5. **OM Explorer** Stock-Rite, Inc., is considering the use of ABC analysis to focus on the most critical items in its inventory. For a random sample of 8 items, the following table shows the item's unit value and annual demand. Categorize these items as A, B, and C classes.

ITEM CODE	UNIT VALUE	DEMAND (units)
A104	$40.25	80
D205	80.75	120
X104	10.00	150
U404	40.50	150
L205	60.70	50
S104	80.20	20
X205	80.15	20
L104	20.05	100

6. **OM Explorer** Yellow Press, Inc., buys slick paper in 1,500-pound rolls for textbook printing. Annual demand is 2,500 rolls. The cost per roll is $800, and the annual holding cost is 15 percent of the cost. Each order costs $50.

a. How many rolls should Yellow Press order at a time?

b. What is the time between orders?

7. **OM Explorer** Babble, Inc. buys 400 blank cassette tapes per month for use in producing foreign language courseware. The ordering cost is $12.50. Holding cost is $0.12 per cassette per year.

a. How many rolls should Babble order at a time?

b. What is the time between orders?

8. **OM Explorer** At Dot Com, a large retailer of popular books, demand is constant at 32,000 books per year. The cost of placing an order to replenish stock is $10, and the annual cost of holding is $4 per book. Stock is received 5 working days after an order has been placed. No back-ordering is allowed. Assume 300 working days a year.

a. What is Dot Com's optimal ordering quantity?

b. What is the optimal number of orders per year?

c. What is the optimal interval (in working days) between orders?

d. What is demand during the lead time?

e. What is the reorder point?

f. What is the inventory position immediately after an order has been placed?

9. **OM Explorer** Leaky Pipe, a local retailer of plumbing supplies, faces demand for one of its inventoried items at a constant rate of 30,000 units per year. It costs Leaky Pipe $10 to process an order to replenish stock and $1 per unit per year to carry the item in stock. Stock is received 4 working days after an order is placed. No back-ordering is allowed. Assume 300 working days a year.

a. What is Leaky Pipe's optimal ordering quantity?

b. What is the optimal number of orders per year?

c. What is the optimal interval (in working days) between orders?

d. What is the demand during the lead time?

e. What is the reorder point?

f. What is the inventory position immediately after an order has been placed?

10. **OM Explorer** Sam's Cat Hotel operates 52 weeks per year, 6 days per week, and uses a continuous review inventory system. It purchases kitty litter for $11.70 per bag. The following information is available about these bags.

Demand = 90 bags/week
Order cost = $54/order
Annual holding cost = 27% of cost
Desired cycle-service level = 80%
Lead time = 3 weeks (18 working days)
Standard deviation of weekly demand = 15 bags

Current on-hand inventory is 320 bags, with no open orders or backorders.

a. What is the EOQ? What would be the average time between orders (in weeks)?

b. What should R be?

c. An inventory withdrawal of 10 bags was just made. Is it time to reorder?

d. The store currently uses a lot size of 500 bags (i.e., $Q = 500$). What is the annual holding cost of this policy? Annual ordering cost? Without calculating the EOQ, how can you conclude from these two calculations that the current lot size is too large?

e. What would be the annual cost saved by shifting from the 500-bag lot size to the EOQ?

11.   **OM Explorer** Consider again the kitty litter ordering policy for Sam's Cat Hotel in Problem 10.

a. Suppose that the weekly demand forecast of 90 bags is incorrect and actual demand averages only 60 bags per week. How much higher will total costs be, owing to the distorted EOQ caused by this forecast error?

b. Suppose that actual demand is 60 bags but that ordering costs are cut to only $6 by using the Internet to automate order placing. However, the buyer does not tell anyone, and the EOQ isn't adjusted to reflect this reduction in S. How much higher will total costs be, compared to what they could be if the EOQ were adjusted?

12.   **OM Explorer** In a Q system, the demand rate for gizmos is normally distributed, with an average of 300 units *per week*. The lead time is 9 weeks. The standard deviation of *weekly* demand is 15 units.

a. What is the standard deviation of demand during the 9-week lead time?

b. What is the average demand during the 9-week lead time?

c. What reorder point results in a cycle-service level of 99 percent?

13.   **OM Explorer** Petromax Enterprises uses a continuous review inventory control system for one of its inventory items. The following information is available on the item. The firm operates 50 weeks in a year.

Demand = 50,000 units per year
Ordering cost = $35 per order
Holding cost = $2 per unit per year
Average lead time = 3 weeks
Standard deviation of weekly demand = 125 units.

a. What is the economic order quantity for this item?

b. If Petromax wants to provide a 90 percent cycle-service level, what should be the safety stock and the reorder point?

14.   **OM Explorer** In a perpetual inventory system, the lead time for dohickies is 5 weeks. The standard deviation of demand during the lead time is 85 units. The desired cycle-service level is 99 percent. The supplier of dohickies has streamlined operations and now quotes a 1-week lead time. How much can safety stock be reduced without reducing the 99 percent cycle-service level?

15.   **OM Explorer** In a two-bin inventory system, the demand for whatchamacallits during the 2-week lead time is normally distributed, with an average of 53 units per week. The standard deviation of weekly demand is 5 units. What cycle-service level is provided when the normal level in the second bin is set at 120 units?

16.   **OM Explorer** Nationwide Auto Parts uses a periodic review inventory control system for one of its stock items. The review interval is 6 weeks, and the lead time for receiving the materials ordered from its wholesaler is 3 weeks. Weekly demand is normally distributed, with a mean of 100 units and a standard deviation of 20 units.

a. What is the average and the standard deviation of demand during the protection interval?

b. What should be the target inventory level if the firm desires 97.5 percent stockout protection?

c. If 350 units were in stock at the time of a certain periodic review, how many units should be ordered?

17.   In a P system, the lead time for gadgets is 2 weeks and the review period is 1 week. Demand during the protection interval averages 218 units, with a standard deviation of 40 units. What is the cycle-service level when the target inventory level is set at 300 units?

18.   **OM Explorer** You are in charge of inventory control of a highly successful product retailed by your firm. Weekly demand for this item varies, with an average of 200 units and a standard deviation of 16 units. It is purchased from a wholesaler at a cost of $12.50 per unit. The supply lead time is 4 weeks. Placing an order costs $50, and the inventory carrying rate per year is 20 percent of the item's cost. Your firm operates 5 days per week, 50 weeks per year.

a. What is the optimal ordering quantity for this item?

b. How many units of the item should be maintained as safety stock for 99 percent protection against stock-outs during an order cycle?

c. If supply lead time can be reduced to 2 weeks, what is the percent reduction in the number of units maintained as safety stock for the same 99 percent stock-out protection?

d. If through appropriate sales promotions, the demand variability is reduced so that the standard deviation of weekly demand is 8 units instead of 16, what is the percent reduction (compared to that in part (b)) in the number of units maintained as safety stock for the same 99 percent stockout protection?

19. 💿 **OM Explorer** Suppose that Sam's Cat Hotel in Problem 10 uses a P system instead of a Q system. The average daily demand is 15 bags (90/6), and the standard deviation of *daily* demand is 6.124 bags $(15/\sqrt{6})$.

a. What P (in working days) and T should be used to approximate the cost trade-offs of the EOQ?

b. How much more safety stock is needed than with a Q system?

c. It's time for the periodic review. How much should be ordered?

20. 💿 **OM Explorer** Your firm uses a continuous review system and operates 52 weeks per year. One of the items handled has the following characteristics.

Demand $(D) = 20,000$ units/year
Ordering cost $(S) = \$40$/order
Holding cost $(H) = \$2$/unit/year
Lead time $(L) = 2$ weeks
Cycle-service level = 95%
Demand is normally distributed, with a standard deviation of *weekly* demand of 100 units.
Current on-hand inventory is 1,040 units, with no scheduled receipts and no backorders.

a. Calculate the item's EOQ. What is the average time, in weeks, between orders?

b. Find the safety stock and reorder point that provide a 95 percent cycle-service level.

c. For these policies, what are the annual costs of (i) holding the cycle inventory and (ii) placing orders?

d. A withdrawal of 15 units just occurred. Is it time to reorder? If so, how much should be ordered?

21. 💿 **OM Explorer** Suppose that your firm uses a periodic review system, but otherwise the data are the same as in Problem 20.

a. Calculate the P that gives approximately the same number of orders per year as the EOQ. Round your answer to the nearest week.

b. Find the safety stock and the target inventory level that provide a 95 percent cycle-service level.

c. How much larger is the safety stock than with a Q system?

22. 💿 **OM Explorer** A company begins a review of ordering policies for its continuous review system by checking the current policies for a sample of items. Following are the characteristics of one item.

Demand $(D) = 64$ units/week (Assume 52 weeks per year.)
Ordering and setup cost $(S) = \$50$/order
Holding cost $(H) = \$13$/unit/year
Lead time $(L) = 2$ weeks
Standard deviation of *weekly* demand = 12 units
Cycle-service level = 88%

a. What is the EOQ for this item?

b. What is the desired safety stock?

c. What is the reorder point?

d. What are the cost implications if the current policy for this item is $Q = 200$ and $R = 180$?

23. 💿 **OM Explorer** Using the same information as in Problem 22, develop the best policies for a periodic review system.

a. What value of P gives the same approximate number of orders per year as the EOQ? Round to the nearest week.

b. What safety stock and target inventory level provide an 88 percent cycle-service level?

24. 💿 **OM Explorer** Wood County Hospital consumes 1,000 boxes of bandages per week. The price of bandages is $35 per box, and the hospital operates 52 weeks per year. The cost of processing an order is $15, and the cost of holding one box for a year is 15 percent of the value of the material.

a. The hospital orders bandages in lot sizes of 900 boxes. What *extra cost* does the hospital incur, which it could save by using the EOQ method?

b. Demand is normally distributed, with a standard deviation of weekly demand of 100 boxes. The lead time is 2 weeks. What safety stock is necessary if the hospital uses a continuous review system and a 97 percent cycle-service level is desired? What should be the reorder point?

c. If the hospital uses a periodic review system, with $P = 2$ weeks, what should be the target inventory level, T?

25. 🌐 **OM Explorer** A golf specialty wholesaler operates 50 weeks per year. Management is trying to determine an inventory policy for its 1-irons, which have the following characteristics:

    Demand (D) = 2,000 units/year
    Demand is normally distributed.
    Standard deviation of *weekly* demand = 3 units
    Ordering cost = $40/order
    Annual holding cost (H) = $5/unit
    Desired cycle-service level = 90%
    Lead time (L) = 4 weeks

    a. If the company uses a periodic review system, what should P and T be? Round P to the nearest week.

    b. If the company uses a continuous review system, what should R be?

Advanced Problems

Problems 28–31 require prior reading of the Simulation supplement.

26. Clone Computer Mart estimates the distribution of demand during the lead time for boxes of diskettes to be as follows:

DEMAND	PROBABILITY
20	0.20
40	0.40
60	0.20
80	0.10
100	0.10
	1.00

    a. If a continuous review system is used, what reorder point, R, provides an 80 percent cycle-service level?

    b. What would be the safety stock?

(*Hint:* Set up the cumulative probability distribution of demand and choose R so that probabilities of demand less than or equal to R sum to 0.80. Safety stock is R minus the average demand during lead time.)

27. Club Hardware estimates the following demand during lead time distribution for crescent wrenches:

DEMAND	PROBABILITY
0	0.20
25	0.20
50	0.20
75	0.20
100	0.10
125	0.10
	1.00

    a. What reorder point R would result in a 90 percent cycle-service level?

    b. How much safety stock would be provided with this policy?

(*Hint:* Set up the cumulative probability distribution of demand and choose R so that probabilities of demand less than or equal to R sum to 0.90.) Safety stock is R minus the average demand during lead time.

28. The Georgia Lighting Center stocks more than 3,000 lighting fixtures, including chandeliers, swags, wall lamps, and track lights. The store sells at retail, operates 6 days per week, and advertises itself as the "brightest spot in town." One expensive fixture is selling at an average rate of 5 units per day. The reorder policy is $Q = 40$ and $R = 15$. A new order is placed on the day the reorder point is reached. The lead time is 3 business days. For example, an order placed on Monday will be delivered on Thursday. Simulate the performance of this Q system for the next 3 weeks (18 workdays). Any stockouts result in lost sales (rather than backorders). The beginning inventory is 19 units, and there are no scheduled receipts. Table 13.1 simulates the first week of operation. Extend Table 13.1 to simulate operations for the next 2 weeks if demand for the next 12 business days is 7, 4, 2, 7, 3, 6, 10, 0, 5, 10, 4, and 7.

TABLE 13.1 *First Week of Operation*

WORKDAY	BEGINNING INVENTORY	ORDERS RECEIVED	DAILY DEMAND	ENDING INVENORY	INVENTORY POSITION	ORDER QUANTITY
1. Monday	19	—	5	14	14	40
2. Tuesday	14	—	3	11	51	—
3. Wednesday	11	—	4	7	47	—
4. Thursday	7	40	1	46	46	—
5. Friday	46	—	10	36	36	—
6. Saturday	36	—	9	27	27	—

	BEGINNING	ORDERS	DAILY	ENDING	INVENTORY	ORDER
WORKDAY	INVENTORY	RECEIVED	DEMAND	INVENORY	POSITION	QUANTITY
1. Monday	40	440	143	337	337	474
2. Tuesday	337	—	82	255	729	—
3. Wednesday	255	—	103	152	626	—
4. Thursday	152	—	127	25	526	—
5. Friday	25	474	85	414	414	397

TABLE 13.2 *First Week of Operation*

a. What is the average daily ending inventory over the 18 days?

b. How many stockouts occurred?

29. Simulate Problem 28 again, but this time use a P system with $P = 8$ and $T = 55$. Let the first review occur on the first Monday. As before, the beginning inventory is 19 units, and there are no scheduled receipts.

    a. What is the average daily ending inventory over the 18 days?

    b. How many stockouts occurred?

30. In Solved Problem 5, a Q system for hand drills was devised, with $Q = 440$ and $R = 373$. Simulate this system for a 21-day period by completing and extending Table 13.2. The daily demand is drawn from a normal distribution with a mean of 100 and standard deviation of 30. The demand for the next 16 business days is 60, 94, 87, 102, 42, 123, 140, 85, 67, 83, 123, 108, 88, 120, 138,

and 74. The on-hand inventory at the start of day 1 is 40 units, and one scheduled receipt of 440 units is to arrive on this first day. The lead time for new orders is 4 business days. If a new order is placed on the first workday (Monday), it will be available on the fifth workday (Friday).

    a. What is the average daily ending inventory over the 21 days?

    b. How many new orders were placed?

31. In Solved Problem 6, a P system for hand drills was devised, with $P = 4$ days and $T = 812$. Simulate this system for a 21-day period, using the same random demands as in Problem 30.

    a. What is the average ending inventory over the 21 days?

    b. How many new orders were placed?

SIMULATION EXERCISES

These simulation exercises require the use of the Extend and SimQuick simulation packages. Extend is on the Student CD-ROM that is packaged with every new copy of the textbook. SimQuick is an optional simulation package that your instructor may or may not have ordered.

1. 💿 **OM Explorer** Ready Hardware is a midsize regional distributor of hardware for construction firms, small manufacturers, and independent retailers. The purchasing manager is reviewing replenishment policies for the different product lines. One particular product is a standard door lockset, which has fairly steady sales with approximately 15 sold each day. Use the Extend simulator to evaluate different lot sizing and replenishment policies. See the *Inventory Management at Ready Hardware* case on the Student CD-ROM, which includes the basic

model and how to use it. Answer the various questions asked in Sections A to D. Section E, on quantity discounts, should be done after reading the Special Inventory Models supplement.

2. **SimQuick** A large electronics superstore sells a popular hand-held computer. Whenever the number of computers in stock reaches 25, the store places an order for 35 to the manufacturer. The time it takes to receive an order varies according to a normal distribution, with a mean of 5 days and a standard deviation of 0.3 days. The mean demand is 5 computers a day. Management would like to maintain a 90 percent service level on its inventory of computers. Use SimQuick to determine the best reorder point and order size. See Example 9 in *SimQuick: Process Simulation* in Excel for more details of this problem and additional exercises.

CASE **PARTS EMPORIUM**

It is June 6, Sue McCaskey's first day in the newly created position of materials manager for Parts Emporium. A recent graduate of a prominent business school, McCaskey is eagerly awaiting her first real-world problem. At approximately 8:30 A.M. it arrives in the form of status reports on inventory and orders shipped. At the top of an extensive computer printout is a handwritten note from Joe Donnell, the purchasing manager: "Attached you will find the inventory and customer service performance data. Rest assured that the individual inventory levels are accurate because we took a complete physical inventory count at the end of last week. Unfortunately, we don't keep compiled records in some of the areas as you requested. However, you're welcome to do so yourself. Welcome aboard!"

A little upset that aggregate information is not available, McCaskey decides to randomly select a small sample of approximately 100 items and compile inventory and customer service characteristics to get a feel for the "total picture." The results of this experiment reveal to her why Parts Emporium decided to create the position she now fills. It seems that the inventory is in all the wrong places. Although there is an *average* of approximately 60 days of inventory, customer service is inadequate. Parts Emporium tries to backorder the customer orders not immediately filled from stock, but some 10 percent of demand is being lost to competing distributorships. Because stockouts are costly relative to inventory holding costs, McCaskey believes that a cycle-service level of at least 95 percent should be achieved.

Parts Emporium, Inc., was formed in 1973 as a wholesale distributor of automobile parts by two disenchanted auto mechanics, Dan Block and Ed Spriggs. Originally located in Block's garage, the firm showed slow but steady growth until 1976, when it relocated to an old, abandoned meat-packing warehouse on Chicago's South Side. With increased space for inventory storage, the company was able to begin offering an expanded line of auto parts. This increased selection, combined with the trend toward longer car ownership, led to an explosive growth of the business. By 1998, Parts Emporium was the largest independent distributor of auto parts in the North Central region.

In 2000, Parts Emporium relocated in a sparkling new office and warehouse complex off Interstate 55 in suburban Chicago. The warehouse space alone occupied more than 100,000 square feet. Although only a handful of new products have been added since the warehouse was constructed, its utilization has increased from 65 percent to more than 90 percent of capacity. During this same period, however, sales growth has stagnated. These conditions motivated Block and Spriggs to hire the first manager from outside the company in the firm's history.

Sue McCaskey knows that although her influence to initiate changes will be limited, she must produce positive results immediately. Thus, she decides to concentrate on two products from the extensive product line: the EG151 exhaust gasket and the DB032 drive belt. If she can demonstrate significant gains from proper inventory management for just two products, perhaps Block and Spriggs will give her the backing needed to change the total inventory management system.

The EG151 exhaust gasket is purchased from an overseas supplier, Haipei, Inc. Actual demand for the first 21 weeks of 2001 is shown in the following table:

WEEK	ACTUAL DEMAND	WEEK	ACTUAL DEMAND
1	104	12	97
2	103	13	99
3	107	14	102
4	105	15	99
5	102	16	103
6	102	17	101
7	101	18	101
8	104	19	104
9	100	20	108
10	100	21	97
11	103		

A quick review of past orders, shown in another document, indicates that a lot size of 150 units is being used and that the lead time from Haipei is fairly constant at two weeks. Currently, at the end of week 21, no inventory is on hand; 11 units are backordered, and there is a scheduled receipt of 150 units.

The DB032 drive belt is purchased from the Bendox Corporation of Grand Rapids, Michigan. Actual demand so far in 2001 is shown in the following table:

WEEK	ACTUAL DEMAND	WEEK	ACTUAL DEMAND
11	18	17	50
12	33	18	53
13	53	19	54
14	54	20	49
15	51	21	52
16	53		

Because this product is new, data are available only since its introduction in week 11. Currently, 324 units are on hand; there are no backorders and no scheduled receipts. A lot size of 1,000 units is being used, with the lead time fairly constant at three weeks.

continued

continued

The wholesale prices that Parts Emporium charges its customers are $12.99 for the EG151 exhaust gasket and $8.89 for the DB032 drive belt. Because no quantity discounts are offered on these two highly profitable items, gross margins based on current purchasing practices are 32 percent of the wholesale price for the exhaust gasket and 48 percent of the wholesale price for the drive belt.

Parts Emporium estimates its cost to hold inventory at 21 percent of its inventory investment. This percent recognizes the opportunity cost of tying money up in inventory and the variable costs of taxes, insurance, and shrinkage. The annual report notes other warehousing expenditures for utilities and maintenance and debt service on the 100,000-square-foot warehouse, which was built for $1.5 million. However, McCaskey reasons that these warehousing costs can be ignored because they will not change for the range of inventory policies that she is considering.

Out-of-pocket costs for Parts Emporium to place an order with suppliers are estimated to be $20 per order for exhaust gaskets and $10 per order for drive belts. On the outbound side, there can be delivery charges. Although most customers pick up their parts at Parts Emporium, some orders are delivered to customers. To provide this service, Parts Emporium contracts with a local company for a flat fee of $21.40 per order, which is added to the customer's bill. McCaskey is unsure whether to increase the ordering costs for Parts Emporium to include delivery charges.

Questions

1. Put yourself in Sue McCaskey's position and prepare a detailed report to Dan Block and Ed Spriggs on managing the inventory of the EG151 exhaust gasket and the DB032 drive belt. Be sure to present a proper inventory system and recognize all relevant costs.
2. By how much do your recommendations for these two items reduce annual cycle inventory, stockout, and ordering costs?

Source: This case was provided by Professor Robert Bregman, University of Houston.

SELECTED REFERENCES

Berlin, Bob. "Solving the OEM Puzzle at Valleylab." *APICS—The Performance Advantage* (March 1997), pp. 58–63.

Chikan, A., A. Milne, and L. G. Sprague. "Reflections on Firm and National Inventories." Budapest: International Society for Inventory Research, 1996.

"Factors That Make or Break Season Sales." *Wall Street Journal* (December 9, 1991).

Greene, James H. *Production and Inventory Control Handbook*, 3d ed. New York: McGraw-Hill, 1997.

Inventory Management Reprints. Falls Church, Va.: American Production and Inventory Control Society, 1993.

Krupp, James A. G. "Are ABC Codes an Obsolete Technology?" *APICS—The Performance Advantage* (April 1994), pp. 34–35.

Silver, Edward A. "Changing the Givens in Modeling Inventory Problems: The Example of Just-In-Time Systems." *International Journal of Production Economics*, vol. 26 (1996) pp. 347–351.

Silver, Edward A., D. F. Pyke, and Rein Peterson. *Inventory Management, Production Planning and Scheduling*, 3d ed. New York: John Wiley & Sons, 1998.

Tersine, Richard J. *Principles of Inventory and Materials Management*, 4th ed. Saddlebrook, NJ: Prentice-Hall, 1994.

Special Inventory Models

Learning Goals

After reading this supplement you will be able to . . .

1. calculate the optimal lot size when replenishment isn't instantaneous.
2. explain the need to acknowledge the cost of material when quantity discounts are available.
3. determine the optimal order quantity when materials are subject to quantity discounts.
4. calculate the order quantity that maximizes expected profits for a one-period inventory decision.

M ANY REAL-WORLD PROBLEMS REQUIRE relaxation of certain assumptions on which the EOQ model is based. This supplement addresses three realistic situations that require going beyond the simple EOQ formulation.

1. *Noninstantaneous Replenishment.*   Particularly in situations where manufacturers use a continuous process to make a primary material such as a liquid, gas, or powder, production isn't instantaneous, and thus inventory is replenished gradually rather than in lots.
2. *Quantity Discounts.*   There are three relevant annual costs: the inventory holding cost, the fixed cost for ordering and setup, and the cost of materials. For service providers and for manufacturers alike, the unit cost of purchased materials sometimes depends on the order quantity.
3. *One-Period Decisions.*   Retailers and manufacturers of fashion goods often face a situation in which demand is uncertain and occurs during just one period or season.

NONINSTANTANEOUS REPLENISHMENT

If an item is being produced internally rather than purchased, finished units may be used or sold as soon as they are completed, without waiting until a full lot has been completed. For example, a restaurant that bakes its own dinner rolls begins to use some of the rolls from the first pan even before the baker finishes a five-pan batch. The inventory of rolls never reaches the full five-pan level, the way it would if the rolls all arrived at once on a truck sent by an external supplier or a cart driven by an internal materials handler.

Figure E.1 depicts the usual case, in which the production rate, p, exceeds the demand rate, d.[1] Cycle inventory accumulates faster than demand occurs; that is, there is a buildup of $p - d$ units during the time when both production and demand occur. For example, if the production rate is 100 units per day and the demand is 5 units per day, the buildup is 95 (or $100 - 5$) units each day. This buildup continues until the lot size, Q, has been produced, after which the inventory depletes at a rate of 5 units per day. Just as the inventory reaches 0, the next production interval begins. To be consistent, both p and d must be expressed in units of the same time interval, such as units per day or units per week. Here, we assume that they are expressed in units per day.

The $p - d$ buildup continues for Q/p days because Q is the lot size and p units are produced each day. In our example, if the lot size is 300 units, the production interval is 3 days (300/100). For the given rate of buildup over the production interval, the maximum cycle inventory, $I_{\max}$, is

$$I_{\max} = \frac{Q}{p}\,(p - d) = Q\left(\frac{p - d}{p}\right)$$

Cycle inventory is no longer $Q/2$, as it was with the basic EOQ method (see the Inventory Management chapter); instead, it is $I_{\max}/2$. Setting up the total cost equation for this production situation, where D is annual demand, as before, and d is daily demand, we get

FIGURE E.1

Lot Sizing with Noninstantaneous Replenishment

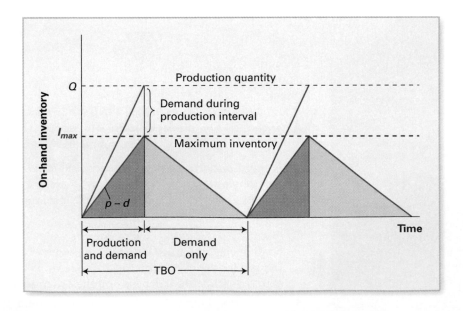

---

[1] If they were equal, production would be continuous with no buildup of cycle inventory. If the production rate is lower than the demand rate, sales opportunities are being missed on an ongoing basis. We assume that $p > d$ in this supplement.

Total cost = Annual holding cost + Annual ordering or setup cost

$$C = \frac{I_{max}}{2}(H) + \frac{D}{Q}(S) = \frac{Q}{2}\left(\frac{p-d}{p}\right)(H) + \frac{D}{Q}(S)$$

economic production lot size (ELS) The optimal lot size in a situation where replenishment is not instantaneous.

Based on this cost function, the optimal lot size, often called the **economic production lot size (ELS)**, is

$$\text{ELS} = \sqrt{\frac{2DS}{H}}\sqrt{\frac{p}{p-d}}$$

Because the second term is a ratio greater than 1, the ELS results in a larger lot size than the EOQ.

| EXAMPLE E.1 | *Finding the Economic Production Lot Size* |

**TUTOR
E.1**

A plant manager of a chemical plant must determine the lot size for a particular chemical that has a steady demand of 30 barrels per day. The production rate is 190 barrels per day, annual demand is 10,500 barrels, setup cost is $200, annual holding cost is $0.21 per barrel, and the plant operates 350 days per year. Determine

    a. The economic production lot size (ELS),

    b. The total annual setup and inventory holding cost for this item,

    c. The TBO, or cycle length, for the ELS,

    d. The production time per lot.

What are the advantages of reducing the setup time by 10 percent?

SOLUTION

a. Solving first for the ELS, we get

$$\text{ELS} = \sqrt{\frac{2DS}{H}}\sqrt{\frac{p}{p-d}} = \sqrt{\frac{2(10,500)(\$200)}{\$0.21}}\sqrt{\frac{190}{190-30}}$$

$$= 4,873.4 \text{ barrels}$$

b. The annual total cost with the ELS is

$$C = \frac{Q}{2}\left(\frac{p-d}{p}\right)(H) + \frac{D}{Q}(S)$$

$$= \frac{4,873.4}{2}\left(\frac{190-30}{190}\right)(\$0.21) + \frac{10,500}{4,873.4}(\$200)$$

$$= \$430.91 + \$430.91 = \$861.82$$

c. Applying the TBO formula (see the Inventory Management chapter) to the ELS, we get

$$\text{TBO}_{ELS} = \frac{\text{ELS}}{D}(350 \text{ days/year}) = \frac{4,873.4}{10,500}(350)$$

$$= 162.4, \quad \text{or} \quad 162 \text{ days}$$

d. The production time during each cycle is the lot size divided by the production rate:

$$\frac{\text{ELS}}{p} = \frac{4,873.4}{190} = 25.6, \quad \text{or} \quad 26 \text{ days}$$

Solver - Economic Production Lot Size

Period used in Calculations	Day
Demand per Day	30
Production Rate/Day	190
Annual Demand	10,500
Setup Cost	$180
Annual Holding Cost ($)	$0.21
Operating Days per Year	350

◉ Enter Holding Cost Manually   ○ Holding Cost as % of Value

Economic Lot Size (ELS)	4,623
Annual Total Cost	$817.60
Time Between Orders (Days)	154.1
Production Time	24.3

FIGURE E.2

Decision Point As OM Explorer shows in Figure E.2, the net effect of reducing the setup cost by 10 percent is to reduce the lot size, time between orders, and production cycle time. Consequently, costs are also reduced. This adds flexibility to the manufacturing process because items can be made quicker with less expense. Management must decide whether the added cost of improving the setup process is worth the added flexibility and inventory cost reductions. ◻

QUANTITY DISCOUNTS

Quantity discounts, which are price incentives to purchase large quantities, create pressure to maintain a large inventory. For example, a supplier may offer a price of $4 per unit for orders between 1 and 99 units, a price of $3.50 per unit for orders between 100 and 199 units, and a price of $3.00 per unit for orders of more than 200 units. The item's price is no longer fixed, as assumed in the EOQ derivation; instead, if the order quantity is increased enough, the price is discounted. Hence, a new approach is needed to find the best lot size—one that balances the advantages of lower prices for purchased materials and fewer orders (which are benefits of large order quantities) against the disadvantage of the increased cost of holding more inventory.

The total annual cost now includes not only the holding cost, $(Q/2)(H)$, and the ordering cost, $(D/Q)(S)$, but also the cost of purchased materials. For any per-unit price level, P, the total cost is

$$\text{Total cost} = \frac{\text{Annual holding}}{\text{cost}} + \frac{\text{Annual ordering}}{\text{cost}} + \frac{\text{Annual cost}}{\text{of materials}}$$

$$C = \frac{Q}{2}(H) + \frac{D}{Q}(S) + PD$$

The unit holding cost, H, usually is expressed as a percent of the unit price because the more valuable the item held in inventory, the higher the holding cost is. Thus, the lower the unit price, P, is, the lower H is. Conversely, the higher P is, the higher H is.

As when we calculated total cost previously (see the Inventory Management chapter), the total cost equation yields U-shaped total cost curves. Adding the annual cost of materials to the total cost equation raises each total cost curve by a fixed amount, as shown in Figure E.3(a). There are three cost curves—one for each price level. The top

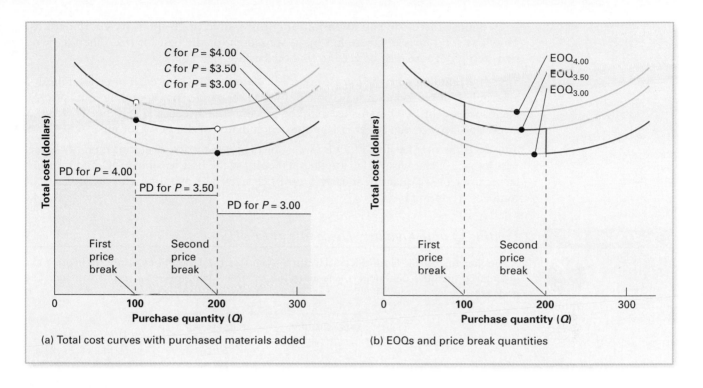

(a) Total cost curves with purchased materials added

(b) EOQs and price break quantities

FIGURE E.3

Total Cost Curves with Quantity Discounts

curve applies when no discounts are received; the lower curves reflect the discounted price levels. No single curve is relevant to all purchase quantities. The relevant, or *feasible*, total cost begins with the top curve, then drops down, curve by curve, at the price breaks. A *price break* is the minimum quantity needed to get a discount. In Figure E.3, there are two price breaks: at $Q = 100$ and $Q = 200$. The result is a total cost curve, with steps at the price breaks.

Figure E.3(b) also shows three additional points—the minimum point on each curve, obtained with the EOQ formula at each price level. These EOQs do not necessarily produce the best lot size for two reasons.

1. The EOQ at a particular price level may not be feasible—the lot size may not lie in the range corresponding to its per-unit price. Figure E.3(b) illustrates two instances of an infeasible EOQ. First, the minimum point for the $3.00 curve appears to be about 175 units. However, the supplier's quantity discount schedule does not allow purchase of that small a quantity at the $3.00 unit price. Similarly, the EOQ for the $4.00 price level is greater than the first price break, so the price charged would be only $3.50.

2. The EOQ at a particular price level may be feasible but may not be the best lot size—the feasible EOQ may have a *higher* cost than is achieved by the EOQ or price break quantity on a *lower* price curve. In Figure E.3(b), for example, the 200-unit price break quantity for the $3.00 price level has a lower total cost than the feasible EOQ for the $3.50 price level. A feasible EOQ always is better than any feasible point on cost curves with higher price levels, but not necessarily those with lower levels. Thus, the only time we can immediately conclude, without comparing total costs, that a feasible EOQ is the best order quantity is when it is on the curve for the *lowest* price level. This conclusion is not possible in Figure E.3(b) because the only feasible EOQ is at the middle price level, $P = \$3.50$.

We must therefore pay attention only to feasible price–quantity combinations, shown as solid lines in Figure E.3(b), as we search for the best lot size. The following two-step procedure may be used to find the best lot size.[2]

Step 1. Beginning with the *lowest* price, calculate the EOQ for each price level until a feasible EOQ is found. It is feasible if it lies in the range corresponding to its price. Each subsequent EOQ is smaller than the previous one because P, and thus H, gets larger and because the larger H is in the denominator of the EOQ formula.

Step 2. If the first feasible EOQ found is for the *lowest* price level, this quantity is the best lot size. Otherwise, calculate the total cost for the first feasible EOQ and for the larger price break quantity at each *lower* price level. The quantity with the lowest total cost is optimal.

EXAMPLE E.2	*Finding Q with Quantity Discounts at LFKHS*

**TUTOR
E.2**

A supplier for Lower Florida Keys Health System (see the Operations Strategy chapter) has introduced quantity discounts to encourage larger order quantities of a special catheter. The price schedule is

ORDER QUANTITY	PRICE PER UNIT
0–299	$60.00
300–499	$58.80
500 or more	$57.00

LFKHS estimates that its annual demand for this item is 936 units, its ordering cost is $45 per order, and its annual holding cost is 25 percent of the catheter's unit price. What quantity of this catheter should the hospital order to minimize total costs? Suppose the price for quantities between 300 and 499 is reduced to $58.00. Should the order quantity change?

SOLUTION

Step 1. Find the first feasible EOQ, starting with the lowest price level:

$$\text{EOQ}_{57.00} = \sqrt{\frac{2DS}{H}} = \sqrt{\frac{2(936)(45)}{0.25(57.00)}}$$
$$= 77 \text{ units}$$

A 77-unit order actually costs $60 per unit, instead of the $57 per unit used in the EOQ calculation, so this EOQ is infeasible. Now try the $58.80 level:

$$\text{EOQ}_{58.80} = \sqrt{\frac{2DS}{H}} = \sqrt{\frac{2(936)(45)}{0.25(58.80)}}$$
$$= 76 \text{ units}$$

This quantity also is infeasible because a 76-unit order is too small to qualify for the $58.80 price. Try the highest price level:

$$\text{EOQ}_{60.00} = \sqrt{\frac{2DS}{H}} = \sqrt{\frac{2(936)(45)}{0.25(60.00)}} = 75 \text{ units}$$

This quantity is feasible, because it lies in the range corresponding to its price, $P = \$60.00$.

---

[2] Another approach which often reduces the number of iterations can be found in Goyal, S. K. "A Simple Procedure for Price Break Models," *Production Planning & Control*, vol. 6, no. 6 (1995), pp. 584–585.

Step 2. The first feasible EOQ of 75 does not correspond to the lowest price level. Hence, we must compare its total cost with the price break quantities (300 and 500 units) at the *lower* price levels ($58.80 and $57.00):

$$C = \frac{Q}{2}(H) + \frac{D}{Q}(S) + PD$$

$$C_{75} = \frac{75}{2}[(0.25)(\$60.00)] + \frac{936}{75}(\$45) + \$60.00(936) = \$57,284$$

$$C_{300} = \frac{300}{2}[(0.25)(\$58.80)] + \frac{936}{300}(\$45) + \$58.80(936) = \$57,382$$

$$C_{500} = \frac{500}{2}[(0.25)(\$57.00)] + \frac{936}{500}(\$45) + \$57.00(936) = \$56,999$$

The best purchase quantity is 500 units, which qualifies for the deepest discount.

Solver - Evaluating Quantity Discounts

Enter data in yellow-shaded areas.

| More | Fewer |

Min. Amount Req'd for Price Point	Lot Sizes	Price/Unit
---	0 - 299	$60.00
300	300 -499	$58.00
500	500 or more	$57.00

Annual Demand	936
Order Cost	$45
Holding Cost (% of Price)	25%

Best Order Quantity	300

	Price Point	EOQ or Req'd Order for Price Point	Inventory Cost	Order Cost	Purchase Cost	Total Cost
	$60.00	75	$562.50	$561.60	$56,160	$57,284
>>	$58.00	300	$2,175	$140.40	$54,288	$56,603 <<
	$57.00	500	$3,563	$84.24	$53,352	$56,999

FIGURE E.4

Decision Point If the price per unit for the range of 300 to 499 units is reduced to $58.00, the best decision is to order 300 catheters, as shown by OM Explorer in Figure E.4. This result shows that the decision is sensitive to the price schedule. A reduction of slightly more than 1 percent is enough to make the difference in this example. In general, however, it is not always the case that you should order more than the economic order quantity when given price discounts. When discounts are small, holding cost H is large, and demand D is small, small lot sizes are better even though price discounts are forgone. ⊐

ONE-PERIOD DECISIONS

One of the dilemmas facing many retailers is how to handle seasonal goods such as winter coats. Often, they can't be sold at full markup next year because of changes in styles. Furthermore, the lead time can be longer than the selling season, allowing no second chance to rush through another order to cover unexpectedly high demand. A similar problem exists for manufacturers of fashion goods.

This type of situation is often called the *newsboy problem*. If the newspaper seller does not buy enough papers to resell on the street corner, sales opportunities are lost. If the seller buys too many, the overage cannot be sold because nobody wants yesterday's newspaper.

The following process is a straightforward way to analyze such problems and decide on the best order quantity.

1. List the different levels of demand that are possible, along with the estimated probability of each.

2. Develop a *payoff table* (see the Decision Making supplement) that shows the profit for each purchase quantity, Q, at each assumed demand level, D. Each row in the table represents a different order quantity, and each column represents a different demand level. The payoff for a given quantity–demand combination depends on whether all units are sold at the regular profit margin during the regular season. There are two possible cases.

   a. If demand is high enough $(Q \leq D)$ that all units are sold at the full profit margin, p, during the regular season,

   $$\text{Payoff} = (\text{Profit per unit})\,(\text{Purchase quantity})$$
   $$= pQ$$

   b. If the purchase quantity exceeds the eventual demand $(Q > D)$, only D units are sold at the full profit margin, and the remaining units purchased must be disposed of at a loss, l, after the season. In this case,

   $$\text{Payoff} = \left(\begin{array}{c}\text{Profit per unit sold}\\\text{during season}\end{array}\right)(\text{Demand}) - \left(\begin{array}{c}\text{Loss per}\\\text{unit}\end{array}\right)\left(\begin{array}{c}\text{Amount disposed of}\\\text{after season}\end{array}\right)$$
   $$= pD - l(Q - D)$$

3. Calculate the expected payoff for each Q (or row in the payoff table) by using the *expected value* decision rule (see the Decision Making supplement). For a specific Q, first multiply each payoff in the row by the demand probability associated with the payoff and then add these products.

4. Choose the order quantity Q with the highest expected payoff.

Using this decision process for all such items over many selling seasons will maximize profits. However, it is not foolproof, and it can result in an occasional bad outcome.

EXAMPLE E.3   *Finding Q for One-Time Inventory Decisions*

**TUTOR
E.3**

One of many items sold at a museum of natural history is a Christmas ornament carved from wood. The gift shop makes a $10 profit per unit sold during the season, but it takes a $5 loss per unit after the season is over. The following discrete probability distribution for the season's demand has been identified:

Demand	10	20	30	40	50
Demand Probability	0.2	0.3	0.3	0.1	0.1

How many ornaments should the museum's buyer order?

SOLUTION

Each demand level is a candidate for best order quantity, so the payoff table should have five rows. For the first row, where $Q = 10$, demand is at least as great as the purchase quantity. Thus, all five payoffs in this row are

$$\text{Payoff} = pQ = (\$10)(10) = \$100$$

This formula can be used in other rows but only for those quantity–demand combinations where all units are sold during the season. These combinations lie in the upper-right portion of the payoff table, where $Q \leq D$. For example, the payoff when $Q = 40$ and $D = 50$ is

$$\text{Payoff} = pQ = (\$10)(40) = \$400$$

The payoffs in the lower-left portion of the table represent quantity–demand combinations where some units must be disposed of after the season ($Q > D$). For this case, the payoff must be calculated with the second formula. For example, when $Q = 40$ and $D = 30$,

$$\text{Payoff} = pD - l(Q - D) = (\$10)(30) - (\$5)(40 - 30) = \$250$$

Using OM Explorer, we obtain the payoff table in Figure E.5.

Solver - One-Period Inventory Decisions

Enter data in yellow-shaded areas.

Profit	$10.00	(if sold during preferred period)
Loss	$5.00	(if sold after preferred period)

Enter the possible demands along with the probability of each occurring. Use the buttons to increase or decrease the number of allowable demand forecasts. NOTE: Be sure to enter demand forecasts and probabilities in all tinted cells, and be sure probabilities add up to 1.

	<	>			
Demand	10	20	30	40	50
Probability	0.2	0.3	0.3	0.1	0.1

Payoff Table

		Demand				
		10	20	30	40	50
Quantity	10	100	100	100	100	100
	20	50	200	200	200	200
	30	0	150	300	300	300
	40	-50	100	250	400	400
	50	-100	50	200	350	500

FIGURE E.5

Now we calculate the expected payoff for each Q by multiplying the payoff for each demand quantity by the probability of that demand and then adding the results. For example, for $Q = 30$,

$$\text{Payoff} = 0.2(\$0) + 0.3(\$150) + 0.3(\$300) + 0.1(\$300) + 0.1(\$300) = \$195$$

Using OM Explorer, Figure E.6 shows the expected payoffs.

Weighted Payoffs

Order Quantity	Expected Payoff		
10	100	Greatest Expected Payoff	195
20	170		
30	195	Associated with Order Quantity	30
40	175		
50	140		

FIGURE E.6

Decision Point Because $Q = 30$ has the highest payoff at \$195, it is the best order quantity. Management can use OM Explorer to do sensitivity analysis on the demands and their probabilities to see how confident they are with that decision. ◻

The need for one-time inventory decisions also can arise in manufacturing plants when (1) customized items (specials) are made (or purchased) to a single order *and* (2) scrap quantities are high.[3] A special item produced for a single order is never intentionally held in stock because the demand for it is too unpredictable. In fact, it may never be ordered again, so the manufacturer would like to make just the amount requested by the customer—no more, no less. The manufacturer also would like to satisfy an order in just one run to avoid an extra setup and a delay in delivering goods ordered. These two goals may conflict if the likelihood of some units being scrapped is high. Suppose that a customer places an order for 20 units. If the manager orders 20 units from the shop or from the supplier, one or two units may have to be scrapped. This shortage will force the manager to place a second (or even third) order to replace the defective units. Replacement can be costly if setup time is high and can also delay shipment to the customer. To avoid such problems, the manager could order more than 20 units the first time. If some units are left over, the customer might be willing to buy the extras or the manager might find an internal use for them. For example, some manufacturing companies set up a special account for obsolete materials. These materials can be "bought" by departments within the company at less than their normal cost, as an incentive to use them.

FORMULA REVIEW

Noninstantaneous Replenishment

1. Economic production lot size: $ELS = \sqrt{\dfrac{2DS}{H}} \sqrt{\dfrac{p}{p-d}}$

2. Maximum inventory: $(I_{max}) = Q\left(\dfrac{p-d}{p}\right)$

3. Total cost = Annual holding cost + Annual setup cost

$$C = \dfrac{Q}{2}\left(\dfrac{p-d}{p}\right)(H) + \dfrac{D}{Q}(S)$$

4. Time between orders, in years: $TBO_{ELS} = \dfrac{ELS}{D}$

Quantity Discounts

5. Total cost = Annual holding cost + Annual setup cost + Annual cost of material

$$C = \dfrac{Q}{2}(H) + \dfrac{D}{Q}(S) + PD$$

One-Period Decisions

6. Payoff matrix: $\text{Payoff} = \begin{cases} pQ & \text{if } Q \le D \\ pD - l(Q - D) & \text{if } Q > D \end{cases}$

---

[3] One goal of TQM is to eliminate scrap. Achievement of that TQM goal makes this discussion moot.

SUPPLEMENT HIGHLIGHTS

☐ When inventory items are made instead of bought, inventory is replenished gradually over some production period. This condition is called *noninstantaneous replenishment.* The amount of inventory accumulated during the production period is reduced by concurrent sales. Hence, the maximum amount in inventory will be less than the production lot size. The economic lot size is a balance between annual holding and annual ordering costs. Sales during the production period have the effect of lowering the average inventory and annual holding costs, so balance is restored by increasing the size of each order. Larger orders reduce the number of orders placed during a year.

☐ When quantity discounts are available, the total relevant cost includes annual holding, ordering, and materials costs. Purchasing larger quantities to achieve price discounts reduces annual ordering and materials costs but usually increases annual holding costs. The order quantity is based on minimizing the total of relevant costs per year, instead of obtaining the minimum purchase price per unit.

☐ Retailers, as well as manufacturers of customized products, often face one-time inventory decisions. Demand uncertainty can lead to ordering too much or too little, which can result in cost or customer service penalties. A straightforward approach to one-time inventory decisions is to calculate the expected payoff over a range of reasonable alternatives and choose the one with the best expected payoff.

KEY TERM

economic production lot size (ELS) *637*

SOLVED PROBLEM 1

Peachy Keen, Inc., makes mohair sweaters, blouses with Peter Pan collars, pedal pushers, poodle skirts, and other popular clothing styles of the 1950s. The average demand for mohair sweaters is 100 per week. Peachy's production facility has the capacity to sew 400 sweaters per week. Setup cost is $351. The value of finished goods inventory is $40 per sweater. The annual per-unit inventory holding cost is 20 percent of the item's value.

a. What is the economic production lot size (ELS)?

b. What is the average time between orders (TBO)?

c. What is the total of the annual holding costs and setup costs?

SOLUTION

a. The production lot size that minimizes total costs is

$$ELS = \sqrt{\frac{2DS}{H}} \sqrt{\frac{p}{p-d}} = \sqrt{\frac{2(100 \times 52)(\$351)}{0.20(\$40)}} \sqrt{\frac{400}{(400-100)}}$$

$$= \sqrt{456,300} \sqrt{\frac{4}{3}} = 780 \text{ sweaters}$$

b. The average time between orders is

$$TBO = \frac{ELS}{D} = \frac{780}{5,200} = 0.15 \text{ year}$$

Converting to weeks, we get

$$\text{TBO} = (0.15 \text{ year}) (52 \text{ weeks/year}) = 7.8 \text{ weeks}$$

c. The minimum total of ordering and holding costs is

$$C = \frac{Q}{2}\left(\frac{p-d}{p}\right)(H) + \frac{D}{Q}(S) = \frac{780}{2}\left(\frac{400-100}{400}\right)(0.20 \times \$40) + \frac{5{,}200}{780}(\$351)$$

$$= \$2{,}340/\text{year} + \$2{,}340/\text{year} = \$4{,}680/\text{year}$$

SOLVED PROBLEM 2

A hospital buys disposable surgical packages from Pfisher, Inc. Pfisher's price schedule is $50.25 per package on orders of 1 to 199 packages, and $49.00 per package on orders of 200 or more packages. Ordering cost is $64 per order, and annual holding cost is 20 percent of the per-unit purchase price. Annual demand is 490 packages. What is the best purchase quantity?

SOLUTION

We first calculate the EOQ at the *lowest* price:

$$\text{EOQ}_{\$49.00} = \sqrt{\frac{2DS}{H}} = \sqrt{\frac{2(490)(\$64)}{0.20(\$49.00)}} = \sqrt{6{,}400} = 80 \text{ packages}$$

This solution is infeasible because, according to the price schedule, we cannot purchase 80 packages at a price of $49 each. Therefore, we calculate the EOQ at the next lowest price ($50.25):

$$\text{EOQ}_{\$50.25} = \sqrt{\frac{2DS}{H}} = \sqrt{\frac{2(490)(\$64)}{0.20(\$50.25)}} = \sqrt{6{,}241} = 79 \text{ packages}$$

This EOQ is feasible, but $50.25 per package is not the lowest price. Hence, we have to determine whether total costs can be reduced by purchasing 200 units and thereby obtaining a quantity discount.

$$C = \frac{Q}{2}(H) + \frac{D}{Q}(S) + PD$$

$$C_{79} = \frac{79}{2}(0.20 \times \$50.25) + \frac{490}{79}(\$64) + \$50.25(490)$$

$$= \$396.98/\text{year} + \$396.96/\text{year} + \$24{,}622.50/\text{year} = \$25{,}416.44/\text{year}$$

$$C_{200} = \frac{200}{2}(0.20 \times \$49) + \frac{490}{200}(\$64) + \$49(490)$$

$$= \$980/\text{year} + \$156.80/\text{year} + \$24{,}010/\text{year} = \$25{,}146.80/\text{year}$$

Purchasing 200 units per order will save about $270/year, compared to buying 79 units at a time.

SOLVED PROBLEM 3

Swell Productions is sponsoring an outdoor conclave for owners of collectible and classic Fords. The concession stand in the T-Bird area will sell T-shirts, poodle skirts, and other souvenirs of the 1950s. Poodle skirts are purchased from Peachy Keen, Inc., for $40 each and are sold during the event for $75 each. If any skirts are left over, they can be returned to Peachy for a refund of $30 each. Poodle skirt sales depend on the weather, attendance, and other variables. The following table shows the probability of various sales quantities. How many poodle skirts should Swell order from Peachy Keen for this one-time event?

SALES QUANTITY	PROBABILITY	SALES QUANTITY	PROBABILITY
100	0.05	400	0.34
200	0.11	500	0.11
300	0.34	600	0.05

SOLUTION

Table E.1 is the payoff table that describes this one-period inventory decision. The upper-right portion of the table shows the payoffs when the demand, D, is greater than or equal to the order quantity, Q. The payoff is equal to the per-unit profit (the difference between price and cost) multiplied by the order quantity. For example, when the order quantity is 100 and the demand is 200,

$$\text{Payoff} = (p - c)Q = (\$75 - \$40)100 = \$3{,}500$$

The lower-left portion of the payoff table shows the payoffs when the order quantity exceeds the demand. Here, the payoff is the profit from sales, pD, minus the loss associated with returning overstock, $l(Q - D)$, where l is the difference between the cost and the amount refunded for each poodle skirt returned and $Q - D$ is the number of skirts returned. For example, when the order quantity is 500 and the demand is 200,

$$\text{Payoff} = pD - l(Q - D) = (\$75 - \$40)200 - (\$40 - \$30)(500 - 200) = \$4{,}000$$

TABLE E.1 *Payoffs*

	DEMAND, D						
Q	100	200	300	400	500	600	EXPECTED PAYOFF
100	$3,500	$3,500	$ 3,500	$ 3,500	$ 3,500	$ 3,500	$ 3,500
200	$2,500	$7,000	$ 7,000	$ 7,000	$ 7,000	$ 7,000	$ 6,775
300	$1,500	$6,000	$10,500	$10,500	$10,500	$10,500	$ 9,555
400	$ 500	$5,000	$ 9,500	$14,000	$14,000	$14,000	$10,805
500	($ 500)	$4,000	$ 8,500	$13,000	$17,500	$17,500	$10,525
600	($1,500)	$3,000	$ 7,500	$12,000	$16,500	$21,000	$ 9,750
Probability	0.05	0.11	0.34	0.34	0.11	0.05	

The highest expected payoff occurs when 400 poodle skirts are ordered:

$$\begin{aligned}\text{Expected payoff}_{400} = &(\$500 \times 0.05) + (\$5{,}000 \times 0.11) + (\$9{,}500 \times 0.34) \\ &+ (\$14{,}000 \times 0.34) + (\$14{,}000 \times 0.11) + (\$14{,}000 \times 0.05) \\ = &\$10{,}805\end{aligned}$$

OM EXPLORER AND INTERNET EXERCISES

Visit our Web site at www.prenhall.com/krajewski for OM Explorer Tutors, which explain quantitative techniques; Solvers, which help you apply mathematical models; and Internet Exercises, including Facility Tours, which expand on the topics in this chapter.

PROBLEMS

1. **OM Explorer** Bold Vision, Inc., makes laser printer and photocopier toner cartridges. The demand rate is 625 EP cartridges per week. The production rate is 1,736 EP cartridges per week, and the setup cost is $100. The value of inventory is $130 per unit, and the holding cost is 20 percent of the inventory value. What is the economic production lot size?

2. **OM Explorer** Sharpe Cutter is a small company that produces specialty knives for paper cutting machinery. The annual demand for a particular type of knife is 100,000 units. The demand is uniform over the 250 working days in a year. Sharpe Cutter produces this type of knife in lots and, on average, can produce 450 knives a day. The cost to set up a production lot is $300, and the annual holding cost is $1.20 per knife. Determine

   a. The economic production lot size (ELS),

   b. The total annual setup and inventory holding cost for this item,

   c. The TBO, or cycle length, for the ELS,

   d. The production time per lot.

3. **OM Explorer** Suds's Bottling Company does bottling, labeling, and distribution work for several local microbreweries. The demand rate for Wortman's beer is 600 cases (24 bottles each) per week. Suds's bottling production rate is 2,400 cases per week, and the setup cost is $800. The value of inventory is $12.50 per case, and the annual holding cost is 30 percent of the inventory value. What is the economic production lot size?

4. **OM Explorer** The Bucks Grande major league baseball team breaks an average of four bats per week. The team orders baseball bats from Corky's, a bat manufacturer noted for its access to the finest hardwood. The order cost is $70, and the annual holding cost per bat per year is 38 percent of the purchase price. Corky's price structure is

ORDER QUANTITY	PRICE PER UNIT
0–11	$54.00
12–143	$51.00
144 or more	$48.50

   a. How many bats should the team buy per order?

   b. What are the total annual costs associated with the best order quantity?

   c. Corky discovers that, owing to special manufacturing processes required for the Bucks' bats, it has underestimated setup costs. Rather than raise prices, Corky adds another category to the price structure to provide an incentive for larger orders and reduce the number of setups required. If the Bucks buy 180 bats or more, the price will drop to $45 each. Should the Bucks revise the order quantity to 180 bats?

5. **OM Explorer** To boost sales, Pfisher (refer to Solved Problem 2) announces a new price structure for disposable surgical packages. Although the price break no longer is available at 200 units, Pfisher now offers an even greater discount if larger quantities are purchased. On orders of 1 to 499 packages, the price is $50.25 per package. For orders of 500 or more, the price per unit is $47.80. Ordering costs, annual holding costs, and annual demand remain at $64 per order, 20 percent of the per-unit cost, and 490 packages per year, respectively. What is the new lot size?

6. **OM Explorer** The University Bookstore at a prestigious private university buys mechanical pencils from a wholesaler. The wholesaler offers discounts for large orders according to the following price schedule:

ORDER QUANTITY	PRICE PER UNIT
0–200	$4.00
201–2,000	3.50
2,001 or more	3.25

The bookstore expects an annual demand of 2,500 units. It costs $10 to place an order, and the annual cost of holding a unit in stock is 30 percent of the unit's price. Determine the best order quantity.

7. 💿 **OM Explorer** Mac-in-the-Box, Inc., sells computer equipment by mail and telephone order. Mac sells 1,200 flat-bed scanners per year. Ordering cost is $300, and annual holding cost is 16 percent of the item's price. The scanner manufacturer offers the following price structure to Mac-in-the-Box:

ORDER QUANTITY	PRICE PER UNIT
0–11	$520.00
12–143	$500.00
144 or more	$400.00

What order quantity minimizes total annual costs?

8. 💿 **OM Explorer** As inventory manager you must decide on the order quantity for an item that has an annual demand of 2,000 units. Placing an order costs you $20 each time. Your annual holding cost, expressed as a percent of average inventory value, is 20 percent. Your supplier has provided the following price schedule:

MINIMUM ORDER QUANTITY	PRICE PER UNIT
1	$2.50
200	$2.40
300	$2.25
1,000	$2.00

What ordering policy do you recommend?

9. 💿 **OM Explorer** National Printing Company must decide how many wall calendars it should produce for sale during the upcoming sale season. Each calendar sells for $8.50 and costs $2.50 to produce. The local school district has agreed to buy all unsold calendars at a unit price of $1.50. National estimates the following probability distribution for the season's demand:

DEMAND	PROBABILITY
2,000	0.05
3,000	0.20
4,000	0.25
5,000	0.40
6,000	0.10

How many calendars should National produce to maximize its expected profit?

10. 💿 **OM Explorer** Dorothy's pastries are freshly baked and sold at several specialty shops throughout Dallas. When they are a day old, they must be sold at reduced prices. Daily demand is distributed as follows:

DEMAND	PROBABILITY
50	0.25
150	0.50
200	0.25

Each pastry sells for $1.00 and costs $0.60 to make. Each one not sold at the end of the day can be sold the next day for $0.30 as day-old merchandise. How many pastries should be baked each day?

11. 💿 **OM Explorer** The Aggies will host Tech in this year's homecoming football game. Based on advance ticket sales, the athletic department has forecast hot dog sales as shown in the following table. The school buys premium hot dogs for $1.50 and sells them during the game at $3.00 each. Hot dogs left over after the game will be sold for $0.50 each to the Aggie student cafeteria to be used in making beanie weenie casserole.

SALES QUANTITY	PROBABILITY
2,000	0.10
3,000	0.30
4,000	0.30
5,000	0.20
6,000	0.10

Use a payoff matrix to determine the number of hot dogs to buy for the game.

SIMULATION EXERCISE

This simulation exercise requires the use of the Extend software, which is on the Student CD-ROM that is packaged with every new copy of the textbook.

1. ● **Extend** Revisit the case on Ready Hardware, a midsize regional distributor of hardware that was introduced in the Simulation Exercise at the end of the Inventory Management chapter. Given the supplier's quantity discount schedule for the lockset, what lot sizing policy do you recommend, using the Extend simulator? See Section E of the *Inventory Management at Ready Hardware* case on the Student CD-ROM, which includes the basic model and how to use it.

SELECTED REFERENCES

"Factors That Make or Break Season Sales." *Wall Street Journal* (December 9, 1991).

Fogerty, Donald W., and Thomas R. Hoffman. *Production and Inventory Management*. Cincinnati: South-Western, 1983.

Greene, James H. *Production and Inventory Control Handbook,* 3d ed. New York: McGraw-Hill, 1997.

Inventory Management Reprints. Falls Church, Va.: American Production and Inventory Control Society, 1993.

Johnson, Lynwood A., and Douglas C. Montgomery. *Operations Research in Production Planning, Scheduling and Inventory Control.* New York: John Wiley & Sons, 1979.

Silver, Edward A., D. F. Pyke, and Rein Peterson. *Inventory Management, Production Planning, and Scheduling,* 3d ed. New York: John Wiley & Sons, 1998.

Sipper, Daniel, and Robert L. Bulfin, Jr. *Production Planning, Control, and Integration.* New York: McGraw-Hill, 1997.

Tersine, Richard J. *Principles of Inventory and Materials Management,* 4th ed. Saddlebrook, NJ: Prentice-Hall, 1994.

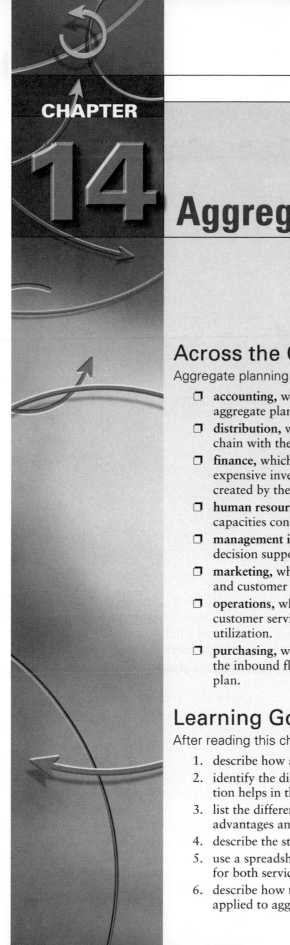

Aggregate Planning

Across the Organization

Aggregate planning is important to . . .

- ❏ **accounting,** which prepares cost accounting information needed to evaluate aggregate plans.
- ❏ **distribution,** which coordinates the outbound flow of materials in the supply chain with the aggregate plan.
- ❏ **finance,** which knows the financial condition of the firm, seeks ways to contain expensive inventory accumulations, and develops plans to finance the cash flows created by the aggregate plan.
- ❏ **human resources,** which is aware of how labor-market conditions and training capacities constrain aggregate plans.
- ❏ **management information systems,** which develops information systems and decision support systems for developing production and staffing plans.
- ❏ **marketing,** which provides demand forecasts and information on competition and customer preferences.
- ❏ **operations,** which develops plans that are the best compromise among cost, customer service, inventory investment, stable workforce levels, and facility utilization.
- ❏ **purchasing,** which provides information on supplier capabilities and coordinates the inbound flow of materials and services in the supply chain with the aggregate plan.

Learning Goals

After reading this chapter, you will be able to . . .

1. describe how aggregate plans relate to a firm's long- and short-term plans.
2. identify the dimensions on which aggregation is done and explain why aggregation helps in the planning process.
3. list the different types of reactive and aggressive alternatives and discuss the advantages and limitations of each.
4. describe the steps involved in developing an acceptable aggregate plan.
5. use a spreadsheet approach to evaluate different level, chase, and mixed strategies for both service providers and manufacturers.
6. describe how the transportation method and linear programming method can be applied to aggregate planning problems.

hirlpool Corporation (www.whirlpool-corp.com/whr) is a leading producer of room air conditioners. The demand for window units is highly seasonal and also depends on variations in the weather. Typically, Whirlpool begins production of room air conditioners in the fall and holds them as anticipation inventory until they are shipped in the spring. Building anticipation inventory in the slack season allows the company to level production rates over much of the year and yet satisfy demand in the peak periods (spring and summer) when retailers are placing most of their orders. However, when summers are hotter than usual, demand increases dramatically and stockouts can occur. If Whirlpool increases

Whirlpool Corporation's La Vergne, Tennessee, manufacturing division produces air conditioners, which are subject to heavy seasonal demand.

output and the summer is hot, it stands to increase its sales and market share. But if the summer is cool, the company is stuck with expensive inventories of unsold machines. Whirlpool prefers to make its production plans based on the average year, taking into account industry forecasts for total sales and traditional seasonalities. Because of Whirlpool's increasingly global operations, its aggregate demand smoothes out regional variations in demand. For example, the particularly strong results in North America and Europe more than offset weak economic and business conditions in Latin America and Asia.

Source: www.whirlpoolcorp.com/whr from January 10, 2000.

---

aggregate plan A statement of a company's production rates, workforce levels, and inventory holdings based on estimates of customer requirements and capacity limitations.

production plan A manufacturing firm's aggregate plan, which generally focuses on production rates and inventory holdings.

staffing plan A service firm's aggregate plan, which centers on staffing and other labor-related factors.

WHIRLPOOL, LIKE MANY OTHER companies, experiences seasonal shifts in demand for its products. Its strategy, called an **aggregate plan,** is a statement of its production rates, workforce levels, and inventory holdings based on estimates of customer requirements and capacity limitations. This statement is time-phased, meaning that the plan is projected for several time periods (such as months) into the future.

A manufacturing firm's aggregate plan, called a **production plan,** generally focuses on production rates and inventory holdings, whereas a service firm's aggregate plan, called a **staffing plan,** centers on staffing and other labor-related factors. For both types of company, the plan must balance conflicting objectives involving customer service, workforce stability, cost, and profit.

Based on the broad, long-term goals of a company, the aggregate plan specifies how the company will work for the next year or so toward those goals within existing equipment and facility capacity constraints. From these medium-range plans, managers prepare detailed operating plans. For manufacturing companies, the aggregate plan links strategic goals and objectives with production plans for individual products and the specific components that go into them. In this chapter and the Resource Planning and Lean Systems chapters, we demonstrate how this linkage is achieved. For service firms the aggregate plan links strategic goals with detailed workforce schedules. We discuss this linkage in the Scheduling chapter.

THE PURPOSE OF AGGREGATE PLANS

In this section, we explain why companies need aggregate plans and how they use them to take a macro, or big-picture, view of their business. We also discuss how the aggregate plan relates to a company's long- and short-term plans.

AGGREGATION

What items should be aggregated?

The aggregate plan is useful because it focuses on a general course of action, consistent with the company's strategic goals and objectives, without getting bogged down in details. For example, it allows Whirlpool's managers to determine whether they can satisfy budgetary goals without having to schedule each of the company's thousands of products and employees. Even if a planner could prepare such a detailed plan, the time and effort required to update it would make it uneconomical. For this reason, production and staffing plans are prepared by grouping, or aggregating, similar products, services, units of labor, or units of time. For instance, a manufacturer of bicycles that produces 12 different models of bikes might divide them into two groups, mountain bikes and road bikes, for the purpose of preparing the aggregate plan. It might also consider its workforce needs in terms of units of labor needed per month. In general, companies aggregate products or services, labor, and time. Managerial Practice 14.1 shows some aggregate planning situations encountered in the auto industry and in package delivery services.

PRODUCT FAMILIES. Recall that a group of products or services that have similar demand requirements and common processing, labor, and materials requirements is called a product family (see the Forecasting chapter). Sometimes, product families relate to market groupings or, in the case of production plans, to specific manufacturing processes. A firm can aggregate its products or services into a set of relatively broad families, avoiding too much detail at this stage of the planning process. Common and relevant measurements, such as units, dollars, standard hours, gallons, or pounds, should be used. For example, consider the bicycle manufacturer that has aggregated all products into two families: mountain bikes and road bikes. This approach aids production planning for the assembly lines in the plant. A firm that specializes in quick oil changes might aggregate the services it offers into two categories: the basic service and special services.

LABOR. A company can aggregate labor in various ways, depending on workforce flexibility. For example, if workers at the bicycle manufacturer are trained to work on either mountain bikes or road bikes, for planning purposes management can consider its workforce to be a single aggregate group, even though the skills of individual workers may differ.

Alternatively, management can aggregate labor along product family lines by splitting the workforce into subgroups and assigning a different group to the production of each product family. Automobile manufacturers, such as Ford use this approach, devoting production lines and even entire plants to separate product families. In service operations, such as a city government, workers are aggregated by the type of service they provide: fire fighters, police officers, sanitation workers, and administrators.

Companies that aggregate labor along product lines must plan for changes in economic conditions and consumer demand that may cause cutbacks in production of some product families and increases in production of others. When such shifts occur, labor may not be interchangeable. For example, in automobile assembly, production of different product families takes place in scattered locations. In such cases, planning for

MANAGERIAL PRACTICE 14.1
Typical Aggregate Planning Problems

Automobile Industry

The peak demands for cars and trucks in 1994 created a problem for the Big Three automakers. With United Automobile Workers (UAW) (www.uaw.org) wages ranging from $18 to $44 an hour, including benefits, achieving high productivity per labor hour was essential. The automakers thus were reluctant to hire more workers, fearing the pension and health care costs they would have to cover during the inevitable downturn. They also wanted to protect productivity gains made over the past decade, when they shrank their payrolls while sales increased. Part of their response was to hire temporary employees in the summer of 1994. However, they made up most of the shortfall by operating at record levels of overtime. Even this amount of overtime production fell short, costing the Big Three as many as 200,000 vehicles in sales in 1994.

General Motors (www.gm.com) faced a particular dilemma in 1994, being pressed by investors to reduce its hourly workforce and bring its productivity into line with Ford's. Its overtime rose at Buick City in Flint, Michigan, to the point where workers were averaging 17 hours of overtime a week. Although the UAW had mostly cooperated with automakers' efforts to shrink payrolls and improve productivity, it contended that its members were being worked too hard and could not sustain the overtime work pace. More than 11,000 workers went on strike. GM settled quickly because of the boom market and the effect the Flint shutdown would have on other GM plants; the company hired nearly 1,000 new workers.

The industry's highest cost producer had to slow its drive to reduce costs because the strike had already cost GM the production of about 10,000 vehicles.

Delivery Services

United Parcel Service (www.ups.com) utilizes a large number of employees for its package-sorting hub. The work is hard and routine, and the hours are long. The high level of productivity demanded by UPS occasionally generates complaints from Teamsters Union members. When faced with the alternatives of hiring full- or part-time employees, UPS managers prefer full-time employees for many jobs so that they can train them and, by means of thoroughly researched process and job designs, instill

FedEx prefers to use large numbers of part-time employees. It is recognized as an employer that offers flexible work schedules, which are particularly valued by working mothers.

a strong sense of teamwork and job satisfaction. At the same time, UPS does have a part-time workforce, which was the cause of a union strike in 1997.

FedEx (www.fedex.com/us) also requires large numbers of employees for its package-sorting facilities. Its managers, however, prefer part-time employees. To enable next-day delivery, FedEx's facilities are designed and staffed to sort more than a million pieces of freight and express mail in only 4 hours during the middle of the night. A full complement of full-time employees could not be effectively utilized all day long, whereas part-time employees, with high energy levels, can be used to meet daily peak demands. College students are a good source of labor for these sorting facilities. So are working mothers. FedEx won an award in 1998 as being a great place for working mothers, who match well with the company's need for part-time workers and a flexible work schedule.

Sources: "Auto Workers Pushed to the Limit." *New York Times* (September 24, 1994); "GM, in a Switch, Agrees to Hire New Workers." *Wall Street Journal* (October 3, 1994); www.upsjobs.com; www.fedex.com/us/about/express/pressreleases/pressrelease090898.html.

---

changes in workforce levels and the use of overtime by aggregating labor around product families is the most practical approach.

planning horizon The length of time covered by an aggregate plan.

TIME. A **planning horizon** is the length of time covered by an aggregate plan. Typically, the planning horizon is one year, although it can differ in various situations. To avoid the expense and disruptive effect of frequent changes in output rates and the workforce, adjustments usually are made monthly or quarterly. In other words, the company looks at time in the aggregate—months, quarters, or seasons, rather than days or hours. Some companies use monthly planning periods for the near portion of the planning horizon and quarterly periods for the later portion. In practice, planning periods reflect a balance between the needs for (1) a limited number of decision points to reduce planning complexity and (2) flexibility to adjust output rates and workforce levels when demand forecasts exhibit seasonal variations. The bicycle manufacturer, for example, may choose monthly planning periods so that timely adjustments to inventory levels can be made without excessively disruptive changes to the workforce.

RELATIONSHIP TO OTHER PLANS

How should an aggregate plan fit with other plans?

business plan A projected statement of income, costs, and profits.

A financial assessment of the organization's near future—that is, for one or two years ahead—is called either a business plan (in for-profit firms) or an annual plan (in non-profit services). A **business plan** is a projected statement of income, costs, and profits. It usually is accompanied by budgets, a projected (pro forma) balance sheet, and a projected cash-flow statement, showing sources and allocations of funds. The business plan unifies the plans and expectations of a firm's operations, finance, sales, and marketing managers. In particular, it reflects plans for market penetration, new product introduction, and capital investment. Manufacturing firms and for-profit service organizations, such as a retail store, firm of attorneys, or hospital, prepare such plans. A nonprofit service organization, such as the United Way or a municipal government, prepares a different type of plan, called an **annual plan** or **financial plan.**

annual plan or financial plan A plan for financial assessment used by a nonprofit service organization.

master production schedule A schedule that specifies the timing and size of production quantities for each product in the product families.

Figure 14.1 illustrates the relationships among the business or annual plan, production or staffing plan (aggregate plan), and detailed production or workforce schedules. In the manufacturing sector, top management sets the company's strategic objectives for at least the next year in the business plan. It provides the overall framework of demand projections, functional area inputs, and capital budget from which the aggregate plan and the master production schedule (MPS) are developed. The production plan specifies corresponding product family production rates, inventory levels, and workforce levels. The **master production schedule,** in turn, specifies the timing and size of production quantities for each product in the product families. Thus, the aggregate plan plays a key role in translating the strategies of the business plan into an operational plan for the manufacturing process.

FIGURE 14.1

Relationship of Production or Staffing Plan (Aggregate Plan) to Other Plans

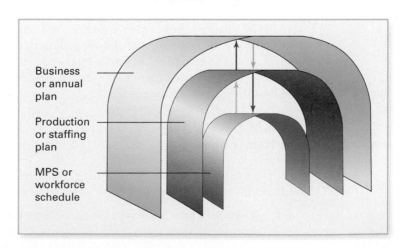

Business or annual plan

Production or staffing plan

MPS or workforce schedule

workforce schedule A schedule that details the specific work schedule for each category of employee.

In the service sector, top management sets the organization's direction and objectives in the business plan (for-profit organization) or annual plan (nonprofit organization). In either case, the plan provides the framework for the staffing plan and workforce schedule. The staffing plan presents the number and types of employees needed to meet the objectives of the business or annual plan. The **workforce schedule**, in turn, details the specific work schedule for each category of employee. For example, a staffing plan might allocate 10 police officers for the day shift in a particular district; the workforce schedule might assign 5 of them to work Monday through Friday and the other 5 to work Wednesday through Sunday to meet the varying daily needs for police protection in that district. Thus, the workforce schedule implements the staffing plan in much the same way that the master production schedule implements the production plan. (We present a more complete discussion of workforce scheduling in the Scheduling chapter.)

As the arrows in Figure 14.1 indicate, information flows in two directions: from the top down (broad to detailed) and from the bottom up (detailed to broad). If an aggregate plan cannot be developed to satisfy the objectives of the business or annual plan, the business or annual plan might have to be adjusted. Similarly, if a feasible master production schedule or workforce schedule cannot be developed, the aggregate plan might have to be adjusted. The planning process is dynamic, with periodic plan revisions or adjustments based on two-way information flows.

An analogy for the three levels of plans in Figure 14.1 is a student's calendar. Basing the choice of a school on career goals—a plan covering 4 or 5 years—corresponds to the highest planning level. Basing the choice of classes on that school's requirements—a plan for the next school year—corresponds to the middle planning level (or aggregate plan). Finally, scheduling group meetings and study times around work requirements in current classes—a plan for the next few weeks—corresponds to the most detailed planning level.

MANAGERIAL IMPORTANCE OF AGGREGATE PLANS

In this section, we concentrate on the managerial inputs, objectives, alternatives, and strategies associated with aggregate plans.

MANAGERIAL INPUTS

What kind of cross-functional coordination is needed?

Figure 14.2 shows the types of information that managers from various functional areas supply to aggregate plans. One way of ensuring the necessary cross-functional coordination and supply of information is to create a committee of functional-area representatives. Chaired by a general manager, the committee has the overall responsibility to make sure that company policies are followed, conflicts are resolved, and a final plan is approved. Coordinating the firm's functions, either in this way or less formally, helps synchronize the flow of materials, services, and information through the supply chain and best meet customer demand.

TYPICAL OBJECTIVES

The many functional areas in an organization that give input to the aggregate plan typically have conflicting objectives for the use of the organization's resources. Six objectives usually are considered during development of a production or staffing plan, and conflicts among them may have to be resolved:

1. *Minimize Costs/Maximize Profits.* If customer demand is not affected by the plan, minimizing costs will also maximize profits.

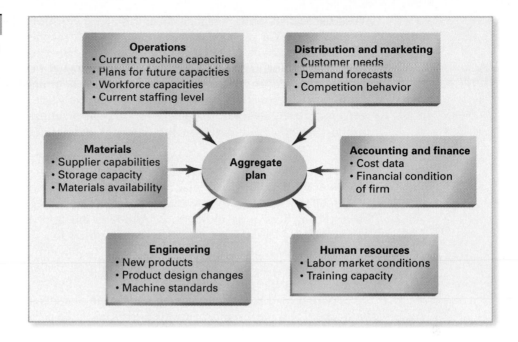

2. *Maximize Customer Service.*   Improving delivery time and on-time delivery may require additional workforce, machine capacity, or inventory resources.

3. *Minimize Inventory Investment.*   Inventory accumulations are expensive because the money could be used for more productive investments.

4. *Minimize Changes in Production Rates.*   Frequent changes in production rates can cause difficulties in coordinating the supplying of materials and require production line rebalancing.

5. *Minimize Changes in Workforce Levels.*   Fluctuating workforce levels may cause lower productivity because new employees typically need time to become fully productive.

6. *Maximize Utilization of Plant and Equipment.* Processes based on a line flow strategy require uniformly high utilization of plant and equipment.

The weight given to each one in the plan involves cost trade-offs and consideration of nonquantifiable factors. For example, maximizing customer service with fast, on-time delivery can be improved by increasing—not minimizing—the stock of finished goods in a production plan. Or, for example, a staffing plan that minimizes costs may not minimize changes in workforce levels or maximize customer service.

Balancing these various objectives to arrive at an acceptable aggregate plan involves consideration of various alternatives. The two basic types of alternatives are reactive and aggressive. Reactive alternatives are actions that respond to given demand patterns, whereas aggressive alternatives are actions that adjust demand patterns.

REACTIVE ALTERNATIVES

reactive alternatives
Actions that can be taken
to cope with demand
requirements.

What options should be
considered in responding to
uneven demand?

Reactive alternatives are actions that can be taken to cope with demand requirements. Typically, an operations manager controls reactive alternatives. That is, the operations manager accepts forecasted demand as a given and modifies workforce levels, overtime, vacation schedules, inventory levels, subcontracting, and planned backlogs to meet that demand.

WORKFORCE ADJUSTMENT.   Management can adjust workforce levels by hiring or laying off employees. The use of this alternative can be attractive if the workforce is largely unskilled or semiskilled and the labor pool is large. However, for a particular company, the size of the qualified labor pool may limit the number of new employees that can be hired at any one time. Also, new employees must be trained, and the capacity of the training facilities themselves might limit the number of new hires at any one time. In some industries, laying off employees is difficult or unusual for contractual reasons (unions); in other industries, such as tourism and agriculture, seasonal layoffs and hirings are the norm.

ANTICIPATION INVENTORY.   A plant facing seasonal demand can stock *anticipation inventory* (see the Inventory Management chapter) during light demand periods and use it during heavy demand periods. Although this approach stabilizes output rates and workforce levels, it can be costly because the value of the product is greatest in its finished state. Stocking components and subassemblies that can be assembled quickly when customer orders come in might be preferable to stocking finished goods.

   Service providers generally cannot use anticipation inventory because services can't be stocked. In some instances, however, services can be performed prior to actual need. For example, telephone company workers usually lay cables for service to a new subdivision before housing construction begins. They can do this work during a period when the workload for scheduled services is low.

WORKFORCE UTILIZATION.   An alternative to workforce adjustment is workforce utilization involving overtime and undertime. **Overtime** means that employees work longer than the regular workday or workweek and receive additional pay for the extra hours. It can be used to satisfy output requirements that cannot be completed on regular time. However, overtime is expensive (typically 150 percent of the regular-time pay rate). Moreover, workers often do not want to work a lot of overtime for an extended period of time, and excessive overtime may result in declining quality and productivity.

overtime The time that employees work that is longer than the regular workday or workweek, for which they receive additional pay for the extra hours.

undertime The situation that occurs when employees do not work *productively* for the regular-time workday or workweek.

   Undertime means that employees do not work *productively* for the regular-time workday or workweek. For example, they do not work productively for eight hours per day or for five days per week. Undertime occurs when labor capacity exceeds a period's demand requirements (net of anticipation inventory) and this excess capacity cannot or should not be used productively to build up inventory or to satisfy customer orders earlier than the delivery dates already promised. When products or services are customized, anticipation inventory isn't usually an option. A product cannot be produced to inventory if its specifications are unknown or if customers are unlikely to want what has been produced in advance because it doesn't meet their exact requirements.

   Undertime can either be paid or unpaid. An example of *unpaid undertime* is when part-time employees are paid only for the hours or days worked. Perhaps they only work during the peak times of the day or peak days of the week. Sometimes, part-time arrangements provide predictable work schedules, such as the same hours each day for five consecutive days each week. At other times, such as with stockpickers at some warehouse operations, worker schedules are unpredictable and depend on customer shipments expected for the next day. If the workload is light, some workers are not called in to work. Such arrangements are more common in low-skill positions or when the supply of workers seeking such an arrangement is sufficient. An example of this arrangement includes college students near a FedEx package-sorting facility (see Managerial Practice 14.1). Although unpaid undertime may minimize costs, the firm must balance cost considerations against the ethical issues of being a good employer.

An example of *paid undertime* is when employees are kept on the payroll rather than being laid off. In this scenario, employees work a full day and receive their full salary but are not as productive because of the light workload. Some companies use paid undertime (though they do not call it that) during slack periods, particularly with highly skilled, hard-to-replace employees or when there are obstacles to laying off workers. The disadvantages of paid undertime include the cost of paying for work not performed and lowered productivity.

VACATION SCHEDULES. A firm can shut down during an annual lull in sales, leaving a skeleton crew to cover operations and perform maintenance. Employees might be required to take all or part of their allowed vacation time during this period. Automakers, such as General Motors, sometimes use this alternative during the Christmas holiday period, not only to do maintenance work or install equipment but also to reduce inventory. Use of this alternative depends on whether the employer can mandate the vacation schedules of its employees. In any case, employees may be strongly discouraged from taking vacations during peak periods or encouraged to take vacations during periods when replacement part-time labor is most abundant.

SUBCONTRACTORS. Subcontractors can be used to overcome short-term capacity shortages, such as during peaks of the season or business cycle. Subcontractors can supply services, make components and subassemblies, or even assemble an entire product. If the subcontractor can supply components or subassemblies of equal or better quality less expensively than the company can produce them itself, these arrangements may become permanent. The major automakers, for example, typically outsource production of underbody frames, steering linkage components, and other items. In the service industry, book publishers are turning increasingly to free lance artists and copy editors as part of a downsizing trend.

BACKLOGS, BACKORDERS, AND STOCKOUTS. Firms that maintain a backlog of orders as a normal business practice can allow the backlog to grow during periods of high demand and then reduce it during periods of low demand. A **backlog** is an accumulation of customer orders that have been promised for delivery at some future date. Firms that use backlogs do not promise instantaneous delivery, as do wholesalers or retailers farther forward in the supply chain. Instead, they impose a lead time between when the order is placed and when it is delivered. Firms that are most likely to use backlogs— and increase the size of them during periods of heavy demand—make customized products and provide customized services. They tend to have a make-to-order or customized services strategy and include job shops, TV repair shops, automobile repair shops, and dental offices. Backlogs reduce the uncertainty of future production requirements and also can be used to level these requirements. However, they become a competitive disadvantage if they get too big. Fast delivery time often is an important competitive priority (see the Operations Strategy chapter), but large backlogs mean long delivery times.

Manufacturers with a make-to-stock strategy, and service providers with a standardized services strategy (see the Operations Strategy chapter), are expected to provide immediate delivery. For them, poor customer service during peak demand periods takes the form of backorders and stockouts, rather than large backlogs. A **backorder** is

backlog An accumulation of customer orders that have been promised for delivery at some future date.

backorder An order that the customer expected to be filled immediately but reluctantly asks that it be delivered as soon as possible.

an order that the customer expected to be filled immediately but reluctantly asks that it be delivered as soon as possible. Although the customer isn't pleased with the delay, the customer order is not lost and is filled at a later date. A **stockout** is much the same, except that the order is lost and the customer goes elsewhere. A backorder adds to the next period's requirement, whereas a stockout doesn't increase future requirements. Backorders and stockouts can lead dissatisfied customers to do their future business with another firm. Generally, backorders and stockouts are to be avoided. Planned stockouts may be used, but only when the expected loss in sales and customer goodwill is less than the cost of using other reactive alternatives or aggressive alternatives, or adding the capacity needed to satisfy demand.

In conclusion, decisions about the use of each alternative for each period of the planning horizon specify the output rate for each period. In other words, the output rate is a function of the choices among these alternatives.

stockout An order that is lost and causes the customer to go elsewhere.

How can demand be leveled to reduce operating costs?

aggressive alternatives Actions that attempt to modify demand and, consequently, resource requirements.

complementary products Products or services having similar resource requirements but different demand cycles.

AGGRESSIVE ALTERNATIVES

Coping with seasonal or volatile demand by using reactive alternatives can be costly. Another approach is to attempt to change demand patterns to achieve efficiency and reduce costs. **Aggressive alternatives** are actions that attempt to modify demand and, consequently, resource requirements. Typically, marketing managers are responsible for specifying these actions in the marketing plan.

COMPLEMENTARY PRODUCTS.   One way a company can even out the load on resources is to produce **complementary products** or services having similar resource requirements but different demand cycles. For example, a company producing garden tractors can also produce snowmobiles, making requirements for major components, such as engines, reasonably uniform year round. In the service sector, city parks and recreation departments can counterbalance seasonal staffing requirements for summer activities by offering ice skating, tobogganing, or indoor activities during the winter months. The key is to find products and services that can be produced with existing resources and can level off the need for resources over the year.

CREATIVE PRICING.   Promotional campaigns are designed to increase sales with creative pricing. Examples include automobile rebate programs, price reductions for winter clothing in the late summer months, reduced prices on airline tickets for travel during off-peak periods, and "two for the price of one" automobile tire sales.

PLANNING STRATEGIES

Managers often combine reactive and aggressive alternatives in various ways to arrive at an acceptable aggregate plan. For the remainder of this chapter, let us assume that the expected results of the aggressive alternatives have already been incorporated into the demand forecasts of product families or services. This assumption allows us to focus on the reactive alternatives that define output rates and workforce levels. Countless aggregate plans are possible even when just a few reactive alternatives are allowed. Four very different strategies, two chase strategies and two level strategies, are useful starting points in searching for the best plan. These strategies can be implemented with a limited or expanded set of reactive alternatives, as shown in the following table. The specific reactive alternatives allowed, and how they are mixed together, must be stated before a chase or level strategy can be translated into a unique aggregate plan.

Strategy	Possible Alternatives During Slack Season	Possible Alternatives During Peak Season
1. **Chase #1:** vary *workforce level* to match demand	Layoffs	Hiring
2. **Chase #2:** vary *output rate* to match demand	Layoffs, undertime, vacations	Hiring, overtime, subcontracting
3. **Level #1:** constant *workforce level*	No layoffs, building anticipation inventory, undertime, vacations	No hiring, depleting anticipation inventory, overtime, subcontracting, backorders, stockouts
4. **Level #2:** constant *output rate*	Layoffs, building anticipation inventory, undertime, vacations	Hiring, depleting anticipation inventory, overtime, subcontracting, backorders, stockouts

chase strategy A strategy that matches demand during the planning horizon by varying either the work-force level or the output rate.

CHASE STRATEGIES. A **chase strategy** *matches* demand during the planning horizon by varying either (1) the workforce level or (2) the output rate. When a chase strategy uses the first method, varying the *workforce level* to match demand, it relies on just one reactive alternative—workforce variation. Sometimes called the *capacity strategy*, it uses hiring and layoffs to keep the workforce's regular-time capacity equal to demand. This chase strategy has the advantages of no inventory investment, overtime, or undertime. However, it has some drawbacks, including the expense of continually adjusting workforce levels, the potential alienation of the workforce, and the loss of productivity and quality because of constant changes in the workforce.

The second chase strategy, varying the *output rate* to match demand, opens up additional reactive alternatives beyond changing the workforce level. Sometimes called the *utilization strategy*, the extent and timing of the workforce's utilization is changed through overtime, undertime, and when vacations are taken. Subcontracting, including temporary help during the peak season, is another way of matching demand.

level strategy A strategy that maintains a constant workforce level or constant output rate during the planning horizon.

LEVEL STRATEGIES. A **level strategy** maintains a (1) constant workforce level or (2) constant output rate during the planning horizon. These two strategies differ from chase strategies not only because either the workforce or output rate is held constant but also because anticipation inventory, backorders, and stockouts are added to the list of possible reactive alternatives. For this reason, they are sometimes called *inventory strategies*.

When a level strategy uses the first method, maintaining a constant *workforce level*, it might consist of not hiring or laying off workers (except at the beginning of the planning horizon), building up anticipation inventories to absorb seasonal demand fluctuations, using undertime in slack periods and overtime up to contracted limits for peak periods, using subcontractors for additional needs as necessary, and scheduling vacation timing to match slack periods.

Even though a constant workforce must be maintained with this first level strategy, many aggregate plans are possible. The constant workforce can be sized many ways. It can be so large as to minimize the planned use of overtime and subcontractors (which creates considerable undertime) or so small as to rely heavily on overtime and subcontractors during the peak seasons (which places a strain on the workforce and endangers quality). Many teaching hospitals throughout the United States currently have small-sized workforces. A review board that accredits residency training programs cited many as overworking their interns and residents, creating a long-term burnout problem. Elsewhere in a hospital's workforce—the nurses—one contentious part of union contracts is the amount of mandatory overtime that is allowed. The Massachusetts Nurses

Overtime and subcontracting (using part-time employees) are two reactive alternatives used extensively in the health industry. However, excessive use of these alternatives is opposed by nurses. Here two nurses jump up and down on the picket line in front of Worcester Medical Center in Worcester, MA, after hearing news that the contract dispute on these issues had been settled, ending the six-week-old nurses' strike.

Association recently praised one hospital's new contract as a huge victory because it limits mandatory overtime to no more than four hours twice every three months or eight times per year. On the other side of the argument, hospital administrators say that overtime offers a safety net when several nurses are out and hospital beds are full. Thus, the advantages of a stable workforce must be weighted against the disadvantages of the other alternatives allowed, such as increased undertime, overtime, and inventory. Managerial Practice 14.2 shows how Hallmark uses a level strategy for competitive advantage.

MANAGERIAL PRACTICE 14.2
Hallmark's Level Strategy

Hallmark (www.hallmark.com), a $2-billion-a-year producer of greeting cards, spends considerable sums to improve efficiency and has made significant gains—all without imposing layoffs. Hallmark has never used layoffs to adjust production rates of greeting cards, even though the business is highly competitive, exhibits little growth, and is very seasonal. Employee flexibility is the key to this strategy. The company's four plants produce millions of cards each day, along with gift wrapping paper and other party goods. Even though technology in the industry has made production processes increasingly more labor efficient, Hallmark's philosophy has been to retrain its employees continually to make them more flexible. For example, a cutting machine operator might also be a custom card imprinter, a painter, or a modular office assembler as needed. To keep workers busy, Hallmark shifts production from its Kansas City plant to branch plants in Topeka, Leavenworth, and Lawrence, Kansas, to keep those plants fully utilized. It uses the Kansas City plant as its

"swing facility"—when demand is down, these employees may take jobs in clerical positions, all at factory pay rates. They might also be in classrooms learning new skills.

According to CEO Irvine O. Hockaday, Hallmark must protect its employees from cyclical markets and other unexpected happenings beyond their control. The added job security, however, carries the expectation that employees' performance will be commensurate with their compensation package. The philosophy has paid dividends. For example, reducing setup times to support short production runs is crucial to keeping inventories and costs low. Employees have suggested ways to cut setup times significantly. A stable workforce policy has been a major factor in allowing Hallmark to capture some 42 percent of the $5.6 billion domestic card market.

Source: "Loyal to a Fault." *Forbes* (March 14, 1994), pp. 58–60.

When a level strategy uses the second method, maintaining a constant *output rate,* it allows hiring and layoffs in addition to the other alternatives of the first level strategy. The output rate can be level even if the workforce fluctuates, depending on the set of alternatives that are used in the strategy. The key to identifying a level strategy is whether the workforce or output rate is constant.

MIXED STRATEGIES.   Used alone, chase and level strategies are unlikely to produce the best acceptable aggregate plan. Improvements are likely by considering plans that are neither pure level nor chase strategies. The workforce (or output rate) is not exactly level, and yet does not exactly match demand. Instead, the best strategy for a process is a **mixed strategy** that considers and implements a fuller range of reactive alternatives and goes beyond a "pure" chase or level strategy. Whether management chooses a pure strategy or some mix, the strategy should reflect the organization's environment and planning objectives. For example, for the municipal street repair department, which faces seasonal demand shifts and needs an ample supply of unskilled labor, possible strategies include varying the workforce level, reducing overtime, and eliminating subcontracting.

mixed strategy A strategy that considers and implements a fuller range of reactive alternatives and goes beyond a "pure" chase or level strategy.

THE PLANNING PROCESS

Figure 14.3 shows the process for preparing aggregate plans. It is dynamic and continuing, as aspects of the plan are updated periodically when new information becomes available and new opportunities emerge.

DETERMINING DEMAND REQUIREMENTS
The first step in the planning process is to determine the demand requirements for each period of the planning horizon using one of the many methods that we have already discussed. For staffing plans, the planner bases forecasts of staff requirements for each workforce group on historical levels of demand, managerial judgment, and existing backlogs for services. For example, a director of nursing in a hospital can develop a direct-care index for a nursing staff and translate a projection of the month-to-month patient census into an equivalent total amount of nursing care time—and thus the number of nurses—required for each month of the year. A police department can

FIGURE 14.3

The Process for Preparing Aggregate Plans

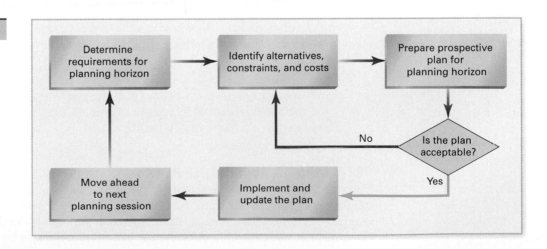

develop a formula for patrol staffing that accounts for the number of calls for service by type, the number of street miles patrolled, and the number of businesses in the community, and other factors to determine weekly or monthly workloads and thus the number of police officers or vehicles required.

For production plans, however, the requirements represent the demand for finished goods and the external demand for replacement parts. The planner can derive future requirements for finished goods from backlogs (for make-to-order operations) or from forecasts for product families made to stock (for make-to-stock operations). Sometimes, distributors or dealers indicate their requirements for finished goods in advance of actual orders, providing a reliable forecast of requirements from those sources.

IDENTIFYING ALTERNATIVES, CONSTRAINTS, AND COSTS

The second step is to identify the alternatives, constraints, and costs for the plan. We presented the reactive alternatives used in aggregate plans earlier, so we now focus on constraints and costs.

Constraints represent physical limitations or managerial policies associated with the aggregate plan. Examples of physical constraints might include training facilities capable of handling only so many new hires at a time, machine capacities that limit maximum output, or inadequate inventory storage space. Policy constraints might include limitations on the amount of backordering or the use of subcontracting or overtime, as well as the minimum inventory levels needed to achieve desired safety stocks.

Typically, many plans can satisfy a specific set of constraints. The planner usually considers several types of costs when preparing aggregate plans:

1. *Regular-Time Costs.*   These costs include regular-time wages paid to employees plus contributions to such benefits as health insurance, dental care, Social Security, and retirement funds and pay for vacations, holidays, and certain other types of absence.

2. *Overtime Costs.*   Overtime wages typically are 150 percent of regular-time wages, exclusive of fringe benefits. Some companies offer a 200 percent rate for working overtime on Sundays and holidays.

3. *Hiring and Layoff Costs.*   Hiring costs include the costs of advertising jobs, interviews, training programs for new employees, scrap caused by the inexperience of new employees, loss of productivity, and initial paperwork. Layoff costs include the costs of exit interviews, severance pay, retraining remaining workers and managers, and lost productivity.

4. *Inventory Holding Costs.*   Inventory holding costs include costs that vary with the *level* of inventory investment: the costs of capital tied up in inventory, variable storage and warehousing costs, pilferage and obsolescence costs, insurance costs, and taxes.

5. *Backorder and Stockout Costs.*   As discussed earlier, the use of backorders and stockouts involves costs of expediting past-due orders, costs of lost sales, and the potential cost of losing the customer's sales to competitors in the future (sometimes called loss of goodwill).

PREPARING AN ACCEPTABLE PLAN

The third step is to prepare the aggregate plan. Developing an acceptable plan is an iterative process; that is, plans may need to go through several revisions and adjustments (see Figure 14.3). A prospective, or tentative, plan is developed to start. A production plan with monthly periods, for example, must specify monthly production rates, inventory and backorder accumulations, subcontracted production, and monthly workforce levels (including hires, layoffs, and overtime). The plan must then be checked against constraints and evaluated in terms of strategic objectives. If the prospective plan is not acceptable for either of those reasons, a new prospective plan must be developed. It may include new alternatives or proposed changes in physical or policy constraints. When the plan is acceptable to the representatives from all functional areas, implementation can begin.

IMPLEMENTING AND UPDATING THE PLAN

The final step is implementing and updating the aggregate plan. Implementation requires the commitment of managers in all functional areas. The planning committee may recommend changes in the plan during implementation or updating to balance conflicting objectives better. Acceptance of the plan does not necessarily mean that everyone is in total agreement, but it does imply that everyone will work to achieve it.

AGGREGATE PLANNING WITH SPREADSHEETS

Should a level workforce strategy or some variable workforce strategy be used in providing services?

Here we use a *spreadsheet* approach of stating a strategy, developing a plan, comparing the developed plan to other plans, and finally modifying the plan or strategy as necessary, until we are satisfied with the results. We demonstrate this approach by developing two staffing plans, the first based on a level strategy and the second on a chase strategy. We then consider two mixed strategies for a manufacturer facing a different demand pattern and cost structure.

After a plan has been formulated, it is evaluated by use of a spreadsheet. One part of the spreadsheet shows the *input values* that give the demand requirements and the reactive alternative choices period by period. Another part shows the *derived values* that must follow from the input values. The final part of the spreadsheet shows the *calculated costs* of the plan. Along with qualitative considerations, the calculated cost of each plan determines whether the plan is satisfactory or whether a revised plan should be considered. When seeking clues about how to improve a plan already evaluated, we identify its highest cost elements. Revisions that would reduce these specific costs might produce a new plan with lower overall costs. Spreadsheet programs make analyzing these plans easy and present a whole new set of possibilities for developing sound aggregate plans.

LEVEL STRATEGY WITH OVERTIME AND UNDERTIME

One possible level strategy, which uses a constant number of employees that will satisfy demand during the planning horizon, is determined by using the maximum amount of overtime in the peak period. Undertime is used in slack periods. The workforce level does not change, except possibly for hiring or layoffs at the beginning of the first period if the current and desired constant workforce levels do not match. The level strategy can lead to considerable undertime, which is the amount of time by which capacity exceeds demand requirements, summed over all periods for the time horizon. The cost of this unused capacity depends on whether undertime is paid or unpaid.

| EXAMPLE 14.1 | *A Level Strategy with Overtime and Undertime* |

The manager of a large distribution center must determine how many part-time stockpickers to maintain on the payroll. She wants to develop a staffing plan with a level workforce, implemented with overtime and undertime. Her objective is to keep the part-time workforce stable

A customer looks inside a tent on display at the REI flagship store in Seattle, Washington. REI employs a high percentage of part-time workers, many of whom are college students, in its retail stores. They tend to be young people who participate in outdoor sports and are very familiar with the equipment that REI sells.

TUTOR 14.1

and to minimize undertime usage. She will achieve this goal by using the maximum amount of overtime possible in the peak period.

The manager divides the next year into 6 time periods, each one 2 months long. Each part-time employee can work a maximum of 20 hours per week on regular time, but the actual number can be less. The distribution center shortens each worker's day during slack periods, rather than pay undertime. Once on the payroll, each worker is used each day, but may work only a few hours. Overtime can be used during peak periods to avoid excessive undertime.

Workforce requirements are shown as the number of part-time employees required for each time period at the maximum regular time of 20 hours per week. For example, in period 3, an estimated 18 part-time employees working 20 hours per week on regular time will be needed.

	TIME PERIOD						
	1	2	3	4	5	6	TOTAL
Requirement*	6	12	18	15	13	14	78

*Number of part-time employees

Currently, 10 part-time clerks are employed. They haven't been subtracted from the requirements shown. Constraints on employment and cost information are as follows:

1. The size of training facilities limits the number of new hires in any period to no more than 10.

2. No backorders are permitted; demand must be met each period.

3. Overtime cannot exceed 20 percent of the regular-time capacity (that is, 4 hours) in any period. Therefore, the most that any part-time employee can work is 1.20 (20) = 24 hours per week.

4. The following costs can be assigned:

Regular-time wage rate	$2,000 per time period at 20 hours per week
Overtime wages	150 percent of the regular-time rate
Hiring	$1,000 per person
Layoffs	$500 per person

SOLUTION

For this particular level strategy, the manager begins by finding the number of part-time employees, at 24 hours per week (20 × 1.20) needed to meet the peak requirement. The most overtime that she can use is 20 percent of the regular-time capacity, w, so

$$1.20w = 18 \text{ employees required in peak period (period 3)}$$

$$w = \frac{18}{1.20} = 15 \text{ employees}$$

A 15 employee staff size minimizes the amount of undertime for this level strategy. As there already are 10 part-time employees, the manager should immediately hire 5 more. The complete plan is shown in Figure 14.4.

The input values are the requirement, a 15-person workforce level, undertime, and overtime for each period. The first row of derived values is called *productive time*, which is that portion of the workforce's regular time that is paid for and used productively. In any period, the productive time equals the workforce level minus undertime. The hires and layoffs rows can be derived from the workforce levels. In this example, the workforce is increased for period 1 from its initial size of 10 employees to 15, which means that 5 employees are hired. Because the workforce size remains constant throughout the planning horizon, there are no other hirings or layoffs.

For this particular example, overtime and undertime can be derived directly from the first two rows of input values. When a period's workforce level exceeds the requirement, overtime is zero and undertime equals the difference. When a period's workforce level is less than the requirements, undertime is zero and overtime equals the difference. For the general case when other alternatives (such as vacations, inventory, and backorders) are possible, however, the overtime and undertime cannot be derived just from information on requirements and workforce levels. Thus, undertime and overtime are shown as input values (rather than derived values) in the spreadsheet, and the user must be careful to specify consistent input values.

Another decision to be made is how to apportion undertime and overtime to employees. Except for periods 3 and 4, the employees will have some undertime or work less than the maximum 20 hours per week, because the requirement for those periods is less than 15 employees. In period 1, for example, 15 employees are on the payroll, but only 120 hours, or 6(20), per week are needed. Consequently, each employee might work only 8 hours per week. Alternatively, the manager could assign 5 employees to 4 hours per week and 10 employees to 10 hours per week. A similar approach can be applied to overtime. For example, in period 3, the overtime worked is the equivalent of 3 employees, or 18 − 15, working 20-hour weeks. This overtime could be apportioned equitably to the 15 employees.

	1	2	3	4	5	6	Total
Requirement	6	12	18	15	13	14	78
Workforce level	15	15	15	15	15	15	90
Undertime	9	3	0	0	2	1	15
Overtime	0	0	3	0	0	0	3
Productive time	6	12	15	15	13	14	75
Hires	5	0	0	0	0	0	5
Layoffs	0	0	0	0	0	0	0
Costs	1	2	3	4	5	6	Totals
Productive time	$12,000	24,000	30,000	30,000	26,000	28,000	$150,000
Undertime	$0	0	0	0	0	0	$0
Overtime	$0	0	9,000	0	0	0	$9,000
Hires	$5,000	0	0	0	0	0	$5,000
Layoffs	$0	0	0	0	0	0	$0
Total cost	$17,000	24,000	39,000	30,000	26,000	28,000	$164,000

FIGURE 14.4

The calculated costs for this plan are $164,000, which seems reasonable because the minimum conceivable cost is only $156,000 (78 periods × $2,000/period). This cost could be achieved only if the manager found a way to cover the requirement for all 78 periods with regular time. This plan seems reasonable primarily because it involves the use of large amounts of undertime (15 periods), which in this example are unpaid. The only ways to reduce costs are somehow to reduce the premium for 3 overtime periods (3 periods × $1,000/period) or to reduce the hiring cost of 5 employees (5 hires × $1,000/person). Nonetheless, better solutions may be possible. For example, undertime can be reduced by delaying the hiring until period 2 because the current workforce is sufficient until then. This delay would decrease the amount of unpaid undertime, which is a qualitative improvement. However, this modification creates mixed strategy rather than a level strategy with a constant workforce out to the horizon, which is the one illustrated here.

Decision Point The manager, now having a point of reference with which to compare other plans, decided to evaluate some other plans before making a final choice, beginning with the chase strategy. ⬚

CHASE STRATEGY WITH HIRING AND LAYOFFS

Consider the chase strategy that adjusts workforce levels as needed to achieve requirements without using overtime, undertime, or subcontractors. This chase strategy can result in a large number of hirings and layoffs. However, many employees, such as college students, prefer part-time work. With this chase strategy, the workforce level row is identical to the requirement row, with no overtime in any period.

EXAMPLE 14.2   *A Chase Strategy with Hiring and Layoffs*

The manager now wants to determine the staffing plan for the distribution center using the chase strategy so as to avoid all overtime and undertime.

SOLUTION

This strategy simply involves adjusting the workforce as needed to meet demand, as shown in Figure 14.5.

**TUTOR
14.2**

The manager should plan to lay off 4 part-time employees immediately because the current staff is 10 and the staff level required in period 1 is only 6. The workforce then should steadily build to 18 by period 3. After that, the manager can reduce the workforce except for the secondary peak in period 6, when she should hire 1 more employee.

	1	2	3	4	5	6	Total
Requirement	6	12	18	15	13	14	78
Workforce level	6	12	18	15	13	14	78
Undertime	0	0	0	0	0	0	0
Overtime	0	0	0	0	0	0	0
Productive time	6	12	18	15	13	14	78
Hires	0	6	6	0	0	1	13
Layoffs	4	0	0	3	2	0	9
Costs	1	2	3	4	5	6	Totals
Productive time	$12,000	24,000	36,000	30,000	26,000	28,000	$156,000
Undertime	$0	0	0	0	0	0	$0
Overtime	$0	0	0	0	0	0	$0
Hires	$0	6,000	6,000	0	0	1,000	$13,000
Layoffs	$2,000	0	0	1,500	1,000	0	$4,500
Total cost	$14,000	30,000	42,000	31,500	27,000	29,000	$173,500

FIGURE 14.5

The $173,500 cost of this plan is considerably higher than for the level strategy. The spreadsheet shows that most of the cost increase comes from frequent hiring and layoffs, which add $17,500 to the cost of productive regular-time costs. Clearly, a low-cost solution must avoid frequent workforce adjustments by using more overtime and undertime, particularly because part-time employees offer flexible work hours and because undertime is not a payroll cost.

Decision Point Having found this chase strategy worse than the level strategy, the manager decided to formulate some mixed strategies that keep more of the elements of a level strategy. ◻

MIXED STRATEGIES

The manager of the distribution center in Example 14.1 might find even better solutions with a mixed strategy, which varies the workforce level or output rate somewhat but not to the extreme of a chase strategy. She might also consider a fuller range of reactive alternatives, such as vacations, subcontracting, and even customer service reductions (increased backlogs, backorders, or stockouts).

Manufacturers often have still another alternative, building up anticipation inventory to help smooth the output rate. When inventory is introduced, however, care must be taken to recognize differences in how requirements and reactive alternatives are measured. The workforce level might be expressed as the number of employees, but the requirements and inventory are expressed as units of the product. Relationships between the requirements and reactive alternatives must account for these differences. The OM Explorer spreadsheets require a common unit of measure, so we must translate some of the data prior to entering the input values. Perhaps the easiest approach is to express the requirements and reactive alternatives as *employee-period equivalents*. If demand requirements are given as units of product, we can convert them to employee-period equivalents by *dividing* them by the productivity of a worker. For example, if the demand is for 1,500 units of product and the average employee produces 100 units in one period, the demand requirement is 15 employee-period equivalents.

This translation from product units to employee-period equivalents also applies to the initial inventory or backorders at the beginning of period 1, if they are given as product units. To convert the spreadsheet results back to product units, we simply *multiply* employee-period equivalents by the productivity rate. For example, an ending inventory of 20 employee-period equivalents would translate back to 2,000 units of product, or 20 × 100. Example 14.3 demonstrates a mixed strategy for a manufacturer and demonstrates the full range of reactive alternatives.

EXAMPLE 14.3 *Mixed Strategies in Manufacturing*

The production planning manager of a small manufacturing firm must determine an aggregate plan for the next year, which is broken into 6 two-month periods. Each employee works 40 hours per week regular time, and undertime is paid. Requirements and all alternatives are to be expressed as employee-period equivalents. The demand requirements for the next year, already translated from product units to employee-period equivalents, are forecast as follows:

	ACCOUNTING PERIOD						
	1	2	3	4	5	6	TOTAL
Requirement	24	142	220	180	136	168	870

Currently, 120 workers are employed. The manager can vary the workforce with hiring and layoffs. Paid undertime, overtime, vacation time, subcontracting, inventory, and backorders are all allowed. There is no beginning inventory and no backorders at the start of period 1. Overtime cannot exceed 20 percent of the regular-time capacity in any period. Because backorders are allowed, stockouts and backlog extensions are not allowed. Usually, only one of the three alternatives applies to any particular situation. A total of 40 employee-period equivalents must be given sometime during the year as paid vacations. The following costs can be assigned.

Regular-time production	$4,000 per employee-period equivalent
Overtime production	150 percent of the regular-time rate
Subcontracting	$7,200 per employee-period equivalent
Hires	$2,400 per person
Layoffs	$400 per person
Inventory	$40 per employee-period equivalent per period
Backorders	$1,000 per employee-period equivalent per period

SOLUTION

Figure 14.6 represents a plan for using all alternatives (except overtime and layoffs) to meet the requirements. The manager uses it as a starting point, with the computer evaluating the merits of the plan. The cost breakdown can help him find ways to improve on the plan in subsequent iterations.

The starting solution relies heavily on inventory to smooth the output rates and expands the workforce in period 2 by hiring 38 more employees. Vacations are planned for periods 1, 2, 5, and 6, when demand is particularly low. Having four different periods also gives the employees some latitude in planning vacations. Paid undertime (period 1), subcontracting (period 6), and backorders (period 4) are also part of the plan.

A period's inventory is equal to the beginning inventory (the ending inventory of the prior period) plus the production from all sources (productive time, overtime, and subcontracting) minus the requirements and any backorders carrying over from the last period. If this difference is negative, the ending inventory is zero and the backorder equals the difference. Either inven-

	1	2	3	4	5	6	Total
Requirement	24	142	220	180	136	168	870
Workforce level	120	158	158	158	158	158	910
Undertime	6	0	0	0	0	0	6
Overtime	0	0	0	0	0	0	0
Vacation time	20	6	0	0	4	10	40
Subcontracting time	0	0	0	0	0	6	6
Backorders	0	0	0	4	0	0	4
Productive time	94	152	158	158	154	148	864
Inventory	70	80	18	0	14	0	182
Hires	0	38	0	0	0	0	38
Layoffs	0	0	0	0	0	0	0

Costs	1	2	3	4	5	6	Totals
Productive time	$376,000	608,000	632,000	632,000	616,000	592,000	$3,456,000
Undertime	$24,000	0	0	0	0	0	$24,000
Overtime	$0	0	0	0	0	0	$0
Vacation time	$80,000	24,000	0	0	16,000	40,000	$160,000
Inventory	$2,800	3,200	720	0	560	0	$7,280
Backorders	$0	0	0	4,000	0	0	$4,000
Hires	$0	91,200	0	0	0	0	$91,200
Layoffs	$0	0	0	0	0	0	$0
Subcontracting	$0	0	0	0	0	43,200	$43,200
Total cost	$482,800	726,400	632,720	636,000	632,560	675,200	$3,785,680

FIGURE 14.6

	1	2	3	4	5	6	Total
Requirement	24	142	220	180	136	168	870
Workforce level	120	152	158	158	158	158	904
Undertime	0	0	0	0	4	0	4
Overtime	0	0	0	4	0	6	10
Vacation time	20	6	0	0	4	10	40
Subcontracting time	0	0	0	0	0	0	0
Backorders	0	0	0	0	0	0	0
Productive time	100	146	158	158	150	148	860
Inventory	76	80	18	0	14	0	188
Hires	0	32	6	0	0	0	38
Layoffs	0	0	0	0	0	0	0
Costs	1	2	3	4	5	6	Totals
Productive time	$400,000	584,000	632,000	632,000	600,000	592,000	$3,440,000
Undertime	$0	0	0	0	16,000	0	$16,000
Overtime	$0	0	0	24,000	0	36,000	$60,000
Vacation time	$80,000	24,000	0	0	16,000	40,000	$160,000
Inventory	$3,040	3,200	720	0	560	0	$7,520
Backorders	$0	0	0	0	0	0	$0
Hires	$0	76,800	14,400	0	0	0	$91,200
Layoffs	$0	0	0	0	0	0	$0
Subcontracting	$0	0	0	0	0	0	$0
Total cost	$483,040	688,000	647,120	656,000	632,560	668,000	$3,774,720

FIGURE 14.7

tory or backorders must be zero for every period. For example, the ending inventory for period 1 is shown to be 70 employee-period equivalents. It equals the beginning inventory (0 in this example) plus the production from all sources [94 (productive time) + 0 (overtime) + 0 (subcontracting)] minus the demand from all sources [24 (requirements) + 0 (backorders)]. Another example is period 5, for which beginning inventory is 0 and the backorder of 4 employee-period equivalents carries forward. Thus, the total demand is 140 [136 (requirements) + 4 (backorder from period 4)].

This plan is reasonably good, with over 91 percent of the $3,785,680 total cost coming from the productive time (the cheapest production option) and vacation time (which is mandated). Further improvements are possible, however. Three possibilities are to

1. eliminate the undertime in period 1 and build more inventory then, which is compensated for by hiring only 32 employees in period 2 and the remaining 6 in period 3;

2. switch from subcontracting to overtime in period 6, which is a less expensive alternative; and

3. use overtime in period 4 and paid undertime in period 5. This tactic eliminates the costly backorder in period 4 and prevents an inventory buildup for the start of the next year, when the demand will be low.

As Figure 14.7 shows, this revised mixed strategy reduces cost to $3,774,720, which saves $10,960.

Decision Point The manager adopted this second mixed strategy, partly because of its lower cost. The one-time expansion in the workforce was also appealing, as was the use of anticipation inventory and no planned backorders or subcontracting. ⊐

AGGREGATE PLANNING WITH MATHEMATICAL METHODS

The major advantage of the spreadsheet approach is its simplicity; however, the planner still must make many choices for each period of the planning horizon. The large costs involved with aggregate plans are a motivation to seek the best possible plan.

Several mathematical methods can help with this search process. We begin with the transportation method.

TRANSPORTATION METHOD OF PRODUCTION PLANNING

In this section, we present and demonstrate the **transportation method of production planning**. Earlier, we applied it to locating a facility within a network of facilities (see the Location chapter). The transportation method, when applied to aggregate planning, is particularly helpful in determining anticipation inventories. Thus, it relates more to manufacturers' production plans than to service providers' staffing plans. In fact, the workforce levels for each period are inputs to the transportation method rather than outputs from it. Different workforce adjustment plans, ranging from the chase strategy to the level strategy must be tried. Thus, several transportation method solutions may be obtained before a final plan is selected.

Use of the transportation method for production planning is based on the assumption that a demand forecast is available for each period, along with a workforce level plan for regular time. Capacity limits on overtime and subcontractor production also are needed for each period. Another assumption is that all costs are linearly related to the amount of goods produced—that is, that a change in the amount of goods produced creates a proportionate change in costs.

With these assumptions, the transportation method yields the optimal mixed-strategy production plan for the planning horizon.

PRODUCTION PLANNING WITHOUT BACKORDERS.   We start with a table—called a *tableau*—of the workforce levels, capacity limits, demand forecast quantities, beginning inventory level, and costs for each period of the planning horizon. Figure 14.8 shows such a tableau for a four-period production plan, where

h = holding cost per unit per period

r = cost per unit to produce on regular time

c = cost per unit to produce on overtime

s = cost per unit to subcontract

u = undertime cost per unit

b = backorder cost per unit per period

I_0 = beginning inventory level

I_4 = desired inventory level at the end of period 4

R_t = regular-time capacity in period t

O_t = overtime capacity in period t

S_t = subcontracting capacity in period t

D_t = forecasted demand for period t

U = total unused capacities

Note that each row in the tableau represents an alternative for supplying output. For example, the first row shows the beginning inventory (the amount currently on hand) for the present time (period 0), which can be used to satisfy demand in any of the four periods. The second row is for regular-time production in period 1, which can also be used to satisfy demand in any of the four periods the plan will cover. The third and fourth rows are for two other production alternatives (overtime and subcontracting) in period 1, for meeting demand in any of the four periods.

Should subcontracting be used to achieve short-term capacity increases or should some combination of inventory accumulation and overtime be used?

transportation method of production planning The use of the transportation method to solve production planning problems, assuming that a demand forecast is available for each period, along with a workforce level plan for regular time.

FIGURE 14.8

Transportation Method of Production Planning

Alternatives		Time Period				Unused Capacity	Total Capacity
		1	2	3	4		
Period	Beginning inventory	0	h	$2h$	$3h$	$4h$	I_0
1	Regular time	r	$r+h$	$r+2h$	$r+3h$	u	R_1
1	Overtime	c	$c+h$	$c+2h$	$c+3h$	0	O_1
1	Subcontract	s	$s+h$	$s+2h$	$s+3h$	0	S_1
2	Regular time	$r+b$	r	$r+h$	$r+2h$	u	R_2
2	Overtime	$c+b$	c	$c+h$	$c+2h$	0	O_2
2	Subcontract	$s+b$	s	$s+h$	$s+2h$	0	S_2
3	Regular time	$r+2b$	$r+b$	r	$r+h$	u	R_3
3	Overtime	$c+2b$	$c+b$	c	$c+h$	0	O_3
3	Subcontract	$s+2b$	$s+b$	s	$s+h$	0	S_3
4	Regular time	$r+3b$	$r+2b$	$r+b$	r	u	R_4
4	Overtime	$c+3b$	$c+2b$	$c+b$	c	0	O_4
4	Subcontract	$s+3b$	$s+2b$	$s+b$	s	0	S_4
Requirements		D_1	D_2	D_3	D_4+I_4	U	

The columns represent the periods that the plan must cover, plus the unused and total capacities available. The box in the upper right-hand corner of each cell shows the cost of producing a unit in one period and, in some cases, carrying the unit in inventory for sale in a future period. For example, in period 1 the regular-time cost to produce one unit is r (column 1). To produce the unit in period 1 for sale in period 2, the cost is $r + h$ (column 2) because we must hold the unit in inventory for one period. Satisfying a unit of demand in period 3 by producing in period 1 on regular time and carrying the unit for two periods costs $r + 2h$ (column 3), and so on. The cells in color at the bottom left of the tableau imply backorders (or producing in a period to satisfy in a past period). We can disallow backorders by making the backorder cost an arbitrarily large number. If backorder costs are so large, the transportation method will try to avoid backorders because it seeks a solution that minimizes total cost. If that is not possible, we increase the staffing plan and the overtime and subcontracting capacities.

The least expensive alternatives are those in which the output is produced and sold in the same period. However, we may not always be able to use those alternatives exclusively because of capacity restrictions. Finally, the per-unit holding cost for the beginning inventory in period 1 is 0 because it is a function of previous production planning decisions. Similarly, the target inventory at the end of the planning horizon is added to the forecasted demand for the last period. No holding cost is charged because we have already decided to have a specified ending inventory; in this regard, it is a sunk cost.[1]

Use the following procedure to develop an acceptable aggregate plan.

Step 1. Select a workforce adjustment plan (or R_t values), using a chase strategy, level strategy, or a mixed strategy. Identify the capacity constraints on overtime (O_t values) and on subcontracting (S_t values). Usually, a period's overtime capacity is a percent of its regular-time capacity. Also identify the on-hand anticipation inventory (I_0 values) currently available before the start of period 1. Input these values to the computer routine, which in turn inserts these values in the last column of the transportation tableau.

Step 2. Input the cost parameters (h, r, c, s, u, and b) for the different reactive alternatives. The computer software uses them to compute the values in the box of the upper right-hand corner of each cell.

Step 3. Forecast the demand for each future period, and insert the forecasts as the values in the tableau's last row. The last period's requirement should be increased to account for any desired inventory at the end of the planning horizon. The unused capacity cell in the last row equals the total demand requirements in the last row, minus the total capacity in the tableau's last column.

Step 4. Solve the transportation problem just formulated with a computer routine to find the optimal solution (based on the workforce adjustment plan). The sum of all entries in a row equals the total capacity for that row, and the sum of all entries in a column must equal the requirements for that column.

Step 5. Return to step 1 and try other staffing plans until you find the solution that best balances cost and qualitative considerations.

EXAMPLE 14.4	*Preparing a Production Plan with the Transportation Method*

**TUTOR
14.3**

The Tru-Rainbow Company produces a variety of paint products for both commercial and private use. The demand for paint is highly seasonal, peaking in the third quarter. Current inventory is 250,000 gallons, and ending inventory should be 300,000 gallons.

Tru-Rainbow's manufacturing manager wants to determine the best production plan using the following demand requirements and capacity plan. Demands and capacities here are expressed in thousands of gallons (rather than employee-period equivalents). The manager knows that the regular-time cost is $1.00 per unit, overtime cost is $1.50 per unit, subcontracting cost is $1.90 per unit, and inventory holding cost is $0.30 per gallon per quarter.

---

[1]If we were analyzing the implications of different ending inventory levels, the holding cost of the ending inventory would have to be added to the costs because ending inventory level would be a decision variable.

	QUARTER				TOTAL
	1	2	3	4	
Demand	300	850	1,500	350	3,000
Capacities					
Regular time	450	450	750	450	2,100
Overtime	90	90	150	90	420
Subcontracting	200	200	200	200	800

The following constraints apply:

1. Maximum allowable overtime in any quarter is 20 percent of the regular-time capacity in that quarter.

2. The subcontractor can supply a maximum of 200,000 gallons in any quarter. Production can be subcontracted in one period and the excess held in inventory for a future period to avoid a stockout.

3. No backorders or stockouts are permitted.

SOLUTION

Figure 14.9 shows graphically the inventory accumulation and consumption over the planning horizon that the tableau solution provides. Inventory accumulates whenever production plus subcontracting exceeds quarterly demand. Conversely, anticipation inventories are consumed when production plus subcontracting is less than quarterly demand. Quarter 2 illustrates this scenario when total production (including subcontracting) is only 740,000 gallons, but requirements are for 850,000 gallons, calling for consumption of 110,000 gallons from inventory.

The tableau solution from which this graph is derived is found using OM Explorer's Tutor 14.3. Figure 14.10 on the following page shows the computer output. The *Results Worksheet* summarizes the costs of this prospective production plan, as shown in the two rows below the tableau. These numbers can be confirmed as the sum of the products calculated by multiplying the allocation in each cell by the cost per unit in that cell. Computing the cost column by column, as done by Tutor 14.3, yields a total cost of $4,010,000, or $4,014 \times 1,000$.

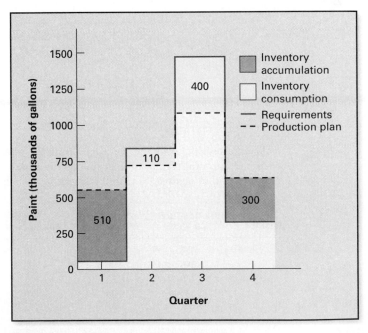

FIGURE 14.9 • Prospective Tru-Rainbow Production Plan

Tutor 14.3 - Transportation Method for Aggregate Planning

Solve

	Period	Quarter 1	Quarter 2	Quarter 3	Quarter 4	Unused Capacity	Total Capacity
1	Beginning Inventory	0 / **250**	$0.30	$0.60	$0.90	0	250
1	Regular Time	$1.00 / **30**	$1.30 / **420**	$1.60 / -	$1.90 / -	-	450
1	Overtime	$1.50 / -	$1.80 / **90**	$2.10 / -	$2.40 / -	-	90
1	Subcontract	$1.90 / **20**	$2.20 / -	$2.50 / -	$2.80 / -	180	200
2	Regular Time	999	$1.00 / **340**	$1.30 / **110**	$1.60 / -	-	450
2	Overtime	999	$1.50 / -	$1.80 / **90**	$2.10 / -	-	90
2	Subcontract	999	$1.90 / -	$2.20 / **200**	$2.50 / -	-	200
3	Regular Time	999	999	$1.00 / **750**	$1.30 / -	-	750
3	Overtime	999	999	$1.50 / **150**	$1.80 / -	-	150
3	Subcontract	999	999	$1.90 / **200**	$2.20 / -	-	200
4	Regular Time	999	999	999	$1.00 / **450**	-	450
4	Overtime	999	999	999	$1.50 / **90**	-	90
4	Subcontract	999	999	999	$1.90 / **110**	90	200
	Requirements	300	850	1500	650	270	3570

	Q1	Q2	Q3	Q4
Costs	68	1,048	2,100	794
Total Cost				4,010

FIGURE 14.10

Quarter 1:	250($0) + 30($1.00) + 20($1.90)	= $ 68
Quarter 2:	420($1.30) + 90($1.80) + 340($1.00)	= 1,048
Quarter 3:	110($1.30) + 90($1.80) + 200($2.20) + 750($1.00) +	
	150($1.50) + 200($1.90)	= 2,100
Quarter 4:	450($1.00) + 90($1.50) + 110($1.90)	= 794
		Total = $4,010

To interpret the solution, we can convert the tableau solution into the following table. For example, the total regular-time production in quarter 1 is 450,000 gallons (30,000 gallons to meet demand in quarter 1 and 420,000 gallons to help satisfy demand in quarter 2).

QUARTER	REGULAR-TIME PRODUCTION	OVERTIME PRODUCTION	SUB-CONTRACTING	TOTAL PRODUCTION	ANTICIPATION INVENTORY
1	450	90	20	560	250 + 560 − 300 = 510
2	450	90	200	740	510 + 740 − 850 = 400
3	750	150	200	1,100	400 + 1,100 − 1,500 = 0
4	450	90	110	650	0 + 650 − 350 = 300
Totals	2,100	420	530	3,050	

Note: Anticipation inventory is the amount at the end of each quarter, where Beginning inventory + Total production − Demand = Ending inventory.

The anticipation inventory held at the end of each quarter is obtained in the last column. For any quarter, it is the quarter's beginning inventory plus total production (regular-time and overtime production, plus subcontracting) minus demand. For example, for quarter 1 the beginning inventory (250,000) plus the total from production and subcontracting (560,000) minus quarter 1 demand (300,000) results in an ending inventory of 510,000, which also is the beginning inventory for quarter 2.

Decision Point This plan requires too much overtime and subcontracting. The manager decided to search for a better capacity plan—with increases in the workforce to boost regular-time production capacity—that could lower production costs, perhaps even low enough to offset the added capacity costs. ◻

ADDITIONAL CAPACITY PLANS.   A series of capacity plans can be tried and compared to find the best plan. Even though this process in itself involves trial and error, the transportation method yields the best mix of regular time, overtime, and subcontracting for each capacity plan.

LINEAR PROGRAMMING FOR PRODUCTION PLANNING

The transportation method just discussed actually is a specialized form of linear programming (see the Linear Programming supplement). Linear programming models for production planning seek the optimal production plan for a linear objective function and a set of linear constraints; that is, there can be no cross products or powers of decision variables or other types of nonlinear terms in the problem formulation. Linear programming models are capable of handling a large number of variables and constraints and, unlike the transportation method, are not limited to the use of a specific capacity plan. Linear programming models can be used to determine optimal inventory levels, backorders, subcontractor quantities, production quantities, overtime production, hires, and layoffs. The main drawbacks are that all relationships between variables must be linear and that the optimal values of the decision variables may be fractional. The assumption of linearity is violated when certain costs (e.g., setup costs) are incurred only when specific product families are produced in a time period and do not get larger as the production quantity increases. Also, fractional values of the decision variables may cause difficulties when the variables represent discrete items, such as workers, bicycles, or trucks.

Suppose that you must plan the production of a certain product family and do not want to use backorders. Each worker produces 5,000 units per month if used productively on regular time or overtime. Subcontracting and overtime production are possible options to supplement regular-time production, and undertime is paid. Overtime is limited to 15 percent of the regular-time production in any month. Let

D_t = demand as product units in month t (presumed known; not a variable)

W_t = workers on hand at the start of month t

H_t = hires at the start of month t

L_t = layoffs at the start of month t

I_t = inventory as product units at the end of month t

S_t = subcontracted production as product units in month t

O_t = overtime production as product units in month t

Then, for each month, the following constraints are required:

$W_t = W_{t-1} + H_t - L_t$ (relationship for the number of workers)

$I_t = I_{t-1} + 5{,}000W_t + O_t + S_t - D_t$ (relationship for the inventory level)

$O_t \le 0.15(5{,}000W_t)$ (relationship for the overtime limit)

There are six variables (D_t is not a decision variable) and three constraints for each month. If the production plan is to cover 12 months, you need 72 decision variables and 36 constraints. In addition, you need to specify an objective function for minimizing costs or maximizing profits. For example, let

c_w = regular-time wages per worker per month

c_h = cost to hire one worker

c_L = cost to lay off one worker

c_I = cost to hold one unit of product for one month

c_s = cost to subcontract one unit of product

c_o = cost to produce one unit of product on overtime

An objective function for minimizing costs would be

$$TC = \sum_{t=1}^{12}(c_wW_t + c_hH_t + c_LL_t + c_II_t + c_sS_t + c_oO_t)$$

Obviously, even for simple problems, this approach requires a considerable number of variables and constraints. Hence, a computer is mandatory for production-planning applications of linear programming. Nonetheless, the method is versatile in its ability to handle a wide variety and large number of variables and constraints.

MANAGERIAL CONSIDERATIONS

Other mathematical techniques, such as linear decision rules (Holt, Modigliani, and Simon, 1955), the search decision rule (Taubert, 1968), goal programming (Lee and Moore, 1974), and simulation (Lee and Khumawala, 1974), are available in addition to those covered here. All can be useful in developing sound aggregate plans, but they are only aids to the planning process. As you have seen in this chapter, the planning process is dynamic and often complicated by conflicting objectives. Analytic techniques can help managers evaluate plans and resolve conflicting objectives, but managers—not techniques—make the decisions.

After arriving at an acceptable production plan, management must implement it. However, the aggregate plan is stated in aggregate terms. The first step in implementation therefore is to disaggregate the plan—that is, break it down into specific products, work centers, and dates (see the Resource Planning chapter, the Scheduling chapter, and the Master Production Scheduling supplement).

AGGREGATE PLANNING ACROSS THE ORGANIZATION

Aggregate planning is meaningful throughout the organization. *First,* the aggregate planning process requires managerial inputs from all of a firm's functions and must reconcile sometimes conflicting needs and objectives. Marketing provides inputs on demand and customer requirements, and accounting provides important cost data and the firm's financial condition. One of finance's objectives might be to cut inventory, whereas operations might argue for a more stable workforce and for less reliance on overtime. *Second,* each function is affected by the plan. An aggregate plan puts into effect decisions on expanding or reducing the size of the workforce, which has a direct impact on the hiring and training requirements for the human resources function. As an aggregate plan is implemented, it creates revenue and cost streams that finance must deal with as it manages the firm's cash flows. *Third,* each department and group in a firm has its own workforce. Managers of its processes must make choices on hiring, overtime, and vacations. Aggregate planning is an activity for the whole organization.

CHAPTER HIGHLIGHTS

❐ Aggregate plans (production plans or staffing plans) are statements of strategy that specify time-phased production or service rates, workforce levels, and (in manufacturing) inventory investment. These plans show how the organization will work toward longer-term objectives while considering the demand and capacity that are likely to exist during a planning horizon of only a year or two. In manufacturing organizations, the plan linking strategic goals to the master production schedule is called the production plan. In service organizations, the staffing plan links strategic goals to the workforce schedule.

❐ To reduce the level of detail required in the planning process, products or services are aggregated into families, and labor is aggregated along product family lines or according to the general skills or services provided. Time is aggregated into periods of months or quarters.

❐ Managerial inputs are required from the various functional areas in the organization. This approach typically raises conflicting objectives, such as high customer service, a stable workforce, and low inventory investment. Creativity and cross-functional compromise are required to reconcile these conflicts.

❐ The two basic types of alternatives are reactive and aggressive. Reactive alternatives take customer demand as a given. Aggressive alternatives attempt to change the timing or quantity of customer demand to stabilize production or service rates and reduce inventory requirements.

❐ Four pure, but generally high-cost planning strategies are the two level strategies, which maintain a constant workforce size or production rate, and the two chase strategies, which vary workforce level or production rate to match fluctuations in demand.

❐ Developing aggregate plans is an iterative process of determining demand requirements; identifying relevant constraints, alternatives, and costs; preparing and approving a plan; and implementing and updating the plan.

❐ Although spreadsheets, the transportation method, and linear programming can help analyze complicated alternatives, aggregate planning is primarily an exercise in conflict resolution and compromise. Ultimately, decisions are made by managers, not by quantitative methods.

KEY TERMS

aggregate plan *652*
aggressive alternatives *660*
annual plan or financial plan *655*
backlog *659*
backorder *659*
business plan *655*
chase strategy *661*
complementary products *660*

financial plan *655*
level strategy *661*
master production schedule *655*
mixed strategy *663*
overtime *658*
planning horizon *654*
production plan *652*
reactive alternatives *657*

staffing plan *652*
stockout *660*
transportation method of production
   planning *672*
undertime *658*
workforce schedule *656*

SOLVED PROBLEM 1

**TUTOR
14.4**

The Cranston Telephone Company employs workers who lay telephone cables and perform various other construction tasks. The company prides itself on good service and strives to complete all service orders within the planning period in which they are received.

Each worker puts in 600 hours of regular time per planning period and can work as much as an additional 100 hours overtime. The operations department has estimated the following workforce requirements for such services over the next four planning periods:

Planning Period	1	2	3	4
Demand (hours)	21,000	18,000	30,000	12,000

Cranston pays regular-time wages of $6,000 per employee per period for any time worked up to 600 hours (including undertime). The overtime pay rate is $15 per hour over 600 hours.

Hiring, training, and outfitting a new employee costs $8,000. Layoff costs are $2,000 per employee. Currently, 40 employees work for Cranston in this capacity. No delays in service, or backorders, are allowed. Use the spreadsheet approach to answer the following questions:

a. Develop a level workforce plan that uses only the overtime and undertime alternatives. Maximize the use of overtime during the peak period so as to minimize the workforce level and amount of undertime.

b. Prepare a chase strategy using only the workforce adjustment alternative of hiring and layoffs. What are the total numbers of employees hired and laid off?

c. Propose an effective mixed-strategy plan.

d. Compare the total costs of the three plans.

SOLUTION

a. The peak demand is 30,000 hours in period 3. As each employee can work 700 hours per period (600 on regular time and 100 on overtime), the level workforce that minimizes undertime is 30,000/700 = 42.86, or 43, employees. The level strategy calls for three employees to be hired in the first quarter and for none to be laid off. To convert the demand requirements into employee-period equivalents, divide the demand in hours by 600. For example, the demand of 21,000 hours in period 1 translates into 35 employee-period equivalents (21,000/600) and demand in the third period translates into 50 employee-period equivalents (30,000/600). Figure 14.11 shows one solution using the "level strategy" option of Tutor 14.4.

b. The chase strategy workforce is calculated by dividing the demand for each period by 600 hours, or the amount of regular-time work for one employee during one period. This strategy calls for a total of 20 workers to be hired and 40 to be laid off during the four period plan. Figure 14.12 shows the "chase strategy" solution that Tutor 14.4 produces.

Tutor 14.4 - Staffing Strategies with Spreadsheets (4 periods)

Enter data in yellow-shaded areas.

Starting workforce	40	Regular-time hrs per worker	600
Regular-time wages	$6,000	Max overtime hrs per worker	100
(per worker per quarter)		Overtime rate ($/hour)	$15
☑ Employees paid for undertime		Cost to hire one worker	$8,000
		Cost to lay off one worker	$2,000
Level Strategy ▼			
Required staff level	43		

	Quarter				
	1	2	3	4	Total
Requirement (hrs)	21,000	18,000	30,000	12,000	81000
Workforce level (workers)	43	43	43	43	172
Undertime (hours)	4,800	7,800	0	13,800	26400
Overtime (hours)	0	0	4,200	0	4200
Productive time (hours)	21,000	18,000	25,800	12,000	76800
Hires (workers)	3	0	0	0	3
Layoffs (workers)	0	0	0	0	0
Costs					
Productive time	$210,000	$180,000	$258,000	$120,000	$768,000
Undertime	48,000	78,000	0	138,000	264,000
Overtime	0	0	63,000	0	63,000
Hires	24,000	0	0	0	24,000
Layoffs	0	0	0	0	0
Total Cost					$1,119,000

FIGURE 14.11

Tutor 14.4 - Staffing Strategies with Spreadsheets (4 periods)

Enter data in yellow-shaded areas.

Starting workforce	40	Regular-time hrs per worker	800
Regular-time wages	$6,000	Max overtime hrs per worker	100
(per worker per quarter)		Overtime rate ($/hour)	$15
☑ Employees paid for undertime		Cost to hire one worker	$8,000
Chase Strategy ▼		Cost to lay off one worker	$2,000
Required staff level	---		

	\multicolumn{4}{c	}{Quarter}	
	1	2	3	4	Total
Requirement (hrs)	21,000	18,000	30,000	12,000	81,000
Workforce level (workers)	35	30	50	20	135
Undertime (hours)	0	0	0	0	0
Overtime (hours)	0	0	0	0	0
Productive time (hours)	21,000	18,000	30,000	12,000	81,000
Hires (workers)	0	0	20	0	20
Layoffs (workers)	5	5	0	30	40
Costs					
Productive time	$210,000	$180,000	$300,000	$120,000	$810,000
Undertime	0	0	0	0	0
Overtime	0	0	0	0	0
Hires	0	0	160,000	0	160,000
Layoffs	10,000	10,000	0	60,000	80,000
Total Cost					$1,050,000

FIGURE 14.12

c. The mixed strategy plan that we propose uses a combination of hires, layoffs, and overtime to reduce total costs. The workforce is reduced by 5 at the beginning of the first period, increased by 8 in the third period, and reduced by 13 in the fourth period. Switching to the general-purpose *Aggregate Planning with Spreadsheets Solver* for this mixed strategy, and hiding any unneeded columns and rows, we get the results shown in Figure 14.13. The solver can evaluate

Solver - Aggregate Planning with Spreadsheets

Enter data in yellow-shaded areas.

☑ Employees Paid for Undertime

	1	2	3	4	Total
Requirement	35	30	50	20	135
Workforce level	35	35	43	30	143
Undertime	0	5	0	10	15
Overtime	0	0	7	0	7
Productive time	35	30	43	20	128
Hires	0	0	8	0	8
Layoffs	5	0	0	13	18
Costs	1	2	3	4	Totals
Productive time	$210,000	180,000	258,000	120,000	$768,000
Undertime	$0	30,000	0	60,000	$90,000
Overtime	$0	0	63,000	0	$63,000
Hires	$0	0	64,000	0	$64,000
Layoffs	$10,000	0	0	26,000	$36,000
Total cost	$220,000	210,000	385,000	206,000	$1,021,000

FIGURE 14.13

any aggregate plan that is proposed. Its format is much the same as that for Tutor 14.4, except that the data in the top half of the spreadsheet (above the cost data) are expressed as employee-period equivalents, rather than as hours.

d. The total cost of the level strategy is $1,119,000. The chase strategy results in a total cost of $1,050,000. The mixed-strategy plan was developed by trial and error and results in a total cost of $1,021,000. Further improvements to the mixed strategy are possible.

SOLVED PROBLEM 2

The Arctic Air Company produces residential air conditioners. The manufacturing manager wants to develop a production plan for the next year based on the following demand and capacity data (in hundreds of product units):

| | PERIOD | | | | | |
	Jan–Feb (1)	Mar–Apr (2)	May–Jun (3)	Jul–Aug (4)	Sep–Oct (5)	Nov–Dec (6)
Demand	50	60	90	120	70	40
Capacities						
Regular time	65	65	65	80	80	65
Overtime	13	13	13	16	16	13
Subcontractor	10	10	10	10	10	10

Undertime is unpaid, and no cost is associated with unused overtime or subcontractor capacity. Producing one air conditioning unit on regular time costs $1,000, including $300 for labor. Producing a unit on overtime costs $1,150. A subcontractor can produce a unit to Arctic Air specifications for $1,250. Holding an air conditioner in stock costs $60 for each two-month period, and 200 air conditioners are currently in stock. The plan calls for 400 units to be in stock at the end of period 6. No backorders are allowed. Use the transportation method to develop the aggregate plan that minimizes costs.

SOLUTION

The following table identifies the optimal production and inventory plans and concludes with a cost summary. Figure 14.14 shows the tableau that corresponds to this solution. An arbitrarily large cost ($99,999 per period) was used for backorders, which effectively ruled them out. Again, all production quantities are in hundreds of units. Note that demand in period 6 is 4,400. That amount is the period 6 demand plus the desired ending inventory of 400. The anticipation inventory is measured as the amount at the end of each period. Cost calculations are based on the assumption that workers are not paid for undertime or are productively put to work elsewhere in the organization whenever they are not needed for this work. The total cost of this plan is $44,287,000.

Production Plan

PERIOD	REGULAR-TIME PRODUCTION	OVERTIME PRODUCTION	SUBCONTRACTING	TOTAL
1	6,500	—	—	6,500
2	6,500	400	—	6,900
3	6,500	1,300	—	7,800
4	8,000	1,600	1,000	10,600
5	7,000	—	—	7,000
6	4,400	—	—	4,400

Anticipation Inventory

PERIOD	BEGINNING INVENTORY PLUS TOTAL PRODUCTION MINUS DEMAND	ANTICIPATION (ENDING) INVENTORY
1	200 + 6,500 − 5,000	1,700
2	1,700 + 6,900 − 6,000	2,600
3	2,600 + 7,800 − 9,000	1,400
4	1,400 + 10,600 − 12,000	0
5	0 + 7,000 − 7,000	0
6	0 + 4,400 − 4,000	400

Alternatives		Time Period						Unused Capacity	Total Capacity
		1	2	3	4	5	6		
Period	I_0	0 / 2	60	120	180	240	300	0	2
1	R_1	1,000 / 48	1,060	1,120 / 17	1,180	1,240	1,300	0	65
	R_1	1,150	1,210	1,270	1,330	1,390	1,450	13	13
	S_1	1,250	1,310	1,370	1,430	1,490	1,550	10	10
2	R_2	99,999	1,000 / 60	1,060 / 5	1,120	1,180	1,240	0	65
	O_2	99,999	1,150	1,210	1,270 / 4	1,330	1,390	9	13
	S_2	99,999	1,250	1,310	1,370	1,430	1,490	10	10
3	R_3	99,999	99,999	1,000 / 65	1,060	1,120	1,180	0	65
	O_3	99,999	99,999	1,150 / 3	1,210 / 10	1,270	1,330	0	13
	S_3	99,999	99,999	1,250	1,310	1,370	1,430	10	10
4	R_4	99,999	99,999	99,999	1,000 / 80	1,060	1,120	0	80
	R_4	99,999	99,999	99,999	1,150 / 16	1,210	1,270	0	16
	S_4	99,999	99,999	99,999	1,250 / 10	1,310	1,370	0	10
5	R_5	99,999	99,999	99,999	99,999	1,000 / 70	1,060	10	80
	O_5	99,999	99,999	99,999	99,999	1,150	1,210	16	16
	S_5	99,999	99,999	99,999	99,999	1,250	1,310	10	10
6	R_6	99,999	99,999	99,999	99,999	99,999	1,000 / 44	21	65
	O_6	99,999	99,999	99,999	99,999	99,999	1,150	13	13
	S_6	99,999	99,999	99,999	99,999	99,999	1,250	10	10
	D	50	60	90	120	70	44	132	566

FIGURE 14.14

DISCUSSION QUESTIONS

1. Quantitative methods can help managers evaluate alternative production plans on the basis of cost. These methods require cost estimates for each of the controllable variables, such as overtime, subcontracting, hiring, firing, and inventory investment. Say that the existing workforce is made up of 10,000 direct-labor employees, each having skills valued at $40,000 per year. The production plan calls for "creating alternative career opportunities"—in other words, laying off 500 employees. List the types of costs incurred when employees are laid off, and make a rough estimate of the length of time required for payroll savings to recover restructuring costs. If business is expected to improve in one year, are layoffs financially justified? What costs are incurred in a layoff that are difficult to estimate in monetary terms?

2. In your community, some employers maintain stable workforces at all costs, and others furlough and recall workers seemingly at the drop of a hat. What are the differences in markets, management, products, financial position, skills, costs, and competition that could explain these two extremes in personnel policy?

3. As the fortunes of the Big Three domestic automakers improved in the mid-1990s, workers at one GM plant went on strike. The striking workers produced transmissions used in other GM plants. Almost immediately, many other GM plants shut down for lack of transmissions. Facing lost production during a hot market, GM management quickly acceded to labor's demands to recall more furloughed workers and schedule less overtime. What production planning decisions regarding the controllable variables (listed in Discussion Question 1) are apparent in this situation?

OM EXPLORER AND INTERNET EXERCISES

Visit our Web site at www.prenhall.com/krajewski for OM Explorer Tutors, which explain quantitative techniques; Solvers, which help you apply mathematical models; and Internet Exercises, including Facility Tours, which expand on the topics in this chapter.

PROBLEMS

An icon next to a problem identifies the software that can be helpful, but not mandatory. The software is available on the Student CD-ROM that is packaged with every new copy of the textbook.

1. **OM Explorer** The Barberton Municipal Division of Road Maintenance is charged with road repair in the city of Barberton and surrounding area. Cindy Kramer, road maintenance director, must submit a staffing plan for the next year based on a set schedule for repairs and on the city budget. Kramer estimates that the labor hours required for the next four quarters are 6,000, 12,000, 19,000, and 9,000, respectively. Each of the 11 workers on the workforce can contribute 500 hours per quarter. Payroll costs are $6,000 in wages per worker for regular time worked up to 500 hours, with an overtime pay rate of $18 for each overtime hour. Overtime is limited to 20 percent of the regular-time capacity in any quarter. Although unused overtime capacity has no cost, unused regular time is paid at $12 per hour. The cost of hiring a worker is $3,000, and the cost of laying off a worker is $2,000. Subcontracting is not permitted.

   a. Find a level workforce plan that allows no delay in road repair and minimizes undertime. Overtime can be used to its limits in any quarter. What is the total cost of the plan and how many undertime hours does it call for?

   b. Use a chase strategy that varies the workforce level without using overtime or undertime. What is the total cost of this plan?

   c. Propose a plan of your own. Compare your plan with those in parts (a) and (b) and discuss its comparative merits.

2. **OM Explorer** Bob Carlton's golf camp estimates the following workforce requirements for its services over the next two years.

Quarter	1	2	3	4
Demand *(hours)*	4,200	6,400	3,000	4,800

Quarter	5	6	7	8
Demand *(hours)*	4,400	6,240	3,600	4,800

Each certified instructor puts in 480 hours per quarter regular time and can work an additional 120 hours overtime. Regular-time wages and benefits cost Carlton $7,200 per employee per quarter for regular time worked up to 480 hours, with an overtime cost of $20 per hour. Unused regular time for certified instructors is paid at $15 per hour. There is no cost for unused overtime capacity. The cost of hiring, training, and certifying a new employee is $10,000. Layoff costs are $4,000 per employee. Currently, eight employees work in this capacity.

a. Find a level workforce plan that allows for no delay in service and minimizes undertime. What is the total cost of this plan?

b. Use a chase strategy that varies the workforce level without using overtime or undertime. What is the total cost of this plan?

c. Propose a low-cost, mixed-strategy plan and calculate its total cost.

3. Continuing Problem 2, now assume that Carlton is permitted to employ some uncertified, part-time instructors, provided they represent no more than 15 percent of the total workforce hours in any quarter. Each part-time instructor can work up to 240 hours per quarter, with no overtime or undertime cost. Labor costs for part-time instructors are $12 per hour. Hiring and training costs are $2,000 per uncertified instructor, and there are no layoff costs.

a. Propose a low-cost, mixed-strategy plan and calculate its total cost.

b. What are the primary advantages and disadvantages of having a workforce consisting of both regular and temporary employees?

4. The Donald Fertilizer Company produces industrial chemical fertilizers. The projected manufacturing requirements (in thousands of gallons) for the next four quarters are 80, 50, 80, and 130, respectively. Stockouts and backorders are to be avoided. A level production strategy is desired.

a. Determine the level quarterly production rate required to meet total demand for the year. Beginning inventory is zero.

b. Specify the anticipation inventories that will be produced.

c. Suppose that the requirements for the next four quarters are revised to 80, 130, 50, and 80, respectively.

If total demand is the same, what level of production rate is needed now?

5. ● **OM Explorer** Management at the Davis Corporation has determined the following demand schedule (in units).

Month	1	2	3	4
Demand	500	800	1,000	1,400

Month	5	6	7	8
Demand	2,000	1,600	1,400	1,200

Month	9	10	11	12
Demand	1,000	2,400	3,000	1,000

An employee can produce an average of 10 units per month. Each worker on the payroll costs $2,000 in regular-time wages per month. Undertime is paid at the same rate as regular time. In accordance with the labor contract in force, Davis Corporation does not work overtime or use subcontracting. Davis can hire and train a new employee for $2,000 and lay one off for $500. Inventory costs $32 per unit on hand at the end of each month. At present, 140 employees are on the payroll.

a. Prepare a production plan with a level workforce strategy. The plan may call for a one-time adjustment of the workforce before month 1.

b. Prepare a production plan with a chase strategy that varies the workforce without undertime, overtime, and subcontracting.

c. Compare and contrast the two pure-strategy plans on the basis of annual costs and other factors that you believe to be important.

d. Propose a mixed-strategy plan that is better than the two pure-strategy plans. Explain why you believe that your plan is better.

6. ● **OM Explorer** The Flying Frisbee Company has forecasted the following staffing requirements for full-time employees. Demand is seasonal, and management wants three alternative staffing plans to be developed.

Month	1	2	3	4
Requirement	2	2	4	6

Month	5	6	7	8
Requirement	18	20	12	18

Month	9	10	11	12
Requirement	7	3	2	1

The company currently has 10 employees. No more than 10 new hires can be accommodated in any month because of limited training facilities. No backorders are allowed, and overtime cannot exceed 25 percent of regular-time capacity in any month. There is no cost for unused overtime capacity. Regular-time wages are $1,500 per month, and overtime wages are 150 percent of regular-time wages. Undertime is paid at the same rate as regular time. The hiring cost is $2,500 per person, and the layoff cost is $2,000 per person.

a. Prepare a staffing plan utilizing a level workforce strategy. The plan may call for a one-time adjustment of the workforce before month 1.

b. Using a chase strategy, prepare a plan that is consistent with the constraint on hiring and minimizes use of overtime.

c. Prepare a low-cost, mixed-strategy plan.

d. Which strategy is most cost-effective? What are the advantages and disadvantages of each plan?

7. 💿 **OM Explorer** The Twilight Clothing Company makes jeans for children. Management has just prepared a forecast of sales (in pairs of jeans) for next year and now must prepare a production plan. The company has traditionally maintained a level workforce strategy. Currently, there are eight workers, who have been with the company for a number of years. Each employee can produce 2,000 pairs of jeans during a two-month planning period. Every year management authorizes overtime in periods 1, 5, and 6, up to a maximum of 20 percent of regular-time capacity. Management wants to avoid stockouts and backorders and will not accept any plan that calls for such shortages. At present, there are 12,000 pairs of jeans in finished goods inventory. The demand forecast is as follows:

Period	1	2	3
Sales	25,000	6,500	15,000

Period	4	5	6
Sales	19,000	32,000	29,000

a. Is the level workforce strategy feasible with the current workforce, assuming that overtime is used only in periods 1, 5, and 6? Explain.

b. Find two alternative plans that would satisfy management's concern over stockouts and backorders, disregarding costs. What trade-offs between these two plans must be considered?

Advanced Problems

Linear programming approaches, including the transportation method, are recommended for solving Advanced Problems 8–10. Additional applications of these production-planning problems may be found in the Linear Programming Supplement, Problems 16, 17, and 20.

8. 💿 **OM Explorer** The Bull Grin Company makes a supplement for the animal feed produced by a number of companies. Sales are seasonal, but Bull Grin's customers refuse to stockpile the supplement during slack sales periods. In other words, the customers want to minimize their inventory investments, insist on shipments according to their schedules, and will not accept backorders.

Bull Grin employs manual, unskilled laborers, who require little or no training. Producing 1,000 pounds of supplement costs $830 on regular time and $910 on overtime. There is no cost for unused regular-time, overtime, or subcontractor capacity. These figures include materials, which account for 80 percent of the cost. Overtime is limited to production of a total of 20,000 pounds per quarter. In addition, subcontractors can be hired at $1,000 per thousand pounds, but only 30,000 pounds per quarter can be produced this way.

The current level of inventory is 40,000 pounds, and management wants to end the year at that level. Holding 1,000 pounds of feed supplement in inventory per quarter costs $100. The latest annual forecast is shown in Table 14.1.

Use the transportation method of production planning to find the optimal production plan and calculate its cost, or use the spreadsheet approach to find good production plan and calculate its cost.

TABLE 14.1   *Forecasts and Capacities*

	PERIOD				
	QUARTER 1	QUARTER 2	QUARTER 3	QUARTER 4	TOTAL
Demand (pounds)	130,000	400,000	800,000	470,000	1,800,000
Capacities (pounds)					
Regular time	390,000	400,000	460,000	380,000	1,630,000
Overtime	20,000	20,000	20,000	20,000	80,000
Subcontract		30,000	30,000	30,000	30,000

9. ● **OM Explorer** The Cut Rite Company is a major producer of industrial lawn mowers. The cost to Cut Rite for hiring a semiskilled worker for its assembly plant is $3,000 and for laying one off is $2,000. The plant averages an output of 36,000 mowers per quarter with its current workforce of 720 employees. Regular-time capacity is directly proportional to the number of employees. Overtime is limited to a maximum of 3,000 mowers per quarter, and subcontracting is limited to 1,000 mowers per quarter. The costs to produce one mower are $2,430 on regular time (including materials), $2,700 on overtime, and $3,300 via subcontracting. Unused regular-time capacity costs $270 per mower. There is no cost for unused overtime or subcontractor capacity. The current level of inventory is 4,000 mowers, and management wants to end the year at that level. Customers do not tolerate backorders, and holding a mower in inventory per quarter costs $300. The demand for mowers this coming year is

Quarter	1	2	3	4
Demand	10,000	41,000	77,000	44,000

Two workforce plans have been proposed, and management is uncertain as to which one to use. The table shows the number of employees per quarter under each plan.

Quarter	1	2	3	4
Plan 1	720	780	920	720
Plan 2	860	860	860	860

a. Which plan would you recommend to management? Explain, supporting your recommendation with an analysis using the transportation method of production planning.

b. If management used creative pricing to get customers to buy mowers in nontraditional time periods, the following demand schedule would result:

Quarter	1	2	3	4
Demand	20,000	54,000	54,000	44,000

Which workforce plan would you recommend now?

10. ● **OM Explorer** Gretchen's Kitchen is a fast-food restaurant located in an ideal spot near the local high school. Gretchen Lowe must prepare an annual staffing plan. The only menu items are hamburgers, chili, soft drinks, shakes, and french fries. A sample of 1,000 customers taken at random revealed that they purchased 2,100 hamburgers, 200 pints of chili, 1,000 soft drinks and shakes, and 1,000 bags of french fries. Thus, for purposes of estimating staffing requirements, Lowe assumes that each customer purchases 2.1 hamburgers, 0.2 pint of chili, 1 soft drink or shake, and 1 bag of french fries. Each hamburger requires 4 minutes of labor, a pint of chili requires 3 minutes, and a soft drink or shake and a bag of fries each take 2 minutes of labor.

The restaurant currently has 10 part-time employees who work 80 hours a month on staggered shifts. Wages are $400 per month for regular time and $7.50 per hour for overtime. Hiring and training costs are $250 per new employee, and layoff costs are $50 per employee.

Lowe realizes that building up seasonal inventories of hamburgers (or any of the products) would not be wise because of shelf-life considerations. Also, any demand not satisfied is a lost sale and must be avoided. Three strategies come to mind.

- Utilize a level workforce strategy and use up to 20 percent of regular-time capacity on overtime.

- Maintain a base of 10 employees, hiring and laying off as needed to avoid any overtime.

- Utilize a chase strategy, hiring and firing employees as demand changes to avoid overtime.

When performing her calculations Lowe always rounds to the next highest integer for the number of employees. She also follows a policy of not using an employee more than 80 hours per month, except when overtime is needed. The projected demand by month (number of customers) for next year is as follows:

Jan.	3,200	July	4,800
Feb.	2,600	Aug.	4,200
Mar.	3,300	Sept.	3,800
Apr.	3,900	Oct.	3,600
May	3,600	Nov.	3,500
June	4,200	Dec.	3,000

a. Develop the schedule of service requirements for the next year.

b. Which of the strategies is most effective?

c. Suppose that an arrangement with the high school enables the manager to identify good prospective employees without having to advertise in the local newspaper. This source reduces the hiring cost to $50, which is mainly the cost of charred hamburgers during training. If cost is her only concern, will this method of hiring change Gretchen Lowe's strategy? Considering other objectives that may be appropriate, do you think she should change strategies?

11. **OM Explorer** The Holloway Calendar Company produces a variety of printed calendars for both commercial and private use. The demand for calendars is highly seasonal, peaking in the third quarter. Current inventory is 165,000 calendars, and ending inventory should be 200,000 calendars.

Ann Ritter, Holloway's manufacturing manager, wants to determine the best production plan for the demand requirements and capacity plan shown in the table on the next page.

Alternatives		Quarter				Unused Capacity	Total Capacity
		1	2	3	4		
Quarter 1	Beginning inventory	0.00 / 200	3.00	6.00	9.00	0	200
	Regular time	10.00 / 350	13.00 / 150	16.00	19.00	0	500
	Overtime	15.00	18.00 / 100	21.00	24.00	0	100
	Subcontract	19.00	22.00 / 50	25.00	28.00	150	200
2	Regular time	999	10.00 / 1,000	13.00	16.00	0	1,000
	Overtime	999	15.00 / 200	18.00	21.00	0	200
	Subcontract	999	19.00 / 200	22.00	25.00	0	200
3	Regular time	999	999	10.00 / 500	13.00	0	500
	Overtime	999	999	15.00 / 100	18.00	0	100
	Subcontract	999	999	19.00 / 100	22.00	100	200
4	Regular time	999	999	999	10.00 / 500	0	500
	Overtime	999	999	999	15.00 / 100	0	100
	Subcontract	999	999	999	19.00 / 50	150	200
Requirements		550	1,700	700	650		

FIGURE 14.15

(Here, demand and capacities are expressed in thousands of calendars rather than employee-period equivalents.) Ritter knows that the regular-time cost is $0.50 per unit, overtime cost is $0.75 per unit, subcontracting cost is $0.90 per unit, and inventory holding cost is $0.10 per calendar per quarter.

	QUARTER				
	1	2	3	4	TOTAL
Demand	250	515	1200	325	2,290
Capacities					
Regular Time	300	300	600	300	1,500
Overtime	75	75	150	75	375
Subcontracting	150	150	150	150	600

a. Recommend a production plan to Ritter, using the transportation method of production planning. (Do not allow any stockouts or backorders to occur.)

b. Interpret and explain your recommendation.

c. Calculate the total cost of your recommended production plan.

12. The Alexis Golf Company produces three major lines of premium golf clubs. The demand for their products is highly seasonal, peaking in the second quarter. Kyle Stone, Alexis's manufacturing manager, has presented the tableau, shown in Figure 14.15, based on the transportation method of production planning. All quantities are in 000s.

Use the information shown in Figure 14.15 to answer the following questions.

a. How much regular-time production is expected during the third period? How much subcontracting is expected during the third period?

b. How much regular-time production is expected during the first period? How much anticipatory inventory is expected to be held at the end of the first period?

c. As shown, the firm has no ending inventory for period 4. If the firm decided to hold 250,000 units in inventory at the end of period 4, how could it do so?

CASE MEMORIAL HOSPITAL

Memorial Hospital is a 265-bed regional health care facility located in the mountains of western North Carolina. The mission of the hospital is to provide quality health care to the people of Ashe County and the six surrounding counties. To accomplish this mission, Memorial Hospital's CEO has outlined three objectives: (1) maximize customer service to increase customer satisfaction, (2) minimize costs to remain competitive, and (3) minimize fluctuations in workforce levels to help stabilize area employment.

The hospital's operations are segmented into eight major wards for the purposes of planning and scheduling the nursing staff. These wards are listed in Table 14.2 along with the number of beds, targeted patient-to-nurse ratios, and average patient census for each ward. The overall demand for hospital services has remained relatively constant over the past few years even though the population of the seven counties served has increased. This stable demand can be attributed to increased competition from other hospitals in the area and the rise in alternative health care delivery systems such as health maintenance organizations (HMOs). However, demand for Memorial Hospital's services does vary considerably by type of ward and time of year. Table 14.3 provides a historical monthly breakdown of the average daily patient census per ward.

The director of nursing for Memorial Hospital is Darlene Fry. Each fall she confronts one of the most challenging aspects of her job: planning the nurse staffing levels for the next calendar year. Although the average demand for nurses has remained relatively stable over the past couple of years, the staffing plan usually changes because of changing work policies, changing pay structures, and temporary nurse availability and cost. With fall quickly approaching, Fry has begun to collect information to plan next year's staffing levels.

The nurses at Memorial Hospital work a regular schedule of four 10-hour days per week. The average regular-time pay across all nursing grades is $12.00 per hour. Overtime may be scheduled when necessary. However, because of the intensity of the demands placed on nurses, only a limited amount of overtime is permitted per week. Nurses may be scheduled for as many as 12 hours per day for a maximum of five days per week. Overtime is compensated at a rate of $18.00 per hour. In periods of extremely high demand, temporary part-time nurses may be hired for a limited period of time. Temporary nurses are paid $15.00 per hour. Memorial Hospital has a policy that limits the proportion of temporary nurses to 15 percent of the total nursing staff.

Finding, hiring, and retaining qualified nurses is a problem that hospitals have been facing for years. One reason is that various forms of private practice are luring many nurses away from hospitals with higher pay and greater flexibility. This situation has caused Memorial to guarantee its full-time staff nurses pay for a minimum of

continued

continued

TABLE 14.2   *Ward Capacity Data*

WARD	NUMBER OF BEDS	PATIENTS PER NURSE	PATIENT CENSUS*	
Intensive care	20	2	10	
Cardiac	25	4	15	
Maternity	30	4	10	
Pediatric	40	4	22	
Surgery	5	†	†	
Post op	15	5	8	(T–F daily equivalent)‡
Emergency	10	3	5	(daily equivalent)‡
General	120	8	98	

* Yearly average per day.
† The hospital employs 20 surgical nurses. Routine surgery is scheduled on Tuesdays and Fridays; five surgeries can be scheduled per day per operating room (bed) on these days. Emergency surgery is scheduled as needed.
‡ Daily equivalents are used to schedule nurses because patients flow through these wards in relatively short periods of time. A daily equivalent of 5 indicates that, throughout a typical day, an average of five patients are treated in the ward.

TABLE 14.3   *Average Daily Patient Census per Month*

	MONTH											
WARD	J	F	M	A	M	J	J	A	S	O	N	D
Intensive care	13	10	8	7	7	6	11	13	9	10	12	14
Cardiac	18	16	15	13	14	12	13	12	13	15	18	20
Maternity	8	8	12	13	10	8	13	13	14	10	8	7
Pediatric	22	23	24	24	25	21	22	20	18	20	21	19
Surgery*	20	18	18	17	16	16	22	21	17	18	20	22
Post op†	10	8	7	7	6	6	10	10	7	8	9	10
Emergency†	6	4	4	7	8	5	5	4	4	3	4	6
General	110	108	100	98	95	90	88	92	98	102	107	94

* Average surgeries per day.
† Daily equivalents.

30 hours per week, regardless of the demand placed on nursing services. In addition, each nurse receives a four-week paid vacation each year. However, vacation scheduling may be somewhat restricted by the projected demand for nurses during particular times of the year.

At present, the hospital employs 130 nurses, including 20 surgical nurses. The other 110 nurses are assigned to the remaining seven major areas of the hospital. The Personnel Department has told Fry that the average cost to the hospital for hiring a new full-time nurse is $400 and for laying off or firing a nurse is $150. Although layoffs are an option, Fry is aware of the hospital's objective of maintaining a level workforce.

After looking over the information that she has collected, Darlene Fry decides that it is time to roll up her sleeves and get started. She wants to consider staffing changes in all areas except the surgery ward, which is already correctly staffed.

Questions

1. Explain the alternatives available to Darlene Fry as she develops a nurse staffing plan for Memorial Hospital. How does each meet the objectives stated by the CEO?
2. Based on the data presented, develop a nurse staffing plan for Memorial Hospital. Explain your rationale for this plan.

Source: This case was prepared by Dr. Brooke Saladin, Wake Forest University, as a basis for classroom discussion.

SELECTED REFERENCES

Armacost, R. L., R. L. Penlesky, and S. C. Ross. "Avoiding Problems Inherent in Spreadsheet-Based Simulation Models—An Aggregate Planning Application." *Production and Inventory Management,* vol. 31 (1990), pp. 62–68.

Bowman, E. H. "Production Planning by the Transportation Method of Linear Programming." *Journal of the Operations Research Society,* vol. 4 (1956), pp. 100–103.

Buxey, G. "Production Planning and Scheduling for Seasonal Demand." *International Journal of Operations and Production Management,* vol. 13, no. 7 (1993), pp. 4–21.

Fisher, M. L., J. H. Hammond, W. R. Obermeyer, and A. Raman. "Making Supply Meet Demand in an Uncertain World." *Harvard Business Review,* vol. 72, no. 3 (1994), pp. 83–93.

Hanssman, F., and S. W. Hess. "A Linear Programming Approach to Production and Employment Scheduling." *Management Technology,* vol. 1 (1960), pp. 46–51.

Heskett, J., W. E. Sasser, and C. Hart. *Service Breakthroughs: Changing the Rules of the Game.* New York: The Free Press, 1990.

Holt, C., C. F. Modigliani, and H. Simon. "A Linear Decision Rule for Production and Employment Scheduling." *Management Science,* vol. 2, no. 2 (1955), pp. 1–30.

Jones, C. H. "Parametric Production Planning." *Management Science,* vol. 15, no. 11 (1967), pp. 843–866.

Krajewski, L., and H. Thompson. "Efficient Employment Planning in Public Utilities." *Bell Journal of Economics and Management Science,* vol. 6, no. 1 (1975), pp. 314–320.

Lee, S. M., and L. J. Moore. "A Practical Approach to Production Scheduling." *Production and Inventory Management* (First Quarter 1974), pp. 79–92.

Lee, W. B., and B. M. Khumawala. "Simulation Testing of Aggregate Production Planning Models in an Implementation Methodology." *Management Science,* vol. 20, no. 6 (1974), pp. 903–911.

Ryan, D. M. "Optimization Earns Its Wings." *OR/MS Today,* vol. 27, no. 2 (2000), pp. 26–30.

Silver, E. A. "A Tutorial on Production Smoothing and Workforce Balancing." *Operations Research* (November–December 1967), pp. 985–1010.

Sipper, D., and R. Bulfin. *Production: Planning, Control, and Integration.* New York: McGraw-Hill, 1997.

Taubert, W. H. "A Search Decision Rule for the Aggregate Scheduling Problem." *Management Science,* vol. 14, no. 6 (1968), pp. 343–359.

Vollmann, T. E., W. L. Berry, and D. C. Whybark. *Manufacturing Planning and Control Systems,* 3d ed. Homewood, Ill.: Irwin, 1992.

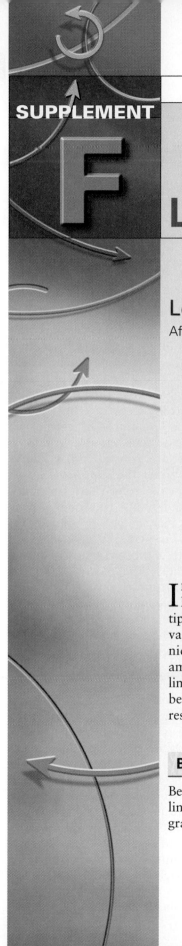

Linear Programming

Learning Goals

After reading this supplement, you will be able to . . .

1. explain the characteristics and assumptions of linear programming models.
2. formulate models for various problems.
3. perform graphic analysis for two-variable problems and find the algebraic solution for the corner point found to be optimal.
4. describe the meaning of slack and surplus variables.
5. discuss the meaning of sensitivity analysis on the objective function coefficients and right-hand-side parameters.
6. interpret the computer output of a linear programming solution.

IN MANY BUSINESS SITUATIONS, resources are limited and demand for them is great. For example, a limited number of vehicles may have to be scheduled to make multiple trips to customers, or a staffing plan may have to be developed to cover expected variable demand with the fewest employees. In this supplement, we describe a technique called **linear programming**, which is useful for allocating scarce resources among competing demands. The resources may be time, money, or materials, and the limitations are known as constraints. Linear programming can help managers find the best allocation solution and provide information about the value of additional resources.

BASIC CONCEPTS

Before we can demonstrate how to solve problems in operations management with linear programming, we must first explain several characteristics of all linear programming models and mathematical assumptions that apply to them:

1. Objective function
2. Decision variables
3. Constraints
4. Feasible region

linear programming A technique that is useful for allocating scarce resources among competing demands.

objective function An expression in linear programming models that states mathematically what is being maximized (e.g., profit or present value) or minimized (e.g., cost or scrap).

decision variables The variables that represent choices the decision maker can control.

constraints The limitations that restrict the permissible choices for the decision variables.

feasible region A region that represents all permissible combinations of the decision variables in a linear programming model.

parameter A value that the decision maker cannot control and that does not change when the solution is implemented.

certainty Used to describe that a fact is known without doubt.

linearity A characteristic of linear programming models that implies proportionality and additivity—there can be no products or powers of decision variables.

5. Parameters

6. Linearity

7. Nonnegativity

Linear programming is an *optimization* process. A single **objective function** states mathematically what is being maximized (e.g., profit or present value) or minimized (e.g., cost or scrap). The objective function provides the scorecard on which the attractiveness of different solutions is judged.

Decision variables represent choices that the decision maker can control. Solving the problem yields their optimal values. For example, a decision variable could be the number of units of a product to make next month or the number of units of inventory to hold next month. Linear programming is based on the assumption that decision variables are *continuous*—they can be fractional quantities and need not be whole numbers. Often, this assumption is realistic, as when the decision variable is expressed in dollars, hours, or some other continuous measure. Even when the decision variables represent nondivisible units such as workers, tables, or trucks, we sometimes can simply round the linear programming solution up or down to get a reasonable solution that does not violate any constraints, or we can use a more advanced technique, called *integer programming*.

Constraints are limitations that restrict the permissible choices for the decision variables. Each limitation can be expressed mathematically in one of three ways: a less-than-or-equal-to ($\leq$), equal-to ($=$), or greater-than-or-equal-to ($\geq$) constraint. A $\leq$ constraint puts an upper limit on some function of decision variables and most often is used with maximization problems. For example, a $\leq$ constraint may specify the maximum number of customers who can be served or the capacity limit of a machine. An $=$ constraint means that the function must equal some value. For example, 100 (not 99 or 101) units of one product must be made. An $=$ constraint often is used for certain mandatory relationships, such as the fact that ending inventory always equals beginning inventory plus production minus sales. A $\geq$ constraint puts a lower limit on some function of decision variables. For example, a $\geq$ constraint may specify that production of a product must exceed or equal demand.

Every linear programming problem must have one or more constraints. Taken together, the constraints define a **feasible region**, which represents all permissible combinations of the decision variables. In some unusual situations, the problem is so tightly constrained that there is only one possible solution—or perhaps none. However, in the usual case the feasibility region contains infinitely many possible solutions, assuming that the feasible combinations of the decision variables can be fractional values. The goal of the decision maker is to find the best possible solution.

The objective function and constraints are functions of decision variables and parameters. A **parameter**, also known as a *coefficient* or *given constant*, is a value that the decision maker cannot control and that doesn't change when the solution is implemented. Each parameter is assumed to be known with **certainty**. For example, a computer programmer may know that running a software program will take three hours—no more, no less.

The objective function and constraint equations are assumed to be linear. **Linearity** implies proportionality and additivity—there can be no products (e.g., $10x_1x_2$) or powers (e.g., x_1^3) of decision variables. Suppose that the profit gained by producing two types of products (represented by decision variables x_1 and x_2) is $2x_1 + 3x_2$. Proportionality implies that one unit of x_1 contributes \$2 to profits and two units contribute \$4, regardless of how much of x_2 is produced. Similarly, each unit of x_2 contributes \$3, whether it is the first or the tenth unit produced. Additivity means that the total objective function value equals the profits from x_1 plus the profits from x_2.

nonnegativity An assumption that the decision variables must be either positive or zero.

Finally, we make an assumption of **nonnegativity,** which means that the decision variables must be positive or zero. A firm making spaghetti sauce, for example, cannot produce a negative number of jars. To be formally correct, a linear programming formulation should show a ≥ 0 constraint for each decision variable.

Although the assumptions of linearity, certainty, and continuous variables are restrictive, linear programming can help managers analyze many complex resource allocation problems. The process of building the model forces managers to identify the important decision variables and constraints, a useful step in its own right. Identifying the nature and scope of the problem represents a major step toward solving it. In a later section, we show how sensitivity analysis can help the manager deal with uncertainties in the parameters and answer "what-if" questions.

FORMULATING A PROBLEM

Linear programming applications begin with the formulation of a *model* of the problem with the general characteristics just described. We illustrate the modeling process here with the **product-mix problem**—a one-period type of aggregate planning problem, the solution of which yields optimal output quantities (or product mix) of a group of products or services, subject to resource capacity and market demand constraints. Formulating a model to represent each unique problem, using the following three-step sequence, is the most creative and perhaps the most difficult part of linear programming.

product-mix problem A one-period type of aggregate planning problem, the solution of which yields optimal output quantities (or product mix) of a group of products or services, subject to resource capacity and market demand constraints.

Step 1. Define the Decision Variables. What must be decided? Define each decision variable specifically, remembering that the definitions used in the objective function must be equally useful in the constraints. The definitions should be as specific as possible. Consider the following two alternative definitions:

x_1 = product 1

x_1 = number of units of product 1 to be produced and sold next month

The second definition is much more specific than the first, making the remaining steps easier.

Step 2. Write Out the Objective Function. What is to be maximized or minimized? If it is next month's profits, write out an objective function that makes next month's profits a linear function of the decision variables. Identify parameters to go with each decision variable. For example, if each unit of x_1 sold yields a profit of \$7, the total profit from product $x_1 = 7x_1$. If a variable has no impact on the objective function, its objective function coefficient is 0. The objective function often is set equal to Z, and the goal is to maximize or minimize Z.

Step 3. Write Out the Constraints. What limits the values of the decision variables? Identify the constraints and the parameters for each decision variable in them. As with the objective function, the parameter for a variable that has no impact in a constraint is 0. To be formally correct, also write out the nonnegativity constraints.

As a consistency check, make sure that the same unit of measure is being used on both sides of each constraint and in the objective function. For example, suppose that the right-hand side of a constraint is hours of capacity per month. Then if a decision variable on the left-hand side of the constraint measures the number of units produced per month, the dimensions of the parameter that is multiplied by the decision variable must be hours per unit because

$$\left(\frac{\text{hours}}{\text{unit}} \right)\left(\frac{\cancel{\text{units}}}{\text{month}} \right) = \left(\frac{\text{hours}}{\text{month}} \right)$$

Of course, you can also skip around from one step to another, depending on the part of the problem that has your attention. If you cannot get past step 1, try a new set of definitions for the decision variables. There may be more than one way to model a problem correctly.

| EXAMPLE F.1 | *Formulating a Linear Programming Model* |

The Stratton Company produces two basic types of plastic pipe. Three resources are crucial to the output of pipe: extrusion hours, packaging hours, and a special additive to the plastic raw material. The following data represent next week's situation. All data are expressed in units of 100 feet of pipe.

| | PRODUCT | | RESOURCE |
RESOURCE	Type 1	Type 2	AVAILABILITY
Extrusion	4 hr	6 hr	48 hr
Packaging	2 hr	2 hr	18 hr
Additive mix	2 lb	1 lb	16 lb

The contribution to profits and overhead per 100 feet of pipe is $34 for type 1 and $40 for type 2. Formulate a linear programming model to determine how much of each type of pipe should be produced to maximize contribution to profits and to overhead.

SOLUTION

Step 1. To define the decision variables that determine product mix, we let

x_1 = amount of type 1 pipe to be produced and sold next week,
measured in 100-foot increments (e.g., $x_1 = 2$ means 200 feet of type 1 pipe)

and

x_2 = amount of type 2 pipe to be produced and sold next week,
measured in 100-foot increments

Step 2. Next, we define the objective function. The goal is to maximize the total contribution that the two products make to profits and overhead. Each unit of x_1 yields $34, and each unit of x_2 yields $40. For specific values of x_1 and x_2, we find the total profit by multiplying the number of units of each product produced by the profit per unit and adding them. Thus, our objective function becomes

$$\text{Maximize:} \quad \$34x_1 + \$40x_2 = Z$$

Step 3. The final step is to formulate the constraints. Each unit of x_1 and x_2 produced consumes some of the critical resources. In the extrusion department, a unit of x_1 requires 4 hours and a unit of x_2 requires 6 hours. The total must not exceed the 48 hours of capacity available, so we use the ≤ sign. Thus, the first constraint is

$$4x_1 + 6x_2 \leq 48 \quad \text{(extrusion)}$$

Similarly, we can formulate constraints for packaging and raw materials:

$$2x_1 + 2x_2 \leq 18 \quad \text{(packaging)}$$
$$2x_1 + x_2 \leq 16 \quad \text{(additive mix)}$$

These three constraints restrict our choice of values for the decision variables because the values we choose for x_1 and x_2 must satisfy all of them. Negative values for x_1 and x_2 don't make sense, so we add nonnegativity restrictions to the model:

$$x_1 \geq 0 \quad \text{and} \quad x_2 \geq 0 \quad \text{(nonnegativity restrictions)}$$

We can now state the entire model, made complete with the definitions of variables.

$$\text{Maximize:} \quad \$34x_1 + \$40x_2 = Z$$
$$\text{Subject to:} \quad 4x_1 + 6x_2 \leq 48$$
$$2x_1 + 2x_2 \leq 18$$
$$2x_1 + x_2 \leq 16$$
$$x_1 \geq 0 \quad \text{and} \quad x_2 \geq 0$$

where

x_1 = amount of type 1 pipe to be produced and sold next week, measured in 100-foot increments

x_2 = amount of type 2 pipe to be produced and sold next week, measured in 100-foot increments □

GRAPHIC ANALYSIS

graphic method of linear programming A type of graphic analysis involving the following five steps: plotting the constraints; identifying the feasible region; plotting an objective function line; finding a visual solution; and finding the algebraic solution.

With the model formulated, we now seek the optimal solution. In practice, most linear programming problems are solved with the computer. However, insight into the meaning of the computer output—and linear programming concepts in general—can be gained by analyzing a simple two-variable problem with the **graphic method of linear programming**. Hence, we begin with the graphic method, even though it is not a practical technique for solving problems having three or more decision variables. The five basic steps are

1. plot the constraints,
2. identify the feasible region,
3. plot an objective function line,
4. find the visual solution, and
5. find the algebraic solution.

PLOT THE CONSTRAINTS

We begin by plotting the constraint equations, disregarding the inequality portion of the constraints ($<$ or $>$). Making each constraint an equality ($=$) transforms it into the equation for a straight line. The line can be drawn as soon as we identify two points on it. Any two points reasonably spread out may be chosen; the easiest ones to find are the *axis intercepts,* where the line intersects each axis. To find the x_1 axis intercept, set x_2 equal to 0 and solve the equation for x_1. For the Stratton Company in Example F.1, the equation of the line for the extrusion process is

$$4x_1 + 6x_2 = 48$$

For the x_1 axis intercept, $x_2 = 0$ and so

$$4x_1 + 6(0) = 48$$
$$x_1 = 12$$

To find the x_2 axis intercept, set $x_1 = 0$ and solve for x_2:

$$4(0) + 6x_2 = 48$$
$$x_2 = 8$$

We connect points (0, 8) and (12, 0) with a straight line, as shown in Figure F.1.

FIGURE F.1

*Graph of the Extrusion
Constraint*

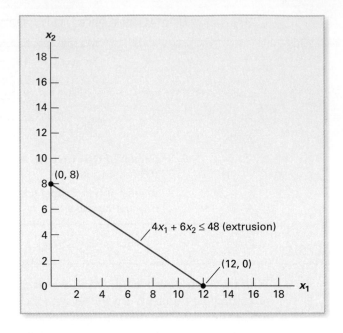

EXAMPLE F.2

Plotting the Constraints

TUTOR
F.1

For the Stratton Company problem, plot the other constraints: one for packaging and one for the
additive mix.

SOLUTION

The equation for the packaging process's line is $2x_1 + 2x_2 = 18$. To find the x_1 intercept, set
$x_2 = 0$:

$$2x_1 + 2(0) = 18$$

$$x_1 = 9$$

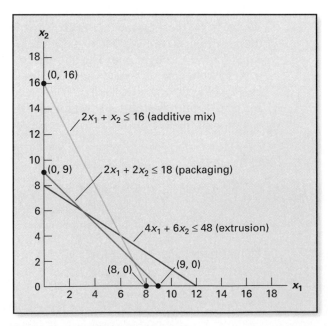

FIGURE F.2 • Graph of the Three Constraints

To find the x_2 axis intercept, set $x_1 = 0$:

$$2(0) + 2x_2 = 18$$
$$x_2 = 9$$

The equation for the additive mix's line is $2x_1 + x_2 = 16$. To find the x_1 intercept, set $x_2 = 0$:

$$2x_1 + 0 = 16$$
$$x_1 = 8$$

To find the x_2 axis intercept, set $x_1 = 0$:

$$2(0) + x_2 = 16$$
$$x_2 = 16$$

With a straight line, we connect points $(0, 9)$ and $(9, 0)$ for the packaging constraint and points $(0, 16)$ and $(8, 0)$ for the additive mix constraint. Figure F.2 shows the graph with all three constraints plotted. ◻

IDENTIFY THE FEASIBLE REGION

The feasible region is the area on the graph that contains the solutions that satisfy all the constraints simultaneously, including the nonnegativity restrictions. To find the feasible region, locate first the feasible points for each constraint and then the area that satisfies all constraints. *Generally* the following three rules identify the feasible points for a given constraint:

1. For the $=$ constraint, only the points on the line are feasible solutions.
2. For the $\leq$ constraint, the points on the line and the points below or to the left are feasible solutions.
3. For the $\geq$ constraint, the points on the line and the points above or to the right are feasible solutions.

Exceptions to these rules occur when one or more of the parameters on the left-hand side of a constraint are negative. In such cases, we draw the constraint line and test a point on one side of it. If the point does not satisfy the constraint, it is in the infeasible part of the graph. Suppose that a linear programming model has the following five constraints plus the nonnegativity constraints:

$$2x_1 + x_2 \geq 10$$
$$2x_1 + 3x_2 \geq 18$$
$$x_1 \leq 7$$
$$x_2 \leq 5$$
$$-6x_1 + 5x_2 \leq 5$$
$$x_1, x_2 \geq 0$$

The feasible region is the shaded portion of Figure F.3. The arrows shown on each constraint identify which side of each line is feasible. The rules work for all but the fifth constraint, which has a negative parameter, -6, for x_1. We arbitrarily select $(2, 2)$ as the test point, which Figure F.3 shows is below the line and to the right. At this point, we find $-6(2) + 5(2) = -2$. Because -2 does not exceed 5, the portion of the figure containing $(2, 2)$ is feasible, at least for this fifth constraint.

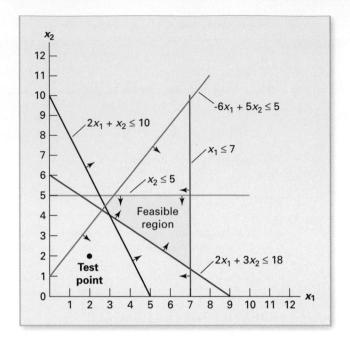

EXAMPLE F.3

Identifying the Feasible Region

Identify the feasible region for the Stratton Company problem.

SOLUTION

Because there are only ≤ constraints and the parameters on the left-hand side of each constraint are not negative, the feasible portions are to the left of and below each constraint. The feasible region, shaded in Figure F.4, satisfies all three constraints simultaneously. ◻

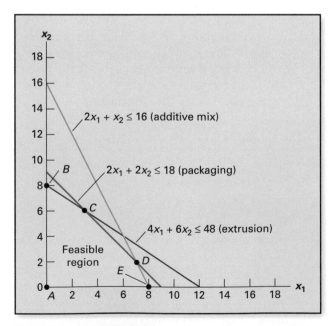

FIGURE F.4 • The Feasible Region

PLOT AN OBJECTIVE FUNCTION LINE

Now we want to find the solution that optimizes the objective function. Even though all the points in the feasible region represent possible solutions, we can limit our search to the corner points. A **corner point** lies at the intersection of two (or possibly more) constraint lines on the boundary of the feasible region. No interior points in the feasible region need be considered because at least one corner point is better than any interior point. Similarly, other points on the boundary of the feasible region can be ignored because there is a corner point that is at least as good as any of them.

corner point A point that lies at the intersection of two (or possibly more) constraint lines on the boundary of the feasible region.

In Figure F.4, the five corner points are marked *A, B, C, D,* and *E*. Point *A* is the origin $(0, 0)$ and can be ignored because any other feasible point is a better solution. We could try each of the other corner points in the objective function and select the one that maximizes *Z*. For example, corner point *B* lies at $(0, 8)$. If we substitute these values into the objective function, the resulting *Z* value is 320:

$$34x_1 + 40x_2 = Z$$
$$34(0) + 40(8) = 320$$

However, we may not be able to read accurately the values of x_1 and x_2 for some of the points (e.g., *C* or *D*) on the graph. Algebraically solving two linear equations for each corner point also is inefficient when there are many constraints and thus many corner points.

The best approach is to plot the objective function on the graph of the feasible region for some arbitrary *Z* values. From these objective function lines, we can spot the best solution visually. If the objective function is profits, each line is called an *iso-profit line* and every point on that line will yield the same profit. If *Z* measures cost, the line is called an *iso-cost line* and every point on it represents the same cost. We can simplify the search by plotting the first line in the feasible region—somewhere near the optimal solution, we hope. For the Stratton Company example, let us pass a line through point *E* $(8, 0)$. This point is a corner point. It might even be the optimal solution because it is far from the origin. To draw the line, we first identify its *Z* value as $34(8) + 40(0) = 272$. Therefore, the equation for the objective function line passing through *E* is

$$34x_1 + 40x_2 = 272$$

Every point on the line defined by this equation has an objective function *Z* value of 272. To draw the line, we need to identify a second point on it and then connect the two points. Let us use the x_2 intercept, where $x_1 = 0$:

$$34(0) + 40x_2 = 272$$
$$x_2 = 6.8$$

Figure F.5 shows the iso-profit line that connects points $(8, 0)$ and $(0, 6.8)$. A series of other dashed lines could be drawn parallel to this first one. Each would have its own *Z* value. Lines above the first one we drew would have higher *Z* values. Lines below it would have lower *Z* values.

FIND THE VISUAL SOLUTION

We now eliminate corner points *A* and *E* from consideration as the optimal solution because better points lie above and to the right of the $Z = 272$ iso-profit line. Our goal is to maximize profits, so the best solution is a point on the iso-profit line *farthest* from the origin but still touching the feasible region. (For minimization problems, it is a point in the feasible region on the iso-cost line *closest* to the origin.) To identify which

*Passing an Iso-Profit
Line Through (8, 0)*

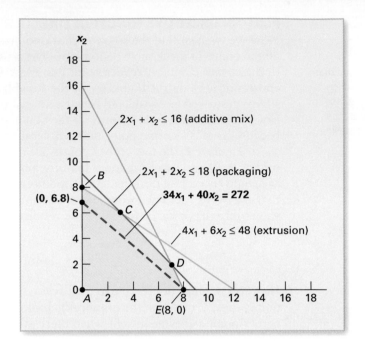

of the remaining corner points is optimal (*B*, *C*, or *D*), we draw, parallel to the first line, one or more iso-profit lines that give better *Z* values (higher for maximization and lower for minimization). The line that just touches the feasible region identifies the optimal solution. For the Stratton Company problem, Figure F.6 shows the second iso-profit line. The optimal solution is the last point touching the feasible region: point *C*. It appears to be in the vicinity of (3, 6), but the visual solution is not exact.

A linear programming problem can have more than one optimal solution. This situation occurs when the objective function is parallel to one of the faces of the feasible

*Drawing the Second
Iso-Profit Line*

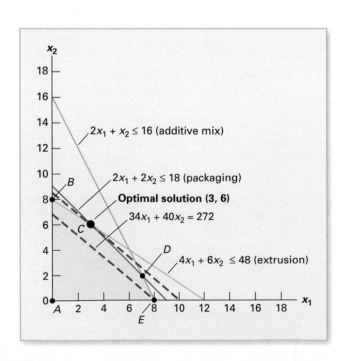

region. Such would be the case if our objective function in the Stratton Company problem were $\$38x_1 + \$38x_2$. Points (3, 6) and (7, 2) would be optimal, as would any other point on the line connecting these two corner points. In such a case, management probably would base a final decision on nonquantifiable factors. It is important to understand, however, that we need to consider only the corner points of the feasible region when optimizing an objective function.

FIND THE ALGEBRAIC SOLUTION

To find an exact solution, we must use algebra. We begin by identifying the pair of constraints that define the corner point at their intersection. We then list the constraints as equations and solve them simultaneously to find the coordinates (x_1, x_2) of the corner point. Simultaneous equations can be solved several ways. For small problems the easiest way is as follows:

Step 1. Develop an equation with just one unknown. Start by multiplying both sides of one equation by a constant so that the coefficient for one of the two decision variables is *identical* in both equations. Then subtract one equation from the other and solve the resulting equation for its single unknown variable.

Step 2. Insert this decision variable's value into either one of the original constraints and solve for the other decision variable.

| EXAMPLE F.4 | *Finding the Optimal Solution Algebracially* |

**TUTOR
F.2**

Find the optimal solution algebraically for the Stratton Company problem. What is the value of Z when the decision variables have optimal values?

SOLUTION

Step 1. Figure F.6 shows that the optimal corner point lies at the intersection of the extrusion and packaging constraints. Listing the constraints as equalities, we have

$$4x_1 + 6x_2 = 48 \qquad \text{(extrusion)}$$
$$2x_1 + 2x_2 = 18 \qquad \text{(packaging)}$$

We multiply each term in the packaging constraint by 2. The packaging constraint now is $4x_1 + 4x_2 = 36$. Next, we subtract the packaging constraint from the extrusion constraint. The result will be an equation from which x_1 has dropped out. (Alternatively, we could multiply the second equation by 3 so that x_2 drops out after the subtraction.) Thus,

$$\begin{aligned} 4x_1 + 6x_2 &= 48 \\ -(4x_1 + 4x_2 &= 36) \\ \hline 2x_2 &= 12 \\ x_2 &= 6 \end{aligned}$$

Step 2. Substituting the value of x_2 into the extrusion equation, we get

$$4x_1 + 6(6) = 48$$
$$4x_1 = 12$$
$$x_1 = 3$$

Thus, the optimal point is (3, 6). This solution gives a total profit of $34(3) + 40(6) = \$342$.

Decision Point Management at the Stratton Company decided to produce 300 feet of type 1 pipe and 600 feet of type 2 pipe for the next week. ▫

SLACK AND SURPLUS VARIABLES

Figure F.6 shows that the optimal product mix will exhaust all the extrusion and packaging resources because at the optimal corner point (3, 6) the two constraints are equalities. Substituting the values of x_1 and x_2 into these constraints shows that the left-hand sides equal the right-hand sides:

$$4(3) + 6(6) = 48 \qquad \text{(extrusion)}$$
$$2(3) + 2(6) = 18 \qquad \text{(packaging)}$$

binding constraint A constraint that helps form the optimal corner point; it limits the ability to improve the objective function.

A constraint (such as the one for extrusion) that helps form the optimal corner point is called a **binding constraint** because it limits the ability to improve the objective function. If a binding constraint is *relaxed*, or made less restrictive, a better solution is possible. Relaxing a constraint means increasing the right-hand-side parameter for a $\leq$ constraint or decreasing it for a $\geq$ constraint. No improvement is possible from relaxing a constraint that is not binding, such as the additive mix constraint in Figure F.6. If the right-hand side were increased from 16 to 17 and the problem solved again, the optimal solution would not change. In other words, there is already more additive mix than needed.

For nonbinding inequality constraints, knowing how much the left and right sides differ is helpful. Such information tells us how close the constraint is to becoming binding. For a $\leq$ constraint, the amount by which the left-hand side falls short of the right-hand side is called **slack**. For a $\geq$ constraint, the amount by which the left-hand side exceeds the right-hand side is called **surplus**. To find the slack for a $\leq$ constraint algebraically, we *add* a slack variable to the constraint and convert it to an equality. Then we substitute in the values of the decision variables and solve for the slack. For example, the additive mix constraint in Figure F.6, $2x_1 + x_2 \leq 16$, can be rewritten by adding slack variable s_1:

slack The amount by which the left-hand side falls short of the right-hand side.

surplus The amount by which the left-hand side exceeds the right-hand side.

$$2x_1 + x_2 + s_1 = 16$$

We then find the slack at the optimal solution (3, 6):

$$2(3) + 6 + s_1 = 16$$
$$s_1 = 4$$

TUTOR
F.3

The procedure is much the same to find the surplus for a $\geq$ constraint, except that we *subtract* a surplus variable from the left-hand side. Suppose that $x_1 + x_2 \geq 6$ was another constraint in the Stratton Company problem, representing a lower bound on the number of units produced. We would then rewrite the constraint by subtracting a surplus variable s_2:

$$x_1 + x_2 - s_2 = 6$$

The slack at the optimal solution (3, 6) would be

$$3 + 6 - s_2 = 6$$
$$s_2 = 3$$

SENSITIVITY ANALYSIS

Rarely are the parameters in the objective function and constraints known with certainty. Often they are just estimates of actual values. For example, the available packaging and extrusion hours for the Stratton Company are estimates that do not reflect the uncertainties associated with absenteeism or personnel transfers, and the required hours per unit to package and extrude may be work standards that essentially are averages. Likewise, profit contributions used for the objective function coefficients do not reflect uncertainties in selling prices and such variable costs as wages, raw materials, and shipping.

Despite such uncertainties, initial estimates are needed to solve the problem. Accounting, marketing, and work-standard information systems often provide these initial estimates. After solving the problem using these estimated values, the analyst can determine how much the optimal values of the decision variables and the objective function value Z would be affected if certain parameters had different values. This type of postsolution analysis for answering "what-if" questions is called *sensitivity analysis*.

One way of conducting sensitivity analysis for linear programming problems is the brute-force approach of changing one or more parameter values and re-solving the entire problem. This approach may be acceptable for small problems but is inefficient if there are many parameters. For example, brute-force sensitivity analysis using 3 separate values for each of 20 objective function coefficients requires 3^{20}, or 3,486,784,401, separate solutions! Fortunately, efficient methods are available for getting sensitivity information without re-solving the entire problem, and they are routinely used in most linear programming computer software packages. Here, we do sensitivity analysis on the objective function coefficients and the right-hand-side parameters of the constraints for a one-parameter-at-a-time change.

OBJECTIVE FUNCTION COEFFICIENTS

We begin sensitivity analysis on the objective function of a two-variable problem by calculating the slope of the iso-profit (or iso-cost) lines. The equation of any straight line can be written as $y = mx + b$, where m is the slope of the line. In our graphic solution in Figure F.6, we used x_2 rather than y, and x_1 rather than x. Thus, the equation that reveals a line's slope will be $x_2 = mx_1 + b$. To put the objective function in this form, we solve the objective function for x_2 in terms of x_1 and Z:

$$34x_1 + 40x_2 = Z$$
$$40x_2 = -34x_1 + Z$$
$$x_2 = -\frac{34x_1}{40} + \frac{Z}{40}$$

Thus, the slope m of the iso-profit lines for Stratton Company is $-34/40$, or -0.85. In general, it is the negative of the ratio found by dividing the objective function coefficient of x_1 by the objective function coefficient of x_2.

Now, let us see what happens when an objective function coefficient changes. We define c_1 to be the profit contribution per 100 feet of x_1 and c_2 to be the profit contribution per 100 feet of x_2. The equation of the iso-profit line becomes

$$x_2 = -\frac{c_1 x_1}{c_2} + \frac{Z}{c_2}$$

If c_1 *increases* while c_2 stays constant, the slope becomes more negative (steeper), and the line rotates clockwise. For example, if c_1 increases to \$40, the slope becomes -1.00, or $-40/40$. But if c_1 *decreases*, the slope becomes less negative and the line rotates counterclockwise. If the reduction is substantial enough, the slope of the objective function will equal the slope of the extrusion constraint. When this happens, point B becomes an optimal corner point. If c_1 instead increases so that the slope of the objective function becomes more negative than the slope of the packaging constraint, corner point D becomes optimal. Similar conclusions also can be drawn about changes in c_2.

Finding the Range of Optimality

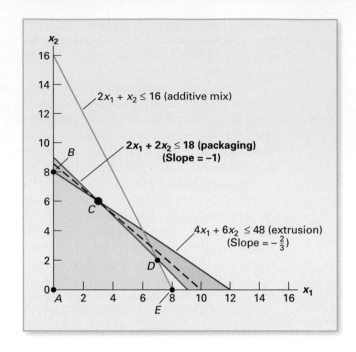

RANGE OF OPTIMALITY. If the objective function coefficient makes the slope of the objective function greater than the slope of the packaging constraint but less than the slope of the extrusion constraint, point C remains the optimal solution. In Figure F.7, the area between the two binding constraints, extrusion and packaging, is shaded. Note that point C remains optimal if the objective function slope is greater than -1.00, the slope of the packaging constraint, and less than $-2/3$, the slope of the extrusion constraint. Thus, the following relationship holds:

$$-1 \leq -\frac{c_1}{c_2} \leq -\frac{2}{3}$$

We use this relationship to find the range over which c_1 can vary without changing the optimality of point C, holding c_2 constant at $40:

$$-1 \leq -\frac{c_1}{40} \leq -\frac{2}{3}$$

Because we seek the range for c_1, rather than $-c_1/40$, we multiply by -40. Multiplying by a negative number reverses the direction of the inequalities, so we get

$$40 \geq c_1 \geq 26.67$$

Rearranging terms for ease of reading yields

$$26.67 \leq c_1 \leq 40$$

range of optimality The lower and upper limit over which the optimal values of the decision variables remain unchanged.

Thus, the objective function coefficient for x_1 ranges from a *lower limit* of $26.67 through an *upper limit* of $40. This **range of optimality** defines a lower and upper limit over which the optimal values of the decision variables remain unchanged. Of course, the value of Z would change as c_1 changed. For example, if c_1 increased from $34 to $40, the value of Z at point C would become 360:

$$40x_1 + 40x_2 = Z$$
$$40(3) + 40(6) = 360$$

| EXAMPLE F.5 | *Finding the Range of Optimality for c_2* |

What is the range of optimality for c_2 in the Stratton Company problem?

SOLUTION

If we hold c_1 constant at \$34, the relationship for the slope of the iso-profit lines is

$$-1 \leq -\frac{34}{c_2} \leq -\frac{2}{3}$$

Because c_2 is in the denominator, defining one limit at a time is easiest. For the limit on the left, we get

$$-1 \leq -\frac{34}{c_2}$$

Multiplying by $-c_2$, we find the lower limit:

$$c_2 \geq 34$$

Now, taking the second relationship on the right, we have

$$-\frac{34}{c_2} \leq -\frac{2}{3}$$

Multiplying by $-c_2$, we obtain the upper limit:

$$34 \geq \frac{2c_2}{3}$$

$$51 \geq c_2$$

Putting both limits into one final expression, we find that c_2 can be as low as \$34 or as high as \$51 without changing the optimality of point C, or

$$34 \leq c_2 \leq 51 \quad \square$$

COEFFICIENT SENSITIVITY. In the Stratton Company problem, the optimal point makes both decision variables greater than 0 (3 and 6). If c_1 were low enough (below 26.67), point B would be optimal, and the optimal value of x_1 would be 0. Sensitivity analysis can give us additional information about variables that have optimal values of 0. **Coefficient sensitivity** measures how much the objective function coefficient of such a decision variable must *improve* (increase for maximization or decrease for minimization) before the optimal solution changes and the decision variable becomes some positive number. The coefficient sensitivity for c_1 can be found in the following manner:

coefficient sensitivity
The measurement of how much the objective function coefficient of a decision variable must improve (increase for maximization or decrease for minimization) before the optimal solution changes and the decision variable becomes some positive number.

Step 1. Identify the direction of rotation (clockwise or counterclockwise) of the iso-profit (or iso-cost) line that improves c_1. Rotate the iso-profit (or iso-cost) line in this direction until it reaches a new optimal corner point that makes x_1 greater than 0.

Step 2. Determine which binding constraint has the same slope as the rotated iso-profit (or iso-cost) line at this new point. Solve for the value of c_1 that makes the objective function slope equal to the slope of this binding constraint.

Step 3. Set the coefficient sensitivity equal to the difference between this value and the current value of c_1.

| EXAMPLE F.6 | *Finding the Coefficient Sensitivity for a Revised Problem* |

Suppose that the Stratton Company problem is changed so that c_1 is $20 rather than $34. Figure F.8 shows that the highest iso-profit line now passes through point B, making it the optimal solution rather than point C. At point B, the optimal value of x_1 is 0. What is the coefficient sensitivity for c_1?

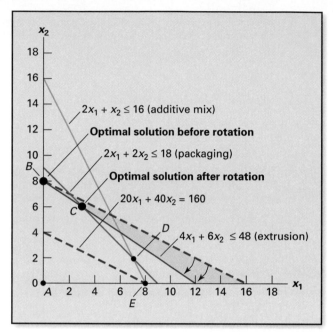

FIGURE F.8 • Coefficient Sensitivity for the Revised Problem

SOLUTION

We apply the three solution steps to the revised Stratton problem.

Step 1. This is a maximization problem, so c_1 improves as it *increases*. Increasing c_1 rotates the iso-profit line clockwise. Rotation continues until point C is reached—a corner point that makes x_1 a positive number (3).

Step 2. The binding constraint that has the same slope is extrusion. Solving for the c_1 that makes the two slopes equal, we get

$$-\frac{c_1}{40} = -\frac{2}{3}$$
$$c_1 = 26.67$$

Step 3. The coefficient sensitivity is $6.67, or $26.67 − $20.

Therefore, c_1 must increase by $6.67 before it is optimal to make x_1 greater than 0. ❑

RIGHT-HAND-SIDE PARAMETERS

Now consider how a change in the right-hand-side parameter for a constraint may affect the feasible region and perhaps cause a change in the optimal solution. Let us return to the original Stratton Company problem, changing c_1 back from $20 to $34. However, we now consider adding one more hour to the packaging resource, increasing it from 18 to 19 hours.

Enlarging the Feasible Region by Relaxing the Packaging Constraint by One Hour

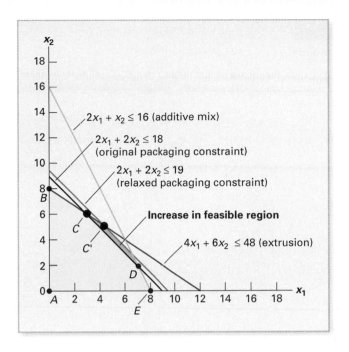

SHADOW PRICES. As Figure F.9 demonstrates, this change expands the feasible region, and the optimal solution changes from point C to point C'. Point C' is better in terms of Z because the added unit of a binding constraint will be used to make more product. To find the amount of improvement, we first find the new values of x_1 and x_2 by simultaneously solving the two binding constraints at point C', where

$$4x_1 + 6x_2 = 48 \qquad \text{(extrusion)}$$
$$2x_1 + 2x_2 = 19 \qquad \text{(packaging)}$$

The optimal values are $x_1 = 4.5$ and $x_2 = 5$, and the new Z value is $34(4.5) + \$40(5) = \$353$. Because the value of Z was $342 with 18 hours of packaging, the value of one more hour of packaging is $11 (or $353 − $342).

The change in Z per unit of change in the value of the right-hand-side parameter of a constraint is called the shadow price. The **shadow price** is the marginal *improvement* in Z (increase for maximization and decrease for minimization) caused by relaxing the constraint by one unit. Relaxation means making the constraint less restrictive, which involves increasing the right-hand side for a $\leq$ constraint or decreasing it for a $\geq$ constraint. The shadow price also is the marginal loss in Z caused by making the constraint more restrictive by one unit. In our example, the shadow price for the packaging resource is $11 per hour. Thus, if scheduling additional packaging hours is possible, Stratton's management should be willing to pay a premium of up to $11 per hour over and above the normal cost for a packaging hour. However, if capacity is cut by one hour, profits will fall by $11.

shadow price The marginal improvement in Z (increase for maximization and decrease for minimization) caused by relaxing the constraint by one unit.

range of feasibility The interval over which the right-hand side parameter can vary while its shadow price remains valid.

RANGE OF FEASIBILITY.   A lower limit and an upper limit define the **range of feasibility**, which is the interval over which the right-hand-side parameter can vary while its shadow price remains valid. If the right-hand side is increased beyond the upper limit or reduced beyond the lower limit, at least one other constraint becomes binding, which in turn alters the rate of change in Z. These two limits are established when, as

Defining the Upper and Lower Limits to Packaging's Range of Feasibility

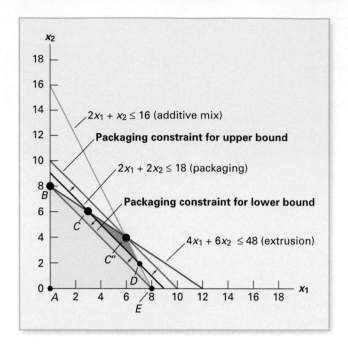

the constraint line is relaxed or tightened, a new corner point on the feasible region is reached that makes a different constraint binding.

With 18 packaging hours, the optimal solution for the Stratton Company is $x_1 = 3$, $x_2 = 6$, 4 pounds of slack in the additive mix, and 0 slack for the other two constraints. We found that each additional packaging hour would increase profit by $11 (minus any premium cost of adding this additional capacity). Similarly, one fewer packaging hour would reduce profits by $11. However, $11 is the shadow price over a limited range of packaging hours. Let's begin by finding the *upper* limit over which this shadow price is valid. Figure F.10 shows the packaging constraint being relaxed and shifted to the right, away from the origin. When it reaches point C'', where it intersects the extrusion and additive mix constraints, the additive mix constraint and the extrusion constraint become binding. Until the packaging constraint reaches C'', relaxing it will expand the feasible region, as shown by the pink shading in the feasible region. With this expansion comes the improvement in Z, which is $11 per packaging hour added. However, any increase in packaging hours beyond what is used at point C'' will be worth $0 because the constraint will no longer be binding.

To find how many hours are used at point C'', we solve the additive mix and extrusion constraints simultaneously because C'' lies at their intersection. Doing so, we get $x_1 = 6$ and $x_2 = 4$. Substituting these values into the packaging constraint, we find that the upper limit on the shadow price of $11 is 20 packaging hours, or $2(6) + 2(4) = 20$.

Finding the Lower Limit on the $11 Shadow Price

What is the lower limit on the $11 shadow price for packaging hours?

SOLUTION

Figure F.10 shows that reducing the packaging hours shifts the constraint to the left, toward the origin, reducing the feasible region and, thus, the value of Z. Eventually the constraint reaches corner point B, defined by the extrusion constraint and the x_1 nonnegativity constraint. Because a new constraint is binding (the x_1 nonnegativity constraint), B defines the lower limit on packaging's shadow price. We found earlier that, at point B, $x_1 = 0$ and $x_2 = 8$. Substituting these values into the packaging constraint, we determine the *lower* limit on the shadow price of $11 to be 16 packaging hours, or $2(0) + 2(8) = 16$. ◻

In some cases, there may be no lower or upper limit to the range of feasibility. The additive mix constraint provides one example. Figure F.6 shows that this constraint is not binding. Shifting the constraint upward still more does not expand the feasible region or improve Z. Thus, the shadow price of the additive mix is $0. The right-hand side can be increased without limit—to infinity—and the shadow price remains at $0.

The additive mix constraint illustrates a final principle that always holds: When a constraint's slack or surplus variable is greater than 0, its shadow price is 0. In every optimal solution, either a constraint's slack (or surplus) variable is 0 or its shadow price is 0. For the additive mix, with its shadow price of $0, there are 4 pounds of slack at the optimal point C. Because $x_1 = 3$ and $x_2 = 6$ at C, only $2(3) + 1(6) = 12$ pounds of the additive mix are needed. The slack is 4 pounds ($16 - 12$), because 16 pounds of the mix are available.

COMPUTER SOLUTION

simplex method An iterative algebraic procedure for solving linear programming problems.

Most real-world linear programming problems are solved on a computer, so we concentrate here on understanding the use of linear programming and the logic on which it is based. The solution procedure in computer codes is some form of the **simplex method,** an iterative algebraic procedure for solving linear programming problems.

SIMPLEX METHOD

The graphic analysis gives insight into the logic of the simplex method, beginning with the focus on corner points. One corner point will always be the optimum, even when there are multiple optimal solutions. Thus, the simplex method starts with an initial corner point and then systematically evaluates other corner points in such a way that the objective function improves (or, at worst, stays the same) at each iteration. In the Stratton Company problem, an improvement would be an increase in profits. When no more improvements are possible, the optimal solution has been found.[1] The simplex method also helps generate the sensitivity analysis information that we developed graphically.

Each corner point has no more than m variables that are greater than 0, where m is the number of constraints (not counting the nonnegativity constraints). The m variables include slack and surplus variables, not just the original decision variables. Because of this property, we can find a corner point by simultaneously solving m constraints, where all but m variables are set equal to 0. For example, point B in Figure F.6 has three nonzero variables: x_2, the slack variable for packaging, and the slack variable for the additive mix. Their values can be found by solving simultaneously the three constraints, with x_1 and the slack variable for extrusion equal to 0. After finding this corner point, the simplex method applies information similar to the coefficient sensitivity to decide which new corner point to find next that gives an even better Z value. It continues in this way until no better corner point is possible. The final corner point evaluated is the optimal one.

---

[1] For more information on how to perform the simplex method manually, see Cook and Russell (1993) or any other current textbook on management science.

COMPUTER OUTPUT

Computer programs dramatically reduce the amount of time required to solve linear programming problems. Special-purpose programs can be developed for applications that must be repeated frequently. Such programs simplify data input and generate the objective function and constraints for the problem. In addition, they can prepare customized managerial reports.

The capabilities and displays of software packages are not uniform. For example, OM Explorer can handle small- to medium-sized linear programming problems. It relies on Microsoft's *Excel Solver* to find the optimal solutions, and, thus, Excel's "Solver Add-In" must be installed to use OM Explorer's linear programming spreadsheet. Solving linear programming problems with OM Explorer, rather than using Excel's *Solver* directly, is more convenient for two reasons. First, inputs are easily made and nonnegativity constraints need not be entered. Second, the output's interpretation and format corresponds exactly to the graphic analysis that we just presented.

OM Explorer has three worksheets of output, which we illustrate for the Stratton Company. The output from the first two worksheets is shown in Figure F.11.

The *Inputs Worksheet* asks for the number of decision variables and constraints, and also whether it is a maximization or minimization problem. After making these inputs and clicking the Setup Problem button, the *Work Area Worksheet* is opened. The user may choose to enter labels for the decision variables, right-hand-side values, objective function, and constraints. Here, the first decision variable is labeled as "X1," the right-hand-side values as "RHV," the objective function as "Max-Z," and the extrusion constraint as "Extrusion." For convenience in specifying the type of constraint ($\leq$, $=$, or $\geq$), just enter "<" for a $\leq$ constraint, and ">" for a $\geq$ constraint. Slack and surplus variables will be added automatically as needed. When all of the inputs are made, click the "Find Optimal Solution" button.

The *Results Worksheet*, shown in Figure F.12, gives the optimal solution for the Stratton Company problem. OM Explorer begins by showing the optimal values of the decision variables (X1 = 3.0000 and X2 = 6.0000), their objective function coeffi-

FIGURE F.11

Inputs Worksheet

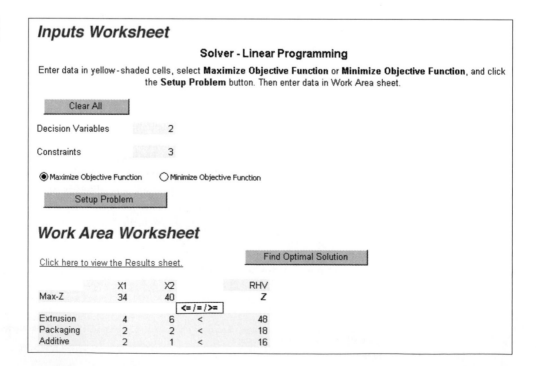

FIGURE F.12

Results Worksheet

Solver - Linear Programming

Solution

Variable Label	Variable Value	Original Coefficient	Coefficient Sensitivity
X1	3.0000	34.0000	0
X2	6.0000	40.0000	0

Constraint Label	Original RHV	Slack or Surplus	Shadow Price
Extrusion	48	0	3.0000
Packaging	18	0	11.0000
Additive	16	4	0

Objective Function Value:	342

Sensitivity Analysis and Ranges

Objective Function Coefficients

Variable Label	Lower Limit	Original Coefficient	Upper Limit
X1	26.66666667	34	40
X2	34	40	51

Right-Hand-Side Values

Constraint Label	Lower Limit	Original Value	Upper Limit
Extrusion	40	48	54
Packaging	16	18	20
Additive	12	16	No Limit

cients, and their coefficient sensitivities. There is a coefficient sensitivity number for each decision variable's objective function coefficient. Two tips on interpreting its value are

1. The sensitivity number is relevant only for a decision variable that is 0 in the optimal solution. If the decision variable is greater than 0, ignore the coefficient sensitivity number.

2. OM Explorer reports the absolute value of the coefficient sensitivity number, ignoring any minus sign. Thus, the value always tells how much the objective function coefficient must *improve* (increase for maximization problems or decrease for minimization problems) before the optimal solution would change. At that point, the decision variable associated with the coefficient

enters the optimal solution at some positive level. To learn the new solution, apply OM Explorer again with a coefficient improved by slightly more than the coefficient sensitivity number.

Thus, for the Stratton Company problem, the coefficient sensitivities provide no new insight because they are always 0 when decision variables have positive values in the optimal solution. Look instead at the lower and upper limits on the objective function coefficients, given in a following output section.

For the constraints, the output shows the original right-hand-side values, the slack or surplus variables, and the shadow prices. There is a shadow price for each right-hand-side value, or more specifically the constraint's slack or surplus variable. Two tips on interpreting its value are

1. The number is relevant only for a binding constraint, where the slack or surplus variable is 0 in the optimal solution. For a nonbinding constraint, the shadow price is 0.

2. OM Explorer reports the absolute value of the shadow price numbers, ignoring any minus sign. Thus, the value always tells how much the objective function's Z value *improves* (increases for maximization problems or decreases for minimization problems) by "relaxing" the constraint by one unit. Relaxing means increasing the right-hand-side value for a $\leq$ constraint, or decreasing it for a $\geq$ constraint. The shadow price can also be interpreted as the marginal loss (or penalty) in Z caused by making the constraint more restrictive by one unit.

Thus, for the Stratton Company problem, there are 4 pounds of the additive mix slack and so the shadow price is $0. Packaging, on the other hand, is a binding constraint because it has no slack. The shadow price of one more packaging hour is $11.

Finally, at the end of the top half of the output, OM Explorer reports the optimal objective function Z value as $342. All output confirms our earlier calculations and the graphic analysis.

The bottom half of the *Results Worksheet* begins with the range over which the objective function coefficients can vary without changing the optimal values of the decision variables. Note that c_1, which currently has a value of $34, has a range of optimality from $26.67 to $40. The objection function's Z value would change with coefficient changes over this range, but the optimal values of the decision variables themselves remain the same. Finally, OM Explorer reports the range of feasibility, over which the right-hand-side parameters can range without changing the shadow prices. For example, the $11 shadow price for packaging is valid over the range from 16 to 20 hours. Again, these findings are identical to the sensitivity analysis done graphically. The difference is that OM Explorer can handle more than two decision variables (up to 99) and can be solved much more quickly.

The number of variables in the optimal solution (counting the decision variables, slack variables, and surplus variables) that are greater than 0 never exceeds the number of constraints. Such is the case for the Stratton Company problem, where there are three constraints (not counting the implicit nonnegativity constraints) and three nonzero variables in the optimal solution (X1, X2, and the additive mix slack variable). On some rare occasions, the number of nonzero variables in the optimal solution can be less than the number of constraints—a condition is called **degeneracy**. When degeneracy occurs, the sensitivity analysis information is suspect. Ignore the sensitivity analysis portion of the OM Explorer's output that is suspect. If you want more "what-if" information, simply run OM Explorer again using the new parameter values that you want to investigate.

degeneracy A condition that occurs when the number of nonzero variables in the optimal solution is less than the number of constraints.

| EXAMPLE F.8 | *Using Shadow Prices for Decision Making* |

The Stratton Company needs answers to three important questions: Would increasing capacities in the extrusion or packaging area pay if it cost an extra $8 per hour over and above the normal costs already reflected in the objective function coefficients? Would increasing packaging capacity pay if it cost an additional $6 per hour? Would buying more raw materials pay?

SOLUTION

Expanding extrusion capacity would cost a premium of $8 per hour, but the shadow price for that capacity is only $3 per hour. However, expanding packaging hours would cost only $6 per hour more than the price reflected in the objective function, and the shadow price is $11 per hour. Finally, buying more raw materials would not pay because there is already a surplus of 4 pounds; the shadow price is 0 for that resource.

Decision Point Management decided to increase its packaging hours capacity, but not to expand extrusion capacity or buy more raw materials. ❑

APPLICATIONS

Many problems in operations management, and in other functional areas, have been modeled as linear programming problems. Knowing how to formulate a problem generally, the decision maker can then adapt it to the situation at hand.

The following list identifies some problems that can be solved with linear programming. Review problems at the end of this supplement and of other chapters illustrate many of these types of problems.

❑ **Aggregate planning**
  Production.   Find the minimum-cost production schedule, taking into account hiring and layoff, inventory-carrying, overtime, and subcontracting costs, subject to various capacity and policy constraints.
  Staffing.   Find the optimal staffing levels for various categories of workers, subject to various demand and policy constraints.
  Blends.   Find the optimal proportions of various ingredients used to make products such as gasoline, paints, and food, subject to certain minimal requirements.

❑ **Distribution**
  Shipping.   Find the optimal shipping assignments from factories to distribution centers or from warehouses to retailers.

❑ **Inventory**
  Stock Control.   Determine the optimal mix of products to hold in inventory in a warehouse.
  Supplier Selection.   Find the optimal combination of suppliers to minimize the amount of unwanted inventory.

❑ **Location**
  Plants or Warehouses.   Determine the optimal location of a plant or warehouse with respect to total transportation costs between various alternative locations and existing supply and demand sources.

❑ **Process management**
  Stock Cutting.   Given the dimensions of a roll or sheet of raw material, find the cutting pattern that minimizes the amount of scrap material.

❐ **Scheduling**

Shifts.   Determine the minimum-cost assignment of workers to shifts, subject to varying demand.

Vehicles.   Assign vehicles to products or customers and determine the number of trips to make, subject to vehicle size, vehicle availability, and demand constraints.

Routing.   Find the optimal routing of a product or service through several sequential processes, each having its own capacity and other characteristics.

SUPPLEMENT HIGHLIGHTS

❐ Linear programming is an effective tool for solving complex resource allocation problems when the objective and constraints can be approximated by linear equations. Skill and creativity often are required to model a situation with a set of linear equations. After the model has been formulated, one of several available computer programs may be used to identify the optimal solution.

❐ Although only simple linear programming problems can be solved by using graphic analysis, the technique provides valuable insight into the way optimal solutions to complex problems are generated.

❐ In addition to identifying the optimal combination of decision variables, analysis of the solution will determine shadow price, coefficient sensitivity, and ranging information. Shadow prices are the values of additional resources. Coefficient sensitivity indicates the penalties associated with nonoptimal solutions. Ranging describes either how much coefficients can change without invalidating the solution or how much of a resource can be acquired without changing the value of its shadow price.

KEY TERMS

binding constraint *704*
certainty *694*
coefficient sensitivity *707*
constraints *694*
corner point *701*
decision variables *694*
degeneracy *714*
feasible region *694*

graphic method of linear
    programming *697*
linear programming *694*
linearity *694*
nonnegativity *695*
objective function *694*
parameter *694*
product-mix problem *695*

range of feasibility *709*
range of optimality *706*
shadow price *709*
simplex method *711*
slack *704*
surplus *704*

SOLVED PROBLEM 1

**TUTOR
F.4**

O'Connel Airlines is considering air service from its hub of operations in Cicely, Alaska, to Rome, Wisconsin, and Seattle, Washington. O'Connel has one gate at the Cicely Airport, which operates 12 hours per day. Each flight requires 1 hour of gate time. Each flight to Rome consumes 15 hours of pilot crew time and is expected to produce a profit of $2,500. Serving Seattle uses 10 hours of pilot crew time per flight and will result in a profit of $2,000 per flight. Pilot crew labor is limited to 150 hours per day. The market for service to Rome is limited to nine flights per day.

a. Use the graphic method of linear programming to maximize profits for O'Connel Airlines.

b. Identify slack and surplus constraints, if any.

c. Find the range of optimality for c_1, the profit per flight to Rome.

d. Chris Hoover says that radio advertising would increase the demand for travel to Rome. What is the value of increasing demand (relaxing the market constraint) by one flight to Rome?

e. By how much would O'Connel's objective function increase if the Cicely Airport operated an extra hour per day? Would increased hours of operation result in increased service to Rome, Seattle, or both?

f. Maurice Foster strongly voices his opinion that O'Connel would benefit from hiring additional experienced pilots. What is the value of one additional hour of flight crew resources? What is the upper limit on the range of feasibility for flight crew time?

SOLUTION

a. The objective function is to maximize profits, Z:

$$\text{Maximize: } \$2{,}500x_1 + \$2{,}000x_2 = Z$$

where

x_1 — number of flights per day to Rome, Wisconsin
x_2 = number of flights per day to Seattle, Washington

The constraints are

$$x_1 + x_2 \le 12 \quad \text{(gate capacity)}$$
$$15x_1 + 10x_2 \le 150 \quad \text{(labor)}$$
$$x_1 \le 9 \quad \text{(market)}$$
$$x_1 \ge 0 \quad \text{and} \quad x_2 \ge 0$$

A careful drawing of iso-profit lines parallel to the one shown in Figure F.13 will indicate that point D is the optimal solution. It is at the intersection of the labor and gate capacity constraints. Solving algebraically, we get

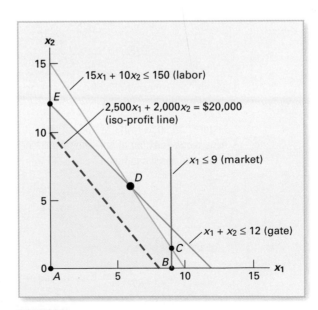

FIGURE F.13

$$15x_1 + 10x_2 = 150 \qquad \text{(labor)}$$
$$\underline{-10x_1 - 10x_2 = -120} \qquad \text{(gate} \times -10)$$
$$5x_1 + 0x_2 = 30$$
$$x_1 = 6$$
$$6 + x_2 = 12 \qquad \text{(gate)}$$
$$x_2 = 6$$

The maximum profit results from making six flights to Rome and six flights to Seattle:

$$\$2,500(6) + \$2,000(6) = \$27,000$$

b. The market constraint has three units of slack, so the demand for flights to Rome is not fully met:

$$x_1 \leq 9$$
$$x_1 + s_3 = 9$$
$$6 + s_3 = 9$$
$$s_3 = 3$$

c. Point *D* remains optimal as long as the objective function slope $(-c_1/c_2)$ is between $-3/2$, the slope of the labor constraint, and -1.00, the slope of the gate capacity constraint, or

$$-\frac{3}{2} \leq -\frac{c_1}{c_2} \leq -1$$

Holding c_2 constant at 2,000 yields

$$-\frac{3}{2} \leq -\frac{c_1}{2,000} \leq -1$$

and multiplying by $-2,000$ gives

$$3,000 \geq c_1 \geq 2,000 \qquad \text{or} \qquad 2,000 \leq c_1 \leq 3,000$$

d. As the market constraint already has slack, the optimal solution would not improve with an increase in demand for service to Rome.

e. Figure F.14 shows what would happen if the gate were open for 13 hours instead of 12 hours. One increased hour of operation would increase service to Seattle from six to nine flights, but decrease service to Rome from six to four flights. The intersecting constraints are

$$x_1 + x_2 \leq 13 \qquad \text{(gate capacity)}$$
$$15x_1 + 10x_2 \leq 150 \qquad \text{(labor)}$$

Solving algebraically, we have

$$15x_1 + 10x_2 = 150 \qquad \text{(labor)}$$
$$\underline{-10x_1 - 10x_2 = -130} \qquad \text{(gate} \times -10)$$
$$5x_1 + 0x_2 = 20$$

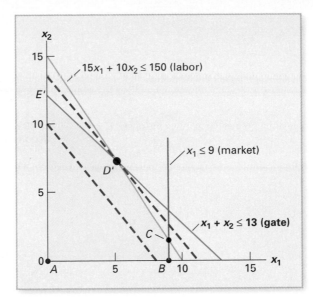

FIGURE F.14

$$x_1 = 4$$
$$4 + x_2 = 13 \qquad \text{(gate)}$$
$$x_2 = 9$$

The objective function would be $2,500(4) + $2,000(9) = $28,000, an increase of $1,000 over the previous solution. The shadow price for gate capacity is $1,000 per hour.

f. The intersecting constraints are

$$x_1 + x_2 \le 12 \qquad \text{(gate capacity)}$$
$$15x_1 + 10x_2 \le 151 \qquad \text{(labor)}$$

Solving algebraically, we get

$$15x_1 + 10x_2 = 151 \quad \text{(labor)}$$

$$\underline{-10x_1 - 10x_2 = -120} \quad \text{(gate} \times -10)$$
$$5x_1 + 0x_2 = 31$$

$$x_1 = 6.2$$
$$6.2 + x_2 = 12 \qquad \text{(gate)}$$
$$x_2 = 5.8$$

The objective function would be $2,500(6.2) + $2,000(5.8) = $27,100, an increase of $100 over the previous solution. The shadow price for flight crew time is $100 per hour. Increasing flight crew time would increase service to Rome and decrease service to Seattle. However, a one-hour change in flight crew time does not result in an integer change in the number of flights.

As more hours of flight crew time become available, the optimal solution shifts toward point *F*. Eventually, as Figure F.15 shows, the market limit on flights to Rome (≤ 9) will bind the solution. Point *F* is at the intersection of the market and gate constraints, located at (9, 3). You may

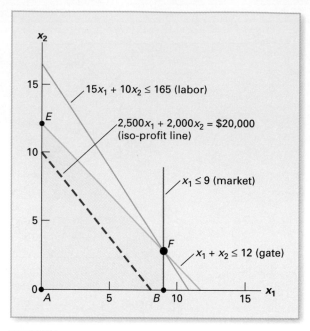

FIGURE F.15

prove this result by algebraically solving for the intersection of those two constraints. Now we find the labor constraint that will also go through that point. When $x_1 = 9$ and $x_2 = 3$,

$$15x_1 + 10x_2 = 15(9) + 10(3) = 165$$

The labor constraint that passes through point (9, 3) is

$$15x_1 + 10x_2 \leq 165$$

The right-hand side of the labor constraint has increased by $(165 - 150) = 15$ hours. Therefore, 15 more flight crew hours would improve the solution by (15)($100 shadow price) = $1,500. Beyond this point, additional flight crew time would merely become a slack resource and not further improve the solution.

SOLVED PROBLEM 2

Holling desires to minimize the cost of preparing at least 750 hors d'oeuvres for a celebration. Holling is considering two recipes: Dave's crabcakes (x_1) and Shelly's seafood surprise (x_2). The cost per unit is $0.30 for the crabcakes and $0.20 for the seafood surprise. Holling has a good supply of Alaskan king crab but must order at least 20 pounds at a time to obtain it at a reasonable price. The crabcake recipe requires 0.02 pound of crabmeat per unit. Seafood surprise requires 0.04 pound per unit. Because of crabmeat's short shelf life, Holling wants to use an entire order of crabmeat in preparing the hors d'oeuvres. Again, at least 20 pounds of crabmeat must be consumed.

a. Use the graphic method of linear programming to minimize Holling's costs.

b. Use coefficient sensitivity to determine the value of c_1, the cost of crabcakes, that would bring x_1 into the solution (make x_1 greater than 0).

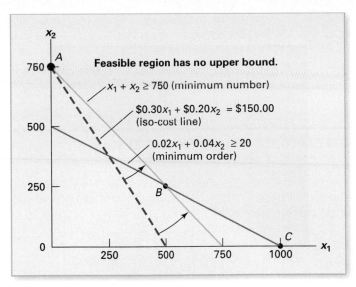

FIGURE F.16

SOLUTION

a. The graphic solution (Figure F.16) shows that the optimal solution occurs at point A. Thus, 750 units of Shelly's seafood surprise and no crabcakes would be produced.

b. The per-unit cost of crabcakes would have to be reduced to $0.20 to bring x_1 into the optimal solution. Improving c_1 results in a counterclockwise rotation of the iso-cost line. The objective function becomes parallel to the quantity constraint (at least 750 hors d'oeuvres produced). The slope of that constraint is -1.00. Solving for the value of c_1 that makes the objective function slope, $-c_1/c_2$, equal to -1.00 yields

$$- \frac{c_1}{c_2} = -1.00$$

$$- \frac{c_1}{\$0.20} = -1.00$$

$$c_1 = \$0.20$$

The coefficient sensitivity equals the difference between this value and the current value of c_1: $0.30 - 0.20 = 0.10$. In other words, forcing the production of one crabcake into the solution incurs a penalty of $0.10.

DISCUSSION QUESTIONS

1. A company wants to use linear programming for production planning but finds that the cost of firing workers isn't linear. Rather, it is approximated by the equation

Firing cost $= \$4,000F^{1.25}$

where F is the number of workers fired during a month. How could this relation be modified to permit linear program formulation and modeling of this situation?

2. A particular linear programming maximization problem has the following less-than-or-equal-to constraints: (1) raw materials, (2) labor hours, and (3) storage space. The optimal solution occurs at the intersection of the raw

materials and labor hours constraints, so those constraints are binding. Management is considering whether to authorize overtime. What useful information could the linear programming solution provide to management in making this decision? Suppose a warehouse becomes available for rent at bargain rates. What would management need to know in order to decide whether to rent the warehouse? How could the linear programming model be helpful?

OM EXPLORER AND INTERNET EXERCISES

Visit our Web site at www.prenhall.com/krajewski for OM Explorer Tutors, which explain quantitative techniques; Solvers, which help you apply mathematical models; and Internet Exercises, including Facility Tours, which expand on the topics in this chapter.

PROBLEMS

An icon next to a problem identifies the software that can be helpful, but not mandatory. The software is available on the Student CD-ROM that is packaged with every new copy of the textbook.

1. **OM Explorer** The Really Big Shoe is a manufacturer of basketball and football shoes. Ed Sullivan, the manager of marketing, must decide the best way to spend advertising resources. Each football team sponsored requires 120 pairs of shoes. Each basketball team requires 32 pairs of shoes. Football coaches receive $300,000 for shoe sponsorship, and basketball coaches receive $1,000,000. Sullivan's promotional budget is $30,000,000. The Really Big Shoe has a limited supply (4 liters or 4000 cubic centimeters) of flubber, a rare and costly compound used in promotional athletic shoes. Each pair of basketball shoes requires 3 cc of flubber, and each pair of football shoes requires 1 cc. Sullivan wants to sponsor as many basketball and football teams as resources allow.

   a. Create a set of linear equations to describe the objective function and the constraints.

   b. Use graphic analysis to find the visual solution.

   c. What is the maximum number of each type of team The Really Big Shoe can sponsor?

2. A business student at Nowledge College must complete a total of 65 courses to graduate. The number of business courses must be greater than or equal to 23. The number of nonbusiness courses must be greater than or equal to 20. The average business course requires a textbook costing $60 and 120 hours of study. Nonbusiness courses require a textbook costing $24 and 200 hours of study. The student has $3,000 to spend on books.

   a. Create a set of linear equations to describe the objective function and the constraints.

   b. Use graphic analysis to find the visual solution.

   c. What combination of business and nonbusiness courses minimizes total hours of study?

   d. Identify the slack or surplus variables.

3. In Problem 2, suppose that the objective is to minimize the cost of books and that the student's total study time is limited to 12,600 hours.

   a. Use graphic analysis to determine the combination of courses that minimizes the total cost of books.

   b. Identify the slack or surplus variables.

4. Mile-High Microbrewery makes a light beer and a dark beer. Mile-High has a limited supply of barley, limited bottling capacity, and a limited market for light beer. Profits are $0.20 per bottle of light beer and $0.50 per bottle of dark beer.

   a. The following table shows resource availability of products at the Mile-High Microbrewery. Use the graphic method of linear programming to maximize profits. How many bottles of each product should be produced per month?

RESOURCE	PRODUCT		RESOURCE AVAILABILITY (PER MONTH)
	Light Beer (x_1)	Dark Beer (x_2)	
Barley	0.1 gram	0.6 gram	2,000 grams
Bottling	1 bottle	1 bottle	6,000 bottles
Market	1 bottle		4,000 bottles

b. Identify any constraints with slack or surplus.

c. Find the range of optimality for c_2, the profit per bottle of dark beer.

d. Beth Richards says that sponsoring sporting events would increase the demand for Mile-High's light beer. What is the value of increasing demand for light beer?

e. Jorge Gallegos suggests that the bottling constraint could be alleviated by subcontracting for additional bottling capacity. By how much would Mile-High's objective function increase if bottling capacity increased by one bottle per month? Would increased hours of operation result in increased production of light beer, dark beer, or both?

f. What is the upper limit on the range of feasibility for bottling capacity?

5. The plant manager of a plastic pipe manufacturer has the opportunity to use two different routings for a particular type of plastic pipe. Routing 1 uses extruder A, and routing 2 uses extruder B. Both routings require the same melting process. The following table shows the time requirements and capacities of these processes:

PROCESS	TIME REQUIREMENTS (hr/100 ft)		CAPACITY (hr)
	ROUTING 1	ROUTING 2	
Melting	1	1	45
Extruder A	3	0	90
Extruder B	0	1	160

Each 100 feet of pipe processed on routing 1 uses 5 pounds of raw material, whereas each 100 feet of pipe processed on routing 2 uses only 4 pounds. This difference results from differing scrap rates of the extruding machines. Consequently, the profit per 100 feet of pipe processed on routing 1 is $60 and on routing 2 is $80. A total of 200 pounds of raw material is available.

a. Create a set of linear equations to describe the objective function and the constraints.

b. Use graphic analysis to find the visual solution.

c. What is the maximum profit?

d. Use coefficient sensitivity to determine the value of c_1, the profit per unit processed on routing 1, that would bring x_1 into the solution (make x_1 greater than 0).

6. A manufacturer of textile dyes can use two different processing routings for a particular type of dye. Routing 1 uses drying press A, and routing 2 uses drying press B. Both routings require the same mixing vat to blend

chemicals for the dye before drying. The following table shows the time requirements and capacities of these processes:

PROCESS	TIME REQUIREMENTS (hr/kg)		CAPACITY (hr)
	ROUTING 1	ROUTING 2	
Mixing	2	2	54
Dryer A	6	0	120
Dryer B	0	8	180

Each kilogram of dye processed on routing 1 uses 20 liters of chemicals, whereas each kilogram of dye processed on routing 2 uses only 15 liters. The difference results from differing yield rates of the drying presses. Consequently, the profit per kilogram processed on routing 1 is $50 and on routing 2 is $65. A total of 450 liters of input chemicals is available.

a. Write the constraints and objective function to maximize profits.

b. Use the graphic method of linear programming to find the optimal solution.

c. Identify any constraints with slack or surplus.

d. What is the value of an additional hour of mixing time? What is the upper limit of the range for which this shadow price is valid?

7. ● **OM Explorer** The Trim-Look Company makes several lines of skirts, dresses, and sport coats. Recently, a consultant suggested that the company reevaluate its South Islander line and allocate its resources to products that would maximize contribution to profits and to overhead. Each product requires the same polyester fabric and must pass through the cutting and sewing departments. The following data were collected for the study:

PRODUCT	PROCESSING TIME (hr)		MATERIAL (yd)
	CUTTING	SEWING	
Skirt	1	1	1
Dress	3	4	1
Sport coat	4	6	4

The cutting department has 100 hours of capacity, sewing has 180 hours of capacity, and 60 yards of material are available. Each skirt contributes $5 to profits and overhead; each dress, $17; and each sport coat, $30.

a. Specify the objective function and constraints for this problem.

b. Use a computer package to solve the problem.

8. 💿 **OM Explorer** Consider Problem 7 further.

    a. How much would you be willing to pay for an extra hour of cutting time? For an extra hour of sewing time? For an extra yard of material? Explain your response to each question.

    b. Determine the range of right-hand-side values over which the shadow price would be valid for the cutting constraint and for the material constraint.

9. 💿 **OM Explorer** Polly Astaire makes fine clothing for big and tall men. A few years ago Astaire entered the sportswear market with the Sunset line of shorts, pants, and shirts. Management wants to make the amount of each product that will maximize profits. Each type of clothing is routed through two departments, A and B. Following are the relevant data for each product.

| | PROCESSING TIME (hr) | | |
PRODUCT	Department A	Department B	MATERIAL (yd)
Shirt	2	1	2
Shorts	2	3	1
Pants	3	4	4

Department A has 120 hours of capacity, department B has 160 hours of capacity, and 90 yards of material are available. Each shirt contributes $10 to profits and overhead; each pair of shorts, $10; and each pair of pants, $23.

    a. Specify the objective function and constraints for this problem.

    b. Use a computer package to solve the problem.

    c. How much should Astaire be willing to pay for an extra hour of department A capacity? Department B capacity? For what range of right-hand values are these shadow prices valid?

10. 💿 **OM Explorer** The Butterfield Company makes a variety of hunting knives. Each knife is processed on four machines. Following are the processing times required; machine capacities (in hours) are 1,500 for machine 1, 1,400 for machine 2, 1,600 for machine 3, and 1,500 for machine 4.

| | PROCESSING TIME (hr) | | | |
KNIFE	Machine 1	Machine 2	Machine 3	Machine 4
A	0.05	0.10	0.15	0.05
B	0.15	0.10	0.05	0.05
C	0.20	0.05	0.10	0.20
D	0.15	0.10	0.10	0.10
E	0.05	0.10	0.10	0.05

Each product contains a different amount of two basic raw materials. Raw material 1 costs $0.50 per ounce, and raw material 2 costs $1.50 per ounce. There are 75,000 ounces of raw material 1 and 100,000 ounces of raw material 2 available.

| | REQUIREMENTS (oz/unit) | | |
KNIFE	Raw Material 1	Raw Material 2	SELLING PRICE ($/unit)
A	4	2	15.00
B	6	8	25.50
C	1	3	14.00
D	2	5	19.50
E	6	10	27.00

    a. If the objective is to maximize profit, specify the objective function and constraints for the problem. Assume that labor costs are negligible.

    b. Solve the problem with a computer package.

11. 💿 **OM Explorer** The Nutmeg Corporation produces five different nut and mixed nut products: almond pack, walnut pack, gourmet pack, fancy pack, and thrifty pack. Each product (individual or mix) comes in a one-pound can. The firm can purchase almonds at $0.80 per pound, walnuts at $0.60 per pound, and peanuts at $0.35 per pound. Peanuts are used to complete each mix, and the company has an unlimited supply of them. The supply of almonds and walnuts is limited. The company can buy up to 3,000 pounds of almonds and 2,000 pounds of walnuts. The resource requirements and forecasted demand for the products follow. Use a computer package to solve this problem.

| | MINIMUM REQUIREMENTS (%) | | |
PRODUCT	Almonds	Walnuts	DEMAND (cans)
Almonds	100	—	1,250
Walnuts	—	100	750
Gourmet	45	45	1,000
Fancy	30	30	500
Thrifty	20	20	1,500

    a. What mix minimizes the cost of meeting the demand for all five products?

    b. What is the impact on the product mix if only 2,000 pounds of peanuts are available?

    c. What is the impact on the product mix if the gourmet pack requires 50 percent almonds and 50 percent walnuts?

    d. What is the impact on the product mix if demand for the fancy pack doubles?

12. **OM Explorer** A problem often of concern to managers in processing industries is blending. Consider the task facing Lisa Rankin, procurement manager of a company that manufactures special additives. She must determine the proper amount of each raw material to purchase for the production of a certain product. Each gallon of the finished product must have a combustion point of at least 220 °F. In addition, the product's gamma content (which causes hydrocarbon pollution) cannot exceed 6 percent of volume, and the product's zeta content (which cleans the internal moving parts of engines) must be at least 12 percent by volume. Three raw materials are available. Each raw material has a different rating on these characteristics.

	RAW MATERIAL		
CHARACTERISTIC	A	B	C
Combustion point (°F)	200	180	280
Gamma content (%)	4	3	10
Zeta content (%)	20	10	8

Raw material A costs $0.60 per gallon; raw materials B and C cost $0.40 and $0.50 per gallon, respectively. The procurement manager wants to minimize the cost of raw materials per gallon of product. Use linear programming to find the optimal proportion of each raw material for a gallon of finished product. (*Hint:* Express the decision variables in terms of fractions of a gallon; the sum of the fractions must equal 1.00.)

13. **OM Explorer** A small fabrication firm makes three basic types of components for use by other companies. Each component is processed on three machines. Following are the processing times; total capacities (in hours) are 1,600 for machine 1, 1,400 for machine 2, and 1,500 for machine 3.

	PROCESSING TIME (hr)		
COMPONENT	Machine 1	Machine 2	Machine 3
A	0.25	0.10	0.05
B	0.20	0.15	0.10
C	0.10	0.05	0.15

Each component contains a different amount of two basic raw materials. Raw material 1 costs $0.20 per ounce, and raw material 2 costs $0.35 per ounce. There are 200,000 ounces of raw material 1 and 85,000 ounces of raw material 2 available.

	REQUIREMENT (oz/unit)		SELLING PRICE
COMPONENT	Raw Material 1	Raw Material 2	($/unit)
A	32	12	40
B	26	16	28
C	19	9	24

a. Assume that the company must make at least 1,200 units of component B, that labor costs are negligible, and that the objective is to maximize profits. Specify the objective function and constraints for the problem.

b. Use a computer package to solve the problem.

14. The following is a linear programming model for analyzing the product mix of Maxine's Hat Company, which produces three hat styles:

Maximize: $\$7x_1 + \$5x_2 + \$2x_3 = Z$

Subject to:
$$3x_1 + 5x_2 + x_3 \leq 150 \quad \text{(machine A time)}$$
$$5x_1 + 3x_2 + 2x_3 \leq 100 \quad \text{(machine B time)}$$
$$x_1 + 2x_2 + x_3 \leq 160 \quad \text{(machine C time)}$$
$$x_1 \geq 0, \quad x_2 \geq 0, \quad \text{and} \quad x_3 \geq 0$$

The OM Explorer printout in Figure F.17 on page 726 shows the optimal solution to the problem. Consider each of the following statements independently, and state whether it is true or false. Explain each answer.

a. If the price of hat 3 were increased to $2.50, it would be part of the optimal product mix.

b. The capacity of machine C can be reduced to 65 hours without affecting profits.

c. If machine A had a capacity of 170 hours, the production output would remain unchanged.

15. **OM Explorer** The Washington Chemical Company produces chemicals and solvents for the glue industry. The production process is divided into several "focused factories," each producing a specific set of products. The time has come to prepare the production plan for one of the focused factories. This particular factory produces five products, which must pass through both the reactor and the separator. Each product also requires a certain combination of raw materials. Production data are shown in Table F.1.

The Washington Chemical Company has a long-term contract with a major glue manufacturer that requires annual production of 3,000 pounds of both products 3 and 4. More of these products could be produced because there is a demand for them.

Solver - Linear Programming

Solution

Variable Label	Variable Value	Original Coefficient	Coefficient Sensitivity
X1	3.1250	7.0000	0
X2	28.1250	5.0000	0
X3	0.0000	2.0000	0.7500

Constraint Label	Original RHV	Slack or Surplus	Shadow Price
Machine A	150	0	0.2500
Machine B	100	0	1.2500
Machine C	160	100.6250	0

Objective Function Value: 162.5

Sensitivity Analysis and Ranges

Objective Function Coefficients

Variable Label	Lower Limit	Original Coefficient	Upper Limit
X1	5.2857	7	8.3333
X2	4.2000	5	11.6667
X3	No Limit	2	2.75

Right-Hand-Side Values

Constraint Label	Lower Limit	Original Value	Upper Limit
Machine A	60	150	166.6667
Machine B	90	100	250
Machine C	59.3750	160	No Limit

FIGURE F.17

TABLE F.1 *Production Data for Washington Chemical*

| | PRODUCT | | | | | TOTAL RESOURCES |
RESOURCE	1	2	3	4	5	AVAILABLE
Reactor (hr/lb)	0.05	0.10	0.80	0.57	0.15	7,500 hr*
Separator (hr/lb)	0.20	0.02	0.20	0.09	0.30	7,500 hr*
Raw material 1 (lb)	0.20	0.50	0.10	0.40	0.18	10,000 lb
Raw material 2 (lb)	—	0.70	—	0.50	—	6,000 lb
Raw material 3 (lb)	0.10	0.20	0.40	—	—	7,000 lb
Profit contribution ($/lb)	4.00	7.00	3.50	4.00	5.70	

*The total time available has been adjusted to account for setups. The five products have a prescribed sequence owing to the cost of changeovers between products. The company has a 35-day cycle (or 10 changeovers per year per product). Consequently, the time for these changeovers has been deducted from the total time available for these machines.

a. Determine the annual production quantity of each product that maximizes contribution to profits. Assume the company can sell all it can produce.

b. Specify the lot size for each product.

16. **OM Explorer** The Warwick Manufacturing Company produces shovels for industrial and home use. Sales of the shovels are seasonal, and Warwick's customers refuse to stockpile them during slack periods. In other words, the customers want to minimize inventory, insist on shipments according to their schedules, and will not accept backorders.

Warwick employs manual, unskilled laborers, who require only very basic training. Producing 1,000 shovels costs $3,500 on regular time and $3,700 on overtime. These amounts include materials, which account for over 85 percent of the cost. Overtime is limited to production of 15,000 shovels per quarter. In addition, subcontractors can be hired at $4,200 per thousand shovels, but Warwick's labor contract restricts this type of production to 5,000 shovels per quarter.

The current level of inventory is 30,000 shovels, and management wants to end the year at that level. Holding 1,000 shovels in inventory costs $280 per quarter. The latest annual demand forecast is

QUARTER	DEMAND
1	70,000
2	150,000
3	320,000
4	100,000
Totals	640,000

Build a linear programming model to determine the *best* regular-time capacity plan. Assume that

- the firm has 30 workers now, and management wants to have the same number in quarter 4,
- each worker can produce 4,000 shovels per quarter, and
- hiring a worker costs $1,000, and laying off a worker costs $600.

17. **OM Explorer** The management of Warwick Company (Problem 16) is willing to give price breaks to its customers as an incentive to purchase shovels in advance of the traditional seasons. Warwick's sales and marketing staff estimates that the demand for shovels resulting from the price breaks would be

QUARTER	DEMAND	ORIGINAL DEMAND
1	120,000	70,000
2	180,000	150,000
3	180,000	320,000
4	160,000	100,000
Totals	640,000	640,000

Calculate the optimal production plan (including the workforce staffing plan) under the new demand schedule. Compare it to the optimal production plan under the original demand schedule. Evaluate the potential effects of demand management.

18. The Bull Grin Company produces a feed supplement for animal foods produced by a number of companies. Sales are seasonal, and Bull Grin's customers refuse to stockpile the supplement during slack sales periods. In other words, the customers want to minimize inventory, insist on shipments according to their schedules, and won't accept backorders.

Bull Grin employs manual, unskilled laborers, who require little or no training. Producing 1,000 pounds of supplement costs $810 on regular time and $900 on overtime. These amounts include materials, which account for over 80 percent of the cost. Overtime is limited to production of 30,000 pounds per quarter. In addition, subcontractors can be hired at $1,100 per thousand pounds, but only 10,000 pounds per quarter can be produced this way.

The current level of inventory is 40,000 pounds, and management wants to end the year at that level. Holding 1,000 pounds of feed supplement in inventory costs $110 per quarter. The latest annual forecast follows:

QUARTER	DEMAND (lb)
1	100,000
2	410,000
3	770,000
4	440,000
Total	1,720,000

The firm currently has 180 workers, a number that management wants to keep in quarter 4. Each worker can produce 2,000 pounds per quarter, so regular-time production costs $1,620 per worker. Idle workers must be paid at that same rate. Hiring one worker costs $1,000, and laying off a worker costs $600.

Write the objective function and constraints describing this production planning problem, after fully defining the decision variables.

19. Inside Traders, Inc., invests in various types of securities. The firm has $5 million for immediate investment and wants to maximize the interest earned over the next year. Four investment possibilities are presented in the following table. To further structure the portfolio, the board of directors has specified that at least 40 percent of the investment must be in corporate bonds and common stock. Furthermore, no more than 20 percent of the investment may be in real estate.

INVESTMENT	EXPECTED INTEREST EARNED (%)
Corporate bonds	8.5
Common stock	9.0
Gold certificates	10.0
Real estate	13.0

Write the objective function and constraints for this portfolio investment problem, after fully defining the decision variables.

20. JPMorgan Chase has a scheduling problem. Operators work eight-hour shifts and can begin work at midnight, 4 A.M., 8 A.M., noon, 4 P.M., or 8 P.M. Operators are needed to satisfy the following demand pattern. Formulate a linear programming model to cover the demand requirements with the minimum number of operators.

TIME PERIOD	OPERATORS NEEDED
Midnight to 4 A.M.	4
4 A.M. to 8 A.M.	6
8 A.M. to noon	90
Noon to 4 P.M.	85
4 P.M. to 8 P.M.	55
8 P.M. to 12 midnight	20

SELECTED REFERENCES

Asim, R., E. De Falomir, and L. Lasdon. "An Optimization-Based Decision Support System for a Product-Mix Problem." *Interfaces*, vol. 12, no. 2 (1982), pp. 26–33.

Bonini, Charles P., Warren H. Hausman, and Harold Bierman, Jr. *Quantitative Analysis for Management*, 9th ed. Chicago: Irwin, 1997.

Cook, Thomas M., and Robert A. Russell. *Introduction to Management Sciences*. Englewood Cliffs, NJ: Prentice-Hall, 1993.

Eppen, G. D., F. J. Gould, C. P. Schmidt, Jeffrey H. Moore, and Larry R. Weatherford. *Introductory Management Science: Decision Modeling with Spreadsheets*, 5th ed. Upper Saddle River, NJ: Prentice-Hall, 1998.

Fourer, Robert. "Software Survey: Linear Programming." *OR/MS Today* (April 1997), pp. 54–63.

Greenberg, H. J. "How to Analyze the Results of Linear Programs— Part 2: Price Interpretation." *Interfaces*, vol. 23, no. 5 (1993), pp. 97–114.

Hess, Rick. *Managerial Spreadsheet Modeling and Analysis*. Chicago, Ill. Irwin, 1997.

Jayaraman, V., R. Srivastava, and W. C. Benton. "Supplier Selection and Order Quantity Allocation." *Journal of Supply Chain Management*, vol. 35, no. 2 (1999), pp. 50–58.

Krajewski, L. J., and H. E. Thompson. *Management Science: Quantitative Methods in Context*. New York: John Wiley & Sons, 1981.

Markland, Robert E., and James R. Sweigart. *Quantitative Methods: Applications to Managerial Decision Making*. New York: John Wiley & Sons, 1987.

Perry, C., and K. C. Crellin. "The Precise Management Meaning of a Shadow Price." *Interfaces*, vol. 12, no. 2 (1982), pp. 61–63.

Ragsdale, Cliff T, and Rick Hess. *Spreadsheet Modeling and Decision Analysis; A Practical Introduction to Management Science*, 2d ed. Cincinnati, OH: South-Western, 1998.

Taylor, Bernard W., III. *Introduction to Management Science*. Needham Heights, MA: Allyn & Bacon, 1990.

Verma, Rohit. "My Operations Management Students Love Linear Programming." *Decision Line* (July 1997), pp. 9–12.

Winston, Wayne L., S. Christian Albright, and Mark Broadie. *Practical Management Science: Spreadsheet Modeling and Applications*. Pacific Grove, CA: Duxbury, 1996.

Resource Planning

Across the Organization

Resource planning is important to . . .

☐ **accounting,** which coordinates the payments to suppliers and billings to customers with the resource plan.

☐ **finance,** which plans for adequate working capital to support the schedules generated in the resource plan.

☐ **human resources,** which determines the implications of the resource plan on personnel requirements.

☐ **management information systems,** which must identify the information requirements of managers and the information that can be generated from the resource plan.

☐ **marketing,** which makes reliable delivery commitments to customers.

☐ **operations,** which is responsible for inventories and the utilization of the resources required by the firm's processes to meet customer demand.

Learning Goals

After reading this chapter, you will be able to . . .

1. distinguish between independent and dependent demand and their differences when planning for the replenishment of materials.

2. explain the logic of material requirements planning, how it can be used to plan distribution inventories, and how to schedule the receipt of materials to meet promised delivery dates.

3. identify the key outputs from the resource planning process and how they are used.

4. provide examples of the effective use of manufacturing resource planning and its benefits to various functional areas of the firm.

5. discuss resource planning for service providers and how it can be accomplished.

What do Wrangler or Lee jeans, Timber Creek khakis, Vanity Fair underwear, Healthtex clothes for kids, Jantzen bathing suits, and JanSport backpacks have in common, other than that you can find them in diverse retail outlets such as Wal-Mart, Target, and Macy's? One-hundred-year-old VF Corp. (www.vfc.com), a $5.5 billion-a-year company in Greensboro, NC, and the world's largest apparel producer, manufactures all of these products and many more. While VF's stock has been a steady performer, its sales were flat and management realized that the corporation needed shaking up. VF's 14 divisions were operated as independent entities, each with its own purchasing, production, marketing, and computer systems. Management initiated a drive to focus its key business processes on identifying and fulfilling customer needs. The restructuring resulted in five "coalitions": Jeanswear, Intimates, Playwear, Knitwear, and International Operations and Marketing. Each coalition will phase into the integrated system over time.

Data on quality are important inputs for VF's ERP system. Here an employee inspects jeans to assure they conform to VF's quality standards and meet customer expectations.

The coalitions need to work together to take advantage of common resources. However, resource planning across such a complex environment poses major challenges. To establish the critical information links between the coalitions, VF decided to install a modified version of the R/3 ERP system from SAP AG specifically designed for apparel and footwear manufacturers as the core integrating system (www.sap.com). However, VF also decided to use the *best of breed* implementation strategy, which allowed VF to choose the best applications modules from any vendor or retain some of its own legacy systems. For example, the heart of the system has only four R/3 modules: order management, production planning, materials management, and finance. However, each coalition has its favorite applications from other vendors that have to be included. Intimates uses WebPDM from Gerber to cut product design costs and Rhythm from i2 to optimize materials utilization and assembly-line space. Information from Rhythm is fed back to the R/3 production planning module. Jeanswear is using software from Logility to make customer forecasts, which are fed back to the production planning and financial modules in R/3. VF's own customized software tracks production in the plants, using information from the R/3 production planning, order management, and materials management modules and then reports back to R/3 for the fine-tuning of production plans. VF also has developed a "micromarketing" system that forecasts the need for a specific size and color of Wrangler jeans (say), for the beginning of summer, at a particular Wal-Mart store.

Key modules in the new system for resource planning are material requirements planning and capacity planning. The material requirements planning system is contained in the production planning module and uses forecasts from the Logility sales and demand planning module to determine the purchase quantities and delivery dates for supplies and materials such as leather, fabric, or linings; the production of finished goods such as jeans, backpacks, or shirts; and the manufacture of assemblies such as shoe soles or bootlegs. The output from material requirements planning is useful for planning production as well as financial resources. For example, the timing of planned-purchase quantities can be translated into the need for funds to pay for them. The output can also be used by the capacity planning module, which facilitates the planning for critical resources such as skilled employees or specialized equipment to support the production plan.

VF has a great start but has a long way to go. Jeanswear was the first to completely implement the common systems platform, and Intimates is the next to go on-line. VF has spent more than $100 million on the new system, which is not unusual for complex environments such as this one.

Sources: Brown, Eryn. "VF Corp. Changes Its Underware." *Fortune* (December 7, 1998), pp. 115–118; "SAP Consumer Products for Apparel & Footwear" (July 2000); VFC Press Release. "VF Corporation Launches First Large Scale Apparel Industry-Specific SAP Solution." (May 31, 2000).

T HE VF CORPORATION DEMONSTRATES that companies can gain a competitive edge by integrating processes through an effective operations information system. Maintaining an efficient flow of materials and services from suppliers and managing internal activities relating to materials and other resources are essential to a profitable operation. Operations management ensures that all resources needed to produce finished products or services are available at the right time. For a manufacturer, this task may mean keeping track of thousands of subassemblies, components, and raw materials. For a service provider, this task may mean keeping track of various materials and supplies and time requirements for many different categories of employees and equipment.

We begin this chapter with a discussion of material requirements planning (MRP), which is a key element of manufacturing resource planning systems. We discuss the important concept of dependent demand and all the information inputs to MRP that are used to generate the reports needed for managing manufacturing and distribution inventories as well as other resources. We also devote an entire section to resource planning for service providers and demonstrate how the concept of dependent demands can be used to manage supplies, human resources, equipment, and financial resources. Resource planning techniques are important elements of ERP systems for manufacturers as well as service providers (see chapter 5).

OVERVIEW OF MATERIAL REQUIREMENTS PLANNING

material requirements planning (MRP) A computerized information system developed specifically to aid in managing dependent demand inventory and scheduling replenishment orders.

Material requirements planning (MRP)—a computerized information system—was developed specifically to aid companies manage dependent demand inventory and schedule replenishment orders. MRP systems have proven to be beneficial to many companies. In this section, we discuss the nature of dependent demands and identify some of the benefits firms have experienced with these systems.

DEPENDENT DEMAND

dependent demand A demand that occurs because the quantity required is a function of the demand for other items held in inventory.

To illustrate the concept of dependent demand, let us consider a Huffy bicycle produced for retail outlets. The bicycle, one of many different types held in inventory at Huffy's plant, has a high-volume demand rate over time. Demand for a final product such as a bicycle is called *independent demand* because it is influenced only by market conditions and not by demand for any other type of bicycle held in inventory (see the Inventory Management chapter). Huffy must *forecast* that demand (see the Forecasting chapter). However, Huffy also keeps many other items in inventory, including handlebars, pedals, frames, and wheel rims, used to make completed bicycles. Each of these items has a **dependent demand** because the quantity required is a function of the demand for other items held in inventory. For example, the demand for frames, pedals, and rims is *dependent* on the production of completed bicycles. Operations can *calculate* the demand for dependent demand items once the bicycle production levels are announced. For example, every bicycle needs two wheel rims, so 1,000 completed bicycles need $1,000(2) = 2,000$ rims. Statistical forecasting techniques aren't needed for these items.

parent Any item manufactured from one or more components.

component An item that may go through one or more operations to be transformed into or become part of one or more parents.

The bicycle, or any other good manufactured from one or more components, is called a **parent**. The wheel rim is an example of a **component**—an item that may go through one or more operations to be transformed into or become part of one or more parents. The rim may have several different parents because it might be used for more than one style of bicycle. The parent–component relationship can cause erratic dependent demand patterns for components. Suppose that every time inventory falls to 500 units (a reorder point), an order for 1,000 more bicycles is placed, as shown in Figure 15.1(a). The assembly supervisor then authorizes the withdrawal of 2,000 rims from inventory, along with other components for the finished product; demand for the

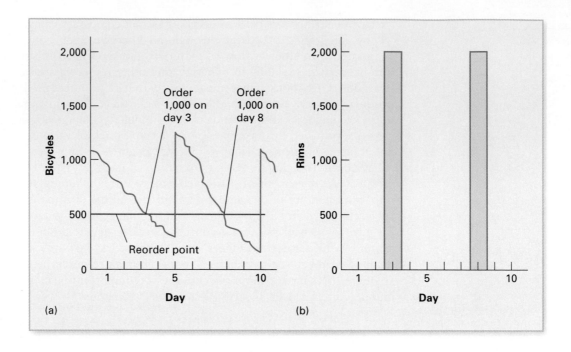

(a)   (b)

FIGURE 15.1

Lumpy Dependent Demand Resulting from Continuous Independent Demand

rim is shown in Figure 15.1(b). So, even though customer demand for the finished bicycle is continuous and uniform, the production demand for wheel rims is "lumpy"; that is, it occurs sporadically, usually in relatively large quantities. Thus, the *production* decisions for the assembly of bicycles, which account for the costs of assembling the bicycles and the projected assembly capacities at the time the decisions are made, determine the demand for rims.

Managing dependent demand inventories is complicated because some components may be subject to both dependent and independent demand. For example, operations needs 2,000 wheel rims for the new bicycles, but the company also sells replacement rims for old bicycles directly to retail outlets. This practice places an independent demand on the inventory of rims. Material requirements planning can be used in complex situations involving components that may have independent demand as well as dependent demand inventories.

BENEFITS OF MATERIAL REQUIREMENTS PLANNING

Why should companies invest in an MRP system?

For years, many companies tried to manage production and delivery of dependent demand inventories with independent demand systems, but the outcome was seldom satisfactory. However, because it recognizes dependent demands, the MRP system enables businesses to reduce inventory levels, utilize labor and facilities better, and improve customer service. For example, when American Sterilizer Company introduced MRP at its Hospital Products and Systems Group, it increased on-time customer deliveries from 70 to 95 percent. It also cut overtime by at least 50 percent, reduced component shortages by more than 80 percent, lowered indirect labor by 24 percent, and reduced direct labor by 7 percent.

Successes such as those at American Sterilizer Company are due to three advantages of material requirements planning.

1. Statistical forecasting for components with lumpy demand results in large forecasting errors. Compensating for such errors by increasing safety stock is costly, with no guarantee that stockouts can be avoided. MRP calculates the dependent

demand of components from the production schedules of their parents, thereby providing a better forecast of component requirements.

2. MRP systems provide managers with information useful for planning capacities and estimating financial requirements. Production schedules and materials purchases can be translated into capacity requirements and dollar amounts and can be projected in the time periods when they will appear. Planners can use the information on parent item schedules to identify times when needed components may be unavailable because of capacity shortages, supplier delivery delays, and the like.

3. MRP systems automatically update the dependent demand and inventory replenishment schedules of components when the production schedules of parent items change. The MRP system alerts the planners whenever action is needed on any component.

INPUTS TO MATERIAL REQUIREMENTS PLANNING

MRP explosion A process that converts the requirements of various final products into a material requirements plan that specifies the replenishment schedules of all the subassemblies, components, and raw materials needed by the final products.

The key inputs of an MRP system are a bill of materials database, master production schedules, and an inventory record database, as shown in Figure 15.2. Using this information, the MRP system identifies actions that operations must take to stay on schedule, such as releasing new production orders, adjusting order quantities, and expediting late orders.

An MRP system translates the master production schedule and other sources of demand, such as independent demand for replacement parts and maintenance items, into the requirements for all subassemblies, components, and raw materials needed to produce the required parent items. This process is called an **MRP explosion** because it converts the requirements of various final products into a *material requirements plan* that specifies the replenishment schedules of all the subassemblies, components, and raw materials needed by the final products.

BILL OF MATERIALS

FIGURE 15.2

Material Requirements Plan Inputs

The replenishment schedule for a component is determined from the production schedules of its parents. Hence, the system needs accurate information on parent–component relationships. A **bill of materials** (BOM) is a record of all the components of an item,

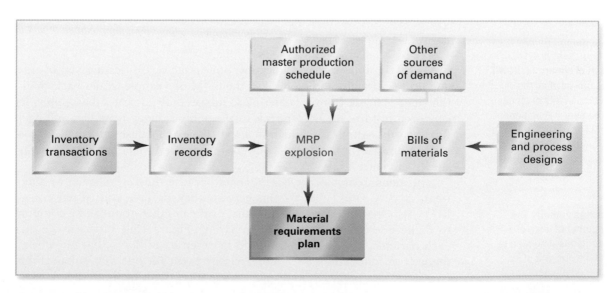

FIGURE 15.3

*Bill of Materials for a
Ladder-Back Chair*

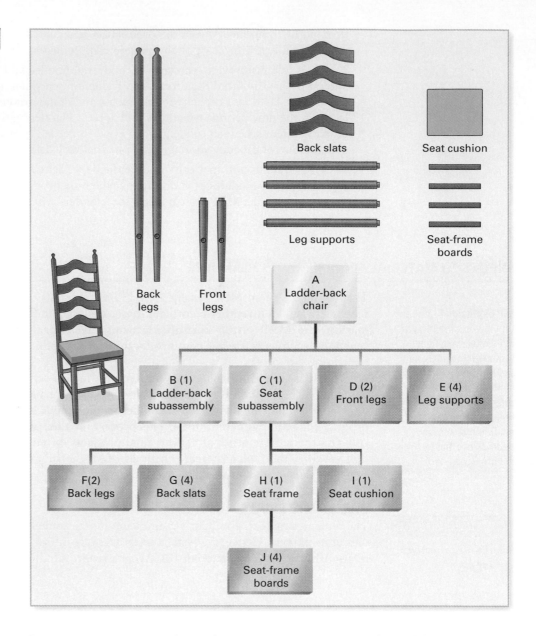

bill of materials (BOM)
A record of all the
components of an item,
the parent–component
relationships, and usage
quantities derived from
engineering and process
designs.

usage quantity The
number of units of a
component needed to
make one unit of its
immediate parent.

the parent–component relationships, and usage quantities derived from engineering and process designs. In Figure 15.3, the BOM of a simple ladder-back chair shows that the chair is made from a ladder-back subassembly, a seat subassembly, legs, and leg supports. In turn, the ladder-back subassembly is made from legs and back slats, and the seat subassembly is made from a seat frame and a cushion. Finally, the seat frame is made from seat-frame boards. For convenience, we refer to these items by the letters shown in Figure 15.3.

All items except A are components because they are needed to make a parent. Items A, B, C, and H are parents because they all have at least one component. The BOM also specifies the **usage quantity,** or the number of units of a component needed to make one unit of its immediate parent. Figure 15.3 shows usage quantities for each parent–component relationship in parentheses. Note that one chair (item A) is made from one ladder-back subassembly (item B), one seat subassembly (item C), two front legs (item D), and four leg supports (item E). In addition, item B is made from two back legs (item F) and four back slats (item G). Item C needs one seat frame (item H) and one seat cushion (item I). Finally, item H needs four seat-frame boards (item J).

Four terms frequently used to describe inventory items are end items, intermediate items, subassemblies, and purchased items. An **end item** typically is the final product sold to the customer; it is a parent but not a component. Item A in Figure 15.3, the completed ladder-back chair, is an end item. Accounting statements classify inventory of end items as either work-in-process (WIP), if work remains to be done, or finished goods. An **intermediate item** is one such as B, C, or H that has at least one parent and at least one component. Some products have several levels of intermediate items; the parent of one intermediate item also is an intermediate item. Inventory of intermediate items—whether completed or still on the shop floor—is classified as WIP. A **subassembly** is an intermediate item that is *assembled* (as opposed to being transformed by other means) from *more* than one component. Items B and C are subassemblies. A **purchased item** has no components because it comes from a supplier, but it has one or more parents. Examples are items D, E, F, G, I, and J in Figure 15.3. Inventory of purchased items is treated as raw materials in accounting statements.

A component may have more than one parent. **Part commonality,** sometimes called *standardization of parts* or *modularity,* is the degree to which a component has more than one immediate parent. As a result of commonality, the same item may appear in several places in the bill of materials for a product, or it may appear in the bills of materials for several different products. For example, the seat assembly in Figure 15.3 is a component of the ladder-back chair and of a kitchen chair that is part of the same family of products. The usage quantity specified in the bill of materials relates to a specific parent–component relationship. The usage quantity for any component can change, depending on the parent item. Part commonality increases volume and repeatability for some items—which has several advantages for process design (see the Process Management chapter)—and helps minimize inventory costs. Today, with the need for greater efficiency in all firms, part commonality is used extensively.

end item The final product sold to a customer.

intermediate item An item that has at least one parent and at least one component.

subassembly An intermediate item that is *assembled* (as opposed to being transformed by other means) from *more* than one component.

purchased item An item that has one or more parents, but no components because it comes from a supplier.

part commonality The degree to which a component has more than one immediate parent.

MASTER PRODUCTION SCHEDULE

The second input into a material requirements plan is the **master production schedule (MPS),** which details how many end items will be produced within specified periods of time. It breaks the aggregate production plan (see the Aggregate Planning chapter) into specific product schedules. Figure 15.4 shows how an aggregate plan for a family of chairs breaks down into the weekly master production schedule for each specific chair type (the time period can be hours, days, weeks, or months). Here, the scheduled quantities are shown in the week they must be released to the shop to start final assembly so as to meet customer delivery promises. We use the MPS "start" quantities throughout this chapter. The chair example demonstrates the following aspects of master scheduling:

1. The sums of the quantities in the MPS must equal those in the aggregate production plan. This consistency between the plans is desirable because of the economic analysis done to arrive at the aggregate plan.

2. The aggregate production quantities must be allocated efficiently over time. The specific mix of chair types—the amount of each type as a percent of the total aggregate quantity—is based on historic demand and marketing and promotional considerations. The planner must select lot sizes for each chair type, taking into

Why is the master production schedule important to the material requirements plan?

master production schedule (MPS) A part of the material requirements plan that details how many end items will be produced within specified periods of time.

FIGURE 15.4

Master Production Schedule for a Family of Chairs

	April				May			
	1	2	3	4	5	6	7	8
Ladder-back chair	150					150		
Kitchen chair				120			120	
Desk chair		200	200		200			200
Aggregate production plan for chair family			670				670	

consideration economic factors such as production setup costs and inventory carrying costs.

3. Capacity limitations, such as machine or labor capacity, storage space, or working capital, may determine the timing and size of MPS quantities. The planner must acknowledge these limitations by recognizing that some chair styles require more resources than others and setting the timing and size of the production quantities accordingly.

The MPS start quantities are used in the MRP system to determine the components needed to support the schedule. Details of how to develop the MPS are contained in the Master Production Scheduling supplement at the end of this chapter.

INVENTORY RECORD

Inventory records are the final input to MRP, and the basic building blocks of up-to-date records are inventory transactions (see Figure 15.2). Transactions include releasing new orders, receiving scheduled receipts, adjusting due dates for scheduled receipts, withdrawing inventory, canceling orders, correcting inventory errors, rejecting shipments, and verifying scrap losses and stock returns. Recording such transactions is essential for maintaining the accurate records of on-hand inventory balances and scheduled receipts necessary for an effective MRP system.

The **inventory record** divides the future into time periods called *time buckets*. In our discussion, we use weekly time buckets for consistency with our MPS example, although other time periods could as easily be used. The inventory record shows an item's lot-size policy, lead time, and various time-phased data. The purpose of the inventory record is to keep track of inventory levels and component replenishment needs. The time-phased information contained in the inventory record consists of

1. gross requirements,
2. scheduled receipts,
3. projected on-hand inventory,
4. planned receipts, and
5. planned order releases.

We illustrate the discussion of inventory records with the seat subassembly, item C, shown in Figure 15.3. It is used in two products: a ladder-back chair and a kitchen chair.

inventory record A record that shows an item's lot-size policy, lead time, and various time-phased data.

FIGURE 15.5

Material Requirements Planning Record for the Seat Subassembly

Item: C					Lot Size: 230 units		
Description: Seat subassembly					Lead Time: 2 weeks		

	Week							
	1	2	3	4	5	6	7	8
Gross requirements	150	0	0	120	0	150	120	0
Scheduled receipts	230	0	0	0	0	0	0	0
Projected on-hand inventory	37 | 117	117	117	–3	–3	–153	–273	–273
Planned receipts								
Planned order releases								

Explanation:
Gross requirements are the total demand for the two chairs. Projected on-hand inventory in week 1 is 37 + 230 – 150 = 117 units.

gross requirements The total demand derived from *all* parent production plans.

GROSS REQUIREMENTS. The **gross requirements** are the total demand derived from *all* parent production plans. They also include demand not otherwise accounted for, such as demand for replacement parts for units already sold. Figure 15.5 shows an inventory record for item C, the seat subassembly. Item C is produced in lots of 230 units and has a lead time of two weeks. The inventory record also shows item C's gross requirements for the next eight weeks, which come from the master production schedules for the ladder-back and kitchen chairs (see Figure 15.4). The MPS start quantities for each parent are added to arrive at each week's gross requirements. The seat subassembly's gross requirements exhibit lumpy demand: Operations will withdraw seat subassemblies from inventory in only four of the eight weeks.

The MRP system works with release dates to schedule production and delivery for components and subassemblies. Its program logic anticipates the removal of all materials required by a parent's production order from inventory at the *beginning* of the parent item's lead time—when the scheduler first releases the order to the shop.

SCHEDULED RECEIPTS. Recall that *scheduled receipts* (sometimes called *open orders*) are orders that have been placed but not yet completed. For a purchased item, the scheduled receipt could be in one of several stages: being processed by a supplier, being transported to the purchaser, or being inspected by the purchaser's receiving department. If production is making the item in-house, the order could be one the shop floor being processed, waiting for components, waiting in queue, or waiting to be moved to its next operation. According to Figure 15.5, one 230-unit order of item C is due in week 1. Given the two-week lead time, the inventory planner released the order two weeks ago.

projected on-hand inventory An estimate of the amount of inventory available each week after gross requirements have been satisfied.

PROJECTED ON-HAND INVENTORY. The **projected on-hand inventory** is an estimate of the amount of inventory available each week after gross requirements have been satisfied. The beginning inventory, shown as the first entry (37) in Figure 15.5, indicates on-hand inventory available at the time the record was computed. As with scheduled receipts, entries are made for each actual withdrawal and receipt to update the MRP database. Then, when the MRP system produces the revised record, the correct inventory will appear.

Other entries in the row show inventory expected in future weeks. Projected on-hand inventory is calculated as

$$\begin{pmatrix} \text{Projected on-hand} \\ \text{inventory balance} \\ \text{at end of week } t \end{pmatrix} = \begin{pmatrix} \text{Inventory on} \\ \text{hand at end of} \\ \text{week } t-1 \end{pmatrix} + \begin{pmatrix} \text{Scheduled} \\ \text{or planned} \\ \text{receipts in} \\ \text{week } t \end{pmatrix} - \begin{pmatrix} \text{Gross} \\ \text{requirements} \\ \text{in week } t \end{pmatrix}$$

planned receipts Orders that are not yet released to the shop or the supplier.

The projected on-hand calculation includes the consideration of **planned receipts**, which are orders not yet released to the shop or the supplier. In any week, there will never be both a scheduled receipt and a planned receipt. In Figure 15.5, the planned receipts are all zero. The on-hand inventory calculations for each week are

$$
\begin{aligned}
\text{Week 1:} \quad & 37 + 230 - 150 = 117 \\
\text{Weeks 2 and 3:} \quad & 117 + 0 - 0 = 117 \\
\text{Week 4:} \quad & 117 + 0 - 120 = -3 \\
\text{Week 5:} \quad & -3 + 0 - 0 = -3 \\
\text{Week 6:} \quad & -3 + 0 - 150 = -153 \\
\text{Week 7:} \quad & -153 + 0 - 120 = -273 \\
\text{Week 8:} \quad & -273 + 0 - 0 = -273
\end{aligned}
$$

In week 4, the balance drops to −3 units, which indicates that a shortage of 3 units will occur unless more seat subassemblies are built. This condition signals the need for a planned receipt to arrive in week 4. In addition, unless more stock is received, the shortage will grow to 273 units in weeks 7 and 8.

PLANNED RECEIPTS. Planning for receipt of new orders will keep the projected on-hand balance from dropping below zero. The planned receipt row is developed as follows:

1. Weekly on-hand inventory is projected until a shortage appears. Completion of the initial planned receipt is scheduled for the week when the shortage is projected. The addition of the newly planned receipt should raise the projected on-hand balance so that it equals or exceeds zero. It will exceed zero when the lot size exceeds requirements in the week it is planned to arrive.

2. Projection of on-hand inventory continues until the next shortage occurs. This shortage signals the need for the second planned receipt.

This process is repeated until the end of the planning horizon by proceeding column by column through the MRP record—filling in planned receipts as needed and completing the projected on-hand inventory row. Figure 15.6 shows the planned receipts for the seat subassembly. In week 4, the projected on-hand inventory will drop below zero, so

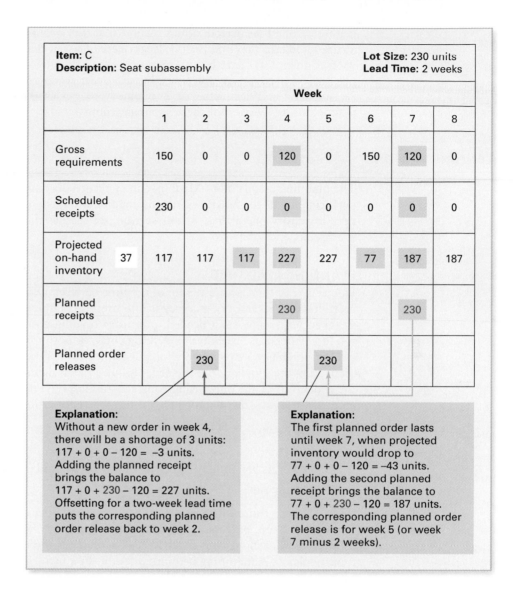

FIGURE 15.6

Completed Inventory Record for the Seat Subassembly

Item: C
Description: Seat subassembly

Lot Size: 230 units
Lead Time: 2 weeks

		Week							
		1	2	3	4	5	6	7	8
Gross requirements		150	0	0	120	0	150	120	0
Scheduled receipts		230	0	0	0	0	0	0	0
Projected on-hand inventory	37	117	117	117	227	227	77	187	187
Planned receipts					230			230	
Planned order releases			230			230			

Explanation:
Without a new order in week 4, there will be a shortage of 3 units: 117 + 0 + 0 − 120 = −3 units. Adding the planned receipt brings the balance to 117 + 0 + 230 − 120 = 227 units. Offsetting for a two-week lead time puts the corresponding planned order release back to week 2.

Explanation:
The first planned order lasts until week 7, when projected inventory would drop to 77 + 0 + 0 − 120 = −43 units. Adding the second planned receipt brings the balance to 77 + 0 + 230 − 120 = 187 units. The corresponding planned order release is for week 5 (or week 7 minus 2 weeks).

a planned receipt of 230 units is scheduled for week 4. The updated inventory on-hand balance is 117 (inventory at end of week 3) + 230 (planned receipts) − 120 (gross requirements) = 227 units. The projected on-hand inventory remains at 227 for week 5 because there are no scheduled receipts or gross requirements. In week 6, the projected on-hand inventory is 227 (inventory at end of week 5) − 150 (gross requirements) = 77 units. This quantity is greater than zero, so no new planned receipt is needed. In week 7, however, a shortage will occur unless more seat subassemblies are received. With a planned receipt in week 7, the updated inventory balance is 77 (inventory at end of week 6) + 230 (planned receipts) − 120 (gross requirements) = 187 units.

planned order release An indication of when an order for a specified quantity of an item is to be issued.

PLANNED ORDER RELEASES. A **planned order release** indicates when an order for a specified quantity of an item is to be issued. We must place the planned order release quantity in the proper time bucket. To do so, we must assume that all inventory flows—scheduled receipts, planned receipts, and gross requirements—occur at the same point of time in a time period. Some firms assume that all flows occur at the beginning of a time period; others assume that they occur at the end of a time period or at the middle of the time period. Regardless of when the flows are assumed to occur, we find the release date by subtracting the lead time from the receipt date. For example, the release date for the first planned order release in Figure 15.6 is: 4 (planned receipt date) − 2 (lead time) = 2 (planned order release date). Figure 15.6 shows the planned order releases for the seat subassembly.

PLANNING FACTORS

The planning factors in an MRP inventory record play an important role in the overall performance of the MRP system. By manipulating these factors, managers can fine-tune inventory operations. In this section, we discuss the planning lead time, the lot-sizing rule, and safety stock.

PLANNING LEAD TIME

Planning lead time is an estimate of the time between placing an order for an item and receiving it in inventory. Accuracy is important in planning lead time. If an item arrives in inventory sooner than needed, inventory holding costs increase. If an item arrives too late, stockouts, excessive expediting costs, or both may occur.

For purchased items, the planning lead time is the time allowed for receiving a shipment from the supplier after the order has been sent, including the normal time to place the order. Often, the purchasing contract stipulates the delivery date. For items manufactured in-house, the planning lead time consists of estimates for

- ❏ setup time,
- ❏ process time,
- ❏ materials handling time between operations, and
- ❏ waiting time.

Each of these times must be estimated for every operation along the item's route. Estimating setup, processing, and materials handling time may be relatively easy, but estimating the waiting time for materials handling equipment or a machine to perform a particular operation may be more difficult. In a facility using a make-to-order strategy, such as a machine shop, the load on the shop varies considerably over time, causing actual waiting times for a particular order to fluctuate widely. Therefore, estimating waiting time in such a facility is very important in estimating the planning lead time. However, in a facility using a make-to-stock strategy, such as an assembly plant, product routings are more standard and waiting time is more predictable; hence, waiting time generally is a less significant proportion of planning lead times.

LOT-SIZING RULES

How important is the choice of lot-sizing rules?

A lot-sizing rule determines the timing and size of order quantities. A lot-sizing rule must be assigned to each item before planned receipts and planned order releases can be computed. The choice of lot-sizing rules is important because they determine the number of setups required and the inventory holding costs for each item. We present three lot-sizing rules: fixed order quantity, periodic order quantity, and lot for lot.

fixed order quantity (FOQ)
A rule that maintains the same order quantity each time an order is issued.

FIXED ORDER QUANTITY. The **fixed order quantity (FOQ)** rule maintains the same order quantity each time an order is issued. For example, the lot size might be the size dictated by equipment capacity limits, as when a full lot must be loaded into a furnace at one time. For purchased items, the FOQ could be determined by the quantity discount level, truckload capacity, or minimum purchase quantity. Alternatively, the lot size could be determined by the economic order quantity (EOQ) formula (see the Inventory Management chapter). Figure 15.6 illustrates the FOQ rule. However, if an item's gross requirement within a week is particularly large, the FOQ might be insufficient to avoid a shortage. In such unusual cases, the inventory planner must increase the lot size beyond the FOQ, typically to a size large enough to avoid a shortage. Another option is to make the order quantity an integer multiple of the FOQ. This option is appropriate when capacity constraints limit production to FOQ sizes (at most) and setup costs are high.

periodic order quantity (POQ) A rule that allows a different order quantity for each order issued but tends to issue the order at predetermined time intervals.

PERIODIC ORDER QUANTITY. The **periodic order quantity (POQ)** rule allows a different order quantity for each order issued but tends to issue the order at predetermined time intervals, such as every two weeks. The order quantity equals the amount of the item needed during the predetermined time between orders and must be large enough to prevent shortages. Specifically, the POQ is

$$\begin{pmatrix} \text{POQ lot size} \\ \text{to arrive in} \\ \text{week } t \end{pmatrix} = \begin{pmatrix} \text{Total gross requirements} \\ \text{for } P \text{ weeks, including} \\ \text{week } t \end{pmatrix} - \begin{pmatrix} \text{Projected on-hand} \\ \text{inventory balance at} \\ \text{end of week } t-1 \end{pmatrix}$$

This amount exactly covers P weeks' worth of gross requirements. That is, the projected on-hand inventory should equal zero at the end of the Pth week.

TUTOR 15.1

Suppose that we want to switch from the FOQ rule used in Figure 15.6 to the POQ rule. Figure 15.7 shows application of the POQ rule, with $P = 3$ weeks, to the seat subassembly inventory. The first order is required in week 4 because that is the first week when the projected inventory balance will fall below zero. The first order using $P = 3$ weeks is

$$\begin{pmatrix} \text{POQ} \\ \text{lot} \\ \text{size} \end{pmatrix} = \begin{pmatrix} \text{Gross requirements} \\ \text{for weeks} \\ 4, 5, \text{ and } 6 \end{pmatrix} - \begin{pmatrix} \text{Inventory at} \\ \text{end of week } 3 \end{pmatrix}$$

$$= (120 + 0 + 150) - 117 = 153 \text{ units}$$

FIGURE 15.7

The POQ (P = 3) Rule for the Seat Subassembly

Solver - Single-Item MRP

Enter data in yellow-shaded areas.

		1	2	3	4	5	6	7	8
Periods	8								
Item Description	Seat Assembly		Period (P) for POQ	3	Lot Size (FOQ)				
POQ Rule						Lead Time		2	
Gross Requirements		150			120		150	120	
Scheduled Receipts		230							
Projected On-Hand Inventory	37	117	117	117	150	150			
Planned Receipts					153			120	
Planned Order Releases			153		120				

The second order must arrive in week 7, with a lot size of $(120 + 0) - 0 = 120$ units. This second order reflects only two weeks' worth of gross requirements—to the end of the planning horizon.

The POQ rule does *not* mean that operations must issue a new order every P weeks. Rather, when an order *is* planned, its lot size must be enough to cover P successive weeks. One way to select a P value is to divide the average lot size desired, such as the EOQ (see the Inventory Management chapter), or some other applicable lot size, by the average weekly demand. That is, express the target lot size as a desired weeks of supply (P) and round to the nearest integer.

lot-for-lot (L4L) A rule under which the lot size ordered covers the gross requirements of a single week.

LOT FOR LOT. A special case of the POQ rule is the **lot-for-lot** (L4L) rule, under which the lot size ordered covers the gross requirements of a single week. Thus, $P = 1$, and the goal is to minimize inventory levels. This rule ensures that the planned order is just large enough to prevent a shortage in the single week it covers. The L4L lot size is

$$\begin{pmatrix} \text{L4L lot size} \\ \text{to arrive in} \\ \text{week } t \end{pmatrix} = \begin{pmatrix} \text{Gross requirements} \\ \text{for week } t \end{pmatrix} - \begin{pmatrix} \text{Projected on-hand} \\ \text{inventory balance at} \\ \text{the end of week } t - 1 \end{pmatrix}$$

The projected on-hand inventory combined with the new order will equal zero at the end of week t. Following the first planned order, an additional planned order will be used to match each subsequent gross requirement.

This time we want to switch from the FOQ rule to the L4L rule. Figure 15.8 shows application of the L4L rule to the seat subassembly inventory. As before, the first order is needed in week 4:

$$\begin{pmatrix} \text{L4L} \\ \text{lot} \\ \text{size} \end{pmatrix} = \begin{pmatrix} \text{Gross requirements} \\ \text{in week 4} \end{pmatrix} - \begin{pmatrix} \text{Inventory balance} \\ \text{at end of week 3} \end{pmatrix}$$

$$= 120 - 117 = 3$$

The stockroom must receive additional orders in weeks 6 and 7 to satisfy each of the subsequent gross requirements. The lot size for week 6 is 150 and for week 7 is 120.

FIGURE 15.8

The Lot-for-Lot (L4L) Rule for the Seat Subassembly

Solver - Single-Item MRP

Enter data in yellow-shaded areas.

Periods	8								
Item	Seat Assembly		Period (P) for POQ			Lot Size (FOQ)			
Description						Lead Time			2
L4L Rule ▼		1	2	3	4	5	6	7	8
Gross Requirements		150			120		150	120	
Scheduled Receipts		230							
Projected On-Hand Inventory	37	117	117	117					
Planned Receipts					3		150	120	
Planned Order Releases			3		150	120			

COMPARISON OF LOT-SIZING RULES. Choosing a lot-sizing rule can have important implications for inventory management. Lot-sizing rules affect inventory costs and setup or ordering costs. The FOQ, POQ, and L4L rules differ from one another in one or both respects. In our example, each rule took effect in week 4, when the first order was placed. Let us compare the projected on-hand inventory averaged over weeks 4 through 8 of the planning horizon. The data are shown in Figure 15.6, 15.7, and 15.8, respectively.

$$\text{FOQ: } \frac{227 + 227 + 77 + 187 + 187}{5} = 181 \text{ units}$$

$$\text{POQ: } \frac{150 + 150 + 0 + 0 + 0}{5} = 60 \text{ units}$$

$$\text{L4L: } \frac{0 + 0 + 0 + 0 + 0}{5} = 0 \text{ units}$$

The performance of the L4L rule with respect to average inventory levels comes at the expense of an additional planned order and its accompanying setup time and cost. We can draw three conclusions from this comparison.

1. The FOQ rule generates a high level of average inventory because it creates inventory *remnants*. A remnant is inventory carried into a week but is too small to prevent a shortage. Remnants occur because the FOQ does not match requirements exactly. For example, according to Figure 15.6, the stockroom must receive a planned order in week 7, even though 77 units are on hand at the beginning of that week. The remnant is the 77 units that the stockroom will carry for three weeks, beginning with receipt of the first planned order in week 4. Although they increase average inventory levels, inventory remnants introduce stability into the production process by buffering unexpected scrap losses, capacity bottlenecks, inaccurate inventory records, or unstable gross requirements.

2. The POQ rule reduces the amount of average on-hand inventory because it does a better job of matching order quantity to requirements. It adjusts lot sizes as requirements increase or decrease. Figure 15.7 shows that in week 7, when the POQ rule has fully taken effect, the projected on-hand inventory is zero. There are no remnants.

3. The L4L rule minimizes inventory investment, but it also maximizes the number of orders placed. This rule is most applicable to expensive items or items with small ordering or setup costs. It is the only rule that can be used for a low-volume item made to order.

By avoiding remnants, both the POQ and the L4L rule may introduce instability by tying the lot-sizing decision so closely to requirements. If any requirement changes, so must the lot size, which can disrupt component schedules. Last-minute increases in parent orders may be hindered by missing components.

SAFETY STOCK

An important managerial issue is the quantity of safety stock to require. It is more complex for dependent demand items than for independent demand items. Safety stock for dependent demand items with lumpy demand (gross requirements) is valuable only when future gross requirements, the timing or size of scheduled receipts, and the amount of scrap are uncertain. Safety stock should be reduced and ultimately removed as the causes of the uncertainty are eliminated. The usual policy is to use safety stock

Tutor 15.1 - FOQ, POQ, and L4L Rules

FOQ Rule								Lot Size	230
								Lead Time	2
								Safety Stock	80
		1	2	3	4	5	6	7	8
Gross Requirements		150	0	0	120	0	150	120	0
Scheduled Receipts		230	0	0	0	0	0	0	0
Projected On-Hand Inventory	37	117	117	117	227	227	307	187	187
Planned Receipts		0	0	0	230	0	230	0	0
Planned Order Releases		0	230	0	230	0	0	0	0

for end items and purchased items to protect against fluctuating customer orders and unreliable suppliers of components and to avoid using it as much as possible for intermediate items. Safety stocks can be incorporated in the MRP logic by scheduling a planned receipt whenever the projected on-hand inventory balance drops below the desired safety stock level (rather than zero as before). The objective is to keep a minimum level of planned inventories equal to the safety stock quantity. Figure 15.9 shows what happens when there is a requirement for 80 units of safety stock for the seat assembly using a FOQ of 230 units. Compare these results to Figure 15.6. The net effect is to move the second planned order release from week 5 to week 4 to avoid going below 80 units in week 6.

OUTPUTS FROM MATERIAL REQUIREMENTS PLANNING

Material requirements planning systems provide many reports, schedules, and notices to help managers control dependent demand inventories, as indicated in Figure 15.10. In this section, we discuss the MRP explosion process, action notices that alert managers to items needing attention, and capacity reports that project the capacity requirements implied by the material requirements plan.

MATERIAL REQUIREMENTS PLANNING EXPLOSION

What information is available from MRP systems that will provide help in managing materials better?

MRP translates, or *explodes*, the master production schedule and other sources of demand into the requirements for all subassemblies, components, and raw materials needed to produce parent items. This process generates the material requirements plan for each component item.

An item's gross requirements are derived from three sources:

1. the MPS for immediate parents that are end items,
2. the planned order releases for parents below the MPS level, and
3. any other requirements not originating in the MPS, such as the demand for replacement parts.

Consider the seat subassembly for which we have developed the inventory record shown in Figure 15.6. The seat subassembly requires a seat cushion and a seat frame, which in turn needs four seat-frame boards. Its BOM is shown in Figure 15.11 (see also Figure 15.3, which shows how the seat subassembly BOM relates to the product as a whole). How many seat cushions should we order from the supplier? How many seat frames should we produce to support the seat subassembly schedule? How many

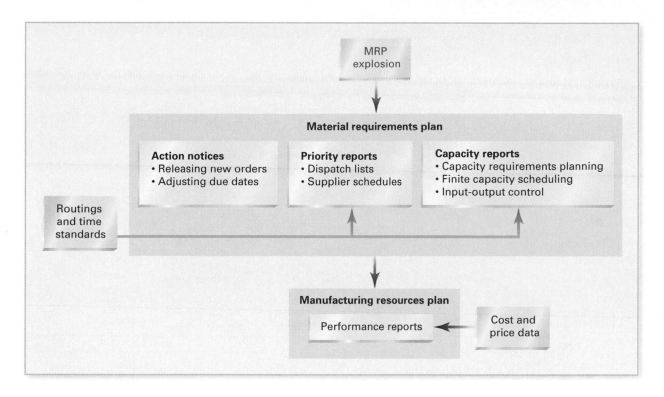

FIGURE 15.10

Material Requirements Planning Outputs

seat-frame boards do we need to make? The answers to these questions depend on the inventories we already have of these items and the replenishment orders already in progress. MRP can help answer these questions through the explosion process.

Figure 15.12 shows the MRP records for the seat subassembly and its components. We have already shown how to develop the MRP record for the seat subassembly. We now concentrate on the MRP records of its components. The lot-size rules are an FOQ of 300 units for the seat frame, L4L for the seat cushion, and an FOQ of 1,500 for the seat-frame boards. All three components have a one-week lead time. The key to the

FIGURE 15.11

Bill of Materials for the Seat Subassembly

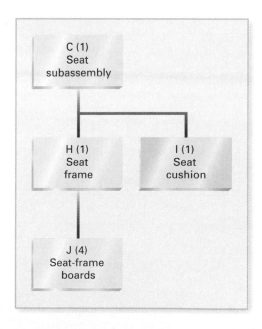

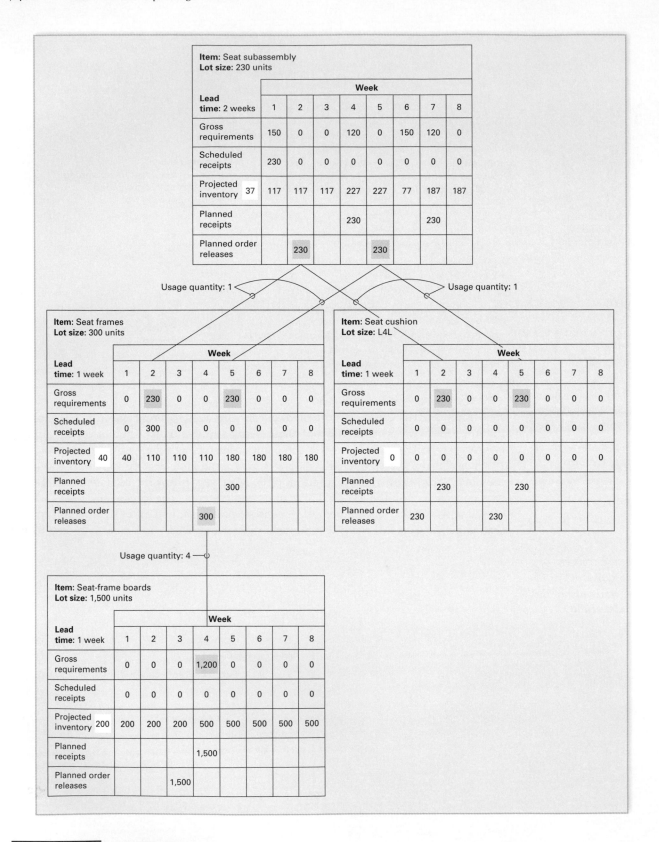

FIGURE 15.12   *MRP Explosion of Seat Assembly Components*

explosion process is to determine the proper timing and size of the gross requirements for each component. When we have done that, we can derive the planned order release schedule for each component by using the logic we have already demonstrated.

In our example, the components have no independent demand for replacement parts. Consequently, in Figure 15.12, the gross requirements of a component come from the planned order releases of its parents. The seat frame and the seat cushion get their gross requirements from the planned order release schedule of the seat subassembly. Both components have gross requirements of 230 units in weeks 2 and 5, the same weeks in which we will be releasing orders to make more seat subassemblies. In week 2, for example, the materials handler for the assembly department will withdraw 230 seat frames and 230 seat cushions from inventory so that the assembly department can produce the seat subassemblies in time to avoid a stockout in week 4. The materials plans for the seat frame and the seat cushion must allow for that.

Using the gross requirements in weeks 2 and 5, we can develop the MRP records for the seat frame and the seat cushion, as shown in Figure 15.12. For a scheduled receipt of 300 in week 2, an on-hand quantity of 40 units, and a lead time of one week, we need to release an order of 300 seat frames in week 4 to cover the assembly schedule for the seat subassembly. The seat cushion has no scheduled receipts and no inventory on hand; consequently, we must place orders for 230 units in weeks 1 and 4, using the L4L logic with a lead time of one week.

Once we have determined the replenishment schedule for the seat frame, we can calculate the gross requirements for the seat-frame boards. We plan to begin producing 300 seat frames in week 4. Each frame requires 4 boards, so we need to have $300(4) = 1,200$ boards available in week 4. Consequently, the gross requirement for seat-frame boards is 1,200 in week 4. Given no scheduled receipts, 200 boards in stock, a lead time of one week, and an FOQ of 1,500 units, we need a planned order release of 1,500 in week 3.

The questions we posed earlier can now be answered. The following orders must be released: 300 seat frames in week 4, 230 seat cushions in each of weeks 1 and 4, and 1,500 seat-frame boards in week 3.

ACTION NOTICES

action notice A computer-generated memo used by inventory planners to make decisions about releasing new orders and adjusting the due dates of scheduled receipts.

Once computed, inventory records for any item appearing in the bills of materials can be printed in hard copy or displayed on a computer video screen. Inventory planners use a computer-generated memo called an **action notice** to make decisions about releasing new orders and adjusting the due dates of scheduled receipts. These notices are generated every time the system is updated. The action notice alerts planners to only the items that need their attention. They can then view the full records for those items and take the necessary actions. An action notice can simply be a list of part numbers for items needing attention. Or it can be the full record for such items, with a note at the bottom identifying the action needed.

action bucket The first week's entry of a planned order release row.

RELEASING NEW ORDERS. When there is a nonzero quantity in the first week's entry of the planned order release row, sometimes called the **action bucket,** the computer issues an action notice. Planned orders in future time periods are not given action notices. An order in the action bucket is the call to release the planned order. When an order is released, paperwork is issued to the shop authorizing the withdrawal of all required materials from the inventory storeroom and the start of production. The date on which production actually begins depends on the amount of work already in the shop. Delaying the release one week will provide *less* than the planned lead time for producing the item. Releasing an order before it gets to the action bucket allows *more* than the planned lead time for production. Action notices are *not* issued for planned order releases outside the action bucket so as to focus attention only on those orders needing immediate attention. Subsequent MRP explosions will generate action notices for future planned orders as they reach the action bucket. Solved Problem 2 provides an example of using action notices to release new orders. There is an action notice for item B, indicating that the planner should release an order of 280 units, and another one for item D, indicating the need to release an order of 500 units.

ADJUSTING DUE DATES OF SCHEDULED RECEIPTS. Action notices are generated any time the system detects a mismatch between a scheduled receipt's due date and the date when the material is needed. If subtracting the scheduled receipt from the projected on-hand inventory for the week in which it is due does not cause a shortage (or the projected on-hand inventory to drop below the desired safety stock, if one is used), the scheduled receipt is arriving too early. In this case, the inventory planner can delay the scheduled receipt. If the projected on-hand balance for the week prior to the arrival of the scheduled receipt indicates a shortage (or is below the desired safety stock), the scheduled receipt is arriving too late. In this case, the planner should expedite the arrival of the scheduled receipt. Mismatches in the planned due dates of scheduled receipts and their actual "need" dates occur because of changes in the item's gross requirements. Figure 15.13 shows an action notice for the seat frames in Figure 15.12 that indicates a need to expedite the scheduled receipt for 300 units so as to cover a projected shortage of 190 units in week 1. The

Action Notice Showing Need to Expedite a Scheduled Receipt

Item: Seat frames   **Lot Size:** 300 units   **Lead Time:** 1 week

				Week				
	1	2	3	4	5	6	7	8
Gross requirements	230				230			
Scheduled receipts		300						
Projected on-hand inventory 40	−190	110	110	110	180	180	180	180
Planned receipts					300			
Planned order releases				300				

Action to be taken:
Stockout projected for week 1.
Reschedule open order In week 2 to week 1.

imbalance in the inventory record is caused by a change in the production schedule for the parent of the seat frames. Expediting an open order that is already in progress makes more sense than releasing a new expedited order. Solved Problem 2, however, shows a reversed situation. There is an action notice for item C suggesting that the scheduled receipt for 200 units could be delayed to week 2 without causing material shortages.

MAKING DECISIONS. Although the computer generates action notices, *decisions* based on them are made by the inventory planner. The planner reviews the item's complete MRP inventory record, along with those of its components. If component inventory is available to support the order, the planner usually decides to release the order as planned. The planner would input an *inventory transaction* to change the computer record file by adding the quantity and due date of a new scheduled receipt. This new order would show up in the scheduled receipts row the next time the system generated the material requirements plan, and it would drop out of the planned order receipt row. When releasing a new order, the computer can also prepare documentation for tool requisitions, routings, or parts lists. For purchased items, a requisition is sent electronically to the appropriate buyer, who in turn places the order with a supplier. These purchasing activities often are automated, particularly when the purchased item is used routinely and a supplier contract has been negotiated.

CAPACITY REPORTS

How can capacity constraints be recognized in the material requirements plan?

By itself, the MRP system does not recognize capacity limitations when computing planned orders. That is, it may call for a planned order release that exceeds the amount that can be physically produced. An essential role of managers is to monitor the capacity requirements of material requirements plans, adjusting a plan when it cannot be met. In this section, we discuss three sources of information for short-term decisions that materials managers continually make: capacity requirements planning reports, finite capacity scheduling reports, and input–output reports.

capacity requirements planning (CRP) A technique used for projecting time-phased capacity requirements for workstations; its purpose is to match the material requirements plan with the plant's production capacity.

CAPACITY REQUIREMENTS PLANNING. One technique for projecting time-phased capacity requirements for workstations is **capacity requirements planning (CRP)**. Its purpose is to match the material requirements plan with the plant's production capacity. The technique is used to calculate workload according to work required to complete the scheduled receipts already in the shop and to complete the planned order releases not yet released. This task involves the use of the inventory records, which supply the planned order releases and the status of the scheduled receipts; the item's routing, which specifies the workstations that must process the item; average lead times between each workstation; and the average processing and setup times at each workstation. Using the MRP dates for arrival of replenishment orders for an item to avoid shortages, CRP traces back through the item's routing to estimate when the scheduled receipt or planned order will reach each workstation. The system uses the processing and setup times to estimate the load that the item will impose on each station for each planned order and scheduled receipt of the item. The workloads for each workstation are obtained by adding the time that each item needs at a particular workstation. Critical workstations are those at which the projected loads exceed station capacities.

Figure 15.14 shows a capacity requirements report for a lathe station that turns wooden table legs. Each of four lathes is scheduled for two shifts per day. The lathe station has a maximum capacity of 320 hours per week. The *planned* hours represent labor requirements for all planned orders for items that need to be routed through the lathe station. The *actual* hours represent the backlog of work visible on the shop floor (i.e., scheduled receipts). Combining requirements from both sources gives *total* hours.

FIGURE 15.14

Capacity Requirements Report

Date: **Week:** 32
Plant 01 Dept. 03: Lathe Station
Capacity: 320 hours per week

	Week					
	32	33	34	35	36	37
Planned hours	90	156	349	210	360	280
Actual hours	210	104	41	0	0	0
Total hours	300	260	390	210	360	280

Explanation:
Projected capacity requirements exceed weekly hours of capacity.

Comparing total hours to actual capacity constraints gives advance warning of any potential problems. The planner must manually resolve any capacity problems uncovered.

For example, the CRP report shown in Figure 15.14 would alert the planner to the need for scheduling adjustments. Unless something is done, the current capacity of 320 hours per week will be exceeded in week 34 and again in week 36. Requirements for all other time periods are well below the capacity limit. Perhaps the best choice is to release some orders earlier than planned so that they will arrive at the lathe station in weeks 32, 33, and 35 rather than weeks 34 and 36. This adjustment will help smooth capacity and alleviate bottlenecks. Other options might be to change the lot sizes of some items, use overtime, subcontract, off-load to another workstation, or simply let the bottlenecks occur.

FINITE CAPACITY SCHEDULING. In large production facilities thousands of orders may be in progress at any one time. Manually adjusting the timing of these orders with the use of spreadsheets or wall-mounted magnetic schedule boards is virtually impossible. The best solutions—those that meet the MRP schedule due dates and do not violate any constraints—may never be identified because of the time needed to explore the alternatives. A useful tool for these situations is a **finite capacity scheduling (FCS)** system, which is an algorithm designed to schedule a group of orders appropriately across an entire shop. The system utilizes routings for the items manufactured, resource constraints, available capacity, shift patterns, and a scheduling rule to be used at each workstation to determine the priorities for orders (see the Scheduling chapter).

finite capacity scheduling (FCS) An algorithm designed to schedule a group of orders appropriately across an entire shop.

To be effective, the FCS system needs to be integrated with MRP. The MRP system can download the orders that need to be scheduled, but the FCS system needs much more than that. An FCS system operates at a finer level of detail than MRP and needs to know the status of each machine and when the current order will finish processing, the maintenance schedule, the routings, the setup times, machine speeds and capabilities, and resource capacities, for example. The FCS system uses that information to determine actual, realistic start and end times of jobs and uploads the results to MRP for subsequent replanning. The FCS system provides a more accurate picture than MRP of when the orders will be completed because MRP uses estimates for job waiting times in job lead times, does not recognize capacities when making the materials plans, and often uses aggregated time buckets (e.g., weeks). If these realistic completion times conflict with the MRP schedule, it may have to be revised and the FCS system rerun. Many companies are using advanced planning and scheduling (APS) systems that link their FCS and MRP systems to their ERP and supply-chain management systems (see the Scheduling chapter).

input–output control report A report that compares planned input (from prior CRP or FCS reports) with actual input and compares planned output with actual output.

INPUT–OUTPUT CONTROL. An **input–output control report** compares planned input (from prior CRP or FCS reports) with actual input and compares planned output with actual output. Inputs and outputs are expressed in common units, usually labor or machine hours. Information in the report indicates whether workstations have been performing as expected and helps management pinpoint the source of capacity problems. Actual outputs can fall behind planned outputs for two reasons:

1. *Insufficient Inputs.* Output may lag when inputs are insufficient to support the planned output rates. The problem can lie upstream at a prior operation, or it may be caused by missing purchased parts. In effect, not enough work arrives to keep the operation busy.

2. *Insufficient Capacity.* Output may lag at the station itself. Even though input rates keep pace, output may slip below expected levels because of absenteeism, equipment failures, inadequate staffing levels, or low productivity rates.

The input–output report shown in Figure 15.15 was prepared for a rough mill workstation at which desk chair components are machined. Management established a tolerance of ±25 hours of cumulative deviations from plans. As long as cumulative deviations do not exceed this threshold, there is no cause for concern. However, the report shows that in week 31 actual outputs fell behind planned outputs by a total

FIGURE 15.15

Input–Output Report

Workstation: Rough Mill					Week: 32
Tolerance: ±25 hours					

	Week Ending				
	28	29	30	31	32
Inputs					
Planned	160	155	170	160	165
Actual	145	160	168	177	
Cumulative deviation	−15	−10	−12	+5	
Outputs					
Planned	170	170	160	160	160
Actual	165	165	150	148	
Cumulative deviation	−5	−10	−20	−32	

Explanation: Cumulative deviations between −25 hours and +25 hours are allowed.

Explanation: Cumulative deviation exceeds lower tolerance limit, indicating actual hours of output have fallen too far below planned hours of output and some action is required.

of 32 hours. This cumulative deviation exceeds the 25-hour tolerance, so there is a problem. Actual inputs are keeping pace with planned inputs, so the lag results from insufficient capacity at the rough mill station itself. Temporary use of overtime may be necessary to increase the output rate.

IMPLEMENTATION ISSUES

Although thousands of firms have tried MRP, not all have applied it successfully. A company can easily invest $500,000 in an MRP system, only to be plagued still by high inventories and late customer deliveries. What goes wrong? Success is not automatic; it is achieved only through the efforts of those involved in making the system function as intended. Top management support is required, and the project implementation team must be selected so that all affected processes and functional areas are represented (see the Managing Project Processes chapter). However, technical issues such as data integrity, BOM structure, magnitude of lot sizes, and environmental volatility can also play a major role in the success of an MRP implementation.

DATA INTEGRITY. To work properly, any decision support system such as MRP must have valid input data from the master production schedule, bills of materials, and inventory records. When MRP fails to live up to expectations, management should look first at these inputs. Are they accurate, timely, and realistic? Data adequacy makes a significant difference in whether MRP implementation is successful.

Cycle counting, or checking items periodically, is one of several ways to improve accuracy (see the Inventory Management chapter). MRP inventory records are checked against actual counts, and corrections are made to the inventory record file in the MRP system. But this activity can keep a group of cycle counters busy full-time if the number of items in stock is large, and it can be tedious and time consuming. Consider the problem of counting thousands of transistors or resistors in a plant producing electronic products. In such cases, sensitive scales can be used to estimate the number of items in stock. Based on the weight of one or a small number of parts and the weight of their container, the scale can estimate the total number of parts in the container, with errors of less than 1 percent.

BOM STRUCTURE. Product engineers develop a product's bill of materials taking advantage of any assemblies or components that are used in other products. Each item shown in a structured BOM such as the one in Figure 15.3 represents an item that has an inventory record. Even if the item is produced or ordered using L4L logic with no planned safety stock inventory, it may temporarily have inventories because of changes to its requirements during its lead time. The structured BOM also recognizes the way the product is manufactured. For example, the seat frame and the seat cushion are joined together in a process to produce a seat assembly. Another process assembles the ladder backs, seats, front legs, and leg supports to make the ladder-back chair. The furniture company has decided that organizing the manufacturing plant with those processes is the most efficient way to produce the mix of products assigned to it.

Designing breaks in a manufacturing process can also take advantage of part commonality. For example, the seat assembly is used in other end items. Stocking the seat assembly allows the MRP system to aggregate the requirements of all the parents of the seat assembly. Rather than making many small runs of the seat assembly in response to each parent's needs, a more efficient batch or line process can be designed.

The bills of materials for the furniture company's products have several levels to reflect the design of its manufacturing process. Other plants may have been able to design their processes so that they only need to stock raw materials, purchased components, and finished goods, avoiding the need to have any intermediate items. Those bills of materials may have only one level. When used as a tool to schedule inventory replenishment orders as we have shown in this chapter, MRP is most useful in managing large numbers of dependent demand items—that is, when there are many levels in the bills of materials. Thus, the greatest numbers of MRP users are in the fabricated metals, machinery, electric, and electronic industries, which tend to have many BOM levels and consequently lumpy demand for components. The average user of MRP has more than six BOM levels.

MAGNITUDE OF LOT SIZES. Even with many levels, though, dependent demand patterns need not be lumpy. Engineers may be able to reduce the time and cost of making setups, thereby enabling efficient production of small lot sizes (see the Inventory Management and Lean Systems chapters). Often, however, firms are forced to work with large lot sizes for at least some of their processes. The relative advantages of MRP are greatest with more BOM levels *and* larger lot sizes. When the firm works with extremely small lot sizes, dependent demands approximate independent demands and the improvements anticipated by the MRP system may not be very pronounced.

OPERATING ENVIRONMENT VOLATILITY. As with any sophisticated information system, MRP operates best when there is only moderate volatility in the operating environment. A basic assumption underlying MRP systems is that projections of gross requirements, scheduled receipts, inventory on hand, and planned order releases are realistic. This assumption is not valid in a highly volatile manufacturing environment with high scrap rates, capacity bottlenecks, last-minute rush jobs, and unreliable suppliers. Before implementing MRP, volatility in the environment must be minimized.

LINKS TO FUNCTIONAL AREAS

The basic MRP system has its roots in the batch manufacturing of discrete parts involving assemblies that must be stocked to support future manufacturing needs. The focus is on producing schedules that meet the materials needs identified in the master production schedule. When managers realized that the information in an MRP system would be useful to functional areas other than operations, MRP evolved into **manufacturing resource planning (MRP II)**, a system that ties the basic MRP system to the company's financial system. Figure 15.16 shows an overview of an MRP II system. The focus of MRP II is to aid the management of a firm's resources by providing information based on the production plan to all functional areas. MRP II enables managers to test "what-if" scenarios by using simulation. For example, managers can see the effect of changing the MPS on the purchasing requirements for certain critical suppliers or the workload on bottleneck work centers without actually authorizing the schedule. In addition, management can project the dollar value of shipments, product costs, overhead allocations, inventories, backlogs, and profits by using the MRP plan along with prices and product and activity costs from the accounting system. Also, information from the MPS, scheduled receipts, and planned orders can be converted into cash flow projections, broken down by product families. For example, the projected on-hand quantities in MRP inventory records allow the computation of future levels of inventory investment. These levels are obtained simply by multiplying the quantities by the

manufacturing resource planning (MRP II)
A system that ties the basic MRP system to the company's financial system.

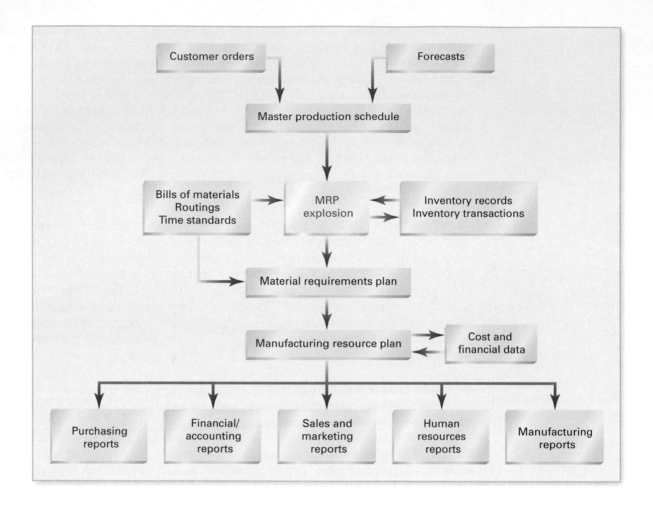

FIGURE 15.16

*Overview of a
Manufacturing
Resource Planning
System*

per-unit value of each item and adding these amounts for all items belonging to the same product family. Similar computations are possible for other performance measures of interest to management.

Information from MRP II is used by managers in manufacturing, purchasing, marketing, finance, accounting, and engineering. MRP II reports help these managers develop and monitor the overall business plan and recognize sales objectives, manufacturing capabilities, and cash flow constraints. MRP II is used extensively and provides benefits beyond that of MRP alone. For example, the Colorado Springs Division of Hewlett-Packard has used MRP II successfully. This division, which makes a variety of complex electronic instruments, modified its MRP system to coordinate its financial reports with its operational plans. As a result, production costs are within 1 percent of predictions. Managerial Practice 15.1 shows how MRP II can support a firm's strategy in the computer industry.

MRP AND THE ENVIRONMENT

Consumer and governmental concern about deterioration of the natural environment has driven manufacturers to reengineer their processes to become more environmentally friendly. Recycling of base materials is becoming more commonplace and products are being designed for ease of remanufacturing after their useful lives. Nonetheless,

MANAGERIAL PRACTICE 15.1
IBM's Rochester Plant Uses MRP to Execute Its Fast Turn-Around Strategy

IBM's Rochester, Minnesota, plant (www.research.ibm.com) is responsible for the final assembly of IBM's AS/400 midrange computers. The complex includes a printed circuit board assembly and testing facility that provides subassemblies to the final assembly lines. Each AS/400 computer is assembled to customer order, which the plant does more than 50,000 times per year. There are more than 10,000 different configurations. The plant must manage over 57,000 parts and assemblies no matter where they might be in the 3.6 million square feet of space the facility occupies, a daunting task without the help of modern systems. To remain competitive in this industry, IBM must promise delivery of complete computers within 96 hours of receiving the order. In addition, because of the short lead times, the plant must procure materials before firm customer orders are received, which requires careful management of inventory levels and shortages.

A core element of the plant's fast turn-around strategy is a MAPICS MRP II system (www.mapics.com), which took 18 months to install. In addition, IBM developed an application called Production Resource Manager (PRM), which interfaces with a firm's MRP II or ERP systems. In addition to typical inputs to an MRP II system, PRM requires *bills of capacity*, production, suppliers and inventory constraints, and optimization objectives such as maximizing profits, minimizing costs, or minimizing inventories. The bills of capacity are analogous to bills of material except they contain the amounts of specific capacities that are needed by a particular configuration of the final product and when they are needed. PRM takes the MRP II plan for component and purchased material replenishment orders and modifies it as needed to account for supply and component availability, capacity constraints, and objectives. The many outputs include a master production schedule, an optimal component production schedule, a revised shipment schedule, and a critical parts list.

IBM's Rochester, Minnesota, plant produces AS/400 computers in more than 10,000 configurations. Management uses an MRP II system to coordinate the production of 50,000 computers a year.

The system has enabled the Rochester plant to improve its inventory accuracy to 99 percent and reduce safety stocks by 15 to 25 percent. The system also includes a cost accounting module, which makes costing information that used to take more than a week to obtain immediately available. In addition, planners can simulate "what-if" scenarios quickly to see the impacts of various events on the production schedule. MRP II and the PRM application have enabled IBM's Rochester plant to execute its fast turn-around strategy.

Sources: "Success Stories: IBM Rochester Minnesota, USA." MAPICS, Inc. (2000), Weaver, Russ. "PRM in Action at Rochester, MN" IBM Corporation (1996), Weaver, Russ. "Production Resource Manager." IBM Corporation (1996).

manufacturing processes often produce a number of wastes that need to be properly disposed of. Wastes come in many forms, including

- ❑ effluents such as carbon monoxide, sulfur dioxide, and hazardous chemicals that are associated with the processes used to manufacture the product;
- ❑ materials such as metal shavings, oils, and chemicals that are associated with specific operations;
- ❑ packaging materials such as unusable cardboard and plastics associated with certain products or purchased items; and
- ❑ scrap associated with unusable product or component defects generated by the manufacturing process.

Companies can modify their MRP systems to assist them in tracking these wastes and planning for their disposition. The type and amount of waste associated with each item can be entered into its bill of materials by treating the waste much like you would a component of the item. When the master production schedule is developed for a product, reports can be generated that project the amount of waste that is expected and when it will occur. Although this approach requires substantial modification of a firm's bills of materials, the benefits are also substantial. Firms can identify their waste problems in advance and consequently plan for the proper disposal of them. The firms also have a means to generate any formal documentation required by the government to verify compliance with environmental laws and policies.

DISTRIBUTION REQUIREMENTS PLANNING

distribution requirements planning (DRP) An inventory control and scheduling technique that applies MRP principles to distribution inventories.

Can MRP be used for distribution inventories?

The principles of MRP can also be applied to distribution inventories, or stocks of items held at retailers and distribution centers. Consider the distribution system in Figure 15.17. The top level represents retail stores at various locations throughout the country. At the middle level are regional distribution centers (DCs) that replenish retail store inventories on request. The bottom level consists of one or more plants that supply the DCs. In the past, plants tended to schedule production to meet the forecasted demand patterns of the DCs. The DCs, in turn, replenished their inventories based on past demand patterns of the retail stores, reordering stocks from the factory whenever the inventory position reached a predetermined reorder point. The retailers followed a similar procedure, ordering stock from the distributor.

To illustrate the shortcomings of this approach, let us suppose that customer demand for a product suddenly increases by 10 percent. What will happen? Because the retailers carry some inventory, there will be some delay before the DCs feel the impact of the full 10 percent increase. Still more time passes before the plants feel the effect of the full increase, reflected as higher demand from the DCs. Thus, for months the plants could continue underproducing at their normal rate. When the deficiency finally becomes apparent, the plants must increase their output by much more than 10 percent to replenish inventory levels.

Distribution requirements planning (DRP) is an inventory control and scheduling technique that applies MRP principles to distribution inventories. It helps avoid self-induced swings in demand. An inventory record is maintained for each item at each location. The planned order releases projected at the retail level are used to derive the gross requirements for each item at the DC level from standard MRP logic and bills of materials. Next, planned order releases at the DC level are computed, from which the

FIGURE 15.17

Distribution System, Showing Supply Links from Plants to Distribution Centers and Retail Stores

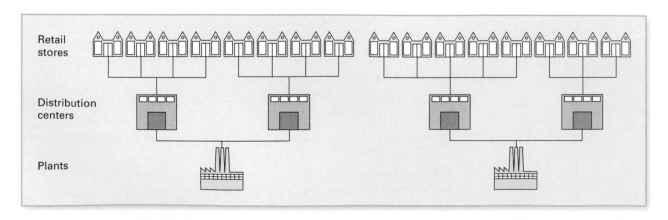

gross requirements for the plant level can be derived. This information provides the basis for updating the master production schedule at the plant.

Use of DRP requires an integrated information system. If the manufacturer operates its own DCs and retail stores, called *forward integration*, gathering demand information and relaying it back to the plants is easy. If the manufacturer does not own the DCs and retail stores, all three levels must agree to convey planned order releases from one level to the next. Open communication can be extended from manufacturers to their suppliers, giving suppliers a better idea of future demand. Reducing demand uncertainty can pay off in lower inventories, better service, or both.

SERVICE RESOURCE PLANNING

Service providers must plan for resources just as manufacturers do. A major difference, however, is that the need for resources in a service company is capacity driven, as opposed to material driven. We have seen how manufacturing companies can disaggregate a master production schedule of finished products into the plans for assemblies, components, and purchased materials, which in turn can be translated into the needs for resources such as staff, equipment, supporting materials, and financial assets. Service providers must plan for the same resources; however, the focus is on maintaining the capacity to serve as opposed to producing a product to stock. Utilization of resources is important because materials are only a fraction of a typical service provider's investment in capital and people. In this section, we will discuss the concept of dependent demands for service providers and the use of a bill of resources.

DEPENDENT DEMAND

How can the concept of dependent demand be useful to service providers?

When we discussed MRP earlier in this chapter, we introduced the concept of *dependent demand,* which is demand for an item that is a function of the demand for some other item the company produces. For service resource planning, it is useful to define the concept of dependent demand to include demands for resources that are driven by forecasts of customer requests for services or by plans for various activities in support of the services the company provides. For example, a resource every service provider manages closely is cash. Forecasts of customer requests for services drive the need to purchase supporting materials and outside services. Staffing levels, a function of the forecasts, and employee schedules, a function of the forecasts and the staffing plan, drive the payroll (see the Aggregate Planning and Scheduling chapters). These actions increase the firm's accounts payable. As services are actually completed the accounts receivable increase. Both the accounts receivable and the accounts payable help predict the amount and timing of cash flows for the firm. Here are some other examples of dependent demands for service providers.

RESTAURANTS. Every time you order from the menu at a restaurant, you initiate the need for supporting materials (uncooked food items, plates, and napkins), staff (chef, servers, and dishwashers), and equipment (stoves, ovens, and cooking utensils). Using a forecast of the demand for each type of meal, the manager of the restaurant can estimate the need for resources. Many restaurants have "specials" on certain days, such as fish frys on Fridays or prime ribs on Saturdays. Specials improve the accuracy of the forecast for meal types and typically signal the need for above-average levels of staff help.

AIRLINES. Whenever an airline schedules a flight, there are requirements for supporting materials (meals, beverages, and fuel), staff (pilots, flight attendants, and airport services), and equipment (plane and airport gate). Forecasts of customer patronage of each flight help determine the amount of supporting materials and the type of plane needed. A master schedule of flights based on the forecasts can be exploded to determine the resources needed to support the schedule.

HOSPITALS. With the exception of the emergency room, appointments, a form of master schedule for specific services, generally drive the short-term need for health care resources in hospitals. Forecasts of requests for various services provided by the hospital drive the long-term needs. When you schedule a surgical procedure, you generate a need for supporting materials (medicines, surgical gowns, and linens), staff (surgeon, nurses, and anesthesiologist), and equipment (operating room, surgical tools, and recovery bed). Hospitals must take care so that certain equipment or personnel do not become overcommitted. That is why an appointment for a hernia operation is put off until the surgeon is available, even though the appropriate operating room, nurses, and other resources are available.

HOTELS. The major fixed assets at a hotel are the rooms where guests stay. Given the high capital costs involved, hotels try to maintain as high a utilization rate as possible by offering group rates or special promotions at certain times of the year. Reservations, supplemented by forecasts of "walk-in" customers, provide a master schedule of needs for the hotel's services. When a traveler makes a reservation at a hotel, a need is generated for supporting materials (soap and towels), staff (front desk, housekeeping, and concierge), and equipment (fax, television, and exercise bicycle). Managerial Practice 15.2 shows that resource planning for a large hotel management and holding company can be a complex problem.

BILL OF RESOURCES

bill of resources (BOR)
A record of all the required materials, equipment time, staff, and other resources needed to provide a service, the parent–component relationships, and the usage quantities.

The service analogy to the BOM in a manufacturing company is the **bill of resources (BOR)**, which is a record of all the required materials, equipment time, staff, and other resources needed to provide a service, the parent–component relationships, and the usage quantities. Given a master schedule of services, the bills of resources can be used to derive the time-phased requirements for the firm's critical resources, as we did for the inventory records in MRP. A BOR for a service provider can be as complex as a BOM for a manufacturer. Consider a hospital that has just scheduled treatment of a patient with an aneurysm. As shown in Figure 15.18, the BOR for treatment of an aneurysm has seven levels, starting at the top (end item): (1) discharge; (2) intermediate

MANAGERIAL PRACTICE 15.2

Resource Planning at Starwood Hotels & Resorts Worldwide

Starwood Hotels & Resorts Worldwide (www.starwood.com) is the largest hotel and gambling company in the world, with more than 650 hotels and resorts in more than 70 countries worldwide. It owns international hotel chains such as Sheraton Hotels, CIGA Hotels, Four Points Hotels, and The Luxury Collection, which includes the St. Regis in New York, the Prince de Gaulle in Paris, the Hotel Gritti Palace in Venice, and the Hotel Imperial in Vienna. It also owns Caesar's Palace in Las Vegas and other casinos in Cairo, Egypt, and Atlantic City. Over 50 million travelers a year visit Starwood's properties.

Resource planning at a company such as Starwood is complex, not only because of the size of the business but also because of the variety of its holdings. As in any service environment, resources such as employees, equipment, and supplies must be managed so as to ensure that the needs and expectations of the customers are met. Information technology can help by providing the means for centralized information flows while allowing decision making to take place at the most appropriate level. An important concept for resource planning in services is *dependent demand* for key resources. Starwood makes use of that concept in two ways. First, Starwood's reservation system builds profiles of its customers' preferences so that they can be better served each time they stay at a hotel or resort. For example, the profile would include information such as whether they like a feather or foam pillow, what types of newspapers they like, whether they want a low floor or a high floor, if they want suites, or even if they are handicapped. The profile is used at the time a reservation is made to estimate the requirements for various types of rooms and locations, newspapers, pillows, and any other resource affected by the customer's preferences. Such a capability provides a "customized" experience for each guest.

A couple enjoys eating at a fine restaurant. Each meal initiates the need to buy supporting supplies, staff, and equipment.

Second, Starwood plans to link its worldwide reservation system to its property management system for resource planning at a particular property. The property management system schedules staff and housekeepers and projects requirements for the food-preparation department. Given expected occupancies for weeks in advance, property managers can plan for the needed resources to make their customers' stay enjoyable.

The ERP system Starwood uses for managing the resources of this worldwide enterprise has a centralized database and common modules, including Payroll, Accounts Payable, General Ledger, and Fixed Assets, from Oracle as well as some legacy systems. Given the enormity of this application, various parts of the enterprise will be phased into the integrated system over time.

Source: Baum, David. "Setting the Standard for Service." *Profit Magazine* (1999), www.oracle.com.

care; (3) postoperative care—step down; (4) postoperative care—intensive; (5) surgery; (6) preoperative care—angiogram; and (7) preoperative care—testing. Each level of the BOR has a set of material and resource requirements and a lead time. For example, at level 6 shown in Figure 15.18(b), the patient needs 6 hours of nurses' time, 1 hour of the primary MD's time, 1 hour of the respiratory therapist's time, 24 hours of bed time, 3 different lab tests, 1 dietary meal, and 10 different medicines from the pharmacy. The lead time for this level is 1 day. The lead time for the entire stay for treatment of the aneurysm is 12.2 days. A master schedule of patient admissions and the BORs for each illness enable the hospital to manage their critical resources. Reports analogous to those we discussed for MRP II can be generated for the managers of the major processes in the hospital.

*Bill of Resources for
Treating an Aneurysm*

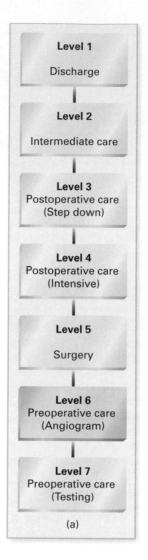

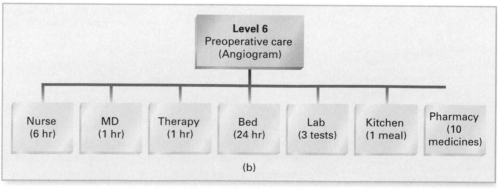

(a)

(b)

RESOURCE PLANNING ACROSS THE ORGANIZATION

Resource planning lies at the heart of any organization. We have seen examples of how traditional bricks-and-mortar organizations such manufacturers, restaurants, airlines, hospitals, and hotels organize their resource planning efforts by utilizing integrated information systems that connect the organization's enterprise processes and functional areas. But what about the so-called dot-coms, which rely extensively on Internet connectivity to customers and suppliers? They too have resource planning concerns that permeate the organization. For example, consider on-line grocers, which do not have the retail outlets and checkout counters their bricks-and-mortar competitors do. What resource planning must on-line grocers do? To be competitive in a very competitive industry where profit margins are low, they must make it easy for the customer to shop on the Internet, provide a wide variety of goods, and make sure the deliveries of groceries are on time and cost efficient. Their Web pages must be designed to keep track of customers' preferences so that weekly shopping is easier and shoppers are apprised of specials and promotions that sometimes are keyed to the availability of goods in stock. The demands for goods at their warehouses are derived from the orders placed by customers at their Web sites. They must manage their resources at the warehouses to ensure a wide variety of grocery options for customers, enough stock to minimize stockouts, and adequate personnel to fill orders. On-line grocers must do the order picking, packing, and handling that customers normally do at traditional supermarkets. In addition, the delivery of customer orders is derived from the delivery time requested by the customers as well as the completion of the packing process. The delivery of groceries is complicated by the fact that they cannot be left at the door if the customer is not home, and rural deliveries are usually far apart from each other and difficult to efficiently schedule. This operation needs a specialized delivery fleet, capable of moving perishable, bulky items over short distances. Effective management of the delivery service is critical to an on-line grocery's success. Finally, on-line grocers are also concerned with planning their cash flows, which are derived from the timing between its sales of groceries and their payments to suppliers and employees. Dot-com companies have very important resource planning problems that affect all the major processes of the firm.

CHAPTER HIGHLIGHTS

☐ Dependent demand for component items can be calculated from production schedules of parent items in a manufacturing company. Dependent demands can be calculated from forecasts and other resource plans in a service company.

☐ Material requirements planning (MRP) is a computerized scheduling and information system that offers benefits in managing dependent demand inventories because it (1) recognizes the relationship between production schedules and the demand for component items, (2) provides forward visibility for planning and problem solving, and (3) provides a way to change materials plans in concert with production schedule changes. MRP has three basic

inputs: bills of materials, the master production schedule, and inventory records.

☐ A bill of materials is a diagram or structured list of all components of an item, the parent–component relationships, and usage quantities.

☐ A master production schedule (MPS) states the number of end items to be produced during specific time periods within an intermediate planning horizon. The MPS is developed within the overall guidelines of the production plan.

☐ The MRP is prepared from the most recent inventory records for all items. The basic elements in each record are gross requirements, scheduled receipts, projected on-hand inventory, planned receipts, and planned order releases. Several quantities must be determined for each inventory record, including lot size, lead time, and safety stock.

❐ The MRP explosion procedure determines the production schedules of the components that are needed to support the master production schedule. The planned order releases of a parent, modified by usage quantities shown in the bill of materials, become the gross requirements of its components.

❐ MRP systems provide outputs such as the material requirements plan, action notices, capacity reports, and performance reports. Action notices bring to a planner's attention new orders that need to be released or items that have open orders with misaligned due dates.

❐ Capacity requirements planning (CRP) is a technique for estimating the workload required by a master schedule. CRP uses routing information to identify the workstations involved and MRP information about existing inventory, lead-time off-

set, and replacement part requirements to calculate accurate workload projections. Finite capacity scheduling (FCS) determines a schedule for production orders that recognizes resource constraints. The input–output control report monitors activity at the workstations and compares actual workloads to those planned by CRP or FCS. Discrepancies between the actual and the plan indicate the need for corrective action.

❐ Manufacturing resource planning (MRP II) ties the basic MRP system to the financial and accounting systems. Advanced systems integrate management decision support for all business functions.

❐ Implementation of MRP systems is widespread. Significant inventory, customer service, and productivity benefits have been reported by many firms. Prerequisites to successful implementation are adequate managerial and computer support, accurate databases, and user knowledge and acceptance. The relative benefits of MRP depend on the number of BOM levels, the magnitude of lot sizes, and environmental volatility.

❐ Service providers can take advantage of MRP principles by developing bills of resources that include requirements for materials, labor, and equipment.

KEY TERMS

action bucket *749*	fixed order quantity (FOQ) *742*	MRP explosion *735*
action notice *749*	gross requirements *739*	parent *733*
bill of materials (BOM) *736*	input–output control report *753*	part commonality *737*
bill of resources (BOR) *760*	intermediate item *737*	periodic order quantity (POQ) *743*
capacity requirements	inventory record *738*	planned order release *741*
planning (CRP) *751*	lot-for-lot (L4L) *744*	planned receipts *740*
component *733*	manufacturing resource planning	projected on-hand inventory *740*
dependent demand *733*	(MRP II) *755*	purchased item *737*
distribution requirements	master production schedule	subassembly *737*
planning (DRP) *758*	(MPS) *737*	usage quantity *736*
end item *737*	material requirements	
finite capacity scheduling (FCS) *752*	planning (MRP) *733*	

SOLVED PROBLEM 1

Refer to the bill of materials for item A shown in Figure 15.19.

If there is no existing inventory, how many units of G, E, and D must be purchased to produce five units of end item A?

SOLUTION

Five units of G, 30 units of E, and 20 units of D must be purchased to make 5 units of A. The usage quantities shown in Figure 15.19 indicate that 2 units of E are needed to make 1 unit of B and that 3 units of B are needed to make 1 unit of A; therefore, 5 units of A require 30 units of E $(2 \times 3 \times 5 = 30)$. One unit of D is consumed to make 1 unit of B, and 3 units of B per unit of A result in 15 units of D $(1 \times 3 \times 5 = 15)$; plus 1 unit of D in each unit of C and 1 unit of C per unit of A result in another 5 units of D $(1 \times 1 \times 5 = 5)$. The total requirements to make 5 units of A are 20 units of D $(15 + 5)$. The calculation of requirements for G is simply $1 \times 1 \times 1 \times 5 = 5$ units.

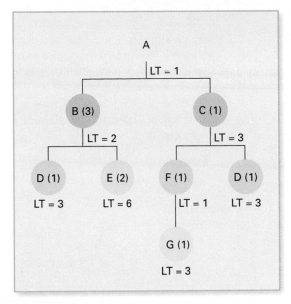

FIGURE 15.19

SOLVED PROBLEM 2

The MPS for product A calls for the assembly department to begin final assembly according to the following schedule: 100 units in week 2; 200 units in week 4; 120 units in week 6; 180 units in week 7; and 60 units in week 8. Develop a material requirements plan for the next eight weeks for items B, C, and D, identifying any action notices that would be provided. The BOM for A is shown in Figure 15.20, and data from the inventory records are shown in Table 15.1.

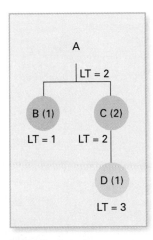

FIGURE 15.20

TABLE 15.1 *Inventory Record Data*

	ITEM		
DATA CATEGORY	**B**	**C**	**D**
Lot-sizing rule	POQ ($P = 3$)	L4L	FOQ $= 500$ units
Lead time	1 week	2 weeks	3 weeks
Scheduled receipts	None	200 (week 1)	None
Beginning (on-hand) inventory	20	0	425

SOLUTION

We begin with items B and C and develop their inventory records, as shown in Figure 15.21. The MPS for item A must be multiplied by 2 to derive the gross requirements for item C because of the usage quantity. Once the planned order releases for item C are found, the gross requirements for item D can be calculated.

An action notice would call for delaying the scheduled receipt for item C from week 1 to week 2. Other action notices would notify planners that items B and D have a planned order release in the action bucket.

Item: B Description:								Lot Size: POQ ($P=3$) Lead Time: 1 week		
					Week					
	1	2	3	4	5	6	7	8	9	10
Gross requirements		100		200		120	180	60		
Scheduled receipts										
Projected on-hand inventory 20	20	200	200	0	0	240	60	0	0	0
Planned receipts		280				360				
Planned order releases	280				360					

Item: C Description:								Lot Size: L4L Lead Time: 2 weeks		
					Week					
	1	2	3	4	5	6	7	8	9	10
Gross requirements		200		400		240	360	120		
Scheduled receipts	200 →									
Projected on-hand inventory 0	200	0	0	0	0	0	0	0	0	0
Planned receipts				400		240	360	120		
Planned order releases		400		240	360	120				

FIGURE 15.21

Item: D Description:							Lot Size: FOQ = 500 units Lead Time: 3 weeks				
		Week									
		1	2	3	4	5	6	7	8	9	10
Gross requirements			400		240	360	120				
Scheduled receipts											
Projected on-hand inventory	425	425	25	25	285	425	305	305	305	305	305
Planned receipts					500	500					
Planned order releases		500	500								

FIGURE 15.21 (*continued*)

DISCUSSION QUESTIONS

1. Form a group with each member representing a different functional area. Identify the nature and importance of the information that a material requirements plan can provide to each of the functional areas.

2. Consider the tours of Lower Florida Keys Health System (LFKHS) and Chapparal Steel in Chapter 2 and the Virtual Text CD. Explain how the concept of a bill of resources (BOR) can help LFKHS plan for medical resources. Could Chapparal Steel use the BOR concept as well?

3. Consider a service provider that is in the delivery business, such as UPS or FedEx. How can the principles of MRP be useful to such a company?

OM EXPLORER AND INTERNET EXERCISES

Visit our Web site at www.prenhall.com/krajewski for OM Explorer Tutors, which explain quantitative techniques; Solvers, which help you apply mathematical models; and Internet Exercises, including Facility Tours, which expand on the topics in this chapter.

PROBLEMS

1. Consider the bill of materials in Figure 15.22 on page 768.

   a. How many immediate parents (one level above) does item I have? How many immediate parents does item E have?

   b. How many unique components does item A have at all levels?

   c. Which of the components are purchased items?

   d. How many intermediate items does item A have at all levels?

   e. Given the lead times noted on Figure 15.22, how far in advance of shipment is the earliest purchase commitment required?

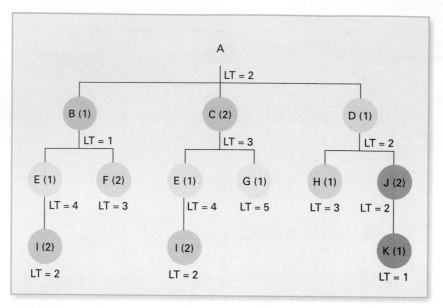

FIGURE 15.22

2. Item A is made from components B, C, and D. Item B is a subassembly that requires 2 units of C and 1 unit of E. Item D also is an intermediate item, made from F. All other usage quantities are 2. Draw the bill of materials for item A.

3. What is the lead time (in weeks) to respond to a customer order for item A, based on the BOM shown in Figure 15.23 and assuming that there are no existing inventories?

4. Item A is made from components B and C. Item B, in turn, is made from D and E. Item C also is an intermediate item, made from F and H. Finally, intermediate item E is made from H and G. Note that item H has two parents. The following are item lead times:

Item	A	B	C	D	E	F	G	H
Lead Time (weeks)	1	2	2	6	5	6	4	3

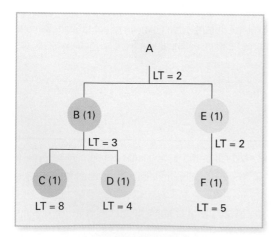

FIGURE 15.23

a. What lead time (in weeks) is needed to respond to a customer order for item A, assuming that there are no existing inventories?

b. What is the customer response time if all purchased items (i.e., D, F, G, and H) are in inventory?

c. If you are allowed to keep just one purchased item in stock, which one would you choose?

5. Refer to Figure 15.19 and Solved Problem 1. If there are 2 units of B, 1 unit of F, and 3 units of G in inventory, how many units of G, E, and D must be purchased to produce 5 units of end item A?

6. A milling machine workstation makes small gears used in a transmission gear box. As of week 22, the capacity requirements planning (CRP) report for the workstation revealed the following information. The planned hours for weeks 22, 23, 24, 25, 26, and 27 were 40, 60, 100, 120, 175, and 160, respectively. The actual hours for the same weeks were 90, 75, 80, 0, 0, and 0. Each of two machines at the workstation is scheduled for two shifts per day. The workstation has a maximum capacity of 160 hours per week. Does the CRP report reveal any problems at the workstation? If so, what are they and what should be done to correct them?

7. The partially completed inventory record in Figure 15.24 shows gross requirements, scheduled receipts, lead time, and current on-hand inventory.

a. Complete the last three rows of the record for an FOQ of 110 units.

b. Complete the last three rows of the record by using the L4L lot-sizing rule.

Item: M405—X Description: Table top assembly		Lot Size: Lead Time: 2 weeks									
		Week									
		1	2	3	4	5	6	7	8	9	10
Gross requirements		90		85		80		45	90		
Scheduled receipts		110									
Projected on-hand inventory	40										
Planned receipts											
Planned order releases											

FIGURE 15.24

c. Complete the last three rows of the record by using the POQ lot-sizing rule, with $P = 2$.

8. 💿 **OM Explorer** The partially completed inventory record in Figure 15.25 shows gross requirements, scheduled receipts, lead time, and current on-hand inventory.

a. Complete the last three rows of the record for an FOQ of 150 units.

b. Complete the last three rows of the record by using the L4L lot-sizing rule.

c. Complete the last three rows of the record by using the POQ lot-sizing rule, with $P = 2$.

Item: Rotor assembly		Lot Size: Lead Time: 2 weeks							
		Week							
		1	2	3	4	5	6	7	8
Gross requirements		65	15	45	40	80	80	80	80
Scheduled receipts		150							
Projected on-hand inventory	20								
Planned receipts									
Planned order releases									

FIGURE 15.25

Item: Driveshaft					Lot Size:			
					Lead Time: 3 weeks			
	Week							
	1	2	3	4	5	6	7	8
Gross requirements	35	25	15	20	40	40	50	50
Scheduled receipts	80							
Projected on-hand inventory 10								
Planned receipts								
Planned order releases								

FIGURE 15.26

9. ● **OM Explorer** The partially completed inventory record in Figure 15.26 shows gross requirements, scheduled receipts, lead time, and current on-hand inventory.

   a. Complete the last three rows of the inventory record for an FOQ of 50 units.

   b. Complete the last three rows of the record by using the L4L lot-sizing rule.

   c. Complete the last three rows of the record by using the POQ lot-sizing rule, with $P = 4$.

10. ● **OM Explorer** Figure 15.27 shows a partially completed inventory record. Gross requirements, scheduled

Item: MQ—09						Lot Size:				
Description: Rear wheel assembly						Lead Time: 1 week				
	Week									
	1	2	3	4	5	6	7	8	9	10
Gross requirements	205		130	85		70	60	95		
Scheduled receipts	300									
Projected on-hand inventory 100										
Planned receipts										
Planned order releases										

FIGURE 15.27

Item: GF—4
Description: Motor assembly

Lot Size:
Lead Time: 3 weeks

	Week											
	1	2	3	4	5	6	7	8	9	10	11	12
Gross requirements		50		35		55		30		10		25
Scheduled receipts		60										
Projected on-hand inventory 40												
Planned receipts												
Planned order releases												

FIGURE 15.28

receipts, lead time, and current on-hand inventory, are shown.

a. Complete the record for an FOQ of 300 units.

b. Complete the record by using the L4L rule.

c. Complete the record by using the POQ rule, with $P = 4$.

11. 💿 **OM Explorer** The inventory record in Figure 15.28 has been partially completed.

a. Complete the last three rows for an FOQ of 60 units. If there are action notices, what factors should you consider in responding to them?

b. Revise the planned order release row by using the L4L rule.

c. Revise the planned order release row by using the POQ rule. Find the value of P that should (in the long run) yield an average lot size of 60 units. Assume that the average weekly demand for the foreseeable future is 15 units.

12. 💿 **OM Explorer** The BOM for product A is shown in Figure 15.29, and data from the inventory records are shown in Table 15.2. In the master production schedule for product A, the MPS start row has 500 units in week 6. The lead time for production of A is two weeks. Develop the material requirements plan for the next six weeks for items B, C, and D.

After completing the plan, identify any action notices that would be issued. (*Hint*: You cannot derive an item's gross requirements unless you know the planned order releases of all its parents.)

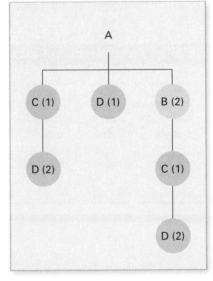

FIGURE 15.29

TABLE 15.2 *Inventory Record Data*

	ITEM		
DATA CATEGORY	B	C	D
Lot-sizing rule	L4L	L4L	FOQ = 2,000
Lead time	3 weeks	1 week	1 week
Scheduled receipts	None	None	2,000 (week 1)
Beginning inventory	0	0	200

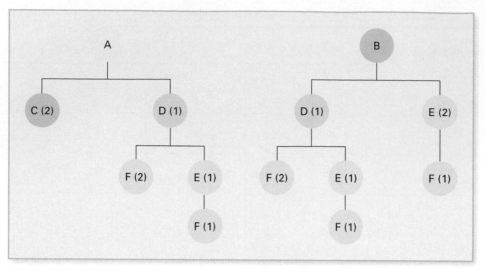

FIGURE 15.30

13. **OM Explorer** The BOMs for products A and B are shown in Figure 15.30. Data from inventory records are shown in Table 15.3. The MPS calls for 85 units of product A to be started in week 3 and 100 units in week 6. The MPS for product B calls for 180 units to be started in week 5. Develop the material requirements plan for the next six weeks for items C, D, E, and F. Identify any action notices.

14. **OM Explorer** Figure 15.31 illustrates the BOM of product A. The MPS start row in the master production schedule for product A calls for 50 units in week 2, 65 units in week 5, and 80 units in week 8. Item C is produced to make A and to meet the forecasted demand for replacement parts. Past replacement part demand has been 20 units per week (add 20 units to C's gross requirements). The lead times for items F and C are one week, and for the other items the lead time is two weeks. No safety stock is required for items B, C, D, E, and F. The L4L lot-sizing rule is used for items B and F; the POQ lot-sizing rule ($P = 3$) is used for C. Item E has an FOQ of 600 units, and D has an FOQ of 250 units. On-hand inventories are 50 units of B, 50 units of C, 120 units of D, 70 units of E, and 250 units of F. Item B has a scheduled receipt of 50 units in week 2.

TABLE 15.3 *Inventory Record Data*

DATA CATEGORY	ITEM			
	C	D	E	F
Lot-sizing rule	FOQ = 220	L4L	FOQ = 300	POQ ($P = 2$)
Lead time	3 weeks	2 weeks	3 weeks	2 weeks
Scheduled receipts	280 (week 1)	None	300 (week 3)	None
Beginning inventory	25	0	150	600

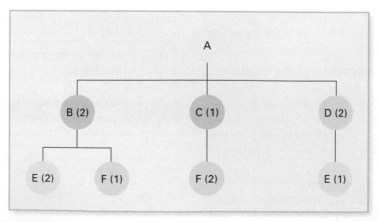

FIGURE 15.31

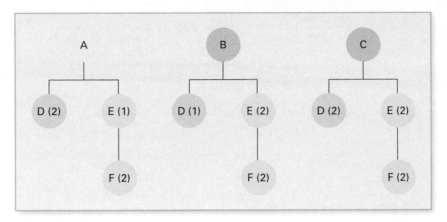

FIGURE 15.32

Develop a material requirements plan for the next eight weeks for items B, C, D, E, and F. What action notices will be generated?

Advanced Problems

15. The following information is available for three MPS items.

    Item A   An 80-unit order is to be started in week 3.
                  A 55-unit order is to be started in week 6.
    Item B   A 125-unit order is to be started in week 5.
    Item C   A 60-unit order is to be started in week 4.

Develop the material requirements plan for the next six weeks for items D, E, and F, identifying any action notices that would be provided. The BOMs are shown in Figure 15.32, and data from the inventory records are shown in Table 15.4. (*Warning*: There is a safety stock requirement for item F. Be sure to plan a receipt for any week in which the projected on-hand inventory becomes less than the safety stock.)

TABLE 15.4 *Inventory Record Data*

DATA CATEGORY	ITEM		
	D	E	F
Lot-sizing rule	FOQ = 150	L4L	POQ ($P = 2$)
Lead time	3 weeks	1 week	2 weeks
Safety stock	0	0	30
Scheduled receipts	150 (week 3)	120 (week 2)	None
Beginning inventory	150	0	100

16. At the beginning of week 45, production schedules at the chair assembly workstation called for the existing 60-hour backlog of work to be gradually reduced to 20 hours by the end of week 48. This reduction was to be accomplished by releasing an average of 310 hours of work per week to chair assembly while providing resources sufficient to complete 320 hours per week. At the beginning of week 49, the input–output report represented by Figure 15.33 is brought to your attention.

Workstation: Chair assembly				**Week:** 49	
Tolerance: ±50 hours					
	Week				
	45	46	47	48	49
Inputs					
Planned	310	310	310	310	320
Actual	305	285	295	270	
Cumulative deviation					
Outputs					
Planned	320	320	320	320	320
Actual	320	305	300	290	
Cumulative deviation					
Planned ending backlog (hr)	50	40	30	20	20
Actual backlog 60 hr					

FIGURE 15.33

Item: A Description:						Lot Size: 90 units Lead Time: 2 weeks	

		Week						
		1	2	3	4	5	6	7
Gross requirements		65		70			110	60
Scheduled receipts		90						
Projected on-hand inventory	20	45	45	65	65	65	45	75
Planned receipts				90			90	90
Planned order releases		90			90	90		

FIGURE 15.34

a. What triggered this report? (*Hint*: Complete the cumulative deviation rows.)

b. What problem is indicated by the data in the input–output control report? (*Hint*: Calculate the actual backlog row and compare it to the planned backlog row.)

c. What might be done to resolve this problem?

17. ● **OM Explorer** Items A and B are dependent demand items. Item B's only parent is A. The current material requirements plans for A is shown in Figure 15.34. Three units of B are needed to make one unit of A. The order policy for B is L4L and the lead time is three weeks. A scheduled receipt of 270 units for B is to arrive in week 2.

a. Today the planner responsible for items A and B learned some good news and some bad news. Although the scheduled receipt of 90 units of A has been finished (the good news), only 45 units were put in the storeroom; the other 45 units were scrapped (the bad news). Prepare the inventory records for A and B to reflect this event. (*Hint*: A scheduled receipt should no longer be shown for A, but its on-hand balance now is 65 units.)

b. What action notices would be issued relative to the new material requirements plan?

18. ● **OM Explorer** Figure 15.35 shows the BOMs for two end items, A and B. Table 15.5 shows the MPS quantity start date for each one. Table 15.6 contains data from inventory records for items C, D, and E. There are no safety stock requirements for any of the items. Determine the material requirements plan for items C, D, and E for the next eight weeks. Identify any action notices that would be provided.

TABLE 15.5 *MPS Quantity Start Dates*

	DATE							
PRODUCT	1	2	3	4	5	6	7	8
A		125		95		150		130
B			80			70		

TABLE 15.6 *Inventory Record Data*

	ITEM		
DATA CATEGORY	C	D	E
Lot-sizing rule	L4L	POQ ($P = 3$)	FOQ = 800
Lead time	3 weeks	2 weeks	1 week
Scheduled receipts	200 (week 2)	None	800 (week 1)
Beginning inventory	85	625	350

19. ● **OM Explorer** The BOM for product A is shown in Figure 15.36. The MPS for product A calls for 120 units to be started in weeks 2, 4, 5, and 8. Table 15.7 shows

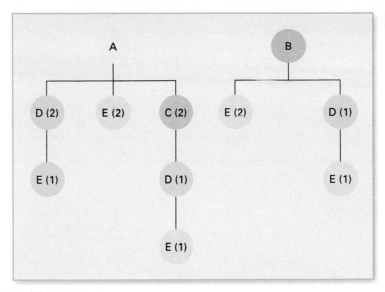

FIGURE 15.35

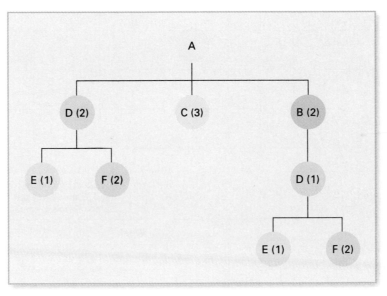

FIGURE 15.36

	TABLE 15.7 *Inventory Record Data*				
	ITEM				
DATA CATEGORY	**B**	**C**	**D**	**E**	**F**
Lot-sizing rule	L4L	FOQ = 700	FOQ = 700	L4L	L4L
Lead time	3 weeks	3 weeks	4 weeks	2 weeks	1 week
Safety stock	0	0	0	50	0
Scheduled receipts	150 (week 2)	450 (week 2)	700 (week 1)	None	1,400 (week 1)
Beginning inventory	125	0	235	750	0

TABLE 15.8 *Inventory Record Data*

DATA CATEGORY	ITEM					
	B	C	D	E	F	G
Lot-sizing rule	L4L	L4L	POQ ($P=2$)	L4L	L4L	FOQ $=100$
Lead time	2 weeks	3 weeks	3 weeks	6 weeks	1 week	3 weeks
Safety stock	30	10	0	0	0	0
Scheduled receipts	150 (week 2)	50 (week 2)	None	400 (week 6)	40 (week 3)	None
Beginning inventory	30	20	60	400	0	0

Item: X
Description:
Lot Size: L4L
Lead Time: 1 week
Safety Stock: 0 units

	Week									
	1	2	3	4	5	6	7	8	9	10
Gross requirements	20	110	50		80	50	100	40		
Scheduled receipts	25									
Projected on-hand inventory	0									
Planned receipts										
Planned order releases										

Item: Y
Description:
Lot Size: POQ ($P=2$ weeks)
Lead Time: 3 weeks
Safety Stock: 0 units

	Week									
	1	2	3	4	5	6	7	8	9	10
Gross requirements										
Scheduled receipts	100									
Projected on-hand inventory	55									
Planned receipts										
Planned order releases										

FIGURE 15.37

data from the inventory records. Develop the material requirements plan for the next eight weeks for each item. Would any action notices be issued? If so, identify them. (*Warning*: Note that item E has a safety stock requirement.)

20. 💿 **OM Explorer** Develop the material requirements plan for all components and intermediate items associated with end item A for the next ten weeks. Refer to Solved Problem 1 (Figure 15.19) for the bill of materials and Table 15.8 for component inventory record informa-

tion. The MPS for product A calls for 50 units to be started in weeks 2, 6, 8, and 9. (*Warning*: Note that items B and C have safety stock requirements.)

21. 💿 **OM Explorer** Items X and Y are dependent demand items. One unit of Y is needed to make one unit of X. Item Y's only parent is X. The current material requirements plans for X and Y are shown in Figure 15.37. Complete the records to determine the planned order releases for items X and Y.

CASE FLASHY FLASHERS, INC.

Jack Jacobs, the P & IM Manager of Flashy Flashers, Inc., stopped for a moment to adjust his tie knot and run his fingers through his hair before entering the office of Ollie Prout, the vice-president of operations. From the tone of Prout's voice over the telephone, Jacobs knew that he was not being called for a social tête-à-tête.

COMPANY BACKGROUND

Flashy Flashers, Inc., is a medium-sized firm employing 500 persons and 75 managerial and administrative personnel. The firm produces a line of automotive electrical components. It supplies about 75 auto parts stores and "Moonbird Silverstreak" car dealers in its region.

Johnny Bennett, who serves as the president, founded the company. Bennett is a great entrepreneur who started producing cable assemblies in his garage. Through hard work, consistent product quality, and high customer service, he expanded his business to produce a variety of electrical components. Bennett's commitment to customer service is so strong that his company motto, "Love Thy Customers As Thyself," is etched on a big cast-iron plaque under his giant oil portrait in the building's front lobby.

The company's two most profitable products are the automotive front sidelamp and the headlamp. With the recent boom in the auto industry and the rising popularity of Eurosport sedans such as the Moonbird Silverstreak, Flashy Flashers has enjoyed substantial demand for these two lamp items.

Last year, on Prout's recommendation—and for better management of the inventory system—Bennett approved the installation of a new MRP system. Prout worked closely with the task force created to bring MRP on-line. He frequently attended the training sessions for selected employees, emphasizing how MRP should help Flashy Flashers secure a better competitive edge. On the day the system "went up," there was an aura of tranquility and good-

will. The days of the informal system of fire fighting were over!

A year later, Prout's mood is quite different. Inventory and overtime levels had not dropped as much as expected, customer service was getting worse, and there were too many complaints about late shipments. Convinced that this should not happen with MRP, Prout is attempting to find out what is going wrong.

THE PROBLEMS

Jacobs had barely taken two steps inside Prout's office when his voice cut across the room. "Jack, what's going on out there? I've just received another call from a customer complaining that we've fallen back on our lamp shipment to them again! This is the umpteenth time I've received complaints about late shipments. Johnny has been on my back about this. Why isn't our system working as it is supposed to and what do we have to do to hold onto valuable customers and stay in business?"

Jacobs gulped and took a moment to regain his composure before answering Prout. "We're trying our best to maintain the inventory records and BOM files. With our system, there's a new explosion each week. This gives us an updated material requirements plan and action notices for launching new orders. Some of my group think we should extend our outputs to get priority and capacity reports. As you know, we decided to get the order-launching capability well established first. However, we don't seem to have a formal system of priority planning, and that's creating scheduling problems on the shop floor.

"I think our purchasing and marketing departments also are at fault. We seem to experience too many stockouts of purchased parts even though we've worked closely with Jayne Spring's group to get realistic lead-time estimates. And marketing keeps taking last-minute orders from favorite customers. This plays havoc with our master production schedule."

continued

continued

"Well, I'm really getting fed up with this," Prout cut in. "Talk with the people concerned and find out what exactly is going wrong. I'll expect a complete report from you in two weeks, giving me all the details and recommendations for improvement."

Jacobs decided to get to the bottom of things, as he walked out of Ollie's office. He first called on Sam McKenzie, the shop superintendent.

PRODUCTION

Jacobs's conversation with McKenzie suggested that the pre-MRP informal system is still alive and well. "I'm starting to wonder about this MRP system, even though it looks great on paper," McKenzie commented. "Last week we hardly had any work, and I was forced to overproduce on several orders just to keep everyone busy. This week is just the opposite, so many new orders were released with short fuses that almost everyone will need to work overtime. It's either feast or famine! Our priority planners don't seem to update the due dates assigned to each order, but things change pretty quickly around here.

"Another thing is the inventory records. When I get an order, I first check the inventory record for that item to find out the current stock situation. More often than not, the actual number of units is less than what the records indicate. This means that I often have to produce more than planned. This plays havoc with our capacity plans. We can't stick to our lead times when things are so fluid around here!"

PURCHASING

Jacobs's next conversation was with Jayne Spring, the purchasing manager. It was equally disconcerting. "Our buyers are really getting frustrated with this new system. There's no time for creative buying. Almost all of their time is spent following up on late orders because of constant expediting notices. For example, the other day we received an action notice to bring in 200 units of part HL222P in just two weeks. We tried all possible vendors, but they said that a delivery in two weeks was impossible. What are the planners doing? The perplexing thing is that the planned lead time in the inventory record for this part is correctly stated as four weeks. Doesn't MRP offset for lead time? On top of this, we also have some problems with unreliable vendor lead times. This requires us to carry more safety stock for some items than is necessary."

Jacobs tried to assimilate all this information. He then proceeded to collect all the required information about the side- and headlamps (shown in Tables 15.9–15.13 and Figure 15.38) and decided to gain further insights into the problem by working out the MRP explosion manually for the next six weeks.

TABLE 15.9 *Part Numbers and Descriptions*

C206P:	Screw
C310P:	Back rubber gasket
HL200E:	Headlamp
HL211A:	Head frame subassembly
HL212P:	Head lens
HL222P:	Headlamp module
HL223F:	Head frame
SL100E:	Sidelamp
SL111P:	Side lens
SL112A:	Side frame subassembly
SL113P:	Side lens rubber gasket
SL121F:	Side frame
SL122A:	Side bulb subassembly
SL123A:	Flasher bulb subassembly
SL131F:	Side cable grommet and receptacle
SL132P:	Side bulb
SL133F:	Flasher cable grommet and receptacle
SL134P:	Flasher bulb

TABLE 15.10 *Master Production Schedule*

The following data show the MPS start dates.

ITEM DESCRIPTION AND PART NUMBER	QUANTITY	MPS START DATE
Sidelamp (SL100E)	100	Week 13
	80	Week 15
	110	Week 16
Headlamp (HL200E)	120	Week 14
	90	Week 15
	75	Week 16

TABLE 15.11 *Replacement Part Demand*

ITEM DESCRIPTION AND PART NUMBER	QUANTITY	DATE
Side lens (SL111P)	40	Week 13
	35	Week 16

YOUR ASSIGNMENT

Put yourself in Jacobs's place and write the report to your boss, Ollie Prout. Specifically, you are required to do a manual MRP explosion for the side- and headlamps for the next six weeks (beginning with the current week). Assume that it is now the start of week 11. Fill in the planned order releases form provided. It should show the

TABLE 15.12 *Selected Data from Inventory Records*

PART NUMBER	LEAD TIME (WEEKS)	SAFETY STOCK (UNITS)	LOT-SIZING RULE	ON-HAND (UNITS)	SCHEDULED RECEIPT (UNITS AND DUE DATES)
C206P	1	30	FOQ = 2500	150	—
C310P	1	20	FOQ = 180	30	180 (week 12)
HL211A	2	0	L4L	10	50 (week 12)
HL212P	2	15	FOQ = 350	15	—
HL222P	4	10	POQ ($P = 4$ week)	50	110 (week 14)
HL223F	1	0	L4L	70	—
SL111P	2	0	FOQ = 350	15	—
SL112A	3	0	L4L	20	100 (week 13)
SL113P	1	20	FOQ = 100	20	—
SL121F	3	0	L4L	0	70 (week 13)
SL122A	1	0	L4L	10	50 (week 12)
SL123A	1	0	L4L	0	—
SL131F	2	0	POQ ($P = 2$ week)	0	—
SL132P	1	25	FOQ = 100	35	100 (week 12)
SL133F	2	0	POQ ($P = 2$ week)	0	180 (week 12)
SL134P	1	25	FOQ = 100	20	100 (week 11)

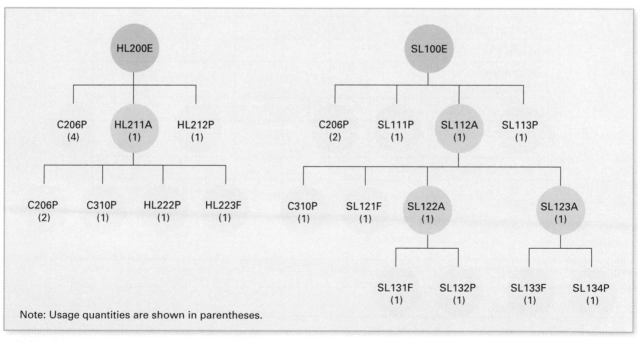

Note: Usage quantities are shown in parentheses.

FIGURE 15.38 • Bills of Materials

planned order releases for all items for the next six weeks. Include it in your report.

Your report should identify the good and bad points of MRP implementation at Flashy Flashers. Supplement your discussion with worksheets on the manual MRP explosion, indicating the types of action notices that should be made for order releases and adjusting priorities. Conclude by making suggestions for change.

continued

continued

TABLE 15.13 *Planned Order Release Form*

(Fill in the planned order releases for all components.)

ITEM DESCRIPTION AND PART NUMBER	WEEK					
	11	12	13	14	15	16
Side lens (SL111P)						
Side lens rubber gasket (SL113P)						
Side frame subassembly (SL112A)						
Side frame (SL121F)						
Side bulb subassembly (SL122A)						
Flasher bulb subassembly (SL123A)						
Side cable grommet and receptacle (SL131F)						
Flasher cable grommet and receptacle (SL133F)						
Side bulb (SL132P)						
Flasher bulb (SL134P)						
Head frame subassembly (HL211A)						
Head lens (HL212P)						
Headlamp module (HL222P)						
Head frame (HL223F)						
Back rubber gasket (C310P)						
Screws (C206P)						

Source: This case was prepared by Professor Soumen Ghosh, Georgia Institute of Technology, for the purpose of classroom discussion only.

SELECTED REFERENCES

Blackstone, J. H. *Capacity Management.* Cincinnati: South-Western, 1989.

Conway, Richard W. "Linking MRP II and FCS." *APICS—The Performance Advantage* (June 1996), pp. 40–44.

Cotten, Jim. "Starting from Scratch." *APICS—The Performance Advantage* (November 1996), pp. 34–37.

Dollries, Joseph. "Don't Pick a Package—Match One." *APICS—The Performance Advantage* (May 1996), pp. 50–52.

Goddard, Walter, and James Correll. "MRP II in the Year 2000." *APICS—The Performance Advantage* (March 1994), pp. 38–42.

Haddock, Jorge, and Donald E. Hubicki. "Which Lot-Sizing Techniques Are Used in Material Requirements Planning?" *Production and Inventory Management Journal,* vol. 30, no. 3 (1989), pp. 53–56.

Hoy, Paul A. "The Changing Role of MRP II." *APICS—The Performance Advantage* (June 1996), pp. 50–53.

Jernigan, Jeff. "Comprehensiveness, Cost-Effectiveness Sweep Aside Operations Challenges." *APICS—The Performance Advantage* (March 1993), pp. 44–45.

Lunn, Terry, and Susan Neff. *MRP: Integrating Material Requirements*

Planning and Modern Business. Homewood, Ill.: Irwin Professional Publication, 1992.

Melnyk, Steven A., Robert Stroufe, Frank Montabon, Roger Calantone, R. Lal Tummala, and Timothy J. Hinds. "Integrating Environmental Issues Into Material Planning. 'Green' MRP." *Production and Inventory Management Journal* (Third Quarter 1999), pp. 36–45.

Orlicky, J. *Material Requirements Planning.* New York: McGraw-Hill, 1975.

Ormsby, Joseph G., Susan Y. Ormsby, and Carl R. Ruthstrom. "MRP II Implementation: A Case Study." *Production and Inventory Management,* vol. 31, no. 4 (1990), pp. 77–82.

Prouty, Dave. "Shiva Finite Capacity Scheduling System." *APICS—The Performance Advantage* (April 1997), pp. 58–61.

Ptak, Carol. *MRP and Beyond.* Homewood, Ill.: Irwin Professional Publication, 1996.

Ritzman, Larry P., Barry E. King, and Lee J. Krajewski. "Manufacturing Performance—Pulling the Right Levers." *Harvard Business Review* (March–April 1984), pp. 143–152.

Roth, Aleda V., and Roland Van Dierdonck. "Hospital Resource Planning: Concepts, Feasibility, and Framework." *Production and Operations Management,* vol. 4, no. 1 (1995), pp. 2–29.

Turbide, David A. "This Is Not Your Father's MRP!" *APICS—The Performance Advantage* (March 1994), pp. 28–37.

Vollmann, T. E., W. L. Berry, and D. C. Whyhark. *Manufacturing Planning and Control Systems,* 4th ed. Homewood, Ill.: Irwin Professional Publications, 1997.

Wallace, Tom. *MRP II: Making It Happen.* Essex Junction, VT: Oliver Wight Ltd. Publishers, 1994.

Wight, Oliver W. *Manufacturing Resource Planning: MRP II.* Essex Junction, VT. Oliver Wight Ltd. Publishers, 1984.

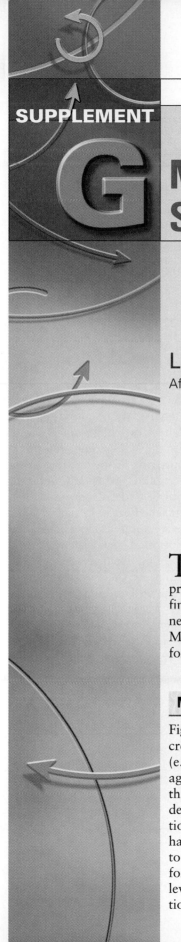

G Master Production Scheduling

Learning Goals

After reading this supplement, you will be able to . . .

1. discuss the importance of the master production schedule (MPS) and the nature of the information that can be derived from it.
2. develop an MPS in a make-to-stock environment.
3. compute available-to-promise quantities for end items.

T HE MASTER PRODUCTION SCHEDULE (MPS) is a link between the firm's broad strategies and tactical plans that enables the firm to achieve its goals. The MPS provides essential information for functional areas such as operations, marketing, and finance. In this supplement, we discuss the master production scheduling process, the need for functional coordination, the way to develop an MPS, the information that an MPS provides to assist in negotiating delivery dates, and the managerial considerations for establishing and stabilizing the MPS.

MASTER PRODUCTION SCHEDULING PROCESS

Figure G.1 shows the master production scheduling process. Operations must first create a prospective MPS to test whether it meets the schedule with the resources (e.g., machine capacities, labor, overtime, and subcontractors) provided for in the aggregate production plan. Operations revises the MPS until it obtains a schedule that satisfies all resource limitations or determines that no feasible schedule can be developed. In the latter event, the production plan must be revised to adjust production requirements or increase authorized resources. Once a feasible prospective MPS has been accepted by plant management, operations uses the authorized MPS as input to material requirements planning. Operations can then determine specific schedules for component production and assembly. Actual performance data such as inventory levels and shortages are inputs to the next prospective MPS, and the master production scheduling process is repeated.

*Master Production
Scheduling Process*

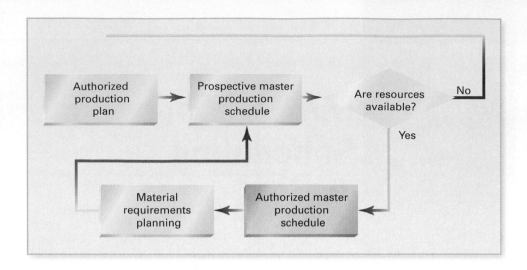

FUNCTIONAL INTERFACES

Operations needs information from other functional areas to develop an MPS that achieves production plan objectives and organizational goals. Although master production schedules are continually subject to revision, changes should be made with a full understanding of their consequences. Often, changes to the MPS require additional resources, as in the case of an increase in the order quantity of a product. Many companies face this situation frequently, and the problem is amplified when an important customer is involved. Unless more resources are authorized for the product, less resources will be available for other products, putting their schedules in jeopardy. Some companies require the vice-presidents of marketing and manufacturing jointly to authorize significant MPS changes to ensure mutual resolution of such issues.

Other functional areas can use the MPS for routine planning. Finance uses the MPS to estimate budgets and cash flows. Marketing can use it to project the impact of product mix changes on the firm's ability to satisfy customer demand and manage delivery schedules. Manufacturing can use it to estimate the effects of MPS changes on loads at critical workstations. Personal computers, with their excellent graphic capabilities, give managers access to many MPS-related reports in readable and useful formats. PC programs allow managers to ask "what-if" questions about the effects of changes to the MPS.

DEVELOPING A MASTER PRODUCTION SCHEDULE

The process of developing a master production schedule includes (1) calculating the projected on-hand inventory and (2) determining the timing and size of the production quantities of specific products. We use the manufacturer of the ladder-back chair (see the Resource Planning chapter) to illustrate the process. For simplicity, we assume that the firm does not utilize safety stocks for end items, even though many firms do. In addition, we use weeks as our planning periods, even though hours, days, or months could be used.

Step 1.   *Calculate Projected On-Hand Inventories.* The first step is to calculate the projected on-hand inventory, which is an estimate of the amount of inventory available each week after demand has been satisfied:

$$\begin{pmatrix} \text{Projected on-hand} \\ \text{inventory at the end} \\ \text{of this week} \end{pmatrix} = \begin{pmatrix} \text{On-hand} \\ \text{inventory at the} \\ \text{end of last week} \end{pmatrix} + \begin{pmatrix} \text{MPS quantity} \\ \text{due at the start} \\ \text{of this week} \end{pmatrix} - \begin{pmatrix} \text{Projected} \\ \text{requirements} \\ \text{this week} \end{pmatrix}$$

This calculation is similar to that for the projected on-hand inventory in an MRP record and serves essentially the same purpose (see the Resource Planning chapter).

In some weeks, there may be no MPS quantity for a product because sufficient inventory already exists. For the projected requirements for this week, the scheduler uses whichever is larger—the forecast or the customer orders booked—recognizing that the forecast is subject to error. If actual booked orders exceed the forecast, the projection will be more accurate if the scheduler uses the booked orders because booked orders are a known quantity. Conversely, if the forecast exceeds booked orders for a week, the forecast will provide a better estimate of requirements for that week because some orders are yet to come in.

The manufacturer of the ladder-back chair produces the chair to stock and needs to develop an MPS for it. Marketing has forecasted a demand of 30 chairs for the first week of April, but actual customer orders booked are for 38 chairs. The current on-hand inventory is 55 chairs. No MPS quantity is due in week 1. Figure G.2 shows an MPS record with these quantities listed. As actual orders for week 1 are greater than the forecast, the scheduler uses that figure for actual orders in calculating the projected inventory balance at the end of week 1:

$$\text{Inventory} = \begin{pmatrix} \text{55 chairs} \\ \text{currently} \\ \text{in stock} \end{pmatrix} + \begin{pmatrix} \text{MPS quantity} \\ \text{(0 for week 1)} \end{pmatrix} - \begin{pmatrix} \text{38 chairs already} \\ \text{promised for} \\ \text{delivery in week 1} \end{pmatrix} = 17 \text{ chairs}$$

FIGURE G.2

Master Production Schedule for Weeks 1 and 2

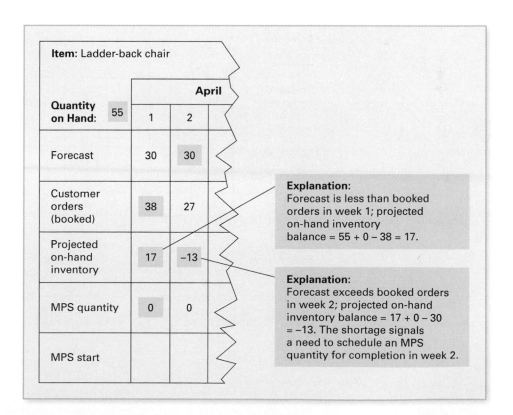

Item: Ladder-back chair

		April		
Quantity on Hand:	55	1	2	
Forecast		30	30	
Customer orders (booked)		38	27	
Projected on-hand inventory		17	−13	
MPS quantity		0	0	
MPS start				

Explanation:
Forecast is less than booked orders in week 1; projected on-hand inventory balance = 55 + 0 − 38 = 17.

Explanation:
Forecast exceeds booked orders in week 2; projected on-hand inventory balance = 17 + 0 − 30 = −13. The shortage signals a need to schedule an MPS quantity for completion in week 2.

In week 2, the forecasted quantity exceeds actual orders booked, so the projected on-hand inventory for the end of week 2 is $17 + 0 - 30 = -13$. The shortage signals the need for more chairs in week 2.

Step 2.   Determine the Timing and Size of MPS Quantities. The goal of determining the timing and size of MPS quantities is to maintain a nonnegative projected on-hand inventory balance. As shortages in inventory are detected, MPS quantities should be scheduled to cover them, much as planned receipts are scheduled in an MRP record (see the Resource Planning chapter). The first MPS quantity should be scheduled for the week when the projected on-hand inventory reflects a shortage, such as week 2 in Figure G.2.[1] The scheduler adds the MPS quantity to the projected on-hand inventory and searches for the next period when a shortage occurs. This shortage signals a need for a second MPS quantity, and so on.

Figure G.3 shows a master production schedule for the ladder-back chair for the next eight weeks. The order policy requires production lot sizes of 150 units, which is the same as FOQ = 150 (see the Resource Planning chapter). A shortage of 13 chairs in week 2 will occur unless the scheduler provides for an MPS quantity for that period.

FIGURE G.3

Master Production Schedule for Weeks 1–8

Item: Ladder-back chair   **Order Policy:** 150 units   **Lead Time:** 1 week

Quantity on Hand: 55	April				May			
	1	2	3	4	5	6	7	8
Forecast	30	30	30	30	35	35	35	35
Customer orders (booked)	38	27	24	8	0	0	0	0
Projected on-hand inventory	17	137	107	77	42	7	122	87
MPS quantity	0	150	0	0	0	0	150	0
MPS start	150	0	0	0	0	150	0	0

Explanation:
The time needed to assemble 150 chairs is one week. The assembly department must start assembling chairs in week 1 to have them ready by week 2.

Explanation:
On-hand inventory balance = $17 + 150 - 30 = 137$. The MPS quantity is needed to avoid a shortage of $30 - 17 = 13$ chairs in week 2.

---

[1] In some cases, new orders will be planned before a shortage is encountered. Two such instances are building safety stocks and building anticipation inventories.

Once the MPS quantity is scheduled, the updated projected inventory balance for week 2 is

$$\text{Inventory} = \begin{pmatrix} 17 \text{ chairs in} \\ \text{inventory at the} \\ \text{end of week 1} \end{pmatrix} + \begin{pmatrix} \text{MPS quantity} \\ \text{of 150 chairs} \end{pmatrix} - \begin{pmatrix} \text{Forecast of} \\ 30 \text{ chairs} \end{pmatrix} = 137 \text{ chairs}$$

The scheduler proceeds column by column through the MPS record until reaching the end, filling in the MPS quantities as needed to avoid shortages. The 137 units will satisfy forecasted demands until week 7, when the inventory shortage in the absence of an MPS quantity is $7 + 0 - 35 = -28$. This shortage signals the need for another MPS quantity of 150 units. The updated inventory balance is $7 + 150 - 35 = 122$ chairs for week 7.

The last row in Figure G.3 indicates the periods in which production of the MPS quantities must *begin* so that they will be available when indicated in the MPS quantity row. This row is analogous to the planned order receipt row in an MRP record (see the Resource Planning chapter). In the upper-right portion of the MPS record, a lead time of one week is indicated for the ladder-back chair; that is, one week is needed to assemble 150 ladder-back chairs, assuming that items B, C, D, and E are available. For each MPS quantity, the scheduler works backward through the lead time to determine when the assembly department must start producing chairs. Consequently, a lot of 150 units must be started in week 1 and another in week 6. These quantities correspond to the gross requirements in the MRP record for item C, the seat subassembly, in Figure 15.6 (see the Resource Planning chapter).

AVAILABLE-TO-PROMISE QUANTITIES

available-to-promise (ATP) inventory The quantity of end items that marketing can promise to deliver on specified dates.

In addition to providing manufacturing with the timing and size of production quantities, the MPS provides marketing with information that is useful in negotiating delivery dates with customers. The quantity of end items that marketing can promise to deliver on specified dates is called **available-to-promise (ATP) inventory**. It is the difference between the customer orders already booked and the quantity that operations is planning to produce. As new customer orders are accepted, the ATP inventory is reduced to reflect commitment of the firm to ship those quantities, but the actual inventory stays unchanged until the order is removed from inventory and shipped to the customer. An available-to-promise inventory is associated with each MPS quantity because the MPS quantity specifies the timing and size of new stock that can be earmarked to meet future bookings.

Figure G.4 shows an MPS record with an additional row for the available-to-promise quantities. The ATP in week 2 is the MPS quantity minus booked customer order until the next MPS quantity, or $150 - (27 + 24 + 8 + 0 + 0) = 91$ units. The ATP indicates to marketing that, of the 150 units scheduled for completion in week 2, 91 units are uncommitted, and total new orders up to that quantity can be promised for delivery as early as week 2. In week 7, the ATP is 150 units because there are no booked orders in week 7 and beyond.

The procedure for calculating available-to-promise information is slightly different for the first (current) week of the schedule than for other weeks because it accounts for the inventory currently in stock. The ATP inventory for the first week equals *current on-hand inventory* plus the MPS quantity for the first week, minus the cumulative total of booked orders up to (but not including) the week in which the next MPS quantity

*MPS Record with
an ATP Row*

Item: Ladder-back chair						Order Policy: 150 units Lead Time: 1 week		
Quantity on Hand: 55	April				May			
	1	2	3	4	5	6	7	8
Forecast	30	30	30	30	35	35	35	35
Customer orders (booked)	38	27	24	8	0	0	0	0
Projected on-hand inventory	17	137	107	77	42	7	122	87
MPS quantity	0	150	0	0	0	0	150	0
MPS start	150	0	0	0	0	150	0	0
Available-to-promise (ATP) inventory	17	91					150	

Explanation:
The total of customer orders booked until the next MPS receipt is 38 units. The ATP = 55 (on-hand) + 0 (MPS quantity) – 38 = 17.

Explanation:
The total of customer orders booked until the next MPS receipt is 27 + 24 + 8 = 59 units. The ATP = 150 (MPS quantity) – 59 = 91 units.

arrives. So, in Figure G.4, the ATP for the first week is $55 + 0 - 38 = 17$. This information indicates to the sales department that it can promise as many as 17 units this week, 91 more units sometime in weeks 2 through 6, and 150 more units in week 7 or 8. If customer order requests exceed ATP quantities in those time periods, the MPS must be changed before the customer orders can be booked or the customers must be given a later delivery date—when the next MPS quantity arrives. See the solved problem at the end of this supplement for an example of decision making using the ATP quantities.

FREEZING THE MPS

The master production schedule is the basis of all end item, subassembly, component, and materials schedules. For this reason, changes to the MPS can be costly, particularly if they are made to MPS quantities soon to be completed. Increases in an MPS quantity may cause delays in shipments to customers or excessive expediting costs because of shortages in materials. Decreases in MPS quantities can result in unused materials or components (at least until another need for them arises) and tying up valuable capacities for something not needed. Similar costs occur when forecasted need dates for MPS quantities are changed. For these reasons, many firms, particularly those with a make-to-stock strategy and a focus on low-cost operations, *freeze*, or disallow changes to, a portion of the MPS.

demand time fence The number of periods (beginning with the current period) during which few, if any, changes can be made to the MPS.

Freezing can be accomplished by specifying a **demand time fence,** which is the number of periods (beginning with the current period) during which few, if any, changes can be made to the MPS (i.e., the MPS is firm). Companies select the demand time fence after considering the costs of making changes to the MPS: The more costly the changes, the more periods are included in the demand time fence. The costs of making changes to the MPS typically go down as the changes occur farther in the future. For example, the Ethan Allen Furniture Company uses a demand time fence of eight weeks. If the current week is week 1, the MPS is frozen for weeks 1 through 8 because the costs of rescheduling the assembly line, the shop, and suppliers' shipments are prohibitive in that time frame. Neither the master scheduler nor the computer can reschedule MPS quantities for this period without management's approval. Making a change to the schedule for week 10, for example, is much less costly because of the lead time that everyone has to react to the change.

planning time fence A time fence that typically covers a longer period than the demand time fence.

Other time fences that allow varying amounts of change can be specified. For example, the **planning time fence** typically covers a longer period than the demand time fence. The master scheduler—but not the computer—can make changes to MPS quantities during this period of time. The cost of making changes to the MPS within the planning time fence is less than making changes to the MPS within the demand time fence. Beyond the planning time fence the computer may schedule the MPS quantities, based on the approved ordering policy that is programmed into the computer. Figure G.5 shows a demand time fence of two weeks and a planning time fence of six weeks for the ladder-back chair MPS. The MPS quantity in week 2 cannot be changed without management's approval. The MPS quantity in week 7 can be changed by the master scheduler without management's approval. The MPS quantities beyond week 8 can be changed by the computer, based on policies approved by management that are programmed into the computer.

The number of time fences can vary. Black & Decker uses three time fences: 8, 13, and 26 weeks. The 8-week fence is essentially a demand time fence. From 8 to 13 weeks, the MPS is quite rigid, but minor changes to model series may be made if components are available. From 13 to 26 weeks, substitution of one end item for another is permitted as long as the production plan is not violated and components are available.

Master Production Schedule Time Fences

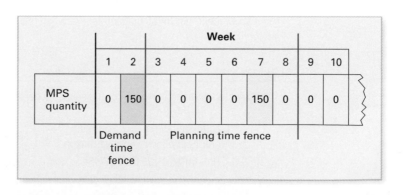

Beyond 26 weeks, marketing can make changes as long as they are compatible with the production plan.

The length of time fences should be reviewed periodically and adjusted as necessary. Although freezing the MPS reduces manufacturing costs and makes life easier for those responsible for scheduling components and materials, it tends to make the MPS less responsive to changes in customer demand. The costs of not being able to satisfy customers who place unexpected orders for delivery within the demand time fence must be weighed against the savings in production costs.

SUPPLEMENT HIGHLIGHTS

❏ The master production schedule is a link between a firm's broad strategies and the tactical plans that enable the firm to achieve its goals. The MPS provides essential information for functional areas such as operations, marketing, and finance.

❏ MPS quantities are scheduled to avoid shortages. A conservative approach to estimating the on-hand inventory in future periods is used: The estimated requirements for any period are the greater of the actual orders booked for that period or the forecast.

❏ Available-to-promise quantities enable the sales department to establish realistic delivery dates with customers.

❏ Firms with a make-to-stock strategy and a focus on low-cost operations often freeze portions of their master production schedules to stabilize operations because unplanned changes to the MPS can be very costly.

KEY TERMS

available-to-promise (ATP)
inventory *787*

demand time fence *789*
planning time fence *789*

SOLVED PROBLEM

**TUTOR
G.1**

The order policy is to produce end item A in lots of 50 units. Using the data shown in Figure G.6 and the FOQ lot-sizing rule, complete the projected on-hand inventory and MPS quantity rows. Then complete the MPS start row by offsetting the MPS quantities for the final assembly lead time. Finally, compute the available-to-promise inventory for item A. If in week 1, a customer requests a new order for 30 units of item A, when is the earliest date the entire order could be shipped?

SOLUTION

The projected on-hand inventory for the second week is

$$\begin{pmatrix} \text{Projected on-hand} \\ \text{inventory at end} \\ \text{of week 2} \end{pmatrix} = \begin{pmatrix} \text{On-hand} \\ \text{inventory in} \\ \text{week 1} \end{pmatrix} + \begin{pmatrix} \text{MPS quantity} \\ \text{due in week 2} \end{pmatrix} - \begin{pmatrix} \text{Requirements} \\ \text{in week 2} \end{pmatrix}$$

$$= 25 + 0 - 20 = 5 \text{ units}$$

Item: A — **Order Policy:** 50 units — **Lead Time:** 1 week

Quantity on Hand: 5	Week 1	2	3	4	5	6	7	8	9	10
Forecast	20	10	40	10	0	0	30	20	40	20
Customer orders (booked)	30	20	5	8	0	2	0	0	0	0
Projected on-hand inventory	25									
MPS quantity	50									
MPS start										
Available-to-promise (ATP) inventory										

FIGURE G.6

where requirements are the larger of the forecast or actual customer orders booked for shipment during this period. No MPS quantity is required.

Without an MPS quantity in the third period, there will be a shortage of item A: $5 + 0 - 40 = -35$. Therefore, an MPS quantity equal to the lot size of 50 must be scheduled for completion in the third period. Then the projected on-hand inventory for the third week will be $5 + 50 - 40 = 15$.

Figure G.7 shows the projected on-hand inventories and MPS quantities from OM Explorer that would result from completing the MPS calculations. The MPS start row is completed by simply shifting a copy of the MPS quantity row to the left by one column to account for the one-week final assembly lead time. Also shown are the available-to-promise quantities. In week 1, the ATP is

$$\begin{pmatrix} \text{Available-to-} \\ \text{promise in} \\ \text{week 1} \end{pmatrix} = \begin{pmatrix} \text{On-hand} \\ \text{quantity in} \\ \text{week 1} \end{pmatrix} + \begin{pmatrix} \text{MPS quantity} \\ \text{in week 1} \end{pmatrix} - \begin{pmatrix} \text{Orders booked up} \\ \text{to week 3 when the} \\ \text{next MPS arrives} \end{pmatrix}$$
$$= 5 + 50 - (30 + 20) = 5 \text{ units}$$

The ATP for the MPS quantity in week 3 is

$$\begin{pmatrix} \text{Available-to-} \\ \text{promise in} \\ \text{week 3} \end{pmatrix} = \begin{pmatrix} \text{MPS quantity} \\ \text{in week 3} \end{pmatrix} - \begin{pmatrix} \text{Orders booked up} \\ \text{to week 7 when the} \\ \text{next MPS arrives} \end{pmatrix}$$
$$= 50 - (5 + 8 + 0 + 2) = 35 \text{ units}$$

Inputs

Solver - Master Production Scheduling
Enter data in yellow-shaded areas.

Lot Size 50
Lead Time 1

Quantity on Hand 5	1	2	3	4	5	6	7	8	9	10	11	12	13	14	15
Forecast	20	10	40	10			30	20	40	20					
Customer Orders (Booked)	30	20	5	8		2									
Projected On-Hand Inventory	25	5	15	5			20		10	40					
MPS Quantity	50		50				50		50	50					
MPS start		50				50		50	50						
Available-to-Promise Inv (ATP) 5		35					50		50	50					

FIGURE G.7

The other ATPs equal their respective MPS quantities because there are no booked orders for those weeks. As for the new order for 30 units, the earliest it can be shipped is week 3 because the ATP for week 1 is insufficient. If the customer accepts the delivery date of week 3, the ATP for week 1 will stay at 5 units and the ATP for week 3 will be reduced to 5 units. This acceptance allows the firm the flexibility to immediately satisfy an order for 5 units or less, if one comes in. The customer orders booked for week 3 would be increased to 35 to reflect the new order's shipping date.

DISCUSSION QUESTIONS

1. Form a group in which each member represents a different functional area of a firm. Provide a priority list of the information that could be generated from an MPS, from the most important to the least important, for each functional area. Rationalize the differences in the lists.

2. Consider the master flight schedule of a major airline, such as Northwest Airlines. Discuss the ways such a schedule is analogous to a master production schedule for a manufacturer.

OM EXPLORER AND INTERNET EXERCISES

Visit our Web site at www.prenhall.com/krajewski for OM Explorer Tutors, which explain quantitative techniques; Solvers, which help you apply mathematical models; and Internet Exercises, including Facility Tours, which expand on the topics in this chapter.

PROBLEMS

1. **OM Explorer** Complete the MPS record in Figure G.8 for a single item.

2. **OM Explorer** Complete the MPS record shown in Figure G.9 for a single item.

3. **OM Explorer** An end item's demand forecasts for the next 10 weeks are 30, 20, 35, 50, 25, 25, 0, 40, 0, and 50 units. The current on-hand inventory is 80 units. The order policy is to produce in lots of 100. The booked customer orders for the item, starting with week 1, are 22, 30, 15, 9, 0, 0, 5, 3, 7, and 0 units. At present, there are no MPS quantities for this item. The lead time is two weeks. Develop an MPS for this end item.

Item: A

Order Policy: 60 units
Lead Time: 1 week

Quantity on Hand: 35

	Week							
	1	2	3	4	5	6	7	8
Forecast	20	18	28	28	23	30	33	38
Customer orders (booked)	15	17	9	14	9	0	7	0
Projected on-hand inventory								
MPS quantity								
MPS start								

FIGURE G.8

Item: A

Order Policy: 100 units
Lead Time: 1 week

Quantity on Hand: 75

	January				February			
	1	2	3	4	5	6	7	8
Forecast	65	65	65	45	50	50	50	50
Customer orders (booked)	40	10	85	0	35	70	0	0
Projected on-hand inventory								
MPS quantity								
MPS start								

FIGURE G.9

4. **OM Explorer** At present, there are 50 units of an end item in inventory. Order policy is fixed at 125 units.

   a. Complete the MPS record in Figure G.10 for this end item.

   b. The MPS in part (a) was not approved. During the approval process, the MPS quantity in week 9 was brought forward to week 2. For this changed MPS, revise the projected on-hand inventory row in Figure G.10, and list the advantages and concerns associated with this change.

5. **OM Explorer** Figure G.11 shows a partially completed MPS record for ball bearings.

   a. Develop the MPS for ball bearings.

   b. Four customer orders arrived in the following sequence:

ORDER	QUANTITY	WEEK DESIRED
1	500	4
2	400	5
3	300	1
4	300	7

Assume that you must commit to the orders in the sequence of arrival and cannot change the desired shipping dates or your MPS. Which orders should you accept?

6. **OM Explorer** Morrison Electronics has forecasted the following demand for one of its products for the next eight weeks: 70, 70, 65, 60, 55, 85, 75, and 85. The booked customer orders for this product, starting in week 1, are 50, 60, 55, 40, 35, 0, 0, and 0 units. The current on-hand inventory is 100 units, the order quantity is 150 units, and the lead time is 1 week.

   a. Develop an MPS for this product.

   b. The marketing department at Morrison has revised its forecasts. Starting with week 1, the new forecasts are 70, 70, 75, 70, 70, 100, 100, and 110 units. Assuming that the prospective MPS you developed in part (a) does not change, prepare a revised MPS record. Comment on the situation that Morrison now faces.

7. **OM Explorer** Figure G.12 on page 796 shows a partially completed MPS record for 2″ pneumatic con-

Item: A							Order Policy: 125 units Lead Time: 1 week				

Quantity on Hand: 50	Week									
	1	2	3	4	5	6	7	8	9	10
Forecast	10	15	20	30	40	60	80	120	120	120
Customer orders (booked)	12	9	11	5	2	0	4	0	0	0
Projected on-hand inventory										
MPS quantity										
MPS start										

FIGURE G.10

Item: Ball bearings						Order Policy: 500 units	Lead Time: 1 week				

Quantity on Hand: 400	Week										
	1	2	3	4	5	6	7	8	9	10	
Forecast	550	300	400	450	300	350	200	300	450	400	
Customer orders (booked)	300	350	250	250	200	150	100	100	100	100	
Projected on-hand inventory											
MPS quantity	500										
MPS start											
Available-to-promise (ATP) inventory											

FIGURE G.11

trol valves. Suppose that you have received the following orders for the valves (shown in the order of their arrival). As they arrive you must decide whether to accept or reject them. Which orders would you accept for shipment?

ORDER	AMOUNT (UNITS)	WEEK REQUESTED
1	15	2
2	30	5
3	25	3
4	75	7

8. ● **OM Explorer** The forecasted requirements for an electric hand drill for the next six weeks are 15, 40, 10, 20, 50, and 30 units. The marketing department has booked orders totaling 20, 25, 10, and 20 units for delivery in the first (current), second, third, and fourth weeks. Currently, 30 hand drills are in stock. The policy is to order in lots of 60 units. Lead time is one week.

a. Develop the MPS record for the hand drills.

b. A distributor of the hand drills places an order for 15 units. What is the appropriate shipping date for the entire order?

9. ● **OM Explorer** A forecast of 240 units in January, 320 units in February, and 240 units in March has been approved for the seismic-sensory product family manufactured at the Rockport facility of Maryland Automated, Inc. Three products, A, B, and C, comprise this family. The product mix ratio for products A, B, and C for the past two years has been 35 percent, 40 percent, and 25 percent, respectively. Management believes that the monthly forecast requirements are evenly spread over the four weeks of each month. Currently, there are 10 units of product C on hand. The company produces product C in lots of 40, and the lead time is 2 weeks. A production quantity of 40 units from the previous period is scheduled to arrive in week 1. The company has accepted orders for product C of 25, 12, 8, 10, 2, and 3 of product C in weeks 1–6, respectively. Prepare a prospective MPS for product C and calculate the available-to-promise inventory quantities.

Item: 2″ Pneumatic control valve						Order Policy: 75 units Lead Time: 1 week		

Quantity on Hand: 10	Week							
	1	2	3	4	5	6	7	8
Forecast	40	40	40	40	30	30	50	50
Customer orders (booked)	60	45	30	35	10	5	5	0
Projected on-hand inventory								
MPS quantity	75	75						
MPS start	75							
Available-to-promise (ATP) inventory								

FIGURE G.12

SELECTED REFERENCE

Bruggeman, J. J., and S. Haythornthwaite. "The Master Schedule." *APICS—The Performance Advantage* (October 1991), pp. 44–46.

Dougherty, J. R., and J. F. Proud. "From Master Schedules to Finishing Schedules in the 1990s." *American Production and Inventory Control Society 1990 Annual Conference Proceedings,* pp. 368–370.

Lunn, Terry, and Susan Neff. *MRP: Integrating Material Requirements Planning and Modern Business.* Homewood, Ill.: Irwin Professional Publication, 1992.

Ptak, Carol. *MRP and Beyond.* Homewood, Ill.: Irwin Professional Publication, 1996.

Vollmann, T. E., W. L. Berry, and D. C. Whybark. *Manufacturing Planning and Control Systems,* 4th ed. Homewood, Ill.: Irwin Professional Publication, 1997.

Wallace, Tom. *MRP II: Making It Happen.* Essex Junction, VT: Oliver Wight Ltd., Publishers, 1994.

Lean Systems

Across the Organization

Lean systems are important to . . .

- ❐ **accounting,** which often must adjust its billing and cost accounting practices to take advantage of lean systems.
- ❐ **engineering,** which must design products that use more common parts so that fewer setups are required and focused factories and group technology can be used.
- ❐ **finance,** which must secure the working capital needed for a lean system.
- ❐ **human resources,** which must recruit, train, and evaluate the employees needed to successfully operate a lean system.
- ❐ **management information systems,** which must integrate the lean system with other information systems in the firm.
- ❐ **marketing,** which relies on lean systems to deliver high-quality products or services on time, at reasonable prices.
- ❐ **operations,** which is responsible for using the lean system in the production of goods or services.

Learning Goals

After reading this chapter, you will be able to . . .

1. identify the characteristics of lean systems that enable the realization of the lean system philosophy.
2. describe how lean systems can facilitate the continuous improvement of operations.
3. calculate the number of containers of a specific part required for a system.
4. explain how the principles of the lean system philosophy can be applied by service providers.
5. discuss the strategic advantages of lean systems and the implementation issues associated with the application of these systems.

f you were to select one company that is exemplary of excellence in automobile manufacturing, it would probably be Toyota (www.toyota.com). Worldwide in its presence, it has a total investment of $12 billion in 10 manufacturing plants that employ 30,500 associates in North America alone. Toyota was at the forefront of firms developing lean systems for manufacturing, and today the Toyota Production System (TPS) is one of the most admired lean manufacturing systems in existence. Replicating the system, however, is fraught with difficulties. What makes the system tick, and why could Toyota employ the system in so many different plants when others have difficulty?

Most outsiders see the Toyota Production System as a set of tools and procedures that are readily visible during a plant tour. While they are important for the success of the TPS, they are not the keys to the heart of the system. What most people overlook is that Toyota has built a learning organization over the course of 50 years. Lean systems require constant improvements to increase efficiency and reduce waste. Toyota has created a system that stimulates employees to experiment with their environment by seeking better ways whenever things go wrong. Toyota sets up all operations as experiments and teaches employees at all levels how to use the scientific method of problem solving.

There are four underlying principles of the Toyota Production System. First, all work must be completely specified as to content, sequence, timing, and outcome. Detail is important, otherwise there is no foundation for improvements. Second, every customer–supplier connection must be direct, unambiguously specifying the people involved, the form and quantity of the goods or services to be provided, the way the requests are made by each customer, and the expected time in which the requests will be met. Customer–supplier connections can be internal—employee to employee— or external—company to company.

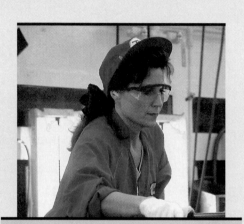

A team member is preparing a vehicle for an application of paint at the Toyota manufacturing facility at Georgetown, Kentucky. Painting is one of the most detailed processes at the plant, using both water-borne and solvent-based paints. The metal of the vehicles is carefully checked for any imperfections before the first coat of paint is ever applied. Note the clothing and gloves that the employee wears, designed to keep the vehicles from being accidentally marred in the painting process.

Third, the pathway for every product and service must be simple and direct. That is, goods and services do not flow to the next available person or machine, but to a *specific* person or machine. With this principle, employees can determine, for example, that there is a capacity problem at a particular workstation and then analyze ways to resolve it.

The first three principles define the system in detail by specifying how employees do work, interact with each other, and design work flows. These specifications actually are "hypotheses" about the way the system should work. For example, if something goes wrong at a workstation enough times, the hypothesis about the methods the employee uses to do work is rejected. The fourth principle, then, is that any improvement to the system must be made in accordance with the scientific method, under the guidance of a teacher, at the lowest possible organizational level. The scientific method involves clearly stating a verifiable hypothesis of the form, "If we make the following specific changes, we expect to achieve this specific outcome." The hypothesis must then be tested under a variety of conditions. Working with a teacher, who is often the employees' supervisor, is a key to becoming a learning organization. Employees learn the scientific method and eventually become teachers of others. Finally, making improvements at the lowest level of the organization means that the employees who are actually doing the work are actively involved in making improvements.

These four principles are deceptively simple; however, they are difficult to replicate. Nonetheless, those organizations that have successfully implemented them have enjoyed the benefits of a lean system that adapts to change.

Source: Spear, Steven and H. Kent Bowen. "Decoding the DNA of the Toyota Production System." *Harvard Business Review* (September–October 1999), pp. 97–106.

lean systems Operations systems that are designed to create efficient processes by taking a total systems perspective.

T HE CONCEPT OF **lean systems** embodies much of what we have already covered in this text. It focuses on operations strategy, processes, technology, quality, capacity, layout, supply chains, inventory, and resource planning. Lean systems "put it all together" to create efficient processes. They are known by many different names, including *zero inventory, synchronous manufacturing, stockless production* (Hewlett-Packard), *material as needed* (Harley-Davidson), and *continuous flow manufacturing* (IBM), each with their own operational differences. In this chapter, however, we will focus on the most popular system that incorporates the generic elements of lean systems—the just-in-time (JIT) system. The **just-in-time (JIT) philosophy** is simple but powerful—*eliminate waste* by cutting unnecessary inventory and removing nonvalue-added activities in operations. The goals are to produce goods and services as needed and to continuously improve the value-added benefits of operations. A **JIT system** is the organization of resources, information flows, and decision rules that can enable an organization to realize the benefits of the JIT philosophy. Often, a crisis (such as being faced with going out of business or closing a plant) galvanizes management and labor to work together to change traditional operating practices. Converting from traditional manufacturing to a just-in-time system brings up not only inventory control issues but also process management and scheduling issues. In this chapter, we identify the characteristics of lean systems as embodied in JIT systems, discuss how they can be used for continuous improvement of operations, and indicate how manufacturing and service operations utilize such systems. We also address the strategic implications of lean systems and some of the implementation issues that companies face.

just-in-time (JIT) philosophy The belief that waste can be eliminated by cutting unnecessary inventory and removing nonvalue-added activities in operations.

JIT system The organization of resources, information flows, and decision rules that enable an organization to realize the benefits of a JIT philosophy.

CHARACTERISTICS OF LEAN SYSTEMS: JUST-IN-TIME OPERATIONS

The just-in-time system, a primary example of lean systems, focuses on reducing inefficiency and unproductive time in processes to improve continuously the process and the quality of the products or services they produce. Employee involvement and the reduction of nonvalue-added activities are essential to JIT operations. In this section, we discuss the following characteristics of JIT systems: pull method of material flow, consistently high quality, small lot sizes, uniform workstation loads, standardized components and work methods, close supplier ties, flexible workforce, line flows, automated production, and preventive maintenance.

PULL METHOD OF MATERIALS FLOW

Just-in-time systems utilize the pull method of materials flow. However, another popular method is the push method. To differentiate between these two systems, let's first consider the production system for a Quarter Pounder at a McDonald's restaurant. There are two workstations. The burger maker is the person responsible for producing this burger: Burger patties must be fried; buns must be toasted and then dressed with ketchup, pickles, mayonnaise, lettuce, and cheese; and the patties must be inserted into buns and put on a tray. The final assembler takes the tray, wraps the burgers in paper, and restocks the inventory. Inventories must be kept low because any burgers left unsold after seven minutes must be destroyed.

The flow of materials is from the burger maker to the final assembler to the customer. One way to manage this flow is by using the **push method,** in which the production of the item begins in advance of customer needs. With this method, management schedules the receipt of all raw materials (e.g., meat, buns, and condiments) and authorizes the start of production, all in advance of Quarter Pounder needs. The burger maker starts production of 24 burgers (the capacity of the griddle) and, when

push method A method in which the production of the item begins in advance of customer needs.

Fast food workers using the pull system to serve their customers at a McDonald's store in Taipei, Taiwan. The burger maker and assembler are behind the racks, which are readily available to the workers at the sales counter.

they are completed, pushes them along to the final assembler's station, where they might have to wait until the final assembler is ready for them. The packaged burgers then wait on a warming tray until a customer purchases one.

pull method A method in which customer demand activates production of the item.

The other way to manage the flow among the burger maker, the final assembler, and the customer is to use the **pull method,** in which customer demand activates production of the item. With the pull method, as customers purchase burgers, the final assembler checks the inventory level of burgers and, when they are almost depleted, orders six more. The burger maker produces the six burgers and gives the tray to the final assembler, who completes the assembly and places the burgers in the inventory for sale. The pull method is better for the production of burgers: The two workers can coordinate the two workstations to keep inventory low, important because of the seven-minute time limit. The production of burgers is a highly repetitive process, setup times and process times are low, and the flow of materials is well defined. There is no need to produce to anticipated needs more than a few minutes ahead.

Under what circumstances can a just-in-time system be used effectively?

Firms that tend to have highly repetitive manufacturing processes and well-defined material flows use just-in-time systems because the pull method allows closer control of inventory and production at the workstations. Other firms, such as those producing a large variety of products in low volumes with low repeatability in the production process, tend to use a push method such as MRP. In this case, a customer order is promised for delivery on some future date. Production is started at the first workstation and pushed ahead to the next one. Inventory can accumulate at each workstation because workstations are responsible for producing many other orders and may be busy at any particular time.

CONSISTENTLY HIGH QUALITY

Just-in-time systems seek to eliminate scrap and rework in order to achieve a uniform flow of materials. Efficient JIT operations require conformance to product or service specifications and implementation of the behavioral and statistical methods of total quality management (TQM) (see the Total Quality Management and Statistical Process Control chapters). JIT systems control quality at the source, with workers acting as their own quality inspectors. For example, a soldering operation at the Texas Instruments antenna department had a defect rate that varied from zero to 50 percent on a daily basis, averaging about 20 percent. To compensate, production planners increased the lot sizes, which only increased inventory levels and did nothing to reduce the number of defective items. Engineers discovered through experimentation that gas temperature was a critical variable in producing defect-free items. They devised statistical control charts for the operators to use to monitor gas temperature and adjust it themselves. Process yields immediately improved and stabilized at 95 percent, eventually enabling management to implement a JIT system.

Management must realize the enormous responsibility this method places on the workers and must prepare them properly, as one GM division quickly learned. When Buick City began using JIT in 1985, management authorized its workers to stop the production line by pulling a cord if quality problems arose at their stations—a practice the Japanese call *andon*. GM also eliminated production-line inspectors and cut the number of supervisors by half. Stopping the line, however, is a costly action that brings a problem to everyone's attention. The workers were not prepared for that responsibility; productivity and quality took a nose-dive. The paint on Le Sabres was not shiny enough. The seams were not straight. The top of the dashboard had an unintended wave. Management, labor, and engineering formed a team to correct the problems. Work methods were changed, and the *andon* system was modified to include a yellow warning cord so that workers could call for help without stopping the line.

SMALL LOT SIZES

Rather than building up a cushion of inventory, users of JIT systems maintain inventory with lot sizes that are as small as possible. Small lot sizes have three benefits. First, small lot sizes reduce *cycle* inventory, the inventory in excess of the safety stock carried between orders (see the Inventory Management chapter). The average cycle inventory equals one-half the lot size: As the lot size gets smaller, so does cycle inventory. Reducing cycle inventory reduces the time and space involved in manufacturing and holding inventory. Figure 16.1 shows the effect on cycle inventory of reducing the lot size from 100 to 50 for a uniform demand of 10 units per hour: Cycle inventory is cut in half.

FIGURE 16.1

Implications of Small and Large Lot Sizes for Cycle Inventory

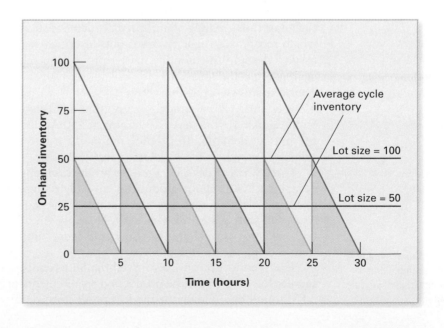

Second, small lot sizes help cut lead times. A decline in lead time in turn cuts pipeline (WIP) inventory because the total processing time at each workstation is greater for large lots than for small lots. Also, a large lot often has to wait longer to be processed at the next workstation while that workstation finishes working on another large lot. In addition, if any defective items are discovered, large lots cause longer delays because the entire lot must be inspected to find all the items that need rework.

Finally, small lots help achieve a uniform operating system workload. Large lots consume large chunks of processing time on workstations and, therefore, complicate scheduling. Small lots can be juggled more effectively, enabling schedulers to utilize capacities more efficiently. In addition, small lots allow workstations to accommodate mixed-model production (more than one item) by reducing waiting-line times for production. We return to this point when we discuss uniform workstation loads.

Although small lot sizes are beneficial to operations, they have the disadvantage of increased setup frequency. In operations where the setup times are normally low, as in the McDonald's example, small lots are feasible. However, in fabrication operations with sizable setup times, increasing the frequency of setups may result in wasting employee and equipment time. These operations must reduce setup times to realize the benefits of small-lot production.

Achieving low setup times often requires close cooperation among engineering, management, and labor. For example, changing dies on large presses to form automobile parts from sheet metal can take three to four hours. At Honda's Marysville, Ohio, plant—where four stamping lines stamp all the exterior and major interior body panels for Accord production—teams worked on ways to reduce the changeover time for the massive dies. As a result, a complete change of dies for a giant 2,400-ton press now takes less than eight minutes. The goal of **single-digit setup** means having setup times of less than 10 minutes. Some techniques to reduce setup times include using conveyors for die storage, moving large dies with cranes, simplifying dies, enacting machine controls, using microcomputers to automatically feed and position work, and preparing for changeovers while the current job is being processed.

single-digit setup The goal of having a setup time of less than ten minutes.

UNIFORM WORKSTATION LOADS

The JIT system works best if the daily load on individual workstations is relatively uniform. Uniform loads can be achieved by assembling the same type and number of units each day, thus creating a uniform daily demand at all workstations. Capacity planning, which recognizes capacity constraints at critical workstations, and line balancing are used to develop the monthly master production schedule. For example, at Toyota the aggregate production plan may call for 4,500 vehicles per week for the next month. That requires two full shifts, five days per week, producing 900 vehicles each day, or 450 per shift. Three models are produced: Camry (C), Avalon (A), and Sienna (S). Suppose that Toyota needs 200 Camrys, 150 Avalons, and 100 Siennas per shift to satisfy market demand. To produce 450 units in one shift of 480 minutes, the line must roll out a vehicle every 480/450 = 1.067 minutes.

Three ways of devising a master production schedule for the vehicles are of interest here. First, with big-lot production, all daily requirements of a model are produced in one batch before another model is started. The sequence of 200 C's, 150 A's, and 100 S's would be repeated once per shift. Not only would these big lots increase the average cycle inventory level but they also would cause lumpy requirements on all the workstations feeding the assembly line.

mixed-model assembly A type of assembly that produces a mix of models in smaller lots.

The second option uses **mixed-model assembly**, producing a mix of models in smaller lots. Note that the production requirements are in the ratio of 4 C's to 3 A's to 2 S's, found by dividing the model's production requirements by the greatest common divisor, or 50. Thus, the Toyota planner could develop a production cycle consisting of 9 units: 4 C's, 3 A's, and 2 S's. The cycle would repeat in $9(1.067) = 9.60$ minutes, for a total of 50 times per shift (480 min/9.60 min = 50).

A sequence of C–S–C–A–C–A–C–S–A, repeated 50 times per shift, would achieve the same total output as the other options. This third option is feasible only if the setup times are very short. The sequence generates a steady rate of component requirements for the various models and allows the use of small lot sizes at the feeder workstations. Consequently, the capacity requirements at those stations are greatly smoothed. These requirements can be compared to actual capacities during the planning phase, and modifications to the production cycle, production requirements, or capacities can be made as necessary.

STANDARDIZED COMPONENTS AND WORK METHODS

The standardization of components, called *part commonality* or *modularity,* increases repeatability. For example, a firm producing 10 products from 1,000 different components could redesign its products so that they consist of only 100 different components with larger daily requirements. Because the requirements per component increase, so does repeatability; that is, each worker performs a standardized task or work method more often each day. Productivity tends to increase because, with increased repetition, workers learn to do the task more efficiently. Standardization of components and work methods aids in achieving the high-productivity, low-inventory objectives of JIT systems.

CLOSE SUPPLIER TIES

Because JIT systems operate with very low levels of inventory, close relationships with suppliers are necessary. Stock shipments must be frequent, have short lead times, arrive on schedule, and be of high quality. A contract might require a supplier to deliver goods to a factory as often as several times per day. Purchasing managers focus on three areas: reducing the number of suppliers, using local suppliers, and improving supplier relations.

Typically, one of the first actions undertaken when a JIT system is implemented is to pare the number of suppliers. Xerox, for example, reduced the number of its suppliers from 5,000 to just 300. This approach puts a lot of pressure on these suppliers to deliver high-quality components on time. To compensate, JIT users extend their contracts with these suppliers and give them firm advance-order information. In addition, they include their suppliers in the early phases of product design to avoid problems after production has begun. They also work with their suppliers' vendors, trying to achieve JIT inventory flows throughout the entire supply chain.

Manufacturers using JIT systems generally utilize local suppliers. For instance, when GM located its Saturn complex in Tennessee, many suppliers clustered nearby. Harley-Davidson reduced the number of its suppliers and gave preference to those close to its plants—for example, three-fourths of the suppliers for the Milwaukee engine plant are located within a 175-mile radius. Geographic proximity means that the company can reduce the need for safety stocks. Companies that have no suppliers close by must rely on a finely tuned supplier delivery system. For example, New United Motor Manufacturing, Incorporated (NUMMI), the joint venture between GM and Toyota in California, has suppliers in Indiana, Ohio, and Michigan. Through a carefully coordinated system involving trains and piggyback truck trailers, suppliers deliver enough parts for exactly one day's production each day.

Users of JIT systems also find that a cooperative orientation with suppliers is essential (see the Supply-Chain Management chapter). The JIT philosophy is to look for ways to improve efficiency and reduce inventories throughout the supply chain. Close cooperation between companies and their suppliers can be a win–win situation for everyone. Better communication of component requirements, for example, enables more efficient inventory planning and delivery scheduling by suppliers, thereby improving supplier profit margins. Customers can then negotiate lower component prices. Suppliers also should be included in the design of new products so that inefficient component designs can be avoided before production begins. Close supplier relations cannot be established and maintained if companies view their suppliers as adversaries whenever contracts are negotiated. Rather, they should consider suppliers to be partners in a venture wherein both parties have an interest in maintaining a long-term, profitable relationship.

FLEXIBLE WORKFORCE

Workers in flexible workforces can be trained to perform more than one job. When the skill levels required to perform most tasks are low—at a McDonald's restaurant, for instance—a high degree of flexibility in the workforce can be achieved with little training. In situations requiring higher skill levels, such as at the Texas Instruments antenna department, shifting workers to other jobs may require extensive, costly training. Flexibility can be very beneficial: Workers can be shifted among workstations to help relieve bottlenecks as they arise without resorting to inventory buffers—an important aspect of the uniform flow of JIT systems. Also, they can step in and do the job for those on vacation or out sick. Although assigning workers to tasks they do not usually perform may reduce efficiency, some rotation relieves boredom and refreshes workers.

LINE FLOWS

Line flows can reduce the frequency of setups. If volumes of specific products are large enough, groups of machines and workers can be organized into a product layout (see the Layout chapter) to eliminate setups entirely. If volume is insufficient to keep a line of similar products busy, *group technology* can be used to design small production lines that manufacture, in volume, families of components with common attributes. Changeovers from a component in one product family to the next component in the same family are minimal.

Another tactic used to reduce or eliminate setups is the one-worker, multiple-machines (OWMM) approach, which essentially is a one-person line. One worker operates several machines, with each machine advancing the process a step at a time. Because the same product is made repeatedly, setups are eliminated. For example, in a McDonald's restaurant, the person preparing fish sandwiches uses the OWMM approach. When the signal is given to produce more fish sandwiches, the employee puts the fish patties into the fish fryer and sets the timer. Then while the fish are frying, he puts the buns into the steamer. When the buns are finished, he puts them on a tray and dresses them with condiments. When the fish patties are ready, he inserts them into the buns. He then places the completed sandwiches on the shelf for the final assembler to package for the customer. The cycle is repeated throughout the day.

AUTOMATED PRODUCTION

Automation plays a big role in JIT systems and is a key to low-cost operations. Money freed up because of JIT inventory reductions or other efficiencies can be invested in automation to reduce costs. The benefits, of course, are greater profits, greater market share (because prices can be cut), or both. Automation should be planned carefully, however. Many managers believe that if some automation is good, more is better. That is not always the case. When GM initiated Buick City, for example, it installed 250 robots,

A robotic hand assembles an electronic curcuit board by inserting microchips. Circuit boards are made up of components such as microchips, diodes, capacitors and resistors, which are linked by electrical pathways. Automation is an important characteristic of JIT systems.

some with vision systems for mounting windshields. Unfortunately, the robots skipped black cars because they could not "see" them. New software eventually solved the problem; however, GM management found that humans could do some jobs better than robots and replaced 30 robots with humans.

PREVENTIVE MAINTENANCE

Because JIT emphasizes finely tuned flows of materials and little buffer inventory between workstations, unplanned machine downtime can be disruptive. Preventive maintenance can reduce the frequency and duration of machine downtime. After performing routine maintenance activities, the technician can test other parts that might need to be replaced. Replacement during regularly scheduled maintenance periods is easier and quicker than dealing with machine failures during production. Maintenance is done on a schedule that balances the cost of the preventive maintenance program against the risks and costs of machine failure.

Another tactic is to make workers responsible for routinely maintaining their own equipment and develop employee pride in keeping their machines in top condition. This tactic, however, typically is limited to general housekeeping chores, minor lubrication, and adjustments. Maintenance of high-tech machines needs trained specialists. Doing even simple maintenance tasks goes a long way toward improving machine performance, though.

CONTINUOUS IMPROVEMENT

How can lean systems facilitate continuous improvement?

By spotlighting areas that need improvement, lean systems lead to continuous improvement in quality and productivity. For example, Figure 16.2 characterizes the philosophy behind continuous improvement with lean systems. In manufacturing, the water surface represents product and component inventory levels. In services, the water surface represents service system capacity, such as staff levels. The rocks represent problems encountered in manufacturing or service delivery. When the water surface is high enough, the boat passes over the rocks because the high level of inventory or capacity

FIGURE 16.2

*Continuous
Improvement
with Lean Systems*

covers up problems. As inventory shrinks, rocks are exposed. Ultimately, the boat will hit a rock if the water surface falls far enough. Through lean systems, workers, supervisors, engineers, and analysts apply methods for continuous improvement to demolish the exposed rock (see the Process Management, Total Quality Management, and Statistical Process Control chapters). The coordination required for the pull system of material flows in lean systems identifies problems in time for corrective action to be taken.

In manufacturing, eliminating the problem of too much scrap might require improving work methods, employee quality training, and supplier quality. The desire to eliminate capacity imbalances might focus attention on the master production schedule and workforce flexibility. Reducing unreliable deliveries calls for cooperating better with suppliers or replacing suppliers. Maintaining low inventories, periodically stressing the system to identify problems, and focusing on the elements of the lean system lie at the heart of continuous improvement. For example, the Kawasaki plant in Nebraska periodically cuts safety stocks almost to zero. Problems are exposed, recorded, and later assigned as improvement projects. After the improvements have been made, inventories are permanently cut to the new level. The Japanese have used this trial-and-error process to develop more efficient manufacturing operations.

Service operations that are integral to both manufacturing and service organizations, including scheduling, billing, order taking, accounting, and financial tasks, also can be improved with lean systems. As in manufacturing, continuous improvement means that employees and managers continue to seek ways to improve operations. However, the mechanics of highlighting the areas needing improvement are different. In service operations, a common approach used by managers to place stress on the system is to reduce the number of employees doing a particular operation or series of operations until the process begins to slow or come to a halt. The problems can be identified, and ways for overcoming them can be explored. We return to the use of lean systems in services later.

THE KANBAN SYSTEM

How is the flow of materials in a factory controlled in a JIT system?

kanban A word meaning "card" or "visible record" in Japanese; refers to cards used to control the flow of production through a factory.

One of the most publicized aspects of lean systems, and the Toyota Production System in particular, is the kanban system developed by Toyota. **Kanban,** meaning "card" or "visible record" in Japanese, refers to cards used to control the flow of production through a factory. In the most basic kanban system, a card is attached to each container of items that have been produced. The container holds a given percent of the daily requirements for an item. When the user of the parts empties a container, the card is removed from the container and put on a receiving post. The empty container is taken to the storage area. The card signals the need to produce another container of the part. When a container has been refilled, the card is put on the container, which is then returned to a storage area. The cycle begins again when the user of the parts retrieves the container with the card attached.

Figure 16.3 shows how a single-card kanban system works when a fabrication cell feeds two assembly lines. As an assembly line needs more parts, the kanban card for those parts is taken to the receiving post and a full container of parts is removed from the storage area. The receiving post accumulates cards for both assembly lines and sequences the production of replenishment parts. In this example, the fabrication cell will produce product 1 before it produces product 2. The cell consists of three different operations, but operation 2 has two workstations. Once production has been initiated in the cell, the product begins on operation 1, but could be routed to either of the workstations performing operation 2, depending on the workload at the time. Finally, the product is processed on operation 3 before being taken to the storage area.

FIGURE 16.3

Single-Card Kanban System

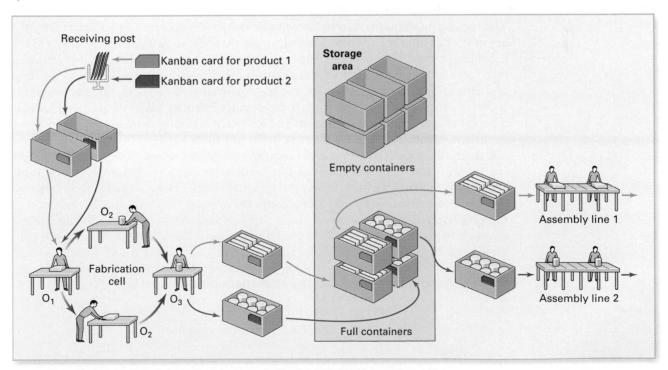

GENERAL OPERATING RULES

The operating rules for the single-card system are simple and are designed to facilitate the flow of materials while maintaining control of inventory levels.

1. Each container must have a card.
2. The assembly line always withdraws materials from the fabrication cell. The fabrication cell never pushes parts to the assembly line because, sooner or later, parts will be supplied that are not yet needed for production.
3. Containers of parts must never be removed from a storage area without a kanban first being posted on the receiving post.
4. The containers should always contain the same number of good parts. The use of nonstandard containers or irregularly filled containers disrupts the production flow of the assembly line.
5. Only nondefective parts should be passed along to the assembly line to make the best use of materials and workers' time.
6. Total production should not exceed the total amount authorized on the kanbans in the system.

Toyota uses a two-card system, based on a withdrawal card and a production-order card, to control withdrawal quantities more closely. The withdrawal card specifies the item and the quantity the user of the item should withdraw from the producer of the item, as well as the stocking locations for both the user and the producer. The production-order card specifies the item and the production quantity to be produced, the materials required and where to find them, and where to store the finished item. Materials cannot be withdrawn without a withdrawal card, and production cannot begin without a production-order card. The cards are attached to containers when production commences.

DETERMINING THE NUMBER OF CONTAINERS

The number of authorized containers in the Toyota Production System determines the amount of authorized inventory. Management must make two determinations: (1) the number of units to be held by each container and (2) the number of containers flowing back and forth between the supplier station and the user station. The first decision amounts to determining the lot size and may be compared to calculating the economic order quantity (EOQ) or specifying a fixed order quantity based on other considerations (see the Inventory Management and Resource Planning chapters).

The number of containers flowing back and forth between two stations directly affects the quantities of work-in-process inventory and safety stock. The containers spend some time in production, in a line waiting, in a storage location, or in transit. The key to determining the number of containers required is to estimate accurately the average lead time needed to produce a container of parts. The lead time is a function of the processing time per container at the supplier station, the waiting time during the production process, and the time required for materials handling. The number of containers needed to support the user station equals the average demand during the lead time plus some safety stock to account for unexpected circumstances, divided by the number of units in one container. Therefore, the number of containers is

$$k = \frac{\text{Average demand during lead time } \textit{plus} \text{ safety stock}}{\text{Number of units per container}}$$

$$= \frac{d(\overline{w} + \overline{p})(1 + \alpha)}{c}$$

where

k = number of containers for a part

d = expected daily demand for the part, in units

$\overline{w}$ = average waiting time during the production process plus materials handling time per container, in fractions of a day

$\overline{p}$ = average processing time per container, in fractions of a day

c = quantity in a standard container of the part

α = a policy variable that reflects the efficiency of the workstations producing and using the part (Toyota uses a value of no more than 10 percent)

The number of containers must, of course, be an integer. Rounding k up provides more inventory than desired, whereas rounding k down provides less.

The kanban system allows management to fine-tune the flow of materials in the system in a straightforward way. For example, removing cards from the system reduces the number of authorized containers of the part, thus reducing the inventory of the part.

The container quantity, c, and the efficiency factor, α, are variables that management can use to control inventory. Adjusting c changes the lot sizes, and adjusting α changes the amount of safety stock. The kanban system actually is a special form of the base-stock system (see the Inventory Management chapter). In this case, the stocking level is $d(\overline{w} + \overline{p})(1 + \alpha)$, and the order quantity is fixed at c units. Each time a container of parts is removed from the base stock, authorization is given to replace it.

| EXAMPLE 16.1 | *Determining the Appropriate Number of Containers* |

**TUTOR
16.1**

The Westerville Auto Parts Company produces rocker-arm assemblies for use in the steering and suspension systems of four-wheel-drive trucks. A typical container of parts spends 0.02 day in processing and 0.08 day in materials handling and waiting during its manufacturing cycle. The daily demand for the part is 2,000 units. Management believes that demand for the rocker-arm assembly is uncertain enough to warrant a safety stock equivalent of 10 percent of its authorized inventory.

    a. If there are 22 parts in each container, how many containers should be authorized?

    b. Suppose that a proposal to revise the plant layout would cut materials handling and waiting time per container to 0.06 day. How many containers would be needed?

Solver - Number of Containers

Enter data in yellow-shaded areas.

Daily Expected Demand	2000
Quantity in Standard Container	22
Container Waiting Time (days)	0.06
Processing Time (days)	0.02
Policy Variable	10%
Containers Required	8

FIGURE 16.4

SOLUTION

a. If $d = 2,000$ units/day, $\overline{p} = 0.02$ day, $\alpha = 0.10$, $\overline{w} = 0.08$ day, and $c = 22$ units,

$$k = \frac{2,000(0.08 + 0.02)(1.10)}{22} = \frac{220}{22} = 10 \text{ containers}$$

b. Figure 16.4 shows that the number of containers drops to 8.

Decision Point The average lead time per container is $\overline{w} + \overline{p}$. With a lead time of 0.10 day, 10 containers are needed. However, if the improved facility layout reduces the materials handling time and waiting time, $\overline{w}$, to 0.06 day, only 8 containers are needed. The maximum authorized inventory of the rocker-arm assembly is kc units. Thus, in part (a), the maximum authorized inventory is 220 units, but in part (b), it is only 176 units. Reducing $\overline{w} + \overline{p}$ by 20 percent has reduced the inventory of the part by 20 percent. Management must balance the cost of the relay-out (a one-time charge) against the long-term benefits of inventory reduction. ❐

OTHER KANBAN SIGNALS

Cards are not the only way to signal the need for more production of a part. Other, less formal, methods are possible, including container and containerless systems.

CONTAINER SYSTEM. Sometimes the container itself can be used as a signal device: An empty container signals the need to fill it. Unisys took this approach for low-value items. The amount of inventory of the part is adjusted by adding or removing containers. This system works well when the container is specially designed for a part and no other parts could accidentally be put in it. Such is the case when the container is actually a pallet or fixture used to position the part during precision processing.

CONTAINERLESS SYSTEM. Systems requiring no containers have been devised. In assembly-line operations, operators having their own workbench areas put completed units on painted squares, one unit per square. Each painted square represents a container, and the number of painted squares on each operator's bench is calculated to balance the line flow. When the subsequent user removes a unit from one of the producer's squares, the empty square signals the need to produce another unit.

McDonald's uses a containerless system. A command from the manager or the final assembler starts production, or the number of hamburgers in the ramp itself signals the need. Either way, the customer dictates production.

JIT II

The JIT II concept was conceived and implemented by the Bose Corporation, producer of high-quality professional sound systems and speaker systems. In a JIT II system, the supplier is brought into the plant to be an active member of the purchasing office of the customer. The *in-plant representative* is on site full-time at the supplier's expense and is empowered to plan and schedule the replenishment of materials from the supplier. This is an example of vendor-managed inventories (see the Supply-Chain Management chapter). Typically, the representative's duties include

❐ issuing purchase orders to his or her own firms on behalf of Bose,

❐ working on design ideas to help save costs and improve manufacturing processes, and

❐ managing production schedules for suppliers, materials contractors, and other subcontractors.

The in-plant representative replaces the buyer, the salesperson, and sometimes the materials planner in a typical JIT arrangement. Thus, JIT II fosters extremely close interaction with suppliers. Bose started the system in 1987, and by 1993, there were 12 in-plant representatives billing about 25 percent of the total purchasing budget. Although more representatives will be added, the qualifications for a supplier to be included in the program are stringent.

In general, JIT II offers the following benefits to the customer:

❏ Liberated from administrative tasks, the purchasing staff is able to work on improving efficiencies in other areas of procurement.

❏ Communication and purchase order placement are improved dramatically.

❏ The cost of materials is reduced immediately, and the savings are ongoing.

❏ Preferred suppliers are brought into the product design process earlier.

❏ A natural foundation is provided for electronic data interchange (EDI), effective paperwork, and administrative savings.

In general, JIT II offers the following benefits to the supplier:

❏ It eliminates sales effort.

❏ Communication and purchase order placement are improved dramatically.

❏ The volume of business rises at the start of the program and continues to grow as new products are introduced.

❏ An evergreen contract is provided, with no end date and no rebidding.

❏ The supplier can communicate with and sell directly to engineering.

❏ Invoicing and payment administration are efficient.

Several large corporations have implemented JIT II in their supply chains. IBM and Intel have more than 50 on-site JIT II suppliers. AT&T, Honeywell, Roadway Express, Ingersoll-Rand, and Westinghouse also use the system. JIT II is an advance over other just-in-time systems because it provides the organizational structure needed to improve supplier coordination by integrating the logistics, production, and purchasing processes.

LEAN SYSTEMS IN SERVICES

How can lean systems be used in a service environment?

Lean systems and the just-in-time philosophy also can be applied to the production of services. We have already discussed some of the elements of the JIT system used in a McDonald's restaurant. In general, service environments may benefit from lean systems such as JIT if their operations are repetitive, have reasonably high volumes, and deal with tangible items such as sandwiches, mail, checks, or bills. In other words, the services must involve "manufacturing-like" operations. Other services involving a high degree of customization, such as haircutting, can also make use of JIT systems but to a lesser degree—basically utilizing elements of the just-in-time philosophy in their operations.

 The focus of JIT systems is on improving the process; therefore, some of the JIT concepts useful for manufacturers are also useful for service providers. These concepts include the following:

❏ *Consistently High Quality.* Benchmarking, service design, and quality function deployment can be used successfully in service operations. Service employees can be taught the value of providing defect-free services.

❏ *Uniform Facility Loads.* Reservation systems and differential pricing are two ways in which service providers can level the loads on their facilities.

❑ *Standardized Work Methods.* In highly repetitive service operations, great efficiencies can be gained by analyzing work methods and standardizing improvements for all employees to use. For example, UPS consistently monitors work methods and revises them as necessary to improve service.

❑ *Close Supplier Ties.* Volume services such as fast-food restaurants and mass merchandisers such as Wal-Mart and Kmart require close supplier contacts to ensure frequent, short lead time and high-quality shipments of supplies.

❑ *Flexible Workforce.* The more customized the service, the greater is the need for a multiskilled workforce. For example, stereo component repair shops require broadly trained personnel who can identify a wide variety of problems and then repair the defective unit. The employees at a sectional center post

MANAGERIAL PRACTICE 16.1
Internet Grocer Webvan Uses JIT for Its Order-Fulfillment Process

Do you have a taste for gourmet and specialty food items but do not have a lot of time to shop? If so, you are among a growing population of consumers who are using the Internet to do their grocery shopping. Webvan, a major competitor in the Internet grocery market, offers full service to its customers 24 hours a day, 7 days a week. Customers can shop for groceries and other household items, including consumer electronics, books, stamps, flowers, and office supplies, using Webvan's Web site (www.webvan.com).

Low cost, high quality, delivery speed, and delivery dependability are key competitive priorities in the Internet grocery market. Webvan guarantees that deliveries will be made within a 30-minute window of time specified by the customer. Webvan's order-fulfillment process must be capable of achieving those competitive priorities. Webvan uses JIT in the following way:

❑ Nothing happens until a customer places an order on the Web site (*pull method*).

❑ A tote with the customer's order is conveyed automatically to a stock picker, who puts items into the tote (*automation*). The tote is then conveyed to other areas of the warehouse housing additional items for the order (*line flow*).

❑ Pickers travel no more than 19.5 feet in any direction to reach 8,000 bins of goods that are brought to the picker on rotating carousels (*automation*). Pickers perform repetitive operations (*standardized work methods*).

❑ The tote is loaded on a refrigerated van, transported to a transfer station, and then delivered to the customer using a three-step, repetitive process (*line flow*).

At Webvan, just-in-time deliveries at any time of the day within a small window of time translate into the need for a sizeable truck fleet.

❑ Orders are checked for accuracy before leaving the warehouse. If something is missing when the order arrives at the customer, the courier who delivers the order contacts the warehouse and the missing items are immediately dispatched at no cost to the customer (*high quality*).

Although the ultimate success of Internet grocers such as Webvan is yet to be determined, the principles of JIT are fundamental to their operations.

Source: Himelstein, Linda, "Can You Sell Groceries Like Books?" *Business Week* (July 26, 1999), pp. EB 44–EB 50.

office have more narrowly defined jobs because of the repetitive nature of the tasks they must perform, and thus they do not have to acquire many alternative skills.

❑ *Automation.*   Automation can play a big role in providing just-in-time services. For example, banks offer ATMs that provide various bank services on demand 24 hours a day.

❑ *Preventive Maintenance.*   Services that are highly dependent on machinery can make good use of routine preventive maintenance. For example, entertainment services such as Walt Disney World must have dependable people-moving apparatus to accommodate large volumes of customers.

❑ *Pull Method of Material Flows.*   Service operations where tangible items are processed, such as fast-food restaurants, can utilize the pull method.

❑ *Line Flows.*   Managers of service operations can organize their employees and equipment to provide uniform flows through the system and eliminate wasted employee time. Banks use this strategy in their check-processing operations, as does UPS in its parcel-sorting process.

Managerial Practice 16.1 shows how Webvan is using JIT to deliver groceries to its customers.

STRATEGIC IMPLICATIONS OF LEAN SYSTEMS

When corporate strategy centers on dramatic improvements in inventory turnover and labor productivity, a just-in-time philosophy can be the solution. For example, lean systems such as just-in-time form an integral part of corporate strategies emphasizing time-based competition because they focus on cutting cycle times, improving inventory turnover, and increasing labor productivity. In this section, we consider competitive priorities and product or service flows, as well as the operational benefits of lean systems as represented by JIT.

COMPETITIVE PRIORITIES

Low cost and consistent quality are the priorities emphasized most often in JIT systems. Superior features and volume flexibility are emphasized less often. The ability to provide product or service variety depends on the degree of flexibility designed into the production system. Such is the case with firms using an assemble-to-order strategy. For example, mixed-model automobile assembly lines allow variety in output in terms of color, options, and even body style. JIT systems such as the Toyota Production System work well in this environment. Production to customized, individual orders, however, usually is not attempted with a JIT system. The erratic demand and last-minute rush jobs of customized orders in make-to-order or customized service environments do not link well with a system designed to produce at a constant daily rate utilizing low inventory or capacity buffers.

FLOWS

A JIT system involves line flows to achieve high-volume, low-cost production of products or services. Workers and machines are organized around product or service flows and arranged to conform to the sequence of work operations. With line flows, a unit of work finished at one station goes almost immediately to the next station, thereby reducing lead time and inventory. Process repetition makes opportunities for methods improvement more visible. Line flows support the make-to-stock, standardized services, and assemble-to-order strategies (see the Operations Strategy chapter).

OPERATIONAL BENEFITS

Just-in-time systems have many operational benefits. They

❑ reduce space requirements;

❑ reduce inventory investment in purchased parts, raw materials, work in process, and finished goods;

❑ reduce lead times;

❑ increase the productivity of direct-labor employees, indirect-support employees, and clerical staff;

❑ increase equipment utilization;

❑ reduce paperwork and require only simple planning systems;

❑ set valid priorities for scheduling;

❑ encourage participation by the workforce; and

❑ increase product or service quality.

One goal is to drive setup times so low that production of one end unit or part becomes economical. Although this goal is rarely achieved, the focus still is on small-lot production. In addition, constant attention is given to removing nonvalue-added activities in processes. The result is less need for storage space, inventory investment, or capacity. Smaller lot sizes and smoothed flows of materials help reduce lead times, increase employee productivity, and improve equipment utilization.

A primary operational benefit is the simplicity of the system. For example, in manufacturing, product mix or volume changes planned by the MPS can be accomplished by adjusting the number of kanbans in the system. The priority of each production order is reflected in the sequence of the kanbans on the post. Production orders for parts that are running low are placed before those for parts that have more supply.

Just-in-time systems also involve a considerable amount of employee participation through small-group interaction sessions, which have resulted in improvements in many aspects of operations, not the least of which is product or service quality. Overall, the advantages of JIT systems have caused many managers to reevaluate their own systems and consider adapting operations to the JIT philosophy.

IMPLEMENTATION ISSUES

What can be done to make employees more receptive to the changes associated with just-in-time systems?

The benefits of lean systems seem to be outstanding, yet problems can arise even after a lean system has long been operational. Even the Japanese, who pioneered JIT practices in the automobile industry, are not immune to problems: Tokyo is experiencing monumental traffic jams owing in large measure to truck deliveries to JIT manufacturers—small trucks make up 47 percent of Tokyo's traffic. In this section, we address some of the issues managers should be aware of when implementing a lean system such as JIT.

ORGANIZATIONAL CONSIDERATIONS

Implementing a JIT system requires management to consider issues of worker stress, cooperation and trust among workers and management, and reward systems and labor classifications.

HUMAN COSTS OF JIT SYSTEMS. Just-in-time systems can be coupled with statistical process control (SPC) to reduce variations in outputs. However, this combination requires a high degree of regimentation and sometimes causes stress in the workforce. In a JIT system, workers must meet specified cycle times, and, with SPC, they must follow prescribed problem-solving methods. Such systems might make workers feel pushed and stressed, causing productivity losses or quality reductions. In addition, workers might feel that they have lost some autonomy because of the close linkages in materials flows between stations with little or no safety stocks. Managers can mitigate some of these effects by allowing slack in the system through the judicious use of safety stock inventories or capacity slack and by emphasizing materials flows instead of worker pace. Managers also can promote the use of work teams and allow them to determine their task assignments or rotations within the team's domain of responsibility.

COOPERATION AND TRUST. In a JIT system workers and first-line supervisors must take on responsibilities formerly assigned to middle managers and support staff. Activities such as scheduling, expediting, and improving productivity become part of the duties of lower-level personnel. Consequently, organizational relationships must be reoriented to build close cooperation and mutual trust between the workforce and management. Such cooperation and trust may be difficult to achieve, particularly in light of the typical adversarial positions taken by labor and management in the past. For example, the Mazda plant in Flat Rock, Michigan, was experiencing quality problems. Greater absenteeism than the Japanese expected and inexperience of the workforce were cited as major contributors. Some people felt that the real problem was a lack of understanding of the American culture by Japanese managers. As the president of UAW Local 3000 put it, "To the Japanese, work is the most important part of life, and they expect everybody to be as dedicated as they are. But to Americans, the job is there to support your life on the outside."

REWARD SYSTEMS AND LABOR CLASSIFICATIONS. In some instances, the reward system must be revamped when a JIT system is implemented. At General Motors, for example, a plan to reduce stock at one plant ran into trouble because the production superintendent refused to cut back production of unneeded parts; his salary was based on his plant's production volume.

The realignment of reward systems is not the only hurdle. Labor contracts traditionally have reduced management's flexibility in reassigning workers as the need arises. A typical automobile plant in the United States has several unions and dozens of labor classifications. To gain more flexibility, management in some cases has obtained union concessions by granting other types of benefits. In other cases, management has relocated plants to take advantage of nonunion or foreign labor. In contrast, at Toyota management deals with only one company union, and there are only eight different labor classifications in a typical plant.

PROCESS CONSIDERATIONS

Firms using JIT systems typically have some dominant work flows. To take advantage of JIT practices, firms might have to change their existing layouts. Certain workstations might have to be moved closer together, and cells of machines devoted to particular families of components may have to be established. A survey of 68 firms using JIT systems indicated that the single most important factor in successful implementation is changing product flows and layout to a cellular design (Billesbach, 1991). However, rearranging a plant to conform to JIT practices can be costly. For example, whereas many plants now receive raw materials and purchased parts by rail, to facilitate smaller, more frequent JIT shipments, truck deliveries would be preferable. Loading docks might have to be reconstructed or expanded and certain operations relocated to accommodate the change in transportation mode and quantities of arriving materials.

INVENTORY AND SCHEDULING

Firms need to have stable master production schedules, short setups, and frequent, reliable supplies of materials and components to achieve the full potential of the JIT concept.

MPS STABILITY. Daily production schedules in high-volume, make-to-stock environments must be stable for extended periods. At Toyota, the master production schedule is stated in fractions of days over a three-month period and is revised only once a month. The first month of the schedule is frozen to avoid disruptive changes in the daily production schedule for each workstation; that is, the workstations execute the same work schedule each day of the month. At the beginning of each month, kanbans are reissued for the new daily production rate. Stable schedules are needed so that production lines can be balanced and new assignments found for employees who otherwise would be underutilized. Just-in-time systems used in high-volume, make-to-stock environments cannot respond quickly to scheduling changes because little slack inventory or capacity is available to absorb these changes.

SETUPS. If the inventory advantages of a JIT system are to be realized, small lot sizes must be used. However, because small lots require a large number of setups, companies must significantly reduce setup times. Some companies have not been able to achieve short setup times and, therefore, have to use large-lot production, negating some of the advantages of JIT practices. Also, JIT systems are vulnerable to lengthy changeovers to new products because the low levels of finished goods inventory will be insufficient to cover demand while the system is down. If changeover times cannot be reduced, large finished goods inventories of the old product must be accumulated to compensate. In the automobile industry, every week that a plant is shut down for new-model changeover costs between $16 million and $20 million in pretax profits.

PURCHASING AND LOGISTICS. If frequent, small shipments of purchased items cannot be arranged with suppliers, large inventory savings for these items cannot be realized. In the United States, such arrangements may prove difficult because of the geographic dispersion of suppliers.

The shipments of raw materials and components must be reliable because of the low inventory levels in JIT systems. A plant can be shut down because of a lack of materials. For example, in 1992, a strike at the GM plant in Lordstown, Ohio, caused the Saturn plant in Spring Hill, Tennessee, to shut down, losing the production of 1,000 cars per day. Lordstown supplies parts to Saturn, which does not stock-pile the parts because of JIT practices.

Managerial Practice 16.2 shows that implementing a lean system can take a long time.

LEAN SYSTEMS ACROSS THE ORGANIZATION

The philosophy of lean systems has application throughout the organization. A theme of this text is that organizations create products or services with processes, which cut across functional boundaries to create value for customers—who can be internal or external. Lean systems focus on efficient value creation, which applies to any process in the organization.

MANAGERIAL PRACTICE 16.2
Implementing Lean Manufacturing Principles at Cessna

Cessna Aircraft (www.cessna.com) is a leading manufacturer of business jets, utility planes, and single-engine piston-powered personal aircraft. Almost half of all the general aviation planes shipped in 1999 were Cessnas. The planes range in price from $150,000 for a single-engine piston-powered aircraft to over $17 million for a business jet. However, 10 years ago, the company decided to abandon the production of single-engine piston-powered planes because of the liability the company incurred for just about any accident involving a Cessna, regardless of the circumstances. After legislation in 1994 limited the liability of aircraft manufacturers, Cessna decided to get back into the manufacture of small planes by building a new plant in Independence, Kansas. It was an opportunity to incorporate a new lean manufacturing system to a product line that had not changed much over the years, with the exception of the avionics in the cockpit and a new, efficient engine, which was outsourced. To do so, however, Cessna had to learn how to go from a craftwork mentality, which is what they had when they last produced small aircraft, to a modern manufacturing mentality that involves a whole new way of doing things.

Cessna adopted three lean manufacturing practices in its new plant. First, management committed to the team concept (see the Process Management and Total Quality Control chapters). Teamwork fosters workforce flexibility because team members learn the duties of other team members and can shift across assembly lines as needed. However, because of a shortage of technically qualified employees, Cessna had to hire employees short on sheet metal skills but willing to work as a team and to assume responsibility. Productivity initially suffered, but retired assembly-line workers were recalled to serve as mentors to teach the new employees the skills and confidence they needed to do their jobs. It has taken four years to bring the teams to the point of learning about conflict resolution, problem solving, and flexibility.

Second, Cessna initiated vendor-managed inventories with several of its suppliers. For example, two Honeywell field engineers who also help with problems after installation maintain a 30-day avionics inventory worth $30 million on-site. In addition, a warehouse nearby was opened to house the inventories of several suppliers. The warehouse operations are being integrated with the plant schedule so that inventory will be delivered daily to the production line. Suppliers initially balked at the idea, but eventually saw its advantages.

Single-engine Cessna airplanes roll off the assembly line at Independence, Kansas. Three versions of single-engine planes are built at the southeast Kansas plant, using the concepts of lean manufacturing systems.

Finally, Cessna has incorporated manufacturing cells and group technology in their manufacturing process and has moved away from a batch process approach that supported a make-to-stock strategy. In the past, Cessna had a network of dealers who took what was sent to them, maintained large inventories to support the dealers, and had to give incentives to get rid of excess inventories. Today, Cessna assembles to order. This change in manufacturing strategy required a change in the manufacturing process as well as a change in the way Cessna does business with its dealers (see the Operations Strategy and Process Management chapters).

Cessna has made the transition from craftwork to modern manufacturing, but not without hard work. Although inventory investment has shown improvement, it still takes twice as many hours to build a model 172 than it did in the 1980s. The theoretical capacity of the plant is 2,000 planes a year, but the annual target four years after the start of operations was only 975 planes a year. Much of the slow start-up was due to initiating a brand-new workforce. This experience at Cessna shows that switching to modern manufacturing methods is a long-term commitment.

Source: Siekman, Phillip. "Cessna Tackles Lean Manufacturing." *Fortune* (May 1, 2000), pp. I222 B–I222 Z.

To take advantage of lean systems, companies must clearly define the value of their products or services as perceived by their customers (see the Total Quality Management chapter). Every product or service category must be carefully scrutinized for excessive complexity or unnecessary features and options. The goal should be to deliver products or services that precisely match the customer's needs without waste. Then, the company must identify the sequence of activities and the processes involved that are *essential* to the creation of the product or service by drawing flow charts and developing process charts (see the Process Management chapter). Activities that are value-added (those tasks that transform the product or service in some measurable way) should be clearly differentiated from those that are nonvalue added (wasted effort that could be eliminated without any impact on the customer).

Once the activities are identified and the flows are charted, the barriers to the flow of value must be eliminated. For example, these barriers can be found in the factory in the form of large batches and excessive inventory; in the product development process in the form of excessive documentation, approvals, and meetings; or in the order-entry process in the form of incomplete product or service information or poorly designed Web pages. These barriers are examples of the rocks in Figure 16.2. Once these rocks are removed, the firm is free to allow its customers to "pull" value, which is the real market demand that becomes the trigger for all activities to follow. Lean systems certainly are important to all processes in the organization.

FORMULA REVIEW

1. Number of containers:

$$k = \frac{\text{Average demand during lead time } + \text{ Safety stock}}{\text{Number of units per container}}$$

$$= \frac{d(\overline{w} + \overline{p})(1 + \alpha)}{c}$$

CHAPTER HIGHLIGHTS

☐ Lean systems focus on the efficient delivery of products or services. A just-in-time system, a popular lean system, is designed to produce or deliver just the right products or services in just the right quantities just in time to serve subsequent processes or customers.

☐ Some of the key elements of JIT systems are a pull method to manage material flow, consistently high quality, small lot sizes, uniform workstation loads, standardized components and work methods, close supplier ties, flexible workforce, line flow strategy, automated production, preventive maintenance, and continuous improvement.

☐ A single-card JIT system uses a kanban to control production flow. The authorized inventory of a part is a function of the number of authorized cards for that item. The number of cards depends on average demand during

manufacturing lead time, the container size, and a policy variable to adjust for unexpected occurrences. Many other methods may be used to signal the need for material replenishment and production.

☐ The JIT II system provides an organizational structure for improved supplier coordination by integrating the logistics, production, and purchasing processes.

☐ Just-in-time concepts can be applied to the production of services. Service organizations that have repetitive operations, maintain reasonably high volume, and deal with some tangible item are most likely to benefit from JIT practices.

☐ For operations competing on the basis of low cost and consistent quality, JIT system advantages include reductions in inventory, space requirements, and paperwork and increases in productivity, employee participation, and quality. JIT systems require fundamental changes in the way *all* of the firm's business functions are performed. Increasing cooperation and trust between management and labor, basing rewards on team rather than individual performance, and replacing adversarial supplier relationships with partnerships arc some of the basic cultural changes involved in JIT system implementation.

KEY TERMS

just-in-time (JIT) philosophy *799*
JIT system *799*
kanban *807*

lean systems *799*
mixed-model assembly *802*
pull method *800*

push method *799*
single-digit setup *802*

SOLVED PROBLEM

A company using a kanban system has an inefficient machine group. For example, the daily demand for part L105A is 3,000 units. The average waiting time for a container of parts is 0.8 day. The processing time for a container of L105A is 0.2 day, and a container holds 270 units. Currently, there are 20 containers for this item.

a. What is the value of the policy variable, α?

b. What is the total planned inventory (work in process and finished goods) for item L105A?

c. Suppose that the policy variable, α, were 0. How many containers would be needed now? What is the effect of the policy variable in this example?

SOLUTION

a. We use the equation for the number of containers and then solve for α:

$$k = \frac{d(\overline{w} + \overline{p})(1 + \alpha)}{c}$$

$$= \frac{3,000(0.8 + 0.2)(1 + \alpha)}{270} = 20$$

and

$$(1 + \alpha) = \frac{20(270)}{3,000(0.8 + 0.2)} = 1.8$$

$$\alpha = 1.8 - 1 = 0.8$$

b. With 20 containers in the system and each container holding 270 units, the total planned inventory is $20(270) = 5,400$ units.

c. If $\alpha = 0$,

$$k = \frac{3,000(0.8 + 0.2)(1 + 0)}{270} = 11.11 \qquad \text{or} \qquad 12 \text{ containers}$$

The policy variable adjusts the number of containers. In this case, the difference is quite dramatic because $\overline{w} + \overline{p}$ is fairly large and the number of units per container is small relative to daily demand.

DISCUSSION QUESTIONS

1. Compare and contrast the following two situations:
   a. A company's JIT system stresses teamwork. Employees feel more involved, and therefore productivity and quality have increased. Yet one of the problems in implementing the JIT system has been the loss of individual autonomy.
   b. A humanities professor believes that all students desire to learn. To encourage students to work together and learn from each other, thereby increasing involvement, productivity, and the quality of the learning experience, the professor announces that all students in the class will receive the same grade and that it will be based on the performance of the group.

2. Which elements of JIT systems would be most troublesome for U.S. manufacturers to implement? Why?

OM EXPLORER AND INTERNET EXERCISES

Visit our Web site at www.prenhall.com/krajewski for OM Explorer Tutors, which explain quantitative techniques; Solvers, which help you apply mathematical models; and Internet Exercises, including Facility Tours, which expand on the topics in this chapter.

PROBLEMS

1. The Harvey motorcycle company produces three models: the Tiger, a sure-footed dirt bike; the LX2000, a nimble cafe racer; and the Golden, a large interstate tourer. This month's master production schedule calls for the production of 54 Goldens, 42 LX2000s, and 30 Tigers per seven-hour shift.
   a. What average cycle time is required for the assembly line to achieve the production quota in seven hours?
   b. If mixed-model scheduling is used, how many of each model will be produced before the production cycle is repeated?
   c. Determine a satisfactory production sequence for the ultimate in small-lot production: one unit.
   d. The design of a new model, the Cheetah, includes features from the Tiger, LX2000, and Golden models. The resulting blended design has an indecisive character and is expected to attract some sales from the other models. Determine a mixed-model schedule resulting in 52 Goldens, 39 LX2000s, 26 Tigers, and 13 Cheetahs per seven-hour shift. Although the total number of motorcycles produced per day will increase only slightly, what problem might be anticipated in implementing this change from the production schedule indicated in part (b)?

2. ● **OM Explorer** A fabrication cell at Spradley's Sprockets uses the pull method to supply gears to an assembly line. George Jitson is in charge of the assembly line, which requires 500 gears per day. Containers typically wait 0.20 day in the fabrication cell. Each container holds 20 gears, and one container requires 1.8 days in machine time. Setup times are negligible. If the policy variable for unforeseen contingencies is set at 5 percent, how many containers should Jitson authorize for the gear replenishment system?

3. ● **OM Explorer** You have been asked to analyze the kanban system of LeWin, a French manufacturer of gaming devices. One of the workstations feeding the assembly line produces part M670N. The daily demand for M670N is 1,800 units. The average processing time per unit is 0.003 day. LeWin's records show that the average container spends 1.05 days waiting at the feeder workstation. The container for M670N can hold 300 units. Twelve containers are authorized for the part. Recall that $\bar{p}$ is the average processing time per container, not per individual part.

a. Find the value of the policy variable, α, that expresses the amount of implied safety stock in this system.

b. Use the implied value of α from part (a) to determine the required reduction in waiting time if one container was removed. Assume that all other parameters remain constant.

4. ⊙ **OM Explorer** An assembly line requires two components: gadjits and widjits. Gadjits are produced by center 1 and widjits by center 2. Each unit of the end item, called a jit-together, requires 3 gadjits and 2 widjits, as shown in Figure 16.5. The daily production quota on the assembly line is 800 jit-togethers.

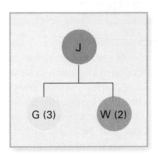

FIGURE 16.5

The container for gadjits holds 80 units. The policy variable for center 1 is set at 0.09. The average waiting time for a container of gadjits is 0.09 day, and 0.06 day is needed to produce a container. The container for widjits holds 50 units, and the policy variable for center 2 is 0.08. The average waiting time per container of widgits is 0.14 day, and the time required to process a container is 0.20 day.

a. How many containers are needed for gadjits?

b. How many containers are needed for widjits?

5. ⊙ **OM Explorer** Gestalt, Inc., uses a kanban system in its automobile production facility in Germany. This facility operates eight hours per day to produce the Jitterbug, a replacement for the obsolete but immensely popular Jitney Beetle. Suppose that a certain part requires 150 seconds of processing at machine cell 33B and a container of parts averages 1.6 hours of waiting time there. Management has allowed a 10 percent buffer for unexpected occurrences. Each container holds 30 parts, and 8 containers are authorized. How much daily demand can be satisfied with this system? (*Hint*: Recall that $\bar{p}$ is the average processing time per container, not per individual part.)

6. ⊙ **OM Explorer** A jittery U.S. Postal Service supervisor is looking for ways to reduce stress in the sorting department. With the existing arrangement, stamped letters are machine canceled and loaded into tubs with 375 letters per tub. The tubs are then pushed to postal clerks, who read and key zip codes into an automated sorting machine at the rate of one tub per 375 seconds. To overcome the stress caused when the stamp canceling machine outpaces the sorting clerks, a pull system is proposed. When the clerks are ready to process another tub of mail, they will pull the tub from the canceling machine area. How many tubs should circulate between the sorting clerks and the canceling machine if 90,000 letters are to be sorted during an eight-hour shift, the safety stock policy variable, α, is 0.18, and the average waiting time plus materials handling time is 25 minutes per tub?

7. ⊙ **OM Explorer** The master schedule at Mazda calls for 1,200 Mazdas to be produced during each of 22 production days in January and 900 Mazdas to be produced during each of 20 production days in February. Mazda uses a kanban system to communicate with Gesundheit, a nearby supplier of tires. Mazda purchases four tires per vehicle from Gesundheit. The safety stock policy variable, α, is 0.15. The container (a delivery truck) size is 200 tires. The average waiting time plus materials handling time is 0.16 day per container. Assembly lines are rebalanced at the beginning of each month. The average processing time per container in January is 0.10 day. February processing time will average 0.125 day per container. How many containers should be authorized for January? How many for February?

8. ⊙ **OM Explorer** Jitsmart uses a special case of the base stock system (see the Inventory Management chapter) to manage inventories of plastic action-figure toys. The action figures are purchased from Tacky Toys, Inc., and arrive in boxes of 48. Full boxes are stored on high shelves out of reach of customers. A small inventory is maintained on child-level shelves. Depletion of the lower-shelf inventory signals the need to take down a box of action figures to replenish the inventory. A reorder card is then removed from the box and sent to Tacky Toys to authorize replenishment of a container of action figures. The average demand rate for a popular action figure, Agent 99, is 36 units per day. The total lead time (waiting plus processing) is 11 days. Jitsmart's safety stock policy variable, α, is 0.25. What is the base stock level for Jitsmart?

SIMULATION EXERCISE

This simulation exercise requires the use of the Extend software, which is on the Student CD-ROM that is packaged with every new copy of the textbook.

1. 🌀 **Extend** Heritage Furniture is a medium-sized regional supplier of bedroom furniture. Heritage's products include the full range of dressers, commonly referred to as case goods in the trade. The plant manager is reviewing the process for manufacturing drawers. The process has nine basic steps, with operations divided between manual steps and more automated operations. Use the Extend simulator to evaluate the impact of adopting a just-in-time (JIT) system, and identify bottlenecks. See the *Just-in-Time Production at Heritage Furniture* case on the Student CD-ROM, which includes the basic model and how to use it. Answer the various questions and indicate how performance changes with the different changes in the system and process.

CASE **COPPER KETTLE CATERING**

Copper Kettle Catering (CKC) is a full-service catering company that provides services ranging from box lunches for picnics or luncheon meetings to large wedding, dinner, or office parties. Established as a lunch delivery service for offices in 1972 by Wayne and Janet Williams, CKC has grown to be one of the largest catering businesses in Raleigh, North Carolina. The Williamses divide customer demand into two categories: *deliver only* and *deliver* and *serve*.

The deliver-only side of the business provides dropoff of boxed meals consisting of a sandwich, salad, dessert, and fruit. The menu for this service is limited to six sandwich selections, three salads or potato chips, and a brownie or fruit bar. Grapes and an orange slice are included with every meal, and iced tea can be ordered to accompany the meals. The overall level of demand for this service throughout the year is fairly constant, although the mix of menu items delivered varies. The planning horizon for this segment of the business is short: Customers usually call no more than a day ahead of time. CKC requires customers to call deliver-only orders in by 10:00 A.M. to guarantee delivery the same day.

The deliver-and-serve side of the business focuses on catering large parties, dinners, and weddings. The extensive range of menu items includes a full selection of hors d'oeuvres, entrées, beverages, and special-request items. The demand for these services is much more seasonal, with heavier demands occurring in the late spring–early summer for weddings and the late fall–early winter for holiday parties. However, this segment also has a longer planning horizon. Customers book dates and choose menu items weeks or months ahead of time.

Copper Kettle Company's food preparation facilities support both operations. The physical facilities layout resembles that of a job shop. There are five major work areas: a stove–oven area for hot food preparation, a cold area for salad preparation, an hors d'oeuvre preparation area, a sandwich preparation area, and an assembly area where deliver-only orders are boxed and deliver-and-serve orders are assembled and trayed. Three walk-in coolers store foods requiring refrigeration, and a large pantry houses nonperishable goods. Space limitations and the risk of spoilage limit the amount of raw materials and prepared food items that can be carried in inventory at any one time. CKC purchases desserts from outside vendors. Some deliver the desserts to CKC; others require CKC to send someone to pick up desserts at their facilities.

The scheduling of orders is a two-stage process. Each Monday, the Williamses develop the schedule of deliver-and-serve orders to be processed each day. CKC typically has multiple deliver-and-serve orders to fill each day of the week. This level of demand allows a certain efficiency in preparation of multiple orders. The deliver-only orders are scheduled day to day owing to the short-order lead times. CKC sometimes runs out of ingredients for deliver-only menu items because of the limited inventory space.

Wayne and Janet Williams have 10 full-time employees: two cooks and eight food preparation workers, who also work as servers for the deliver-and-serve orders. In periods of high demand, the Williamses hire additional part-time servers. The position of cook is specialized and requires a high degree of training and skill. The rest of the employees are flexible and move between tasks as needed.

The business environment for catering is competitive. The competitive priorities are high-quality food, delivery reliability, flexibility, and cost—in that order. "The quality of the food and its preparation is paramount," states Wayne Williams. "Caterers with poor-quality food will not stay in business long." Quality is measured by both freshness and taste. Delivery reliability encompasses both on-time delivery and the time required to respond to customer orders (in effect, the order lead time). Flexibility focuses on both the range of catering requests that a company can satisfy and menu variety.

Recently, CKC has begun to feel the competitive pressures of increasingly demanding customers and several new specialty caterers. Customers are demanding more menu flexibility and faster response times. Small specialty caterers have entered the market and have targeted specific well-defined market segments. One example is a small caterer called Lunches-R-US, which located a facility in the middle of a large office complex to serve the lunch trade and competes with CKC on cost.

Wayne and Janet Williams have been impressed by the concepts of just-in-time operating systems, especially the ideas of increasing flexibility, reducing lead times, and lowering costs. They sound like what CKC needs to do to remain competitive. But the Williamses wonder whether JIT concepts and practices are transferable to a service business.

Questions

1. Are the operations of Copper Kettle Catering conducive to the application of JIT concepts and practices? Explain.
2. What, if any, are the major barriers to implementing a JIT system at Copper Kettle Catering?
3. What would you recommend that Wayne and Janet Williams do to take advantage of JIT concepts in operating CKC?

Source: This case was prepared by Dr. Brooke Saladin, Wake Forest University, as a basis for classroom discussion.

SELECTED REFERENCES

Beckett, W. K., and K. Dang. "Synchronous Manufacturing, New Methods, New Mind Set." *Journal of Business Strategy,* vol. 12 (1992), pp. 53–56.

Billesbach, Thomas J. "A Study of the Implementation of Just-in-Time in the United States." *Production and Inventory Management Journal* (Third Quarter 1991), pp. 1–4.

Billesbach, Thomas J., and M. J. Schniederjans. "Applicability of Just-in-Time Techniques in Administration." *Production and Inventory Management Journal* (Third Quarter 1989), pp. 40–44.

Dixon, Lance. "Tomorrow's Ideas Take Flight in Today's Leading Edge Corporations." *APICS—The Performance Advantage* (July 1996), p. 60.

Ellis, Scott, and Bill Conlon. "JIT Points the Way to Gains in Quality, Cost and Lead Time." *APICS—The Performance Advantage* (August 1992), pp. 16–19.

Golhar, D. Y., and C. L. Stam. "The Just-in-Time Philosophy: A Literature Review." *International Journal of Production Research,* vol. 29 (1991), pp. 657–676.

Greenblatt, Sherwin. "Continuous Improvement in Supply Chain Management." *Chief Executive* (June 1993), pp. 40–43.

Hall, Robert W. "The Americanization of the Toyota System." *Target,* vol. 15, no. 1 (First Quarter 1999), pp. 52–54.

Hall, R. W. *Driving the Productivity Machine.* Falls Church, VA: The American Production and Inventory Control Society, 1981.

Karmarkar, U. "Getting Control of Just-in-Time." *Harvard Business Review* (September–October 1989), pp. 123–131.

Klein, J. A. "The Human Costs of Manufacturing Reform." *Harvard Business Review* (March–April 1989), pp. 60–66.

Mascitelli, Ron. "Lean Thinking: It's About Efficient Value Creation." *Target,* vol. 16, no. 2 (Second Quarter 2000), pp. 22–26.

McClenahen, John S. "So Long, Salespeople, and Good-bye, Buyers—JIT II Is Here." *Industry Week* (February 18, 1991), pp. 48–65.

Millstein, Mitchell. "How to Make Your MRP System Flow." *APICS—The Performance Advantage* (July 2000), pp. 47–49.

Moody, Patricia E. "Bose Corporation: Hi-Fi Leader Stretches to Meet Growth Challenges." *Target* (Winter 1991), pp. 17–22.

Syberg, Keith. "Best Practices (BP) Program: Honda of America Manufacturing." *Target,* vol. 15, no. 2 (Second Quarter 1999), pp. 46–48.

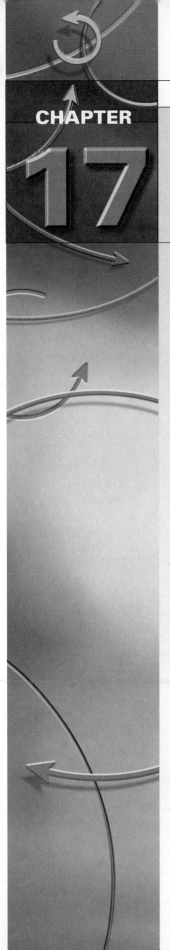

Scheduling

Across the Organization

Scheduling is important to . . .

- ☐ **accounting,** which administers the billing process that is driven by the scheduling of products or services.
- ☐ **finance,** which manages the cash flows in the firm which in turn are a function of the effectiveness of product and service scheduling.
- ☐ **human resources,** which hires and trains employees needed to support workforce schedules.
- ☐ **marketing,** which depends on meeting due dates promised to customers.
- ☐ **management information systems,** which designs the software and databases to support the scheduling process.
- ☐ **operations,** which is responsible for effective scheduling of production systems.

Learning Goals

After reading this chapter, you will be able to . . .

1. explain the importance of scheduling to the performance of a firm.
2. identify the performance measures that are important in selecting a schedule.
3. create schedules for single and multiple workstations.
4. distinguish between the ways that service managers schedule customers to provide timely service and utilize fixed capacity.
5. schedule a workforce to allow each employee to have two consecutive days off.

How important is scheduling to an airline company? Certainly, customer satisfaction regarding on-time schedule performance is critical in a highly competitive industry such as air transportation. In addition, airlines lose a lot of money when expensive equipment such as an aircraft is idle. Flight and crew scheduling, however, is a very complex process. For example, Air New Zealand (www.airnz.com) has 8,000 employees and operates 85 domestic and 50 international flights daily. Scheduling begins with a 5-year market plan that identifies the new and existing flight segments that are needed to remain competitive in the industry. This general plan is further refined to a 3-year plan, and then put into an annual budget where the flight segments have specific departure and arrival times.

Next, crew availability must be matched to the flight schedules. There are two types of crews—pilots and attendants—each with their own set of constraints. Pilots, for example, cannot be scheduled for more than 35 hours in a 7-day week and no more than 100 hours in a 28-day cycle and must have a 36-hour break every 7 days and 30 days off in an 84-day cycle. Sophisticated optimization models are used to design generic minimum-cost tours of duty that cover every flight and recognize all the constraints. Each tour of duty begins and ends at a crew base and consists of an alternating sequence of duty periods and rest periods with duty periods including one or more flights. The tours of duty are posted and crew members bid on them within a specified period of time. Actual crew rosters are constructed from the bids received. The roster must ensure that each flight has a qualified crew complement and that each crew member has a feasible line of work over the roster period.

From the crew's point of view, it is also important to satisfy as many crew requests and preferences as possible.

Scheduling does not end with the definition of the flights and crew rosters. Daily disruptions such as severe weather conditions or mechanical failures can cause schedule changes to crews, pilots, and even aircraft. Customers expect a fast resolution of the problem, and the company needs to find the least-cost solution. In the airline industry, the scheduling process can determine a company's long-term competitive strength.

Pilot training in the B747 simulator at New Zealand Airlines. Refresher training "duties" occur at specific frequencies and have to be built into flight crew rosters. Good flight and crew schedules are vital to on-time performance. Sophisticated scheduling techniques are used to handle the complexities of these scheduling problems.

Sources: Ryan, David M. "Optimization Earns Its Wings." *OR/MS Today* (April 2000), pp. 26–30; "Service Scheduling at Air New Zealand." *Operations Management In Action Video Series*. Upper Saddle River, NJ: Prentice-Hall, 2000.

scheduling The allocation of resources over time to accomplish specific tasks.

As THE CREW SCHEDULING example demonstrates, effective scheduling is essential to successful operations. **Scheduling** allocates resources over time to accomplish specific tasks. Normally, scheduling is done after many other managerial decisions have been made. For example, planning emergency services such as fire protection first requires an analysis of the best location for fire stations, decisions about the type and quantity of fire-fighting equipment at each location, and a staffing plan for each station. Only then can specific work schedules for fire fighters be determined. Sound scheduling can help an organization achieve its strategic goals. For this reason, scheduling applications are becoming more common in ERP systems.

In this chapter, we discuss scheduling in both manufacturing and service organizations and some useful techniques for generating schedules. Two basic types of scheduling are used: **workforce scheduling,** which determines when employees work, and **operations scheduling,** which assigns jobs to machines or workers to jobs. At Air New Zealand, managers work with crew members to develop their workforce schedules. In manufacturing, operations scheduling is crucial because many performance measures, such as on time delivery, inventory levels, the manufacturing cycle time, cost, and quality, relate directly to the scheduling of each production lot. Workforce scheduling is equally crucial because measures of performance such as customer waiting time, waiting-line length, utilization, cost, and quality are related to the availability of the servers.

workforce scheduling
A type of scheduling that determines when employees work.

operations scheduling
A type of scheduling that assigns jobs to machines or workers to jobs.

SCHEDULING IN MANUFACTURING

Operations schedules are short-term plans designed to implement the master production schedule. Operations scheduling focuses on how best to use existing capacity, taking into account technical production constraints. Often, several jobs (e.g., open orders for components) must be processed at one or more workstations. Typically, a variety of tasks can be performed at each workstation. If schedules are not carefully planned to avoid bottlenecks, waiting lines may develop. For example, Figure 17.1 depicts the complexity of scheduling a manufacturing process. When a job order is received for a part, the raw materials are collected and the batch is moved to its first operation. The colored arrows show that jobs follow different routes through the manufacturing process, depending on the product being made. At each workstation someone must determine which job to process next because the rate at which jobs arrive at

FIGURE 17.1

Diagram of a Manufacturing Process

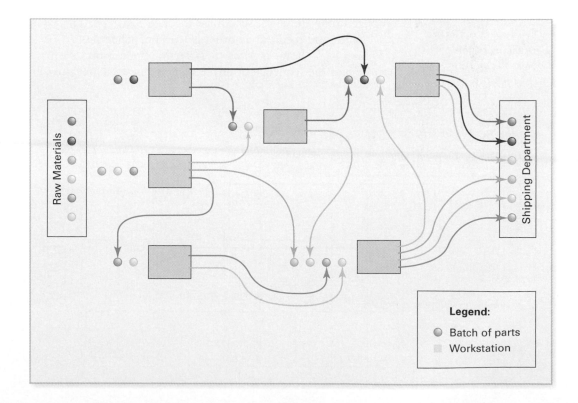

a workstation often differs from the rate at which the workstation can process them, thereby creating a waiting line. In addition, new jobs can enter the manufacturing process at any time, thereby creating a dynamic environment. Such complexity puts pressure on managers to develop scheduling procedures that will handle efficiently the production stream.

In this section, we introduce the problem of scheduling by presenting a traditional manual tool for scheduling called the Gantt chart and then identifying the performance measures used for evaluating schedules. Next, we focus on scheduling approaches used in two basic manufacturing environments: job shops and flow shops. A **job shop** is a firm that specializes in low- to medium-volume production utilizing job or batch processes (see the Process Management chapter). Tasks in this type of flexible flow environment are difficult to schedule because of the variability in job routings and the continual introduction of new jobs to be processed. A **flow shop** specializes in medium- to high-volume production and utilizes line or continuous processes. Tasks are easier to schedule because in a line flow facility the jobs have a common flow pattern through the system. Nonetheless, scheduling mistakes can be costly in either situation.

GANTT CHARTS

The Gantt chart, which we introduced in the Managing Project Processes chapter, can be used as a tool for sequencing work on machines and monitoring its progress. The chart takes two basic forms: the job or activity progress chart and the machine chart. Both types of Gantt charts present the ideal and the actual use of resources over time. The *progress chart* graphically displays the current status of each job relative to its scheduled completion date. For example, suppose that an automobile parts manufacturer has three jobs under way, one each for Ford, Plymouth, and Pontiac. The actual status of these orders is shown by the colored bars in Figure 17.2, the red lines indicate the desired schedule for the start and finish of each job. For the current date, April 21, this Gantt chart shows that the Ford order is behind schedule because operations has completed only the work scheduled through April 18. The Plymouth order is exactly on schedule, and the Pontiac order is ahead of schedule.

Figure 17.3 shows a *machine chart* for the automobile parts manufacturer. This chart depicts the sequence of future work at the two machines and also can be used to

job shop A firm that specializes in low- to medium-volume production utilizing job or batch processes.

flow shop A firm that specializes in medium- to high-volume production and utilizes line or continuous processes.

FIGURE 17.2

Gantt Chart of Job Progress for an Auto Parts Company

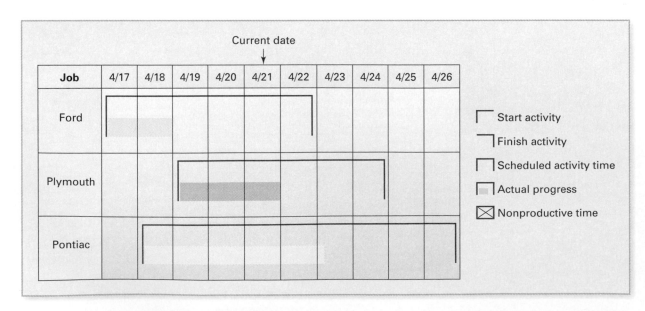

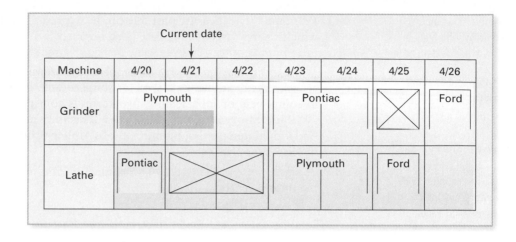

Gantt Chart for Machines at an Auto Parts Company

monitor progress. Using the same notation as in Figure 17.2, the chart shows that for the current date of April 21, the Plymouth job is on schedule at the grinder because the actual progress coincides with the current date. The Pontiac order has finished at the lathe, which is now idle. The plant manager can easily see from the Gantt machine chart the consequence of juggling the schedules. The usual approach is to juggle the schedules by trial and error until a satisfactory level of selected performance measures is achieved.

PERFORMANCE MEASURES

The example of the auto parts manufacturer demonstrates a common problem in scheduling operations—in this case, how to schedule three jobs on two machines. In general, for n jobs, each requiring m machines, there are $(n!)^m$ possible schedules. In the case of the auto parts company, there are $(3!)^2 = 36$ possible schedules. Some might not be feasible because of individual job routings or because some jobs depend on the completion of others. Even so, in a typical job shop hundreds of scheduling decisions must be made every day.

From the manager's perspective, identifying the performance measures to be used in selecting a schedule is important. If the overall goals of the organization are to be achieved, the schedules should reflect managerially acceptable performance measures. The following list describes the most common performance measures used in operations scheduling. Each of these measures can be expressed as a statistical distribution having a mean and variance.

job flow time The amount of shop time for the job.

❐ *Job Flow Time.*   The amount of shop time for the job is called **job flow time.** It is the sum of the moving time between operations, waiting time for machines or work orders, process time (including setups), and delays resulting from machine breakdowns, component unavailability, and the like.

$$\text{Job flow time} = \text{Time of completion} - \begin{array}{l}\text{Time job was available for first}\\ \text{processing operation}\end{array}$$

Note that the starting time is the time the job was *available* for its first processing operation, not necessarily when the job began its first operation. Job flow time is sometimes referred to as **throughput time.**

throughput time See **Job flow time.**

makespan The total amount of time required to complete a group of jobs.

❐ *Makespan.*   The total amount of time required to complete a *group* of jobs is called **makespan.**

$$\text{Makespan} = \text{Time of completion of last job} - \text{Starting time of first job}$$

past due The amount of time by which a job missed its due date or the percentage of total jobs processed over some period of time that missed their due dates.

tardiness See **Past due.**

work-in-process (WIP) inventory Any job in a waiting line, moving from one operation to the next, being delayed for some reason, being processed, or residing in component or subassembly inventories.

total inventory The sum of scheduled receipts and on-hand inventories.

❏ *Past due.*   The measure **past due** can be expressed as the *amount of time* by which a job missed its due date (also referred to as **tardiness**) or as the *percent of total jobs* processed over some period of time that missed their due dates.

❏ *Work-in-Process Inventory.*   Any job in a waiting line, moving from one operation to the next, being delayed for some reason, being processed, or residing in component or subassembly inventories is considered to be **work-in-process (WIP) inventory** or *pipeline inventory*. This measure can be expressed in units (individual items only), number of jobs, dollar value for the entire system, or weeks of supply.

❏ *Total Inventory.*   The sum of scheduled receipts and on-hand inventories is the **total inventory.**

$$\text{Total inventory} = \text{Scheduled receipts for all items} + \begin{array}{c}\text{On-hand inventories}\\\text{of all items}\end{array}$$

This measure could be expressed in weeks of supply, dollars, or units (individual items only).

❏ *Utilization.*   The percent of work time productively spent by a machine or worker is called utilization (see the Capacity chapter).

$$\text{Utilization} = \frac{\text{Productive work time}}{\text{Total work time available}}$$

Utilization for more than one machine or worker can be calculated by adding the productive work times of all machines or workers and dividing by the total work time they are available.

These performance measures often are interrelated. For example, in a job shop, minimizing the mean job flow time tends to reduce work-in-process inventory and increase utilization. In a flow shop, minimizing the makespan for a group of jobs tends to increase facility utilization. An understanding of the interactions of job flow time, makespan, past due, WIP inventory, total inventory, and utilization can make scheduling easier.

JOB SHOP DISPATCHING

dispatching procedures A method of generating schedules in job shops that allows the schedule for a workstation to evolve over a period of time.

Which jobs should have top priority?

priority sequencing rules The rules that specify the job processing sequence when several jobs are waiting in line at a workstation.

Just as there are many feasible schedules for a specific group of jobs on a particular set of machines, there also are many ways to generate schedules. They range from straightforward manual methods, such as manipulating Gantt charts, to sophisticated computer models for developing optimal schedules. One way of generating schedules in job shops—**dispatching procedures**—allows the schedule for a workstation to evolve over a period of time. The decision about which job to process next (or whether to let the station remain idle) is made with simple priority rules whenever the workstation becomes available for further processing. One advantage of this method is that last-minute information on operating conditions can be incorporated into the schedule as it evolves.

Dispatching procedures determine the job to process next with the help of **priority sequencing rules.** When several jobs are waiting in line at a workstation, priority rules specify the job processing sequence. These rules can be applied by a worker or incorporated into a computerized scheduling system that generates a dispatch list of jobs and priorities for each workstation. The following priority sequencing rules are commonly used in practice.

critical ratio (CR) A ratio calculated by dividing the time remaining until a job's due date by the total shop time remaining for the job, including the setup, processing, move, and expected waiting times of all remaining operations, including the operation being scheduled.

earliest due date (EDD) A priority sequencing rule which specifies that the job that has the earliest due date is the next job to be processed.

first come, first served (FCFS) A priority sequencing rule which states that the job that arrived at the workstation first has the highest priority.

shortest processing time (SPT) A priority sequencing rule which states that the job requiring the shortest processing time is the next job to be processed.

slack per remaining operations (S/RO) A priority sequencing rule that determines priority by dividing the slack by the number of operations that remain, including the one being scheduled.

❑ *Critical Ratio.* The **critical ratio (CR)** is calculated by dividing the time remaining to a job's due date by the total shop time remaining for the job, including the setup, processing, move, and expected waiting times of all remaining operations, including the operation being scheduled. The formula is

$$CR = \frac{\text{Due date} - \text{Today's date}}{\text{Total shop time remaining}}$$

The difference between the due date and today's date must be in the same time units as the total shop time remaining. A ratio less than 1.0 implies that the job is behind schedule, and a ratio greater than 1.0 implies that the job is ahead of schedule. The job with the lowest CR is scheduled next.

❑ *Earliest Due Date.* The job with the **earliest due date (EDD)** is scheduled next.

❑ *First Come, First Served.* The job that arrived at the workstation first has the highest priority under a **first come, first served (FCFS)** rule.

❑ *Shortest Processing Time.* The job requiring the **shortest processing time (SPT)** at the workstation is processed next.

❑ *Slack per Remaining Operations.* Slack is the difference between the time remaining to a job's due date and the total shop time remaining, including that of the operation being scheduled. A job's priority is determined by dividing the slack by the number of operations that remain, including the one being scheduled, to arrive at the **slack per remaining operations (S/RO)**.

$$S/RO = \frac{(\text{Due date} - \text{Today's date}) - \text{Total shop time remaining}}{\text{Number of operations remaining}}$$

The job with the lowest S/RO is scheduled next.

There are many ways to break ties if two or more jobs have the same top priority. One way is to arbitrarily choose one of the tied jobs for processing next.

Although the priority sequencing rules seem simple, the actual task of scheduling hundreds of jobs through hundreds of workstations requires intensive data gathering and manipulation. The scheduler needs information on each job's processing requirements: the job's due date; its routing; the standard setup, processing, and expected waiting times at each operation; whether alternative machines could be used at each operation; and the components and raw materials needed at each operation. In addition, the scheduler needs to know the job's current status: its location (in line for a machine or being processed on a machine), how much of the operation has been completed, the actual arrival and departure times at each operation or waiting line, and the actual processing and setup times. The scheduler uses the priority sequencing rules to determine the processing sequence of jobs at a workstation and the remaining information for estimating job arrival times at the next workstation, determining whether an alternative machine should be used when the primary one is busy, and predicting the need for materials-handling equipment. Because this information may change throughout the day, computers are needed to track the data and to maintain valid priorities.

SEQUENCING OPERATIONS FOR ONE MACHINE

Any priority sequencing rule can be used to schedule any number of workstations with the dispatching procedure. For the purpose of illustrating the rules, however, we focus

single-dimension rules
A set of rules that base the priority of a job on a single aspect of the job, such as arrival time at the workstation, the due date, or the processing time.

on scheduling several jobs on a single machine. We divide the rules into two categories: single- and multiple-dimension rules.

SINGLE-DIMENSION RULES.   Some priority rules (e.g., FCFS, EDD, and SPT) base a job's priority assignment only on information on the jobs waiting for processing at the individual workstation. We call these rules **single-dimension rules** because they base the priority on a single aspect of the job, such as arrival time at the workstation, the due date, or the processing time. We begin with an example of single-dimension rules.

EXAMPLE 17.1

Comparing the EDD and SPT Rules

TUTOR
17.1

The Taylor Machine Shop rebores engine blocks. Currently, five engine blocks are waiting for processing. At any time, the company has only one engine expert on duty who can do this type of work. The engine problems have been diagnosed, and processing times for the jobs have been estimated. Times have been agreed upon with the customers as to when they can expect the work to be completed. The accompanying table shows the situation as of Monday morning. As Taylor is open from 8 A.M. until 5 P.M. each weekday, plus weekend hours as needed, the customer pickup times are measured in business hours from Monday morning. Determine the schedule for the engine expert by using (a) the EDD rule and (b) the SPT rule. For each, calculate the average hours early, hours past due, work-in-process inventory, and total inventory. If low job flow times and WIP inventories are critical, which rule should be chosen?

ENGINE BLOCK	PROCESSING TIME, INCLUDING SETUP (hr)	SCHEDULED CUSTOMER PICKUP TIME (business hr from now)
Ranger	8	10
Explorer	6	12
Bronco	15	20
Econoline 150	3	18
Thunderbird	12	22

SOLUTION

a. The EDD rule states that the first engine block in the sequence is the one with the closest due date. Consequently, the Ranger engine block is processed first. The Thunderbird engine block, with its due date furthest in the future, is processed last. The sequence is shown in the following table, along with the job flow times, the hours early, and the hours past due.

ENGINE BLOCK SEQUENCE	BEGIN WORK		PROCESSING TIME (hr)		JOB FLOW TIME (hr)	SCHEDULED CUSTOMER PICKUP TIME	ACUTAL CUSTOMER PICKUP TIME	HOURS EARLY	HOURS PAST DUE
Ranger	0	+	8	=	8	10	10	2	
Explorer	8	+	6	=	14	12	14		2
Econoline 150	14	+	3	=	17	18	18	1	
Bronco	17	+	15	=	32	20	32		12
Thunderbird	32	+	12	=	44	22	44		22

The flow time for each job equals the waiting time plus the processing time. For example, the Explorer engine block had to wait 8 hours before the engine expert started to work on it. The process time for the job is 6 hours, so its flow time is 14 hours. The average flow time and the other performance measures for the EDD schedule for the five engine blocks are

$$\text{Average job flow time} = \frac{8 + 14 + 17 + 32 + 44}{5} = 23 \text{ hours}$$

$$\text{Average hours early} = \frac{2 + 0 + 1 + 0 + 0}{5} = 0.6 \text{ hour}$$

$$\text{Average hours past due} = \frac{0 + 2 + 0 + 12 + 22}{5} = 7.2 \text{ hours}$$

$$\text{Average WIP inventory} = \frac{\text{Sum of flow times}}{\text{Makespan}} = \frac{8 + 14 + 17 + 32 + 44}{44}$$

$$= 2.61 \text{ engine blocks}$$

You might think of the sum of flow times as the total *job hours* spent by the engine blocks waiting for the engine expert and being processed. (In this example, there are no component or subassembly inventories, so WIP inventory consists only of those engine blocks waiting or being processed.) Dividing this sum by the makespan, or the total elapsed time required to complete work on all the engine blocks, provides the average work-in-process inventory.

Finally,

$$\text{Average total inventory} = \frac{\text{Sum of time in system}}{\text{Makespan}} = \frac{10 + 14 + 18 + 32 + 44}{44}$$

$$= 2.68 \text{ engine blocks}$$

Total inventory is the sum of the work-in-process inventory and the completed jobs waiting to be picked up by customers. The average total inventory equals the sum of the times each job spent in the shop—in this example, the total job hours spent waiting for the engine expert, being processed, and waiting for pickup—divided by the makespan. For example, the first job to be picked up is the Ranger engine block, which spent 10 hours in the system. Then the Explorer engine block is picked up, after spending 14 job hours in the system. The time spent by any job in the system equals its actual customer pickup time because all jobs were available for processing at time zero.

b. Under the SPT rule, the sequence starts with the engine block having the shortest processing time, the Econoline 150, and ends with the one having the longest processing time, the Bronco. The sequence, along with the job flow times, early hours, and past due hours, is contained in the following table.

ENGINE BLOCK SEQUENCE	BEGIN WORK		PROCESSING TIME (hr)		JOB FLOW TIME (hr)	SCHEDULED CUSTOMER PICKUP TIME	ACUTAL CUSTOMER PICKUP TIME	HOURS EARLY	HOURS PAST DUE
Econoline 150	0	+	3	=	3	18	18	15	
Explorer	3	+	6	=	9	12	12	3	
Ranger	9	+	8	=	17	10	17		7
Thunderbird	17	+	12	=	29	22	29		7
Bronco	29	+	15	=	44	20	44		24

The performance measures are

$$\text{Average job flow time} = \frac{3 + 9 + 17 + 29 + 44}{5} = 20.4 \text{ hours}$$

$$\text{Average hours early} = \frac{15 + 3 + 0 + 0 + 0}{5} = 3.6 \text{ hours}$$

$$\text{Average past due hours} = \frac{0 + 0 + 7 + 7 + 24}{5} = 7.6 \text{ hours}$$

$$\text{Average WIP inventory} = \frac{3 + 9 + 17 + 29 + 44}{44} = 2.32 \text{ engine blocks}$$

$$\text{Average total inventory} = \frac{18 + 12 + 17 + 29 + 44}{44}$$

$$= 2.73 \text{ engine blocks}$$

Decision Point   The SPT rule is clearly superior to the EDD rule with respect to average job flow time and average WIP inventory. If these criteria outweigh all others, management should use SPT. ⊓

How important is the choice of priority dispatching rules to the effectiveness of the operating system?

As the solution of Example 17.1 shows, the SPT schedule provided a lower average job flow time and lower work-in-process inventory. The EDD schedule, however, gave better customer service, as measured by the average hours past due, and a lower maximum hours past due (22 versus 24). It also provided a lower total inventory because fewer job hours were spent waiting for customers to pick up their engine blocks after they had been completed. The SPT priority rule will push jobs through the system to completion more quickly than will the other rules. Speed can be an advantage—but only if jobs can be delivered sooner than promised and revenue collected earlier. If they cannot, the completed job must stay in finished inventory, canceling the advantage of minimizing the average work-in-process inventory. Consequently, the priority rule chosen can help or hinder the organization in meeting its competitive priorities.

In Example 17.1, SPT and EDD provided schedules that resulted in different values for the performance criteria; however, both schedules have the same makespan of 44 hours. This result always will occur in single-operation scheduling for a *fixed number* of jobs available for processing—regardless of the priority rule used—because there are no idle workstation times between any two jobs.

Researchers have studied the implications of the single-dimension rules for various performance measures. In most of these studies, all jobs were considered to be independent, and the assumption was made that sufficient capacity generally was available. These studies found that the EDD rule performs well with respect to the percent of jobs past due and the variance of hours past due. For any set of jobs to be processed on a single machine, it minimizes the maximum of the past due hours of any job in the set. It is popular with firms that are sensitive to due date changes, although it does not perform very well with respect to flow time, work-in-process inventory, or utilization.

Often referred to as the *world champion*, the SPT rule tends to minimize mean flow time, work-in-process inventory, and percent of jobs past due and to maximize shop utilization. For the single-machine case, the SPT rule always will provide the lowest mean flow time. However, it could increase total inventory because it tends to push all work to the finished state. In addition, it tends to produce a large variance in past due hours because the larger jobs might have to wait a long time for processing. Also, it provides no opportunity to adjust schedules when due dates change. The advantage of this rule over others diminishes as the load on the shop increases.

Finally, though the first-come, first served rule is considered fair to the jobs (or customers), it performs poorly with respect to all performance measures. This result is to be expected because FCFS does not acknowledge any job (or customer) characteristics.

MULTIPLE-DIMENSION RULES.   Priority rules such as CR and S/RO incorporate information about the remaining workstations at which the job must be processed, in addition to the processing time at the present workstation or the due date considered by single-dimension rules. We call these rules **multiple-dimension rules** because they apply to more than one aspect of the job. Example 17.2 demonstrates their use for sequencing jobs.

multiple-dimension rules
A set of rules that apply to more than one aspect of a job.

| EXAMPLE 17.2 | *Sequencing with the CR and S/RO Rules* |

The first five columns of the following table contain information about a set of four jobs presently waiting at an engine lathe. Several operations, including the one at the engine lathe, remain to be done on each job. Determine the schedule by using (a) the CR rule and (b) the S/RO rule. Compare these schedules to those generated by FCFS, SPT, and EDD.

JOB	OPERATION TIME AT ENGINE LATHE (hr)	TIME REMAINING TO DUE DATE (days)	NUMBER OF OPERATIONS REMAINING	SHOP TIME REMAINING (days)	CR	S/RO
1	2.3	15	10	6.1	2.46	0.89
2	10.5	10	2	7.8	1.28	1.10
3	6.2	20	12	14.5	1.38	0.46
4	15.6	8	5	10.2	0.78	−0.44

SOLUTION

a. Using CR to schedule the machine, we divide the time remaining to the due date by the shop time remaining to get the priority index for each job. For job 1,

$$CR = \frac{\text{Time remaining to due date}}{\text{Shop time remaining}} = \frac{15}{6.1} = 2.46$$

By arranging the jobs in sequence with the lowest critical ratio first, we determine that the sequence of jobs to be processed by the engine lathe is 4–2–3–1, assuming that no other jobs arrive in the meantime.

b. Using S/RO, we divide the difference between the time remaining to the due date and the shop time remaining by the number of remaining operations. For job 1,

$$S/RO = \frac{\text{Time remaining to due date} - \text{Shop time remaining}}{\text{Number of operations remaining}}$$
$$= \frac{15 - 6.1}{10} = 0.89$$

Arranging the jobs by starting with the lowest S/RO yields a 4–3–1–2 sequence of jobs.

Decision Point Note that application of the two priority rules gives two different schedules. Moreover, the SPT sequence, based on operation times (measured in hours) at the engine lathe only, is 1–3–2–4. No preference is given to job 4 in the SPT schedule, even though it may not be finished by its due date. The FCFS sequence is 1–2–3–4, and the EDD sequence is 4–2–1–3. The following table shows the comparative performance of the five dispatching rules at the engine lathe.

Priority Rule Summary

	FCFS	SHORTEST PROCESSING TIME	EARLIEST DUE DATE	CRITICAL RATIO	SLACK PER REMAINING OPERATIONS
Avg. flow time	17.175	16.100	26.175	27.150	24.025
Avg. early time	3.425	6.050	0	0	0
Avg. past due	7.350	8.900	12.925	13.900	10.775
Avg. WIP	1.986	1.861	3.026	3.139	2.777
Avg. total inv.	2.382	2.561	3.026	3.139	2.777

The S/RO rule is better than the EDD rule and the CR rule but much worse than the SPT rule and the FCFS rule for this example. However, the S/RO has the advantage of allowing schedule changes when due dates change. These results cannot be generalized to other situations because only four jobs are being processed. □

Research studies have shown that S/RO is better than EDD with respect to the percent of jobs past due but worse than SPT and EDD with respect to average job flow times. These studies also indicate that CR results in longer job flow times than SPT but less variance in the distribution of past due hours. Consequently, even though use of the multiple-dimension rules requires more information, there is no clear-cut best choice. Each rule should be tested in the environment for which it is intended.

MULTIPLE-WORKSTATION SCHEDULING

Priority sequencing rules may be used to schedule more than one operation with the dispatching procedure. Each operation is treated independently. When a workstation becomes idle, the priority rule is applied to the jobs waiting for that operation, and the one with the highest priority is selected. When that operation is finished, the job is moved to the next operation in its routing, where it waits until it again has the highest priority. At any workstation, the jobs in the waiting line change over a period of time, so the choice of a priority rule can make quite a difference in processing sequence. Schedules can be evaluated with the performance measures already discussed.

Identifying the best priority rule to use at a particular operation in a manufacturing process is a complex problem because the output from one operation becomes the input to another. The priority rule at an operation determines the sequence of work the operation will perform, which in turn determines the arrival of work at the next operation downstream. Computer simulation models are effective tools to determine which priority rules work best in a given situation (see the Simulation supplement). Once the current process is modeled, the analyst can make changes to the priority rules at various operations and measure the impact on performance measures such as past due, work-in-progress, job flow time, and utilization. Example 17.3 demonstrates the use of simulation using Extend, simulation software that is on the Student CD-ROM packaged with each new textbook. To learn more about Extend, see its tutorials and work through the simulation exercises with the preprogrammed model at the end of this chapter.

| EXAMPLE 17.3 | *Simulation of Precision AutoBody Operations* |

Precision AutoBody has an excellent reputation in the local market for doing high-quality auto-body repair work. Repair of a vehicle body consists of two general steps: body repair and finishing. For body repair, vehicles are classified as having either minor or major damage. Those with minor damage require, on average, one eight-hour day to complete, and two-thirds of the vehicles serviced by Precision fell into this category. In contrast, vehicles with major damage require more extensive repairs that extend beyond the surface sheet metal, and damages often include hidden problems that are not evident when fist inspected. As a result, this repair work averages two days. Of those vehicles with major damage, about half need to have the underlying frame of the vehicle straightened on special hydraulic equipment in a dedicated area adjacent to the repair bays. This extra operation tends to add an average of one additional day to the completion time.

After body repair, the vehicle is moved to the finishing area. A small percent of vehicles, 25 percent of those with minor damage, move directly to the finishing area. Here, an apprentice prepares the vehicle by doing final sanding and masking off areas that are not to be painted. Next, the vehicle is moved to one of several paint booths, where the painter mixes the paint color to match the vehicle, taking into account any fading that has occurred. Virtually all vehicles require two coats, a colored base coat followed by a clear coat applied the next day. After completion, the vehicle's exterior and interior are thoroughly cleaned to give that "just new" impression to the customer when the vehicle is delivered. The times to complete each operation are summarized in the following table.

Precision AutoBody Process Times

OPERATION	TIME TO PERFORM	
	Average (hr)	Standard Deviation
1. Frame straightening*	8	2
2a. Body repair, major damage*	16	4
2b. Body repair, minor damage*	8	2
3. Paint preparation	$1\frac{1}{4}$	$\frac{1}{3}$
4. Paint application (two coats)	$1\frac{1}{2}$	$\frac{1}{2}$
6. Clean up	3	$\frac{1}{2}$

*Not necessary for all vehicles.

The operations times all can be approximated by a log-normal distribution.

Bill Curtis, manager at Precision, schedules each vehicle at the body repair and paint operations on a first come, first served basis—an equitable approach—with a quoted delivery time of about one week (i.e., five business days), plus any lead time needed for delivery of the parts. A review of the last month's data indicated that 18.17 percent of the jobs were delivered late and the average throughput time (flow time) per auto was 30.49 hours. In addition, the average number of vehicles in the system (work-in-process) was 9.6 autos. Curtis wanted to know if the SPT rule applied to the body repair and paint operations would improve delivery performance and reduce flow times and work-in-process.

SOLUTION

The Extend software, contained on the Student CD-ROM, is used to model and simulate the Precision AutoBody operations. Figure 17.4 shows the simulation model. The five operations are

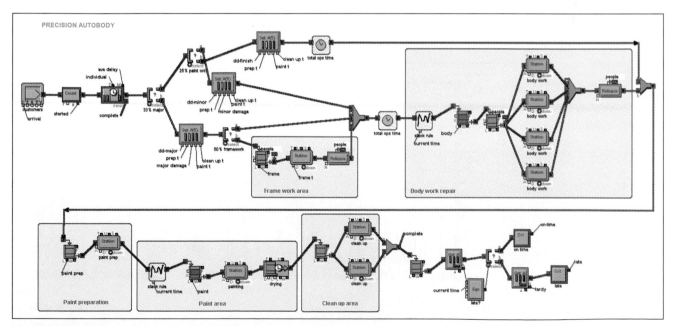

FIGURE 17.4

```
           DELIVERY PERFORMANCE

  Late (%)                        17.35

  Average tardiness (hr)          7.896


              System performance

  Average number of              9.422
    vehicles in system

  Overall throughput time (hr)

     average                     29.67

     standard deviation          18.92


              Operation utilization

  Body repair                   0.8338

  Paint operation               0.7687
```

FIGURE 17.5

boxed in the diagram. As the simulation proceeds, vehicles arrive and require major repair with a 33 percent chance. If major repair is needed, there is a 50 percent chance that the vehicle will need the framework operation before the body repair operation. If minor repair is needed, there is a 25 percent chance that the vehicle will go straight to the paint preparation operation. After body repair, all vehicles go through paint preparation, painting, and clean up. The activities after clean up are needed to gather the statistics for each vehicle before it exits the simulation. The SPT priority rule for each operation was selected in the Controls box (not shown).

The results of the simulation using the SPT rule for the body repair operation and the finishing operations (paint preparation, paint, and clean up) are shown in Figure 17.5, using the Notebook feature of Extend. Notice that the percent of late deliveries, the average number of vehicles in the system, and the average throughput time have been improved with the use of SPT.

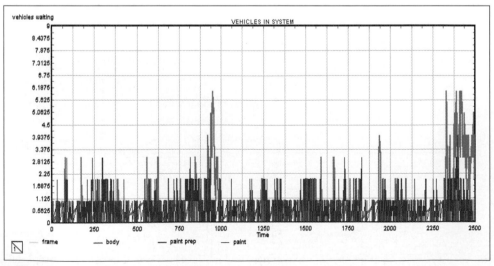

FIGURE 17.6

The average tardiness statistic, shown in Figure 17.5, is another form of the past due measure of performance. It is the average number of hours past the due date for those vehicles that were delivered late.

Figure 17.6 shows the number of vehicles in the system for a simulated period of 2,500 hours. Each of the operations is color coded to show how the work-in-process at each operation changes over the time period simulated.

Decision Point   The results show that SPT is superior to the FCFS priority rule for Precision AutoBody. Curtis should consider changing the priority rule. However, Figure 17.6 indicates that the body repair operation will have sizeable swings in work-in-process inventory. Management should explore increasing resources at that operation. Further improvements in the percent of late deliveries might be achieved by increasing the lead time in setting the due dates or changing the priority rules. The simulation model can help determine the best solution.

Source: This case and simulation experience was provided by Professor Robert Klassen, University of Western Ontario. ❐

SEQUENCING OPERATIONS FOR A TWO-STATION FLOW SHOP

Suppose that a flow shop has several jobs ready for processing at two workstations and that the routings of all jobs are identical. Whereas in single-machine scheduling the makespan is the same regardless of the priority rule chosen, in the scheduling of two or more operations in a flow shop the makespan varies according to the sequence chosen. Determining a production sequence for a group of jobs so as to minimize the makespan has two advantages.

1. The group of jobs is completed in minimum time.
2. Utilization of the two-station flow shop is maximized. Utilizing the first workstation continuously until it processes the last job minimizes the idle time on the *second* workstation.

Johnson's rule
A procedure that minimizes makespan in scheduling a group of jobs on two workstations.

Johnson's rule is a procedure that minimizes makespan in scheduling a group of jobs on two workstations. S. M. Johnson showed that the sequence of jobs at the two stations should be identical and that therefore the priority assigned to a job should be the same at both. The procedure is based on the assumption of a known set of jobs, each with a known processing time and available to begin processing on the first workstation. The procedure is as follows.

Step 1.   Scan the processing times at each workstation and find the shortest processing time among the jobs not yet scheduled. If there is a tie, choose one job arbitrarily.

Step 2.   If the shortest processing time is on workstation 1, schedule the corresponding job as early as possible. If the shortest processing time is on workstation 2, schedule the corresponding job as late as possible.

Step 3.   Eliminate the last job scheduled from further consideration. Repeat steps 1 and 2 until all jobs have been scheduled.

EXAMPLE 17.4

Scheduling a Group of Jobs on Two Workstations

TUTOR 17.3

The Morris Machine Company just received an order to refurbish five motors for materials handling equipment that were damaged in a fire. The motors will be repaired at two workstations in the following manner.

Workstation 1   Dismantle the motor and clean parts.

Workstation 2   Replace parts as necessary, test the motor, and make adjustments.

The customer's shop will be inoperable until all the motors have been repaired, so the plant manager is interested in developing a schedule that minimizes the makespan and has authorized round-the-clock operations until the motors have been repaired. The estimated time for repairing each motor is shown in the following table.

MOTOR	TIME (hr)	
	Workstation 1	Workstation 2
M1	12	22
M2	4	5
M3	5	3
M4	15	16
M5	10	8

SOLUTION

The logic for the optimal sequence is shown in Table 17.1.

TABLE 17.1 *Establishing a Job Sequence*

ITERATION	JOB SEQUENCE					COMMENTS
1					M3	Shortest processing time is 3 hours for M3 at workstation 2. Therefore, M3 is scheduled as late as possible.
2	M2				M3	Eliminate M3's time from the table of estimated times. The next shortest processing time is 4 hours, for M2 at workstation 1. M2 is therefore scheduled first.
3	M2			M5	M3	Eliminate M2 from the table. The next shortest processing time is 8 hours for M5 at workstation 2. Therefore, M5 is scheduled as late as possible.
4	M2	M1		M5	M3	Eliminate M5 from the table. The next shortest processing time is 12 hours for M1 at workstation 1. M1 is scheduled as early as possible.
5	M2	M1	M4	M5	M3	The last motor to be scheduled is M4. It is placed in the last remaining position, in the middle of the schedule.

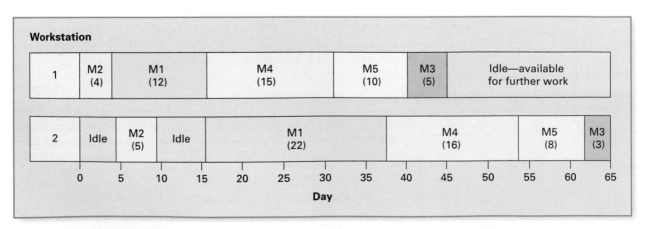

FIGURE 17.7 • Machine Chart for the Morris Machine Company Repair Schedule

Decision Point No other sequence of jobs will produce a lower makespan. To determine the makespan, we have to draw a Gantt chart, as shown in Figure 17.7. In this case, refurbishing and reinstalling all five motors will take 65 hours. This schedule minimizes the idle time of workstation 2 and gives the fastest repair time for all five motors. Note that the schedule recognizes that a job cannot begin at workstation 2 until it has been completed at workstation 1. ☐

LABOR-LIMITED ENVIRONMENTS

Thus far, we have assumed that a job never has to wait for lack of a worker; that is, the limiting resource is the number of machines or workstations available. More typical, however, is a **labor-limited environment** in which the resource constraint is the amount of labor available, not the number of machines or workstations. In this case, workers are trained to work on a variety of machines or tasks to increase the flexibility of operations.

In a labor-limited environment, the scheduler not only must decide which job to process next at a particular workstation but also must assign workers to their next workstations. The scheduler can use priority rules to make these decisions, as we used them to schedule engine blocks in Example 17.1. In labor-limited environments, the labor-assignment policies, as well as the dispatching priority rules, affect performance. The following are some examples of labor-assignment rules.

> ❏ Assign personnel to the workstation having the job that has been in the system longest.
>
> ❏ Assign personnel to the workstation having the most jobs waiting for processing.
>
> ❏ Assign personnel to the workstation having the largest standard work content.
>
> ❏ Assign personnel to the workstation having the job that has the earliest due date.

LINKING MANUFACTURING SCHEDULING TO THE SUPPLY CHAIN

In the Supply-Chain Management chapter, we discussed how firms design and manage the linkages between customers and suppliers with the concept of an integrated supply chain. True integration requires the manipulation of large amounts of complex data in real time because the customer order work flow must be synchronized with the required material, manufacturing, and distribution activity. Attempting to accomplish this integration with piecemeal systems can be resource-intensive and ultimately less than satisfactory. The Internet, new computer software, and improved data storage and manipulation methods have given rise to **advanced planning and scheduling (APS) systems,** which seek to optimize resources across the supply chain and align daily operations with strategic goals. These systems typically have four major components:

> ❏ *Demand Planning.*   This capability enables companies in a supply chain to share demand forecasts, thereby providing more visibility of future requirements. A broad range of forecasting techniques is provided (see the Forecasting chapter).
>
> ❏ *Supply Network Planning.*   Optimization models based on linear programming can be used to make long-term decisions such as the number and location of plants and distribution centers, which suppliers to use, and the optimal location and amounts of inventory (see the Location chapter and the Linear Programming supplement).
>
> ❏ *Available-to-Promise.*   Firms can use this capability to promise delivery to customers by checking the availability of components and materials at its

---

labor-limited environment
An environment in which the resource constraint is the amount of labor available, not the number of machines or workstations.

advanced planning and scheduling (APS) systems
Systems that seek to optimize resources across the supply chain and align daily operations with strategic goals.

suppliers, who may be located anywhere in the world (see the Master Production Scheduling supplement). Variants of this capability include *capable-to-promise*—for suppliers who produce to customer order and reserve capacity—and *capable-to-deliver*—for suppliers of transportation services.

❑ *Manufacturing Scheduling.*   This module attempts to determine an optimal grouping and sequencing of manufacturing orders based on detailed product attributes, production line capacities, and material flows. In some applications, schedules for material, labor, and equipment can be determined minute-by-minute. Gantt charts can be used to view the schedule and make adjustments (see Figs. 17.2 and 17.3). The schedules are "constraint-based" and use the *theory of constraints* to schedule bottlenecks in the manufacturing process (see the Capacity chapter).

MANAGERIAL PRACTICE 17.1
Real-Time Scheduling in Chrysler's APS System

Vehicle painting operations are typically a bottleneck to the assembly process. Every auto must go through the paint process, which involves special application sequences depending on the required finish. When an auto requires a different color than the auto just before it in sequence, the paint guns must be purged and cleaned with special solvents. The time to accomplish this activity depends on the sequence of colors. Typically, production orders are sequenced from lighter to darker colors to minimize the time to clean the paint guns between color changes. The problem is much more complex than simply deciding how many autos should be included in each batch of a particular color. Each auto has particular options selected by the customer that have to be assembled to the auto after the paint operation. Disregarding the implications of the paint schedule on the other processes can cause bottlenecks elsewhere in the plant. For example, a batch of blue cars ordered by a governmental agency might all be ordered with diesel engines. If all of these cars are included in the same batch of blue cars, an overload may occur on the limited manpower available to mount diesel engines. Delays in mounting diesel engines may cause delays in the entire production line, which in turn can affect global supplies of autos. The challenge is to optimize the paint sequence while recognizing the constraints imposed by other processes in the plant.

At Chrysler, (daimlerchrysler.com) the vehicle painting operations were a major bottleneck that affected operations throughout the plant. Operations at the paint booth had to be optimized; however, overloading or underutilizing other parts of the production line had to be avoided. Chrysler developed its own paint sequencing application as part of an advanced planning and scheduling system and employed it in 18 assembly plants. The

Chrysler cars are coming off the assembly line in Sterling Heights, Michigan. Chrysler developed its own software to sequence cars along the assembly line, with particular attention to the painting process.

new system eliminated the bottleneck at the paint operations, reducing paint purges in the 18 plants from 383 to 191 per day, resulting in more than $7 million in savings per year. In addition, the time to produce a one-day schedule of 1,200 vehicles was cut from four to six hours to only 2 and one-half minutes. This capability allows Chrysler to adjust schedules in real time, making the production process much more responsive to customer needs and supply chain constraints.

Source: Berger, Llana. "Optimizing the Supply Chain with APS." *APICS— The Performance Advantage* (December 1999), pp. 24–27.

The manufacturing scheduling process is a key element of an integrated supply chain. APS systems attempt to link to the scheduling process demand data and forecasts, supply-chain facility and inventory decisions, and the capability of suppliers so that the entire supply chain can operate as efficiently as possible. The ability to change schedules quickly while recognizing the implications on the rest of the supply chain can provide a competitive edge. Managerial Practice 17.1 demonstrates the advantages of real-time scheduling at Chrysler.

SCHEDULING IN SERVICES

What scheduling methods can be used to manage the capacity of a service system?

One important distinction between manufacturing and services that affects scheduling is that service operations cannot create inventories to buffer demand uncertainties. A second distinction is that in service operations demand often is less predictable. Customers may decide on the spur of the moment that they need a hamburger, a haircut, or a plumbing repair. Thus capacity, often in the form of employees, is crucial for service providers. In this section, we discuss various ways in which scheduling systems can facilitate the capacity management of service providers.

SCHEDULING CUSTOMER DEMAND

One way to manage capacity is to schedule customers for arrival times and definite periods of service time. With this approach, capacity remains fixed and demand is leveled to provide timely service and utilize capacity. Three methods are commonly used: appointments, reservations, and backlogs.

APPOINTMENTS. An appointment system assigns specific times for service to customers. The advantages of this method are timely customer service and high utilization of servers. Doctors, dentists, lawyers, and automobile repair shops are examples of service providers that use appointment systems. Doctors can use the system to schedule parts of their day to visit hospital patients, and lawyers can set aside time to prepare cases. If timely service is to be provided, however, care must be taken to tailor the length of appointments to individual customer needs rather than merely scheduling customers at equal time intervals.

RESERVATIONS. Reservation systems, although quite similar to appointment systems, are used when the customer actually occupies or uses facilities associated with the service. For example, customers reserve hotel rooms, automobiles, airline seats, and concert seats. The major advantage of reservation systems is the lead time they give service managers to plan the efficient use of facilities. Often, reservations require some form of down payment to reduce the problem of no-shows.

BACKLOGS. A less precise way to schedule customers is to allow backlogs to develop; that is, customers never know exactly when service will commence. They present their service request to an order taker, who adds it to the waiting line of orders already in the system. TV repair shops, restaurants, banks, grocery stores, and barber shops are examples of the many types of businesses that use this system. Various priority rules can be used to determine which order to process next. The usual rule is first come, first served, but if the order involves rework on a previous order, it may get a higher priority.

SCHEDULING THE WORKFORCE

Another way to manage capacity with a scheduling system is to specify the on-duty and off-duty periods for each employee over a certain time period, as in assigning postal clerks, nurses, pilots, attendants, or police officers to specific workdays and shifts. This approach is used when customers demand quick response and total demand can be forecasted with reasonable accuracy. In these instances, capacity is adjusted to meet the expected loads on the service system.

Recall that workforce schedules translate the staffing plan into specific schedules of work for each employee (see the Aggregate Planning chapter). Determining the workdays for each employee in itself does not make the staffing plan operational. Daily workforce requirements, stated in aggregate terms in the staffing plan, must be satisfied. The workforce capacity available each day must meet or exceed daily workforce requirements. If it does not, the scheduler must try to rearrange days off until the requirements are met. If no such schedule can be found, management might have to change the staffing plan and authorize more employees, overtime hours, or larger backlogs.

CONSTRAINTS.   The technical constraints imposed on the workforce schedule are the resources provided by the staffing plan and the requirements placed on the operating system. However, other constraints, including legal and behavioral considerations, also can be imposed. For example, Air New Zealand is required to have at least a minimum number of flight attendants on duty at all times. Similarly, a minimum number of fire and safety personnel must be on duty at a fire station at all times. Such constraints limit management's flexibility in developing workforce schedules.

The constraints imposed by the psychological needs of workers complicate scheduling even more. Some of these constraints are written into labor agreements. For example, an employer may agree to give employees a certain number of consecutive days off per week or to limit employees' consecutive workdays to a certain maximum. Other provisions might govern the allocation of vacation, days off for holidays, or rotating shift assignments. In addition, preferences of the employees themselves need to be considered.

rotating schedule
A schedule that rotates employees through a series of workdays or hours.

One way that managers deal with certain undesirable aspects of scheduling is to use a **rotating schedule,** which rotates employees through a series of workdays or hours. Thus, over a period of time, each person has the same opportunity to have weekends and holidays off and to work days, as well as evenings and nights. A rotating schedule gives each employee the next employee's schedule the following week. In contrast, a **fixed schedule** calls for each employee to work the same days and hours each week.

fixed schedule
A schedule that calls for each employee to work the same days and hours each week.

How can an effective workforce schedule be developed for a service system?

DEVELOPING A WORKFORCE SCHEDULE. Suppose that we are interested in developing an employee schedule for a company that operates seven days a week and provides each employee two consecutive days off. In this section, we demonstrate a method that recognizes this constraint.[1] The objective is to identify the two consecutive days off for each employee that will minimize the amount of total slack capacity. The work schedule for each employee, then, is the five days that remain after the two days off have been determined. The procedure involves the following steps.

Step 1.   From the schedule of net requirements for the week, find all the pairs of consecutive days that exclude the maximum daily requirements. Select the unique pair that has the lowest total requirements for the two days. In some unusual situations, all

---

[1]See Tibrewala, Philippe, and Brown (1972) for an optimizing approach.

pairs may contain a day with the maximum requirements. If so, select the pair with the lowest total requirements. Suppose that the numbers of employees required are

Monday:	8	Friday:	7
Tuesday:	9	Saturday:	4
Wednesday:	2	Sunday:	2
Thursday:	12		

The maximum capacity requirement is 12 employees, on Thursday. The pair having the lowest total requirements is Saturday–Sunday, with $4 + 2 = 6$.

Step 2. If a tie occurs, choose one of the tied pairs, consistent with provisions written into the labor agreement, if any. Alternatively, the tie could be broken by asking the employee being scheduled to make the choice. As a last resort, the tie could be broken arbitrarily. For example, preference could be given to Saturday–Sunday pairs.

Step 3. Assign the employee the selected pair of days off. Subtract the requirements satisfied by the employee from the net requirements for each day the employee is to work. In this case, the employee is assigned Saturday and Sunday off. After requirements are subtracted, Monday's requirement is 7, Tuesday's is 8, Wednesday's is 1, Thursday's is 11, and Friday's is 6. Saturday's and Sunday's requirements do not change because no employee is yet scheduled to work those days.

Step 4. Repeat steps 1–3 until all requirements have been satisfied or a certain number of employees have been scheduled.

This method reduces the amount of slack capacity assigned to days having low requirements and forces the days having high requirements to be scheduled first. It also recognizes some of the behavioral and contractual aspects of workforce scheduling in the tie-breaking rules. However, the schedules produced might *not* minimize total slack capacity. Different rules for finding the days-off pair and breaking ties are needed to ensure minimal total slack capacity.

EXAMPLE 17.5   *Developing Workforce Schedule*

TUTOR 17.4

The Amalgamated Parcel Service is open seven days a week. The schedule of requirements is

Day	M	T	W	Th	F	S	Su
Number of employees	6	4	8	9	10*	3	2

The manager needs a workforce schedule that provides two consecutive days off and minimizes the amount of total slack capacity. To break ties in the selection of off days, the scheduler gives preference to Saturday–Sunday if it is one of the tied pairs. If not, she selects one of the tied pairs arbitrarily.

SOLUTION

Friday contains the maximum requirements (designated by an *), and the pair S–Su has the lowest total requirements. Therefore, employee 1 is scheduled to work Monday–Friday. The revised set of requirements, after scheduling employee 1, is

Day	M	T	W	Th	F	S	Su
Number of employees	5	3	7	8	9*	3	2

TABLE 17.2 *Scheduling Days Off*

M	T	W	Th	F	S	Su	EMPLOYEE	COMMENTS
4	2	6	7	8*	3	2	3	S–Su has the lowest total requirements. Reduce the requirements to reflect a M–F schedule for employee 3.
3	1	5	6	7*	3	2	4	M–T has the lowest total requirements. Assign employee 4 to a W–Su schedule and update the requirements.
3	1	4	5	6*	2	1	5	S–Su has the lowest total requirements. Assign employee 5 to a M–F schedule and update the requirements.
2	0	3	4	5*	2	1	6	M–T has the lowest total requirements. Assign employee 6 to a W–Su schedule and update the requirements.
2	0	2	3	4*	1	0	7	S–Su has the lowest total requirements. Assign employee 7 to a M–F schedule and update the requirements.
1	0	1	2	3*	1	0	8	Three pairs have the minimum requirement and the lowest total: S–Su, M–T, and T–W. Choose S–Su according to the tie-breaking rule. Assign employee 8 a M–F schedule and update the requirements.
0	0	0	1	2*	1	0	9	Arbitrarily choose Su–M to break ties because S–Su does not have the lowest total requirements. Assign employee 9 to a T–S schedule.
0	0	0	0	1*	0	0	10	Choose S–Su according to the tie-breaking rule. Assign employee 10 a M–F schedule.

Note that Friday still has the maximum requirements and that the requirements for S–Su are carried forward because these are employee 1's days off. These updated requirements are the ones the scheduler uses for the next employee.

The unique minimum again is on S–Su, so the scheduler assigns employee 2 to a M–F schedule. She then reduces the requirements for M–F to reflect the assignment of employee 2.

The day-off assignments for the remaining employees are shown in Table 17.2. In this example, Friday always has the maximum requirements and should be avoided as a day off. The schedule for the employees is shown in Table 17.3.

TABLE 17.3 *Final Schedule*

EMPLOYEE	M	T	W	Th	F	S	Su	TOTAL
1	X	X	X	X	X	off	off	
2	X	X	X	X	X	off	off	
3	X	X	X	X	X	off	off	
4	off	off	X	X	X	X	X	
5	X	X	X	X	X	off	off	
6	off	off	X	X	X	X	X	
7	X	X	X	X	X	off	off	
8	X	X	X	X	X	off	off	
9	off	X	X	X	X	X	off	
10	X	X	X	X	X	off	off	
Capacity, C	7	7	10	10	10	3	2	50
Requirements, R	6	4	8	9	10	3	2	42
Slack, $C - R$	1	3	2	1	0	0	1	8

Decision Point With its substantial amount of slack capacity, the schedule is not unique. Employee 9, for example, could have Su–M, M–T, or T–W off without causing a capacity shortage. Indeed, the company might be able to get by with one fewer employee because of the total of eight slack days of capacity. However, all 10 employees are needed on Fridays. If the manager were willing to get by with only 9 employees on Fridays or if someone could work one day of overtime on a rotating basis, he would not need employee 10. As indicated in the table, the net requirement left for employee 10 to satisfy amounts to only one day, Friday. Thus, employee 10 can be used to fill in for vacationing or sick employees. ◻

COMPUTERIZED WORKFORCE SCHEDULING SYSTEMS. Workforce scheduling often entails myriad constraints and concerns. In some types of firms, such as telephone companies, mail-order catalog houses, or emergency hotline agencies, employees must be on duty 24 hours a day, seven days a week. Sometimes a portion of the staff is part-time, allowing management a great deal of flexibility in developing schedules but adding considerable complexity to the requirements. The flexibility comes from the opportunity to match anticipated loads closely by using overlapping shifts or odd shift lengths; the complexity comes from having to evaluate the numerous possible alternatives. Management also must consider the timing of lunch breaks and rest periods, the number and starting times of shift schedules, and the days off for each employee. An additional typical concern is that the number of employees on duty at any particular time be sufficient to answer calls within a reasonable amount of time.

Computerized scheduling systems are available to cope with the complexity of workforce scheduling. For example, L. L. Bean's telephone service center must be staffed with telephone operators 7 days a week, 24 hours a day. The company uses 350

Utility companies must schedule their repair workforce so that someone is available at all times in case of unexpected failures. Here a lineman works atop a telephone pole standing in water on Smith Island, Maryland. The workers move from pole to pole by motorboat until the repair is completed.

MANAGERIAL PRACTICE 17.2
Course Scheduling at the University of California, Los Angeles

Manually scheduling undergraduate, MBA, and doctoral courses at the Anderson Graduate School of Management at the University of California, Los Angeles (www.agsm.ucr.edu), used to take two people as many as three days each quarter. The complexity comes from myriad faculty preferences and facility and administrative constraints. For example, teachers may prefer to teach their assigned courses back-to-back, on the same days, and in the afternoon. In addition, there are only eight time slots in a day to start core MBA classes and limits to the number of rooms that can handle case discussion, large lectures, or computer access. Courses taught by the same instructor must not overlap, and courses must be scheduled at times so that students can take all required courses offered each quarter. Scheduling the 25 core MBA courses and 120 noncore courses to maximize faculty preferences, meet student needs, and satisfy all the constraints obviously is difficult.

Scheduling of the courses is now done with computer assistance. Core courses are scheduled first because they have limited starting times and all MBA students must enroll in them. Data on the number of sections of the core courses to be offered, facility and administrative constraints, and the teaching preferences of the faculty who will teach the core courses are entered into a com-

puter model that assigns faculty to courses and courses to time slots that maximizes teaching preferences and meets all constraints. Not all teaching preferences can be satisfied. If the teacher's time preferences can be changed, however, the model can be used again to produce a completely new schedule in seconds.

Another model was developed to assign noncore courses to times and teachers to courses so that faculty preferences are maximized. Inputs to the model include the teaching assignments of the core courses, as a teacher can teach both a core and noncore course, the schedule of the core courses, classroom availability, and faculty preferences.

The system has been implemented and is running smoothly. The scheduling system improves the quality of the final course schedule and saves time. The entire schedule of courses can now be produced in only three hours, which includes time needed to resolve conflicts with faculty preferences.

Source: Stallaert, Jan. "Automated Timetabling Improves Course Scheduling at UCLA." *Interfaces*, vol. 27, no. 4 (July–August 1997), pp. 67–81.

permanent and temporary employees. The permanent workers are guaranteed a minimum weekly workload apportioned over a 7-day week on a rotating schedule. The temporary staff works a variety of schedules, ranging from a full six-day week to a guaranteed weekly minimum of 20 hours. The company uses a computer program to forecast the hourly load for the telephone service center, translate the workload into capacity requirements, and then generate week-long staffing schedules for the permanent and temporary telephone operators to meet these demand requirements. The program selects the schedule that minimizes the sum of expected costs of over- and understaffing. Managerial Practice 17.2 describes the computerized scheduling system used by the Anderson Graduate School of Management at UCLA.

SCHEDULING ACROSS THE ORGANIZATION

In this chapter, we have shown the importance of the scheduling process for manufacturing and service processes. Whether the business is an airline, hotel, computer manufacturer, or university, schedules are a part of everyday life. Schedules involve an enormous amount of detail and affect every process in a firm. For example, product, service, and employee schedules determine specific cash flow requirements, trigger the billing process into action, and initiate requirements for the employee training process. The order-fulfillment process depends on good performance in terms of due dates for promised products or services, which is the result of a good scheduling process. In addition, when customers place orders using a Web-based order-entry process, the scheduling process determines when they can expect to receive the product or service. Certainly, regardless of the discipline, schedules affect everyone in a firm.

Given the development of computer hardware and software and the availability of the Internet, firms have elevated the scheduling process to a level where it can be used as a competitive weapon. As we have seen in Managerial Practice 17.1, Chrysler used the scheduling process to decrease costs and improve responsiveness to supply-chain dynamics by finding the way to produce complex schedules quickly. These schedules affect operations in plants worldwide. The scheduling process can provide any firm with a capability it can use to compete successfully, whether it is in manufacturing or services.

FORMULA REVIEW

1. Performance measures:

$$\text{Job flow time} = \text{Time of completion} - \begin{array}{l}\text{Time job was available for}\\\text{first processing operation}\end{array}$$

$$\text{Makespan} = \text{Time of completion of last job} - \text{Starting time of first job}$$

$$\text{Average WIP inventory} = \frac{\text{Sum of flow times}}{\text{Makespan}}$$

$$\text{Average inventory} = \frac{\text{Sum of time in system}}{\text{Makespan}}$$

$$\text{Total inventory} = \text{Scheduled receipts for all items} + \text{On-hand inventories of all items}$$

$$\text{Utilization} = \frac{\text{Productive work time}}{\text{Total work time available}}$$

2. Critical ratio:

$$\text{CR} = \frac{\text{Due date} - \text{Today's date}}{\text{Total shop time remaining}}$$

3. Slack per remaining operations:

$$\text{S/RO} = \frac{(\text{Due date} - \text{Today's date}) - \text{Shop time remaining}}{\text{Number of operations remaining}}$$

CHAPTER HIGHLIGHTS

❏ Scheduling is the allocation of resources over a period of time to accomplish a specific set of tasks. Two basic types of scheduling are workforce scheduling and operations scheduling. Scheduling applications are becoming more common in ERP systems.

❏ Gantt charts are useful for depicting the sequence of work at a particular workstation and for monitoring the progress of jobs in the system.

❏ No approach to scheduling is best for all situations. Performance measures that can be used to evaluate schedules include average job flow time, makespan, percent of jobs past due, average amount of time past due per job, average work-in-process inventory, average investment in total inventory, and utilization of equipment and workers.

❐ Dispatching procedures allow a schedule to evolve from new information about operating conditions. Priority rules are used to make these decisions. The choice of priority rule can affect the schedule performance measures that are of concern to management.

❐ Labor-limited systems add another dimension to operations scheduling. In addition to determining which job to process next, the scheduler also must assign the work to an available operator having the required skills.

❐ The impact of scheduling can be increased by focusing on the schedules of bottleneck resources so as to maximize the flow of total value-added funds.

❐ Capacity considerations are important for scheduling services. If the capacity of the operating system is fixed, loads can be leveled by using approaches such as appointments, reservations, and backlogs. If service is determined by labor availability, workforce scheduling may be appropriate.

❐ A workforce schedule translates a staffing plan into a specific work schedule for each employee. Typical workforce scheduling considerations include capacity limits, service targets, consecutive days off, maximum number of workdays in a row, type of schedule (fixed or rotating), and vacation and holiday time.

KEY TERMS

advanced planning and scheduling (APS) systems *841*
critical ratio (CR) *831*
dispatching procedures *830*
earliest due date (EDD) *831*
first come, first served (FCFS) *831*
fixed schedule *844*
flow shop *828*
job flow time *829*
job shop *828*

Johnson's rule *839*
labor-limited environment *841*
makespan *829*
multiple-dimension rules *834*
operations scheduling *827*
past due *830*
priority sequencing rules *830*
rotating schedule *844*
scheduling *826*
shortest processing time (SPT) *831*

single-dimension rules *832*
slack per remaining operations (S/RO) *831*
tardiness *830*
throughput time *829*
total inventory *830*
workforce scheduling *827*
work-in-process (WIP) inventory *830*

SOLVED PROBLEM 1

The Neptune's Den Machine Shop specializes in overhauling outboard marine engines. Some engines require replacement of broken parts, whereas others need a complete overhaul. Currently, five engines with varying problems are awaiting service. The best estimates for the labor times involved and the promise dates (in number of days from today) are shown in the following table. Customers usually do not pick up their engines early.

ENGINE	ESTIMATED LABOR TIME (days)	PROMISE DATE (days from now)
50-hp Evinrude	5	8
7-hp Chrysler	4	15
100-hp Mercury	10	12
4-hp Sportsman	1	20
75-hp Nautique	3	10

a. Develop separate schedules by using the SPT and EDD rules. Compare the two schedules on the basis of average job flow time, percent of past due jobs, and maximum past due days for any engine.

b. For each schedule, calculate average work-in-process inventory (in engines) and average total inventory (in engines).

SOLUTION

a. Using the shortest processing time (SPT) rule, we obtain the following schedule:

REPAIR SEQUENCE	PROCESSING TIME	JOB FLOW TIME	PROMISE DATE	ACTUAL PICKUP DATE	DAYS EARLY	DAYS PAST DUE
4-hp Sportsman	1	1	20	20	19	
75-hp Nautique	3	4	10	10	6	
7-hp Chrysler	4	8	15	15	7	
50-hp Evinrude	5	13	8	13		5
100-hp Mercury	10	23	12	23		11
Total		49		81		

Using the earliest due date (EDD), we come up with this schedule:

REPAIR SEQUENCE	PROCESSING TIME	JOB FLOW TIME	PROMISE DATE	ACTUAL PICKUP DATE	DAYS EARLY	DAYS PAST DUE
50-hp Evinrude	5	5	8	8	3	
75-hp Nautique	3	8	10	10	2	
100-hp Mercury	10	18	12	18		6
7-hp Chrysler	4	22	15	22		7
4-hp Sportsman	1	23	20	23		3
Total		76		81		

Average job flow time is 9:8 (or 49/5) days for SPT and 15.2 (or 76/5) days for EDD. Percent of past due jobs is 40 percent (2/5) for SPT and 60 percent (3/5) for EDD. The EDD schedule minimizes the maximum days past due but has a greater flow time and causes more jobs to be past due.

b. For SPT, inventory averages are as follows:

$$\text{Average WIP inventory} = \frac{\text{Sum of flow times}}{\text{Makespan}} = \frac{49}{23} = 2.13 \text{ engines}$$

$$\text{Average total inventory} = \frac{\text{Sum of time in system}}{\text{Makespan}} = \frac{81}{23} = 3.52 \text{ engines}$$

For EDD, they are

$$\text{Average WIP inventory} = \frac{76}{23} = 3.30 \text{ engines}$$

$$\text{Average total inventory} = \frac{81}{23} = 3.52 \text{ engines}$$

SOLVED PROBLEM 2

The following data were reported by the shop floor control system for order processing at the edge grinder. The current date is day 150. The number of remaining operations and the total work remaining include the operation at the edge grinder. All orders are available for processing, and none have been started yet.

CURRENT ORDER	PROCESSING TIME (hr)	DUE DATE (day)	REMAINING OPERATIONS	SHOP TIME REMAINING (days)
A101	10	162	10	9
B272	7	158	9	6
C105	15	152	1	1
D707	4	170	8	18
E555	8	154	5	8

a. Specify the priorities for each job if the shop floor control system uses slack per remaining operations (S/RO) or critical ratio (CR).

b. For each priority rule, calculate the average job flow time per job at the edge grinder.

SOLUTION

a. We specify the priorities for each job using the two dispatching rules.

$$S/RO = \frac{(\text{Due date} - \text{Today's date}) - \text{Shop time remaining}}{\text{Number of operations remaining}}$$

$$\text{E555:} \quad S/RO = \frac{(154 - 150) - 8}{5} = -0.80 \quad [1]$$

$$\text{B272:} \quad S/RO = \frac{(158 - 150) - 6}{9} = 0.22 \quad [2]$$

$$\text{D707:} \quad S/RO = \frac{(170 - 150) - 18}{8} = 0.25 \quad [3]$$

$$\text{A101:} \quad S/RO = \frac{(162 - 150) - 9}{10} = 0.30 \quad [4]$$

$$\text{C105:} \quad S/RO = \frac{(152 - 150) - 1}{1} = 1.00 \quad [5]$$

The sequence of production for S/RO is shown above in brackets.

$$CR = \frac{\text{Due date} - \text{Today's date}}{\text{Shop time remaining}}$$

$$\text{E555:} \quad CR = \frac{154 - 150}{8} = 0.50 \quad [1]$$

$$\text{D707:} \quad CR = \frac{170 - 150}{18} = 1.11 \quad [2]$$

$$\text{B272:} \quad CR = \frac{158 - 150}{6} = 1.33 \quad [3]$$

$$\text{A101:} \quad CR = \frac{162 - 150}{9} = 1.33 \quad [4]$$

$$\text{C105:} \quad CR = \frac{152 - 150}{1} = 2.00 \quad [5]$$

The sequence of production for CR is shown above in brackets.

b. We are looking for the flow time of a set of jobs at a single machine, so each job's flow time equals the flow time of the job just prior to it in sequence plus its own processing time. Consequently, the average flow times are

$$\text{S/RO:} \quad \frac{8 + 15 + 19 + 29 + 44}{5} = 23.0 \text{ hours}$$

$$\text{CR:} \quad \frac{8 + 12 + 19 + 29 + 44}{5} = 22.4 \text{ hours}$$

In this example, the average flow time per job is lower for the critical ratio rule, which is not always the case. For example, the critical ratios for B272 and A101 are tied at 1.33. If we arbitrarily assigned A101 before B272, the average flow time would increase to (8 + 12 + 22 + 29 + 44)/5 = 23.0 hours.

SOLVED PROBLEM 3

The Rocky Mountain Arsenal, formerly a chemical warfare manufacturing site, is said to be one of the most polluted locations in the United States. Cleanup of chemical waste storage basins will involve two operations.

Operation 1:   Drain and dredge basin.
Operation 2:   Incinerate materials.

Management has estimated that each operation will require the following amounts of time (in days):

	STORAGE BASIN									
	A	B	C	D	E	F	G	H	I	J
Dredge	3	4	3	6	1	3	2	1	8	4
Incinerate	1	4	2	1	2	6	4	1	2	8

Because of the health danger, human access to the area has been severely restricted for decades. As an unintended result, the Rocky Mountain Arsenal has now become a prolific wildlife refuge, which now supports several endangered species. Management's objective is to clean up the area while minimizing disruption to wildlife. This objective can be translated as minimizing the makespan of the cleanup operations. First, find a schedule that minimizes the makespan. Then, calculate the average job flow time of a storage basin through the two operations. What is the total elapsed time for cleaning all 10 basins? Display the schedule in a Gantt machine chart.

SOLUTION

We can use Johnson's rule to find the schedule that minimizes the total makespan. Four jobs are tied for the shortest process time: A, D, E, and H. We arbitrarily choose to start with basin E, the first on the list for the drain and dredge operation. The 10 steps used to arrive at a sequence are as follows:

Select basin E first (tied with basin H); put at the front.	E	—	—	—	—	—	—	—	—	—
Select basin H next; put toward the front.	E	H	—	—	—	—	—	—	—	—
Select basin A next (tied with basin D); put at the end.	E	H	—	—	—	—	—	—	—	A
Put basin D toward the end.	E	H	—	—	—	—	—	—	D	A
Put basin G toward the front.	E	H	G	—	—	—	—	—	D	A
Put basin C toward the end.	E	H	G	—	—	—	—	C	D	A
Put basin I toward the end.	E	H	G	—	—	—	I	C	D	A
Put basin F toward the front.	E	H	G	F	—	—	I	C	D	A
Put basin B toward the front.	E	H	G	F	B	—	I	C	D	A
Put basin J in the remaining space.	E	H	G	F	B	J	I	C	D	A

There are several optimal solutions to this problem because of the ties at the start of the scheduling procedure. However, all have the same makespan. The schedule would be as follows:

	OPERATION 1		OPERATION 2	
BASIN	**Start**	**Finish**	**Start**	**Finish**
E	0	1	1	3
H	1	2	3	4
G	2	4	4	8
F	4	7	8	14
B	7	11	14	18
J	11	15	18	26
I	15	23	26	28
C	23	26	28	30
D	26	32	32	33
A	32	35	35	<u>36</u>
			Total	200

The makespan is 36 days. The average job flow time is the sum of incineration finish times divided by 10, or 200/10 = 20 days. The Gantt machine chart for this schedule is given in Figure 17.8.

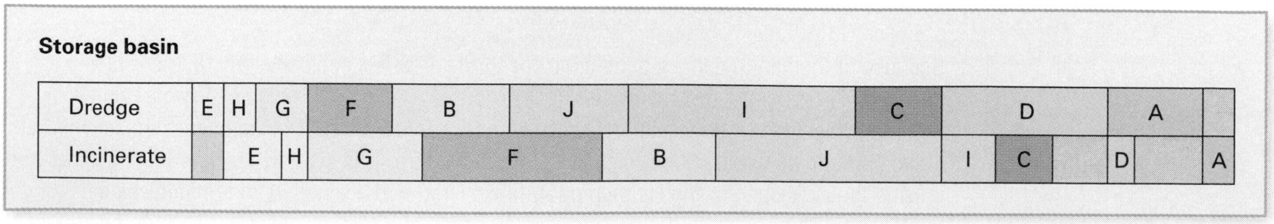

FIGURE 17.8

SOLVED PROBLEM 4

The Food Bin grocery store operates 24 hours per day, seven days per week. Fred Bulger, the store manager, has been analyzing the efficiency and productivity of store operations recently. Bulger decided to observe the need for checkout clerks on the first shift for a one-month period. At the end of the month, he calculated the average number of checkout registers that should be open during the first shift each day. His results showed peak needs on Saturdays and Sundays.

Day	M	T	W	Th	F	S	Su
Number of employees	3	4	5	5	4	7	8

Bulger now has to come up with a workforce schedule that guarantees each checkout clerk two consecutive days off but still covers all requirements.

a. Develop a workforce schedule that covers all requirements while giving two consecutive days off to each clerk. How many clerks are needed? Assume that the clerks have no preference regarding which days they have off.

b. Plans can be made to use the clerks for other duties if slack or idle time resulting from this schedule can be determined. How much idle time will result from this schedule and on what days?

SOLUTION

a. We use the method demonstrated in Example 17.5 to determine the number of clerks needed.

				DAY			
	M	T	W	Th	F	S	Su
Requirements	3	4	5	5	4	7	8*
Clerk 1	off	off	X	X	X	X	X
Requirements	3	4	4	4	3	6	7*
Clerk 2	off	off	X	X	X	X	X
Requirements	3	4	3	3	2	5	6*
Clerk 3	X	X	X	off	off	X	X
Requirements	2	3	2	3	2	4	5*
Clerk 4	X	X	X	off	off	X	X
Requirements	1	2	1	3	2	3	4*
Clerk 5	X	off	off	X	X	X	X
Requirements	0	2	1	2	1	2	3*
Clerk 6	off	off	X	X	X	X	X
Requirements	0	2*	0	1	0	1	2*
Clerk 7	X	X	off	off	X	X	X
Requirements	0	1*	0	1*	0	0	1*
Clerk 8	X	X	X	X	off	off	X
Requirements	0	0	0	0	0	0	0

*Maximum requirements.

The minimum number of clerks is eight.

b. Based on the results in part (a) the number of clerks on duty minus the requirements is the number of idle clerks available for other duties:

				DAY			
	M	T	W	Th	F	S	Su
Number on duty	5	4	6	5	5	7	8
Requirements	3	4	5	5	4	7	8
Idle clerks	2	0	1	0	1	0	0

The slack in this schedule would indicate to Bulger the number of employees he might ask to work part-time (fewer than five days per week). For example, clerk 7 might work Tuesday, Saturday, and Sunday, and clerk 8 might work Tuesday, Thursday, and Sunday. That would eliminate slack from the schedule.

DISCUSSION QUESTIONS

1. Suppose that two alternative approaches for determining machine schedules are available. One is an optimizing approach that can be run once a week on the computer. The other is a dispatching approach that utilizes priority rules to determine the schedule as it evolves. Discuss the advantages and disadvantages of each approach and the conditions under which each approach is likely to be better.

2. Explain why management should be concerned about priority systems in manufacturing and service organizations.

OM EXPLORER AND INTERNET EXERCISES

Visit our Web site at www.prenhall.com/krajewski for OM Explorer Tutors, which explain quantitative techniques; Solvers, which help you apply mathematical models; and Internet Exercises, including Facility Tours, which expand on the topics in this chapter.

PROBLEMS

1. **OM Explorer** The Hickory Company manufactures wooden desks. Management schedules overtime every weekend to reduce the backlog on the most popular models. The automatic routing machine is used to cut certain types of edges on the desktops. The following orders need to be scheduled for the routing machine:

ORDER	ESTIMATED MACHINE TIME (hr)	DUE DATE (hr from now)
1	10	12
2	3	8
3	15	18
4	9	20
5	7	21

The due dates reflect the need for the order to be at its next operation.

a. Develop separate schedules by using the FCFS, SPT, and EDD rules. Compare the schedules on the basis of average flow time, the average early time, and average past due hours for any order.

b. For each schedule, calculate average work-in-process inventory (in orders) and average total inventory (in orders).

c. Comment on the performance of the two rules relative to these measures.

2. **OM Explorer** The drill press is a bottleneck operation in a production system. Currently, five jobs are waiting to be processed. Following are the available operations data. Assume that the current date is week 5 and that the number of remaining operations and the shop time remaining include the operation at the drill press.

JOB	PROCESSING TIME	DUE DATE	OPERATIONS REMAINING	SHOP TIME REMAINING (wk)
AA	4	10	3	4
BB	8	16	4	6
CC	13	21	10	9
DD	6	23	3	12
EE	2	12	5	3

a. Specify the priority for each job if the shop floor control system uses each of the following priority rules: SPT, S/RO, EDD, and CR.

b. For each priority rule, calculate the average flow time per job at the drill press.

TABLE 17.4	*Manufacturing Data*				
JOB	**RELEASE TIME**	**LOT SIZE**	**PROCESSING TIME (hr/unit)**	**SETUP TIME (hr)**	**DUE DATE**
1	9:00 A.M. Monday	50	0.06	4	9:00 P.M. Monday
2	10:00 A.M. Monday	120	0.05	3	10:00 P.M. Monday
3	11:00 A.M. Monday	260	0.03	5	11:00 P.M. Monday
4	12:00 P.M. Monday	200	0.04	2	2:00 A.M. Tuesday

c. Which of these priority rules would work best for priority planning with an MRP system? Why?

3. The machine shop at Bycraft Enterprises operates 24 hours a day and uses a numerically controlled (NC) welding machine. The load on the machine is monitored, and no more than 24 hours of work is released to the welding operators in one day. The data for a typical set of jobs are shown in Table 17.4. Management has been investigating scheduling procedures that would reduce inventory and increase customer service in the shop. Assume that at 8:00 A.M. on Monday the NC welding machine was idle.

a. Develop schedules for SPT and EDD priority rules, and draw a Gantt machine chart for each schedule.

b. For each schedule in part (a), calculate the average past due hours per job and the average flow time per job. Keep in mind that the jobs are available for processing at different times.

c. Comment on the customer service and inventory performance of the two rules. What trade-offs should management consider in selecting rules for scheduling the welding machine in the future?

4. **OM Explorer** Refer to the Gantt machine chart in Figure 17.9.

a. Suppose that a routing requirement is that each job must be processed on machine A first. Can the makespan be improved? If so, draw a Gantt chart with the improved schedule. If not, state why not.

b. Suppose that there is no routing restriction on machine sequence, and that jobs can be processed in any sequence on the machines. Can the makespan in the chart be improved in this case? If so, draw a Gantt chart with your schedule. If not, state why not.

5. **OM Explorer** A manufacturer of sails for small boats has a group of custom sails awaiting the last two processing operations before the sails are sent to the customers. Operation 1 must be performed before operation 2, and the jobs have different time requirements for each operation. The hours required are as follows:

					JOB					
	1	**2**	**3**	**4**	**5**	**6**	**7**	**8**	**9**	**10**
Operation 1	1	5	8	3	9	4	7	2	4	9
Operation 2	8	3	1	2	8	6	7	2	4	1

a. Use Johnson's rule to determine the optimal sequence.

b. Draw a Gantt chart for each operation.

6. **OM Explorer** McGee Parts Company is under tremendous pressure to complete a government contract

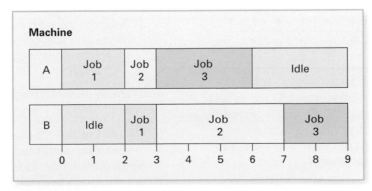

FIGURE 17.9

for six orders in 31 working days. The orders are for spare parts for highway maintenance equipment. According to the government contract, a late penalty of $1,000 is imposed each day the order is late. Owing to a nation-wide increase in highway construction, McGee Parts has received many orders for spare parts replacement and the shop has been extremely busy. To complete the government contract, the parts must be deburred and heat treated. The production control manager has suggested the following schedule:

	DEBURR		HEAT TREAT	
JOB	Start	Finish	Start	Finish
1	0	2	2	8
2	2	5	8	13
3	5	12	13	17
4	12	15	17	25
5	15	16	25	30
6	16	24	30	32

a. Use Johnson's rule to determine the optimal sequence.

b. Draw a Gantt chart for each operation.

7. ● **OM Explorer** Carolyn Roberts is the operations manager of the machine shop of Reliable Manufacturing. She has to schedule eight jobs that are to be sent to final assembly for an important customer order. Currently, all eight jobs are in department 12 and must be routed to department 22 next. Jason Mangano, supervisor for department 12, is concerned about keeping his work-in-process inventory low and is adamant about processing the jobs through his department on the basis of shortest processing time. Pat Mooney, supervisor for department 22, pointed out that if Mangano were more flexible the orders could be finished and shipped earlier. The processing times (in days) for each job in each department follow:

	JOB							
	1	2	3	4	5	6	7	8
Department 12	2	4	7	5	4	10	8	2
Department 22	3	6	3	8	2	6	6	5

a. Determine a schedule for the operation in each department. Use SPT for department 12 and the same sequence for department 22. What is the average job flow time for department 12? What is the makespan through both departments? What is the sum of jobs times days spent in the system?

b. Find a schedule that will minimize the makespan through both departments, and then calculate the

average job flow time for department 12. What is the sum of jobs times days spent in the system?

c. Discuss the trade-offs represented by these two schedules. What implications do they have for centralized scheduling?

8. ● **OM Explorer** Gerald Glynn manages the Michaels Distribution Center. After careful examination of his data-base information, he has determined the daily requirements for part-time loading dock personnel. The distribution center operates seven days a week, and the daily part-time staffing requirements are

Day	M	T	W	Th	F	S	Su
Requirements	6	3	5	3	7	2	3

Find the minimum number of workers Glynn must hire. Prepare a workforce schedule for these individuals so that each will have two consecutive days off per week and all staffing requirements will be satisfied. Give preference to the pair S–Su in case of a tie.

9. Cara Ryder manages a ski school in a large resort and is trying to develop a schedule for instructors. The instructors receive little salary and work just enough to earn room and board. They do receive free skiing, spending most of their free time tackling the resort's notorious double black diamond slopes. Hence, the instructors work only four days a week. One of the lesson packages offered at the resort is a four-day beginner package. Ryder likes to keep the same instructor with a group over the four-day period, so she schedules the instructors for four consecutive days and then three days off. Ryder uses years of experience with demand forecasts provided by management to formulate her instructor requirements for the upcoming month.

Day	M	T	W	Th	F	S	Su
Requirements	7	5	4	5	6	9	8

a. Determine how many instructors Ryder needs to employ. Give preference to Saturday and Sunday off. (*Hint*: Look for the group of three days with lowest requirements.)

b. Specify the work schedule for each employee. How much slack does your schedule generate for each day?

10. ● **OM Explorer** The mayor of Massilon, Ohio, wanting to be environmentally progressive, has decided to implement a recycling plan. All residents of the city will receive a special three-part bin to separate their glass, plastic, and aluminum, and the city will be responsible for

picking up the materials. A young city and regional planning graduate, Michael Duffy, has been hired to manage the recycling program. After carefully studying the city's population density, Duffy decides that the following numbers of recycling collectors will be needed.

Day	M	T	W	Th	F	S	Su
Requirements	12	7	9	9	5	3	6

The requirements are based on the populations of the various housing developments and subdivisions in the city and surrounding communities. To motivate residents of some areas to have their pickups scheduled on weekends, a special tax break will be given.

a. Find the minimum number of recycling collectors required if each employee works five days a week and has two consecutive days off. Give preference to S–Su when that pair is involved in a tie.

b. Specify the work schedule for each employee. How much slack does your schedule generate for each day?

c. Suppose that Duffy can smooth the requirements further through greater tax incentives. The requirements then will be 8 on Monday and 7 on the other days of the week. How many employees will be needed now? Find the optimal solution in terms of minimal total slack capacity. Does smoothing of requirements have capital investment implications? If so, what are they?

Advanced Problems

11. **OM Explorer** The repair manager at Standard Components needs to develop a priority schedule for repairing eight Dell PCs. Each job requires analysis using the same diagnostic system. Furthermore, each job will require additional processing after the diagnostic evaluation. The manager does not expect any rescheduling delays, and the jobs are to move directly to the next process after the diagnostic work has been completed. The manager has collected the following processing time and scheduling data for each repair job:

JOB	WORK TIME (days)	DUE DATE (days)	SHOP TIME REMAINING (days)	OPERATIONS REMAINING
1	1.25	6	2.5	5
2	2.75	5	3.5	7
3	2.50	7	4.0	9
4	3.00	6	4.5	12
5	2.50	5	3.0	8
6	1.75	8	2.5	6
7	2.25	7	3.0	9
8	2.00	5	2.5	3

a. Compare the relative performance of the FCFS, SPT, EDD, S/RO, and CR rules.

b. Discuss the selection of one of the rules for this company. What criteria do you consider most important in the selection of a rule in this situation?

12. **OM Explorer** Penultimate Support Systems makes fairly good speaker and equipment support stands for music groups. The assembly process involves two operations: (1) fabrication, or cutting aluminum tubing to the correct lengths, and (2) assembly, with purchased fasteners and injection-molded plastic parts. Setup time for assembly is negligible. Fabrication setup time and run time per unit, assembly run time per unit, and the production schedule for next week follow. Organize the work to minimize makespan, and create a Gantt chart. Can this work be accomplished within two 40-hour shifts?

MODEL	QUANTITY	FABRICATION Setup (hr)	FABRICATION Run Time (hr/unit)	ASSEMBLY Run Time (hr/unit)
A	200	2	0.050	0.04
B	300	3	0.070	0.10
C	100	1	0.050	0.12
D	250	2	0.064	0.60

13. **OM Explorer** Little 6, Inc., an accounting firm, forecasts the following weekly workload during the tax season:

	M	T	W	Th	F	S	Su
Personal tax returns	24	14	18	18	10	28	16
Corporate tax returns	18	10	12	15	24	12	4

Corporate tax returns each require 4 hours of an accountant's time, and personal returns each require 90 minutes. During tax season, each accountant can work up to 10 hours per day. However, error rates increase to unacceptable levels when accountants work more than five consecutive days per week.

a. Create an effective and efficient work schedule.

b. Assume that Little 6 has three part-time employees available to work three days per week. How could these employees be effectively utilized?

14. Eight jobs must be processed on three machines in the sequence M1–M2–M3. The processing times (in hours) are

	JOB							
	1	**2**	**3**	**4**	**5**	**6**	**7**	**8**
Machine 1	2	5	2	3	1	2	4	2
Machine 2	4	1	3	5	5	6	2	1
Machine 3	6	4	5	2	3	2	6	2

Machine M2 is a bottleneck, and management wants to maximize its use. Consequently, the schedule for the eight jobs, through the three machines, was based on the SPT rule on M2. The proposed schedule is 2–8–7–3–1–4–5–6.

a. It is now 4 P.M. on Monday. Suppose that processing on M2 is to begin at 7 A.M. on Tuesday. Use the proposed schedule to determine the schedules for M1 and M3 so that job 2 begins processing on M2 at 7 A.M. on Tuesday. Draw Gantt charts for M1, M2, and M3. What is the makespan for the eight jobs?

b. Find a schedule that utilizes M2 better and yields a shorter makespan.

15. The last few steps of a production process require two operations. Some jobs require processing on M1 before processing on M3. Other jobs require processing on M2 before M3. Currently, six jobs are waiting at M1 and four jobs are waiting at M2. The following data have been supplied by the shop floor control system:

	PROCESSING TIME (hr)			
JOB	**M1**	**M2**	**M3**	**DUE DATE (hr from now)**
1	6	—	4	13
2	2	—	1	18
3	4	—	7	22
4	5	—	3	16
5	7	—	4	30
6	3	—	1	29
7	—	4	6	42
8	—	2	10	31
9	—	6	9	48
10	—	8	2	40

a. Schedule this shop by using the following rules: SPT, EDD, S/RO, and CR.

b. Discuss the operating implications of each of the schedules you developed in part (a).

16. Return to Problem 8 and the workforce schedule for part-time loading dock workers. Suppose that each part-time worker can work only three days, but the days must be consecutive. Devise an approach to this workforce scheduling problem. Your objective is to minimize total slack capacity. What is the minimum number of clerks needed now and what are their schedules?

SIMULATION EXERCISES

These simulation exercises require the use of the Extend and SimQuick simulation packages. Extend is on the Student CD-ROM that is packaged with every new copy of the textbook. SimQuick is an optional simulation package that your instructor may or may not have ordered.

1. **Extend** Recall Precision AutoBody in Example 17.3. Customers are increasingly frustrated with long delivery times and unmet delivery promises. Use the Extend simulator to evaluate the current process and other priority dispatching rules such as first come, first served (FCFS), shortest process time (SPT), earliest due date (EDD), and minimum slack time. See the *Scheduling Vehicle Repair at Precision AutoBody* case on the Student CD-ROM, which includes the basic model and how to use it. Answer the various questions about scheduling rules, increased customer demand, and adjusted due dates.

2. **SimQuick** A small company has a single machine that processes four types of products, each with its own processing time distributions and arrival time distributions. It is important to schedule the machine so as to reduce the average work-in-process of the products and the tardiness in delivering the products to the customers. Use SimQuick to determine the mean flow time and overall tardiness of the products processed by the machine when the shortest processing time (SPT) and the earliest due date (EDD) rules are used to schedule the machine. See Example 16 in *SimQuick: Process Simulation in Excel* for more details about this problem and additional exercises.

CASE FOOD KING

Based in Charlotte, North Carolina, the Food King grocery supermarket chain stretches from the Virginias down the East Coast into Florida. As in the rest of the country, the grocery supermarket industry in the Southeast is very competitive, with average profit margins running at about 2 percent of revenues. Historically, the overriding competitive priority for all grocery chains was low prices. With profit margins so small, stores were continually looking for ways to reduce costs and utilize facilities efficiently. Several grocery chains still focus on low prices as their main competitive priority.

Food King, however, recently decided to focus its competitive positioning on enhancing the consumer's shopping experience. Food King's target market is the upscale food shopper, who has the following shopping priorities:

1. *Cleanliness.* The facility is clean and orderly, with items well marked and easy to find.

2. *Availability.* The selection of items is broad, and the customer has several choices for any one item.

3. *Timely Service.* The store is open at convenient times, and customers do not have to wait in long checkout lines.

4. *Reasonable Prices.* Although customers are willing to pay a small premium for cleanliness, availability, and good service, prices still must be competitive.

Marty Moyer had been the store manager of the Food King supermarket in Rock Hill, South Carolina, for the past three years. He had worked his way up from stockboy to manager of this medium-sized facility. Because of his success managing the Rock Hill facility, Moyer was promoted to the store manager's position at the large, flagship Food King store in Columbia. This facility had just instituted 24-hours-per-day, 7-days-a-week hours in response to competitive pressures.

After a month as manager at the Columbia store, Moyer has become familiar with the local market characteristics, store operations, and store personnel. His major challenge for the future is to align the store with the new competitive priorities established for the chain. An area he has identified as a particular concern is the scheduling of stockers and baggers. The cleanliness, availability, and service time priorities put added pressure on Moyer to have the appropriate number of stocking and bagging personnel available. Maintaining a high level of cleanliness requires more stocking personnel to keep the stock orderly on the shelves and the aisles clear and swept. The availability priority requires more frequent replenishment of shelves

because the greater selection of items means less space is allocated to any one brand or item. Finally, the need for fast service requires baggers to be available to assist the cashier in serving customers quickly, especially during peak shopping periods when long waits could occur if cashiers had to bag and ring up the groceries.

Moyer knows that he cannot solve the cleanliness, availability, and timely service issues just by adding stocking and bagging personnel to the payroll. To make a profit in a low-margin business environment, he has to control costs so that prices remain competitive. The trick is to develop a work schedule for the stocking and bagging personnel that satisfies competitive requirements, conforms to a reasonable set of work policies, and utilizes the personnel efficiently to minimize labor costs.

Moyers begins to address this problem by collecting information on existing scheduling policies and procedures along with a forecasted level of demand for personnel. The stocking and bagging positions can be filled with either full- or part-time employees. Full-time employees work eight hours per day five days a week, with two consecutive days off each week. The eight-hour shifts usually are scheduled as consecutive eight-hour blocks of time; however, he can schedule an employee to two four-hour time blocks (with four hours off between them) within a particular day if there is a stocker and a bagger for the four-hour period between scheduled blocks of time.

All part-time employees are scheduled in four-hour blocks of time for up to 20 hours per week. Food King limits the number of part-time employees to 50 percent of the total number of full-time employees for each category of worker. Most of the part-time employees are utilized as baggers because they tend to be retired people who have difficulty with the heavy lifting required in stocking shelves. Food King likes to hire retired people because they are dependable, reliable, and more willing to work weekends than are teenagers. Full-time employees earn $5.25 per hour; part-time employees earn only $4.50 per hour.

For scheduling purposes, each day is divided into six four-hour time blocks beginning with 8:00 A.M. to 12:00 noon. Demand for stocking and bagging personnel varies quite a bit within a 24-hour period. Moyer developed a forecast of personnel needs by four-hour time blocks by analyzing customer activity data and supplier delivery schedules. The following table gives his estimate of the total number of stockers and baggers required for each four-hour block of time starting at the time indicated:

continued

continued

HOUR	DAY						
	M	**T**	**W**	**Th**	**F**	**S**	**Su**
8:00 A.M.	6	8	5	5	8	15	4
12:00 P.M.	6	8	5	5	10	15	6
4:00 P.M.	5	6	5	5	15	15	6
8:00 P.M.	4	4	4	4	8	6	4
12:00 A.M.	4	4	4	4	5	4	4
4:00 A.M.	8	4	4	8	5	4	4

The peak requirements occur during the heavy shopping periods on Friday and Saturday. More stocking personnel are required on Monday and Thursday evenings because of the large number of supplier deliveries on those days.

Moyer wants to determine the number of stocking and bagging personnel needed, the appropriate mix of full-time and part-time employees, and the work schedule for each employee. Going to a 24-hours-a-day operation has certainly complicated the scheduling task. He knows that younger, full-time employees probably will be best for the late night and early morning blocks of time. But the younger employees dislike working these hours. Somehow the schedule has to convey fairness for all.

Questions

1. Translate the four priorities of the shoppers into a set of competitive priorities for operations at the Rock Hill Food King store.
2. Develop a schedule of full-time and part-time stockers and baggers for Marty Moyer. Explain the strategy you used and the trade-offs you made to satisfy the Rock Hill store's competitive priorities.
3. What measures would you take to ensure that the schedule is fair to all employees?

Source: This case was prepared by Dr. Brooke Saladin, Wake Forest University, as a basis for classroom discussion.

SELECTED REFERENCES

Andrews, B. H., and H. L. Parsons. "L. L. Bean Chooses a Telephone Agent Scheduling System." *Interfaces* (November–December 1989), pp. 1–9.

Ashton, James E., and Frank X. Cook, Jr. "Time to Reform Job Shop Manufacturing." *Harvard Business Review* (March–April 1989), pp. 106–111.

Baker, K. R. *Elements of Sequencing and Scheduling.* Hanover, NH: Baker Press, 1995.

Buyer's Guide. "Scheduling Software." *IIE Solutions* (September 1995), pp. 46–53.

Browne, J. J. "Simplified Scheduling of Routine Work Hours and Days Off." *Industrial Engineering* (December 1979), pp. 27–29.

Browne, J. J., and J. Prop. "Supplement to Scheduling Routine Work Hours." *Industrial Engineering* (July 1989), p. 12.

Dillon, Jeffrey E., and Spyros Kontogiorgis. "US Airways Optimizes the Scheduling of Reserve Flight Crews." *Interfaces* (September–October 1999), pp. 123–131.

Johnson, S. M. "Optimal Two Stage and Three Stage Production Schedules with Setup Times Included." *Naval Logistics Quarterly,* vol. 1, no. 1 (1954), pp. 61–68.

Kiran, Ali S., and Thomas H. Willingham. "Simulation: Help for Your Scheduling Problems." *APICS—The Performance Advantage* (August 1992), pp. 26–28.

LaForge, R. Lawrence, and Christopher W. Craighead. "Computer-Based Scheduling in Manufacturing Firms: Some Indicators of Successful Practice." *Production and Inventory Management Journal* (First Quarter 2000), pp. 29–34.

Lesaint, David, Christos Voudouris, and Nader Azarmi. "Dynamic Workforce Scheduling for British Telecommunications plc." *Interfaces* (January–February 2000), pp. 45–56.

Port, Otis. "Customers Move Into the Driver's Seat." *Business Week* (October 4, 1999), pp. 103–106.

Rhodes, Phillip. "Modern Job Shop Manufacturing Systems." *APICS— The Performance Advantage* (January 1992), pp. 27–28.

Simons, Jacob, Jr., and Wendell P. Simpson III, "An Exposition of Multiple Constraint Scheduling as Implemented in the Goal System (Formerly Disaster™)." *Production and Operations Management,* vol. 6, no. 1 (Spring 1997), pp. 3–22.

Suresh, V., and D. Chaudhuri. "Dynamic Scheduling—A Survey of Research." *International Journal of Production Economics,* vol. 32 (1993), pp. 52–63.

Tibrewala, R. K., D. Philippe, and J. J. Browne. "Optimal Scheduling of Two Consecutive Idle Periods." *Management Science,* vol. 19, no. 1 (1972), pp. 71–75.

Treleven, M. D. "The Timing of Labor Transfers in Dual Resource-Constrained Systems: Push versus Pull Rules." *Decision Sciences,* vol. 18, no. 1 (1987), pp. 73–88.

Voet, M., and P. Dewilde. "Choosing a Scheduling Package." *APICS— The Performance Advantage* (November 1994), pp. 28–31.

Vollmann, Thomas E., William Berry, and D. Clay Whybark. *Manufacturing Planning and Control Systems,* 4th ed. Homewood, Ill.: Irwin Professional Publication, 1997.

Appendix 1: Normal Distribution

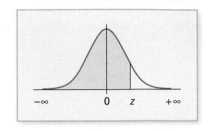

	.00	.01	.02	.03	.04	.05	.06	.07	.08	.09
.0	.5000	.5040	.5080	.5120	.5160	.5199	.5239	.5279	.5319	.5359
.1	.5398	.5438	.5478	.5517	.5557	.5596	.5636	.5675	.5714	.5753
.2	.5793	.5832	.5871	.5910	.5948	.5987	.6026	.6064	.6103	.6141
.3	.6179	.6217	.6255	.6293	.6331	.6368	.6406	.6443	.6480	.6517
.4	.6554	.6591	.6628	.6664	.6700	.6736	.6772	.6808	.6844	.6879
.5	.6915	.6950	.6985	.7019	.7054	.7088	.7123	.7157	.7190	.7224
.6	.7257	.7291	.7324	.7357	.7389	.7422	.7454	.7486	.7517	.7549
.7	.7580	.7611	.7642	.7673	.7704	.7734	.7764	.7794	.7823	.7852
.8	.7881	.7910	.7939	.7967	.7995	.8023	.8051	.8078	.8106	.8133
.9	.8159	.8186	.8212	.8238	.8264	.8289	.8315	.8340	.8365	.8389
1.0	.8413	.8438	.8461	.8485	.8508	.8531	.8554	.8577	.8599	.8621
1.1	.8643	.8665	.8686	.8708	.8729	.8749	.8770	.8790	.8810	.8830
1.2	.8849	.8869	.8888	.8907	.8925	.8944	.8962	.8980	.8997	.9015
1.3	.9032	.9049	.9066	.9082	.9099	.9115	.9131	.9147	.9162	.9177
1.4	.9192	.9207	.9222	.9236	.9251	.9265	.9279	.9292	.9306	.9319
1.5	.9332	.9345	.9357	.9370	.9382	.9394	.9406	.9418	.9429	.9441
1.6	.9452	.9463	.9474	.9484	.9495	.9505	.9515	.9525	.9535	.9545
1.7	.9554	.9564	.9573	.9582	.9591	.9599	.9608	.9616	.9625	.9633
1.8	.9641	.9649	.9656	.9664	.9671	.9678	.9686	.9693	.9699	.9706
1.9	.9713	.9719	.9726	.9732	.9738	.9744	.9750	.9756	.9761	.9767
2.0	.9772	.9778	.9783	.9788	.9793	.9798	.9803	.9808	.9812	.9817
2.1	.9821	.9826	.9830	.9834	.9838	.9842	.9846	.9850	.9854	.9857
2.2	.9861	.9864	.9868	.9871	.9875	.9878	.9881	.9884	.9887	.9890
2.3	.9893	.9896	.9898	.9901	.9904	.9906	.9909	.9911	.9913	.9916
2.4	.9918	.9920	.9922	.9925	.9927	.9929	.9931	.9932	.9934	.9936
2.5	.9938	.9940	.9941	.9943	.9945	.9946	.9948	.9949	.9951	.9952
2.6	.9953	.9955	.9956	.9957	.9959	.9960	.9961	.9962	.9963	.9964
2.7	.9965	.9966	.9967	.9968	.9969	.9970	.9971	.9972	.9973	.9974
2.8	.9974	.9975	.9976	.9977	.9977	.9978	.9979	.9979	.9980	.9981
2.9	.9981	.9982	.9982	.9983	.9984	.9984	.9985	.9985	.9986	.9986
3.0	.9987	.9987	.9987	.9988	.9988	.9989	.9989	.9989	.9990	.9990
3.1	.9990	.9991	.9991	.9991	.9992	.9992	.9992	.9992	.9993	.9993
3.2	.9993	.9993	.9994	.9994	.9994	.9994	.9994	.9995	.9995	.9995
3.3	.9995	.9995	.9995	.9996	.9996	.9996	.9996	.9996	.9996	.9997
3.4	.9997	.9997	.9997	.9997	.9997	.9997	.9997	.9997	.9997	.9998

Appendix 2: Table of Random Numbers

71509	68310	48213	99928	64650	13229	36921	58732	13459	93487
21949	30920	23287	89514	58502	46185	00368	82613	02668	37444
50639	54968	11409	36148	82090	87298	41396	71111	00076	60029
47837	76716	09653	54466	87987	82362	17933	52793	17641	19502
31735	36901	92295	19293	57582	86043	69502	12601	00535	82697
04174	32342	66532	07875	54445	08795	63563	42295	74646	73120
96980	68728	21154	56181	71843	66134	52396	89723	96435	17871
21823	04027	76402	04655	87276	32593	17097	06913	05136	05115
25922	07122	31485	52166	07645	85122	20945	06369	70254	22806
32530	98882	19105	01769	20276	59401	60426	03316	41438	22012
00159	08461	51810	14650	45119	97920	08063	70819	01832	53295
66574	21384	75357	55888	83429	96916	73977	87883	13249	28870
00995	28829	15048	49573	65277	61493	44031	88719	73057	66010
55114	79226	27929	23392	06432	50200	39054	15528	53483	33972
10614	25190	52647	62580	51183	31338	60008	66595	64357	14985
31359	77469	58126	59192	23371	25190	37841	44386	92420	42965
09736	51873	94595	61367	82091	63835	86858	10677	58209	59820
24709	23224	45788	21426	63353	29874	51058	29958	61220	61199
79957	67598	74102	49824	39305	15069	56327	26905	34453	53964
66616	22137	72805	64420	58711	68435	60301	28620	91919	96080
01413	27281	19397	36231	05010	42003	99865	20924	76151	54089
88238	80731	20777	45725	41480	48277	45704	96457	13918	52375
57457	87883	64273	26236	61095	01309	48632	00431	63730	18917
21614	06412	71007	20255	39890	75336	89451	88091	61011	38072
26466	03735	39891	26361	86816	48193	33492	70484	77322	01016
97314	03944	04509	46143	88908	55261	73433	62538	63187	57352
91207	33555	75942	41668	64650	38741	86189	38197	99112	59694
46791	78974	01999	78891	16177	95746	78076	75001	51309	18791
34161	32258	05345	79267	75607	29916	37005	09213	10991	50451
02376	40372	45077	73705	56076	01853	83512	81567	55951	27156
33994	56809	58377	45976	01581	78389	18268	90057	93382	28494
92588	92024	15048	87841	38008	80689	73098	39201	10907	88092
73767	61534	66197	47147	22994	38197	60844	86962	27595	49907
51517	39870	94094	77092	94595	37904	27553	02229	44993	10468
33910	05156	60844	89012	21154	68937	96477	05867	95809	72827
09444	93069	61764	99301	55826	78849	26131	28201	91417	98172
96896	43760	72890	78682	78243	24061	55449	53587	77574	51580
97523	54633	99656	08503	52563	12099	52479	74374	79581	57143
42568	30794	32613	21802	73809	60237	70087	36650	54487	43718
45453	33136	90246	61953	17724	42421	87611	95369	42108	95369
52814	26445	73516	24897	90622	35018	70087	60112	09025	05324
87318	33345	14546	15445	81588	75461	12246	47858	08983	18205
08063	83575	25294	93027	09988	04487	88364	31087	22200	91019
53400	62078	52103	25650	75315	18916	06809	88217	12245	33053
90789	60614	20862	34475	11744	24437	55198	55219	74730	59820
73684	25859	86858	48946	30941	79017	53776	72534	83638	44680
82007	12183	89326	53713	77782	50368	01748	39033	47042	65758
80208	30920	97774	41417	79038	60531	32990	57770	53441	58732
62434	96122	63019	58439	89702	38657	60049	88761	22785	66093
04718	83199	65863	58857	49886	70275	27511	99426	53985	84077

Name Index

Subject Index

Photo Credits

SITE LICENSE AGREEMENT AND LIMITED WARRANTY

READ THIS LICENSE CAREFULLY BEFORE USING THIS PACKAGE. BY USING THIS PACKAGE, YOU ARE AGREEING TO THE TERMS AND CONDITIONS OF THIS LICENSE. IF YOU DO NOT AGREE, DO NOT USE THE PACKAGE. PROMPTLY RETURN THE UNUSED PACKAGE AND ALL ACCOMPANYING ITEMS TO THE PLACE YOU OBTAINED. *THESE TERMS APPLY TO ALL LICENSED SOFTWARE ON THE DISK EXCEPT THAT THE TERMS FOR USE OF ANY SHAREWARE OR FREEWARE ON THE DISKETTES ARE AS SET FORTH IN THE ELECTRONIC LICENSE LOCATED ON THE DISK:*

1. GRANT OF LICENSE and OWNERSHIP: The enclosed computer programs and data ("Software") are licensed, not sold, to you by Prentice-Hall, Inc. ("We" or the "Company") and in consideration of your purchase or adoption of the accompanying Company textbooks and/or other materials, and your agreement to these terms. We reserve any rights not granted to you. You own only the disk(s) but we and/or licensors own the Software itself. This license allows you to use and display the enclosed copy of the Software on up to 1 computer at a single campus or branch or geographic location of an educational institution, for academic use only, so long as you comply with the terms of this Agreement. You may make one copy for back up only.

2. RESTRICTIONS: You may not transfer or distribute the Software or documentation to anyone else. Except for backup, you may not copy the documentation or the Software. You may not reverse engineer, disassemble, decompile, modify, adapt, translate, or create derivative works based on the Software or the Documentation. You may be held legally responsible for any copying or copyright infringement which is caused by your failure to abide by the terms of these restrictions.

3. TERMINATION: This license is effective until terminated. This license will terminate automatically without notice from the Company if you fail to comply with any provisions or limitations of this license. Upon termination, you shall destroy the Documentation and all copies of the Software. All provisions of this Agreement as to limitation and disclaimer of warranties, limitation of liability, remedies or damages, and our ownership rights shall survive termination.

4. LIMITED WARRANTY AND DISCLAIMER OF WARRANTY: Company warrants that for a period of 60 days from the date you purchase this Software (or purchase or adopt the accompanying textbook), the Software, when properly installed and used in accordance with the Documentation, will operate in substantial conformity with the description of the Software set forth in the Documentation, and that for a period of 30 days the disk(s) on which the Software is delivered shall be free from defects in materials and workmanship under normal use. The Company does not warrant that the Software will meet your requirements or that the operation of the Software will be uninterrupted or error-free. Your only remedy and the Company's only obligation under these limited warranties is, at the Company's option, return of the disk for a refund of any amounts paid for it by you or replacement of the disk. THIS LIMITED WARRANTY IS THE ONLY WARRANTY PROVIDED BY THE COMPANY AND ITS LICENSORS, AND THE COMPANY AND ITS LICENSORS DISCLAIM ALL OTHER WARRANTIES, EXPRESS OR IMPLIED, INCLUDING WITHOUT LIMITATION, THE IMPLIED WARRANTIES OF MERCHANTABILITY AND FITNESS FOR A PARTICULAR PURPOSE. THE COMPANY DOES NOT WARRANT, GUARANTEE OR MAKE ANY REPRESENTATION REGARDING THE ACCURACY, RELIABILITY, CURRENTNESS, USE, OR RESULTS OF USE, OF THE SOFTWARE.

5. LIMITATION OF REMEDIES AND DAMAGES: IN NO EVENT, SHALL THE COMPANY OR ITS EMPLOYEES, AGENTS, LICENSORS, OR CONTRACTORS BE LIABLE FOR ANY INCIDENTAL, INDIRECT, SPECIAL, OR CONSEQUENTIAL DAMAGES ARISING OUT OF OR IN CONNECTION WITH THIS LICENSE OR THE SOFTWARE, INCLUDING FOR LOSS OF USE, LOSS OF DATA, LOSS OF INCOME OR PROFIT, OR OTHER LOSSES, SUSTAINED AS A RESULT OF INJURY TO ANY PERSON, OR LOSS OF OR DAMAGE TO PROPERTY, OR CLAIMS OF THIRD PARTIES, EVEN IF THE COMPANY OR AN AUTHORIZED REPRESENTATIVE OF THE COMPANY HAS BEEN ADVISED OF THE POSSIBILITY OF SUCH DAMAGES. IN NO EVENT SHALL THE LIABILITY OF THE COMPANY FOR DAMAGES WITH RESPECT TO THE SOFTWARE EXCEED THE AMOUNTS ACTUALLY PAID BY YOU, IF ANY, FOR THE SOFTWARE OR THE ACCOMPANYING TEXTBOOK. SOME JURISDICTIONS DO NOT ALLOW THE LIMITATION OF LIABILITY IN CERTAIN CIRCUM-STANCES, THE ABOVE LIMITATIONS MAY NOT ALWAYS APPLY.

6. MICROSOFT PROJECT SOFTWARE: This program is distributed by PRENTICE HALL under a special arrangement with Microsoft Corporation. For this reason, PRENTICE HALL is responsible for the product warranty and for support. If your diskette is defective, please return it to PRENTICE HALL, which will arrange for its replacement. DO NOT RETURN THE SOFTWARE TO MICROSOFT CORPORA-TION. Any product support will be provided, if at all, by PRENTICE HALL. DO NOT CONTACT MICROSOFT CORPORATION FOR PRODUCT SUPPORT. End users of this Microsoft program shall not be considered "registered owners" of a Microsoft product and therefore shall not be eligible for upgrades, promotions or other benefits available to "registered owners" of Microsoft products.

7. GENERAL: THIS AGREEMENT SHALL BE CONSTRUED IN ACCORDANCE WITH THE LAWS OF THE UNITED STATES OF AMER-ICA AND THE STATE OF NEW YORK, APPLICABLE TO CONTRACTS MADE IN NEW YORK, AND SHALL BENEFIT THE COMPANY, ITS AFFILIATES AND ASSIGNEES. This Agreement is the complete and exclusive statement of the agreement between you and the Company and supersedes all proposals, prior agreements, oral or written, and any other communications between you and the company or any of its representatives relating to the subject matter. If you are a U.S. Government user, this Software is licensed with "restricted rights" as set forth in subparagraphs (a)-(d) of the Commercial Computer-Restricted Rights clause at FAR 52.227-19 or in subparagraphs (c)(1)(ii) of the Rights in Technical Data and Computer Software clause at DFARS 252.227-7013, and similar clauses, as applicable.

Should you have any questions concerning this agreement or if you wish to contact the Company for any reason, please contact in writing:

Director, Media Production

Pearson Education

1 Lake Street

Upper Saddle River, NJ 07458